W9-CEX-018

Mobil ✦✦ Travel Guide

Southwest 2004

Arizona

Colorado

Nevada

New Mexico

Utah

Ex╳onMobil Travel Publications

Maps by ✦ **RAND MCNALLY**

Acknowledgements

We gratefully acknowledge the help of our representatives for their efficient and perceptive inspections of the lodging and dining establishments listed; the establishments' proprietors for their cooperation in showing their facilities and providing information about them; the many users of previous editions who have taken the time to share their experiences; and for their time and information, the thousands of chambers of commerce, convention and visitors bureaus, city, state, and provincial tourism offices, and government agencies who assisted in our research.

Mobil Travel Guide is also grateful to all the highly talented writers who contributed entries to this book.

Maps Copyright © 2004 Rand McNally & Company

Printing Acknowledgement: North American Corporation of Illinois

www.mobiltravelguide.com

The information contained herein is derived from a variety of third-party sources. Although every effort has been made to verify the information obtained from such sources, the publisher assumes no responsibility for inconsistencies or inaccuracies in the data or liability for any damages of any type arising from errors or omissions.

Neither the editors nor the publisher assumes responsibility for the services provided by any business listed in this guide or for any loss, damage, or disruption in your travel for any reason.

ISBN: 0-7627-2890-6

Manufactured in the United States of America.

10 9 8 7 6 5 4 3 2 1

Contents

MAP SYMBOLS

━━━━	Free limited-access highway
- - -	New — under construction
━━━━	Toll limited-access highway
- - -	New — under construction
━━━━	Other multilane highway
───	Principal highway
───	Other through highway
───	Other road
- - -	Unpaved road
········	Ferry
90 190 80	Interstate highway
41 183 18	U.S. highway
8 18 14 83	State or provincial highway
4 43 147	Other highway
⊢9⊣	Miles between arrows One mile or less not shown
2 □○ 10	Interchanges and interchange numbers
-------	Time zone boundary
▦	Urbanized area in state maps; in city maps Separate cities within metro area
⊛ ⊗ ● ○ ○	National capital; state capital; cities; towns (size of type indicates relative population)
▦	U.S. or Canadian National Park
▦	State/Provincial Park or Recreation Area
▦	National Forest or Grassland, city park
▪	Point of interest
⊞	Hospital, medical center
········	Continental divide

© 2003 Rand McNally

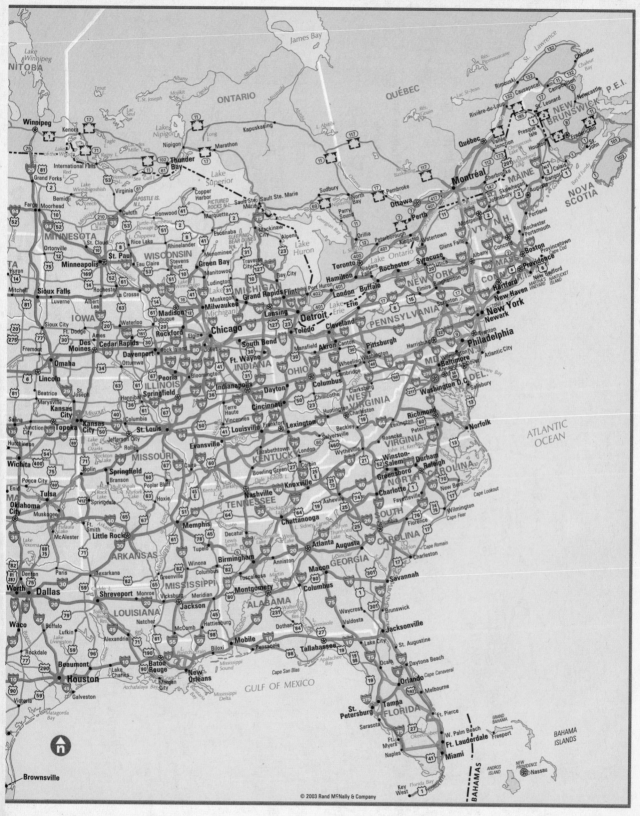

© 2003 Rand McNally & Company

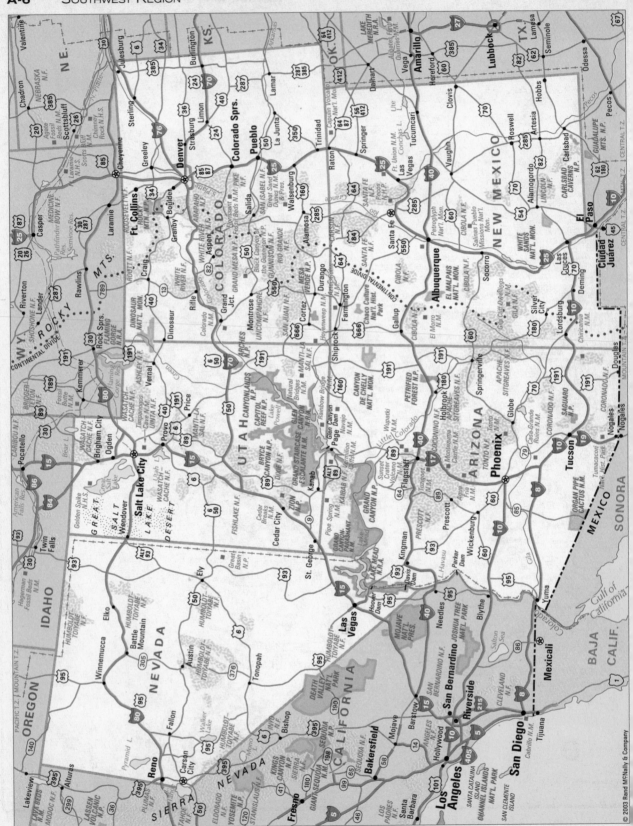

© 2003 Rand McNally & Company

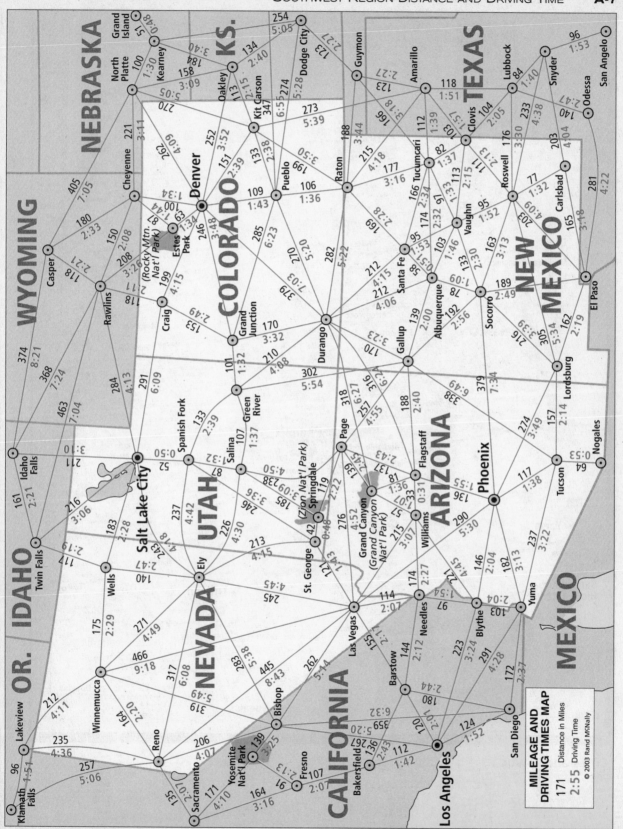

MILEAGE AND
DRIVING TIMES MAP

171   Distance in Miles
2:55   Driving Time

© 2003 Rand McNally

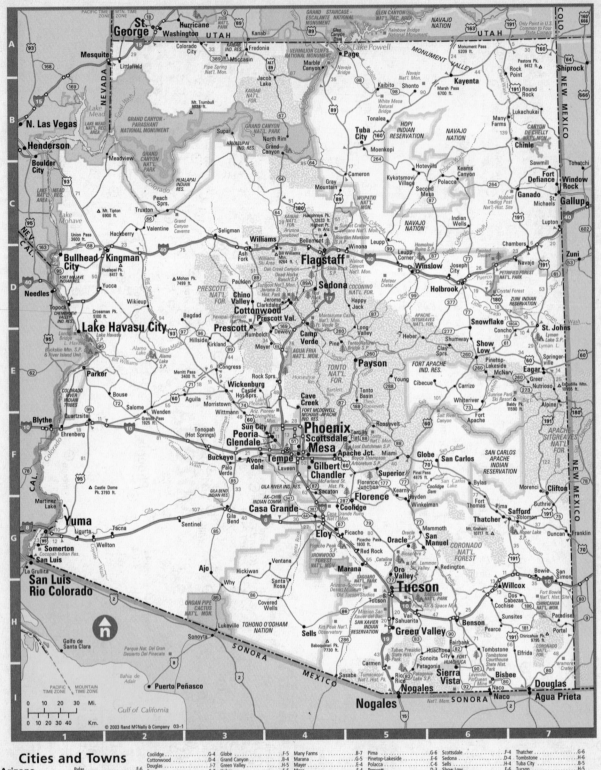

Cities and Towns

Arizona

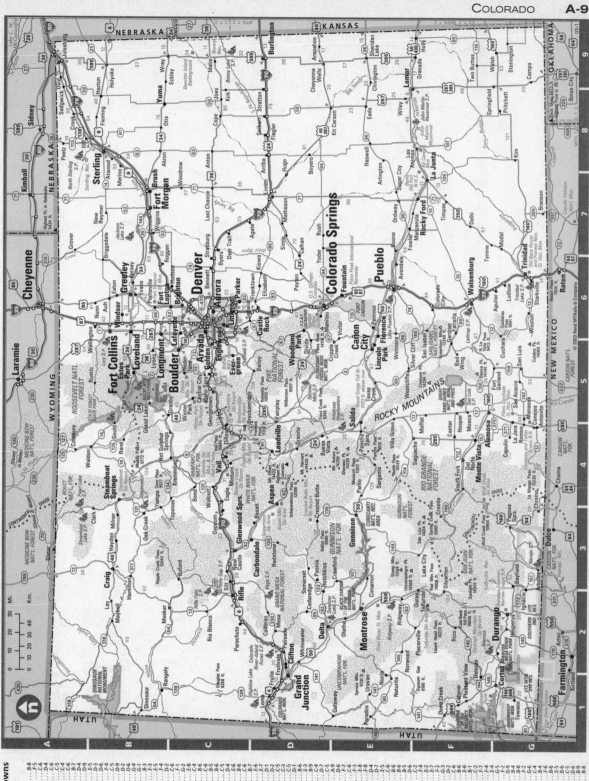

Cities and Towns

Nevada

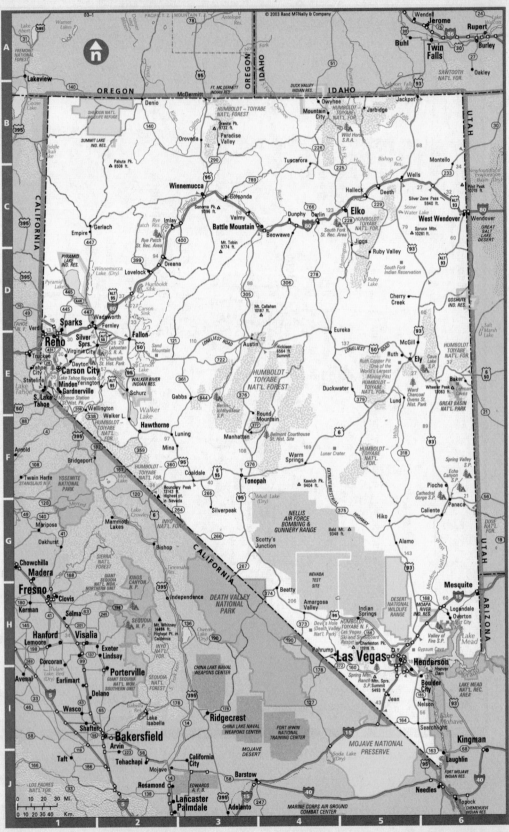

© 2003 Rand McNally & Company

© 2003 Rand McNally & Company

Cities and Towns
New Mexico

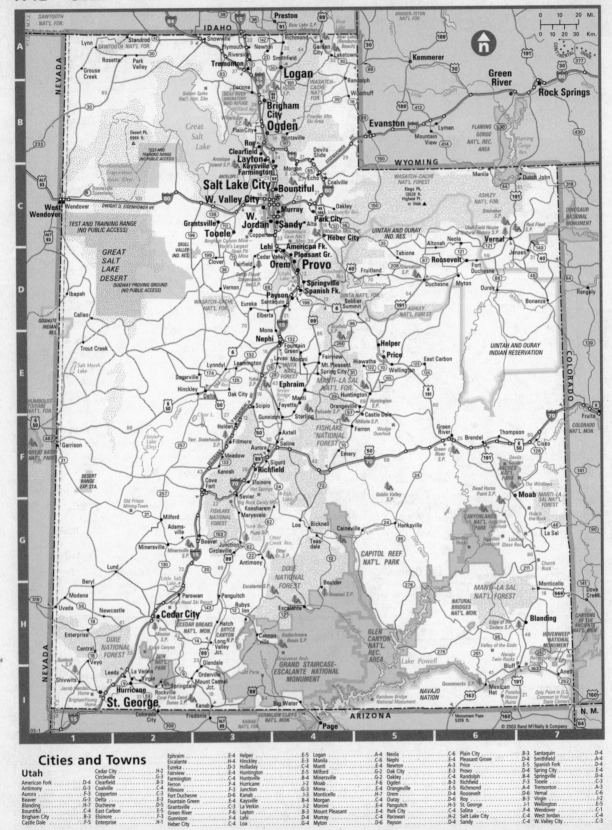

Cities and Towns

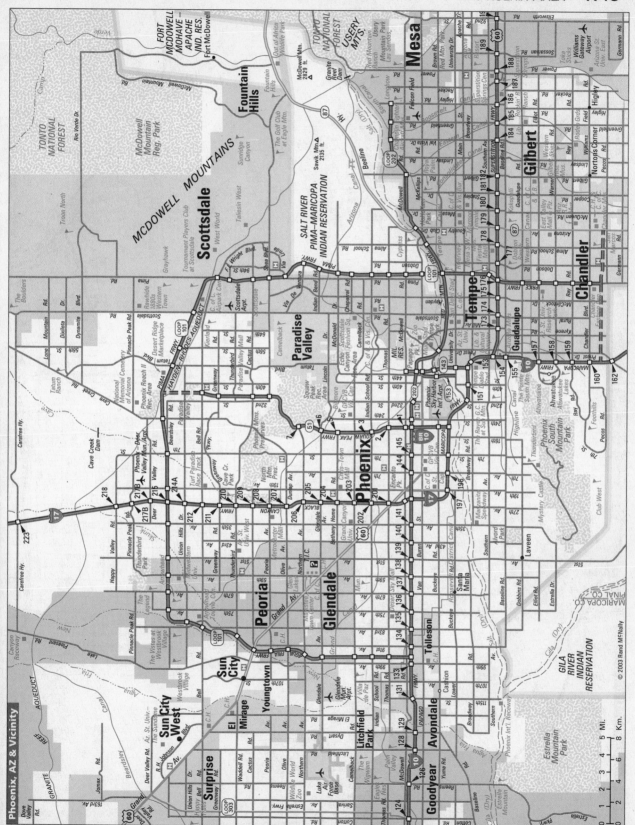

Phoenix, AZ & Vicinity

Flagstaff, AZ

© 2003 Rand McNally

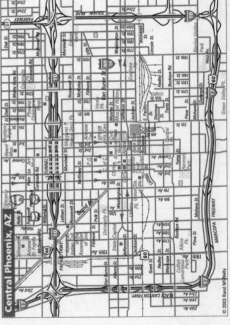

Central Phoenix, AZ

© 2003 Rand McNally

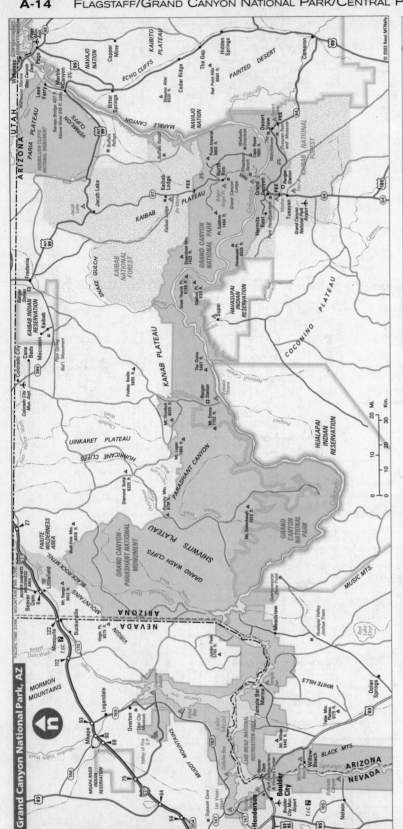

Grand Canyon National Park, AZ

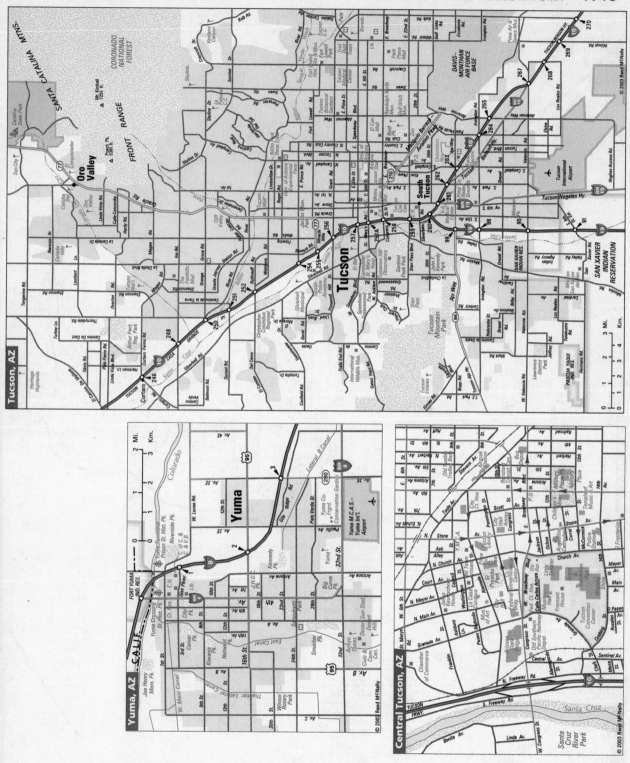

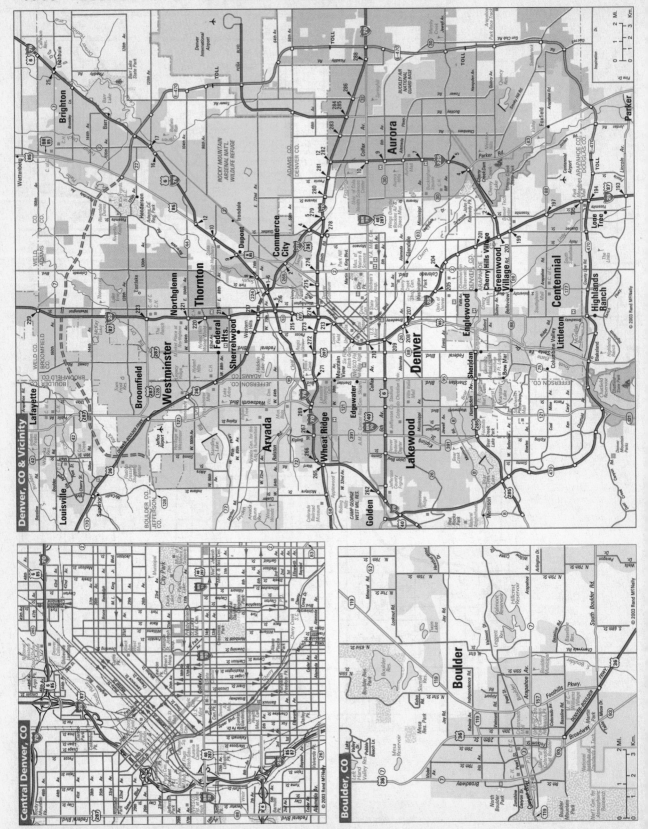

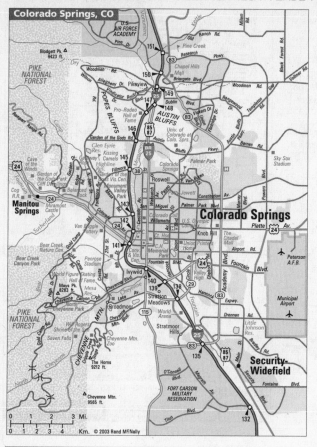

Colorado Springs, CO

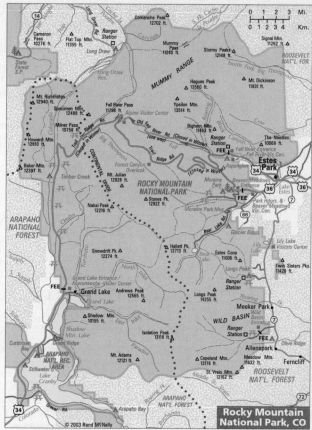

Rocky Mountain National Park, CO

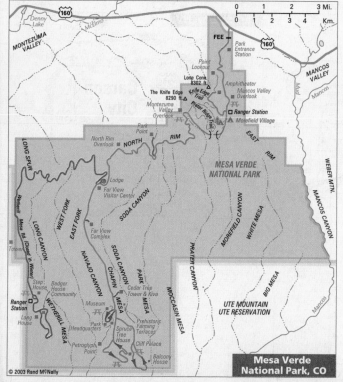

Mesa Verde National Park, CO

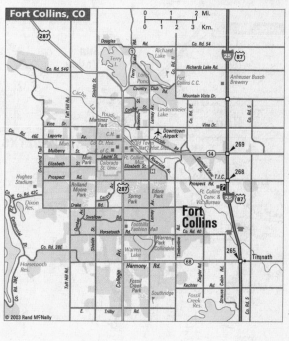

Fort Collins, CO

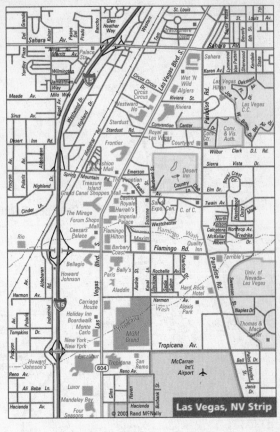

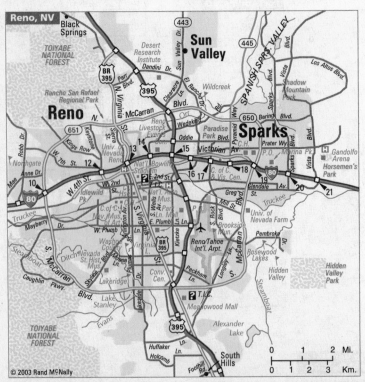

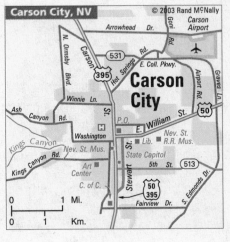

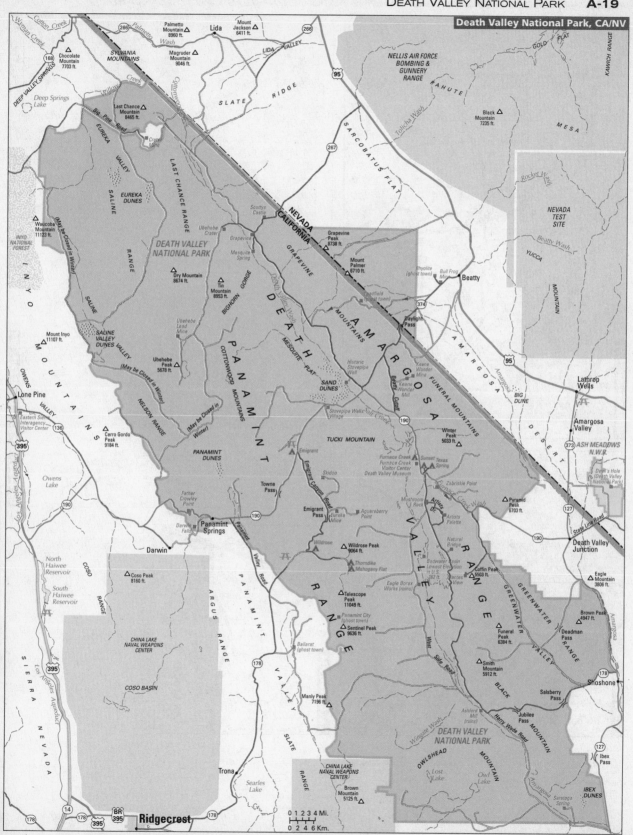

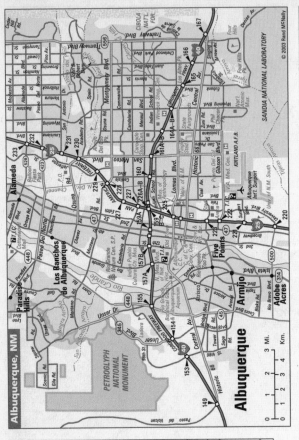

Albuquerque, NM

Albuquerque

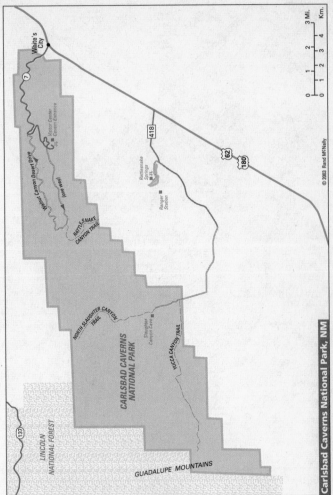

Carlsbad Caverns National Park, NM

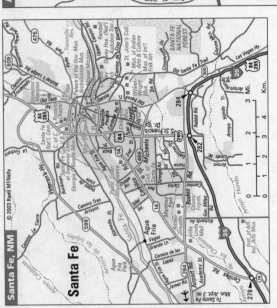

Santa Fe, NM

Santa Fe

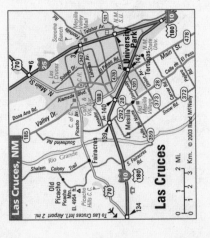

Las Cruces, NM

Las Cruces

© 2003 Rand McNally

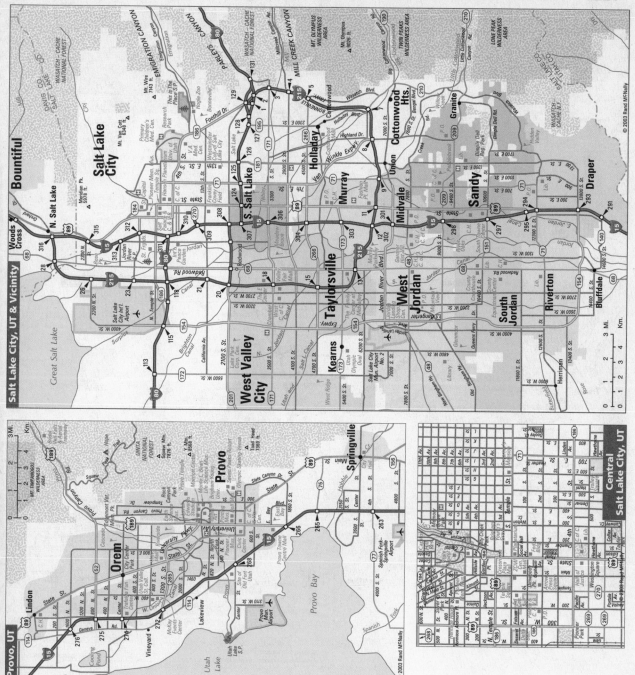

Arches National Park, UT

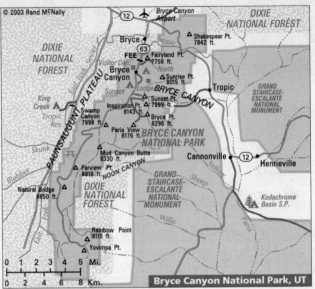

Bryce Canyon National Park, UT

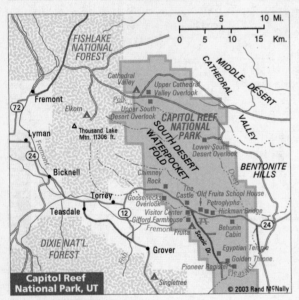

Capitol Reef National Park, UT

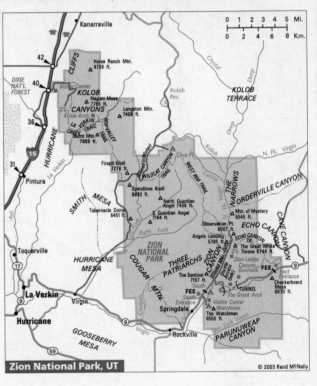

Zion National Park, UT

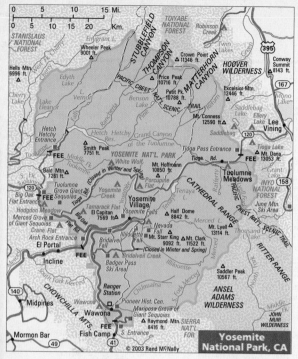

Yosemite National Park, CA

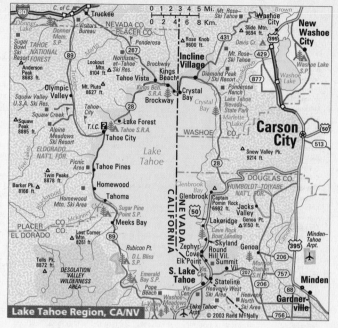

Lake Tahoe Region, CA/NV
© 2003 Rand McNally

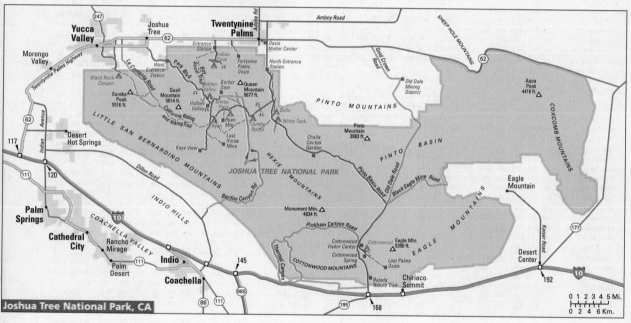

Joshua Tree National Park, CA

	Atlanta, GA	Billings, MT	Boston, MA	Charlotte, NC	Chicago, IL	Cincinnati, OH	Cleveland, OH	Dallas, TX	Denver, CO	Detroit, MI	Houston, TX	Indianapolis, IN	Kansas City, MO	Los Angeles, CA	Memphis, TN	Miami, FL	Milwaukee, WI	Minneapolis, MN	New Orleans, LA	New York, NY	Omaha, NE	Philadelphia, PA	Phoenix, AZ	Pittsburgh, PA	Portland, OR	St. Louis, MO	Salt Lake City, UT	San Francisco, CA	Seattle, WA	Tulsa, OK	Washington, D.C.	Wichita, KS
Albany, NY	1014	2076	166	777	820	727	478	1682	1814	648	1770	791	1287	2833	1230	1407	921	1236	1441	153	1274	238	2544	472	2927	1040	2206	2953	2899	1433	365	1477
Albuquerque, NM	1406	994	2247	1629	1341	1397	1606	644	439	1591	890	1290	783	799	1014	1960	1424	1222	1170	2019	979	1939	463	1649	1385	1041	626	1097	1456	650	1886	593
Amarillo, TX	1121	971	1962	1344	1056	1112	1321	359	424	1306	605	1005	604	1084	729	1675	1139	1043	885	1734	716	1654	748	1364	1666	756	911	1382	1737	365	1601	417
Atlanta, GA		1890	1100	243	712	463	715	791	1415	723	797	529	810	2205	393	661	811	1132	468	896	1000	816	1862	686	2604	556	1883	2503	2675	798	635	972
Baltimore, MD	673	1960	407	436	704	523	379	1366	1693	532	1454	592	1088	2681	914	1080	805	1120	1125	203	1158	102	2345	251	2811	841	2090	2837	2783	1234	38	1278
Billings, MT	1890		2242	2055	1247	1547	1598	1429	555	1534	1676	1433	1078	1239	1606	2551	1176	843	1954	2067	896	2017	1206	1716	891	1333	549	1179	821	1238	1961	1064
Birmingham, AL	148	1839	1185	391	661	467	719	647	1364	727	671	478	759	2058	246	783	760	1081	342	981	949	901	1722	753	2553	505	1832	2356	2624	651	743	825
Bismarck, ND	1558	417	1828	1610	833	1133	1184	1274	709	1120	1521	1019	790	1595	1318	2219	762	429	1709	1653	608	1603	1515	1302	1310	1045	927	1598	1240	1037	1547	802
Boise, ID	2184	621	2673	2349	1702	1959	2029	1704	830	1965	1951	1852	1372	846	1900	2845	1741	1466	2229	2498	1233	2448	995	2147	425	1627	338	648	496	1513	2392	1339
Boston, MA	1100	2242		863	986	893	644	1768	1980	814	1856	957	1453	2999	1316	1483	1087	1402	1527	211	1440	313	2710	586	3093	1206	2372	3119	3065	1599	441	1643
Buffalo, NY	896	1787	461	659	531	438	189	1376	1525	359	1495	502	998	2544	924	1381	632	947	1243	417	985	412	2255	216	2638	751	1917	2664	2610	1144	388	1188
Charleston, SC	321	2196	966	207	911	619	721	1112	1721	850	1113	730	1116	2526	714	580	1010	1325	784	762	1306	661	2183	654	2910	862	2189	2824	2981	1119	525	1306
Charlotte, NC	243	2055	863		770	478	516	1034	1580	645	1040	589	975	2428	617	724	869	1184	711	659	1165	534	2092	449	2769	721	2048	2726	2840	1021	398	1165
Cheyenne, WY	1450	455	1939	1615	968	1225	1295	974	100	1231	1221	1118	638	1102	1166	2111	1007	878	1499	1764	499	1714	906	1413	1155	893	434	1181	1226	783	1658	609
Chicago, IL	712	1247	986	770		293	342	933	1009	278	1089	179	529	2028	536	1373	92	407	927	811	469	761	1804	460	2122	300	1401	2148	2070	693	705	719
Cincinnati, OH	463	1547	893	478	293		252	938	1208	260	1057	112	603	2196	486	1124	392	707	805	660	726	580	1860	290	2379	356	1658	2405	2370	749	524	793
Cleveland, OH	715	1598	644	516	342	252		1190	1336	170	1309	316	812	2355	738	1238	443	758	1057	486	796	436	2069	135	2449	565	1728	2475	2421	958	380	1002
Columbus, OH	574	1606	783	433	352	111	142	1049	1276	204	1168	175	671	2264	597	1155	451	766	916	553	794	473	1928	183	2447	424	1726	2473	2429	817	417	861
Dallas, TX	791	1429	1768	1034	933	938	1190		882	1198	247	882	552	1440	454	1316	1016	991	526	1564	664	1484	1069	1228	2124	633	1403	1741	2195	262	1326	365
Davenport, IA	792	1166	1135	898	175	421	491	915	843	427	1095	314	363	1862	550	1453	214	359	941	960	303	910	1609	609	1956	266	1235	1982	1989	612	854	553
Denver, CO	1415	555	1980	1580	1009	1208	1336	882		1272	1129	1101	605	1022	1097	2076	1048	919	1407	1805	540	1750	809	1460	1250	858	529	1276	1321	691	1694	517
Des Moines, IA	961	997	1304	1067	333	590	660	746	674	596	926	483	194	1693	623	1622	372	243	1014	1129	134	1079	1440	778	1787	350	1066	1813	1820	443	1023	384
Detroit, MI	723	1534	814	645	278	260	170	1198	1272		1317	310	792	2291	746	1367	379	694	1065	639	732	589	2054	288	2385	550	1664	2411	2357	943	533	955
Duluth, MN	1189	861	1459	1241	464	764	815	1145	1073	751	1325	650	593	2092	965	1850	393	157	1356	1284	533	1234	1839	933	1754	681	1465	2042	1684	842	1178	783
El Paso, TX	1426	1178	2394	1669	1488	1544	1753	633	623	1738	753	1437	930	807	1087	1939	1571	1369	1100	2197	1016	2117	436	1796	1627	1188	868	1188	1698	797	1959	740
Fargo, ND	1369	607	1639	1421	644	944	995	1087	901	931	1334	830	603	1785	1131	2030	573	240	1522	1464	421	1414	1707	1113	1500	858	1117	1788	1430	850	1358	725
Flagstaff, AZ	1733	1070	2574	1956	1668	1724	1933	971	673	1918	1217	1617	1110	472	1341	2287	1751	1549	1497	2346	1210	2266	136	1976	1279	1368	520	770	1350	977	2213	920
Houston, TX	797	1676	1856	1040	1089	1057	1309	247	1129	1317		1025	732	1560	573	1190	1179	1171	351	1652	911	1572	1189	1347	2371	837	1650	1941	2442	505	1414	612
Indianapolis, IN	529	1433	957	589	179	112	316	882	1101	310	1025		496	2089	472	1190	278	593	816	729	619	649	1753	359	2272	249	1551	2298	2256	642	593	686
Jackson, MS	383	1817	1424	626	747	692	944	408	1225	952	442	683	737	1850	212	908	837	1119	180	1220	927	1140	1479	982	2467	495	1746	2149	2538	534	982	708
Jacksonville, FL	346	2236	1142	383	1058	795	897	1001	1761	1026	875	875	1156	2431	712	341	1157	1478	546	938	1346	837	2060	830	2950	902	2229	2742	3021	1117	701	1291
Kansas City, MO	810	1078	1453	975	529	603	812	552	605	792	732	496		1626	526	1471	568	439	917	1225	188	1145	1246	855	1792	253	1071	1818	1863	249	1089	190
Knoxville, TN	215	1826	928	229	542	250	502	840	1351	510	928	361	746	2199	388	876	641	956	599	724	936	644	1863	496	2540	492	1819	2497	2611	792	486	936
Las Vegas, NV	1982	966	2726	2205	1755	1956	2082	1220	749	2018	1466	1849	1353	275	1590	2536	1794	1665	1746	2551	1286	2498	292	2208	1021	1606	416	569	1122	1226	2462	1265
Lexington, KY	386	1669	935	401	375	83	335	874	1194	343	993	188	589	2175	422	1047	474	789	741	731	779	645	1839	373	2383	335	1662	2409	2454	728	543	779
Little Rock, AR	531	1513	1453	754	655	623	875	315	966	883	434	591	389	1682	139	1165	745	826	441	1249	577	1169	1346	913	2208	403	1487	1980	2279	275	1011	449
Los Angeles, CA	2205	1239	2999	2428	2028	2196	2355	1440	1022	2291	1560	2089	1626		1813	2746	2067	1938	1907	2824	1559	2738	371	2448	967	1840	689	381	1141	1449	2685	1392
Louisville, KY	415	1595	996	475	297	103	355	835	1120	363	954	114	515	2101	383	1076	396	711	702	763	705	683	1765	393	2309	261	1588	2335	2380	654	617	705
Memphis, TN	393	1606	1316	617	536	486	738	454	1097	746	573	472	526	1813		1027	626	908	392	1112	716	1032	1477	776	2320	284	1599	2111	2391	406	874	580
Miami, FL	661	2551	1483	724	1373	1124	1238	1316	2076	1367	1190	1190	1471	2746	1027		1472	1793	861	1279	1661	1178	2375	1171	3265	1217	2544	3057	3336	1432	1042	1606
Milwaukee, WI	811	1176	1087	869	92	392	443	1016	1048	379	1179	278	568	2067	626	1472		336	1017	912	508	862	1887	561	2069	383	1440	2187	1999	776	806	758
Minneapolis, MN	1132	843	1402	1184	407	707	758	991	919	694	1171	593	439	1938	908	1793	336		1299	1227	379	1177	1685	876	1736	624	1311	2058	1666	688	1121	629
Mobile, AL	329	2003	1429	572	920	726	978	598	1415	986	472	737	923	2028	398	718	1019	1305	143	1225	1113	1145	1657	1009	2657	681	1936	2339	2728	724	964	898
Montréal, QC	1227	1909	324	990	848	829	590	1767	1842	575	1886	879	1362	2861	1315	1632	949	1264	1654	384	1302	463	2632	617	2955	1128	2234	2981	2732	1521	590	1525
Nashville, TN	242	1650	1106	407	472	278	530	663	1175	538	782	289	570	2022	211	903	571	892	527	902	760	822	1686	568	2364	316	1643	2320	2435	615	664	760
New Orleans, LA	468	1954	1527	711	927	805	1057	526	1407	1065	351	816	917	1907	392	861	1017	1299		1323	1107	1243	1536	1095	2649	675	1928	2267	2720	679	1085	890
New York, NY	896	2067	211	659	811	660	486	1564	1805	639	1652	729	1225	2824	1112	1279	912	1227	1323		1265	109	2482	388	2918	978	2197	2944	2890	1371	237	1415
Norfolk, VA	557	2147	577	320	891	601	566	1348	1781	719	1384	713	1176	2729	918	948	992	1307	1055	373	1366	276	2393	438	2970	922	2249	2996	3041	1315	196	1366
Odessa, TX	1147	1204	2122	1390	1244	1292	1509	354	649	1494	546	1193	792	1088	808	1672	1327	1231	882	1918	904	1838	717	1552	1784	944	1025	1469	1855	553	1680	605
Oklahoma City, OK	862	1221	1702	1085	796	852	1061	208	674	1046	455	745	344	1343	470	1496	879	783	733	1474	456	1394	1007	1104	1916	496	1195	1641	1987	105	1342	157
Omaha, NE	1000	896	1440	1165	469	726	796	664	540	732	911	619	188	1559	716	1661	508	379	1107	1265		1215	1346	914	1653	443	932	1679	1724	435	1159	302
Orlando, FL	440	2330	1284	525	1152	903	1039	1095	1855	1163	969	969	1250	2525	806	229	1251	1572	640	1080	1440	979	2154	972	3044	996	2323	2836	3115	1211	843	1385
Philadelphia, PA	816	2017	313	534	761	580	436	1484	1750	589	1572	649	1145	2738	1032	1178	862	1177	1243	109	1215		2402	308	2868	898	2147	2894	2840	1291	136	1335
Phoenix, AZ	1862	1206	2710	2092	1804	1860	2069	1069	809	2054	1189	1753	1246	371	1477	2375	1887	1685	1536	2482	1346	2402		2112	1338	1504	656	752	1486	1113	2349	1056
Pittsburgh, PA	686	1716	586	449	460	290	135	1228	1460	288	1347	359	855	2448	776	1171	561	876	1095	388	914	308	2112		2567	608	1846	2593	2539	1001	252	1045
Portland, ME	1229	2343	117	964	1087	994	745	1897	2081	915	1985	1058	1554	3100	1445	1584	1188	1503	1656	312	1541	414	2811	687	3194	1307	2473	3220	3166	1700	542	1744
Portland, OR	2604	891	3093	2769	2122	2379	2449	2124	1250	2385	2371	2272	1792	967	2320	3265	2069	1736	2649	2918	1653	2868	1338	2567		2047	758	636	174	1933	2812	1759
Rapid City, SD	1521	373	1904	1686	909	1209	1260	1069	400	1196	1316	1095	709	1312	1237	2182	838	609	1628	1729	527	1679	1206	1378	1266	964	644	1391	1196	878	1623	704
Reno, NV	2406	955	2895	2571	1924	2181	2251	1665	1052	2187	1911	2074	1594	473	2122	3067	1963	1834	2193	2720	1455	2670	735	2369	578	1849	522	224	752	1735	2614	1561
Roanoke, VA	430	1917	678	193	663	370	429	1098	1550	558	1186	482	945	2457	646	915	762	1077	857	474	1135	394	2121	365	2739	691	2018	2765	2810	1050	236	1135
St. Louis, MO	556	1333	1206	721	300	356	565	633	858	550	837	249	253	1840	284	1217	383	624	675	978	443	898	1504	608	2047		1326	2073	2118	393	878	443
Salt Lake City, UT	1883	549	2372	2048	1401	1658	1728	1403	529	1664	1650	1551	1071	689	1599	2544	1440	1311	1928	2197	932	2147	656	1846	758	1326		746	829	1212	2091	1038
San Antonio, TX	992	1483	2051	1235	1210	1215	1467	277	936	1475	199	1159	817	1365	731	1385	1293	1256	546	1847	929	1767	994	1505	2100	910	1341	1746	2171	539	1609	630
San Diego, CA	2154	1299	3064	2397	2088	2214	2423	1361	1082	2351	1481	2107	1600	124	1831	2667	2127	1998	1828	2836	1619	2756	354	2466	1091	1858	749	505	1265	1467	2703	1410
San Francisco, CA	2503	1179	3119	2726	2148	2405	2475	1741	1276	2411	1941	2298	1818	381	2111	3057	2187	2058	2267	2944	1679	2894	752	2593	636	2073	746		810	1747	2838	1785
Sault Ste Marie, ON	1047	1282	943	960	452	584	506	1357	1446	350	1510	537	966	2465	957	1708	404	549	1347	939	906	925	2228	624	2175	724	1838	2585	2105	1117	869	1129
Seattle, WA	2675	821	3065	2840	2070	2370	2421	2195	1321	2357	2442	2256	1863	1141	2391	3336	1999	1666	2720	2890	1724	2840	1486	2539	174	2118	829	810		2004	2784	1830
Shreveport, LA	605	1614	1646	848	851	819	1071	186	1067	1079	239	787	566	1628	335	1130	941	1005	347	1442	752	1362	1257	1109	2309	599	1588	1927	2380	339	1204	550
Sioux Falls, SD	1177	717	1564	1342	569	876	920	849	654	856	1096	769	365	1673	893	1838	498	269	1284	1389	183	1339	1460	1038	1610	620	989	1736	1540	612	1283	487
Spokane, WA	2431	539	2783	2596	1788	2088	2139	1970	1096	2075	2217	1974	1619	1215	2147	3092	1717	1384	2495	2608	1437	2558	1377	2257	352	1874	720	885	282	1779	2502	1605
Springfield, MO	684	1247	1418	849	512	568	777	423	761	762	666	461	169	1630	283	1345	595	606	674	1190	357	1110	1294	820	1961	212	1240	1928	2032	183	1090	263
Tallahassee, FL	270	2143	1301	470	965	733	985	839	1668	993	713	782	1063	2269	550	478	1064	1385	384	1097	1253	996	1898	917	2857	809	2136	2580	2928	955	860	1129
Tampa, FL	458	2348	1340	581	1170	921	1095	1113	1873	1181	987	987	1268	2543	824	273	1269	1590	658	1136	1458	1035	2172	1028	3062	1014	2341	2854	3133	1229	899	1403
Toronto, ON	961	1773	566	766	517	498	296	1436	1511	244	1555	548	1031	2530	984	1488	618	933	1303	528	971	517	2301	323	2624	797	1903	2650	2596	1190	495	1194
Tulsa, OK	798	1238	1599	1021	693	749	958	262	691	943	505	642	249	1449	406	1432	776	688	679	1371	435	1291	1113	1001	1933	393	1212	1747	2004		1271	174
Washington, D.C.	635	1961	441	398	705	524	380	1326	1694	533	1414	593	1089	2685	874	1042	806	1121	1085	237	1159	136	2349	252	2812	878	2091	2838	2784	1271		1279
Wichita, KS	972	1064	1643	1165	719	793	1002	365	517	955	612	686	190	1392	580	1606	758	629	890	1415	302	1335	1056	1045	1759	443	1038	1785	1830	174	1279	

Making road trips easy is our driving ambition.

Come and see how easy and convenient our Exxon and Mobil locations are. Before you head off for your next road trip, stop into your local Exxon or Mobil retailer and fill up on the essentials: film, batteries, cold soda for your thirst, salty snacks and candy for your hunger and, of course, automotive services and quality fuels. With over 16,000 locations nationwide, we make it effortless.

 And don't forget to use your *Speedpass*™ to get back on the road even faster. After all, getting there is half the fun. How do we know? We're drivers too.

We're drivers too.

Meet The Stars

Mobil Travel Guide 2004 *Five-Star* Award Winners

LODGINGS

California
The Beverly Hills Hotel, *Beverly Hills*
Chateau du Sureau, *Oakhurst*
Four Seasons, San Francisco, *San Francisco*
Hotel Bel-Air, *Los Angeles*
The Peninsula Beverly Hills, *Beverly Hills*
Raffles L'Ermitage Beverly Hills, *Beverly Hills*
The Ritz-Carlton San Francisco, *San Francisco*

Colorado
The Broadmoor, *Colorado Springs*
The Little Nell, *Aspen*

Connecticut
The Mayflower Inn, *Washington*

Florida
Four Seasons Resort Palm Beach, *Palm Beach*
The Ritz-Carlton, Naples, *Naples*
The Ritz-Carlton, Palm Beach, *Palm Beach*

Georgia
Four Seasons Hotel Atlanta, *Atlanta*
The Lodge at Sea Island Golf Club, *Sea Island*

Illinois
Four Seasons Hotel Chicago, *Chicago*
Peninsula Chicago, *Chicago*
The Ritz-Carlton, A Four Seasons Hotel, *Chicago*

Massachusetts
Four Seasons Hotel Boston, *Boston*
Blantyre, *Lenox*

New York
Four Seasons Hotel New York, *Manhattan*
The Point, *Saranac Lake*
The Ritz-Carlton New York Central Park, *Manhattan*
The St. Regis, *Manhattan*

North Carolina
Fearrington House, *Pittsboro*

South Carolina
Woodlands Resort and Inn, *Summerville*

Texas
The Mansion on Turtle Creek, *Dallas*

Vermont
Twin Farms, *Woodstock*

Virginia
The Inn at Little Washington, *Washington*
The Jefferson Hotel, *Richmond*

RESTAURANTS

California
The Dining Room at The Ritz-Carlton San Francisco, *San Francisco*
The French Laundry, *Yountville*
Gary Danko, *San Francisco*

Georgia
The Dining Room, *Atlanta*
Seeger's, *Atlanta*

Illinois
Charlie Trotter's, *Chicago*
Trio, *Evanston*

New York
Alain Ducasse, *Manhattan*
Jean Georges, *Manhattan*

Ohio
Maisonette, *Cincinnati*

Pennsylvania
Le Bec-Fin, *Philadelphia*

South Carolina
The Dining Room at Woodlands, *Summerville*

Virginia
The Inn at Little Washington, *Washington*

The Mobil Travel Guide has been rating establishments with a One- to Five-Star system since 1958. Each establishment awarded the Mobil Five-Star rating is "one of the best in the country." Detailed information on each award winner can be found in the corresponding regional edition listed on the back cover.

Welcome

Dear Traveler,

Since its inception in 1958, Mobil Travel Guide has served as a trusted advisor to auto travelers in search of value in lodging, dining, and destinations. Now in its 46th year, the Mobil Travel Guide is the hallmark of our ExxonMobil family of travel publications, and we're proud to offer an array of products and services from our Mobil, Exxon, and Esso brands in North America to facilitate life on the road.

Whether you're looking for business or pleasure venues, our nationwide network of independent, professional evaluators offers their expertise on thousands of travel options, allowing you to plan a quick family getaway, a full-service business meeting, or an unforgettable Five-Star celebration.

Your feedback is important to us as we strive to improve our product offerings and better meet today's travel needs. Whether you travel once a week or once a year, please take the time to contact us at www.mobiltravelguide.com. We hope to hear from you soon.

Best wishes for safe and enjoyable travels.

Lee R Raymond

Lee R. Raymond
Chairman and CEO
Exxon Mobil Corporation

A Word to Our Readers

Travelers are on the roads in great numbers these days. They're exploring the country on day trips, weekend getaways, business trips, and extended family vacations, visiting major cities and small towns along the way. Because time is precious and the travel industry is ever-changing, having accurate, reliable travel information at your fingertips is critical. Mobil Travel Guide has been providing invaluable insight to travelers for more than 45 years, and we are committed to continuing this service well into the future.

The Mobil Corporation (known as Exxon Mobil Corporation since a 1999 merger) began producing the Mobil Travel Guide books in 1958, following the introduction of the US highway system in 1956. The first edition covered only five southwestern states. Since then, our books have become the premier travel guides in North America, covering the 48 contiguous states and Canada. Now, ExxonMobil presents the latest editions of our annual travel guides, with a fresh new look. We also recently introduced road atlases and specialty publications, a robust new Web site, as well as the first fully integrated, auto-centric travel support program called MobilCompanion, the driving force in travel. (See the inside back cover for more information).

Since its founding, Mobil Travel Guide has served as an advocate for travelers seeking knowledge about hotels, restaurants, and places to visit. Based on an objective process, we make recommendations to our customers that we believe will enhance the quality and value of their travel experiences. Our trusted One- to Five-Star rating system is the oldest and most respected lodging and restaurant inspection and rating program in North America. Most hoteliers, restaurateurs, and industry observers favorably regard the rigor of our inspection program and understand the prestige and benefits that come with receiving a Mobil Travel Guide star rating.

The Mobil Travel Guide process of rating each establishment includes:

- Unannounced facility inspections
- Incognito service evaluations for Mobil Four- and Five-Star properties
- A review of unsolicited comments from the general public
- Senior management oversight

For each property, more than 450 attributes, including cleanliness, physical facilities, employee attitude, and courtesy, are measured and evaluated to produce a mathematically derived score, which is then blended with the other elements to form an overall score. These quantifiable scores allow comparative analysis among properties and form the basis that Mobil Travel Guide uses to assign its Mobil One- to Five-Star ratings.

This process focuses largely on guest expectations, guest experience, and consistency of service, not just physical facilities and amenities. It is fundamentally a relative rating system that rewards those properties that continually strive for and achieve excellence each year. Indeed, the very best properties are consistently raising the bar for those that wish to compete with them. These properties proactively respond to consumers' needs even in today's uncertain times.

Only facilities that meet Mobil Travel Guide's standards earn the privilege of being listed in the guide. Deteriorating, poorly managed establishments are deleted. A Mobil Travel Guide listing constitutes a positive quality recommendation; every listing is an accolade, a recognition of achievement. Our One- to Five-Star rating system highlights its level of service. Extensive in-house research is constantly underway to determine new additions to our lists.

- The Mobil Five-Star Award indicates that a property is one of the very best in the country and consistently provides gracious and courteous service, superlative quality in its facility, and a unique ambience. The lodgings and restaurants at the Five-Star level consistently and proactively respond to consumers' needs and continue their commitment to excellence, doing so with grace and perseverance.
- Also highly regarded is the Mobil Four-Star Award, which honors properties for outstanding achievement in overall facility and for providing very strong service levels in all areas. These award-winners provide a distinctive experience for the ever-demanding and sophisticated consumer.
- The Mobil Three-Star Award recognizes an excellent property that provides full services and amenities. This category ranges from exceptional hotels with limited services to elegant restaurants with a less-formal atmosphere.

○ A Mobil Two-Star property is a clean and comfortable establishment that has expanded amenities or a distinctive environment. A Two-Star property is an excellent place to stay or dine.

○ A Mobil One-Star property is limited in its amenities and services but focuses on providing a value experience while meeting travelers' expectations. The property can be expected to be clean, comfortable, and convenient.

Allow us to emphasize that we do not charge establishments for inclusion in our guides. We have no relationship with any of the businesses and attractions we list and act only as a consumer advocate. In essence, we do the investigative legwork so that you won't have to.

Keep in mind, too, that the hospitality business is ever-changing. Restaurants and lodgings—particularly small chains and standalone establishments—change management or even go out of business with surprising quickness. Although we make every effort to double-check information during our annual updates, we nevertheless recommend that you call ahead to make sure the place you've selected is still open and offers all the amenities you're looking for. We've provided phone numbers; when available, we also list fax numbers and Web site addresses.

We hope that your travels are enjoyable and relaxing and that our books help you get the most out of every trip you take. If any aspect of your accommodation, dining, or sightseeing experience motivates you to comment, please drop us a line. We depend a great deal on our readers' remarks, so you can be assured that we will read your comments and assimilate them into our research. General comments about our books are also welcome. You can write to us at Mobil Travel Guide, 1460 Renaissance Drive, Suite 401, Park Ridge, IL 60068, or send an e-mail to info@mobiltravelguide.com.

Take your Mobil Travel Guide books along on every trip you take. We're confident that you'll be pleased with their convenience, ease of use, and breadth of dependable coverage.

Happy travels!

How to Use This Book

The Mobil Travel Guide travel planners are designed for ease of use. The book begins with a general introduction that provides a geographical and historical orientation to the state and gives basic statewide tourist information, from climate to popular highways to seatbelt laws. The remainder is devoted to travel destinations within the state—mainly cities and towns, but also national and state parks and tourist areas—which are arranged alphabetically.

The following sections explain the wealth of information you'll find about those travel destinations: information about the area, things to see and do there, and where to stay and eat.

Maps and Map Coordinates

At the front of this book in the full-color section, we have provided state maps as well as maps of selected larger cities to help you find your way around once you leave the highway. You'll find a key to the map symbols on the Contents page at the beginning of the map section.

Next to most cities and towns throughout the book, you'll find a set of map coordinates, such as C-2. These coordinates reference the maps at the front of this book and help you find the location you're looking for quickly and easily.

Destination Information

Because many travel destinations are close to other cities and towns where travelers might find additional attractions, accommodations, and restaurants, we've included cross-references to those cities and towns when it makes sense to do so. We also list addresses and phone numbers for travel information resources—usually the local chamber of commerce or office of tourism—as well as pertinent statistics and, in many cases, a brief introduction to the area.

Information about airports, ground transportation, and suburbs is included for large cities.

Driving and Walking Tours

The driving tours that we include for many states are usually day trips that make for interesting side excursions, although they can be longer. They offer you a way to get off the beaten path and visit an area that travelers often overlook. These trips frequently cover areas of natural beauty or historical significance.

Each walking tour focuses on a particularly interesting area of a city or town. Again, these tours can provide a break from everyday tourist attractions. The tours often include places to stop for meals or snacks.

What to See and Do

The Mobil Travel Guide offers information about nearly 20,000 museums, art galleries, amusement parks, historic sites, national and state parks, ski areas, and many other types of attractions. A white star on a black background ✪ signals that the attraction is a must-see—one of the best in the state. Because municipal parks, public tennis courts, swimming pools, and small educational institutions are common to most towns, they generally are not mentioned.

In an attraction's description, you'll find the months, days, and, in some cases, hours of operation; the address/directions, telephone number, and Web site (if there is one); and the admission price category. The following are the ranges we use for admission fees:

- ✪ **FREE**
- ✪ **$** = Up to $5
- ✪ **$$** = $5.01-$10
- ✪ **$$$** = $10.01-$15
- ✪ **$$$$** = Over $15

Special Events

Special events are either annual events that last only a short time, such as festivals and fairs, or longer, seasonal events such as horseracing, summer theater and concerts, and professional sports. The Mobil Travel Guide Special Events listings also include infrequently occurring occasions that mark certain dates or events, such as a centennial or other commemorative celebration.

Side Trips

We recognize that your travels don't always end where state lines fall, so we've included some side trips that technically fall outside the scope of this book but that travelers frequently visit when they're in this region. Nearby national park, major cities, and other major draws fall into this category. You'll find side trips for a particular area at the end of that state's city listings.

Lodging and Restaurant Listings

Lodgings and restaurants are usually listed under the city or town in which they are located. Make sure to check the related cities and towns that appear right beneath the city heading for additional options, especially if you're traveling to a major metropolitan area that includes many suburbs. In large cities, lodgings located within 5 miles of major commercial airports are listed under a separate "Airport Area" heading that follows the city section.

LODGINGS

Travelers have different wants and needs when it comes to accommodations. To help you pinpoint properties that meet your particular needs, each lodging property is classified by type according to the following characteristics:

⊙ **Motels/Motor Lodges.** These accommodations are in low-rise structures with rooms that are easily accessible to parking, which is usually free. Properties have small, functional lobbies, and guests enter their rooms from the outdoors. Service is often limited, and dining may not be offered in lower-rated motels. Shops and businesses are generally found only in higher-rated properties, as are bell staff, room service, and restaurants serving three meals daily.

⊙ **Hotels.** A hotel is an establishment that provides lodging in a clean, comfortable environment. Guests can expect private bathrooms as well as some measure of guest services, such as luggage assistance, room service, and daily maid service.

⊙ **Resorts.** A resort is an establishment that provides lodging in a facility that is typically located on a larger piece of land. Recreational activities are emphasized and often include golf, spa, and tennis. Guests can expect more than one food and beverage establishment on the property, which aims to provide a variety of food choices at a variety of price points.

⊙ **All Suites.** In an all suites property, guest accommodations consist of two rooms: a bedroom and a living room. Higher-rated properties offer facilities and services comparable to regular hotels.

⊙ **B&Bs/Small Inns.** The hotel alternative for those who prefer the comforts of home and a personal touch. It may be a structure of historic significance and often is located in an interesting setting. Breakfast is usually included and often is treated as a special occasion. Cocktails and refreshments may be served in the late afternoon or evening. Rooms are often individually decorated, but telephones, televisions, and private bathrooms may not be available in every room.

⊙ **Boutique Hotels.** Frequently a small hotel of fewer than 150 guest rooms, a boutique hotel is more about décor than about functionality and service. In many cases, the unique décor is trendsetting and hip, but don't let it fool you…there are, more often than not, inherent weaknesses in the facility with regard to size of the guest rooms, bathrooms, and so on. Services offered usually match those of a larger hotel but are done on a more personal and, often, more interesting manner.

⊙ **Guest Ranches.** Like resorts, guest ranches specialize in stays of three days or more. These lodgings also offer meal plans and extensive outdoor activities. Horseback riding is usually a feature; stables and trails are found on the ranch property, and trail rides and daily instruction are part of the program. Many guest ranches are working ranches, ranging from casual to rustic, and guests are encouraged to participate in ranch life. Eating is often family style and may include cookouts. Western saddles are assumed; phone ahead to inquire about English saddle availability.

⊙ **Extended Stay.** These hotels specialize in stays of three days or more and usually offer weekly room rates. Service is often limited, and dining may not be offered at lower-rated properties.

⊙ **Casino Hotels.** Casino hotels incorporate areas that offer games of chance such as blackjack, poker, and slot machines and are found only in states where gambling is legal. These hotels offer a wide range of services and amenities comparable to regular hotels.

Because most lodgings offer the following features and services, information about them does not appear in the listings unless exceptions exist:

⊙ Year-round operation with a single rate structure

⊙ Major credit cards accepted (note that Exxon or Mobil Corporation credit cards cannot be used to pay for room or other charges)

⊙ Air-conditioning and heat, often with individual room controls

⊙ Bathroom with tub and/or shower in each room

⊙ Cable television

⊙ Cots and cribs available

⊙ Daily maid service

⊙ Elevators

⊙ In-room telephones

Each lodging listing gives the name, address/location (when no street address is available), neighborhood and/or directions from downtown (in major cities), phone number(s), fax number, total number of guest rooms, and seasons open (if not year-round). Also included are details on business, luxury, recreational, and dining facilities on the property or nearby. A key to the symbols at the end of each listing can be found on the inside front cover of this book.

For every property, we also provide pricing information. Because lodging rates change frequently, we often opt to list a pricing category rather than specific prices; however, we provide specific room rates wherever possible. The pricing categories break down as follows:

- ☼ **$** = Up to $150
- ☼ **$$** = $151-$250
- ☼ **$$$** = $251-$350
- ☼ **$$$$** = $351 and up

All prices quoted by the Mobil Travel Guide are in effect at the time of publication; however, prices cannot be guaranteed. In some locations, short-term price variations may exist because of special events or holidays. Whenever possible, these price variations are noted. Certain resorts have complicated rate structures that vary with the time of year; always confirm rates when making your plans.

RESTAURANTS

All dining establishments listed in our books have a full kitchen and offer table service and a complete menu. Parking on or near the premises, in a lot or garage, is assumed. If parking is not available, we note that fact in the listing.

Each listing also gives the cuisine type, address (or directions if no street address is available), neighborhood and/or directions from downtown (in major cities), phone and fax numbers, Web site (if available), meals served, days of operation (if not open daily year-round), reservation policy, and pricing category or, whenever possible, specific à la carte entrée prices. We also indicate if a child's menu is offered. The price categories are defined as follows per diner and assume that you order an appetizer, entrée, and one drink:

- ☼ **$** = $15 and under
- ☼ **$$** = $16-$35
- ☼ **$$$** = $36-$85
- ☼ **$$$$** = $86 and up

QUALITY RATINGS

The Mobil Travel Guide has been rating lodgings and restaurants in the United States since the first edition was published in 1958. For years, the guide was the only source of such ratings, and it remains among the few guidebooks to rate restaurants across the country and in Canada.

All listed establishments have been inspected by experienced field representatives and/or evaluated by a senior staff member. Our ratings are based on detailed inspection reports of the individual properties, on written evaluations of staff members who stay and dine anonymously, and on an extensive review of reader comments. Rating categories reflect both the features a property offers and its quality in relation to similar establishments.

Here are the definitions for the star ratings for lodgings:

- ☼ ★ : A Mobil One-Star lodging is a limited-service hotel, motel, or inn that is considered a clean, comfortable, and reliable establishment.
- ☼ ★★ : A Mobil Two-Star lodging is considered a clean, comfortable, and reliable establishment that has expanded amenities, such as a full-service restaurant on the premises.
- ☼ ★★★ : A Mobil Three-Star lodging is well appointed, with a full-service restaurant and expanded amenities, such as a fitness center, golf course, tennis courts, 24-hour room service, and optional turndown service.
- ☼ ★★★★ : A Mobil Four-Star lodging provides a luxury experience with expanded amenities in a distinctive environment. Services may include, but are not limited to, automatic turndown service, 24-hour room service, and valet parking.
- ☼ ★★★★★ : A Mobil Five-Star lodging provides consistently superlative service in an exceptionally distinctive luxury environment, with expanded services. Attention to detail is evident throughout the hotel, resort, or inn, from bed linens to staff uniforms.

The Mobil Travel Guide star ratings for restaurants are defined as follows:

- ☼ ★ : A Mobil One-Star restaurant provides a distinctive experience through culinary specialty, local flair, or individual atmosphere.
- ☼ ★★ : A Mobil Two-Star restaurant serves fresh food in a clean setting with efficient service. Value is considered in this category, as is family friendliness.
- ☼ ★★★ : A Mobil Three-Star restaurant has good food, warm and skillful service, and enjoyable décor.
- ☼ ★★★★ : A Mobil Four-Star restaurant provides professional service, distinctive presentations, and wonderful food.
- ☼ ★★★★★ : A Mobil Five-Star restaurant offers one of few flawless dining experiences in the country. These establishments consistently provide their guests with exceptional food, superlative service, elegant décor, and exquisite presentations of each detail surrounding a meal.

TERMS AND ABBREVIATIONS IN LISTINGS

The following terms and abbreviations are used throughout the Mobil Travel Guide lodging and restaurant listings to indicate which amenities and services are available at each establishment. We've done our best to provide accurate and up-to-date information, but things do change, so if a particular feature is essential to you, please contact the establishment directly to make sure that it is available.

Complete meal Soup and/or salad, entrée, and dessert, plus a nonalcoholic beverage.

Continental breakfast Usually coffee and a roll or doughnut.

D Followed by a price, indicates the room rate for a double room—two people in one room in one or two beds (the charge may be higher for two double beds).

Each additional The extra charge for each additional person beyond the stated number of persons.

In-room modem link Every guest room has a connection for a modem that's separate from the main phone line.

Kitchen(s) A kitchen or kitchenette that contains a stove or microwave, sink, and refrigerator and is either part of the room or a separate, adjoining room. If the kitchen is not fully equipped, the listing will indicate "no equipt" or "some equipt."

Laundry service Either coin-operated laundry facilities or overnight valet service is available.

Luxury level A special section of a lodging, spanning at least an entire floor, that offers increased luxury accommodations. Management must provide no less than three of these four services: separate check-in and check-out, concierge, private lounge, and private elevator service (with key access). Complimentary breakfast and snacks are commonly offered.

Movies Prerecorded videos are available for rental or check-out.

Prix fixe A full, multicourse meal for a stated price; usually available at finer restaurants.

Valet parking An attendant is available to park and retrieve your car.

VCR VCRs are present in all guest rooms.

VCR available VCRs are available for hookup in guest rooms.

SPECIAL INFORMATION FOR TRAVELERS WITH DISABILITIES

The Mobil Travel Guide D symbol indicates establishments that are at least partially accessible to people with mobility problems. Our criteria for accessibility are unique to our publications. Please do not confuse them with the universal symbol for wheelchair accessibility.

When the D symbol follows a listing, the establishment is equipped with facilities to accommodate people using wheelchairs or crutches or otherwise needing easy access to doorways and rest rooms. Travelers with severe mobility problems or with hearing or visual impairments may or may not find the facilities they need. Always phone ahead to make sure that an establishment can meet your needs.

All lodgings bearing our D symbol have the following facilities:

- ISA-designated parking near access ramps
- Level or ramped entryways to buildings
- Swinging building entryway doors a minimum of 39 inches wide
- Public rest rooms on the main level with space to operate a wheelchair and handrails at commode areas
- Elevator(s) equipped with grab bars and lowered control buttons
- Restaurant(s) with accessible doorway(s), rest rooms with space to operate a wheelchair, and handrails at commode areas
- Guest room entryways that are at least 39 inches wide
- Low-pile carpet in rooms
- Telephones at bedside and in the bathroom
- Beds placed at wheelchair height
- Bathrooms with a minimum doorway width of 3 feet
- Bath with an open sink (no cabinet) and room to operate a wheelchair
- Handrails at commode areas and in the tub
- Wheelchair-accessible peepholes in room entry door
- Wheelchair-accessible closet rods and shelves

All restaurants bearing our D symbol offer the following facilities:

- ISA-designated parking beside access ramps
- Level or ramped front entryways to the building
- Tables that accommodate wheelchairs
- Main-floor rest rooms with an entryway that's at least 3 feet wide
- Rest rooms with space to operate a wheelchair and handrails at commode areas

Making the Most of Your Trip

A few hardy souls might look back with fondness on a trip during which the car broke down, leaving them stranded for three days, or a vacation that cost twice what it was supposed to. For most travelers, though, the best trips are those that are safe, smooth, and within budget. To help you make your trip the best it can be, we've assembled a few tips and resources.

Saving Money

ON LODGING

Many hotels and motels offer discounts—for senior citizens, business travelers, families, you name it. It never hurts to ask—politely, that is. Sometimes, especially in the late afternoon, desk clerks are instructed to fill beds, and you might be offered a lower rate or a nicer room to entice you to stay. Simply ask the reservation agent for the best rate available. Also, make sure to try both the toll-free number and the local number. You may be able to get a lower rate from one than the other.

Becoming a member of MobilCompanion will entitle you to discounted rates at many well-known hotels around the country. For more information, call 877/ 785-6788 or visit www.mobilcompanion.com.

Timing your trip right can cut your lodging costs as well. Look for bargains on stays over multiple nights, in the off-season, and on weekdays or weekends, depending on the location. Many hotels in major metropolitan areas, for example, have special weekend packages that offer considerable savings on rooms; they may include breakfast, cocktails, and dinner discounts.

Another way to save money is to choose accommodations that give you more than just a standard room. Rooms with kitchen facilities enable you to cook some meals yourself, reducing your restaurant costs. A suite might save money for two couples traveling together. Even hotel luxury levels can provide good value, as many include breakfast or cocktails in the price of a room.

State and city taxes, as well as special room taxes, can increase your room rate by as much as 25 percent per day. We are unable to include information about taxes in our listings, but we strongly urge you to ask about taxes when making reservations so that you understand the total cost of your lodgings before you book.

Watch out for telephone-usage charges that hotels frequently impose on long-distance, credit-card, and other calls. Before phoning from your room, read the information given to you at check-in, and then be sure to review your bill carefully when checking out. You won't be expected to pay for charges that the hotel didn't spell out. Consider using your cell phone if you have one; or, if public telephones are available in the hotel lobby, your cost savings may outweigh the inconvenience of using them.

Here are some additional ways to save on lodgings:

- Stay in B&B accommodations; they're generally less expensive than standard hotel rooms, and the complimentary breakfasts cut down on food costs.
- If you're traveling with children, find lodgings at which kids stay free.
- When visiting major cities, stay just outside the city limits; these rooms are usually less expensive than those in downtown locations.
- Consider visiting national parks during the low season, when prices of lodgings near the parks drop 25 percent or more.
- When calling a hotel, ask whether it is running any special promotions or if any discounts are available; many times reservationists are told not to volunteer deals unless specifically asked about them.
- Check for hotel packages; some offer nightly rates that include a rental car or discounts on major attractions.

ON DINING

There are several ways to get a less expensive meal at a more expensive restaurant. Early-bird dinners are popular in many parts of the country and offer considerable savings. If you're interested in sampling a Mobil Four- or Five-Star establishment, consider going at lunchtime. Although the prices are probably still relatively high at midday, they may be half of those at dinner, and you'll experience the same ambience, service, and cuisine.

As a member of MobilCompanion, you can enroll in iDine. This program earns you up to 20 percent cash back at more than 1,900 restaurants on meals purchased with the credit card you register; the rebate appears on your credit card bill. For more information about MobilCompanion and iDine, call 877/785-6788 or go to www.mobilcompanion.com.

ON ENTERTAINMENT

Although many national parks, monuments, seashores, historic sites, and recreation areas may be used free of charge, others charge an entrance fee (ranging from $1 to $6 per person or $5 to $20 per carload) and/or a usage fee for special services and facilities. If you plan to make several visits to national recreation areas, consider one of the following money-saving programs offered by the National Park Service:

- ✪ National Parks Pass. This annual pass is good for entrance to any national park that charges an entrance fee. If the park charges a per-vehicle fee, the pass holder and any accompanying passengers in a private noncommercial vehicle may enter. If the park charges a per-person fee, the pass applies to the holder's spouse, children, and parents as well as the holder. It is valid for entrance fees only; it does not cover parking, camping, or other fees. You can purchase a National Parks Pass in person at any national park where an entrance fee is charged; by mail from the National Park Foundation, PO Box 34108, Washington, DC 20043-4108; by calling 888/GO-PARKS; or at www.nationalparks.org. The cost is $50.

- ✪ Golden Eagle. When affixed to a National Parks Pass, this sticker, available to people who are between 17 and 61 years of age, extends coverage to sites managed by the US Fish and Wildlife Service, the US Forest Service, and the Bureau of Land Management. It is good until the National Parks Pass to which it is affixed expires and does not cover usage fees. You can purchase one at National Park Service, Fish and Wildlife Service, and Bureau of Land Management fee stations. The cost is $15.

- ✪ Golden Age Passport. Available to citizens and permanent US residents 62 and older, this passport is a lifetime entrance permit to fee-charging national recreation areas. The fee exemption extends to those accompanying the permit holder in a private noncommercial vehicle or, in the case of walk-in facilities, to the holder's spouse and children. The passport also entitles the holder to a 50 percent discount on federal usage fees charged in park areas, but not on concessions. Golden Age Passports must be obtained in person and are available at most National Park Service units that charge an entrance fee. The applicant must show proof of age, such as a driver's license or birth certificate (Medicare cards are not acceptable proof). The cost is $10.

- ✪ Golden Access Passport. Issued to citizens and permanent US residents who are physically disabled or visually impaired, this passport is a free lifetime entrance permit to fee-charging national recreation areas. The fee exemption extends to those accompanying the permit holder in a private noncommercial vehicle or, in the case of walk-in facilities, to the holder's spouse and children. The passport also entitles the holder to a 50 percent discount on usage fees charged in park areas, but not on concessions. Golden Access Passports must be obtained in person and are available at most National Park Service units that charge an entrance fee. Proof of eligibility to receive federal benefits (under programs such as Disability Retirement, Compensation for Military Service-Connected Disability, and the Coal Mine Safety and Health Act) is required, or an affidavit must be signed attesting to eligibility.

A money-saving move in several large cities is to purchase a CityPass. If you plan to visit several museums and other major attractions, CityPass is a terrific option because it gets you into several sites for one substantially reduced price. Currently, CityPass is available in Boston, Chicago, Hollywood, New York, Philadelphia, San Francisco, Seattle, and southern California (which includes Disneyland, Sea World, and the San Diego Zoo). For more information or to buy one, call 888/330-5008 or visit www.citypass.net. You can also buy a CityPass from any participating CityPass attraction.

Here are some additional ways to save on entertainment and shopping:

- ✪ Check with your hotel's concierge for various coupons and special offers; they often have two-for-one tickets for area attractions and coupons for discounts at area stores and restaurants.

- ✪ Purchase same-day concert or theater tickets for half-price through the local cheap-tickets outlet, such as TKTS in New York City or Hot Tix in Chicago.

- ✪ Visit museums on their free or "by donation" days, when you can pay what you wish rather than a specific admission fee.

- ✪ Save receipts from purchases in Canada; visitors to Canada can get a rebate on federal taxes and some provincial sales taxes.

ON TRANSPORTATION

Transportation is a big part of any vacation budget. Here are some ways to reduce your costs:

- ✪ If you're renting a car, shop early over the Internet; you can book a car during the low season for less, even if you'll be using it in the high season.

- ✪ Rental car discounts are often available if you rent for one week or longer and reserve in advance.

- ✪ Get the best gas mileage out of your vehicle by making sure that it's properly tuned up and keeping your tires properly inflated. If your tires need to be replaced, you can save money on a new set of Michelins by becoming a member of MobilCompanion.

○ Travel at moderate speeds on the open road; higher speeds require more gasoline.

○ Fill the tank before you return your rental car; rental companies charge to refill the tank and do so at prices of up to 50 percent more than at local gas stations.

○ Make a checklist of travel essentials and purchase them before you leave; don't get stuck buying expensive sunscreen at your hotel or overpriced film at the aiport.

FOR SENIOR CITIZENS

Look for the senior-citizen discount symbol **SC** in this book's lodging and restaurant listings. Always call ahead to confirm that a discount is being offered, and be sure to carry proof of age. At places not listed in this book, it never hurts to ask if a senior-citizen discount is offered. Additional information for mature travelers is available from the American Association of Retired Persons (AARP), 601 E St NW, Washington, DC 20049; phone 202/434-2277; www.aarp.org.

Tipping

Tips are expressions of appreciation for good service. However, you are never obligated to tip if you receive poor service.

IN HOTELS

○ Door attendants usually get $1 for hailing a cab.

○ Bell staff expect $2 per bag.

○ Concierges are tipped according to the service they perform. Tipping is not mandatory when you've asked for suggestions on sightseeing or restaurants or for help in making dining reservations. However, a tip of $5 is appropriate when a concierge books you a table at a restaurant known to be difficult to get into. For obtaining theater or sporting event tickets, $5 to $10 is expected.

○ Maids should be tipped $1 to $2 per day. Hand your tip directly to the maid, or leave it with a note saying that the money has been left expressly for the maid.

IN RESTAURANTS

Before tipping, carefully review your check for any gratuity or service charge that is already included in your bill. If you're in doubt, ask your server.

○ Coffee shop and counter service waitstaff usually receive 15 percent of the bill, before sales tax.

○ In full-service restaurants, tip 18 percent of the bill, before sales tax.

○ In fine restaurants, where gratuities are shared among a larger staff, 18 to 20 percent is appropriate.

○ In most cases, the maitre d' is tipped only if the service has been extraordinary, and only on the way out. At upscale properties in major metropolitan areas, $20 is the minimum.

○ If there is a wine steward, tip $20 for exemplary service and beyond, or more if the wine was decanted or the bottle was very expensive.

○ Tip $1 to $2 per coat at the coat check.

AT AIRPORTS

Curbside luggage handlers expect $1 per bag. Car-rental shuttle drivers who help with your luggage appreciate a $1 or $2 tip.

Staying Safe

The best way to deal with emergencies is to avoid them in the first place. However, unforeseen situations do happen, so you should be prepared for them.

IN YOUR CAR

Before you head out on a road trip, make sure that your car has been serviced and is in good working order. Change the oil, check the battery and belts, make sure that your windshield washer fluid is full and your tires are properly inflated (which can also improve your gas mileage). Other inspections recommended by the vehicle's manufacturer should also be made.

Next, be sure you have the tools and equipment needed to deal with a routine breakdown:

○ Jack

○ Spare tire

○ Lug wrench

○ Repair kit

○ Emergency tools

○ Jumper cables

○ Spare fan belt

○ Fuses

○ Flares and/or reflectors

○ Flashlight

○ First-aid kit

○ In winter, a windshield scraper and snow shovel

Many emergency supplies are sold in special packages that include the essentials you need to stay safe in the event of a breakdown.

Also bring all appropriate and up-to-date documentation—licenses, registration, and insurance cards—and know what your insurance covers. Bring an extra set of keys, too, just in case.

En route, always buckle up! In most states, wearing a seatbelt is required by law.

If your car does break down, do the following:
- Get out of traffic as soon as possible—pull well off the road.
- Raise the hood and turn on your emergency flashers or tie a white cloth to the roadside door handle or antenna.
- Stay in your car.
- Use flares or reflectors to keep your vehicle from being hit.

If you are a member of MobilCompanion, remember that En Route Support is always ready to help when you need it. Just give us a call and we'll locate and dispatch an emergency roadside service to assist you, as well as provide you with significant savings on the service.

IN YOUR HOTEL OR MOTEL

Chances are slim that you will encounter a hotel or motel fire, but you can protect yourself by doing the following:
- Once you've checked in, make sure that the smoke detector in your room is working properly.
- Find the property's fire safety instructions, usually posted on the inside of the room door.
- Locate the fire extinguishers and at least two fire exits.
- Never use an elevator in a fire.

For personal security, use the peephole in your room door and make sure that anyone claiming to be a hotel employee can show proper identification. Call the front desk if you feel threatened at any time.

PROTECTING AGAINST THEFT

To guard against theft wherever you go:
- Don't bring anything of more value than you need.
- If you do bring valuables, leave them at your hotel rather than in your car.
- If you bring something very expensive, lock it in a safe. Many hotels put one in each room; others will store your valuables in the hotel's safe.
- Don't carry more money than you need. Use traveler's checks and credit cards or visit cash machines to withdraw more cash when you run out.

For Travelers with Disabilities

To get the kind of service you need and have a right to expect, don't hesitate when making a reservation to question the management about the availability of accessible rooms, parking, entrances, restaurants, lounges, or any other facilities that are important to you, and confirm what is meant by "accessible."

The Mobil Travel Guide D symbol indicates establishments that are at least partially accessible to people with special mobility needs (people using wheelchairs or crutches or otherwise needing easy access to buildings and rooms). Keep in mind that our criteria for accessibility are unique to our publication and should not be confused with the universal symbol for wheelchair accessibility. Further information about these criteria can be found in the earlier section "How to Use This Book."

A thorough listing of published material for travelers with disabilities is available from the Disability Bookshop, Twin Peaks Press, Box 129, Vancouver, WA 98666; phone 360/694-2462; disabilitybookshop. virtualave.net. Another reliable organization is the Society for Accessible Travel & Hospitality (SATH), 347 Fifth Ave, Suite 610, New York, NY 10016; phone 212/447-7284; www.sath.org.

Border Crossing Regulations

Proof of citizenship—a passport or a certified birth certificate—is required for travel into Mexico. A driver's license is not acceptable. Aliens must carry their alien registration cards, and naturalized citizens should carry their naturalization certificates. If you are planning to stay for more than 24 hours or if you are a naturalized citizen or a resident alien, get a copy of current border regulations from the nearest Mexican consulate or tourism office before crossing, and make sure that you understand them. A helpful booklet, *Know Before You Go*, may be obtained free of charge from the nearest office of the US Customs Service.

If you take your car for the day, you may find it more convenient to unload all baggage before crossing than to go through a thorough customs inspection upon your return. You will not be permitted to bring any plants, fruits, or vegetables into the United States. Federal regulations permit each US citizen 21 years of age or older to bring back 1 quart of alcoholic beverage duty free. However, state regulations vary; check locally before entering Mexico. New regulations may be issued at any time.

Your automobile insurance is not valid in Mexico; for short visits, get a one-day policy before crossing. US currency is accepted in all border cities. Mexico does not observe Daylight Savings Time.

For more information about traveling to Mexico, including safety information, look for the US State Department's Consular Information Sheet at travel.state.gov/mexico.html, or request it by fax by calling 202/647-3000.

Important Toll-Free Numbers and Online Information

Hotels and Motels

Adams Mark 800/444-2326
www.adamsmark.com
AmericInn 800/634-3444
www.americinn.com
AmeriHost Inn Hotels 800/434-5800
www.amerihostinn.com
Amerisuites 800/833-1516
www.amerisuites.com
Baymont Inns 877/BAYMONT
www.baymontinns.com
Best Inns & Suites 800/237-8466
www.bestinn.com
Best Value Inns 888/315-BEST
www.bestvalueinn.com
Best Western International 800/WESTERN
www.bestwestern.com
Budget Host Inn 800/BUDHOST
www.budgethost.com
Candlewood Suites 888/CANDLEWOOD
www.candlewoodsuites.com
Clarion Hotels 800/252-7466
www.choicehotels.com
Comfort Inns and Suites 800/252-7466
www.choicehotels.com
Country Hearth Inns 800/848-5767
www.countryhearth.com
Country Inns & Suites 800/456-4000
www.countryinns.com
Courtyard by Marriott 888/236-2437
www.courtyard.com
Cross Country Inn 800/621-1429
www.crosscountryinns.com
Crowne Plaza Hotels and Resorts 800/227-6963
www.crowneplaza.com
Days Inn 800/544-8313
www.daysinn.com
Delta Hotels 800/268-1133
www.deltahotels.com
Destination Hotels & Resorts 800/434-7347
www.destinationhotels.com
Doubletree Hotels 800/222-8733
www.doubletree.com
Drury Inns 800/378-7946
www.druryinn.com
Econolodge 800/553-2666
www.econolodge.com
Economy Inns of America 800/826-0778
www.innsofamerica.com

Embassy Suites 800/362-2779
www.embassysuites.com
ExelInns of America 800/FOREXEL
www.exelinns.com
Extended StayAmerica 800/EXTSTAY
www.extstay.com
Fairfield Inn by Mariott 800/228-2800
www.fairfieldinn.com
Fairmont Hotels 800/441-1414
www.fairmont.com
Four Points by Sheraton 888/625-5144
www.starwood.com
Four Seasons 800/545-4000
www.fourseasons.com
Hampton Inn/Hampton Inn and Suites 800/426-7866
www.hamptoninn.com
Hard Rock Hotels, Resorts and Casinos 800/HRDROCK
www.hardrock.com
Harrah's Entertainment 800/HARRAHS
www.harrahs.com
Harvey Hotels 800/922-9222
www.bristolhotels.com
Hawthorn Suites 800/527-1133
www.hawthorn.com
Hilton Hotels and Resorts (US) 800/774-1500
www.hilton.com
Holiday Inn Express 800/HOLIDAY
www.sixcontinentshotel.com
Holiday Inn Hotels and Resorts 800/465-4329
www.holiday-inn.com
Homestead Studio Suites 888/782-9473
www.stayhsd.com
Homewood Suites 800/225-5466
www.homewoodsuites.com
Howard Johnson 800/406-1411
www.hojo.com
Hyatt 800/633-7313
www.hyatt.com
Ian Schrager . . . .
www.inaschragerhotels.com
Inter-Continental 888/567-8725
www.intercontinental.com
Joie de Vivre 800/738-7477
www.jdvhospitality.com
Kimpton Hotels 888/546-7866
www.kimptongroup.com
Knights Inn 800/843-5644
www.knightsinn.com

La Quinta 800/531-5900
www.laquinta.com
Le Meridien 800/543-4300
www.lemeridien.com
Leading Hotels of the World 800/223-6800
www.lhw.com
Loews Hotels 800/235-6397
www.loewshotels.com
MainStay Suites 800/660-6246
www.choicehotels.com
Mandarin Oriental 800/526-6566
www.mandarin-oriental.com
Marriott Conference Centers 800/453-0309
www.conferencecenters.com
Marriott Hotels, Resorts, and Suites 888/236-2427
www.marriott.com
Marriott Vacation Club International 800/845-5279
www.marriott.com/vacationclub
Microtel Inns & Suites 800/771-7171
www.microtelinn.com
Millennium & Copthorne Hotels 866/866-8086
www.mill-cop.com
Motel 6 . . . . .800/4MOTEL6
www.motel6.com
Omni Hotels 800/843-6664
www.omnihotels.com
Pan Pacific Hotels and Resorts 800/327-8585
www.panpac.com
Park Inn & Park Plaza 888/201-1801
www.parkhtls.com
The Peninsula Group . . . .
www.peninsula.com
Preferred Hotels & Resorts Worldwide 800/323-7500
www.preferredhotels.com
Quality Inn 800/228-5151
www.qualityinn.com
Radisson Hotels 800/333-3333
www.radisson.com
Raffles International Hotels and Resorts 800/637-9477
www.raffles.com
Ramada International 888/298-2054
www.ramada.com
Ramada Plazas, Limiteds, and Inns 800/2RAMADA
www.ramadahotels.com
Red Lion Inns 800/733-5466
www.redlion.com
Red Roof Inns 800/733-7663
www.redroof.com
Regal Hotels 800/222-8888
www.regal-hotels.com
Regent International 800/545-4000
www.regenthotels.com
Relais & Chateaux 800/735-2478
www.relaischateaux.com

Renaissance Hotels 888/236-2427
www.renaissancehotels.com
Residence Inns 888/236-2427
www.residenceinn.com
Ritz-Carlton 800/241-3333
www.ritzcarlton.com
Rockresorts 888/FORROCKS
www.rockresorts.com
Rodeway Inns 800/228-2000
www.rodeway.com
Rosewood Hotels & Resorts 888/767-3966
www.rosewood-hotels.com
Scottish Inn 800/251-1962
www.bookroomsnow.com
Select Inn 800/641-1000
www.selectinn.com
Sheraton 888/625-5144
www.sheraton.com
Shilo Inns 800/222-2244
www.shiloinns.com
Shoney's Inns 800/552-4667
www.shoneysinn.com
Signature/Jameson Inns 800/822-5252
www.jamesoninns.com
Sleep Inns 800/453-3746
www.sleepinn.com
Small Luxury Hotels of the World 800/525-4800
www.slh.com
Sofitel 800/763-4835
www.sofitel.com
SpringHill Suites 888/287-9400
www.springhillsuites.com
SRS Worldhotels 800/223-5652
www.srs-worldhotels.com
St. Regis Luxury Collection 888/625-5144
www.stregis.com
Staybridge Suites by Holiday Inn 800/238-8000
www.staybridge.com
Summerfield Suites by Wyndham 800/833-4353
www.summerfieldsuites.com
Summit International 800/457-4000
www.summithotels.com
Super 8 Motels 800/800-8000
www.super8.com
The Sutton Place Hotels 866/378-8866
www.suttonplace.com
Swissotel 800/637-9477
www.swissotel.com
TownePlace Suites 800/257-3000
www.towneplace.com
Travelodge 800/578-7878
www.travelodge.com
Universal 800/23LOEWS
www.loewshotel.com

Vagabond Inns 800/522-1555
www.vagabondinns.com
W Hotels 888/625-5144
www.whotels.com
Wellesley Inn and Suites 800/444-8888
www.wellesleyinnandsuites.com
WestCoast Hotels 800/325-4000
www.westcoasthotels.com
Westin Hotels & Resorts 800/937-8461
www.westin.com
Wingate Inns 800/228-1000
www.wingateinns.com
Woodfin Suite Hotels 800/966-3346
www.woodfinsuitehotels.com
Wyndham Hotels & Resorts 800/996-3426
www.wyndham

Airlines

Air Canada 888/247-2262
www.aircanada.ca
Alaska 800/252-7522
www.alaskaair.com
American 800/433-7300
www.aa.com
America West 800/235-9292
www.americawest.com
ATA . . . . : 800/435-9282
www.ata.com
British Airways 800/247-9297
www.british-airways.com
Continental 800/523-3273
www.flycontinental.com
Delta 800/221-1212
www.delta-air.com
Island Air 800/323-3345
www.islandair.com
Mesa 800/637-2247
www.mesa-air.com
Northwest 800/225-2525
www.nwa.com
Southwest 800/435-9792
www.southwest.com
United 800/241-6522
www.ual.com
US Airways 800/428-4322
www.usairways.com

Car Rentals

Advantage 800/777-5500
www.arac.com
Alamo 800/327-9633
www.goalamo.com
Allstate 800/634-6186
www.bnm.com/as.htm

Avis 800/831-2847
www.avis.com
Budget 800/527-0700
www.budgetrentacar.com
Dollar 800/800-4000
www.dollarcar.com
Enterprise 800/325-8007
www.pickenterprise.com
Hertz 800/654-3131
www.hertz.com
National 800/227-7368
www.nationalcar.com
Payless 800/729-5377
www.800-payless.com
Rent-A-Wreck.com 800/535-1391
www.rent-a-wreck.com
Sears 800/527-0770
www.budget.com
Thrifty 800/847-4389
www.thrifty.com

Four-Star and Five-Star Establishments in the Southwest

Arizona
★★★★ Lodgings
The Boulders Resort and Golden Door® Spa, *Carefree*
Four Seasons Resort Scottsdale at Troon North, *Scottsdale*
The Phoenician, *Scottsdale*
The Ritz-Carlton, *Phoenix*

★★★★ Restaurants
Acacia, *Scottsdale*
Arizona Kitchen, *Litchfield Park*
Golden Swan, *Scottsdale*
The Gold Room, *Tucson*
Mary Elaine's, *Scottsdale*
The Ventana Room, *Tucson*

Colorado
★★★★★ Lodgings
The Broadmoor, *Colorado Springs*
The Little Nell, *Aspen*

★★★★ Lodgings
The Brown Palace Hotel, *Denver*
C Lazy U Ranch, *Granby*
The Ritz-Carlton, Bachelor Gulch, *Avon*
The St. Regis, Aspen, *Aspen*
Tall Timber Resort, *Durango*
Vista Verde Guest and Ski Ranch, *Steamboat Springs*

★★★★ Restaurants
Flagstaff House Restaurant, *Boulder*
Kevin Taylor Restaurant, *Denver*
Mirabelle at Beaver Creek, *Vail*
Montagna, *Aspen*
Penrose Room, *Colorado Springs*
Q's, *Boulder*
Renaissance, *Aspen*
Tante Louise, *Denver*

Nevada
★★★★ Lodgings
Bellagio Las Vegas, *Las Vegas*
Four Seasons Hotel, *Las Vegas*
The Venetian Resort Hotel Casino, *Las Vegas*

★★★★ Restaurants
Aqua, *Las Vegas*
Aureole, *Las Vegas*
Lutece, *Las Vegas*
Nobu, *Las Vegas*
Picasso, *Las Vegas*
Renoir, *Las Vegas*

New Mexico
★★★★ Lodgings
Inn of the Anasazi, *Santa Fe*

★★★★ Restaurants
Geronimo, *Santa Fe*

Utah
★★★★ Lodgings
The Grand America Hotel, *Salt Lake City*
Stein Eriksen Lodge, *Park City*

★★★★ Restaurants
Riverhorse Cafe, *Park City*

Arizona

This rapidly growing state has more than tripled its population since 1940. Its irrigated farms grow citrus fruits, cotton, vegetables, and grain on lush green lands that contrast sharply with the surrounding desert. It also produces 60 percent of the nation's copper.

As a vacation state, its progress has been spectacular. In winter, the areas around Phoenix, Tucson, and Yuma offer sunshine, relaxation, and informal Western living. Air-conditioning and swimming pools make year-round living pleasant. In summer, the northern mountains, cool forests, spectacular canyons, trout streams, and lakes offer a variety of vacation activities, including hunting and fishing camps, ghost and mining towns, meadows filled with wildflowers, intriguing ancient Native American villages, cliff dwellings, and dude ranches.

Francisco Vasquez de Coronado crossed the area in 1540 on his ill-fated search for the non-existent gold of Cibola. Grizzled prospectors panned for gold in mountain streams and hit pay dirt. The missions built by Father Kino and his successors date back as far as 1692. Irrigation ditches, built by the Hohokam people hundreds of years earlier, have been incorporated into modern systems.

The state has 23 reservations and one of the largest Native American populations in the United States. More than half of the Native American population is Navajo. Craft specialties include basketry, pottery, weaving, jewelry, and kachina dolls.

Arizona is a state of contrasts. It has modern and prehistoric civilizations, mountains, deserts, and modern agriculture. Arizona offers fascinating adventures for everyone.

When to Go/Climate

We recommend visiting Arizona in the spring or fall, when the temperatures are milder and the heavy tourist traffic is over.

Population: 5,130,632
Area: 113,642 square miles
Elevation: 70-12,633 feet
Peak: Humphreys Peak (Coconino County)
Entered Union: February 14, 1912 (48th state)
Capital: Phoenix
Motto: God enriches
Nickname: Grand Canyon State
Flower: Saguaro (sah-WAH-ro) Cactus Blossom
Bird: Cactus Wren
Tree: Palo Verde
Time Zone: Mountain
Website: www.arizonaguide.com
Fun Facts:
  Among all the states, Arizona has the largest percentage of its land set aside and designated as Indian lands.

AVERAGE HIGH/LOW TEMPERATURES (°F)

Flagstaff

Jan 42/15	May 67/33	Sept 74/41
Feb 45/18	June 78/41	Oct 63/31
Mar 49/21	July 82/51	Nov 51/22
Apr 58/27	Aug 79/49	Dec 43/16

Phoenix

Jan 66/49	May 94/64	Sept 98/73
Feb 71/45	June 104/73	Oct 88/61
Mar 76/49	July 106/81	Nov 75/49
Apr 85/55	Aug 104/79	Dec 66/42

Parks and Recreation

Water-related activities, hiking, riding, various other sports, picnicking, camping, and visitor centers are available at all parks. There is a $5/car day-use fee at state parks; $45 and $75 annual day-use permits are available. Camping costs $10-$16/day. Arizona also has 9 state historic parks ($3-$6; guided tours

Calendar Highlights

JANUARY

Fiesta Bowl *(Tempe). ASU Sun Devil Stadium. Phone 480/350-0900.* College football.

Native American Festival *(Litchfield Park). Phone West Valley Fine Arts Council 623/935-6384.* Approximately 100 Native American craft vendors. Native American dancing and other authentic entertainment.

Touchstone Energy Tucson Open *(Tucson). Omni Tucson National Golf Resort & Spa and The Gallery Golf Club. Phone 800/882-7660.* $3-million tournament featuring top pros.

FEBRUARY

Winter Fest *(Flagstaff). Phone 800/842-7293.* Features art contest and exhibit, theater performances, workshops, sled dog and other races, and games; Winterfaire with arts and crafts; entertainment.

Arabian Horse Show *(Scottsdale). WestWorld. Phone 480/515-1500.* The largest Arabian horse show in the world. More than 2,000 champion horses. Barn parties and more than 300 commercial vendors.

Arizona Renaissance Festival *(Apache Junction). Phone 520/463-2700.* Hundreds of participants enjoy music, theater, crafts exhibits, and games. Concessions. Jousting tournament at King's Jousting Arena.

MARCH

Spring Festival of the Arts *(Tempe). Downtown. Phone Mill Avenue Merchants Association 480/967-4877.* Artists' exhibits, food, entertainment, family activities.

SEPTEMBER

Southwestern Navajo Nation Fair *(Dilkon). Navajo Nation Fairgrounds. Phone 520/657-3376.* Navajo traditional song and dance; Inter-tribal powwow; All-Indian Rodeo; parade, concerts, exhibits.

Sedona Jazz on the Rocks *(Sedona). Phone 520/282-1985.* More than 5,000 people attend this outdoor jazz festival, featuring internationally renowned artists.

OCTOBER

Arizona State Fair *(Phoenix). State Fairgrounds. Phone 602/252-6771.*

DECEMBER

Tostitos Fiesta Bowl Block Party *(Tempe). Phone 480/784-4444.* Includes games, rides, entertainment, pep rally, fireworks, and food.

---

additional fee). For further information, contact Arizona State Parks, Public Information Officer, 1300 W Washington, Phoenix 85007; 602/542-1996.

FISHING AND HUNTING

Both are excellent in a number of sections of the state. Nonresident fishing licenses: 1-day (except Colorado River), $12.50; 5-day, $26; 4-month, $37.50; general, $51.50; Colorado River, all species, $42.50; trout stamp, $49.50. Urban fishing (for 14 lakes in 6 cities), $16. Inquire for fees to fish on Native American reservations. Nonresident hunting licenses: 3-day small game, $38; general, $85.50. Tags cost from $50.50 for turkey to $3,755 for buffalo. Permits for most big-game species available by drawing only. Combination nonresident licenses (fishing and hunting), $177.50 (includes a trout stamp). Fees subject to change. For updated information, contact the Arizona Game & Fish Department, 2222 W Greenway Rd, Phoenix 85023; 602/942-3000.

Driving Information

Safety belts are mandatory for all persons in the front seat of a vehicle. Children under 4 years or under 40 pounds in weight must be in approved safety seats anywhere in the vehicle. For further information, phone 602/223-2000.

INTERSTATE HIGHWAY SYSTEM

Use the following list as a guide to access interstate highways in Arizona. Always consult a map to confirm driving routes.

Highway Number	Cities/Towns within ten miles
Interstate 8	Casa Grande, Gila Bend, Yuma
Interstate 10	Casa Grande, Chandler, Glendale, Litchfield Park, Mesa, Phoenix, Scottsdale, Tempe, Tucson, Willcox

YOU'VE SEEN THE GRAND CANYON—NOW WHAT?

This loop drive, a side trip for visitors to the South Rim of Grand Canyon National Park, combines scenic beauty with archeological, historical, geologic, and scientific sites. It can be done in one full day or divided into a day and a half with an overnight stop in Flagstaff.

From Grand Canyon Village head south on AZ 64/US 180, turning southeast on US 180 at Valle for a slow but beautiful drive through the San Francisco Mountains. Those interested in the history of the area, including prehistoric peoples and more recent American Indians, will want to stop at the Museum of Northern Arizona. Then continue along US 180 to the turnoff to Lowell Observatory, which has been the site of many important astronomical discoveries since its founding in 1894. Guided tours of the facilities are offered, and there's a public observatory. Kids especially like the interactive displays in the exhibit hall and the Pluto Walk, a trip through the Solar System.

You are now on the north edge of Flagstaff, and the city is a good spot to spend the night. Flagstaff's top attractions include Riordan Mansion State Historic Park, where you'll step back into the early 20th century to the rustic elegance of the home of two wealthy brothers, Tim and Mike Riordan, who were very successful in the timber industry. Actually two homes in one large log building, the mansion is somewhat unique among historic homes in that it contains practically all of its original furnishings—the exact pieces bought by the Riordan brothers and their wives (also two siblings) in 1904. The mansion was constructed and then furnished in American Arts and Crafts style, also called Craftsman, a style of furniture that was simple, well-made, and durable.

From Flagstaff go east on I-40, and take the turnoff to Walnut Canyon National Monument to see dozens of small cliff dwellings built by the Sinagua people some 800 years ago. You'll explore the monument on two trails. One is a fairly easy walk along a mesa-top; the other is a bit more strenuous, but provides a much closer look at the cliff dwellings as it drops about 400 feet into Walnut Canyon.

Leaving the monument, head back toward Flagstaff on I-40 and go north on US 89 to the Sunset Crater Volcano/ Wupatki national monuments loop road, where you'll find an extinct volcano, fields of lava rock, and ruins of prehistoric stone pueblos. Wupatki National Monument's main attraction is Wupatki Pueblo, a 100-room dwelling, three stories high in places, built in the 12th century by the Sinaguans. This handsome apartment house was constructed of red sandstone slabs, blocks of pale beige limestone, and chunks of brown basalt, cemented together with clay. Nearby, Sunset Crater Volcano National Monument offers an intimate look at a dormant volcano, with its rugged landscape of jet black basalt, twisted into myriad shapes ranging from humorous to grotesque. Sunset Crater's primary eruption was in the winter of 1064-1065, and archeologists continue to speculate as to how this tremendous event affected the people who lived in this area at the time, primarily the Sinagua at nearby Wupatki and Walnut Canyon.

After rejoining US 89, continue north into the Navajo Reservation and the community of Cameron, with the historic but still operating Cameron Trading Post, which sells museum-quality items as well as more affordable rugs, baskets, jewelry, and other American Indian crafts. From Cameron, head west on AZ 64 back into the national park. **(Approximately 215 miles)**

Interstate 17	Cottonwood, Flagstaff, Glendale, Phoenix, Scottsdale, Sedona, Tempe
Interstate 19	Nogales, Tucson
Interstate 40	Flagstaff, Holbrook, Kingman, Seligman, Williams, Winslow

Additional Visitor Information

Arizona Highways is an excellent monthly magazine; contact 2039 W Lewis Ave, Phoenix 85009. Several informative booklets may be obtained from the Arizona Office of Tourism, 2702 N 3rd St, Suite 4015, Phoenix 85004; phone 602/230-7733 or 888/520-3434.

Bisbee (I-6)

See also Douglas, Sierra Vista, Tombstone

Founded 1880 **Pop** 6,090 **Elev** 5,400 ft **Area code** 520 **Zip** 85603

Information Greater Bisbee Chamber of Commerce, 7 Main St, Box BA; 520/432-5421

Nestled in the foothills of the Mule Mountains of southeastern Arizona, Bisbee once was a tough mining town known as "Queen of the Copper Camps." Today, Bisbee is rich in architecture and culture with many art galleries, period hotels, and bed and breakfasts.

What to See and Do

Bisbee Mining and Historical Museum. *5 Copper Queen Plaza. Phone 520/432-7071; 520/432-7848.* Housed in the 1897 office building of the Copper Queen Consolidated Mining Company. Depicts early development of this urban center through displays on mining, minerals, social history, and period offices; historical photographs. Shattuck Memorial Research Library. (Daily; closed Jan 1, Thanksgiving, Dec 25) 207B Youngblood Hill. Also operates Muheim Heritage House (early 1900s). (Fri-Tues) **$$**

Bisbee Restoration Association & Historical Museum. *37 Main St. Phone 520/432-4106; 520/432-2386.* Local historical and pioneer artifacts; Native American relics. (Mon-Sat; closed holidays) **DONATION**

Mine tours. *118 Arizona St. On US 80 near Old Bisbee. For information on all tours, phone 520/432-2071.* The tours include

Lavender Pit. *37 Main St.* A 340-acre open-pit copper mine, now inactive. Approximately one-hour van tour of surface mine and historic district (daily; closed Thanksgiving, Dec 25). Lavender Viewpoint (daily; free). **$$$**

Queen Mine. *118 Arizona St (85603).* Approximately one-hour guided tour on mine train; takes visitors 1,800 feet into mine tunnel. Mine temperature 47°F-49°F; jacket recommended. (Daily; closed Thanksgiving, Dec 25). **$$$**

Hotel

★ ★ **COPPER QUEEN HOTEL.** *11 Howell Ave (85603). Phone 520/432-2216; toll-free 800/247-5829; fax 520/432-4298. www.copperqueen.com.* 47 rooms, 4 story. S, D $70-$105; each additional $10. Crib $10. TV; cable. Heated pool. Restaurant 7 am-2:30 pm, 5:30-9 pm. Bar 11-1 am; entertainment Fri-Sat. Check-out 11 am. Meeting room. Business services available. Built in 1902. Cr cds: A, C, D, DS, MC, V.

D ⬛ ⬛

B&B/Small Inns

★ ★ **CALUMET AND ARIZONA GUEST HOUSE.** *608 Powell St (85603). Phone 520/432-4815.* 6 rooms, 2 story. No room phones. S $45-$65; D $70-$80; each additional $15. Complimentary full breakfast. Check-out 11 am. TV in sitting room; VCR (movies). Restaurant nearby. Concierge service. Totally nonsmoking. Cr cds: MC, V.

⬛

★ **HOTEL LA MORE/THE BISBEE INN.** *45 Ok St (85603). Phone 520/432-5131; fax 520/432-5343. www.bisbeeinn.com.* 20 rooms, 2 story. S $45-$60; D $75-$85; each additional $15. Pet accepted. Deposit $40. Complimentary full breakfast. Check-out 11 am, check-in 3 pm. TV in sitting room. Restored 1917 hotel. Totally nonsmoking. Cr cds: A, D, DS, ER, MC, V.

🐾 ⬛

★ **SCHOOL HOUSE INN.** *818 Tombstone Canyon (85603). Phone 520/432-2996.* 9 rooms, 3 suites, 2 story. No A/C. No room phones. S $50-$60; D $65-$95; each additional $10; suites $70-$75. Children over 13 years only. Complimentary full breakfast. Check-out 11 am, check-in 3-5 pm. TV in den; cable. Restaurant nearby. Concierge service. Totally nonsmoking. Cr cds: A, C, D, DS, JCB, MC, V.

D ⬛

Bullhead City (D-1)

See also Kingman, Needles, Laughlin, NV

Founded 1946 **Pop** 21,951 **Elev** 540 ft **Area code** 928

Information Chamber of Commerce, 1251 US 95, 86429; 928/754-4121

Bullhead City was established in 1945 as a construction camp for Davis Dam, a reclamation facility located three miles to the north. The name is derived from its proximity to Bullhead Rock, now largely concealed by the waters of Lake Mojave. Bullhead City is across the Colorado River from Laughlin, Nevada (see) and its casinos.

What to See and Do

Davis Dam and Power Plant. *Davis Dam (86429). 4 miles N on Colorado River. Phone 928/754-3628.* Dam (200-feet high, 1,600-feet long) impounds Lake Mohave, which has a surface area of 28,500 acres and reaches 67 miles upstream to Hoover Dam. Self-guided tour through power plant (daily). **FREE**

Fishing, camping. *Phone 928/754-3245.* Trout, bass, bluegill, crappie, and catfish. Campsites, picnic grounds at

Katherine, 5 miles N, a part of the Lake Mead National Recreation Area (see NEVADA). Standard fees.

Motels/Motor Lodges

★ **BEST WESTERN BULLHEAD CITY INN.** *1126 Hwy 95 (86429). Phone 928/754-3000; toll-free 800/780-7234; fax 928/754-5234. www.bestwestern.com.* 88 rooms, 2 story. S, D $45-$75; under 12 free; higher rates during special events. Pet accepted; fee. Complimentary continental breakfast. Check-out noon. TV; cable (premium). Pool, whirlpool. Cr cds: A, C, D, DS, MC, V.

[D] 🐾 🏊 ⊠ SC

★ **LAKE MOHAVE RESORT.** *Katherines Landing (86430). Phone 928/754-3245; fax 928/754-1125. www.sevencrowns.com.* 49 rooms, 1-2 story, 14 kitchens. S, D $80-$90; each additional $6; kitchen units $100-$110; under 5 free. Pet accepted, some restrictions; $5. Restaurant 7 am-9 pm mid-Apr-Nov. Bar 4-10 pm. Check-out 11 am. Business services available. Boat rental. Private patios, balconies. Spacious grounds. View of lake. Cr cds: DS, MC, V.

[D] 🐾 ⚓ 🏄 ⊠ ⊠

★ **LODGE ON THE RIVER.** *1717 Hwy 95 (86503). Phone 928/758-8080; toll-free 888/200-7855; fax 928/758-8283.* 64 rooms, 13 suites, 2 story. S $30-$65; D $35-$78; each additional $6; suites $49-$95; under 12 free; weekly rates. Crib $6. Check-out 11 am. TV; cable. Microwaves available. Some refrigerators. Restaurant nearby. Pool. On river. Cr cds: A, D, DS, MC, V.

[D] 🏊 ⊠

Restaurant

★ **EL ENCANTO.** *1884 S Hwy 95 (86442). Phone 928/754-5100.* Mexican, American menu. Closed some major holidays. Lunch, dinner. Bar. Children's menu. Outdoor seating. Cr cds: A, MC, V.

[D]

Canyon de Chelly National Monument (B-7)

See also Ganado

(In NE corner of the state at Chinle)

The smooth red sandstone walls of the canyon extend straight up as much as 1,000 feet from the nearly flat sand bottom. When William of Normandy defeated the English at the Battle of Hastings in 1066, the Pueblo had already built apartment houses in these walls. Many ruins are still here.

The Navajo came long after the original tenants had abandoned these structures. In 1864, Kit Carson's men drove nearly all the Navajo out of the area, marching them on foot 300 miles to the Bosque Redondo in eastern New Mexico. Since 1868, Navajo have returned to farming, cultivating the orchards, and grazing their sheep in the canyon. In 1931, Canyon de Chelly (pronounced "de-SHAY") and its tributaries, Canyon del Muerto and Monument Canyon, were designated a national monument.

There are more than 60 major ruins, some dating from circa A.D. 300, in these canyons. White House, Antelope House, and Mummy Cave are among the most picturesque. Most ruins are inaccessible but can be seen from either the canyon bottom or from the road along the top of the precipitous walls. Two spectacular, 16-mile rim drives can be made by car in any season. Lookout points, sometimes a short distance from the road, are clearly marked. The only self-guided trail (2 1/2-miles round trip) leads to the canyon floor and White House ruin from White House Overlook. Other hikes can be made only with a National Park Service permit and an authorized Navajo guide (fee). Only four-wheel drive vehicles are allowed in the canyons; each vehicle must be accompanied by an authorized Navajo guide (fee) and requires a National Park Service permit obtainable from a ranger at the visitor center.

The visitor center has an archaeological museum and rest rooms. (Daily; free) Rim drive guides and White House Trail guides at visitor center bookstore. Picnic areas and campgrounds (free).

What to See and Do

⭐ **Canyon Tours.** *US 191 and RR 7, 3 mi E. Phone 928/674-5841; 800/679-2473.* Offered by Thunderbird Lodge (see MOTELS/MOTOR LODGES). Lodge personnel conduct jeep tours into the canyons; half-day (daily) and full-day (Apr-Oct, daily) trips. **$$$$**

Motels/Motor Lodges

★★ **BEST WESTERN CANYON DE CHELLY INN.** *100 Main St (Rte 7), Chinle (86503). Phone 928/674-5874; toll-free 800/327-0354; fax 928/674-3715. www.bestwestern.com.* 99 rooms. Early May-Oct: S $108; D $112; each additional $4; under 12 free; lower rates rest of year. Crib free. Pet accepted. Complimentary coffee in rooms. Check-out 11 am. TV; cable. Restaurant 6:30 am-10 pm; Nov-Mar to 9 pm. Indoor pool. Picnic tables. Gift shop. Navajo décor. Cr cds: A, C, D, DS, MC, V.

🐾 📶 🏄 🏊

★★ **HOLIDAY INN GARCIA TRADING POST.** *Indian Rte 7; PO Box 1889, Chinle (86503). Phone 928/674-5000; toll-free 800/465-4329; fax 928/674-8264. www.holiday-inn.com.* 108 rooms, 2 story. May-Oct: S, D $69-$109; under 18 free; lower rates rest of year. Crib free. Check-out noon. TV; cable (premium). Balconies. Restaurant 6 am-2 pm, 5-10 pm; winter hours vary. Room service. Heated pool. Meeting rooms, Business services available. Sundries, gift shop. Cr cds: A, C, D, DS, JCB, MC, V.

D ⛵ ⛴ SC

Hotel

★★ **THUNDERBIRD LODGE.** *Hwy 191 and Rte 7, Chinle (86503). Phone 928/674-5841; toll-free 800/ 679-2473; fax 928/674-5844. www.tbirdlodge.com.* 72 rooms in motel, lodge. Mar-Oct: S $65-$97; D $70-$106; each additional $4; lower rates rest of year. Crib $6. TV; cable. Restaurant 6:30 am-9 pm; winter hours vary. Check-out 11 am. Meeting room. Business services available. Airport transportation. Canyon tours available. Cr cds: A, C, D, DS, MC, V.

D ⛴

Carefree

See also Chandler, Mesa, Phoenix, Scottsdale, Tempe

Pop 2,927 **Elev** 2,389 ft **Area code** 480 **Zip** 85377

Information Carefree/Cave Creek Chamber of Commerce, 748 Easy St, Marywood Plaza, Box 734; 480/488-3381

The immense Tonto National Forest (see PAYSON) stretches to the north and east; the Ranger District office for the forest's Cave Creek District is located here. Located in the center of town is the largest and most accurate sundial in the Western Hemisphere.

Special Events

Carefree Fine Art and Wine Festivals. *Downtown. On Easy and Ho Hum sts. Phone 480/837-5637.* At each of these pleasant outdoor festivals, held three times a year, more than 150 booths feature the work of nationally recognized artists. You'll find a wide range of mediums—from paintings and pottery to sculptures and stained glass—in all price ranges. In the wine pavilion, host to Arizona's largest wine-tasting event, visitors can sample vintages from around the world. The popular festivals draw more than 180,000 art lovers each year. (Daily 10 am-5 pm)**$**

Fiesta Days. *Memorial Arena. Phone 480/488-4043.* PRCA rodeo, parade. Usually first weekend in Apr.

Resort

★★★★ **THE BOULDERS RESORT AND GOLDEN DOOR® SPA.** *34631 N Tom Darlington Dr (85377). Phone 480/488-9009; toll-free 800/553-1717; fax 480/488-4118. www.wyndham.com/boulders.* Nestled in the foothills of the Sonoran Desert near Scottsdale, The Boulders Resort and Golden Door Spa is a most unusual place, with a flair for the dramatic. Mimicking the natural landscape in its architecture, it teases the eye as it blends perfectly with its surroundings of rock outcroppings, ancient boulders, and saguaro cactus plants. The adobe casitas make wonderful homes and are distinguished by overstuffed leather chairs, exposed beams, and Mexican tiles, while one-, two-, and three-bedroom Pueblo Villas are ideal for families traveling together or for those on longer visits. The resort boasts a first-rate tennis facility, and two 18-hole championship golf courses. The Golden Door Spa, an outpost of the famous California spa, is simply divine, and is particularly notable for its hot rock massage. A cavalcade of flavors is discovered at the six restaurants, from Mexican and Spanish to Southwestern and continental. 205 rooms, also patio homes; 1-2 story. S, D $495-$985; each additional $25; under 18 free; MAP available. Service charge $27/day. Pet accepted; fee. Check-out noon, check-in 4 pm. TV; cable (premium), VCR. In-room modem link. Fireplaces. Dining rooms (public by reservation) 6 am-10 pm. Bar 11-1 am. Entertainment. Room service. Exercise room, spa, massage, sauna, steam room. 4 heated pools; whirlpool, poolside service. Golf, greens fee $230. Tennis. Business center. Cr cds: A, C, D, DS, ER, JCB, MC, V.

D 🐾 🏌 🎿 ⛵ 🚶 ⛴ 🏃

Restaurants

★★ **CANTINA DEL PEDREGAL.** *34505 N Scottsdale Rd, Scottsdale (85602). Phone 480/488-0715.* Mexican menu. Closed Thanksgiving, Dec 25. Lunch, dinner. Bar. Children's menu. Outdoor seating. Cr cds: A, D, DS, ER, JCB, MC, V. **$$**

D

★★★ **THE LATILLA ROOM.** *34631 N Tom Darlington Dr (85377). Phone 480/488-9009; fax 480/488-4113. www.wyndham.com/boulders.* Regional American fare is served with understated elegance at the Boulders Resort's Latilla Room, a glass-walled space tucked into the Sonoran Desert and surrounded by 12-million-year-old granite boulder formations. The menu here is a zesty blend of Louisiana Creole and Arizona Southwestern fare, which means that dishes pack a serious punch of flavor. Timid palates need not apply. The rustic, cozy dining room is decorated with Native American weavings, and, as its name suggests, the main room's ceiling is crafted from Ocotillo branches (called *latilla*, which means "little sticks" in Spanish). The outdoor patio, which is warmed by a blazing fire, is an ideal spot to have a drink before or after dinner or simply to soak up the views at twilight. (See also RESORT.) Regional American menu. Hours: 6-10 pm; Sun brunch (Dec-May) 11:30 am-2 pm. Dinner $24-$34. Sun brunch (Dec-May). Bar 11-1 am. Entertainment. Jacket required. Outdoor dining. Totally nonsmoking. Cr cds: A, C, D, DS, ER, JCB, MC, V.

D

Casa Grande (G-4)

See also Florence, Gila Bend, Phoenix

Pop 25,224 **Elev** 1,405 ft **Area code** 520 **Zip** 85222

Information Chamber of Commerce, 575 N Marshall St; 520/836-2125 or 800/916-1515

Web www.casagrandechamber.org

Named for the Hohokam ruins 20 miles northeast of town, Casa Grande is situated in an agricultural and industrial area.

What to See and Do

Casa Grande Ruins National Monument *(see) Approximately 14 miles E on AZ 84, 287, then 4 miles N on AZ 87.*

Casa Grande Valley Historical Society & Museum. *110 W Florence Blvd. Phone 520/836-2223.* Exhibits tracing Casa Grande Valley growth from prehistoric times to present with emphasis on farm, ranch, mining, and domestic life. Gift shop. (Mid-Sept-Memorial Day weekend, Tues-Sun; closed holidays) **$**

Factory outlet stores. Two different outlet malls: Factory Stores of America, 440 N Camino Mercado; 602/986-7616; and Tanger Factory Outlet Center, 2300 E Tanger Dr; 520/836-9663.

Picacho Peak State Park. *24 miles SE off I-10, Picacho Peak exit. Phone 520/466-3183.* This 3,400-acre park includes a sheer-sided peak rising 1,500 feet above the desert floor, which was a landmark for early travelers. The only Civil War battle in Arizona was fought near here. Colorful spring wildflowers; desert nature study. Hiking, picnicking (shelter). Interpretive center programs (seasonal).

Special Event

O'Odham Tash-Casa Grande's Indian Days. *1201 Pinal Ave (85230). Phone 520/836-4723.* Rodeo, parades, ceremonial dances, arts and crafts, chicken scratch dance and bands; Native American foods, barbecue. Reservations advised. Phone 520/836-4723. Mid-Feb.

Casa Grande Ruins National Monument (G-4)

See also Casa Grande, Chandler, Florence, Phoenix

(33 miles SE of Chandler on AZ 87, 1 mile N of Coolidge)

The Hohokam people existed in the Salt and Gila river valleys for hundreds of years before abandoning the region sometime before 1450. They built irrigation canals in order to grow beans, corn, squash, and cotton. Casa Grande (Big House) was built during the 14th century.

Casa Grande was constructed of caliche-bearing soil (a crust of calcium carbonate on stony soil) and is four stories high (although the first story was filled in with dirt). The top story probably provided an excellent view of the surrounding country and may have been used for astronomical observations.

After being occupied for some 100 years, Casa Grande was abandoned. Father Kino, the Jesuit missionary and explorer, sighted and named it Big House in 1694.

Casa Grande is the only structure of its type and size in southern Arizona. It is covered by a large protective roof. There is a museum with archaeological exhibits (daily); self-guided tours. Contact Superintendent, 1100 Ruins Dr. Coolidge 85228; phone 520/723-3172. **$**

Chandler (F-4)

See also Mesa, Phoenix, Scottsdale, Tempe

Pop 176,581 **Elev** 1,213 ft **Area code** 480

Information Chandler Chamber of Commerce, 25 S Arizona Pl, 85225; 480/963-4571 or 800/963-4571

Web www.chandlerchamber.com

Cotton, citrus fruits, pecans, and sugar beets are grown in the surrounding area. A growing number of high-technology companies have facilities here including Intel, Motorola, and Microchip Technologies.

What to See and Do

Gila River Arts & Crafts Center. *15 miles S via AZ 93 at junction I-10 (exit 175), on Gila River Indian Reservation. Phone 480/963-3981.* Gallery featuring the works of outstanding Native American artists and artisans from more than 30 tribes. Restaurant features Native American food. Museum preserves cultural heritage of Pima and Maricopa tribes. Gila Heritage Park features five Native American villages. (Daily; closed holidays) **FREE**

Special Events

ASA Amateur Softball National Tournament. *Snedigar Sportsplex (85225). Phone 480/782-2000 or 480/782-2727.* Sept.

Chandler Jazz Festival. *Downtown. Phone 480/786-4424.* Each year, during the last weekend of April (Fri-Sun), downtown Chandler transforms itself into New Orleans's Bourbon Street for a lively salute to jazz. But this festival showcases the modern version, not the traditional one that rings through the Crescent City. So the 20-plus bands that perform play mostly swing music featuring the sweet sounds of the piano, saxophone, trumpet, and upright bass. The event attracts about 6,000 jazz lovers, and the beat goes on for three days at a price that can't be beat. **FREE**

Chandler Ostrich Festival. *44 S San Marcos Pl (85225). Phone 480/963-0571.* Features ostrich racing, food, entertainment, and arts and crafts. Early Mar.

Motels/Motor Lodges

★ **FAIRFIELD INN BY MARRIOTT.** *7425 W Chandler Blvd (85226). Phone 480/940-0099; fax 480/940-7336. www.fairfieldinn.com.* 84 rooms, 3 story. S, D $49-$99. Complimentary continental breakfast. Check-out noon, check-in 3 pm. TV; cable (premium). In-room modem link. Whirlpool. Cr cds: A, C, D, DS, MC, V.

★ **HAMPTON INN.** *7333 W Detroit St (85226). Phone 480/753-5200; fax 480/753-5100. www.hamptoninn.com.* 101 rooms, 6 story. S, D $49-$129; under 18 free. Complimentary continental breakfast. Check-out noon, check-in 3 pm. TV; cable (premium). In-room modem link. Pool, whirlpool. Airport transportation (Mon-Fri). Cr cds: A, C, D, DS, JCB, MC, V.

★★ **WYNDHAM GARDEN.** *7475 W Chandler Blvd (85226). Phone 480/961-4444; fax 480/940-0269. www.wyndham.com/chandler.* 178 rooms, 4 story. S, D $89-$159; each additional $10. Check-out noon, check-in 3 pm. TV. Restaurant 6:30 am-2 pm, 5-10 pm.

Bar 4-11 pm. Room service. Exercise equipment. Whirlpool, poolside service. Cr cds: A, C, D, DS, MC, V.

Resort

★★★ **SHERATON SAN MARCOS GOLF RESORT AND CONFERENCE CENTER.** *One San Marcos Pl (85225). Phone 480/812-0900; toll-free 800/528-8071; fax 480/963-6777. www.sanmarcosresort.com.* Located just minutes from Phoenix, this historic resort marries both business and pleasure into a desert oasis. Golf, tennis, and horseback riding are available on site, with great shopping and excursions close by, insuring that there's something for everyone. 307 rooms, 4 story. S, D $49-$169, each additional $10; under 18 free; weekend, holiday rates; golf plans. Pet accepted; fee. Check-out noon, check-in 3 pm. TV; cable (premium). Restaurant 6:30 am-10 pm. Bar 11-1 am. Exercise equipment. Pool, children's pool, whirlpool, poolside service. Greens fee $109 with cart. Lighted tennis, pro. Business center. Concierge. Cr cds: A, C, D, DS, ER, JCB, MC, V.

Restaurant

★★ **C-FU GOURMET.** *2051 W Warner (85224). Phone 480/899-3888; fax 602/899-1388.* Chinese menu. Hours: 10 am-2:30 pm, 4:30-9:30 pm. Dinner $4.95-$10.95. Bar. Casual attire. Cr cds: A, MC, V.

Chiricahua National Monument (H-7)

See also Willcox

(32 miles SE of Willcox on AZ 186, then 3 miles E on AZ 181)

This national monument features 20 square miles of picturesque natural rock sculptures and deep twisting canyons.

The Chiricahua (Cheer-a-CAH-wah) Apaches hunted in the Chiricahua Mountain range. Cochise, Geronimo, "Big Foot" Massai, and other well-known Apaches undoubtedly found their way into this region during the 1870s and 1880s. A visitor center, two miles from the entrance, has geological, zoological, and historical displays. (Daily)

At Massai Point Overlook, geologic exhibits explain the volcanic origin of the monument. The road up Bonita Canyon leads to a number of other outlook points; there are also 20 miles of excellent day-use trails to points of special interest.

Picnicking and camping sites are located within the national monument. Campground/night; 26-foot limit on trailers. Contact Superintendent, HCR #2, Box 6500, Willcox 85643; phone 520/824-3560.

Clifton (F-7)

See also Safford

Settled 1872 **Pop** 2,596 **Elev** 3,468 ft **Area code** 520 **Zip** 85533

The scenic Coronado Trail (US 666) begins here and continues north 90 miles to Alpine. The Apache National Forest (see SHOW LOW) stretches north and east of Clifton; the Clifton Ranger District office of the Apache-Sitgreaves National Forest is located here.

What to See and Do

Old Jail & Locomotive. *S Coronado Blvd. Phone 520/824-3560.* Jail blasted out of mountainside; first occupied by the man who built it.

Cottonwood (D-4)

See also Flagstaff, Prescott, Sedona

Pop 9,179 **Elev** 3,314 ft **Area code** 928 **Zip** 86326

Information Chamber of Commerce, 1010 S Main St; 928/634-7593

This town is in the beautiful Verde Valley, an area offering many opportunities for exploration.

What to See and Do

Dead Horse Ranch State Park. *675 Dead Horse Ranch Rd (86326). At Verde River, N of town on 10th St. Phone 928/634-5283.* This 320-acre park offers fishing; nature trails, hiking, picnicking (shelter), camping (dump station). Visitor center. Standard fees.

Fort Verde State Historic Park. *125 E Hollamon (86322). 15 miles SE on AZ 279/260 in town of Camp Verde. Phone 928/567-3275.* Four original buildings of US Army fort, a major base during the campaigns of 1865-1890; museum; two furnished officers' quarters; post doctor's quarters; military artifacts. Picnicking. (Daily; closed Dec 25) **$$**

Jerome. *310 N Hull Ave (86331). 8 miles W on US 89A. Phone 928/634-2900.* 3,200-5,200 feet almost straight up. Historic old copper-mining town with cobblestone streets and renovated structures now housing gift, jewelry, antique, and pottery shops; art galleries; restaurants; and hotels. Views of Verde Valley and the Mogollon Rim.

Jerome State Historic Park. *Douglas Rd. Off US 89A. Phone 928/634-5381.* Douglas Memorial Mining Museum depicts history of Jerome, mining in Arizona; housed in former house of "Rawhide" Jimmy Douglas (fee). Picnicking. No overnight facilities. (Daily; closed Dec 25) **$$**

Montezuma Castle National Monument. *2800 Montezuma Castle Hwy, Campe Verde (86322). 20 miles SE of Cottonwood on AZ 260, then N and E off I-17. Phone 928/567-3322.* This five-story, 20-room structure was built by Native Americans more than 800 years ago and is one of the most remarkable cliff dwellings in the United States. Perched under a protective cliff, which rises 150 feet, the dwelling is 70 feet straight up from the talus.

Visitors are not permitted to enter the castle, but there is a self-guided trail offering a good view of the structure and of other ruins in the immediate area. Castle "A," a second ruin, is nearby. Montezuma Well, about 11 miles northeast, is a 470-foot-wide limestone sinkhole, with a lake 55 feet deep. Around the rim are well-preserved cliff dwellings. An irrigation system built by the inhabitants about 800 years ago leads from the spring. Limited picnicking; no camping. The Castle Visitor Center and a self-guided trail are both accessible to wheelchairs. (Daily) Contact the Chief Ranger, Box 219, Camp Verde 86322 **$**

Verde Canyon Railroad. *2 miles NW via US 89A. Phone 928/639-0010 or 800/293-7245.* Contact 300 N Broadway, Clarkdale 86324. Scenic excursion train takes passengers through the Verde Canyon on a four-hour round trip from Clarkdale to Perkinsville. Panoramic views of rugged, high-desert area; Verde River; Native American ruins. Some open-air viewing cars. Starlight rides (summer). (Daily, schedule varies; closed Jan 1, Thanksgiving, Dec 25) **$$$$**

Special Events

Fort Verde Days. *125 E Hollomon St (86322). Phone 928/567-9294. In Camp Verde.* Parade, dancing, barbecue, reenactments. Second weekend in Oct.

Paseo de Casas. *200 Main St (86331). Phone 928/634-5477. In Jerome.* Tour of unique old homes. Third weekend in May.

Verde Valley Fair. *Fairgrounds. 800 E Cherry St (86326). Phone 928/634-3290.* First weekend in May.

Motels/Motor Lodges

★ ★ **BEST WESTERN COTTONWOOD INN.** *993 S Main St (86326). Phone 928/634-5575; fax 928/634-5576. www.cottonwoodinn-az.com.* 77 rooms, 2 story. Mar-Oct:

S, D $69-$109; each additional $6; suites $89-$109; under 12 free; lower rates rest of year. Crib free. Complimentary continental breakfast. Check-out 11 am. TV; cable. Some refrigerators. Coffee in rooms. Coin laundry. Restaurant 6 am-10 pm. Room service. Heated pool, whirlpool. Meeting rooms, business services available. Cr cds: A, C, D, DS, V.

⊟ ⊠ SC

★ ★ **QUALITY INN.** *301 W Hwy 89A (86326). Phone 928/634-4207; toll-free 800/228-5151; fax 928/634-5764. www.qualityinn-az.com.* 52 rooms, 2 story. Mar-May, Sept-Oct: S $59-$99; D $65-$109; each additional $5; under 18 free; lower rates rest of year. Crib free. Complimentary continental breakfast. Check-out 11 am. TV; cable (premium). Coffee in rooms. Restaurant 11 am-9 pm. Bar. Heated pool, whirlpool. Meeting rooms, business services available. Cr cds: A, C, D, DS, JCB, MC, V.

D ⊟ ⊠ SC

Douglas (I-7)

Founded 1901 **Pop** 14,312 **Elev** 3,990 ft **Area code** 520 **Zip** 85607

Information Chamber of Commerce, 1125 Pan American; 520/364-2477

Located on the Mexican border, this diversified manufacturing town is a warm, sunny place abounding in Western hospitality. A Ranger District office of the Coronado National Forest (see TUCSON) is located here.

Special Events

Cinco de Mayo. Mexican independence festival. Early May.

Cochise County Fair & College Rodeo. *3677 N Leslie Canyon Rd (85607). Phone 520/364-3819.* Cochise County Fairgrounds. Third weekend in Sept.

Douglas Fiestas. Mid-Sept.

Horse races. *Cochise County Fairgrounds. 3677 N Leslie Canyon Rd (85607). Phone 520/364-3819.* Mid-Apr-mid-Sept.

Flagstaff (D-4)

See also Sedona, Williams, Winslow

Settled 1876 **Pop** 52,894 **Elev** 6,910 ft **Area code** 928

Information Chamber of Commerce, 101 W Rte 66, 86001; 928/774-4505

Web www.flagstaffchamber.org

In 1876, the Boston Party, a group of men who had been lured west, made camp in a mountain valley on the Fourth of July. They stripped a pine tree of its branches and hung a flag at its top. Afterward, the tree was used as a marker for travelers who referred to the place as the spring by the flag staff. In 1882, Flagstaff became a railroad town when the Atlantic and Pacific Railroad (now the Santa Fe) was built.

Flagstaff, home of Northern Arizona University (1899), is an educational and cultural center. Tourism is Flagstaff's main industry; the city is a good place to see the Navajo country, Oak Creek Canyon, the Grand Canyon (see), and Humphreys Peak (12,670 feet), the tallest mountain in Arizona. Tall pine forests of great beauty abound in the surrounding area. A Ranger District office of the Coconino National Forest is located here.

What to See and Do

Arizona Historical Society Pioneer Museum. *2340 N Fort Valley Rd (86001). 2 1/2 miles NW on Fort Valley Rd (US 180). Phone 928/774-6272.* History of northern Arizona. (Mon-Sat; closed holidays) **FREE**

Arizona Snowbowl Ski & Summer Resort. *6355 US 180 (86004). 7 miles NW off US 180 at Snowbowl Rd in Coconino National Forest. Phone 928/779-1951.* Resort has two triple, two double chairlifts; patrol, school, rentals; restaurants, bars, lounge; lodges. Thirty-two trails, longest run more than two miles; vertical drop 2,300 feet. (Mid-Dec-mid-Apr, daily) Skyride (Memorial Day-Labor Day; fee) takes riders to 11,500-feet elevation. **$$$$**

Coconino National Forest. *2322 E Greenlaw Ln (86004). Phone 928/527-3600.* Surrounds city of Flagstaff and the community of Sedona (see). Outstanding scenic areas including Humphreys Peak, Arizona's highest point; parts of the Mogollon Rim and the Verde River Valley; the red rock country of Sedona and Oak Creek Canyon, where Zane Grey wrote *Call of the Canyon;* the San Francisco Peaks; seven wilderness areas; the eastern portions of Sycamore Canyon and Kendrick wilderness areas and the northern portion of Mazatzal Wilderness area; extinct volcanoes; high country lakes. Fishing; hunting on almost two million acres, winter sports, picnicking, camping (fee). Standard fees.

Lowell Observatory. *1400 Mars Hill Rd. 1 mile W on Mars Hill Rd, off Santa Fe Ave. Phone 928/774-2096.* Established by Percival Lowell in 1894; the planet Pluto was discovered from this observatory in 1930. Guided tours; slide presentations; telescope viewing (seasonal). Museum, gift shop. Telescope domes are unheated; appropriate clothing advised. **$$**

Mormon Lake Ski Center. *28 miles SE off Lake Mary Rd on Mormon Lake Rd. Phone 928/354-2240.* Terrain includes snowy meadows, huge stands of pine, oak, and aspen, old logging roads, and turn-of-the-century railroad grades.

School. Has 21 miles of marked, groomed trails; restaurant, bar; motel, cabins. Rentals. Guided tours. **$$$**

Museum of Northern Arizona. *3101 N Fort Valley Rd (86001). 3 miles NW on US 180. Phone 928/774-5213.* Exhibits on the archaeology, geology, biology, paleontology, and fine arts of the Colorado Plateau; offers Hispanic, Hopi, Navajo, Zuni, and Pai exhibits and summer marketplaces, revealing the region's artistic traditions, native cultures, and natural sciences. (Daily; closed Jan 1, Thanksgiving, Dec 25) **$$**

Oak Creek Canyon. *14 miles S on US 89A. Phone 928/ 282-3034.* This spectacular gorge may look familiar to you. It's a favorite location for western movies. The northern end of the road starts with a lookout point atop the walls and descends nearly 2,000 feet to the stream bed. The creek has excellent trout fishing. At the southern mouth of the canyon is Sedona (see), a resort town.

Riordan State Historic Park. *409 Riordan Rd. W on I-40, exit Flagstaff/Grand Canyon, then N on Milton Rd; turn right at sign past second light. Phone 928/779-4395.* Features a mansion built in 1904 by Michael and Timothy Riordan. The brothers played a significant role in the development of Flagstaff and northern Arizona. Original artifacts, handcrafted furniture, mementos. Picnic area; no overnight facilities. Guided tours. (Daily; closed Dec 25) **$$$**

Sunset Crater Volcano National Monument. *(see) 7133 N US 89 (86004). 15 miles N of Flagstaff on US 89, then 2 miles E on Sunset Crater/Wupatki Loop Road. Phone 520/526-0502.*

Walnut Canyon National Monument. *Walnut Canyon Rd (86004). Phone 520/526-3367.* **$**

Wupatki National Monument. *2717 N Steves Blvd, Suite 3 (86004). 35 miles N of Flagstaff on US 89. Phone 520/ 556-7152.* The nearly 2,600 archeological sites of the Sinagua and Anasazi cultures were occupied between 1100 and 1250. The largest of them, Wupatki Pueblo, was 3 stories high, with about 100 rooms. The eruption of nearby Sunset Crater (see) spread volcanic ash over an 800-square-mile area and for a time made this an active farming center. The half-mile ruins trail is self-guided; books are available at its starting point. The visitor center and main ruin are open daily (closed December 25). Rangers on duty. Wupatki National Monument and Sunset Crater Volcano National Monument (see) are located on a 35-mile paved loop off of US 89. Nearest camping at Bonito Campground (May-October; phone 520/526-0866). Contact the Superintendent, 6400 US 89A, Flagstaff 86004; phone 520/526-1157. **$$**

Special Events

Coconino County Fair. *Fort Tuthill County Park HCR 30 Box 3A (86001). Phone 928/774-5139.* Labor Day weekend.

Flagstaff Festival of the Arts. *Northern Arizona University campus, SW edge of city. Phone 520/774-7750; 800/266-7740.* Symphonic/pops concerts, chamber music; theater; dance; art exhibits; poetry; film classics. July-early Aug.

Hopi Artists' Exhibition. *3101 N Fort Valley Rd (86001). Phone 928/774-5213.* The Museum of Northern Arizona. Late June-early July.

Navajo Artists' Exhibition. *3101 N Fort Valley Rd (86001). Phone 928/774-5213.* The Museum of Northern Arizona. Last weekend in July-first weekend in Aug.

Winter Festival. *Phone 520/774-4505.* Features art contest and exhibit; theater performances; workshops; sled dog and other races, games; Winterfaire, with arts and crafts; entertainment. Feb.

Zuni Artists' Exhibition. *3101 N Fort Valley Rd (86001). Phone 928/774-5213.* The Museum of Northern Arizona. Five days beginning the Sat before Memorial Day.

Motels/Motor Lodges

★ **BEST WESTERN PONY SOLDIER INN & SUITES.** *3030 E Rte 66 (86004). Phone 928/ 526-2388; toll-free 800/356-4143; fax 928/527-8329. www. bestwesternponysoldier.com.* 92 rooms, 2 story. S, D $50-$99; each additional $5; under 18 free. Complimentary continental breakfast. Check-out 11 am, check-in 2 pm. TV; cable (premium). Restaurant 4:30-9:30 pm; Fri, Sat to 10 pm. Indoor pool. Downhill ski 15 miles. Cr cds: A, C, D, DS, MC, V.

⊡ ⌦ ⊠ ⊠

★ **DAYS INN HIGHWAY 66.** *1000 W Rte 66 (86001). Phone 928/774-5221; toll-free 800/329-7466; fax 928/521-0228. www.daysinnflagstaff.com.* 158 rooms, 2 story. S, D $35-$99; under 18 free. Pet accepted, some restrictions; fee. Complimentary continental breakfast. Check-out 11 am, check-in 3 pm. TV; cable (premium). Pool. Cr cds: A, C, D, DS, JCB, MC, V.

⊡ ⌦ ⊠ ⊠ **SC**

★ **DAYS INN EAST.** *3601 E Lockett Rd (86004). Phone 928/527-1477; toll-free 800/435-4363; fax 928/527-0228. www.daysinnflagstaffeast.com.* 69 rooms, 3 story. S, D $39-$139; under 18 free. Complimentary continental breakfast. Check-out 11 am, check-in 3 pm. TV. Indoor pool, whirlpool. Cr cds: A, C, D, DS, JCB, MC, V.

⊡ ⊠ ⊠

★ **FAIRFIELD INN.** *2005 S Milton Rd (86001). Phone 928/773-1300; toll-free 800/574-6395; fax 928/773-1462. www.fairfieldinn.com.* 134 rooms, 3 story. S, D $59-$119; under 18 free. Complimentary continental breakfast. Check-out noon, check-in 3 pm. TV; cable (premium). In-room modem link. Pool. Downhill/cross-country ski 15 miles. Cr cds: A, C, D, DS, JCB, MC, V.

⊡ ⌦ ⊠ ⊠

★ **HAMPTON INN & SUITES.** *2400 S Beulah Blvd (86001). Phone 928/913-0900; toll-free 800/426-7866; fax 928/913-0800. www.flagstaffhampton.com.* 126 rooms, 39 kitchen units, 5 story. June-Aug: S, D $69-$99; kitchen suites $99-$129; under 18 free; higher rates during graduation; lower rates rest of year. Crib free. Complimentary continental breakfast. Check-out noon. TV; cable (premium). In-room modem link. Many fireplaces, some in-room whirlpools, microwaves, refrigerators; VCRs in suites. Valet services, coin laundry. Restaurant adjacent 10 am-10 pm. Exercise equipment, sauna. Heated indoor pool, whirlpool. Meeting rooms. Business services available. Bellhops. Sundries. Coffee in suites. Cr cds: A, C, D, DS, MC, V.

⊡ ⊠ ⊠ ⊠ ⊠

★ **HAMPTON INN.** *3501 E Lockett Rd (86004). Phone 928/526-1885; toll-free 800/453-4363; fax 928/526-9885. www.hamptoninnflagstaff.com.* 52 rooms, 3 story. S, D $59-$149; under 18 free. Complimentary continental breakfast. Check-out 11 am, check-in 3 pm. TV; cable (premium). Indoor pool, whirlpool. Downhill ski 15 miles. Cr cds: A, C, D, DS, MC, V.

⊡ ⊠ ⊠ ⊠ ⊠ ⊠ SC

★★ **HILTON GARDEN INN.** *350 W Forest Meadows St (86001). Phone 928/226-8888; toll-free 800/333-0785; fax 928/556-9059. www.hiltongardeninn.com.* Near Northern Arizona University, this hotel is more of a budget property than the typical Hilton branch. Guests can head to Grand Canyon National Park, albeit an 80-mile drive, or stay nearby for various outdoor activities including snow skiing, hiking and golfing. 90 rooms, 3 story. Apr-Oct: S, D $69-$139; each additional $10; under 18 free; package plans; higher rates special events; lower rates rest of year. Check-out noon. TV; cable (premium). In-room modem link. Room service 11 am-10 pm. Exercise equipment, sauna. Whirlpool. Downhill/cross-country ski 15 miles. Cr cds: A, C, D, DS, ER, JCB, MC, V.

⊡ ⊠ ⊠ ⊠ ⊠

★★ **HOLIDAY INN.** *2320 E Lucky Ln (86004). Phone 928/714-1000; toll-free 800/533-2754; fax 928/779-2610. www.holiday-inn.com/flagstaffaz.* 157 rooms, 5 story. S, D $49-$109; each additional $10; under 18 free. Pet accepted; fee. Check-out noon, check-in 3 pm. TV. In-room modem link. Restaurant 6-9 am, 5-10 pm. Bar 5-10 pm. Room service. Exercise equipment. Indoor pool, whirlpool. Downhill ski 11 miles. Free airport transporation. Cr cds: A, C, D, DS, JCB, MC, V.

⊡ ⊠ ⊠ ⊠ ⊠ ⊠

★ **QUALITY INN FLAGSTAFF.** *2000 S Milton Rd (86001). Phone 928/774-8771; toll-free 800/228-5151; fax 928/773-9382. www.qualityinnflagstaffaz.com.* 96 rooms, 2 story. S, D $49-$89; each additional $5; under 18 free. Pet accepted; fee. Complimentary continental breakfast.

Check-out 11 am, check-in 2 pm. TV. Downhill ski 15 miles. Airport transportation. Cr cds: A, C, D, DS, JCB, MC, V.

⊡ ⊠ ⊠ ⊠ ⊠ SC

★ **RAMADA LIMITED WEST.** *2755 Woodlands Village Blvd (86001). Phone 928/773-1111; toll-free 877/703-0291; fax 928/774-1449. www.ramada.com.* 89 suites, 2 story. S, D $39-$129; each additional $10; under 17 free. Pet accepted; fee. Complimentary continental breakfast. Check-out 11 am, check-in 3 pm. TV; cable (premium). Exercise equipment, sauna. Whirlpool. Cr cds: A, C, D, DS, JCB, MC, V.

⊡ ⊠ ⊠ ⊠ ⊠ SC

Hotels

★★ **LITTLE AMERICA HOTEL.** *2515 E Butler Ave (86004). Phone 928/779-7900; toll-free 800/352-4386; fax 928/779-7983. www.littleamerica.com.* Located on 500 acres of beautiful ponderosa pine forest, this hotel offers luxurious amenities with all the cultural and natural riches of northern Arizona. Private hiking trails and complimentary hors d'oeuvers served nightly are sure to delight guests. 256 rooms, 2 story. S, D $79-$129; each additional $10; under 12 free. Check-out 1 pm, check-in 4 pm. TV; cable (premium), VCR available. In-room modem link. Some fireplaces. Restaurant 6 am-midnight. Bar 11-1 am; entertainment. Room service 6 am-11 pm; Fri, Sat to midnight. Exercise equipment. Whirlpool. Downhill ski 15 miles. Lawn games. Concierge. Cr cds: A, C, D, DS, JCB, MC, V.

⊠ ⊠ ⊠

★★ **RADISSON WOODLANDS HOTEL.** *1175 W Rte 66 (86001). Phone 928/773-8888; fax 928/773-0597. www.radisson.com.* 200 rooms, 4 story. S, D $69-$149; each additional $8; under 12 free; ski plans. Check-out noon, check-in 4 pm. TV; cable (premium). In-room modem link. Restaurant (See also SAKURA). Bar. Room service. Exercise equipment, sauna. Whirlpool. Downhill/cross-country ski 11 miles. Cr cds: A, C, D, DS, ER, JCB, MC, V.

⊡ ⊠ ⊠ ⊠ ⊠

All Suites

★ **AMERISUITES FLAGSTAFF.** *2455 S Beulah Blvd (86001). Phone 928/774-8042; fax 928/774-5524. www.amerisuites.com.* 117 kitchen suites, 5 story. May-Sept: S $109-$149; D $119-$159; each additional $10; under 18 free; higher rates during special events; lower rates rest of year. Crib free. Pet accepted, some restrictions. TV; cable, VCR. Heated indoor pool; whirlpool. Complimentary continental breakfast, coffee in rooms. Check-out noon. Coin laundry. Business center. In-room modem link. Valet service. Free airport, train station, bus depot transportation. Exercise equipment. Refrigerators. Cr cds: A, C, D, DS, ER, JCB, MC, V.

⊡ 🛎 🏊 🏃 ✈ 🍽 SC 🏃

★ ★ **EMBASSY SUITES HOTEL.** *706 S Milton Rd (86001). Phone 928/774-4333; toll-free 800/774-4333; fax 928/774-0216. www.embassysuitesflagstaff.com.* Within walking distance of historic Flagstaff, this hotel offers a complimentary made-to-order breakfast each morning. 119 suites, 3 story. Mid-Apr-mid-Sept: suites $89-$179; each additional $10; ski, holiday rates; lower rates rest of year. Pet accepted, some restrictions; fee. Check-out noon. TV; cable (premium). In-room modem link. Exercise equipment. Whirlpool. Downhill ski 12 miles. Cr cds: A, C, D, DS, MC, V.

⊡ 🛎 🏊 🏖 🏃 🍽

B&B/Small Inn

★ ★ ★ **INN AT 410 BED & BREAKFAST.** *410 N Leroux St (86001). Phone 928/774-0088; toll-free 800/774-2008; fax 928/774-6354. www.inn410.com.* Known as the place with the personal touch, this charming 1907 Craftsman home offers fresh-baked cookies in the evenings. 9 rooms, 1 with shower only, 2 story, 4 suites. No room phones. Mar-Oct: S, D, suites $135-$190; each additional $25; weekends Apr-late-Oct (2-day minimum), holidays. Complimentary full breakfast; afternoon refreshments. Coffee in rooms. Restaurant nearby. Check-out 11 am, check-in 4-6 pm. Luggage handling. Concierge service. Downhill ski 14 miles; cross-country ski 7 miles. Refrigerators. Picnic tables. Built in 1907; antiques. Some fireplaces. Totally nonsmoking. Cr cds: MC, V.

🏖 🍽

Restaurants

★ ★ **BUSTER'S.** *1800 S Milton Rd (86001). Phone 928/774-5155; fax 928/774-5156.* Seafood menu. Closed Thanksgiving, Dec 25. Lunch, dinner. Bar. Children's menu. Cr cds: A, D, DS, MC, V. **$$**

⊡

★ ★ **COTTAGE PLACE.** *126 W Cottage Ave (86001). Phone 928/774-8431. www.cottageplace.com.* Continental menu. Closed Mon. Dinner. Children's menu. Intimate dining in 1909 cottage. Cr cds: A, MC, V. **$$**

⊡

★ **KACHINA DOWNTOWN.** *522 E Rte 66 (86001). Phone 928/779-1944; fax 928/773-7826.* Mexican menu. Hours: 11 am-9 pm; Sun to 8 pm. Closed some major holidays. Reservations accepted. Bar. Children's menu. Lunch, dinner $6-$18. Cantina decor. Cr cds: A, D, DS, ER, JCB, MC, V.

⊡

★ ★ **MAMMA LUISA.** *2710 N Steves Blvd (86004). Phone 928/526-6809.* Italian, vegetarian menu. Hours: 5-10 pm. Closed Thanksgiving, Dec. 25. Reservations accepted. Service bar. Dinner $7.95-$15.95. Children's menu. Specialties: chicken rollantini, veal saltimbocca, fresh-baked garlic bread. Cr cds: A, D, DS, MC, V.

⊡

★ ★ **SAKURA.** *1175 W US 66 (86001). Phone 928/773-9118; fax 928/773-0597. www.radisson.com.* Japanese menu. Lunch, dinner. Bar. Children's menu. Cr cds: A, D, DS, JCB, MC, V. **$$$**

⊡ SC

★ **SALSA BRAVA.** *1800 S Milton Rd (86001). Phone 520/774-1083; fax 520/779-5216.* Mexican menu. Hours: 11 am-9 pm; Fri to 10 pm; Sat, Sun 8 am-10 pm. Closed major holidays. Bar. Breakfast $3.29-$6.95, lunch $4.95-$6.95, dinner $5.95-$8.50. Children's menu. Specializes in carnitas. Outdoor dining. Casual atmosphere. Salsa bar. Cr cds: A, MC, V.

⊡

Florence (G-5)

See also Casa Grande

Pop 17,054 **Elev** 1,490 ft **Area code** 520 **Zip** 85232

Information Chamber of Commerce, Box 929; 520/868-9433 or 800/437-9433; or the Pinal County Visitor Center, PO Box 967; 520/868-4331

Web www.florenceaz.org

Set in the desert amid multicolored mountains, the seat of Pinal County is the fifth oldest pioneer settlement in the state. Florence has many early houses still standing, making the town something of a living relic of pioneer days.

What to See and Do

Casa Grande Ruins National Monument (see). *10 miles W via AZ 287, then S on A287.*

McFarland State Historic Park. *Ruggles Ave and Main St. Phone 520/868-5216.* (1878) First of three courthouses built here; restored adobe building with interpretive center, displays of early Arizona and US legal history, and the personal collections of Governor Ernest McFarland, also a US Senator and state supreme court justice. (Thurs-Mon; closed Dec 25) **$**

Pinal County Historical Society Museum. *715 S Main St. Phone 520/868-4382.* Exhibits depict early life in the area. (Tues-Sat, Sun afternoons; closed holidays, also mid-July-Aug) **DONATION**

Special Event

Junior Parada. *291 N Bailey St (85232). Phone 520/868-9433.* Three-day celebration features parade and rodeo. Sat of Thanksgiving weekend.

B&B/Small Inn

★★**RANCHO SONORA INN & RV PARK.** *9198 N Hwy 79 (85232). Phone 520/868-8000; toll-free 800/205-6817. www.ranchosonora.com.* 11 rooms, 3 casitas. Some room phones. S, D $74-$79; casitas $105-$150; under 5 free. Pet accepted, some restrictions. TV; cable (premium); VCR available (free movies). Complimentary continental breakfast. Restaurant nearby. Check-out 11 am, check-in 2 pm. Business services available. Coin laundry. Pool; whirlpool. Some refrigerators, microwaves. Picnic tables, grills. Built in 1930. Original adobe, western and traditional decor. Courtyard. Cr cds: A, D, DS, MC, V.

[D] [icons]

Ganado (C-7)

See also Canyon de Chelly National Monument, Window Rock

Pop 1,505 **Elev** 6,386 ft **Area code** 928 **Zip** 86505

What to See and Do

Hubbell Trading Post National Historic Site. *Hwy 264. 1 mile W on AZ 264. Phone 928/755-3475 or 928/755-3477.* The oldest continuously operating trading post (1878) on the Navajo Reservation; named for founder John Lorenzo Hubbell, who began trading with the Navajo in 1876. Construction of the present-day post began in 1883. The visitor center houses exhibits; Navajo weavers and a silversmith can be observed at work; tours of the Hubbell house, containing paintings, Navajo rugs, and Native American arts and crafts; self-guided tour of the grounds (ranger-conducted programs in summer). (Daily; closed Jan 1, Thanksgiving, Dec 25) **FREE**

Gila Bend (G-3)

See also Casa Grande

Pop 1,980 **Elev** 736 ft **Area code** 520 **Zip** 85337

Located on a desert plain near a sharp bend in the Gila River, Gila Bend was home to a flourishing Native American community prior to the arrival of Spanish explorers in the 17th century.

Motel/Motor Lodge

★★**BEST WESTERN SPACE AGE LODGE.** *401 E Pima St (85337). Phone 520/683-2273; toll-free 800/780-7234. www.bestwestern.com.* 41 rooms. Jan-Apr: S $60-$70; D $65-$85; each additional $4; under 17 free; lower rates rest of year. Crib free. Pet accepted. Check-out noon. TV; cable (premium). Some refrigerators. Coffee in rooms. Restaurant 24 hours. Pool, whirlpool. Cr cds: A, C, D, DS, MC, V.

[D] [icons] [SC]

Glendale (F-4)

See also Litchfield Park, Mesa, Phoenix, Scottsdale, Tempe

Founded 1892 **Pop** 218,812 **Elev** 1,150 ft **Area code** 623

Information Chamber of Commerce, 7105 N 59th Ave, Box 249, 85311; 623/937-4754 or 800/437-8669

Located just west of Phoenix in the beautiful and scenic Valley of the Sun, Glendale shares all of the urban advantages of the area. Luke Air Force Base is located here.

What to See and Do

Arizona's Antique Capital. *5850 W Glendale Ave (85301). Phone 623/930-4500.* Shopping area in downtown Glendale including antique stores, specialty shops, and candy factory. (Most stores open Mon-Sat)

Bo's Funky Stuff. *5605 W Glendale Ave (85301). Phone 623/842-0220.* No run-of-the-mill antique store, this offbeat emporium proves the old adage that one man's junk is another man's treasure. Two side-by-side rooms are crammed with old advertising signs, housewares, and '50s furniture, all of it fun, and all of it funky. Sure, some items are pure kitsch, but some are one-of-a-kind collectibles. Prices range from under a dollar to several thousand. (Sept-May: daily, noon-5 pm; June-Aug: Thurs-Sun, noon-5 pm)

Motels/Motor Lodges

★**HAMPTON INN.** *8408 W Paradise Ln (85382). Phone 623/486-9918; toll-free 800/426-7866; fax 623/486-4842. www.hamptoninn.com.* 112 rooms, 5 story. S, D $53-$125; each additional $10; under 18 free; golf plans. Complimentary continental breakfast. Check-out noon, check-in 3 pm. TV; cable (premium), VCR available. In-room modem link. Coin laundry. Exercise equipment. Pool, whirlpool. Cr cds: A, C, D, DS, JCB, MC, V.

[D] [icons] [SC]

★ **HOLIDAY INN EXPRESS.** *7885 W Arrowhead Towne Center Dr (85308). Phone 623/412-2000; fax 623/412-5522. www.holiday-inn.com.* 60 rooms, 2 story. S, D $59-$139; each additional $10; under 18 free. Complimentary continental breakfast. Check-out 11 am, check-in 3 pm. TV; cable (premium). Exercise equipment. Whirlpool. Cr cds: A, D, DS, JCB, MC, V.

🄳 🏊 ⚓ 🏋 🆇 SC

★ **LA QUINTA PHOENIX INN AND SUITES.** *16321 N 83 Ave, Peoria (85382). Phone 623/487-1900; toll-free 800/687-6667; fax 623/487-1919. www.laquinta.com.* 113 rooms, 5 story. S, D $65.99-$95.99; each additional $10; under 18 free; golf plans. Pet accepted, some restrictions; fee. Complimentary continental breakfast. Check-out noon, check-in 3 pm. TV; cable (premium). In-room modem link. Exercise equipment. Pool, whirlpool. Cr cds: A, C, D, DS, MC, V.

🄳 🏊 ⚓ 🏋 🆇 SC

All Suite

★ **SPRINGHILL SUITES BY MARRIOTT.** *7810 W Bell Rd (85308). Phone 623/878-6666; fax 623/878-6611. www.springhillsuites.com.* 89 suites, 4 story. $59-$129; under 18 free. Complimentary continental breakfast. Check-out noon, check-in 3 pm. TV; cable (premium). In-room modem link. Pool, whirlpool. Lighted tennis privileges, pro. Cr cds: A, C, D, DS, MC, V.

🄳 🎿 ⚓ 🆇

★ **WINDMILL SUITES SUN CITY WEST.** *12545 W Bell Rd (85374). Phone 623/583-0133; fax 623/583-8366. www.windmillinns.com.* 127 rooms, 3 story. S, D $53-$153; each additional $6; under 18 free. Pet accepted, some restrictions. Complimentary continental breakfast. Check-out 11 am, check-in 4 pm. TV; cable (premium). Whirlpool. Golf privileges. Cr cds: A, D, DS, MC, V.

🄳 🏊 🎿 ⚓ 🆇

Globe (F-5)

See also San Carlos

Settled 1876 **Pop** 7,486 **Elev** 3,509 ft **Area code** 928 **Zip** 85501

Information Greater Globe-Miami Chamber of Commerce, 1360 N Broad St, Box 2539, 85502; 928/425-4495 or 800/804-5623

A silver strike settled Globe, but copper made the town what it is today. One of the original copper mines, Old Dominion, is no longer worked; however, other mines are still in operation. Cattle ranching also contributes to the economy. A Ranger District office for the Tonto National Forest (see PAYSON) is located here.

What to See and Do

Besh-Ba-Gowah Indian Ruins. *150 N Pine St (85501). From end of S Broad St turn right across bridge, continue on Jess Hayes Rd. Phone 928/425-0320.* Ruins of a village inhabited by the Salado from 1225-1400. More than 200 rooms. Visitor center, museum. 15-minute video presentation.(Daily; closed Jan 1, Thanksgiving, Dec 25) **$$**

Boyce Thompson Southwestern Arboretum. *37615 US 60 (85273). 28 miles W on US 60; 3 miles W of Superior. Phone 928/689-2811.* Large collection of plants from arid parts of world added to native flora in high Sonoran Desert setting at foot of Picket Post Mountain; labeled plants in 39-acre garden. Picnicking. Book store. Visitor center features biological and historical displays. (Daily; closed Dec 25) **$$$**

Gila County Historical Museum. *1330 N Broad St (85502). 1 mile N on US 60. Phone 928/425-7385.* Exhibit of artifacts of Gila County, including those of the Apache. (Mon-Sat; closed holidays) **DONATION**

Special Events

Apache Days. Fourth weekend in Oct.

Gila County Fair. *Hwy 60 and Hwy 70 (85502). Phone 520/476-3587.* Four days in mid-Sept.

Motel/Motor Lodge

★ **TRAVELODGE MOTEL.** *2119 Old West Hwy 60 (85502). Phone 928/425-7008; fax 928/425-6410.* 45 rooms, 2 story. S, D $56-$70; each additional $7; under 18 free. Crib free. Pet accepted. TV; cable (premium). Complimentary continental breakfast. Restaurant opposite 11 am-9 pm. Check-out noon. Meeting rooms. Business services available. Coin laundry. Some refrigerators. Cr cds: A, C, D, DS, JCB, MC, V.

🄳 🐾 🆇

Grand Canyon National Park (B-4)

See also Flagstaff, Williams

Approximately 50 miles N on US 180 (AZ 64) to South Rim

Every minute of the day, the light changes the colors and form of this magnificent spectacle. Sunrises and sunsets are particularly superb.

In 1540, Spanish explorer de Cardenas became the first European to see this canyon of the Colorado River, but he and his party were unable to cross and soon left. In 1857, American Lieutenant Joseph Ives said the region was "altogether valueless. . . . Ours has been the first and will doubtless be the last party of whites to visit this profitless locality."

As much as 18 miles wide and about a mile deep, the canyon has wildlife that includes at least 287 different species of birds, 76 species of mammals, 35 species of reptiles, and 6 species of amphibians.

The South Rim (see), open all year, has the greatest number of services and is the most popular to visit. The North Rim (see), blocked by heavy snows in winter, is open from mid-May-mid-Oct. One rim can be reached from the other by a 220-mile drive. The South Rim has an altitude of about 7,000 feet; the North Rim is about 8,100 feet. The river is some 4,600 feet below the South Rim. It is 7 miles via the South Kaibab Trail and 9 miles via the Bright Angel Trail from the South Rim to the bottom of the canyon.

The park encompasses more than 1 million acres. Of the Grand Canyon's 277-mile length, the first 50 or so miles along the Colorado River comprise what is known as Marble Canyon, where 3,000-foot near-vertical walls of sandstone and limestone may be seen. US 89A crosses Navajo Bridge 467 feet above the Colorado River.

Pets must be on a leash and are not allowed on trails below the rim. For further information, contact Trip Planner, Grand Canyon National Park, PO Box 129, Grand Canyon 86023; phone 928/638-7888. Per vehicle over $15.

North Rim (Grand Canyon National Park) (B-4)

220 miles NW of Flagstaff: 116 miles N via US 89, 58 miles W via US 89A, then 46 mi S via AZ 67

What to See and Do

Camping. *Phone 800/365-2267.* Campsites, trailer parking space at North Rim Campground (seven-day limit; no hookups). **$$$$**

⭐ **Drive to Cape Royal.** *About 23 miles from Bright Angel Point over paved road.* Several good viewpoints along the way. Many think the view from here is better than from the South Rim. Archaeology and geology talks in summer and fall.

Hiking. Six trails (1/4 mile to 10 miles); some are self-guided.

Muleback trips. *280 W Bryce Way. Phone 520/638-9875 (summer).* Into canyon (daytime only). Also horseback trips (along rim only, not into canyon).

Programs. *Consult information board at Grand Canyon Lodge for schedule.* By naturalists; occasionally other events. **FREE**

Motel/Motor Lodge

★ ★ **GRAND CANYON LODGE.** *Phone 520/638-2611; fax 520/638-2554. www.grandcanyonnorthrim.com.* 201 units; 161 cabins, 40 motel rooms. May-Oct: S, D $55-$91; each additional $5; under 16 free. Closed rest of year. Crib $5. Restaurant 6:30-10 am, 11:30 am-2:30 pm, 5-9:30 pm. Bar 11:30 am-10:30 pm. Check-out 11 am. Business services available. Bellhops. Sundries. Gift shop. Game room. View of canyon. Cr cds: A, D, DS, JCB, MC, V.

🄳 🎿 🐾 🚫 🖼

South Rim (Grand Canyon National Park) (B-4)

Approximately 80 miles NW of Flagstaff vis US 180

What to See and Do

Camping. *Phone 800/365-2267.* Sites (no hookups) at Mather Campground (fee); reservations can be made through BIOSPHERICS. **$$$$**

⭐ **Drives to viewpoints.** There are West Rim and East Rim drives out from Grand Canyon Village; each is rewarding. Grandview Point and Desert View on the East Rim Drive are especially magnificent. West Rim Drive is closed to private vehicles early Apr-early Oct. Free shuttle buses serve West Rim and Village area during this period.

Evening programs. Every night all year by Park Service ranger-naturalist in outdoor amphitheater; inside Shrine of the Ages Building during the colder months; daytime talks given all year at Yavapai Observation Station and at Visitor Center. **FREE**

Gand Canyon IMAX Theatre. *Hwy 64 and 180, 1 mile S of park entrance. Phone 928/638-2203.* Large screen film (35-minutes) highlighting features of Grand Canyon. (Daily) **$$$**

Guided river trips. Reservations should be made well in advance. There are

Multiday trips. *Phone 928/638-7888 for a written list of commercial outfitters.* Within the park.

One-day trips. *50 S Lake Powell Blvd, Page. Phone 928/645-3279.* Available from Page to Lees Ferry, in Glen Canyon National Recreation Area.

Hiking down into the canyon. Not recommended except for those in good physical condition, because heat and the 4,500-foot climb back are exhausting. Consult Backcountry Office staff before attempting this. (**Caution:** always carry sufficient water and food; neither is available along trails.) Reservations and fees required for camping below the rim; by mail from the Backcountry Office, PO Box 129, Grand Canyon 86023, or in person at the Backcountry Office, located adjacent to Maswik Lodge.

Kaibab National Forest. *800 S 6th St, Williams. Phone 928/638-2443.* Adjacent to both North and South rims are units of this 1 1/2 million-acre forest (see WILLIAMS). The Ranger District office for the Tusayan District is located in Tusayan, four miles south of the park.

Mule trip into the canyon. *Phone 303/297-2757.* Easier than walking and quite safe; a number of trips are scheduled, all with guides. There are some limitations. Trips take one, two, or three days. Reservations should be made several months in advance (preferably one year prior).

Scenic flights over the Grand Canyon. Many operators offer air tours of the Canyon. Flights out of many different airports. For a partial list of companies, contact the Grand Canyon Chamber of Commerce, PO Box 3007, Grand Canyon 86023.

Tusayan Museum. *East Rim Dr, 22 miles E of Grand Canyon Village.* Exhibits on prehistoric man in the Southwest. Excavated pueblo ruin (circa 1185) nearby. (Daily, weather permitting) **FREE**

Yavapai Observation Station. *On rim, 1 mile E of Grand Canyon Village.* Scenic views, exhibits, information. (Daily) **FREE**

Motels/Motor Lodges

★ ★ **BEST WESTERN GRAND CANYON SQUIRE INN.** *Hwy 64 (86023). Phone 928/638-2681; toll-free 800/622-6966; fax 928/638-2782. www.bestwestern.com.* 250 rooms, 3 story. Apr-Oct: S, D $150-$175; each additional $10; under 12 free; lower rates rest of year. Crib free. Check-out noon. TV; cable (premium). Coin laundry. Restaurant 6:30 am-10 pm. Bar 10 am-midnight. Exercise equipment, sauna. Game room, recreation room. Heated pool, whirlpool. Bowling alley on premises. Beauty shop. Business services available. Convention center/facilities. Concierge. Sundries, gift shop. Cowboy museum, mural of Grand Canyon. Cr cds: A, DS, MC, V.

★ **BRIGHT ANGEL LODGE.** *1 Main St (86023). Phone 928/638-2631; fax 928/638-9247. www.xanterra.com.* 89 rooms: 39 in lodge, 15 with bath; 50 cabins. No A/C. S, D $58-$114; each additional $7; suite $227. Crib free. TV in some rooms. Restaurant 6:30 am-10 pm. Bar 11-1 am; Sun from noon. Check-out 11 am. Bellstaff. Sundries. Gift shop. Barber, beauty shop. Fireplace in some cabins. Some canyon-side rooms. Canyon tour service. Cr cds: A, C, D, DS, JCB, MC, V.

★ **KACHINA LODGE.** *1 Main St (86023). Phone 928/638-2631; fax 928/638-9247. www.xanterra.com.* 49 air-cooled rooms, 2 story. S, D $107-$117; each additional $9. Crib free. TV; cable. Restaurant adjacent 6:30 am-2 pm, 5-10 pm. Check-out 11 am. Bellstaff. Canyon tour service. Cr cds: A, C, D, DS, JCB, MC, V.

★ ★ **QUALITY INN.** *AZ 64 Grand Canyon (86023). Phone 928/638-2673; toll-free 800/221-2222; fax 928/638-9537. www.grandcanyonqualityinn.com.* 232 rooms, 3 story. Apr-Oct: S, D $73-$118; each additional $10; under 18 free; lower rates rest of year. Crib $10. Check-out 11 am. TV; cable. In-room modem link. Balconies, Some minibars. Complimentary coffee in rooms. Restaurant 6 am-10 pm. Pool, whirlpool. Gift shop. Atrium. Cr cds: A, C, D, DS, ER, JCB, MC, V.

★ **RODEWAY INN RED FEATHER LODGE.** *Hwy 64 (86023). Phone 928/638-2414; toll-free 800/538-2345; fax 928/638-2707. www.redfeatherlodge.com.* 234 rooms, 2-3 story. May-Oct: S, D $100-$175; each additional $10; under 18 free; lower rates rest of year. Crib free. Pet accepted; $45. Check-out 11 am. TV; cable. Restaurant adjacent 6 am-10 pm. Exercise equipment. Business services available. Cr cds: A, C, D, DS, JCB, MC, V.

★ **THUNDERBIRD LODGE.** *1 Main St (86023). Phone 928/638-2631; fax 928/638-9247. www.xanterra.com.* 55 air-cooled rooms, 2 story. S, D $102-$112; each additional $9. Crib free. TV; cable. Restaurant adjacent 6:30 am-10 pm. Check-out 11 am. Meeting rooms. Bellstaff. Some canyon-side rooms. Canyon tour service. Cr cds: A, C, D, DS, JCB, MC, V.

★ **YAVAPAI LODGE.** *1 Main St (86023). Phone 928/638-2631; fax 928/638-9247. www.xanterra.com.* 358 rooms, 2 story. No A/C. S, D $83-$98; each additional $9. Crib free. TV; cable. Restaurant 6 am-9 pm. Check-out 11 am. Bellstaff. Gift shop. Sundries. Canyon tour service. Cr cds: A, C, D, DS, JCB, MC, V.

Hotel

★ ★ ★ **EL TOVAR.** *1 Main St (86023). Phone 928/638-2631; fax 928/638-9247. www.grandcanyonlodges.com.* The premier lodging facility at the Grand Canyon, El Tovar Hotel—named in honor of the Spanish explorer Don Pedro de Tovar, who reported the existence of the Grand Canyon to fellow explorers—opened its doors in 1905 and was dubbed "the most expensively constructed and appointed log house in America." Just 20 feet from the edge of the Canyon's South Rim, the building is a little Swiss, vaguely Scandinavian, and charmingly rustic. Upon entering, guests are greeted by a roaring fire, striking paintings of the Canyon, copper statues depicting the American West, and a bustling peacefulness that ensures a remarkable stay. The hotel features a fine dining room, lounge, and a gift shop highlighting Native American artisans. With so much to do right at your doorstep—hiking, mule rides, train excursions, interpretive walks, cultural activities—El Tovar offers the best of the Grand Canyon, combining turn-of-the-century lodge ambience with the highest standard of service on the Canyon's edge. Advance reservations are recommended, especially for the summer season, which is usually booked up a year in advance. 78 rooms, 4 story. S, D $112-$169; each additional $11; suites $192-$277. Check-out 11 am. TV; cable. Restaurant (See also EL TOVAR DINING ROOM). Bar 11 am-11 pm. Concierge. Cr cds: A, C, D, DS, JCB, MC, V.

D ⊠

Restaurants

★ ★ ★ **EL TOVAR DINING ROOM.** *1 Main St (86023). Phone 928/638-2631.* Located 20 feet from the South Rim of the Grand Canyon, the El Tovar Dining Room in the spectacularly rustic and historic El Tovar Hotel is considered the premier dining establishment at the Grand Canyon. It provides a memorable experience thanks to the spicy regional cuisine and spectacular Canyon views. The atmosphere is casually elegant with native stone fireplaces, Oregon pine vaulted ceilings, Native American artwork, and Mission-style accents. Diners can select from a well-rounded menu that blends regional flavors and contemporary techniques and offers many vegetarian options. The menu is unique and the wine list extensive. Southwestern menu. Hours: 6:30 am-2 pm, 5-10 pm. Breakfast, lunch, dinner. Children's menu. Reservations required for dinner. Totally nonsmoking. Cr cds: A, C, D, DS, ER, MC, V. **$$**

D

★ **STEAKHOUSE AT THE GRAND CANYON.** *AZ 64 and US 180 (86023). Phone 928/638-2780; fax 520/638-0331. www.kaibab.org/gc/serv/gc_or_ts.htm.* Vegetarian menu. Hours: 11 am-10 pm. Dinner $7.95-$22.95. Bar. Children's menu. Hayrides, stagecoach rides Mar-Oct. Covered wagon in front yard. Cr cds: MC, V.

D

Greer (E-7)

See also McNary, Pinetop, Springerville

Pop 125 **Elev** 8,380 ft **Area code** 520 **Zip** 85927

Within the Apache-Sitgreaves National Forests, this town is 18 miles southwest of Springerville (see) on AZ 273. Cross-country and downhill skiing are available nearby from December to March; fishing, hunting, backpacking, bicycling, and camping are popular at other times of year.

Motel/Motor Lodge

★ **GREER LODGE.** *44 Main St (85927). Phone 520/735-7516; toll-free 888/475-6343; fax 520/735-7720. www.greerlodge.com.* 8 rooms in main lodge, 3 cabins, 3 story. No A/C, no elevator, no room phones. S $90; D $150; each additional $15; kitchen units $75-$110; each additional $15; package plans. Crib available. Pet accepted in cabins; $10/day. Check-out 11 am. TV in lobby and lounge. Fireplace, piano in living room. Restaurant (public by reservation) 7-10 am, 11:30 am-2:30 pm, 5-8:30 pm. Bar 10 am-10 pm. Cross-country ski 5 miles. Picnic tables, grills. Ice skating; skates provided. Sleighing/sleigh rides. Meeting rooms. Sun deck. Stocked trout pond. On 9 acres; overlooks Little Colorado River. Cr cds: A, D, DS, MC, V.

D ◓ ⏁ ⚡ ⊠ ⊠

B&B/Small Inn

★ ★ ★ **RED SETTER INN.** *8 County Rd 1120 (85927). Phone 520/735-7441; toll-free 888/994-7337; fax 520/735-7425. www.redsetterinn.com.* Picnic sack lunches are included for guest stays of two nights or more. 12 rooms, 3 story. S, D $125-$195; each additional $25; weekends (2-day minimum); holidays (3-day minimum). Children over 16 years only. Complimentary full breakfast, complimentary afternoon refreshments. Check-out 10:30 am, check-in 3-7 pm. TV in common room; VCR (movies). Many balconies. Fireplaces, some in-room whirlpools. Restaurant nearby. Downhill ski 15 miles, cross-country ski 5 miles. Business services available. Luggage handling. Concierge service. Antiques; Irish Setter theme. On river. Totally nonsmoking. Cr cds: A, MC, V.

⊠ ⊠

Restaurant

★ **MOLLY BUTLER.** *109 Main St (85927). Phone 520/735-7226; fax 520/735-7538. www.mollybutlerlodge.com.* Specializes in steak, seafood. Hours: 5-9 pm. Reservations accepted. No A/C. Bar 8- 1 am. Dinner $6.95-$32.50. Old West atmosphere; 2 dining areas; rustic decor. Scenic view of valley meadows, mountains. Cr cds: MC, V.

D

Holbrook (D-6)

See also Hopi Indian Reservation, Navajo Indian Reservation, Winslow

Pop 4,917 **Elev** 5,083 ft **Area code** 928 **Zip** 86025

Information Chamber of Commerce, 100 E Arizona St; 928/524-6558 or 800/524-2449

What to See and Do

Apache-Sitgreaves National Forests (see). 46 miles S on AZ 77 to Show Low (see).

Navajo County Historical Museum. *100 E Arizona, in Old County Courthouse. Phone 928/524-6558.* Exhibits on Navajo, Apache, Hopi, and Hispanic culture; petrified forest; local history; dinosaurs. (May-Sept, Mon-Sat; rest of year, Mon-Fri; closed holidays) **DONATION**

Petrified Forest National Park. (see). *North entrance: 25 miles E of Holbrook on I-40; South entrance: 19 miles E of Holbrook on US 180. Phone 928/524-6228.*

Special Events

Navajo County Fair. *402 E Hopi Dr (86025). Phone 928/ 524-6407.* Mid-Sept.

Old West Celebration. *100 E Arizona St (86025). Phone 928/524-6558.* Second week in June.

Motels/Motor Lodges

★ ★ **BEST WESTERN ARIZONIAN INN.** *2508 Navajo Blvd (86025). Phone 928/524-2611; toll-free 877/ 280-7300; fax 928/524-2253. www.bestwestern.com.* 70 rooms, 2 story. June-Aug: S $46-$63; D $50-$69; each additional $4; under 17 free; lower rates rest of year. Crib $5. Pet accepted, some restrictions. Complimentary coffee in lobby. Check-out 11 am. TV; cable (premium). Microwaves, Some refrigerators. Restaurant 24 hours. Heated pool. Cr cds: A, C, D, DS, MC, V.

★ **COMFORT INN HOLBROOK.** *2602 E Navajo Blvd (86025). Phone 928/524-6131; toll-free 800/228-5150; fax 928/524-2281. www.comfortinn.com.* 60 rooms, 2 story. May-Sept: S $60; D $65; each additional $5; under 18 free; weekly, weekend rates; lower rates rest of year. Crib free. Pet accepted, some restrictions. Complimentary coffee in lobby. Check-out 11 am. TV; cable (premium). Microwaves, some refrigerators. Coin laundry. Restaurant adjacent open 24 hours. Pool. Cr cds: A, C, D, DS, JCB, MC, V.

★ **ECONO LODGE.** *2596 Navajo Blvd (86001). Phone 928/524-1448; toll-free 800/446-6900; fax 928/524-1493.*

www.econolodge.com. 63 rooms, 2 story. June-Aug: S $44; D $50; each additional $5; under 18 free; lower rates rest of year. Crib free. Pet accepted. Complimentary breakfast. Check-out 11 am. TV; cable (premium). Some refrigerators. Coin laundry. Restaurant adjacent. Heated pool. Picnic tables. Cr cds: A, C, D, DS, ER, JCB, MC, V.

★ **HOLIDAY INN EXPRESS.** *1308 Navajo Blvd (86025). Phone 928/524-1466; fax 928/524-1788. www.holiday-inn.com.* 59 rooms, 2 story. Late May-late Aug: S $59; D $63; each additional $4; suites $69-$83; under 17 free; lower rates rest of year. Crib $4. Pet accepted. Complimentary continental breakfast. Check-out 11 am. TV; cable. Microwave in suites. Refrigerator in suites. Coin laundry. Restaurant nearby. Indoor pool, whirlpool. Meeting rooms. Cr cds: A, C, D, DS, JCB, MC, V.

Restaurant

★ ★ **MESA ITALIANA.** *2318 N Navajo Blvd (86025). Phone 928/524-6696; fax 928/524-3130.* Italian menu. Closed Mon. Lunch, dinner. Bar. Children's menu. Cr cds: A, DS, MC, V. **$$$**

Hopi Indian Reservation (B-5)

See also Canyon de Chelly National Monument, Holbrook, Kayenta, Page

Completely surrounded by the Navajo Indian Reservation (see) is the 1 1/2 million-acre Hopi Indian Reservation. The Hopi are pueblo people of Shoshonean ancestry who have lived here for more than 1,000 years. The Hopi have a complex religious system. Excellent farmers, they also herd sheep, as well as craft pottery, silver jewelry, kachina dolls, and baskets. They live in some of the most intriguing towns on the North American continent.

Both the Navajo and Hopi are singers and dancers—each in their own style. The Hopi are most famous for their Snake Dance, which may not be viewed by visitors, but there are dozens of other beautiful ceremonies that visitors are allowed to watch. However, the photographing, recording, or sketching of any events on the reservation is prohibited.

All major roads leading into and across the Navajo and Hopi Reservations are paved. Do not venture off the main highways.

The Hopi towns are located, for the most part, on three mesas. On the first mesa is Walpi, founded around 1680, one of the most beautiful Hopi pueblos. It is built on the tip of a narrow, steep-walled mesa, along with its companion villages, Sichomovi and Hano, which are inhabited by the Tewa and the Hano. Hanoans speak a Tewa language as well as Hopi. You can drive to Sichomovi and walk along a narrow connecting mesa to Walpi. Only passenger cars are allowed on the mesa; no RVs or trailers. Individuals of Walpi and First Mesa Villages offer Hopi pottery and kachina dolls for sale; inquire locally.

The second mesa has three towns: Mishongnovi, Shipaulovi, and Shongopovi, each fascinating in its own way. The Hopi Cultural Center, located on the second mesa, includes a museum and craft shops (daily), a restaurant serving both Hopi and American food, and a motel; reservations (phone 520/734-2421) for May-August should be made at least three months in advance. Near the Cultural Center is a primitive campground (free). The third mesa has Oraibi, the oldest Hopi town, and its three offshoots, Bacabi, Kyakotsmovi, and Hotevilla, a town of considerable interest. A restaurant, a small motel, and tent and trailer sites can be found at Keams Canyon. There are not many places to stay, so plan your trip carefully.

Kayenta (B-6)

See also Hopi Indian Reservation,
Navajo Indian Reservation

Pop 4,922 **Elev** 5,641 ft **Area code** 928 **Zip** 86033

Located in the spectacular Monument Valley, Kayenta's (Kay-en-TAY) surrounding area offers some of the most memorable sightseeing in the state; the great tinted monoliths are spectacular.

What to See and Do

Crawley's Monument Valley Tours, Inc. *Hwy 160 and 163. Phone 928/697-3734; 928/697-3463.* Guided tours in backcountry vehicles to Monument Valley, Mystery Valley, and Hunt's Mesa. Half- and full-day rates. (Daily) **$$$$**

Guided tours. Available through **Bennett Tours,** *phone 800/862-8270;* **Daniel's Guided Tours,** *Phone 800/596-8427;* **Totem Pole Tours,** *Phone 800/345-8687;* **Goulding's Monument Valley Lodge,** *Phone 801/727-3231.* Fees and schedules vary.

Monument Valley Navajo Tribal Park. *25 miles NE off US 163. Phone 801/727-3287.* Self-guided tours of the valley (road conditions vary, inquire locally). Camping (at Park Headquarters only; fee). (Daily; closed Jan 1, Dec 25) **$$**

Navajo National Monument (see). *19 miles SW of Kayenta on US 160, then 9 miles N on paved road AZ 564 to Visitor Center. Phone 928/672-2366.* **FREE**

Motel/Motor Lodge

★ ★ **HOLIDAY INN.** *Jct US 160 and 163 (86033). Phone 928/697-3221; toll-free 800/465-4329; fax 928/697-3349. www.holiday-inn.com.* 162 rooms, 2 story. Apr-Nov: S, D $89-$150; each additional $10; suites $120-$160; under 19 free; lower rates rest of year. Crib free. TV; cable. Pool; wading pool. Restaurant 6 am-10 pm. Room service. Check-out noon. Business services available. Coin laundry. Sundries. Gift shop. Cr cds: A, C, D, DS, JCB, MC, V.

[D] [symbols]

Resort

★ ★ **GOULDING'S LODGE.** *P.O. Box 36001, Monument Valley, UT 84536. Phone 435/727-3231; fax 435/727-3344. www.gouldings.com.* 19 rooms in lodge, 41 rooms in 2-story motel; 2 cabins. S, D, cabins $62-$148; each additional $6. Pet accepted; fee. TV, VCR (movies). Indoor pool. Restaurant 7 am-9 pm. Check-out 11 am. Coin laundry. Sundries. Gift shop. Refrigerators. Private patios, balconies. Guided jeep tours. One building is old trading post; now museum. John Wayne movies filmed here. Cr cds: A, C, D, DS, JCB, MC, V.

[D] [symbols]

Kingman (D-2)

See also Bullhead City, Lake Havasu City

Pop 20,069 **Elev** 3,341 ft **Area code** 928 **Zip** 86401

Information Chamber of Commerce, 333 W Andy Devine, Box 1150, 86402; 928/753-6106

Web www.kingmanchamber.org

Kingman is the seat of Mohave County. It lies at the junction of two transcontinental highways, I-40 reaching from the East to the West coast, and US 93 from Fairbanks, Alaska, to Guatemala, Mexico. It is a convenient stop on the way to the Grand Canyon, Las Vegas, or Los Angeles. Nearby are Lakes Mead, Mohave, and Havasu, with year-round swimming, waterskiing, fishing, and boating. To the south are the beautiful Hualapai Mountains. This city lies at the heart of historic Route 66 and once was a rich silver and gold mining area; several ghost towns are nearby.

What to See and Do

Bonelli House. *430 E Spring St. Phone 928/753-1413; 928/753-3195.* (1894) One of the earliest permanent structures in the city. Restored and furnished with many original pieces. (Mon, Thurs-Sun afternoons; closed holidays) **FREE**

Mohave Museum of History & Art. *400 W Beale St, 1/4 mile E of I-40, Beale St/Las Vegas exit. Phone 928/753-3195.* Exhibits trace local and state history; portrait collection of US presidents and first ladies; Andy Devine display; turquoise display; rebuilt 1926 pipe organ; Native American displays. Local artists' gallery. (Daily; closed holidays) **$$**

Oatman. *Oatman Rd (86433). 28 miles SW, located on old US 66. Phone 928/768-6222.* In the 1930s, this was the last stop in Arizona before entering the Mojave Desert in California. Created in 1906 as a tent camp, it flourished as a gold mining center until 1942, when Congress declared that gold mining was no longer essential to the war effort. The ghost town has been kept as authentic as possible; several motion pictures have been filmed here. Wild burros abound, many roaming streets that are lined with historic buildings, former mine sites, old town jail, old and modern hotels, museum, turquoise and antique shops. Gunfights staged (daily). Contact the Oatman Chamber of Commerce. **FREE**

Powerhouse Visitor Center. *120 W Andy Devine Ave. Phone 928/753-6106.* Renovated power generating station (1907). Houses Historic Route 66 Association of Arizona, Tourist Information Center, Carlos Elmer Memorial Photo Gallery, model railroad shop, gift shop, deli. (Daily; closed holidays) **FREE**

Special Events

Andy Devine Days & PRCA Rodeo. *2600 Fairgrounds Blvd (86401). Phone 928/753-6106.* Sports tournaments, parade, other events. Two days in late Sept.

Mohave County Fair. *2600 Fairgrounds Blvd (86401). Phone 928/753-2636.* First weekend after Labor Day.

Motels/Motor Lodges

★ **BEST WESTERN WAYFARER'S INN.** *2815 E Andy Devine Ave (86041). Phone 928/753-6271; toll-free 800/548-5695; fax 928/753-9608. www.bestwestern.com.* 101 rooms, 2 story. Mid-May-Sept: S $60-$65; D $67-$70; suites $90; under 12 free; lower rates rest of year. Pet accepted. Check-out noon. TV; cable (premium). Cr cds: A, C, D, DS, MC, V.

★ **DAYS INN WEST.** *3023 E Andy Devine Ave (86401). Phone 928/753-7500; toll-free 800/329-7466; fax 928/753-4686. www.daysinn.com.* 60 rooms, 40 kitchen units, 2 story. May-Sept: S, D $55-$75; kitchen units $60; higher rates during holidays; lower rates rest of year. Crib free. Pet accepted; $3. TV; cable (premium). In-room modem link. Microwaves available. Coin laundry. Restaurant opposite 6 am-11 pm. Heated pool, whirlpool. Business services available. Coffee in lobby. Cr cds: A, C, D, DS, JCB, MC, V.

★ **QUALITY INN.** *1400 E Andy Devine Ave (86401). Phone 928/753-4747; toll-free 800/869-3252; fax 928/753-5175. www.qualityinn.com.* 98 rooms, 1-2 story. June-Aug: S, D, kitchen units $54-$69; each additional $10; under 18 free; lower rates rest of year. Pet accepted. Complimentary continental breakfast. Check-out noon. TV; cable (premium). Exercise equipment, sauna. Pool, whirlpool. Free airport transportation. Cr cds: A, C, D, DS, JCB, MC, V.

Lake Havasu City (E-1)

See also Kingman, Parker, Needles

Settled 1964 **Pop** 41,938 **Elev** 600 ft **Area code** 928 **Zip** 86403

Information Lake Havasu Tourism Bureau, 314 London Bridge Rd; 928/855-4115 or 800/242-8278

Web www.havasuchamber.com

This is the center of a year-round resort area on the shores of 45-mile-long Lake Havasu. London Bridge, imported from England and reassembled here as part of a recreational area, was designed by John Rennie and built from 1824-31; it spanned the Thames River in London until 1968. It now connects the mainland city with a three-square-mile island that has a marina, golf course, tennis courts, campgrounds, and other recreational facilities.

> ### City Fun Facts—Lake Havasu City
> The original London Bridge was shipped—stone by stone—and reconstructed in Lake Havasu City.

What to See and Do

Lake Havasu State Park. *699 London Bridge Rd. Phone 928/855-1223.* There are 13,000 acres along 23 miles of shoreline. Windsor Beach Unit, 2 miles N on old US 95 (London Bridge Rd), has swimming, fishing, boating (ramps); hiking, ramadas, camping (dump station). Phone 928/855-2784. Cattail Cove Unit, 15 miles S, 1/2 mile W of US 95, has swimming, fishing, boating (ramps); camping (including some water-access sites; fee). Standard fees.

London Bridge Resort & English Village. *1477 Queens Bay. Phone 928/855-0888; 928/855-0880.* English-style village on 21 acres; home of the world-famous London Bridge. Specialty shops, restaurants, boat rides, nine-hole golf course, accommodations. Village (daily). **$**

Sightseeing. Outback Off-Road Adventures, *Phone 928/ 680-6151;* **Lake Havasu Boat Tours,** *phone 928/855-7979;* **Bluewater Jet Boat Tours,** *phone 928/855-7171;* **Dixie Bell Boat Tours,** *phone 928/453-6776;* **London Jet Boat Tours,** *phone 888/505-3545.* **$$$$**

Topock Gorge. *10 miles N on lake (accessible only by boat), S boundary of Havasu National Wildlife Refuge.* Scenic steep volcanic banks along Colorado River. Migratory birds winter here; herons, cormorants, and egrets nest (Apr-May). Fishing; picnicking. **FREE**

Motel/Motor Lodge

★ ★ **HOLIDAY INN.** *245 London Bridge Rd (85204). Phone 928/855-4071; toll-free 888/428-2465; fax 928/ 855-2379. www.holiday-inn.com.* 162 rooms, 4 story. Feb-Nov: S $49-$78; D $57-$84; each additional $8; suites $97-$135; under 18 free; weekly rates; golf plan; higher rates: holidays, special events; lower rates rest of year. Crib free. Pet accepted, some restrictions. Check-out noon. TV; cable (premium). In-room modem link. Balconies, refrigerators. Coin laundry. Restaurant 6 am-10 pm. Bar 11-1 am; Sun from noon. Room service. Game room. Heated pool. Free airport transportation. Meeting rooms. Business services available. Cr cds: A, C, D, DS, JCB, MC, V.

D 🐾 🛄 🏊 🏊

Restaurant

★ ★ **SHUGRUE'S.** *1425 McCulloch Blvd (86403). Phone 928/453-1400; fax 928/453-3577. www.shugrues.com.* Hours: 11 am-10 pm. Closed Dec 25. Reservations accepted. Bar to 1 am. Lunch $5.25-$7.95, dinner $9.95-$32.95. Children's menu. Specializes in fresh seafood, steak, chicken. Multi-level dining. Nautical décor. Overlooks London Bridge. Cr cds: A, MC, V.

D

Litchfield Park

See also Glendale, Mesa, Phoenix, Scottsdale, Tempe

Pop 3,810 **Elev** 1,027 ft **Area code** 623 **Zip** 85340

Information Southwest Valley Chamber of Commerce, 289 N Litchfield Rd, Goodyear 85338; 623/932-2260.

Web www.southwestvalleychamber.org

In 1916, the Goodyear Tire and Rubber Company purchased and leased two tracts of land to grow Egyptian cotton. One tract was west of the Agua Fria River and was, for a short time, referred to as the Agua Fria Ranch. In 1926, the name was changed to Litchfield in honor of Paul W. Litchfield, vice president of the company.

What to See and Do

Duncan Family Farms. *5 miles S in Goodyear; off of Cotton Ln at 17203 W Indian School Rd.* Phone 623/853-9880. Two-thousand-acre working fruit and vegetable farm allows guests to pick their own organic produce. Petting zoo; farm play yard with "kittie kattle train," swings, giant maze. Country market and bakery. Seasonal festivals. (Fri-Sun; closed holidays) **FREE**

Wildlife World Zoo. *16501 W Northern Ave. 3 miles W on Northern Ave. Phone 623/935-9453.* White tigers. African lions. Dromedary camels. White rhinos. Go wild on these 55 acres and feast your eyes on Arizona's largest collection of exotic animals—about 1,300, representing nearly 320 species. But do more than just hoof it from one exhibit to the next. Get a bird's-eye view from high above on a brand-new sky ride. Feed giraffes, lemurs, and touracos. Take a safari through Africa on a train. Ride a pontoon through the Australian Outback. And much more. (Daily) **$$$**

Special Events

Billy Moore Days. *Coldwater Park. Phone 623/932-2260. Held in Avondale and Goodyear.* Carnival, entertainment, parade, other events. Mid-Oct.

Goodyear Rodeo Days. *Estrella Mountain Regional Park. Phone 623/932-2260. In Goodyear.* Includes entertainment, family games, dancing. Late Feb.

Native American Festival. *387 E Indian School Rd.* Approximately 100 Native American craft vendors. Native American dancing and other authentic entertainment both days. Third weekend in Jan.

Motel/Motor Lodge

★ **HOLIDAY INN EXPRESS.** *1313 N Litchfield Rd (85338). Phone 623/535-1313; fax 623/535-0950. www.holiday-inn.com.* 90 rooms, 3 story. Jan-May: S, D $129-$149; each additional $10; family rates; higher rates special events; lower rates rest of year. Crib free. Pet accepted. TV; cable (premium). Complimentary continental breakfast. Restaurant adjacent 6:30 am-10 pm. Check-out noon. Meeting rooms. Business services available. In-room modem link. Valet service. Coin laundry. Exercise equipment. Pool; whirlpool. Game room. Many in-room whirlpools, refrigerators, microwaves, wet bars. Cr cds: A, C, D, DS, JCB, MC, V.

D 🐾 🏊 🏋 🏊

Resort

★ ★ ★ **THE WIGWAM RESORT AND GOLF CLUB.** *300 Wigwam E Blvd (85340). Phone 623/935-3811; toll-free 800/935-3737; fax 623/ 856-1081. www.wigwamresort.com.* Once a private club for executives of the Goodyear Tire Company, The Wigwam Resort is one of Arizona's finest. Located in the village of Litchfield Park, it is only 20 minutes from downtown Phoenix. The rooms and suites highlight authentic regional design. Whitewashed wood furniture, slate floors, Mexican ceramic tiles, and traditional Southwestern colors distinguish the accommodations. Comfortable and spacious, the rooms could convince some guests to remain within, yet the tempting array of outdoor pursuits lures visitors from their hideaways. Three award-winning golf courses, nine tennis courts, two pools with a waterslide, and a fitness center with spa keep adults satisfied, while Camp Pow Wow puts a smile on the faces of the youngest guests. Five restaurants and bars have something for everyone, from continental cuisine and live entertainment to regional dishes in a traditional Southwestern kitchen. 331 rooms, 1-2 story. S, D $369-$429; each additional $25; suites $429-$539; under 18 free; golf plan; AP and MAP available. Pet accepted, some restrictions. Check-out noon, check-in 4 pm. TV; cable (premium). Some fireplaces. Dining rooms (public by reservation) 6:30-10:30 am, 11:30 am-2:30 pm, 5-10 pm. Bar 11-1 am. Room service 24 hours. Supervised children's activities (June-Sept and holidays); ages 5-12. Exercise room, sauna, steam room. 2 pools; whirlpool, poolside service. Golf, greens fee $120 (including cart). Tennis, lighted courts. Skeet, trapshooting. Entertainment. Bicycles. Airport transportation. Business center. Concierge. Cr cds: A, C, D, DS, MC, V.

Restaurant

★ ★ ★ ★ **ARIZONA KITCHEN.** *300 Wigwam E Blvd (85340). Phone 623/935-3811. www.wigwamresort.com.* Given The Arizona Kitchen's adobe fireplace, red brick flooring, wood-beamed ceilings, and a stunning exhibition kitchen featuring a mesquite-wood fired hearth and grill, seekers of authentic Arizona cuisine and atmosphere should feel quite rewarded after an evening here. Located just 20 minutes from Phoenix in the historic Wigwam Resort (See also THE WIGWAM), this perpetually packed Southwestern restaurant is a showcase for the fiery culinary techniques and flavors of the region. Using herbs grown just steps from the door, the kitchen pays homage to local ingredients with signature dishes like smoked corn chowder, grilled sirloin of buffalo with sweet potato pudding, and mesquite-dusted Chilean sea bass. If you're searching for a place to feast on terrific, authentic Arizona-style fare, look no further. This is the real thing. Southwestern menu. Hours: 6-10 pm. Dinner $19-$33. Bar 4 pm-midnight. Reservations required.Cr cds: A, D, DS, MC, V.

Marble Canyon (A-4)

See also Page

Pop 150 **Elev** 3,580 ft **Area code** 928 **Zip** 86036

What to See and Do

Marble Canyon. *Phone 800/433-2543.* Part of Grand Canyon National Park (see).

River-running trips. *Hwy 180. Phone 928/638-7888.* Multiday trips on the Colorado River. For a list of commercial operators contact Grand Canyon National Park, PO Box 129, Grand Canyon 86023.

Motels/Motor Lodges

★ **CLIFF DWELLERS LODGE.** *Hwy 89A (85321). Phone 928/355-2228; toll-free 800/433-2543; fax 928/355-2271. www.leesferry.com.* 20 rooms. S, D $60-$82. Restaurant 5 am-10 pm (winter hours may vary). Check-out 11 am. Business services available. Gift shop. Hiking, fishing; river raft trips. Cr cds: A, DS, MC, V.

★ **MARBLE CANYON LODGE.** *Hwy 89A (86036). Phone 928/355-2225; toll-free 800/726-1789; fax 928/355-2227.* 58 rooms, some kitchens May-Aug: S $45; D $55-$60; suites $125; kitchen units $55; under 12 free; some lower rates rest of year. Crib free. Pet accepted. Complimentary coffee in rooms. Restaurant 6 am-9 pm; Dec-Mar from 6:30 am. Bar 6 am-9 pm. Check-out 11 am. Coin laundry. Meeting rooms. Business services available. Sundries. Hiking. 3,500-foot paved landing strip. Shuttle service for river rafting. Cr cds: A, DS, MC, V.

McNary (E-6)

See also Greer, Pinetop, Show Low, Springerville

Pop 349 **Elev** 7,316 ft **Area code** 928 **Zip** 85930

McNary is in the northeastern section of the Fort Apache Indian Reservation. "Hon-dah" is Apache for "be my guest," and visitors find a warm welcome here. The White Mountain Apaches have a number of recreation areas on their reservation. Trout fishing, exploring, and camping are available. For further information contact White Mountain Recreation Enterprise, Game & Fish Department, Box 220, Whiteriver 85941; 928/338-4385.

What to See and Do

Hawley Lake. *12 miles E on AZ 260, then S 11 miles on AZ 473. Phone 928/335-7511 or 928/338-4417.* Summer activities including fishing; camping, hiking, and cabin rental. (May-Oct)

Sunrise Park Resort. *20 miles E on AZ 260, then S on AZ 273, on Fort Apache Indian Reservation. Phone 928/735-7669 or 800/772-7669.* Resort has two quad, four triple, double chairlift, three rope tows; patrol, school, rentals; cafeteria, restaurants, bars. Sixty-five runs. Also snowboarding. (Nov-mid-Apr, daily) Summer activities include swimming, fishing, canoeing; hiking, horseback riding, tennis. Camping. **$$$$**

Mesa (F-4)

See also Casa Grande, Chandler, Phoenix, Scottsdale, Tempe

Settled 1878 **Pop** 396,375 **Elev** 1,241 ft

Information Convention & Visitors Bureau, 120 N Center, 85201; 480/827-4700 or 800/283-6372

Web www.mesachamber.org

Mesa, Spanish for "table," sits atop a plateau overlooking the Valley of the Sun and is one of the state's largest and fastest-growing cities. Mesa offers year-round golf, tennis, hiking, and water sports. It also provides easy access to other Arizona and Southwest attractions.

What to See and Do

Arizona Museum for Youth. *35 N Robson. Phone 480/644-2467.* Fine arts museum with changing hands-on exhibits for children. (Tues-Sun; closed holidays) **$$**

Arizona Temple Visitor Center. *525 E Main St. Phone 480/964-7164.* Murals; ten-foot replica of Thorvaldsen's *Christus* statue; history of prehistoric irrigation; films; dioramas; information. Temple gardens (site of concert series) have large variety of trees, cacti, and shrubs collected from all over the world; extensive light display during Christmas season. The Church of Jesus Christ of Latter-day Saints (Mormon) Arizona Temple is located just south of visitor center (not open to the public). Tours of the visitor center (Daily). **FREE**

Boyce Thompson Southwestern Arboretum. *37615 Hwy 60. E via US 60 to Superior. Phone 520/689-2811.* Three hundred acres of gardens and natural areas include cacti, streamside forest, desert lake, hidden canyon, herb garden. Bookstore. Miles of nature trails. (Daily; closed Dec 25) **$$$**

Champlin Fighter Museum. *Falcon Field, 4636 Fighter Aces Dr. Phone 480/830-4540.* Large vintage fighter aircraft collection of WWI, WWII, Korean, and Vietnam War planes; also art gallery with paintings of aircraft in combat; extensive collection of photos of fighter aces from WWI to Vietnam. (Daily) **$$$**

Dolly Steamboat Cruises. *16802 NE Hwy 88. Phone 480/827-9144; fax 480/671-0483.* Narrated tours and twilight dinner cruises of Canyon Lake, following the original path of the Salt River. **$$$$**

Factory Stores of America. *2050 S Roslyn Pl (85208). Phone 480/984-0697.* If you can't get your fill of good deals, check out all the bargains just waiting for you and your shopping bags at this factory-outlet mall. The price is usually right at any of its 25 stores, which include All-Star Music, Book Warehouse, Casual Corner Outlet, Factory Brand Shoes, KB Toy Liquidators, Assonate, and Wallet Works. (Mon-Sat 10 am-8 pm, Sun noon-5 pm)

Lost Dutchman State Park. *6109 N Apache Tr. 14 miles E via US 60/89 to Apache Junction, then 5 miles NE via AZ 88 (Apache Tr Hwy). Phone 480/982-4485.* A 300-acre park in the Superstition Mountains area. Hiking, picnicking (shelter), improved camping (dump station). Interpretive trails and access to nearby forest service wilderness area. (Daily; closed Dec 25) Standard fees.

Mesa Southwest Museum. *53 N MacDonald St. Phone 480/644-2230.* At this natural history museum, you'll have only one thing on your mind: the Southwest, from the past to the present. You'll learn about the dinosaurs that once walked this very land and the Native Americans who lived off of it. You'll also see art of the ancient Americas, a replica of a Spanish mission, territorial jail cells from the Old West, and much more, as you explore this 80,000-square-foot regional resource. At the Adventure Center, interactive exhibits stimulate the young and curious. (Tues-Sun; closed major holidays) **$$**

River tubing. Salt River Recreation Inc. *N Bush Hwy (85215). 15 miles NE in Tonto National Forest (see PAYSON): E on US 60 to Power Rd, then N to junction Usery Pass Hwy. Phone 480/984-3305.* Fee includes tube rental and shuttle bus service to various points on the Salt River. (Mid-Apr-Sept) **$$$$**

Special Events

Arizona Renaissance Festival. *12601 E Hwy 60 (85219). Phone 520/463-2700.* Weekends Feb-mid-Mar.

Chicago Cubs Spring Training. *1235 N Center St (85201). Ho Ho Kam Park. Phone 480/964-4467.* Chicago Cubs baseball spring training, exhibition games. Late Feb-late Mar.

Mesa Territorial Day Festival. *Sirrine House, 160 N Center. Phone 480/644-2760.* Arizona's birthday party celebrated in Old West style. Western arts and crafts, music, food. Second Sat in Feb.

Motels/Motor Lodges

★★ **BEST WESTERN DOBSON RANCH INN & RESORT.** *1666 S Dobson Rd (85202). Phone 480/831-7000; toll-free 800/528-1356. www.dobsonranchinn.com.* 225 rooms, 2 story. S, D $60-$140; each additional $15; under 12 free; weekend rates. Complimentary full breakfast, newspaper. Check-out noon, check-in 2 pm. TV; cable (premium). In-room modem link. Restaurant 6:30 am-10 pm. Bar 10-1 am. Room service. Exercise equipment. Whirlpool. Cr cds: A, C, D, DS, MC, V.

D ⌨ 🏊 ⛵ SC

★ **BEST WESTERN SUPERSTITION SPRINGS INN.** *1342 S Power Rd (85206). Phone 480/641-1164; toll-free 800/780-7234; fax 480/641-7253. www.bestwestern.com.* 59 rooms, 2 story. S, D $49-$129; each additional $10; under 15 free. Pet accepted, some restrictions; fee. Complimentary continental breakfast. Check-out 11 am, check-in 2 pm. TV; cable (premium). In-room modem link. Exercise equipment. Pool, whirlpool. Cr cds: A, C, D, DS, JCB, MC, V.

D ⌨ 🍴 🏊 ⛵

★★ **COURTYARD BY MARRIOTT.** *1221 S Westwood Ave (85210). Phone 480/461-3000; toll-free 800/321-2211; fax 480/461-0179. www.marriotthotels.com.* 149 units, 3 story. Jan-Apr: S, D $109-$169; suites $159-$169; weekend rates (off-season); lower rates rest of year. Crib free. TV; cable (premium). Heated pool; whirlpool. Complimentary coffe in rooms. Restaurant 6-10 am; Fri to 10pm; Sat, Sun 7am-noon. Bar 5-10 pm. Check-out noon. Coin laundry. Meeting rooms. Business services available. In-room modern link. Valet service. Sundries. Exercise equipment. Refrigerator, microwave in suites. Many balconies. Cr cds: A, C, D, DS, MC, V.

D 🏊 ⛵

★ **FAIRFIELD INN BY MARRIOTT.** *1405 S Westwood (85210). Phone 480/668-8000; fax 480/668-7313. www.fairfieldinn.com.* 80 rooms, 3 story. S, D $59-$109; under 18 free. Complimentary continental breakfast. Check-out noon, check-in 3 pm. TV; cable (premium). In-room modem link. Pool, whirlpool. Cr cds: A, C, D, DS, MC, V.

D 🏊 ⛵ SC

★ **HAMPTON INN.** *1563 S Gilbert Rd (85204). Phone 480/926-3600; toll-free 800/426-7866; fax 480/926-4892. www.arizonahamptoninns.com.* 118 rooms, 4 story. S, D $49-$114; under 18 free. Pets accepted. Complimentary continental breakfast. Check-out noon, check-in 3 pm. TV; cable (premium). In-room modem link. Health club privileges. Whirlpool. Cr cds: A, C, D, DS, MC, V.

D ⌨ 🏊 ⛵ SC

★ **LA QUINTA INN AND SUITES.** *6530 E Superstition Springs Blvd (85206). Phone 480/654-1970; fax 480/654-1973. www.laquinta.com.* 113 rooms, 6 story. S, D $59-$119; suites $175; under 18 free. Pet accepted, some restrictions. Complimentary continental breakfast. Check-out noon, check-in 2 pm. TV; cable (premium). In-room modem link. Exercise equipment. Pool, whirlpool. Cr cds: A, C, D, DS, MC, V.

D ⌨ 🍴 🏊 ⛵

★ **DAYS INN EAST.** *5531 E Main St (85205). Phone 480/981-8111; fax 480/396-8027. www.daysinn.com.* 61 rooms, 2 story. S, D $49-$79; under 12 free. Complimentary continental breakfast. Check-out 11 am, check-in noon. TV. Whirlpool. Cr cds: A, C, D, DS, JCB, MC, V.

D ⌨ 🏊 ⛵ SC

★ **DAYS INN.** *333 W Juanita Ave (85210). Phone 480/844-8900; fax 480/844-0973. www.daysinn.com.* 128 rooms. S, D $39-$89; each additional $6; under 18 free. Complimentary continental breakfast. Check-out 11 am, check-in 2 pm. TV; cable (premium), VCR available (movies). Coin laundry. Exercise equipment, sauna. Whirlpool. Cr cds: A, C, D, DS, JCB, MC, V.

D 🏊 ⛵

Hotels

★★★ **HILTON EAST/MESA.** *1011 W Holmes Ave (85210). Phone 480/833-5555; toll-free 800/544-5266; fax 480/649-1886. www.mesapavilion.hilton.com.* 314 rooms, 8 story. S, D $59-$119; each additional $15; under 18 free; some weekend rates. Check-out noon, check-in 3 pm. TV; cable (premium), VCR available. In-room modem link. Restaurant 6:30 am-10 pm. Bar 11-1 am; seasonal entertainment. Exercise equipment. Poolside service (in season). Golf privileges. Business center. Luxury level. Cr cds: A, C, D, DS, MC, V.

D 🍴 🏋 🏊 ⛵ 🏃

★★★ **SHERATON MESA HOTEL AND CONVENTION CENTER.** *200 N Centennial Way (85201). Phone 480/898-8300; toll-free 800/456-6372; fax 480/964-9279. www.sheratonmesa.com.* 282 rooms, 12 story. D $89-$179; each additional $10; under 18 free. Pet accepted; fee. Check-out noon, check-in 3 pm. TV; cable (premium), VCR available. Restaurant 6 am-10 pm. Bar 4 pm-1 am. Exercise equipment. Whirlpool. Luxury level. Elaborate landscaping with palm trees, fountain. Cr cds: A, C, D, DS, JCB, MC, V.

[icons]

Resorts

★ ★ ★ **ARIZONA GOLF RESORT & CONFERENCE CENTER.** *425 S Power Rd (85206). Phone 480/832-3202; toll-free 800/528-8282; fax 480/981-0151. www.azgolfresort.com.* Tropical palms and beautiful lakes are the setting at this 150-acre golf resort. Guest suites, designed in clusters, have BBQs and heated spas. 285 kitchen units, 1-2 story. S, D $79-$159; each additional $15-$25; under 16 free; golf plans. Pets accepted. Check-out noon, check-in 3 pm. TV; cable (premium), VCR available. Dining room 6 am-9 pm. Bar 10 am-midnight. Exercise equipment. Lighted tennis. Cr cds: A, C, D, DS, ER, JCB, MC, V.

[icons]

★ ★ ★ **GOLD CANYON GOLF RESORT.** *6100 S Kings Ranch Rd (85218). Phone 480/982-9090; toll-free 800/624-6445; fax 480/983-9554. www.gcgr.com.* Whether taking in beautiful sunsets or hitting the driving range, guests at this golf resort will experience attentive service. 101 rooms, 1 story. S, D $69-$305; each additional $10; under 18 free. Pets accepted; fee. Check-out 11 am, check-in 4 pm. TV; VCR available. In-room modem link. Fireplaces; many whirlpools. Dining room 6:30 am-10 pm. Bar 10:30-1 am. Room service. Whirlpool, poolside service. 36-hole golf, greens fee $80-$135 (including cart). Lighted tennis. Bicycle rentals. Concierge. In foothills of Superstition Mountains on 3,300 acres. Cr cds: A, C, D, DS, JCB, MC, V.

[icons]

Restaurants

★ ★ **LANDMARK.** *809 W Main St (85201). Phone 480/962-4652; fax 480/962-1124. www.lmrk.com.* Specializes in seafood, beef, chicken. Hours: 11 am-9 pm, Sun to 7 pm. Closed July 4, Thanksgiving, Dec 25. Lunch $5.95-$11.95, dinner $9.95-$24.95. Service bar. Salad bar. Children's menu. Former Mormon church (circa 1905). Totally nonsmoking. Cr cds: A, DS, MC, V.

[icon]

★ ★ **MICHAEL MONTI'S MESA GRILL.** *1233 S Alma School Rd (85210). Phone 480/844-1918; fax 480/834-5317. www.montis.com.* Hours: 11 am-4 pm, 5-10 pm; Sat from noon; Sun 5-9 pm. Closed Dec 25. Lunch $5.29-$9.95, dinner $8.95-$33. Bar. Children's menu. Reservations accepted. Totally nonsmoking. Cr cds: A, D, DS, JCB, MC, V.

[icon]

Montezuma Castle National Monument (D-4)

See also Cottonwood, Flagstaff

(20 miles SE of Cottonwood on AZ 260, then N and E off I-17)

This 5-story, 20-room structure was built by Native Americans more than 800 years ago and is one of the most remarkable cliff dwellings in the United States. Perched under a protective cliff, which rises 150 feet, the dwelling is 70 feet straight up from the talus.

Visitors are not permitted to enter the castle, but there is a self-guided trail offering a good view of the structure and of other ruins in the immediate area. Castle "A," a second ruin, is nearby. Montezuma Well, about 11 miles northeast, is a 470-foot-wide limestone sinkhole, with a lake 55 feet deep. Around the rim are well-preserved cliff dwellings. An irrigation system built by the inhabitants about 800 years ago leads from the spring. Limited picnicking; no camping. The Castle Visitor Center and a self-guided trail are both accessible to wheelchairs. (Daily) Contact the Chief Ranger, Box 219, Camp Verde 86322; phone 520/567-3322.

Navajo Indian Reservation

See also Holbrook, Kayenta, Page, Winslow

The Navajo Nation is the largest Native American tribe and reservation in the United States. The reservation covers more than 25,000 square miles within three states: the larger portion in northeast Arizona and the rest in New Mexico and Utah.

More than 400 years ago, the Navajo people (the Dineh) moved into the arid southwestern region of the United States and carved out a way of life that was in harmony with the natural beauty of present-day Arizona, New Mexico, and Utah. In the 1800s, this harmonious life was interrupted by westward-moving settlers and the marauding cavalry. For the Navajo, this conflict resulted in their forced removal from their ancestral land and the "Long Walk" to Fort Sumner, New Mexico. This forced removal of the Navajo was judged a failure; in 1868, they were allowed to return to their homeland.

Coal, oil, and uranium have been discovered on the reservation. The income from these, which is handled democratically by the tribe, has helped improve its economic and educational situation.

The Navajo continue to practice many of their ancient ceremonies, including the Navajo Fire Dance and the Yei-bi-chei (winter) and Enemy Way Dances (summer). Many ceremonies are associated with curing the sick and are primarily religious in nature. Visitors must obtain permission to view these events; photography, recording, and sketching are prohibited.

Most of the traders on the reservation are friendly and helpful. Do not hesitate to ask them when and where the dances take place. Navajo Tribal rangers, who patrol tribal parks, also are extremely helpful and can answer almost any question that may arise.

There are a number of paved roads across the Navajo and Hopi Reservations (see)—as well as some unpaved gravel and dirt roads. During the rainy season (mostly August to September), the unpaved roads are difficult or impassable; it is best to stay off them.

Some of the most spectacular areas in Navajoland are Canyon de Chelly National Monument (see); Navajo National Monument (see); Monument Valley Navajo Tribal Park, north of Kayenta (see); Four Corners Monument; and Rainbow Bridge National Monument (see Utah). Hubbell Trading Post National Historic Site is in Ganado (see).

Accommodations on the reservation are limited; reservations are needed months in advance. For information contact the Navajoland Tourism Dept, Box 663, Window Rock 86515; phone 520/871-6436 or 520/871-7371.

Navajo National Monument (B-5)

See also Kayenta

19 miles SW of Kayenta on US 160, then 9 miles N on paved road AZ 564 to Visitor Center)

This monument comprises three scattered areas totaling 600 acres and is surrounded by the Navajo Nation. Each area is the location of a large and remarkable prehistoric cliff dwelling. Two of the ruins are accessible by guided tour.

Headquarters for the monument and the visitor center are near Betatakin, the most accessible of the three cliff dwellings. Guided tours, limited to 25 people (Betatakin tour), are arranged on a first-come, first-served basis (May-September; tours sometimes possible earlier in spring and late in fall; phone for schedule). Hiking distance is five miles round-trip including a steep 700-foot trail and takes five to six hours. Because of hot temperatures, high elevations, and rugged terrain, this tour is recommended only for those in good physical condition. Betatakin may also be viewed from the Sandal Trail overlook—a 1/2-mile, one-way, self-guided trail. (Daily)

The largest and best preserved ruin, Keet Seel (Memorial Day-Labor Day, phone for schedule), is 8 1/2 miles one-way by foot or horseback from headquarters. A permit is required either way, and reservations can be made up to two months in advance. Primitive campground available for overnight hikers. The horseback trip takes all day; horses should be reserved when making reservations (fee for horses and for guide; no children under 12 without previous riding experience).

The visitor center has a museum and film program. There are picnic tables, a campground, and a craft shop at the headquarters area. (Daily; closed Jan 1, Thanksgiving, Dec 25) Contact the Superintendent, HC-71, Box 3, Tonalea 86044-9704; phone 928/672-2367. **FREE**

Nogales (I-5)

See also Patagonia, Tucson

Founded 1880 **Pop** 20,878 **Elev** 3,869 ft **Area code** 520 **Zip** 85621

Information Nogales-Santa Cruz County Chamber of Commerce, 123 W Kino Park Pl; 520/287-3685

Web www.nogaleschamber.com

This is a pleasant city and port of entry directly across the border from Nogales, Mexico. (For Border Crossing Regulations, see MAKING THE MOST OF YOUR TRIP.) A Ranger District office of the Coronado National Forest (see TUCSON) is located here.

What to See and Do

Pimeria Alta Historical Society Museum. *136 N Grand Ave, in former City Hall.* Phone 520/287-4621. History of southern Arizona and northern Sonora, from A.D. 1000-present. Photo collection; library; archives; self-guided walking tours. (Tues-Sat; closed holidays) **FREE**

Tubac Presidio State Historic Park. *20 miles N off I-19.* Phone 520/398-2252. Arizona's first European settlement, where a presidio (military post) was built in 1752. Spanish colonial and territorial ruins. Picnicking. Museum with exhibits and underground view of the remains of the presidio's main building. (Daily; closed Dec 25) **$$**

Motel/Motor Lodge

★ **SUPER 8 MOTEL.** *547 W Mariposa Rd (85621). Phone 520/281-2242; fax 520/281-0125. www.super8.com.* 117 rooms, 3 story. No elevator. S $45-$55; D $56-$65; under 12 free. Crib $10. Pet accepted; $5 a day. Check-out noon. TV; cable. Refrigerators, microwaves. Valet services, coin laundry. Restaurant 6 am-9 pm. Bar 3-11 pm. Pool, whirlpool. Meeting rooms. Business services available. Cr cds: A, C, D, DS, MC, V.

[D] [🐾] [≈] [⊠] [SC]

Resort

★ ★ ★ **RIO RICO RESORT AND COUNTRY CLUB.** *Phone 520/281-1901; toll-free 800/288-4746; fax 520/281-7132. www.rioricoresort.com.* Go back in time with the Old West feel of this picturesque resort with its very own ghost town. 180 units, 2-3 story. No elevator. Jan-Apr: S, D $180; each additional $15; suites $250-$1,000; under 18 free; golf, tennis, horseback riding plans; lower rates mid-Apr-Sept. Crib free. Pet accepted; $50 refundable. TV; cable (premium). Heated pool; whirlpool, poolside service. Coffee in rooms. Dining room 6 am-2 pm, 5-9 pm. Box lunches, picnics. Room service. Bar 11-1 am; entertainment weekends. Check-out noon, check-in 4 pm. Grocery 1/2 mile. Meeting rooms. Business center. Valet service. Gift shop. Airport transportation. Lighted tennis. 18-hole golf, $85 with cart, pro, putting green, driving range. Stables. Exercise equipment; sauna. Lawn games. Some microwaves, refrigerators. Private patios, balconies. Western cook-outs. On mesa top with scenic view. Cr cds: A, C, D, DS, ER, JCB, MC, V.

[🐾] [🚶] [⛷] [≈] [🎿] [🏃]

Restaurant

★ **MR C'S.** *282 W View Point Dr (85621). Phone 520/281-9000; fax 520/281-1220.* Continental menu. Closed Jan 1, Dec 25; also Sun. Lunch, dinner. Children's menu. Hilltop location; supper club atmosphere. Cr cds: A, C, D, DS, MC, V. **$$**

Organ Pipe Cactus National Monument (H-3)

(Park entrance 15 miles S of Ajo on AZ 85; Visitor Center 35 miles S of Ajo on AZ 85)

This 516-square-mile Sonoran desert area on the Mexican border is Arizona's largest national monument. The organ pipe cactus grows as high as 20 feet and has 30 or more arms, which resemble organ pipes. The plant blooms in May and June. Blossoms, usually at branch tips, are white with pink or lavender touches. During February and March, depending on the rainfall, parts of the area may be covered with Mexican goldpoppy, magenta owl clover, blue lupine, and bright orange mallow. Mesquite, saguaro, several species of cholla, barrel cacti, paloverde trees, creosote bush, ocotillo, and other desert plants thrive here.

There are two graded scenic drives, which are self-guided: the 53-mile Puerto Blanco and the 21-mile Ajo Mountain drives. There is a 208-site campground near headquarters (May-mid-January, 30-day limit; mid-January-April, 14-day limit; 35-foot RV limit; fee), no reservations; groceries (5 miles). Information service and exhibits are at the visitor center (daily). Standard fees. Contact the Superintendent, Rte 1, Box 100, Ajo 85321; phone 520/387-6849.

B&B/Small Inn

★ ★ **GUEST HOUSE INN.** *700 Guest House Rd (85321). Phone 520/387-6133; fax 520/387-3995. www.guesthouseinn.biz.* 4 rooms. No room phones. Sept-May: S $59-$69; D $89; each additional $10; lower rates rest of year. Complimentary full breakfast. Check-out 11 am, check-in 2 pm. TV in sitting room; VCR available. Restaurant nearby. Former executive guest house built in 1925; stately dining room. Bird watching. Totally non-smoking. Cr cds: D, MC, V.

[⊠]

Page (A-4)

See also Marble Canyon, Navajo Indian Reservation

Pop 6,809 **Elev** 4,000 ft **Area code** 520 **Zip** 86040

Information Page/Lake Powell Chamber of Commerce, 644 N Navajo, Tower Plaza, Box 727; 520/645-2741 or 888/261-7243.

Web www.powellguide.com

Page is at the east end of the Glen Canyon Dam, on the Colorado River. The dam, 710 feet high, forms Lake Powell, a part of the Glen Canyon National Recreation Area. The lake, 186 miles long with 1,900 miles of shoreline, is the second-largest man-made lake in the United States.

The dam was built for the Bureau of Reclamation for water storage and the generation of electric power. The lake is named for John Wesley Powell, the intrepid and brilliant geologist who lost an arm at the Battle of Shiloh, led an expedition down the Colorado in 1869, and was later director of the US Geological Survey.

What to See and Do

Boat trips on Lake Powell. *100 Lake Shore Dr (86040). 6 miles N on US 89 at Wahweap Lodge and Marina. Phone 602/278-8888 ; 800/528-6154.* One-hour to one-day trips, some including Rainbow Bridge National Monument. Houseboat and powerboat rentals. Reservations advised.

Glen Canyon National Recreation Area. *PO Box 1507. Phone 928/608-6404.* More than one million acres including Lake Powell. Campfire program (Memorial Day-Labor Day). Swimming, waterskiing, fishing, boating (ramps, marina); hiking, picnicking, restaurants, lodge, camping. Developed areas in Utah include Bullfrog, Hite, Halls Crossing, Dangling Rope (accessible by boat only); many of these have ranger stations, marinas, boat rentals and trips, supplies, camping, and lodging. Lees Ferry on Colorado River (approximately 15 miles downstream from dam, but a 45-mile drive SW from Page) has a launch ramp and camping. Visitor center on canyon rim, adjacent to Glen Canyon Bridge on US 89, has historical exhibits. Ranger station, 7 miles N of dam at Wahweap. (Daily; closed Jan 1, Dec 25) Guided tours (summer). **$$$**

John Wesley Powell Memorial Museum. *6 N Lake Powell Blvd. Phone 928/645-9496.* Fluorescent rock collection, Native American artifacts; books, videos; replica of Powell's boat. (Mid-Mar-mid-Dec, schedule varies) **$**

Rainbow Bridge National Monument. *Box 1507. Approximately 60 miles NE in Utah, NW of Navajo Mountain. Phone 928/608-6404.* (see UTAH)

Scenic flights over area. *Page Airport in Classic Helicopter Building, 1/2 mile NE on US 89. For fee information contact Scenic Air, Box 1385. Phone 928/645-2494.* Trips vary from 30 minutes to more than two hours. (Daily; closed Jan 1, Thanksgiving, Dec 25)

Wilderness River Adventures. *2040 E Frontage Rd. Phone 800/528-6154.* Half-day smoothwater trip on the Colorado River in Glen Canyon in raftlike neoprene boats. (Mar-Oct) **$$$$**

Motels/Motor Lodges

★ ★ **BEST WESTERN ARIZONA INN.** *716 Rim View Dr (86040). Phone 928/645-2466; toll-free 800/826-2718; fax 928/645-2053.* 103 units, 3 story. Apr-Oct: S $62-$92; D $79-$92; each additional $5; suites $125; under 18 free; lower rates rest of year. Crib free. Pet accepted. Check-out noon. TV; cable, VCR (movies). Restaurant 6 am-10 pm. Bar. Pool, whirlpool. Airport transportation. Meeting rooms. Business services available. Cr cds: A, D, DS, MC, V.

★ **BEST WESTERN PAGE INN.** *207 N Lake Powell Blvd (86040). Phone 928/645-2451; toll-free 800/637-9183; fax 928/645-9552. www.bwwestoninn.domainvalet.com.* 90 rooms, 3 story. S $58-$62; D $63-$150; each additional $5; under 17 free. Pet accepted, some restrictions; fee. Complimentary continental breakfast. Check-out 11 am. TV; cable (premium), VCR available (movies). In-room modem link. Heated pool, whirlpool. Free airport transportation. Cr cds: A, C, D, DS, MC, V.

★ ★ **QUALITY INN AT LAKE POWELL.** *287 N Lake Powell Blvd (86040). Phone 520/645-8851; fax 520/645-2523.* 130 rooms, 3 story. Mid-Apr-Oct: S, D $85-$106; each additional $7; under 18 free; lower rates rest of year. Crib free. Pet accepted. TV; cable. Heated pool. Restaurant 6 am-10 pm (summer); 6:30 am-2 pm, 5-9 pm (winter). Room service from 7 am. Bar 4 pm-1 am (summer). Check-out 11 am. Coin laundry. Meeting rooms. Business services available. Bellstaff. Sundries. Gift shop. Private patios, balconies. Picnic tables, grills. Cr cds: A, C, D, DS, JCB, MC, V.

★ ★ ★ **WAHWEAP LODGE.** *100 Lakeshore Dr (86040). Phone 928/645-2433; toll-free 800/528-6154; fax 928/645-1031. www.visitlakepowell.com.* Located on beautiful Lake Powell, enjoy the spectacular atmosphere this homey lodge has to offer. Guestrooms include lake or resort views to enjoy. 350 rooms in 8 buildings, 2 story. May-Oct: S, D $125-$149; each additional $10; suites $227; under 18 free; lower rates rest of year. Crib free. Pet accepted. Check-out 11 am. TV; cable. Balconies, private patios. Coin laundry. Restaurant 6 am-10 pm. Bar 11-1 am; Sun from noon. Exercise equipment. 2 pools, whirlpool, poolside service. Golf privileges. Boats, motorboats, scenic boat trips. Host for national bass fishing tournaments. Free airport transportation. Meeting rooms, business services available. Bellstaff, concierge. Sundries, gift shop. Cr cds: A, C, D, DS, MC, V.

Restaurants

★ ★ **BELLA NAPOLI.** *810 N Navajo Dr (86040). Phone 928/645-2706; fax 928/645-2554.* Italian menu. Hours: 5-10 pm. Dinner $7-$18.95. Cr cds: A, DS, MC, V.

★ **KEN'S OLD WEST.** *718 Vista (86040). Phone 928/645-5160; fax 928/645-3349.* Specializes in steak, barbecued ribs. Hours: 4-11 pm. Closed Jan 1, Thanksgiving, Dec 25. Dinner $5.95-$26. Bar to 1 am. Salad bar. Children's menu. Patio dining. Cr cds: A, D, DS, MC, V.

Paradise Valley

Restaurant

★ ★ ★ **LON'S.** *5532 N Palo Cristi Rd (85253). Phone 602/955-7878; fax 602/955-7893. www.lons.com.* Built by southwestern artist Lon Megargee in the 1930s, the inn's adobe design and rustic furnishings are a fitting setting for some of the best American comfort food in Phoenix. Fresh fruits, vegetables and herbs from the chef's on-site garden make up the seasonal specials. Contemporary American menu. Hours: 11:30 am-2 pm, 6-10 pm; Sun brunch 10 am-2 pm. Closed Jan 1, Memorial Day, July 4, Labor Day. Dinner $18-$28. Bar. Children's menu. Casual attire. Outdoor dining. Cr cds: A, MC, V.

D

Parker (E-1)

See also Lake Havasu City

Founded 1908 **Pop** 3,140 **Elev** 413 ft **Area code** 520 **Zip** 85344

Information Chamber of Commerce, 1217 California Ave; 520/669-2174

Web www.coloradoriverinfo.com/parker

Parker is located on the east bank of the Colorado River, about 16 miles south of Parker Dam (320 feet high, 856 feet long), which forms Lake Havasu. Popular recreational activities in the area include fishing, frogging, boating, jet and water skiing, hunting, golfing, rock hunting, and camping. The town has become the trade center for surrounding communities and the Colorado Indian Reservation.

What to See and Do

Buckskin Mountain State Park. *5476 AZ 95. 11 miles NE on AZ 95. Phone 928/667-3231.* On 1,676 acres. Scenic bluffs overlooking the Colorado River. Swimming, fishing, boating (ramp, marina); nature trails, hiking, picnicking (shelter), concession, camping (electric hookups, dump station), riverside cabanas (fee). **River Island Unit** has boating (ramp); picnicking (shelter), camping (water hook-ups). (Daily) Standard fees. 1/2 mile N of main unit. Phone 928/667-3386 or 928/667-3231.

★ **Colorado River Indian Tribes Museum, Library, and Gaming Casino.** *Rodeo Dr. 928/669-9211.* Museum contains exhibits that interpret the history of the four Colorado River Tribes: Mohave, Chemehuevi, Navajo, and Hopi. Authentic Native American arts and crafts for sale. Bluewater Casino is open 24 hours; slots, poker, bingo.

Operated by the Colorado River Indian Tribes. (Mon-Sat; closed holidays) **FREE** The museum is part of the

Colorado River Indian Tribes Reservation. *Rodeo Dr. Phone 928/669-9211.* More than 278,000 acres in Arizona and California. Fishing, boating, waterskiing; hunting (tribal permit required), camping (fee).

La Paz County Park. *7350 Riverside Dr. 8 1/2 miles N on AZ 95. Phone 928/667-2069.* A 540-acre park with 4,000 feet of Colorado River beach frontage. Swimming, water-skiing, fishing, boating (ramps); tennis court, golf course, driving range, picnicking (shelter), playground, camping (electric hookups, dump station). Fee for some activities.

Parker Dam & Power Plant. *17 miles N via AZ 95, Riverside Dr exit. Phone 760/663-3712.* One of the deepest dams in the world, 65 percent of its structural height of 320 feet is below the riverbed. Only 85 feet of the dam is visible while another 62 feet of its superstructure rises above the roadway, across the top of the dam. (Daily) **FREE**

Special Events

Holiday Lighted Boat Parade. Decorated boats parade on the 11-mile strip to a selected site for trophy presentation; viewing from both sides of the river. Late Nov.

La Paz County Fair. *13991 2nd Ave (85344). Phone 928/669-8100.* Carnival, livestock auction, farm olympics, entertainment. Mid-Mar.

Parker 400 Off Road Race. *1217 S California Ave. Phone 928/669-2174.* Three Arizona loops. Four hundred miles of desert racing. Late Jan.

Parker Enduro-Aquasports Weekend. *One Park Dr (85344). Phone 928/669-2174 or 928/855-2208.* Longest and oldest boat racing event in the country. May.

Motel/Motor Lodge

★ **KOFA INN.** *1700 S California Ave (85344). Phone 928/669-2101; toll-free 800/742-6072; fax 928/669-6902.* 41 rooms, 1-2 story. S $41; D $45; each additional $4. Check-out noon. TV; cable. Restaurant adjacent open 24 hours. Pool. Sundries. Cr cds: A, C, D, MC, V.

D

Patagonia (I-5)

See also Nogales, Sierra Vista

Pop 881 **Elev** 4,057 ft **Area code** 520 **Zip** 85624

Information Information/Visitors Center, Horse of a Different Color Emporium, Box 241; 520/394-0060 or 888/794-0060

A small cattle town with a distinct mining flavor, Patagonia is surrounded by beautiful mountains and Hollywood-style Western scenery.

What to See and Do

Patagonia Lake State Park. *400 Patagonia Lake Rd. 8 miles S on AZ 82, then 4 miles N on Patagonia Lake Rd. Phone 520/287-6965.* A 265-acre park with a lake. Swimming beach, fishing, boating (ramp, rentals, marina); hiking, picnicking, concession, ramadas, camping (dump station). Standard fees.

Patagonia-Sonoita Creek Preserve. *150 Salero Canyon Rd. Along AZ 82; watch for directional signs to the entrance. Phone 520/394-2400.* The 312 acres extend downstream along Sonoita Creek for more than one mile. Bordered by willows, cottonwoods, and ash, it provides a perfect sanctuary for more than 250 species of birds.

Payson (E-5)

See also Phoenix

Founded 1882 **Pop** 13,620 **Elev** 5,330 ft **Area code** 520 **Zip** 85541

Information Chamber of Commerce, Box 1380, 85547; 520/474-4515 or 800/6-PAYSON

Web www.rimcountry.com

Payson, in the heart of the Tonto National Forest, provides many outdoor recreational activities in a mild climate.

What to See and Do

Tonto National Forest. *2324 E McDowell Rd. Phone 602/225-5200.* This area includes almost three million acres of desert and mountain landscape. Six lakes along the Salt and Verde rivers offer opportunities for fishing, boating, hiking, and camping. Seven wilderness areas are located within the forest's boundaries, providing hiking and bridle trails. The forest also features Tonto Natural Bridge, the largest natural travertine bridge in the world. Scenic attractions include the Apache Trail, Four Peaks, the Mogollon Rim, and Sonoran Desert country.

Special Events

Old-Time Fiddler's Contest & Festival. *Multi-Event Center/Rumsey Park. Phone 928/474-3398.* Late Sept.

World's Oldest Continuous PRCA Rodeo. *Multi-Event Center. Phone 928/474-4515.* Third weekend in Aug.

Motel/Motor Lodge

★ **HOLIDAY INN EXPRESS.** *206 S Beeline Hwy (85541). Phone 928/472-7484; fax 928/472-6283.* *www.holiday-inn.com.* 44 rooms, 3 story. June-Aug: S $89-$109; D $99-$119; each additional $10; suites $119-$169; under 19 free; higher rates during special events; lower rates rest of year. Crib free. Complimentary continental breakfast. Complimentary afternoon refreshments. Check-out 11 am. TV. Refrigerator in suites, microwave available. Coin laundry. Restaurant nearby. Indoor pool, whirlpool. Meeting rooms. Business services available. Sundries. Cr cds: A, D, DS, JCB, MC, V.

Hotels

★ ★ **BEST WESTERN PAYSON INN.** *801 N Beeline Hwy (85541). Phone 928/474-3241; toll-free 800/247-9477; fax 928/472-6564. www.innofpayson.com.* 99 rooms, 2 story. May-Sept: S, D $59-$89; each additional $10; apartment (2 bedroom) $149; under 16 free; lower rates rest of year. Crib $10. Pet accepted; $10-day. Complimentary continental breakfast. Check-out 11 am. TV; cable (premium). Private patios. Refrigerators, some in-room fireplaces. Complimentary coffee in rooms. Restaurant 11 am-2 pm, 5-9 pm, Fri-Sat to 10 pm. Bar from 4 pm. Heated pool, whirlpool. Meeting rooms. Business services available. Cr cds: A, C, D, DS, JCB, MC, V.

★ ★ **MAJESTIC MOUNTAIN INN.** *602 E Hwy 260 (85541). Phone 928/474-0185; toll-free 800/408-2442; fax 928/472-6097. www.majesticmountaininn.com.* 50 rooms, 1 story. Feb-Nov: S $55-$99; D $64-$99; each additional $6; lower rates rest of year. Crib free. Check-out 11 am. TV; cable (premium), VCR available (movies). Refrigerators, some fireplaces, in-room whirlpools. Complimentary coffee in rooms. Restaurant adjacent 10:30 am-9 pm. Health club privileges. Pool. Picnic tables, grills. Meeting rooms. Cr cds: A, C, D, DS, MC, V.

Restaurants

★ **LA CASA PEQUENA.** *911 S Beeline Hwy (85541). Phone 928/474-6329.* Mexican, American menu. Hours: 11 am-10 pm. Closed Thanksgiving, Dec 25. Bar to 1 am. Lunch $4.25-$7.95, dinner $5.50-$13.95. Specialties: La Casa chimichanga, chicken Acapulco, chicken fajitas. Entertainment Fri, Sat. Mexican décor; large collection of wheeled decanters. Surrounded by gardens. Cr cds: MC, V.

★ **MARIO'S.** *600 E AZ 260 (85541). Phone 928/474-5429.* American, Italian menu. Hours: 10:30 am-9 pm; Fri, Sat to 10 pm. Closed Memorial Day, Dec 25. Lunch $8-$12, dinner $10-$12. Bar. Entertainment weekends. Children's menu. Cr cds: DS, MC, V.

Peoria (F-4)

Restaurant

★ ★ **LE RHONE.** *9401 W Thunderbird Rd (85381). Phone 623/933-0151; fax 623/933-7187.* Swiss, continental menu. Closed Mon; Jan 1. Dinner. Bar. Cr cds: A, D, DS, MC, V.

D

Petrified Forest National Park (D-6)

See also Holbrook

(North entrance: 25 miles E of Holbrook on I-40; south entrance: 19 miles E of Holbrook on US 180)

These 93,532 acres include one of the most spectacular displays of petrified wood in the world. The trees of the original forest may have grown in upland areas and then washed down onto a floodplain by rivers. Subsequently, the trees were buried under sediment and volcanic ash, causing the organic wood to be filled gradually with mineral compounds, especially quartz. The grain, now multicolored by the compounds, is still visible in some specimens.

The visitor center is located at the entrance off I-40. The Rainbow Forest Museum (off US 180) depicts the paleontology and geology of the Triassic Era (daily; closed Dec 25). Service stations and cafeteria at the north entrance; snacks only at south entrance. Prehistoric Pueblo inhabitants left countless petroglyphs of animals, figures, and symbols carved on sandstone throughout the park.

The park contains a portion of the Painted Desert, a colorful area extending 200 miles along the north bank of the Little Colorado River. This highly eroded area of mesas, pinnacles, washes, and canyons is part of the Chinle formation, a soft shale, clay, and sandstone stratum of the Triassic age. The sunlight and clouds passing over this spectacular scenery create an effect of constant, kaleidoscopic change. There are very good viewpoints along the park road.

Picnicking facilities at Rainbow Forest and at Chinle Point on the rim of the Painted Desert; no campgrounds. Important: It is forbidden to take even the smallest piece of petrified wood or any other object from the park. Nearby curio shops sell wood taken from areas outside the park. (Daily; closed Dec 25) Standard fees. Contact the Superintendent, Box 2217, Petrified Forest National Park 86028; phone 520/524-6228.

Phoenix (F-4)

See also Major Cities

Settled 1864 **Pop** 1,321,045 **Elev** 1,090 ft **Area code** 602

Information Greater Phoenix Convention & Visitors Bureau, One Arizona Center, 400 E Van Buren St, Suite 600, 85004; 602/254-6500

Web www.visitphoenix.com

Suburbs Glendale, Mesa, Scottsdale, Tempe.

The capital of Arizona lies on flat desert, surrounded by mountains and green irrigated fields of cotton, lettuce, melons, and alfalfa and groves of oranges, grapefruit, lemons, and olives. It is a resort area as well as an industrial area. It is also the home of Grand Canyon University (1949). The sun shines practically every day. Most rain falls in December, with some precipitation in summer. There is swimming, fishing, boating, horseback riding, golf, and tennis. Phoenix, like Tucson, is a health center, known for its warm temperatures and low humidity. As a vacation spot, it is both sophisticated and informal.

What to See and Do

Antique Gallery/Central Antiques. *5037 N Central Ave (85012). Phone 602/241-1174; 602/241-1636.* As you browse through these two appealing galleries, sister stores in the same upscale shopping center, you'll be oohing and ahhing every step of the way. In 30,000 square feet of retail space, about 150 dealers showcase heirloom-quality antiques. No collectibles, no kitsch. We're talking period furniture, American and English silver, European porcelain, and much more. Even if the prices top your budget, you'll be glad you stopped in for a look-see. (Daily; closed major holidays)

Arizona Diamondbacks (MLB). *401 E Jefferson. Bank One Ballpark. Phone 602/462-6000.*

Arizona Mining & Mineral Museum. *1502 W Washington. Phone 602/255-3791.* Collections of minerals, ores, gems; petrified wood; mining exhibits. Maintained by the Arizona Department of Mines and Mineral Resources. (Mon-Sat; closed holidays) **FREE**

Arizona Science Center. *600 E Washington St (85004). Phone 602/716-2000.* People of all ages tote their curiosity to this cavernous learning center and have a field day getting smarter. More than 300 hands-on exhibits give the serious and mysterious world of science a fun twist and help teach inquiring minds about topics ranging from geology and weather to healing and information technology. See the universe up close in a planetarium and stare wide-eyed at science films in a theater with a five-story screen. (Daily; closed Thanksgiving, Dec 25) **$$**

Arizona State Capitol Museum. *1700 W Washington St (85007). Phone 602/542-4675 or 602/542-4581.* Built in 1899, this stately building first served as the capitol for the territorial government, and then the state capitol beginning in 1912, when Arizona was admitted to the Union. In need of more space, the state moved to adjacent office buildings in the 1970s, and this original structure has operated as a museum since its restoration in 1981. Wander through its history-filled halls and you'll see offices with period furniture and the House and Senate chambers exactly as they looked in early statehood. Don't miss the mosaic Arizona state seal on the rotunda floor and Winged Victory, a 16-foot zinc weather vane standing tall atop the capitol's copper dome. Guided tours are offered daily at 10 am and 2 pm. A landscaped area includes a variety of native trees, shrubs, and cacti. (Mon-Fri 8 am-5 pm, Sat 10 am-3 pm, closed Sun) **FREE**

Biltmore Fashion Park. *2502 E Camelback Rd (85016). Phone 602/955-1963.* If you have expensive taste, take your designer pocketbook here for high-end shopping in a low-key, relaxed outdoor setting. The more than 40 stores include A-list retailers such as Cartier, Christofle, Escada, Gucci, and Saks Fifth Avenue and a few less pricey options—Banana Republic, Chico's, Macy's, and Talbots among them. The merchants line a red-brick walkway that's colorfully landscaped and dotted with soothing water fountains. Dine in one of several restaurants, some with alfresco seating perfect for fashionista watching. (Daily; closed Thanksgiving, Dec 25)

Camelback Mountain. *Trailheads at Echo Canyon Pkwy, south of McDonald Dr; and Cholla Ln, east of 64th St. Phone 602/262-8318.* Its distinctive hump makes this mountain a very visible local landmark—and a very popular spot for hiking and toning those thighs. Go and enjoy its trails, which wind through desert flora and fauna, but don't be overzealous: the two strenuous summit trails, 1.2 and 1.5 miles one way, gain more than 1,200 feet in elevation and aren't for the out of shape. Two shorter ones at the base provide much easier trekking, with elevation gains of only 100 and 200 feet. (Daily dawn-dusk)

Celebrity Theatre. *440 N 32nd St (85008). Phone 602/267-1600.* The stargazing's stellar in the wide-open Arizona desert, but you can get front-row views of shining stars without ever leaving the busy streets of Phoenix. Some of the entertainment industry's biggest names bring their music and comedy to this theater. And even though the venue holds more than 2,000, no seat is more than 75 feet from center stage, a guarantee that you'll like what you see. Plus, the stage revolves, so you see a show from all angles.

Char's Has the Blues. *4631 N 7th Ave (85013). Phone 602/230-0205.* At this small, nothing-fancy joint, bands sing the blues every night—and that's nothing to cry in your beer about. All the wailing makes for very good listening if these typically sad songs touch your soul. New Times, the weekly alternative newspaper in Phoenix, named Char's the city's best blues club for 11 consecutive years. A diverse crowd spans all ages. (Daily) **$$**

Desert Botanical Gardens. *1201 N Galvin Pkwy (86008). Phone 480/941-1217 or 480/941-1225.* Includes 150 acres of plants from the world's deserts; self-guided nature walk; public lectures; Cactus Show (Apr). (Daily; closed July 4, Dec 25) **$$$**

Dog racing. *3801 E Washington St. Phoenix Greyhound Park. Phone 602/273-7181.* (Daily)

Encanto Park and Recreation Area. *Encanto Blvd (85007). Between 7th and 15th aves. Phone 602/261-8993.* Pack up the family and head to this 222-acre park for lots of fun in the sun just minutes from downtown. Active kids with energy to burn can fish in a small lake, feed ducks in a pond, ride in boats, frolic on playground equipment, cool off in the swimming pool, hop aboard a train and eight other rides geared toward 2- to 10-year-olds at the Enchanted Island amusement park (Wed-Sun; **$$**), and more. Two public golf courses (18 holes and 9 holes; **$$-$$$$**) appeal to the older crowd. (Daily) **FREE**

⭐ **The Heard Museum.** *2301 N Central Ave (85004). Phone 602/252-8848 or 602/252-8840.* At this stellar museum, which has won international accolades, immerse yourself in the cultures and art of Native Americans of the Southwest. The 130,000-square-foot attraction has nearly 30,000 square feet of exhibit space in 10 galleries (and a working-artist studio)—all packed with must-sees that attract nearly 250,000 visitors each year. Its collection of 32,000 works of art and ethnographic objects includes 3,600 pieces of contemporary Native-American fine art, 437 historic Hopi katsina dolls, more than 500 pieces of important Navajo and Zuni jewelry, and 90 prize-winning documented Navajo textiles. As part of its year-round education program, the Heard also offers artist demonstrations, music and dance performances, and many classes and workshops. An 8,500-square-foot branch location in north Scottsdale (34505 N Scottsdale Rd; 480/488-9817) features changing exhibitions by Native-American artists. (Daily 9:30 am-5 pm; closed holidays) **$$$**

Heritage Square. *115 N Sixth St. Phone 602/262-5071 or 602/262-5029.* Historical city park has eight turn-of-the-century houses, including restored 1895 Victorian Rosson House (Wed-Sun; fee) and Arizona Doll & Toy Museum. Also open-air Lath House Pavilion. (Daily) **FREE**

MercBar. *2525 E Camelback Rd (85016). Phone 602/508-9449.* The beautiful people who come to this ultrachic bar to see and be seen know the drink of choice: the martini, which the Merc shakes up in 13 different ways. Its various takes on this classic cocktail rate among the best in the Valley—as well they should at $9 to $10 a glass. Patrons savor the pricey drinks in their best attire; this is not the place to dress down. Dark wood and leather seating give this hotspot a sophisticated, worldly look that clashes with casual. (Daily)

Mr. Lucky's. *3660 NW Grand Ave (85019). Phone 602/246-0686.* Cowboys and cowgirls have been slippin' into their boots and slidin' over to this old-fashioned country dance hall for serious two-steppin' to live music since 1966. Come join in the foot-shufflin' even if you're a city slicker frettin' about steppin' on toes; instructors will teach you all the right moves. Try the live bull-riding in the parking lot, too. Bring the kids on Friday night for mutton-bustin' (sheep-riding) at 7:30, just before the kids' talent show. (Wed-Sat) Wed and Thurs no cover charge. **$$**

★ **Mystery Castle.** *800 E Mineral Rd (85066). Seven miles S via Central Ave, E on Baseline Rd, S on 7th St, then E on Mineral Rd. Phone 602/268-1581.* Some dads build dreamy playhouses for their little girls, but Boyce Luther Gulley fashioned an 18-room castle with 13 fireplaces for his daughter Mary Lou. It's how Gulley marked time between 1930 and 1945 after being diagnosed with tuberculosis and abandoning his family in Washington State to try beating his disease in barren Arizona. Mary Lou learned about her dad's labor of love after his death in the 1940s and has been keeping up appearances there ever since. If you're lucky, the lady of the house will lead your tour herself, as she often does. Architectural Digest it's not. Quirky best describes what you'll see in this unconventional, imaginative desert manor made of native stone and found objects and furnished with Southwestern antiques. (Thurs-Sun; closed July-Sept) **$**

Papago Park. *625 N Galvan Pkwy (85086). Phone 602/262-4837.* This 1,200-acre park with sandstone buttes is flatter than many others in the area, so it doesn't offer serious fitness buffs strenuous hiking. But the terrain appeals to novice hikers and mountain-bikers, who like to pedal its 10 miles of trails. And because it's close to the Phoenix Zoo, families often come to enjoy its many picnic areas and fishing lagoon. The golf course lures duffers. All park visitors get good views of the city, especially at sunset from the Hole-in-the-Rock Archaeological Site, a naturally eroded rock formation. (Daily 6 am-11 pm) **FREE**

Phoenix Art Museum. *1625 N Central Ave (85004). Phone 602/257-1880.* At more than 160,000 square feet, this spectacle of color is one of the largest art museums in the Southwest. Its collection spans the centuries and exceeds 17,000 works, about 1,000 on display at any given time in several galleries divided into three main sections: Art of Asia, Art of the Americas and Europe to 1900, and Art of Our Time: 1900 to the Present. Major traveling exhibits also hang here. Every third Sunday of each month, the museum sponsors Family Sundays for children ages 5-12 and the adults in their lives who want to encourage their creative development. The participatory fun includes imaginative art projects and self-guided explorations of the galleries. (Tues-Sun; closed major holidays) Free admission Thurs. **$$**

Phoenix Coyotes (NHL). *9375 E Bell Rd, Scottsdale. Phone 480/784-4444. America West Arena, ALLTEL Ice Den.*

Phoenix International Raceway. *7602 S 115th Ave (85323). Avondale. Phone 602/252-2227.* If you've seen Days of Thunder, starring Tom Cruise, you've seen this high-octane attraction on the big screen. On six weekends spread throughout the year, big-name drivers fire up their souped-up engines and go for speedy spins on its 1-mile track. The NASCAR Weekend in late fall generates the most sparks, with more than 100,000 fans lapping up all the fast-forward action, which features the Winston Cup Series, the Busch Series, and the Craftsman Truck Series. Other events that zoom into town and onto the track include the Rolex Grand American Sports Car Series and the IRL Indy Car Series. No other speedways in Arizona open their greasy pits to so many different classes of cars. But it also hosts plenty of non-racing events, a large Fourth of July celebration, festivals, arts and crafts fairs, and one of the Southwest's largest chili cook-offs. **$$$$**

Phoenix Mercury (WNBA). *201 E Jefferson St. Phone 602/252-WNBA. America West Arena.*

Phoenix Mountains Preserve. *16th St and Greenway Rd. Phone 602/262-6861.* Located in both the northern and southern parts of the city, the parks offer more than 23,500 acres of unique desert mountain recreational activities. Hiking, riding, and picnicking daily. **FREE** Located here are

Echo Canyon. *E McDonald and Tatum Blvd. Phone 602/256-3220.* (Camelback Mountain) Hiking trails, including trail to top of Camelback Mountain.

North Mountain Recreation Area. *10600 N 7th St. Phone 602/262-7901.* Hiking on mountain trails. Picnicking (shelter).

South Mountain. *10919 S Central. Phone 602/262-6111.* Offers 16,000 acres in a rugged mountain range. Hiking trails, park drives to scenic overlooks, picnicking (shelter).

Squaw Peak Park. *2701 E Squaw Peak Dr (85016). Phone 602/262-7901.* When you want to get your heart pumping, go trailblazing on this craggy pinnacle. When you do, you'll probably have plenty of company, and it will soon become apparent why. Besides a calorie-busting workout, this vertical climb delivers views that may take your breath away as much as the hiking does. The demanding, 1.2-mile trek up the Summit

Trail will test you every step of the way. For an easier go, opt for the Circumference Trail. (Daily)

Phoenix Museum of History. *105 N 5th St. Phone 602/253-2734.* More than 2,000 years of Arizona history; changing exhibits. (Daily; closed holidays) **$$**

Phoenix Suns (NBA). *201 E Jefferson. Phone 602/379-7867. America West Arena.*

Phoenix Zoo. *455 N Galvin Pkwy (85008). In Papago Park. Phone 602/273-1341.* Now that the Arabian oryx—the flagship species at this animal attraction—have moved into a new home at the zoo, visitors get even better views of these desert bighorn sheep. You don't want to butt heads with them, of course, but you'll be glad to get good glimpses of them. In all, you'll see more than 400 mammals, 500 birds, and 500 reptiles and amphibians. Walk (or hop, if you like) among the wallabies in a new exhibit coming December 2003. (Daily; closed Dec 25)**$$$** Opposite the zoo is

Hall of Flame Firefighting Museum. *6101 E Van Buren St (85008). Phone 602/275-3473.* So many kids dream of someday sliding down a firehouse pole, climbing aboard a bright red firetruck, and rushing off to battle a three-alarm blaze. So it's no wonder that this smokin' museum, believed to be the largest of its kind in the world, brings big, wide smiles to kids' faces. Its four galleries are packed with more than 90 pieces of awe-inspiring firefighting equipment, from antique, hand-drawn pumps dating as far back as the 1700s to snazzy, motorized fire engines. (Daily; closed Jan 1, Thanksgiving, Dec 25) **$$**

Pioneer Living History Museum. *3901 W Pioneer Rd (85086). Phone 623/465-1052.* Escape the freeways of modern-day Phoenix and experience city life as pioneers in the Old West knew it, sans cars. On these 90 acres celebrating the 1800s, you can belly up to the bar in the saloon, check out the chiseling in the blacksmith shop, eye the vintage fashions in the dress store, say a little prayer in the community church, and more. While in town, mind your manners: say howdy to the manly cowboys and tip your hat to the lovely Victorian ladies. (Wed-Sun) **$$**

Pueblo Grande Museum and Archaeological Park. *4619 E Washington St. Approximately 1 mile NE of Sky Harbor International Airport. Phone 602/495-0901.* At the ruins of a Hohokam village, you can revisit the past and learn how these prehistoric people lived in Arizona 1,500 years ago. You'll see an old platform mound that the Hohokam probably used for ceremonies or as an administrative center, an excavated ball court, reproductions of adobe homes, and irrigation canals used for farming. Make the rounds of this 102-acre park on your own, or take a guided tour on Saturday at 11 am or 1 pm or on Sunday at 1:30 pm. (Daily; closed major holidays) Free admission Sun. **$**

Roadrunner Park Farmers' Market. *3501 Cactus Rd (85032). Phone 623/848-1234.* On Saturday mornings, up to 5,000 people shop at this outdoor market to stock up on fresh produce grown in the Arizona desert. As many as 60 vendors sell melons, onions, peppers, squash, tomatoes, and other fresh-from-the-farm crops (though a few peddle arts and crafts, instead). The same association that operates this food fest also runs seven smaller ones in the area, including two downtown at Heritage Square (Thurs, 10 am-2 pm, Oct-May) and Patriot Square (Wed, 10 am-2 pm, Oct-Apr). (Sat 8 am-noon; closed Jan 1, Dec 25) **FREE**

The Shops at Arizona Center. *Van Buren St between 3rd and 5th sts. Phone 602/271-4000.* Tucked behind two downtown office buildings—One Arizona Center and Two Arizona Center—sits this parklike plaza for your entertainment pleasure. Even though the plaza is attractively landscaped with palm trees, gardens, and pools, you may not notice it from the street, but you'd be wise to look for it. While you're there, you can shop at about 15 stores and kiosks, including Copper Square Clothing Company, where nothing sells for more than $12.99. Who can resist a good bargain? The hungry break bread in seven restaurants, while revelers whoop it up in four nightclubs. The more sedate sit back, relax, and take in the latest Hollywood flicks at a 24-screen theater. (Daily; closed Jan 1, Thanksgiving, Dec 25)

Thoroughbred Horse Racing. *Turf Paradise, 1501 W Bell Rd, 10 miles N on I-17 to Bell Rd exit. Phone 602/942-1101.* (Late Sept-early May, Mon, Tues, Fri-Sun; closed holidays)

Vans Skatepark. *9617 N Metro Pkwy W, Suite 2129 (85051). Phone 602/944-2204.* If you or your family members like to skateboard or go in-line skating, this is the place to spin your wheels in Phoenix. The riding areas and obstacles include a street course with birch ramps and a wooden bowl with swimming-pool tiles and coping. The park accommodates all skill levels, so don't worry if you're not up for a challenge. Three days a week, it also offers sessions for BMX bikers. (Mon-Thurs 10 am-10 pm, Fri 10 am-midnight, Sat-Sun 10 am-9:45 pm)

Special Events

Arizona Opera. *225 E Adams St (85004). Phone 602/266-7464.* The high notes of arias have been ringing across the Arizona wilderness for more than 25 years, prompting many a bravo. So if the passionate music of opera lights your fire, you'll likely be drawn to the Phoenix Symphony Hall, where this company produces five operas each season. Between October 2003 and March 2004, it will stage The Pearl Fishers, The Mikado, Don Pasquale, Sweeney Todd, and La Boheme in both Phoenix and Tucson. Fri-Sun, Oct-Mar.

Arizona State Fair. *1826 W McDowell Rd (85007). Phone 602/252-6771.* This annual event attracts big, big crowds—and with good reason. It's fun and entertaining, and has everything you'd expect at a good ol' state fair: a busy midway packed with exciting rides and games; high-decibel concerts, some featuring marquis names such as country crooners Mark Chesnutt, Joe Diffie, and Tracy Lawrence; gooey cotton candy and other carnival fare; animal and 4-H exhibits; all-Indian rodeo action; cooking contests guaranteed to whet any appetite, and much, much more. Early-mid Oct.

Arizona Theatre Company. *502 W Roosevelt. Phone 602/256-6899 or 602/256-6995.* Professional regional company performs both classic and contemporary works. Oct-May.

Cowboy Artists of America Sale and Exhibition. *1625 N Central Ave # 1 (85004). Phone 602/257-1880.* Members of Cowboy Artists of America—a select group of 20-plus who produce fine Western American art—are considered the most prestigious in this genre. At this annual event, they offer more than 100 of their new, never-before-viewed works for sale, but not at Old West prices. Indeed, some of the art commands six figures. Whoa! But don't worry if that's way more bucks than you can wrangle. All the paintings, drawings, and sculptures, remain on exhibit for several weeks before buyers claim them, so you can appreciate these colorful pieces without having to pony up a cattle baron's pay. Late Oct-mid-Nov.

Fiesta Bowl. *120 S Ash Ave (85281). Phone 480/350-0900.* College football classic game. Early Jan.

Firecracker Sports Festival. *9833 N 25th Ave (85021). Phone 602/262-6483.* About 140 teams from throughout Arizona come to play ball during this annual event, the state's largest and longest-running softball tournament. The action features adult slow pitch and youth (girls) fast pitch in up to 13 divisions (based on age, sex, and skill level of players). The Ross Mofford Sports Complex hosts the opening-night party and colorful fireworks display that launch the tourney each year, but three other venues also host all the pitching, hitting, and fielding. Last weekend in June.

Indian Fair and Market. *2301 N Central Ave (85004). Heard Museum (see). Phone 602/252-8840.* Native American artisans, demonstrations, dances, native foods. First weekend in Mar.

The New Works Festival. *100 E McDowell Rd (85004). Phone 602/254-2151.* Want to see plays and musicals staged in their early phases? This festival does just that, as actors perform works-in-progress with "books in hand" and with minimal set decorations. Ultimately, some of those put to the test get further developed and fine-tuned, then get produced as part of Phoenix Theatre's regular

season. But you can brag you saw them first. Mid-July-early Aug.

The Phoenix Symphony. *225 E Adams St. Symphony Hall. Phone 602/495-1999.* May.

Yaqui Indian Holy Week Ceremonials. *Yaqui Temple and Ceremonial Grounds. Phone 602/883-2838.* Fri evenings prior to Easter, beginning the first Fri after Ash Wednesday.

Motels/Motor Lodges

★★ **BEST WESTERN EXECUTIVE PARK HOTEL.** *1100 N Central Ave (85004). Phone 602/252-2100; fax 602/340-1989. www.bestwestern.com.* 113 rooms, 8 story. S, D $55-$129; each additional $10; under 18 free; weekend rates. Check-out noon, check-in 3 pm. TV. In-room modem link. Restaurant 6:30 am-10 pm. Bar 11 am-11 pm, room service. Exercise equipment, sauna. Whirlpool, poolside service. Panoramic mountain views. Free airport transportation. Cr cds: A, C, D, DS, MC, V.

🅓 🏊 ✈ 🏌

★★ **BEST WESTERN GRACE INN AT AHWATUKEE.** *10831 S 51st St (85044). Phone 480/893-3000; toll-free 800/843-6010; fax 480/496-8303. www.bestwestern.com.* 175 rooms, 6 story. S, D $59-$169; each additional $10; under 17 free. Check-out noon, check-in 3 pm. TV; cable (premium). Restaurant 6 am-10 pm. Bar 11:30-1 am; Sun from noon, entertainment. Room service. Poolside service. Lighted tennis. Lawn games. Luxury level. Free airport transportation. Cr cds: A, C, D, DS, JCB, MC, V.

🅓 🏊 ✈ 🏌 SC

★ **BEST WESTERN INN SUITES HOTEL.** *1615 E Northern Ave (85020). Phone 602/997-6285; toll-free 800/752-2204; fax 602/943-1407. www.bestwestern.com.* 105 rooms, 2 story. S, D $69.99-$199.99; under 19 free. Pet accepted, some restrictions; fee. Complimentary continental breakfast. Check-out noon, check-in 2 pm. TV; cable (premium). In-room modem link. Health club privileges, exercise equipment. Whirlpool. Cr cds: A, C, D, DS, MC, V.

🅓 🐾 🏊 🏌 SC

★★ **COURTYARD BY MARRIOTT.** *2101 E Camelback Rd (85016). Phone 602/955-5200; fax 602/955-1101. www.courtyard.com.* 167 rooms, 4 story. S, D $79-$169; under 13 free; weekend, weekly, holiday rates. Check-out noon, check-in 3 pm. TV; cable (premium). In-room modem link. Restaurant 6:30-10:30 am; Sat, Sun 7 am-noon. Bar 4-11 pm. Room service. Exercise equipment. Whirlpool. Cr cds: A, C, D, DS, MC, V.

🅓 🏊 🏌 SC

★ ★ **COURTYARD BY MARRIOTT.** *2621 S 47th St (85034). Phone 480/966-4300; fax 480/966-0198. www.courtyard.com.* 145 units, 4 story. Jan-early May: S, D $159-$169; each additional $10; suites $179-$189; weekend, weekly rates; lower rates rest of year. Crib free. TV; cable (premium). Heated pool; whirlpool. Complimentary coffee in rooms. Restaurant 6 am-2 pm, 5-10 pm; weekends 7 am-noon, 5-10 pm. Bar 4-11 pm. Check-out noon. Coin laundry. Meeting rooms. Business services available. In-room modem link. Valet service. Free airport transportation. Exercise equipment. Health club privileges. Refrigerator in suites. Many balconies. Cr cds: A, C, D, DS, MC, V.

★ ★ **COURTYARD BY MARRIOTT METRO CENTER MALL.** *9631 N Black Canyon Hwy (85021). Phone 602/944-7373; fax 602/944-0079. www.courtyard.com/phxmc.* 146 rooms, 3 story. Jan-mid-Apr: S, D $149-$159, suites $169-$179; under 18 free; weekend rates; lower rates rest of year. Crib free. Check-out noon. TV; cable (premium). In-room modem link. Balconies. Some refrigerators, microwaves available. Complimentary coffee in rooms. Valet services, coin laundry. Restaurant 5-10 pm. Exercise equipment. Heated pool, whirlpool. Business services available. Cr cds: A, C, D, DS, JCB, MC, V.

★ **FAIRFIELD INN BY MARRIOTT AIRPORT.** *4702 E University Dr (85034). Phone 480/829-0700; fax 480/829-8068. www.marriott.com.* 108 rooms, 3 story. S, D $49-$119; under 18 free. Complimentary continental breakfast. Check-out noon, check-in 3 pm. TV; cable (premium), VCR available. In-room modem link. Pool, whirlpool. Cr cds: A, C, D, DS, MC, V.

★ **HAMPTON INN.** *8101 N Black Canyon Hwy (85021). Phone 602/864-6233; fax 602/995-7503. www.hamptoninn.com.* 147 rooms, 3 story. Jan-mid-Apr: S, D $79-$99; under 18 free; higher rates during special events; lower rates rest of year. Crib free. Pet accepted, some restrictions; $25. Complimentary continental breakfast. Check-out noon. TV; cable (premium). In-room modem link. Heated pool, whirlpool. Grills. Meeting rooms. Business services available. Cr cds: A, C, D, DS, ER, JCB, MC, V.

★ ★ **HOLIDAY INN.** *1500 N 51st Ave (85043). Phone 602/484-9009; toll-free 800/465-4329; fax 602/484-0108. www.holiday-inn.com.* 147 rooms, 4 story. S, D $69-$139; each additional $10; under 18 free. Pet accepted; fee. Check-out noon, check-in 2 pm. TV; cable (premium), VCR available. Restaurant 6 am-10 pm; weekend hours vary. Bar 11 pm-1 am. Exercise equipment, sauna. Pool, whirlpool, poolside service. Golf privileges. Cr cds: A, C, D, DS, JCB, MC, V.

★ ★ **HOLIDAY INN SELECT AIRPORT.** *4300 E Washington St (85034). Phone 602/273-7778; toll-free 800/465-4329; fax 602/275-5616. www.holiday-inn.com/phx-airport.* 299 rooms, 10 story. S, D $59-$159; each additional $10; under 18 free. Pet accepted, fee. Check-out noon, check-in 3 pm. TV; cable (premium). In-room modem link. Restaurant 6 am-10 pm. Bar 11-1 am; entertainment Fri, Sat. Exercise equipment. Game room. Whirlpool, poolside service. Free airport transportation. Cr cds: A, C, D, DS, JCB, MC, V.

★ **HOMEWOOD SUITES.** *2001 E Highland Ave (85016). Phone 602/508-0937; fax 602/508-0854. www.homewood-suites.com.* 124 kitchen units, 4 story. Suites $99-$169; each additional $10; under 18 free; weekly, weekend, holiday rates. Pet accepted, some restrictions; fee. Complimentary continental breakfast. Check-out noon, check-in 3 pm. TV; cable (premium), VCR available. In-room modem link. Some fireplaces. Health club privileges, exercise equipment. Pool. Business center. Cr cds: A, C, D, DS, MC, V.

★ **LA QUINTA INNS.** *2725 N Black Canyon Hwy (85009). Phone 602/258-6271; toll-free 800/531-5900; fax 602/340-9255. www.laquinta.com.* 141 rooms, 2 story. S, D $49-$109; each additional $10; under 18 free. Pet accepted, some restrictions. Complimentary continental breakfast. Check-out noon, check-in 1 pm. TV; cable (premium). Cr cds: A, C, D, DS, MC, V.

★ ★ **WYNDHAM GARDEN.** *2641 W Union Hills Dr (85027). Phone 602/978-2222; fax 602/588-9972. www.wyndham.com.* 182 rooms, 2 story. D $39-$159; each additional $10; under 18 free. Check-out noon, check-in 3 pm. TV; cable (premium). In-room modem link. Restaurant 6:30 am-10 pm. Bar 4:30-11 pm. Room service 5-10 pm. Exercise equipment. Heated pool; whirlpool, poolside service. Cr cds: A, C, D, DS, MC, V.

★ **PHOENIX INN SUITES.** *2310 E Highland Ave (85016). Phone 602/956-5221; toll-free 800/956-5221; fax 602/468-7220. www.phoenixinnsuites.com.* 123 rooms, 4 story. D $109-$185; each additional $10; under 18 free.

Complimentary continental breakfast. Check-out noon, check-in 4 pm. TV; cable (premium), VCR available. In-room modem link. Health club privileges, exercise equipment. Whirlpool. Free airport transportation. Cr cds: A, C, D, DS, MC, V.

⊡ ⇌ 🏃 ⤨ SC

★ ★ **QUALITY INN SOUTH MOUNTAIN.** *5121 E Lapuente Ave (85044). Phone 480/893-3900; toll-free 800/562-3332; fax 480/496-0815. www.qualityinn.com.* 182 rooms, 4 story. S, D $49-$129; under 17 free. Pet accepted; fee. Complimentary continental breakfast. Check-out noon, check-in 3 pm. TV. In-room modem link. Restaurant 6:30-10 am, 5-10 pm. Whirlpool. Cr cds: A, C, D, DS, JCB, MC, V.

🐾 ⇌

★ ★ **RED LION.** *12027 N 28th Dr (85029). Phone 602/ 866-7000; fax 602/942-7512. www.redlion.com.* 174 rooms, 4 story. S, D $49-$129; each additional $10; under 18 free. Pet accepted, some restrictions; fee. Check-out noon, check-in 3 pm. TV; cable (premium). In-room modem link. Restaurant 6 am-10 pm. Bar 4-11 pm. Room service. Exercise equipment. Whirlpool, poolside service. Cr cds: A, C, D, DS, MC, V.

🐾 ⇌ 🏃

Hotels

★ ★ **HILTON PHOENIX AIRPORT.** *2435 S 47th St (85034). Phone 480/894-1600; toll-free 800/728-6357; fax 480/921-7844. www.hilton.com.* 261 rooms, 4 story. S, D $69-$239; each additional $15; under 18 free. Check-out noon, check-in 3 pm. TV; cable (premium), VCR available. In-room modem link. Restaurant 6 am-2 pm, 5-10 pm; Sun 5-9 pm. Bar 11 am-midnight. Room service to midnight. Exercise equipment. Pool, whirlpool, poolside service. Business center. Concierge, luxury level. Free airport transportation. Cr cds: A, C, D, DS, ER, JCB, MC, V.

⊡ ⇌ 🏃 ✈ ⤨ 🏃

★ ★ ★ **HYATT REGENCY.** *122 N 2nd St (85004). Phone 602/252-1234; toll-free 800/233-1234; fax 602/254-9472. www.hyatt.com.* 742 rooms, 21 story. S, D $99-$295; under 18 free; weekend rates. Check-out noon, check-in 3 pm. TV; cable (premium), VCR available. Restaurant 5:30 am-midnight (See also COMPASS). Bar 11-1 am. Health club privileges, exercise equipment. Whirlpool, poolside service. Business center. Concierge. Cr cds: A, C, D, DS, ER, JCB, MC, V.

⊡ ⇌ 🏃 ⤨ 🏃

★ ★ **MARRIOTT PHOENIX AIRPORT.** *1101 N 44th St (85008). Phone 602/273-7373; fax 602/273-7333. www.marriott.com.* 349 rooms, 12 story. S, D $139-$229; under 18 free. Check-out 11 am, check-in 3 pm. TV; cable

(premium). In-room modem link. Restaurant 6:30 am-10 pm. Bar to 11 pm. Room service 24 hours. Exercise equipment. Pool, whirlpool. Business center. Concierge. Cr cds: A, C, D, DS, ER, JCB, MC, V.

⊡ ⇌ 🏃 ⤨ SC 🏃

★ ★ **RADISSON HOTEL PHOENIX AIRPORT.** *3333 E University Dr (85034). Phone 602/437-8400; toll-free 800/333-3333; fax 602/470-0998. www.radisson.com.* 176 rooms, 6 story. S, D $69-$149; each additional $10; under 18 free; holiday rates. Check-out noon, check-in 3 pm. TV; cable (premium). Restaurant 6 am-10 pm. Bar 11-1 am. Room service. Exercise equipment, sauna. Whirlpool, poolside service. Free airport transportation. Cr cds: A, C, D, DS, ER, JCB, MC, V.

⊡ ⇌ 🏃 ✈ ⤨ SC

★ ★ ★ ★ **THE RITZ-CARLTON.** *2401 E Camelback (85016). Phone 602/468-0700; fax 602/468-0713. www.ritzcarlton.com.* The Ritz-Carlton is the premier address in Phoenix. Not far from the airport, the hotel is located in the city's Camelback Corridor, known for its shopping, dining, and businesses, and all of Phoenix is within reach from here. The 11-story hotel is home to 281 rooms and suites. All accommodations are graciously styled with classic décor. Discerning travelers appreciate the views of the skyline or the Squaw Peak Mountain Range. A fitness center keeps guests in tiptop shape, and the outdoor pool is a splendid spot for reflection and relaxation. Winning accolades for its high levels of personal service, the hotel consistently exceeds guests' expectations. Dining is always a pleasure, whether in the comfort and privacy of a guest room or in the vibrant setting of Bistro 24 (See also BISTRO 24). Festive and stylish, the restaurant is commended for its modern take on French classics. 281 rooms, 11 story. S, D $199-$355; under 12 free. Check-out noon, check-in 3 pm. TV; cable (premium), VCR available. Bar 5 pm-1 am; Sat, Sun from 11 am. Room service 24 hours. Restaurant. Exercise room; sauna, Spa. Massage. Pool, poolside service. Bicycle rentals. Covered parking. Airport transportation. Business center. Concierge. Luxury level. Cr cds: A, C, D, DS, ER, JCB, MC, V.

⊡ ⇌ 🏃 ⤨ 🏃

★ ★ ★ **SHERATON CRESCENT HOTEL.** *2620 W Dunlap Ave (85021). Phone 602/943-8200; toll-free 800/ 423-4126; fax 602/371-2856. www.sheratoncrescent.com.* Imagine luxury and fun as the setting at this hotel in the heart of downtown Phoenix. Guests can enjoy suites that include Italian marble bathrooms and splash it up at the new 166-foot Monsoon Mountain water slide. 354 rooms, 8 story. D $69-$269; some weekend rates. Pet accepted, some restrictions; fee. Check-out noon, check-in 3 pm. TV; cable (premium), VCR available. Some fireplaces.

Restaurant 6 am-10 pm. Bar 11-1 am. Exercise room, sauna, steam room. Whirlpool, poolside service. Lighted tennis. Lawn games. Business center. Luxury level. Cr cds: A, C, D, DS, ER, JCB, MC, V.

★★ **WYNDHAM AIRPORT HOTEL.** *427 N 44th St (85008). Phone 602/220-4400; fax 602/231-8703. www.wyndham.com.* 234 rooms, 7 story. S, D $159-$229; each additional $10; under 18 free. Pets accepted. Check-out noon, check-in 3 pm. TV. Restaurant 6:30 am-2 pm, 5-10 pm; Sat, Sun from 7 am. Bar 4 pm-midnight. Room service 6:30 am-10 pm. Exercise equipment. Whirlpool, poolside service. Business center. Free airport transportation. Cr cds: A, C, D, DS, JCB, MC, V.

Resorts

★★★ **ARIZONA BILTMORE RESORT AND SPA.** *2400 E Missouri Rd (85016). Phone 602/955-6600; fax 602/954-2571. www.arizonabiltmore.com.* Earning the moniker "the Jewel of the Desert," the venerated Arizona Biltmore Resort and Spa opened to great fanfare in 1929. This resort bears the distinction of being the only existing hotel touched by the hands of Frank Lloyd Wright. The architect's influence is also evident in the private spaces, where Mission-style furnishings, neutral tones, and unique lamps honor the 1930s heritage. Eight pools keep the warm rays of the Arizona sun at bay; golfers have their choice of more than 30 courses in the valley, in addition to the resort's adjacent course; and tennis players are well cared for with 18 courts. From desert Jeep and Grand Canyon tours to horseback riding and hot-air ballooning, this resort truly has something for everyone. Native American wisdom is employed at the 22,000-square-foot spa, while Southwestern, French, and Asian flavors tempt diners in the four restaurants. 736 rooms, 2-4 story. Jan-May: S, D $395-$495; each additional $30; suites $620-$1,745; golf plan; lower rates rest of year. Check-out noon, check-in 4 pm. TV; cable (premium). Restaurant 5:30 am-midnight. Bar 10-1 am. Supervised children's activities. Fitness center; sauna. Spa. 8 heated pools; whirlpool, poolside service. 36-hole golf, greens fee $165 (including cart). Tennis, lighted courts. Bicycle rentals. Concierge. Cr cds: A, C, D, DS, JCB, MC, V.

★★ **THE LEGACY GOLF RESORT.** *6808 S 32nd St (85042). Phone 602/305-5500; toll-free 888/828-3673; fax 602/305-5501. www.legacygolfresort.com.* 328 rooms, 2 story. S, D $199-$249; under 18 free. Crib available. Check-out 11 am. TV; cable (premium). Balconies, refrigerators, microwaves. Restaurant 6:30 am-10 pm. Bar

to 10 pm. Exercise room. Pool, whirlpool. Golf, 18 holes. Lighted tennis. Concierge. Cr cds: A, C, D, DS, MC, V.

★★★ **POINTE HILTON SQUAW PEAK RESORT.** *7677 N 16th St (85020). Phone 602/997-2626; fax 602/395-9604. www.pointehilton.com.* Families will love this all-suite, desert resort with 8-acres of pool area, mountain views and creative kid's programs. At the base of the 300-acre Squaw Peak mountain preserve, there are plenty of outdoor activities in a Spanish Mediterranean-style setting. 563 suites, 4 story. S, D $99-$309; under 18 free; golf plans; holidays (4-day minimum). Pet accepted; fee. Check-out noon, check-in 4 pm. TV; cable (premium), VCR available. Restaurant 6 am-11 pm. Bar 11-2 am. Room service 6 am-midnight. Supervised children's activities; ages 4-12. Exercise room, massage, sauna, steam room. Children's pool, whirlpool, poolside service. Greens fee $119. Lighted tennis. Bicycle rentals. Airport transportation. Business center. Concierge. Cr cds: A, C, D, DS, ER, JCB, MC, V.

★★★ **POINTE HILTON TAPATIO CLIFFS RESORT.** *11111 N 7th St (85020). Phone 602/866-7500; fax 602/993-0276. www.hilton.com.* Architectural wonder terraces the slopes of the Phoenix North Mountain Preserve. The highlight of the property is a 40-foot waterfall and open-air bar/restaurant pavilion. 585 suites, 2-4 story. S, D $89-$109; each additional $15-$25; under 18 free; weekend, holiday rates; golf plan. Pet accepted, some restrictions; fee. Check-out noon, check-in 4 pm. TV; cable (premium), VCR available. In-room modem link. Fireplaces. Restaurant (See also DIFFERENT POINTE OF VIEW). Bar 10-1 am, entertainment. Supervised children's activities May-Sept; ages 3-12. Health club privileges, exercise room, sauna, steam room. Game room. Pool, whirlpool, poolside service. Greens fee $130-$140. Lighted courts. Bicycle rentals. Horse stables. Business center. Concierge, luxury level. Cr cds: A, C, D, DS, ER, JCB, MC, V.

★★★ **POINTE SOUTH MOUNTAIN RESORT.** *7777 S Pointe Pkwy (85044). Phone 602/438-9000; toll-free 877/800-4888; fax 602/431-6535. www.pointesouthmtn.com.* With 700 acres of breathtaking landscape, this resort has fun for all. Don't miss the tin slide and cowboy poetry at Rustler's Rooste. 640 suites, 2-5 story. Jan-mid-May: S, D $155-$325; each additional $15; under 18 free; higher rates rest of year. Check-out noon, check-in 4 pm. TV; cable (premium). Balconies, private patios, minibars, Complimentary coffee in rooms. Coin laundry. Dining room (See also RUSTLER'S ROOSTE). Bar 11-1 am.

Room service. Supervised child's activities; ages 5-12. Exercise room, massage, sauna. Social/Activities/Sports Director, recreation room. 6 heated pools, wading pool, whirlpool, poolside service. 18-hole golf, greens fee $135 (including cart), pro, putting green. Lighted tennis, pro. Bicycles. Beauty shop. Business center, convention center/facilities. Cr cds: A, C, D, DS, JCB, MC, V.

★ ★ ★ ROYAL PALMS HOTEL AND CASITAS.

5200 E Camelback Rd (85018). Phone 602/840-3610; toll-free 800/672-6011; fax 602/840-6927. www.royalpalms hotel.com. Royal Palms Hotel and Casitas is an intriguing and intimate hideaway. Constructed in the late 1920s as a private mansion, this hotel brings a bit of the Mediterranean to the Sonoran desert. Graceful palm trees reign over the entrance to this convenient, yet secluded, place halfway between the Biltmore area and downtown Scottsdale. The casitas and guest rooms are light-filled and extraordinary. Rich details, jewel tones, and unique accents create a wondrous ambience. Fireplaces, balconies, and patios complete the experience. Great care is paid to the grounds, where fragrant blossoms, stone walkways, and well-tended courtyards are de rigueur. Set against a backdrop of the Camelback Mountains, the pool is dreamy, and the spa induces a trancelike state with its wonderful offerings. The Bar and Cigar Room are ideal for lingering, but the pièce de résistance is T. Cook's (See also T. COOK'S), where the rustic elegance is a perfect setting for the award-winning cuisine. 116 rooms, 1-2 story. S, D $365; each additional $25; under 18 free. Service charge $18/day. Check-out noon. TV; cable (premium). Bar 11 am-midnight; Fri, Sat to 1 am. Room service 24 hours. Restaurant. Exercise room, spa. Pool; poolside service. Tennis. Business center. Totally nonsmoking. Cr cds: A, C, D, DS, MC, V.

All Suites

★ ★ DOUBLETREE GUEST SUITES GATEWAY CENTER.

320 N 44th St (85008). Phone 602/225-0500; toll-free 800/800-3098; fax 602/231-0957. www.doubletree.com. Enjoy the convenience of this hotel's location, just two miles north of Sky Harbor Airport and minutes from shopping, sporting events, and casinos. 242 suites, 6 story. S, D $59-$219; each additional $10; weekend rates. Check-out noon, check-in 3 pm. TV; cable (premium), VCR available. Restaurant 6 am-10 pm; Sat, Sun from 7 am. Bar 11 am-midnight. Exercise equipment. Whirlpool, poolside service. Free airport transportation. Business center. Cr cds: A, C, D, DS, ER, JCB, MC, V.

★ ★ EMBASSY SUITES HOTEL.

2630 E Camelback Rd (85016). Phone 602/955-3992; toll-free 800/362-2779; fax 602/955-6479. www.embassysuites.com. Waterfalls cascade and Koi fish splash as guests enter the lobby of this hotel tucked in Phoenix's most renowned residential area. 232 kitchen units, 5 story. S, D $109-$289; each additional $15; under 13 free. Complimentary full breakfast. Check-out 1 pm, check-in 3 pm. TV; cable (premium). In-room modem link. Restaurant 11 am-10 pm. Bar to midnight. Health club privileges, exercise equipment. Whirlpool, poolside service. Golf privileges. Cr cds: A, C, D, DS, JCB, MC, V.

★ EMBASSY SUITES HOTEL.

2577 W Greenway Rd (85023). Phone 602/375-1777; toll-free 800/527-7715; fax 602/993-5963. www.embassysuites.com. In northwest Phoenix, this hotel is conveniently located to nearby sporting events, shopping, and much more. 314 suites, 3 story. Jan-mid-May: S, D $119-$169; under 18 free; lower rates rest of year. Complimentary full breakfast. Check-out noon. TV; cable (premium). In-room modem link. Restaurant 6 am-10 pm. Bar 11-1 am. Room service. Exercise equipment. Children's pool, whirlpool. Lighted tennis. Lawn games. Cr cds: A, C, D, DS, MC, V.

★ ★ EMBASSY SUITES AIRPORT.

1515 N 44th St (85008). Phone 602/244-8800; fax 602/244-8114. www.embassysuites.com. 229 suites, 4 story. S, D $79-$219; each additional $10; under 18 free. Pet accepted, fee. Complimentary full breakfast. Check-out noon, check-in 3 pm. TV; cable (premium). Restaurant 11 am-10 pm. Bar. Whirlpool, poolside service. Airport transportation. Cr cds: A, C, D, DS, ER, JCB, MC, V.

★ ★ HILTON SUITES.

10 E Thomas Rd (85012). Phone 602/222-1111; toll-free 800/932-3322; fax 602/212-9537. www.phoenixsuites.hilton.com. This high-rise suite hotel is conveniently located near museums, shopping and many PGA golf courses. Ideal for families and small groups. 226 suites, 11 story. S, D $79-$249; each additional $15; under 18 free; weekend, holiday rates. Pet accepted; fee. Complimentary full breakfast. Check-out noon, check-in 3 pm. TV; cable (premium), VCR available. In-room modem link. Restaurant 11 am-2 pm, 5:30-10 pm; Sat, Sun from 5:30 pm. Bar 4 pm-midnight. Health club privileges, exercise equipment, sauna. Indoor pool, whirlpool. Business center. Concierge. Cr cds: A, C, D, DS, ER, JCB, MC, V.

B&B/Small Inn

★ ★ **MARICOPA MANOR B & B.** *15 W Pasadena Ave (85013). Phone 602/274-6302; toll-free 800/292-6403; fax 602/266-3904. www.maricopamanor.com.* This historic Spanish-style bed and breakfast, built in 1928, provides a quiet oasis within a large city. Its staff caters to a guest's every need. Have the Breakfast in a Basket delivered each morning for an intimate in-room dining experience. 7 suites, 1 story. S, D $99-$219; each additional $25. Complimentary continental breakfast in rooms. Check-out 11 am, check-in 4-6 pm. TV; cable (premium). Health club privileges. Pool, whirlpool. Restored Spanish mission-style mansion (1928). Totally nonsmoking. Cr cds: A, C, D, DS, MC, V.

Extended Stay

★ ★ **RESIDENCE INN BY MARRIOTT AIRPORT.** *801 N 44th St (85008). Phone 602/273-9220. www.residenceinn.com.* Guests can take advantage of the on-site sport court, or unwind in the Southwestern-style guest rooms featuring separate living and sleeping areas. 200 kitchen suites, 4 story. Kitchen suites $129-$229. Pet accepted, some restrictions. Complimentary continental breakfast. Check-out noon, check-in 3 pm. TV; cable (premium). In-room modem link. Some fireplaces. Coin laundry, laundry valet. Exercise room. Outdoor pool. Golf nearby. Tennis on premise. Cr cds: A, C, D, DS, ER, JCB, MC, V.

Restaurants

★ ★ ★ **AVANTI OF PHOENIX.** *2728 E Thomas Rd (85016). Phone 602/956-0900; fax 602/468-1913. www.avanti-az.com.* A stark Art Deco interior of black and white is the backdrop for this romantic restaurant. Fresh pasta with rich sauces are the mainstay of this 25-year-old operation. Continental, Italian menu. Specialty: osso buco. Own desserts. Hours: 11 am-2 pm, 5-10 pm; Sat, Sun from 5:30 pm. Closed July 4, Dec 25. Lunch $8.95-$15.95, dinner $17.95-$35.95. Bar, wine list. Entertainment Thurs-Sat. Reservations accepted. Valet parking. Patio dining in season. Cr cds: A, D, DS, MC, V.

★ **BABY KAY'S CAJUN KITCHEN.** *2119 E Camelback Rd (85016). Phone 602/955-0011; fax 602/955-2288. www.babykays.com.* Cajun menu. Closed Thanksgiving, Dec 25. Lunch, dinner. Bar. Outdoor seating. Cr cds: A, D, DS, MC, V. **$$**

★ ★ ★ **BISTRO 24.** *2401 E Camelback Rd (85016). Phone 602/952-2424; fax 602/468-0793. www.ritzcarlton.com.* A classic French bistro, complete with wicker chairs and soft lighting, this popular new restaurant is all that it promises to be. Entrees are hearty and succulent, yet unassuming, served by debonair waiters. A great spot for a night cap or light bite. American menu. Breakfast, lunch, dinner, Sun brunch. Bar. Children's menu. Valet parking. Outdoor seating. Cr cds: A, D, DS, JCB, MC, V. **$$$**

★ **CHOMPIE'S.** *3202 E Greenway Rd (85032). Phone 602/971-8010; fax 602/941-2343. www.chompies.com.* Kosher deli menu. Hours: 6 am-9 pm; Mon to 8 pm; Fri to 9:30 pm; Sun 6:30 am-8 pm. Breakfast $2.50-$6, lunch $3.50-$7, dinner $5.95-$10.95. Children's menu. Cr cds: A, MC, V.

★ ★ ★ **CHRISTOPHER'S FERMIER BRASSERIE.** *2584 E Camelback Rd (85016). Phone 602/522-2344; fax 602/468-0314. www.fermier.com.* Chef Christopher Gross has created a winning combination of casual French bistro ambience, knowledgeable attentive service and wonderful cuisine. Save room for the irresistable desserts. French menu. Menu changes daily. Hours: 11 am-3 pm, 5-10 pm. Sat, Sun from noon. Closed holidays. Reservations accepted. Specialty: truffle-infused sirloin. Lunch $9.95-$14; dinner $16.95-$26.95. Cr cds: A, D, DS, JCB, MC, V.

★ ★ **COMPASS.** *122 N 2nd St (85004). Phone 602/440-3166; fax 602/256-0801. www.hyatt.com.* Lunch, dinner, Sun brunch. Bar. Children's menu. Valet parking. Totally nonsmoking. Cr cds: A, D, DS, MC, V. **$$$**

★ ★ ★ **DIFFERENT POINTE OF VIEW.** *11111 N 7th St (85020). Phone 602/863-0912; fax 602/866-6358. www.hilton.com.* Innovative continental cuisine is the result of the chef's flair for mixing fresh-from-the-garden herbs and vegetables with wild game and hearty meats. A spectacular view of the city accompanies the chic menu. French, Italian, Mediterranean menu. Hours: 5:30-10 pm. Closed Sun, Mon (mid-June-Oct). Dinner $26-$39. Bar 5 pm-1 am. Entertainment Wed-Sat. Children's menu. Casual attire. Valet parking. Outdoor dining. Totally nonsmoking. Cr cds: A, D, DS, MC, V.

★ **DUCK AND DECANTER.** *1651 E Camelback Rd (85016). Phone 602/274-5429; fax 602/274-5672. www.duckanddecanter.com.* Closed some major holidays. Lunch, dinner. Bar. Children's menu. Outdoor seating. Totally nonsmoking. Cr cds: A, D, DS, MC, V. **$**

D

★★ **FISH MARKET.** *1720 E Camelback Rd (85016). Phone 602/277-3474; toll-free 800/730-3474; fax 602/277-2543. www.thefishmarket.com.* Specializes in fresh fish, live shellfish, smoked fish. Hours: 11 am-9:30 pm; Fri, Sat to 10 pm; Sun noon-9:30 pm. Closed Thanksgiving, Dec 25. Reservations accepted. Bar. Lunch $8-$20, dinner $10-$49.50. Children's menu. Oyster bar. Outdoor dining. Nautical decor. Retail fish market. Sushi bars. Cr cds: A, D, DS, MC, V. **$**

D

★★★ **GREEKFEST.** *1940 E Camelback Rd (85016). Phone 602/265-2990; fax 602/265-3036. www.thegreekfest.com.* A merry, family atmosphere and authentic decor transport guests to the Mediterranean for a feast of Greek foods! Greek menu. Hours: 11 am-2:30 pm, 5-10 pm; Fri, Sat to 11 pm; Sun 5-9 pm. Closed Sun; Jan 1, Dec 25. Lunch $4.95-$12, dinner $8.50-$25. Bar. Children's menu. Reservations accepted. Outdoor dining. Greek décor. Cr cds: A, D, DS, MC, V.

D

★★★ **HARRIS'.** *3101 E Camelback Rd (85016). Phone 602/508-8888; fax 602/508-8868. www.harrisrestaurantphx.com.* Guests dine in intimate booths or on the garden patio at this upscale steakhouse. Top quality beef is aged and carved on the premises by the restaurant's own butchers, then grilled and served sizzling. The house martini, listed as an appetizer, is hailed as the best in town. Hours: 11:30 am-2 pm, 5:30-10 pm. Closed Dec 25, also Sun (summer). Reservations accepted. Bar 11 am-10 pm; Sat, Sun 5-10 pm. Wine cellar. Lunch $8.95-$10.95, dinner $14-$34. Specializes in dry-aged Angus beef. Pianist Thurs-Sat. Valet parking. Outdoor dining. Southwestern décor. Cr cds: A, D, DS, MC, V.

D

★★ **HAVANA CAFE.** *4225 E Camelback Rd (85018). Phone 602/952-1991.* Cuban, Spanish menu. Hours: 11:30 am-10 pm; Sun 4-9 pm. Closed some major holidays. Dinner $8.95-$25. Bar. Casual attire. Patio dining. Totally nonsmoking. Cr cds: A, D, DS, MC, V.

★★★ **LA FONTANELLA.** *4231 E Indian School Rd (85018). Phone 602/955-1213; fax 602/955-1491. www.lafontanella.com.* A local favorite, this fine Italian restaurant is renowned for its warm atmosphere and elaborate dishes. Italian menu. Specialties: rack of lamb, osso buco, pasta with seafood. Hours: 4:30 pm-9:30 pm,

closed Dec 25. Dinner $11.75-$23.75. Bar. Reservations accepted. Cr cds: A, D, DS, MC, V.

D

★★ **LOMBARDI'S.** *455 N 3rd St (85004). Phone 602/257-8323; fax 602/257-0591. www.lombardisrestaurant.com.* Italian menu. Specialty: frutti de mar. Hours: 11 am-11 pm; Sun to 10 pm. Closed some holidays. Reservations accepted. Bar. A la carte entrees: lunch $8-$14.95, dinner $10-$18. Children's menu. Patio dining. Open kitchen. Cr cds: A, D, MC, V.

D

★★ **MONTI'S.** *12025 N 19th Ave (85029). Phone 602/997-5844; fax 602/997-0060.* Steak menu. Hours: 11 am-10 pm; Fri, Sat to 11 pm; early-bird dinner 3-6:30 pm. Closed Dec 25. Dinner $15-$22. Bar. Children's menu. Casual attire. Outdoor dining. Cr cds: A, D, DS, MC, V.

D

★★ **PIZZERIA BIANCO.** *623 E Adams St (85004). Phone 602/258-8300.* Italian menu. Closed Mon. Lunch, dinner. Bar. Totally nonsmoking. Own dough, mozzarella. Cr cds: MC, V. **$$**

D

★★ **PRONTO RISTORANTE.** *3950 E Campbell (85018). Phone 602/956-4049; fax 602/956-4460. www.prontoristorante.com.* Regional Italian menu. Hours: 11:30 am-2:30 pm, 5:30-10 pm; Fri, Sat to 10:30 pm. Closed Sun; Thanksgiving, Dec 25. Dinner $10-$22. Dinner theater Fri, Sat. Bar. Casual attire. Cr cds: A, D, DS, MC, V.

D

★★★ **ROXSAND.** *2594 E Camelback Rd (85016). Phone 602/381-0444; fax 602/957-7558. www.roxsand.net.* The acclaimed chef and proprietor is a master of fusion cuisine, bringing flavors from around the world together in daring combinations. These bold dishes are served in an edgy atmosphere that continues to impress the locals. Hours: 11 am-10 pm; Fri, Sat to 10:30 pm; Sun noon-9:30 pm. Closed most major holidays. Reservations accepted. Bar. Wine list. Children's menu. Specialty: Chilean sea bass with horseradish crust. Lunch $8.25-$11.95, dinner $17.95-$33. Menu changes seasonally. Valet parking. Outdoor dining. Cr cds: A, MC, V.

D

★★ **RUSTLER'S ROOSTE.** *7777 S Pointe Pkwy (85044). Phone 602/431-6474; fax 602/431-6529. www.rustlersrooste.com.* Steak menu. Dinner. Bar. Entertainment. Children's menu. Valet parking available. Outdoor seating. Cr cds: A, D, DS, MC, V. **$$**

D

★ ★ ★ **RUTH'S CHRIS STEAK HOUSE.** *2201 E Camelback Rd (85016). Phone 602/957-9600; fax 602/224-1948. www.ruthschris.com.* Steak menu. Closed Thanksgiving, Dec 25. Dinner. Bar. Valet parking. Outdoor seating. Cr cds: A, D, DS, JCB, MC, V. **$$$**

Ⓓ

★ ★ **STEAMERS SEAFOOD AND RAW BAR.** *2576 E Camelback Rd (85016). Phone 602/956-3631; fax 602/957-7847. www.steamersgenuineseafood.com* Seafood menu. Closed Thanksgiving, Dec 25. Lunch, dinner. Bar. Children's menu. Valet parking. Outdoor seating. Bright and colorful, spacious dining area. Cr cds: A, D, DS, MC, V. **$$$**

Ⓓ

★ ★ ★ **T. COOK'S.** *5200 E Camelback Rd (85018). Phone 602/808-0766; fax 602/808-3115. www.royalpalmshotel.com.* Tucked away in the Royal Palms Hotel and Casitas (See also ROYAL PALMS HOTEL AND CASITAS) is a jewel of a restaurant, stylishly decorated with deep cherry wood, hand-painted Italian frescos, and artisan-carved and -painted wooden shelves. The menu has a decidedly Mediterranean slant and includes dishes inspired by Spain, Tuscany, and the south of France, accented with Arizona's regional flair. Ingredients are organic whenever possible, and the kitchen has a knack for preparing simple yet elegant plates that easily inspire love at first bite. For those who enjoy a stogie and whiskey as well as a terrific meal, T. Cook's Cigar Room is luxuriously appointed with deep red leather custom-made upholstery and antique lamps, making it the perfect place to unwind after a long day. Hours: 6 am-2 pm, 6-10 pm; Sun brunch 10 am-2 pm. Dinner $18-$30. Sun brunch. Bar 10 am-midnight; Fri, Sat to 1 am. Piano. Valet parking. Outdoor dining. Cr cds: A, D, DS, MC, V.

Ⓓ

★ ★ ★ **TARBELL'S.** *3213 E Camelback Rd (85018). Phone 602/955-8100; fax 602/955-8181. www.tarbells.com.* This world-class restaurant maintains a friendly, neighborhood charm with a sophisticated, yet relaxed atmosphere. Fresh, seasonal dishes of "refined" comfort food are whisked from the open-view kitchen to guests' tables by attentive, well-trained servers. Specialties: grilled salmon on a crispy potato cake. Hours: 5-11 pm; Sun to 10 pm. Closed most major holidays. Reservations accepted. Bar. Wine cellar. Dinner $17-$33. Own baking. Open kitchen with woodburning oven. Cr cds: A, D, DS, JCB, MC, V.

Ⓓ

★ ★ **TOMASO'S.** *3225 E Camelback Rd (85016). Phone 602/956-0836; fax 602/956-0842.* Italian cuisine made of the finest ingredients, keeps guests coming back to this upscale restaurant. The pace is leisurely, and the atmosphere relaxed. Closed Super Bowl Sun. Lunch, dinner. Bar. Cr cds: A, D, DS, MC, V. **$$**

Ⓓ

★ ★ **TOP OF THE MARKET.** *1720 E Camelback Rd (85016). Phone 602/277-3474; fax 602/227-2543. www.thefishmarket.com.* American menu. Closed Thanksgiving, Dec 25. Dinner. Bar. Children's menu. Cr cds: A, C, D, DS, MC, V. **$$$**

Ⓓ

★ **TUCCHETTI.** *2135 E Camelback Rd (85016). Phone 602/957-0222; fax 602/381-1950. www.tucchetti.com.* Italian menu. Closed Thanksgiving, Dec 25. Lunch, dinner. Bar. Children's menu. Outdoor seating. Cr cds: A, D, DS, JCB, MC, V. **$$**

Ⓓ

★ ★ ★ **VINCENT GUERITHAULT ON CAMELBACK.** *3930 E Camelback Rd (85018). Phone 602/224-0225; fax 602/956-5400. www.vincentsoncamelback.com.* This intimate restaurant, which fearlessly combines hearty Southwest flavors with elegant French cuisine, spawned Phoenix's culinary reputation 15 years ago. The flawless waitstaff and enduring menu continue to impress. Southwestern, American menu. Closed major holidays; also on Sun during June-Sept. Lunch, dinner. Bar. Valet parking. Cr cds: A, D, MC, V. **$$$**

Ⓓ

★ ★ ★ **WRIGHT'S.** *2400 Missouri Rd (85016). Phone 602/954-6600; fax 602/381-7600. www.arizonabiltmore.com.* A homage to the celebrated Frank Lloyd Wright, the dining room reflects the architect's penchant for stark angles and contrast. Innovative cuisine is served for dinner and the unparalleled Sunday brunch. Be sure to sample one of the delectable chocolate desserts! Contemporary Mediterranean menu. Hours: 11 am-2 pm; 6 pm-10 pm; Sun brunch 10am-2pm. Dinner $22-$30. Casual attire. Valet parking. Cr cds: A, D, DS, MC, V.

Ⓓ

★ ★ **ZEN 32.** *3160 E Camelback (85016). Phone 602/954-8700; fax 602/667-9510. www.zen32.com.* Japanese menu. Hours: 11 am-midnight. Dinner $9-$19. Entertainment: Japanese animation. Casual attire. Cr cds: A, C, D, MC, V.

Ⓓ ⬛

Pinetop (E-6)

See also McNary, Show Low

Pop 3,582 **Elev** 6,959 ft **Area code** 520 **Zip** 85935

Information Pinetop-Lakeside Chamber of Commerce, 102-C W White Mountain Blvd, PO Box 4220; 520/367-4290

Web www.pinetoplakesidechamber.com

Trout fishing, horseback riding, hiking, biking, and golfing are popular summer activities here; skiing and snowmobiling draw many winter visitors.

Motels/Motor Lodges

★ **BEST WESTERN INN OF PINETOP.** *404 S White Mountain Blvd (85935). Phone 520/367-6667; toll-free 800/780-7234; fax 520/367-6672. www.innofpinetop.com.* 41 rooms, 2 story. June-mid-Sept, mid-Dec-Mar: S, D $69-$99; suite $199; each additional $5; under 12 free; higher rates: holidays, special events; lower rates rest of year. Complimentary continental breakfast. Check-out 11 am. TV; cable (premium). Cr cds: A, C, D, DS, ER, JCB, MC, V.

D ⟲ ⚡ ⊠ SC

★ **PINETOP COMFORT INN.** *1637 E White Mountain Blvd (85044). Phone 520/368-6600; toll-free 800/843-4792. www.comfortinn.com.* 55 rooms, 2 story. May-Oct, Dec-Mar: S, D $55-$69; each additional $8; under 18 free; higher rates during holiday weekends (2-day minimum); lower rates rest of year. Complimentary continental breakfast. Check-out 11 am. TV; cable, VCR available. In-room modem link. Refrigerators, some fireplaces. Meeting rooms. Business services available. Cr cds: A, D, DS, JCB, MC, V.

D ⟲ ⚡ ⊠ SC

Pipe Spring National Monument (A-3)

See also Kanab, UT

(14 miles W of Fredonia on spur off AZ 389)

Located on the Kaibab-Paiute Indian Reservation, the focal point of this monument is a beautifully built sandstone Mormon fort, dating back to 1870. Several years earlier, Brigham Young had ordered the exploration of this region north of the Grand Canyon. According to legend, rifleman William "Gunlock Bill" Hamblin gave the place its name by shooting the bottom out of a smoking pipe at 50 paces.

The fort, actually a fortified ranchhouse, was built under the direction of Bishop Anson P. Winsor to protect the families caring for the church's cattle. Cattle drives, headed for the railroad in Cedar City, Utah, began here.

Guide service (daily); living history demonstrations (June-Sept). Kaibab Paiute Campground (fee), 1/2 mile N of access road to visitor center. Area closed Jan 1, Thanksgiving, Dec 25. Contact the Superintendent, HC 65, Box 5, Fredonia 86022; phone 928/643-7105. **$**

Prescott (D-3)

Founded 1864 **Pop** 33,938 **Elev** 5,368 ft **Area code** 928

Information Chamber of Commerce, 117 W Goodwin St, PO Box 1147, 86302; 928/445-2000 or 800/266-7534

Web www.prescott.org

When President Lincoln established the territory of Arizona, Prescott became the capital. In 1867, the capital was moved to Tucson and then back to Prescott in 1877. After much wrangling, it was finally moved to Phoenix in 1889.

Tourism and manufacturing are now Prescott's principal occupations. The climate is mild during summer and winter. The Prescott National Forest surrounds the city; its headquarters are located here.

What to See and Do

Arcosanti. *2 1/2 miles W of Cordes Jct NE (86333). 36 miles SE on AZ 69 to Cordes Jct, then 2 miles E on unnumbered road (follow signs or inquire locally for directions). Phone 928/632-7135.* Architectural project by Paolo Soleri and the Cosanti Foundation. This prototype town is being constructed as a functioning example of "arcology," a fusion of architecture and ecology. Guided tours. (Daily; closed holidays) **DONATION**

Prescott National Forest. *344 S Cortez St. 20 miles NE on US 89A or 1 mile SW on US 89. Phone 928/445-1762.* Minerals and varied vegetation abound in this forest (more than one million acres). Within the forest are Juniper Mesa, Apache Creek, Granite Mountain, Castle Creek, Woodchute, and Cedar Bench wilderness areas, and parts of Sycamore Canyon and Pine Mountain wilderness areas. Fishing (Granite Basin, Lynx lakes); hunting, picnicking, camping.

Sharlot Hall Museum. *415 W Gurley St. Phone 928/445-3122.* Period houses including the Territorial Governor's Mansion (1864), restored in 1929 by poet-historian

Sharlot Hall; Fort Misery (1864); William Bashford house (1877); and John C. Fremont house (1875). Period furnishings. Museum, library, and archives. Also on grounds are grave of Pauline Weaver; rose and herb garden; pioneer schoolhouse. All buildings (daily; closed Jan 1, Thanksgiving, Dec 25). **$**

Smoki Museum. *147 N Arizona St. Phone 928/445-1230.* Native American artifacts, ancient and modern. (May-Sept, daily; rest of year, Mon, Tues, Thurs; also Sun afternoons) **$$**

Special Events

Bluegrass Festival. *130 N Cortez St (86301). Courthouse Plaza. Phone 928/445-0204.* Mid-June.

Phippen Museum Fine Art Show & Sale. *4701 N US Hwy 89 (86301). Phone 928/778-1385.* Over 50 artists. Memorial Day weekend.

Prescott Frontier Days Rodeo. *828 Rodeo Dr (86305). Fairgrounds on Miller Valley Rd. Phone 928/445-3103.* Also parade and laser show. Late-June-July 4.

Territorial Prescott Days. *130 N Cortez St (86301). Courthouse Plaza, and throughout city. Phone 928/445-0204.* Art show, craft demonstrations, old-fashioned contests, home tours. Early June.

Motels/Motor Lodges

★ ★ **BEST WESTERN PRESCOTTONIAN.** *1317 E Gurley St (86301). Phone 928/445-3096; fax 928/778-2976. www.bestwestern.com.* 121 rooms, 2-3 story. No elevator. S, D $59-$89; each additional $10. Pet accepted. Check-out noon, check-in 2 pm. TV; cable. In-room modem link. Laundry services. Restaurant 6 am-10 pm. Bar 11 am-10 pm. Pool, whirlpool. Cr cds: A, C, D, DS, MC, V.

D 🐾 🏊 🏧 SC

★ **COMFORT INN.** *1290 White Spar Rd (86303). Phone 928/778-5770; toll-free 800/889-9774; fax 928/771-9373. www.comfortinn.com.* 61 rooms, 2 story. S, D $67.99-$159.99; each additional $10; under 18 free. Complimentary continental breakfast. Check-out 11 am, check-in 3 pm. TV. Cr cds: A, C, D, DS, JCB, MC, V.

D 🛬 🏧

★ **DAYS INN.** *7875 E Hwy 69 (86314). Phone 928/772-8600; fax 928/772-0942. www.daysinn.com.* 59 rooms, 2 story. S $59-$69; D $69-$79; each additional $10; suites $99-$109; under 12 free; holidays (2-day minimum); higher rates during special events. Crib free. Pet accepted; $50. TV; cable (premium). Complimentary continental breakfast. Restaurant adjacent open 24 hours. Check-out 11 am. Meeting room. Business services available. Pool; whirlpool. Some refrigerators; microwave, wet bar in suites. Cr cds: A, C, D, DS, JCB, MC, V.

D 🐾 🏊 🏧 SC

★ **HOLIDAY INN EXPRESS.** *3454 Ranch Dr (86303). Phone 928/445-8900; fax 928/778-2629. www.hiexpress.com/prescottaz.* 79 rooms, 3 story. S, D $99-$109; each additional $10; under 17 free; holidays (2-day minimum). Complimentary continental breakfast. Check-out 11 am, check-in 2 pm. TV; cable (premium). In-room modem link. Exercise equipment. Indoor pool, whirlpool. Cr cds: A, C, D, DS, JCB, MC, V.

🏊 🏋 🏧

Hotels

★ ★ **FOREST VILLAS HOTEL.** *3645 Lee Circle (86301). Phone 928/717-1200; toll-free 800/223-3449; fax 928/717-1400. www.forestvillas.com.* This property has flowing fountains and a panoramic view of the Prescott Mountains. Wine and champagne are served nightly in the elegant Mediterranean-style lobby, which features oversized chairs and crystal chandeliers. 76 rooms, 2 story. S, D $79-$95; each additional $10; under 13 free. Complimentary continental breakfast. Check-out 11 am, check-in 3 pm. TV; cable (premium). Whirlpool. Free garage parking. European décor with grand staircase. Cr cds: A, C, D, DS, MC, V.

D 🏊 🏧

★ ★ **HASSAYAMPA INN.** *122 E Gurley St (86301). Phone 928/778-9434; toll-free 800/322-1927; fax 928/445-8590. www.hassayampainn.com.* 68 rooms, 4 story. S, D $49-$139; each additional $15; under 6 free. Complimentary full breakfast. Check-out noon, check-in 3 pm. TV; VCR available. Restaurant 6:30 am-2 pm, 5-9 pm; Fri, Sat to 9:30 pm. Bar 11 am-11 pm. On National Register of Historic Places. Cr cds: A, D, DS, MC, V.

D 🏧

★ ★ **HOTEL VENDOME.** *230 S Cortez St (86303). Phone 928/776-0900; toll-free 888/468-3583; fax 928/771-0395. www.vendomehotel.com.* 20 rooms, 2 story. S, D $79-$199; under 18 free. Complimentary continental breakfast. Check-out 11 am, check-in 2 pm. TV; cable. Bar 10-1 am. Vintage (1917) lodging house. Cr cds: A, C, D, DS, MC, V.

D 🏧

Resort

★ ★ **PRESCOTT RESORT CONFERENCE CENTER & CASINO.** *1500 Hwy 69 (86301). Phone 928/776-1666; toll-free 800/967-4637; fax 928/776-8544. www.prescottresort.com.* 240 rooms, 5 story. S, D $79-$145; under 18 free; golf plans. Check-out noon, check-in 3 pm. TV; cable (premium). Restaurant 6:30 am-9:30 pm. Bar 11-12:30 am, entertainment Fri-Sat. Exercise equipment, sauna. Indoor pool, outdoor pool, whirlpool, poolside service. Lighted tennis. Racquetball court. Casino. Cr cds: A, C, D, DS, JCB, MC, V.

🅳 ⛷ ⚓ 🍴 🏊

B&B/Small Inn

★ ★ **PLEASANT STREET INN B&B.** *142 S Pleasant St (86303). Phone 928/445-4774; toll-free 877/226-7128; fax 928/777-8696. www.pleasantstreetinn-bb.com.* 6 rooms, 2 story. S, D $95; holidays (2-day minimum). Complimentary full breakfast. Check-out 11 am, check-in 2-5 pm. Street parking. Built in 1906; Victorian décor. Totally nonsmoking. Cr cds: A, DS, MC, V.

🏊

Restaurants

★ ★ **GURLEY STREET GRILL.** *230 W Gurley St (86301). Phone 928/445-3388; fax 928/445-8412.* American menu. Hours: 11-1 am. Closed Dec 25. Dinner $6.25-$16.95. Bar. Children's menu. Casual attire. Patio dining. Cr cds: A, DS, MC, V.

🅳

★ ★ **MURPHY'S.** *201 N Cortez (86301). Phone 928/445-4044; fax 928/778-4844. www.murphysrestaurants.com.* American, seafood, steak menu. Hours: 11 am-11 pm; winter hours vary; early-bird dinner Sun-Thurs 4:30-6 pm, closed day after Labor Day, Dec 25. Dinner $11-$49.95. Bar to 1 am. Children's menu. Memorabilia from turn-of-the-century on display. Restored (circa 1890) mercantile building. Casual attire. Cr cds: A, DS, MC, V.

🅳

★ **PINE CONE INN.** *1245 White Spar Rd (86303). Phone 928/445-2970.* American menu. Hours: 11 am-10:30 pm; Sun from 8 am; early-bird dinner 4-6 pm. Closed Dec 24-26. Dinner $8-$45. Bar to midnight. Entertainment Tues-Sun. Children's menu. Casual attire. Cr cds: A, DS, MC, V.

🅳

Safford (G-7)

See also Willcox

Founded 1874 **Pop** 9,232 **Elev** 2,920 ft **Area code** 928 **Zip** 85546

Information Graham County Chamber of Commerce, 1111 Thatcher Blvd; 928/428-2511

Web www.graham-chamber.com

Safford is a marketplace for cotton, alfalfa, grain, vegetables, and fruit produced on 35,000 acres irrigated by waters from the Gila River. It is the trade center for a wide area. Nearby is Aravaipa Canyon, a designated primitive area. A Ranger District office for the Coronado National Forest (see TUCSON) is located here.

What to See and Do

Roper Lake State Park. *101 E Roper Lake Rd. 6 miles S, 1/2 mile E of US 666. Phone 928/428-6760.* This 320-acre park includes a small artificial lake, a swimming beach, and natural hot springs with tubs for public use; fishing (dock), boat launch (no gas-powered motors); nature trails, hiking, picnicking (shelter), camping, tent and trailer sites (hook-ups, dump station). Fishing dock accessible to the disabled. Dankworth Unit, 6 miles S, is a day-use area with fishing and picnicking. Standard fees.

The Swift Trail. *504 S 5th Ave (85545). Phone 928/428-4150.* AZ 366 snakes its way 36 miles SW from Safford to the high elevations of the Pinaleño Mountains in Coronado National Forest; splendid view from the top, where Mount Graham towers 10,713 feet. There are five developed campgrounds (mid-Apr-mid-Nov, weather permitting); trout fishing at Riggs Flat Lake and in the streams. The upper elevations of AZ 366 are closed from mid-Nov-mid-Apr. **$$$**

Special Events

Fiesta de Mayo. *311 S Central Ave (85546). Phone 928/428-4920.* Mexican-American commemoration of *Cinco de Mayo* (May 5th), date of Mexican independence from Europe. First weekend in May.

Graham County Fair. *527 E Armory Rd (85546). Phone 928/428-6240.* Mid-Oct.

Pioneer Days. Commemorates Mormon settlement. Late July.

Motels/Motor Lodges

★ **BEST WESTERN DESERT INN.** *1391 Thatcher Blvd (85546). Phone 928/428-0521; toll-free 800/707-2336; fax 928/428-7653. www.bestwestern.com.* 70 rooms, 2 story. S $59-$80; D $65; each additional $6; under 17 free. Pet accepted. Check-out 11 am. TV. Restaurant adjacent 6 am-10:30 pm. Bar 11 am-11 pm; Sun from noon. Cr cds: A, C, D, DS, MC, V.

🅳 🐾 🎾 🏊 🏊

★ **COMFORT INN.** *1578 W Thatcher Blvd (85546). Phone 928/428-5851; fax 928/428-4968. www.comfortinn.com.* 45 rooms, 2 story. S $58; D $68; each additional $5; under 18 free; golf plans. Crib $3. Pet accepted, some restrictions. TV; cable (premium). Heated pool. Complimentary continental breakfast. Coffee in rooms. Check-out 11 am. Business services available.

In-room modem link. Some refrigerators, microwaves. Cr cds: A, C, D, DS, JCB, MC, V.

D 🐾 🏋 🕭 🏊 🚶 ⛽

Restaurant

★ **CASA MAÑANA.** *502 1st Ave (85546). Phone 928/ 428-3170.* Mexican, American menu. Closed Dec 25. Lunch, dinner. Totally nonsmoking. Cr cds: DS, MC, V. **$$**

D 🚭 SC

Saguaro National Park (H-5)

See also Tuscon

(Rincon Mountain District: 17 miles E of Tucson via Broadway and Old Spanish Tr. Tucson Mountain District: 16 miles W of Tucson via Speedway and Gates Pass Rd)

The saguaro (sah-WAH-ro) cactus may grow as high as 50 feet and may live to be 200 years old. The fluted columns, spined with sharp, tough needles, sometimes branch into fantastic shapes. During the rainy season, large saguaros can absorb enough water to sustain themselves during the dry season.

The saguaro's waxy, white blossoms (Arizona's state flower), which open at night and close the following afternoon, bloom in May and June; the red fruit ripens in July. The Tohono O'Odham eat this fruit fresh and dried; they also use it to make jellies, jams, and wines.

Wildlife is abundant. Gila woodpeckers and gilded flickers drill nest holes in the saguaro trunks. Once vacated, these holes become home to many other species of birds, including the tiny elf owl. Peccaries (piglike mammals), coyotes, mule deer, and other animals are often seen. Yuccas, agaves, prickly pears, mesquite, paloverde trees, and many other desert plants grow here.

The Rincon Mountain District offers nature trails, guided nature walks (winter), eight-mile self-guided drive (fee), mountain hiking, bridle trails, picnicking (no water), back-country camping. Visitor center with museum and orientation film.

The Tucson Mountain District offers nature trails, a six-mile self-guided drive, and hiking and bridle trails. Five picnic areas (no water). Visitor center; exhibits, slide program (daily). Contact the Superintendent, 3693 S Old Spanish Tr, Tucson 85730; phone 520/733-5100 or 520/733-5153. **FREE**

Scottsdale (F-4)

See also Chandler, Glendale, Mesa, Phoenix, Tempe

Pop 202,705 **Elev** 1,250 ft **Area codes** 602/480

Information Chamber of Commerce, 7343 Scottsdale Mall, 85251; 480/945-8481 or 800/877-1117

Web www.scottsdalechamber.com

Scottsdale is a popular resort destination located on the eastern border of Phoenix. It is renowned for outstanding art galleries, excellent shopping and dining, lush golf courses, abundant recreational activities, and Western and Native American heritage.

What to See and Do

Cosanti Foundation. *6433 Doubletree Ranch Rd. Phone 480/948-6145 or 800/752-3187.* Earth-formed concrete structures and studios by Italian architect Paolo Soleri; constructed by Soleri's students. Soleri windbells made in crafts areas. (Daily; closed holidays) **FREE**

Gray Line sightseeing tours. *1243 S. 7th St. #2. Phone 602/ 495-9100.* Contact PO Box 21126, Phoenix (85036).

Hot Air Expeditions. *2243 E Rose Garden Loop # 1. Phone 480/502-6999; 800/831-7610.* See this beautiful desert region from on high, in a hot-air balloon. For up to an hour, float above this barren land for gorgeous 360-degree views. You'll likely catch glimpses of its animal life—jackrabbits, quails, roadrunners, coyote, maybe even deer and javelina—and descend close to its trees, cacti, and other plants. The trip ends with a champagne breakfast or hors d'oeuvres on the desert floor.

Kierland Commons. *15054 N Scottsdale Rd (85254).* This 38-acre urban village bills itself as "today's version of yesterday, given its Main Street feel and pedestrian friendly layout. Its well-landscaped streets are lined with offices and more than 50 upscale specialty retailers, including Agata Boutique, Chocolates by Bernard Callebaut, Crate and Barrel, Optical Shop of Aspen, Smith and Hawken, and Z Gallerie. Among its dining options are Morton's Steak House, News Cafe, and P.F. Chang's China Bistro. Do hang out here if you like hangin' with the trendy crowd. (Mon-Sat 10 am-9 pm, Sun noon-6 pm; closed Easter, Thanksgiving, Dec 25)

McCormick-Stillman Railroad Park. *7301 E Indian Bend Rd. Phone 480/312-2312. www.therailroadpark.com.* Watch your little ones smile as they climb on the fast track and loop this 30-acre city park aboard the Paradise and Pacific Railroad, a miniature reproduction of a Colorado narrow-gauge railroad. After circling on the choo-choo, they'll want to head over to the 1950s carousel for a bumpier ride, then to one of two well-equipped playgrounds. Be sure to tour the Roald Amundsen Pullman Car, used by four US presidents: Herbert Hoover, Franklin Roosevelt, Harry Truman, and Dwight Eisenhower. (Daily; closed Thanksgiving, Dec 25) Fee for rides. **$**

Scottsdale Center for the Arts. *7380 E 2nd St. Phone 480/994-2787.* Offers theater, dance; classical, jazz and popular music; lectures; outdoor festivals and concerts. Sculpture garden; art exhibits (daily; closed holidays). **$$$**

⭐ **Taliesin West.** *12621 N Frank Lloyd Wright Blvd (85261). Phone 480/860-2700 or 480/860-8810 (recording).* Take a guided tour of this amazing compound and see for yourself Frank Lloyd Wright's architectural genius at work, and his passion for "organic architecture." In the late 1930s, Wright and his apprentices literally built this winter camp out of the Sonoran desert, using rocks and sand they gathered from the rugged terrain. In true Wright fashion, the architect designed the various buildings with terraces, gardens, and walkways that link the outdoors with the indoors. To help ensure Wright's legacy lives on, Taliesin West still functions as a school for 20-plus architectural students who subscribe to his philosophies about the craft he loved and mastered. (Daily) **$$$$**

WestWorld of Scottsdale. *16601 N Pima Rd. Phone 480/312-6802.* A 360-acre recreation park and event facility at the base of the McDowell Mountains. Hosts concerts, sports competitions, special events. (Daily)

Wild West Jeep Tours. *7343 Scottsdale Mall. Phone 480/922-0144.* Four-hour guided desert tour. Explore an ancient ruin. (Daily) **$$$$**

Special Events

Arabian Horse Show. *WestWorld. 16601 N Pima Rd. Phone 480/515-1500.* Two weeks in mid-Feb.

ArtWalk. *Along Main Street and Marshall Way in downtown Scottsdale. Phone 480/990-3939.* Locals brag that Scottsdale has more art galleries per capita than most any other US city. To get a good taste of this thriving scene, stroll the downtown streets during ArtWalk, a weekly Thursday night tradition for more than 20 years. For two hours, galleries host special exhibits, demonstrations, and meet-the-artist receptions, complete with wine, champagne, and tasty hors d'oeuvres. You'll almost feel like an insider yourself, not a potential buyer. Thurs evenings. **FREE**

Parada del Sol & Rodeo. *8102 E Jackrabbit Rd. Phone 480/990-3179. Phone 480/990-3179 (parade) or 480/502-5600 (rodeo).* Mid-Feb.

San Francisco Giants Spring Training. *Scottsdale Stadium. 7408 E Osborn Rd (85251). Phone 480/312-2586.* San Francisco Giants baseball spring training, exhibition games. Early Mar-early Apr.

Scottsdale Culinary Festival. *Scottsdale League for the Arts (85251). Phone 480/945-7193.* If you appreciate mouthwatering cuisine, then savor some of the tastiest dishes imaginable at this hot culinary adventure that mixes the Southwest's best chefs with food lovers from the Valley and way beyond. Choose from any of nine individual events ranging from casual to black-tie-only. In most cases, wine and music spice up the menu to set just the right mood. Proceeds benefit area charities. Mid-Mar and mid-Apr.

The Tradition at Superstition Mountain. *Superstition Mountain Golf & Country Club, 8000 E Club Village Dr. Phone 800/508-9999.* Senior PGA Tour golf tournament. Early Apr.

Motels/Motor Lodges

⭐⭐ **BEST WESTERN PAPAGO INN AND RESORT.** *7017 E McDowell Rd (85257). Phone 480/947-7335; fax 480/994-0692. www.papagoinn.com.* 58 rooms, 2 story. S, D $69-$139; each additional $5; under 17 free. Check-out noon, check-in 2 pm. TV; cable (premium). Restaurant, bar 10-1 am. Room service. Exercise equipment, sauna. Poolside service. Free airport transportation. Cr cds: A, C, D, DS, JCB, MC, V.

⭐⭐ **BEST WESTERN AIRPARK SUITES.** *7515 E Butherus Dr (85260). Phone 480/951-4000; toll-free 800/334-1977; fax 480/483-9046. www.scottsdalebestwestern.com.* 236 suites, 4 story. S, D $115-$159; under 12 free; golf plans. Pet accepted, some restrictions; fee. Complimentary full breakfast. Check-out noon, check-in 3 pm. TV; cable. In-room modem link. Laundry services. Restaurant 6 am-10 pm. Bar 3 pm-10 pm. Room service. Exercise equipment. Whirlpool, poolside service. Cr cds: A, C, D, DS, MC, V.

⭐ **COMFORT INN.** *7350 E Gold Dust Ave (85258). Phone 480/596-6559; toll-free 888/296-9776; fax 480/596-0554. www.comfortinn.com.* 124 rooms, 3 story. S, D $49-$109; each additional $10; under 18 free; golf plans. Complimentary continental breakfast. Check-out noon, check-in 3 pm. TV; cable (premium). In-room modem link. Laundry services. Room service 11 am-9 pm. Health club privileges. Pool, whirlpool. Business center. Cr cds: A, C, D, DS, JCB, MC, V.

⭐ **COUNTRY INN & SUITES BY CARLSON.** *10801 N 89th Pl (85260). Phone 480/314-1200; toll-free 800/456-4000; fax 480/314-7367. www.countryinns.com/scottsdaleaz_central.* 163 rooms, 92 suites, 3 story. Jan-May: S, D $49-$139; each additional $10; suites $159-$189; under 18 free; lower rates rest of year. Pet accepted; fee. Complimentary continental breakfast. Check-out noon. TV; cable (premium). In-room modem link. Exercise equipment. Children's pool, whirlpool. Cr cds: A, D, DS, MC, V.

★ **FAIRFIELD INN BY MARRIOTT SCOTTSDALE NORTH.** 13440 N Scottsdale Rd (85254). Phone 480/483-0042; toll-free 800/228-2800; fax 480/483-3715. www.fairfieldinn.com. 132 rooms, 3 story. S, D $59-$139; under 18 free. Complimentary continental breakfast. Check-out noon, check-in 3 pm. TV; cable (premium). In-room modem link. Pool, whirlpool. Cr cds: A, C, D, DS, MC, V.

★ **HAMPTON INN.** 4415 N Civic Center Plaza (85251). Phone 480/941-9400; fax 480/675-5240. www.hamptoninnoldtown.com. 135 rooms, 5 story. S, D $49-$129; under 18 free. Pet accepted; fee. Complimentary continental breakfast. Check-out noon, check-in 3 pm. TV; cable (premium). Pool. Cr cds: A, C, D, DS, MC, V.

★ **HAWTHORN SUITES.** 7445 E Chapparral Rd (85250). Phone 480/994-5282; fax 480/994-5625. www.hotelwaterfrontivy.com. 175 rooms, 2 story. S, D $79-$189; package plans. Complimentary breakfast buffet. Check-out noon, check-in 3 pm. TV; cable (premium), VCR available (movies). Exercise equipment. 5 pools. Outdoor tennis. Cr cds: A, C, D, DS, ER, JCB, MC, V.

★ ★ ★ **HILTON GARDEN INN.** 7324 E Indian School Rd (85251). Phone 480/481-0400; toll-free 800/HILTONS; fax 480/481-0800. www.scottsdale.gardeninn.com. Conveniently situated near Old Town Scottsdale, major shopping centers, and numerous restaurants, this modern hotel is designed for the business traveler. In addition to a host of amenities, it offers attractive public areas and large, well-furnished guestrooms. 248 rooms, 7 story. S, D $89-$199; under 18 free. Check-out noon, check-in 3 pm. TV; cable (premium). Restaurant 6:30 am-10 pm. Bar. Exercise equipment. Pool, whirlpool. Business center. Cr cds: A, C, D, DS, ER, JCB, MC, V.

★ ★ **HOLIDAY INN SUNSPREE RESORT.** 7601 E Indian Bend Rd (85250). Phone 480/991-2400; fax 480/998-2261. www.holiday-inn.com. 216 rooms, 3 story. S, D $49-$149; each additional $10; under 18 free; package plans. Check-out noon, check-in 3 pm. TV; cable (premium). Dining room 6:30 am-10 pm. Bar 11-1 am. Room service. Supervised children's activities (May-Aug). Exercise equipment. Poolside service. Golf on premises. Lighted tennis, pro. Lawn games, Bicycles (rentals). Cr cds: A, D, DS, ER, JCB, MC, V.

★ ★ **HOMEWOOD SUITES.** 9880 N Scottsdale Rd (85253). Phone 480/368-8705; fax 480/368-8725. www.homewoodsuites.com. 114 suites, 3 story. S, D $159-$259; under 18 free. Complimentary continental breakfast. Check-out noon. TV; cable (premium), VCR available. In-room modem link. Exercise equipment. Pool. Cr cds: A, C, D, DS, MC, V.

★ ★ **HOSPITALITY SUITE RESORT.** 409 N Scottsdale Rd (85257). Phone 480/949-5115; fax 480/941-8014. www.hospitalitysuites.com. 210 rooms, 3 story. S, D $49-$129; under 18 free. Pet accepted, some restrictions; fee. Complimentary full breakfast. Check-out 11 am, check-in 2 pm. TV; cable (premium). Restaurant 6:30 am-10 pm. Bar 11-1 am. Room service. Health club privileges. Whirlpool, poolside service. Lighted tennis. Lawn games. Free airport transportation. Cr cds: A, C, D, DS, MC, V.

★ **LA QUINTA INN AND SUITES.** 8888 E Shea Blvd. (85260). Phone 480/614-5300; fax 480/614-5333. www.laquinta.com. 140 rooms, 3 story. Jan-Apr: S $69-$119; D $79-$129; each additional $10; under 18 free; lower rates rest of year. Crib free. Pet accepted, some restrictions. Complimentary continental breakfast. Complimentary coffee in rooms. Check-out noon. TV; cable (premium). Some refrigerators, some microwaves. Coin laundry. Restaurant adjacent 7 am-11 pm. Exercise equipment. Pool, whirlpool. Meeting rooms, business services available. Cr cds: A, C, D, DS, MC, V.

★ **SPRINGHILL SUITES BY MARRIOTT.** 17020 N Scottsdale Rd (85255). Phone 480/922-8700; fax 480/948-2276. www.springhillsuites.com. 123 rooms, 4 story. S, D $65-$149; under 18 free. Complimentary continental breakfast. Check-out noon, check-in 3 pm. TV; cable (premium), VCR available. In-room modem link. Room service 5-10 pm. Pool, whirlpool. Cr cds: A, C, D, DS, MC, V.

Hotels

★ ★ **COURTYARD BY MARRIOTT.** 13444 E Shea Blvd (85259). Phone 480/860-4000; fax 480/860-4308. www.courtyard.com. 124 rooms, 8 suites, 2 story. Jan-mid-May: S, D $89-$159; suites $109-$179; lower rates rest of year. Crib free. Check-out noon. TV; cable (premium). Many balconies. Refrigerators available. Microwaves available. Complimentary coffee in rooms. Valet services, coin laundry. Restaurant 6:30 am-9 pm; Sat, Sun 7 am-2 pm, 5-9 pm. Bar 4-11 pm. Room service. Exercise equipment. Heated pool, whirlpool. Meeting rooms. Business services available. Cr cds: A, C, D, DS, MC, V.

★ ★ **COURTYARD BY MARRIOTT.** *17010 N Scottsdale Rd (85255). Phone 480/922-8400; toll-free 800/321-2211; fax 480/948-3481. www.courtyard.com.* 153 rooms, 3 story. S, D $79-$189; under 18 free; golf plans. Check-out noon, check-in 3 pm. TV; cable (premium), VCR available. In-room modem link. Restaurant 6 am-11 pm. Bar 5-11 pm. Room service 6-11 am, 5-10 pm. Exercise equipment. Pool, whirlpool. Cr cds: A, C, D, DS, MC, V.

D ⊠ 🏃 ⊠ SC

★ ★ ★ **HILTON SCOTTSDALE RESORT AND VILLAS.** *6333 N Scottsdale Rd (85250). Phone 480/ 948-7750; toll-free 800/528-3119; fax 480/948-2232. www.scottsdaleresort.hilton.com.* Conveniently located near major shopping areas, restaurants and attractions, this resort offers standard guestrooms as well as one and two bedroom villas with full kitchens, fireplaces, washers and dryers. The hotel has recently been renovated and provides a number of amenities including two pools, a wading pool, restaurants, an exercise room and a gift shop. 195 rooms, 2-3 story. S, D $69-$279; under 18 free. Check-out noon, check-in 4 pm. TV; cable (premium), VCR available. In-room modem link. Restaurant 7 am-10 pm. Bar to midnight. Business center. Concierge. Cr cds: A, C, D, DS, ER, JCB, MC, V.

D ⊠ 🏃 ⊠ 🏃

Resorts

★ ★ **DOUBLETREE LA POSADA RESORT.** *4949 E Lincoln Dr (85253). Phone 602/952-0420; toll-free 800/222-8733; fax 602/840-8576. www.doubletree.com.* Camelback Mountain is a beautifully striking backdrop at this Hilton chain. On-site recreations include a 1-million-gallon lagoon pool, but shopping, golf and the famed Biltmore Country Club Resort are also nearby. 262 rooms, 1 story. S, D $79-$239; each additional $20; under 18 free; package plan. Pet accepted, some restrictions. Check-out noon, check-in 4 pm. TV; cable (premium). Restaurant 6 am-10 pm; Fri, Sat to 11 pm. Bar noon-1 am. Room service. Exercise equipment, sauna. 2 heated pools, whirlpool, poolside service. Golf on premises. Lighted tennis. Lawn games. Bicycle rentals. Racquetball. Cr cds: A, C, D, DS, ER, JCB, MC, V.

🏊 🏇 🏌 ⊠ 🏃

★ ★ **DOUBLETREE RESORT SCOTTSDALE/ PARADISE VALLEY.** *5401 N Scottsdale Rd (85250). Phone 480/947-5400; fax 480/946-1524. www.doubletree.com.* Guests will savor freshly baked chocolate chip cookies, as they are welcomed to this 22-acre resort. Relax in the sun, stroll nearby through historic downtown Scottsdale, or enjoy a refreshing "Prickly Pear Margarita" at the hotel's main bar, Loggia. 399 rooms, 2 story. S, D $69-$249; each additional $10; under 18 free;

weekend rates; golf plans. Check-out noon, check-in 4 pm. TV; cable (premium). Restaurant 6:30 am-11 pm. Bar 11-1 am. Room service. Exercise room, massage, sauna, steam room. Whirlpool, poolside service. Golf privileges. 2 lighted tennis courts. Concierge. Cr cds: A, C, D, DS, ER, JCB, MC, V.

D ⊠ 🏇 ⊠ 🏃 ⊠

★ ★ ★ **THE FAIRMONT SCOTTSDALE PRINCESS.** *7575 E Princess Dr (85255). Phone 480/585-4848; fax 480/585-0086. www.fairmont.com.* The Fairmont Scottsdale Princess is a cosmopolitan oasis snuggled on 450 lush acres overlooking Scottsdale and the majestic McDowell Mountains. The pink Spanish Colonial buildings are just the beginning at this comprehensive resort, where recreational opportunities are plentiful. Two championship golf courses, one of which hosts the PGA Tour's Phoenix Open; seven tennis courts; and an extensive fitness center please the active minded, while the Willow Stream Spa soothes the weary with its serene design and balancing principles. Four pools cool guests, and adults and children alike are tickled pink by the aquatic recreation area complete with two waterslides. The rooms and suites are a blend of Mediterranean design interspersed with Southwestern accents. Spacious and comfortable, the accommodations have fantastic views. Diners traverse the world at the six restaurants and bars, where dishes hailing from the Italian Riviera, Mexico, and the American heartland delight guests. 650 rooms, 3-4 story. S, D $479-$539; each additional $30; under 16 free; golf, tennis, spa, holiday plans. Check-out noon, check-in 4 pm. TV; cable; VCR available. Some fireplaces. Dining rooms 6:30 am-11 pm (see also LA HACIENDA and MARQUESA). Bar 11-1 am. Room service 24 hours. Supervised children's activities (Memorial Day-Labor Day and holidays); ages 5-12. Exercise room, sauna, steam room. Spa. Massage. 3 pools; whirlpool, poolside service. 36-hole golf, greens fee $91-$214. Tennis, lighted courts. Lawn games. Valet parking. Business center. Concierge. Cr cds: A, C, D, DS, JCB, MC, V.

D 🏇 🏌 ⊠ 🏃 ⊠ 🏃

★ ★ ★ **FOUR SEASONS RESORT SCOTTSDALE AT TROON NORTH.** *10600 E Crescent Moon Dr (85255). Phone 480/515-5700; fax 480/ 515-5599. www.fourseasons.com.* The Four Seasons Resort Scottsdale at Troon North basks in the abundant golden sunshine synonymous with the Southwest. Blending with the natural surroundings, this two-story resort rests within a 40-acre nature preserve. The rooms and suites are housed in 25 casitas clustered around the grounds. Native American pottery and textiles add local flavor and set a sense of place in the rooms, where fireplaces warm the interiors and windows frame expansive views of the stunning desert. Extra luxuries like plunge pools, alfresco garden showers, and outdoor kiva fireplaces characterize the gracious suites. Influenced by the location, the spa offers desert nectar facials and moonlight massages, and the landscaped pool deck provides a pleasurable place for relaxation. Three restaurants reflect the resort's casually elegant attitude in their ambience and menu. A veritable mecca for golfers, the resort grants priority tee times at Troon North's two courses, considered among the best in the world. 210 rooms, 2 story. Jan-June: S, D $425-$650; under 17 free; golf plan. Pet accepted, some restrictions. Check-out noon, check-in 4 pm. TV; cable (premium), VCR available. In-room modem link. Restaurant 7 am-10 pm. Bar to midnight. Room service 24 hours. Exercise room, spa, massage, sauna, steam room. Pool, whirlpool, poolside service. Golf, greens fee $248. Tennis, lighted courts. Business center. Concierge. Cr cds: A, C, D, DS, ER, JCB, MC, V.

⬛ 🏌 🚴 ⛷ 🏊 🧍 🏃

★ ★ ★ **HYATT REGENCY SCOTTSDALE.** *7500 E Doubletree Ranch Rd (85258). Phone 480/991-3388; toll-free 800/233-1234; fax 480/483-5550. www.hyatt.com.* The Hyatt Regency Scottsdale Resort at Gainey Ranch enjoys a truly spectacular setting. Set against the backdrop of the McDowell Mountains, the resort is nestled on 560 acres filled with shimmering pools, trickling fountains, and cascading waterfalls. Neutral tones and regional furnishings create serene havens in the rooms and suites. This is a desert playground for the whole family, with exceptional golf, tennis, and other recreational facilities. The resort is committed to preserving the integrity of its home, from the innovative environmental conservation techniques to the cultural programming on the Southwest's indigenous people. A wide variety of restaurants take guests on a culinary journey, and in the case of Ristorante Sandolo, a gondola ride. Diners can feast on Northern Italian specialties, continental cuisine, and Southwestern dishes in refined or casual settings. 486 rooms; 4 story. 7 casitas (1-4 bedroom) on lake. Jan-mid-June: S, D $350-$525; under 18 free; golf plans. Check-out noon, check-in 4 pm. TV; cable (premium), VCR available. In-room modem link. Fireplace in casitas. Restaurant (public by reservation) 6:30 am-10:30 pm (See also GOLDEN SWAN). Bar noon-1 am. Room service 24 hours. Supervised children's activities; ages 3-5, 6-12. Exercise room, massage, sauna, steam room. 10 pools; poolside service. 27-hole golf, greens fee $160. Tennis, lighted courts. Bicycles. Free valet parking. Business center. Concierge, luxury level. Cr cds: A, C, D, DS, JCB, MC, V.

⬛ 🏌 ⛷ 🏊 🧍 🚴 SC 🏃

★ ★ ★ **MARRIOTT CAMELBACK INN RESORT GOLF CLUB & SPA.** *5402 E Lincoln Dr (85253). Phone 480/948-1700; toll-free 800/242-2635; fax 480/951-8469. www.marriott.com.* Since the 1930s, the Camelback Inn has appealed to travelers seeking the very best in the American Southwest. This special hideaway, reminiscent

of a hacienda, is situated on 125 acres in Arizona's beautiful Sonoran Desert. Supremely comfortable, the rooms and suites share the distinctive charms of the region while providing modern luxuries. To further indulge guests, the suites even offer private pools. Outdoor enthusiasts explore the region on horseback, enjoy the thrill of whitewater rafting, or marvel at the view from above in a hot-air balloon, while tennis courts, three heated pools, and a comprehensive fitness center keep guests occupied closer to home. Set at the base of Mummy Mountain, the spa is a peaceful retreat. All cravings are satisfied here, with a total of seven dining venues ranging from quick and casual to more formal settings ideal for lingering over sensational meals. 453 rooms, 1-2 story. S, D $399-$450; under 18 free; golf, tennis, spa, package plans. Pet accepted. Check-out noon, check-in 4 pm. TV; cable (premium), VCR available. In-room modem link. Dining rooms 6:30 am-10 pm. Bar 11-1 am. Room service to midnight. Supervised children's activities holidays only; ages 5-12. Exercise room, spa, sauna, steam room. 3 pools; whirlpool, poolside service. Golf, greens fee $90-$155 (including cart). Tennis, lighted courts. Lawn games. Entertainment. Bicycle rental. Business center. Concierge. Cr cds: A, C, D, DS, ER, JCB, MC, V.

⬛ 🏌 🚴 ⛷ 🏊 🧍 🚴 🏃

★ ★ ★ **MARRIOTT MOUNTAIN SHADOWS RESORT AND GOLF CLUB.** *5641 E Lincoln Dr (85253). Phone 480/948-7111; toll-free 800/782-2123; fax 480/951-5430. www.mountainshadows.net.* 369 rooms, 1-2 story. S, D $79-$229; under 18 free. Check-out noon, check-in 4 pm. TV; cable (premium). Dining rooms 6:30 am-midnight. Bar 11-1 am. Room service. Exercise room, sauna. 3 heated pools, whirlpool. 54-hole golf, greens fee $60-$105 (including cart), driving range. Lighted tennis. Lawn games. Business center. Cr cds: A, C, D, DS, ER, JCB, MC, V.

⬛ 🏌 🚴 ⛷ 🏊 🧍 🚴 🏃

★ ★ ★ **MILLENNIUM RESORT SCOTTSDALE, MCCORMICK RANCH.** *7401 N Scottsdale Rd (85253). Phone 480/948-5050; toll-free 800/243-1332; fax 480/948-9113. www.millennium-hotels.com/scottsdale.* At Scottsdale's single lakeside resort, enjoy a day on the lake with paddleboats or sailing, complimentary for resort guests only. 128 rooms, villas, 3 story. S, D $55-$285; each additional $10; under 18 free; golf, tennis plans. Check-out noon, check-in 3 pm. TV; cable (premium). Fireplace in villas. Dining room 6:30 am-10 pm. Bar 11-1 am. Room service. Health club privileges, exercise equipment. Whirlpool, poolside service. Lighted tennis. Lawn games. Dock; sailboats, paddleboats. Valet parking. Business center. Concierge. Cr cds: A, C, D, DS, MC, V.

⬛ 🚴 🏌 ⛷ 🏊 🧍 🏃

★ ★ ★ **ORANGE TREE GOLF AND CONFERENCE CENTER.** *10601 N 56th St (85254). Phone 480/948-6100; toll-free 800/228-0386; fax 480/483-6074. www.orangetree.com.* A luscious landscape and a championship 18-hole golf course set the stage for this desert resort that was once an orange orchard. Spacious and cozy suites have French door openings to private terraces. 160 suites, 2 story. Jan-May: S, D $150-$275; under 18 free; golf plan; lower rates rest of year. Crib free. Check-out 11 am, check-in 4 pm. TV; cable (premium), VCR (movies). Balconies, private patios, refrigerators, microwaves, bathroom phones. Coffee in rooms. Valet services, coin laundry. Dining room 6 am-10 pm. Bar 11-1 am, entertainment Wed-Sat. Room service, box lunches. Supervised children's activities. Exercise equipment, massage. Sports director. Heated pool, wading pool, whirlpool, poolside service. Golf resort with country club atmosphere. 18-hole golf, greens fee $100 (including cart), pro. Picnics/tables. Meeting rooms. Business services available. Bellhops, concierge. Gift shop. Grocery, package store 1 mile. Cr cds: A, D, DS, MC, V.

★ ★ ★ ★ **THE PHOENICIAN.** *6000 E Camelback Rd (85251). Phone 480/941-8200; fax 480/947-4311. www.thephoenician.com.* The world-class Phoenician rests at the base of Camelback Mountain in Scottsdale's Valley of the Sun. This patrician resort almost defies belief with nine pools, 11 restaurants and lounges, and 654 guest accommodations. Home to an $8 million art collection, this resort embodies sophistication in the desert and stands out for its European panache. Aubusson tapestries and antiques in the lobby impart a continental feeling, yet the expansive, unobstructed views of the striking desert firmly root visitors in the Southwest. The rooms and suites are elegantly appointed, and meticulous attention to detail is a hallmark of this resort. Every imaginable recreational opportunity is available here, from championship golf and tennis to desert hikes. Swimmers can take a dip in one of the many pools and enjoy the thrill of the 165-foot waterslide. The impressive spa nurtures the spirit, while the fabulous restaurants feed the soul and garner praise from gourmets. 654 rooms, casitas. 4-6 story. S, D $525-$695; each additional $50; under 17 free; golf plans. Check-out noon, check-in 4 pm. TV; cable (premium), VCR available (movies). In-room modem link. Dining rooms (public by reservation) 6 am-10 pm. Bar 11-1 am; entertainment. Room service 24 hours. Supervised children's activities; ages 5-12. Exercise room, spa, sauna, steam room. 9 pools; whirlpool, poolside service. Golf, greens fee $90-$175. Tennis, lighted courts. Lawn games. Bicycle rentals. Hiking. Airport transportation. Business center. Concierge. Cr cds: A, C, D, DS, JCB, MC, V.

★ ★ ★ **RADISSON RESORT & SPA.** *7171 N Scottsdale Rd (85253). Phone 480/991-3800; fax 480/948-1381. www.radisson.com.* A perfect retreat for business or pleasure, this desert resort is located in Scottsdale's cultural district. 352 rooms, 2 story. S, D $89-$229; each additional $20; under 18 free. Check-out noon, check-in 4 pm. TV; cable (premium). Dining rooms 6:30 am-10 pm. Bar 11-1 am. Room service. Supervised children's activities (Late June-mid-Sept); ages 4-12. Exercise equipment, sauna. Whirlpool, poolside service. Lighted tennis, pro. Business center. Concierge. Cr cds: A, C, D, DS, ER, JCB, MC, V.

★ ★ ★ **RENAISSANCE SCOTTSDALE RESORT.** *6160 N Scottsdale Rd (85253). Phone 480/991-1414; fax 480/951-3350. www.renaissancehotels.com.* Nestled in the famous Camelback Mountain, this 25-acre oasis is a beautifully intimate experience. Whether shopping at the Borgata, shaping up with Splash Aerobics or chowing down at a private western-style dinner, guests will enjoy a variety of southwestern flair. 171 rooms, 1 story. S, D $79-$219; each additional $10; under 18 free; package plans. Pet accepted, some restrictions; fee. Complimentary continental breakfast. Check-out noon, check-in 4 pm. TV; cable (premium), VCR available (movies). Fireplaces. Restaurant 7 am-10:30 pm. Bar noon-11 pm. Room service 24 hours. Health club privileges. Poolside service. Golf privileges. Lighted tennis. Lawn games, bicycle rentals. Concierge. Cr cds: A, C, D, DS, ER, JCB, MC, V.

★ ★ ★ **SANCTUARY AT CAMELBACK MOUNTAIN.** *5700 E McDonald Dr, Paradise Valley (85253). Phone 480/948-2100; fax 480/483-7314. www.sanctuaryaz.com.* 159 rooms, 1 story. S, D $135-$530. Check-out noon, check-in 4 pm. TV; cable (premium). In-room modem link. Restaurant 6:30 am-10 pm. Bar to midnight. Exercise room. Pool, whirlpool. Business center. Concierge. Cr cds: A, C, D, DS, MC, V.

★ ★ ★ **SCOTTSDALE PLAZA RESORT.** *7200 N Scottsdale Rd (85253). Phone 480/948-5000; fax 480/998-5971. www.scottsdaleplaza.com.* This Mediterranean-style desert resort is a truly luxurious experience. 404 rooms, 2 story. S, D $115-$290; each additional $10; golf, pkg plans; under 17 free; weekend rates. Check-out noon, check-in 3 pm. TV; VCR available. Fireplaces in suites. Dining rooms 6 am-11 pm (See also REMINGTON). Bar 11-1 am, entertainment, room service. Exercise equipment, sauna. Poolside service. Lighted tennis. Lawn games, bike rentals. Racquetball. Business center. Concierge. Spanish Colonial-style buildings on 40 acres; waterfall. Cr cds: A, D, DS, JCB, MC, V.

★ ★ ★ **SUNBURST RESORT.** *4925 N Scottsdale Rd (85251). Phone 480/945-7666; toll-free 800/528-7867; fax 480/946-4056. www.sunburstresort.com.* A Mediterranean-like escape in the middle of the southwestern desert, describes the garden courtyard and the sandy pool area. Nearby to many PGA golf courses and shopping, it's representative of the charm and hospitality of the Old West. 218 rooms, 2 story. S, D $89-$210; each additional $10; under 18 free; family, weekend, holiday rates; golf plans. Check-out noon, check-in 3 pm. TV; cable (premium). In-room modem link. Restaurant 6 am-10 pm. Bar 10-1 am. Room service. Exercise equipment. Whirlpool, poolside service. Concierge. Cr cds: A, C, D, DS, MC, V.

[D] [≈] [⅄] [≈] [SC]

All Suite

★ **AMERISUITES.** *7300 E 3rd Ave (85251). Phone 480/423-9944; toll-free 800/833-1516; fax 480/423-2991. www.amerisuites.com.* 128 suites, 6 story. Suites $79-$169; each additional $10; under 18 free. Pet accepted, some restrictions; fee. Complimentary continental breakfast. Check-out noon, check-in 3 pm. TV; cable (premium), VCR available. Exercise equipment. Pool. Parking lot. Business center. Cr cds: A, C, D, DS, ER, JCB, MC, V.

[D] [≈] [≈] [⅄] [≈] [⅄]

★ ★ **CHAPARRAL SUITES RESORT.** *5001 N Scottsdale Rd (85250). Phone 480/949-1414; toll-free 800/528-1456; fax 480/947-2675. www.chaparralsuites.com.* 311 suites, 4 story. S, D $69-$189; each additional $10; under 18 free. Pet accepted, some restrictions. Complimentary full breakfast. Check-out noon, check-in 3 pm. TV; cable (premium), VCR available (movies). Restaurant 11 am-2:30 pm, 5-10 pm; Fri, Sat to 11 pm. Bar to 1 am. Exercise equipment. Game room. Poolside service. Lighted tennis. Concierge. Free airport transportation. Cr cds: A, C, D, DS, JCB, MC, V.

[D] [≈] [⊱] [≈] [⅄] [≈]

★ **GAINEY SUITES.** *7300 E Gainey Suites Dr (85258). Phone 480/922-6969; toll-free 800/970-4666; fax 480/922-1689. www.gaineysuiteshotel.com.* 162 rooms, 3 story. S, D $59-$399. Complimentary continental breakfast. Check-out noon, check-in 3 pm. TV. Exercise equipment. Pool, whirlpool. Hiking trail. Business center. Concierge. Cr cds: A, C, D, DS, MC, V.

[D] [⚓] [⅄] [≈] [⅄] [≈] [SC] [⅄]

★ ★ ★ **MARRIOTT SCOTTSDALE AT MCDOWELL MOUNTAIN.** *16770 N Perimeter Dr (85260). Phone 480/502-3836; toll-free 800/288-6127; fax 480/502-0653. www.marriottscottsdale.com.* This all-suite hotel is located in north Scottsdale. The colorful attractive public areas and well-furnished guestrooms are designed for both families and the business traveler. Some rooms have views of the TPC-Scottsdale golf course. 270 rooms, 5 story. S, D $79-$320. Check-out noon, check-in 4 pm. TV; cable (premium), VCR available. Dry cleaning, coin laundry. Restaurant 6:30 am-10 pm. Bar. Exercise room, steam room. Pool, whirlpool. Golf. Hiking trail. Valet parking available. Business center. Concierge service. Cr cds: A, C, D, DS, ER, JCB, MC, V.

[D] [⅄] [⚓] [≈] [⅄] [✈] [≈] [⅄]

★ ★ ★ **MARRIOTT SUITES SCOTTSDALE OLD TOWN.** *7325 E 3rd Ave (85251). Phone 480/945-1550; toll-free 800/228-9290; fax 480/945-2005. www.marriott.com.* Having everything for the business traveler, the suites at this hotel come fully loaded with the latest in office amenities, as well as plenty of recreational facilities to help wind down from the day. 251 suites, 7 story. S, D $79-$249. Check-out noon, check-in 3 pm. TV; cable (premium). Restaurant 6:30 am-10 pm; Sat, Sun 7 am-11 pm. Bar 5-11 pm. Exercise equipment, sauna. Whirlpool, poolside service. Valet parking. Business center. Cr cds: A, C, D, DS, ER, JCB, MC, V.

[≈] [⅄] [⅄]

★ **SUMMERFIELD SUITES.** *4245 N Drinkwater Blvd (85251). Phone 480/946-7700; toll-free 800/833-4353; fax 480/946-7711. www.wyndham.com.* This all-suite property has numerous amenities that make this an ideal location for families and extended-stay guests. 164 suites, 3 story. Suites $69-$199. Pet accepted, some restrictions, fee. Complimentary full breakfast. Check-out noon, check-in 4 pm. TV; cable (premium), VCR available. Exercise equipment. Pool, whirlpool. Golf on premises. Bike rentals. Concierge. Cr cds: A, C, D, DS, JCB, MC, V.

[D] [⚓] [≈] [⅄] [✈] [≈]

B&B/Small Inns

★ ★ ★ **THE HERMOSA INN.** *5532 N Palo Cristi Rd (85253). Phone 602/955-8614; toll-free 800/241-1210; fax 602/955-8299. www.hermosainn.com.* Accommodations range from spacious villas to cozy adobe casitas. Sitting on a half-acre marked by gracious olive and mesquite trees, towering palms, and brilliant flowers, this inn occasionally gets ghostly visits from its original owner. 42 rooms, 1 story. S, D $105-$355; each additional $25; under 6 free. Complimentary continental breakfast. Check-out noon, check-in 3 pm. TV. Many fireplaces. Restaurant (See also LON'S). Room service. Whirlpool. Tennis on premises. Concierge. Cr cds: A, C, D, DS, MC, V.

[⅄] [⅄] [≈] [≈] [SC]

★ ★ ★ **INN AT CITADEL.** *8700 E Pinnacle Peak Rd (85255). Phone 480/585-6133; toll-free 800/927-8367; fax 480/585-3436. www.citadelinn.com.* This unique bed and breakfast located in north Scottsdale is a quiet mix of luxury and comfort. 11 suites. Jan-Mid-May: S, D $79-$249; lower rates rest of year. Crib free. Pet accepted. TV; cable (premium). Complimentary continental breakfast. Coffee in rooms. Restaurant adjacent 6 am-11 pm. Room service. Check-out noon, check-in 3 pm. Business services available. Some balconies, minibars. Each room individually decorated with antiques, artwork. View of Sonoran Desert, city. Cr cds: A, D, DS, MC, V.

★ ★ ★ **SOUTHWEST INN AT EAGLE MOUNTAIN.** *9800 N. Summer Hill Blvd, Fountain Hill (85268). Phone 480/816-3000; toll-free 800/992-8083; fax 480/816-3090. www.southwestinn.com.* Located on the 18th fairway with views of Red Mountain, each room includes plush robes. 42 rooms, 2 story, 11 suites. Jan-May: S, D $109-$199; each additional $10; suites $149-$259; under 13 free; package plans; lower rates rest of year. Crib free. TV; cable (premium), VCR. Complimentary continental breakfast. Complimentary coffee in rooms. Check-out 11 am, check-in 3 pm. Meeting rooms. Business services available. In-room modem link. Bellstaff. Concierge service. Gift shop. Lighted tennis privileges, pro. 18-hole golf privileges, pro, putting green, driving range. Heated pool; whirlpool. Bathroom phones, in-room whirlpools, refrigerators, fireplaces. Balconies. Totally nonsmoking. Cr cds: A, D, DS, MC, V.

Extended Stay

★ ★ **RESIDENCE INN BY MARRIOTT.** *6040 N Scottsdale Rd (85253). Phone 480/948-8666; toll-free 800/ 331-3131; fax 480/443-4869. www.residenceinn.com.* 122 kitchen units, 2 story. S, D $79-$179; weekly, monthly rates. Pet accepted; fee. Complimentary continental breakfast. Check-out noon, check-in 3 pm. TV; cable (premium), VCR available. Exercise equipment. Whirlpool, poolside service. 36-hole golf privileges. Cr cds: A, C, D, DS, ER, JCB, MC, V.

Restaurants

★ ★ ★ ★ **ACACIA.** *10600 E Crescent Moon Dr (85255). Phone 480/515-5700; fax 480/515-5599. www.fourseasons.com.* If you happen to find yourself nibbling on artistic, up-to-the-minute American fare under a vast, dark sky carpeted with stars, faced with stunning views of the McDowell Mountains and with the twinkle of city lights around you, chances are you are at The Four Seasons Resort Scottsdale at Troon North (See also FOUR SEASONS RESORT SCOTTSDALE AT TROON NORTH), dining at its flagship eatery, Acacia. Decked out in glossy wood floors, wood-beamed ceilings, and serene earth tones, and warmed with light from wrought-iron alabaster chandeliers and a two-way fireplace the size of a small home, Acacia is one of the most beautiful places to sink into for an evening of dining and atmosphere. Entrées are divided among steaks and chops (USDA Prime and certified Angus), seafood, and poultry. Signatures include five-spiced tuna with soy sauce, wasabi, and pickled ginger; and grilled, dry-rubbed, double-cut lamb chops, making Acacia a perfect place for all sorts of eaters and appetites. Hours: 6-10 pm, Fri, Sat to 10:30 pm. Dinner $22-$34. Cr cds: A, C, D, DS, ER, JCB, MC, V.

★ ★ **BANDERA.** *3821 N Scottsdale Rd (85251). Phone 480/922-7775; fax 480/922-7775. www.houstons.com.* American menu. Hours: 5-10 pm; Fri to 11 pm; Sat 4:30-11 pm; Sun from 4:30 pm. Closed Thanksgiving, Dec 25. Dinner $14-$24. Bar. Children's menu. Casual attire. Cr cds: A, D, MC, V.

★ ★ **BUSTER'S.** *8320 N Hayden (85258). Phone 480/ 951-5850. www.bustersrestaurant.com.* American menu. Closed Dec 25. Lunch, dinner. Bar. Children's menu. Outdoor seating. Cr cds: A, D, DS, MC, V. **$$**

★ ★ **CHAPARRAL DINING ROOM.** *5402 E Lincoln Dr (85253). Phone 480/948-1700; fax 480/905-7948. www.camelbackinn.com.* This Scottsdale landmark sports excellent views of the Camelback Mountain, creating a breathtaking ambiance. American menu, continental menu. Hours: 5:30-10 pm; Fri, Sat from noon. Dinner $20-$35. Bar to midnight. Casual attire. Valet parking. Cr cds: A, D, DS, ER, JCB, MC, V. **$$**

★ ★ **CHART HOUSE.** *7255 McCormick Pkwy (85258). Phone 480/951-2250; fax 480/951-1733. www. scottsdalecharthouse.com.* Dinner. Bar. Children's menu. Outdoor seating. Cr cds: A, D, DS, MC, V. **$$$**

★ **CHOMPIE'S.** *9301 E Shea Blvd (85260). Phone 480/ 860-0475; fax 480/860-8422. www.chompies.com.* Kosher deli menu. Breakfast, lunch, dinner. Cr cds: A, MC, V. **$$**

★ ★ **CREW.** *34505 N Scottsdale Rd, Suite 32 (85262). Phone 480/488-8840; fax 480/488-6830. www.creweats.com.* Closed Thanksgiving, Dec 25. Lunch, dinner. Entertainment. Children's menu. Cr cds: A, D, DS, MC, V. **$$**

★ ★ **DON AND CHARLIE'S AMERICAN RIB AND CHOP HOUSE.** 7501 E Camelback Rd (85251). Phone 480/990-0900; fax 480/947-3464. www.donandcharlies.com. American menu. Hours: 5-10 pm; Fri, Sat to 10:30 pm; Sun 4:30-9 pm. Closed Thanksgiving. Dinner $10.95-$36.95. Bar. Children's menu. Casual attire. Totally nonsmoking. Cr cds: A, D, DS, MC, V.

D

★ ★ **EL CHORRO LODGE.** 5550 E Lincoln Dr (85253). Phone 480/948-5170; fax 480/483-2283. www.elchorro.com. American menu. Hours: 11 am-4 pm, 6-10 pm; Sat, Sun from 6 pm. Dinner $9.95-$62. Bar. Piano, guitar Thurs-Sat. Casual attire. Valet parking. Outdoor dining. Fireplaces. Cr cds: A, D, DS, MC, V.

D

★ ★ ★ **ELEMENTS.** 5700 E McDonald Rd (85253). Phone 480/607-2300. American menu. Breakfast, lunch, dinner. Bar. Casual attire. **$$$**

D

★★★★**GOLDEN SWAN.** 7500 E Doubletree Rd (85258). Phone 480/483-5572; fax 480/483-5550. www.scottsdale.hyatt.com. Modern, upscale Southwestern fare is the culinary theme at The Golden Swan, a stone-floored, desert-toned dining room set in the Hyatt Regency's Scottsdale Resort (see also HYATT REGENCY SCOTTSDALE RESORT AT GAINEY RANCH). The kitchen is known for adding spark to the plate with the heat of the region's indigenous chilies, barbecue sauces, and spices; free-range chicken baked in Arizona red rock clay and grilled Pacific salmon with mesquite-honey barbecue sauce are signatures. The food here is fantastic, which is part of the explanation behind the restaurant's unstoppable popularity. With its movie-set views of the lake and gazebo, it is not surprising to learn that the restaurant boasts four or five marriage proposals per week. If you have room in your schedule on a Sunday, make a point of getting to the Sunday Chef's Brunch. It includes a belt-busting numbers of selections: salads, shellfish, sushi, pastas, breakfast pastries, fresh-baked breads, and hand-carved meats, and the added bonus of ordering your meal in the kitchen directly from the chef. Southwestern gourmet cuisine. Hours: 6-10 pm; Sun brunch 9:30 am-2:30 pm. Closed Sun, Mon (July 4-Labor Day). Dinner $28-$31. Sun brunch. Bar. Valet parking. Totally nonsmoking. Cr cds: A, D, DS, JCB, MC, V.

D

★ ★ ★ **HAPA.** 6204 N Scottsdale Rd (85253). Phone 480/998-8220; fax 480/998-2355. www.restauranthapa.com. Hapa is Hawaiian slang for half and refers to the Asian-American ancestry of chef James McDevitt. With wife Stacey creating splendid desserts, like warm chocolate cake with mango sauce, this Pacific Rim menu is interesting from start to finish. Asian American menu. Hours: 11:30 am-2:30 pm, 5:30-10 pm. Closed Sun; most major holidays; 2 weeks in summer. Dinner $18-$34. Bar to midnight. Casual attire. Outdoor dining. Cr cds: A, MC, V.

D

★ ★ ★ **L'ECOLE.** 8100 E Camelback Rd (85251). Phone 480/990-7639; fax 480/990-3773. www.scichefs.com. You can be sure that the food is top-of-the-line at this "training ground" for the Scottsdale Culinary Institute. This student-operated restaurant is set in a lovely dining room that is booked weeks in advance. Diners also enjoy the patio setting with colorful awnings. American menu. Closed Sat, Sun. Lunch, dinner. Reservations required. Cr cds: A, DS, MC, V. **$$**

D

★ ★ ★ **LA HACIENDA.** 7575 E Princess Dr (85255). Phone 480/585-4848; fax 480/585-2613. www.fairmont.com. Housed in a turn-of-the-century Mexican ranch house on the lush grounds of the Fairmont Scottsdale Princess, a notable southwestern resort and spa (See also THE FAIRMONT SCOTTSDALE PRINCESS), La Hacienda offers traditional Mexican specialties. Signatures like filete a la parrilla—grilled filet mignon with corn, poblano salsa, and cascabel glaze—and cochinillo asado—a barbacoa-style suckling pig that is spit-roasted and stuffed with homemade chorizo sausage and carved tableside—are prepared with care and the technique of generations past. Strolling mariachis, flagstone flooring, wood-beamed ceilings, hurricane lamps, tapestry-upholstered seating, assorted artifacts from Mexico, and magnificent views make this an alluring spot to dine and watch the sun go down. Like any respectable authentic Mexican eatery, La Hacienda makes killer margaritas, served with crisp, golden tortilla chips to keep you thirsting for more. Hours: 6-10 pm. Closed Wed. Dinner $22-$31. Bar from 5 pm. Strolling mariachis. Children's menu. Valet parking. Outdoor dining. Cr cds: A, D, DS, MC, V.

D

★ ★ **LANDRY'S PACIFIC FISH COMPANY.** 4321 N Scottsdale Rd (85251). Phone 480/941-0602; fax 480/941-1518. www.landrysseafood.com. Closed Thanksgiving, Dec 25. Lunch, dinner. Bar. Entertainment weekends. Children's menu. Free valet parking. Outdoor seating. Cr cds: A, D, DS, MC, V. **$$$**

D

★ ★ ★ **MANCUSO'S.** 6166 N Scottsdale Rd (85253). Phone 480/948-9988; fax 480/948-6011. www.mancusosrestaurant.com. Delicate piano music sets the mood at this very polished Italian restaurant, which reflects the richness of the Renaissance period. Guests sip cappuccinos in the espresso bar after dinner. Continental menu. Closed Dec 25. Dinner. Bar. Piano. Valet parking. Cr cds: A, C, D, DS, MC, V. **$$**

D

★ ★ **MARCO POLO SUPPER CLUB.** *8608 E Shea Blvd (85260). Phone 480/483-1900; fax 480/483-9752. www.marcopolosupperclub.com.* Continental menu. Specialties: lobster spedini with penne alfredo and spinach. Hours: 5-10 pm; Fri, Sat to 11 pm. Reservations accepted. Bar to 1 am. A la carte entrees: dinner $11.95-$30. Musicians. Valet parking. Outdoor dining. Family photographs adorn walls. Cr cds: A, DS, MC, V.
Ⓓ

★ ★ ★ **MARIA'S WHEN IN NAPLES.** *7000 E Shea Blvd (85254). Phone 480/991-6887; fax 480/483-3818. www.mariaswheninnaples.com.* Handmade pasta and fresh sauces are served in traditional Italian decor that exudes a casual elegance. A local favorite. Italian menu. Hours: 11:30 am-2:30 pm, 5-10 pm; Sat, Sun from 5 pm. Closed most major holidays. Dinner $13-$23. Bar. Casual attire. Outdoor dining. Cr cds: A, D, DS, MC, V.
Ⓓ

★ ★ ★ **MARQUESA.** *7575 E Princess Dr (85255). Phone 480/585-4848; fax 480/585-2613. www.fairmont.com.* Marquesa is one of those restaurants that can be habit forming. Lucky for you, in terms of addictions, this one is not detrimental to your health but actually has health benefits. Marquesa features the wonderful foods of the Mediterranean Riviera. The kitchen stays true to the peasant dishes of Italy, France, and Spain but also offers a selection of more innovative creations, which means that classic dishes like bouillabaisse and paella share menu space with more extravagant dishes like duck and squab with pistachio, caramelized pears, turnip gratin, and fruit reduction. The soothing dining room is all atmosphere—appointed with wildflowers, brocade tapestries, rich leather, magnificent paintings, and antiques from the 16th and 17th centuries. Dining under the stars with a bird's-eye view of the McDowell Mountains is made possible in chilly weather thanks to a stone fireplace. Hours: 6-10 pm; Sun brunch 10:30 am-2:30 pm. Closed Sun, Mon. Dinner $27-$42. Flamenco guitarist Sun brunch. Bar. Entertainment. Children's menu. Valet parking. Outdoor dining. Cr cds: A, D, DS, MC, V.
Ⓓ

★ ★ ★ ★ **MARY ELAINE'S.** *6000 E Camelback Rd (85251). Phone 480/423-2444; fax 480/423-2516. www.thephoenician.com.* Never mind the extraordinary prices: this bastion of luxury is worth the price tag. The impeccable service staff will anticipate your every need, whether it's a stool on which to rest your handbag or guidance navigating the impressive wine list. Seafood is the specialty, with heavenly choices including pan-seared New Zealand John Dory, Sea of Cortez scallops, and roasted American red snapper. French menu. Specializes in fresh seafood from around the world, rack of lamb, veal, Artisan game. Hours: 6-10 pm; Fri, Sat to 11 pm. Closed Sun, Mon. Bar. Wine cellar. Reservations accepted.

A la carte entrees: dinner $40-$45. Complete meals: dinner $70-$100. Children's menu. Entertainment. Valet parking. Jacket. Cr cds: A, D, DS, JCB, MC, V.
Ⓓ

★ ★ ★ **MICHAEL'S.** *8700 E Pinnacle Peak Rd (85255). Phone 480/515-2575; fax 480/515-1451. www.michaelsrestaurant.com.* This namesake restaurant of Michael DeMaria is in The Citadel resort in the Sonoran Desert. Signature features are a demonstration cooking studio and a chef's table with kitchen views. The bright dining room is a great space to showcase contemporary American cuisine. Specialties: seared Chilean sea bass. Hours: 6-10 pm. Closed some holidays. Reservations accepted. Bar 5 pm-midnight. Wine cellar. A la carte entrees: dinner $17.95-$27.95. Jazz Fri, Sat. Outdoor dining. Unique décor with waterfall. Cr cds: A, D, MC, V.
Ⓓ

★ ★ **OCEANA.** *8900 E Pinnacle Peak Rd (85255). Phone 480/515-2277; fax 480/515-3532. www.restaurantoceana.com.* Skeptical of seafood in the middle of the desert? Don't be. Near The Boulders resort, this cozy spot offers inspired, strikingly fresh seafood creations from a small, daily changing menu. Tasting menus are also offered for a more involved dining experience. Closed most major holidays; Sun (May-Aug); 1st 2 weeks of Aug. Dinner. Bar. Outdoor seating. Cr cds: A, D, DS, MC, V. **$$**
Ⓓ

★ ★ ★ **PALM COURT.** *7700 E McCormick Pkwy (85258). Phone 480/596-7700; fax 480/596-7427.* This candlelit restaurant maintains the classic traditions of fine dining with lavish continental fare prepared tableside in a dazzling production. Dapper, tuxedo-clad waiters serve decadent mainstays. Breakfast, lunch, dinner, Sun brunch. Bar. Piano. Children's menu. Jacket required (dinner). Valet parking. Totally nonsmoking. Cr cds: A, D, DS, MC, V. **$$$**

★ **PISCHKE'S PARADISE.** *7217 E 1st St (85251). Phone 480/481-0067. www.pischkesparadise.com.* American menu. Hours: 7 am-11 pm; Sun 8 am-10 pm. Closed most major holidays. Dinner $8-$18. Bar. Casual attire. Outdoor dining. Cr cds: A, DS, MC, V.
Ⓓ

★ **QUILTED BEAR.** *6316 N Scottsdale Rd (85253). Phone 480/948-7760; fax 480/948-1080.* Breakfast, lunch, dinner. Children's menu. Outdoor seating. Cr cds: A, D, DS, MC, V. **$$**
Ⓓ

★ ★ ★ **RAZZ'S.** *10315 N Scottsdale Rd (85253). Phone 480/905-1308; fax 480/607-6698. www.razzsrestaurant.com.* Chef Razz Kamnitzer is the Wolfgang Puck of the Southwest, setting the pace for innovative cuisine in Scottsdale. He combines edible flowers, fresh herbs and vegetables from his own garden with familiar dishes from around the world to create a dazzling, unpredictable menu. Contemporary international menu. Hours: 5-10 pm. Closed Sun, Mon; most major holidays; also July-Aug. Dinner $15.95-$22.95. Bar. Children's menu. Casual attire. Reservations required Fri, Sat. Cr cds: A, D, DS, MC, V.

D

★ ★ ★ **REMINGTON.** *7200 N Scottsdale Rd (85253). Phone 480/951-5101; fax 480/951-5108.* A handpainted skyscape creates a unique indoor ambiance or enjoy patio dining with a fantastic view of Camelback Mountains. Located in the Scottsdale Plaza Hotel. Lunch, dinner. Bar. Outdoor seating. Cr cds: A, D, DS, MC, V. **$$$**

D

★ ★ ★ **ROARING FORK.** *4800 N Scottsdale Rd (85251). Phone 480/947-0795; fax 480/994-1102. www.roaringfork.com.* One of the founders of southwestern cuisine, chef Robert McGrath turns out American western cooking at this rustic yet refined dining room filled with exposed brick and blond wood. The adjacent J-Bar is a fun place to congregate for a drink. American menu. Hours: 11 am-3 pm, 6-10 pm; Fri to 11 pm; Sat 6-11 pm. Closed Sun; most major holidays; hours vary June-Aug. Dinner $16-$35. Bar. Children's menu. Casual attire. Valet parking Fri, Sat. Outdoor dining. Cr cds: A, D, DS, MC, V.

D

★ ★ ★ **RUTH'S CHRIS STEAK HOUSE.** *7001 N Scottsdale Rd (85253). Phone 480/991-5988; fax 480/991-6850. www.ruthschris.com.* White tablecloths and finely dressed waiters create an atmosphere of elegance at this cosmopolitan steak house. Hours: 5-10 pm; Fri, Sat to 10:30 pm. Closed Thanksgiving, Dec 25. Dinner $18.95-$33.95. Bar. Casual attire. Outdoor dining. Cr cds: A, D, DS, MC, V.

D

★ ★ **SALT CELLAR.** *550 N Hayden Rd (85257). Phone 480/947-1963. www.saltcellarrestaurant.com.* Closed Dec 25. Dinner. Bar. Children's menu. Restaurant located underground, in former salt cellar. Cr cds: A, MC, V. **$$**

★ ★ **SUSHI ON SHEA.** *7000 E Shea Blvd (85254). Phone 480/483-7799; fax 480/483-7779. www.sushionshea.com.* Japanese menu. Hours: 11:30 am-2:30 pm, 5:30-10 pm; Fri, Sat to 11 pm; Sun from 5:30 pm. Closed most major holidays. Dinner $8.95-$45. Bar. Aquarium; sushi bar. Children's menu. Casual attire. Cr cds: A, D, DS, MC, V.

D

★ ★ ★ **THE TERRACE DINING ROOM.** *6000 E Camelback Rd (85251). Phone 480/423-2530; fax 480/423-2640. www.thephoenician.com.* Inside or outside, The Terrace Dining Room is a majestic and breathtaking (not to mention very tasty) place to dine. The glowing indoor space is lined with picture windows, floral murals, and creamy Frette-topped tables, while the stunning outdoor terrace is enveloped in picturesque views of the Phoenician's croquet fields, and the resort's beautifully landscaped grounds, including a turquoise pool inlaid with mother of pearl. To add to the visual pleasure, The Terrace's new American menu of pastas, fish, poultry, and steaks cut at the in-house butcher shop is impeccably prepared using the finest products. A live orchestra plays nightly to make every evening an enchanted one. Try to pry yourself out of bed if you are there on a Sunday for their fabulous feast commonly known as brunch. (See also THE PHOENICIAN.) Continental, American menu. Hours: 6 am-10 pm; Sun brunch 10 am-2 pm. Dinner $19-$35. Sun brunch. Entertainment. Children's menu. Valet parking. Cr cds: A, D, DS, MC, V.

D

★ ★ **VIC'S AT PINNACLE PEAK.** *8711 E Pinnacle Peak Rd (85255). Phone 480/998-2222; fax 480/585-6635. www.vicsrestaurant.com.* Lunch, dinner. Bar. Children's menu. Outdoor seating. Cr cds: A, MC, V. **$$$**

D

Sedona (D-4)

See also Cottonwood, Flagstaff

Founded 1902 **Pop** 10,192 **Elev** 4,400 ft **Area code** 928

Information Sedona-Oak Creek Canyon Chamber of Commerce, PO Box 478, 86339; 928/282-7722 or 800/288-7336

Web www.sedonachamber.com

Known worldwide for the beauty of the red rocks surrounding the town, Sedona has grown from a pioneer settlement into a favorite film location. This is a resort area with numerous outdoor activities, including hiking, fishing, and biking, that can be enjoyed all year. Also an art and shopping destination, Sedona boasts Tlaquepaque (T-lock-ay-POCK-ay), a 4 1/2-acre area of gardens, courtyards, fountains, galleries, shops, and restaurants. A Ranger District office of the Coconino National Forest is here.

What to See and Do

Chapel of the Holy Cross. *780 Chapel Rd. 2 1/2 miles S on AZ 179. Phone 928/282-4069.* Chapel perched between two pinnacles of uniquely colored red sandstone. Open to all for prayer and meditation. (Daily) **FREE**

Jeep tours. *270 N US 89A. Phone 800/8-SEDONA.* Two-hour back country trips. (Daily) Other tours also available. Contact Red Rock Jeep Tours, phone 928/282-6826. **$$$$**

Oak Creek Canyon. *Phone 928/282-2085.* A beautiful drive along a spectacular fishing stream, north toward Flagstaff (see). Also in the canyon is

> **Slide Rock State Park.** *270 N US 89A. 7 miles N on US 89A. Phone 928/282-3034.* A 43-acre day-use park on Oak Creek. Swimming, natural sandstone waterslide, fishing; hiking, picnicking. Concessions. Standard fees. **$$**

Sedona Cultural Park. *1725 W Hwy 89A (86336). Cultural Park Pl, off US 89A. Phone 928/282-0747.* A 5-acre park that is home to the Georgia Frontiere Performing Arts Pavilion (seating 1,200-5,500), plus nature trails, picnic areas, and splendid views of the surrounding red rock country. Performing arts season (May-Oct) features classical, jazz, country, and popular music, plus live theater and outdoor cinema. (Daily) **$$$$**

Tlaquepaque. *336 Hwy 179. On AZ 179. Phone 928/282-4838.* Consists of 40 art galleries and stores set in a Spanish-style courtyard; cafés. (Daily except holidays) **FREE**

Verde Canyon Railroad. *300 N Broadway. 20 miles SW via US 89A, in Clarkdale. (See COTTONWOOD) Phone 800/293-7245.*

Special Events

Red Rock Fantasy of Lights. *160 Portal Ln (86336). Phone 928/282-1777.* Late Nov-mid-Jan.

Sedona Film Festival. *1725 W Hwy 89A # 2 (86336). Phone 928/282-0747.* First full weekend in Mar.

Sedona Jazz on the Rocks. *250 Cultural Park Pl (86336). Phone 928/282-1985.* Late Sept.

Motels/Motor Lodges

★ **BEST WESTERN ARROYO ROBLE HOTEL AND CREEKSIDE VILLAS.** *400 N Hwy 89A (86336). Phone 928/282-4001; toll-free 800/773-3662. www.bestwesternsedona.com.* 66 rooms, 5 story. Mid-Feb-Nov: S, D $100-$149; each additional $10; suite $159-$179; cottage $179; villas $299; under 12 free; lower rates rest of year. Complimentary continental breakfast. Check-out 11 am. TV; cable (premium). In-room modem link. Fireplaces. Exercise equipment, sauna, steam room. Lighted tennis $5/person. Racquetball. Views of red sandstone buttes. Cr cds: A, C, D, DS, MC, V.

[D] [icons] SC

★ **BEST WESTERN INN OF SEDONA.** *1200 W Hwy 89A (86336). Phone 928/282-3072; toll-free 800/292-6344; fax 928/282-7218. www.innofsedona.com.* 110 rooms, 3 story. Mar-May, Sept-Oct: S, D $79-$179; suite $189; each additional $10; under 12 free; holidays (2-day minimum); lower rates rest of year. Pet accepted; fee. Complimentary continental breakfast, coffee in rooms. Check-out 11 am. TV; cable (premium). In-room modem link. Many refrig-

erators; some fireplaces, balconies. Exercise equipment. Heated pool, whirlpool. Airport transportation. Concierge. Cr cds: A, C, D, DS, MC, V.

[D] [icons] SC

★ **DESERT QUAIL INN.** *6626 State Rte 179 (86351). Phone 928/284-1433; toll-free 800/385-0927; fax 928/284-0487. www.desertquailinn.com.* 41 rooms, 1 suite, 2 story. S, D $69-$149; suite $139-$169; each additional $10; under 13 free; golf plan; higher rates: holidays (2-day minimum), special events. Pet accepted, some restrictions; fee. Check-out 11 am. TV. In-room modem link. Some fireplaces. Restaurant nearby. Pool. Golf privileges. Cr cds: A, C, D, DS, MC, V.

[D] [icons]

★**HAMPTON INN.** *1800 W Hwy 89A (86336). Phone 928/282-4700; fax 928/282-0004. www.sedonahamptoninn.com.* 56 rooms, 2 story. Sept-Oct: S, D $89-$129; suites $129-$159; under 18 free; lower rates rest of year. Crib free. TV; cable (premium). Complimentary continental breakfast, coffee in rooms. Restaurant nearby. Check-out noon. Meeting room. In-room modem link. Valet service. Heated pool; whirlpool. Refrigerators, microwaves; in-room whirlpool. Cr cds: A, C, D, DS, JCB, MC, V.

[D] [icons] SC

★ **LOS ABRIGADOS LODGE.** *270 N Hwy 89A (86336). Phone 928/282-7125; fax 928/282-1825. www.ilxresorts.com.* 32 rooms, 7 suites, 2 story. Mar-Dec: S, D $119-$139; suites $169. Check-out 11 am. TV; cable (premium), VCR (movies). In-room modem link. Fireplaces. Laundry services. Exercise equipment. Heated pool, whirlpool, poolside services available. Concierge. Cr cds: A, D, DS, MC, V.

[D] [icons]

★**SKY RANCH LODGE.** *1105 Airport Rd (86339). Phone 928/282-6400; toll-free 888/708-6400; fax 928/282-7682. www.skyranchlodge.com.* 94 rooms, 20 kitchen units, 2 cottages, 1-2 story. S, D, $80-$149; each additional $8; cottages $179; under 12 free. Pet accepted, some restrictions; fee. Check-out 11 am. TV; cable. Some refrigerators, fireplaces. Laundry services. Pool, whirlpool. Cr cds: A, MC, V.

[D] [icons]

Resorts

★ ★ ★ **ENCHANTMENT RESORT.** *525 Boynton Canyon Rd (86336). Phone 928/282-2900; toll-free 800/826-4180; fax 928/282-9249. www.enchantmentresort.com.* Travelers check out of the world when checking in at Enchantment Resort, where Sedona's rugged natural beauty revives the spirit and soothes the soul. Scenery is paramount at this resort, nestled within the spectacular Boynton Canyon. Whether they're dining with 180-degree views or enjoying the sights from private decks, guests are treated to unforgettable vistas. This resort is full of Southwestern character, from the Native American furnishings and decorative accents in the accommodations to the regional kick of the sensational dining. Tennis, croquet, swimming, and pitch-and-putt golf are just some of the activities available for adults, while Camp Coyote entertains young guests with arts and crafts and special programs. Sybarites head straight for the Mii Amo Spa, a destination unto itself with 16 casitas for the total spa experience. Often considered one of the best spas in the country, this facility is guaranteed to recharge and rejuvenate. 220 rooms. S, D $175-$375. Check-out noon, check-in 4 pm. TV; cable (premium), VCR available (movies). In-room modem link. Some fireplaces. Laundry services. Restaurant, bar; entertainment. Room service. Supervised children's activities; ages 4-12. Exercise room, steam room, sauna, spa, massage. Pool, whirlpool, poolside service. Golf. Lighted tennis. Lawn games, bicycles, hiking. Valet parking available. Business center. Concierge. Cr cds: A, C, D, DS, MC, V.

★ ★ ★ **L'AUBERGE DE SEDONA.** *301 L'Auberge Ln (86336). Phone 928/282-1661; toll-free 800/272-6777; fax 928/282-2885. www.lauberge.com.* This country French inn with gourmet cuisine offers traditional comforts along the banks of the Oak Creek. Choose from private cottages, the cozy lodge with a large fireplace and reading room, to rooms in the hillside orchards overlooking the colorful red rocks. 26 rooms, 2 story; 34 cottages. S, D $230-$275; cottage $280-$450; each additional $20; under 12 free. Crib free. TV; cable. Heated pool; whirlpool; poolside service. Complimentary coffee in rooms, library. Dining room (See also L'AUBERGE). Room service. Bar 11 am-10 pm. Coffee in rooms. Check-out 11 am. Concierge. Bellstaff. Gift shop. Business services available. In-room modem link. Valet service. Free airport transportation. Lawn games. Refrigerators, minibars, fireplaces. Some balconies. Romantic atmosphere; on Oak Creek. Cr cds: A, D, DS, MC, V.

★ ★ **LOS ABRIGADOS RESORT AND SPA.** *160 Portal Ln (86336). Phone 928/282-1777; toll-free 800/521-3131; fax 928/282-0199. www.ilxresorts.com.* 175 suites, 2 story. S, D $190-$285; each additional $20; under 16 free. Check-out noon, check-in 4 pm. TV; cable (premium), VCR. Some fireplaces. Laundry services. Dining room (See also JOEY BISTRO). Bar 11-1 am. Room service. Exercise room, sauna, steam room. 2 pools, whirlpool, poolside service. Outdoor tennis. Lawn games. Fishing in Oak Creek. Concierge. Spanish-style stucco and tile-roofed buildings set among buttes of Oak Creek Canyon. Cr cds: A, C, D, DS, MC, V.

★ ★ **RADISSON POCO DIABLO RESORT.** *1752 S Hwy 179 (86336). Phone 928/282-7333; toll-free 800/333-3333; fax 928/282-9712. www.radisson.com.* 137 rooms, 2 story. S, D $109-$209; each additional $20; under 18 free. Crib free. TV; cable (premium). Heated pool; whirlpool, poolside service. Coffee in rooms. Dining room (public by reservation) 7 am-9 pm; Fri, Sat to 11 pm. Room service. Bar 11-1 am. Check-out 11 am. Meeting rooms. Business services available. In-room modem link. Valet service. Concierge. Lighted tennis, pro. 9-hole, par-3 golf, greens fee $10. Playground. Hiking. Basketball. Racquetball. Game room. Massage. Coin laundry. Exercise equipment. Refrigerators; some in-room spas, fireplaces, balconies. Views of Red Rock mountains. Cr cds: A, C, D, DS, ER, JCB, MC, V.

All Suite

★ ★ ★ **HILTON SEDONA RESORT AND SPA.** *90 Ridge Trail Dr (86351). Phone 928/284-4040; fax 928/284-6940. www.hiltonsedona.com.* 219 rooms, 3 story. S, D $109-$249; special events (2-day minimum); under 18 free. Crib available. Pet accepted; $50. TV; cable (premium). Heated pool; wading pool; whirlpool; poolside services available. Supervised children's activities. Restaurant 6:30 am-10 pm. Room service. Bar 11 am-11 pm; Fri, Sat to midnight. Coffee in rooms. Check-out noon. Meeting rooms. Business services available. In-room modem link. Bellstaff. Valet service. Concierge. Gift shop. Coin laundry. Exercise room. 18-hole golf; greens fee $59-$109, pro, pro shop, cart available. Lighted tennis. Spa. Massage. Fireplaces. Minibars. Balconies. Cr cds: A, C, D, DS, ER, JCB, MC, V.

★ **KOKOPELLI SUITES.** *3119 W AZ 89 (86336). Phone 928/204-1146; toll-free 800/789-7393; fax 928/204-5851. www.kokopellisuites.com.* 46 suites, 2 story. Mar-May, Sept-Nov: suites $69-$239; under 12 free; special events (2-day minimum); lower rates rest of year. Complimentary continental breakfast. Check-out 11 am. TV; cable. In-room modem link. Fireplaces. Laundry services. Heated pool, whirlpool. Cr cds: A, C, D, DS, MC, V.

★ ★ **SEDONA REAL INN.** *95 Arroyo Piñon Dr (86336). Phone 928/282-1414; toll-free 800/353-1239; fax 928/282-0900. www.sedonareal.com.* Resort-like amenities are included in this all-suite inn. Surrounded by the majestic red rocks and near the Grand Canyon, you will find spacious rooms with separate sitting areas along with personal attention. 47 suites, 2 story. Mar-Nov, Dec-Jan: S, D $120-$250; each additional $10; under 12 free; golf plans; lower rates rest of year. Complimentary continental breakfast. Check-out 11 am. TV; cable (premium),

VCR available. In-room modem link. Fireplaces. Exercise equipment. Whirlpool. Concierge. Cr cds: A, DS, MC, V.

D ⇌ 🏋 🏊 SC

B&B/Small Inns

★ ★ ★ **ADOBE VILLAGE GRAHAM INN.** *150 Canyon Circle Dr (86351). Phone 928/284-1425; toll-free 800/228-1425; fax 928/284-0767. www.sedonasfinest.com.* Bake bread in your own private casita with a king bed and a waterfall shower! The beautifully landscaped pool and courtyard are delightful. 7 rooms in inn, 2 story; 4 kitchen casitas. Inn: S $184-$454, D $199-$469; suite S $354-$554, D $369-$569; casitas: S $414-$424, D $429-$439; each additional $20; weekends 2-day minimum, holidays 3-day minimum. Crib free. TV; cable, VCR (movies). CD player. Heated pool; whirlpool. Complimentary drinks in casitas and sitting room. Complimentary full breakfast; afternoon refreshments. Dining room opposite 8-9:30am. Check-out 11 am, check-in 3-6 pm. Business center. In-room modem link. Coin laundry. Luggage handling. Concierge service. Gift shop. Valet service. Bicycles available. Fireplaces, in-room whirlpools. Bathroom phone, refrigerator, microwave, wet bar, fireplace in casitas. Balconies. Guest library. Totally nonsmoking. Cr cds: A, D, DS, JCB, MC, V.

D ⇌ 🏊

★ ★ ★ **APPLE ORCHARD INN.** *656 Jordan Rd (86336). Phone 928/282-5328; toll-free 800/663-6968; fax 928/204-0044. www.appleorchardbb.com.* Personal service awaits guests at this inn that has a charming southwestern atmosphere. It has easily accessible hiking trails with spectacular views of Wilson Mountain and Steamboat Rock. 6 rooms, 2 story. S, D $135-$230; each additional $20; holidays, weekends 2-day minimum. Children over 12 years only. TV; cable, VCR (movies). Heated pool; whirlpool. Complimentary full breakfast. Restaurant nearby. Check-out 11 am, check-in 3-6 pm. Business services available. Coin laundry. Luggage handling. Valet service. Refrigerators; many in-room whirlpools. Some fireplaces, balconies. Totally nonsmoking. Cr cds: A, MC, V.

D ⇌ 🏊

★ ★ **A TOUCH OF SEDONA B&B.** *595 Jordan Rd (86336). Phone 928/282-6462; toll-free 800/600-6462; fax 928/282-1534. www.touchsedona.com.* 5 rooms, 3 with shower only. No room phones. Apr-June, Aug-Nov: S, D $119-$169; each additional $15; weekends, holidays (2-3 day minimum); lower rates rest of year. Crib free. TV; cable (premium), VCR available. Complimentary full breakfast; afternoon refreshments. Restaurant nearby. Check-out 11 am, check-in 4-6 pm. Luggage handling. Concierge service. Valet service. Refrigerators. Balconies. Picnic tables. Totally nonsmoking. Cr cds: A, DS, MC, V.

D 🐾 🏊

★ ★ ★ **CANYON VILLA BED AND BREAKFAST INN.** *125 Canyon Circle Dr (86351). Phone 928/284-1226; toll-free 800/453-1166; fax 928/284-2114. www.canyonvilla.com.* The Canyon Villa Bed and Breakfast Inn opens its arms to travelers longing for the comforts of home. All guests feel like family here, where the warm, friendly innkeepers personally welcome each visitor. Charming and intimate, the inn mesmerizes its guests with staggering views of Sedona's renowned red rock formations. Nearly all of the guest rooms frame unparalleled vistas, with French doors opening out onto private patios or decks for even better viewing. English country meets the American Southwest in the interiors. Four-poster beds and floral patterns add a romantic touch, while Indian rugs and iron furnishings reflect a regional flavor. No alarm clocks are necessary here, where the wonderful aroma of freshly baked cinnamon buns gently coaxes guests from deep slumber. Every delicious morsel of the inn's gourmet breakfast is savored, and the gracious poolside hors d'oeuvre service offers visitors a chance to make new friends. 11 rooms, 2 story. D $189-$279. Children over 11 years only. Complimentary full breakfast. Check-out 11 am, check-in 3-6 pm. TV; cable (premium). In-room modem link. Some fireplaces. Heated pool. Totally nonsmoking. Cr cds: A, DS, MC, V.

D ⇌ 🏊

★ ★ ★ **CASA SEDONA BED AND BREAKFAST.** *55 Hozoni Dr (86336). Phone 928/282-2938; toll-free 800/525-3756; fax 928/282-2259. www.casasedona.com.* Guests will experience rooms decorated with traditional and contemporary furnishings and art. 16 rooms, 2 story. S $170-$250; D $180-$260; each additional $30; weekend, holidays (2-day minimum). Children over 12 only. TV; cable (premium), VCR (movies). Whirlpool. Complimentary full breakfast. Check-out 11 am, check-in 3-6 pm. Meeting room. Business services available. In-room modem link. Bellstaff. Concierge service. Valet service. Refrigerators, fireplaces. Balconies. Picnic tables. Each room with view of Red Rocks. Totally nonsmoking. Cr cds: MC, V.

D 🐾 🏊

★ ★ ★ **THE INN ON OAK CREEK.** *556 Hwy 179 (86336). Phone 928/282-7896; toll-free 800/499-7896; fax 928/282-0696. www.sedona-inn.com.* This former art gallery turned inn is as exquisite as the view. Family designed and built, it sits on Oak Creek, near Indian reservations and fantastic shopping. A professional cooking staff prepares different breakfasts and hors d'oeuvres daily. 13 rooms, 2 story. S, D $165-$260; each additional $20; weekends, holidays (2-day minimum). Children over 10 years only. Complimentary full breakfast. Check-out 11 am, check-in 3-6 pm. TV; cable (premium), VCR (movies). In-room modem link. In-room whirlpools, fireplaces. Concierge service. Totally nonsmoking. Cr cds: A, DS, MC, V.

★★★ **THE LODGE AT SEDONA.** *125 Kallof Pl (86336). Phone 928/204-1942; toll-free 800/619-4467; fax 928/204-2128. www.lodgeatsedona.com.* Two hours south of the Grand Canyon, this lodge is situated on wooded acres with rustic timber and red sandstone decor. A labyrinth of rocks on a clearing of red earth creates a quiet place to meditate. 14 rooms, 2 story. D $140-$275; weekends (2-day minimum); each additional $30. TV; cable (premium) in sitting room. Complimentary full breakfast; afternoon refreshments. Check-out 11 am, check-in 4-8 pm. Concierge service. Gift shop. Meeting room. Business services available. Lawn games. Health club privileges. Some in-room whirlpools, fireplaces. Picnic tables. Antiques. Library. Located on 2 1/2 acres. Gardens, labyrinth. Totally nonsmoking. Cr cds: DS, MC, V.

★★★ **SOUTHWEST INN AT SEDONA.** *3250 W Hwy 89A (86336). Phone 928/282-3344; toll-free 800/483-7422; fax 928/282-0267. www.swinn.com.* This Santa Fe-style inn offers the best of Sedona with all the amenities of home. Relax with a breathtaking view from your room or soak in the beautifully landscaped pool. 28 rooms, 2 story. Mid-Mar-May, Sept-Oct: S, D $139-$199; each additional $10; suites $189-$239; under 13 free; weekends, holidays, special events (2-day minimum); lower rates rest of year. Crib free. Complimentary continental breakfast. Check-out 11 am. TV; cable (premium), VCR (movies). In-room modem link. Balconies, refrigerators, microwaves available. Fireplaces. Complimentary coffee in rooms. Restaurant opposite 11:30 am-9 pm. Exercise equipment. Heated pool, whirlpool. Golf nearby. Meeting rooms. Business services available. Bellstaff, concierge. Totally nonsmoking. Cr cds: A, C, D, DS, MC, V.

★★★ **TERRITORIAL HOUSE B&B.** *65 Piki Dr (86336). Phone 928/204-2737; toll-free 800/801-2737; fax 928/204-2230. www.territorialhousebb.com.* The Old West comes alive with the sounds of the wild, and with tastefully decorated rooms reminiscent of the old western movies. Deliciously hearty breakfasts and late day snacks are just part of the hospitality guests find here. 4 rooms, 2 with shower only, 1 suite, 2 story. No A/C. S $105-$170; D $115-$185; each additional $20; suite $175-$250; minimum stay weekends, holidays. Complimentary full breakfast. Complimentary afternoon refreshments. Check-out 11 am, check-in 4-6 pm. TV; cable (premium), VCR (movies). Some balconies. Refrigerators available. Microwaves available. Converted Western ranch house; stone fireplace.

Coin laundry. Business services available. 3 room phones. Totally nonsmoking. Cr cds: A, DS, MC, V.

Restaurants

★★ **COWBOY CLUB.** *241 N AZ 89A (86336). Phone 928/282-4200; fax 928/204-5985. www.cowboyclub.com.* Closed Thanksgiving, Dec 25. Lunch, dinner. Bar. Children's menu. Cr cds: A, DS, MC, V. **$$$**

★★★ **HEARTLINE CAFE.** *1610 W AZ 89A (86336). Phone 928/282-0785; fax 928/204-9206. www.heartlinecafe.com.* This intimate and cozy restaurant showcases daily unique chef specialties. Eclectic menu. Specialties: mesquite-crusted rack of lamb, pecan-crusted local trout, crab cakes. Hours: 11:30 am-3 pm, 5-9:15 pm; Tues, Wed from 5 pm. Reservations accepted. Bar. Wine cellar. Lunch $6.95-$13.50, dinner $15-$27. Children's menu. Patio dining. Cottage surrounded by English garden. Smoking on patio only. Cr cds: A, D, DS, MC, V.

★ **HIDEAWAY.** *179 Country Sq (86336). Phone 928/282-4204; fax 928/282-7583. www.sedona.net/hideaway.* Italian menu. Closed Thanksgiving, Dec 24, 25. Lunch, dinner. Bar. Outdoor seating. Cr cds: A, C, D, DS, MC, V. **$**

★★★ **L'AUBERGE.** *301 L'Auberge Ln (86339). Phone 928/282-1667; fax 928/282-2885. www.lauberge.com.* Overlooking Oak Creek, the room is decorated with imported fabrics and fine china. French menu. Breakfast, lunch, dinner, Sun brunch. Bar. Children's menu. Jacket (dinner). Outdoor seating. Totally nonsmoking. Cr cds: A, D, DS, MC, V. **$$**

★★★ **PIETRO'S.** *2445 W AZ 89A # 3 (86336). Phone 928/282-2525. www.pietrossedona.com.* This charming little cafe serves dinner nightly and has a cozy bar, wine cellar and enclosed patio. The menu features simple but elegant northern Italian cuisine. Guests can try the early bird menu, which offers six entree selections. Closed Dec 25. Dinner. Bar. Totally nonsmoking. Cr cds: A, C, DS, MC, V. **$$$**

★★★ **RENE AT TLAQUEPAQUE.** *AZ 179 (86336). Phone 928/282-9225; fax 928/282-5629. www.rene-sedona.com.* Hours: 11:30 am-2:30 pm, 5:30-8:30 pm, Fri, Sat to 9 pm. Closed Dec 25. Reservations accepted. Continental menu. Specializes in Colorado rack of lamb. Bar. Lunch $7.95-$11.95, dinner $18.95-$27.95. Outdoor dining. Casual, elegant dining. Totally nonsmoking. Cr cds: MC, V.

★★★**SHUGRUE'S HILLSIDE GRILL.** *671 AZ 179 (86336). Phone 928/282-5300; fax 928/282-7379. www.shugrues.com.* Hours: 11:30 am-3 pm, 5-9:30 pm. Closed Dec 25. Reservations accepted. Continental menu. Bar. Lunch $7-$13, dinner $16-$28. Children's menu. Specializes in steak, seafood, lamb, seared ahi tuna. Jazz Fri-Sat. Parking. Outdoor dining. Located high upon a hill; commanding view of rock formations. Cr cds: A, D, MC, V.
D

★ **WILD TOUCAN.** *2081 W Hwy 89A (86340). Phone 928/284-1604; fax 928/284-0517. www.wildtoucan.com.* Closed Thanksgiving, Dec 25. Lunch, dinner. Bar. Children's menu. Cr cds: A, D, DS, MC, V. **$$**
D

★ ★ **YAVAPAI.** *525 Boynton Canyon Rd (86336). Phone 928/204-6000; fax 928/282-1370. www.enchantmentresort.com.* At this fine-dining restaurant, guests watch the breathtaking Boynton Canyon through large windows that provide a 180-degree view. Guests can enjoy the sunset while dining on the terrace. Southwestern menu. Breakfast, lunch, dinner, Sun brunch. Bar. Entertainment Fri-Sun. Children's menu. Reservations required. Outdoor seating. Cr cds: A, C, D, DS, MC, V. **$$$**
D

Seligman (C-3)

See also Flagstaff, Williams

Pop 456 **Elev** 5,242 ft **Area code** 928 **Zip** 86337

Information Chamber of Commerce, Box 65, 86337; 928/422-3939

What to See and Do

Grand Canyon Caverns. *Old Rte 66, mile marker 115. 25 miles NW on AZ 66. Phone 928/422-3223.* Includes the 18,000-square-foot "Chapel of Ages" and other rooms and tunnels; 3/4 mile trail; temperature 56°F. Elevator takes visitors 210 feet underground; 50-minute guided tours. Motel, restaurant; western-style cookouts (May-Sept). (Daily; closed Dec 25) Golden Age Passport accepted. **$$$$**

Sells (H-4)

See also Tucson

Pop 2,799 **Elev** 2,360 ft **Area code** 520 **Zip** 85634

Information Tohono O'Odham Nation Executive Office, Box 837; 520/383-2028

This is the headquarters of the Tohono O'Odham Indian Reservation (almost 3 million acres). The Papagos farm, raise cattle, and craft pottery and baskets. The main road (AZ 86) passes through the reservation, and side roads lead to other villages. The older houses are made of saguaro ribs plastered with mud. More recently, burnt adobe (mud brick) construction and conventional housing have been adopted.

What to See and Do

Kitt Peak National Observatory. *Approximately 36 miles NE on AZ 86, then 12 miles S on AZ 386, in the Quinlan Mountains of the Sonoran Desert (elevation 6,882 feet). Phone 520/318-8600. (National Optical Astronomy Observatories)* Site of world's largest collection of ground-based optical telescopes; 36-, 50-, 84-, and 158-inch stellar telescopes; world's largest solar telescope (60 inches). Visitor center with exhibits. Tours. Observatory (daily; closed holidays). **DONATION**

Show Low (E-6)

See also McNary, Pinetop

Pop 7,695 **Elev** 6,347 ft **Area code** 928 **Zip** 85901

Information Show Low Regional Chamber of Commerce, 951 W Deuce of Clubs, PO Box 1083, 85902; 928/537-2326 or 888-SHOW-LOW

Web www.showlowchamberofcommerce.com

This town, astride the Mogollon Rim on US 60, is a good stop for the golf enthusiast, angler, photographer, or nature lover.

What to See and Do

Apache-Sitgreaves National Forests. *309 S Mountain Ave. Phone 928/333-4301 or 800/280-2267 (reservations).* Combined into one administrative unit, these two forests (see SPRINGERVILLE) encompass more than 2 million acres of diverse terrain. The Sitgreaves Forest (AZ 260) is named for Captain Lorenzo Sitgreaves, conductor of the first scientific expedition across the state in the 1850s; part of the General George Cook military trail is here. Fishing; hunting, self-guided nature hikes, picnicking, camping (dump station; fee). Sat evening programs in summer.

Fishing. Rainbow Lake. *915 W Deuce of Clubs (85901). Phone 928/537-2326. 8 miles SE on AZ 260.* **Show Low Lake.** *4 miles SE off AZ 260.* **Fool Hollow Lake.** *3 miles NW.* Many others in area. Boat rentals at some lakes.

Hunting. *915 W Deuce of Clubs (85901). Phone 928/537-2326.* Elk, deer, turkey, bear, mountain lion, bighorn sheep, and antelope.

Motels/Motor Lodges

★★**BEST WESTERN PAINT PONY LODGE.** *581 W Deuce of Clubs Ave (85901). Phone 928/537-5773; fax 928/537-5766. www.bestwestern.com.* 50 rooms, 2 story. Mid-May-mid-Sept: S $69-$79; D $74-$84; each additional $5; suites $129-$139; higher rates holidays; lower rates rest of year. Crib $5. Pet accepted. TV; cable (premium). Complimentary continental breakfast. Restaurant 11 am-2 pm, 5-9 pm; weekend hours vary. Room service. Bar. Check-out 11 am. Meeting rooms. Business services available. In-room modem link. Sundries. Free airport transportation. Cross-country ski 17 miles. Refrigerators; some fireplaces; microwaves available. Cr cds: A, C, D, DS, MC, V.

🔄

★ **DAYS INN.** *480 W Deuce of Clubs Ave Hwy 60 (85901). Phone 928/537-4356; fax 928/537-8692. www.daysinn.com.* 122 rooms, 2 story. S $54-$65; D $69-$74; each additional $10; higher rates during special events. Crib free. Pet accepted, some restrictions. TV; cable (premium). Heated pool. Complimentary full breakfast. Restaurant 6 am-10 pm. Check-out noon. Coin laundry. Meeting rooms. Business services available. Beauty shop. Free airport transportation. Refrigerators, microwaves. Cr cds: A, C, D, DS, JCB, MC, V.

D 🔄 ➿ ⛷

Restaurant

★**BRANDING IRON STEAK HOUSE.** *1261 E Deuce of Clubs Ave (85901). Phone 928/537-5151.* Hours: 11 am-2 pm, 5-10 pm; early-bird dinner Sun-Fri 5-7 pm. Closed Dec 25. Reservations accepted. Bar. Lunch $4.50-$9, dinner $10-$28. Children's menu. Specializes in steak, beef, seafood. Salad bar. Western saloon. Cr cds: C, D, DS, ER, MC, V.

D

Sierra Vista (I-6)

See also Patagonia

Pop 37,775 **Elev** 4,623 ft **Area code** 520 **Zip** 85635

Information Chamber of Commerce, 21 E Wilcox; 520/458-6940

What to See and Do

Coronado National Forest. *300 W Congress St. Phone 520/670-4552. (see TUCSON)* One of the larger sections of the forest lies to the south and west of Fort Huachuca Military Reservation. Picnicking, camping (fee). Parker Canyon Lake offers boating, fishing; camping (fee). A Ranger District office is located in Sierra Vista.

Coronado National Memorial. *16 miles S via AZ 92 to Coronado Memorial Rd then W on Montezuma Canyon Rd. Phone 520/366-5515.* Commanding view of part of Coronado's route through the Southwest in 1540-1542. Hiking trails, picnic grounds. Visitor center (daily; closed Jan 1, Dec 25). **FREE**

Fort Huachuca. *21 E Wilcox Dr (85635). Phone 520/538-7111.* Founded by the US Army in 1877 to protect settlers and travelers from hostile Apache raids, the fort is now the home of the US Army Intelligence Center, the Information Systems Command, and the Electronic Proving Ground. A historical museum is on the "Old Post," Boyd and Grierson aves (daily; closed holidays). The historic Old Post area (1885-95) is typical of frontier post construction and is home to the post's ceremonial cavalry unit; open to public. Directions and visitor's pass at main gate, just west of Sierra Vista. Bronze statue of buffalo soldier. **FREE**

Motel/Motor Lodge

★ **SUPER 8 MOTEL.** *100 Fab Ave (85635). Phone 520/459-5380; fax 520/459-6052. www.innworks.com.* 52 rooms, 2 story. S $38-$48; D $42-$52; each additional $5; under 12 free; golf plans. Crib $4. Pet accepted; $10. Complimentary continental breakfast. Check-out 11 am. TV; cable. Refrigerators. Coin laundry. Restaurant nearby. Pool. Business services available. Cr cds: A, C, D, DS, MC, V.

D 🔄 ➿ ⛷ SC

Hotel

★**WINDEMERE HOTEL AND CONFERENCE CENTER.** *2047 S Hwy 92 (85635). Phone 520/459-5900; toll-free 800/825-4656; fax 520/458-1347. www.windemere-hotel.com.* 149 rooms, 3 story. S $78; D $86; each additional $8; suites $150-$200; under 18 free; golf plans. Crib free. Pet accepted, some restrictions; $50 refundable. Complimentary breakfast. Check-out 11 am. TV; cable. Some refrigerators, microwaves. Coffee in rooms. Valet services, coin laundry. Restaurant 6 am-2 pm, 4:30-9 pm. Bar 4-9 pm; entertainment. Room service. Health club privileges. Heated pool, whirlpool. Meeting rooms. Business services available. Cr cds: A, C, D, DS, ER, JCB, MC, V.

D 🔄 ➿ ⛷ SC

B&B/Small Inn

★ ★ **RAMSEY CANYON INN.** *29 E Ramsey Canyon Rd, Hereford (85638) Phone 520/378-3010; fax 520/378-1480. www.nature.org/arizona.com.* 8 units, 6 rooms, 2 cottages. No A/C, no room phones. S, D $110. Children under 16 years cottages only. Complimentary full breakfast (except cottages). Complimentary afternoon refreshments. Check-out 11 am, check-in 3 pm. Charming country inn with antiques throughout; bounded on 2 sides by Coronado National Forest. Situated on a winding mountain stream, in a wooded canyon, this is a hummingbird haven; peak season is Mar-Oct (2-day minimum). More than 10 species visit the inn's feeders during the year. Totally nonsmoking. Cr cds: MC, V.

D ⊠

Restaurant

★ ★ **MESQUITE TREE.** *AZ 92S and Carr Canyon Rd (85635).* Phone 520/378-2758. Eclectic decor. Specialties: prime rib, steak, Gulf shrimp scampi. Hours: Hours: 5-9 pm; Sun, Mon to 8 pm. Closed Mon. Thanksgiving, Dec 25. Dinner $7.25-$17.95. Bar. Children's menu. Reservations accepted. Outdoor dining. Cr cds: A, C, DS, ER, MC, V.

D SC

Springerville (E-7)

See also Greer, McNary

Pop 1,972 **Elev** 6,968 ft **Area code** 928 **Zip** 85938

Information Round Valley Chamber of Commerce, 318 E Main St, PO Box 31; 928/333-2123

The headquarters for the Apache-Sitgreaves National Forests is located here.

What to See and Do

Apache-Sitgreaves National Forests. *309 S Mountain Ave.* Phone 928/333-4301. Combined into one administrative unit, these two forests (see SHOW LOW) encompass more than two million acres of diverse terrain. The Apache Forest (on US 180/666) features the Mount Baldy, Escudilla, and Bear Wallow wilderness areas and Blue Range Primitive Area, which are accessible only by foot or horseback, and the Coronado Trail (US 666), the route followed by the explorer in 1540. Lake and stream fishing; big-game hunting, picnicking, camping (fee charged in some campgrounds).

Lyman Lake State Park. *38147 AZ 81, Saint Johns (85936). 18 miles N on US 180/666.* Phone 928/337-4441. There are 1,180 acres bordering a 1,500-acre reservoir near headwaters of the Little Colorado River; high desert, juniper country. Swimming, waterskiing, fishing (walleye, trout, channel and blue catfish), boating (ramps); hiking, picnicking (shelter), tent and trailer sites (dump station). Standard fees.

Madonna of the Trail. *S Mountain and Hwy 60 (85938).* Phone 928/333-2123. Erected in 1927, the statue is one of 12 identical monuments placed in states along the National Old Trails Highway to commemorate pioneer women who trekked west.

Sunset Crater Volcano National Monument (C-4)

See also Flagstaff

(15 miles N of Flagstaff on US 89, then 2 miles E on Sunset Crater/Wupatki Loop Road)

Between the growing seasons of 1064 and 1065, violent volcanic eruptions built a large cone-shaped mountain of cinders and ash called a cinder cone volcano. Around the base of the cinder cone, lava flowed from cracks, creating the Bonito Lava Flow on the west side of the cone and the Kana'a Lava Flow on the east side. The approximate date of the initial eruption was determined by examining tree rings of timber found in the remains of Native American pueblos at Wupatki National Monument (see).

This cinder cone, now called Sunset Crater, stands about 1,000 feet above the surrounding terrain. Mineral deposits around the rim stained the cinders, giving the summit a perpetual sunset hue, thus the name Sunset Crater. Along the Lava Flow Trail at the base of the cone, visitors will find "squeeze-ups" and other geologic features related to lava flows.

Park rangers are on duty all year. Do not attempt to drive off the roads; the cinders are soft, and the surrounding landscape is very fragile. The US Forest Service maintains a campground (May-mid-September; fee) opposite the visitor center. Guided tours and naturalist activities are offered during the summer. Visitor center (daily; closed December 25). A 20-mile paved road leads to Wupatki National Monument (see). Phone 520/556-7042.

Tempe (F-4)

See also Chandler, Glendale, Mesa, Phoenix, Scottsdale

Founded 1871 **Pop** 158,625 **Elev** 1,160 ft **Area code** 480

Information Chamber of Commerce, 909 E Apache Blvd, PO Box 28500, 85285; 480/967-7891

Web www.tempechamber.org

Founded as a trading post by the father of former Senator Carl Hayden, this city is now the site of Arizona State University, the state's oldest institution of higher learning.

What to See and Do

Arizona Cardinals (NFL). *8701 S Hardy Dr (85284). Sun Devil Stadium, Mill at University Dr, ASU campus. Phone 800/999-1402.*

Arizona Historical Society Museum. *1300 N College Ave (85281). Phone 480/939-0292.* Wander through this regional museum to learn more about 20th-century life in the Salt River Valley. The 28,000 items in its collection include about 14,000 pieces in a country store and 2,800 stage props and sets from the 37-year run of the Wallace and Ladmo Show on KPHO Television. Another exhibit focuses on the many ways World War II transformed Arizona. (Tues-Sat 10 am-4 pm, Sun noon-4 pm; closed Mon) **FREE**

Arizona State University. *University Dr and Mill Ave. In town center on US 60/80/89. Phone 480/965-4980 (tours).* (1885) (52,000 students.) Divided into 13 colleges. Included on the 700-acre main campus are several museums and collections featuring meteorites; anthropology and geology exhibits; the Charles Trumbull Hayden Library, the Walter Cronkite School of Journalism, and the Daniel Noble Science and Engineering Library. Also located here are

Grady Gammage Memorial Auditorium. *Mill and Apache Blvd (85287). Phone 480/965-4050 (tours); 480/965-3434 (box office).* (1964) Last major work designed by Frank Lloyd Wright. Guided tours (Mon-Fri). **FREE**

Nelson Fine Arts Center and Ceramics Reserach Center. *Phone 480/965-ARTS.* Exhibits of American paintings and sculpture; Latin American art; comprehensive print collection; American crockery and ceramics. Tours available.

The Improvisation. *901 E University Dr (85281). Phone 480/921-9877.* If you need a few laughs, take a seat here and listen to some of the country's best stand-up comedians say the darnedest things. Unless you're a real sourpuss, these foolish folks will surely crack you up with their zaniness. An optional dinner precedes the 8 pm shows. (Thurs-Sun; major holidays) **$$$$**

Niels Petersen House Museum. *1414 W Southern Ave. Phone 480/350-5151.* Built in 1892 and remodeled in the 1930s. Restoration retains characteristics of both the Victorian era and the 1930s. Half-hour, docent-guided tours available. (Tues-Thurs, Sat) **FREE**

Tempe Bicycle Program. *Phone 480/350-2739.* For a change of pace, two-wheel your way around Tempe. This bicycle friendly city has more than 150 miles of bikeways along its streets and through its parks. For your convenience, most major destinations provide bicycle racks, some particularly eye-catching ones designed by local artists. If you get tired and want to hitch a ride, city buses are also equipped with racks. Several bicycle shops offer rentals for as little as $15 per day—and they also have free bikeway maps to keep you on the right path.

Tempe Historical Museum. *809 E Southern. Phone 480/350-5100.* Exhibits relating the history of Tempe from the prehistoric Hohokam to the present; artifacts, videos, interactive exhibits. Research library. Gift shop. (Mon-Thurs; Sat-Sun; closed holidays) **FREE**

Special Events

Anaheim Angels Spring Training. *2200 W Alameda Dr (85282). Tempe Diablo Stadium. Phone 888/99-HALOS.* Anaheim Angels baseball spring training, exhibition games. Early Mar-early Apr.

Spring Festival of the Arts. *804 St. Germanine St. Phone 480/965-2278.* Last weekend in Mar.

Tempe Festival of the Arts. *On Mill Ave in downtown Tempe. Phone 480/967-4877.* When a three-day event attracts nearly a quarter-million people, you know that it belongs at the top of your to-do list, too. For this blast of a street party, Mill Avenue in downtown Tempe closes to traffic so that fun-loving people of all ages can have a good time milling around. They buy handmade goods from more than 500 artisans, chow down on tasty food from around the world, quench their thirst with ice-cold beer and other beverages, and rock to live bands amped up on multiple stages. In an area just for them, youngsters make their own fun creating crafts and taking part in activities designed to make any kid smile. The best news: this party gets crankin' twice a year, in spring and fall. Late Mar and early Dec.

Tostitos Fiesta Bowl. *120 S Ash Ave (85281). ASU Sun Devil Stadium. ASU Sun Devil Stadium. Phone 480/350-0900.* College football. Early Jan.

Tostitos Fiesta Bowl Block Party. *120 S Ash Ave (85281). Phone 480/350-0900.* Includes games, rides, entertainment, pep rally, fireworks, food. Dec 31.

Motels/Motor Lodges

★ **COUNTRY INN & SUITES BY CARLSON.** *1660 W Elliot (85284). Phone 480/345-8585; fax 480/345-7461. www.countryinns.com.* 139 kitchen units, 3 story. Kitchen suites $49-$129, each additional $10; under 18 free. Pet accepted, some restrictions; fee. Complimentary continental breakfast. Check-out noon, check-in 3 pm. TV; cable (premium). Health club privileges. Pool, children's pool, whirlpool. Free airport transportation. Cr cds: A, D, DS, MC, V.

D 🐾 ➗ ⬇ SC

★ ★ **COURTYARD BY MARRIOTT.** *601 S Ash Ave (85281). Phone 480/966-2800; toll-free 800/321-2211; fax 480/829-8446. www.courtyard.com.* 160 rooms, 3 story. Jan-mid-May: S, D $89-$169; suites $169-$179; under 18 free; lower rates rest of year. Crib free. Complimentary coffee in rooms. Check-out noon. TV; cable (premium). In-room modem link. Some balconies. Refrigerators, some in-room whirlpools, wet bar in suites. Valet services, coin laundry. Restaurant 6-10 am; Sat, Sun 7-11 am. Bar 4-11 pm. Exercise equipment. Heated pool, whirlpool. Airport transportation. Meeting rooms. Business services available. Cr cds: A, C, D, DS, MC, V.

★ **HOLIDAY INN EXPRESS.** *5300 S Priest Dr (85283). Phone 480/820-7500; toll-free 800/465-4329; fax 480/730-6626. www.holiday-inn.com.* 160 rooms, 4 story. S, D $89-$129; each additional $5; under 18 free. Pet accepted; fee. Complimentary continental breakfast. Check-out noon, check-in 2 pm. TV; cable (premium). Exercise equipment. Pool, whirlpool. Cr cds: A, C, D, DS, JCB, MC, V.

★ ★ **HOLIDAY INN PHOENIX-TEMPE/ASU.** *915 E Apache Blvd (85281). Phone 480/968-3451; toll-free 800/553-1826; fax 480/968-6262. www.holiday-inn.com/phx-tempeasu.* 194 rooms, 4 story. S, D $64-$139; under 19 free. Pet accepted. Check-out 1 pm, check-in 1 pm. TV; cable (premium). Free laundry facilities. Restaurant 6 am-10 pm. Bar 11-1 am. Room service. Health club privileges, exercise equipment. Whirlpool, poolside service. Free airport transportation. Cr cds: A, C, D, DS, JCB, MC, V.

★ **LA QUINTA INN PHOENIX/TEMPE SKY HARBOR AIRPORT.** *911 S 48th St (85281). Phone 480/967-4465; toll-free 800/531-5900; fax 480/921-9172. www.laquinta.com.* 131 rooms, 3 story. S, D $60-$99; each additional $6; under 18 free. Pet accepted, some restrictions. Complimentary continental breakfast. Check-out noon, check-in 1 pm. TV; cable (premium). Exercise room. Free airport transportation. Cr cds: A, C, D, DS, MC, V.

★ **RODEWAY INN.** *1550 S 52nd St (85281). Phone 480/967-3000; fax 480/966-9568. www.rodewayinn.com.* 100 rooms, 2 story. S, D $39-$99; under 18 free. Pet accepted, some restrictions; fee. Complimentary continental breakfast. Check-out noon, check-in 3 pm. TV; cable (premium). Whirlpool. Free airport transportation. Cr cds: A, C, D, DS, JCB, MC, V.

Hotels

★ ★ **SHERATON PHOENIX AIRPORT HOTEL.** *1600 S 52nd St (85281). Phone 480/967-6600; toll-free 800/346-3049; fax 480/966-2392. www.sheraton.com/phoenixairport.* 210 rooms, 4 story. S, D $69-$194; each additional $10; under 18 free. Check-out noon, check-in 3 pm. TV; cable (premium). Restaurant 6 am-10 pm. Bar 11 am-midnight. Room service. Exercise room. Pool, whirlpool, poolside service. Free airport transportation. Cr cds: A, C, D, DS, MC, V.

★ **TWIN PALMS HOTEL.** *225 E Apache Blvd (85281). Phone 480/967-9431; toll-free 800/367-0835; fax 480/968-1877. www.twinpalmshotel.com.* 140 rooms, 7 story. S, D $69-$159; each additional $10; under 18 free. Check-out noon, check-in 3 pm. TV; cable (premium). Bar 4 pm-1 am. Health club privileges. Pool. Free airport transportation. Cr cds: A, C, D, DS, JCB, MC, V.

★ ★ **THE WYNDHAM BUTTES RESORT.** *2000 Westcourt Way (85282). Phone 602/225-9000; toll-free 800/843-1986; fax 602/438-8622. www.wyndham.com.* 353 rooms, 4-5 story. Jan-May: S, D $175-$325; each additional $10; suites $425-$700; under 18 free; golf, weekend plans; lower rates rest of year. Crib $10. TV; cable (premium). 2 pools; poolside service. Complimentary coffee in rooms. Restaurants 6 am-10 pm; Fri, Sat to 11 pm (See also TOP OF THE ROCK). Room service 5:30 am-midnight. Bar 5 pm-1 am. Check-out noon. Meeting rooms. Business center. Concierge. Gift shop. Lighted tennis. Exercise equipment; sauna. Massage. Minibars. Some private patios. Large resort built into mountainside. Heliport. Luxury level. Cr cds: A, C, D, DS, ER, JCB, MC, V.

Resorts

★ ★ ★ **FIESTA INN.** *2100 S Priest Dr (85282). Phone 480/967-1441; toll-free 800/501-7590; fax 480/967-0224. www.fiestainnresort.com.* Frank Lloyd Wright's design influence is evident from the landscape and lobby to the guestrooms at this beautiful inn. 271 rooms, 3 story. S, D $65-$179; each additional $10; under 18 free. Check-out 11 am, check-in 2 pm. TV; VCR available. Restaurant 6:30 am-10 pm. Bar 11-1 am. Room service. Exercise equipment, sauna. Whirlpool, poolside service. Lighted tennis. Business center. Concierge. Free airport transportation. Cr cds: A, C, D, DS, MC, V.

★ ★ ★ **TEMPE MISSION PALMS HOTEL.** *60 E 5th St (85281). Phone 480/894-1400; toll-free 800/547-8705; fax 480/968-7677. www.missionpalms.com.* This southwestern-style hotel is located in Old Town Tempe, within walking distance of the Sun Devil Stadium. 309 rooms, 4 story. S, D $85-$285; each additional $10; under 18 free; golf packages. Check-out noon, check-in 3 pm. TV; cable (premium). In-room modem link. Restaurant 6:30 am-9:30 pm. Bar 11-1 am. Health club privileges, exercise equipment. Whirlpool, poolside service. Lighted tennis. Free airport transportation. Business center. Cr cds: A, C, D, DS, JCB, MC, V.

All Suite

★ ★ **EMBASSY SUITES HOTEL PHOENIX-TEMPE.** *4400 S Rural Rd (85282). Phone 480/897-7444; toll-free 800/362-2779; fax 480/897-6112. www.embassysuitestempe.com.* This hotel is only 3 miles from Arizona State University. 224 suites, 3 story. S, D $79-$199; each additional $10; under 18 free; weekend rates. Complimentary full breakfast. Check-out 1 pm, check-in 3 pm. TV; cable (premium). Restaurant 11 am-10 pm; Fri, Sat to 11 pm. Bar 11-1 am. Exercise equipment, sauna. Game room. Whirlpool, poolside service. Free airport transportation. Cr cds: A, C, D, DS, JCB, MC, V.

★ ★ **INNSUITES HOTELS TEMPE.** *1651 W Baseline Rd (85283). Phone 480/897-7900; fax 480/491-1008. www.innsuites.com.* 103 rooms, 67 kitchen units, 2 story. S, D $59-$99; suites, kitchen units $109; under 18 free. Pet accepted; fee. Complimentary continental breakfast. Check-out noon, check-in 2 pm. TV; cable (premium). In-room modem link. Restaurant 6 am-2 pm, 4-10 pm; Oct-Apr 6 am-10 pm. Exercise equipment. Whirlpool. Lighted tennis. Business center. Free airport transportation. Cr cds: A, C, D, DS, JCB, MC, V.

Restaurants

★ ★ **BYBLOS.** *3332 S Mill Ave (85282). Phone 480/894-1945; fax 480/829-8022.* Mediterranean menu. Hours: 11 am-3 pm, 5-10 pm; Fri, Sat to 10:30 pm; Sun 4-9:30 pm. Closed Mon; Jan 1, Dec 25; 1st 2 weeks in July. Lunch $4.75-$6.95, dinner $7.95-$16.95. Bar. Children's menu. Reservations accepted. Non-smoking seating. Belly dancing last Sun of the month. Cr cds: A, D, DS, MC, V.

★ ★ **HOUSE OF TRICKS.** *114 E 7th St (85281). Phone 480/968-1114; fax 480/968-0080. www.houseoftricks.com.* Hours: 11 am-10 pm. Closed Sun; most major holidays; also first 2 weeks in Aug. Reservations accepted. Contemporary American menu. Patio bar. A la carte entrees: lunch $5.95-$8.50, dinner $12.75-$20. Parking. Outdoor dining. Restored cottage (1918); hardwood and tile floors, stone fireplace. Cr cds: A, D, DS, MC, V.

★ **MACAYO.** *300 S Ash Ave (85281). Phone 480/966-6677; fax 480/894-9196. www.macayo.com.* Mexican menu. Hours: 11 am-11 pm; Fri, Sat to midnight. Lunch

$4.99-$6.95, dinner $7.25-$11.50. Bar. Children's menu. Reservations accepted. Outdoor dining. Old Mexican-style cantina, located in a converted train station. Cr cds: A, D, DS, MC, V.

★ ★ **MARCELLO'S PASTA GRILL.** *1701 E Warner Rd (85284). Phone 480/831-0800; fax 480/831-5745. www.marcellospastagrill.com.* Italian menu. Hours: 11 am-10 pm; Fri to 11 pm; Sat 4-11 pm; Sun 4-9 pm. Closed some major holidays. Dinner $8.95-$15.95. Bar. Children's menu. Casual attire. Outdoor dining. Cr cds: A, D, MC, V.

★ **SIAMESE CAT.** *5034 S Price Rd (85282). Phone 480/820-0406. www.thesiamesecat.com.* Thai menu. Hours: 11 am-2 pm, 5-9 pm; Fri, Sat to 10 pm. Closed some major holidays. Dinner $6.25-$9.95. Casual attire. Cr cds: A, MC, V.

Tombstone (H-6)

See also Bisbee

Settled 1879 **Pop** 1,504 **Elev** 4,540 ft **Area code** 520 **Zip** 85638

Information Tombstone Chamber of Commerce, PO Box 995; 888/457-3929.

Web www.tombstone.org

Shortly after Ed Schieffelin discovered silver, Tombstone became a rough-and-tumble town with saloons, bawdy-houses, and lots of gunfighting. Tombstone's most famous battle was that of the O.K. Corral, between the Earps and the Clantons in 1881. Later, water rose in the mines and could not be pumped out; fires and other catastrophes occurred, but Tombstone was "the town too tough to die." Now a health and winter resort, it is also a museum of Arizona frontier life. In 1962, the town was designated a National Historic Landmark by the US Department of the Interior.

What to See and Do

Bird Cage Theatre. *517 E Allen. Phone 520/457-3421.* Formerly a frontier cabaret (1880s), this famous landmark has seen many of the West's most famous characters. In its heyday it was known as "the wildest and wickedest nightspot between Basin Street and the Barbary Coast." The upstairs "cages," where feathered girls plied their trade, inspired the refrain, "only a bird in a gilded cage." Original fixtures, furnishings. (Daily) **$$**

Gunfights and Saloons

Begin exploring "The Town Too Tough to Die" on Toughnut Street. At the corner of Third and Toughnut, explore the gorgeous Cochise County Courthouse, now a museum and state historic park. Built in 1882, it's a beautiful testament to Victorian Neoclassical architecture; check out the town gallows in the courtyard, and browse the book shop. To the west a few steps, Victoria's B&B Wedding Chapel (on Toughnut between Second and Third) is located in an 1880s home. To the east one block, the Rose Tree Museum at Fourth and Toughnut occupies another 1880s home; inside its courtyard is a century-old rose tree that blooms every April and covers an 8,000-square-foot space. At Fifth and Toughnut streets, Nellie Cashman's is the oldest restaurant in town, specializing in homemade pies.

Now follow Third Street north one block to Allen Street, essentially the main drag of historic Tombstone. Stop in between Third and Fourth streets on Allen, where the Historama offers a 30-minute presentation (narrated by Vincent Price) that tells the town story in film and animated figures. Next door, see life-size figures in the OK Corral, the alleged site of the legendary gunfight between the Earp and Clanton brothers and Doc Holliday. (Actually, it took place on nearby Fremont Street.) Across the street, Tombstone Art Gallery offers works by local artisans and crafters.

On the corner of Allen and Fifth streets, the Crystal Palace Saloon has been restored to its 1879 glory, looking every bit the lusty watering hole and gambling den of legend. In the block of Allen between Fifth and Sixth streets, the Prickly Pear Museum is chock-full of military history; on Allen at Sixth, find the famous old Bird Cage Theater Museum. The Pioneer Home Museum, between Eighth and Ninth streets, continues telling the rowdy-days story.

From Fifth and Allen, walk north a half-block to the Tombstone Epitaph Museum to see an 1880s printing press and newsroom equipment and buy a copy of the 1881 Epitaph report of the OK Corral shoot-out. Continue walking north of Fifth, crossing Fremont Street and turning left onto Safford Street. Walk west on Safford three blocks to Second and Safford, where the two-story adobe called Buford House B&B occupies an 1880s home bearing a National Historic Landmark plaque.

Boothill Graveyard. *Boothill. NW on US 80 W. Phone 520/457-9344.* About 250 marked graves, some with unusual epitaphs, many of famous characters.

Crystal Palace Saloon. *5th and Allen sts. Phone 520/457-3611.* Restored. Dancing Fri-Sun evenings. (Daily)

Office of the *Tombstone Epitaph*. *9 S 5th St (85638). Phone 520/457-2211.* The oldest continuously published newspaper in Arizona, founded in 1880; it is now a monthly journal of Western history. Office houses collection of early printing equipment. (Daily) **FREE**

O.K. Corral. *308 Allen St E (85638). Phone 520/457-3456.* Restored stagecoach office and buildings surrounding gunfight site; life-size figures; Fly's Photography Gallery (adjacent) has early photos. (Daily; closed Dec 25) **$$$**

Rose Tree Inn Museum. *116 S 4th St. Phone 520/457-3326.* Largest rose bush in the world, spreading over 9,000 square feet; blooms in Apr. Museum in 1880 boarding house (oldest house in town); original furniture, documents. (Daily; closed Dec 25) **$$**

St. Paul's Episcopal Church. *3rd and Stafford sts (85638).* (1882) Oldest Protestant church still in use in state; original fixtures.

Tombstone Courthouse State Historic Park. *219 E Toughnut St (85638). Off US 80. Phone 520/457-3311.* (1882) Victorian building houses exhibits recalling Tombstone in the turbulent 1880s. Tombstone and Cochise County history. (Daily; closed Dec 25) **$$**

Tombstone Historama. *308 Allen St E. Adjacent to O.K. Corral. Phone 520/457-3456.* Electronic diorama and film narrated by Vincent Price tell the story of Tombstone. (Daily; hourly showings; closed Dec 25) **$$**

Special Events

Helldorado. Three days of reenactments of Tombstone events of the 1880s. Third weekend in Oct.

Territorial Days. *4th and Fremont (85638). Phone 520/457-9317.* Commemorates formal founding of the town. Fire-hose cart races and other events typical of a celebration in Arizona's early days. Second weekend in Mar.

Wild West Days and Rendezvous of Gunfighters. *O.K. Corral. Phone 520/457-9465.* Labor Day weekend.

Wyatt Earp Days. *108 W Allen (85638). Phone 520/457-3434.* Also fiddlers' contests. Memorial Day weekend.

Motel/Motor Lodge

★★**BEST WESTERN LOOKOUT LODGE.** *US Hwy 80 (85638). Phone 520/457-2223; toll-free 877/652-6772; fax 520/457-3870. www.bestwestern.com.* 40 rooms, 2 story. S $58-$65; D $62-$69; each additional $5; under 12 free; higher rates special events. Crib free. Pet accepted, some restrictions; $50 and $5/day. TV; cable. Heated pool. Complimentary continental breakfast. Restaurant nearby. Check-out 11 am. Business services available. Cr cds: A, C, D, DS, MC, V.

Restaurants

★ **BIG NOSE KATE'S SALOON.** *417 E Allen St (85638). Phone 520/457-3107; fax 520/457-3424. www.bignosekates.com.* Hours: 11 am-8 pm. Closed Thanksgiving, Dec 25. Mexican menu. No A/C. Bar 10 am-10 pm; Thurs-Sat to midnight. Lunch, dinner $2.50-$16.95. Children's menu. Specializes in authentic Mexican entrees, burgers, pizza. Entertainment. Street parking. Outdoor dining. Original 1880 building; mine shaft at basement level; retail Western wear. Cr cds: MC, V.

★ **LONGHORN.** *501 E Allen (85638). Phone 520/457-3405; fax 520/457-3803. www.bignosekates.com.* American menu. Closed Thanksgiving, Dec 25. Breakfast, lunch, dinner. Totally nonsmoking. Cr cds: MC, V. **$$**

★ **NELLIE CASHMAN'S.** *117 S 5th (85638). Phone 520/457-2212.* American menu. Breakfast, lunch, dinner. In historic adobe building (1879); established in 1882 by Nellie Cashman, "the angel of Tombstone," at height of silver boom. Totally nonsmoking. Cr cds: A, DS, MC, V. **$$**

Tucson (H-5)

See also Nogales

Founded 1775 **Pop** 486,669 **Elev** 2,386 ft **Area code** 520

Information Metropolitan Tucson Convention & Visitors Bureau, 110 S Church Ave, #7199, 85701; 520/624-1817

Web www.visittucson.org

Tucson (TOO-sahn) offers a rare combination of delightful Western living, colorful desert and mountain scenery, and cosmopolitan culture.

It is one of several US cities that developed under four flags. The Spanish standard flew first over the Presidio of Tucson, built to withstand Apache attacks in 1776. Later, Tucson flew the flags of Mexico, the Confederate States and, finally, the United States.

Today, Tucson is a resort area, an educational and copper center, a cotton and cattle market, headquarters for the Coronado National Forest, and a place of business for several large industries. Health-seekers, under proper medical advice, nearly always find relief. The city's shops, restaurants, resorts, and points of interest are varied and numerous.

What to See and Do

Arizona Historical Society Fort Lowell Museum. *2900 N Craycroft Rd; in Fort Lowell County Park, N end of Craycroft Rd. Phone 520/885-3832.* Reconstruction of commanding officer's quarters. Exhibits, period furniture. (Wed-Sat; closed holidays) **FREE**

Arizona Historical Society Fremont House Museum. *151 S Granada Ave (85701). In the Tucson Community Center Complex, downtown. Phone 520/622-0956.* (circa 1880) Adobe house restored and furnished in period style. Once occupied by John C. Frémont's daughter, Elizabeth, when he was territorial governor (1878-1881). Special programs all year, including slide shows on Arizona history (Sat; free) and walking tours of historic sites (Nov-Mar, Sat; fee; registration in advance). Museum (Wed-Sat).

Arizona Historical Society Museum, Library, and Archives. *949 E 2nd St (85719). Phone 520/628-5774.* Exhibits depicting state history from the Spanish colonial period to present; Arizona mining hall; photography gallery. Research library (Mon-Sat) contains collections on Western history; manuscripts. (Mon-Sat, also Sun afternoons; closed holidays) **DONATION**

Catalina State Park. *11570 N Oracle Rd. 9 miles N on US 77. Phone 520/628-5798.* A 5,500-acre desert park with a vast array of plants and wildlife; bird area (nearly 170 species). Nature and horseback riding trails, hiking, trail access to adjacent Coronado National Forest; picnicking, camping (dump station). Standard fees. **$$**

Colossal Cave. *16711 E Colossal Cave Rd. 19 miles SE on I-10 to Vail, exit 279, then 7 miles N on Colossal Cave Rd. Phone 520/647-7275.* Fossilized marine life provides evidence of ocean that once covered Arizona desert. 70°F year-round. Forty-five-minute to one-hour guided tours. (Daily) **$$$**

Columbia University's Biosphere 2 Center. *32540 S Biosphere Rd (85623). 35 miles N on US 89 to AZ 77 milepost 96.5, then 1/2 mile N to Biosphere 2 Rd. Phone 520/896-6200.* An ambitious attempt to learn more about our planet's ecosystems began in Sept 1991 with the first of a series of missions in this 3 1/2-acre, glass-enclosed, self-sustaining model of Earth. Isolated from the outside, a rotating crew of researchers rely entirely on the air, water, and food generated and recycled within the structure. It contains over 3,500 species of plants and animals in multiple ecosystems, including a tropical rain forest with an 85-foot-high mountain. Visitors are permitted within the biospherian living areas of the enclosure. They may also view the interior from outside as well as enjoy many other exhibits located throughout the campus. Because of variance in research schedule, the biospherian crew may not always be present. Walking tours (wear comfortable shoes) include multimedia introduction to Biosphere 2. Visitor center, gift shop, restaurant. (Daily; closed Dec 25) **$$$$**

Coronado National Forest. *300 W Congress St Fl 6. Phone 520/670-4552.* Mt Lemmon Recreation Area, part of this forest (almost 2 million acres), offers fishing; bird-watching, hiking, horseback riding, picnicking, skiing, camping (fee). Madera Canyon offers recreation facilities, lodge. Peña Blanca Lake and Recreation Area (see NOGALES) and the Chiricahua Wilderness area in the southeast corner of the state are part of the 12 areas that make up the forest. The Santa Catalina Ranger District, located in Tucson (phone 520/749-8700), has its headquarters at Sabino Canyon, 12 miles NE on Sabino Canyon Rd; a 1/4-mile nature trail begins at the headquarters, as does a shuttle ride almost 4 miles into Sabino Canyon (fee). Northeast, east and south of city.

Gray Line bus tours. *181 W Broadway Blvd. Contact PO Box 1991, 85702. Phone 520/622-8811.*

Greyhound racing. *2601 S 3rd Ave. Tucson Greyhound Park. Phone 520/884-7576.* Pari-mutuel wagering.

International Wildlife Museum. *4800 W Gates Pass Rd, on Speedway 5 miles W of I-10. Phone 520/617-1439.* Includes hundreds of wildlife exhibits from around the world; hands-on, interactive computer displays; videos; cafe. (Daily; closed Thanksgiving, Dec 25) **$$$**

Mount Lemmon Ski Valley. *35 miles NE via Mt Lemmon Hwy. Phone 520/576-1400.* Double chairlift, two tows; patrol, school, rentals; snack bar, restaurant. Fifteen runs, longest run one mile; vertical drop 900 feet. (Late Dec-mid-Apr, daily) Chairlift operates rest of year (daily; fee). Nature trails.

Old Town Artisans. *186 N Meyer Ave. Phone 520/623-6024.* (Daily; closed holidays)

Pima Air & Space Museum. *6000 E Valencia Rd; I-10 to exit 267 (Valencia Rd), then E. Phone 520/574-0462.* Aviation history exhibits with an outstanding collection of more than 250 aircraft, both military and civilian. (Daily; closed Thanksgiving, Dec 25) **$$**

Reid Park. *900 S Randolph Way. Phone 520/791-4873 or 520/791-3204 (zoo).* Picnicking; zoo; rose garden; outdoor performance center. (Daily except Dec 25) **$$**

Titan Missile Museum. *1580 W Duval Mine Rd. Located in Green Valley, approximately 20 miles S via I-19, exit 69 (Duval Mine Rd), then W, past La Canada, turn right and*

follow signs. Phone 520/625-7736. Deactivated Titan II missile on display; memorabilia, models, rocket engine that powered the missile, support vehicles, UH1F helicopter, various exhibits. A one-hour guided tour begins with a briefing and includes a visit down into the missile silo (may be strenuous; comfortable walking shoes required in the missile silo). The silo may also be viewed from a glass observation area located at the museum level. (Nov-Apr, daily; rest of year, Wed-Sun). **$$$**

Tohono Chul Park. *Ina and Oracle rds, entrance at 7366 N Paseo del Norte. Phone 520/575-8468.* A 37-acre preserve with more than 400 species of arid climate plants; nature trails; demonstration garden; geology wall; recirculating stream; ethnobotanical garden. Many varieties of wild birds visit the park. Exhibits, galleries, tea room, and gift shops in restored adobe house (Daily; closed July 4). **DONATION**

Tucson Botanical Gardens. *2150 N Alvernon Way. Phone 520/326-9255.* Gardens include Mediterranean and landscaping plants; native wildflowers; tropical greenhouse; xeriscape/solar demonstration garden. Tours, botanical classes; special events. Picnic area (free). (Daily; closed holidays) **$$**

Tucson Mountain Park. *1204 W Silverlake Rd. 12 miles W, via AZ 86 (Ajo Way) about 6 miles to Kinney Rd, turn right. Phone 520/883-4200 or 520/740-2690.* More than 18,000 acres of saguaro cactus and mountain scenery. Picnic facilities. Gilbert Ray Campground (electric hookups, dump station; fee). Also located here is

Arizona-Sonora Desert Museum. *2021 N Kinney Rd (85743). Phone 520/883-2702.* Live desert creatures: mountain lions, beavers, bighorn sheep, birds, tarantulas, prairie dogs, snakes, otters, and many others. Nature trails through labeled desert botanical gardens. Underground earth sciences center with limestone caves; geological, mineral, and mining exhibits. Orientation room provides information on natural history of deserts. (Daily) **$$$**

★ **Tucson Museum of Art.** *140 N Main Ave. Phone 520/624-2333.* Housed in six renovated buildings within the boundaries of El Presidio Historic District (circa 1800). Pre-Columbian, Spanish colonial, and Western artifacts; decorative arts and paintings; art of the Americas; contemporary art and crafts; changing exhibits. Mexican heritage museum; historic presidio room; 6,000-volume art resource library; art school. (Labor Day-Memorial Day, Mon-Sat, also Sun afternoons; rest of year, Tues-Sun; closed holidays) Free admission Sun. **$$**

University of Arizona. *2501 E Elm St (85716). Phone 520/621-5130.* (1885) (35,000 students.) The 343-acre campus is beautifully landscaped, with handsome buildings.

Visitor center, located at University Blvd and Cherry Ave, has campus maps and information on attractions and activities. Tours (Mon-Sat). Also located here is

Arizona State Museum. *Park Ave and University Blvd (85721). Phone 520/621-6281.* Exhibits on the Native American cultures of Arizona and the Southwest from 10,000 years ago to the present. (Daily; closed holidays) **FREE**

Center for Creative Photography. *1030 N Olive Rd. S of pedestrian underpass on Speedway Blvd, 1 block E of Park Ave. Phone 520/621-7968.* Archives, museum, and research center including archives of Ansel Adams and Richard Avedon, collection of works by more than 2,000 photographers; changing exhibits. (Mon-Fri, also Sat-Sun afternoons; closed holidays) **FREE**

Flandrau Science Center & Planetarium. *1601 E University Blvd (85719). Phone 520/621-7827.* Interactive, hands-on science exhibits (Tue-Sun; closed holidays; free); planetarium shows (limited hours). Nightly telescope viewing (Wed-Sat). **$$**

Mineral Museum. *N Cherry Ave and E University Blvd (85721). Basement of Flandrau Science Center. Phone 520/621-4227.* Rocks, minerals, gemstones, and cuttings; paleontological materials. Meteorite exhibit. (Tues-Sun; closed holidays) **$$**

Museum of Art. *N Park Ave and E Speedway Blvd. Phone 520/621-7567.* Art museum (free) with extensive collection, including Renaissance, baroque, and contemporary art; changing exhibits. (Mon-Fri, Sun; closed holidays) Music building and theater, in which plays are produced by students. Inquire locally for programs.

Special Events

Arizona Opera. *260 S Church Ave. Phone 602/266-7464.* The high notes of arias have been ringing across the Arizona wilderness for more than 25 years, prompting many a bravo. So if the passionate music of opera lights your fire, you'll likely be drawn to the Tucson Convention Center, where this company produces five operas each season. Between October 2003 and March 2004, it will stage *The Pearl Fishers, The Mikado, Don Pasquale, Sweeney Todd,* and *La Boheme* in both Tucson and Phoenix. Fri-Sun, Oct-Mar. **$$$$**

Arizona Theatre Company. *330 S Scott Ave (85701). The Temple of Music & Art. Phone 520/622-2823.* The State Theatre of Arizona performs both classic and contemporary works. Evening performances Tues-Sun; matinees Wed, Sat, and Sun. Phone 520/622-2823. Sept-May.

Baseball. *Hi Corbett Field, Tucson Electric Park, 2500 E Ajo Way (85713). Phone 520/434-1111.* Colorado Rockies, Chicago White Sox, and Arizona Diamondbacks baseball spring training, exhibition games; late Feb-late Mar. Also

the home of the Arizona Diamondbacks' minor league team, the Tucson Sidewinders; Apr-Sept.

Chrysler Classic of Tucson. *2727 West Club Dr (85742). Phone 520/297-2271. Omni Tucson National Golf Resort & Spa* and *The Gallery Golf Club.* $3-million tournament featuring top pros. Late-Feb-early-Mar.

Fiesta del Presidio. *140 N Main Ave (85701). Phone 520/624-2333. Tucson Museum of Art Plaza.* Low-rider car show, dancing, Mexican fiesta events, costumes, food.

Gem & Mineral Show. *260 S Church Ave (85701). Phone 520/322-5773. Tucson Convention Center.* Displays of minerals; jewelry; lapidary skills; Smithsonian Institution collection. Mid-Feb.

Tucson: Meet Yourself. *El Presidio Park. Downtown. Phone 520/882-3060.* Commemorates Tucson's cultural and historic heritage with a torchlight pageant, Native American dances, children's parade, Mexican fiesta, frontier encampment, and other events. Oct.

Tucson Symphony Orchestra. *2175 N 6th Ave. Phone 520/882-8585.* Sept-May.

Motels/Motor Lodges

★ **BEST WESTERN INN SUITES HOTEL AND SUITES.** *6201 N Oracle Rd (85704). Phone 520/297-8111; toll-free 888/554-4535; fax 520/297-2935. www.bestwestern.com.* 159 rooms, 2 story. S, D $59.99-$129; under 18 free; weekend, weekly rates. Pet accepted, some restrictions; fee. Complimentary breakfast buffet. Check-out noon, check-in 2 pm. TV; cable (premium). Laundry services. Room service. Whirlpool. Lighted tennis. Cr cds: A, C, D, DS, MC, V.

⊡ 🛏 ⛷ 🛌 🕴 ⊠ SC

★ ★ **BEST WESTERN ROYAL SUN INN AND SUITES.** *1015 N Stone Ave (85705). Phone 520/622-8871; toll-free 800/545-8858; fax 520/623-2267. www.bestwestern.com.* 99 rooms, 2 story. S, D $69-$149; each additional $10. Check-out 1 pm, check-in 10 am. TV; cable (premium), VCR (movies). Restaurant 6 am-9 pm. Bar 4 pm-1 am. Room service. Heated pool, whirlpool, poolside service. Cr cds: A, C, D, DS, MC, V.

⊡ 🛌 ⊠ SC

★ ★ **CLARION HOTEL AIRPORT TUCSON.** *6801 S Tucson Blvd (85706). Phone 520/746-3932; toll-free 800/526-0550; fax 520/889-9934. www.choicehotels.com.* 190 rooms, 2 story. S, D $99-$139; under 18 free; weekend rates. Complimentary breakfast. Check-out noon, check-in 2 pm. TV; cable (premium). In-room modem link. Restaurant 6 am-11 pm. Bar. Room service. Exercise equipment. Whirlpool, poolside service. Free airport transportation. Business center. Cr cds: A, C, D, DS, ER, JCB, MC, V.

⊡ 🛌 🕴 ✈ ⊠ 🕴

★ **CLARION HOTEL RANDOLPH PARK.** *102 N Alvernon Way (85711). Phone 520/795-0330; toll-free 800/227-6086; fax 520/326-2111. www.clarionhotel.com.* 174 rooms, 3 story. S, D $59-$119; each additional $10; under 18 free. Pet accepted, fee. Complimentary breakfast. Check-out noon, check-in 3 pm. TV; cable (premium). In-room modem link. Exercise equipment. Children's pool. Business center. Cr cds: A, C, D, DS, ER, JCB, MC, V.

▣ 🐾 🏊 🏃 🏖 SC 🏋

★ **COUNTRY INN & SUITES BY CARLSON.** *7411 N Oracle Rd (85704). Phone 520/575-9255; toll-free 800/456-4000; fax 520/575-8671. www.countryinns.com.* 247 kitchen units, 3 story. S, D $59.99-$99.95; under 18 free. Complimentary continental breakfast. Check-out noon, check-in 3 pm. TV; cable (premium). In-room modem link. Health club privileges. Whirlpool. Free airport transportation. Cr cds: A, D, DS, MC, V.

▣ 🏊 ✈ 🏖 SC

★★ **COURTYARD BY MARRIOTT TUCSON AIRPORT.** *2505 E Executive Dr (85706). Phone 520/573-0000; toll-free 800/321-2211; fax 520/573-0470. www.marriott.com.* 165 rooms, 3 story. S, D $59-$104; under 12 free. Check-out noon, check-in 3 pm. TV; cable (premium). In-room modem link. Restaurant 6-10 am, 5-10 pm; Sat, Sun 7-11 am. Bar 4-11 pm. Exercise room. Whirlpool. Airport transportation. Cr cds: A, C, D, DS, MC, V.

▣ 🏊 🏃 ✈

★★ **COURTYARD BY MARRIOTT TUCSON WILLIAMS CENTER.** *201 S Williams Blvd (85711). Phone 520/745-6000; toll-free 800/228-9290; fax 520/745-2393. www.courtyard.com.* 159 rooms, 3 story. S, D $59-$139; higher rates special events (2-3-day minimum). Check-out noon, check-in 3 pm. TV; cable (premium). In-room modem link. Restaurant 6-10 am, 5-10 pm. Bar 4-11 pm. Room service from 5 pm. Pool, whirlpool, poolside service. Cr cds: A, C, D, DS, MC, V.

▣ 🏊 🏃 🏖 SC

★ **HAMPTON INN.** *6971 S Tucson Blvd (85706). Phone 520/918-9000; fax 520/889-4002. www.hamptoninn.com.* 129 rooms, 4 story. S, D $54-$129; under 18 free. Complimentary continental breakfast. Check-out noon, check-in 3 pm. TV; cable (premium). Whirlpool. Free airport transportation. Cr cds: A, C, D, DS, MC, V.

▣ 🏊 🏖

★★ **HOLIDAY INN.** *4550 S Palo Verde Rd (85714). Phone 520/746-1161; fax 520/741-0036. www.holiday-inn.com.* 352 rooms, 6 story. S, D $79-$111; each additional $10; under 18 free. Pets accepted; fee. Check-out noon, check-in 1 pm. TV; cable (premium), VCR available. Coin laundry. Restaurant 6 am-2:30 pm, dining room 5-10 pm. Bar 4 pm-1 am, Sun noon-10 pm. Room service. Exercise room. Outdoor pool, whirlpool, poolside service. Lighted tennis. Free parking. Free airport transportation. Cr cds: A, C, D, DS, JCB, MC, V.

▣ 🐾 🏌 🏊 🏃 ✈ 🏖

★ **RAMADA FOOTHILLS INN & SUITES.** *6944 E Tanque Verde Rd (85715). Phone 520/886-9595; fax 520/721-8466. www.ramadafoothillstucson.com.* 176 rooms, 2 story. S, D $49-$139; each additional $10; under 18 free. Pet accepted, some restrictions; fee. Complimentary continental breakfast. Check-out noon, check-in 3 pm. TV; cable (premium). In-room modem link. Outdoor pool, whirlpool. Free parking. Cr cds: A, C, D, DS, JCB, MC, V.

▣ 🐾 🏊 🏖 SC

★★ **SMUGGLER'S INN.** *6350 E Speedway Blvd (85710). Phone 520/296-3292; toll-free 866/517-6870; fax 520/722-3713. www.smugglersinn.com.* 150 rooms, 2 story. S, D $69-$119; each additional $10; suites, kitchen units $89-$139; under 15 free. Pets accepted. Complimentary continental breakfast. Check-out noon, check-in 4 pm. TV; cable (premium), VCR available. Coin laundry. Restaurant 6:30 am-9:30 pm. Bar 1:30 pm-1 am; Sun from noon. Room service. Outdoor pool, whirlpool. Free parking. Cr cds: A, C, D, DS, MC, V.

▣ 🐾 🏊 🏖

Hotels

★★ **CLARION HOTEL & SUITES SANTA RITA.** *88 E Broadway (85701). Phone 520/622-4000; fax 520/620-0376. www.clarionhotel.com.* 184 rooms, 8 story. S, D $55-$94; each additional $10; under 18 free. Pet accepted, some restrictions; fee. Complimentary breakfast. Check-out noon, check-in 2 pm. TV; cable (premium). In-room modem link. Restaurant (See also CAFE POCA COSA). No room service. Exercise equipment. Pool, whirlpool. Business center. Cr cds: A, C, D, DS, JCB, MC, V.

🐾 🏃 🏖 🏋

★★ **DOUBLETREE REID PARK.** *445 S Alvernon Way (85711). Phone 520/881-4200; fax 520/323-5225. www.doubletreehotels.com.* Ten minutes from downtown and the airport, this Hilton chain is a nice resting place for business and leisure travelers alike. Directly across the street is the expansive Reid Park. 302 rooms, 2-9 story. S, D $89-$169; each additional $20; under 18 free. Pet accepted, some restrictions; fee. Check-out noon, check-in 3 pm. TV; cable (premium), VCR available. Restaurant 6 am-11 pm. Bar 11-1 am, Sun from noon. Room service. Exercise equipment. Whirlpool, poolside service. Lighted tennis. Business center. Cr cds: A, C, D, DS, ER, JCB, MC, V.

▣ 🐾 🏌 🏊 🏃 ✈ 🏖 🏋

★★ **FOUR POINTS BY SHERATON.** *1900 E Speedway Blvd (85719). Phone 520/327-7341; toll-free 800/325-3535; fax 520/327-0276. www.fourpoints.com.* 151 rooms, 7 story. S, D $69-$129; each additional $10; under 16 free. Check-out noon, check-in 3 pm. TV; cable (premium). Restaurant 6:30 am-10 pm. Bar 11-1 am; Sun to 8 pm. Room service. Whirlpool. Cr cds: A, C, D, DS, JCB, MC, V.

🄳 ⌷ 🛏

★★ **HILTON TUCSON EAST.** *7600 E Broadway (85710). Phone 520/721-5600; toll-free 800/445-8667; fax 520/721-5696. www.tucsoneast.hilton.com.* Located on the trendy East side of Tucson, this property is convenient to shopping, the University of Arizona, and tourist attractions like Old Tucson. The lush vegetation and the mountain views are sure to relax visitors. 241 rooms, 7 story. S, D $49-$200; each additional $14; under 18 free. Pets accepted. Check-out noon, check-in 3 pm. TV; cable (premium). Restaurant 6 am-10 pm; Sat, Sun from 6:30 am. Bar 11 am-11 pm. Room service 6 am-11 pm. Exercise room. Outdoor pool, whirlpool, poolside service. Free parking. Airport transportation. Concierge. Luxury level. Cr cds: A, C, D, DS, JCB, MC, V.

🄳 ⌷ 🛏 ✈ 🛏 🛏

★★★ **MARRIOTT TUCSON UNIVERSITY PARK.** *880 E 2nd St (85719). Phone 520/792-4100; fax 520/882-4100. www.marriott.com.* Just off of the University of Arizona's campus, this property provides the comfort and convenience demanded by business and leisure travelers alike. 267 rooms, 9 story. S, D $79-$209; each additional $15; under 18 free; weekend rates; golf plans. Check-out noon, check-in 3 pm. TV; cable (premium). In-room modem link. Restaurant 6 am-10 pm, bar 11 am-10 pm. Exercise room, sauna. Outdoor pool, whirlpool, poolside service. Valet parking. Business center. Concierge. Luxury level. Cr cds: A, C, D, DS, JCB, MC, V.

🄳 ⌷ 🛏 🛏 🛏

★★ **RADISSON HOTEL CITY CENTER.** *181 W Broadway Blvd (85701). Phone 520/624-8711; toll-free 800/333-3333; fax 520/624-9963. www.radisson.com.* 309 rooms, 12 story. S, D $109-$149; each additional $10; under 18 free. Pet accepted, some restrictions; fee. Check-out noon, check-in 3 pm. TV; cable (premium). Restaurant 6 am-2 pm, 5-10 pm. Bar 4 pm-10 pm; weekends to 1 am. Exercise room. Outdoor pool, poolside service. Free garage parking. Airport transportation. Concierge. Cr cds: A, C, D, DS, ER, JCB, MC, V.

🄳 🐾 ⌷ 🛏 ✈ 🛏

★★ **SHERATON TUCSON HOTEL AND SUITES.** *5151 E Grant Rd (85712). Phone 520/323-6262; fax 520/325-2989. www.sheraton.com.* 216 rooms, 4 story. S, D $69-$229; under 18 free; weekend rates. Pets accepted;

fee. Complimentary continental breakfast. Check-out noon, check-in 3 pm. TV; cable (premium). Coin laundry. Restaurant 11:30 am-11 pm. Bar 11-1 am. Exercise room, steam room. Outdoor pool, poolside service. Free parking. Cr cds: A, C, D, DS, MC, V.

🄳 ⌷ 🛏 🛏

Resorts

★★★ **ARIZONA INN.** *2200 E Elm St (85719). Phone 520/325-1541; toll-free 800/933-1093; fax 520/881-5830. www.arizonainn.com.* This family-owned inn was built in 1930 and features the ultimate quiet comforts. Guestrooms have been individually decorated. 101 rooms, 3 houses, 2 story. S, D $129-$239; houses $595-$2,500; each additional $15; under 2 free (summer). Check-out noon, check-in 3 pm. TV; VCR available. In-room modem link. Dining room 6-10 am, 11 am-2 pm, 6-10 pm. Room service. Exercise equipment. Lighted tennis. Concierge service. Adobe-style buildings (1930) on 15 acres of landscaped lawns and gardens. Pianist 6-10 pm. Cr cds: A, D, MC, V.

🄳 ⚑ ⌷ 🛏 🛏 🛏

★★★ **THE GOLF VILLAS.** *10950 N La Canada (85737). Phone 520/498-0098; toll-free 888/388-0098; fax 520/498-5150. www.thegolfvillas.com.* Luxury one-,two- and three-bedroom villas afford golf course views. Guests have use of an extensive array of recreational facilities at El Conquistador Country Club across the street. 79 rooms, 2 story. Suites $109-$499. Pet accepted. Check-out noon, check-in 3 pm. TV; cable (premium), VCR available. Exercise equipment, sauna. Pool. Hiking trail. Valet parking available. Business center. Concierge service. Cr cds: A, C, D, DS, JCB, MC, V.

🄳 🐾 🍴 ⌷ 🛏 🛏 🛏 🛏

★★★ **HILTON EL CONQUISTADOR.** *10000 N Oracle Rd (85737). Phone 520/544-5000; fax 520/544-1222. www.hilton.com.* This resort and country club lures visitors with its extensive golf and tennis facilities, including 45 holes and 31 lighted courts, but just gazing at the sunsets and spectacular Santa Catalina Mountain views is therapeutic. The grounds, 2,000 feet below the Pusch Ridge cliffs, feature five restaurants, and 45,000 square feet of meeting space. Jan-May: S, D $230-$300; suites, studio rooms $275-$610; under 17 free; golf, tennis plans; lower rates rest of year. Crib free. Pet accepted, some restrictions. TV; cable (premium), VCR available. Pools; whirlpools, poolside service. Supervised child's activities; ages 5-12. Coffee in rooms. Dining rooms 6 am-11 pm (See also LAST TERRITORY). Room service to 2 am. Bar to 1 am; Sun from 10:30 am; entertainment. Check-out noon, check-in 4 pm. Convention facilities. Business center. Bellstaff. Valet service. Concierge. Shopping arcade. Beauty shop. Pro shop. Sports director. Lighted tennis, pro.

45-hole golf, greens fee (includes cart) $95-$135 ($48-$60 in summer), pro, putting green, driving range. Bicycles. Breakfast and evening horseback rides; hayrides. Exercise room; sauna. Massage. Lawn games. Basketball. Hiking and nature trails. Minibars; some bathroom phones, wet bars, fireplaces; microwaves available. Private patios, balconies. Cr cds: A, C, D, DS, ER, JCB, MC, V.

★★★ THE LODGE AT VENTANA CANYON RESORT.

6200 N Clubhouse Ln (85750). Phone 520/577-1400; toll-free 800/828-5701; fax 520/577-4065. www.wyndham.com. The Lodge at Ventana Canyon is a desert paradise. Nestled in the foothills of the Santa Catalina Mountains on a 600-acre desert preserve, the Lodge is a peaceful getaway for tennis players, golfers, and those in pursuit of nothing more challenging than a day at the pool. Two 18-hole Tom Fazio-designed golf courses wind their way through the stunning landscape of wild brush and giant saguaros. The 12 hard-surface tennis courts are perfect for matches, and the Dennis Ralston Tennis Camp helps guests master their serves or perfect their backhands. Whether horseback riding through the canyon or lounging by the Olympic-size pool, visitors reap the rewards of this idyllic setting. Mission-style furniture, fully stocked kitchens, and even old-fashioned freestanding bathtubs create a sense of luxurious comfort in the guest accommodations. Regional cuisine is highlighted at Hearthstone Restaurant, and dining under the stars at Sabino Terrace is a romantic treat. 50 rooms, 2 story. $345-$495; under 18 free. Service charge $20/day. Check-out noon, check-in 4 pm. TV; cable; VCR available. Laundry services. Restaurant, bar. Room service. Exercise room, massage, sauna, steam room. Pool, children's pool, whirlpool, poolside service. Golf; greens fee $56-$199. Outdoor tennis, lighted courts. Lawn games, bicycles. Concierge. Cr cds: A, C, D, DS, JCB, MC, V.

★★★ LOEWS VENTANA CANYON RESORT.

7000 N Resort Dr (85750). Phone 520/299-2020; toll-free 800/234-5117; fax 520/299-6832. www.loewshotels.com. Loews Ventana Canyon Resort is a lush oasis in the Sonoran Desert. Set on 93 acres near Tucson, this splendid resort caters to a sophisticated clientele seeking the finest accommodations, fresh cuisine, and world-class amenities. Drenched in glorious sunlight, the grounds exude tranquility and are perfect for activities like guided hikes and biking excursions. The award-winning designs of Tom Fazio beckon golfers, eight tennis courts call out to players, and two pools cool off guests in superb style. Visitors preferring hydrotherapy to hot-air ballooning take advantage of the spa's complete services. The guest rooms are furnished in a luxurious continental style, and many rooms feature fireplaces. Five restaurants and lounges offer a taste of everything in a variety of settings, from poolside cafés to refined dining rooms. Ventana Room grabs the attention of epicureans with its artfully presented, elegant cuisine. 398 rooms, 4 story. S, D $249-$409; under 18 free. Check-out noon, check-in 3 pm. TV; VCR available. In-room modem link. Room service 24 hours. Dining room, bar. Supervised children's activities; ages 4-12. Exercise room, sauna, steam room, spa. Pool, whirlpool, poolside service. Golf; greens fee $80-$169. Outdoor tennis, lighted courts. Lawn games, bicycles. Business center. Concierge. Cr cds: A, C, D, DS, JCB, MC, V.

★★★ OMNI TUCSON NATIONAL GOLF RESORT/SPA.

2727 W Club Dr (85742). Phone 520/297-2271; toll-free 800/528-4856; fax 520/297-7544. www.omnihotels.com. Breathtaking views, championship golf, and first-class service make the Omni Tucson National Golf Resort & Spa a favorite of leisure travelers. Just outside Tucson, the resort enjoys a peaceful location in the Sonoran Desert. Golf is the centerpiece here, where the 27-hole course is the home of the annual PGA Tucson Open; however, all guests are well taken care of with two pools, a comprehensive fitness center, and tennis, basketball, and sand volleyball courts, as well as a 13,000-square-foot spa featuring the finest therapies and treatments. The rich colors of the Southwest dictate a soothing ambience in the guest rooms. These comfortable retreats are enhanced by expansive views of the verdant golf course or majestic mountains. Some accommodations feature full kitchens, but with four grills, lounges, and restaurants turning out delicious meals, most guests leave the cooking to the resort's talented professionals. 167 rooms, 2 story. S, D $229-$274; under 18 free. Pet accepted, some restrictions; deposit. Check-out noon, check-in 4 pm. TV; cable (premium), VCR available. Wet bars, mini bars; many fireplaces. Restaurant, bar; entertainment. Exercise room, massage, sauna, steam room. Pool, whirlpool, poolside service. Golf; greens fee $85-$179. Outdoor tennis, lighted courts. Lawn games. Concierge. Cr cds: A, C, D, DS, JCB, MC, V.

★★★ THE WESTIN LA PALOMA RESORT AND SPA.

3800 E Sunrise Dr (85718). Phone 520/742-6000; toll-free 800/937-8461; fax 520/577-5878. www.westinlapalomaresort.com. Visitors will stay in one of the luxurious guestrooms located within this Sonora Desert resort. With the 27-hole Jack Nicklaus Signature course nearby, golfers are sure to be pleased! 487 units, 3 story. Jan-May: S, D $319-$480; each additional $30; suites $445-$1,995; under 18 free; golf, tennis plans; lower rates rest of year. Crib free. Service charge $10/day. Check-out noon, check-in 4 pm. TV; cable (premium). Microwaves available, Some fireplaces. Coffee in rooms. Valet services. Dining room 6:30 am-10 pm (See also JANOS). Bar 11-1 am. Room service 24 hours. Box lunches, snack bar, picnics. Supervised children's activities; ages 3-12 years. Exercise room, massage, sauna in suites. Steam room. Recreation room. 2 pools; water slide, whirlpool, poolside service. 27-hole golf (Jack Nicklaus Signature Design), greens fee $185-$205, pro, putting green, driving range. 10 lighted tennis courts (4 clay), pro. Lawn games, Horseback privileges 15 miles. Valet parking. Business center. Convention center/facilities. Bellstaff. Concierge. Shopping arcade. Package store 2 miles. Cr cds: A, C, D, DS, JCB, MC, V.

★ ★ ★ WESTWARD LOOK RESORT. 245 E Ina Rd (85704). Phone 520/297-1151; toll-free 800/722-2500; fax 520/297-9023. www.westwardlook.com. This oasis in the Sonoran Desert features suite-size accommodations in a breath-taking setting, combining historic ambiance with contemporary luxury. 246 rooms, 2 story. S, D $89-$369; each additional $10; under 16 free; golf plans; holiday rates. Pet accepted, some restrictions; fee. Check-out noon, check-in 4 pm. TV; cable (premium). Restaurant 6 am-10 pm (See also THE GOLD ROOM). Bar 4 pm-1 am; entertainment Thurs-Sat. Room service. Exercise room. Spa, massage. 3 heated pools; whirlpools. Lighted tennis. Lawn games. Bicycles. Free parking. Business center. Concierge. Cr cds: A, C, D, DS, JCB, MC, V.

All Suite

★ ★ DOUBLETREE GUEST SUITES. 6555 E Speedway Blvd (85710). Phone 520/721-7000; fax 520/721-1991. www.doubletreetucson.com. Located in the city's upscale neighborhood, this Hilton chain is just 20 minutes from Tucson International Airport and Restaurant Row. Most suites have mountain-view courtyards. 304 suites, 5 story. S, D $59-$144; Jan-mid-Apr: under 18 free; package plans. Pet accepted, some restrictions; fee. Check-out noon, check-in 3 pm. TV; cable (premium). Restaurant 6 am-11 pm. Bar. Exercise equipment. Whirlpool, poolside service. Business center. Cr cds: A, C, D, DS, ER, JCB, MC, V.

★ EMBASSY SUITES HOTEL TUCSON-BROADWAY. 5335 E Broadway (85711). Phone 520/745-2700; fax 520/790-9232. www.embassysuites.com. 142 suites, 3 story. No elevator. S, D $79-$179; each additional $10; under 18 free. Pet accepted, some restrictions. Complimentary full breakfast. Check-out noon, check-in 3 pm. TV; cable (premium). Room service. Whirlpool. Cr cds: A, C, D, DS, JCB, MC, V.

★ ★ EMBASSY SUITES HOTEL TUCSON-INTERNATIONAL AIRPORT. 7051 S Tucson Blvd (85706). Phone 520/573-0700; toll-free 800/362-2779; fax 520/741-9645. www.embassysuites.com. 204 suites, 3 story. S, D $149-$199; each additional $10; under 12 free; weekend rates.

Pet accepted, fee. Complimentary full breakfast. Check-out 1 pm, check-in 3 pm. TV; cable (premium). Restaurant 11 am-10 pm; Fri, Sat to 11 pm. Bar to midnight. Exercise equipment. Whirlpool, poolside service. Free airport transportation. Cr cds: A, C, D, DS, JCB, MC, V.

★ WINDMILL SUITES AT ST. PHILLIPS PLAZA. 4250 N Campbell Ave (85718). Phone 520/577-0007; toll-free 800/547-4747; fax 520/577-0045. www.windmillinns.com. 122 suites, 3 story. Jan-Apr: suites $135-$395; each additional $10; under 18 free; lower rates rest of year. Pet accepted, some restrictions. Complimentary continental breakfast. Check-out 11 am. TV; cable (premium). Whirlpool. Bicycles. Cr cds: A, D, DS, MC, V.

B&B/Small Inns

★★ADOBE ROSE INN BED AND BREAKFAST. 940 N Olsen Ave (85719). Phone 520/318-4644; toll-free 800/328-4122; fax 520/325-0055. www.aroseinn.com. 7 rooms, 2 story. S, D $65-$135; each additional $15; weekly rates. Children over 10 years only. Complimentary full breakfast. Check-out 11 am, check-in 3-6 pm. TV. Restaurant nearby. Pool, whirlpool. Concierge service. 4 room phones; phones in suites. Totally nonsmoking. Cr cds: A, MC, V.

★★★CAR-MAR'S SOUTHWEST B & B. 6766 W Oklahoma St (85735). Phone 520/578-1730; toll-free 888/578-1730; fax 520/578-7272. www.members.aol.com/carmarbb. 4 rooms, 2 share bath. Jan-Apr: S, D $75-$145; under 5 free; weekly rates; lower rates rest of year. Complimentary full breakfast. Check-out 11 am, check-in 4-6 pm. TV in some rooms; cable (premium), VCR available (movies). Some refrigerators, some microwaves. Complimentary coffee in rooms. Restaurant nearby. Pool, whirlpool. Picnic tables, grills. Business services available. Luggage handling. Concierge service. Antiques, hand-made furniture. Totally nonsmoking. Cr cds: MC, V.

★ ★ CASA ALEGRE BED AND BREAKFAST INN. 316 E Speedway Blvd (85705). Phone 520/628-1800; toll-free 800/628-5654; fax 520/792-1880. www.casaalegreinn.com. 4 rooms, 1 story. No room phones. S, D $80-$135; under 12 free; weekly, monthly rates. Complimentary full breakfast. Check-out 11 am, check-in 4-6 pm. TV; VCR (free movies). Pool, whirlpool. Covered parking. Totally nonsmoking. Cr cds: DS, MC, V.

★ ★ CATALINA PARK INN. 309 E 1st St (85705). Phone 520/792-4541; toll-free 800/792-4885. www.catalinaparkinn.com. 6 rooms, 2 story. Dec-Apr:

S, D $114-$144; weekly, monthly rates; special events (2-day minimum); lower rates rest of year. Closed mid June-Aug. Children over 10 years only. Complimentary full breakfast, complimentary afternoon refreshments. Check-out 11 am, check-in 4-6 pm. TV; cable, VCR available. Luggage handling. Concierge service. House built in 1927 detailed with Mexican mahogany; unique antiques. Totally nonsmoking. Cr cds: A, DS, MC, V.

★ **PEPPERTREE'S BED AND BREAKFAST INN.** *724 E University Blvd (85719). Phone 520/622-7167; toll-free 800/348-5763. www.peppertreesinn.com.* 12 rooms, 2 story. S, D $80-$108. Complimentary full breakfast. Check-out 11 am, check-in 3-6 pm. TV in sitting room; VCR. Coin laundry. Free parking. Concierge service. Totally nonsmoking. Cr cds: DS, MC, V.

★★ **SUNCATCHER BED AND BREAKFAST TUCSON DESERT RETREAT.** *105 N Avenida Javalina (85748). Phone 520/885-0883; toll-free 877/775-8355; fax 520/885-0883. www.thesuncatcher.com.* Guests looking for gracious hospitality in a peaceful and serene desert setting, find their desires fulfilled at this charming bed and breakfast. Gourmet breakfasts and beautiful rooms await you in this architecturally stunning home on four unspoiled acres. 4 rooms, 1 story. S, D $80-$145. Complimentary full breakfast. Check-out noon, check-in 3 pm. TV; VCR (movies). Outdoor pool. Free parking. Concierge. Totally nonsmoking. Cr cds: A, DS, MC, V.

Guest Ranches

★★★ **TANQUE VERDE GUEST RANCH.** *14301 E Speedway Blvd (85748). Phone 520/296-6275; toll-free 800/234-3833; fax 520/721-9426. www.tanqueverderanch.com.* Guests have the opportunity to explore the uniqueness of the Sonoran desert. This ranch offers rooms and suites that include gorgeous views. 94 rooms, 1 story. S, D $270-$465; each additional $90-$100. Service charge 15%. Complimentary full breakfast. Check-out noon, check-in 2 pm. TV available; VCR available. Internet access. Many fireplaces. Coin laundry. Dining room (public by reservation) 8-9 am, noon-1:30 pm, 6-8 pm. Entertainment. Supervised children's activities; ages 4-11. Exercise room, sauna, steam room. 1 indoor, children's pool. Tennis on premises. Free parking. Free airport transportation (4-night minimum). Cr cds: A, DS, MC, V.

★★★ **WHITE STALLION RANCH.** *9251 W Twin Peaks Rd (85743). Phone 520/297-0252; toll-free 888/977-2624; fax 520/744-2786. www.wsranch.* Guests are sure to enjoy the Southwest-ranch style rooms. This ranch is located only 17 miles from Tucson. 41 rooms in cottages.

AP, mid-Dec-May: S $156-$165; S, D $240-$310; suites $312-$368; each additional $89; weekly rates; lower rates Sept-mid-Dec. Closed June-Aug. Crib free. Petting zoo. Check-out 11 am, check-in 2 pm. Refrigerators, fireplaces. Coin laundry. Bar. Breakfast rides, hayrides, rodeos, bonfires with entertainment. Box lunches, cookouts. Recreation room. Heated pool. Tennis. Lawn games. Free airport, train station, bus depot transportation (4 night minimum). Meeting rooms. Business services available. Gift shop. Library. Family-style meals. Informal ranch on 3,000 acres. Team penning (working cattle in the arena).

Restaurants

★ **BLUE WILLOW.** *2616 N Campbell Ave (85719). Phone 520/327-7577; fax 520/327-9585.* Hours: 8 am-10 pm; Thur, Fri, Sat to midnight; Sun to 9 pm. Closed Thanksgiving, Dec 25. Breakfast $2.25-$6.75, lunch $3.50-$7.95, dinner $3.50-$10.50. Outdoor dining. Totally nonsmoking. Cr cds: A, DS, MC, V.

★★ **CAFE POCA COSA.** *88 E Broadway (85701). Phone 520/622-6400.* Mexican menu. Menu changes daily. Hours: 11 am-9 pm; Fri, Sat to 10 pm. Closed Sun; most major holidays. Dinner $14-$20. Bar. Casual attire. Outdoor dining. Totally nonsmoking. Cr cds: MC, V.

★★ **CAPRICCIO.** *4825 N 1st Ave (85718). Phone 520/887-2333; fax 520/887-0385.* Continental menu. Hours: 5:30-9:30 pm. Closed Sun; Jan 1, Thanksgiving, Dec 25; also Mon mid-May-Aug. Dinner $15-$24.50. Reservations accepted. Cr cds: A, DS, MC, V.

★★ **CHAD'S STEAKHOUSE.** *3001 N Swan (85712). Phone 520/881-1802.* Seafood, steak menu. Closed Thanksgiving, Dec 25. Dinner, dinner. Bar. Children's menu. Reservations accepted. Cr cds: A, C, D, DS, ER, MC, V. **$$**

★★ **CITY GRILL.** *6464 E Tanque Verde (85715). Phone 520/733-1111; fax 520/733-1933. www.metrorestaurants.com.* American menu. Hours: 11 am-10 pm; Fri, Sat to 11 pm; Sun to 9 pm. Closed most major holidays. Dinner $11.99-$17.99. Bar to midnight; weekends to 1 am. Children's menu. Casual attire. Outdoor dining. Cr cds: A, C, D, DS, MC, V.

★ **DELECTABLES.** *533 N 4th Ave (85705). Phone 520/884-9289; fax 520/628-7948. www.delectables.com.* Cafe menu. Hours: 11 am-9 pm; Fri, Sat to 11 pm, closed major holidays. Dinner $8.50-$12.95. Bar. Children's menu. Casual attire. Outdoor dining. Cr cds: A, C, D, DS, JCB, MC, V.

D **SC**

★ ★ ★ **EVANGELOS SCORDATO'S.** *4405 W Speedway Blvd (85745). Phone 520/792-3055; fax 520/ 792-9808.* Two-time recipient of the Golden Plate award, this is the place to get your favorite Italian veal dish and enjoy a beautiful view of the Tucson Mountains. Italian, Continental menu. Hours: 5-10 pm; Sun 4-9 pm. Closed Sun, Mon (June-Aug); July 4, Thanksgiving, Dec 25. Dinner $17-$25. Bar. Children's menu. Casual attire. Outdoor dining. Cr cds: A, C, D, DS, MC, V.

D

★ ★ ★ **FUEGO.** *6958 E Tanque Verde Rd (85715). Phone 520/886-1745; fax 520/886-6084. www.fuegorestaurant.com.* Southwestern menu. Hours: 5-10 pm; Fri, Sat to 11 pm; hours vary June-Sept. Closed some major holidays. Dinner $8.50-$22. Bar. Children's menu. Casual attire. Outdoor dining. Southwestern décor. Cr cds: A, D, MC, V.

D **SC**

★ ★ ★ ★ **THE GOLD ROOM.** *245 E Ina Rd (85704). Phone 520/297-1151; fax 520/297-9023. www.westwardlook.com.* Set high in the foothills overlooking Tucson, The Gold Room features both regional Southwestern fare and traditional American cuisine, combining the simplicity of steaks and seafood with more intricate and robust dishes that reflect the region's local color. Native produce—assorted chilies, beans, squash, and the like—are cultivated in the chef's on-site garden and are winningly blended into entrées like mesquite-grilled buffalo sirloin with chipotle maple glaze and mesquite-grilled lamb, ostrich, and venison with green chile mashed potatoes. Wraparound windows afford spectacular views of the mountains and desert. A jazz brunch on Sundays features a weekly changing menu of inspired regional dishes like blue corn pancakes with prickly pear syrup and Sonoran Caesar salad with smoked duck. Contemporary American menu. Hours: 6 am-4 pm, 5:30-10 pm. Dinner $19.75-$38. Sun brunch. Children's menu. Valet parking. Outdoor dining. Totally nonsmoking. Cr cds: A, C, D, DS, ER, JCB, MC, V.

D

★ ★ ★ **THE GRILL AT HACIENDA DEL SOL.** *5601 N Hacienda del Sol Rd (85718). Phone 520/529-3500; fax 502/299-5554. www.haciendadelsol.com.* Rustic Spanish-Colonial architecture, fine pottery, and Mexican art adorn this beautifully restored Tucson landmark. Several tables afford diners spectacular valley views and the award-winning New American cuisine is complemented by a superlative wine list and excellent service. The creative menu, including roasted tomato and basil soup with garlic and chevre croustade, makes this one of Tucson's favorite dining destinations. Contemporary American menu. Menu changes seasonally. Dinner, Sunday brunch. Children's menu. Reservations accepted. Cr cds: A, C, D, DS, MC, V. **$$$**

D ▨

★ ★ ★ **JANOS RESTAURANT.** *3770 E Sunrise Dr (85718). Phone 520/615-6100; fax 520/615-3334. www.janos.com.* The legendary Janos Wilder presides over this French-inspired Southwestern masterpiece 30 minutes northeast of town on the grounds of the Westin La Paloma Resort & Spa. Diners are surrounded by original artwork and romatic decor, and enjoy a view overlooking the Tucson valley. Features both tasting and a la carte menus, which are constantly changing and are inspired by diverse influences from around the world. French, Southwestern menu. Closed Sun; Jan 1, Dec 25; also Mon mid-May-Nov. Dinner. Bar. Reservations accepted. Outdoor seating. Cr cds: A, D, MC, V. **$$$**

D

★ ★ ★ **KINGFISHER.** *2564 E Grant (85716). Phone 520/323-7739; fax 520/795-7810. www. kingfisherbarandgrill.com.* A full-service raw oyster bar with fifteen varieties of oysters is a prominent aspect of this restaurant. American, seafood menu. Hours: 11 am-midnight; weekends from 5 pm. Closed some major holidays. Dinner $13-$21. Bar. Children's menu. Casual attire. Cr cds: A, C, D, DS, ER, MC, V.

D

★ ★ **LA FUENTE.** *1749 N Oracle Rd (85705). Phone 520/623-8659; fax 520/623-6188.* Mexican menu. Hours: 11 am-10 pm; Fri-Sun to 11 pm; Sat from noon; Sun brunch 11:30 am-2 pm. Closed most major holidays. Dinner $8.95-$20. Entertainment. Children's menu. Cr cds: A, D, MC, V.

D

★ ★ **LA PLACITA CAFE.** *2950 N Swan Rd (85712). Phone 520/881-1150; fax 520/881-3922.* Mexican menu. Hours: 11:30 am-2:30 pm, 5-9:30 pm; Sun from 5 pm. Closed Jan 1, Thanksgiving, Dec 25. Dinner $5.99-$16.99. Sonoran décor; turn-of-the-century Tucson prints, raised-hearth tile fireplace, serape drapes. Outdoor dining. Cr cds: A, C, D, DS, ER, MC, V.

D

★ ★ **LE BISTRO.** *2574 N Campbell Ave (85719). Phone 520/327-3086; fax 520/327-3412. www.lebistrotucson.com.* French, Italian menu. Hours: 11 am-2:30 pm; 5-9:30 pm; Fri to 11 pm; Sat 5-11 pm; Sun from 5 pm. Closed Thanksgiving, Dec 25. Dinner $12.95-$22.95. Cr cds: A, C, DS, ER, MC, V.

D

★ ★ **METROPOLITAN GRILL.** *7892 N Oracle Rd (85704). Phone 520/531-1212; fax 520/297-3750. www. metrorestaurants.com.* American menu. Hours: 11 am-10 pm; Fri, Sat to 10:30 pm. Closed Dec 25. Dinner $8-$19. Bar to 1 am. Children's menu. Outdoor dining. Cr cds: A, C, D, DS, ER, MC, V.

D

★ ★ ★ **OLIVE TREE.** *7000 E Tanque Verde Rd (85715). Phone 520/298-1845; fax 520/298-1846.* This local favorite serves the freshest and most generous Greek food in town. Hours: 5-10 pm. Closed Mon (June-Sept); also some major holidays. Dinner $13.95-$26.95. Bar. Children's menu. Courtyard dining. Cr cds: A, MC, V.

D

★ **PINNACLE PEAK.** *6541 E Tanque Verde Rd (85715). Phone 520/296-0911; fax 520/298-3614.* Steak menu. Hours: 5-10 pm. Closed Thanksgiving, Dec 25. Dinner $5.50-$13.95. Bar. Children's menu. Cr cds: A, DS, MC, V.

D

★ ★ **PRESIDIO GRILL.** *3352 E Speedway (85716). Phone 520/327-4667; fax 520/323-2037. www.dotucson.com.* American menu. Hours: 11 am-10 pm; Fri, Sat to midnight; Sun from 10 am. Closed most major holidays. Dinner $12-$22. Bar. Children's menu. Casual attire. Cr cds: A, C, D, DS, ER, MC, V.

D

★ **SERI MELAKA.** *6133 E Broadway (85711). Phone 520/747-7811; fax 520/790-2707. www.serimelaka.com.* Malaysian, Chinese menu. Hours: 11 am-9:30 pm; weekends to 10 pm; early-bird dinner Mon-Fri 4:30-6 pm. Dinner $10.95-$28.95. Casual attire. Cr cds: A, DS, MC, V.

D

★ ★ ★ **SOLEIL.** *3001 E Skyline Dr (85718). Phone 520/299-3345; fax 520/232-0815.* Mediterranean menu. Menu changes seasonally. Hours: 11 am-10 pm; hours vary in summer. Closed Mon. Dinner $14-$29. Casual attire. Cr cds: A, C, D, DS, JCB, MC, V.

D ⊠

★ **TOHONO CHUL TEA ROOM.** *7366 N Paseo del Norte (85704). Phone 520/797-1222; fax 520/797-7598. www.tohonochulpark.org.* Hours: 8 am-5 pm. Closed most major holidays. Breakfast $2.50-$8.95, lunch $6.95-$9.95. Children's menu. Outdoor dining. Adobe house in park dedicated to arid flora and landscape. Cr cds: A, MC, V.

D

★ ★ ★ **THE VENTANA ROOM.** *7000 N Resort Dr (85750). Phone 520/299-2020; fax 520/299-6832. www.ventanaroom.com.* Intimate and romantic, The Ventana Room offers the perfect balance of rustic charm and upscale elegance. The airy, windowed restaurant is appointed with tall floral arrangements, wine cases, a dramatic front entryway with striking, angled doors, and tables lit with candles of different heights. The restaurant's upper-tier fireplace is open on both sides for warm and cozy dining, and the glass-enclosed room, with southern exposure, offers panoramic views on either side of the lights of Tucson or the Catalina Mountains. The meticulously prepared continental menu stays true to regional ingredients and features wild cuts of game as well as a wide variety of seafood and locally farmed poultry, veal, and lamb, each prepared in harmony with the seasons. For those who love cheese after dinner, the restaurant offers more than 50 imported and domestic cheeses, including several varieties that are made and aged in house. Contemporary American menu. Hours: 6-9 pm; Fri, Sat to 10 pm. Dinner $32-$45. Bar. Valet parking. Totally nonsmoking. Cr cds: A, D, DS, JCB, MC, V.

D

★ ★ ★ **VIVACE.** *4310 N Campbell Rd (85718). Phone 520/795-7221.* Italian menu. Closed Sun; Thanksgiving, Dec 25. Lunch, dinner. Bar. Children's menu. Casual attire. Outdoor seating. Cr cds: A, D, DS, MC, V. **$$**

D

Tumacacori National Historical Park (I-5)

See Nogales, Patagonia, Tucson

(Exit 29 on I-19, 48 miles S of Tucson, 18 miles N of Nogales)

Father Kino, a Jesuit missionary, visited the Pima village of Tumacacori in 1691. Work began on the present historic mission church in 1800. It was completed in 1822, but was abandoned in 1848.

There is a beautiful patio garden and a museum with fine dioramas (daily; closed Thanksgiving, December 25). Self-guided trail; guided tours (December-April, daily; advance notice needed rest of year). There is a fiesta held on the first weekend in December with entertainment, music, and food. Contact the Superintendent, PO Box 67, Tumacacori 85640; Phone 520/398-2341.

Resort

★ ★ **TUBAC GOLF RESORT.** *1 Otero Rd, Tubac (85646). Phone 520/398-2211; fax 520/398-9261.* 46 rooms, 10 kitchens. Mid-Jan-mid-Apr: S, D $140-$150; each additional $15; suites $170-$235; lower rates rest of year. Crib free. TV. Heated pool. Complimentary coffee in rooms. Restaurant 7 am-9 pm. Bar to 10 pm. Checkout noon. Coin laundry. Meeting room. Tennis. 18-hole golf, greens fee $63 (includes cart), pro, putting green, pro shop. Refrigerators. Many fireplaces, private patios. Contemporary Southwest décor. Pool area has mountain view. Credit cards accepted.

🐾 D 🐾 🏊 🐾

Walnut Canyon National Monument (D-4)

(see Flagstaff)

Wickenburg (E-3)

See also Phoenix

Founded 1863 **Pop** 5,082 **Elev** 2,070 ft **Area code** 928

Information Chamber of Commerce, Santa Fe Depot, 216 N Frontier St, 85390; 928/684-5479 or 928/684-0977

Web www.wickenburgchamber.com

Wickenburg was first settled by early Hispanic families who established ranches in the area and traded with the local Native Americans. The town was relatively unpopulated until a Prussian named Henry Wickenburg picked up a rock to throw at a stubborn burro and stumbled onto the richest gold find in Arizona, the Vulture Mine. His find began a $30-million boom and the birth of a town. Today, Wickenburg is the oldest town north of Tucson and is well-known for its area dude ranches.

What to See and Do

Desert Caballeros Western Museum. *21 N Frontier St. Phone 928/684-2272.* Western art gallery; diorama room; street scene (circa 1915); period rooms; mineral display; Native American exhibit. (Daily; closed holidays) **$$**

Frontier Street. *Phone 928/684-5479.* Preserved in early 1900s style. Train depot (houses Chamber of Commerce), brick Hassayampa building (former hotel) and many other historic buildings.

The Jail Tree. *Tegner and Wickenburg Way (85390). Phone 928/684-5479.* This tree was used from 1863-1890 (until the first jail was built) to chain rowdy prisoners. Friends and relatives visited the prisoners and brought picnic lunches. Escapes were unknown.

Little Red Schoolhouse. *245 N Tegner (85390). Four blocks N of Wickenburg Way on Tegner. Phone 928/684-5479.* Pioneer schoolhouse.

Old 761 Santa Fe Steam Locomotive. *At Apache and Tegner, behind Town Hall. Phone 928/684-5479.* This engine and tender ran the track between Chicago and the West.

Special Events

Bluegrass Music Festival. *Bowman Rodeo Grounds. Phone 928/684-5479.* Four-Corner States Championship. Second full weekend in Nov.

Gold Rush Days. *120 N Valentine St (85390). Phone 928/ 684-5479.* Bonanza days revived, with chance to pan for gold and keep all you find. Rodeo; parade. Second full weekend in Feb.

Septiembre Fiesta. *120 N Valentine St (85390). Phone 928/684-5479.* Celebration of Hispanic heritage. First Sat in Sept.

Motels/Motor Lodges

★ ★ **AMERICINN.** *850 E Wickenburg Way (85358). Phone 928/684-5461; toll-free 800/634-3444; fax 928/ 684-5461. www.americinn.com.* 29 rooms, 2 story. Nov-May: S $53-$62; D $59-$68; each additional $6; under 16 free; lower rates rest of year. Crib free. Check-out 11 am. TV; cable (premium). Balconies, private patios, some microwaves. Restaurant 7 am-1:30 pm, 5-8:30 pm; closed Mon. Bar (except Mon). Room service. Heated pool, whirlpool. Business services available. Cr cds: A, C, D, DS, MC, V.

D ⌘ ⌘

★ ★ **BEST WESTERN RANCHO GRANDE.** *293 E Wickenburg Way (85390). Phone 928/684-5445; toll-free 800/ 528-1234; fax 928/684-7380. www.bwranchogrande.com.* 80 rooms, 1-2 story, 24 kitchens Nov-Apr: S $63-$94; D $66-$104; each additional $3; suites $94-$115; higher rates special events; lower rates rest of year. Crib $3. Pet accepted. TV; cable, VCR available (movies). Heated pool; whirlpool. Playground. Complimentary coffee in rooms. Restaurant nearby. Check-out noon. Business services available. Bellstaff. Valet service. Free airport transportation. Tennis. Refrigerators; some bathroom phones, microwaves. Some private patios, balconies. Cr cds: A, C, D, DS, ER, JCB, MC, V.

D ⌘ ⌘ ⌘ ⌘

Guest Ranches

★ ★ **FLYING E RANCH.** *2801 W Wickenburg Way (85390). Phone 928/684-2690; toll-free 888/684-2650; fax 928/684-5304. www.flyingeranch.com.* 17 units. AP (3-day minimum), Nov-Apr: S $145-$185; D $230-$295; each additional $40-$100; family rates. Closed rest of year. Check-out 11 am, check-in varies. TV; VCR available. Refrigerators. Occasional entertainment; square, line dancing. Exercise equipment, sauna. Heated pool. Lighted tennis. Trail rides (fee); hay rides. Business services available. Family-style meals. Breakfast cookouts, chuckwagon dinners. On 20,000-acre cattle ranch in shadow of Vulture Peak. No credit cards accepted. Shuffleboard.

⌘ ⌘ ⌘ ⌘

★ ★ ★ **RANCHO DE LOS CABALLEROS.** *1551 S Vulture Mine Rd (85390). Phone 928/684-5484; toll-free 800/684-5030; fax 928/684-2267. www.sunc.com.* Experience the Old West like never before in this historic guest ranch and golf club. Visit ghost towns and gold mines. Ride in a rodeo and dine by campfire. 79 rooms, 33 kitchen units. AP, Feb-mid-May: S $239-$299; D $379-$439; under 5 free; golf plans; holiday rates; lower rates Oct-Jan. Closed rest of year. Crib free. Check-out 1 pm, check-in 4 pm. TV. Some refrigerators, microwaves. Complimentary coffee in rooms. Coin laundry. Restaurant 7-9 am, 12:30 am-1:30 pm, 6:30-8:30 pm. Bar 10:30 am-midnight; entertainment Wed, Fri, Sat. Box lunches, snacks. Free supervised children's activities; ages 5-12. Playgrounds. Massage. Social/Activities/Sports Director. Pool, poolside service. 18-hole, greens fee $75, putting green, driving range, pro shop. Tennis, pro. Bicycles, hiking, horse stables. Hot air ballooning. Airport transportation. Meeting rooms; Business services available. Bellstaff. Grocery 2 miles. Trap and skeet shooting.

D ⌘ ⌘ ⌘ ⌘ ⌘ ⌘

Willcox (H-6)

See also Safford

Pop 3,733 **Elev** 4,200 ft **Area code** 520 **Zip** 85643

Information Chamber of Commerce, Cochise Information Center, 1500 N Circle I Rd; 520/384-2272 or 800/ 200-2272

What to See and Do

Amerind Foundation. *2100 N Amerind Rd. Approximately 1 mile SW via I-10, exit 318 on Dragoon Rd in Dragoon. Phone 520/586-3666.* Amerind (short for American Indian) Museum contains one of the finest collections of archaeological and ethnological artifacts in the country. Displayed in the art gallery are paintings by Anglo and Native American artists. Picnic area, museum shop. (Sept-May, daily; rest of year, Wed-Sun; closed holidays) **$$**

Chiricahua National Monument. *(32 miles SE of Willcox on AZ 186, then 3 miles E on AZ 181) Phone 520/824-3560.* This national monument features 20 square miles of picturesque natural rock sculptures and deep twisting canyons.

The Chiricahua (Cheer-a-CAH-wah) Apaches hunted in the Chiricahua Mountain range. Cochise, Geronimo, "Big Foot" Massai, and other well-known Apaches undoubtedly found their way into this region during the 1870s and 1880s. A visitor center, 2 miles from the entrance, has geological, zoological, and historical displays. (Daily)

At Massai Point Overlook, geologic exhibits explain the volcanic origin of the monument. The road up Bonita Canyon leads to a number of other outlook points; there are also 20 miles of excellent day-use trails to points of special interest.

Picnicking and camping sites are located within the national monument. Campground/night; 26-foot limit on trailers. Contact Superintendent, HCR #2, Box 6500, Willcox 85643; phone 520/824-3560. **$$$**

Cochise Information Center. *1500 N Circle I Rd. 1 mile N via Circle I Rd just off Fort Grant Rd, exit from I-10. Phone 520/384-2272 or 800/200-2272.* (Daily; closed Jan 1, Thanksgiving, Dec 25) **FREE**

Cochise Stronghold. *1500 N Circle I Rd (85643). SW via I-10 to US 191 S, then W on Ironwood Rd. Phone 520/364-3468.* Rugged canyon once sheltered Chiricahua Apache; unique rock formations provided protection and vantage points. Camping, picnicking; nature, hiking, horseback, and history trails. (Daily)

Fort Bowie National Historic Site. *Apache Pass Rd. 22 miles SE on AZ 186, then 6 miles NE on graded road leading east into Apache Pass and two miles to trailhead, then walk 1 1/2 miles on foot trail to the fort ruins. Phone 520/847-2500.* Visitors pass ruins of Butterfield Stage Station, post cemetery, Apache Spring, and the first Fort Bowie on the way to ruins of the second Fort Bowie. Visitor center. Carry water in summer, beware of flash floods and rattlesnakes. Do not climb on ruins or disturb any of the site's features. **FREE**

The Rex Allen Arizona Cowboy Museum & Cowboy Hall of Fame. *150 N Railroad Ave. Phone 520/384-4583.* Museum dedicated to Willcox-native Rex Allen, the "last of the Silver Screen Cowboys." Details his life from ranch life in Willcox to radio, TV, and movie days. Also special exhibits on pioneer settlers and ranchers. Cowboy Hall of Fame pays tribute to real cattle industry heroes. Gift shop. (Daily; closed Jan 1, Thanksgiving, Dec 25) **$**

Special Events

Rex Allen Days. *150 N Railroad Ave (85643). Phone 520/384-2272.* PRCA Rodeo, concert by Rex Allen, Jr., parade, country fair, Western dances, softball tournament. First weekend in Oct.

Wings Over Willcox/Sandhill Crane Celebration. *1500 N Circle I Rd (85643). Phone 520/384-2272.* Tours of birdwatching areas, trade shows, seminars, workshops. Third weekend in Jan.

Motels/Motor Lodges

★ ★ **BEST WESTERN PLAZA INN.** *1100 W Rex Allen Dr (85643). Phone 520/384-3556; toll-free 800/528-1234; fax 520/384-2679. www.bestwestern.com.* 91 rooms, 2 story. S, D $59-$109; each additional $10; under 12 free. Crib free. Pet accepted, some restrictions; $8. TV; cable. Heated pool. Complimentary full breakfast. Coffee in rooms. Restaurant 6 am-9 pm; Fri, Sat to 10 pm. Room service. Bar 4 pm-1 am. Check-out noon. Coin laundry.

Meeting rooms. Business services available. Many refrigerators. Cr cds: A, C, D, DS, MC, V.

★ **DAYS INN.** *724 N Bisbee Ave (85643). Phone 520/384-4222; toll-free 800/329-7466; fax 520/384-3785. www.daysinn.com.* 73 rooms, 2 story. June-Aug and Nov-Feb: S $40-$42; D $45-$52; each additional $5; under 13 free; lower rates rest of year. Pet accepted, some restrictions; fee. Complimentary continental breakfast. Check-out 11 am. TV; cable (premium). Cr cds: A, C, D, DS, MC, V.

B&B/Small Inn

★ ★ **CHIRICAHUA FOOTHILLS.** *9920 Pinery Canyon Road (85643). Phone 520/824-3632.* 5 air-cooled rooms. No room phones. S, D $70; under 12 free. Complimentary breakfast. Check-out 11 am, check-in 3 pm. 2 TV rooms; VCR available (movies). Totally nonsmoking.

Williams (D-4)

See also Flagstaff, Seligman

Settled 1880 **Pop** 2,842 **Elev** 6,750 ft **Area code** 928 **Zip** 86046

Information Williams-Grand Canyon Chamber of Commerce, 200 W Railroad Ave; 928/635-4061

This town lies at the foot of Bill Williams Mountain (named for an early trapper and guide) and is the principal entrance to the Grand Canyon (see). It is a resort town in the midst of Kaibab National Forest, which has its headquarters here. There are seven small fishing lakes in the surrounding area.

What to See and Do

Grand Canyon National Park. (see). *Hwy 180. Phone 928/638-7888.* **$$$$**

Kaibab National Forest. *Phone 928/635-2681.* More than 1 1/2 million acres; one area surrounds Williams and including Sycamore Canyon and Kendrick Mountain wilderness areas and part of National Historic Rte 66; a second area is 42 miles N on US 180 (AZ 64) near the South Rim of Grand Canyon; a third area lies north of the Grand Canyon (outstanding views of the canyon from seldom-visited vista points in this area) and includes Kanab Creek and Saddle Mountain wilderness areas, the Kaibab Plateau, and the North Rim Parkway National

Scenic Byway. The forest is home for a variety of wildlife unique to this area, including mule deer and the Kaibab squirrel. Fishing (trout); hunting, picnicking, camping (fee). Also located here is

Williams Ski Area. *4 miles S of town, on the N slopes of Bill Williams Mountain. Phone 928/635-9330.* Pomalift, rope tow; patrol, school, rentals; snack bar. Vertical drop 600 feet. (Mid-Dec-Easter, Mon, Thurs-Sun) Sledding slopes and cross-country trails nearby. **$$$$**

Special Events

Bill Williams Rendezvous Days. Black powder shoot, carnival, street dances, pioneer arts and crafts. Memorial Day weekend.

Labor Day Rodeo. *Phone 928/635-4061.* Professional rodeo and Western celebration. Labor Day weekend.

Motels/Motor Lodges

★ **BEST VALUE INN.** *1001 W Rte 66 (86046). Phone 928/635-2202; fax 928/635-9202. www.bestvalueinn.com.* 33 rooms. May-Sept: S $26-$59; D $30-$77; each additional $5; under 12 free; ski plans; lower rates rest of year. Crib $7. Complimentary coffee in lobby. Check-out 11 am. TV; cable (premium). In-room modem link. Refrigerators, microwaves available. Restaurant nearby. Pool. Golf privileges. Downhill ski 4 miles. Grills. Free train station transportation. Business services available. Cr cds: A, DS, MC, V.

★ **BEST WESTERN INN OF WILLIAMS.** *2600 W Rte 66 (86046). Phone 928/635-4400; toll-free 800/635-4445; fax 928/635-4488. www.bestwestern.com.* 79 rooms, 10 suites, 2 story. Mid-May-Aug: S $79-$135; D $89-$135; each additional $10; suites $125-$181; under 12 free; ski plan; lower rates rest of year. Complimentary full breakfast. Check-out noon. TV; cable (premium). In-room modem link. Bar 5-10 pm. Pool, whirlpool. Downhill ski 5 miles. Cr cds: A, C, D, DS, MC, V.

★ **EL RANCHO MOTEL.** *617 E Rte 66 (86046). Phone 928/635-2552; toll-free 800/228-2370; fax 928/635-4173. www.thegrandcanyon.com\elrancho.* 25 rooms, 2 suites, 2 story. Mid-May-Sept: S, D $52-$73; each additional $5; suites $95-$105; lower rates rest of year. Crib $3. Complimentary coffee in rooms. Check-out 11 am. TV; cable (premium), VCR available. Refrigerators, microwaves. Restaurant opposite 6 am-2 pm; 5-10 pm. Heated pool. Downhill ski 4 miles. Cr cds: A, DS, MC, V.

★ ★ **HOLIDAY INN.** *950 N Grand Canyon Blvd (86046). Phone 928/635-4114; toll-free 800/465-4329;* *fax 928/635-2700. www.holiday-inn.com.* 120 rooms, 2 story, 12 suites. S, D $79-$99; each additional $10; suites $99-$119; under 19 free; higher rates holidays; lower rates rest of year. Crib free. Pet accepted. TV; cable. Complimentary coffee in lobby. Restaurant 6-10 am, 5-10 pm; summer hours 6 am-10 pm. Room service. Bar from 5 pm. Check-out 11 am. Meeting room. Business services available. Bellstaff. Gift shop. Coin laundry. Downhill ski 5 miles. Indoor pool; whirlpool. Some refrigerators. Wet bars in suites. Cr cds: A, C, D, DS, JCB, MC, V.

★ **MOTEL 6.** *831 W Bill Williams Ave (86046). Phone 928/635-9000; fax 928/635-2300. www.motel6.com.* 52 rooms, 2 story. June-Sept: S, D $45-$69; each additional $6; under 18 free; higher rates holidays; lower rates rest of year. Crib free. Pet accepted. Check-out 11 am. TV; cable. In-room modem link. Coin laundry. Restaurant opposite 11 am-9 pm. Indoor pool, whirlpool. Business services available. Cr cds: A, D, DS, MC, V.

★ **MOUNTAINSIDE INN.** *642 E Rte 66 (86046). Phone 928/635-4431; fax 928/635-2292. www.mtnsideinn.com.* 96 rooms, 2 story. Apr-Oct: S, D $95-$125; each additional $10; under 18 free; 2-day minimum stay holidays; lower rates rest of year. Crib free. Pet accepted. Check-out noon. TV; cable. Microwaves available. Restaurant 6 am-2 pm, 4-10 pm. Bar. Room service (evening only). Heated pool, whirlpool. Downhill ski 4 miles. Picnic tables. Gift shop. Cr cds: A, D, DS, MC, V.

Resort

★ ★ **FRAY MARCOS HOTEL.** *235 N Grand Canyon Blvd (86046). Phone 928/635-4010; toll-free 800/843-8724; fax 928/635-2180. www.thetrain.com.* 89 rooms, 2 story. Apr-mid-Sept: S, D $79-$119; each additional $10; under 16 free; lower rates rest of year. Crib free. Complimentary coffee in lobby. Check-out 11 am. TV; cable (premium). Restaurant 4-10 pm. Bar. Business services available. Bellstaff. Sundries, gift shop. Cr cds: A, DS, MC, V.

B&B/Small Inn

★ ★ **TERRY RANCH BED AND BREAKFAST.** *701 Quarterhorse Rd (86046). Phone 928/635-4171; toll-free 800/210-5908; fax 928/635-2488. www.terryranchbnb.com.* 4 rooms. No A/C. No room phones. May-Sept: S, D $110-$155; each additional $15; lower rates rest of year. Complimentary full breakfast; afternoon refreshments. Check-out 10 am, check-in 4-6 pm. TV in common room; cable (premium), VCR available (movies). Some in-room fireplaces, whirlpools. Restaurant nearby. Concierge service. Country Victorian log house. Totally nonsmoking. Cr cds: A, DS, MC, V.

Restaurant

★ **ROD'S STEAK HOUSE.** *301 E Bill Williams Ave (86046). Phone 928/635-2671; fax 928/635-9557. www.rods-steakhouse.com.* Specialties: mesquite-broiled steak, prime rib. Hours: 11:30 am-9:30 pm. Closed Thanksgiving, Dec 24, 25. Reservations accepted. Bar. Lunch $3.50-$7.50, dinner $7-$23. Children's menu. Paintings of the Old West, stained-glass windows. Cr cds: MC, V.

Window Rock (C-7)

Pop 3,059 **Elev** 6,880 ft **Area code** 928

Information Navajoland Tourism Department, PO Box 663; 928/871-6436 or 928/871-7371

This is the headquarters of the Navajo Nation. The 88-member tribal council, democratically elected, meets in an octagonal council building; tribal officials conduct tribal business from Window Rock.

Behind the town is a natural bridge that looks like a window. It is in the midst of a colorful group of sandstone formations called "The Window Rock."

What to See and Do

Canyon de Chelly National Monument. (see). *Phone 928/674-5500*

Guided tours of Navajoland. *Phone 928/871-6436.* Various organizations and individuals offer walking and driving tours of the area. Fees and tours vary; phone for information.

Hozhoni Tours. *Phone 520/697-8198.* Contact PO Box 1995, Kayenta 86033.

Roland's Navajo Land Tours. *N Hwy 163 Milepost 394 (86033). Phone 928/697-8198.* Contact PO Box 1995, Kayenta 86033.

Stanley Perry, Step-On Tours. *Phone 520/871-2484* (after 7 pm). Contact PO Box 2381.

Navajo Nation Museum. *HC-71 Box 3. E of junction AZ 264 and Indian Rte 12, on AZ 264 in Navajo Arts & Crafts Enterprise Center. Phone 520/871-6673.* Established in 1961 to preserve Navajo history, art, culture, and natural history; permanent and temporary exhibits. Literature and Navajo Information available. (Mon-Fri; closed tribal and other holidays) **DONATION**

Navajo Nation Zoological and Botanical Park. *E of junction AZ 264 and Indian Rte 12, on AZ 264. Phone 928/871-6573.* Features a representative collection of animals and plants of historical or cultural importance to the Navajo people. (Daily; closed Jan 1, Dec 25) **FREE**

St. Michael's. *S of AZ 264, and 4 mi W of Window Rock. Phone 928/871-4172.* Catholic mission, established in 1898, which has done much for the education and health of the tribe. Original mission building now serves as a museum depicting history of the area. Gift shop. (Memorial Day-Labor Day, daily) **FREE**

Special Events

Navajo Nation Fair. *Navajo Nations Fairgrounds. Phone 928/871-6478.* Navajo traditional song and dance; Intertribal powwow; all-Indian Rodeo; parade; concerts; exhibits. Early Sept.

Pow Wow and PRCA Rodeo. *Navajo Nations Fairgrounds. Phone 928/871-6478.* July 4.

Winslow (D-5)

See also Holbrook, Hopi Indian Reservation, Navajo Indian Reservation

Founded 1880 **Pop** 9,520 **Elev** 4,880 ft **Area code** 928 **Zip** 86047

Information Chamber of Commerce, 300 W North Rd, PO Box 460; 928/289-2434 or 928/289-2435

A railroad town, Winslow is also a trade center and convenient stopping point in the midst of a colorful and intriguing area; a miniature painted desert lies to the northeast. The Apache-Sitgreaves National Forests, with the world's largest stand of ponderosa pine, lie about 25 miles to the south.

What to See and Do

Homolovi Ruins State Park. *N Hwy 87. 3 miles E on I-40, then 1 mile N on AZ 87. Phone 928/289-4106.* This park contains six major Anasazi ruins dating from A.D. 1250-1450. Arizona State Museum conducts occasional excavations (June, July). Trails. Visitor center; interpretive programs. Standard fees. (Daily; closed Dec 25)

Meteor Crater. *I-40 and exit 233 (86002). 20 miles W on I-40, then 5 miles S on Meteor Crater Rd. Phone 928/289-2362.* Crater is one mile from rim to rim and 560 feet deep. The world's best preserved meteorite crater was used as a training site for astronauts. Museum, lecture; Astronaut Wall of Fame; telescope on highest point of the crater's rim offers excellent view of surrounding area. (Daily) **$$$**

Old Trails Museum. *212 N Kinsley Ave. Phone 928/289-5861.* Operated by the Navajo County Historical Society; exhibits and displays of local history, Native American artifacts, and early Americana. (Apr-Oct, Tues-Sat; rest of year, Tues, Thurs, and Sat; closed holidays) **FREE**

Motels/Motor Lodges

★ ★ **BEST WESTERN ADOBE INN.** *1701 N Park Dr (86047). Phone 928/289-4638; fax 928/289-5514. www.bestwestern.com.* 72 rooms, 2 story. June-Aug: S $50-$56; D $54-$58; suites $68; under 18 free; lower rates rest of year. Crib $4. Pet accepted, some restrictions. Check-out 11 am. TV; cable (premium), VCR available. Coin laundry. Restaurant 6 am-2 pm, 4-10 pm; Sun to 9 pm. Bar 4-11 pm, Sun to 10 pm. Room service. Indoor pool, whirlpool. Free airport, train station, bus depot transportation. Meeting rooms. Business services available. Cr cds: A, C, D, DS, MC, V.

◧ ⬧ ▨

★ **ECONO LODGE.** *1706 N Park Dr (86047). Phone 928/289-4687; toll-free 800/228-5050; fax 928/289-9377. www.econolodge.com.* 73 rooms, 2 story. Late May-Sept: S, D $45-$59; under 18 free; lower rates rest of year. Pet accepted; $5 a day. TV; cable (premium), VCR available. Pool. Complimentary coffee in rooms. Check-out 11 am. Coin laundry. Business services available. Some refrigerators, microwaves. Cr cds: A, C, D, DS, JCB, MC, V.

D ◧ ▨ ⬓ SC

Wupatki National Monument (C-5)

See also Flagstaff

(35 miles N of Flagstaff on US 89)

The nearly 2,600 archeological sites of the Sinagua and Anasazi cultures were occupied between 1100 and 1250. The largest of them, Wupatki Pueblo, was three stories high, with about 100 rooms. The eruption of nearby Sunset Crater (see) spread volcanic ash over an 800-square-mile area and for a time made this an active farming center.

The half-mile ruins trail is self-guided; books are available at its starting point. The visitor center and main ruin are open daily (closed December 25). Rangers on duty. Wupatki National Monument and Sunset Crater Volcano National Monument (see) are located on a 35-mile paved loop off of US 89. Nearest camping at Bonito Campground (May-October) *Phone 520/526-0866. Contact the Superintendent, 6400 US 89A, Flagstaff 86004; phone 520/526-1157.*

Yuma (G-1)

Founded 1849 **Pop** 77,515 **Elev** 138 ft **Area code** 928

Information Convention & Visitors Bureau, 377 Main St, PO Box 11059, 85366; 928/783-0071

Web www.visityuma.com

Hernando de Alarcón, working with the Coronado Expedition, passed this point on the Colorado River in 1540. Father Kino came into the area in 1699. Padre Francisco Tomas Garces established a mission in 1780, which was destroyed a year later. The Yuma Crossing, where the Colorado River narrows between the Yuma Territorial Prison and Fort Yuma (one of Arizona's oldest military posts), was made a historic landmark in recognition of its long service as a river crossing for many peoples.

Yuma's air-conditioned stopping places are a great comfort to motorists crossing the desert. If the scenery looks familiar, it may be because movie producers have used the dunes and desert for location shots.

Irrigation from the Colorado River makes it profitable to raise cattle, alfalfa, cotton, melons, lettuce, citrus fruits, and other crops here. A Marine Corps Air Station and an army proving ground are adjacent to the town.

What to See and Do

Arizona Historical Society Sanguinetti House. *240 Madison Ave. Phone 928/782-1841.* Former home of E. F. Sanguinetti, pioneer merchant; now a division of the Arizona Historical Society. Artifacts from Arizona Territory, including documents, photographs, furniture, and clothing. Gardens and exotic birds surround museum. Historical library open by appointment. (Tues-Sat; closed holidays) **FREE**

Fort Yuma-Quechan Museum. *488 S Maiden Ln (85366). Fort Yuma. Phone 619/572-0661.* Part of one of the oldest military posts (1855) associated with the Arizona Territory; offered protection to settlers and secured the Yuma Crossing. Fort Yuma is headquarters for the Quechan Tribe. Museum houses tribal relics of southwestern Colorado River Yuman groups. (Daily; closed holidays) **$**

Imperial National Wildlife Refuge. *100 Red Cloud Mine Rd. 40 miles N via US 95. Phone 928/783-3371.* Bird-watching; photography. Fishing; hunting, hiking. Interpretive center/office (Mon-Fri). **FREE**

Yuma River Tours. *1920 Arizona Ave. Phone 928/783-4400.* Narrated historical tours on the Colorado River; half- and full-day trips. Sunset dinner cruise. Also jeep tours to sand dunes. (Mon-Fri; fees vary)

Yuma Territorial Prison State Historic Park. *1 Prison Hill Rd. Off I-8, Giss Pkwy exit. Phone 928/783-4771.* Remains of 1876 prison; museum, original cell blocks. Southwest artifacts and prison relics. (Daily; closed Dec 25) **$$**

Yuma Valley Railway. *980 S Palm Ave. Levee at 8th St. Phone 928/783-3456.* Tracks run 12 miles through fields along the Colorado River levee and Morelos Dam. Two-hour trips; dinner trips. (Nov-Mar, Sat and Sun; Apr-May, Oct, Sat only; June by appointment only; closed July-Sept) **$$$**

Special Events

Midnight at the Oasis Festival. *Desert Sun Stadium. Phone 928/343-1715.* First full weekend in Mar.

Yuma County Fair. *2520 E 32nd St (85365). Phone 928/726-4420.* Five days in early Apr.

Motels/Motor Lodges

★ **INTERSTATE 8 INN.** *2730 S 4th Ave (85364). Phone 928/726-6110; toll-free 800/821-7465; fax 928/726-7711.* 120 rooms, 2 story. Jan-Mar: S $26-$39; D $34-$56; each additional $6; under 13 free; higher rates special events; lower rates rest of year. Crib free. Pet accepted, some restrictions. Complimentary coffee in lobby. Check-out 11 am. TV; cable (premium), VCR available (movies). Refrigerators, microwaves available. Coin laundry. Restaurant adjacent 6 am-11 pm. Pool, whirlpool. Picnic tables, grills. Business services available. Cr cds: A, C, D, DS, JCB, MC, V.

★ **LA FUENTE INN & SUITES.** *1513 E 16th St (85365). Phone 928/329-1814; fax 928/343-2671. www.lafuenteinn.com.* 50 rooms, 46 suites, 2 story. Jan-May: S $68-$80; D $78-$90; suites $95; under 12 free; higher rates special events; lower rates rest of year. Complimentary continental breakfast. Check-out noon. TV; cable (premium), VCR available (movies). Health club privileges, exercise equipment. Whirlpool. Airport transportation. Near Yuma Airport. Cr cds: A, D, DS, MC, V.

★★ **SHILO INN.** *1550 S Castle Dome Ave (85365). Phone 928/782-9511; toll-free 800/222-2244; fax 928/783-1538. www.shiloinns.com.* 134 rooms, 16 kitchen units, 4 story. S, D $89-$159; each additional $12; kitchen units $109-$260; under 12 free. Crib free. Pet accepted, some restrictions; $10 a day. Complimentary full breakfast. Check-out noon. TV; cable (premium), VCR available. In-room modem link. Balconies, private patios, refrigerators,

microwaves available. Coin laundry. Restaurant 6 am-10 pm. Bar to midnight. Exercise equipment, sauna, steam room. Heated pool, whirlpool, poolside service. Airport transportation. Meeting rooms. Business services available. Cr cds: A, D, DS, MC, V.

★ **YUMA AIRPORT TRAVELODGE.** *711 E 32nd St (85365). Phone 928/726-4721; toll-free 800/835-1132; fax 928/344-0452. www.travelodge.com.* 80 rooms, 2 story. S $54; D $62; each additional $5; suites $78; under 14 free; higher rates special events (2-day minimum); lower rates rest of year. Crib free. Pet accepted, some restrictions; $25 deposit. Complimentary continental breakfast, coffee in rooms. Check-out noon. TV; cable (premium), VCR available (movies). Refrigerators, microwaves available. Wet bar in suites. Coin laundry. Restaurant 11 am-10 pm. Bar. Health club privileges. Whirlpool; pool. Picnic tables, grills. Business services available. Cr cds: A, C, D, DS, JCB, MC, V.

All Suites

★★ **BEST WESTERN INN SUITES.** *1450 S Castle Dome Ave (85365). Phone 928/783-8341; toll-free 800/922-2034; fax 928/783-1349. www.bestwestern.com.* 166 rooms. Jan-Apr: S, D $99; 2-room suites $94-$139; under 20 free; higher rates opening week dove season; lower rates rest of year. Crib free. Pet accepted. Complimentary continental breakfast. Check-out noon. TV; cable (premium), VCR available. In-room modem link. Refrigerators, microwaves, coffee in rooms. Valet services, coin laundry. Exercise equipment. Heated pool, whirlpool. Lighted tennis. Business center. Library. Cr cds: A, C, D, DS, MC, V.

★ **RADISSON SUITES INN.** *2600 S 4th Ave (85364). Phone 928/726-4830; fax 928/341-1152. www.radisson.com.* 164 suites, 13 story. Oct-Apr: S $106; D $116; each additional $10; under 16 free; lower rates rest of year. Pet accepted. Complimentary continental breakfast. Check-out noon. TV; cable (premium). Health club privileges. Whirlpool. Free airport transportation. Cr cds: A, C, D, DS, ER, JCB, MC, V.

Restaurants

★ **THE CROSSING.** *2690 S 4th Ave (85364). Phone 928/726-5551; fax 928/726-6064.* Italian, American menu. Specialties: in prime rib, catfish, buffalo wings. Hours: 11 am-9:30 pm; Sun to 8:30 pm. Lunch, dinner $3.95-$14.95. Beer, wine. Children's menu. Casual dining. Reservations accepted. Cr cds: A, C, DS, MC, V.

★★ **HUNTER STEAKHOUSE.** *2355 S 4th Ave (85364).* Phone 928/782-3637; fax 928/329-8129. Hours: 11:30 am-2 pm, 5-9 pm; Sat, Sun from 4 pm. Early-bird dinner Mon-Sat 5-6 pm, Sun 4-6 pm. Closed Dec 25. Bar to 11 pm. Lunch $5-$8, dinner $10-$30. Children's menu. Specializes in beef, steak, fresh seafood. Reservations accepted. Cr cds: A, C, D, DS, ER, MC, V.

★★ **MANDARIN PALACE.** *350 E 32nd St (85364).* Phone 928/344-2805; fax 928/344-1350. Hours: 11 am-10 pm; Fri, Sat to 11 pm. Chinese, American menu. Bar. A la carte entrees: lunch $5.50-$6.95, dinner $7.25-$24.95. Specializes in crispy beef a la Szechwan, rainbow shrimp, crispy Mandarin duck. Elegant Oriental décor. Reservations accepted. Cr cds: A, C, D, DS, ER, MC, V.

D

After exploring the Phoenix area, head over to California to check out one of the most interesting national parks in the United States: Joshua Tree. The park preserves sections of two deserts, the Mojave and the Colorado, with terrain ranging from mountains to desert flats. The temperature also ranges from sweltering in the summer to freezing in the winter. This is a fine of example of extremes.

Joshua Tree National Park, CA

5 hours, 300 miles from Phoenix, AZ

(Entrances: 25 miles E of Indio on I-10 or S of Joshua Tree, Yucca Valley, and Twentynine Palms on CA 62)

Covering more than 1,236 square miles, this park preserves a section of two deserts: the Mojave and the Colorado. Particularly notable are the variety and richness of desert vegetation. The park shelters many species of desert plants. The Joshua tree, which gives the park its name, was christened by the Mormons because of its upstretched "arms." A member of the Lily family, this giant yucca attains heights of more than 40 feet. The area consists of a series of block mountains ranging in altitude from 1,000 to 5,800 feet and separated by desert flats. The summer gets

very hot, and the temperature drops below freezing in the winter. Water is available only at the Black Rock Canyon Visitor Center/Campground, Cottonwood Campground, the Indian Cove Ranger Station, and the Twenty-nine Palms Visitor Center. Pets are permitted on leash only; pets are not allowed on trails. Guided tours and campfire programs (Feb-May and Oct-Dec). Picnicking is permitted in designated areas and campgrounds, but no fires may be built outside the campgrounds. For additional information, contact *74485 National Park Dr. Twentynine Palms, 92277; Phone 760/367-5500.*

What to See and Do

Camping. Restricted to nine campgrounds with limited facilities; bring own firewood and water. Thirty-day limit, July-Sept; 14-day limit rest of year. Cottonwood, Black Rock Canyon, and Indian Cove Campgrounds (fee); other campgrounds free. Group camping at Cottonwood, Indian Cove, and Sheep Pass. Campgrounds are operated on a first-come, first-served basis except for Indian Cove, Sheep Pass, and Black Rock Canyon. Phone 800/365-2267.

Hidden Valley Nature Trail. One-mile loop; access from picnic area across Hidden Valley Campground. Valley enclosed by wall of rocks.

Keys View. (5,185 feet) Sweeping view of Coachella valley, desert, and mountain. A paved path leads off the main road.

Lost Palms Canyon. Eight-mile round-trip hike. Reached by four-mile trail from Cottonwood Spring. Shelters largest group of palms (120) in the park. Day use only.

⭐ **Oasis Visitor Center.** *Park headquarters, just N of park at Twentynine Palms entrance.* Exhibits; self-guided nature trail through the Oasis of Mara, discovered by a government survey party in 1855. (Daily)

Strands of Joshua Trees. In Queen and Lost Horse valleys.

Special Event

Pioneer Days. *Twentynine Palms, 5 mi N.* Phone 760/367-3445. Carnival, parade, rodeo, food, games. Third weekend in Oct.

Motels/Motor Lodges

★★ **BEST WESTERN GARDEN INN & SUITES.** *71487 Twentynine Palms Hwy (92277).* Phone 760/367-9141; fax 760/367-2584. www.bestwestern.com. 84 rooms, 2 story, 12 kitchen suites. S, D $79-$85; each additional $10; kitchen suites $98-$119; under 12 free. Crib free. Pet accepted, some restrictions; $10 a day. TV. Heated pool; whirlpool. Complimentary continental breakfast. Restaurant nearby. Check-out 11 am. Business services available. In-room modem link. Exercise room. Refrigerators, microwaves. Grill. Cr cds: A, C, D, DS, MC, V.

⊡ ⬛ ⬛ ⬛ ⬛

★★ **CIRCLE C LODGE.** *6340 El Rey Ave (92277). Phone 760/367-7615; fax 760/361-0247. www. circleclodge.com.* 12 kitchen units. S $74; D $90; each additional $10; under 15 free. Pet accepted; $10/day. TV; cable (premium), VCR. Heated pool; whirlpool. Continental breakfast. Restaurant nearby. Check-out 11 am. Meeting room. Business services available. Refrigerators, microwaves. Picnic tables, grills. Cr cds: A, D, DS, MC, V.

⬛ ⬛ ⬛ ⬛

Hotel

★★ **OASIS OF EDEN INN & SUITES.** *56377 29 Palms Hwy (92284). Phone 760/365-6321; toll-free 800/606-6686; fax 760/365-9592. www.oasisofeden.com.* 39 rooms, 14 theme rooms, 1-2 story, 6 kitchen units. Jan-May: S, D $59-$89; each additional $5; kitchen units $69-$99; theme rooms $99-$299; family, weekly, monthly rates; lower rates rest of year. Crib free. Pet accepted, some restrictions; $10. Complimentary continental breakfast. Check-out 11 am. TV; cable (premium), VCR available (movies). Microwaves available. Theme rooms with refrigerators, VCR, in-room whirlpools. Restaurant opposite 7 am-10 pm. Heated pool, whirlpool. Meeting rooms. Business services. Cr cds: A, C, D, DS, ER, JCB, MC, V.

⊡ ⬛ ⬛ ⬛ ⬛ **SC**

B&B/Small Inns

★★ **JOSHUA TREE INN.** *61259 29 Palms Hwy (92252). Phone 760/366-1188; fax 760/366-3805. www.joshuatreeinn.com.* 10 rooms, shower only, 1 with A/C, 2 suites. Oct-mid-June: S $95; suites $145; each additional $10; under 10 free; lower rates rest of year. Pet accepted, some restrictions; $10. Complimentary breakfast. Check-out 11 am, check-in 3 pm. TV; cable (premium), VCR available. Some refrigerators. Microwaves available. Pool. Business services. Concierge. Cr cds: A, C, D, DS, MC, V.

⬛ ⬛ ⬛

Colorado

From the eastern plains westward through the highest Rockies, Colorado's terrain is diverse, fascinating, and spectacularly beautiful. The highest state in the Union, with an average elevation of 6,800 feet and with 53 peaks above 14,000 feet, Colorado attracts sports enthusiasts and vacationers as well as high-technology research and business.

When gold was discovered near present-day Denver in 1858, an avalanche of settlers poured into the state; when silver was discovered soon afterward, a new flood came. Mining camps, usually crude tent cities clinging to the rugged slopes of the Rockies, contributed to Colorado's colorful, robust history. Some of these mines still operate, but most of the early mining camps are ghost towns today. Thousands of newcomers arrive yearly, drawn to Colorado's Rockies by the skiing, hunting, fishing, and magnificent scenery.

Throughout the state there are deep gorges, rainbow-colored canyons, mysterious mesas, and other strange and beautiful landmass variations carved by ancient glaciers and eons of erosion by wind, rain, and water. Great mountains of shifting sand lie trapped by the Sangre de Cristo Mountains in Great Sand Dunes National Monument (see also); fossils 140 million years old lie in the quarries of Dinosaur National Monument (see also).

Spaniards penetrated the area by the mid-1500s. American exploration of the area first took place in 1806, three years after a good portion of the region became American property through the Louisiana Purchase. The leader of the party was Lieutenant Zebulon M. Pike, for whom Pikes Peak is named. Pike pronounced the 14,110-foot mountain unclimbable. Today, one may drive to the top on a good gravel highway (first 5 miles paved). Colorado became a territory in 1861 and earned its "Centennial State" nickname by becoming a state in 1876, 100 years after the signing of the Declaration of Independence.

Colorado produces more tin, molybdenum, uranium, granite, sandstone, and basalt than any other state. The

Population: 4,301,261
Area: 104,100 square miles
Elevation: 3,350-14,433 feet
Peak: Mount Elbert (Lake County)
Entered Union: August 1, 1876 (38th state)
Capital: Denver
Motto: Nothing without providence
Nickname: Centennial State, Silver State
Flower: Rocky Mountain Columbine
Bird: Lark Bunting
Tree: Colorado Blue Spruce
Fair: August in Pueblo
Time Zone: Mountain
Website: www.colorado.com

mountain area also ranks high in production of coal, gold, and silver; the state as a whole has vast deposits of brick clay and oil. Its extensively irrigated plateaus and plains are good grazing lands for stock and rich producers of potatoes, wheat, corn, sugar beets, cauliflower, fruit, and flowers.

When to Go/Climate

Most of Colorado falls in a semiarid climate zone. Springs are short; summers are dry. Winters are surprisingly mild along the Front Range, but annual snowfall in the mountains often exceeds 20 feet.

AVERAGE HIGH/LOW TEMPERATURES (°F)

Colorado Springs

Jan 41/16	May 69/42	Sept 74/47
Feb 45/19	June 79/51	Oct 64/36
Mar 50/25	July 84/57	Nov 51/25
Apr 60/33	Aug 81/55	Dec 42/17

Denver

Jan 43/16	May 71/44	Sept 77/48
Feb 47/20	June 81/52	Oct 66/36
Mar 52/26	July 88/59	Nov 53/25
Apr 62/35	Aug 86/57	Dec 45/17

Calendar Highlights

JANUARY

National Western Livestock Show, Horse Show & Rodeo (Denver). National Western Complex and Coliseum. Phone 303/297-1166.

Winterskol Carnival (Aspen). Phone 970/925-1940. Parade, fireworks, skiing, and ice skating.

MAY

Bolder Boulder (Boulder). Phone 303/444-7223. Ten-kilometer race. Includes a citizens race and world-class heats.

JUNE

FIBArk River International Whitewater Boat Race (Salida). Phone 719/539-2068. 26-mile kayak race. Other events include slalom, raft, foot, and bicycle races.

Colorado Stampede (Grand Junction). Phone 970/245-7723. Rodeo.

AUGUST

Pikes Peak Marathon (Colorado Springs). Phone 719/473-2625. Footrace on Barr's Trail from cog depot to the top of Pikes Peak and back.

Jazz (Telluride). Phone 800/525-3455. Town Park and local nightclubs. Mainstream jazz with international flavors, performed in various locales throughout the city.

Boulder County Fair & Rodeo (Longmont). Fairgrounds. Phone 303/441-3927.

Colorado State Fair (Pueblo). Phone 800/876-4567. Fairgrounds, Prairie Ave. PRCA rodeo, grandstand and amphitheater entertainment, livestock and agricultural displays, industrial and high technology displays, arts and crafts, and a carnival.

SEPTEMBER

Vintage Auto Race & Concours d'Elegance (Steamboat Springs). Phone 970/879-3120. Mt Werner Circle and downtown. Vintage auto racing, exhibition of restored vintage automobiles, and an art show of works by automotive artists.

Telluride Airmen's Rendezvous & Hang Gliding Festival (Telluride). Pilots phone 970/728-5793. Pilots converge on Telluride for a week of hang gliding and paragliding. Climax is the World Aerobatic Hang Gliding Championship in Town Park.

Parks and Recreation

Water-related activities, hiking, riding, various other sports, picnicking, and visitor centers, as well as camping, are available in many of Colorado's parks. Interpretive and watchable wildlife programs are available as well. A parks pass is required, good for driver and passengers; annual pass, $50; 1-day pass, $3-$6/car. Passes are available at self-service dispensers at all state parks and park offices. Camping is available in most parks. Reservations can be made by phoning 303/470-1144 or 800/678-2267 from 8 am to 4:30 pm, Mon-Fri. Reservations cost $7 and a campground fee of $6-$16 is charged, depending on the services offered. Electrical hookups are $5-$8 per night.

Fishing, camping, and picnicking are possible in most parks. For further information or a free Colorado State Parks Guide, contact Colorado State Parks, 1313 Sherman #618, Denver 80203; phone 303/866-3437.

FISHING AND HUNTING

Nonresident fishing licenses: annual $40.25; 5-day, $18.25; 1-day, $5.25; additional 1-day stamp, $5; second-rod stamp, $4. Many varieties of trout can be found in Colorado: rainbow and brown in most streams, lakes, and western Colorado River, brook in all mountain streams, and cutthroat in most mountain lakes. Mackinaw can be found in many lakes and reservoirs. Kokanee salmon are also found in many reservoirs.

Nonresident hunting licenses: elk, $250.25; deer, $150.25; small game, $40.25. For information about regulations, write to the Division of Wildlife, 6060 Broadway, Denver 80216; or phone 303/297-1192.

Driving Information

Safety belts are mandatory for all persons in the front seat of a vehicle. Children under 4 years and under 40 pounds in weight must be in approved safety seats anywhere in the vehicle. Phone 303/239-4500 for more information.

INTERSTATE HIGHWAY SYSTEM

The following alphabetical listing of Colorado towns in this book shows that these cities are within 10 miles of the indicated interstate highways. Check a highway map for the nearest exit.

Highway Number	Cities/Towns within 10 Miles
Interstate 25	Colorado Springs, Denver, Englewood, Fort Collins, Lakewood, Longmont, Loveland, Manitou Springs, Pueblo, Trinidad, Walsenburg.
Interstate 70	Breckenridge, Burlington, Central City, Denver, Dillon, Evergreen, Georgetown, Glenwood Springs, Golden, Grand Junction, Idaho Springs, Lakewood, Limon, Vail.
Interstate 76	Denver, Fort Morgan, Sterling.

Additional Visitor Information

Colorado Outdoors magazine is published six times a year by the State Department of Wildlife, 6060 Broadway, Denver 80216; phone 303/297-1192. *Colorado, Official State Vacation Guide* is available from the Colorado Travel & Tourism Authority, PO Box 3524, Englewood 80155; phone 800/COLORADO. A pamphlet on guest ranches is available from the Colorado Dude & Guest Ranch Association, PO Box 2120, Granby 80446; phone 970/724-3653.

Seven welcome centers in Colorado provide brochures and travel information. They are located at I-70 westbound in Burlington, I-70 eastbound in Fruita, US 40 eastbound in Dinosaur, I-25 northbound in Trinidad, US 160/666 northbound in Cortez, US 50 westbound in Lamar, and I-76 westbound in Julesburg.

Gold mining towns abound in Colorado, as they do in many western states. Though not all towns can be reached by passenger cars, Colorado has developed the Jeep tour to great advantage. Information about ghost towns and Jeep trips is listed under Breckenridge, Gunnison, Ouray, Salida, and Silverton.

COLORADO'S GOLD MINES

The San Juan Skyway is a spectacular scenic 236-mile loop out of Durango that ranges over five mountain passes as it wanders through the San Juan Mountains. From Durango, head west on US 160 to Hesperus, where you can take a side trip into La Plata Canyon to see mining ruins and a few ghost towns. Continuing west, you'll pass Mesa Verde National Park and come to CO 145 shortly before Cortez. Head north to the town of Dolores and the Anasazi Heritage Center, which features a large display of artifacts, most more than 1,000 years old. The road now follows the Dolores River, a favorite of trout anglers, and climbs the 10,222-foot Lizard Head Pass, named for the imposing rock spire looming overhead. Descending from the pass, take a short side trip into Telluride, a historic mining town and ski resort nestled in a beautiful box canyon. Follow the San Miguel River valley to CO 62, and turn north to cross the 8,970-foot Dallas Divide. After the historic railroad town of Ridgway and Ridgway State Park, where you might stop for a swim or picnic, turn south on US 550 and drive to Ouray, a picturesque old mining town. Continue over the 11,008-foot Red Mountain Pass; there is a monument here dedicated to snowplow operators who died while trying to keep the road open during winter storms. Next stop is Silverton, a small mining town and the northern terminus of the Durango and Silverton Narrow Gauge Railroad. South of Silverton is the 10,910-foot Molas Divide, after which the road almost parallels the rails as they follow the Animas River back to Durango. This tour can be done in one long day by those who want to see only the mountain scenery, but is better over two or three days, with stops at Mesa Verde National Park and the historic towns along the way.

(Approximately 236 miles)

Alamosa (F-5)

See also Monte Vista

Founded 1878 **Pop** 7,960 **Elev** 7,544 ft **Area code** 719 **Zip** 81101

Information Alamosa County Chamber of Commerce, Cole Park; 719/589-3681 or 800/BLU-SKYS

Web www.alamosachamber.com

The settlers who came to the center of the vast San Luis Valley were pleased to find a protected area on the Rio Grande shaded by cottonwood trees and named their new home Alamosa, Spanish for "cottonwood." The little town quickly became a rail, agricultural, mining, and educational center. A Ranger District office of the Rio Grande National Forest (see SOUTH FORK) is located in La Jara, 14 miles south on US 285.

What to See and Do

Cole Park. *425 4th St, on Rio Grande River.* Old Denver and Rio Grande Western narrow-gauge train on display. Chamber of Commerce located in old train station. Tennis, bicycle trails, picnicking, playgrounds. **FREE**

Cumbres & Toltec Scenic Railroad, Colorado Limited. *500 S Terrace Ave (87520). 28 miles S in Antonito. Contact Box 789, Chama, NM 87520, 505/756-2151; or Box 668, Antonito, CO 81120, 719/376-5483.* Round-trip excursion to Osier on 1880s narrow-gauge steam railroad. Route passes through backwoods country and mountain scenery, including the Phantom Canyon and the Toltec Gorge. Warm clothing advised due to sudden weather changes. (Memorial Day-mid-Oct, daily) Also trips to Chama, NM, via the **New Mexico Express** with van return. Reservations advised. **$$$$**

Fort Garland Museum. *25 miles E on US 159 at Fort Garland. Phone 719/379-3512.* Army post (1858-1883) where Kit Carson held his last command. Restored officers' quarters; collection of Hispanic folk art. (Apr-Oct, daily; rest of year, Mon, Thurs-Sun) **$$**

Great Sand Dunes National Monument (see). *Phone 505/479-6124. 9 miles on Rte 145 just outside East Durham.*

Special Events

Early Iron Festival. *425 4th St (81101). Phone 719/589-6077.* Auto show. Labor Day weekend.

Sunshine Festival. *425 5th St (81101). Phone 719/589-6077. Cole Park.* Arts, crafts, food booths, bands, horse rides, parade, pancake breakfast, contests. First full weekend in June.

Motels/Motor Lodges

★★ **BEST WESTERN INN.** *1919 Main St (81101). Phone 719/589-2567; toll-free 800/459-5123; fax 719/589-0767. www.bestwestern.com/alamosainn.* 53 rooms, 2 story. Pet accepted, some restrictions. Complimentary continental breakfast. Check-out 11 am, check-in 2 pm. TV; cable (premium). Restaurant, bar. Indoor pool, whirlpool. Airport transportation. Cr cds: A, C, D, DS, MC, V. **$**

D 🐾 ☒ ✈ ☒

★★ **HOLIDAY INN.** *333 Santa Fe Ave (81101). Phone 719/589-5833; toll-free 800/669-1658; fax 719/589-4412. www.holiday-inn.com.* 126 rooms, 2 story. Pet accepted. Check-out noon, check-in 3 pm. TV; VCR available. In-room modem link. Restaurant, bar. Room service. Sauna. Game room. Indoor pool, whirlpool. Airport transportation. Business center. Cr cds: A, D, DS, JCB, MC, V. **$**

D 🐾 ☒ ☒ 🚶

B&B/Small Inns

★★★ **COTTONWOOD INN.** *123 San Juan Ave (81101). Phone 719/589-3882; toll-free 800/955-2623; fax 719/589-6437. www.cottonwoodinn.com.* With easy access to Sedona and the Grand Canyon, this inn features a lovely courtyard setting. 10 rooms, 2 story. Pet accepted. Complimentary continental breakfast. Check-out 11 am, check-in 4 pm. TV. Whirlpool. Totally nonsmoking. Cr cds: A, DS, MC, V. **$**

🐾 ☒

Restaurant

★ **TRUE GRITS STEAKHOUSE.** *100 Santa Fe Ave (81101). Phone 719/589-9954.* Steak menu. Closed Thanksgiving, Dec 25. Lunch, dinner. Bar. Children's menu. Casual attire. John Wayne memorabilia. Cr cds: DS, MC, V. **$$**

D

Aspen (D-4)

See also Snowmass Village

Settled 1879 **Pop** 5,914 **Elev** 7,908 ft **Area code** 970 **Zip** 81611

Information Aspen Chamber Resort Association, 425 Rio Grande Place; 970/925-1940 or 800/26-ASPEN

Web www.aspen.com

Seven great silver mines made Aspen a booming camp of 12,000 in 1893. From the Molly Gibson Mine came a nugget of 93 percent pure silver that weighed 1,840 pounds. The boom ended with the collapse of silver prices in the early 1890s. Aspen nearly became a ghost town when the population at one time dropped to about 700. Largely through the efforts of Walter P. Paepcke, a Chicago industrialist, the city experienced a rebirth as a recreational and cultural center in the late 1940s. Today's resident population is reinforced by thousands of visitors each year. A Ranger District office of the White River National Forest (see GLENWOOD SPRINGS) is located in Aspen.

What to See and Do

Ashcroft Ghost Town. *620 W Bleeker St. 10 miles S. Phone 970/925-3721.* Partially restored ghost town and mining camp features 1880s buildings, hotel. Guided tours (June-Aug 11 am and 2 pm, daily) Self-guided tours available daily. **$$**

Aspen Highlands. *1 1/2 miles SW on Maroon Creek Rd in White River National Forest (see GLENWOOD SPRINGS). Phone 970/925-1220 or toll-free 800/525-6200.* Three quad, triple chairlift; patrol, school, rentals, snowmaking; three restaurants, bar. One hundred twelve runs; longest run 3 1/2 miles; vertical drop 3,635 feet. (Dec-mid-Apr, daily) Snowboarding. Shuttle bus service to and from Aspen. Half-day rates.

Aspen Mountain. *55 E Durant Ave (81611). Phone 970/925-1220; 800/525-6200.* Three quad, four double chairlifts; gondola; patrol, school, snowmaking; restaurants, bars. Seventy-six runs; longest run 3 miles; vertical drop 3,267 feet. (Dec-mid-Apr, daily) Shuttle bus service to Buttermilk, Aspen Highlands, and Snowmass. **$$$$**

Blazing Adventures. *407 E Hyman Ave (81611). Phone 800/282-7238.* Half-day, full-day, and overnight river rafting trips on the Arkansas, Roaring Fork, Colorado, and Gunnison rivers. Trips range from scenic floats for beginners to exciting runs for experienced rafters. (May-Oct; reservations required) Transportation to site. **$$$$**

Buttermilk. *806 W Hallam (81611). 2 miles W on CO 82. Phone 800/525-6200; 970/925-1221.* Quad, five double chairlifts, surface lift; patrol, school, rentals, snowmaking; cafeteria, restaurants, bar, nursery. Forty-three runs; longest run 3 miles; vertical drop 2,030 feet. Snowboarding. (Dec-mid-Apr, daily) Shuttle bus service from Ajax and Snowmass. **$$$$**

HeritageAspen. *620 W Bleeker St. Phone 970/925-3721. www.aspenhistory.org.* Exhibits depict Aspen area history. (Early June-Sept and mid-Dec-mid-Apr, Tues-Fri; rest of year by appointment; closed Dec 25) **$$$$**

Independence Pass. *Rte 82 from US 24 to Aspen. Phone 970/925-3445.* A route to be shunned if you are afraid of heights, Route 82 through Independence Pass is, nevertheless, a spectacular visual treat, not to mention an adrenaline rush. The winding, cliff-hanging road between US 24 and Aspen is among the nation's highest, reaching 12,095 feet at its rocky summit. It offers beautiful vistas of Colorado's

majestic forests and snow-covered peaks at every hair-raising turn. Stop at the top for the views and a short trail hike. The pass is closed between Nov and May.

Recreation. Swimming, fishing, river rafting; hunting (deer, elk), hiking, climbing, horseback riding, golf, tennis, ice skating, camping, pack trips, kayaking, hanggliding, paragliding, sailplaning, and ballooning. There are 1,000 miles of trout streams and 25 lakes within a 20-mile radius of Aspen, plus many more in the surrounding mountains. More than 10 public campgrounds. Contact the Aspen Chamber Resort Association for details.

Snowmass. *12 miles NW (see SNOWMASS VILLAGE).*

Special Events

Aspen Music Festival. *2 Music School Rd (81611). Phone 970/925-3254.* Aspen Music Tent, Wheeler Opera House, and Harris Concert Hall. Symphonies, chamber music concerts, opera, and jazz. June-Aug.

Aspen Theater in the Park. *2 Music School Rd (81611). Phone 970/925-3254.* Performances nightly and afternoons. June-Aug.

Winterskol Carnival. *N Mill St (81611). Phone 970/925-1940.* Mid-Jan.

Motel/Motor Lodge

★★ **INNSBRUCK INN.** *233 W Main St (81611). Phone 970/925-2980; fax 970/925-6960. www.preferred lodging.com.* 30 rooms, some A/C, 2 kitchen units, 2 story. Mid-Nov-mid-Apr: S, D $139-$399; each additional $20; under 16, $10; higher rates during the Christmas holidays; lower rates rest of year. Pet accepted. Complimentary continental breakfast. Check-out 11 am, check-in 3 pm. TV; cable (premium), VCR available. In-room modem link. Restaurant nearby. Whirlpool. Downhill, cross-country ski 1/2 mile. Cr cds: A, D, DS, MC, V.

Hotels

★ **ASPEN MOUNTAIN LODGE.** *311 W Main St (81611). Phone 970/925-7650; fax 970/925-5744. www. aspenmountainlodge.com.* 38 rooms, 4 story. No elevator. Closed late Apr-mid-May. Pet accepted. Complimentary buffet breakfast. Check-out 11 am, check-in 4 pm. TV. In-room modem link. Outdoor pool, whirlpool. Downhill, cross-country ski 6 blocks. Four-story river rock fireplace. Cr cds: A, D, DS, MC, V.

★★ **ASPEN SQUARE CONDOMINIUM HOTEL.** *617 E Cooper Ave (81611). Phone 970/925-1000; toll-free 800/862-7736; fax 970/925-1017. www.aspensquarehotel. com.* 104 air-cooled condo apartments with kitchen,

3-4 story. Late Nov-Apr: S, D $165-$295; each additional (after fourth person) $15; under 12 free; higher rates at Christmas time; lower rates rest of year. Check-out 10 am, check-in 4 pm. TV; cable (premium), VCR available. In-room modem link. Fireplaces. Restaurant adjacent 7:30 am-3:30 pm. Health club privileges, exercise equipment. Whirlpool. Downhill ski adjacent, cross-country ski 1 mile. Cr cds: A, MC, V.

★ ★ **HOTEL ASPEN.** *110 W Main St (81611). Phone 970/925-3441; toll-free 800/527-7369; fax 970/920-1379. www.aspen.com/ha.* 45 rooms, 2-3 story. No elevator. Mid-Feb-late-Mar: S, D $149-$399; each additional $20; under 13 free; higher rates holidays; lower rates rest of year. Pet accepted; $20/day. Complimentary continental breakfast. Check-out 11 am, check-in 4 pm. TV; cable (premium), VCR available. In-room modem link. Fireplaces. Health club privileges. Whirlpool. Downhill ski 8 blocks. Free ski shuttle. Parking $1/day. Totally nonsmoking. Cr cds: A, D, DS, MC, V.

★ ★ ★ **HOTEL JEROME.** *330 E Main St (81611). Phone 970/920-1000; toll-free 800/331-7213; fax 970/925-2784. www.hoteljerome.com.* Built to rival the Ritz in Paris, the Hotel Jerome has been an Aspen landmark since 1889. Located in the heart of downtown, this historic hotel is within walking distance of the town's boutiques and restaurants, yet only minutes from the slopes (with complimentary transportation a nice bonus). Guests feel cosseted here; the general concierge meets every demand, and the ski concierge assists with rentals, tickets, and insight on the trails. The boutique-style rooms are magnificent, reflecting the hotel's Victorian heritage with carved armoires and beautiful beds. Every amenity is supplied here, and after a long day of skiing or hiking, guests appreciate the extra touches. From the fabric-covered banquettes to the stained-glass ceiling, the Century Room restaurant embodies the best of the Victorian age. The dashing J Bar, a popular watering hole since the 1890s, is still one of the hottest places in town. 91 rooms, 3-4 story. Pet accepted. Parking. Check-out 11 am, check-in 4 pm. TV; cable (premium), VCR (movies fee). In-room modem link. Room service 24 hours. Restaurant, bar. Babysitting services available. In-house fitness room, massage. Pool, whirlpool, poolside service. Downhill ski 4 blocks, cross-country ski 1 mile. Free airport transportation. Concierge. Cr cds: A, D, MC, V. **$$$$**

★ ★ **MOLLY GIBSON LODGE.** *101 W Main St (81611). Phone 970/925-3434; toll-free 800/356-6559; fax 970/925-2582. www.mollygibson.com.* 58 rooms, 2 story. Feb-Mar: S, D $95-$425; each additional $10; lower rates rest of year. Complimentary continental breakfast. Check-out 10 am, check-in 3 pm. TV; cable (premium),

VCR (movies). In-room modem link. Some fireplaces. Restaurant nearby. Bar 4-9 pm in winter. Exercise equipment. Downhill, cross-country ski 6 blocks. Free bicycle rentals. Free airport transportation. Business center. Cr cds: A, C, D, DS, MC, V.

★ ★ ★ ★ **THE ST. REGIS, ASPEN.** *315 E Dean St (81611). Phone 970/920-3300; toll-free 888/454-9005; fax 970/925-8998. www.stregisaspen.com.* The St. Regis radiates luxury in its superb location at the base of Aspen Mountain. From its elegant interpretation of Western style to its white-glove service, this hotel is the very definition of refinement. Memorable skiing is guaranteed here, with a terrific location between the gondola and lift, gracious shuttles from door to door, and easy transportation to nearby Aspen Highlands, Buttermilk Mountain, and Snowmass. Aspen's picture-perfect vistas attract hikers, while its clear streams appeal to anglers. The sparkling outdoor pool and accompanying lounge are ideal for whiling away warm afternoons. Well-heeled guests succumb to the sumptuous accommodations, where overstuffed leather chairs and stunning appointments create cocoonlike shelters. Guests beat a path to Olives (see also OLIVES), where renowned chef Todd English creates his inspired dishes from the Mediterranean. Live entertainment is enjoyed in the Lobby Lounge, and Whiskey Rocks is a hip gathering place, perfect after a long day spent in the great outdoors. 257 rooms, 6 story. Closed late Oct-mid-Nov. Pet accepted. Valet parking. Check-out noon, check-in 3 pm. TV; cable (premium), VCR available (movies). In-room modem link. Room service 24 hours. Restaurant, bar; entertainment. Babysitting services available. In-house fitness room, sauna, steam room, massage. Outdoor pool, children's pool, whirlpool, poolside service (summer). Downhill ski 1 block, cross-country ski 1 1/2 miles. Bicycles, hiking. Business center. Concierge. Luxury level. Cr cds: A, C, D, DS, JCB, MC, V. **$$$**

Resorts

★ ★ ★ **ASPEN MEADOWS.** *845 Meadows Rd (81611). Phone 970/925-4240; toll-free 800/452-4240; fax 970/925-7790. www.dolce.com.* Six buildings are nestled into this 40-acre mountain retreat, host to leaders from around the world since 1949. Touted as a nonprofit and nonpartisan forum for exchanging ideas, the Institute has a graceful, Bauhaus-inspired style. 98 suites. No A/C. Check-out 11 am, check-in 4 pm. TV; cable (premium), VCR (movies, fee). In-room modem link. Coin laundry. Restaurant. Room service. Babysitting services available. In-house fitness room, Massage. Steam room. Outdoor pool, whirlpool. 18-hole golf privileges. Outdoor tennis. Downhill skiing, cross-country skiing. Mountain bike rentals. Parking. Free airport transportation. Business center. Cr cds: A, C, D, DS, MC, V.

★ **LIMELITE LODGE.** 228 E Cooper St (81611). Phone 970/925-3025; toll-free 800/433-0832; fax 970/925-5120. www.aspen.com/limelite. 63 rooms, 1-3 story. No elevator. Mid-Dec-Mar: D $137-$147; each additional $15; kitchen units $118-$350; under 12 free; ski plans; higher rates holidays; lower rates rest of year. Pet accepted. Complimentary continental breakfast. Check-out 11 am. TV; cable (premium), VCR available. In-room modem link. Sauna. 2 whirlpools. Downhill ski 3 blocks. Cr cds: A, C, D, DS, MC, V.

★ ★ ★ ★ ★ **THE LITTLE NELL.** 675 E Durant Ave (81611). Phone 970/920-4600; toll-free 800/525-6200; fax 970/920-6345. www.thelittlenell.com. Tucked away at the base of a mountain, The Little Nell provides its guests with a perfect location either to hit the slopes for a day of skiing or to pound the streets in search of Aspen's latest fashions. Offering unparalleled luxury, it captures the essence of an elegant private hideaway while maintaining the services usually associated with larger resorts. Romantic in winter, The Little Nell delights visitors throughout the year with its European savoir faire and breathtaking views. The rooms and suites are heavenly cocoons with fireplaces, overstuffed furniture, and luxurious bathrooms. Some suites feature vaulted ceilings showcasing glorious mountainside views, while others overlook the charming former mining town. A well-equipped fitness center challenges guests to vigorous workouts, while the outdoor pool and Jacuzzi soothe tired muscles. The Little Nell's Montagna (see also MONTAGNA) is one of the hottest tables in town with its inventive reinterpretation of American cuisine. 92 rooms, 4 story. Closed late Apr-mid-May. Pet accepted. Check-out noon, check-in 4 pm. TV; cable (premium), VCR available. In-room modem link. Fireplaces. Restaurant, bar; entertainment. In-house fitness room, massage, steam room. Outdoor pool, children's pool, whirlpool, poolside service. Downhill ski on site. Parking. Free airport transportation. Business center. Concierge. Cr cds: A, D, DS, ER, MC, V. **$$$$**

B&B/Small Inns

★ **BOOMERANG LODGE.** 500 W Hopkins Ave (81611). Phone 970/925-3416; toll-free 800/992-8852; fax 970/925-3314. www.boomeranglodge.com. 34 rooms, 2-3 story. Complimentary continental breakfast. Check-out 11 am. Check-in 3 pm. TV; VCR available. In-room modem link. Fireplaces. Guest laundry. Sauna. Outdoor pool, children's pool, whirlpool. Downhill, cross-country ski 5 blocks. Cr cds: A, D, DS, MC, V. **$$**

★ ★ ★ **HOTEL LENADO.** 200 S Aspen St (81611). Phone 970/925-6246; toll-free 800/321-3457; fax 970/925-3840. www.hotellenado.com. Located in the heart of Aspen, this hotel offers personalized touches and a comfortable retreat for travelers year-round. Four-poster beds adorn each room. 19 rooms, 3 story. D $425-$485. Pet accepted; fee. Complimentary full breakfast (in season), continental breakfast (off season). Check-out noon, check-in 4 pm. TV; cable (premium), VCR available. In-room modem link. Bar 4 pm-midnight. Downhill, cross-country ski 6 blocks. Cr cds: A, D, MC, V.

★ ★ ★ **INN AT ASPEN.** 38750 Hwy 82 (81611). Phone 970/925-1500; toll-free 800/952-1515; fax 970/925-9037. www.eastwestresorts.com. This inn is located at the base of Buttermilk Mountain. 144 rooms, 2 story. D $109-$349; each additional $20; under 12 free. Check-out 11 am, check-in 4 pm. TV; cable; VCR available. Restaurant 7 am-10 pm. Bar. Exercise room. Pool. Golf, 18 holes. Downhill skiing. Hiking trail. Free airport transportation. Cr cds: A, D, DS, MC, V.

Restaurants

★ ★ **AJAX TAVERN.** 685 E Durant (81611). Phone 970/920-9333. www.ajaxtavern.com. At the foot of the gondola, this restaurant features a seasonal menu. Italian, seafood menu. Closed mid-Apr-mid-May. Lunch, dinner. Bar. Casual attire. Valet parking available. Outdoor seating. Cr cds: A, C, D, DS, MC, V. **$$$**

★ **BOOGIE'S DINER.** 534 E Cooper Ave (81611). Phone 970/925-6610; fax 970/920-1560. www.boogiesaspen.com. Closed mid-Apr-mid-June. Lunch, dinner. Bar. Children's menu. Casual attire. Cr cds: A, MC, V. **$$**

★ ★ **CANTINA.** 411 E Main St (81611). Phone 970/925-3663. Mexican menu. Lunch, dinner. Bar. Children's menu. Casual attire. Outdoor dining. Cr cds: A, D, DS, MC, V. **$$**

★ ★ ★ **JIMMY'S AN AMERICAN RESTAURANT.** 205 S Mill St (81611). Phone 970/925-6020; fax 970/925-6048. American menu. Closed Thanksgiving, Dec 25. Dinner. Bar. Children's menu. Casual attire. Reservations accepted. Outdoor seating. Totally nonsmoking. Cr cds: A, MC, V. **$$$**

★ ★ **LA COCINA.** *308 E Hopkins (81611). Phone 970/ 925-9714.* Mexican menu. Closed Dec 25; also mid-Apr-mid June. Dinner. Bar. Children's menu. Outdoor seating. Cr cds: MC, V. **$**

★ ★ **L'HOSTARIA.** *620 E Hyman Ave (81611). Phone 970/925-9022; fax 970/925-5868. www.lhostaria.com.* Italian menu. Closed mid-Apr-mid May. Dinner. Bar. Children's menu. Casual attire. Reservations required. Outdoor dining. Cr cds: A, D, MC, V. **$$$**

D

★ ★ **MATSUHISA.** *303 E Main St (81611). Phone 970/544-6628; fax 970/544-6630.* This outpost of Nobu Matsuhisa's LA sushi-shrine is every bit as good as the original; amazing given that it is 9,000 feet above sea level. Creative dishes reflect a thoughtful mind, and the service is arguably among the best in town. Japanese menu. Dinner. Bar. Casual attire. Cr cds: A, D, DS, MC, V. **$$$$**

D

★ ★ **MEZZALUNA.** *624 E Cooper Ave (81611). Phone 970/925-5882; fax 970/925-3423. www.mezzalunaaspen.com.* Italian menu. Lunch, dinner. Entertainment. Casual attire. Reservations accepted. Cr cds: A, D, DS, MC, V. **$$$**

D

★ ★ ★ ★ **MONTAGNA.** *675 E Durant Ave (81611). Phone 970/920-6313; fax 970/920-4670. www.thelittlenell. com.* The Little Nell is one of the most picturesque spots in Aspen, filled with guests who are often as stunning to look at as the breathtaking views of the mountains (see also THE LITTLE NELL). It's no surprise, then, that The Little Nell's contemporary American restaurant, Montagna, is a coveted dining spot. With its glossy, buttery walls, rustic wood, iron chandeliers, and deep picture windows, the restaurant has the feeling of chic Swiss chalet. The food is perfect for satiating post-ski hunger pangs, and the staff will graciously accommodate any special requests. The wine service is especially attentive and is sensitive to the high-altitude effects of alcohol. Montagna has the ability to be simultaneously casual and elegant, proving itself equally appropriate for a family gathering or a romantic meal. American menu. Closed late Apr-mid-May. Dinner, Sun brunch. Bar. Children's menu. Casual attire. Valet parking. Outdoor seating. Cr cds: A, D, DS, MC, V. **$$$**

D

★ ★ **MOTHERLODE.** *314 E Hyman Ave (81611). Phone 970/925-7700; fax 970/925-7197. www.mother loderestaurant.com.* Italian, seafood menu. Closed mid-Apr-June. Dinner. Bar. Casual attire. Outdoor seating. Cr cds: A, C, D, DS, MC, V. **$$**

D

★ ★ ★ **OLIVES.** *315 E Dean St (81611). Phone 970/ 920-7356; toll-free 888/920-7356. www.stregisaspen.com.* Located in the St. Regis Hotel and featuring famed Boston chef Todd English's Mediterranean-influenced cuisine, this casually elegant restaurant is alive with warm woods, rich fabrics, and an open kitchen. Stellar entrées include pecorino-stuffed lamb ribs with mushroom bordelaise and creamy polenta. Lunch $9.75-$19, dinner $20-$35. Children's menu. Reservations accepted. Cr cds: A, C, D, DS, MC, V.

D ✉

★ ★ **PACIFICA.** *307 S Mill St (81611). Phone 970/ 920-9775; fax 970/920-9773.* Lunch, dinner. Bar. Children's menu. Outdoor seating. Cr cds: A, MC, V. **$$**

D

★ ★ ★ **PINE CREEK COOKHOUSE.** *12500 Castle Creek Rd (81611). Phone 970/925-1044; fax 970/ 925-7939. www.pinecreekcookhouse.com.* American, Continental/wildgame menu. Closed mid-Apr-mid June, mid-Sept-mid-Nov. Lunch, dinner. Bar. Unique dining in cabin located in a scenic valley in the Elk Mountains (elevation 9,800 feet); overlooks Castle Creek. Casual attire. Reservations required. Outdoor seating. Totally nonsmoking. Cr cds: A, MC, V. **$$$$**

✉

★ ★ ★ **PIÑON'S.** *105 S Mill St (81611). Phone 970/ 920-2021.* If you find yourself having dinner at Piñon's, make a point of stopping for a moment between sumptuous bites of the restaurant's wonderfully prepared American fare to express your thanks to the person at your table responsible for making your reservation. Sincere gratitude is required because a place at a table at Piñon's is one of the most sought-after seats in Aspen. Hidden away on the second floor of a shop in downtown Aspen, the restaurant is light, contemporary, and decorated in a tropical theme. The service is warm; the innovative, seasonal menu approachable; and the music upbeat and festive, perfect for lively conversation of the personal or business variety. American menu. Closed early Apr-early June, Oct-Nov. Dinner. Bar. Casual attire. Totally nonsmoking. Cr cds: A, MC, V. **$$$**

D ✉

★ ★ ★ ★ **RENAISSANCE.** *304 E Hopkins (81611). Phone 970/925-2402; fax 970/925-6634. www.renaissance restaurant.com.* "Cuisine of the Moment" is the theme of Renaissance, a warm, elegant, and acclaimed restaurant that allows and encourages diners to focus on the art of eating. Renaissance offers both an a la carte menu and a tasting menu, each featuring chef-owner Charles Dale's distinctive brand of inventive regional American fare. The menus change daily, treating diners to a taste of the day's best produce, fowl, game, and seafood. Signatures include the Colorado corn chowder with king crab and potato hash, and the Renaissance chocolate soufflé. American menu. Closed mid-Apr-May. Dinner. Bar. Children's menu. Casual attire. Outdoor seating. Cr cds: A, D, MC, V. **$$$$**

D

★ ★ ★ **RESTAURANT CONUNDRUM.** *325 E Main St (81611). Phone 970/925-9969; fax 970/925-7808. Flavorful, stylish, appealing, delicious,* and *wow* are words that come to mind when describing the menu here. Closed mid-Apr-May. Dinner. Bar. Casual attire. Reservations required. Outdoor seating. Cr cds: A, MC, V. **$$**

D

★ ★ ★ **SYZYGY.** *520 E Hyman Ave (81611). Phone 970/925-3700; fax 970/925-5593.* American menu. Closed mid-Apr-May. Dinner. Bar. Children's menu. Casual attire. Cr cds: A, D, DS, MC, V. **$$$**

D

★ ★ **TAKAH SUSHI.** *420 E Hyman Ave (81611). Phone 970/925-8588; fax 970/925-4255. www.takahsushi.com.* Japanese/ Sushi. Closed Thanksgiving; mid Apr-May, late Oct-late Nov. Dinner. Bar. Children's menu. Cr cds: A, D, DS, MC, V. **$$**

★ ★ **UTE CITY.** *501 E Hyman Ave (81611). Phone 970/920-4699; fax 970/544-9463.* Bar 11:30-2 am. Lunch $8.25-$12.25, dinner $15-$42. Specialties: crab cakes, wild game, home-smoked salmon. Cr cds: A, DS, MC, V. **$$**

D

★ ★ **WIENERSTUBE.** *633 E Hyman Ave (81611). Phone 970/925-3357; fax 970/925-2572.* Austrian/ American menu. Closed Mon. Breakfast, lunch. Bar. Children's menu. Cr cds: A, C, D, DS, MC, V. **$$**

D

Avon

Resorts

★ ★ ★ ★ **THE RITZ-CARLTON, BACHELOR GULCH.** *0130 Daybreak Ridge (81620). Phone 970/748-6200; toll-free 800/241-3333; fax 970 748-6300. www.ritzcarlton.com.* Rugged meets refined at The Ritz-Carlton, Bachelor Gulch. From the doorman who greets you with a ten-gallon hat and sweeping capelike coat to the rustic great room, this resort captures the spirit of the Old West while incorporating the polished style that is synonymous with Ritz-Carlton hotels. Located at the base of the mountain at Beaver Creek, this resort offers a true alpine getaway. The rooms are comfortably stylish. Leather chairs and fireplaces highlight the rustic elegance of the resort. The public spaces proudly show off their Western roots with iron chandeliers and twig furnishings. Attentive and friendly, the service at The Ritz-Carlton is exemplary. 237 rooms. Eight story. Some fireplaces. Pet accepted. Valet parking. Check-out 12, check-in 3. TV; cable (premium). In-room modem link. Room service, 24 hours. Restaurant. Bar. Babysitting services available. In-house fitness room, spa. Outdoor pool, poolside service. Downhill and cross-country skiing. Business center. Concierge. Cr cds: A, C, D, DS, ER, JCB, MC, V. **$$$$**

D

Black Canyon of the Gunnison National Monument (E-2)

See also Montrose

(15 miles NE of Montrose via US 50, CO 347)

Within this monument, 12 of the most spectacular miles of the rugged gorge of the Gunnison River slice down to a maximum depth of 2,660 feet.

Piñon trees, some more than 800 years old, add to the spectacular scenery, along with numerous mule deer. There are scenic drives along the South Rim (the road is plowed to Gunnison Point in winter) and the North Rim (approximately May-Oct). There are also hiking areas and concessions (June-Labor Day). The visitor center is located at Gunnison Point on the South Rim. A descent into the canyon requires a free hiking permit from the visitor center. Cross-country skiing is open in winter. Contact the Superintendent, 102 Elk Creek, Gunnison 81230; phone 970/641-2337. Per vehicle **$**

Black Hawk

What to See and Do

Black Hawk Casino by Hyatt. *1 mile N of Central City, 30 miles W of Denver on Hwy 119. Phone 303/567-1234.* Once a boom-to-bust mining town, Black Hawk is experiencing a new rush of fortune-seekers with the 1990 introduction of limited-stakes gambling in Colorado. Of the 25 casinos that have taken up residence in Black Hawk and nearby Central City, the 55,000-square-foot Black Hawk by Hyatt is by far the largest and most elaborate. Boasting 1,332 slot machines and video poker terminals, 22 poker and blackjack game tables, and 3 restaurants, the property is centered around a 5,000-square-foot circular lounge with 7-story, 2-sided fireplaces; a circular bar; and a stage for live entertainment. Other fees vary by game. (Daily) **FREE**

Boulder (C-5)

See also Denver, Longmont, Lyons

Settled 1858 **Pop** 94,673 **Elev** 5,344 ft **Area code** 303

Information Convention & Visitors Bureau, 2440 Pearl St, 80302; 303/442-2911 or 800/444-0447

Web www.ci.boulder.co.us

This is the only city in the United States that obtains part of its water supply from a city-owned glacier, Arapaho Glacier, 28 miles west. Boulder's location at the head of a rich agricultural valley and the base of the Rocky Mountains gives it an ideal year-round climate. The city's unique greenbelt system serves as both a buffer to preserve its picturesque setting and as an extensive park system for outdoor enthusiasts.

Considered the technical and scientific center of Colorado, Boulder is home to the laboratories of the National Institute of Standards and Technology, the National Center for Atmospheric Research, and many private high-tech companies.

Like many cities in Colorado, Boulder enjoys a wealth of cultural activity, including a symphony, music and dance festivals, and outdoor performances of Shakespeare on summer evenings.

A Ranger District office of the Roosevelt National Forest (see ESTES PARK) is located in Boulder.

What to See and Do

Boulder Creek Path. *From 55th St and Pearl Pkwy to Boulder Canyon. Phone 303/413-7200.* A nature and exercise trail that runs some 16 miles through the city and into the adjacent mountains, with no street crossings, leading past a sculpture garden, restored steam locomotive, and several city parks. (Daily) **FREE**

Boulder History Museum. *Harbeck House (1899), 1206 Euclid Ave. Phone 303/449-3464.* Collections of Boulder history from 1858 to the present including 20,000 artifacts, 111,000 photographs, and 486,000 documents; permanent and rotating interpretive exhibits; and educa-

tional programs. (Tues-Fri 10 am-4 pm; Sat, Sun noon-4 pm) **$$**

Boulder Museum of Contemporary Art. *1750 13th St. Phone 303/443-2122.* Exhibits of contemporary and regional painting, sculpture, and other media; experimental performance series (Thurs, fee); changing exhibits with local, domestic, and international artists. Lectures, workshops, and special events. (Tues-Sun; closed holidays) **$$**

Boulder Reservoir. *5100 51st St (80301). 2 miles N on CO 119. Phone 303/441-3461; 303/441-3468.* Swimming (Memorial Day-Labor Day, daily), waterskiing, fishing, boating (daily; get permit for power boat at main gate), rentals; picnicking. (Daily) **$$**

Celestial Seasonings Industrial Tour. *4600 Sleepytime Dr. Phone 303/530-5300.* This maker of herbal and black teas gives tours covering the history of the company, its product line, and a walk-through of the manufacturing plant.

Eldora Mountain Resort. *2861 Eldora Ski Rd #140 (80466). 21 miles W on CO 119 near Nederland. Phone 303/440-8700.* Two quad, two triple, four double chairlifts; four surface lifts; patrol, school, rentals, snowmaking; cafeteria, bar, nursery. Fifty-three runs; longest run 3 miles; vertical drop 1,400 feet. (Mid-Nov-early Apr) Cross-country skiing (27 miles). **$$$$**

Leanin' Tree Museum of Western Art. *6055 Longbow Dr. Phone 303/530-1442.* Museum displaying the original works of art used in many of the greeting cards produced by Leanin' Tree, a major greeting card publisher. (Daily) **FREE**

National Center for Atmospheric Research. *1850 Table Mesa Dr. Phone 303/497-1174 (recording).* Designed by I. M. Pei. Exhibits on global warming, weather, the sun, aviation hazards, and supercomputing. Also a 400-acre nature preserve on site. Guided tours (summer, Mon-Sat afternoons; rest of year, Wed). (Daily) **FREE**

Pearl Street Mall. *900 to 1500 Pearl St (80302). Phone 303/449-3774.* At Pearl Street Mall, locals and visitors gather to enjoy the unique character—and some of the unique characters—of Boulder. Open year-round, this open-air retail and restaurant district is particularly appealing in the summer with its brick walkways, Victorian storefronts, lush landscaping, and parade of colorful personalities. Offering four blocks of mostly upscale restaurants, galleries, bars, and boutiques, the mall beckons visitors to conclude a day of shopping with a meal, al fresco, at one of its many European-style cafés while taking in the impromptu performances of street musicians, jugglers, artists, and mimes.

University of Colorado. *914 Broadway St (80302). Phone 303/492-1411.* (1876) 25,000 students. Tours of campus. Also here are

Fiske Planetarium and Science Center. *914 Broadway St (80302).* Phone 303/492-5001. Programs using a new computerized control system giving a three-dimensional effect; science classes for all ages, special events (fees). Lobby exhibits. **$$$**

Macky Auditorium Concert Hall. *17th St and University Ave.* Phone 303/492-6309. Artist Series, guest artists, Boulder Philharmonic Orchestra. Concerts during the academic year.

Sommers-Bausch Observatory. *914 Broadway St.* Phone 303/492-6732. Stargazing. (Weather permitting, school year; closed school holidays) Reservations required Fri. **FREE**

University of Colorado Museum. *Broadway and 15th St, in Henderson Building.* Phone 303/492-6892. Displays relics and artifacts of early human life in the area, plus regional geological, zoological, and botanical collections. Changing exhibits. (Daily; closed school holidays) **FREE**

Special Events

Bolder Boulder. *4571 Broadway St (80304).* Phone 303/444-7223. Whether you are one of the 45,000 racers or among the 100,000 spectators, just being in Boulder on Memorial Day is a chance to be part one of the largest road races in the world. The popular 10K Bolder Boulder race through town and the surrounding neighborhoods draws participants of all abilities, from professional runners vying for a prize purse to casual walkers enjoying the race-day festivities and camaraderie. Live music and entertainment along the route add to the enjoyment of this family-centered celebration. Memorial Day. **$**

Boulder Bach Festival. *St (80306).* Phone 303/494-3159. Concerts of the music of Johann Sebastian Bach. Late Jan.

Colorado Music Festival. *1525 Spruce St (80302).* Phone 303/449-1397. Entertainment, lectures. Eight weeks in June-Aug.

Colorado Shakespeare Festival. *4780 Pearl E Cir (80301).* Phone 303/492-7355. Mary Rippon Outdoor Theater, University of Colorado. Three Shakespeare plays in repertory. June-Aug.

Kinetic Conveyance Sculpture Challenge. *2500 Pearl St (80302).* Phone 303/444-5600. People-powered sculpture race across land and water. Early May.

Motels/Motor Lodges

★ ★ **COURTYARD BY MARRIOTT.** *4710 Pearl E Cir (80301).* Phone 303/440-4700; fax 303/440-8975. www.courtyard.com. 161 rooms, 3 story. May-Oct: S, D $139-$159; suites $155-$179; under 12 free; weekly rates; lower rates rest of year. Check-out noon, check-in 3 pm. TV; cable (premium). In-room modem link. Restaurant 6:30-10 am, 6-10 pm; Fri to 10 am, Sat to 11 am; Sun 7 am-noon, 6-10 pm. Bar 5-10:30 pm. Exercise equipment. Heated indoor pool, whirlpool. Airport transportation. Cr cds: A, C, D, DS, JCB, MC, V.

⊡ ≈ ⋊ ⊠

★ **HAMPTON INN.** *912 W Dillon Rd (80027).* Phone 303/666-7700; fax 303/666-7374. www.stonebridgecompanies .com. 80 rooms, 3 story. Late May-Sept: S, D $89-$109; each additional $10; under 18 free; higher rates special events; lower rates rest of year. Crib free. Complimentary continental breakfast. Complimentary coffee in rooms. Check-out 11 am. TV; cable (premium). In-room modem link. Refrigerators, microwaves, bathroom phones. Valet services, coin laundry. Restaurant nearby. Exercise equipment. Indoor pool, whirlpool. Airport transportation. Meeting rooms. Business center. Cr cds: A, C, D, DS, JCB, MC, V.

⊡ ≈ ⋊ ⊠ **SC** ⋊

Hotels

★ ★ **BOULDER BROKER INN.** *555 30th St (80303).* Phone 303/444-3330; toll-free 800/338-5407; fax 303/444-6444. www.boulderbrokerinn.com. The Victorian-style guest rooms of this small inn are spacious and bright. Close to the University of Colorado. 118 rooms, 4 story. May-Sept: S, D $75-$159; each additional $6; suites $199-$299; under 18 free; weekend rates; lower rates rest of year. Crib free. Pet accepted. Complimentary breakfast Mon-Fri. Check-out noon. TV; cable (premium). In-room modem link. Refrigerators available. Bathroom phone in suites. Coffee in rooms. Valet services. Restaurant 6:30-10:30 am, 11 am-2 pm, 5-10 pm; Sat-Sun from 7:30 am. Bar 11-2 am, Sun to midnight; entertainment. Room service. Health club privileges. Heated pool, whirlpool, poolside service. Airport transportation. Meeting rooms. Business center. Bellhops. Concierge. Cr cds: A, C, D, DS, MC, V.

⊡ ⋐ ≈ ⊠ **SC** ⋊

★ ★ ★ **HOTEL BOULDERADO.** *2115 13th St (80302).* Phone 303/442-4344; toll-free 800/433-4344; fax 303/442-4378. www.boulderado.com. This historic hotel in downtown Boulder was built in 1909 and has been fully restored and modernized. 160 rooms, 5 story. S $135-$185; D $235-$325; each additional $12; suites $275; under 12 free. Crib free. Check-out 11 am. TV; cable (premium), VCR available. In-room modem link. Some balconies. Many refrigerators. Coffee in rooms. Valet services, coin laundry. Restaurant (see Q's). Bar 10:30-1 am; entertainment. Room service. Health club privileges. Meeting rooms. Business center. Bellhops. Gift shop. Authentic Victorian furnishings. Cr cds: A, C, D, DS, ER, JCB, MC, V.

⊡ ⊠ ⋊

★ ★ ★ **MARRIOTT BOULDER.** *2660 Canyon Blvd (80302).* Phone 303/440-8877. www.marriott.com. 155

rooms, 5 story. S, D $179-$209; under 18 free. Check-out noon, check-in 4 pm. TV; cable (premium). In-room modem link. Restaurant 6:30 am-10 pm. Bar to midnight. Room service. Exercise equipment. Heated indoor pool, whirlpool. Valet parking. Business center. Concierge. Cr cds: A, C, D, DS, ER, JCB, MC, V.

⬛ 🏊 🏋 📶 🏃

★ ★ ★ **MILLENNIUM HARVEST HOUSE.** *1345 28th St (80302). Phone 303/443-3850; toll-free 800/545-6285; fax 303/443-1480.* Overlooking the Rockies, this mountain lodge supplies both comfort and elegance. Just 40 miles from Denver, it is convenient to many business destinations such as the University of Colorado, as well as many tourist attractions. 277 rooms, 4-5 story. S, D $130-$230; suites $220-$550; family rates. Check-out noon, check-in 3 pm. TV; cable (premium), VCR available. In-room modem link. Coffee in lobby. Restaurant 6:30 am-10 pm. Bar 5-11 pm. Exercise equipment. Children's pool, whirlpool, poolside service. Tennis on premise. Lawn games. Business center. Cr cds: A, C, D, DS, JCB, MC, V.

⬛ 🎾 🏊 🏋 📶 🏃

B&B/Small Inns

★ ★ ★ **ALPS BORDER CANYON INN.** *38619 Boulder Canyon Dr (80302). Phone 303/444-5445; toll-free 800/414-2577; fax 303/444-5522. www.alpsinn.com.* Located five minutes from downtown Boulder, this charming inn was originally built in the 1870s and reopened in 1983. The rooms are all charmingly appointed with furniture brought over from Scotland and England. From the antique furnishings to the Victorian fireplace and stained-glass windows, guests will experience a truly unique and delightful stay. 12 rooms, 2 story. No A/C. S, D $119-$225; each additional $35; lower rates Jan-May. Children over 12 years only. Complimentary full breakfast, refreshments in sitting room. Check-out 11 am, check-in 4-9 pm. TV in sitting room; cable (premium), VCR (movies). In-room modem link. Some balconies, in-room whirlpools. Fireplaces, many antiques. Restaurant nearby. Game room. Downhill, cross-country ski 18 miles. Hiking trails. Business services. Totally nonsmoking. Cr cds: A, C, D, DS, MC, V.

🏂 📶

★ ★ **BRIAR ROSE BED & BREAKFAST.** *2151 Arapahoe Ave (80302). Phone 303/442-3007; fax 303/786-8440. www.briarrosebb.com.* Feel right at home in this beautiful bed-and-breakfast. Each room is individually decorated with antique appointments, and a stroll through the gardens is like a stroll back through time. 9 rooms, 8 A/C, 2 story. May-Dec: S $90-$165; D $165-$199; each additional $15; lower rates rest of year. Children over 6 years only; $15, Crib available. Complimentary continental breakfast, afternoon refreshments. Check-out noon, check-in 3-9 pm. TV in living room.

In-room modem link. Some balconies, fireplaces. Business services. English country-style home (1897). Totally nonsmoking. Cr cds: A, C, D, MC, V.

🛄 📶 📶

★ **SANDY POINT INN.** *6485 Twin Lakes Rd (80301). Phone 303/530-2939; toll-free 800/322-2939; fax 303/530-9101. www.sandypointinn.com.* 35 kitchen units, 2 story. June-Aug: D $89-$99; each additional $10; under 12 free; weekly rates; higher rates special events; lower rates rest of year. Complimentary continental breakfast. Check-out 11 am, check-in 3 pm. TV; cable (premium), VCR available. In-room modem link. Restaurant nearby. Health club privileges. Totally nonsmoking. Cr cds: A, D, DS, ER, MC, V.

⬛ 📶 **SC**

Extended Stay

★ **RESIDENCE INN BY MARRIOTT.** *3030 Center Green Dr (80301). Phone 303/449-5545; toll-free 800/331-3131; fax 303/449-2452. www.residenceinn.com.* 224 suites, 2 story. S, D $89-$220; weekly rates. Pet accepted; $50 (nonrefundable). Complimentary continental breakfast. Check-out noon. Check-in 3 pm. TV; cable (premium). In-room modem link. Some fireplaces. Health club privileges. Whirlpool. Lighted tennis. Cr cds: A, C, D, DS, ER, JCB, MC, V.

⬛ 🐾 🎾 📶

Restaurants

★ **ANTICA ROMA CAFFE.** *1308 Pearl St (80302). Phone 303/442-0378; fax 303/449-3876. www.anticaroma.com.* Italian menu. Hours: 11:30 am-3:30 pm, 5-10 pm. Closed Dec 25. Bar. A la carte entrées: lunch $4-$8, dinner $10-$18. Children's menu. Specialties: il cioppino, saltimbocca alla romana, frutti di mare. Entertainment Tues. Outdoor dining. Totally nonsmoking. Cr cds: A, D, DS, MC, V.

⬛ 📶

★ ★ **EUROPEAN CAFE.** *2460 Arapahoe (80302). Phone 303/938-8250; fax 303/444-8770.* American, French menu. Hours: 11 am-2 pm; 5:30-10 pm; Sat from 5:30 pm. Closed Sun, Memorial Day, July 4, Labor Day. Dinner $14-$26. Casual attire. Cr cds: A, MC, V.

⬛

★ ★ ★ **FLAGSTAFF HOUSE RESTAURANT.** *1138 Flagstaff Rd (80302). Phone 303/442-4640; fax 303/442-8924. www.flagstaffhouse.com.* From its perch on Flagstaff Mountain, the Flagstaff House Restaurant is easily one of the most amazing spots to watch the sun drift down the horizon in an orange haze. But try to tear your eyes away from the view to check out what's on your plate: it's worth a look and then some. The wine list is massive (the restaurant has a 20,000-bottle wine cellar), so enlist the assistance of the attentive sommelier for guidance. The upscale and inspired menu changes daily and is impressive in style and substance. Classic plates like beef Wellington dressed up with black truffle sauce share menu space with more modern, global dishes like Hawaiian ono with ginger, scallions, and soft-shell crabs. The restaurant is owned by the Monette family, which means that dining here is a delight from start to finish, as you are pampered with refined service and homegrown hospitality. If you can, plan on arriving early and have a seat at the stunning mahogany bar for a pre-dinner cocktail. American menu. Hours: 5-10 pm. Closed holidays. Dinner $24-$52; prix fixe $65. Bar 5 pm-midnight. Valet parking. Cr cds: A, D, DS, MC, V.

D

★ ★ **FULL MOON GRILL.** *2525 Arapahoe Ave (80302). Phone 303/938-8800; fax 303/938-5926. www.fullmoongrill.com.* Northern Italian menu. Hours: 11:30 am-2 pm, 5-9:30 pm; Fri to 10 pm; Sat 5-10 pm; Sun 5-9:30 pm. Closed most major holidays. Reservations accepted. Bar. Lunch $7.95-$10.95, dinner $9.95-$19.95. Specializes in fresh seafood, pasta. Outdoor dining. Contemporary atmosphere. Totally nonsmoking. Cr cds: A, DS, MC, V.

D

★ ★ ★ **THE GREENBRIAR INN.** *8735 N Foothills Hwy (US 36) (80302). Phone 303/440-7979; fax 303/449-2054. www.greenbriarinn.com.* This restaurant offers a gourmet getaway in a mountainside setting. Hours: 5-10 pm; Sun brunch 11 am-2:30 pm. Closed Mon; Jan 1. Reservations accepted. Bar to 2 am. Wine list. A la carte entrées: dinner $18-$32. Sun brunch $20. Specialties: rack of Colorado lamb, fresh seafood, venison. Patio dining. Gardens. Cr cds: A, C, D, MC, V.

D

★ ★ ★ **JOHN'S RESTAURANT.** *2328 Pearl St (80302). Phone 303/444-5232. www.johnsrestaurantboulder. com.* Open for dinner Tues-Sat, this restaurant features classic and contemporary dishes from France, Italy, Spain, and America. Their specials include smoked Scottish salmon, filet mignon with Stilton and ale sauce, and for dessert, Italian-style gelato. Continental menu. Hours: 5:30-10 pm. Closed Sun, Mon, July 4, Dec 25. Reservations accepted. Service bar. Dinner $15.50-$24. Own sauces, ice cream. Located in cottage. Totally nonsmoking. Cr cds: A, DS, MC, V.

D

★ ★ **LAUDISIO.** *2785 Iris (80304). Phone 303/442-1300; fax 303/442-6617. www.laudisio.com.* Italian menu. Hours: 11:30 am-2 pm; 5:30-9:30 pm; Fri to 10 pm; Sat 5:30-10 pm; Sun 5:30-9:30 pm. Closed major holidays. Reservations accepted. Bar. A la carte entrées: lunch $6-$9.50,

dinner $10-$24. Children's menu. Specialties: polenta Boulder, chicken scarpariello, zuppa di pesce. Outdoor dining. Cr cds: A, C, D, DS, ER, MC, V.

D SC

★ ★ **THE MEDITERRANEAN.** *1002 Walnut St (80302). Phone 303/444-5335; fax 303/444-6451. www.themedboulder.com.* Mediterranean menu. Hours: 11:30 am-10 pm; Fri, Sat to 11 pm; Sun from 5 pm. Closed most major holidays. Lunch $4.95-$9.95, dinner $7-$17. Bar. Children's menu. Outdoor dining. Cr cds: A, D, MC, V.

D

★ ★ ★ ★ **Q'S.** *2115 13th St (80302). Phone 303/442-4880; fax 303/442-4378.* If you dine out often enough, you may find, on occasion, that menu items seem recycled and tired. But this is not the case at Q's, a cozy, welcoming, bistro-style restaurant in the Hotel Boulderado (see also HOTEL BOULDERADO). At Q's, bold, contemporary American cuisine is created with spark, style, creativity, and a healthy dose of culinary passion. Digging into the region's best local ingredients, the kitchen offers a spectacular selection of seafood, meat, game, and produce. The international wine collection is eclectic and includes small barrel and boutique selections as well as a proprietor's reserve list. The service is delightful and efficient, making dining here a complete pleasure. Contemporary American menu. Hours: 6:30 am-2 pm, 5-10 pm; Sat, Sun brunch 7 am-2 pm. Dinner $17-$27. Sat, Sun brunch. Bar. Children's menu. Totally nonsmoking. Cr cds: A, C, D, DS, MC, V.

★ ★ **RHUMBA.** *950 Pearl St (80302). Phone 303/442-7771; fax 303/448-1185. www.rhumbarestaurant.com.* Caribbean menu. Hours: 11:30 am-10 pm; Fri, Sat to 11 pm. Reservations accepted. Wine list. Lunch $5.95-$9.95; dinner $6.95-$20.95. Children's menu. Entertainment Sat, Sun. Cr cds: A, D, MC, V.

D

★ **ROYAL PEACOCK.** *5290 Arapahoe Ave (80303). Phone 303/447-1409; fax 303/447-0781.* East Indian menu. Hours: 11:30 am-2:30 pm, 5:30-10:30 pm; Sat from 5:30 pm; Sun 5-10 pm. Reservations accepted. Bar. Lunch $6.25-$11, dinner $7-$22. Lunch buffet $6.95. Specializes in curry, tandoori, wild game. Parking. Outdoor dining. Cr cds: A, C, D, DS, ER, MC, V.

D

★ ★ ★ **TRIO'S.** *1155 Canyon Blvd (80302). Phone 303/442-8400; fax 303/442-8730. www.triosgrille.com.* Contemporary American menu. Hours: 11 am-midnight; Fri, Sat to 2 am; Sun brunch 10 am-3 pm. Closed most major holidays. Reservations accepted. Bar. Lunch $6-$11, dinner $18-$25. Sun brunch $5-$11. Specialties: crayfish hash, wood-oven pizza, smoked salmon. Jazz Mon-Sat. Gallery adjacent. Cr cds: A, C, D, DS, MC, V.

D

Breckenridge (C-4)

See also Dillon, Fairplay

Settled 1859 **Pop** 2,408 **Elev** 9,602 ft **Area code** 970 **Zip** 80424

Information Breckenridge Resort Chamber, 311 S Ridge St, PO Box 1909, phone 970/453-2913; or Guest Services and Activities Center, 137 S Main St, phone 970/453-5579

Web www.gobreck.com

Gold was first panned in the Blue River in 1859; by the following year Breckenridge was a booming gold rush town. More recently, it has become a thriving resort area, with skiing, summer activities, and ghost towns to explore.

What to See and Do

Breckenridge Ski Area. *Ski Hill Rd, 1 mile W off CO 9. Phone 970/453-5000; 800/221-1091(lodging information and reservations).* Six high-speed quad, triple, seven double chairlifts; five surface lifts, six carpet lifts; school, rentals, snowmaking; four cafeterias, five restaurants on mountain, picnic area; four nurseries (from 2 months old). One hundred twelve runs on three interconnected mountains; longest run 3 miles; vertical drop 3,398 feet. (Mid-Nov-early May, daily) Cross-country skiing (23 kilometers), heliskiing, ice skating, snowboarding, sleigh rides. Shuttle bus service. Multiday, 1/2-day, and off-season rates. Chairlift and alpine slide operate in summer (mid-June-mid-Sept). **$$$$**

Ghost towns. Lincoln City, Swandyke, Dyersville, others. Some can be reached only by Jeep or on horseback; inquire locally.

Summit County Biking Tour. The Summit County region in northwest Colorado is a mountain biker's dream with its diverse terrain, spectacular scenery, and Wild West heritage. Hundreds of miles of wilderness roads and trails, many left over from the days when miners crisscrossed the land in search of gold and silver, draw cyclists into an unforgettable exploration of Colorado's high country. A good place to begin is Breckenridge, which is traversed by numerous trails through densely forested valleys, along sparkling lake and riverfronts, and into the peaks of the Continental Divide. A ride over the Argentine Pass, at an elevation of over 13,207 feet, is the ultimate conquest for experienced bikers. Those who enjoy the thrill without the work can opt to ride a ski lift up the mountain for some awe-inspiring views of the Ten Mile Range, followed by

a breathtaking, one-way plunge back to the valley below. Check out area visitor centers, bike shops, and ski resorts for tips and trail maps. (Mar-Nov)

Walking tours. *111 N Ridge Rd (80424). Phone 970/453-9022.* Through historic district; also tours to abandoned mines, gold panning, and assay demonstrations. Led by Summit Historical Society. (Mon-Sat) **$$**

Special Events

Backstage Theatre. *355 Village Rd (80424). Phone 970/453-0199. www.backstagetheatre.org.* Melodramas, musicals, comedies. July-Labor Day, mid-Dec-Mar.

Breckenridge Music Festival. *150 W Adams (80424). Phone 970/547-3100.* Some of the best classical music in the country is showcased at one of the most beautiful spots on Earth—Breckenridge, Colorado—during the annual Breckenridge Festival of Music. This eight-week summer celebration includes regular full orchestra performances by Breckenridge's own, highly acclaimed National Repertory Orchestra. Performances are held at Riverwalk Center in the heart of downtown Breckenridge. The center is an 800-seat, tented amphitheater opening in back to allow lawn seating for an additional 1,500-2,000 symphony lovers who come to picnic and enjoy music under the stars. (Late Jun-mid Aug; most concerts begin at 7:30 pm)

International Snow Sculpture Championships. Teams from around the world create works of art from 12-feet-tall, 20-ton blocks of artificial snow. Jan.

No Man's Land Day Celebration. Celebrates the time when Colorado became a state of the Union, while the Breckenridge area was mistakenly forgotten in historic treaties. This area became part of Colorado and the US at a later date. Celebration features emphasis on Breckenridge life in the 1880s; parade, dance, games. Second weekend in Aug.

Ullr Fest & World Cup Freestyle. Honoring Norse god of snow. Parades, fireworks, Nordic night, and ski competition. Seven days in mid-Jan.

Resorts

★ ★ ★ **BEAVER RUN RESORT AND CONFERENCE CENTER.** *620 Village Rd (80424). Phone 970/453-6000; toll-free 800/288-1282; fax 970/453-4284. www.beaverrun.com.* The largest self-contained resort in the area, this picturesque property nestled in the mountains is popular with families in both winter and summer. 567 kitchen suites, 8 story. Mid-Nov-mid-Apr: kitchen suites $210-$710; lower rates rest of year. Crib free. Complimentary coffee in rooms. Check-out 11 am. TV; cable (premium). Balconies. Fireplaces, some in-room whirlpools. Coin laundry. Restaurant 7 am-10 pm. Bar 11-2 am, seasonal entertainment. No room service. Exercise equipment, sauna. Recreation room. 2 heated pools, 1 indoor/outdoor, whirlpool, poolside service. Miniature golf. Tennis. Downhill ski on site, cross-country ski 1 mile. Business center. Convention center/facilities. Concierge. Shopping arcade. Cr cds: A, D, MC, V.

★ ★ ★ **GREAT DIVIDE LODGE.** *550 Village Rd (80424). Phone 970/453-4500; toll-free 800/321-8444; fax 970/453-1983. www.greatdividelodge.com.* Located just 50 yards from the base of Peak 9 and two blocks from Main Street, this property is excellent for winter or summer vacationing. 208 rooms, 10 story. Mid-Dec-mid-Apr: S, D $155-$299; suites $300-$500; children free; ski plans; higher rates special events; lower rates rest of year. TV; cable (premium). Indoor pool; whirlpool. Coffee in rooms. Restaurant 7 am-10 pm. Bar 11 am-11 pm. Check-out 10 am. Meeting rooms. Business services available. Concierge. Sports shop. Garage. Airport, bus depot transportation. Downhill/cross-country ski 1/2 block. Exercise equipment; sauna. Massage. Refrigerators, wet bars. Some balconies. Cr cds: A, C, D, DS, JCB, MC, V.

★ ★ ★ **LODGE & SPA AT BRECKENRIDGE.** *112 Overlook Dr (80424). Phone 970/453-9300; toll-free 800/736-1607; fax 970/453-0625. www.thelodgeatbreck.com.* With exposed wood beams and richly colored fabrics, the décor of this small, full-service spa is sophisticatedly rustic. 47 rooms, 4 story. Feb-Apr: S, D $135-$275; each additional $25; under 16 free; package plans; holidays 5-day minimum; higher rates at Christmas time; lower rates rest of year. Pet accepted, some restrictions; $25. Check-out 11 am. TV; cable (premium), VCR available. In-room modem link. Fireplaces. Restaurant, bar 5 pm-midnight. Room service. Exercise room, massage, sauna, steam room. Indoor pool, whirlpool, poolside service. Greens fee $90 (with cart). Downhill, cross-country ski 2 miles. Free valet parking. Business center. Concierge. Cr cds: A, D, DS, MC, V.

★ ★ **RIVER MOUNTAIN LODGE.** *100 S Park Ave (80424). Phone 970/453-4711; toll-free 800/627-3766; fax 970/453-1763.* 150 kitchen condos, 3-4 story. S, D $89-$599. Check-out 10 am. TV; cable, VCR available (movies $6). Refrigerators, microwaves, some fireplaces. Guest laundry in condos. Coffee in lobby. Restaurant. Exercise equipment, sauna. Pool, whirlpool. Downhill, cross-country ski 1 mile. Covered parking. Airport, bus depot transportation. Meeting rooms. Business services. Concierge. Cr cds: A, DS, MC, V.

B&B/Small Inns

★ ★ ★ **ALLAIRE TIMBERS INN.** *9511 Hwy 9 (80424). Phone 970/453-7530; toll-free 800/624-4904; fax 970/453-8699. www.allairetimbers.com.* The log cabin construction of this charming bed-and-breakfast at the south end of Main Street is made from local pine. Innkeepers Jack and Kathy Gumph welcome you with hearty homemade breakfasts, afternoon snacks, and warm hospitality. 10 rooms, 2 suites, 2 story. Mid-Feb-Mar: S, D $145-$160; suites $220-$250; ski, golf plans; lower rates rest of year. Children over 13 years only. Complimentary full breakfast. Check-out 11 am, check-in 3-7 pm. TV; cable. Balconies. Restaurant nearby. Downhill, cross-country ski 2 miles. Business services. Concierge. Rooms named for historic mountain passes. Totally nonsmoking. Cr cds: A, MC, V.

★ ★ ★ **BED & BREAKFAST ON NORTH MAIN ST.** *303 N Main St (80424). Phone 970/453-2975; toll-free 800/795-2975; fax 970/453-5258. www.breckenridge-inn.com.* Innkeepers Fred Kinat and Diane Jaynes welcome guests to one of the three historic inns that comprise this bed-and-breakfast enterprise. The individually decorated rooms are comfortable. 12 rooms. No A/C. Some room phones. Feb-Mar: S, D $89-$289; higher rates Dec 25-Jan 1; lower rates rest of year. Closed 3 weeks in May, last week in Oct, first 2 weeks of Nov. Adults only. Complimentary full breakfast. Check-out 11 am, check-in by appointment. TV in some rooms. Antiques, fireplaces. Health club privileges. Downhill, cross-country ski 1 mile. Concierge service. Totally nonsmoking. Cr cds: A, DS, MC, V.

★ ★ **EVANS HOUSE BED & BREAKFAST.** *102 S French St (80424). Phone 970/453-5509. www.coloradoevanshouse.com.* 6 rooms, 2 suites, 2 story. No A/C. Dec-Mar: S, D $100-$140; each additional $30; lower rates rest of year. Crib $30. Complimentary full breakfast. Check-out 10 am, check-in 4-6 pm. TV; cable. Restaurant nearby. Whirlpool. Health club privileges, exercise equipment. Downhill, cross-country ski 1 mile. Picnic table. Business services. Luggage handling. House built in 1886. Totally nonsmoking. Cr cds: A, D, DS, MC, V.

★ ★ ★ **HUNT PLACER INN.** *275 Ski Hill Rd (80424). Phone 970/453-7573; toll-free 800/472-1430; fax 970/453-2335. www.huntplacerinn.com.* Individually designed rooms with mountain views and hearty, homemade breakfasts distinguish this romantic bed-and-breakfast. Located just blocks from Main Street. 8 rooms, 3 suites, 3 story. No room phones. Mid-Feb-Mar (4-day minimum): S, D $135-$199; suites $179-$189; 5-day minimum late Dec-early Jan; lower rates rest of year. Children over 12 years only. Complimentary full breakfast. Check-out 11 am, check-in 4-6 pm. TV; VCR available. Fireplaces. Game room. Downhill ski 1 mile, cross-country ski on site. Chalet-style inn. Totally nonsmoking. Cr cds: A, C, D, DS, MC, V.

★ ★ **RIDGE STREET INN.** *212 N Ridge St (80424). Phone 970/453-4680; toll-free 800/452-4680; fax 970/547-1477. www.colorado.net/ridge.* 6 rooms, 2 share bath, 2 story. No A/C. No room phones. Nov-Mar: S, D $98-$150; lower rates rest of year. Children over 6 years only. Complimentary full breakfast. Downhill/cross-country ski 3 miles. Health club privileges. Victorian house; view of mountains. Totally nonsmoking. Cr cds: MC, V.

★ ★ **SWAN MOUNTAIN INN.** *16172 CO 9 (84035). Phone 970/453-7903. www.swanmountaininn.com.* 4 rooms, 1 share bath, 2 story. Late Dec-early Jan, Mar (3-day minimum): S, D $70-$145; under 3 free; MAP available; weekend, holiday rates; lower rates rest of year. Crib free. Complimentary full breakfast. Check-out 11 am, check-in 4 pm. TV; cable, VCR (movies). Restaurant (see SWAN MOUNTAIN INN). Bar. Whirlpool. Downhill ski 5 miles, cross-country ski 1 mile. Picnic tables. Meeting rooms. Rustic log cabin with front porch. Totally nonsmoking. Cr cds: DS, MC, V.

Restaurants

★ **BRECKENRIDGE BREWERY.** *600 S Main St (80424). Phone 970/453-1550; fax 970/453-0928. www.breckenridgebrewery.com.* Hours: 11 am-midnight. Closed Dec 25. Bar to 2 am. Lunch $5.95-$8, dinner $7.95-$18. Children's menu. Specializes in baby-back ribs, fish and chips, fajitas. Parking. Outdoor dining. Microbrewery; tours weekends. Second-story dining arranged around brew kettles. Cr cds: A, D, DS, MC, V.

★ **BRIAR ROSE.** *109 E Lincoln St (80424). Phone 970/453-9948; fax 970/453-2630.* Continental menu. Hours: 5-10 pm; summer from 6 pm. Reservations accepted. Bar 4:30 pm-2 am. Dinner $15-$50. Children's menu. Specializes in prime rib, game, steak. Entertainment (ski season). 1890s Victorian décor; on site of old mining boarding house. Cr cds: A, DS, MC, V.

★ ★ **CAFE ALPINE.** *106 E Adams (80424). Phone 970/453-8218; fax 970/453-6936. www.cafealpine.com.* Continental menu. Hours: 11 am-10 pm. Reservations accepted. Bar. Lunch $5-$9, dinner $12-$24. Children's

menu. Specializes in regional cuisine, tapas. Outdoor dining. Cozy, informal dining in three rooms. Totally nonsmoking. Cr cds: A, D, DS, MC, V.

★ ★ **HEARTHSTONE.** *130 S Ridge St (80424). Phone 970/453-1148; fax 970/453-0247. www.stormrestaurants.com.* Hours: 11:30 am-10 pm; winter from 3 pm. Reservations accepted. No A/C. Bar. Lunch $4.95-$7.95 (summer only), dinner $12.50-$21.95. Children's menu. Specializes in prime rib, fresh seafood. Parking. Outdoor dining. In Victorian house (1886). View of mountains and ski area. Cr cds: A, MC, V.

★ ★ **HORSESHOE 2.** *115 S Main (80424). Phone 970/453-7463; fax 970/453-6223.* American menu. Hours: 11 am-10 pm; Fri-Sun from 8 am. Dinner $6.95-$27. Bar to 2 am. No A/C. Children's menu. Former miners' supply store (1880). Casual attire. Outdoor dining. Totally nonsmoking. Cr cds: A, MC, V.

★ ★ **MI CASA MEXICAN CANTINA.** *600 S Park St (80424). Phone 970/453-2071; fax 970/453-0249. www.stormrestaurants.com.* Mexican menu. Specialties: chimichanga, fajitas, fresh seafood, deep-fried ice cream. Hours: 11:30 am-9 pm. Dinner $5.95-$14.95. Bar. Children's menu. Outdoor dining. Cr cds: A, D, MC, V.

★ ★ ★ **PIERRE'S RIVERWALK CAFE.** *137 S Main (80424). Phone 970/453-0989.* American, French menu. Hours: 11:30 am-2:30 pm, 5:30-10 pm; winter hours vary. Closed Dec 25; also May and Oct; first 2 weeks in Nov. Lunch $6.25-$9, dinner $15-$26. Bar. Reservations accepted. Outdoor dining. Cr cds: D, MC, V.

★ **POIRRIER.** *224 S Main (80424). Phone 970/453-1877. www.poirrierscajuncafe.com.* Cajun menu. Hours: 11:30 am-2:30 pm, 5:30-9:30 pm. No A/C. Bar. Lunch $4.95-$9, dinner $8.95-$19.95. Children's menu. Specializes in seafood platter, crawfish, gumbos. Outdoor dining. Family-owned. Totally nonsmoking. Cr cds: A, D, DS, MC, V.

★ ★ **SALT CREEK.** *110 E Lincoln Ave (80424). Phone 970/453-4949; fax 970/453-7945.* Barbecue, steak menu. Hours: 11:30 am-2 pm, 5-10 pm; hours extended ski season. Lunch $4.95-$7.95, dinner $9.95-$42.95. Bar. Children's menu. Casual Western atmosphere. Outdoor dining. Cr cds: D, DS, MC, V.

★★ **ST. BERNARD INN.** *103 S Main St (80424). Phone 970/453-2572. www.thestbernard.com.* Continental, Northern Italian menu. Hours: 5:30-10 pm. Closed May. Dinner $10-$23. Bar. Children's menu. In historic mercantile building. Reservations accepted. Old mining memorabilia. Cr cds: A, D, DS, MC, V.

[D]

★★ **SWAN MOUNTAIN INN.** *16172 CO 9 (80424). Phone 970/453-7903. www.swanmountaininn.com.* Continental menu. Hours: 7:30-10 am, 11:30 am-2 pm, 5:30-9 pm; Sat, Sun 7:30 am-2 pm, 5:30-9 pm; winter hours vary. Reservations accepted. No A/C. Bar. Breakfast $6.50-$9.50, lunch $6.95-$7.95, dinner $9.95-$20.95. Children's menu. Parking. Outdoor dining. Log structure; view of mountains. Cr cds: A, MC, V.

[SC]

★★ **TOP OF THE WORLD.** *112 Overlook Dr (80424). Phone 970/453-9300; fax 970/453-0625. www.colorado.net/thelodge.* American menu. Hours: 7-10 am, 5-10 pm. Dinner $18-$25. Bar 5 pm-midnight. Children's menu. Casual attire. Cr cds: A, D, MC, V.

[D]

Buena Vista (D-4)

See also Leadville, Salida

Founded 1879 **Pop** 2,195 **Elev** 7,955 ft **Area code** 719 **Zip** 81211

Information Chamber of Commerce, 343 S US 24, Box 2021; 719/395-6612

Web www.fourteenernet.com/buenavista

Lying at the eastern edge of the Collegiate Range and the central Colorado mountain region, Buena Vista is a natural point of departure for treks into the mountains. Within 20 miles are 12 peaks with elevations above 14,000 feet, four rivers, and more than 500 mountain lakes and streams.

What to See and Do

Hiking, camping, mountain biking, snowmobiling, and cross-country skiing. *Phone 719/395-8001.* Equipment rentals, supplies, maps, and information on trails and routes may be obtained from Trailhead Ventures.

River rafting.

Arkansas River Tours. *126 S Main St (93545). Phone 800/321-4352.* The upper Arkansas River in south central Colorado offers some of the nation's most beautiful and challenging rafting experiences. With its long, placid stretches of scenic wilderness punctuated by hair-raising plunges through dramatic whitewater canyons, it accommodates all levels of river-rafting thrill-seekers. Experienced rafters won't want to miss an adrenaline-pumping ride through the magnificent Royal George Canyon. Families, on the other hand, will love a scenic float through the gently rolling Cottonwood Rapid. Arkansas River Tours is one of several rafting outfitters along Highway 50 offering a variety of outings, from 1/4-day trips to multiple-day high-adventure expeditions. (Daily; weather permitting) **$$$$**

Bill Dvorak's Kayak & Rafting Expeditions. *Phone 719/539-6851; 800/824-3795.* Half-day to 12-day trips on the Arkansas, Colorado, Dolores, Green, Gunnison, North Platte, Rio Chama, Rio Grande, and San Miguel rivers. Guided fishing trips; kayak instruction. (Mid-Apr-early Oct) **$$$$**

Noah's Ark Whitewater Rafting Company. *23910 US Hwy 285 S (81211). Phone 719/395-2158.* Half-day to 3-day trips on the Arkansas River. (Mid-May-late Aug) **$$$$**

Wilderness Aware. *12600 US 24/285 (81211). Phone 719/395-2112; 800/462-7238.* Half-day to 10-day river rafting trips on the Arkansas, Colorado, Dolores, North Platte, and Gunnison rivers. (May-Sept) **$$$$**

St. Elmo Ghost Town. The abandoned remains of once-thriving Colorado mining towns stand as melancholy testimony to fortunes made and lost. A visit to one of these ghostly ruins is a trip back in time, filled with enticing secrets that only the imagination can unlock. All it takes is a flexible schedule, a four-wheel drive vehicle, sturdy shoes, and a sense of adventure. Among the most accessible and best-preserved ghost towns is St. Elmo, just west of Buena Vista in the south-central part of the state. With 24 original buildings still standing, it entices visitors to take a walk along its wood-plank sidewalks and contemplate, in the silence, what it must have been like in the high-spirited gold frenzy days of the late 1800s. Just outside St. Elmo are the abandoned ruins of the Mary Murphy gold mine. Those with four-wheel-drive vehicles can traverse the rocky terrain to the mine for a closer look. Caution is advised!

Motels/Motor Lodges

★ **BEST WESTERN VISTA INN.** *733 US Hwy 24 N (81211). Phone 719/395-8009; toll-free 800/809-3495; fax 719/395-6025. www.bestwestern.com.* 41 rooms, 2 story. Pet accepted. Check-out 11 am. Check-in 2 pm. TV; cable (premium). In-room modem link. Whirlpool. Cross-country ski 1 mile. Bicycles, fishing, hiking. Cr cds: A, C, D, DS, MC, V. **$**

[icons]

★ **GREAT WESTERN SUMAC LODGE.** *428 Hwy 24 S (81212). Phone 719/395-8111; toll-free 888/786-2290; fax 719/395-2560.* 30 rooms, 2 story. Late-May-Sept: S, D $56-$73; each additional $5; lower rates rest of year. Pet accepted; $5. Complimentary coffee in lobby. Check-out 11 am. TV; cable (premium). In-room modem link. Restaurant nearby. Mountain view. Cr cds: A, C, DS, MC, V.

Restaurants

★ ★ **BUFFALO BAR & GRILL.** *710 US 24 N (81211). Phone 719/395-6472.* Seafood, steak menu. Closed Sun. Dinner $6.50-$18.95. Bar. Children's menu. Reservations accepted. Cr cds: A, DS, MC, V.

★ **CASA DEL SOL.** *333 US 24 N (81211). Phone 719/395-8810.* Mexican menu. Closed late May-Labor Day. Lunch, dinner. Children's menu. In 1880 miner's cabin. Casual attire. Outdoor seating. Totally nonsmoking. Cr cds: DS, MC, V. **$$**

Burlington (D-9)

Pop 3,678 **Elev** 4,160 ft **Area code** 719 **Zip** 80807

Information Chamber of Commerce, 415 15th St, PO Box 62; 719/346-8070

What to See and Do

Bonny Lake State Park. *23 miles N on US 385, near Idalia. Phone 303/354-7306.* A 2,000-acre lake has swimming, waterskiing, fishing, boating (ramps); picnicking, concession, camping. Standard fees. (Daily) **$$**

Kit Carson County Carousel. *Fairgrounds. Colorado Ave and 15th St. Fee for 20-minute tour and 4-minute ride.* Built in 1905, this restored carousel houses a 1912 Wurlitzer Monster Military Band organ. (Memorial Day-Labor Day, daily, afternoon-mid-evening) **$**

Old Town. *420 S 14th St. Phone 719/346-7382; 800/288-1334.* Historical village with 20 buildings reflects Colorado prairie heritage. Also cancan shows, gunfights, and melodramas (summer); 2-day hoedown (Labor Day weekend). (Daily; closed holidays) **$$**

Special Events

Kit Carson County Fair & Rodeo. *Fairgrounds. 251 16th St #200. Phone 719/346-8133.* Early Aug.

Little Britches Rodeo. *Fairgrounds. 1045 W Rio Grande (80906). Phone 719/389-0333.* Late May.

Motels/Motor Lodges

★ **BEST VALUE INN.** *1901 Rose Ave (80807). Phone 719/346-5333; toll-free 800/362-0464; fax 719/346-9536.* 29 rooms, 1-2 story. S $31-$36; D $35-$45; each additional $3. Crib free. Check-out 10:30 am. TV; cable (premium). Refrigerators, microwaves available. Restaurant nearby. Pool. Bus depot transportation. Cr cds: A, C, D, DS, MC, V.

★ **CHAPARRAL MOTOR INN.** *405 S Lincoln (80807). Phone 719/346-5361; toll-free 800/456-6206; fax 719/346-8502.* 39 rooms. June-Sept: S $33-$43; D $34-$44; each additional $4; under 12 free; lower rates rest of year. Crib $5. Pet accepted, some restrictions. Check-out 11 am. TV; cable (premium). Restaurant adjacent 6 am-11 pm. Playground. Heated pool, whirlpool. Cr cds: A, C, D, DS, MC, V.

Cañon City (E-5)

See also Colorado Springs, Cripple Creek, Pueblo

Founded 1859 **Pop** 15,431 **Elev** 5,332 ft **Area code** 719 **Zip** 81212

Information Chamber of Commerce, 403 Royal Gorge Blvd, PO Bin 749; 719/275-2331 or 800/876-7922

Web www.canoncitychamber.com

Lieutenant Zebulon Pike, in 1807, was one of the first white men to camp on this site, which was long a favored spot of the Ute Indians. Cañon (pronounced Canyon) City is located at the mouth of the Royal Gorge, ringed by mountains. The poet Joaquin Miller, as town judge, mayor, and minister during the early gold-mining days, once proposed renaming the town Oreodelphia, but the horrified miners protested that they could neither spell nor pronounce it. Legend has it that the same earthy logic prevailed when, in 1868, Cañon City was offered either the state penitentiary or the state university. The miners chose the former, pointing out that it was likely to be the better attended institution. A Ranger District office of the San Isabel National Forest (see PUEBLO) is located in Cañon City; phone 719/269-8500.

What to See and Do

Cañon City Municipal Museum. *612 Royal Gorge Blvd (US 50). Phone 719/276-5279.* The complex includes outdoor buildings; Rudd Cabin, a pioneer log cabin constructed in 1860, and Stone House, built in 1881. Second-floor Municipal Building galleries display minerals and rocks, artifacts from settlement of the Fremont County region, and guns. (Early May-Labor Day, Tues-Sun; rest of year, Tues-Sat; closed holidays) **$**

Colorado Territorial Prison Museum and Park. *1st and Macon aves. Phone 719/269-3015.* Housed in the women's prison facility (1935), this museum and resource center displays exhibits and memorabilia of the Colorado prison system. Picnicking is permitted on the grounds. Adjacent is an active medium-security prison. (Summer, daily; winter, Thurs-Sun; closed holidays) **$$**

Fremont Center for the Arts. *505 Macon Ave. Phone 719/275-2790.* Community art center; features visual art exhibits, cultural programs. (Tues-Sat; closed holidays) **$**

Rafting. *Phone 800/876-7922.* There are many rafting companies in the area. For information, contact the Cañon City Chamber of Commerce.

⭐ **Royal Gorge.** *8 miles W on US 50, then 4 miles SW. Phone 719/275-7507.* Magnificent canyon with cliffs rising more than 1,000 feet above the Arkansas River. Royal Gorge Suspension Bridge, 1,053 feet above the river, is highest in the world (recreational vehicles larger than small van or small camper not permitted on bridge). Royal Gorge Incline Railway, the world's steepest, takes passengers 1,550 feet to bottom of canyon. A 2,200-feet aerial tramway glides across the spectacular canyon. Theater; entertainment gazebo; petting zoo; restaurants; gift shops. (Daily)

Royal Gorge Frontier Town and Railway. *8 miles W via US 50, 1 mile S to Royal Gorge. Phone 719/275-5149; 719/275-5485.* Old West theme park includes an old Western town with 30 authentic buildings; restaurant and saloon. Other activities here are daily gunfights, horse-drawn trolley ride, magic shows, and entertainment. Also 3-mile, 30-minute train ride to rim of Royal Gorge. Railway (Mar-Dec, daily). Park (May-Sept, daily). **$$$$**

Royal Gorge Route. *Phone 888/RAILS-4U.* Travel by train through the Royal Gorge on two-hour round-trip departing from Cañon City. (Summer; daily)

Special Events

Blossom & Music Festival. *Phone 719/569-2403.* First weekend in May.

Royal Gorge Rodeo. First weekend in May.

Motels/Motor Lodges

★★ **BEST WESTERN ROYAL GORGE.** *1925 Fremont Dr (81212). Phone 719/275-3377; toll-free 800/231-7317; fax 719/275-3931. www.bestwestern.com.* 67 rooms, 2 story. May-Sept: S $44-$69; D $49-$89; each additional $5; under 12 free; lower rates rest of year. Crib free. Pet accepted, some restrictions; $15 (nonrefundable). TV; cable (premium). Heated pool; whirlpool, poolside service. Playground. Restaurant. Bar. Check-out 11 am. Coin laundry. In-room modem link. Some refrigerators; microwaves available. Picnic tables. Cr cds: A, C, D, DS, MC, V.

D ⬛ ⬛ ⬛

★★★ **CAÑON INN.** *3075 E US 50 (81212). Phone 719/275-8676; toll-free 800/525-7727; fax 719/275-8675. www.canoninn.com.* Located at the mouth of Royal Gorge, this simple hotel offers spectacular vistas. 152 rooms, 2 story. May-Sept: S $65-$90; D $80-$100; each additional $7; under 16 free; lower rates rest of year. Crib free. Pet accepted; $50. TV; cable (premium). Heated pool; whirlpools. Restaurant. Room service. Bar. Check-out 11 am. Coin laundry. Meeting rooms. Business services available. Valet service. Free airport, bus depot transportation. Some bathroom phones, refrigerators; microwaves available. Cr cds: A, C, D, DS, MC, V. **$$**

D ⬛ ⬛ ⬛

Restaurant

★★ **MERLINO'S BELVEDERE.** *1330 Elm Ave (81212). Phone 719/275-5558; toll-free 800/625-2526; fax 719/275-8980. www.belvedererestaurant.com.* American, Italian menu. Closed Thanksgiving, Dec 25. Dinner. Bar. Children's menu. Cr cds: A, D, DS, MC, V. **$$**

D

Castle Rock (D-6)

Special Event

The International at Castle Pines Golf Club. *1000 Hummingbird Dr (80104). Phone 303/688-6000.* The International is a week-long, world-class golf event that attracts some of the top professional golfers to Castle Pines Golf Club in Castle Rock, 29 miles south of Denver. The Jack Nicklaus-designed course is renowned for the beauty of its pine-strewn mountain setting and the challenge of its terrain. The tournament begins in earnest on Thursday, but spectators are welcome to watch practice rounds as well as the junior and pro-am tournaments held earlier in the week. Aug. **$$$$**

Central City (C-5)

See also Denver, Georgetown, Golden, Idaho Springs

Settled 1859 **Pop** 515 **Elev** 8,496 ft **Area code** 303 **Zip** 80427

Perched along steep Gregory Gulch, Central City's precarious location did not prevent it from becoming known as "the richest square mile on earth" when the first important discovery of gold in Colorado was made here in 1859. More than $75 million worth of metals and minerals have come from Central City and neighboring settlements.

What to See and Do

Central City Opera House. *124 Eureka St (80427). 35 miles W of Denver, 1 mile W of Blackhawk on Hwy 279. Phone 303/292-6700; toll-free 800/851-8175.* Established at the site of Colorado's first major gold strike, Central City gained prominence in the 1860s as the financial and cultural center of the state. Though it's now a center for gambling, Central City preserves the riches of its cultural past in the form of a beautiful Opera House. Designed by Denver architect Robert S. Roeschlaub, this lavish, 1878 Historic Landmark building hosts an annual summer opera festival (June-Aug) that draws audiences from around the world to experience its historic charm and acoustic perfection. Tours (fee). Fees vary for performances. **$$$$**

Gilpin County Historical Society Museum. *228 E High St. Phone 303/582-5283.* Exhibits, housed in an early schoolhouse (1870) under continuing restoration, re-create early gold-mining life in Gilpin County; replicas of a Victorian house and period shops with authentic furnishings; collection of antique dolls; personal effects of sheriff gunned down in 1896. (Memorial Day weekend-Labor Day, daily; or by appointment) Also located here is

The Thomas House Museum. *209 Eureka St. Phone 303/582-5283.* (1874) On display are the belongings of one family who lived in this house. (Memorial Day weekend-Labor Day, Thurs-Sun; rest of year, by apppointment) **$$**

Gold Belt Loop. Remnants of the glorious, raucous gold rush days can still be found scattered throughout the Colorado landscape. The unexpected discovery of an abandoned mine shaft, rail track, mining camp, or prospector's shack conjures visions of those who were willing to risk it all in the Colorado wilderness for the promise of fame and fortune. Take the time to explore all or part of the Gold Belt Loop, a designated backcountry byway west of Colorado Springs that connects some of the state's most scenic roadway with some of its most historic locales. A good starting point is Cripple Creek or Victor, both located on Highway 67. These former boomtowns grew up around the most prolific gold mine in the country. Today, they continue to lure fortune seekers with their thriving casino businesses. For a more family-friendly 1800s mining town experience, visit charming Leadville, located northwest of Cripple Creek at the headwaters of the Arkansas River. With 70 square blocks of restored Victorian buildings, its former saloons, boardinghouses, banks, and theaters now house antique stores, restaurants, hotels, and specialty shops. A designated Historic National Landmark District and the home of the National Mining Hall of Fame Museum, Leadville is a great base from which to explore the surrounding mining district as well as its numerous outdoor recreation offerings, including skiing, hiking, mountain biking, horseback riding, rock climbing, hunting, and fishing.

Site of First Gold Lode Discovery in Colorado. *Boundary of Central City and Black Hawk.* Granite monument marks spot where John H. Gregory first found gold on May 6, 1859.

Special Event

Central City Music Festival. Three days of great sounds. Late Aug.

Restaurant

★ ★ ★ **BLACK FOREST RESTAURANT.** *24 Big Springs Dr, Nederland (80466). Phone 303/279-2333; fax 303/258-3005.* German, seafood, steak menu. Hours: 8 am-10 pm; Sun to 9 pm. Dinner $13-$24. Bar to 1 am. Entertainment Fri-Sun. Casual attire. Cr cds: C. Ⓓ

Colorado National Monument (D-1)

See also Grand Junction

(5 miles W of Grand Junction, off CO 340)

Wind, water, a 10-mile fault, and untold eons have combined to produce spectacular erosional forms. In the 32-square-mile monument, deep canyons with sheer walls form amphitheaters for towering monoliths, rounded domes, and other geological features. Wildlife includes deer, foxes, coyotes, porcupines, and a growing herd of desert bighorn sheep. Rim Rock Drive, accessible from either Fruita or Grand Junction, is a spectacular 23-mile road along the canyon rims. There are picnicking and camping facilities within the monument (all year; fee for camping). The Saddlehorn Visitor Center has geology and natural history exhibits (daily). Interpretive programs are offered in summer. Hiking and cross-country skiing trails are open in season. For detailed information contact Superintendent, Fruita, CO 81521; phone 970/858-3617. Per vehicle $2-$5. **$$**

Colorado Springs (D-6)

See also Cañon City, Cripple Creek, Manitou Springs

Founded 1871 **Pop** 360,890 **Elev** 6,035 ft **Area code** 719

Information Convention & Visitor Bureau, 515 S Cascade, Suite 104, 80903; 719/635-7506 or 800/368-4748

Web www.coloradosprings-travel.com

Colorado Springs, at the foot of Pikes Peak, is surrounded by areas containing fantastic rock formations. It was

Exploring the Saratoga of the West

Nestled at the foot of Pikes Peak a mere 7 miles west of downtown Colorado Springs, Manitou Springs is one of the state's definitive—and most accessible—mountain communities. A walking tour of Manitou Avenue, a bustling boulevard rife with artists' studios, restaurants, and boutiques that is one of the country's largest historic districts, is a good place to begin. Start at Memorial Park on the town's east side (Manitou and Deer Path avenues), which is surrounded by ample parking and centered around Seven Minute Springs, one of ten named mineral springs in the area that are renowned for their cool, drinkable water. (As a result, Manitou has been called "The Saratoga of the West.") From the park, walk west two blocks on Manitou Avenue to the Canon Avenue intersection. This is the central business district, and most of the restaurants and galleries are within a 3-block radius. One can't-miss establishment is Arcade Amusements (930 Manitou Avenue), one of the West's oldest amusement arcades, featuring an array of antique coin-operated games. The downtown area is also ground zero for the Manitou Art Project, an annually rotating installation of 20 outdoor sculptures. Just west of the Canon-Manitou intersection is the Jerome Wheeler Town Clock, a landmark named for its eponymous donor, the onetime president of Macy's Department Stores who brought his ailing wife to the area in the 19th century. Continuing west on Manitou Avenue, it's a short walk to Ruxton Avenue, which will be on the left. Head southwest on Ruxton to the Miramont Castle (9 Capitol Hill Avenue, immediately adjacent to Ruxton), one of the architectural gems of Manitou Springs. Built as a home for a Catholic priest in 1895, the castle features English Tudor and Byzantine motifs in its eclectic design. After touring Miramont Castle, you might want to continue up Ruxton Avenue on a steep, 2-mile hike to the Manitou & Pikes Peak Railway Depot (515 Ruxton Avenue), the departure point for a rail trip to the pinnacle of Pikes Peak (open daily in the summertime). However, Miramont is also a good place to backtrack to your car for a drive to Manitou Springs attractions that are less accessible by foot, such as the railway, the Cliff Dwellings Museum, and the Cave of the Winds.

founded by General William J. Palmer and the Denver and Rio Grande Railroad as a summer playground and health resort. The headquarters of Pike National Forest is Colorado Springs.

What to See and Do

Broadmoor-Cheyenne Mountain Area. *1 Lake Ave (80906). 4 miles S on Nevada Ave, then W on Lake Ave to Broadmoor Hotel.* Also located here are

Broadmoor-Cheyenne Mountain Highway. Zig-zags up the east face of Cheyenne Mountain; view of plains to the east. Round-trip to Shrine of the Sun (see) is 6 miles. (Daily; weather permitting) Toll (includes zoo, Shrine of the Sun) **$$$**

Cheyenne Mountain Zoological Park. *4250 Cheyenne Mountain Zoo Rd (80906). Phone 719/633-9925 (recording).* This little gem located on the side of the Cheyenne Mountains in Colorado Springs is known for the diversity of its animal collection and the beauty of its setting. Six hundred fifty animals, including many endangered species, make their home here. The most popular exhibits are the monkey house, the birds of prey, and a herd of giraffe that welcome feedings from visitors. Admission includes access to the Will Rogers Shrine of the Sun, from which you can marvel at the spectacular panoramic view of the Colorado Springs and Pikes Peak regions. (Daily; early closing on Thanksgiving, Dec 24-25) **$$$**

El Pomar Carriage Museum. *10 Lake Circle (80906). Lake Ave and Lake Circle. Phone 719/577-5710.* Collection of fine carriages, vehicles, Western articles of 1890s. (Daily; closed holidays) **FREE**

Shrine of the Sun. *4250 Cheyenne Mountain Zoo (80906).* Memorial to Will Rogers. Built of Colorado pink granite and steel. Contains Rogers memorabilia. (Daily)

Colorado Springs Fine Arts Center. *30 W Dale St. Phone 719/634-5581.* Permanent collections include Native American and Hispanic art, Guatemalan textiles, 19th- and 20th-century American Western paintings, graphics, and sculpture by Charles M. Russell and other American artists. Changing exhibits; painting and sculpture classes; repertory theater performances; films. (Tues-Sun; closed holidays) **$$**

Colorado Springs Pioneer Museum. *215 S Tejon St. Phone 719/385-5990.* Exhibits portray the history of Pikes Peak region. (Tues-Sat, also Sun afternoons in the summers; closed holidays) **FREE**

Flying W Ranch. *3330 Chuckwagon Rd (80906). 8 miles NW on 30th St, 2 miles W of I-25 on Garden of the Gods Rd. Phone 719/598-4000 or toll-free 800/232-FLYW. www.flyingw.com.* A working cattle and horse ranch with chuckwagon suppers and a Western stage show. More than 12 restored buildings with period furniture. Reservations required. (Mid-May-Sept, daily; rest of year, Fri and Sat; closed Dec 25-Feb) **$$$$**

Focus on the Family. *8685 Explorer Dr (I-25 exit 151). Phone 719/531-3328.* Welcome center with interactive displays, a 20-minute video, and a children's play area, at the headquarters of this popular Christian ministry. (Mon-Sat; closed holidays) **FREE**

⭐ **Garden of the Gods.** *1805 N 30th St (80904). Hwy 24 W from I-25 to Ridge Rd exit, or W from I-25 on Garden of the Gods Rd, left of 30th St. Phone 719/634-6666.* This 1,350-acre park at the base of Pike's Peak is a showcase of geological wonders. It's best known for its outstanding red sandstone formations, which include the famous Balanced Rock and Kissing Camels. A hiker's delight, the park offers 8 miles of well-groomed trails that provide easy access to its geological treasures, plants, and wildlife. Other favorite activities include horseback riding and rock climbing (by permit only). Try to plan a visit at sunrise or sunset, when you'll get a true understanding of where the name "Garden of the Gods" came from. **FREE** Also here is

> **Garden of the Gods Trading Post.** *324 Beckers Ln (80829). Near Balanced Rock, at south end of park. Phone 719/685-9045 or 800/874-4515.* Established in 1900. Southwestern art gallery displays contemporary Native American jewelry, Santa Clara pottery, Hopi kachinas. Gift shop. (Daily) **FREE**

Van Briggle Art Pottery Company Tour. *600 S 21st St at W US 24. Phone 719/633-7729; 800/847-6341.* Exhibitions of "throwing potter's wheel"; self-guided tours. (Mon-Sat; closed Jan 1, Thanksgiving, Dec 25) **FREE**

Gray Line bus tours. *Contact 3704 W Colorado Ave (80904). Phone 719/633-1747 or toll-free 800/345-8197.*

Magic Town. *2418 W Colorado Ave. Phone 719/471-9391.* Theatrical sculpture, created by sculptor Michael Garman, is a combination of miniature cityscapes and characters together with theater techniques. Gift shop. (Daily) **$$**

May Natural History Museum. *710 Rock Creek Canyon Rd (80926). 9 miles SW on CO 115. Phone 719/576-0450; 800/666-3841.* Collection of more than 7,000 invertebrates from the tropics. Also here is **Museum of Space Exploration** with hundreds of models and NASA space photos and movies. (May-Sept, daily) Campground (fee). **$$**

McAllister House Museum. *423 N Cascade Ave. Phone 719/635-7925.* (1873) Six-room, Gothic-style cottage; Victorian furnishings. Carriage house. Guided tours. (May-Aug, Wed-Sun; rest of year, Thurs-Sat; closed Jan) **$$**

Museum of the American Numismatic Association. *818 N Cascade Ave. Phone 719/632-2646; 800/367-9723.* Displays and research collections of coins, tokens, medals, paper money; changing exhibits; library. (Mon-Sat; closed holidays) **FREE**

Old Colorado City. *111 S 25th St (80904). 3 miles W on US 24. Phone 719/577-4112.* Renovated historic district features more than 100 quaint shops, art galleries, and restaurants. (Daily) **FREE**

Palmer Park. *On Maizeland Rd off N Academy Blvd.* Magnificent views from scenic roads and trails among its 710 acres on Austin Bluffs. Picnic areas. **FREE**

Peterson Air & Space Museum. *150 E Ent Ave (80914). Main gate, off US 24. Phone 719/556-4915.* Display of 17 historic aircraft from WWII-present, plus exhibits on the history of the Air Force base. (open on restricted basis, call for times) **FREE**

Pike National Forest. *1920 Valley Dr, Pueblo (81008). Phone 719/545-8737.* The more than 1,100,000 acres N and W of town via US 24 include the world-famous Pikes Peak; picnic grounds, campgrounds (fee); Wilkerson Pass (9,507 feet), 45 miles W on US 24, with a visitor information center (Memorial Day-Labor Day); Lost Creek Wilderness, NW of Lake George; and Mount Evans Wilderness, NW of Bailey. Contact the Supervisor, 1920 Valley Dr, Pueblo 81008. There is also a Ranger District office in Colorado Springs at 601 S Weber; phone 719/636-1602.

⭐ **Pikes Peak.** *10 miles W on US 24 to Cascade, then 19 miles on toll road to summit. Phone 719/684-9383.* (14,110 feet) Toll road climbs 7,309 feet. (Daily; weather permitting) Closed during annual Hill Climb in July (see SPECIAL EVENTS). **$$$** Also here is

> **Cog railway.** *515 Ruxton Ave in Manitou Springs, 5 miles W on US 24. Phone 719/685-5401.* Up to eight trips daily (May-Oct, inquire for schedule). Reservations required. **$$$$**

Pikes Peak Auto Hill Climb Educational Museum. *135 Manitou Ave. Phone 719/685-4400.* More than two dozen race cars plus numerous exhibits on the Pikes Peak race, considered America's second-oldest auto race. (Daily, shorter hours in winter; closed holidays) **$$**

Pikes Peak Ghost Town. *US 24 W at 400 S 21st St. Phone 719/634-0696.* Authentic Old West town under one roof in an 1899 railroad building. Includes antique-furnished buildings such as general store, livery, jail, saloon, and re-created Victorian home. Also horseless carriages and buggies and a 1903 Cadillac. Old-time nickelodeons, player pianos, arcade "movies", and shooting gallery. (Daily) **$$$**

Pro Rodeo Hall of Fame and American Cowboy Museum. *101 Pro Rodeo Dr (I-25 exit 147 Rockrimmon Blvd). Phone*

719/528-4764. Traces the rodeo lifestyle and its development over more than 100 years. Multimedia presentation documents rodeo's evolution from its origins in 19th-century ranch work to its present status as a major spectator sport. More than 90 exhibits of historic and modern cowboy and rodeo gear; changing Western art exhibits. The outdoor exhibits include live rodeo animals and a replica rodeo arena. (Daily; closed holidays) **$$$**

Rock Ledge Ranch Historic Site. *3202 Chambers Way, 4 miles W via I-25, Garden of Gods exit to 30th St, S to Gateway Rd at E entrance of Garden of the Gods. Phone 719/578-6777.* A living history program demonstrating everyday life in the region; 1868 homestead, 1895 working ranch, 1907 Orchard House. Braille nature trail. (June-Labor Day, Wed-Sun; after Labor Day-Dec 25, weekends) **$$**

Seven Falls. *2850 S Cheyenne Canyon Rd (80906). 7 miles SW on Cheyenne Blvd in south Cheyenne Canyon. Phone 719/632-0765.* Only completely lighted canyon and waterfall in the world. Best seen from Eagle's Nest, reached by mountain elevator. Native American dance interpretations (summer, daily). Night lighting (summer). **$$$**

US Air Force Academy. *2160 Vickers Dr Suite G (80918). N on I-25 exit 150 B (South Gate) or 156 B (North Gate). Phone 719/333-7742; 800/955-4438.* (1955) (4,200 cadets.) On 18,500 acres at foot of Rampart Range of Rocky Mountains where cadets undergo four-year academic, military, and physical training. Striking, modern cadet chapel (daily; closed for private services; Sunday service open to public.) Cadet Wing marches to lunch may be watched from wall near Chapel (academic year). Planetarium programs for public (free). Visitor center has self-guided tour brochures, theater, and exhibits on cadet life and academy history (Daily; closed Jan 1, Thanksgiving, Dec 25). **FREE**

US Olympic Complex and Visitor Center. *One Olympic Plaza, 2 blocks N of Platte Ave (US 24 E), at Union Blvd. Phone 719/866-4618.* National headquarters of the US Olympic Committee, 15 national sports governing bodies, and Olympic Training Center, where more than 15,000 athletes train each year. Guided tours include film and walking tour of training center. (Daily) **FREE**

World Figure Skating Hall of Fame and Museum. *20 First St, off Lake Ave. Phone 719/635-5200.* Exhibits on history of figure skating; art, memorabilia, library, skate gallery, video collection. (May-Sept, Mon-Sat; rest of year, Mon-Fri; closed holidays) **$$**

Special Events

Colorado Springs Balloon Classic. *Memorial Park. Hancock and Union sts (80910).* Labor Day weekend.

Greyhound racing. *Post Time Greyhound Park. 3701 N Nevada Ave (80907). E of I-25 between Garden of the Gods and Fillmore. Phone 719/632-1391.* Apr-late Sept.

Motor sports. *Pikes Peak International Raceway. 16650 Midway Ranch Rd (80817). S on I-25 in Fountain. Phone 719/382-RACE, 888/306-RACE, or 800/511-PPIR.* May-Sept.

Pikes Peak International Hill Climb. *Last 12 miles of Pikes Peak Hwy. Phone 719/685-4400.* The "Race to the Clouds" has been a part of Colorado Springs' July 4 celebration for more than 80 years. Spectators of all ages marvel at the fine skill and sheer gutsiness of those who dare speed their racecars, trucks, and motorcycles along the final 12.4 miles of Pikes Peak Highway, a gravel route with 156 turns and a 5,000-foot rise in elevation. Vehicles can reach more than 130 mph on straightaways, and there isn't a guardrail in sight. Spectators need to be on the mountain at the crack of dawn to catch the action. Those who don't take advantage of the overnight parking the evening before the race can arrive as early as 4 am to stake out a good spot. The road closes to additional spectators at 8 am, so plan to spend the day here. Those who park above the start line won't be able to leave until late afternoon when the race is over—otherwise, they could become part of the race. The best views are above the tree line, so dress warmly. Late June-early-July. **$$$$**

Pikes Peak Marathon. *Phone 719/473-2625.* Footrace from cog depot to summit and back. Aug.

Pikes Peak or Bust Rodeo. *Spencer Penrose Stadium. Phone 719/635-3547.* First full week in Aug.

Motels/Motor Lodges

★ **COMFORT INN.** *2115 Aerotech Dr (80916). Phone 719/380-9000; fax 719/596-4738. www.comfortinn.com.* 42 rooms, 2 story. S $50-$119; D $60-$129; under 18 free. Crib free. Complimentary continental breakfast. Check-out noon. TV; cable (premium), VCR available. In-room modem link. Coffee in rooms. Coin laundry. Restaurant nearby. Exercise equipment. Indoor pool, whirlpool. Free airport transportation. Meeting rooms. Business services. Cr cds: A, C, D, DS, JCB, MC, V.

🄳 🛇 🏊 🕇 🛇

★ **COMFORT INN NORTH.** *6450 Corporate Center Dr (80210). Phone 719/262-9000; fax 719/262-9900. www.comfortinn.com.* 70 rooms, 4 story. S $59-$95; D $69-$105; each additional $10; under 18 free. TV; cable (premium). Complimentary continental breakfast, coffee in rooms. Restaurant nearby. Check-out 11 am. Meeting rooms. In-room modem link. Coin laundry. Exercise equipment. Indoor pool; whirlpool. Bathroom phones, refrigerators, microwaves. Cr cds: A, C, D, DS, JCB, MC, V.

🄳 🏊 🕇 🔧 🛇 🆂🄲

★ **DRURY INN.** *8155 N Academy Blvd (80920). Phone 719/598-2500; toll-free 800/325-8300. www.drury-inn.com.* 118 rooms, 4 story. May-early Sept: S, D $74-$109; each additional $10; under 18 free; lower rates rest of year. Pet accepted, some restrictions. Complimentary continental breakfast. Check-out noon. TV. In-room modem link. Exercise equipment. Whirlpool. Cr cds: A, C, D, DS, MC, V.

[D] [symbols] [SC]

★ **FAIRFIELD INN.** *7085 Commerce Center Dr (80919). Phone 719/533-1903; toll-free 800/228-2800. www.fairfieldinn.com.* 67 rooms, 4 story. May-early Oct: S $84; D $91; each additional $8; under 18 free; lower rates rest of year. Crib free. TV; cable (premium). Complimentary continental breakfast, coffee in rooms. Restaurant nearby. Check-out 11 am. Meeting room. Business services available. Indoor pool; whirlpool. Game room. Some refrigerators, microwaves. Cr cds: A, C, D, DS, ER, JCB, MC, V.

[D] [symbols] [SC]

★ **FAIRFIELD INN.** *2725 Geyser Dr (80906). Phone 719/576-1717; fax 719/576-4747. www.fairfieldinn.com.* 85 rooms, 3 story. Mid-May-mid-Oct: S, D $99-$139; under 18 free; lower rates rest of year. Complimentary continental breakfast. Check-out noon. TV; cable (premium). In-room modem link. Restaurant nearby. Exercise equipment. Indoor pool, whirlpool. Cr cds: A, C, D, DS, MC, V.

[D] [symbols]

★ **HOLIDAY INN EXPRESS.** *1815 Aeroplaza Dr (80916). Phone 719/591-6000; toll-free 800/465-4329; fax 719/591-6100. www.holiday-inn.com.* 94 rooms, 4 story, 15 suites. S $59-$95; D $69-$105; suites $119-$129; under 19 free; weekend, holiday rates. Crib free. TV; cable (premium). Complimentary continental breakfast. Complimentary coffee in rooms. Restaurant nearby. Check-out noon. Meeting rooms. Business center. In-room modem link. Sundries. Coin laundry. Free airport transportation. Exercise equipment. Bathroom phones. Refrigerator, microwave, wet bar in suites. Some balconies. Cr cds: A, C, D, DS, JCB, MC, V.

[D] [symbols] [SC] [symbol]

★ **MICROTEL INN & SUITES.** *7265 Commerce Center Dr (80919). Phone 719/598-7500; toll-free 800/964-8396; fax 719/598-4975. www.microtelinnco.com.* 105 rooms, 69 suites, 4 story. Mid-May-mid-Sept: S $49-$79; D $89-$120; each additional $10; suites $89; under 16 free; lower rates rest of year. Crib free. Complimentary continental breakfast. Complimentary coffee in rooms. Check-out 11 am. TV; cable (premium). In-room modem link. Refrigerator, microwave in suites. Coin laundry. Restaurant nearby. Exercise equipment. Indoor pool, whirlpool. Cr cds: A, C, D, DS, MC, V.

[D] [symbols] [SC]

★ ★ **RAMADA INN.** *3125 N Sinton Rd (80907). Phone 719/633-5541; fax 719/633-3870. www.ramada.com.* 215 rooms, 2 story. May-Aug: S $89; D $99; suites $175-$225;

under 18 free; lower rates rest of year. Crib free. TV; cable (premium). Complimentary coffee in lobby, rooms. Restaurant 6 am-1:30 pm, 5:30-10 pm. Room service. Bar 5-10 pm. Check-out noon. Meeting rooms. Business services available. In-room modem link. Valet service. Coin laundry. Free airport transportation. Indoor pool. Game room. Health club privileges. Cr cds: A, C, D, DS, ER, JCB, MC, V.

[D] [symbols] [SC]

★ **VILLAGER PREMIER.** *725 W Cimarron St (80905). Phone 719/473-5530; fax 719/473-8763.* 208 rooms, 2 story. Mid-May-mid-Sept: S, D $75-$105; each additional $10; suites $225; under 19 free; family, weekly rates; lower rates rest of year. Pet accepted; fee. Complimentary continental breakfast. Check-out noon. TV; cable (premium). In-room modem link. Cr cds: A, C, D, DS, MC, V.

[D] [symbols]

Hotels

★ ★ ★ **THE ANTLERS ADAM'S MARK HOTEL.** *4 S Cascade (80903). Phone 719/473-5600; fax 719/389-0259. www.adamsmark.com.* Though no longer housed in the original, historic building which opened in 1883 and was destroyed by fire, this modern rendition attempts to re-create the hospitable feel of the original. There is much to do in the area, and many rooms have views of the main attraction, Pikes Peak. 298 rooms, 13 story. D $95-$125; each additional $15; suites $200-$825; under 18 free; weekend rates. Pet accepted, some restrictions. Check-out noon. TV; cable (premium), VCR available. Restaurant 6:30 am-midnight; Fri, Sat to 1 am. Bar 11-1 am, Sun to midnight. Exercise equipment. Indoor pool, whirlpool, poolside service. Valet parking. Concierge. Cr cds: A, C, D, DS, MC, V.

[D] [symbols]

★ ★ ★ **DOUBLETREE HOTEL.** *1775 E Cheyenne Mt Blvd (80906). Phone 719/576-8900; toll-free 800/222-8733; fax 719/576-4450. www.doubletree.com.* This contemporary hotel is situated at the base of the mountains in Colorado Springs. There is access to many of the recreational activities in the area. 299 rooms, 5 story. S, D $59-$169; each additional $15; suites $375-$475; under 18 free; weekend rates. Pet accepted; $10. Check-out noon. TV; cable (premium). In-room modem link. Restaurant 6 am-10 pm. Bar 11-2 am, Tues-Sat. Room service. Exercise equipment, sauna. Indoor pool, whirlpool. Airport transportation. Cr cds: A, C, D, DS, ER, JCB, MC, V.

[D] [symbols]

★ ★ **RADISSON INN & SUITES.** *1645 Newport Rd (80916). Phone 719/597-7000; fax 719/597-4308.*

www.radisson.com. Adjacent to the municipal airport and 10 minutes from downtown, this full-service hotel affords a comfortable stay. 200 rooms, 2 story. May-Sept: S, D $109-$129; each additional $15; suites $160; under 18 free; weekly rates; lower rates rest of year. Pet accepted, some restrictions; fee. Complimentary full breakfast. Check-out noon. TV; cable (premium). In-room modem link. Room service 24 hours. Restaurant 6 am-10 pm. Bar. Exercise equipment. Game room. Indoor pool, whirlpool, poolside service. Free airport transportation. Business center. Concierge. Cr cds: A, C, D, DS, ER, JCB, MC, V.

⊡ 🐾 🏊 🍴 ✈ 🏊 SC 🏃

★★ **RADISSON INN.** *8110 North Academy Blvd (80920). Phone 719/598-5770; fax 719/598-3434. www.radisson.com.* This hotel is the closest option to the U.S. Air Force Academy. 200 rooms, 2-4 story. May-Sept: S $119-$149; D $129-$159; each additional $10; suites $159-$259; under 18 free; weekend rates; lower rates rest of year. Pet accepted, some restrictions. Check-out noon. TV; cable (premium). In-room modem link. Restaurant 6:30 am-10 pm. Bar rom 11 am. Room service. Exercise equipment, sauna. Indoor pool, whirlpool. Free airport transportation. Cr cds: A, C, D, DS, ER, JCB, MC, V.

⊡ 🐾 🏊 🍴 ✈ 🏊 SC

★★★ **SHERATON HOTEL.** *2886 S Cir Dr (80905). Phone 719/576-5900; toll-free 800/981-4012; fax 719/576-7695. www.sheraton.com.* This hotel is near the airport, Pikes Peak, U.S. Airforce Academy, and the Olympic training facility. 500 rooms, 2-4 story. Mid-May-mid-Sept: S, D $105-$155; suites $250; under 18 free; weekend rates; lower rates rest of year. Crib $5. Pet accepted. TV; cable (premium), VCR available. 2 pools, 1 indoor; wading pool, whirlpool. Playground. Coffee in rooms. Restaurant 6 am-10 pm. Room service 24 hours. Bars 11-2 am; entertainment Fri, Sat. Check-out 11 am. Convention facilities. Business center. In-room modem link. Bellhops. Valet. Concierge. Gift shop. Airport transportation. Lighted tennis. Putting green. Exercise equipment; steam room, sauna. Game room. Some refrigerators; microwaves available. Private patios, balconies. Cr cds: A, C, D, DS, JCB, MC, V.

⊡ 🐾 🏊 🏊 🍴 🏊 SC 🏃

★★ **WYNDHAM COLORADO SPRINGS HOTEL.** *5580 Tech Center Dr (80919). Phone 719/260-1800; fax 719/260-1492. www.wyndham.com.* 311 rooms, 9 story. S $129-$159; D $149-$179; suites $275-$350; under 18 free. Crib free. Check-out noon. TV; cable (premium), VCR available. In-room modem link. Laundry facilities. Restaurant 6:30 am-2 pm, 5-11 pm. Bar 11 am-midnight. Exercise equipment, sauna. 2 pools, 1 indoor, poolside service. Business services. Convention center/facilities. Gift shop. Cr cds: A, C, D, DS, ER, JCB, MC, V.

⊡ ⛄ 🏊 🏊 🍴 🏊

Resort

★★★★★ **THE BROADMOOR.** *1 Lake Ave (80906). Phone 719/634-7711; toll-free 800/634-7711; fax 719/577-5700. www.broadmoor.com.* Located at the foot of the Rocky Mountains and surrounded by the sparkling beauty of Cheyenne Lake, The Broadmoor has been one of America's favorite resorts since 1918. This paradise for outdoor enthusiasts is close to Colorado Springs, yet feels a million miles away with its verdant fields carpeted in brilliant wildflowers, perfectly manicured golf courses, and opulent accommodations. This all-season resort is grand in scale, and the accommodations are at once lavish and comfortable. The Broadmoor's myriad recreational opportunities include tennis, golf on three championship courses, horseback riding through old mining claims, fly fishing in pristine streams, and hot air ballooning over the Colorado countryside. Incorporating indigenous botanicals, pure spring water, and natural elements, the spa offers a variety of soothing treatments. Others seek a different kind of therapy in the resort's unique shops, while 11 restaurants and bars cater to all moods. 700 rooms. Mid-May-mid-Oct: S, D $190-$425; suites $450-$2,000; package plans; lower rates rest of year. Check-out noon, check-in 4 pm. TV; cable (premium), VCR available. In-room modem link. Dining room (see PENROSE ROOM). Bar noon-1 am; Sun to midnight. Entertainment, dancing, movie theater. Room service 24 hours. Supervised children's activities (June-Labor Day and Dec 25 holidays); ages 3-12. Exercise room, sauna. Health spa, massage. 4 heated pools, 1 indoor; whirlpool, wading pool, poolside service, lifeguard. Three 18-hole golf courses, greens fee. Tennis (indoor in winter). Bicycles, boats, Fishing/hunting guide service. Horses/riding. Airport, railroad station, bus depot transportation. Business center. Concierge. Cr cds: A, C, D, DS, JCB, MC, V.

⊡ ⛄ 🏌 🍴 🏊 🍴 🏊 🍴 ✈ 🏊 🏃

All Suite

★ **AMERISUITES.** *503 W Garden of the Gods Rd (80907). Phone 719/265-9385; toll-free 800/833-1516; fax 719/532-9514. www.amerisuites.com.* 126 suites, 4 story. Apr-Sept: D $89-$109; suites $149; each additional $10; under 18 free; weekend rates; lower rates rest of year. Complimentary continental breakfast. Check-out noon. TV; cable (premium). In-room modem link. Restaurant adjacent 11 am-11 pm. Exercise equipment. Pool. Cr cds: A, D, DS, MC, V.

⊡ 🏊 🍴 🏊 SC

★★ **EMBASSY SUITES HOTEL COLORADO SPRINGS.** *7290 Commerce Center Dr (80919). Phone 719/599-9100; fax 719/599-4644. www.embassysuites.com.* Located in the northwest end of the city, this hotel has good views of the Rocky Mountains. 207 suites, 4 story.

Mid-Apr-Sept: S, D $99-$169; each additional $10; under 12 free; lower rates rest of year. Complimentary full breakfast. Check-out noon. TV; cable (premium). In-room modem link. Restaurant 11:30 am-2:30 pm, 6-10 pm. Bar to midnight. Room service. Exercise equipment, sauna. Game room. Indoor pool, whirlpool. Cr cds: A, C, D, DS, JCB, MC, V.

B&B/Small Inns

★ ★ ★ **CHEYENNE CAÑON INN.** *2030 W Cheyenne Blvd (80906). Phone 719/633-0625; fax 719/633-8826. www.cheyennecanoninn.com.* Built in 1921 for Colorado Spring's elites, this resort was originally an upscale bordello and gambling hall. This restored Mission-style mansion, with spectacular views of the mountains and Cheyenne Cañon and warm, professional service, is an exceptional find. 10 rooms, 2 story. S, D $95-$200. Complimentary full breakfast. TV; cable (premium). In-room modem link. Whirlpool. Cr cds: A, DS, MC, V.

★ ★ ★ **HEARTHSTONE INN.** *506 N Cascade Ave (80903). Phone 719/473-4413; toll-free 800/521-1885; fax 719/473-1322. www.hearthstoneinn.com.* Each of the rooms in this romantic Victorian inn is uniquely decorated. The yesteryear atmosphere is enhanced by the croquet lawn, roaring fireplace, and other Victorian amenities. 28 rooms, 3 story. No room phones. D $69-$199; each additional $15; under 4 free. Complimentary full breakfast. Check-out 11 am, check-in 2-10 pm. Fireplaces. Restored Victorian mansion (1885); brass fixtures, carved beds, many antique furnishings. Some rooms with view of Pikes Peak. Totally nonsmoking. Cr cds: A, D, DS, MC, V.

★ ★ ★ **HOLDEN HOUSE 1902 BED & BREAKFAST.** *1102 W Pikes Peak Ave (80904). Phone 719/471-3980; toll-free 888/565-3980; fax 719/471-4740. www.holdenhouse.com.* Located in a historic house and carriage house dating from 1902, this inn has modern guest rooms with Victorian charm. Two pure-bred Siamese cats stand guard. 5 suites, 2 story. S, D $135. Adults only. Complimentary full breakfast, afternoon refreshments. Check-out 11 am, check-in 4-6 pm. TV in sitting room. Fireplaces, antique furnishings. Restaurant nearby. Victorian house (1902). Totally nonsmoking. Cr cds: A, C, D, DS, MC, V.

★ ★ ★ **OLD TOWN GUEST HOUSE.** *115 S 26th St (80904). Phone 719/632-9194; toll-free 888/375-4210; fax 719/632-9026. www.oldtown-guesthouse.com.* Built in 1997, this bed-and-breakfast has all of the amenities of a modern hotel, including an elevator, but it is located in the heart of Old Colorado City. 8 rooms, 3 story. S, D

$95-$175. TV; cable (premium), VCR (movies). Complimentary full breakfast. Complimentary coffee in rooms. Restaurant adjacent 6 am-9 pm. Check-out 11 am, check-in 4-6 pm. In-room modem link. Luggage handling. Valet service. Exercise equipment. Game room. Refrigerators. Many fireplaces and balconies. Totally nonsmoking. Cr cds: A, DS, MC, V.

★ ★ ★ **ROOM AT THE INN.** *618 N Nevada Ave (80903). Phone 719/442-1896; toll-free 800/579-4621; fax 719/442-6802. www.roomattheinn.com.* This bed-and-breakfast is housed in a turn-of-the-century Queen Anne Victorian house and carriage house. Original murals and working fireplaces provide the romantic ambiance right in the heart of the historic city. 7 rooms, 1 with shower only, 3 story. S, D $89-$135; each additional $15. Children over 12 years only. Complimentary full breakfast, afternoon refreshments. Check-out 11 am, check-in 4-6 pm. Restaurant nearby. Whirlpool. Luggage services, concierge. Queen Anne Victorian home built in 1896; 3-story turret, wraparound porch. Totally nonsmoking. Cr cds: A, DS, MC, V.

Guest Ranch

★ ★ ★ **LOST VALLEY RANCH.** *29555 Goose Creek Rd (80135). Phone 303/647-2311; fax 303/647-2315. www.lostvalleyranch.com.* Set upon 40,000 acres of the Pike National Forest, this dude ranch, owned by the Foster family, is a perfect getaway spot for corporate retreats or family vacations. 24 (1-3 bedroom) cabins. No A/C. No room phones. Mid-June-Labor Day, AP, weekly: $1,690 each; family rates; lower daily rates rest of year. Check-out Sun 10 am, check-in Sun 2 pm. Coffee in cabins. Private porches, balconies. Refrigerators, fireplaces. Coin laundry. Box lunches, picnics, cookouts. Free supervised children's activities (Memorial Day-Labor Day); ages 3-18. Playground. Social director, entertainment, square dancing. Recreation room. Pool; whirlpools. Tennis. Lawn games. Fishing school; fish cleaning, storage, cooking. Hayrides, wagon rides. Meeting rooms. Business services. Trap shooting. Spring and fall cattle round-ups. Beautiful view of mountains. Authentic working ranch. Homesteaded in 1883.

Restaurants

★ ★ ★ **CHARLES COURT.** *1 Lake Ave (80906). Phone 719/577-5774; toll-free 800/634-7711; fax 719/577-5738. www.broadmoor.com.* One of nine restaurants at the luxurious Broadmoor Hotel, Charles Court offers progressive American fare in a relaxed, open, airy, and contemporary setting. In warm weather, alfresco dining with lakeside views can't be beat. The American-style menu features fresh, seasonal ingredients and borrows influences from Asia, Italy, and Mexico. While there are global accents on the menu, the kitchen also offers a selection of regional Rocky Mountain fare, such as Colorado rack of lamb and the signature Charles Court Game Grill. The restaurant's wine list boasts more than 800 selections from America, France, Italy, Germany, Australia, and New Zealand. For special occasions, head inside to the kitchen for dinner. At the Chef's Table in the kitchen (four guests minimum), you can sit down and have the chef cook the multicourse meal of your choosing. Continental menu. Hours: 7-11 am, 6-9:30 pm. Breakfast $9-$13, dinner $28-$45. Bar. Jacket required. Reservations accepted. Valet parking. Cr cds: A, C, D, DS, ER, JCB, MC, V.

★ ★ **EDELWEISS.** *34 E Ramona Ave (80906). Phone 719/633-2220; fax 719/471-8413. www.restauranteur.com/edelweiss.* American, German menu. Hours: 11:30 am-2 pm, 5-9 pm; Fri, Sat to 9:30 pm; Sun 5-9 pm. Closed Dec 25. Lunch $5.50-$8.75, dinner $9.75-$18.75. Bar. German music and entertainment Fri, Sat. Former schoolhouse (1890). Outdoor dining. Cr cds: A, D, DS, MC, V.

★ **GIUSEPPE'S OLD DEPOT.** *10 S Sierra Madre (80903). Phone 719/635-3111; fax 719/444-0857. www.giuseppes-depot.com.* American, Italian menu. Salad bar. Hours: 11 am-9:30 pm; Fri, Sat to 11 pm. Closed Thanksgiving, Dec 25. Dinner $5.95-$16.50. Bar. Children's menu. In historic railroad depot (1887); railroad memorabilia on display. Patio dining. Cr cds: A, C, D, DS, ER, MC, V.

★ ★ **HATCH COVER.** *252 E Cheyenne Mountain Blvd (80906). Phone 719/576-5223; fax 719/576-3557.* Hours: 11 am-2 pm, 5-10 pm; Sat, Sun from 5 pm. Reservations accepted. Bar to 2 am. Lunch $3.95-$11.95, dinner $10-$35. Specializes in fresh seafood, prime rib, pasta. Parking. Aquariums. Cr cds: D, DS, MC, V.

★ **LA CREPERIE.** *204 N Tejon (80903). Phone 719/632-0984. www.restauranteur.com/lacreperie.* Continental menu. Hours: 10 am-9 pm; Sun, Mon to 3 pm. Closed most major holidays. Lunch $6-$14, dinner $7-$24. Former streetcar horse stable (1892). Cr cds: A, D, MC, V.

★ ★ **LA PETITE MAISON.** *1015 W Colorado Ave (80904). Phone 719/632-4887; fax 719/632-0343. www.restauranteur.com/maison.* Hours: 5-10 pm; early-bird dinner to 6:30 pm. Closed Sun, Mon; Jan 1, July 4, Dec 24-25. Dinner $11.50-$29. Service bar. In renovated house (1894). Reservations accepted. Totally nonsmoking. Cr cds: A, D, DS, MC, V.

★ ★ **MACKENZIE'S CHOP HOUSE.** *128 S Tejon (80903). Phone 719/635-3536 www.mackenzieschophouse.com; fax 719/635-1225.* Steak menu. Specializes in steaks, chops, seafood. Hours: 11 am-2 pm, 5-10 pm; Fri to 11 pm; Sat 5-11 pm, closed Dec 25. Lunch $6.95-$15.95, dinner $10.95-$34.95. Bar. Built 1890. Reservations accepted. Outdoor dining. Totally nonsmoking. Cr cds: A, MC, V.

★ **MAGGIE MAE'S.** *2405 E Pikes Peak Ave (80909). Phone 719/475-1623; fax 719/475-8593.* American, Mexican menu. Hours: 6 am-10 pm; Sat, Sun to 9 pm. Closed Dec 25. Dinner $5.95-$12.95. Bar to 2 am. Children's menu. Cr cds: A, C, D, DS, ER, MC, V.

★ **OLD CHICAGO.** *7115 Commerce Center Dr (80919). Phone 719/593-7678; fax 719/593-2914. www.oldchicago.com.* American, Italian menu. Hours: 11-2 am; Sun to midnight. Closed Thanksgiving, Dec 25. Lunch $4.95-$7.95, dinner $5.95-$15.95. Bar. Sports bar atmosphere. Children's menu. Cr cds: A, D, MC, V.

★ **OLD CHICAGO PASTA & PIZZA.** *118 N Tejon (80903). Phone 719/634-8812; fax 719/634-0629.* Italian menu. Closed Thanksgiving, Dec 25. Lunch, dinner. Bar. Children's menu. Outdoor seating. Cr cds: A, C, D, ER, MC, V.

★ ★ ★ **PENROSE ROOM.** *1 Lake Ave (80906). Phone 719/634-7711; fax 719/577-5700. www.broadmoor.com.* With panoramic views of the city lights and surrounding mountains, dinner at The Penrose Room is a visually thrilling event. The glamorous room, appointed with glittering crystal chandeliers, vintage carpets, tufted armchairs, and luxurious linen tabletops, is steeped in old-world charm. The Penrose Room, which opened its doors in 1918, transports you back to a time when women wore long gloves to dinner and men checked their top hats at the door. But the thrills are not limited to the sense of sight; your sense of taste is also in for a treat. The menu is French contemporary and includes Francophile favorites such as escargots, Coquilles St. Jacques, foie gras terrine, and Chateaubriand of beef (carved tableside), in addition to more modern global fare like Colorado lamb chop with a clover blossom honey glaze. Don't worry about calories here; a big band plays nightly, so you can revive the waltz or the foxtrot on the spacious dance floor to work off your decadent dinner. Hours: 6-10 pm. Dinner $23-$35. Bar. Live music. Jacket required. Cr cds: A, D, MC, V.

Copper Mountain (C-4)

(See Dillon)

Cortez (G-1)

Settled 1890 **Pop** 7,977

Information Cortez/Mesa Verde Visitor Info Bureau, PO Box HH; 970/565-8227 or 800/253-1616

Originally a trading center for sheep and cattle ranchers whose spreads dot the plains to the south, Cortez now accommodates travelers visiting Mesa Verde National Park (see) and oil workers whose business takes them to the nearby Aneth Oil Field. The semidesert area 38 miles southwest of Cortez is the only spot in the nation where one can stand in four states (Colorado, Utah, Arizona, New Mexico) and two Native American nations (Navajo and Ute) at one time; a simple marker located approximately 100 yards from the Four Corners Highway (US 160) indicates the exact place where these areas meet. There are many opportunities for hunting and fishing in the Dolores River valley.

What to See and Do

Anasazi Heritage Center and Escalante. *27501 CO 184 (81323). 8 miles N on CO 145, then 2 miles NW on CO 184. Phone 970/882-4811.* Museum of exhibits, artifacts, and documents from excavations on public lands in southwest Colorado, including the Dolores Archaeological Program. Represents the Northern San Juan Anasazi Tradition (A.D. 1 to 1300). Within 1/2 mile of the center are the Dominguez and Escalante sites—the latter discovered by a Franciscan friar in 1776. Excavations revealed kivas and other structures, pottery, and ceremonial artifacts. (Daily; closed Jan 1, Thanksgiving, Dec 25) **$$**

Hovenweep National Monument. *McElmo Rte (81321). 20 miles NW on US 666 to Pleasant View and follow signs 5 miles W on County BB, then 20 miles S on County 10. Phone 970/562-4282.* Monument consists of six units of prehistoric ruins; the best preserved is at Square Tower, which includes the remains of pueblos and towers. Self-guided trail, park ranger on duty; visitor area (daily). **$$$**

Lowry Pueblo. *110 W 11th St. 21 miles NW on US 666 to Pleasant View, then 9 miles W on County Road CC. Phone 970/247-4874.* Constructed by the Anasazi (circa 1075). Forty excavated rooms including one great and seven smaller kivas. Picnic facilities. No camping. (Daily, weather and road conditions permitting) **FREE**

Mesa Verde National Park (see). *10 miles E on US 160.*

Ute Mountain Tribal Park. *Phone 970/565-9653 or 800/847-5485.* The Ute Mountain Tribe developed this 125,000-acre park on their tribal lands, opening hundreds of largely unexplored 800-year-old Anasazi ruins to the public. Tours begin at the Ute Mountain Visitor Center/Museum, 19 miles S via US 666 (daily); reservations required. Backpacking trips in summer. Primitive camping available. **$$$$**

Special Events

Montezuma County Fair. *30100 Hwy 160 (81321). Phone 970/565-1000.* First week in Aug.

Ute Mountain Rodeo. *Phone 970/565-4485.* Early-mid June.

Motels/Motor Lodges

★ **BEST WESTERN TURQUOISE INN & SUITES.** *535 E Main St (81321). Phone 970/565-3778; toll-free 800/547-3376; fax 970/565-3439. www.cortezbestwestern.com.* 77 rooms, 33 suites, 2 story. Pet accepted. Complimentary continental breakfast. Check-out 11 am, check-in 3 pm. TV; cable (premium). In-room modem link. Fireplaces. Outdoor pool, whirlpool. Free airport transportation. Cr cds: A, C, D, DS, MC, V. **$**

★ **HOLIDAY INN EXPRESS.** *2121 E Main St (81321). Phone 970/565-6000; toll-free 800/626-5652; fax 970/565-3438. www.coloradoholiday.com.* 100 rooms, 3 story. Pet accepted. Complimentary continental breakfast. Check-out 11 am. Check-in 3 pm. TV; cable (premium), VCR available. In-room modem link. Coin laundry. In-house fitness room, sauna. Indoor pool, whirlpool. Free airport transportation. Cr cds: A, D, DS, JCB, MC, V. **$**

Restaurant

★ ★ **HOMESTEADERS.** *45 E Main St (81321). Phone 970/565-6253; fax 970/564-9217.* American, Southwestern menu. Closed major holidays; also Sun, Jan 1, Thanksgiving, Dec 25. Lunch, dinner. Bar. Children's menu. Casual attire. Reservations accepted. Nonsmoking seating. Cr cds: MC, V. **$$**

Craig (B-3)

See also Steamboat Springs

Pop 9,189 **Elev** 6,186 ft **Area code** 970 **Zip** 81625

Information Greater Craig Area Chamber of Commerce, 360 E Victory Way; 970/824-5689 or 800/864-4405

Web www.craig-chamber.com

Craig is known for excellent big-game hunting for elk, deer, and antelope, and bass fishing in Elkhead Reservoir. The Yampa River area draws float-boaters, hikers, and wildlife photographers in summer and cross-country skiers and snowmobilers in winter.

What to See and Do

Dinosaur National Monument (see). *Exit 21 off CO State Thruway, W on CO 23 to CO 145W, 1 mile off CO 145 on Shady Glen Rd in East Durham. Phone 518/239-4559.* **$$$$**

Marcia. *360 E Victory Way. City Park, US 40. Phone 970/824-5689.* Private, luxury Pullman railroad car of David Moffat. Tours available through Moffat County Visitors Center. **FREE**

Museum of Northwest Colorado. *590 Yampa Ave, Old State Armory, center of town. Phone 970/824-6360.* Local history, Native American artifacts; wildlife photography. Cowboy and gunfighter collection. Also the Edwin C. Johnson Collection (Johnson was governor of Colorado and a US senator). (Mon-Sat). **DONATION**

Save Our Sandrocks Nature Trail. *900 Alta Vista Dr. Phone 970/824-6673.* This sloped, 3/4-mile trail provides a view of Native American petroglyphs on the sandrocks. Trail guide available at the Cooperative Extension Office, 200 W Victory Way. (May-Nov) **FREE**

Motel/Motor Lodge

★★ **HOLIDAY INN.** *300 S Hwy 13 (81625). Phone 970/824-4000; toll-free 800/465-4329; fax 970/824-3950. www.holiday-inn.com.* 152 rooms, 2 story. S $59-$79; D $69-$89; each additional $10; suites $84-$109; under 19 free. Crib free. Pet accepted. TV; cable (premium), VCR available. Indoor pool; whirlpool, poolside service. Coffee in rooms. Restaurant 6 am-2 pm, 5-10 pm. Room service. Bar 4 pm-midnight. Check-out 11 am. Coin laundry. Meeting rooms. Business services available. Valet service. Holidome. Exercise equipment. Game room. Refrigerators. Microwaves available. Cr cds: A, D, DS, JCB, MC, V.

🄳 🦮 🏊 🖼️

Crested Butte (D-3)

See also Gunnison

Founded 1880 **Pop** 1,529 **Elev** 8,908 ft **Area code** 970 **Zip** 81224

Information Crested Butte Vacations, 500 Gothic Road, PO Box A, Mount Crested Butte 81225; 800/544-8448

Web www.crestedbutteresort.com

Crested Butte is a remarkably picturesque mining town in the midst of magnificent mountain country. Inquire locally for information on horseback pack trips to Aspen (see) through the West Elk Wilderness. Guided fishing trips are available on the more than 1,000 miles of streams and rivers within a two-hour drive of Crested Butte.

What to See and Do

Crested Butte Mountain Resort Ski Area. *12 Snowmass Rd (81224). 3 miles N on county road in Gunnison National Forest (see GUNNISON). Phone 800/810-SNOW.* Three high-speed quad, three triple, three double chairlifts, four surface lifts, two magic carpets; patrol, school, rentals, snowmaking; cafeteria, restaurant, bar, nursery. Eighty-five runs; longest run 2 1/2 miles; vertical drop 3,062 feet. (Late Nov-mid-Apr, daily) Multiday, half-day rates. Nineteen miles of groomed cross-country trails, 100 miles of wilderness trails; snowmobiling, sleigh rides. **$$$$**

B&B/Small Inns

★★ **CRESTED BUTTE ATHLETIC CLUB.** *512 2nd Ave (81224). Phone 970/349-6655; toll-free 800/815-CLUB; fax 970/349-7580.* 8 rooms, 2 story. Mid-Nov-mid-Apr (2-day minimum): S, D $125-$250; each additional $30; ski, golf plans; lower rates rest of year. Complimentary breakfast buffet. Check-out 11 am, check-in 3 pm. TV; cable (premium). Restaurant opposite 5-10 pm. Bar 7 am-10 pm. Exercise equipment, massage, steam room. Heated indoor pool, whirlpool. Downhill ski 2 miles, cross-country 1 block. Built in 1886; many family heirlooms, fireplaces. Totally nonsmoking. Cr cds: DS, MC, V.

🏊 🕴️ 🛏️ 🏃 🖼️

★★ **THE NORDIC INN.** *14 Treasury Rd (80216). Phone 970/349-5542; toll-free 800/542-7669; fax 970/349-6487. www.nordicinncb.com.* 27 rooms, 2 story. No A/C. Thanksgiving-Apr: S, D $88-$152; each additional $10; kitchen units $125-$175; chalets $230-$315; under 12 free (summer); family, weekly rates (summer); ski plans; lower rates rest of year. Closed May. Complimentary continental breakfast. Check-out 11 am. TV; cable (premium), VCR available. In-room modem link. Fireplace in lobby. Restaurant nearby. Downhill ski 1 block. Cr cds: A, MC, V.

🄳 🖼️ 🖼️

★ **OLD TOWN INN.** *201 6th St (81625). Phone 970/349-6184; fax 970/349-1946. www.toski.com/oti.* 32 rooms, 2 story. D $83-$112; each additional $8; higher rates: spring break, week of Dec 25. Complimentary continental breakfast. Check-out 11 am. TV; cable (premium). Laundry services. Restaurant nearby. Cr cds: A, D, DS, MC, V.

🄳 🖼️ 🖼️ 🆂🅲

Restaurants

★ **DONITA'S CANTINA.** *330 Elk Ave (81224). Phone 970/349-6674; fax 970/349-6817.* Hours: 5:30-9:30 pm. Closed Thanksgiving, Dec 25, last 2 weeks in April. No A/C. Mexican menu. Dinner $8.50-$21.95. Children's menu. Specializes in Tex-Mex, vegetarian cuisine. Own desserts. Mexican décor. Former hotel (1881) with original pressed tin ceiling. Totally nonsmoking. Cr cds: A, D, DS, MC, V.

D ⊠

★ ★ **LE BOSQUET.** *6th and Belleview (81224). Phone 970/349-5808; fax 970/349-5677.* French menu. Hours: 6-10 pm; winter from 5:30 pm. Closed mid-Apr-mid-May. Dinner $12.95-$36.95. Bar. No A/C. Outdoor dining. Totally nonsmoking. Cr cds: A, DS, MC, V.

D ⊠

Cripple Creek (E-5)

See also Cañon City, Colorado Springs, Manitou Springs

Settled 1891 **Pop** 1,115 **Elev** 9,494 ft **Area code** 719 **Zip** 80813

Information Chamber of Commerce, PO Box 650; 719/689-2169 or 800/526-8777

Web www.cripple-creek.co.us

Long considered worthless by mining experts despite frequent reports of gold, the "$300 million cow pasture" was finally developed by tenderfeet, who did their prospecting with pitchforks.

At its height, Cripple Creek and the surrounding area produced as much as $25 million in gold in a single year (at $20 per ounce). Few "Wild West" towns experienced a more colorful past. Jack Johnson and Jack Dempsey both worked here, the latter once fighting a long, bloody battle for $50. Texas Guinan, the speakeasy hostess, started her career here. In 1900, the town had a population of more than 25,000 with more than 500 gold mines in operation. Today, only a handful of people live in the shadow of 10,400-foot Mount Pisgah. The town has been designated a National Historic Mining District. The present buildings were built after a great fire in 1896 destroyed the old town.

What to See and Do

Cripple Creek Casinos. *A 48-mile drive from Colorado Springs. Take Hwy 24 west, Colorado Hwy 67 south. Phone 800/235-2922.* Historic Cripple Creek has managed to preserve some of its Old West charm despite the frenzied arrival of legalized gambling in the 1990s. More family friendly than the big casino center of Black Hawk, Cripple Creek nevertheless has nearly 20 limited-stakes ($5 bet limit) casinos along its Victorian storefront main street

area. The massive Imperial Palace Hotel (123 N 3rd St, 800/235-2922) built in 1896, offers a multi-tiered gambling parlor with antique décor—and a good night's sleep in one of its lovely, turn-of-the-century hotel rooms. For a more Vegas-style experience, check out the glitzy, noisy Double Eagle Hotel & Casino (422 E Bennett Ave, 800/711-7234), with more than 600 slot machines, poker, and blackjack tables under a vaulted stained-glass ceiling and a modern, 158-room hotel attached. Both establishments include restaurants or buffets and offer live entertainment. (Daily) **FREE**

Cripple Creek District Museum. *On CO 67. Phone 719/689-2634.* Artifacts of Cripple Creek's glory; pioneer relics, mining and railroad displays; Victorian furnishings. Heritage Art Gallery and Assay Office. Extensive activities for research. (Memorial Day-mid-Oct, daily; winter and early spring, weekends only) **$$**

Cripple Creek-Victor Narrow Gauge Railroad. *520 Carr St. On CO 67. Phone 719/689-2640.* An authentic locomotive and coaches depart from Cripple Creek District Museum. Four-mile round-trip past many historic mines. (Late May-early Oct, daily, departs every 45 minutes) **$$$**

Imperial Casino Hotel. *123 N 3rd St (80813). Phone 719/689-7777; 800/235-2922.* (1896) (see HOTELS) This hotel was constructed shortly after the town's great fire. **$$$**

Mollie Kathleen Gold Mine. *Hwy 67. 1 mile N on CO 67. Phone 719/689-2465.* Descend 1,000 feet on a 40-minute guided tour through a gold mine. (May-Oct, daily) **$$$**

Victor. *5 miles S on CO 67.* Victor, the "city of mines," actually does have streets paved with gold (low-grade ore was used to surface streets in the early days).

Special Events

Donkey Derby Days. *Phone 719/689-3315.* Last full weekend in June.

Veteran's Memorial Rally. *City Park (80813). Phone 719/487-8005.* Mid-Aug.

Motel/Motor Lodge

★ **HOLIDAY INN EXPRESS CRIPPLER.** *601 E Galena Ave (80813). Phone 719/689-2600; toll-free 800/445-3607; fax 719/689-3426. www.holidayinncc.com.* 67 rooms, 3 story. S, D $68-$99; each additional $5; under 18 free. Crib free. Complimentary continental breakfast. Check-out 11 am. TV; cable (premium). Coin laundry. Restaurant nearby. Picnic tables. Meeting rooms. Concierge. Cr cds: A, C, D, DS, JCB, MC, V.

D ⏪ ⛾ ⊠

Hotels

★ ★ **DOUBLE HOTEL & CASINO.** *442 E Bennett Ave (80813). Phone 719/689-5000; toll-free 800/711-7234; fax 719/689-5050. www.decasino.com.* 157 air-cooled rooms, 5 story. S, D $59-$99; each additional $15; suites $129-$500. Crib free. Complimentary full breakfast. Check-out 11 am. TV; cable. Restaurant 6 am-10 pm. Meeting rooms. Business services. Gift shop. Cr cds: A, D, DS, MC, V.

D ⊠

★ **IMPERIAL CASINO HOTEL.** *123 N 3rd St (80813). Phone 719/689-7777; toll-free 800/235-2922; fax 719/689-1008. www.imperialcasinohotel.com.* 29 rooms, 3 story. No A/C. D $65-$80. Check-out 11 am. Restaurant, bar 10-2 am. Built 1896. Victorian décor; antiques. Gold Bar Room Theatre. Cr cds: A, DS, MC, V.

D ♿ ⚙ ⊠

B&B/Small Inn

★ ★ **VICTOR HOTEL.** *4th St and Victor Ave (80860). Phone 719/689-3553; toll-free 800/713-4595; fax 719/689-4197. www.victorhotel.com.* 20 air-cooled rooms, 4 story. D $69.95-$79.95; under 12 free. Complimentary continental breakfast. Check-out 11 am. Check-in noon. TV; cable (premium). Restaurant May-Sept 11 am-2 pm; Fri-Sat to 9 pm. Room service. Cr cds: A, DS, MC, V.

D ♿ ⚙ ⊠

Restaurant

★ ★ **STRATTON DINING ROOM.** *123 N 3rd St (80813). Phone 719/689-7777; fax 719/689-1008.* Hours: Hours: 7-10 am, 11 am-2 pm, 5-9 pm; Sun brunch 11 am-2 pm. A la carte entrees: breakfast $1.25-$4.95, lunch $5.95, dinner $11.95-$25.95. Bars 8-2 am. Authentic Old West Victorian décor. Valet parking. Cr cds: A, DS, MC, V.

D

Delta (D-2)

See also Montrose

Settled 1880 **Pop** 6,400 **Elev** 4,953 ft **Area code** 970 **Zip** 81416

Information Chamber of Commerce, 301 Main St; 970/874-8616

Situated in Colorado's largest fruit-growing area, Delta annually produces millions of dollars worth of apples, peaches, and cherries. For information on Gunnison National Forest (see GUNNISON), Uncompahgre National Forest (see NORWOOD), and Grand Mesa National Forest (see GRAND JUNCTION), write the Supervisor, 2250 US 50 in Delta.

What to See and Do

Crawford State Park. *4050 Hwy 92 (81415). 20 miles E to Hotchkiss, then 11 miles S on CO 92. Phone 970/921-5721.* Swimming, waterskiing, fishing, boating (ramps); winter sports, picnicking, camping. Standard fees. (Daily) **$$**

Sweitzer State Park. *1735 East Rd (81416). 3 miles SE off US 50. Phone 970/874-4258.* Swimming, waterskiing, fishing, boating (ramps); picnicking, bird-watching. Standard fees. (Daily) **$$**

Special Event

Deltarado Days. *Delta Round-Up Club. 301 Main St (81416). Phone 970/874-8616.* Parade, barbecue, craft booths, games, square dancing, PRCA Rodeo. Last weekend in July.

Motels/Motor Lodges

★ ★ **BEST WESTERN SUNDANCE.** *903 Main St (81416). Phone 970/874-9781; toll-free 800/626-1994; fax 970/874-5440. www.bestwesternsundance.com.* 41 rooms, 2 story. May-Sept: S, D $50-$80; each additional $10; under 12 free; lower rates rest of year. Pet accepted; some restrictions; $5. Complimentary full breakfast. Check-out 11 am. TV; cable (premium). In-room modem link. Bar 11-2 am. Restaurant. Room service. Exercise equipment. Whirlpool. Cr cds: A, C, D, DS, MC, V.

D ♨ 🏋 ⊠ SC

★ **COMFORT INN.** *180 Gunnison River Dr (81416). Phone 970/874-1000; toll-free 800/228-5150; fax 970/874-4154. www.comfortinn.com.* 47 rooms, 4 suites, 2 story. June-Sept: S, D $74-$89; each additional $5; suites $89-$99; under 18 free; higher rates special events; lower rates rest of year. Pet accepted; $5. Complimentary continental breakfast. Check-out 11 am. Check-in 2 pm. TV; cable (premium), VCR available (movies). Restaurant opposite 6 am-10 pm. Health club privileges, sauna. Game room. Pool privileges, whirlpool. Cr cds: A, C, D, DS, JCB, MC, V.

D ♨ 🏊 ⊠ SC

Denver (C-6)

Settled 1858 **Pop** 544,636 **Elev** 5,280 ft **Area code** 303

Information Denver Metro Convention & Visitors Bureau, 1555 California St, Suite 300, 80202; 303/892-1112 or 800/233-6837

Web www.denver.org

Suburbs Boulder, Central City, Englewood, Evergreen, Golden, Idaho Springs, Lakewood. (See individual alphabetical listings.)

Transportation

Airport. See DENVER INTERNATIONAL AIRPORT AREA.

Car Rental Agencies. See IMPORTANT TOLL-FREE NUMBERS.

Public Transportation. Buses (Regional Transportation District), phone 303/299-6000.

Rail Passenger Service. Amtrak 800/872-7245.

Airport Information

Denver International Airport Area. For additional accommodations, see DENVER INTERNATIONAL AIRPORT AREA, which follows DENVER.

The Mile High City, capital of Colorado, began as a settlement of gold seekers, many of them unsuccessful. Denver almost lost out to several booming mountain mining centers. In 1858, the community (together with Auraria—the two were consolidated in 1860) consisted of some 60 raffish cabins, plus Colorado's first saloon. With the opening of silver mines in the 1870s Denver came into its own. By 1890, the population had topped 100,000. Nourished by the wealth that poured in from the silver districts, Denver rapidly became the most important city in the state. Today, with the Great Plains sweeping away to the east, the foothills and the Front Range of the Rocky Mountains immediately to the west, and a dry, mild climate, Denver is a thriving transportation, industrial, commercial, cultural, and vacation center. It has also become a headquarters for energy research and production.

The Denver Mountain Park System is unique in the Rocky Mountain foothills. It covers 13,448 acres, scattered over 380 square miles. The chain begins 15 miles west of the city and extends to Summit Lake (12,740 feet), 60 miles west. A Ranger District office of the Arapaho National Forest is located in Denver.

City Fun Fact—Denver

Denver lays claim to the invention of the cheeseburger. The trademark for the name "cheeseburger" was awarded in 1935 to Louis Ballast.

What to See and Do

16th Street Mall. *16th St, between Market St and Broadway (80202).* This tree-lined pedestrian promenade of red and gray granite runs through the center of Denver's downtown shopping district; outdoor cafes, shops, restaurants, hotels, fountains, and plazas line its mile-long walk. European-built shuttle buses offer transportation from either end of the promenade. Also located here are

Larimer Square. *Larimer and 14th St (80202). Phone 303/534-2367.* Restoration of the first street in Denver, this collection of shops, galleries, nightclubs, and restaurants is set among Victorian courtyards, gaslights, arcades, and buildings; carriage rides around square. (Daily)

Tabor Center. *1201 16th St (80202). Phone 303/572-6868.* The Mall at Tabor Center is a sophisticated urban shopping, dining, and lodging center in the heart of downtown Denver's retail district. Though smaller than outlying malls, Tabor Center nevertheless provides a full array of name-brand men's and women's apparel, gift and jewelry stores, a food court, and three full-service restaurants: The Cheesecake Factory, Big Bowl, and ESPN Zone. The center recently underwent a $26 million renovation. (Mon-Sat; closed Sun, Jan 1, Dec 25)

Antique Row. *400-1800 S Broadway (80210).* Denver's largest concentration of antique dealers can be found along a 14-block stretch of South Broadway. More than 400 shops sell everything old, from books to music, vintage Western wear to museum-quality furniture. Take the light rail to Broadway and I-25 to begin your antiquing tour. Most dealers are located between the 400 and 1800 blocks of South Broadway and 25 and 27 blocks of East Dakota Avenue. (Daily)

Arvada Center for the Arts & Humanities. *6901 Wadsworth Blvd, NW in Arvada. Phone 303/431-3080.* Performing arts center with concerts, plays, classes, demonstrations, art galleries, banquet hall. Amphitheater seats 1,200 (June-early Sept). Historical museum with old cabin and pioneer artifacts. (Daily) Museum and gallery. **FREE**

Brown Palace Hotel. *321 17th St (80202). One block from the 16th St pedestrian mall. Phone 303/297-3111.* Located in the heart of downtown Denver, this stunning landmark hotel has played gracious host to presidents, princesses, and countless celebrities in the 110 years since it was built by noted Colorado architect Frank E. Edbrooke. With its unique triangle shape and 9-story atrium lobby, it is worth a visit, if only to experience the sheer opulence of its interior details and lush décor. For a real taste of turn-of-the-century elegance, stay for afternoon tea, served daily from noon to 4 pm in the atrium lobby. Reservations are recommended.

Byers-Evans House Museum. *1310 Bannock St. Phone 303/620-4933.* Restored Victorian house featuring the history of two noted Colorado pioneer families. Guided tours available. (Tues-Sun; closed holidays) **$$**

Chatfield State Park. *11500 N Roxborough Park Rd (80125). 1 mile S of C-470 on Wadsworth St, near Littleton. Phone 303/791-7275.* Swimming beach, bathhouse, waterskiing, fishing, boating (rentals, dock), marina; hiking, biking, bridle trails; picnicking, snack bar, camping (electrical hookups, dump station). Nature center; interpretive programs. Standard fees. (Daily) **$$**

Cherry Creek State Park. *1 mile S of I-225 on Parker Rd (CO 83), near south Denver. Phone 303/699-3860.* Swimming, bathhouse, waterskiing, fishing, boating (ramps, rentals); horseback riding, picnicking (shelters), concession, camping. Model airplane field, shooting range. (Daily) Per vehicle **$$**

The Children's Museum of Denver. *2121 Children's Museum Dr, off I-25 exit 211. Phone 303/433-7433.* 24,000-square-foot, 2-story hands-on environment allows children to learn and explore the world around them. Exhibits include a room with thousands of plastic balls; Kidslope, a year-round ski slope; science center, educational programs; grocery store. (June-Aug, daily; rest of year, Tues-Sun; closed holidays Children's Museum Theater (weekends) and special events. First Fri of every month is free for seniors (60+) **$$$**

Civic Center. *100 W 14th Ave Pkwy (80209). West of Capitol Complex.* Located here are

> **Denver Art Museum.** *100 W 14th Ave Pkwy, south side of Civic Center. Phone 720/865-5000.* Houses collection of art objects representing almost every culture and period, including a fine collection of Native American arts; changing exhibits. (Tues-Sun; closed holidays) Free admission Sat for Colorado residents. **$$$**

> **Denver City and County Buildings.** *100 W 14th Ave Pkwy (80209). West side of Center. Phone 303/866-2604.* Courts, municipal council, and administrative offices.

> **Denver Public Library.** *10 W 14th Ave Pkwy. Phone 720/865-1351.* First phase of new library opened in 1995; it encompasses the old library. Largest public library in Rocky Mountain region with nearly four million items; outstanding Western History collection, Patent Depository Library, genealogy collections, and branch library system. Programs, exhibits. (Daily; closed holidays) **FREE**

> **Greek Theater.** *100 W 14th Ave Pkwy (80209). South side of Center.* Outdoor amphitheater, summer folk dancing.

Colorado's Ocean Journey. *700 Water Street (80211). Located in the Central Platte Valley on the northeast corner of I-25 and 23rd Avenue. Phone 303/561-4450.* This world-class, 106,500-square-foot aquarium brings visitors face to face with more than 300 species of fish, birds, mammals, and invertebrates from around the world. Exhibits follow the re-creation of water's journey from river to ocean, showcasing the varied and often exotic variety of habitats and creatures found along the way. Several areas encourage hands-on encounters between visitors and animals, including the Critters Up Close demonstrations, the Tide Pool Treasures touchable tide pool display, and the Parade of Rays pool stocked with pettable stingrays. Additional attractions include the Seafoam Fun Zone play area for young children and the "AquaPod" virtual aquatic adventure ride. Upon your arrival, check out the daily presentation notice for times and locations of special exhibits. (Daily, hours are subject to change without notice). **$$$$**

Colorado Avalanche (NHL). *Pepsi Center. 1000 Chopper Circle. Phone 303/405-1100.*

Colorado Bug Tours. *Phone 888/528-5285.* Auto tours in classic Volkswagen convertible.

Colorado History Tours. *Phone 303/866-4686.* Two-hour guided walking tours; three-hour guided step-on bus tours. Reservations required; ten people minimum. Prices and schedules vary.

Colorado Rapids (MLS). *Mile High Stadium, 2755 W 17th Ave. Phone 800/844-7777.*

Colorado Rockies (MLB). *Coors Field, 2001 Blake St. Phone 303/292-0200.*

Comanche Crossing Museum. *30 miles E in Strasburg. Phone 303/622-4322.* Memorabilia of the completion of the transcontinental railway, artifacts pertaining to area history; two buildings with period rooms; restored schoolhouse (1891); Strasburg Union Pacific Depot; caboose, wood-vaned windmill (1880), and homestead on landscaped grounds. (June-Aug, afternoons daily) **DONATION**

Denver Botanic Gardens. *1005 York St (80206). Phone 720/865-3500.* This tropical paradise in the middle of the Rockies is home to more than 15,000 plant species from around the world. Located ten minutes east of downtown Denver, the Denver Botanic Gardens beckons visitors to explore its 23 acres of beautiful outdoor and indoor displays. The Conservatory, with more than 850 tropical and subtropical plants in an enclosed rain forest setting, is a soothing retreat for midwinter guests. New in 2003 is the 20-x-40-foot Cloud Forest Tree covered with hundreds of orchids and rare tropical plants. Other gardens include alpine, herb, Japanese, shade, and wildflower displays. Children particularly enjoy navigating the mazes in the Secret Path garden and climbing the resident banyan tree. (Daily; closed Jan 1, Dec 25). **$$$**

Denver Broncos (NFL). *INVESCO Field at Mile High. 1900 Eliot St. Phone 303/433-7466 or 720/258-3333.*

Denver Firefighters Museum. *1326 Tremont Pl. Phone 303/892-1436.* Housed in Fire House No. 1; maintains atmosphere of working firehouse; firefighting equipment from mid-1800s. (Mon-Sat)

Denver Museum of Nature and Science. *2001 Colorado Blvd, in City Park. Phone 303/322-7009.* Ninety habitat exhibits from four continents displayed against natural backgrounds; Prehistoric Journey exhibit displays dinosaurs in re-created environments; earth sciences lab; gems and minerals; Native American collection. (Daily; closed Dec 25) **$$$** Also here are

Charles C. Gates Planetarium. *2001 Colorado Blvd (80205). Phone 303/322-7009 (schedule and fees).* Contains a Minolta Series IV star projector; presents a variety of star and laser light shows daily. The **Phipps IMAX Theater** has an immense motion picture system projecting images on screen 4 1/2 stories tall and 6 1/2 stories wide. Daily showings. **$$$**

Hall of Life. *2001 Colorado Blvd (80205). Phone 303/322-7009.* Health education center has permanent exhibits on genetics, fitness, nutrition, and the five senses. Classes and workshops (fee). (Daily)

Denver Nuggets (NBA). *Pepsi Center, 1000 Chopper Circle. Phone 303/405-1212.*

Denver Performing Arts Complex. *1245 Champa St (80204). Phone 303/893-4100.* One of the most innovative and comprehensive performing arts centers in the country. With the addition of the Temple Hoyne Buell Theatre, the complex is the second largest in the nation. The complex also contains shops and restaurants.

Denver Zoo. *2300 Steele St (80205). Phone 303/376-4800.* Among Colorado's most popular city attractions is the Denver Zoo. Located in City Park just east of downtown, this 80-acre zoological wonderland is home to more than 4,000 animals representing 700 species. Founded in 1896, the zoo has evolved into one of the nation's premier animal exhibits, noted for its beautiful grounds, innovative combination of outdoor and enclosed habitats, and world-class conservation and breeding programs. Don't miss the Primate Panorama, a 7-acre showcase of rare monkeys and apes. Visit the 22,000-square-foot, glass-enclosed Tropical Discovery and feel what it's like to walk into a tropical rain forest complete with caves, cliffs, waterfalls, and some of the zoo's most exotic (and dangerous!) creatures. Equally popular is the Northern Shores Arctic wildlife habitat, which provides a nose-to-nose underwater look at swimming polar bears and sea lions. Be sure to check out the feeding schedule posted just inside the zoo's entrance. During the evenings throughout December, millions of sparkling lights and holiday music transform the zoo as part of the traditional "Wonderlights" festival. (Daily) **$$$**

Elitch Gardens. *2000 Elitches Cir (80204). Platte River Valley. Phone 303/595-4386.* Relocated into the downtown area in 1995. Amusement park with over 48 major rides. Observation tower, 100-foot-high Ferris wheel, outdoor waterpark. Flower gardens, lakes, and waterfalls. (Memorial Day-Labor Day, daily) **$$$$**

Forney Transportation Museum. *4303 Brighton Blvd. Phone 303/297-1113.* Collection of more than 300 antique cars, carriages, cycles, sleighs, steam locomotives and coaches; Costumed figures. (Mon-Sat) **$$$**

Four Mile Historic Park. *Located east of Colorado Boulevard between Cherry Creek Dr S and Alameda. Phone 303/399-1859.* Take a stroll through Denver history at Four Mile Historic Park. Once a stage stop, this 14-acre living history museum encompasses the oldest house still standing in Denver (circa 1859), plus other outbuildings and farm equipment from the late 1800s. Guides in period costume reenact life on a farmstead. It's a great place for a picnic. Kids particularly enjoy chasing the chickens, visiting with the draft horses, and riding on a real stagecoach (weekends only). (Daily) **$**

Gray Line bus tours. *5855 E 56th Ave. Phone 303/289-2841.* Contact PO Box 17646, 80217.

Hyland Hills Adventure Golf. *9650 N Sheridan Blvd (80030). Phone 303/650-7587.* It's miniature golf on a mega scale. Located 15 minutes north of downtown Denver, Hyland Hills Adventure Golf puts your putting skills, and your imagination, to the test with 54 stunningly landscaped holes in a fantasy setting of cliffs, caves, and waterfalls. (Closed during winter months) **$$$**

Hyland Hills Water World. *1800 W 89th Ave (80260). Located 15 minutes north of downtown Denver. Phone 303/427-7873.* Ranked among the nation's largest water parks, this 64-acre aquatic extravaganza is not a place for the faint of heart—but it's a great spot for the young at heart and a terrific good time for all ages. One admission fee provides unlimited access to 40 amusement and water thrill rides. Water World's beautifully landscaped grounds include a wave pool the size of a football field, 16 water slides, nine inner-tube rides, and a splash pool for tots. Older kids won't want to miss the Lost River of the Pharaohs, a whitewater rafting trip through a mummy-filled pyramid and down a spiraling slide. Younger visitors will enjoy Voyage to the Center of the Earth, a gentler ride featuring close encounters with animatronic dinosaurs. Hours vary according to season and weather, so be sure to call ahead. (Daily; closed Memorial Day to Labor Day) **$$$$**

Molly Brown House Museum. *1340 Pennsylvania St (80203). Phone 303/832-4092.* The Molly Brown House Museum stands as an enduring tribute to one of Denver's most prominent architects, William Lang, and one of its most colorful characters: Margaret "Molly" Brown. A spectacular example of Colorado Victorian design, the fully restored 1880s sandstone and lava stone mansion now serves as a museum, filled with many of the lavish furnishings and personal possessions of its most famous occupant. Anyone interested in the story of the Titanic and the heroics of its "Unsinkable" survivor should take a moment to step back in time and enjoy a tour of her home. (June-Aug, daily; Sept-May; Tues-Sun) **$$**

Park system. *2300 15th St #150 (80202). Phone 303/964-2500.* More than 200 parks within city provide approximately 4,400 acres of facilities for boating, fishing, and other sports. The system includes six golf courses. There are also 27 mountain parks within 72 miles of the city covering 13,448 acres of land in the Rocky Mountain foothills. Also located here are

Cheesman Park. *1177 Race St (80206). Phone 303/322-0066.* This park has excellent views of nearby mountain peaks with aid of dial and pointers. Congress Park swimming pool (fee) is adjacent. Located between Cheesman and Congress parks is the Denver Botanic Gardens (fee), with the Boettcher Memorial Conservatory.

City Park. *Colorado Blvd and York St (80205). Runs between 17th and 26th aves. Phone 303/331-4113.* Contains the Denver Museum of Natural History, an 18-hole golf course, and the Denver Zoo. Animals in natural habitats; primates, felines, and giraffes; aviary, children's zoo, miniature railroad. (Daily) Children under 16 must be accompanied by adult at zoo. **$$$**

⭐ **Red Rocks Park.** *12700 W Alameda Pkwy (80465). 12 miles SW, off CO 26 between I-70 and US 285. Phone 303/697-8801.* Amphitheater (9,500-seat) in natural setting of huge red rocks. Site of Easter sunrise service and summer concerts (fee).

Washington Park. *Louisiana Ave and Downing (80209). Park runs between S Downing and S Franklin sts, E Louisiana and E Virginia aves. Phone 303/698-4930.* Large recreation center with indoor pool (fee). Floral displays include a replica of George Washington's gardens at Mount Vernon.

Pearce-McAllister Cottage. *1880 N Gaylord St. Phone 303/322-3704.* (1899) Dutch Colonial Revival house contains original furnishings. Guided tours give insight into upper middle-class lifestyle of the 1920s. Second floor houses Denver Museum of Dolls, Toys, and Miniatures. (Tues-Sat, also Sun afternoons) **$$**

Pint's Pub Brewery and Freehouse. *211 W Thirteenth Ave (80204). Phone 303/534-7570.* Just south of Civic Center Park on 13th and Broadway, Pint's Pub and Brewery brings a bit of old England to downtown Denver. Bright, lively, and distinctively British, this traditional brewpub offers a wide variety of handcrafted ales on tap, many found nowhere else in the US, plus what they claim is the largest selection of single malt whiskeys in the country. Sit down to an order of fish and chips or sheepherder's stew to go with your brew selection and make a night of it. Look for the red English-style phone booth and British flag at the front entrance.

Sakura Square. *1255 19th St. Lawrence to Larimer sts. Phone 303/295-0305.* Denver's Japanese Cultural and Trade Center features Asian restaurants, shops, businesses; authentic Japanese gardens. Site of famed Buddhist Temple.

Six Flags Elitch Gardens. *2000 Elitches Cir (80204). Phone 303/595-4386.* If you're into adrenaline overload, then Six Flags Elitch Gardens is your kind of place. This grand-daddy of amusement parks in downtown Denver features more than 45 rides sure to satisfy even the most experienced coasterhead. The park is best known for its extreme roller coaster rides; other favorites include a 22-story freefall in the Tower of Doom, Disaster Canyon whitewater rafting, and the new Flying Coaster, which simulates the experience of flying. Six Flags includes a kiddie park for younger children, the popular Island Kingdom water park, and live entertainment nightly. (May-Sept) **$$$$**

Ski Train. *555 17th St (80202). Phone 303/296-4754.* A ride on the Ski Train from Denver to Winter Park has long been a favorite day trip for skiers, hikers, bikers, and family vacationers. Operating weekends year-round, the train takes its passengers on a spectacular wilderness ride through the Rockies and then drops them off at the front entrance of beautiful Winter Park Resort. Tickets are for round-trip, same-day rides only—reservations are highly recommended to assure a seat. (Sat-Sun, winter; June-Aug, Sat) **$$$$**

State Capitol. *200 E Colfax Ave (80203). Phone 303/866-2604.* This magnificent edifice overlooking Civic Center Park is a glorious reminder of Denver's opulent past. Today, it serves as Colorado's legislative center. Designed by architect Elijah Myers in the classical Corinthian style, it was 18 years in the making before its official dedication in 1908. The building is renowned for its exquisite interior details and use of native materials such as gray granite, white marble, pink Colorado onyx, and, of course, the gold that covers its dome. Tours include a climb to the dome, 272 feet up, for a spectacular view of the surrounding mountains. Make sure that the kids find the special marker on the steps outside noting that they are, indeed, a mile high. (Mon-Fri, some Sat in summer; closed holidays) **FREE** Also here is

Colorado History Museum. *1300 Broadway. Phone 303/866-3682.* Permanent and rotating exhibits on people and history of Colorado. Dioramas, full-scale mining equipment, Native American artifacts, photographs; sodhouse. Headquarters of Colorado Historical Society. (Daily; closed Jan 1, Thanksgiving, Dec 25) **$$**

University of Denver. *2199 S University Blvd (80210). Phone 303/871-2711.* (1864) 8,500 students. Handsome 125-acre main campus with Penrose Library, Harper Humanities Gardens, Shwayder Art Building, Seely G. Mudd Building (science), William T. Driscoll University Center, and historic buildings dating from the 1800s. The 33-acre Park Hill campus at Montview Blvd and Quebec St is the site of the University of Denver Law School (Lowell Thomas Law Building) and the Lamont School of Music (Houston Fine Arts Center; for schedule phone 303/871-6400). Campus tours. The university maintains

Chamberlin Observatory. *Observatory Park, 2930 E Warren Ave. Phone 303/871-5172.* Houses large telescope in use since 1894; lectures. Tours (Tues and

Thurs; closed holidays, Christmas week; reservations required). **$**

Special Events

Cherry Creek Arts Festival. *2 Steele St (80206).* Features works by 200 national artists. July 4 weekend.

Denver Film Festival. *900 Auraria Pkwy (80204). Phone 303/595-3456.* Movie junkies will get more than their fill of flicks at the 10-day Denver International Film Festival in October. Showcasing 175 films while playing host to many of their stars, the festival includes international feature releases, independent fiction and documentaries, experimental productions, and children's programs. All films are shown at the Starz Encore Film Center at the Tivoli. It's best to order tickets ahead of time, as many of the features sell out. Oct. **$$**

Denver Lights and Parade of Lights. *Phone 720/913-4900.* From early December through January, downtown Denver is ablaze with what is very possibly the largest holiday light show in the world. Locals and tourists alike drift down to Civic Center Park after dark to view the incredible rainbow display covering the buildings. A spectacular Parade of Lights that winds for 2 miles through Denver's downtown kicks off the holiday season.

Furry Scurry. *Phone 303/964-2522.* The Furry Scurry is a 2-mile walk/fun-run through Denver's Washington Park. Featuring a 2.6-mile jogging trail, several picnic areas, large flower gardens, and two lakes, the park is the perfect spot for an outdoor-loving family to spend the day. The race is a fundraiser for the Denver Dumb Friends League, and most participants bring their dogs as racing companions. The event typically attracts more than 6,000 two- and four-legged participants and raises $400,000 for the league. Early May. **$**

Greyhound racing. *Mile High Greyhound Park. 6200 Dahlia St, Commerce City. Phone 303/288-1591. 7 miles NE at junction I-270 and Vasquez Blvd;* Pari-mutuels. Mid-June-mid-Feb, nightly Tues-Sat; matinee racing Mon, Fri-Sat. Satellite "off-track" betting all year.

National Western Livestock Show, Horse Show & Rodeo. *Located east of I-25 on I-70. Phone 303/297-1166, x 810.* If you are in Denver in the middle of January, you'd better hang onto your Stetson, because that's when the National Western Stock Show and Rodeo comes to town—along with 600,000 rootin' tootin' exhibitors and spectators. Billed as the largest livestock exhibition in the world, this two-week extravaganza is packed with nonstop shows and demonstrations, from sheep shearing to steer wrestling. Daily rodeos showcase the horse and bull-riding skills of some of the best riders in the country before cheering, sellout crowds in the Denver Coliseum. Other favorites include barrel races, show-horse contests, a junior rodeo

(where some of the riders are 3 years old!), Wild West shows, and the colorful Mexican Rodeo Extravaganza. Take a break from the action and tour the exhibition hall for demonstrations in wool spinning and goat milking, or walk the grounds to see what a yak looks like up close. Mid-Jan. **$$**

Motels/Motor Lodges

★ **COMFORT INN.** *401 17th St (80202). Phone 303/296-0400; toll-free 800/252-7466; fax 303/297-0774. www.comfortinn.com.* 231 rooms, 22 suites, 22 story. Check-out noon, check-in 3 pm. TV; cable (premium), VCR available. In-room modem link. Room service 24 hours. Restaurant, bar. In-house fitness room. Valet parking. Cr cds: A, C, D, DS, JCB, MC, V. **$$**

🄳 🕆 ⊠ 🆂🅲

★★ **COURTYARD BY MARRIOTT DENVER STAPLETON.** *7415 E 41st Ave (80216). Phone 303/333-3303; fax 303/399-7356. www.courtyard.com.* 146 rooms, 12 suites, 3 story. S, D $49-$69; each additional $10; suites $95-$105; under 18 free; weekend rates. Crib free. Complimentary coffee in rooms. Check-out noon. TV; cable (premium). In-room modem link. Balconies. Refrigerator in suites. Microwaves available. Valet services, coin laundry. Restaurant 6-10 am, 5-10 pm; Sat, Sun 7-11 am. Bar 4-10 pm. Exercise equipment. Indoor pool, whirlpool. Meeting rooms. Business services. Cr cds: A, C, D, DS, ER, JCB, MC, V.

🄳 ⇌ 🕆 ⊠

★★ **HOLIDAY INN NORTHGLENN.** *10 E 120th Ave (80233). Phone 303/452-4100; fax 303/457-1741. www.holiday-inn.com.* 235 rooms, 12 suites, 6 story. Apr-Sept: S, D $89-$125; each additional $10; suites $150-$175; under 17 free; weekend rates; lower rates rest of year. Crib available. Pet accepted, some restrictions. Check-out noon. TV; cable. In-room modem link. Coffee in rooms. Valet services, coin laundry. Restaurant 6 am-11 pm. Bar 11 am-11 pm. Health club privileges, exercise equipment. Indoor pool, whirlpool. Business services. Convention center/facilities. Gift shop. Cr cds: A, C, D, DS, JCB, MC, V.

🄳 🐾 ⇌ 🕆 ⊠

★ **LA QUINTA INN AIRPORT SOUTH.** *3975 Peoria Way (80239). Phone 303/371-5640; toll-free 800/687-6667; fax 303/371-7015. www.laquinta.com.* 112 rooms, 2 story. S, D $69-$89; under 18 free. Pet accepted, some restrictions. Complimentary continental breakfast. Check-out noon. TV; cable (premium). In-room modem link. Free airport transportation. Cr cds: A, C, D, DS, JCB, MC, V.

🄳 🐾 ⊠ 🆂🅲

★ **LA QUINTA INN DOWNTOWN.** *3500 Park Ave W (80216). Phone 303/458-1222; fax 303/433-2246. www.laquinta.com.* 106 rooms, 3 story. S, D $65-$95; each additional $10; under 18 free. Crib free. Pet accepted. Complimentary continental breakfast. Check-out noon. TV; cable (premium). In-room modem link. Valet services, coin laundry. Restaurant adjacent open 24 hours. Pool. Business services. Cr cds: A, C, D, DS, MC, V.

D 🐾 ⚊ ⊠

★ ★ **QUALITY INN & SUITES.** *4590 Quebec St (80216). Phone 303/320-0260; fax 303/320-7595. www.qualityinn.com.* 200 rooms, 5 story. May-Sept: S $75-$80; D $80-$85; each additional $7; suites $115-$135; under 18 free; lower rates rest of year. Crib free. Complimentary continental breakfast. Coffee in rooms. Check-out noon. TV; cable (premium). In-room modem link. Refrigerators, microwaves. Valet services, coin laundry. Restaurant 6-10 am, 5:30-10 pm; Sat, Sun from 6:30 am. Bar 4 pm-midnight; Sat, Sun from 5 pm. Room service. Exercise equipment. Pool, whirlpool. Free airport transportation. Meeting rooms. Business services. Gift shop. Cr cds: A, C, D, DS, JCB, MC, V.

D ⚊ 大 ⊠

★ ★ **QUALITY INN SOUTH.** *6300 E Hampden Ave (80222). Phone 303/758-2211; toll-free 800/647-1986; fax 303/753-0156. www.qualityinndtc.com.* 182 rooms, 1-2 story. S $74-$79; D $79-$89; each additional $10; under 18 free. Crib free. Pet accepted; $6/day. Complimentary continental breakfast. Coffee in rooms. Check-out 11 am. TV; cable (premium). In-room modem link. Private patios, balconies. Some refrigerators. Coin laundry. Restaurant 6 am-11 pm. Bar from 4 pm. Room service. Health club privileges, sauna. Pool, whirlpool, poolside service. Picnic tables. Lawn games. Meeting rooms. Business services. Cr cds: A, C, D, DS, ER, JCB, MC, V.

D 🐾 ⚊ ⊠ SC

★ ★ **QUALITY INN WEST.** *12100 W 44th Ave (80033). Phone 303/467-2400; toll-free 800/449-0003; fax 303/467-0198. www.qualityinn.com.* 108 rooms, 5 story. May-Aug: S $54; D $69; under 18 free; lower rates rest of year. Crib free. Pet accepted, some restrictions; $50 deposit. Complimentary coffee in lobby. Check-out 11 am. TV; cable (premium). Refrigerators. Restaurant 7 am-10 pm. Bar 11 am-2 am. Room service. Whirlpool. Exercise equipment. Meeting room. Business services. On lake. Cr cds: A, C, D, DS, JCB, MC, V.

D 🐾 大 ⊠ SC

Hotels

★ ★ **ADAM'S MARK.** *1550 Court Pl (80202). Phone 303/893-3333; fax 303/626-2542. www.adamsmark.com.* 1,225 rooms, 2 buildings, 8 and 22 story. S, D $175-$185; each additional $15; suites $375-$1,200; under 18 free; weekend rates. Crib free. Pet accepted, some restrictions; $100 deposit. Check-out noon. TV; cable (premium). In-room modem link. Microwaves available. Coin laundry. Restaurant 6:30 am-11 pm. Bar 11-2 am, entertainment. Room service 24 hours. Health club privileges, exercise equipment, sauna, steam room. Pool, poolside service. Garage $15; in/out privileges. Airport transportation. Business center. Convention center/facilities. Concierge. Gift shops. Luxury level. Cr cds: A, D, DS, MC, V. **$$$**

D 🐾 ⚊ 大 ⊠ 大

★ ★ ★ **THE BROWN PALACE HOTEL.** *321 17th St (80202). Phone 303/297-3111; toll-free 800/321-2599; fax 303/293-9204. www.brownpalace.com.* Occupying a corner of downtown Denver, the Brown Palace Hotel is one of the city's treasures. This historical landmark has been hosting visitors since 1892, and many presidents, monarchs, and celebrities have graced its halls. The hotel retains a regal feel, especially in the lobby, where a magnificent stained-glass ceiling tops off six levels of cast-iron balconies. Marvelous details meet the eye no matter where you direct your gaze. Victorian and Art Deco sensibilities dominate the rooms and suites. The award-winning Palace Arms (see also PALACE ARMS) restaurant delights diners with its formal setting and delicious menu, including signature favorites like rack of lamb and pan-roasted veal. Cigar aficionados flock to the library ambience of the Churchill Bar, while the Ship Tavern appeals to lovers of the sea. Ellygnton's remains the place to be seen in Denver, and its Sunday brunch is legendary. 241 rooms, 10 story. Check-out noon, check-in 3 pm. TV; cable (premium), VCR available. In-room modem link. Room service 24 hours. Restaurant, bar; entertainment. In-house fitness room, health club privileges, massage. Valet parking. Business center. Concierge. Cr cds: A, C, D, DS, ER, JCB, MC, V. **$$$**

D 大 ⊠ 大

★ **CAMBRIDGE HOTEL.** *1560 Sherman St (80203). Phone 303/831-1252; toll-free 800/877-1252; fax 303/831-4724.* 31 suites, 3 story. S, D $129-$139; under 12 free. Crib $10. Complimentary continental breakfast. Check-out noon. TV; cable (premium). In-room modem link. Refrigerators, minibars. Microwaves available. Valet service. Health club privileges. Valet parking $10. Meeting rooms. Business services. Luggage services. Concierge. Antique furnishings, oil paintings, original prints. Cr cds: A, D, DS, MC, V.

D ⊠

★ ★ **HOTEL MONACO.** *1717 Champa St (80202). Phone 303/296-1717; toll-free 800/397-5380; fax 303/296-1818. www.monaco-denver.com.* This yearling boutique hotel has a cool feel and a fun, comfortable design. The guest rooms resemble Mackenzie-Childs pottery, with swirls of patterns and other colorful touches. The feel of the hotel is small and comfortable. Amenities are somewhat limited, but arrangements can be made for most needs. 189 rooms, 32 suites, 7 story. S, D $159-$259; under 18 free. Crib available. Pet accepted. Complimentary coffee in rooms. Check-out noon. TV; cable (premium), VCR available. Restaurant 7 am-11 pm. Room service 24 hours. Bar. Exercise equipment. Bike rental. Valet parking $21/day. Business center. Bellhops. Concierge. Gift shop. Cr cds: A, C, D, DS, ER, JCB, MC, V.

★ ★ ★ **HOTEL TEATRO.** *1100 14th St (80202). Phone 303/228-1100; toll-free 888/727-1200; fax 303/228-1101. www.hotelteatro.com.* This downtown boutique hotel is located in a historic landmark building adjacent to the theatre district. Handsome guest rooms are designed for the business traveler with printers, copiers, and fax machines as well as three telephones in each room. Large, luxurious bathrooms and a sophisticated décor make this an ideal location for both business and leisure guests. 111 rooms, 8 suites, 9 story. S, D $255-$295; suites $1,450; under 18 free. Crib available. Pet accepted. Complimentary coffee in rooms. Check-out noon, check-in 3 pm. TV; cable (premium). In-room modem link. Some balconies. Refrigerators. Valet services. Restaurant 7 am-11 pm. Room service 24 hours. Bar. Supervised children's activities. Health club privileges, exercise equipment. Golf privileges. Tennis privileges. Valet parking $24/day. Meeting rooms. Business services. Bellhops. Concierge. Cr cds: A, C, D, DS, ER, JCB, MC, V.

★ ★ ★ **HYATT REGENCY.** *1750 Welton St (80202). Phone 303/295-1234; toll-free 800/233-1234; fax 303/292-2472. www.denver.regency.hyatt.com.* The 20-foot sandstone fireplace is the focal point of this hotel's lobby, which is warm and inviting. The central location is near many of Denver's top attractions. 511 rooms, 26 story. S, D $85-$275; each additional $25; suites $350-$1,000; weekend rates. Check-out noon. TV; cable (premium). In-room modem link. Restaurant 6 am-11 pm. Bar 10:30-2 am. Health club privileges, exercise equipment. Indoor pool. Tennis. Business center. Concierge. Luxury level. Cr cds: A, D, DS, MC, V.

★ ★ ★ **HYATT REGENCY TECH CENTER.** *7800 E Tufts Ave (80237). Phone 303/779-1234; toll-free 800/233-1234; fax 303/850-7164. www.techcenter.hyatt.com.* Set in the Denver Technological Center, the guest rooms at this property offer some incredible views of the Rocky Mountains. Downtown Denver is a short ten-minute drive from the hotel. 450 rooms, 11 story. S, D $200; each additional $25; suites $350-$1,500; under 18 free; weekend plans. Crib free. Complimentary coffee in rooms. Check-out

noon. TV; cable (premium), VCR available (movies). In-room modem link. Refrigerators, some bathroom phones. Microwaves available. Restaurant 6:30 am-11 pm. Bar 3 pm-1 am; Sun to midnight. Health club privileges, exercise equipment, sauna. Indoor pool, whirlpool, poolside service. Lighted tennis. Valet parking. Airport transportation. Business center. Convention center/facilities. Concierge. Gift shop. Luxury level. Cr cds: A, C, D, DS, ER, JCB, MC, V.

★ ★ ★ **LOEWS HOTEL.** *4150 E Mississippi Ave (80246). Phone 303/782-9300; fax 303/758-6542. www.loewshotels.com.* Pretty flower arrangements and furniture adorn the entrance of this hotel in the Cherry Creek section of Denver. 183 rooms, 11 story. S $199-$229; D $219-$249; each additional $20; suites $259-$900; under 18 free; weekend rates from $79. Crib free. Pet accepted, some restrictions. Complimentary coffee in rooms. Check-out 11 am. TV; cable (premium), VCR available (movies). Bathroom phones, minibars, some refrigerators. Microwaves available. Restaurant (see TUSCANY). Bar noon-1 am. Room service 24 hours. Health club privileges, exercise equipment. Valet parking. Meeting rooms. Business center. Concierge. Gift shop. Library. Cr cds: A, C, D, DS, MC, V.

★ ★ ★ **THE MAGNOLIA HOTEL.** *818 17th St (80202). Phone 303/607-9000; toll-free 888/915-1110; fax 303/607-0101. www.themagnoliahotel.com.* 244 rooms, 10 story. S, D $175-$250; suites $275; under 18 free. Crib available. Pet accepted. Complimentary continental breakfast. Check-out 11 am. TV; cable (premium). In-room modem link. Exercise equipment. Valet parking $21/day. Airport transportation. Meeting rooms. Business center. Concierge. Cr cds: A, C, D, DS, JCB, MC, V.

★ ★ ★ **MARRIOTT CITY CENTER.** *1701 California St (80202). Phone 303/297-1300; toll-free 800/228-9290; fax 303/298-7474. www.marriott.com.* Located in downtown Denver, this property is within walking distance of Coors Field, and several restaurants and shops. 614 rooms, 19 story. S, D $169-$195; suites $225-$825; under 18 free; weekend plans. Crib free. Pet accepted, some restrictions. Check-out noon. TV; cable (premium), VCR available. In-room modem link. Bathroom phones. Refrigerators available. Coffee in rooms. Restaurant 6:30 am-10 pm. Bar 11-2 am. Room service to midnight. Exercise equipment, sauna. Indoor pool, whirlpool. Valet parking; fee. Business center. Convention center/facilities. Concierge. Shopping arcade. Luxury level. Cr cds: A, C, D, DS, ER, JCB, MC, V.

★ ★ ★ **MARRIOTT SOUTHEAST.** *6363 E Hampden Ave (80222). Phone 303/758-7000; toll-free 800/228-9290; fax 303/691-3418. www.marriott.com.* 607 rooms, 11 story. D $69-$129; under 18 free; weekend package plan. Pet accepted, some restrictions. Check-out noon, check-in 4 pm. TV; cable (premium), VCR available. In-room modem link. Laundry services. Restaurant 6 am-11 pm. Bar 11 am-midnight. Exercise equipment. Game room. 2 pools, 1 indoor, whirlpool, poolside service. Covered parking. Airport transportation. Business center. Concierge. Luxury level. Cr cds: A, C, D, DS, ER, JCB, MC, V.

★ ★ ★ **MARRIOTT TECH CENTER.** *4900 S Syracuse St (80237). Phone 303/779-1100; toll-free 800/228-9290; fax 303/740-2523. www.marriott.com.* A block of rooms are designated for business travelers and the hotel will even provide secretarial services. 626 rooms, 2-10 story. S, D $179; suites $260-$500; under 18 free; weekend plans. Crib free. Pet accepted. Check-out noon. TV; cable (premium), VCR available. In-room modem link. Some balconies. Refrigerators. Coffee in rooms. Restaurant 5:30-1 am. Bar 11 am-midnight. Health club privileges, exercise equipment, sauna. 2 pools, 1 indoor, whirlpool. Valet parking. Business center. Convention center/facilities. Shopping arcade. Cr cds: A, C, D, DS, ER, JCB, MC, V.

★ ★ **OXFORD HOTEL.** *1600 17th St (80202). Phone 303/628-5400; toll-free 800/228-5838; fax 303/628-5413. www.theoxfordhotel.com.* Built in 1891 next to Union Station, this luxurious restored property has become a national landmark in Denver, touted as the city's "oldest grand hotel." Centrally located, it is near many attractions including Coors Field, the 16th Street Mall, Larimer Square, and many shops and galleries. 80 rooms, 9 suites, 5 story. S, D $149-$369; each additional $10; suites from $275; under 12 free. Crib available. Complimentary continental breakfast. Check-out 1 pm. TV; cable (premium), VCR available. In-room modem link. Minibars. Restaurant 11 am-2 pm, 5-10 pm; Fri, Sat to 11 pm; Sun 7 am-10 pm. Room service 24 hours. Bar. Whirlpool. Exercise room, spa, steam room. Barber, beauty shop. Valet parking $12. Meeting rooms. Business services. Concierge. First luxury hotel built in Denver. Elegant, European style; many antiques. Cr cds: A, C, D, DS, MC, V.

★ ★ **RADISSON HOTEL STAPLETON PLAZA.** *3333 Quebec St (80207). Phone 303/321-3500; toll-free 800/333-3333; fax 303/322-7343. www.radisson.com.* All rooms in this 11-story atrium hotel have been recently renovated and many have views of the Rocky Mountains and downtown Denver. 304 rooms, 11 story. S, D $69-159; each additional $10; suites $175-$350; under 18 free; weekly, weekend package plans. Check-out noon.

TV; cable (premium). In-room modem link. Restaurant 6 am-11 pm. Bar from 4 pm. Room service. Exercise room, sauna, steam room. Heated pool, whirlpool, poolside service. Free airport transportation. Business center. Cr cds: A, C, D, DS, ER, JCB, MC, V.

★ ★ ★ **RENAISSANCE HOTEL.** *3801 Quebec St (80207). Phone 303/399-7500; toll-free 800/468-3571; fax 303/321-1966. www.renaissancehotels.com.* This atrium hotel boasts breathtaking Rocky Mountain views. 422 rooms, 12 story. S, D $79-$125; each additional $10; suites $150-$600; under 18 free. Check-out noon, check-in 2 pm. TV; cable (premium), VCR available. In-room modem link. Restaurant 6 am-10 pm. Bar 11-1 am. Room service. Exercise equipment, steam room. 2 pools, 1 indoor; whirlpool, poolside service. Airport transportation. Business center. Concierge. Luxury level. Cr cds: A, C, D, DS, JCB, MC, V.

★ ★ ★ **WARWICK HOTEL.** *1776 Grant St (80203). Phone 303/861-2000; toll-free 800/525-2888; fax 303/832-0320. www.warwickdenver.com.* The combination of European-style hospitality and service and traditional American décor make this property warm and inviting. Convenient to many of Denver's major attractions, this hotel is ideally located for both business and leisure travelers and has some spectacular views of the Rocky Mountains. 263 rooms, 16 story. S, D $195-$210; each additional $15; suites $225-$240; under 18 free. Pet accepted. Check-out noon, check-in 3 pm. TV; cable (premium). In-room modem link. Restaurant 6 am-10 pm; Sat, Sun 7 am-11 pm. Bar 10:30 am-11 pm. Room service 6 am-11 pm. Health club privileges. Pool, poolside service. Concierge. Cr cds: A, C, D, DS, JCB, MC, V.

★ ★ ★ **THE WESTIN TABOR CENTER.** *1672 Lawrence St (80202). Phone 303/572-9100; toll-free 800/937-8461; fax 303/572-7288. www.westin.com/taborcenter.* Centrally located to downtown Denver and adjacent to the 16th Street Mall, this hotel boasts some of the largest guest rooms in the city. Many of the rooms have views of the nearby Rocky Mountains. 430 rooms, 19 story. S, D $205; each additional $15; suites $425-$1,200; under 18 free. Crib free. Pet accepted, some restrictions. Check-out 1 pm. TV; cable (premium), VCR available. In-room modem link. Some balconies. Refrigerators, minibars, some bathroom phones. Restaurant 6 am-11 pm. Bar 5 pm-1:30 am; pianist Tues-Sat. Room service 24 hours. Health club privileges, exercise equipment, sauna, steam room. Indoor/outdoor pool, whirlpool, poolside service. Garage $10-$15. Business center. Convention center/facilities. Shopping arcade. Luxury level. Cr cds: A, C, D, DS, ER, JCB, MC, V.

★ ★ ★ **THE WESTIN WESTMINSTER.** *10600 Westminster Blvd, Westminster (80020). Phone 303/410-5000; toll-free 800/937-8461; fax 303/410-5005. www.westin.com.* 369 rooms, 6 suites, 14 story. S, D $99-$269; suites $300-$900; each additional $20; under 18 free. Crib available. Pet accepted, some restrictions. Complimentary coffee in rooms. Check-out noon. TV; cable (premium). In-room modem link. Fireplace, wet bar in suites. Valet services. Restaurant 6:30 am-10:30 pm. Room service 24 hours. Bar. Supervised children's activities. Exercise equipment, sauna. Heated indoor pool, whirlpool, poolside service. Hiking trail. Valet parking. Business center. Conference center/facilities. Concierge. Gift shop. Cr cds: A, C, D, DS, JCB, MC, V.

D ⬛ ⬛ ⬛ ⬛ ⬛ ⬛ ⬛

All Suites

★ ★ ★ **THE BURNSLEY ALL-SUITE HOTEL.** *1000 Grant St (80203). Phone 303/830-1000; toll-free 800/231-3915; fax 303/830-7676. www.burnsley.com.* Stay in one of the suites at this Victorian property and enjoy all the comforts of home. Just minutes away from downtown Denver. 80 kitchen suites, 16 story. S, D $119-$149; suites $149-$189; each additional $15. Complimentary full breakfast. Complimentary coffee in rooms. Check-out noon. TV; cable (premium). Balconies. Microwaves. Restaurant 6:30 am-2 pm, 6-9 pm. Bar from 11 am. Room service to 11 pm. Health club privileges. Pool. Garage parking. Meeting rooms. Business center. Converted apartment building in residential area, near State Capitol. Cr cds: A, D, DS, MC, V.

D ⬛ ⬛ ⬛ ⬛

★ ★ ★ **EMBASSY SUITES SOUTHEAST.** *7525 E Hampden Ave (80231). Phone 303/696-6644; toll-free 800/362-2779; fax 303/337-6202. www.winhotel.com.* This all-suites hotel is conveniently located near many of the area's attractions including the downtown Convention Center and Mile High Stadium. 206 suites, 7 story. S $139-$169; each additional $10; under 18 free; weekend rates. Crib free. Complimentary full breakfast. Check-out 1 pm. TV; cable (premium), VCR available. In-room modem link. Balconies. Refrigerators, microwaves, minibars. Coin laundry. Restaurant 11:30 am-2 pm, 5-10 pm. Bar to 2 am; Sun to midnight. Exercise equipment, sauna, steam room. Indoor pool, whirlpool. Meeting rooms. Business center. Gift shop. Cr cds: A, C, D, DS, JCB, MC, V.

D ⬛ ⬛ ⬛ SC ⬛

★ ★ ★ **EMBASSY SUITES AIRPORT SOUTH.** *4444 Havana St (80239). Phone 303/375-0400; toll-free 800/345-0087; fax 303/371-4634. www.embassysuites.com.* This property is located just 15 miles from the Denver International Airport. 210 suites, 7 story. Suites $124-$145; each additional $12; under 12 free; ski plans, weekend package.

Crib free. Pet accepted, some restrictions; $50 deposit. Complimentary full breakfast. Check-out 1 pm. TV; cable (premium), VCR available. In-room modem link. Refrigerators, microwaves, minibars. Coin laundry. Restaurant 11 am-11 pm. Bar to 1 am. Exercise equipment, sauna, steam room. Indoor pool, whirlpool. Free airport transportation. Meeting rooms. Business services. Gift shop. Cr cds: A, C, D, DS, ER, JCB, MC, V.

D ⬛ ⬛ ⬛ ⬛

Resort

★ ★ ★ **OMNI INTERLOCKEN RESORT.** *500 Interlocken Blvd, Broomfield (80021). Phone 303/438-6600; toll-free 800/843-6664; fax 303/438-7224. www.omnihotels.com.* Metropolitan Denver is home to the wonderful Omni Interlocken Resort. Situated midway between Denver and Boulder in the area's technology corridor, the resort is part of the Interlocken Advanced Technology Park. Sharing space with leading businesses and the FlatIron Crossings shopping center, this all-season resort is a premier recreational destination. Set against the backdrop of the Rocky Mountains, the 300-acre property has something for everyone. Golfers needing to brush up on their game head for the L. A. W.s Academy of Golf for its celebrated instruction before hitting the three 9-hole courses. The well-equipped fitness center and pool keep guests active, while the full-service spa attends to every need. Indigenous Colorado materials are used throughout the resort, enhancing the local flavor of the design. The guest rooms are comfortably elegant and include 21st-century amenities like WebTV and high-speed Internet connections. Three restaurants run the gamut from traditional to pub style. 390 rooms, 13 suites, 11 story. S, D $109-$199; suites $239-$550; each additional $20. Pet accepted; $50 refundable deposit. Complimentary valet parking. Check-out noon. TV; cable (premium), VCR available. In-room modem link. Restaurant 6:30 am-10 pm. Bar. Room service 24 hours. Supervised children's activities (summer). Exercise room; sauna, steam room. Massage. Game room. Heated pool; whirlpool, poolside services available. 27-hole golf; greens fee $65-$105 (including cart). Bike rentals. Hiking trail. Business center. Concierge. Cr cds: A, C, D, DS, ER, JCB, MC, V.

D ⬛ ⬛ ⬛ ⬛ ⬛ ⬛ ⬛

B&B/Small Inns

★ ★ ★ **CAPITOL HILL MANSION B&B.** *1207 Pennsylvania St (80203). Phone 303/839-5221; toll-free 800/839-9329; fax 303/839-9046. www.capitolhillmansion.com.* With its ruby sandstone exterior and dramatic entrance, this 1891 mansion offers a romantic getaway for couples. Rooms feature fresh flowers, soft lighting, and antique furniture. Be sure to have the owners arrange a horse-drawn carriage ride. 8 rooms, 7 with A/C, 3 story, 3 suites.

S, D $85-$95; each additional $10; suites $105-$165. Complimentary full breakfast. Complimentary coffee in rooms. Check-out 11 am, check-in 4:30-8 pm. TV; cable (premium). Some balconies. Some in-room whirlpools, fireplaces. Restaurant nearby. Business services. Concierge service. Built in 1891; Romanesque style with turrets, chimneys and curved porch. Totally nonsmoking. Cr cds: A, C, D, DS, ER, JCB, MC, V.

★ ★ ★ **HAUS BERLIN BED & BREAKFAST.** *1651 Emerson St (80218). Phone 303/837-9527; toll-free 800/659-0253. www.hausberlinbandb.com.* This inn was built in 1892 and features original art and many antiques. Listed on the National Register of Historic Places, it is conveniently located five minutes from downtown. This elegant property is a favorite with business travelers. 4 rooms, 1 suite, 3 story. S $95-$115; D $100; suite $140. Complimentary full breakfast. Check-out 11 am, check-in 4-8 pm. TV (in 3 rooms); cable (premium). Restaurant nearby. Built in 1892 for Reverend Thomas N. Haskell, founder of Colorado College. Totally nonsmoking. Cr cds: A, C, D, MC, V.

★ ★ ★ **HISTORIC CASTLE MARNE INN.** *1572 Race St (80206). Phone 303/331-0621; toll-free 800/926-2763; fax 303/331-0623. www.castlemarne.com.* 10 rooms, 3 story. S, D $85-$250. Complimentary full breakfast. Check-out 11 am, check-in 4 pm. In-room modem link. Health club privileges. Game room. Business center. Concierge. Built 1889; Romanesque mansion was residence of museum curator. Cheesman Park 3 blocks. Totally nonsmoking. Cr cds: A, C, D, DS, MC, V.

★ **HOLIDAY CHALET.** *1820 E Colfax Ave (80218). Phone 303/321-9975; toll-free 800/626-4497; fax 303/377-6556.* 10 kitchen units, 3 story. S, D $94; each additional $5; under 12 free; weekly rates. Crib free. Pet accepted; $50 deposit and $5/day. Complimentary breakfast. Complimentary coffee in rooms. Check-out noon. TV; VCR. Microwaves available. Restaurant nearby. Garage parking $10/day. Concierge. Antique furniture; library; patio; 1880 saltwater fish prints. Restored brownstone built in 1896. Totally nonsmoking. Cr cds: A, C, D, DS, MC, V.

★ ★ **THE LUMBER BARON INN.** *2555 W 37th Ave (80211). Phone 303/477-8205; toll-free 800/697-6552; fax 303/477-0269. www.lumberbaron.com.* Named for its original owner, an immigrant who made his fortune in lumber, this mansion blends old-style architecture and décor with modern conveniences. Function areas include the third floor, which features a 20-foot pyramid

ceiling. 5 rooms, 3 story. S, D $145-$235; weekend rates. Complimentary full breakfast. Complimentary coffee in rooms. Check-out 11 am, check-in 4 pm. TV; VCR available (movies). Fireplaces. Restaurant nearby. Lawn games. Street parking. Business services. Luggage handling. Built in 1890. Ballroom. Totally nonsmoking. Cr cds: A, DS, MC, V.

★ ★ ★ **QUEEN ANNE B&B.** *2147-2151 Tremont Pl (80205). Phone 303/296-6666; toll-free 800/432-4667; fax 303/296-2151. www.queenannebnb.com.* Built in the 1800s, this bed-and-breakfast faces the Benedict Fountain Park in the Clement Historic District of downtown Denver. Four of the 2-room gallery suites are named for famous painters and display samples of their work. The Aspen Room is spectacular, with a mural of an aspen forest that covers both the walls and the ceiling that rises to the top of the Victorian turret. 14 rooms, 3 story. S, D $75-$145; each additional $25; suites $145-$175. Complimentary full breakfast, afternoon refreshments. Check-out noon, check-in 3 pm. In-room modem link. Some in-room whirlpools. Health club privileges. Business services. Built in 1879; antiques; garden; fountain. Totally nonsmoking. Cr cds: A, D, DS, MC, V.

Restaurants

★ **ANNIE'S CAFE.** *4012 E 8th Ave (80220). Phone 303/355-8197.* Hours: 6:30 am-9 pm; Sat 8 am-9 pm; Sun 8 am-3 pm. Closed major holidays. Dinner $4.25-$8.95. Bar. Children's menu. Totally nonsmoking. Cr cds: A, DS, MC, V.

★ ★ **BABY DOE'S MATCHLESS MINE.** *2520 W 23rd Ave (80211). Phone 303/433-3386; fax 303/433-2041.* Hours: 11 am-2:30 pm, 4:30-10 pm; Fri, Sat to 11 pm; Sun 4-10 pm; Sun brunch 9 am-2:30 pm. Closed Mon. Dinner $15-$36. Sun brunch. Children's menu. Replica of Matchless Mine in Leadville; memorabilia of era. Cr cds: A, D, DS, MC, V.

★ ★ **BAROLO GRILL.** *3030 E 6th Ave (80206). Phone 303/393-1040; fax 303/333-9240.* Northern Italian menu. Hours: 5-10:30 pm. Closed Sun, Mon; major holidays. Reservations accepted. Bar. A la carte entrees: dinner $17-$27. Complete meal: dinner $38.95. Children's menu. Specialties: wine-marinated duck, tuna puttanesca, lamb chops. Free valet parking. Outdoor dining. Paintings. Cr cds: A, D, DS, MC, V.

★ ★ **BENNY'S.** *301 E 7th Ave (80203). Phone 303/894-0788; fax 303/839-5488. www.bennysrestaurant.com.* Mexican menu. Closed Thanksgiving, Dec 25. Lunch, dinner. Bar. Casual attire. Outdoor seating, non-smoking seating. Cr cds: A, D, DS, MC, V. **$**

D ☒

★ ★ ★ **BROKER.** *821 17th St (80202). Phone 303/292-5065; fax 303/292-2652. www.brokerrestaurant.com.* Built inside a former turn-of-the-century bank vault, the restaurant's trademark is its free bowls of steamed shrimp for every diner. Hours: 11 am-2:30 pm, 5-11 pm; Sat, Sun from 5 pm. Closed Dec 25. Reservations accepted. Continental menu. Bar. Lunch $6.95-$19.95, dinner $24-$39. Specialties: prime rib, filet Wellington. In vault and board rooms of converted bank (1903). Cr cds: A, D, DS, MC, V.

★ ★ **BUCKHORN EXCHANGE.** *1000 Osage St (80204). Phone 303/534-9505; fax 303/534-2814. www.buckhorn.com.* The Buckhorn Exchange, Denver's oldest (and most famous) restaurant, is part dining establishment, part saloon, and part museum. It's worth a visit, if only to marvel at the collection of more than 500 wall-mounted big-game hunting trophies, as well as photos and artifacts from the many dignitaries who have dined here. Its casual Western charm has been honed through 100 years of continuous service. Take the opportunity to sample buffalo sausage, fried alligator tail, or marinated rattlesnake before digging into one of Buckhorn's famous steaks. On weekends, live music and dancing liven up the Lounge. Hours: 11 am-2 pm, 5:30-9 pm; Fri, Sat 5-10 pm; Sun 5-9 pm. Closed major holidays. Dinner $17-$39. Bar. Historical landmark and museum, built in 1893. Rooftop garden seating. Cr cds: A, C, D, DS, MC, V.

★ ★ **COOS BAY BISTRO.** *2076 S University Blvd (80210). Phone 303/744-3591; fax 303/744-6246. www.coosbaybistro.com.* French, Italian menu. Specialties: Thai pasta, marinated duck breast with blackberry sauce, seared ahi tuna. Hours: 11:15 am-2 pm, 5:30-10 pm; Fri, Sat 5-10:30 pm. Closed major holidays. Dinner $15-$22. Bar. Reservations accepted. Outdoor dining. Totally non-smoking. Cr cds: A, D, MC, V.

D ☒

★ ★ **DENVER CHOPHOUSE & BREWERY.** *1735 19th St (80202). Phone 303/296-0800; fax 303/296-2800. www.chophouse.com.* Hours: 11 am-2:30 pm, 4:30 pm-midnight; Sun 4:30-10 pm. Reservations accepted. Bar. Lunch $7.25-$13.95, dinner $9-$24.95. Specializes in steaks, seafood. Jazz Thurs-Sat. Outdoor dining. Historic warehouse converted into restaurant; microbrewery. Cr cds: A, D, MC, V.

D

★ **EMPRESS SEAFOOD.** *2825 W Alameda Ave (80219). Phone 303/922-2822; fax 303/922-2810.* Hours: 11 am-9 pm; Sat, Sun from 10:30 am. Chinese menu. Bar. A la carte entrees: lunch $4.25-$13, dinner $6-$13. Specializes in seafood. Oriental artwork. Cr cds: A, D, DS, MC, V.

D

★ ★ **FOURTH STORY.** *2955 E 1st Ave (80206). Phone 303/322-1824; fax 303/399-2279. www.fourthstory.com.* American menu. Hours: 11 am-4 pm, 5-10 pm; Sun brunch 11 am-3 pm. Closed some major holidays. Dinner $14-$28. Sun brunch. Bar. Entertainment Sun, Mon. Children's menu. Cr cds: A, D, DS, MC, V.

D

★ ★ ★ **HIGHLANDS GARDEN CAFE.** *3927 W 32nd Ave (80212). Phone 303/458-5920; fax 303/477-6695.* This top-tier new-American restaurant has beautiful Victorian architecture and a wonderful, rose-filled garden. Hours: 11 am-2 pm, 5-9 pm; Sun brunch 10 am-2 pm. Closed Mon; major holidays. Dinner $16-$32. Two Victorian houses converted into restaurant. Outdoor seating. Cr cds: A, MC, V.

D

★ ★ **IL FORNAIO.** *1631 Wazee St (80202). Phone 303/573-5050. www.ilfornaio.com.* Hours: 11:30 am-11 pm; Fri, Sat to midnight. Closed July 4, Thanksgiving, Dec 25. Reservations accepted. Italian menu. Bar. A la carte entrees: lunch $7.95-$21.50, dinner $8.95-$21.50. Children's menu. Menu changes monthly. Valet parking. Outdoor dining. Totally nonsmoking. Cr cds: A, D, MC, V.

D ☒

★ ★ ★ **IMPERIAL CHINESE.** *431 S Broadway (80209). Phone 303/698-2800; fax 303/698-2820. www.imperialchinese.com.* Contemporary Chinese décor with many artifacts. Chinese menu. Closed July 4, Thanksgiving, Dec 25. Lunch, dinner. Bar. Casual attire. Non-smoking seating. Cr cds: A, C, D, MC, V. **$**

D ☒

★ ★ **INDIA'S RESTAURANT.** *3333 S Tamarac (80231). Phone 303/755-4284; fax 303/752-9814. www.indiasrestaurant.com.* Northern Indian menu. Hours: 11:30 am-2:15 pm, 5:30-9:30 pm; Fri to 10 pm; Sat noon-2:15 pm, 5:30-10 pm; Sun 5:30-9 pm. Dinner $9.95-$15.95. Bar. Cr cds: A, D, DS, MC, V.

D

★ **JAPON RESTAURANT.** *1028 S Gaylord St (80209). Phone 303/744-0330; fax 303/715-0336. www.japonsushi. com.* Japanese menu. Hours: 11:30 am-2 pm, 5-10 pm; Fri, Sat to 11:30 pm; Sun from 5 pm. Closed Dec 25. Dinner $10-$25. Totally nonsmoking. Cr cds: A, D, DS, MC, V.

★ **JAX FISH HOUSE.** *1539 17th St (80202). Phone 303/292-5767; fax 303/292-0530. www.jaxfishhousedenver. com.* Hours: 4-10 pm; Fri, Sat to 11 pm; Sun to 9 pm. Closed most major holidays. Seafood menu. Bar. Dinner $8.95-$24.50. Children's menu. Specialties: filet mignon of tuna, oyster bar, cioppino. Jazz Tues. Street parking. Totally nonsmoking. Cr cds: A, D, MC, V.

★ ★ ★ **KEVIN TAYLOR RESTAURANT.** *1106 14th St (80202). Phone 303/820-2600; fax 303/893-1293.* Frequently hailed as one of Denver's best, Kevin Taylor is the flagship eatery of the chic Hotel Teatro, located in the heart of Denver (see also HOTEL TEATRO). A luxurious sense of Parisian elegance is achieved with earth-toned walls, stunning floral arrangements, alabaster chandeliers, Versailles mirrors, original artwork, and cushy, striped silk-covered chairs. Like the décor, the menu is inspired by France, with an emphasis on local, seasonal ingredients that, thanks to chef-owner Kevin Taylor's kitchen magic, dazzle the taste buds. A tasting menu and à la carte selections are available, with a wide variety of choices to suit any craving. Equal in quality to the menu is the wine list, which includes 900 bottles. Hours: 5:30-10:30 pm. Closed Sun; holidays. Dinner $25-$36. Cr cds: A, D, MC, V.

★ **LAS DELICIAS.** *439 E 19th Ave (80203). Phone 303/839-5675; fax 303/839-5859.* Hours: 8 am-9 pm; Fri, Sat to 10 pm; Sun from 9 am. Closed Thanksgiving, Dec 25. Reservations accepted. Mexican menu. Breakfast $1.99-$6, lunch, dinner $2.25-$9.25. Specialties: carnitas estilo michoacan, fajitas estilo michoacan. Street parking. Family-owned since 1976. Cr cds: A, D, DS, MC, V.

★ ★ **LE CENTRAL.** *112 E 8th Ave (80203). Phone 303/ 863-8094; fax 303/863-0219. www.lecentral.com.* French menu. Closed Dec 25. Lunch, dinner, Sat, Sun brunch. Bar. Casual attire. Non-smoking seating. Cr cds: A, MC, V. $

★ ★ **MEL'S.** *235 Fillmore (80206). Phone 303/333-3979; fax 303/355-7005. www.melsbarandgrill.com.* Continental menu. Hours: 11:30 am-2:30 pm, 5:30-9:30 pm; Sun from 5 pm. Closed Easter, Thanksgiving, and Dec 25. Dinner $12-$27. Bar. Live music. Outdoor seating. Cr cds: A, D, DS, MC, V.

★ ★ ★ **MORTON'S OF CHICAGO.** *1710 Wynkoop St (80202). Phone 303/825-3353; fax 303/825-1248. www.mortons.com.* One of the few places left where one can light up a cigar without interference, this national chain fits right into the upscale Denver meat-and-potatoes scene. The martinis are top-notch (as is the beef, naturally). Hours: 5:30-11 pm; Sun 5-10 pm. Closed major holidays. Bar from 5 pm. Wine list. A la carte entrees: dinner $18.95-$29.95. Specializes in steak, lobster. Valet parking. Menu recited. Cr cds: A, D, MC, V.

★ ★ ★ **PALACE ARMS.** *321 17th St (80202). Phone 303/297-3111; fax 303/297-3928. www.brownpalace.com.* The Palace Arms opened its doors in 1892. Granted, 111 years is a long time to carry on culinary excellence, but the task is achieved gracefully and winningly here. This century-old restaurant is a treasure of history and gastronomy. Located in the Brown Palace Hotel (see also THE BROWN PALACE HOTEL), the majestic Palace Arms dining room has a unique western charisma, with rich wood, brocade-upholstered seating, and 17th-century antiques. Just as refined as the atmosphere is the delicious contemporary French cuisine, prepared with regional accents and served with impeccable care. The Palace Arms offers guests a rare opportunity to dine in historically opulent surroundings on a menu of magnificent fare. American menu. Closed major holidays. Dinner. Jacket required. Reservations required. Valet parking. Cr cds: A, D, DS, ER, JCB, MC, V. $$$

★ **POTAGER.** *1109 Ogden St (80218). Phone 303/ 832-5788. www.coloradocuisine.com.* Hours: 5-11 pm. Closed Mon, Sun; also major holidays. Wine, beer. A la carte entrees: dinner $10-$20. Specialties: roasted chicken, grilled salmon, twice-baked cheese souffle. Parking. Outdoor dining. Totally nonsmoking. Cr cds: A, MC, V.

★ ★ **REDFISH.** *1701 Wynkoop (80202). Phone 303/ 595-0443; fax 303/595-8858. www.redfishamerica.com.* Cajun menu. Hours: 11:30 am-midnight; Fri to 1 am; Sat 4 pm-1 am; Sun to 9 pm. Closed Sun; major holidays. Dinner $7.95-$18.95. Entertainment: jazz. Cr cds: A, DS, MC, V.

★ **ROCKY MOUNTAIN DINER.** *800 18th St (80202). Phone 303/293-8383. www.rockymountaindiner.com.* Hours: 11 am-11 pm; Sun 10 am-9 pm. Closed most major holidays. Reservations accepted (dinner). Bar. Lunch, dinner $4.95-$18.95. Children's menu. Specialties: buffalo meatloaf, duck enchiladas. Outdoor dining. Saloon-style décor, Western motif. Cr cds: A, D, DS, MC, V.

★ ★ ★ **STRINGS.** *1700 Humboldt St (80218). Phone 303/831-7310; fax 303/860-8812. www.stringsrestaurant.com.* This casual restaurant attracts celebrities for power lunching. The presentation can be jaw-droppingly good. Hours: 11 am-10 pm; Fri, Sat to 11 pm; Sun 5-10 pm. Closed some major holidays. Reservations accepted. Bar. Wine list. Lunch $10-$17, dinner $18-$30. Children's menu. Specializes in pastas, daily menu. Valet parking. Outdoor dining. Six dining areas, each with its own décor and ambience. Cr cds: A, D, DS, MC, V.

D

★ ★ ★ ★ **TANTE LOUISE.** *4900 E Colfax Ave (80220). Phone 303/355-4488; fax 303/321-6312. www.tantelouise.com.* If you have a romantic evening in Denver planned, there's little reason to dine anywhere other than Tante Louise. This country inn-style restaurant, equipped with a blazing fire and vintage wall coverings, is the ideal spot for soft, intimate conversations and long, luxurious dinners. Even if you are not in love with your dinner companion when you get there, the mood here is so perfect that you'll leave enamored, if not with each other, then at least with the food and the tranquil, charming setting. The artistic cuisine at Tante Louise features playful and surprising twists on classic French dishes prepared with impressive local ingredients. To match the ambience and the cuisine, the wine list boasts an incredible selection of 600 domestic and imported wines and sparkling wines, perfect for keeping the romance going. Continental menu. Hours: 5:30-10 pm. Closed Sun. Dinner $19-$32.95. Bar. Valet parking. Outdoor dining. Cr cds: A, D, DS, MC, V.

D

★ ★ **THREE SONS.** *2915 W 44th Ave (80211). Phone 303/455-4366; fax 303/433-2664.* Italian menu. Hours: 11 am-9:30 pm; Sun from 4 pm; early-bird dinner Tues-Thurs 4-7 pm. Closed Mon; also most major holidays. Bar. Lunch $6.95-$10.25, dinner $10.95-$17.95. Children's menu. Parking. Romanesque décor. Family-owned since 1951. Cr cds: MC, V.

D

★ ★ **TOMMY TSUNAMI'S.** *1432 Market St (80202). Phone 303/534-5050; fax 303/534-3030. www.tommytsunamis.com.* Hours: 11 am-11 pm; Thurs to midnight; Fri to 1 am; Sat 4:30 pm-1 am; Sun 4:30-11 pm. Closed Thanksgiving, Dec 25. Reservations accepted. Pacific Rim menu. Bar. Lunch $6.75-$17.95, dinner $13.95-$23.95. Specializes in sushi, teriyaki, noodles. Outdoor dining. Japanese-influenced modern décor; sushi bar. Totally nonsmoking. Cr cds: A, DS, MC, V.

D

★ **TRINITY GRILLE.** *1801 Broadway (80202). Phone 303/293-2288; fax 303/293-3817. www.trinitygrille.com.* Hours: 11 am-2:30 pm, 5:30-10 pm; Sat from 5:30 pm.

Closed Sun; most major holidays. Dinner $25-$30. Bar. Cr cds: A, D, DS, MC, V.

D

★ ★ ★ **TUSCANY.** *4150 E Mississippi Ave (80246). Phone 303/782-9300; fax 303/758-6542.* Within the walls of the Loews Hotel is one of Denver's top Italian restaurants, where executive chef John P. Mertes supervises the creation of all sorts of regional wonders. Northern Italian menu. Hours: 6 am-10 pm; Sat, Sun from 7 am. Breakfast $2.50-$12.50, lunch $8.25-$16, dinner $12.50-$25. Sun brunch $31.95. Bar noon-midnight. Children's menu. Reservations accepted; required Sun, holidays. Valet parking available. Outdoor dining. Braille menu. Cr cds: A, D, DS, MC, V.

D

★ **WAZEE SUPPER CLUB.** *1600 15th St (80202). Phone 303/623-9518. www.wazeesupperclub.com.* Hours: 11-2 am; Sun noon-midnight. Closed Jan 1, Dec 25. Reservations accepted (Mon-Thurs). Bar. A la carte entrees: lunch, dinner $3.75-$19.45. Specializes in pizza, sandwiches. Sat night entertainment. Street parking. Cr cds: A, MC, V.

D

★ ★ ★ **WELLSHIRE INN.** *3333 S Colorado Blvd (80222). Phone 303/759-3333; fax 303/759-3487. www.wellshireinn.com.* With its lavish décor, the inn's dining room is a perfect choice for special occasions. Hours: 7-10 am, 11:30 am-2:30 pm, 5-10 pm; Fri to 11 pm; Sat 11:30 am-2:30 pm, 5-11 pm; Sun 10 am-2 pm (brunch), 5-9 pm. Closed Jan 1, Memorial Day, Labor Day. Reservations accepted. Bar. Breakfast $4.75-$9.75, lunch $8.25-$12.95, dinner $14.95-$28. Sun brunch $6.95-$12.95. Specializes in salmon, rack of lamb, steak. Outdoor dining. Tudor-style inn. Totally nonsmoking. Cr cds: A, D, DS, MC, V.

D

★ **WYNKOOP BREWING COMPANY.** *1634 18th St (80202). Phone 303/297-2700; fax 303/297-2958. www.wynkoop.com.* Hours: 11-2 am; Sun 10 am-midnight. Closed Thanksgiving, Dec 25. Dinner $5.95-$18.95. Bar. Brewery kettles displayed; beer brewed on premises. Outdoor seating. In J. S. Brown Mercantile Building (1899). Cr cds: A, D, DS, MC, V.

D

★ **ZAIDY'S DELI.** *121 Adams St (80206). Phone 303/333-5336; fax 303/333-4118. www.zaidysdeli.com.* Hours: 7 am-8 pm; Mon, Tues to 3 pm; Sat, Sun 8 am-7 pm. Closed Thanksgiving, Rosh Hashanah, Yom Kippur. Reservations accepted. Bar. Breakfast $3.25-$8.50, lunch $4.50-$8, dinner $5.95-$9. Children's menu. Specializes in blintzes, deli sandwiches. Own baking, soups. Outdoor dining. Totally nonsmoking. Cr cds: A, MC, V.

D

Denver International Airport Area (C-6)

See also Denver

Services and Information

Information. 800/AIR-2-DEN.

Lost and Found. 303/342-4062.

Weather. 303/337-2500.

Airlines. Air Canada, America West, American, Continental, Delta, Frontier, Lone Star, Lufthansa, Martinair Holland, Mexicana, Midwest Express, Northwest, Reno Air, United, USAir, Vanguard.

Motels/Motor Lodges

★ **HAMPTON INN.** *1500 S Abilene St (80012). Phone 303/369-8400; toll-free 800/426-7866; fax 303/369-0324. www.hampton-inn.com.* 132 rooms, 4 story. S $69-$78; D $74-$88; under 18 free. Crib free. TV; cable (premium). Heated pool. Complimentary buffet breakfast. Restaurants nearby. Coffee in rooms. Check-out noon. Coin laundry. Meeting rooms. Business services available. In-room modem link. Valet service. Health club privileges. Some refrigerators; microwaves available. Cr cds: A, C, D, DS, MC, V.

Hotels

★ ★ ★ **DOUBLETREE HOTEL.** *3203 Quebec St (80207). Phone 303/321-3333; fax 303/329-5233. www.doubletree.com.* This Hilton-chain property is located just 20 minutes from Denver International Airport and 6 minutes from downtown. 571 rooms, 9 story. S, D $59-$149; suites $350-$500; each additional $10; under 18 free; weekend rates. Crib available. Pet accepted; $50 deposit. Check-out noon, check-in 3 pm. TV; cable, VCR available. In-room modem link. Some balconies. Refrigerators available. Coffee in rooms. Restaurant 6 am-11 pm. Bar 5 pm-2 am, Sun to midnight. Room service 24 hours. Exercise equipment, sauna. Indoor pool, whirlpool. Free airport transportation. Business center. Convention center/facilities. Sun deck. Cr cds: A, C, D, DS, ER, JCB, MC, V.

★ ★ ★ **DOUBLETREE HOTEL SOUTHEAST.** *13696 E Iliff Pl, Aurora (80014). Phone 303/337-2800; toll-free 800/528-0444; fax 303/752-0296. www.doubletree.com.* Each room at this property is spacious and provides all the comforts of home. 248 rooms, 6 story. S $130; D $150; each additional $10; suites $150; under 18 free; weekend rates. Crib free. TV; cable (premium), VCR available. Indoor pool; poolside service. Restaurant 6:30 am-10 pm. Bar 11-2 am. Check-out noon. Business center. In-room modem link. Gift shop. Tennis privileges. Golf privileges. Exercise equipment. Health club privileges. Cr cds: A, C, D, DS, ER, JCB, MC, V.

Restaurant

★ **LA CUEVA.** *9742 E Colfax Ave, Aurora (80010). Phone 303/367-1422; fax 303/367-4071. www.lacueva.net.* Mexican menu. Hours: 11 am-9 pm. Closed Jan 1, Thanksgiving, Dec 25. Dinner $7-$15. Bar. Casual attire. Cr cds: A, MC, V.

Dillon (C-4)

See also Breckenridge, Georgetown, Leadville, Vail

Pop 802 **Elev** 8,858 ft **Area code** 970 **Zip** 80435

Information Summit County Chamber of Commerce, PO Box 214, Frisco 80443; 800/530-3099

Web www.summitnet.com

The entire town was moved in the early 1960s to make way for Dillon Lake, a reservoir for the Denver water system. The new Dillon, a modern, planned community, has become a popular resort area in the midst of wonderful mountain scenery. Ranger District offices of the Green Mountain Reservoir (see KREMMLING) and the White River National Forest, Arapaho division, (see GLENWOOD SPRINGS) are located in Dillon.

What to See and Do

Arapaho National Forest. *1311 S College Ave. N, S, and E via US 6, CO 9. For information contact the Visitor Center, Arapaho and Roosevelt national forests, 1311 S College, Fort Collins 80526. Phone 970/498-2770.* Campgrounds, picnic grounds, and winter sports areas on more than one million acres. Of special interest are Lake Dillon, Arapaho

National Recreation Area with five reservoirs, and Mount Evans Wilderness Area with the 14,264-foot-high Mount Evans, which has the highest auto road in the US. **$$$**

Copper Mountain Resort Ski Area. *9 miles SW at junction I-70 and CO 91.* Phone 970/968-2882 or 800/458-8386. Six-person, four high-speed quad, five triple, five double chairlifts; six surface lifts; patrol, school, rentals, snow-making; cafeteria, restaurants, bar, nursery. One hundred twenty-six runs; longest run approximately 3 miles; vertical drop 2,601 feet. (Nov-Apr, daily) Cross-country skiing. Half-day rates. Athletic club. Summer activities include boating, sailing, rafting; hiking, bicycling, horse-back riding, golf; Jeep tours. Chairlift also operates to summit of mountain (late June-Sept, daily).

Keystone Resort Ski Area. *1254 Soda Ridge Rd. 6 miles E on US 6.* Phone 800/222-0188. Four ski mountains. Patrol, school, rentals. Snowmaking at Keystone, North Peak, and The Outback. Cafeteria, restaurant, bar, nursery, lodge. (Late Oct-early May) Cross-country skiing, night skiing, ice skating, snowmobiling, sleigh rides. Shuttle bus service. Combination and 1/2-day ski rates; package plans. Summer activities include boating and rafting, gondola rides; golf, tennis, horseback riding, bicycling, and Jeep riding. **$$$$** The four ski mountains here are

Arapahoe Basin. *US Hwy 6 (80435).* Triple, four double chairlifts. Sixty-one runs; longest run 1 1/2 miles; vertical drop 1,670 feet. (Mid-Nov-June) **$$$$**

Keystone Mountain. Six-passenger gondola; two triple, eight double, four quad, two high-speed chairlifts; four surface lifts. Fifty-three runs; longest run 3 miles; vertical drop 2,340 feet. (Late Oct-early May) Night skiing on 13 runs (mid-Nov-early Apr).

North Peak. High-speed gondola; quad and triple chairlifts. Nineteen runs; longest run 2 1/2 miles; vertical drop 1,620 feet. (Mid-Nov-late Apr) **$$$$**

The Outback. High-speed quad chairlift. Seventeen runs; longest run 2 1/2 miles, vertical drop 1,520 feet. (Mid-Nov-late Apr) **$$$$**

Lake Dillon. *680 Blue River Pkwy. Just S of town in Arapaho National Forest on 3,300 acres.* Phone 970/468-5400. Fishing, boating, rafting (ramps, rentals, marinas); hiking, picnicking, camping. Jeep tours (fee). (Daily) **FREE**

Silverthorne Factory Stores. *145 Stephens Way #M. 2 miles N to I-70, exit 205, in Silverthorne.* Phone 970/468-9440. Mall contains more than 45 outlet stores. Snack bars. (Daily)

Special Event

Mountain Community Fair. *Silverthorne.* Phone 970/513-8081. Second weekend in July.

Motels/Motor Lodges

★★ **BEST WESTERN PTARMIGAN LODGE.** *652 Lake Dillon Dr (80435).* Phone 970/468-2341; toll-free 800/842-5939; toll-free 800/780-7234; fax 970/468-6465. www.bestwestern.com. 69 rooms, 4 kitchen units, 1-2 story. No A/C. Late Dec-early Apr: S, D $110-$130; each additional $5-$10; under 12 free; kitchen units $10 additional; lower rates rest of year. Crib free. Pet accepted; $50 deposit, $15. Complimentary continental breakfast. Check-out 11 am. TV; cable (premium). Some balconies, refrigerators. Microwaves available. Coin laundry. Restaurant adjacent 7 am-2:30 pm, 5-10 pm. Bar. Whirlpool. Sauna. Downhill, cross-country ski 5 1/2 miles. Boating. Free ski area transportation. Meeting room. Business services. On lake. Cr cds: A, C, D, DS, MC, V.

★ **DAYS INN.** *580 Silverthorne Ln, Silverthorne (80498).* Phone 970/468-8661; toll-free 800/520-4267; fax 970/468-1421. www.daysinn.com. 73 rooms, 15 kitchen units, 4 story. Nov-Apr: S, D $89-$129; suites, kitchen units $99-$199; under 18 free; lower rates rest of year. Pet accepted; $10. Complimentary continental breakfast. Check-out 11 am. TV; cable (premium). Some fireplaces, wetbars; refrigerators, microwaves available. Coin laundry. Restaurant nearby. Sauna. Wading pool, whirlpool. Golf nearby. Tennis nearby. Downhill, cross-country skiing 6 miles. Cr cds: A, C, D, DS, JCB, MC, V.

★★ **FOUR POINTS BY SHERATON.** *560 Silverthorne Ln (80498).* Phone 970/468-6200; toll-free 800/321-3509; fax 970/468-7829. www.sunstonehotels.com. 160 rooms, 18 suites, 6 story. Nov-Mar: S, D $79-$169; suites $209-$279; ski plans; holidays (7-day minimum); lower rates rest of year. Complimentary continental breakfast. Check-out 10 am. TV; cable (premium). Restaurant 11:30 am-11 pm; Sat, Sun to 3:30 pm. Bar. Room service. Game room. Pool, whirlpool. Downhill, cross-country ski 4 miles. Ski, bicycle rental. Cr cds: A, C, D, DS, MC, V.

★★ **HOLIDAY INN.** *1129 N Summit Blvd (80443).* Phone 970/668-5000; toll-free 800/782-7669; fax 970/668-0718. www.holiday-inn.com/summitcounty. 217 rooms, 3-6 story. Late Dec-Mar: S, D $62-$149; lower rates rest of year. TV; cable (premium). Indoor pool; whirlpool. Restaurant 6:30 am-2 pm, 5-10 pm. Room service. Bar 5-10 pm; Fri, Sat to 11 pm. Coffee in rooms. Check-out 11 am. Coin laundry. Meeting rooms. Business services available. In-room modem link. Valet service. Gift shop. Downhill/cross-country ski 10 miles. Exercise equipment; sauna. Massage. Game room. Recreation room. Some refrigerators. Balconies. Cr cds: A, C, D, DS, JCB, MC, V.

★ **SNOWSHOE MOTEL.** *521 Main St (80443). Phone 970/668-3444; toll-free 800/445-8658; fax 970/668-3883. www.snowshoemotel.com.* 37 rooms, 9 kitchen units, 2 story. No A/C. Late Dec-Mar: S, D $90; kitchen units $5-$7 additional; lower rates rest of year. Complimentary continental breakfast. Check-out 10 am. TV; cable (premium), VCR available. Some refrigerators, microwaves. Restaurant nearby. Whirlpool. Sauna. Downhill ski 6 miles, cross-country ski 1 mile. Business services. Cr cds: A, D, DS, MC, V.

Resorts

★★★ **COPPER MOUNTAIN RESORT.** *509 Copper Rd (80443). Phone 970/968-2882; toll-free 800/458-8386; fax 970/968-6227. www.ski-copper.com.* Guests flock to this resort for one reason—it's all about the slopes. Serious ski buffs will be in heaven with all the facilities one could hope for. 1-7 story. S, D $99-$225; each additional $15; full condo units (1-2 bedroom) $129-$545; under 14 free; higher rates in late Dec (5-day minimum); 3-day minimum early Mar-early Apr; AP, MAP available; package plans. Check-out 11 am, check-in 4 pm. TV; cable (premium), VCR available (movies $4). In-room modem link. Fireplaces. Dining room. Bar 11-2 am. Room service. Supervised children's activities; ages 3-12. Exercise room, massage, sauna, steam room. Indoor pool, whirlpool. Indoor tennis. Downhill, cross-country skiing on site. Entertainment. Lawn games. Bicycle rentals. Paddleboats. Ice skating, sleigh rides. Business center. Concierge. Some services limited in summer. Extensive grounds on 250 acres. Guides. Cr cds: A, D, DS, MC, V.

★★★ **KEYSTONE LODGE.** *22101 US Hwy 6 (80435). Phone 970/496-4202.* 152 rooms, 5 story. S, D $300-$425; each additional $25; suites $500-$1,800; under 12 free. Crib free. Check-out 11 am. TV; cable (premium), VCR (free movies). In-room modem link. Coffee in rooms. Restaurant 7 am-10 pm. Bar 4-11 pm, entertainment. Fitness center. Heated pool, whirlpool, poolside service. Golf privileges. Downhill, cross-country ski. Meeting rooms. Business services. Concierge. Cr cds: A, MC, V.

B&B/Small Inns

★★★ **CREEKSIDE INN.** *51 W Main St, Frisco (80443). Phone 970/668-5607; toll-free 800/668-7320; fax 970/668-8635. www.creeksideinn-frisco.com.* This inn provides a quiet getaway for nature lovers. Afternoon tea and refreshments are included with your stay. 7 rooms, 2 story. No A/C. Room phone available. Late Dec-early Jan: S $125-$155; D $100-$160; each additional $15; higher rates week of Dec 25; lower rates rest of year.

Complimentary full breakfast. Check-out 11 am, check-in 4-7 pm. TV; cable in common area. Restaurant nearby. Whirlpool. Downhill, cross-country ski 2 miles. Business services. Gift shop. View of mountains; Ten Mile Creek at edge of backyard. Totally nonsmoking. Cr cds: DS, MC, V.

★★ **LARK MOUNTAIN INN B&B.** *109 Granite St, Frisco (80443). Phone 970/668-5237; toll-free 800/668-5275; fax 970/668-1988. www.toski.com/lark.* 7 air-cooled rooms, 2 share bath, 1 with shower only, 2 story. No room phones. Mid-Feb-Apr: S, D $130-$160; family, weekend, weekly rates; ski plans; higher rates holidays (5-day minimum); lower rates rest of year. Children over 8 years only. Complimentary full breakfast. Check-out 10 am, check-in 3-6 pm. TV; cable, VCR available (movies). Some balconies. Microwaves available. Restaurant adjacent 6 am-11 pm. Whirlpool. Downhill ski 7 mi, cross-country ski 2 miles. Picnic tables. Business services. Luggage handling. Log timber inn with over 400 hand-stripped rails used in the porch. Totally nonsmoking. Cr cds: A, MC, V.

★ **NEW SUMMIT INN.** *1205 N Summit Blvd (80443). Phone 970/668-3220; toll-free 800/745-1211; fax 970/668-0188. www.newsummitinn.com.* 31 rooms, 2 story. Jan-Apr: S $40-$100; D $49-$139; under 18 free; higher rates late-Dec-early Jan. Crib $5. Pet accepted; $20 deposit and $5/day. TV; cable. Complimentary continental breakfast. Whirlpool. Restaurant adjacent 7 am-9 pm. Check-out 10 am. Coin laundry. Sauna. Refrigerators; microwaves available. Cr cds: A, C, D, DS, MC, V.

★★ **SKI TIP LODGE.** *764 Montezuma Rd, Keystone (80435). Phone 970/496-4950; fax 970/496-4940.* 11 rooms, 2 share bath, 2 story, 2 suites. No A/C. No room phones. Late Dec-early Jan: S, D $70-$174; suites $144-$204; weekly rates; ski plans; lower rates rest of year. Crib free. Complimentary breakfast in summer. Restaurant (see SKI TIP LODGE). Bar. Whirlpool. Health club privileges. Tennis. Downhill, cross-country ski on site. Business services. Mid-1800s stagecoach stop. Totally nonsmoking. Cr cds: A, C, D, DS, JCB, MC, V.

Restaurants

★★ **BLUE SPRUCE INN.** *20 Main St, Frisco (80443). Phone 970/668-5900; fax 970/668-8574. www.thebluespruce.com.* Continental menu. Hours: 5-10 pm. Dinner $16-$30. Bar. Cr cds: A, C, D, DS, ER, MC, V.

★★★ **SKI TIP LODGE.** *764 Montezuma Rd, Keystone (80435). Phone 970/468-4202; fax 970/496-4940. www.skitiplodge.com.* For more than 50 years, this charming bed-and-breakfast has been serving American regional cuisine. Hours: 5:45-9 pm. Complete meal: dinner $63. Bar. Children's menu. Totally nonsmoking. Cr cds: A, C, D, DS, ER, MC, V.

Dinosaur National Monument (A-1)

(88 miles W of Craig on US 40 to monument headquarters)

This 325-square-mile monument in the northwest corner of the state holds one of the largest concentrations of fossilized Jurassic-era dinosaur bones in the world. Visitors can get a close-up view of a quarry wall containing at least 1,500 fossil bones dating back 150 million years. The wall, enclosed in an information-packed Dinosaur Quarry Visitors Center, was once part of an ancient riverbed. The monument itself, spanning more than 300 square miles on the Colorado/Utah border, is distinguished by its ruggedly beautiful landscape of high plateaus and river-carved canyons. Access to the Colorado backcountry section, a land of fantastic, deeply eroded canyons of the Green and Yampa rivers, is via the Harpers Corner Road, starting at monument headquarters on US 40, 2 miles east of Dinosaur. At Harpers Corner, the end of this 32-mile surfaced road, a 1-mile foot trail leads to a promontory overlooking the Green and Yampa rivers.

The entrance to the Dinosaur Quarry section in Utah is at the junction of US 40 and UT 149 in Jensen, Utah, 13 miles east of Vernal. Seven miles north on UT 149 is the Dinosaur Quarry; 4 to 5 miles farther is the Green River campground. No lodgings are available other than at campgrounds.

The visitor centers and one quarry-section campground are open all year; the remainder are often closed by snow approximately mid-November to mid-April.

What to See and Do

Camping, picnicking. Green River campground near Dinosaur Quarry in Utah (Memorial Day-Labor Day; fee); Lodore and Echo Park (fee), Deerlodge campgrounds in Colorado; Harpers Corner has picnic facilities.

Dinosaur Quarry. *7 miles N of Jensen, UT, on UT 149.* Remarkable fossil deposit; exhibit of 150-million-year-old dinosaur remains; preparation laboratory on display. (Daily; extended hours in summer; closed Jan 1, Thanksgiving, Dec 25). Per vehicle **$$$**

Fishing. Utah or Colorado license required.

Monument Headquarters and Information Center. *At park entrance in Colorado.* Display panels; audiovisual

program, talks. (June-Labor Day, daily; rest of year, Mon-Fri; closed holidays) **FREE**

Other Activities. Self-guided nature trails (all year), evening campfire programs, guided nature walks, children's programs, dinosaur talks (summer). Backpacking on marked trails; obtain permit at visitor centers.

River rafting. Permit must be obtained in advance from National Park Service. Guided trips from various concessionaires. Obtain list at visitor centers or from the superintendent.

Durango (G-2)

See also Cortez

Founded 1880 **Pop** 13,922 **Elev** 6,523 ft **Area code** 970 **Zip** 81301

Information Durango Area Chamber Resort Association, 111 S Camino Del Rio, PO Box 2587; 970/247-0312, 800/525-8855, or 800/GO-DURANGO

Web www.durango.org

Will Rogers once said of Durango, "It's out of the way and glad of it." For more than 100 years, this small Western city has profited from its "out of the way" location at the base of the San Juan Mountains. Durango has been the gateway to Colorado's riches for Native Americans, fur traders, miners, prospectors, ranchers, and engineers.

Founded by the Denver & Rio Grande Railroad, Durango was a rowdy community during its early days. The notorious Stockton-Eskridge gang once engaged local vigilantes in an hour-long gun battle in the main street. A local expedition to New Mexico to "dig up Aztecs" in 1885 was supplied with "5 cases of chewing tobacco, 3 cases of beer, 10 gallons of heavy liquids, 4 burro-loads of the stuff that busted Parliament, 7 reels of fuse, a box of soap, 2 boxes of cigars, a fish line, 20 pairs of rubber boots, 200 loaves of bread, a can of lard, and one pound of bacon." In the 1890s, the Durango *Herald-Democrat* was noted for the stinging, often profane, wit of pioneer editor "Dave" Day, who once had 42 libel suits pending against him. Headquarters of San Juan National Forest is in Durango, as well as a District Ranger office for the forest.

What to See and Do

Big-game hunting in season. Vallecito Lake Resort Area. San Juan National Forest. Also on Bureau of Land Mangement.

Diamond Circle Theatre. *PO Box 3041 (81302). In Strater Hotel (see HOTELS). Phone 907/247-3400.* Professional turn-of-the-century melodrama and vaudeville performances (June-Sept, nightly; closed Sun). Advance reservations advised. **$$$$**

⭐ **Durango & Silverton Narrow Gauge Railroad.** *Depot, 479 Main Ave. For details, check with the passenger agent. Phone 970/247-2733 or 800/TRAIN-07.* This historic Narrow Gauge Railroad, in operation since 1881, links Durango in southwest Colorado with the Victorian-era mining town of Silverton, 45 miles away. A journey on this coal-fired, steam-powered locomotive up the Animas River and through the mountainous wilderness of the San Juan National Forest gives you the chance to relive history while taking in some of the most breathtaking scenery Colorado has to offer. Round-trip travel takes approximately nine hours. Same-day travelers may opt to return by bus; others can stay overnight in historic Silverton (see also SILVERTON) with a return train ride the next day. During the winter season, the train makes a shorter, round-trip journey to and from Cascade Canyon. Wheelchair accessible cars are available; reservations for all riders are highly recommended. (May-Oct; shorter routes during the winter months) **$$$$** Also located here is

> **Durango & Silverton Narrow Gauge Railroad Museum.** *479 Main Ave. Phone 970/247-2733.* Museum in conjunction with Durango & Silverton Narrow Gauge Railroad that contains exhibits on steam trains, historic photos, railroad art, and restored railroad cars and a locomotive that can be entered. (Hours correspond to the train depot hours) **$$**

Fishing. *Lemon Dam, 12 miles NE on Florida Rd. Vallecito Lake, 18 miles NE on Florida Rd.* Also Pine, Animas, Dolores rivers.

Mesa Verde National Park. (see). *37 miles W on US 160.*

Purgatory Resort. *1 Skier Pl (81301). 25 miles N on US 550, in San Juan National Forest. Phone 970/247-9000 or 800/982-6103.* Quad, three triple, five double chairlifts; patrol, school, rentals; five restaurants, five bars, nursery, lodge, specialty stores. Seventy runs; longest run 2 miles; vertical drop 2,029 feet. (Late Nov-early Apr) Cross-country skiing. Multiday, half-day rates. Chairlift and alpine slide also operate mid-June-Labor Day (daily; fee); other summer activities. **$$$$**

San Juan National Forest. *N on US 550; E and W on US 160. Phone 970/247-4874.* This forest of nearly 2 million acres include the Weminuche Wilderness, Colorado's largest designated wilderness, with several peaks topping 14,000 feet, as well as the South San Juan and Lizard Head wildernesses. The Colorado Trail begins in Durango and traverses the backcountry all the way to Denver. Recreation includes fishing in high mountain lakes and streams, boating, whitewater rafting; hiking, biking, camping, and four-wheel driving. The San Juan Skyway is a 232-miles auto loop through many of these scenic areas. (Daily)

Southern Ute Indian Cultural Museum. *23 miles SE via US 160 and CO 172 in Ignacio. Phone 970/563-9583.* Historical museum contains archival photos, turn-of-the-century Ute clothing, tools, and accessories. Multimedia presentation. Gift shop. (Mon-Sat; closed holidays)

Special Events

Durango Cowboy Gathering. First weekend in Oct.

Iron Horse Bicycle Classic. *346 S Camino Del Rio (81301). Phone 970/259-4621.* Memorial Day weekend.

Snowdown Winter Carnival. *Phone 970/247-8163.* Last week in Jan.

Motels/Motor Lodges

★ ★ **BEST WESTERN DURANGO INN AND SUITES.** *21382 US Hwy 160 (81301). Phone 970/247-3251; toll-free 800/547-9090; fax 970/385-4835. www.durangoinn.com.* 71 rooms, 2 story. Pet accepted. Check-out 11 am, check-in 2 pm. TV; cable (premium), VCR available. In-room modem link. Restaurant, bar. Sauna. Game room. Indoor pool, children's pool, whirlpool. Cr cds: A, C, D, DS, MC, V. **$**

D 🛄 ⚓ ➳ 🏊

★ ★ **BEST WESTERN LODGE AT DURANGO MOUNTAIN.** *49617 Hwy 550 N (81301). Phone 970/247-9669; toll-free 800/637-7727; fax 970/247-9681. www.bestwestern.com.* 32 air-cooled rooms, 25 kitchen units, 2 story. Pet accepted. Complimentary continental breakfast. Check-out 11 am. Check-in 3 pm. TV; cable (premium), VCR available (movies fee). In-room modem link. Restaurant. In-house fitness room. Game room. Indoor pool, whirlpool. Downhill, cross-country ski adjacent. Cr cds: A, C, D, DS, MC, V. **$**

D 🛄 ⚓ 🏋 ➳ 🏊 🎿 🖼

★ **DAYS INN.** *1700 County Rd 203 (81301). Phone 970/259-1430; toll-free 866/338-1116; fax 970/259-5741. www.daysinndurango.com.* 94 rooms, 3 story. Pet accepted. Complimentary continental breakfast, coffee in rooms. Check-out 11 am, check-in 2 pm. TV; cable (premium). In-room modem link. Coin laundry. In-house fitness room, spa, massage, sauna. Indoor pool, whirlpool. Cr cds: A, C, D, DS, JCB, MC, V. **$**

D 🛄 ➳ 🎿 🖼

★ **DURANGO LODGE.** *150 E 5th St (81301). Phone 970/247-0955; fax 970/385-1882. www.durangolodge.com.* 39 rooms, 2 story. Complimentary continental breakfast, coffee in rooms. Check-out noon, check-in 3 pm. TV; cable. Outdoor pool, whirlpool. Cr cds: A, C, D, DS, MC, V. **$**

➳ 🖼

★ **ECONO LODGE.** *2002 Main Ave (81301). Phone 970/247-4242; toll-free 800/424-4777; fax 970/385-4713. www.econolodge.com.* 43 rooms, 2 story. Complimentary continental breakfast. Check-out 11 am, check-in 2 pm. TV; cable (premium). In-room modem link. Outdoor pool, whirlpool. Cr cds: A, C, D, DS, JCB, MC, V. **$**

D ⩆ ⩗ SC

★ **HAMPTON INN.** *3777 Main Ave (81301). Phone 970/247-2600; toll-free 800/426-7866; fax 970/259-8012. www.hamptoninn.com.* 76 rooms, 3 story. Complimentary continental breakfast. Check-out 11 am, check-in 3 pm. TV; cable (premium), VCR available (movies). In-room modem link. Outdoor pool, whirlpool. Cr cds: A, C, D, DS, MC, V. **$**

⩆ ⩗

★ **RAMADA LIMITED.** *3030 N Main Ave (81301). Phone 970/259-1333; toll-free 800/252-8853; fax 970/247-3854. www.ramada.com.* 48 rooms, 2 story. No elevator. Complimentary continental breakfast. Check-out noon, check-in 2 pm. TV; cable (premium). In-room modem link. Sauna. Outdoor pool, whirlpool. Skiing nearby. Cr cds: A, C, D, DS, MC, V. **$**

⩗ ⩆ ⩗ SC

★ **RODEWAY INN.** *2701 N Main Ave (81301). Phone 970/259-2540; toll-free 800/752-6072; fax 970/247-9642. www.rodewayinndurango.com.* 30 rooms, 2 story. Pet accepted, some restrictions; $7. Complimentary continental breakfast. Check-out 11 am, check-in 2 pm. TV; cable (premium). In-room modem link. Laundry services. Indoor pool, whirlpool. Cr cds: A, C, D, DS, JCB, MC, V. **$**

⩗ ⩆ ⩗

Hotels

★ ★ ★ **DOUBLETREE HOTEL.** *501 Camino Del Rio (81301). Phone 970/259-6580; fax 970/259-4398. www.doubletree.com.* Overlooking the magnificent Animas River, this hotel is just 2 blocks from the historic Durango and Silverton Train and the downtown entertainment center. 159 rooms, 3 story. Pet accepted; fee. Check-out noon, check-in 3 pm. TV; cable (premium). In-room modem link. Restaurant, bar. Room service. In-house fitness room, sauna. Indoor pool, whirlpool. Airport transportation. Concierge. Cr cds: A, C, D, DS, ER, JCB, MC, V. **$**

D ⩗ ⩆ ⩔ ⩘ ⩗

★ ★ ★ **STRATER HOTEL.** *699 Main Ave (81301). Phone 970/247-4431; toll-free 800/247-4431; fax 970/259-2208. www.strater.com.* Henry H. Strater built this Victorian hotel in 1887 when he was just 20 years old. Restored to its original grandeur, the guest rooms are all impeccably adorned with period pieces and modern day amenities. Visit one the most famous ragtime piano bars,

"The Diamond Belle Saloon"; it's like going back in time. 93 rooms, 4 story. Pet accepted. Complimentary breakfast. Check-out 11 am, check-in 4 pm. TV; cable (premium). In-room modem link. Restaurant, bar. Entertainment. Room service. Whirlpool. Valet parking. Concierge. Cr cds: A, C, D, DS, MC, V. **$**

D ⩗ ⩗ SC

All Suite

★ ★ **JARVIS SUITE HOTEL.** *125 W 10th St (81301). Phone 970/259-6190; toll-free 800/824-1024; fax 970/259-6190. www.durangohotel.com.* 21 kitchen suites, 3 story. Complimentary continental breakfast. Check-out 11 am, check-in 3 pm. TV; cable (premium), VCR available. Whirlpool. Restored historic hotel (1888). Cr cds: A, C, D, DS, MC, V.

⩗ ⩗

Resorts

★ **IRON HORSE INN & CONFERENCE CENTER.** *5800 N Main Ave (81301). Phone 970/259-1010; toll-free 800/748-2990; fax 970/385-4791. www.ironhorseinndurango.com.* 143 bilevel rooms. Pet accepted. Complimentary continental breakfast. Check-out 11 am. Check-in 3 pm. TV; cable (premium). In-room modem link. Fireplaces. Restaurant. In-house fitness room, sauna. Game room. Indoor pool, whirlpool. Lawn games. Free airport transportation. Cr cds: A, C, D, DS, MC, V.

D ⩗ ⩔ ⩙ ⩆ ⩘ ⩘ ⩗

★ ★ ★ ★ **TALL TIMBER RESORT.** *1 Silverton Star Rte (80901). Phone 970/259-4813. www.talltimberresort.com.* Accessible exclusively by train or helicopter, Tall Timber Resort is the perfect getaway for alpine Robinson Crusoes. This unique resort rests on 180 private acres rimmed by the San Juan National Forest. There are no televisions, radios, or telephones to distract visitors from the majestic beauty of Tall Timber's crashing waterfalls, majestic evergreens, and mesmerizing canyons. The spirit of the Old West is revived, from the still-visible mining spurs to the Silverton train, the last scheduled narrow-gauge train in the United States. Only 30 guests are treated to this singular experience at one time. The resort's 2-story, ski condo-like accommodations feature simple, rustic décor with stone fireplaces and faux wood paneling, while the casual ease in Tall Timber's dining room permeates its way into the kitchen's basic cooking. Tall Timber lures the entire family with its variety of leisurely pursuits, from trout fishing and trail hiking to helicopter touring and streamside napping. 10 suites, 2 story. No A/C, room phones. AP, July 2-Sept and mid-Dec-early Jan, weekly: 7 days, 6 nights: S $4,300; D $4,600; 4 days, 3 nights: S $3,200; D $3,600; 3-12 years 50 percent less; under 3 years $400; transfer from Durango included; lower rates mid-May-July 1, Oct. Closed rest of year. Check-out 10:30 am, check-in 3:30 pm. Dining room 7:30-9:30 am, 12:30-1:30 pm, 6:30-7:30 pm. Massage. Sauna. Indoor/outdoor pool; whirlpools. 9-hole, par-3 golf, putting green, driving range. Tennis. Downhill ski 3 minutes by air, cross-country ski on site. Totally nonsmoking. Cr cds: MC, V.

★ ★ ★ **TAMARRON RESORT.** *40292 US 550 N (81301). Phone 970/259-2000; toll-free 800/678-1000; fax 970/382-7822. www.lodgeattamarron.com.* Pine trees surround this scenic resort, located on a 750-acre site in the San Juan Mountains. 210 rooms, 4 story. Pet accepted. Check-out 11 am, check-in 4 pm. TV; cable (premium), VCR available. In-room modem link. Room service 24 hours. Restaurant, bar. Supervised children's activities (Memorial Day-Labor Day); ages 4-15. In-house fitness room, spa, massage, sauna, steam room. Game room. Indoor, outdoor pool, whirlpool, poolside service. Golf; greens fee $75. Downhill ski 15 miles, cross-country ski on site; rental equipment available. Bicycle rentals. Fishing/hunting guides. Hiking, sleighing, tobogganing, snowmobiles. Valet parking. Airport transportation. Concierge. Cr cds: A, D, DS, MC, V.

B&B/Small Inns

★ ★ ★ **APPLE ORCHARD INN.** *7758 County Rd 203 (81301). Phone 970/247-0751; toll-free 800/426-0751; fax 970/385-6976. www.appleorhcardinn.com.* 10 rooms, 1-2 story. Complimentary full breakfast. Check-out 11 am, check-in 4-7 pm. TV; cable (premium), VCR available. In-room modem link. Downhill ski 20 miles. Totally nonsmoking. Cr cds: A, DS, MC, V. **$$**

★ ★ **COUNTRY SUNSHINE BED & BREAKFAST.** *35130 US 550 N (81301). Phone 970/247-2853; toll-free 800/383-2853; fax 970/247-1203. www.countrysunshine. com.* 6 air-cooled rooms, 2 story. No room phones. Mid-May-Oct: S, D $95-$125; each additional $15; ski packages; lower rates rest of year. Complimentary full breakfast. Check-out 10:30 am, check-in 4-6 pm. TV; cable (premium), VCR in common room. Whirlpool. Downhill ski 12 miles, cross-country ski on site. Picnic tables, grills. Business services. Library/sitting room. Totally nonsmoking. Cr cds: A, C, D, DS, MC, V.

★ ★ **LELAND HOUSE BED & BREAKFAST SUITES.** *721 E 2nd Ave (81301). Phone 970/385-1920; toll-free 800/664-1920; fax 970/385-1967. www.leland-house. com.* 10 air-cooled rooms, 2 story. Pet accepted. Complimentary full breakfast. Checkout 11 am, check-in 3 pm. TV; cable (premium), VCR available. In-room modem

link. Fireplaces. Restored apartment building (1927); many antiques. Totally nonsmoking. Cr cds: A, C, D, DS, MC, V. **$$**

★ ★ ★ **LIGHTNER CREEK INN.** *999 County Rd 207 (81301). Phone 970/259-1226; toll-free 800/268-9804; fax 970/259-9526. www.lightnercreekinn.com.* A mountain getaway located only five minutes from downtown and fine dining. This inn resembles a French country manor and offers finely decorated rooms. 10 rooms, 2 story. No A/C. Children over 6 years only. Check-out 11 am, check-in 4 pm. Country French house built in 1903. Totally nonsmoking. Cr cds: A, MC, V. **$$**

★ ★ ★ **NEW ROCHESTER HOTEL.** *726 E 2nd Ave (81301). Phone 970/385-1920; toll-free 800/664-1920; fax 970/385-1967. www.rochesterhotel.com.* Built in 1892, this hotel offers guest rooms named after historic figures from the Old West. 15 rooms, 2 story. Pet accepted, some restrictions. Complimentary continental breakfast. Check-out 11 am, check-in 3 pm. TV; cable (premium), VCR available. Totally nonsmoking. Cr cds: A, C, D, DS, MC, V. **$$**

Guest Ranches

★ ★ **COLORADO TRAILS RANCH.** *12161 County Rd 240 (81301). Phone 970/247-5055; toll-free 800/323-3833; fax 970/385-7372. www.coloradotrails.com.* 33 air-cooled rooms in 13 cabins. No room phones. AP, weekly: $1,175-$1,600/person; family rates. Closed Oct-May. Heated pool; whirlpool. Free supervised children's activities from 5 years. Teen club. Dining room (3 sittings): 7:30-9 am, 12:30 pm, 6:30 pm. Box lunches, snack bar, picnics. Check-out 10 am, check-in 2 pm. Laundry facilities. Meeting rooms. Business services available. Gift shop. Free airport transportation. Sports director. Waterskiing. Hiking. Trap shooting. Hayrides. Archery. Lawn games. Entertainment. Game room. Fishing guides. On 450 acres; adjacent to San Juan National Forest. Cr cds: A, D, DS, MC, V.

★ ★ **LAKE MANCOS RANCH.** *42688 County Rd N (81328). Phone 970/533-7900; toll-free 800/325-9462; fax 970/533-7858. www.lakemancosranch.com.* 13 cabins, 4 rooms in lodge. No A/C. No room phones. Early June-Aug, AP, weekly (from Sun): S, D $1,150/person; family rates; lower rates Sept-early Oct. Closed rest of year. Crib free. Heated pool; whirlpool. Free supervised children's activities (mid-June-late Aug); from 4 years. Dining room. Box lunches; snacks. Check-out 10 am, check-in 2 pm. Coin laundry. Business services available. Airport, bus depot transportation. Sports director. Lawn games. Social director; entertainment. Jeep tours, hayrides. Recreation room. Refrigerators. Private patios. Cr cds: DS, MC, V.

⊡ ⬚ ⬚ ⬚ ⬚ ⬚ ⬚

★★★ **WILDERNESS TRAILS GUEST RANCH.** *23486 County Rd 501 (81122). Phone 970/247-0722; toll-free 800/527-2624; fax 970/247-1006. www.wildernesstrails .com.* Owned and operated by the Roberts since 1970 and located in the Pine River Valley, this guest ranch's cozy and rustic cabins are tucked in among pine trees. 20 rooms in 10 cabins. No A/C. No room phones. AP, June-late Aug, weekly: S $1,900; D $2,960; family rates; lower rates early-mid-June and Sept. Closed rest of year. Adults only (Sept). Check-out 10 am, check-in 3 pm. Porches, patios. Fireplace in lounge. Coin laundry. Dining room: breakfast 7:30-9 am, lunch noon, dinner from 6 pm. Box lunches, picnics, cookouts. Free supervised children's activities from age 3. Playground. Game room, recreation room. Heated pool, whirlpool. Picnic tables, grills. Lawn games. Waterskiing, rafting, boats, motor boats. Overnight camping. Fishing guide. Entertainment; line dancing, movies. Hayrides. Four-wheel driving trips. Airport, bus depot transportation. Meeting rooms. Gift shop. Mountain resort. Totally nonsmoking. Cr cds: DS, MC, V.

⬚ ⬚ ⬚ ⬚ ⬚

★★★ **WIT'S END GUEST RANCH AND RESORT.** *254 County Rd 500 (81122). Phone 970/ 884-4113; toll-free 800/236-9483; fax 970/884-3261.* Attractive cabins await you at this leisure getaway home. 35 kitchen cabins, 1-2 story. No A/C. AP, Memorial Day-Labor Day (7-day minimum): D, cabins $3,500-$4,000; under 5 free; lower rates rest of year. Crib free. TV; VCR (free movies). Heated pool; whirlpool. Free supervised children's activities (June-Labor Day); from 5 years. Dining room 7 am-3 pm, 5-9 pm. Room service. Box lunches. Bar; entertainment. Check-out 10 am, check-in 4 pm. Free laundry. Meeting rooms. Business services available. In-room modem link. Gift shop. Airport, bus depot transportation. Tennis. Cross-country ski on site. Horse stables. Hay rides. Snowmobiles, sleighing. Mountain bikes. Social director. Fishing/hunting guides. Microwaves available. Picnic tables, grills. In valley on 550 acres; all cabins are adjacent to a river or pond. Stone fireplaces, knotty pine interiors. Totally nonsmoking. Cr cds: A, DS, MC, V.

⊡ ⬚ ⬚ ⬚ ⬚ ⬚ ⬚

Restaurants

★★ **ARIANO'S ITALIAN RESTAURANT.** *150 E College Dr (81301). Phone 970/247-8146.* Northern Italian menu. Closed Thanksgiving, Dec 25. Dinner. Bar. Children's menu. Turn-of-the-century building originally was a saloon and brothel. Casual attire. Totally nonsmoking. Cr cds: A, C, MC, V. **$$**

⬚

★ **CARVER BREWING CO.** *1022 Main Ave (81301). Phone 970/259-2545; fax 970/385-7268.* American, Southwestern menu. Closed Jan 1, Thanksgiving, Dec 25. Breakfast, lunch, dinner. Bar, brewery. Children's menu. Casual attire. Cr cds: A, MC, V. **$**

⬚

★★ **FRANCISCO'S.** *619 Main Ave (81301). Phone 970/247-4098; fax 970/247-1373.* Mexican, American menu. Lunch, dinner. Bar. Children's menu. Casual attire. Cr cds: A, C, D, DS, MC, V. **$$**

⬚ ⬚

★★ **PALACE.** *505 Main Ave (81301). Phone 970/247-2018; fax 970/247-0231. www.palacerestaurants.com.* American menu. Closed Sun Nov-May; Dec 25. Lunch, dinner. Bar. Casual attire. Reservations accepted. Outdoor dining. Cr cds: A, D, DS, MC, V. **$$**

⬚

★★ **RED SNAPPER.** *144 E 9th St (81301). Phone 970/259-3417; fax 970/259-3441. www.frontier.net/~theredsnapper.* Seafood, steak menu. Closed Thanksgiving, Dec 25. Dinner. Bar. Children's menu. Turn-of-the-century building (1904). Casual attire. Totally nonsmoking. Cr cds: A, DS, MC, V. **$$**

⬚ ⬚

Englewood (C-6)

See also Denver, Lakewood

Pop 31,727 **Elev** 5,369 ft **Area code** 303

Information Greater Englewood Chamber of Commerce, 770 W Hampden Ave, #110, 80110; 303/789-4473; or the South Metro Denver Chamber of Commerce, 7901 S Park Plaza #110, Littleton 80120; 303/795-0142

Englewood is located in Denver's south metro area, which is home to the Denver Technological Center.

What to See and Do

Castle Rock Factory Shops. *5050 Factory Shops Blvd (80104). Approximately 24 miles S on I-25, exit 184, in Castle Rock. Phone 303/688-4494.* More than 40 outlet stores; food court. (Daily)

The Museum of Outdoor Arts. *7600 E Orchard Rd (80111). 1 mile S on S Broadway, then 4 miles E on E Arapahoe Rd, then N on Greenwood Plaza Blvd. Phone 303/741-3609.* Outdoor sculpture garden on 400 acres. Guided tours available (fee). Lunchtime summer performance series (Wed). (Daily; closed holidays) **FREE** The museum includes

Fiddler's Green Amphitheater. *6350 Greenwood Plaza Blvd (80111). Phone 303/220-7000.* Fiddler's Green

Amphitheatre is located 15 minutes south of downtown Denver. The parklike setting is an inviting venue for a wide variety of musical performances during the summer months, from up-and-comers to marquee names, classical orchestras to rock and roll, single acts to all-day festivals. Come early to enjoy the mountain sunset. Bring a blanket or tarp (no lawn chairs are allowed), a picnic dinner, and the kids. Or reserve an indoor seat, purchase dinner from one of the many vendors, and watch the acts up close. More than 16,000 patrons regularly pack the park for shows. (June-Aug)

Motel/Motor Lodge

★ **HAMPTON INN.** *9231 E Arapahoe Rd (80112). Phone 303/792-9999; fax 303/790-4360. www.hamptoninn.com.* 150 rooms, 5 story. S $69-$89; D $79-$99; under 18 free. Pet accepted. Complimentary continental breakfast. Check-out noon, check-in 3 pm. TV; cable (premium), VCR available. In-room modem link. Restaurant nearby. Health club privileges, exercise equipment. Pool. Cr cds: A, C, D, DS, MC, V.

D 🐾 🏊 🏃 🚭 SC

Hotels

★★★ **HILTON DENVER TECH SOUTH.** *7801 E Orchard Rd (80111). Phone 303/779-6161; toll-free 800/327-2242; fax 303/689-7080. www.hilton.com.* This centrally located hotel is convenient to the Denver Tech Center and is just 15 minutes from downtown Denver. The property offers some wonderful southwestern views of the Rocky Mountains. In-room modem link. Balconies. Coffee in rooms. Valet services. Restaurant 6 am-10 pm. Bar 11 am-midnight. Room service 24 hours. Exercise equipment, sauna. Indoor/outdoor pool. Business services. Convention center/facilities. Bellhops. Gift shop. Atrium. Cr cds: A, C, D, DS, ER, JCB, MC, V.

D 🏋 🏊 🏃 🚭 SC

★★★ **SHERATON DENVER TECH CENTER.** *7007 S Clinton (80112). Phone 303/799-6200; fax 303/799-4828. www.sheraton.com.* The spacious guest rooms at this hotel suit the needs of both business and leisure travelers. Nearby attractions include the Denver Musuem of Natural History, the Denver Zoo, and the Coors Brewery. Complimentary shuttle service is provided within a 5 mile radius. 266 rooms, 10 story. S, D $115-$224; each additional $10; under 12 free. Check-out noon, check-in 3 pm. TV; cable (premium). In-room modem link. Restaurant 6:30 am-10 pm. Bar 11:30-2 am. Exercise equipment. Pool; whirlpool, poolside service. Airport transportation. Business center. Concierge. Luxury level. Cr cds: A, C, D, DS, MC, V.

D 🏊 🏃 🚭 🏋

Resort

★★★ **INVERNESS HOTEL AND GOLF CLUB.** *200 Inverness Drive W (80112). Phone 303/799-5800. www.invernesshotel.com.* A terrific choice for corporate retreats, this hotel and conference center has over 60,000 square feet of function space and is well suited to productive meetings with naturally lit board rooms, "fatigue-free" chairs, built-in audiovisual equipment, and more. 302 rooms, 5 story. S, D $159-$279; each additional $10; suites $259-$379; under 18 free; golf plans. Crib free. Check-out noon. TV; cable (premium), VCR available. In-room modem link. Balconies. Minibars. Restaurant. Bar 11-1 am. Health club privileges, exercise room, sauna. Recreation room. 2 pools, 1 indoor, whirlpool, poolside service. 18-hole golf, greens fee $110, putting green, driving range. Pro shop. Lighted tennis. Valet parking. Airport, train, bus depot transportation. Business center. Convention center/facilities. Concierge. Gift shop. Luxury level. Near Centennial Airport. Cr cds: A, D, DS, JCB, MC, V.

🏌 🏃 🏊 🏃 🚭 🏃

All Suite

★★ **EMBASSY SUITES DENVER TECH CENTER.** *10250 E Costilla Ave (80112). Phone 303/792-0433; toll-free 800/654-4810; fax 303/790-1944. www.embassysuitesdenver.com.* Located in the south Denver Metro Denver Tech Center area, this hotel is convenient for business travelers. 236 suites, 9 story. Suites $79-$199; each additional $10; under 12 free; weekend rates. Complimentary full breakfast. Check-out noon. Check-in. TV; cable (premium). In-room modem link. Restaurant 11 am-10 pm. Bar. Exercise equipment. Game room. Indoor pool, whirlpool. Cr cds: A, C, D, DS, ER, JCB, MC, V.

D 🏊 🏃 🚭

Restaurants

★ **COUNTY LINE SMOKEHOUSE & GRILL.** *8351 Southpark Ln, Littleton (80120). Phone 303/797-3727; fax 303/795-1576.* Hours: 11 am-2 pm, 5-9 pm; Sat, Sun to 10 pm. Closed Thanksgiving, Dec 24-25. Bar. Lunch $5.95-$9.50, dinner $8.95-$15.95. Children's menu. Specializes in baby back ribs, mixed barbecue platter, grilled items. Own ice cream. Parking. Covered deck dining with view of mountains and McClellan Lake. Rustic décor; 40s and 50s memorabilia. Totally nonsmoking. Cr cds: A, C, D, DS, ER, MC, V.

D 🚭

★ ★ ★ **Z' TEJAS GRILL.** *8345 S Park Meadows Center Dr, Littleton (80124). Phone 303/768-8191; fax 303/768-8185. www.ztejas.com.* Jalapenos and habaneros spice up the food at this casual, friendly Mexican grill. Southwestern menu. Hours: 11 am-10 pm; Fri, Sat to 11 pm; Sat, Sun brunch 11 am-3 pm. Closed Thanksgiving, Dec 25. Reservations accepted. Bar. Lunch $6-$12, dinner $8-$16. Sat, Sun brunch $6-$8. Children's menu. Specialties: voodoo tuna, mashed potato relleno, stuffed pork tenderloin. Parking. Southwestern atmosphere. Cr cds: A, DS, MC, V.
D

Estes Park (B-5)

See also Fort Collins, Granby, Grand Lake, Loveland, Lyons

Settled 1875 **Pop** 5,413 **Elev** 7,522 ft **Area code** 970 **Zip** 80517

Information Information Center at the Chamber of Commerce, 500 Big Thompson Ave, PO Box 3050; 970/586-4431 or 800/443-7837

Web www.rockymtntrav.com/estes/

Rimmed by snow-capped mountains, Estes Park is the gateway to Rocky Mountain National Park (see) and a resort area that offers a wide variety of activities throughout the year.

What to See and Do

⭐ **Aerial Tramway.** *420 Riverside Dr, 2 blocks S of Elkhorn St. Phone 970/756-6921.* Two cabins, suspended from steel cables, move up or down Prospect Mountain at 1,400 feet per minute. Superb view of Continental Divide during trip; picnic facilities at 8,896-feet summit; panoramic dome shelter; snack bar. (Mid-May-mid-Sept, daily) **$$$**

Big Thompson Canyon. *E on US 34.* One of the most beautiful canyon drives in the state.

Enos Mills Original Cabin. *6760 Hwy 7 (80517). 8 miles S on CO 7. Phone 970/586-4706.* (1885) On this family-owned 200-acre nature preserve stands the cabin of Enos Mills, regarded as the "Father of Rocky Mountain National Park." In the shadow of Longs Peak, the cabin contains photos, notes, and documents of the famed naturalist. Nature guide (fee) and self-guided nature trails. (May-Oct, daily; rest of year, by appointment) **FREE**

Estes Park Area Historical Museum. *200 Fourth St, across from lake. Phone 970/586-6256.* Three facilities including a building that served as headquarters of Rocky Mountain National Park from 1915-1923. Exhibits on history of the park, the town, and surrounding area. (Apr-Sept, daily; Oct-Mar, weekends only) **$$**

Estes Park Ride-a-Kart. *2250 Big Thompson Ave, 1 mile E on US 34. Phone 970/586-6495.* Go-karts, bumper boats and cars, mini-golf, and mini-train in miniature Western town. Separate fees. (May-Sept, daily)

Fishing, boating, hiking, horseback riding, mountain climbing. *US 34 and 36 (80517).* Fishing for trout in local lakes and streams. Fishing license needed at Estes Park. Boating on Lake Estes; motors, boats for rent; permit required for private boats; docks (mid-May-early Sept, daily). More than 1,500 mountain-trained horses and ponies are used for breakfast rides, pack trips. National Park Service conducts guided hikes in Rocky Mountain National Park (see); climbers attempt Longs Peak (14,255 feet). Certified guides also available in town.

Fun City Amusement Park. *455 Prospect. Phone 970/586-2070.* Bumper cars (fee); 15-lane giant slide and spiral slide (fee); arcade; miniature golf; two 18-hole golf courses; go-karts. (Mid-May-mid-Sept, daily)

Rocky Mountain National Park. (see). *3 miles W on US 34, 36.*

Roosevelt National Forest. *240 W Prospect Rd.* Surrounds town on north, east, and south. For information, contact the Visitor Center, 1311 S College, Fort Collins 80526. Phone 970/498-1100. More than 780,000 acres of icy streams, mountains, and beautiful scenery. Trout fishing; hiking trails, winter sports area, picnicking, camping. Of special interest are the Cache la Poudre River, five wilderness areas, and the Peak to Peak Scenic Byway. **FREE**

Special Events

Estes Park Music Festival. *Rocky Ridge Music Center. Elkhorn Ave and Wonderview Ave. Phone 970/586-9203.* Chamber, symphonic, and choral concerts. Early June-late Aug.

Horse shows. Weekends in June-Sept.

Rooftop Rodeo. Rodeo parade, nightly dances, kids jamboree. Five days in mid-July.

Scottish-Irish Highland Festival. *Phone 970/586-6104.* Athletic and dance competitions, arts and crafts shows, magic shows, folk dancing. Weekend after Labor Day.

Motels/Motor Lodges

⭐ **ALPINE TRAIL RIDGE INN.** *927 Moraine Ave (80517). Phone 970/586-4585; toll-free 800/233-5023; fax 970/586-6249. www.alpinetrailridgeinn.com.* 48 rooms, 1 kitchen suite. No A/C. June-early Sept: S $52-$102; D $58-$107; each additional $8; kitchen suite $138; golf plans; lower rates May-mid-June, early Sept-mid-Oct. Closed rest of year. Crib $8. TV; cable. Heated pool. Coffee in lobby. Restaurant 7 am-9 pm. Bar. Check-out

10:30 am. Business services available. Airport transportation. Refrigerators; microwaves available. Some balconies. Mountain views. Cr cds: A, C, D, DS, MC, V.

[D] [icons]

★ **ASPEN WINDS.** *1051 Fall River Ct (80517). Phone 970/586-6010; toll-free 800/399-6010; fax 970/586-3626. www.estes-park.com/aspenwinds.* 16 units, 2 story. Late May-mid-Sept: S, D $125-$169; each additional $10; weekly rates; lower rates rest of year. Check-out 10 am. TV; cable (premium), VCR. Fireplaces. Mountain view. On river. Cr cds: A, DS, MC, V.

[D] [icons] [SC]

★**BEST WESTERN SILVER SADDLE.** *1260 Big Thompson Ave (80517). Phone 970/586-4476; fax 970/586-5530. www.bestwestern.com.* 55 rooms, 1 story. June-late Aug: S, D $109-$199; lower rates rest of year. Crib free. Complimentary continental breakfast. Complimentary coffee in rooms. Check-out 10 am. TV; cable (premium), VCR available. In-room modem link. Balconies. Refrigerators, microwaves; some fireplaces. Coin laundry. Restaurant nearby. Playground. Heated pool, whirlpool. Picnic tables, grills. Business services. Cr cds: A, C, D, DS, MC, V.

[D] [icons] [SC]

★ ★ ★ **BOULDER BROOK ON FALL RIVER.** *1900 Fall River Rd (80517). Phone 970/586-0910; toll-free 800/238-0910; fax 970/586-8067. www.estes-park.com/boulderbrook.* Fall asleep listening to the Fall River gurgle outside your back door or watch it from the "Spa Room." Fishing is widely available in the lake, river, stream, or creek. 19 air-cooled kitchen suites, 1-2 story. May-Oct (3-day minimum): suites $99-$230; each additional $10; weekly rates; lower rates rest of year. Check-out 10 am, check-in 2:30 pm. TV; cable (premium), VCR. In-room modem link. Some fireplaces. Cross-country ski 7 miles. Airport transportation. On banks of Fall River. Totally nonsmoking. Cr cds: A, DS, MC, V.

[icons] [SC]

★ **COMFORT INN.** *1450 Big Thompson Ave (80517). Phone 970/586-2358; fax 970/586-4473. www.comfortinn.com.* 75 rooms, 1-2 story. June-Aug: S, D $85-$190; each additional $8; under 18 free; 2-day minimum stay weekends; lower rates rest of year. Closed Nov-Apr. Crib $3. Complimentary continental breakfast. Complimentary coffee in rooms. Check-out 10:30 am. TV; cable. Some balconies. Some refrigerators. Microwaves available. Restaurant nearby. Heated pool, whirlpool. Cross-country ski 8 miles. Picnic tables. Airport transportation. Business services. Cr cds: A, C, D, DS, ER, JCB, MC, V.

[D] [icons]

★ **DEER CREST.** *1200 Fall River Rd (80517). Phone 970/586-2324; toll-free 800/331-2324; fax 970/586-8693. www.estes-park.com/deercrest.* 26 air-cooled rooms.

8 suites, 6 kitchen units, 2 story. S $59-$79; D $64-$89; June-Sept: S, D, suites, kitchen units $85-$120; each additional $20; lower rates rest of year. Adults only. Check-out 10 am. TV; cable (premium). Heated pool, whirlpool. Cross-country ski 7 miles. Airport transportation. On Fall River. Totally nonsmoking. Cr cds: MC, V.

[icons] [SC]

★ ★ **FAWN VALLEY INN.** *2760 Fall River Rd (80517). Phone 970/586-2388; toll-free 800/525-2961; fax 970/586-0394. www.fawnvalleyinn.com.* 25 condos (1-2 bedrooms), 1-2 story. No A/C. S, D $110-$180; 3-day minimum in season. TV; cable (premium). Heated pool; whirlpool. Restaurant. Bar. Check-out 11 am. Meeting rooms. In-room modem link. Refrigerators, microwaves; many fireplaces. Balconies. Picnic tables, grills. Golf nearby. 8 acres on Fall River. Cr cds: A, DS, MC, V.

[D] [icons]

★ ★ **HOLIDAY INN.** *101 S St. Vrain (80517). Phone 970/586-2332; toll-free 800/803-7837; fax 970/586-2038. www.holiday-inn.com.* 150 rooms, 5 suites, 3-4 story. Mid-June-late Aug: S, D $98-$129; each additional $8; suites $229; under 18 free; lower rates rest of year. Crib free. Check-out 11 am. TV; cable (premium). Coin laundry. Restaurant 7 am-1:30 pm, 5-9 pm. Bar 3 pm-2 am; Sun to midnight. Room service. Exercise equipment. Game room. Indoor pool, whirlpool. Cross-country ski 7 miles. Airport transportation. Meeting rooms. Business services. Bellhops. Holidome. Cr cds: A, C, D, DS, JCB, MC, V.

[D] [icons]

★ **MCGREGOR MOUNTAIN LODGE.** *2815 Fall River Rd (80517). Phone 970/586-3457; toll-free 800/835-8439; fax 970/586-4040. www.mcgregormountainlodge.com.* No A/C. No room phones. June-Sept: S, D $49-$99; each additional $10; kitchen cottages $115-$265; weekly rates; lower rates rest of year. Check-out 11 am, check-in 3 pm. TV; VCR. Fireplaces. Lawn games. Airport transportation. On 10 acres overlooking Fall River Canyon. Rocky Mountain National Park adjacent. Cr cds: DS, MC, V.

[D] [icons]

★ ★ **OLYMPUS MOTOR LODGE.** *2365 Big Thompson Hwy 34 (80517). Phone 970/586-8141; toll-free 800/248-8141; fax 970/586-8143. www.estes-park.com/olympus.* 17 rooms. Memorial Day-mid-Sept: S, D $85-$175; each additional $8; weekly rates; lower rates, family rates rest of year. Pet accepted, some restrictions. Check-out 10 am. TV; cable. Restaurant 11 am-8 pm. Lawn games. Airport transportation. Cr cds: A, C, D, DS, MC, V.

[D] [icons]

★ **PONDEROSA LODGE.** *1820 Fall River Rd (80517). Phone 970/586-4233; toll-free 800/628-0512. www.estes-park.com/ponderosa.* 23 rooms, 2 story. No A/C.

No room phones. Mid-June-Sept: S, D $81-$250; each additional $5; kitchens $117-$250; under 6 free; package plans; summer 2-, 3-, 5-day minimum; lower rates rest of year. Check-out 10 am. Check-in 2 pm. TV; cable (premium). Fireplaces. Restaurant nearby. Cross-country ski 2 miles. Fishing, hiking. Cr cds: A, DS, MC, V.

D ⬚ ⬚ ⬚ ⬚

★ **SUNNYSIDE KNOLL RESORT.** *1675 Fall River Rd (80517). Phone 970/586-5759; toll-free 800/586-5212. www.sunnysideknoll.com.* This property is located in Fall River Valley, just a few miles from downtown Estes Park and Rocky Mountain National Park. Designed for the ultimate experience in privacy, the resort caters to couples and persons wishing to "get away from it all." 17 rooms, 7 kitchen units. No A/C. No room phones. June-Sept: S, D $75-$149; kitchen units $92-$239 (3-day minimum); weekly rates; lower rates rest of year. Children over 12 years only. Check-out 11 am, check-in 2 pm. TV; cable (premium), VCR (movies). Fireplaces. Cross-country ski 2 miles. Cr cds: DS, MC, V.

⬚ ⬚

★ **TRAPPERS MOTOR INN.** *553 W Elkhorn Ave (80517). Phone 970/586-2833; toll-free 800/552-2833. www.estes-park.com/trappers.* 20 rooms, 2 story. Mid-June-early Sept: S, D $52-$72; under 10 free; lower rates rest of year. TV; cable (premium). Playground. Complimentary coffee in lobby. Restaurant nearby. Check-out 10 am. Lawn games. Whirlpool. Some refrigerators; microwaves available. Picnic tables. Cr cds: A, MC, V.

⬚ ⬚

Hotels

★ ★ **NICKY'S RESORT.** *1350 Fall River Rd (80517). Phone 970/586-5376; toll-free 800/323-0031; fax 970/586-0132.* 34 rooms, 2 story. Check-out noon, check-in 11 am. TV; cable (premium). Laundry services. Restaurant, bar. Outdoor pool, whirlpool. Outdoor tennis. Cr cds: A, C, D, DS, ER, JCB, MC, V. **$**

D ⬚ ⬚ ⬚

★ ★ ★ **STANLEY HOTEL.** *333 Wonderview Hotel (80517). Phone 970/586-3371; toll-free 800/976-1377; fax 970/586-4964. www.stanleyhotel.com.* The property that inspired Stephen King's novel *The Shining* is located less than two hours northwest of Denver in the Rocky Mountains. This hotel has 35 acres of sprawling grounds. 162 rooms, 4 story. Mid-May-mid-Oct: D $99-$169; each additional $20; suites $159; under 18 free. Check-out 11 am, check-in 4 pm. TV; cable (premium). Some fireplaces. Restaurant 7 am-9 pm. Bar; entertainment Fri-Sat. Room service. Tennis. Built in 1909 by automaker F. O. Stanley. Cr cds: A, D, DS, MC, V.

D ⬚ ⬚

Resort

★ **BIG THOMPSON TIMBERLANE LODGE.** *740 Moraine Ave (80517). Phone 970/586-3137; toll-free 800/898-4373; fax 970/586-3719. www.bigthompsontimberlane lodge.com.* 54 rooms, 36 kitchen units. June-early Sept: S, D, cottages $89-$315; each additional $20; 1-3-bedroom cabins $89-$315; weekly rates; lower rates rest of year. Crib $10. Complimentary coffee. Check-out 10 am. TV; cable (premium), VCR available. Refrigerators. Microwaves available. Coin laundry. Restaurant adjacent 7 am-10 pm. Playground. Pool, wading pool, whirlpool. Picnic tables, grills. On Big Thompson River. Cr cds: A, D, DS, MC, V.

D ⬚ ⬚ SC

B&B/Small Inn

★ ★ ★ **ROMANTIC RIVERSONG INN.** *1765 Lower Broadview Rd (80517). Phone 970/586-4666; fax 970/577-0699. www.romanticriversong.com.* A gurgling trout stream, gazebo, and pond add to the charm of this bed- and-breakfast (all rooms are named after wildflowers). Located on 27 acres adjacent to Rocky Mountain National Park, the property offers some breathtaking views. 16 rooms, 1-2 story. No A/C. No room phones. S, D $150-$295; each additional $50, suites $160-$275. Children over 12 years only. Complimentary full breakfast. Check-out noon, check-in 4-7 pm. Fireplaces. Airport transportation. Built in 1928; decorated with a blend of antique and modern country furnishings. Dinner with advance reservation. Many ponds, trails. Totally nonsmoking. Cr cds: DS, MC, V.

D ⬚

Guest Ranches

★ ★ **ASPEN LODGE RANCH.** *6120 Hwy 7 (80517). Phone 970/586-8133.* 59 units, 36 rooms in lodge, 23 cottages. No A/C. S, D $185-$260, weekly rates; family rates; AP June-Aug. Crib free. Check-out 11 am, check-in 4 pm. TV in lobby. Dining room (public by reservation) 7 am-10 pm. Box lunches, barbecue, breakfast rides. Bar. Free supervised children's activities (June-Sept), ages 3-12. Playground. Exercise room, sauna. Sports director. Game room, recreation room. Pool, whirlpool. Tennis. Cross-country ski on site. Picnic tables, grills. Lawn games, handball. Paddle boats. Entertainment. Hayrides, overnight cookouts. Ice skating, snowshoeing. Mountain bike rentals. Airport transportation. Meeting rooms. Business center. Concierge. Gift shop. Petting zoo (summer). Cr cds: A, D, DS, MC, V.

D ⬚ ⬚ ⬚ ⬚ ⬚ ⬚ ⬚ ⬚

★ **WIND RIVER RANCH.** *5770 S St. Vrain (80517). Phone 970/586-4212; toll-free 800/523-4212; fax 970/586-2255. www.windriverranch.com.* 15 units, 4 rooms in lodge, 13 (1-3 bedroom) cottages. June-Aug, AP (3-day minimum): S $200; D $400; $850-$1,350/week. Closed rest of year. No room phones. Check-out 10 am, check-in 3 pm. Many private porches. Many fireplaces. Grocery, coin laundry, package store 7 miles. Dining room: 8-9 am, 12:30-1:30 pm, 6-7 pm. Box lunches. Free supervised children's activities (June-Aug). Playground. Heated pool, whirlpool. Hiking, rafting. Airport, bus depot transportation. Meeting rooms. Business center. Cr cds: A, DS, MC, V.

🅳 ⛷ 👯 ✈ 🏊 🎿

Restaurants

★ ★ ★ **BLACK CANYON INN.** *800 MacGregor Ave (80517). Phone 970/586-9344. www.estespark.com/blackcanyon.* Continental menu. Hours: 11:30 am-2 pm, 5-9 pm. Closed Mon. Reservations accepted. Bar. Lunch $6.95-$9.95, dinner $14.95-$25.95. Children's menu. Specializes in seafood, wild game. Parking. Built in 1927 of rough-cut logs. Two-story moss and rock fireplace. Cr cds: A, DS, MC, V.

🅳

★ ★ ★ **FAWN BROOK INN.** *CO 7 Business Loop (80510). Phone 303/747-2556.* Continental menu. Hours: Mid-May-Aug: 5-8:30 pm; off-season hours vary. Closed Mon. Dinner $26.50-$44. Bar. Children's menu. Reservations accepted. Cr cds: A, MC, V.

★ **MAMA ROSE'S.** *338 E Elkhorn Ave (80517). Phone 970/586-3330.* Italian menu. Hours: 7-11 am, 4-9 pm; winter from 4 pm. Closed major holidays; Jan, Feb; also Mon-Wed (winter). Bar. Buffet: breakfast $5.95. Dinner $6.95-$14.95. Children's menu. Specialties: veal Parmesan, chicken Parmesan, fettucine Alfredo. Outdoor dining. Victorian décor; large fireplace. Totally nonsmoking. Cr cds: A, C, DS, ER, MC, V.

🅳 🚭

★ ★ **NICKY'S.** *1350 Fall River Rd (80517). Phone 970/586-5376. www.nickysresort.com.* Continental menu. Hours: 7 am-10 pm. Dinner $14.75-$55.75. Bar 11 am-midnight. Children's menu. Outdoor seating. Cr cds: A, C, DS, ER, MC, V.

🅳

Evergreen (C-5)

See also Central City, Denver, Golden, Idaho Springs

Pop 9,216 **Elev** 7,040 ft **Area code** 303 **Zip** 80439

Information Evergreen Area Chamber of Commerce, 29029 Upper Bear Creek Rd #202, PO Box 97; 303/674-3412

Web www.evergreenchamber.org

What to See and Do

Hiwan Homestead Museum. *4208 S Timbervale Dr. Phone 303/674-6262.* Restored 17-room log lodge (1880); Native American artifacts, changing exhibits. Tours (Tues-Sun; closed holidays). **FREE**

International Bell Museum. *30213 Upper Bear Creek Rd, off CO 74. Phone 303/674-3422.* More than 5,000 bells of widely varying sizes and ages, many historic, artistic, or unusual. (Memorial Day-Labor Day, Tues-Sun) **$$**

Special Events

Mountain Rendezvous. *At Hiwan Homestead Museum (see). 4208 S Timbervale Dr (80439). Phone 303/674-6262.* Craft and trapping demonstrations by mountain men; food, entertainment, and old-fashioned games. First Sat in Aug.

Rodeo Weekend. *Phone 303/298-0220.* Rodeo, parade. Father's Day weekend.

B&B/Small Inn

★ ★ ★ **HIGHLAND HAVEN CREEKSIDE INN.** *4395 Independence Trail (80439). Phone 303/674-3577; toll-free 800/459-2406; fax 303/674-9088. www.highlandhaven.com.* This inn is located only a short walk away from the main street in town where guests can enjoy shopping in local galleries and stores. The inn is perfect for a romantic getaway and a great place to relax. 16 rooms, 9 with shower only, 1-2 story, 6 suites, 6 kitchen cottages. No A/C. S, D $95-$275; suites $150-$270; kitchen cottages $130-$220; under 12 free; weekly rates. Complimentary full breakfast. Check-out 11 am, check-in 3 pm. TV; cable (premium), VCR available. Some balconies. Some fireplaces, in-room whirlpools. Microwaves available. Restaurant nearby. Health club privileges, massage. On Bear Creek. Cr cds: A, D, DS, MC, V.

⛷ 🚭

Fairplay (D-4)

See also Breckenridge, Buena Vista

Settled 1859 **Pop** 610 **Elev** 9,920 ft **Area code** 719
Zip 80440

Information Town Clerk, 400 Front St, PO Box 267; 719/
836-2622

This broad valley, known for many years as South Park, was called "Bayou Salado" or "Salt Creek" by early French trappers. The Ute prized the valley for summer trapping and as a hunting ground. In 1859, gold was discovered and several towns, including Fairplay, sprang up overnight. Now the county seat, Fairplay was founded with the slogan, "In this camp we will have fair play; no man can have more ground than he can work." Within the valley, which is larger than the state of Rhode Island, nearly every kind of recreational opportunity is available to visitors.

What to See and Do

Monument to Prunes, a Burro. *7th and Front St (80440). Phone 719/836-2622.* In memory of a faithful burro named Prunes who packed supplies to every mine in Fairplay for more than 60 years.

Pike National Forest. *601 S Weber St (80903). Phone 719/836-2031.* (see COLORADO SPRINGS) Camping. A Ranger District office is located at the junction of US 285 and CO 9. (Daily) **FREE**

South Park City Museum. *100 4th St. Phone 719/836-2387.* Restoration of mining town includes 42 original buildings, 60,000 artifacts (circa 1860-1900); exhibits on trading, mining, and social aspects of era. (Mid-May-mid-Oct, daily; rest of year, by appointment) **$$**

South Park Historical Foundation, Inc. *100 4th St (80440). Phone 719/836-2387.* More than 30 historic buildings are included in this painstaking restoration of a 19th-century boomtown in Colorado. Mid-May-mid-Oct.

Special Events

Fairplay Burro Race. *Phone 719/836-2233.* For one weekend of the year, the normally quiet little town of Fairplay becomes the site of Colorado's most uproarious athletic event: the annual Pack Burro Race. Held the last Sunday in July, the festival draws 15,000 participants and spectators to see which team of runner and burro will be the first to complete a 29-mile race to the top of Mosquito Pass and back—together. The greatest challenge for the contestants is not the steep and treacherous course, but the tendency of the burros to go their own way. Food booths, crafts, music, and a parade are all part of the festivities. Last Sun in July. **FREE**

World's Championship Pack Burro Race. Commemorating the burros who packed supplies for the miners; 28-mile course uphill to Mosquito Pass and return. Last full weekend in July.

Florissant Fossil Beds National Monument (D-5)

See also Colorado Springs, Cripple Creek, Manitou Springs

(22 miles W of Manitou Springs on US 24)

Florissant Fossil Beds National Monument consists of 6,000 acres once partially covered by a prehistoric lake. Thirty-five million years ago, ash and mud flows from volcanoes in the area buried a forest of redwoods, filling the lake and fossilizing its living organisms. Insects, seeds, and leaves of the Eocene Epoch are preserved in perfect detail, along with remarkable samples of standing petrified sequoia stumps. On the grounds are nature trails, picnic areas, and a restored 19th-century homestead. Guided tours are available. The visitor center is 2 miles south on Teller County Rd 1 (daily; closed Jan 1, Thanksgiving, Dec 25). Contact the Superintendent, PO Box 185, Florissant 80816; phone 719/748-3253. Per family $5; per person $2.

Fort Collins (B-6)

See also Greeley, Loveland

Settled 1864 **Pop** 118,652 **Elev** 5,003 ft **Area code** 970

Information Fort Collins Convention & Visitors Bureau, 3745 E Prospect Rd, Suite 200; 970/491-3388

Web www.ftcollins.com

A favorite camping ground for pioneers, Fort Collins is now an educational, recreational, and industrial community. Headquarters for the Roosevelt National Forest (see ESTES PARK) and the Arapaho National Forest (see DILLON) are located in Fort Collins.

What to See and Do

Anheuser-Busch Brewery Tour. *2351 Busch Dr (80524). Take I-25 to Mountain Vista Dr (exit 271) and turn right onto Busch Dr. Phone 970/490-4691.* A tour of the Anheuser-Busch Brewery in Fort Collins is bound to leave an impression—any operation that can produce

2.6 million cans of beer daily is worthy of note. The presentation includes an overview of the company's history (which dates back to the mid-1800s), a walking tour of the brewing and control rooms, and a visit with the famous Budweiser Clydesdales, housed with their Dalmatian companions in picturesque historic-landmark stables on the beautiful Busch estate. Those of legal drinking age can enjoy complimentary tastings at the end of the tour. (June-Sept, daily; Oct-May, Thurs-Mon) **FREE**

Colorado State University. *Main entrance at W Laurel and Howes sts, W of College Ave. Phone 970/491-1101.* (1870) 24,500 students. Land-grant institution with an 833-acre campus. Pingree Park at 9,500 feet, adjacent to Rocky Mountain National Park, is the summer campus for natural resource science education and forestry.

Discovery Center Science. *703 E Prospect Rd. Phone 970/472-3990. www.dcsm.org.* Hands-on science and technology museum features more than 70 educational exhibits. (Tues-Sat, Sun afternoons; closed holidays) **$$**

Fort Collins Museum. *200 Mathews St. Phone 970/221-6738.* Exhibits include a model of the city's namesake, the army post Fort Collins; a fine collection of Folsom points and Native American beadwork; display of historic household, farm, and business items; and three historic cabins. (Tues-Sun; closed holidays) **FREE**

Lincoln Center. *417 W Magnolia. Phone 970/221-6730.* Includes theater for the performing arts, concert hall, sculpture garden, art gallery, and display areas with changing exhibits. (Daily)

Lory State Park. *9 miles NW in Bellvue. Phone 970/493-1623.* Approximately 2,500 acres. Nearby is Horsetooth Reservoir. Waterskiing, boating (ramps, rentals); nature trails, hiking, stables, picnicking. (Daily) **$$**

Scenic circle drives. Eleven colorful drives, from 50 to 200 miles, includes trip through beautiful Poudre Canyon and Cameron Pass (10,285 feet) in Roosevelt National Forest (see ESTES PARK). Inquire at Fort Collins Convention & Visitors Bureau.

Motels/Motor Lodges

★ **BEST WESTERN KIVA INN.** *1638 E Mulberry St (80524). Phone 970/484-2444; toll-free 888/299-5482; fax 970/221-0967. www.bestwestern.com.* 62 rooms, 1-2 story. S, D $81-$109; each additional $10; under 17 free; higher rates during special events. Complimentary continental breakfast. Check-out 11 am, check-in 1 pm. TV; cable (premium). In-room modem link. Exercise equipment, sauna. Heated pool; whirlpool. Cr cds: A, C, D, DS, MC, V.

D ⊷ ⌨ 🏊 ⊠ SC

★ **BEST WESTERN UNIVERSITY INN.** *914 S College Ave (80524). Phone 970/484-1984; fax 970/484-1987. www.bestwestern.com.* 75 rooms, 2 story. May-Sept: D $65-$115; under 12 free. Pet accepted; fee. Complimentary continental breakfast. Check-out 11 am, check-in 3 pm. TV; cable (premium). Heated pool; whirlpool. In-room modem link. Exercise equipment. Cr cds: A, C, D, DS, MC, V.

D ⊷ ⌨ 🏊 ⊠

★★ **HOLIDAY INN.** *3836 E Mulberry St (80524). Phone 970/484-4660; fax 970/484-2326. www.holiday-inn.com.* 198 rooms, 4 story. D $59-$99; each additional $10; under 18 free. Pet accepted. Check-out noon, check-in 4 pm. TV; cable (premium), VCR available. In-room modem link. Laundry services. Restaurant 6 am-2 pm, 5-10 pm. Bar 4 pm-2 am; Sun to 10 pm. Room service. Exercise equipment, sauna. Game room. Indoor pool, children's pool, whirlpool. Golf on premise. Tennis nearby. Cr cds: A, C, D, DS, JCB, MC, V.

D ⊷ 🏌 🍴 ⌨ 🏊 ⊠

Hotel

★★★ **MARRIOTT FORT COLLINS.** *350 E Horsetooth Rd (80525). Phone 970/226-5200; fax 970/282-0561. www.marriott.com.* Located just 3 miles from Colorado State University, the Marriott is a great place to stay during parent's weekend. 256 rooms, 6 story. S, D $69-$179; suites $159; under 18 free. Pet accepted; $10/day. Check-out noon, check-in 4 pm. TV; cable (premium), VCR available. In-room modem link. Restaurant 6 am-2 pm, 5-9 pm. Bar 4:30 pm-1 am. Room service. Exercise equipment. Heated indoor/outdoor pool, whirlpool. Cross-country ski 15 miles. Business center. Concierge. Luxury level. Cr cds: A, C, D, DS, ER, JCB, MC, V.

D ⊷ 🏊 ⌨ ⊠ ✈

B&B/Small Inn

★★ **PORTER HOUSE B&B INN.** *530 Main St (80550). Phone 970/686-5793; toll-free 888/686-5793; fax 970/686-7046. www.bbonline.com/co/porterhouse.* 4 rooms, 2 with shower only. D $95-$155; each additional $15; golf plans. Children over 12 only. Complimentary full breakfast. Check-out 11 am, check-in 4-6 pm. TV; cable (premium). In-room modem link. Microwaves available. Restaurant nearby. Whirlpool. Golf privileges. Picnic tables, grills. Street parking. Airport transportation. Meeting room. Business services. Luggage handling. Built in 1898. Totally nonsmoking. Cr cds: A, D, DS, MC, V.

D 🏌 ⊠

Fort Morgan (B-7)

See also Sterling

Pop 11,034 **Elev** 4,330 ft **Area code** 970 **Zip** 80701

Information Fort Morgan Area Chamber of Commerce, 300 Main St, PO Box 971; 970/867-6702 or 800/354-8660

Web www.fortmorganchamber.com

What to See and Do

Fort Morgan Museum. *414 Main St. Phone 970/867-6331.* Permanent and changing exhibits depicting history of northeast Colorado. Pamphlet for self-guided walking tour of historic downtown. (Mon-Sat) **FREE**

Jackson Lake State Park. *I-76 W to CO 39, 7 1/4 miles N to County Y5, then 2 1/2 miles W to County Rd 3. Phone 970/645-2551.* Swimming, waterskiing, fishing, boating (rentals, ramps); picnicking (shelters), concession, groceries, camping, wildlife watching. (Daily) **$$**

Special Events

Colorado Rodeo. *10 miles E in Brush.* World's largest amateur rodeo. Weekend in early July.

Festival in the Park. *1600 N Main St (80701). Phone 970/867-3808.* Arts, crafts, parade, pancake breakfast. Third weekend in July.

Glenn Miller Festival. *400 Main St (80701). Phone 970/867-6702.* Big band music. Third weekend in June.

Motels/Motor Lodges

★ **BEST WESTERN PARK TERRACE INN.** *725 Main (80701). Phone 970/867-8256; toll-free 888/593-5793; fax 970/867-8257. www.bestwestern.com.* 24 rooms, 2 story. Mid-May-Sept: S, D $54-$75; special events (2-day minimum); lower rates rest of year. Pet accepted; fee. Check-out 11 am. TV; cable (premium). In-room modem link. Heated pool, whirlpool, poolside service available. Cr cds: A, C, D, DS, MC, V.

★ **CENTRAL MOTEL.** *201 W Platte Ave (80701). Phone 970/867-2401.* 19 rooms. May-Sept: S, D $39-$74; each additional $5; suites from $59.95; under 10 free; lower rates rest of year. Pet accepted, some restrictions. Check-out 11 am, check-in 2 pm. TV; cable (premium). Restaurant nearby. Cr cds: A, D, DS, MC, V.

Georgetown (C-5)

See also Central City, Dillon, Golden, Idaho Springs, Winter Park

Founded 1859 **Pop** 1,088 **Elev** 8,512 ft **Area code** 303 **Zip** 80444

Information Town of Georgetown Visitor Information, PO Box 426; 303/569-2555

Georgetown is named for George Griffith, who discovered gold in this valley in 1859 and opened up the area to other gold seekers. The area around Georgetown has produced almost $200 million worth of gold, silver, copper, lead, and zinc. Numerous 19th-century structures remain standing. Georgetown's famous Hotel de Paris was run by a Frenchman, Louis Dupuy, who, though charming, was very cavalier to any guest who did not please him.

What to See and Do

Hamill House Museum. *305 Argentine St. Phone 303/569-2840.* (1867) Early Gothic Revival house acquired by William A. Hamill, Colorado silver magnate and state senator; period furnishings. Partially restored carriage house and office. (Late May-Sept, daily; rest of year, by appointment) **$$**

Hotel de Paris Museum. *409 6th St. Phone 303/569-2311.* (1875) Internationally known hostelry built and operated by Louis Dupuy; elaborately decorated; original furnishings; courtyard. (Memorial Day-Labor Day, daily; rest of year, Sat and Sun) **$$**

Loveland Ski Area. *Loveland Pass. 12 miles W on I-70, exit 216. Phone 303/569-3203 or 303/571-5580 (Denver direct).* Quad, two triple, five double chairlifts, Pomalift, Mightymite; patrol, school, rentals, snowmaking; cafeteria, restaurants, bars, nursery. Sixty runs; longest run 1 1/2 miles; vertical drop 1,680 feet. (Mid-Oct-mid-May, daily) **$$$$**

Special Event

Georgetown Christmas Market. *45 miles west of Denver on I-70. Phone 303/569-2840.* For a delightful old-fashioned Christmas experience, visit the pretty little Victorian hamlet of Georgetown during the first two weekends in December. The streets and shops come alive with holiday lights, music, dancing, and strolling carolers. Old Kris Kringle is on hand to hear the wishes of young believers, while Mom and Dad will enjoy browsing through the European-style open market for food and handcrafted gifts from around the world. Early Dec.

B&B/Small Inns

★ **HARDY HOUSE BED AND BREAKFAST.** *605 Brownell (80444). Phone 303/569-3388; toll-free 800/490-4802. www.entertain.com/wedgewood/hardy.* 4 air-cooled rooms, 2 story. No room phones. Dec-Mar: S, D $80-$95; suites $80-$150; ski, package plans; lower rates rest of year. Children over 12 years only. TV; cable (premium), VCR (movies). Complimentary full breakfast; afternoon refreshments. Restaurant nearby. Check-out 10:30 am, check-in 3-6 pm. Luggage handling. Downhill ski 10 miles. Whirlpool. Some fireplaces, balconies. Built in 1880; many antiques. Totally nonsmoking. Cr cds: MC, V.

★ **MAD CREEK BED & BREAKFAST.** *167 Park Ave (80438). Phone 303/569-2003; toll-free 888/266-1498. www.madcreekbnb.com.* 3 rooms, 2 story. No A/C. No room phones. D $85-$105; each additional $10. Children over 10 years only. TV in main room; VCR. Complimentary full breakfast; afternoon refreshments. Check-out 4 pm, check-in 11 am. Downhill/cross-country ski 20 miles. Victorian cottage built in 1881; stone fireplace. Totally nonsmoking. Cr cds: MC, V.

Guest Ranch

★★ **NORTH FORK.** *55395 US 285 (80475). Phone 303/838-9873; toll-free 800/843-7895; fax 303/838-1549.* 6 rooms, 3 cottages. No A/C. No room phones. AP, July-Aug, weekly: S $1,295; 6-12 years, $1,095; 2-6 years, $300-$895; lower rates late May-June, early-mid-Sept. Closed rest of year. Crib free. Complimentary coffee in rooms. Check-out 10 am, check-in 3 pm. Some porches. Refrigerator in cottages. Free guest laundry. Dining room 7:30-8:30 am, 12:30 pm and 6:30 pm sittings. Box lunches. Picnics. Free supervised children's activities (June-Aug); ages 1-6. Massage. Game room. Heated pool, whirlpool. Picnic tables, grills. Lawn games. Fishing guides, clean and store. Hiking. Horse stables. Airport transportation. Meeting rooms. Gift shop. Grocery, package store 6 miles. On South Platte River.

Restaurant

★ **HAPPY COOKER.** *412 6th St (80444). Phone 303/569-3166; fax 303/569-0429.* Hours: 7 am-4 pm; Sat, Sun to 5 pm. Closed Thanksgiving, Dec 25. Wine, beer. Breakfast, lunch $3.50-$7.95. Children's menu. Specializes in waffles, chili, cinnamon rolls. Outdoor dining. Homestyle atmosphere. Cr cds: A, D, DS, MC, V.

Glenwood Springs (C-3)

See also Aspen, Snowmass Village

Settled 1885 **Pop** 7,736 **Elev** 5,763 ft **Area code** 970 **Zip** 81601

Information Chamber Resort Association, 1102 Grand Ave; 970/945-6589 or 888/4-GLENWOOD

Web www.glenscape.com

Doc Holliday, the famous gunman, died here in 1887. His marker bears the wry inscription, "He died in bed."

Today, Glenwood Springs is a popular year-round health spa resort where the visitor may both ski and swim in a single day. The town is the gateway to White River National Forest. Aspen and Vail (see both) are less than an hour's drive. Excellent game and fishing country surrounds Glenwood Springs, and camping areas are sprinkled throughout the region.

What to See and Do

Glenwood Hot Springs Pool. *415 6th St (81602). I-70 W exit 116. Phone 970/945-6571; toll-free 800/537-7946. www.hotspringspool.com.* For centuries, visitors have traveled to the hot springs in Colorado to soak in their soothing and, many say, healing mineral-rich waters. Today, those same legendary springs feed the world's largest hot spring pool. Located between Aspen and Vail on the forested banks of the Colorado River, historic Glenwood Hot Springs Lodge and Pool is a great mini-escape for visitors just stopping through, as well as for those looking for a unique resort getaway. The main pool, over 2 blocks long, circulates 3.5 million gallons of naturally heated, spring-fed water each day. The complex includes lap lanes, a shallow play area, diving area, two water slides (summer only), and a therapy pool. The nearby town of Glenwood Springs offers museums, art galleries, specialty shops, and restaurants in a relaxed, western-style setting. (Daily) **$$$$**

River rafting, kayaking, hunting, fishing, camping, hiking, biking, golf, horseback riding, pack trips. *Chamber of Commerce, 1102 Grand Ave (81601).* For details and locations, inquire at the Chamber.

Scenic drives. *On CO 133, visit Redstone, Marble, and Maroon peaks. I-70 provides access to Lookout Mountain and Glenwood Canyon. Beautiful Hanging Lake and Bridal Veil Falls are a 2-mile hike from the road. The marble quarries in the Crystal River Valley are the source of stones for the Lincoln Memorial in Washington, D.C., and the Tomb of the Unknown Soldier in Arlington National Cemetery.*

Sunlight Mountain Resort. *10901 County Rd 117 (81601). Phone 970/945-7491 or 800/445-7931.* Triple, two double chairlifts; surface tow; patrol, school, rentals; cafeteria, bar, nursery. Sixty-seven runs; longest run 2 1/2 miles; vertical drop 2,010 feet. Snowmobiling (Late Nov-early Apr, daily) Half-day rates. Also cross-country touring center, 10 miles. **$$$$**

White River National Forest. *N, W, E, and S of town. Contact the Supervisor's Office, Old Federal Building, 9th and Grand, PO Box 948. Phone 970/945-2521.* More than 2,500,000 acres in the heart of the Colorado Rocky Mountains. Recreation at 70 developed sites with boat ramps, picnicking, campgrounds (fee), and observation points; Holy Cross, Flat Tops, Eagles Nest, Maroon Bells-Snowmass, Raggeds, Collegiate Peaks, and Hunter-Frying Pan wildernesses (check with local ranger for information before entering wildernesses or any backcountry areas). Many streams and lakes with trout fishing; large deer and elk populations; Dillon, Green Mountain, and Ruedi reservoirs. Winter sports at 11 ski areas.

Special Events

Garfield County Fair & Rodeo. *1001 Railroad Ave (81650). Phone 970/625-2514.* 27 miles W in Rifle. Late Aug.

Strawberry Days Festival. Arts and crafts fair, rodeo. Third weekend in June.

Motels/Motor Lodges

★ **BEST WESTERN ANTLERS.** *171 W Sixth St (81601). Phone 970/945-8535; toll-free 800/626-0609; fax 970/945-9388. www.bestwestern.com.* 100 rooms, 1-2 story. Complimentary continental breakfast. Check-out 11 am. Check-in 2 pm. TV; cable (premium). In-room modem link. Outdoor pool, whirlpool. Downhill, cross-country ski 10 miles. Lawn games. Cr cds: A, C, D, DS, ER, JCB, MC, V. **$**

★ **HAMPTON INN.** *401 W 1st St (81601). Phone 970/947-9400; fax 970/947-9440. www.hamptoninn.com.* 70 rooms, 3 story. Complimentary continental breakfast. Check-out 11 am, check-in 3 pm. TV; cable (premium). In-room modem link. Coin laundry. In-house fitness room. Indoor pool, whirlpool. Downhill/cross-country ski 10 miles. Cr cds: A, C, D, DS, JCB, MC, V. **$**

★ **HOT SPRINGS LODGE.** *415 E 6th St (81602). Phone 970/945-6571; toll-free 800/537-7946; fax 970/947-2950. www.hotspringspool.com.* 107 units, 5 story. Complimentary continental breakfast. Check-out noon, check-in. TV; cable (premium). In-room modem link. Coin laundry. Massage, sauna, steam room. Outdoor pool. Downhill/cross-country ski 10 miles. Parking.

Airport, train station, bus depot transportation. Cr cds: A, C, D, DS, MC, V. **$**

★ **RUSTY CANNON MOTEL.** *701 Taughenbaugh Blvd (81650). Phone 970/625-4004; fax 970/625-3604. www.rustycannonmotel.com.* 89 rooms, 2 story. Pet accepted. Check-out 11 am, check-in 3 pm. TV; cable (premium). In-room modem link. Sauna. Outdoor pool. Ski privileges. Horseback riding. Cr cds: A, C, D, DS, MC, V. **$**

Restaurants

★ **CRYSTAL CLUB CAFE.** *467 Redstone Blvd (81623). Phone 970/963-9515.* Hours: 11:30 am-10 pm. Closed Mon-Thurs, Nov-May. No A/C. Italian, American menu. Bar. Lunch $5.50-$8, dinner $5.50-$15.75. Children's menu. Specializes in chicken Marsala, soups, homeade bread. Parking. Outdoor dining. Country mountain décor; stone fireplace. Overlooks Crystal River. Cr cds: MC, V.

★ ★ **FLORINDO'S.** *721 Grand Ave (81601). Phone 970/945-1245; fax 970/876-2024.* Italian menu. Dinner. Bar. Children's menu. Casual attire. Totally nonsmoking. Cr cds: MC, V. **$$**

★ **LOS DESPERADOS.** *55 Mel Rey Rd (81601). Phone 970/945-6878.* Mexican menu. Mexican décor. Lunch, dinner. Bar. Children's menu. Casual attire. Outdoor seating. Non-smoking seating. Cr cds: A, C, DS, MC, V. **$**

★ ★ **RIVER'S RESTAURANT.** *2525 S Grand Ave (81601). Phone 970/928-8813; fax 970/928-8814. www.theriversrestaurant.com.* American menu. Closed Dec 25. Dinner, Sun brunch. Bar. Children's menu. Casual attire. Outdoor seating. Non-smoking seating. Cr cds: A, MC, V. **$$**

Golden (C-5)

See also Central City, Denver, Evergreen, Idaho Springs

Founded 1859 **Pop** 17,159

Information Greater Golden Chamber of Commerce, PO Box 1035, 80402; 303/279-3113 or 800/590-3113

Once a rival of Denver, Golden was capital of the Colorado Territory from 1862-1867.

What to See and Do

Armory Building. *1301 Arapahoe St (80401).* Largest cobblestone building in the US. Approximately 3,000 wagon loads of cobblestones were used in the construction. The rocks are from Clear Creek and the quartz from Golden Gate Canyon.

Astor House Hotel Museum. *822 12th St. Phone 303/278-3557.* (1867) First stone hotel west of the Mississippi. Period furnishings. Self-guided and guided tours (reservations required) Victorian gift shop. (Tues-Sat; closed holidays) **$$**

Colorado Railroad Museum. *17155 W 44th Ave. Phone 303/279-4591 or 800/365-6263.* An 1880-style railroad depot houses memorabilia and operating model railroad. More than 50 historic locomotives and cars from Colorado railroads displayed outside. (Daily; closed Thanksgiving, Dec 25) **$$$**

Colorado School of Mines. *1500 Illinois St (80401). Main entrance at 19th and Elm sts. Phone 303/273-3000; 800/446-9488.* (1874) 3,150 students. World-renowned institution devoted exclusively to education of mineral, energy, and material engineers and applied scientists. Tours of campus. Also see

Edgar Mine. *365 8th Ave. Located in Idaho Springs (see). Phone 303/567-2911.* Experimental mine operated by Colorado School of Mines, state government, and by manufacturers for equipment testing. (Mon-Fri, by apppointment) **$$$**

Geology Museum. *16th and Maple sts. Phone 303/273-3815.* Mineral and mining history exhibits. (Mon-Sat) **FREE** Located off campus is

USGS National Earthquake Information Center. *Illinois and 17th sts. Phone 303/273-8500.* (Mon-Fri, by appointment; closed holidays) **FREE**

Golden Gate Canyon State Park. *3873 CO 46 (80403). 2 miles N via CO 93, then left on Golden Gate Canyon Rd and continue W for 15 miles. Phone 303/582-3707.* On 12,000 acres. Nature and hiking trails, cross-country skiing, picnicking, camping (dump station, electrical hookups). Visitor center. Panorama Point Overlook provides 100-mile view of the Continental Divide. Standard fees. (Daily) **$$**

Golden Pioneer Museum. *923 10th St. Phone 303/278-7151.* Houses more than 4,000 items dating from Golden's territorial capital days; including household articles, clothing, furniture; mining, military, and ranching equipment; unique Native American doll collection. (Mon-Sat) Wheelchair accessible. **DONATION**

Heritage Square. *18301 W Colfax Ave (80401). 1 mile S of 6th Ave on Hwy 40. Phone 303/279-2789.* Located 15 minutes from downtown Denver in the foothills of Golden, Colorado, Heritage Square family entertainment park is reminiscent of an 1870s Colorado mining town with its Old West streetscapes and Victorian facades. In addition to specialty shops, restaurants, museums, and theater, there are amusement rides for the younger children, a water slide, a 70-foot bungee tower, go-karts, and a miniature golf course. Heritage Square is also home to Colorado's longest, 1/2-mile Alpine slide. The slide is particularly popular with teenagers, or anyone else who enjoys the feeling of plunging down a mountainside track on a small fiberglass sled with wheels. The sleds do have handbrakes, so moms and dads can go a little slower. (Daily)

★ **Industrial tour. Coors Brewing Company.** *13th and Ford sts. Phone 303/277-2337.* Tours of Coors brewing and malting processes. Tours for hearing impaired and foreign guests may be arranged. Children welcome when accompanied by an adult. (Mon-Sat) **FREE**

Lariat Trail. *Phone 800/590-3113.* Leads to Denver Mountain Parks. Lookout Mountain, 5 miles W off US 6, is the nearest peak. At the summit are

Buffalo Bill Grave and Museum. *987 Lookout Mountain Rd (80401). Phone 303/526-0747.* Lookout Mountain, 30 minutes west of downtown Denver, is the final resting place of the man who virtually defined for the world the spirit of the Wild West. A born adventurer, William F. "Buffalo Bill" Cody's life included stints as a cattle driver, fur trapper, gold miner, Pony Express rider, and scout for the US cavalry. He became world famous with his traveling "Buffalo Bill's Wild West Show." At the Buffalo Bill Grave and Museum, Cody still draws crowds who come to see the museum's western artifacts collection, take advantage of the beautiful hilltop vistas, and pay homage to this most legendary of Western heroes. May-Oct, daily; Nov-Apr, Tues-Sun; closed Dec 25) **$$**

Rocky Mountain Quilt Museum. *1111 Washington Ave. Phone 303/277-0377.* Houses more than 250 quilts. Five exhibits each year. (Tues-Sat) **$$**

Special Event

Buffalo Bill Days. Parade, golf tournament. July.

Motels/Motor Lodges

★ **LA QUINTA INN.** *3301 Youngfield Service Rd (80401). Phone 303/279-5565; toll-free 800/687-6667; fax 303/279-5841. www.laquinta.com.* 129 rooms, 3 story. S, D $79-$99; under 18 free. Crib free. Pet accepted. TV; cable (premium). Pool. Complimentary continental breakfast. Coffee in rooms. Restaurant nearby. Check-out noon. Coin laundry. Meeting rooms. Business services available. In-room modem link. Valet service. Health club privileges. Cr cds: A, C, D, DS, MC, V.

D 🐾 🏊 ⛷ **SC**

★ ★ ★ **TABLE MOUNTAIN INN.** *1310 Washington Avenue (80401). Phone 303/277-9898; toll-free 800/762-9898; fax 303/271-0298. www.tablemountaininn.com.* 32 rooms, 3 suites, 2 story. S, D $87-$105; each additional $5; suites $130-$145; under 12 free; weekend rates. Crib free. Complimentary coffee in rooms. Check-out 11 am. TV; cable (premium), VCR available. In-room modem link. Balconies. Refrigerators. Microwaves available. Restaurant (see TABLE MOUNTAIN INN). Bar from 11 am. Room service. Health club privileges. Airport transportation. Meeting rooms. Business services. Southwestern décor. Cr cds: A, C, D, DS, JCB, MC, V.

✈ SC

Hotel

★ ★ ★ **MARRIOTT DENVER WEST.** *1717 Denver West Blvd (80401). Phone 303/279-9100; fax 303/271-0205. www.marriott.com.* This property is centrally located near many attractions like the Coors Brewery and Red Rocks Amphitheater. 307 rooms, 6 story. June-Sept: S, D $71-$139; suites $275-$350; under 18 free; package plans; lower rates rest of year. Crib free. Complimentary coffee in rooms. Check-out noon. TV; cable (premium). In-room modem link. Bathroom phones. Wet bar in suites. Microwaves available. Coin laundry. Restaurant 6 am-2 pm, 5-10 pm. Bar from 2 pm. Room service 5-2 am. Exercise equipment, sauna. Game room. Indoor/outdoor pool, whirlpool. Business services. Convention center facilities. Bellhops. Sundries, gift shop. Cr cds: A, C, D, DS, ER, JCB, MC, V.

D ♿ ⚡ ➰ ✈ ⛷

Restaurants

★ ★ **CHART HOUSE.** *25908 Genesee Trail Rd (80401). Phone 303/526-9813; fax 303/526-0753.* Hours: 5-10 pm; Sun 4:30-9 pm. Reservations accepted. Bar to 11 pm; weekends to midnight. Dinner $15-$26.95. Children's menu. Specializes in beef, seafood. Salad bar. Nautical décor. View of mountains and city. Cr cds: A, D, DS, MC, V.

D

★ **CODY INN CONTINENTAL CUISINE.** *866 Lookout Mountain Rd (80401). Phone 303/526-0232.* Continental menu. Specializes in veal, duck, steak. Hours: 5-11 pm; Sun brunch 11 am-2 pm. Closed Mon; Dec 25. Dinner $14-$21, Sun brunch $12. Bar. Children's menu. Reservations accepted. Cr cds: DS, MC, V.

D

★ ★ **SIMMS LANDING.** *11911 W 6th Ave (80401). Phone 303/237-0465; fax 303/237-6993. www.simmslanding.com.* Specializes in prime rib, steak, fresh seafood. Hours: 11 am-10 pm; Fri, Sat to 11 pm; Sun brunch 9 am-2 pm , closed Dec 25. Lunch $6-$14. Buffet: lunch $7.99. Dinner $18-$19, Sun brunch $7. Children's

menu. Valet parking available. Outdoor dining. Cr cds: A, DS, MC, V.

D SC

★ ★ **TABLE MOUNTAIN INN.** *1310 Washington Ave (80401). Phone 303/216-8020; fax 303/271-0298. www.tablemountaininn.com.* Hours: 6:30 am-11 pm; Sat from 7 am; Sun from 8 am; Sun brunch to 2 pm. Reservations accepted. Southwestern menu. Bar to 11 pm. Breakfast $5-$7, lunch $6-$8.50, dinner $7.95-$18.95. Sun brunch $6-$9. Children's menu. Specializes in chicken tortilla soup, buffalo. Own baking. Outdoor dining. Southwestern décor. Cr cds: A, C, D, DS, ER, MC, V.

D

Granby (C-5)

See also Grand Lake, Kremmling, Winter Park

Pop 1,525 **Elev** 7,939 ft **Area code** 970 **Zip** 80446

Information Greater Granby Area Chamber of Commerce, PO Box 35; 970/887-2311 or 800/325-1661

Web www.rkymtnhi.com/granbycoc

Immediately northeast of Granby is the Arapaho National Recreation Area, developed by the Department of Interior as part of the Colorado-Big Thompson Reclamation Project. There is swimming and mineral bathing at Hot Sulphur Springs. Several national forests, lakes, and big-game hunting grounds are within easy reach. Two ski areas are nearby (also see WINTER PARK) and a Ranger District Office of the Arapaho National Forest (see DILLION) is located in Granby.

What to See and Do

Arapaho National Recreation Area. *9 Ten Mile Dr. 6 miles NE on US 34. Phone 970/887-4100.* Includes Shadow Mountain, Willow Creek, Monarch, Grand, and Granby lakes. Boating, fishing; hunting, camping (fee), picnicking, horseback riding. (Daily) **$$**

Grand County Historical Association. *5950 County Rd 5. 10 miles W via US 40 in Hot Sulphur Springs. Phone 970/725-3939.* Museum exhibits depict the history of skiing, ranching, and Rocky Mountain railroads; archaeological finds; reconstructed old buildings, wagons, and tools. (Memorial Day-Labor Day, Tues-Sat, Sun afternoons)

SilverCreek Ski Area. *1000 Village Rd. 3 miles SE on US 40. Phone 970/887-3384, 303/629-1020 (Denver direct), or 800/448-9458.* Two triple, double chairlifts; Pomalift; patrol, school, rentals, snowmaking; concession, cafeteria, bar, nursery, day-lodge. Twenty-two runs; longest run 6,100 feet; vertical drop 1,000 feet. (Dec-mid-Apr) Snowboarding, sleigh rides. Health club. **$$$$**

Motel/Motor Lodge

★**TRAIL RIDERS.** *215 E Agate Ave (80446). Phone 970/ 887-3738.* 11 rooms, 5 suites. S $35, D $45; suites $49-$65. Crib available. Pet accepted, some restrictions. Check-out 10 am. TV; cable (premium). Refrigerators, microwaves. Coffee in rooms. Restaurant adjacent 11 am-10 pm. Free train station transportation. Cr cds: A, DS, MC, V.

Resort

★★**INN AT SILVERCREEK.** *62927 US 40, Silver Creek (80451). Phone 970/887-2131; toll-free 800/927- 4386; fax 970/887-4083. www.silvercreeklodging.com.* 342 rooms, 252 kitchen units, 3 story. No A/C. Feb-Mar: S, D $89; kitchen units $119-$299; ski plan; higher rates late Dec; lower rates rest. of year. Pets accepted. Check-out 11 am, check-in 4 pm. TV; cable (premium). Fireplaces. Bar 4-11 pm, Fri, Sat to 1 am. Exercise equipment, sauna. Pool, whirlpool. Lighted tennis. Downhill ski 1 mile. Fishing. Hot-air balloon rides. Mountain bikes. Racquetball. Sleigh rides. Whitewater rafting. Cr cds: A, C, D, DS, MC, V.

Guest Ranches

★★★★**C LAZY U RANCH.** *3640 CO 125 (80446). Phone 970/887-3344; fax 970/887-3917. www.clazyu.com.* Since the 1940s, C Lazy U Ranch has been offering families a taste of life on a Western ranch. Situated just under 100 miles west of Denver, the ranch enjoys the beautiful Colorado countryside as its backdrop. Visitors come here to return to a simpler time; outside distractions are eliminated with the banishment of televisions and telephones in all accommodations. The guest rooms are decorated with a distinctively Western décor, and nearly all have fireplaces. The rustic design of the Main Lodge belies the sophisticated cooking featured within. Meals are served family style, and afterward, visitors are encouraged to join the fireside sing-a-long. During winter months, snowshoeing, cross-country skiing, sleigh rides, and nearby downhill skiing are popular activities, while hiking, biking, and swimming are pursued during warmer months. The horsemanship program is the centerpiece of the ranch, however, and guests are matched with one horse for the duration of their stay. 41 one- to five-room units in cottages, 3 lodge rooms. No A/C. No room phones. AP (7-day minimum), June-Aug, weekly: S, D $2,070-$3,680/person; ski plan; lower rates early June, Sept, and mid-Dec-Mar. Closed rest of year. Check-out 10 am, check-in 3 pm. TV in game room; VCR available (free movies). Some fireplaces. Free laundry facilities. Dining room (guests only). Bar 11-12:30 am. Entertainment. Free supervised children's activities; ages 3-18. Exercise equipment, sauna. Massage. Heated pool; whirlpool, poolside service. Tennis. Downhill ski 20 miles; cross-country ski on

site. Lawn games. Paddle boats. Fishing guides; cleaning and storage. Sleighing, tubing, tobogganing, winter horseback riding, ice skating, Racquetball. Barbecues, outdoor buffets. Skeet, trap range. Trail rides. No cr cds accepted.

★★**DROWSY WATER RANCH.** *County Rd 219 (80446). Phone 970/725-3456; toll-free 800/845-2292; fax 970/725-3611. www.drowsywater.com.* 8 rooms in lodge, 9 cottages. No A/C. AP, June-mid-Sept, weekly: S $1,230; D $1,150/person; each additional $1,000; under 5, $520; 3-day rates Sept. Closed rest of year. Crib free. Check-out 11 am, check-in 2:30 pm. Some private porches. Coin laundry 7 miles. Free supervised children's activities (June-Aug); ages 1-13. Playground. Social director. Heated pool, whirlpool. Family-style meals in lodge; also trail breakfast, buffets, cookouts, picnicking. Lawn games. Fishing, hunting guides. Optional whitewater rafting ($40/person), pack ($35/person) trips. Hayrides. Riding, hiking trails. Free local train station, bus depot transportation. Meeting rooms. Business services. Gift shop. Rodeo events. Staff show. Square dancing.

Restaurants

★**LONGBRANCH & SCHATZI'S PIZZA.** *165 E Agate Ave (80446). Phone 970/887-2209.* Hours: 11 am-9 pm, Fri, Sat to 9:30 pm; Sun 5-9 pm. Closed Thanksgiving, Dec 25; also mid-Apr-mid-May and mid-Oct-mid-Nov. Reservations accepted. Eclectic menu. Bar. Lunch $4.50-$7.50, dinner $5.50-$17.50. Children's menu. Specializes in German dishes. Own baking, pasta. Street parking. Western atmosphere; wagon-wheel lights, brick fireplace. Totally nonsmoking. Cr cds: C, D, DS, ER, MC, V.

★**PAUL'S CREEKSIDE GRILL.** *62927 US 40 (80451). Phone 970/887-2484.* American menu. Breakfast, lunch, dinner. Bar. Children's menu. Casual attire. Outdoor seating. Cr cds: A, DS, MC, V. **$**

Grand Junction (D-1)

Settled 1881 **Pop** 41,986 **Elev** 4,597 ft **Area code** 970

Information Visitor & Convention Bureau, 740 Horizon Dr, 81506; 970/244-1480 or 800/962-2547

Web www.visitgrandjunction.com

Grand Junction's name stems from its location at the junction of the Colorado (formerly the Grand) and Gunnison rivers. The altitude and warm climate combine to provide a rich agricultural area, which produces peaches, pears, and grapes for the local wine industry. The city serves as a trade and tourist center for western Colorado and eastern Utah as well as a gateway to two national parks, six national forests, and 7 million acres of public land. Fishing, hunting, boating, and hiking may all be enjoyed in the nearby lakes and mountain streams.

What to See and Do

Colorado River. *15 miles E, off I-70 exit 47. Phone 970/ 464-0548; 970/434-3388.* Swimming, fishing; picnicking, camping. Grocery nearby. Standard fees.

Cross Orchards Historic Farm. *3079 Patterson Rd. Phone 970/434-9814.* Operated 1896-1923 by owners of Red Cross shoe company. Living history farm with historically costumed guides interprets the social and agricultural heritage of western Colorado. Restored buildings and equipment on display; narrow gauge railroad exhibit and country store. Demonstrations, special events. (Tues-Sun) **$$**

Dinosaur Hill. *5 miles W, 1 1/2 miles S of Fruita on CO 340.* Self-guided walking trail interprets quarry of paleontological excavations. (Daily) **FREE**

★ **Grand Mesa National Forest.** *Approximately 40 miles E via I-70 and CO 65. Forest Supervisor, 2250 US 50. (81416). Phone 970/874-7691.* This 346,221-acre alpine forest includes a flat-top, basalt-capped tableland at 10,500 feet. There are more than 300 alpine lakes and reservoirs, many with trout; boat rentals are available. The mesa is also a big-game hunting area, with horses available for rent. There are excellent areas for cross-country skiing, snowmobiling, picnicking, and camping (fee at some campgrounds); there is also a lodge and housekeeping cabins. From the rim of Lands End, the westernmost spot on Grand Mesa, there is a spectacular view of much of western Colorado. Also located within the forest is Powderhorn Ski Resort and the Crag Crest National Recreational Trail. Ranger District offices are located in Grand Junction and Collbran and for Uncompaghre Forest to the southwest, as well.

Highline Lake. *1800 11 8/10 Rd. 18 miles NW on I-70 to Loma, then 6 miles N on CO 139. Phone 970/858-7208.* Swimming, waterskiing, fishing, boat ramps, shelters; waterfowl hunting, picnicking, camping. Standard fees.

Museum of Western Colorado. *248 S 4th St. Phone 970/ 242-0971.* Features exhibits on regional, social, and natural history of the Western Slope; collection of small weapons; wildlife exhibits. (Mon-Sat) Tours by appointment. **$**

Powderhorn Ski Resort. *20 miles E via I-70, exit 49. E on CO 65. Phone 970/268-5700 or 800/241-6997.* Quad, two double chairlifts; surface lift; patrol, school, rentals, snowmaking; snack bar, restaurants, bar, day-lodge. Twenty-nine runs; longest run 2 miles; vertical drop 1,650 feet. (mid-Dec-mid-Apr, daily) Cross-country trails (7 miles), snowboarding, snowmobiling, sleigh rides. Half-day rates. Summer activities include fishing, rafting trips, biking, horseback riding, western cookouts. **$$$$**

Rabbit Valley Trail Through Time. *30 miles W on I-70, 2 miles from UT border. Phone 970/241-9210.* A 1 1/2 mile self-guided walking trail through a paleontologically significant area. Fossilized flora and fauna from the Jurassic Age. No pets allowed. (Daily) **FREE**

Riggs Hill. *S Broadway and Meadows Way. Phone 970/ 241-9210.* A 3/4 mile, self-guided walking trail in an area where bones of the Brachiosaurus dinosaur were discovered in 1900. (Daily) **FREE**

River Rafting. *Phone 970/241-5633 or 800/423-4668.* On the Colorado, Green, and Yampa rivers. Two-day to 5-day whitewater raft trips. Contact Adventure Bound, Inc., 2392 H Rd, 81505. **$$$$**

Special Events

Colorado Mountain Winefest. *2785 US 50 (81503). Phone 970/256-1531.* Wine tastings, outdoor events. Late Sept.

Colorado Stampede. Rodeo. Third week in June.

Motels/Motor Lodges

★ **BEST WESTERN SANDMAN MOTEL.** *708 Horizon Dr (81506). Phone 970/243-4150; toll-free 800/780-7234; fax 970/243-1828. www.bestwestern.com.* 80 rooms, 2 story. Check-out 11 am, check-in 3 pm. TV; cable. In-room modem link. Coin laundry. Pool, whirlpool. Free airport transportation. Cr cds: A, C, D, DS, MC, V. **$**

D 🛌 🏊 SC

★ **BUDGET HOST INN.** *721 Horizon Dr (81506). Phone 970/243-6050; toll-free 800/888-5736; fax 970/ 243-0310. www.budgethost.com.* 54 rooms, 2 story. Pet accepted. Complimentary continental breakfast. Check-out 11 am, check-in 3 pm. TV; cable (premium). Coin laundry. Pool. Cr cds: A, C, D, DS, MC, V **$**.

D 🐾 🛌 🏊

★ ★ **HOLIDAY INN.** *755 Horizon Dr (81506). Phone 970/243-6790; toll-free 888/489-9796. www.holiday-inn.com.* 292 rooms. Pet accepted. Check-out 11 am, check-in 4 pm. TV; cable (premium), VCR available. In-room modem link. Restaurant. Bar; entertainment. Room service. In-house fitness room, sauna. Game room. Indoor pool; outdoor pool, children's pool; whirlpool. Airport transportation. Cr cds: A, C, D, DS, ER, JCB, MC, V. **$**

D 🐾 🛌 🏋 🏊 SC

★ ★ **RAMADA INN.** *752 Horizon Dr (81506). Phone 970/243-5150; fax 970/242-3692. www.ramadagj.com.* 100 rooms, 2 story. Pet accepted. Check-out noon, check-in 3 pm. TV; cable (premium), VCR available (movies). In-room modem link. Coin laundry. Restaurant. Outdoor pool, whirlpool. Free airport, train station, bus depot transportation. Cr cds: A, C, D, DS, ER, JCB, MC, V. **$**

D 🐾 ♨ 🛌 🏊 SC

Hotels

★ ★ **ADAM'S MARK.** *743 Horizon Dr (81506). Phone 970/241-8888; fax 970/242-7266. www.adamsmark.com.* 273 rooms, 8 story. Pet accepted. Check-out noon, check-in 3 pm. TV; cable (premium). Restaurant, bar. In-house fitness room. Game room. Outdoor pool, whirlpool, poolside service. Lighted Tennis courts. Lawn games. Free airport. Luxury level. Cr cds: A, D, DS, MC, V. **$**

D ⬛ ⬛ ⬛ ⬛ ⬛ ⬛ ⬛ ⬛ ⬛

★ ★ **GRAND VISTA HOTEL.** *2790 Crossroads Blvd (81506). Phone 970/241-8411; toll-free 800/800-7796; fax 970/241-1077. www.grandvistahotel.com.* 158 rooms, 6 story. Pet accepted. Check-out noon, check-in 3 pm. TV; cable (premium). In-room modem link. Restaurant. Bar. Room service. Health club privileges. Indoor pool, whirlpool. Free airport, train station, bus depot transportation. Cr cds: A, C, D, DS, MC, V. **$**

D ⬛ ⬛ ⬛ ⬛ SC

Restaurants

★ ★ **FAR EAST RESTAURANT.** *1530 North Ave (81501). Phone 970/242-8131; fax 970/242-8170.* Chinese, American menu. Closed major holidays. Lunch, dinner. Bar. Children's menu. Nonsmoking seating. Cr cds: A, C, D, DS, ER, MC, V. **$$**

D ⬛

★ **STARVIN' ARVIN'S.** *752 Horizon Dr (81506). Phone 970/241-0430.* American menu. Closed Thanksgiving, Dec 25. Breakfast, lunch, dinner. Bar. Children's menu. Casual atmosphere; antique photographs. Nonsmoking seating. Cr cds: A, C, D, DS, ER, MC, V. **$**

D SC ⬛

★ ★ **WINERY RESTAURANT.** *642 Main St (81501). Phone 970/242-4100; fax 970/242-3618. www. wineryrestaurant.com.* Hours: 5-10 pm. Closed Dec 25. Dinner $10.95-$26.90. Bar from 4:30 pm. Restored 1890s building. Totally nonsmoking. Cr cds: A, D, DS, MC, V.

D ⬛

Grand Lake (B-5)

See also Estes Park, Granby

Pop 447 **Elev** 8,380 ft **Area code** 970 **Zip** 80447

Information Grand Lake Area Chamber of Commerce, PO Box 57; 970/627-3402 or 800/531-1019

Web www.grandlakechamber.com

Grand Lake is on the northern shore of the largest glacial lake in Colorado, source of the Colorado River. The Ute shunned the vicinity because, according to legend,

mists rising from the lake were the spirits of women and children killed when Cheyenne and Arapahoe attacked a Ute village on the shore.

As one of the state's oldest resort villages, Grand Lake boasts the world's highest yacht club, a full range of water recreation, and horseback riding and pack trips on mountain trails. Grand Lake is at the terminus of Trail Ridge Road at the west entrance to Rocky Mountain National Park.

What to See and Do

Hiking, fishing, boating, horseback riding. *Phone 970/627-3220 (Gala Marina); 970/627-3215 (Winding River Resort).* Boat rentals available from Gala Marina. Horseback riding can be scheduled with Winding River Resort. Other outdoor activities abound in summer at Grand Lake, Shadow Mountain Lake, and Lake Granby.

Snowmobiling and cross-country skiing. Back areas of Arapaho National Forest (see DILLON), portion of Trail Ridge Rd, and local trails around Grand Lake, Shadow Mountain, and Granby Lakes. (Nov-May) Inquire locally for details.

Special Events

Buffalo Barbecue & Western Week Celebration. Parade, food; Spirit Lake Mountain Man rendezvous. Third week in July.

Lipton Cup Sailing Regatta. Early Aug.

Rocky Mountain Repertory Theatre. *Community Building, Town Square.* Three musicals change nightly, Mon-Sat. Reservations advised. For schedule, phone Chamber of Commerce or 970/627-3421 (during event). Late June-late Aug.

Winter Carnival. Ice skating, snowmobiling, snow sculptures, ice-fishing derby, ice-golf tournament. Last weekend in Jan and first weekend in Feb.

Motels/Motor Lodges

★ **BIGHORN LODGE.** *613 Grand Ave (80447). Phone 970/627-8101; toll-free 888/315-2378; fax 970/627-3771. www.rkymtnhi.com/bighorn.* 20 rooms, 2 story. Jan-May, mid-Oct-mid-Dec: S, D $55-$80; each additional $10; higher rates special events. Crib $5. TV; cable. Whirlpool. Restaurant nearby. Check-out 10 am. Business services available. Downhill ski 18 miles; cross-country ski 1 mile. Some refrigerators, microwaves. Cr cds: A, C, D, DS, MC, V.

D ⬛ ⬛ ⬛

★ **DRIFTWOOD LODGE.** *12255 US 34 (80447). Phone 970/627-3654; toll-free 800/766-1123. www.rkymtnhi.com/driftwood.* 26 kitchen units. No A/C. Mid-May-Sept, mid-Dec-early Jan: D $55-$105; each additional $5; 2-room units $65-$86; lower rates rest of year. Check-out 10 am, check-in 2 pm. TV. In-room modem link. Sauna.

Children's pool, whirlpool. Downhill ski 16 miles, cross-country ski 4 miles. Lawn games. Snowmobiling. Cr cds: D, DS, MC, V.

★ **WESTERN RIVIERA.** *419 Garfield St (80447). Phone 970/627-3580; fax 970/627-3320. www.westernriv.com.* 25 rooms, 2 story, 6 kitchen cabins. Mid-June-mid-Sept: S, D $65-$95; each additional $5; family units $95; cabins (3-day minimum) $100; lower rates rest of year. Check-out 10 am. TV. Fireplace in lobby. Downhill ski 18 miles, cross-country ski 1 mile. On lakefront; scenic view. Cr cds: A, C, D, DS, MC, V.

Resort

★ **GRAND LAKE LODGE.** *15500 US 34 (80447). Phone 970/627-3967; fax 970/627-9495. www.grandlakelodge.com.* 56 kitchen units, 1-2 story story. No room phones. June-mid-Sept: S, D, kitchen units, cottages $75-$550. Closed rest of year. Check-out 10 am. Check-in 4 pm. Laundry services. Dining room 7:30-10 am, 11:30 am-2:30 pm, 5:30-9 pm; Sun 9:30 am-1:30 pm. Bar 11 am-midnight, entertainment Wed-Sun. Game room. Heated pool, whirlpool. Lawn games. Cr cds: A, D, DS, MC, V.

B&B/Small Inn

★ ★ **SPIRIT MOUNTAIN RANCH.** *3863 County Rd 41 (80447). Phone 970/887-3551. www.fcinet.com/spirit.* 4 air-cooled rooms, 2 story. No room phones. S, D $130; each additional $30. Children over 10 years only. Complimentary full breakfast, afternoon refreshments. Check-out 11 am, check-in 4 pm. Whirlpool. Game room. Downhill ski 15 miles, cross-country ski on site. Picnic tables, grills. Lawn games. Bicycles. Business services. Luggage handling. Totally nonsmoking. Cr cds: DS, MC, V.

Restaurants

★ ★ ★ **CAROLINE'S CUISINE.** *9921 US 34 #27 (80447). Phone 970/627-9404; fax 970/627-9424. www.sodaspringsranch.com.* Large windows offer views of either the mountain or the hills. Hours: 5-9 pm; Fri, Sat to 9:30 pm. Closed 2 weeks in Apr, 2 weeks in Nov. Reservations accepted. French, American menu. Bar. Wine list. Dinner $13.95-$21.95. Children's menu. Pianist Sat. Parking. Outdoor dining. 3 dining rooms; European décor. Art gallery upstairs. Cr cds: A, DS, MC, V.

★ **E. G.'S GARDEN GRILL.** *1000 Grand Ave (80447). Phone 970/627-8404; fax 970/627-0118. www.egscountry inn.com.* Hours: 11 am-10 pm; hours vary by season. Closed Dec 25. Reservations accepted. No A/C. Bar. Lunch $5.95-$11.95, dinner $6.95-$21. Children's menu. Specializes in baby back ribs, shrimp enchiladas. Street parking. Outdoor dining. Totally nonsmoking. Cr cds: A, D, MC, V.

★ ★ **GRAND LAKE LODGE RESTAURANT.** *15500 US 34 (80447). Phone 970/627-3967.* Steak menu. Closed Mid-Sept-May. Breakfast, lunch, dinner. Bar. Children's menu. Casual attire. Outdoor seating. Cr cds: A, D, DS, MC, V. **$$**

Great Sand Dunes National Monument

See also Alamosa

(35 miles NE of Alamosa, CO, reached by US 160 and CO 150 from the S or from CO 17 and County Six Mile Ln from the W)

Boasting the tallest sand dunes in North America, the 33-square-mile Great Sand Dunes National Monument and Preserve is a fun and fascinating place to visit. The kids will love running and rolling on the sides of sand mountains, some rising over 700 feet. The park is a geological and botanical showcase and a hiker's delight with its alpine lakes and tundras, groves of ancient spruce and pine, grasslands and wetlands, and diversity of wildlife. Kite flying is a favorite activity here, as is, of course, building sand castles. Monument (daily). Visitor center (daily; closed Jan 1, Dec 25).

What to See and Do

Great Sand Dunes Four-Wheel Drive Tour. *5400 CO 150.* A 12-mile, two-hour round-trip tour through Great Sand Dunes National Monument; spectacular scenery; stops for short hikes on dunes. (May-Oct, daily) Five-person minimum. For information contact Great Sand Dunes Oasis, Mosca 81146. **$$$$**

Greeley (B-6)

See also Fort Collins, Loveland

Founded 1870 **Pop** 76,930 **Elev** 4,664 ft **Area code** 970 **Zip** 80631

Information Convention & Visitors Bureau, 902 7th Ave; 970/352-3566 or 800/449-3866

Web www.greeleycvb.com

Horace Greeley conceived of "Union Colony" as a Utopian agricultural settlement similar to the successful experiment at Oneida, New York. The town was founded by Nathan Meeker, agricultural editor of *Greeley's New York Tribune.* Thanks to irrigation, the region today is rich and fertile and sustains a thriving community. Greeley is the seat of Weld County. A Ranger District office of the Roosevelt National Forest (see ESTES PARK) is located in Greeley.

What to See and Do

Centennial Village. *1475 A St. Phone 970/350-9220 or 970/350-9224.* Restored buildings show the growth of Greeley and Weld County from 1860 to 1920; period furnishings; tours, lectures, special events. (Apr-Oct, Tues-Sun) **$$**

Fort Vasquez. *13412 Hwy 85 (80651). 18 miles S on US 85 near Platteville. Phone 970/785-2832.* Reconstructed adobe fur trading post of the 1830s contains exhibits of Colorado's fur trading and trapping industries, the Plains Indians, and archaeology of the fort. (Wed-Sat, Sun afternoons; Memorial Day-Labor Day, Sun afternoons) **FREE**

Meeker Home. *1324 9th Ave. Phone 970/350-9220.* (1870) The house of city founder Nathan Meeker contains many of his belongings, as well as other historical mementos. (Apr-Oct, Tues-Sat; closed holidays) **$$**

Municipal Museum. *919 7th St. Phone 970/350-9220.* County history archives, pioneer life exhibits; library; tours. (Tues-Sat; closed holidays) **FREE**

University of Northern Colorado. *501 20th St (80631). Phone 970/351-1890 or 970/351-1889.* (1889) 10,500 students. On the 236-acre campus are

James A. Michener Library. *1400 22nd Ave (80639). Phone 970/351-1890.* Colorado's largest university library. Collection includes materials owned by Michener while writing the book *Centennial.*

Mariani Art Gallery. *1819 8th Ave (80639). Phone 970/351-4890.* Features faculty, student, and special exhibitions. Multipurpose University Center. **FREE**

Special Events

Greeley Independence Stampede. *600 N 14th Ave (80631). Phone 970/356-2855; toll-free 800/982-BULL.* For one week each summer, the Old West meets the New West at the Greeley Independence Stampede, a spirited, week-long town celebration culminating in the "World's Largest 4th of July Rodeo." In addition to classic rodeo events, the Stampede features nightly stage shows including country & western and classic rock concerts by top-name entertainers, a bull-riding and -fighting event, a kids' rodeo, and the ever-popular demolition derby. The midway carnival is open daily. Fees vary per event. Late June-early July.

Weld County Fair. *501 N 14th St (80631). Phone 970/356-4000.* First week in Aug.

Motel/Motor Lodge

★ ★ **BEST WESTERN REGENCY HOTEL.** *701 8th St (80631). Phone 970/353-8444; toll-free 800/780-7234; fax 970/353-4269. www.bestwestern.com.* 148 rooms, 3 story. S, D $78-$138; each additional $10; suites $125-$155; under 18 free. Crib free. Pet accepted; $50. Complimentary continental breakfast, coffee in rooms. Check-out 11 am. TV; cable (premium). In-room modem link. Some balconies. Refrigerators, microwaves. Valet services. Restaurant 6 am-10 pm. Bar 11 am-midnight. Room service. Health club privileges. Heated indoor pool. Meeting rooms. Business services. Cr cds: A, C, D, DS, MC, V.

D 🐾 ⛱ 🏊 SC

B&B/Small Inn

★ ★ ★ **SOD BUSTER INN.** *1221 9th Ave (80631). Phone 970/592-1221; toll-free 888/300-1221. www.sodbusterinn.com.* 10 rooms, 2 story. Check-out 11 am, check-in 4 pm. TV; VCR available. Internet access. **$**

D

Gunnison (E-3)

See also Crested Butte

Settled 1874 **Pop** 5,409 **Elev** 7,703 ft

Information Gunnison Country Chamber of Commerce, 500 E Tomichi Ave, Box 36; 970/641-1501

Web www.gunnison-co.com

With 2,000 miles of trout-fishing streams, and Colorado's largest lake within easy driving range, Gunnison has long been noted as an excellent fishing center.

What to See and Do

Alpine Tunnel. *500 E Tomichi Ave (81230). 36 miles NE via US 50, County 765, 3 miles E of Pitkin on dirt road.* Completed by Denver, South Park & Pacific Railroad in 1881 and abandoned in 1910, this railroad tunnel, 11,523 feet above sea level, is 1,771 feet long. (July-Oct)

Cumberland Pass. *Chamber of Commerce, 500 E Tomichi Ave (81230). 36 miles NE via US 50, County 765.* (12,200 feet) Gravel road linking the towns of Pitkin and Tincup. (July-Oct)

Curecanti National Recreation Area. *5 miles W on US 50. Contact Superintendent, 102 Elk Creek. Phone 970/641-0406 or 970/641-2337.* Named for the Ute Chief Curicata, who roamed and hunted in this territory. This area along the Gunnison River drainage includes Blue Mesa, Morrow Point, and Crystal reservoirs. Elk Creek Marinas, Inc., offers boat tours on Morrow Point Lake (Memorial Day-Labor Day, daily); phone 970/641-0402 for reservations. Blue Mesa Lake has waterskiing, windsurfing, fishing, boating (ramps, rentals); picnicking, camping (fee). The Elk Creek Visitor Center is 16 miles W (mid-Apr-Oct, daily). **FREE**

Gunnison National Forest. *216 N Colorado St (81230). N, E, and S on US 50. A Ranger District office is located in Gunnison. Phone 970/641-0471.* Forest contains 27 peaks more than 12,000 feet high within 1,662,839 acres of magnificent mountain scenery. Activities include fishing; hiking, picnicking, camping. A four-wheeling and a winter sports area is nearby (see CRESTED BUTTE). Also within the forest are West Elk Wilderness and portions of the Maroon Bells-Snowmass, Collegiate Peaks, La Garita, and Raggeds wilderness areas.

Gunnison Pioneer Museum. *S Adams and Tomico US 50. E edge of town on US 50. Phone 970/641-4530 or 970/641-0740.* County and area history; pioneer items, narrow-gauge railroad, 1905 school house. (Memorial Day-Labor Day, Sun afternoons) **$$**

Old mining town of Tincup. *40 miles NE on County Rd 765. Phone 970/641-1501.* Inquire locally about other mining towns; "20-Circle Tour" ghost town maps provided free at the Visitor Center, 500 E Tomichi Ave (US 50).

Taylor Park Reservoir. *216 N Colorado St (81230). 10 miles N on CO 135 to Almont, then 22 miles NE on County Rd 742 (CO 59) in Gunnison National Forest. Phone 970/641-2922.* Road runs through 20-mile canyon of Taylor River. Fishing, boating; hunting, camping (fee). (Memorial Day-Sept, daily) **FREE**

Tincup, Colorado. *Drive east from Gunnison on Hwy 50 to Parlin, north on Quartz Creek Rd to Pitkin, north on Cumberland Pass Rd to Tincup—also accessible from Taylor Canyon east of Almont and from Cottonwood Pass west of Buena Vista.* For a trip back in time, drive north from Pitkin over the beautiful Cumberland Pass and into the fascinating little town of Tincup. Once a notorious rough-and-tumble mining community known for gambling, brothels, saloons, and shootouts, Tincup is now a sleepy near-ghost town that has preserved a piece of its heritage in a collection of rustic buildings restored to their original 1850s condition. An exploration of the town and surroundings reveals a number of ruins from Tincup's lawless past, including the graves of its earliest inhabitants and abandoned mines. Don't miss a chance to eat at the restored Frenchy's Café, known for its rustic charm and hearty, home-cooked meals. **FREE**

Western State College of Colorado. *909 Escalante Dr. Phone 970/943-2103.* (1901) 2,500 students. In the college library is the Jensen Western Colorado Room containing a collection of books and materials relating to western Colorado history and culture.

Special Event

Cattlemen's Days, Rodeo, and County Fair. Third full weekend in July.

Motels/Motor Lodges

★ ★ **BEST WESTERN TOMICHI VILLAGE.** *41883 E US Hwy 50 (81230). Phone 970/641-1131; toll-free 800/641-1131; fax 970/641-9554. www.bestwestern.com/tomichivillageinn.* 49 rooms, 2 story. June-Sept: S, D $80-$130; each additional $5; higher rates special events; lower rates rest of year. Crib $5. TV; cable (premium). Heated indoor pool; whirlpool. Complimentary continental breakfast, coffee in rooms, lobby. Restaurant 6:30-9:30 am, 5-9 pm. Check-out 11 am. Coin laundry. Meeting rooms. In-room modem link. Free airport transportation. Exercise equipment. Refrigerators, balconies. Corral facilities in hunting season. Cr cds: A, C, D, DS, MC, V.

⊞ 🏌 ⛷ ✈ ⬀ SC

★ **HOLIDAY INN EXPRESS.** *400 E Tomichi Ave (81230). Phone 970/641-1288; toll-free 800/486-6476; fax 970/641-1332. www.holiday-inn.com.* 54 rooms, 1-2 story. June-Sept: S, D $90-$110; each additional $5; under 19 free; ski plans; lower rates rest of year. Crib free. TV; cable (premium). Heated indoor pool; whirlpool. Complimentary continental breakfast. Restaurant nearby. Check-out noon. Meeting room. Business services available. In-room modem link. Valet service. Free airport, bus depot transportation. Exercise equipment. Cr cds: A, C, D, DS, JCB, MC, V.

⊞ 🏌 ⬀ SC

★ **RAMADA.** *1011 W Rio Grande Ave (81230). Phone 970/641-2804; fax 970/641-1420. www.ramada.com.* 36 rooms, 2 story. Late-May-mid-Oct: S, D $59-$99; each additional $6; under 19 free; lower rates rest of year. Pet accepted; fee. Complimentary continental breakfast. Check-out 11 am, check-in 3 pm. TV. Indoor pool, whirlpool. Cr cds: A, D, DS, MC, V.

D 🐾 ⊞ ⬀ SC

★ **SUPER 8 MOTEL.** *411 E Tomichi Ave (81230). Phone 970/641-3068; toll-free 800/800-8000; fax 970/641-1332. www.super8.com.* 52 rooms, 2 story. Mid-June-Sept: S, D $71.88-$78.88; each additional $5; ski plan. Crib $5. TV; cable (premium). Complimentary continental breakfast, coffee in lobby. Restaurant adjacent 6 am-9 pm. Check-out 11 am. In-room modem link. Free airport transportation. Horseback riding. Skiing nearby. Cr cds: A, C, D, DS, MC, V.

⚲ ✈ ⬀ SC

★ **WATER WHEEL INN.** *37478 Hwy 50 (81230). Phone 970/641-1650; toll-free 800/642-1650.* 54 rooms, 2 story. Mid-June-Sept: S, D $85; each additional $5; suites $100; lower rates rest of year. Complimentary continental breakfast. Check-out 11 am, check-in 1 pm. TV; cable (premium). In-room modem link. Exercise equipment. Free airport transportation. Cr cds: A, D, DS, MC, V.

⬚ ⬚ ⬚ ⬚

B&B/Small Inn

★★ **MARY LAWRENCE INN.** *601 N Taylor St (81230). Phone 970/641-3343; toll-free 888/331-6863; fax 970/641-6719. www.commerceteam.com/mary.html.* 7 rooms, 2 story. No A/C. No room phones. S, D $85-$135; each additional $15; ski plan. Complimentary full breakfast. Check-out 11 am, check-in 4-6 pm. TV in suites. Some fireplaces. Whirlpool. Free airport transportation. Many antiques. Italianate inn built 1885 was women's boarding house. Totally nonsmoking. Cr cds: A, MC, V.

⬚ ⬚

Guest Ranches

★★ **HARMEL'S RANCH RESORT.** *6748 County Rd 742 (81210). Phone 970/641-1740; toll-free 800/235-3402; fax 970/641-1944.* 37 rooms. No A/C. No room phones. Mid-June-Aug, AP: D $270-$400; each additional $60; lower rates mid-May-mid-June, Sept, Oct. Closed rest of year. Complimentary full breakfast. Check-out 10 am, check-in 2 pm. TV in recreation room. Dining room 7:30-9:30 am, noon-1 pm, 6-9 pm. Bar 4-10 pm. Free supervised children's activities. Massage, sauna. Game room. Whirlpool. Lawn games. Bicycles (rentals). Hayrides. Horseback riding. Free airport. Tackle store. Whitewater rafting. Square dancing. Trap shooting. 300 acres on Taylor River. Cr cds: A, MC, V.

⬚ ⬚ ⬚ ⬚

★★ **POWDERHORN GUEST RANCH.** *1525 County Rd 27 (81243). Phone 970/641-0220; fax 970/642-1399.* 14 air-cooled (1-2-bedroom) cabins. AP, June-late Sept, weekly: cabins $1,295/person; under 12 $995/week. Closed rest of year. Check-out noon, check-in 2 pm. Coin laundry. Whirlpool. Lawn games. Rafting. Hiking. Horse trail rides. Free airport transportation. Family-oriented ranch in remote area along Cebolla Creek. Cr cds: A, D, DS, MC, V.

⬚ ⬚

★ **WAUNITA HOT SPRINGS RANCH.** *8007 County Rd 887 (81230). Phone 970/641-1266; toll-free 888/232-9337; fax 970/641-0650. www.waunita.com.* 18 rooms, 1-2 story. AP, weekly, June-mid-Sept: S $1,400; D $700-$1,300; lower group rates mid-Dec-Mar. Closed rest of year. Crib free. Complimentary full breakfast. Check-out noon, check-in 2-5 pm. TV in lobby; VCR available (movies). Coin laundry. Dining room 7:30-9 am; lunch (1 sitting) 12:30 pm, dinner (1 sitting) 6:30 pm. Supervised children's activities. Playground. Massage, steam room. Game room. Hot spring-fed pool, whirlpool. Fishing/hunting guides; fish cleaning and storage. Hayrides, Jeep trips, rafting. Petting zoo. Square dancing. Overnight camping. Free local airport, bus depot transportation. Cr cds: A, DS, MC, V.

⬚ ⬚ ⬚

Restaurant

★★ **TROUGH.** *US 50 (81230). Phone 970/641-3724.* Hours: 5:30-10 pm; Fri, Sat to 10:30 pm. Closed Easter, Thanksgiving, Dec 25. Reservations accepted. No A/C. Bar 4 pm-2 am. Dinner $10.95-$31.95. Children's menu. Specializes in steak, prime rib, fresh seafood. Totally nonsmoking. Cr cds: A, C, D, DS, MC, V.

⬚ ⬚

Idaho Springs (C-5)

See also Central City, Denver, Dillon, Georgetown, Golden

Settled 1859 **Pop** 1,889 **Elev** 7,524 ft **Area code** 303 **Zip** 80452

Information Visitors Center, PO Box 97; 303/567-4382 or 800/685-7785

Idaho Springs, the site of Colorado's earliest gold strikes (1859), is today a tourist resort as well as the urban center for more than 200 mines, from which uranium, molybdenum, tungsten, zinc, lead, and gold are pulled from the earth. The town is named for the famous hot springs, first known and used by the Ute; bathing in the springs is still considered beneficial. The world's longest mining tunnel (5 miles) once ran from Idaho Springs through a mountain to Central City (see); only a portion remains (not open to visitors). The road to Mount Evans (elevation 14,260 feet) is the highest paved driving road in North America. A Ranger District office of the Arapaho National Forest (see DILLON) is located in Idaho Springs.

What to See and Do

Argo Town, USA. *2350 Riverside Dr. Phone 303/567-2421.* Reproduction of Western mining town; includes shops and **Argo Gold Mill.** This mill was first operated in 1913 to support mines intersected by the "mighty Argo" Tunnel; today it offers guided tours that unfold the history of the mill and the story of mining. **Clear Creek Mining and Milling Museum** illustrates the role of mining in the past. **Double Eagle Gold Mine** is an authentic and truly representative gold mine with direct access from the Argo Gold Mill. (Daily) **$$$**

Colorado School of Mines-Edgar Mine. *365 8th Ave. Phone 303/567-2911.* Experimental mine operated by students, also by government for training and by manufacturers for equipment testing; one-hour guided tour hourly (mid-June-mid-Aug, Tues-Sat; rest of year, by appointment). **$$**

Jackson Monument. *Colorado Blvd and Miner St (80452). Hwy 103 in front of Clear Creek Secondary School. Phone 800/685-7785.* George J. Jackson made the first major gold discovery in Colorado here on Jan 1, 1859. **FREE**

Phoenix Gold Mine. *834 Country Rd 136. Approximately 2 1/2 miles SW via Stanley Rd to Trail Creek Rd. Phone 303/567-0422; 800/685-7785.* The only working gold mine in the state that is open to the public. (Daily; closed Dec 25) **$$$**

St. Mary's Glacier. *12 miles NW via I-70, Fall River Rd to Alice, a ghost town.* Park car approximately 1 mile NW of Alice, then proceed 1/2 mile on foot.

Special Event

Gold Rush Days. Parades, picnic, foot races, mining contests, arts and crafts. Aug.

B&B/Small Inn

★ ★ ★ **ST. MARY'S GLACIER BED AND BREAKFAST.** *336 Crest Dr (80452). Phone 303/567-4084.* Looking to ski in July? Visit North America's highest bed-and-breakfast, where the snow stays year-round! Only an hour from Denver, this log retreat borders the Arapaho National Forest. Romantic guest rooms feature hand-sewn quilts and many have private decks with spectacular views. 7 rooms, 3 story, 1 suite. No A/C. No elevator. S, D $89-$139; suites $159; package plan. Crib free. Pet accepted, some restrictions. TV in common room; VCR available (movies). Complimentary full breakfast. Check-out 11 am, check-in 4-7 pm. In-room modem link. Game room. Some in-room whirlpools. Some balconies. Totally nonsmoking. Cr cds: A, DS, MC, V.

Kremmling (C-4)

See also Granby

Pop 1,578 **Elev** 7,360 ft **Area code** 970 **Zip** 80459

A Ranger District office of the Arapaho National Forest (see DILLON) is located in Kremmling.

What to See and Do

Green Mountain Reservoir. *680 Blue River Pkwy. 16 miles S on CO 9. Contact Dillon Ranger District, Box 620, Silverthorne 80498. Phone 970/468-5400.* Waterskiing, fishing, boating (ramps); picnicking, groceries, camping (fee). (Daily)

Guest Ranch

★ ★ **LATIGO RANCH.** *201 County Rd 1911 (80459). Phone 970/724-9008; toll-free 800/227-9655. www.latigotrails.com.* 10 air-cooled cottages. AP, June-Aug, weekly: cottages $1,600/person; family rates; lower rates Sept-mid-Nov, mid-Dec-Mar. Closed rest of year. Crib free. Check-out 4 pm, check-in 2 pm. Porches. Refrigerators. Complimentary coffee in rooms. Coin laundry. Dining room 7:30-9 am, 12:30-1:30 pm, 6:30-8 pm. Free supervised children's activities (June-Sept); ages 3-14. Playground. Social director. Game room, recreation room. Heated pool, whirlpool. Cross-country ski on site. Tobogganing. Picnic tables. Lawn games. Entertainment nightly. Fishing/hunting guides, clean and store. Hiking. Picnics. Horse stables. Airport transportation. Meeting rooms. Business services. Gift shop. On lake.

La Junta (F-7)

Settled 1875 **Pop** 7,568 **Elev** 4,066 ft **Area code** 719 **Zip** 81050

Information Chamber of Commerce, 110 Santa Fe Ave; 719/384-7411

La Junta (la HUN-ta, Spanish for "the Junction") is at a junction of the old Navajo and Santa Fe trails. The town is known for its Koshare Indian Dancers, a group of Explorer Scouts who perform authentic Native American dances here and throughout the country.

This is the center of an irrigated farming area, producing melons and commercial vegetables. Cattle auctions are held throughout the year. The Holbrook Lake area has become a popular recreational center.

What to See and Do

Bent's Old Fort National Historic Site. *35110 CO 194 E (81050). 8 miles NE of CO 109 and 194 E. Phone 719/838-5010.* The fort has been reconstructed as accurately as possible to its appearance in 1845-1846; the furnishings are antique and reproductions. The original structure, located on the Mountain Branch of the Santa Fe Trail, was built as a privately-owned frontier trading post (circa 1833). The old fort played a central role in the "opening of the west." For 16 years, until its abandonment in 1849, the fort was an important frontier hub of American trade and served as a rendezvous for trappers, Native Americans, and Hispanic traders on the Santa Fe Trail. It also served as the center of Army operations to protect the traders using the Santa Fe Trail. Self-guided tour. Summer "living history" programs. (Daily; closed Jan 1, Thanksgiving, Dec 25) **$**

⭐ **Koshare Indian Kiva Museum.** *115 W 18th St. Phone 719/384-4411.* Housed in a domed building, a copy of ceremonial kivas in the Southwest, the museum features Native American baskets, arrowheads, paintings, and carvings, as well as paintings by Southwestern artists. (Daily; closed holidays) **$**

Otero Museum. *218 Anderson. Phone 719/384-7500.* History of Otero County and surrounding areas. Santa Fe Railroad history; artifacts. (June-Sept, Mon-Sat) **FREE**

Special Events

Arkansas Valley Fair and Exposition. *Rocky Ford. 105 N Main St. Phone 719/254-7483.* Fairgrounds, grandstand. Colorado's oldest continuous fair. Highlight is "watermelon day," when every visitor receives free watermelon. One week in late Aug.

Early Settlers Day. Fiddlers contest, crafts, parade. Sat after Labor Day.

Koshare Indian Dances. *Kiva Museum. 115 W 18th St (81050). Phone 719/384-4411.* Dances by nationally famous Boy Scout troop. Sat evenings. Late June-early Aug.

Koshare Winter Night Ceremonial. *Kiva Museum. 115 W 18th St (81050). Phone 719/384-4111.* Nightly performances. Week of Dec 25 and first weekend in Jan.

Motels/Motor Lodges

★ ★ **BEST WESTERN BENT FORT'S INN.** *10950 US 50 (81054). Phone 719/456-0011; fax 719/456-2550. www.bestwestern.com.* 38 rooms, 2 story. S $49; D $59; each additional $6; under 18 free. Pet accepted, some restrictions. TV; cable. Pool. Restaurant 6 am-8 pm. Room service. Bar 5-10 pm. Complimentary full breakfast, coffee in rooms. Check-out 11 am. Meeting rooms. Business services available. In-room modem link. Free airport, bus depot transportation. Cr cds: A, C, D, DS, MC, V.

🅳 🐾 🏊 🎣 ⊠

★ ★ **QUALITY INN.** *1325 E Third St (81050). Phone 719/384-2571; toll-free 800/525-8682; fax 719/384-5655.* 76 rooms, 2 story. S $44-$58; D $52-$70; each additional $4; suites $79; under 18 free. Crib $5. Pet accepted, some restrictions. TV; cable (premium), VCR available (movies). Heated indoor/outdoor pool; whirlpool, poolside service. Complimentary breakfast, coffee in rooms. Restaurant 6 am-9 pm. Room service. Bar. Meeting rooms. Business services available. Free airport, train station transportation. Exercise equipment. Refrigerator in suites. Cr cds: A, C, D, DS, ER, JCB, MC, V.

🅳 🐾 🏊 🏃 ⊠

Restaurant

★ **CHIARAMONTE'S.** *27696 Harris Rd (81050). Phone 719/384-8909; fax 719/853-6619.* Hours: 11 am-2 pm, 5-9 pm; Sat from 5 pm; Sun to 2 pm. Closed major holidays. Reservations accepted. Continental menu. Bar. Lunch $4.35-$7.95, dinner $6.75-$14.75. Specializes in steak, seafood. Own soups. Cr cds: A, DS, MC, V.

Lake City (F-3)

Pop 375 **Elev** 8,671 ft **Area code** 970 **Zip** 81235

Information Chamber of Commerce, PO Box 430; 970/944-2527 or 800/569-1874

Web www.hinsdale-county.com

Lake City teemed with gold seekers in the 1870s. Now empty cabins and entire ghost towns dot the hills above the town. Among Lake City's 75 historic homes and buildings are the first church and bank on the Western Slope. Lake San Cristobal and the Lake Fork of the Gunnison River offer excellent fishing.

In the winter of 1873-1874, Alferd Packer led a group of gold prospectors into the San Juan Mountains above Lake City. Emerging from the mountains in the spring, only Packer survived, claiming his companions had abandoned him. For the next ten years, Packer was a fugitive. However, in 1883, he was convicted of murder and cannibalism. The victims' grave sites are located on the south edge of town.

What to See and Do

Alpine Triangle Recreation Area. *216 N Colorado St. South and west of town; access by the Alpine Loop National Backcountry Byway (four-wheel drive necessary in some places). Phone 970/641-0471.* Approximately 250,000 acres administered by Bureau of Land Management and the US Forest Service for primitive and motorized recreation, mining, grazing, and watershed protection. The area has five peaks that are more than 14,000 feet high; excellent backpacking and fishing; habitat for deer, elk, mountain sheep, black bear. Many historical mining tramways, stamp mills, and ghost towns are scattered throughout the area. Mill Creek Campground (14 miles SW) has a picnic area and 22 tent and trailer sites with water (Memorial Day-Oct, daily, weather permitting; fee for camping). Lake San Cristobal (3 miles south of town), the second-largest natural lake in the state, was formed by the Slumgullion earthflow 700 years ago. Williams Creek (10 miles southwest) has picnic areas and 21 tent and trailer sites with water (Memorial Day-Oct, daily; fee for camping). Southwest of town is the site where Alferd Packer murdered and mutilated five prospectors in the winter of 1873-1874.

Hinsdale County Historical Society Tours. *130 Silver St. Phone 970/944-2050.* Weekly guided walking tours, about two hours long, to historic homes, the local cemetery, and "ghostly" sites. (Mid-June-Labor Day; call for specific dates and times). **$$**

Hinsdale County Museum. *130 Silver St. Phone 970/944-2050.* Small museum with exhibits on the trial of notorious cannibal Alferd Packer and the area's silver-mining history, plus a furnished 1870s-era Victorian home. (Daily mid-June-Labor Day; varied hours rest of year) **$**

Special Events

Alferd Packer Barbeque Cookoff. Late May.

Ghost Town Narration Tours. Aug.

Motel/Motor Lodge

★ ★ **MELODY C. CRYSTAL LODGE.** *2175 US 149 S (81235). Phone 970/944-2201; toll-free 800/984-1234; fax 970/944-2503. www.crystallodge.net.* 28 rooms, 1-2 story, 5 suites. No A/C. No room phones. Memorial Day-Sept (2-day minimum): S, D $75-$115; each additional $10; suites, cottages $75-$120; under 2 free; ski rates; lower rates rest of year. Pet accepted, some restrictions; $25. Check-out 10 am, check-in noon. TV; cable (premium), VCR available. Restaurant. Cross-country ski 1 mile. Surrounded by San Juan Mountains. Totally nonsmoking. Cr cds: MC, V.

Lake George

What to See and Do

Lake George (Eleven Mile State Park) Ice Fishing. *38 miles west of Colorado Springs. Phone 719/748-3401.* The fish are biting year-round in Colorado, and the Lake George Eleven Mile Reservoir at Eleven Mile State Park is one of the best spots to experience the unique appeal of ice fishing. Offering 3,400 surface acres, the reservoir is fully stocked with hungry kokanee salmon, carp, trout, and northern pike. A number of local outfitters, such as 11 Mile Sports, Inc. (phone 877/725-3172) can supply the necessary equipment as well as a guide. (Daily) **$$**

Lakewood

See also Denver, Englewood, Golden

Pop 144,126 **Elev** 5,450 ft **Area code** 303

Information West Chamber Serving Jefferson County, PO Box 280748, 80228-0748; 303/233-5555

This suburban community west of Denver was once dotted with farms and fruit orchards and with the summer houses of wealthy Denver residents.

What to See and Do

Bear Creek Lake Park. *15600 W Morrison Rd (80465). 1/4 mile E of CO 470. Phone 303/697-6159.* Approximately 2,600 acres. Waterskiing school, fishing, boating (10 hp limit, rentals, marina); hiking, bicycle trails, picnicking, camping (no electricity). Archery. View of downtown Denver from Mount Carbon. (Daily; closed Jan 1, Thanksgiving, Dec 25) **$**

Crown Hill Park. *W 26th Ave at Kipling St (CO 391). Phone 303/271-5925.* This 168-acre nature preserve includes Crown Hill Lake and a wildlife pond. Fishing; hiking, bicycle, bridle trails. (Daily) **FREE**

Lakewood's Heritage Center. *797 S Wadsworth Blvd (CO 121), just S of Alameda Blvd (CO 26). Phone 303/987-7850.* Nature, art, and historical exhibits in 127-acre park. Turn-of-the-century farm; one-room schoolhouse; vintage farm machinery; Barn Gallery with permanent and changing exhibits, interpretive displays. Lectures, workshops; visitor center. (Tues-Sun) **$$**

Motels/Motor Lodges

★ **COMFORT INN.** *3440 S Vance St (80227). Phone 303/989-5500; toll-free 800/228-5150; fax 303/989-2981. www.comfortinn.com.* 123 rooms, 4 suites, 2 story. S $70; D $78; each additional $10; suites $110; under 18 free; weekly, weekend rates. Crib free. Pet accepted; $50 refundable. Complimentary continental breakfast, coffee in rooms. Check-out noon. TV; cable (premium). In-room modem link. Some refrigerators. Microwaves available. Valet services, coin laundry. Restaurant opposite open 24 hours. Health club privileges, exercise equipment. Heated pool, whirlpool. Airport transportation. Meeting room. Business services. Cr cds: A, C, D, DS, ER, MC, V.

★ **HAMPTON INN.** *3605 S Wadsworth Blvd (80235). Phone 303/989-6900; toll-free 800/426-7866; fax 303/985-4730. www.hamptoninn.com.* 150 rooms, 4 story. S, D $59; each additional $10-$13; under 18 free. Crib available. Complimentary continental breakfast, coffee in rooms. Check-out noon. TV; cable (premium). In-room modem link. Some refrigerators. Microwaves available. Valet services, coin laundry. Restaurant adjacent 11-1 am. Exercise equipment. Heated pool. Meeting rooms. Business services. Cr cds: A, C, D, DS, ER, JCB, MC, V.

★ ★ **HOLIDAY INN.** *7390 W Hampden Ave (80227). Phone 303/980-9200; toll-free 800/465-4329; fax 303/980-6423. www.holiday-inn.com.* 190 rooms, 6 story. S, D $105; each additional $10; suites $150; under 19 free. Crib free. Pet accepted; $50 deposit. Complimentary coffee in rooms. Check-out noon. TV; cable (premium). In-room modem link. Some refrigerators. Valet services, coin laundry. Restaurant 6-11 am, 5-10 pm. Bar 4 pm-midnight. Room service. Health club privileges, exercise equipment, sauna. Heated pool, whirlpool. Meeting rooms. Business services. Gift shop. Cr cds: A, C, D, DS, JCB, MC, V.

★★ **STONEBRIDGE HOTEL.** *137 Union Blvd (80226). Phone 303/969-9900; fax 303/989-9847.* 170 rooms, 6 story. S $79-$99; D $89-$109; each additional $10; under 18 free; weekend rates. Crib free. Complimentary full breakfast, coffee in rooms. Check-out noon. TV; cable (premium), VCR available. In-room modem link. Some refrigerators. Restaurant 6 am-2 pm, 4:30-10 pm. Bar. Health club privileges, exercise equipment, sauna. Heated pool, whirlpool. Meeting rooms. Business services. Cr cds: A, C, D, DS, ER, JCB, MC, V.

Hotel

★★★ **SHERATON DENVER WEST HOTEL.** *360 Union Blvd (80228). Phone 303/987-2000; toll-free 800/525-3966; fax 303/969-0263. www.sheraton.com.* 242 rooms, 12 story. S, D $140-$175; each additional $15; under 18 free; package plans; weekend rates. Crib free. Check-out 1 pm. TV; cable (premium), VCR available. In-room modem link. Some refrigerators. Coffee in rooms. Valet services. Restaurant 6:30 am-9:30 pm. Bar 11-2 am; Sun to midnight. Exercise room, massage, sauna, steam room. Indoor pool, whirlpool. Barber, beauty shop. Business center. Convention center/facilities. Concierge. Gift shop. Luxury level. Cr cds: A, C, D, DS, JCB, MC, V.

Restaurants

★★★ **240 UNION.** *240 Union (80228). Phone 303/989-3562; fax 303/989-3565. www.240union.com.* Hours: 11 am-10 pm; Fri to 10:30 pm; Sat 5-10:30 pm; Sun 5-9 pm. Closed major holidays. Reservations accepted. Continental menu. Bar. Lunch $9-$12, dinner $9-$24. Children's menu. Specializes in seafood, chicken, lamb. Parking. Outdoor dining. Cr cds: A, C, D, DS, ER, MC, V.

★ **CASA BONITA OF DENVER.** *6715 W Colfax Ave (80214). Phone 303/232-5115; fax 303/232-7801. www.casabonitadenver.com.* Mexican, American menu. Hours: 11 am-9:30 pm; Fri, Sat to 10 pm. Closed Thanksgiving, Dec 25. Lunch $6.49-$8.89, dinner $6.49-$8.89. Entertainment: musicians, divers, gunfights, magician, puppet show, dancing monkeys in costume. Children's menu. Cr cds: A, C, D, DS, ER, MC, V.

★ **DARDANO'S.** *11968 W Jewell Ave (80228). Phone 303/988-1991. www.dardanosrestaurant.com.* American, Italian menu. Italian décor. Hours: 5-9 pm; Fri to 10 pm; Sat 4-10 pm; Sun from 4 pm. Closed Mon; Thanksgiving, Dec 24, 25. Lunch $4-$12, dinner $6-$16. Bar. Children's menu. Reservations accepted. Cr cds: A, D, DS, MC, V.

★★★ **THE FORT.** *19192 CO 8 (80465). Phone 303/697-4771; fax 303/697-9310. www.thefort.com.* In an accurate adobe recreation of the historic Bent's Fort, Sam Arnold's popular, kitschy restaurant, southwest of Denver, has been serving the food of the early West for more than 30 years. Southwestern menu. Hours: 5:30-10 pm; Sat from 5 pm; Sun 4-9 pm. Closed Dec 25. Dinner $16.63-$39.95. Bar. Children's menu. Reservations accepted. Outdoor dining. Multiple dining areas in adobe building patterned after Bent's Fort. Cr cds: A, C, D, DS, ER, MC, V.

★★ **GRADY'S AMERICAN GRILL.** *5140 S Wadsworth Blvd (80123). Phone 303/973-5140; fax 303/973-4129.* Hours: 11 am-10 pm; Fri, Sat to 11 pm; Sun to 10 pm. Closed Thanksgiving, Dec 25. Lunch $6-$10, dinner $12-$22. Bar. Children's menu. Reservations accepted. Outdoor dining. Three dining areas on two levels. Cr cds: A, C, D, DS, ER, MC, V.

Lamar (E-8)

Pop 8,869 **Elev** 3,622 ft **Area code** 719 **Zip** 81052

Information Chamber of Commerce, 109A E Beech St; 719/336-4379

What to See and Do

Big Timbers Museum. *7517 US 50. Phone 719/336-2472.* Named for the giant cottonwoods on the banks of the Arkansas River. Museum with newspapers, art, drawings, artifacts of area history. (Daily, afternoons; closed holidays) **FREE**

Motels/Motor Lodges

★★ **BEST WESTERN COW PALACE INN.** *1301 N Main St (81052). Phone 719/336-7753; toll-free 800/678-0344; fax 719/336-9598. www.bestwestern.com.* 95 rooms, 2 story. June-Aug: S $84-$94; D $89-$99; each additional $5; lower rates rest of year. Crib free. Pet accepted. Complimentary breakfast buffet. Check-out 11 am. TV; cable (premium), VCR available. Refrigerators, microwaves. Coffee in rooms. Restaurant 5 am-10 pm. Bar 11-2 am; Sun to midnight. Room service. Health club privileges. Indoor pool, whirlpool, poolside service. Golf privileges;

greens fee $4, driving range. Barber, beauty shop. Free airport transportation. Meeting rooms. Business services. Gift shop. Cr cds: A, C, D, DS, MC, V.

D 🔌 🍴 🚭 ✈ 🆘 SC

★**BLUE SPRUCE.** *1801 S Main St (81052). Phone 719/336-7454; fax 719/336-4729.* 30 rooms. S $30; D $36-$38; each additional $4. Crib free. Pet accepted. TV; cable (premium). Pool. Complimentary continental breakfast. Restaurant nearby. Check-out 11 am. Free airport, train station, bus depot transportation. Cr cds: A, D, DS, MC, V.

🐾 🏊 🚶 🆘

Leadville (D-4)

See also Buena Vista, Dillon, Vail

Settled 1860 **Pop** 2,821 **Elev** 10,430 ft **Area code** 719 **Zip** 80461

Information Greater Leadville Area Chamber of Commerce, 809 Harrison Ave, PO Box 861; 719/486-3900 or 888/264-5344

Web www.leadvilleusa.com

Located just below the timberline, Leadville's high altitude contributes to its reputation for excellent skiing, cool summers, and beautiful fall colors. First a rich gold camp, then an even richer silver camp, the town boasts a lusty, brawling past in which millionaires were made and destroyed in a single day, a barrel of whiskey could net $1,500, tents pitched on the main street were advertised as "the best hotel in town," and thousands of dollars could be—and were—lost on the turn of a card in the town's iniquitous saloons and smoky gambling halls.

Leadville's lively history is intertwined with the lives of Horace Tabor and his two wives, Augusta and Elizabeth Doe, whose rags-to-riches-to-rags story is the basis of the American opera *The Ballad of Baby Doe.* The famed "unsinkable" Molly Brown made her fortune here, as did David May, Charles Boettcher, Charles Dow, and Meyer Guggenheim.

Until 1950, Leadville was a decaying mining town. However, a burst of civic enthusiasm rejuvenated it in the following years. Today it is filled with attractions that date back to the town's glory days, including several museums and a Victorian downtown area.

A Ranger District office of the San Isabel National Forest (see PUEBLO) is located in Leadville.

What to See and Do

Earth Runs Silver. *809 Harrison Ave. Phone 719/486-3900 or 800/933-9301.* Video presentation featuring Leadville's legendary mining camp with music and narration. (Daily; closed Jan 1, Thanksgiving, Dec 25) **$$**

Healy House-Dexter Cabin. *912 Harrison Ave. Phone 719/486-0487.* The restored Healy House, built in 1878, contains many fine Victorian-era furnishings. Dexter Cabin, built by early mining millionaire James V. Dexter, appears on the outside to be an ordinary two-room miner's cabin; built as a place to entertain wealthy gentlemen, the cabin's interior is surprisingly luxurious. (Memorial Day-Labor Day, daily) **$$**

Heritage Museum and Gallery. *9th St and Harrison Ave. Phone 719/486-1878.* Diorama and displays depict local history; scale-model replica of Ice Palace, Victorian costumes, memorabilia of mining days. Changing exhibits of American art. (Mid-May-Oct, daily) **$$**

Leadville, Colorado & Southern Railroad Train Tour. *326 E 7th St. Phone 719/486-3936.* Departs from old depot for 23-mile round-trip scenic ride following the headwaters of the Arkansas River through the Rocky Mountains. (Memorial Day-Oct, daily) **$$$$**

Leadville National Fish Hatchery. *2844 Hwy 300. 7 miles SW via US 24, CO 300. Phone 719/486-0189.* The original hatchery building constructed in 1889 is still in use. Approximately 45 tons of brook, lake, brown, and cutthroat trout are produced here annually. Hiking and ski-touring trails are nearby. (Daily) **FREE**

The Matchless Mine. *1 1/4 miles E on E 7th St. Phone 719/486-1899.* When H. A. W. Tabor died in 1899, his last words to his wife, Baby Doe, were "Hold on to the Matchless," which had produced as much as $100,000 a month in its bonanza days. Faithful to his wish and ever hopeful, the once fabulously rich Baby Doe lived on in poverty in the little cabin next to the mine for 36 years; in it, she was found frozen to death in 1935. The cabin is now a museum. (June-Labor Day, daily) **$$**

National Mining Hall of Fame and Museum. *120 W 9th St. Phone 719/486-1229.* History and technology exhibits of the mining industry. Hall of Fame dedicated to those who have made significant contributions to the industry. (May-Oct, daily; rest of year, Mon-Fri; closed winter holidays) **$$**

Ski Cooper. *Summit of Tennessee Pass, 10 miles N on US 24. Phone 719/486-3684.* Triple, double chairlift; Pomalift, T-bar; patrol, school, rentals; snowcat tours; cafeteria, nursery. Twenty-six runs; longest run 1 1/2 miles; vertical drop 1,200 feet. (Late Nov-early Apr, daily) Groomed cross-country skiing (15 miles). **$$$$**

⭐**Tabor Opera House.** *308 Harrison Ave. Phone 719/486-8409. (1879)* Now a museum, this theater was elegantly furnished at the time of construction. At the time, Leadville had a population of 30,000. The theater was host to the Metropolitan Opera, the Chicago Symphony, and most of the famous actors and actresses of the period. Their pictures line the corridors. Many of the original furnishings, much of the scenery, and the dressing areas are still in use and on display. The Tabor box, where many dignitaries were Tabor's guests, is part of the theater tour. Summer shows (inquire locally). Self-guided tours (Memorial Day-Sept, daily) **$$**

Special Events

Boom Days & Burro Race. First full weekend in Aug.

Crystal Carnival. First weekend in Mar.

Victorian Christmas & Home Tour. First Sat in Dec.

Motel/Motor Lodge

★ **SUPER 8 MOTEL.** *1128 S Hwy 24 (80461). Phone 719/486-3637; toll-free 800/261-3637. www.super8.com.* 58 rooms, 3 story. No A/C. No elevator. Complimentary continental breakfast. Check-out 10 am, check-in 2 pm. TV; cable (premium). In-room modem link. Sauna. Game room. Cr cds: A, C, D, DS, MC, V. **$**

Hotel

★ ★ **DELAWARE HOTEL.** *700 Harrison Ave (80461). Phone 719/486-1418; toll-free 800/748-2004; fax 719/486-2214. www.delawarehotel.com.* 36 rooms, 4 suites, 3 story. No elevator, A/C. Complimentary continental breakfast. Check-out 11 am, check-in 2 pm. TV; cable (premium). Restaurant. Whirlpool. Historic hotel (1886); Victorian lobby. Cr cds: A, DS, MC, V. **$**

B&B/Small Inn

★ ★ **ICE PALACE INN BED & BREAKFAST.** *813 Spruce St (80461). Phone 719/486-8272; toll-free 800/ 754-2840; fax 719/486-0345. www.icepalaceinn.com.* 5 air-cooled rooms, 2 story. No room phones. Pet accepted. Complimentary full breakfast. Check-out 11 am, check-in 4 pm. TV; VCR (movies). Fireplaces. Whirlpool. Built in 1879. Totally nonsmoking. Cr cds: A, C, D, DS, MC, V. **$**

Restaurant

★ **HIGH COUNTRY.** *115 Harrison Ave (80461). Phone 719/486-3992.* American menu. Closed some major holidays. Lunch, dinner. Bar. Children's menu. Casual attire. Outdoor seating. Three dining areas. Mounted wildlife. Cr cds: C, MC, V. **$**

Limon (D-7)

Pop 2,071 **Elev** 5,365 ft **Area code** 719 **Zip** 80828

Motels/Motor Lodges

★ **BEST WESTERN LIMON INN.** *925 T Ave (80828). Phone 719/775-0277; fax 719/775-2921. www.bestwestern.com.* 47 rooms, 2 story. S $50-$65; D $65-$75; each additional $5; under 12 free; family rates. Pet accepted; fee. Complimentary continental breakfast, coffee in lobby. Check-out 11 am. TV; cable (premium). In-room modem link. Indoor pool. Cr cds: A, C, D, DS, MC, V.

★ **PREFERRED MOTOR INN.** *158 E Main (80828). Phone 719/775-2385; fax 719/775-2901.* 57 rooms. S $28-$38; D $46-$62; each additional $4; suites $65-$100. Crib $4. Pet accepted; $4. Check-out 10 am. TV; cable (premium). Balconies. Restaurant nearby. Indoor pool, whirlpool. Free airport transportation. Meeting rooms. Cr cds: A, D, DS, MC, V.

★ **SAFARI MOTEL.** *637 Main St (80828). Phone 719/ 775-2363; toll-free 800/330-7021; fax 719/775-2316.* 28 rooms, 1-2 story. June-Sept: S, D $40-$67; each additional $4; suites $70; lower rates rest of year. Pet accepted; $5. Complimentary coffee in rooms. Check-out 10 am. TV; cable (premium). In-room modem link. Private patios. Coin laundry. Restaurant opposite. Playground. Pool. Cr cds: A, D, DS, MC, V.

B&B/Small Inn

★ ★ **MIDWEST COUNTRY INN.** *795 Main St (80828). Phone 719/775-2373; toll-free 888/610-6683; fax 719/775-8808.* 32 rooms, 2 story. D $58; each additional $4. Check-out 10 am, check-in anytime. TV; cable. Restaurant nearby. Coffee in lobby. Cr cds: A, D, DS, MC, V.

Restaurant

★ **FIRESIDE JUNCTION.** *2295 9th St (80828). Phone 719/775-2396; fax 719/775-2398.* American, Mexican menu. Specializes in chicken-fried steak. Hours: 6 am-10 pm. Closed Dec 24-25. Breakfast $3-$9.99, dinner $6.39-$29.99. Bar. Salad bar. Children's menu. Reservations accepted. Cr cds: A, DS, MC, V.

Longmont (B-6)

See also Boulder, Denver, Loveland, Lyons

Founded 1870 **Pop** 71,093 **Elev** 4,979 ft **Area code** 303

Information Chamber of Commerce, 528 Main St, 80501; 303/776-5295

Web www.longmontchamber.org

What to See and Do

Longmont Museum. *400 Quail Rd. Phone 303/651-8374.* Changing and special exhibits on art, history, space, and science; permanent exhibits on the history of Longmont and the St. Vrain Valley. (Tues-Sat, Sun afternoons) **FREE**

Special Events

Boulder County Fair and Rodeo. *Fairgrounds. Phone 303/ 441-3927; 303/772-7170.* Nine days in early Aug.

Rhythm on the River. *St. Vrain Greenway, Roger's Grove. Phone 303/776-6050.* Sept.

Hotel

★★**RAINTREE PLAZA HOTEL.** *1900 Ken Pratt Blvd (80501). Phone 303/776-2000; toll-free 800/843-8240; fax 303/678-7361. www.raintreeplaza.com.* 211 rooms, 2 story. S, D $129-$145; each additional $10; suites $225-$275; under 18 free. Crib free. Pet accepted; $50 (nonrefundable). Complimentary continental breakfast. Check-out noon. TV; cable (premium). In-room modem link. Refrigerators. Coffee in rooms. Valet services, free laundry facilities. Restaurant 6 am-2 pm, 5-10 pm; Sat 6 am-1 pm, 5-10 pm. Bar. Room service. Exercise equipment, sauna, steam room. Heated pool. Valet parking. Airport transportation. Meeting rooms. Business services. Cr cds: A, C, D, DS, ER, JCB, MC, V.

D ⬚ ⬚ ⬚ ⬚ ⬚

Loveland (B-6)

See also Estes Park, Fort Collins, Greeley, Longmont, Lyons

Founded 1877 **Pop** 50,608 **Elev** 4,982 ft **Area code** 970

Information Visitor Center/Chamber of Commerce, 5400 Stone Creek Circle, 80538; 970/667-5728 or 800/258-1278

Web www.loveland.org

In recent years, more than 300,000 valentines have been remailed annually by the Loveland post office, stamped in red with the "Sweetheart Town's" cachet, a different valentine verse each year.

What to See and Do

Boyd Lake State Park. *3720 N Country Rd (80538). 1 mile E on US 34, then 2 miles N. Phone 970/669-1739.* Swimming, waterskiing, fishing, boating (ramps, rentals); picnicking (shelters, showers), camping (dump station). Standard fees. (Daily) **$$$**

Special Events

Dog racing. *Cloverleaf Kennel Club. 2577 NW Frontage Rd (80538). 4 miles E at junction US 34, I-25. Phone 970/667-6211.* Races nightly. Matinees Mon, Wed, Sat, and Sun. Pari-mutuel betting. No minors. Mar-June.

Larimer County Fair and Rodeo. *700 S Railroad Ave (80537).* Mid-Aug.

B&B/Small Inn

★★★**CATTAIL CREEK INN BED & BREAKFAST.** *2665 Abarr Dr (80538). Phone 970/667-7600; toll-free 800/ 572-2466; fax 970/667-8968. www.cattailcreekinn.com.* Located on the Cattail Creek Golf Course, this luxury inn offers views of Lake Loveland and the Rocky Mountains. The open guest rooms have cherry woodwork and ceiling fans. Delicious breakfasts include dishes like Belgian pecan waffles with sautéed peaches. 8 rooms, 2 story. S, D $105-$170; each additional $10; golf plans; package plans. Children over 14 years only. Complimentary full breakfast. Check-out 11 am, check-in 4-9 pm. TV; cable (premium). Balconies. 27-hole golf privileges. Totally nonsmoking. Cr cds: A, DS, MC, V.

D ⬚ ⬚

Guest Ranch

★★★**SYLVAN DALE GUEST RANCH.** *2939 N County Rd 31 D (80538). Phone 970/667-3915; toll-free 877/667-3999; fax 970/635-9336. www.sylvandale.com.* Owned and operated by the Jessup family, this dude ranch was established in the 1920s and is proud to still be a working cattle and horse ranch. Located in a river valley at the mouth of Colorado's Big Thompson Canyon, the ranch has over 3,000 acres to enjoy, with elevations ranging from 5,325 feet to 7,500 feet at "Cow Camp." 23 rooms, 1-2 story. No A/C in cabins. Mid-June-early Sept: AP $89-$389; lower rates rest of year. Complimentary full breakfast. Check-out 11 am, check-in 3 pm. Some fireplaces. Dining room (public by reservation). Free supervised children's activities (mid-June-Labor Day). Cookouts, breakfast rides, overnight packtrips. Heated pool. Tennis. Lawn games. Entertainment, square dancing. Hayrides, hiking, horses/riding. Free airport transportation. Business center. Working ranch on 3,000 acres bordered by Roosevelt National Forest. Totally nonsmoking. Cr cds: C.

Restaurant

★ **CACTUS GRILL NORTH.** *281-A E 29th St (80538). Phone 970/663-1550.* American menu. Hours: 11 am-10 pm; Sun-Tues to 9 pm. Closed Dec 25. Dinner $5-$17. Bar. Children's menu. Reservations accepted. Outdoor seating. Cr cds: A, D, DS, MC, V.

Lyons (B-5)

See also Boulder, Estes Park, Longmont, Loveland

Pop 1,585 **Elev** 5,360 ft **Area code** 303 **Zip** 80540

Information Chamber of Commerce, PO Box 426; 303/823-5215. The Visitors Center at 4th and Broadway is staffed Memorial Day-Labor Day, daily; phone 303/823-6640

Special Event

Good Old Days Celebration. *350 Broadway Ave. Phone 303/823-5215.* Midway, parade, flea market, craft fair, food. Last weekend in June.

Guest Ranch

★ ★ **PEACEFUL VALLEY RANCH.** *475 Peaceful Valley Rd (80540). Phone 303/747-2881; toll-free 800/955-6343; fax 303/747-2167. www.peacefulvalley.com.* 42 rooms in 3 lodges, 10 cabins. No A/C. Many room phones. AP, Memorial Day-Labor Day: S $1,300-$1,560; D $1,210-$1,460/person/week; family rates; lower rates rest of year. Check-out 10 am, check-in 2-4 pm. TV in lounge. Some fireplaces. Coin laundry. Dining room (public by reservation) 8-9 am, noon, 6 pm. Supervised children's activities (Memorial Day-Labor Day); ages 3-18. Playground. Social director; entertainment, square dancing (summer), campfires. Picnics, barbecues. Recreation room. Sauna. Indoor pool, wading pool, whirlpool. Downhill, cross-country ski 1/2 mile. Mountain biking. Backcountry tours; overnight pack trips. Petting zoo. Sleigh rides, snowmobiling, snowshoeing. Denver airport transportation. Meeting rooms.

Business center. Gift shop. Varied social program. Mountain setting on 300 acres. Cr cds: A, D, DS, MC, V.

Restaurants

★ **ANDREA'S GERMAN CUISINE.** *216 E Main St (80540). Phone 303/823-5000; fax 303/823-0860.* Hours: 8 am-9 pm. Closed Wed; Dec 25. Reservations accepted. German menu. Bar. Breakfast $2.95-$7.95, lunch $4.95-$12.95, dinner $6.95-$18.95. Specializes in pepper steak, sauerbraten. Bavarian folk music Fri, Sat. Bavarian décor. Cr cds: A, C, D, DS, ER, MC, V.

★ ★ ★ **BLACK BEAR INN.** *42 E Main St (80540). Phone 303/823-6812; fax 303/823-5953. www.blackbearinn.com.* Since 1977, owners Hand and Annalies Wyppler have welcomed guests to their cozy Alpine-style restaurant just outside of Lyons. Continental menu. Hours: 11 am-2:30 pm, 5:30-10 pm; Sat from 5:30 pm, Sun noon-9 pm. Closed Mon, Tues; also Jan-mid-Feb. Dinner $23-$63. Bar. Outdoor seating. Cr cds: A, C, D, DS, ER, MC, V.

★ ★ **LA CHAUMIERE.** *CO 36 (80540). Phone 303/823-6521.* Hours: 5:30-10 pm; Sun 2-9 pm. Closed Mon. Reservations accepted. Continental menu. Service bar. A la carte entrees: dinner $12.50-$23.50. Complete meals: $17. Children's menu. Specializes in sweetbreads, wild game, seafood. Own ice cream. Fireplace. European-style atmosphere. View of mountains. Cr cds: A, C, MC, V.

Manitou Springs (D-6)

See also Colorado Springs

Founded 1872 **Pop** 4,980 **Elev** 6,320 ft **Area code** 719 **Zip** 80829

Information Chamber of Commerce, 354 Manitou Ave; 719/685-5089 or 800/642-2567

Web www.manitousprings.org

Manitou Springs's many mineral springs, familiar to the Native Americans, gave nearby Colorado Springs its name. The natives, attributing supernatural powers to the waters (Manitou is a Native American word for "Great Spirit"), once marked off the surrounding area as a sanctuary. Today, the town is a National Historic District and a popular tourist resort.

What to See and Do

Cave of the Winds. *W US 24. From Manitou Ave and US 24, go 6 miles W on US 24 to Cave of the Winds Rd; turn right and continue 1/2 mile to visitor center. Phone 719/685-5444.* Fascinating 45-minute guided tour through underground passageways filled with beautiful stalactites, stalagmites, and flowstone formations created millions of years ago. Tours leave every 15 minutes (daily). Light jacket and comfortable shoes recommended. Laser light show in canyon (May-Sept, Fri, Sat evenings; rest of year, daily) is 15 stories high and is accompanied by music. (May-Sept, daily) **$$$$**

Florissant Fossil Beds National Monument. *22 miles W of Manitou Springs on US 24.* Florissant Fossil Beds National Monument consists of 6,000 acres once partially covered by a prehistoric lake. Thirty-five million years ago, ash and mud flows from volcanoes in the area buried a forest of redwoods, filling the lake and fossilizing its living organisms. Insects, seeds, and leaves of the Eocene Epoch are preserved in perfect detail, as well as remarkable samples of standing petrified sequoia stumps. On the grounds are nature trails, picnic areas, and a restored 19th-century homestead. Guided tours are available. The visitor center is 2 miles south on Teller County Road 1 (daily; closed January 1, Thanksgiving, December 25). Contact the Superintendent, PO Box 185, Florissant 80816; phone 719/748-3253. **$$**

Iron Springs Chateau. *444 Ruxton Ave. Phone 719/685-5104.* Melodrama dinner theater featuring a traditional "olio" show. Named for the mineral-rich water beneath the ground. (Mon-Sat) **$$$$**

Manitou Cliff Dwellings Museum. *W on US 24. Phone 719/685-5242.* Outdoor southwestern Native American preserve; architecture of the cliff-dwelling natives, A.D. 1100-1300. Native American dancing (June-Aug). Museum (Mar-Nov, daily). **$$$**

Miramont Castle Museum. *9 Capitol Hill Ave. Phone 719/685-1011.* (circa 1895) A 46-room, four-story Victorian house featuring nine styles of architecture, miniatures and doll collection, tea room, soda fountain, gardens. (Tues-Sun; closed Easter, Thanksgiving, Dec 25) **$$**

Pikes Peak Cog Railway. *515 Ruxton Ave (80829). Phone 719/685-5401.* (See COLORADO SPRINGS)

Motels/Motor Lodges

★ **BEST VALUE INN VILLA MOTEL.** *481 Manitou Ave (80829). Phone 719/685-5492; fax 719/685-4143. www.villamotel.com.* 47 rooms, 7 kitchen units, 2 story. Memorial Day-Labor Day: S $46-$89; D $55-$89; kitchens $98-$103; lower rates rest of year. Crib free. Complimentary coffee in lobby. Check-out 11 am. TV; cable (premium). Coin laundry. Restaurant opposite 7 am-10 pm. Heated pool, whirlpool. Picnic tables. Cr cds: A, C, D, DS, MC, V.

★ **REDWING MOTEL.** *56 El Paso Blvd (80829). Phone 719/685-5656; toll-free 800/733-9547; fax 719/685-9547. www.pikes-peak.com/redwing.* 27 rooms, 11 kitchen units, 2 story. S $30-$49; D $38-$64; kitchen units $10 additional. Crib free. Pet accepted. Complimentary coffee in rooms. Check-out 10 am. TV; cable. Some refrigerators. Microwaves available. Restaurant nearby. Playground. Heated pool. Cr cds: A, DS, MC, V.

★ **SILVER SADDLE MOTEL.** *215 Manitou Ave (80829). Phone 719/685-5611; toll-free 800/772-3353. www.silver-saddle.com.* 54 rooms, 1-2 story. Mid-May-mid-Sept: S $69-$79; D $79-$84; under 18 free; each additional $6; suites $99.50-$129.50; lower rates rest of year. Crib free. TV; cable (premium), VCR available. Pool; whirlpool. Complimentary coffee. Restaurant nearby. Check-out 10:30 am. Some in-room whirlpools. Cr cds: A, C, D, DS, MC, V.

B&B/Small Inns

★★ **BLACK BEAR INN OF PIKES PEAK.** *5250 Pikes Peak Hwy (80809). Phone 719/684-0151; toll-free 877/732-5232. www.blackbearinnpikespeak.com.* 9 rooms, shower only, 2 story. S $70; D $85; each additional $10. Children over 10 years only. Complimentary full breakfast. Check-out 10:30 am, check-in 4-6 pm. TV; cable. Restaurant opposite 5:30-9 pm. Whirlpool. Cross-country ski 8 miles. View of mountains. Totally nonsmoking. Cr cds: DS, JCB, MC, V.

★★ **EASTHOLME IN THE ROCKIES.** *4445 Haggerman Ave (80809). Phone 719/684-9901; toll-free 800/672-9901. www.eastholme.com.* 6 rooms, 3 with shower only, 1 share bath, 3 story, 2 cottages. No A/C. No room phones. S $75; D $99; each additional $15; cottage $135. Complimentary full breakfast. Check-out 11 am, check-in 4 pm. Restaurant nearby. Originally a hotel built in 1885. Totally nonsmoking. Cr cds: A, DS, MC, V.

★★★ **RED CRAGS BED & BREAKFAST INN.** *302 El Paso Blvd (80829). Phone 719/685-1920; toll-free 800/721-2248; fax 719/685-1073. www.redcrags.com.* 8 air-cooled rooms, 4 story. S, D $85-$185; each additional $20. Children over 10 years only. Complimentary full breakfast. Check-out 11 am, check-in 4-6 pm. Fireplaces. Restaurant nearby. Mansion (1870) originally built as a clinic. On bluff with view of Pikes Peak, Garden of the Gods. Totally nonsmoking. Cr cds: A, DS, MC, V.

▨

Restaurants

★ ★ ★ **BRIARHURST MANOR.** *404 Manitou Ave (80829). Phone 719/685-1864; fax 719/685-9638. www.briarhurst.com.* Located in a Tudor manor house built in 1876 by the founder of Manitou Springs, William Bell, this elegant fine-dining restaurant has been under the control of chef/owner Sigi Krauss since 1975. Continental menu. Dinner. Bar. Children's menu. Homegrown fresh vegetables and herbs. Outdoor dining. Cr cds: A, MC, V. **$$$**

D SC

★ ★ ★ **CRAFTWOOD INN.** *404 El Paso Blvd (80829). Phone 719/685-9000; fax 719/685-9088. www.craftwood.com.* This romantic restaurant is located in a Tudor manor house dating from 1912. Closed Jan 1, Dec 25. Dinner. Bar. Built in 1912 on 1 1/2 acres of landscaped gardens; view of Pikes Peak. Outdoor dining. Totally nonsmoking. Cr cds: A, D, DS, MC, V. **$$$**

D ▨

★ ★ **MISSION BELL INN.** *178 Crystal Park Rd (80829). Phone 719/685-9089; fax 719/685-9317. www.missionbellinn.com.* Mexican menu. Closed Jan 1, Thanksgiving, Dec 25; also Mon Oct-May. Dinner. Service bar. Outdoor dining. Cr cds: MC, V. **$$**

D

★ ★ **STAGE COACH.** *702 Manitou Ave (80829). Phone 719/685-9400; fax 719/685-1216. www.stagecoachinn.com.* Steak menu. Closed Jan 1, Dec 25. Dinner. Bar. Children's menu. Historic log stage stop built 1881. Outdoor dining. Cr cds: A, DS, MC, V. **$$**

D ▨ SC

Mesa Verde National Park (G-2)

See also Cortez, Durango

(8 miles E of Cortez, 36 miles W of Durango, on US 160 to park entrance, then 15 miles S to visitor center)

In the far southwest corner of Colorado exists the largest—and arguably the most fascinating—archaeological preserve in the nation. Mesa Verde National Park, with 52,000 acres encompassing 4,000 known archaeological sites, is a treasure trove of ancestral Pueblo cultural artifacts, including the magnificent, mysterious Anasazi cliff dwellings. Constructed in the 13th century, these huge, elaborate stone villages built into the canyon walls are spellbinding. To fully appreciate their significance, first take a walk through the park's Chapin Mesa Museum for a historical overview. A visit to the actual sites can be physically challenging but is well worth the effort. Several of the sites can be explored year-round, free of charge; others require tickets for ranger-guided tours in summer months only. Tour tickets can be purchased at the park's Far View Visitor Center. (Daily) **$$**

What to See and Do

Cliff Dwelling Tours. *Administration Building 15 (81330). Phone 970/529-4461.* The cliff dwellings can be entered *only* while rangers are on duty. During the summer, five cliff dwellings may be visited at specific hours; during the winter there are trips to Spruce Tree House only, weather permitting. Obtain daily tickets for Cliff Palace, Balcony House, and Long House tours at Far View Visitor Center. Balcony House tours are limited to 50 persons; Cliff Palace tours are limited to the first 60; and Long House tours are limited to 40 persons. The cliff dwellings that are open to the public are

Balcony House. *On Cliff Palace Loop Rd, 25-minute drive from visitor center. Phone 970/529-4461.* Noted for ladder and tunnel features; accessible only by 32-foot-long ladder. Ranger-guided mid-May to mid-Oct.

Cliff Palace. *On Cliff Palace Loop Rd, 20-minute drive from visitor center. Phone 970/529-4461.* First major dwelling to be discovered (1888). More than 200 living rooms, 23 kivas, numerous storage rooms. Guided tours in summer, fall, and spring; closed winter.

Long and Step Houses and Badger House Community. *On Wetherill Mesa, 12 miles from visitor center. Phone 970/529-4461.* Ranger-conducted (Long) and self-guided (Step) trips (Memorial Day-Labor Day) inquire at visitor center or museum for details.

Spruce Tree House. *In canyon behind museum. Phone 970/529-4461.* Best preserved in Mesa Verde; contains 114 living rooms and eight ceremonial rooms, called kivas. Self-guided tour to site in summer; ranger-guided rest of year.

⭐ **Far View Visitor Center.** *15 miles S of park entrance. Phone 970/529-4461.* All visitors are recommended to stop at center first. (May-Sept, daily)

Mesa Top Loop and Cliff Palace Loop. *Enter at crossroads near museum.* Two 6-mile, self-guided loops afford visits to ten excavated mesa-top sites illustrating 700 years of architectural development; views of 20 to 30 cliff dwellings from canyon rim vantage points. (Daily; closed during heavy snowfalls)

Museum. *Park headquarters, 21 miles S of park entrance. Phone 970/529-4461.* Exhibits tell story of Mesa Verde people: their arts, crafts, industries. (Daily)

Park Point Fire Lookout. *Halfway between park entrance and headquarters. Phone 970/529-4461.* Elevation, 8,572 feet. Spectacular views of entire Four Corners area of Colorado, Arizona, New Mexico, and Utah. Access road closed in winter.

Picnic areas. *Phone 970/529-4461.* One at headquarters and one on each loop of Mesa Top Loop Rd.

Motel/Motor Lodge

★ ★ **FAR VIEW LODGE IN MESA VERDE.** *Navajo Hill, Mile 15 (81328). Phone 970/529-4421; fax 970/533-7831.* 150 rooms, 1-2 story. No A/C. No room phones. Late Apr-late Oct: S, D $83-$103; each additional $8; under 12 free. Closed rest of year. Pet accepted, some restrictions. Check-out 11 am. Restaurant 6:30 am-9 pm, dining room 5-9:30 pm. Bar 4-11 pm. Room service 24 hours. Hiking trails. Mesa Verde tours available. General store, take-out service, coin showers. Educational programs. Camping sites, trailer facilities. View of canyon. Totally nonsmoking. Cr cds: A, D, DS, JCB, MC, V.

D 🔜 🔄 SC

Monte Vista (F-4)

See also Alamosa

Pop 4,529 **Elev** 7,663 ft **Area code** 719 **Zip** 81144

Information Chamber of Commerce, 1035 Park Ave; 719/852-2731 or 800/562-7085

Web www.monte-vista.org

Located in the heart of the high-altitude San Luis Valley, Monte Vista means "mountain view" in Spanish.

What to See and Do

Historical Society Headquarters. *110 Jefferson St.* In 1875 library; information about history of Monte Vista. (Apr-Dec, Mon-Fri afternoons) **FREE**

Monte Vista National Wildlife Refuge. *9383 El Rancho Ln. 6 miles S via CO 15. Phone 719/589-4021.* Created as a nesting, migration, and wintering habitat for waterfowl and other migratory birds. Marked visitor tour road. **FREE**

Special Events

Monte Vista Crane Festival. *Ski-Hi Park. 2345 Sherman Ave (81144). Phone 719/852-3552 or 719/852-2692.* Tours of refuge to view cranes and other wildlife. Arts, crafts, workshops. Mid-Mar.

San Luis Valley Fair. *Ski-Hi Park. 2345 Sherman Ave (81144). Phone 719/589-2271 or 719/852-2692.* Mid-Aug.

Ski-Hi Stampede. *Ski-Hi Park. 835 1st Ave (81144). Phone 719/852-2055.* Rodeo, carnival, arts and crafts show, street parade, barbecue, Western dances. Last weekend in July.

Motels/Motor Lodges

★ ★ **BEST WESTERN MOVIE MANOR.** *2830 W US 160 (81144). Phone 719/852-5921; toll-free 800/771-9468; fax 719/852-0122. www.bestwestern.com.* 60 rooms, 2 story. Pet accepted. Check-out 11 am, check-in noon. TV; cable (premium). Restaurant, bar. Drive-in movies visible from rooms; speakers in most rooms. Cr cds: A, C, D, DS, MC, V. **$**

D 🔜 🐾 🏊

★ **COMFORT INN MONTE VISTA.** *1519 Grand Ave (81144). Phone 719/852-0612; fax 719/852-3585. www.comfortinn.com.* 44 rooms, 2 story. Pet accepted. Complimentary continental breakfast. Check-out 11 am, check-in noon. TV; cable (premium). In-room modem link. Indoor pool, whirlpool. Cr cds: A, C, D, DS, JCB, MC, V. **$**

D 🔜 🐾 🏊

Montrose (E-2)

See also Delta, Ouray

Founded 1882 **Pop** 12,344 **Elev** 5,806 ft **Area code** 970 **Zip** 81401

Information Chamber of Commerce, 1519 E Main St; 970/249-5000 or 800/923-5515

Web www.montrosechamber.com

Montrose is a trading center for a rich mining, agricultural, and recreational area in the Uncompahgre Valley, irrigated by diversion of the waters of the Gunnison River to the Uncompahgre. It is headquarters for the operation and maintenance of all generating and transmission facilities of the Colorado River Storage Project stemming from the Power Operations Center. Several fishing areas are nearby, including the Gunnison River east of town and Buckhorn Lakes southeast. A Ranger District office of the Uncompahgre National Forest (see NORWOOD) is located in Montrose.

What to See and Do

Black Canyon of the Gunnison National Monument. (see) *15 miles NE of Montrose via US 50, CO 347.* **$$$**

Montrose County Historical Museum. *Depot Building. 21 N Rio Grande (81402). Phone 970/249-2085.* Collections of antique farm machinery; archaeological artifacts; pioneer cabin with family items; tool collection; early electrical equipment; Montrose newspapers 1896-1940. (May-Sept, daily) **$**

Ridgway State Park. *28555 US 550 (81432). 20 miles S on US 550. Phone 970/626-5822.* This 2,320-acre park includes four recreational areas and a reservoir. Swimming, waterskiing, scuba diving, sailing, sailboarding, boating (marina); hiking, bicycling, cross-country skiing, sledding, picnicking, playground, improved camping, laundry, concession. Standard fees. (Daily) **$$**

Scenic Drive. Owl Creek Pass. Drive 23 miles S on US 550 to the left-hand turnoff for Owl Creek Pass, marked by a US Forest Service sign, then E 7 miles along Cow Creek to Debbie's Park. In this meadow, Debbie Reynolds was filmed in the wild west breakfast scene in *How the West Was Won.* The next 8 miles, climb to the crest of Owl Creek Pass at 10,114 feet. Fifteen miles from the pass is **Silver Jack Reservoir,** an area with good fishing and scenic hiking trails. About 20 miles N, the road joins US 50 at Cimarron. The road is not recommended for large trucks or RVs and may be impassable in inclement weather.

Ute Indian Museum and Ouray Memorial Park. *17253 Chipeta Dr, 3 miles S on US 550. Phone 970/249-3098.* On home grounds of Chief Ouray and his wife, Chipeta. History of the Utes in artifacts and objects of 19th- and early 20th-century Ute craftsmanship, clothing, dioramas, photographs. Self-guided tours. (Daily; Nov-May, Mon-Sat) **$$**

Motels/Motor Lodges

★ **BEST WESTERN RED ARROW.** *1702 E Main St (81402). Phone 970/249-9641; toll-free 800/468-9323; fax 970/249-8380. www.bestwestern.com/redarrow.* 62 rooms, 2 story. May-Oct: S, D $89-$109; suites $109-$125; children free; lower rates rest of year. Pet accepted; fee. Check-out 11 am. TV; cable (premium), VCR available. In-room modem link. Restaurant. Exercise equipment. Pool; whirlpool. Lawn games. Free airport transportation. Business center. Concierge. Cr cds: A, C, D, DS, MC, V.

★ **BLACK CANYON.** *1605 E Main St (81401). Phone 970/249-3495; toll-free 800/348-3495; fax 970/249-0990. www.toski.com/black-canyon.com.* 49 rooms, 1-2 story. Pet accepted. Check-out 11 am, check-in. TV; cable (premium). Outdoor pool. Cr cds: A, C, D, DS, MC, V. **$**

★ **COUNTRY LODGE.** *1624 E Main St (81401). Phone 970/249-4567; fax 970/249-3082. www.countrylodge.com.* 23

rooms, 1 cabins. Check-out 11 am, check-in 1 pm. TV; cable. Outdoor pool, whirlpool. Cr cds: A, C, D, DS, MC, V. **$**

★ **SAN JUAN INN.** *1480 S Townsend (81401). Phone 970/249-6644; toll-free 888/681-4159; fax 970/249-9314. www.sanjuaninn.com.* 51 rooms, 2 story. Pet accepted. Complimentary continental breakfast. Check-out 11 am, check-in 2 pm. TV; cable (premium). Indoor pool, whirlpool. Free airport transportation. Cr cds: A, C, D, DS, MC, V. **$**

Restaurants

★ ★ **GLENN EYRIE RESTAURANT.** *2351 S Townsend Ave (81401). Phone 970/249-9263; fax 970/240-6002.* American menu. Closed 5-9 pm; Closed Sun, Mon; Jan 1, July 4, Dec 25. Lunch, dinner. Bar. Children's menu. Casual attire. Non-smoking seating. Cr cds: A, DS, MC, V. **$$**

★ **WHOLE ENCHILADA.** *44 S Grand Ave (81401). Phone 970/249-1881.* Mexican menu. Closed Sun. Lunch, dinner. Bar. Casual attire. Outdoor seating. Cr cds: A, DS, MC, V. **$**

Morrison

What to See and Do

Red Rocks Park and Amphitheater. *Phone 303/640-2637.* Red Rocks Amphitheater is located in the majestic 816-acre Red Rocks Park, 15 miles west of Denver. Once the playground of dinosaurs, the naturally created open-air arena is formed by two 300-foot sandstone monoliths that serve as stadium walls. During the summer months, the 8,000-seat amphitheater, with its perfect acoustical conditions, awe-inspiring beauty, and panoramic view of Denver, serves as a stunning stage for performers ranging from chart-topping rock bands to world-renowned symphony orchestras. Call for schedules and to reserve tickets. Performance price varies. **FREE**

Norwood (F-2)

See also Telluride

Pop 438 **Elev** 7,006 ft **Area code** 970 **Zip** 81423

Near the edge of the Uncompahgre National Forest, this ranching community sits atop Wright's Mesa. This mesa and surrounding national forests contain a wide variety of wildlife that makes this one of the most popular hunting areas in Colorado.

What to See and Do

Miramonte Lake. *USFS Rd 610. 18 miles SW.* Fishing, boating, windsurfing. Fishing also in San Miguel River, Gurley Lake, Ground Hog Reservoir, and nearby streams and mountain lakes. Inquire locally for information, permits.

Uncompahgre National Forest. *N, E and S of town. Contact the Forest Service, 1150 Forest St, PO Box 388. Phone 970/327-4261.* More than 940,000 acres of alpine forest ranging in elevation from 7,500 to 14,000 feet, with many peaks higher than 13,000 feet. Fishing; hunting, hiking, picnicking, camping (fee at some campgrounds). Four-wheel drive areas. Snowmobiling, cross-country skiing. Within the forest are Big Blue and Mount Sneffles wilderness areas and portions of Lizard Head Wilderness Area. Also within the forest is a portion of the San Juan Skyway.

Special Event

San Miguel Basin Fair and Rodeo. *Fairgrounds. 1120 Summit. Phone 970/327-4393.* Fair and rodeo. Last full weekend in July.

Ouray (F-2)

See also Montrose, Silverton

Settled 1876 **Pop** 813 **Elev** 7,811 ft **Area code** 970 **Zip** 81427

Information Ouray Chamber Resort Assn, PO Box 145; 970/325-4746 or 800/228-1876

Web www.ouraycolorado.com

The average 19th-century traveler found the gold and silver mines around Ouray of greater interest than the town's setting. In the 20th century, with the mining boom days over, Ouray's location in a natural basin surrounded by majestic 12,000- to 14,000-foot peaks of the San Juan Mountains has finally gained the appreciation of the visitor. Ouray, named for a Ute chief, is reached by the magnificent Million Dollar Highway section of the San Juan Skyway, which was blasted from sheer cliff walls high above the Uncompahgre River.

What to See and Do

Bachelor-Syracuse Mine Tour. *1222 County Rd 14 (81427). 1 mile N via US 550, Dexter Creek Rd exit. Phone 970/325-0220.* Mine in continuous operation since 1884. Guided tour aboard a mine train, advances 3,350 feet horizontally into Gold Hill (mine temperature 47°F). Within the mine, visitors see mining equipment, visit work areas, and learn how explosives are used. Gold panning. Outdoor cafe. (Late May-Sept, daily; closed July 4)

Bear Creek Falls. *1230 Main, Box 145 (81427). 3 miles S on US 550. Phone 970/325-4746.* Road crosses bridge over 227-foot falls; an observation point is nearby.

Box Cañon Falls Park. *1/2 mile S on US 550. Phone 970/325-4464.* Canyon Creek has cut a natural canyon 20 feet wide, 400 feet deep. View of thundering falls from floor of canyon is reached by stairs and suspended bridge. Picnic tables are available in beautiful settings. Children must be accompanied by an adult. (Daily)

Fishing. In lakes and streams. **Hunting, riding, biking, hiking** in surrounding mountains. **Ski** course with rope tow at edge of town; designed for children and beginners (free).

Hot Springs Pool. *1200 Main. (81427). Ouray City Park, US 550 N. Phone 970/325-4638.* Outdoor, million-gallon pool fed by natural mineral hot springs; sulphur-free. Bathhouse; spa. (Daily) **$$**

Jeep trips. *710 Main. (81427). Phone 970/325-4746.* Guides take visitors to ghost towns, mountain passes, and mines, many above the timberline; some full-day trips. (Mid-May-mid-Oct, daily) Also Jeep rentals. **$$$$**

Ouray County Historical Museum. *420 6th Ave. Phone 970/325-4576.* Former hospital constructed in 1887 now houses artifacts; mining, ranching, and Ute relics. (Daily) **$$**

Special Events

Artists' Alpine Holiday & Festival. *476 Main St (81427). Phone 970/626-3611.* National exhibit, competition in all media. One week in mid-Aug.

Imogene Pass Mountain Marathon. *100 5th St (81427). Phone 970/255-1002.* The 18-mile course starts at Ouray's 7,800-foot elevation, crosses over Imogene Pass (13,114 feet), and ends at Main St, Telluride (8,800 feet). Race route follows old mining trail. Sat after Labor Day.

Ouray County Fair & Rodeo. *Hwy 550 at 62. 12 miles N in Ridgway.* Labor Day weekend.

Motels/Motor Lodges

★ **BOX CANYON LODGE & HOT SPRING.** *45 Third Ave (81427). Phone 970/325-4981; toll-free 800/327-5080; fax 970/325-0223. www.boxcanyonouray.com.* 38 rooms, 2 story. No A/C. Mid-June-Sept: D $100; each additional $10; suites $115-$165; higher rates Christmas holidays; lower rates rest of year. Check-out 11 am. TV; cable (premium). Fireplace in suites. At mouth of canyon; scenic view. Near river. Cr cds: A, D, DS, MC, V.

★ **CASCADE FALLS LODGE.** *120 6th Ave (81427). Phone 970/325-4394; toll-free 888/466-8729; fax 970/325-4947.* 19 rooms, 1-2 story. No A/C. Apr-Oct: S, D $40-$94; each additional $5. Closed mid-Oct-mid-Apr. Crib free. Complimentary continental breakfast, coffee in rooms. Check-out 10:30 am. TV; cable (premium). Balconies. Refrigerators, microwaves. Restaurant nearby. Playground. Whirlpool. Picnic tables. Cr cds: DS, MC, V.

⬛⬛⬛ SC

★ **COMFORT INN.** *191 5th Ave (81427). Phone 970/325-7203; toll-free 800/438-5713; fax 970/325-4840. www.ouraycomfortinn.com.* 33 rooms, 2 story. June-mid-Sept: S, D $59-$107; each additional $6; under 18 free; lower rates rest of year. Crib $3. Complimentary continental breakfast, coffee in rooms. Check-out 11 am. TV; cable (premium). In-room modem link. Refrigerators available. Coin laundry. Restaurant nearby. Whirlpool. Business services. Mountain views. Cr cds: A, C, D, DS, JCB, MC, V.

⬛ SC

★ **MATTERHORN MOTEL.** *201 6th Ave (81427). Phone 970/325-4938; toll-free 800/334-9425; fax 970/325-7335. www.ouraycolorado.com/matthorn.html.* 25 air-cooled rooms, 3 suites, 2 story. Late June-Sept: S, D $77-$97; each additional $6; suites $99; lower rates Apr-early June, Oct. Closed rest of year. Check-out 11 am. TV; cable (premium). In-room modem link. Pool; whirlpool. Cr cds: D, DS, MC, V.

⬛⬛⬛⬛

★ ★ **OURAY VICTORIAN INN & TOWNHOMES.** *50 3rd Ave (81427). Phone 970/325-7222; toll-free 800/846-8729; fax 970/325-7225. www.ouraylodging.com.* 38 rooms, 4 suites, 2 story. No A/C. Late-June-Sept: S, D $65-$100; each additional $6; suites $120; under 6 free; ski plans; lower rates rest of year. Crib free. Pet accepted. Complimentary continental breakfast (Oct-May), coffee in rooms. Check-out 11 am. TV; cable (premium). In-room modem link. Restaurant nearby. Playground. 2 whirlpools. Picnic tables. Meeting rooms. Business services. On river. Cr cds: A, C, D, DS, MC, V.

⬛⬛⬛⬛

★ **SUPER 8 MOTEL.** *373 Palomino Trail (81432). Phone 970/626-5444; toll-free 800/368-5444; fax 970/626-5888. www.super8.com.* 52 rooms, 2 story. Mid-June-Labor Day: S, D $55-$75; each additional $7; under 13 free; ski plan; higher rates some holidays; lower rates rest of year. Crib $5. Pet accepted; $25 deposit. Check-out 11 am. TV; cable (premium). In-room modem link. Refrigerator in suites. Coin laundry. Restaurant nearby. Sauna. Heated pool, whirlpool. Business services. Mountain views. Cr cds: A, C, D, DS, MC, V.

⬛⬛⬛⬛⬛

B&B/Small Inns

★ ★ ★ **CHINA CLIPPER BED BREAKFAST INN.** *525 2nd St (81427). Phone 970/325-0565; toll-free 800/315-0565; fax 970/325-4190. www.chinaclipperinn.com.* No matter what the season, this property offers a relaxing experience. Each guest room has a view of the magnificent San Juan Mountains. Winter guests receive half-price coupons to the nearby million-gallon, natural Hot Springs Pool. 12 air-cooled rooms, 3 with shower only, 2 story. Memorial Day-mid-Oct: S, D $75-$175; each additional $10; package plans; holidays 2-day minimum; lower rates rest of year. Crib free. Children over 15 years only. Complimentary full breakfast. Check-out 10:30 am, check-in 2 pm. TV in 9 rooms; cable (premium), VCR available. In-room modem link. Some balconies. Some refrigerators, microwaves, fireplaces, in-room whirlpools. Coin laundry. Restaurant nearby. Whirlpool. Cross-country ski 5 miles. Elegant décor. Totally nonsmoking. Cr cds: DS, MC, V.

⬛⬛⬛⬛

★ ★ ★ **DAMN YANKEE COUNTRY INN.** *100 6th Ave (81427). Phone 970/325-4219; toll-free 800/845-7512; fax 970/325-4339. www.montrose.net/users/damnyank.* This inn is located in the San Juan Mountains. Rooms are furnished with ceiling fans, two-person whirlpools and gas fireplaces with remote control. There is a natural hot springs pool. 10 air-cooled rooms, 3 suites, 3 story. June-Sept: S, D $81-$190; each additional $15; suites $145-$185; special rates (winter); ski plans; lower rates rest of year. Children over 16 years only. Complimentary full breakfast. Check-out 11 am, check-in 3 pm. TV; cable (premium), VCR available. Balconies. Some fireplaces, in-room whirlpools. Restaurant nearby. Whirlpool in gazebo. Street parking. Surrounded by San Juan Mountains. Totally nonsmoking. Cr cds: DS, MC, V.

⬛⬛⬛⬛

★ ★ ★ **ST. ELMO HOTEL.** *426 Main St (81427). Phone 970/325-4951; fax 970/325-0348. www.stelmohotel.com.* 9 rooms, 2 story. No room phones. Mid-May-mid-Oct: D $85-$135; each additional $20; package plans; lower rates rest of year. Complimentary full breakfast. Check-out 11 am, check-in 1 pm. TV in sitting room; cable (premium). Restaurant (see BON TON). Bar. Whirlpool. Sauna. Business services. Restored 1898 hotel. Totally nonsmoking. Cr cds: A, D, DS, MC, V.

⬛⬛⬛

Restaurants

★ ★ **BON TON.** *426 Main St (81427). Phone 970/325-4951; fax 970/325-0348. www.stelmohotel.com.* Italian menu. Hours: 5-10 pm; winter 5:30-9 pm; Sun brunch 9:30 am-1 pm. Closed Dec 25. Dinner $12-$25. Sun brunch. Bar. Children's menu. Built 1898. Outdoor seating. Totally nonsmoking. Cr cds: A, D, DS, MC, V.

D ▨

★ **BUEN TIEMPO.** *515 Main St (81427). Phone 970/325-4544; fax 970/325-0348. www.stelmohotel.com.* Hours: 4-10 pm; winter 5:30-9 pm. Closed Dec 25. No A/C. Mexican, Southwestern menu. Bar. Dinner $5-$15. Specializes in carne adovada, carne asada. Outdoor dining. Casual dining. In 1891 building, originally a hotel. Totally nonsmoking. Cr cds: A, DS, MC, V.

D ▨

★ **CECILIA'S.** *630 Main St (81427). Phone 970/325-4223; fax 970/325-4208.* Hours: 6:30 am-9 pm. Closed mid-Oct-mid-May. American menu. Breakfast $3.80-$6.75, lunch $4.50-$6.65, dinner $6.30-$15.75. Children's menu. Specializes in homemade soup, pastries. Entertainment. In vintage movie theater. Cr cds: MC, V.

D

Pagosa Springs (G-3)

Founded 1880 **Pop** 1,207 **Elev** 7,105 ft **Area code** 970 **Zip** 81147

Information Chamber of Commerce, 402 San Juan St, PO Box 787; 970/264-2360 or 800/252-2204

Web www.pagosa-springs.com

These remarkable mineral springs (153°F) are used for bathing and to heat houses and buildings. Deer and elk hunting are popular activities. The town is surrounded by the San Juan National Forest (see DURANGO). A Ranger District office of the forest is located in Pagosa Springs.

What to See and Do

Chimney Rock Archaeological Area. *180 N Pagosa Blvd. SE via US 151. Phone 970/883-5359; 970/264-2268.* Area features twin pinnacles, held sacred by the Anasazi; Fire Tower, which offers a spectacular view of ruins; and Great House, which sits atop a mesa accessible only by a steep-walled narrow causeway. Guided tours only (four scheduled tours daily). **$$**

Fred Harman Art Museum. *2560 W Hwy 160 (81147). 2 miles W on US 160, across from junction Piedra Rd. Phone 970/731-5785.* Displays of original paintings by Fred Harman, Western artist and comic illustrator best remembered for his famous Red Ryder and Little Beaver comic strip. Also rodeo, movie, and Western memorabilia. (Late May-early Oct, daily; rest of year, Mon-Fri; closed July 4) **$$**

Navajo State Park. *17 miles W on US 160, then 18 miles S on CO 151 near Arboles. Phone 970/883-2208.* Waterskiing, fishing, boating (ramps, rentals); picnicking (shelters), groceries, restaurant, camping (dump station). Visitor center. Standard fees. (Daily) **$$**

Rocky Mountain Wildlife Park. *4821 Hwy 84 (81147). 5 miles S on US 84. Phone 970/264-4515.* Zoo exhibits animals indigenous to the area; wildlife museum; wildlife photography displays. (May-Nov, daily; rest of year, Mon-Tues, Thurs-Sat afternoons) **$$**

Wolf Creek Pass. *20 mi NE of US 160 and US 84 (81147). Phone 970/264-5639.* (10,857 feet) Scenic drive across the Continental Divide. The eastern approach is through the Rio Grande National Forest (see SOUTH FORK), the western approach through the San Juan National Forest (see DURANGO). Best time to drive through is Sept; spectacular views of aspens changing color. Drive takes approximately one hour. Nearby is

Treasure Mountain. Begin at top of Wolf Creek Pass, just east of summit marked where Continental Divide Trail winds southward and connects with Treasure Mountain Trail. Legend states that in 1790, 300 men mined five million dollars in gold and melted it into bars, but were forced to leave it behind. The gold has never been found.

Wolf Creek Ski Area. *20 mi NE of US 160 and US 84 (81147). Phone 970/264-5629 (snow conditions and off-season).* Two triple, two double chairlifts; Pomalift; patrol, school, rentals; cafeteria, restaurant, bar, day lodge. Fifty runs; longest run 2 miles; vertical drop 1,425 feet. (Early Nov-Apr, daily) Shuttle bus service. **$$$$**

Special Event

Winter Fest. *Chambers of Commerce, 800 Goodnight Avenue (81005). Phone 970/264-2360.* Winter carnival, individual and team events for all ages. Early Feb.

Motels/Motor Lodges

★ ★ **BEST VALUE HIGH COUNTRY LODGE.** *3821 E Hwy 160 (81147). Phone 970/264-4181; toll-free 800/862-3707; fax 970/264-4185. www.highcountrylodge. com.* 35 rooms, 2 story. Pet accepted. Complimentary continental breakfast. Check-out 11 am, check-in 2:30 pm. TV. In-room modem link. Restaurant. Whirlpool. Downhill ski 20 miles, cross-country ski 3 miles. Cr cds: A, C, D, DS, MC, V. **$**

D 🐾 ▨ ▨

★ **RED LION INN & SUITES.** *3565 Hwy 60 W (81147). Phone 970/731-3400; toll-free 888/221-8088; fax 970/731-3402. www.pagosaspringsinn.com.* 97 rooms, 3 story. Pet accepted. Check-out noon, check-in 3 pm. TV; cable (premium). In-house fitness room. Game room. Indoor pool, whirlpool. Cross-country ski 3 miles. Cr cds: A, D, DS, MC, V. **$**

D 🐾 ▨ ▨ 🧍 ▨

Resorts

★★**PAGOSA LODGE.** *3505 W Hwy 160 (81147). Phone 970/731-4141; toll-free 800/523-7704; fax 970/731-4343. www.pagosalodge.com.* 101 rooms, 2-3 story. Check-out 11 am, check-in 4 pm. TV. Restaurant, bar. Sauna, steam room. Indoor pool, whirlpool. Cross-country ski on site. Lawn games, bicycles, canoes. Whitewater rafting. Jeep tours. Sleigh rides. Airport transportation. 6,500-foot private airstrip. Cr cds: A, C, D, DS, MC, V. **$**

D ✈ ⊠

★**THE SPRING INN.** *165 Hot Springs Blvd (81147). Phone 970/264-4168; toll-free 800/225-0934; fax 970/264-4707. www.pacosahotsprings.com.* 37 rooms. Pet accepted. Check-out noon, check-in 4 pm. TV; cable (premium), VCR. Spa. Game room. Outdoor pool, whirlpool. Hot springs; unlimited use to guests. Cr cds: D, DS, MC, V. **$**

D 🐾 ⚓ 🔦 ⊠ 🏊

Restaurant

★★**TEQUILA'S.** *439 San Juan St (81157). Phone 970/264-2175; fax 970/264-6149.* Mexican menu. Lunch, dinner. Children's menu. Casual attire. Outdoor seating. Cr cds: A, DS, MC, V. **$$**

D SC

Palisade (D-2)

Special Event

Colorado Mountain Winefest. *12 miles east of Grand Junction, exit 42 or 44 off of I-70. Phone 970/464-7458.* For a taste of Colorado's softer side, plan a visit to the Western Slopes region east of Grand Junction, where numerous wineries have established themselves on the gentle hills between Grand Rapids and Glenwood Springs. At the heart of Colorado's wine country is the charming valley town of Palisade, home of the annual Colorado Mountain Winefest. This colorful weekend harvest celebration in mid-September begins on a Friday with elaborate harvest banquets served at several area restaurants. The next morning, riders embark on a 25-mile bicycle tour thorough the region while winemakers and wine lovers converge for the lively Festival in the Park. As wineries from throughout Colorado present their favorite vintages for sampling, festivalgoers enjoy food, music, contests, demonstrations, and a chance to try their hand (or toes) at grape-stomping. The festival concludes with a wine-tasting tour of the Grand Valley vineyards. Many of the larger wineries are open for tours year-round. For a listing of local wineries and tour hours, contact the Palisades Chamber of Commerce. Mid-Sept, Fri-Sun. **$$$$**

Pueblo (E-6)

See also Cañon City, Colorado Springs

Settled 1842 **Pop** 102,121 **Elev** 4,695 ft **Area code** 719

Information Chamber of Commerce, PO Box 697, 81002; 719/542-1704; or the Pueblo Visitors Information Center, 302 N Santa Fe Ave, 81003. The Visitors Information Center is open daily.

Web www.pueblochamber.org

Pueblo began as a crossroad for Native Americans, Spaniards, and fur traders. When the Rio Grande Railroad reached here in 1872, Pueblo was the leading center for steel and coal production west of the Mississippi. Today, Pueblo is a major transportation and industrial center; more than half of all goods manufactured in Colorado are produced in Pueblo.

What to See and Do

City parks. Approximately 700 acres of parks within city.

City Park. *Pueblo Blvd and Goodnight Ave (81004). Phone 719/542-1704.* Swimming pool (Memorial Day-Labor Day, daily; fee), children's fishing; 9-hole, 18-hole golf and driving range (fee); tennis, picnicking, zoo (fee); herds of wildlife, children's farm, Eco Center, Rainforest. Historical carousel area (Memorial Day-Labor Day, daily; fee). Thirty-five-mile river trail system. Park (daily). **FREE**

Mineral Palace Park. *1500 N Santa Fe (81003). Phone 719/566-1745 or 719/542-1704.* Swimming pool (fee), children's fishing; picnicking. Rose garden, greenhouse. Pueblo Art Guild Gallery with local artists exhibits (Sat and Sun; closed Dec-Feb). **FREE**

El Pueblo Museum. *324 W First St. Phone 719/583-0453.* Full-sized replica of Old Fort Pueblo, which served as a base for fur traders and other settlers from 1842-1855. Exhibits on the Anasazi, steel and ore production, and narrow-gauge railroads. (Daily; closed Thanksgiving, Dec 25) **$$**

Fred E. Weisbrod Aircraft Museum. *31001 Magnuson Ave. Pueblo Memorial Airport. Phone 719/948-3355 or 719/948-9219.* Outdoor museum features static aircraft display. Adjacent is the B-24 Aircraft Memorial Museum, with indoor displays of the history of the B-24 bomber. Guided tours. (Daily; closed holidays) **$$**

The Greenway and Nature Center of Pueblo. *5200 Nature Center Rd, 5 miles W via US 50. Phone 719/549-2414.* Small reptile exhibit and Raptor Center, special nature programs (by appointment). Also 36 miles of hiking and biking trails (rentals). Café. (Tues-Sun; closed Jan 1, Thanksgiving, Dec 25)

Lake Pueblo State Park. *640 Pueblo Reservoir Rd. 6 miles W via CO 96 or US 50 W. Phone 719/561-9320.* Swimming, waterskiing, boating; hiking, camping (dump station). Standard fees. (Daily) **$$**

Rosemount Victorian House Museum. *419 W 14th St. Phone 719/545-5290.* This 37-room mansion contains original Victorian furnishings and the McClelland Collection of world curiosities. (Tues-Sun; closed holidays; also closed Jan) **$$$**

Sangre de Cristo Arts and Conference Center. *210 N Santa Fe Ave. Phone 719/295-7200.* Four art galleries include the Francis King Collection of Western Art on permanent display; changing art exhibits; children's museum, workshops, dance studios, theater; gift shop. (Mon-Sat; closed holidays) **$**

San Isabel National Forest. *NW and W via US 50. Contact the Supervisor, 2840 Kachina Dr. Phone 719/545-8737.* On 1,109,782 acres. Three sections of forest lie adjacent to this highway with picnicking, camping, and two winter sports areas: Monarch and Ski Cooper. In the southern part of the forest is the Spanish Peaks National Natural Landmark. Collegiate Peaks, Mount Massive, and Holy Cross Wilderness areas are also within the forest, as well as four wilderness study areas. Colorado's highest peak, Mount Elbert (14,433 feet), is within the forest south of Leadville (see). Also in forest is

Lake Isabel. *43 miles SW via I-25, CO 165 or 32 miles SW on CO 76.* A 310-acre recreation area. Fishing, boating (no motors); picnicking, camping. No swimming.

University of Southern Colorado. *2200 Bonforte Blvd. Campus tours (Mon-Fri, by appointment), contact Admissions Office, Administration Building. Phone 719/549-2461.* (1975) 4,000 students. Developed from Pueblo Junior College established in 1933. Chemistry Building has Geological Museum with mineral, rock, and fossil exhibits, maps (academic year, Mon-Fri; closed holidays; free).

Special Events

Colorado State Fair. *Fairgrounds. 1001 Beulah Ave (81004). Phone 719/561-8484 or 800/444-FAIR.* PRCA rodeo, grandstand and amphitheater entertainment, livestock and agricultural displays, industrial and high technology displays, home arts, fine arts and crafts, carnival. Aug-Sept.

Pueblo Greyhound Park. *3215 Lake Ave. Phone 719/566-0370.* Pari-mutuel betting. Satellite betting Apr-Sept. Live racing Oct-Mar.

Motels/Motor Lodges

★★ **BEST WESTERN INN AT PUEBLO WEST.** *201 S McCulloch Blvd (81007). Phone 719/547-2111; toll-free 800/448-1972; fax 719/547-0385. www.bestwestern.com/innatpueblow.* 79 rooms, 2 story. June-Sept: S $50-$69; D $55-$74; each additional $5; under 12 free; lower rates rest of year. Crib free. Pet accepted, some restrictions. Check-out 11 am. TV; cable (premium). Private patios. Coffee in rooms. Restaurant 6 am-10 pm. Exercise equipment. Pool. Meeting room. Business services. Gift shop. Cr cds: A, C, D, DS, MC, V.

★ **COMFORT INN.** *4645 N Freeway Rd (I-25) (81008). Phone 719/542-6868. www.comfortinn.com.* 60 rooms, 2 story. Memorial Day-Aug: S, D $60-$85; each additional $5; lower rates rest of year. Complimentary continental breakfast. Check-out 11 am. TV; cable (premium). In-room modem link. Coin laundry. Restaurant nearby. Indoor pool. Business services. Cr cds: A, C, D, DS, JCB, MC, V.

★ **DAYS INN.** *4201 N Elizabeth (81008). Phone 719/543-8031; fax 719/546-1317. www.daysinn.com.* 58 rooms, 2 story. S $45-$59; D $55-$69; each additional $6; suites $75-$135; under 13 free. Crib free. Complimentary continental breakfast. Check-out 11 am. TV; cable (premium). Refrigerator, microwave in suites. Coin laundry. Restaurant nearby. Exercise equipment. Indoor pool, whirlpool. Business services. Cr cds: A, C, D, DS, MC, V.

★ **HAMPTON INN.** *4703 N Freeway (81008). Phone 719/544-4700; toll-free 800/972-0165; fax 719/544-6526. www.sunstonehotels.com.* 111 rooms, 2 story. S $59-$79; D $79-$99; under 19 free; golf plans. Crib available. Complimentary breakfast buffet. Check-out noon. TV; cable (premium), VCR available. Some refrigerators, microwaves. Coffee in rooms. Valet services, coin laundry. Exercise equipment. Heated pool. Meeting room. Business services. Cr cds: A, C, D, DS, MC, V.

★★ **HOLIDAY INN.** *4001 N Elizabeth St (81008). Phone 719/543-8050; toll-free 800/465-4329; fax 719/545-2271. www.holiday-inn.com.* 193 rooms, 2 story. S $59-$99; D $69-$109; each additional $10; suites $150-$250; under 17 free. Crib free. Check-out 11 am. TV; cable. In-room modem link. Coffee in rooms. Coin laundry. Restaurant 6 am-2 pm, 5-10 pm. Bar 4 pm-2 am, Sun to midnight. Room service. Exercise equipment. Game room. Indoor pool, whirlpool. Free airport transportation. Meeting rooms. Business center. Cr cds: A, C, D, DS, JCB, MC, V.

★ **WINGATE INN.** *4711 N Elizabeth St (81008). Phone 719/586-9000; toll-free 800/993-7232. www.wingateinns.com.* 84 rooms, 3 story. Mid-May-Labor Day: S $69-$79; D $79-$89; each additional $10; suites $119; under 18 free; lower rates rest of year. Complimentary continental breakfast. Check-out 11 am. TV; cable (premium). In-room modem link. Exercise equipment. Indoor pool, whirlpool. Business center. Cr cds: A, C, D, DS, JCB, MC, V.

D 🏃 ➾ 🖘 🏃

Hotel

★ ★ ★ **MARRIOTT PUEBLO CONVENTION CENTER.** *110 W First St (81003). Phone 719/542-3200. www.marriott.com.* 164 rooms, 7 story. S, D $150-$225; under 17 free. Check-out noon, check-in 3 pm. TV; cable (premium). In-room modem link. Restaurant 6:30 am-10 pm. Bar to midnight. Exercise equipment. Indoor pool, whirlpool. Business center. Concierge. Cr cds: A, C, D, DS, MC, V.

D ➾ 🏃 🖘 🏃

B&B/Small Inn

★ ★ ★ **ABRIENDO INN.** *300 W Abriendo Ave (81004). Phone 719/544-2703; fax 719/542-6544.* 10 rooms, 1 suite, 3 story. S, D $110-$115; each additional $15; suite $84. Children over 6 years only. Complimentary full breakfast. Check-out 11 am, check-in 3:30-9 pm. TV; cable, VCR. In-room modem link. Restaurant nearby. Business services. Built in 1906. Totally nonsmoking. Cr cds: A, D, MC, V.

🖘

Restaurants

★ ★ **CAFE DEL RIO.** *5200 Nature Center Rd (81003). Phone 719/549-2029; fax 719/549-2547.* Hours: 11 am-9 pm; Sun brunch 10 am-2 pm. Closed Mon. Reservations accepted. Service bar. Lunch $4.25-$9.95, dinner $9.95-$18.95. Sun brunch $12.95. Children's menu. Specializes in steak, seafood, chicken. Own soups. Parking. Outdoor dining. Scenic view of Arkansas river; adobe building built by volunteers. Cr cds: A, D, DS, MC, V.

D

★ ★ **GAETANO'S.** *910 Hwy 50 W (81008). Phone 719/546-0949; fax 719/546-1636.* American, Italian menu. Specializes in steak, seafood, lasagne. Hours: 11 am-10 pm; Sat from 4 pm; early-bird dinner 4-6 pm. Closed Sun; Jan 1, Dec 25. Lunch $4.95-$8.95. Dinner, complete meals: $6.95-$17.95. Bar. Children's menu. Casual dining. Reservations accepted. Outdoor dining. Cr cds: A, C, D, DS, ER, MC, V.

D SC

★ ★ ★ **LA RENAISSANCE.** *217 E Routt Ave (81004). Phone 719/543-6367; fax 719/543-6374.* Continental menu. Hours: 5-9 pm; Sat from 5 pm. Closed Sun; some major holidays. Dinner, complete meals: $9.95-$22.95. Bar. Church built in 1886; garden room. Reservations accepted. Totally nonsmoking. Cr cds: A, D, DS, MC, V.

D 🖘

Rocky Mountain National Park (B-5)

See also Estes Park, Granby, Grand Lake, Loveland, Lyons

(Park headquarters is 3 miles W of Estes Park on US 36; western entrance at Grand Lake)

More than 100 years ago, Joel Estes built a cabin on Fish Creek, one of the higher sections of north-central Colorado. Although the Estes family moved away, more settlers soon followed, and the area became known as Estes Park. Described by Albert Bierstadt, one of the great 19th-century landscape artists of the West, as America's finest composition for the painter, the land west of where Estes settled was set aside as Rocky Mountain National Park in 1915. Straddling the Continental Divide, with valleys 8,000 feet in elevation and 114 named peaks more than 10,000 feet high, the 415-square-mile park contains a staggering profusion of peaks, upland meadows, sheer canyons, glacial streams, and lakes. Dominating the scene is Longs Peak, with its east face towering 14,255 feet above sea level. The park's forests and meadows provide sanctuary for more than 750 varieties of wildflowers, more than 260 species of birds, and such indigenous mammals as deer, wapiti (American elk), bighorn sheep, beaver, and other animals. There are five campgrounds, two of which take reservations from May to early Sept (fee; write to Destinet, 9450 Carroll Park Dr, San Diego CA, 92121-2256; phone 800/365-2267). Some attractions are not accessible during the winter months. $10 per car per week; Golden Eagle Passports are accepted (see MAKING THE MOST OF YOUR TRIP). Contact the Superintendent, Rocky Mountain National Park, Estes Park 80517-8397; phone 970/586-1206.

What to See and Do

Bear Lake Road. Scenic drive (plowed in winter months) into high mountain basin is rimmed with precipitous 12,000- to 14,000-foot peaks. At the end of the road, self-guided nature trail circles Bear Lake. Other trails lead to higher lakes, gorges, glaciers. Bus service (summer).

★ **Headquarters Building.** *Just outside east entrance station on US 36 approach.* Information (publications sales, maps); program on park (daily); guided walks and illustrated evening programs (summer only; daily).

Moraine Park Museum. *One mile inside park from Beaver Meadows entrance.* Exhibits, information, publications sales, maps. (May-Sept, daily)

Never Summer Ranch. *Phone 970/627-3471. 10 miles N of Grand Lake entrance on Trail Ridge Rd.* Historic pioneer homestead and preserved 1920s dude ranch. (Weather permitting, mid-June-Labor Day, daily)

Trail Ridge Road. *1000 US Hwy 36 (80517). Phone 970/586-1363.* Among the most scenic drives in Colorado is the Trail Ridge Road between Grand Lake and Estes Park. Winding through 53 miles of beautiful alpine forest and tundra in the heart of Rocky Mountain National Park, the road reaches an elevation of 12,183 feet to offer stunning vistas of the southern Rockies. In mid-July, wildflowers blanket the tundra, while elk, deer, mountain sheep, and moose are often seen along the route. The drive without stopping takes approximately two hours, but the experience would be lost without stops to take in the views or explore the numerous hiking paths along the way.

Salida (E-4)

See also Buena Vista

Founded 1880 **Pop** 5,504 **Elev** 7,036 ft **Area code** 719 **Zip** 81201

Information Heart of the Rockies Chamber of Commerce, 406 W US 50; 719/539-2068

On the eastern slope of the Rocky Mountains, Salida is a town surrounded by San Isabel National Forest (see PUEBLO). A pleasant climate (thus Salida's nickname "the banana belt") makes Salida ideal for recreational activities throughout the year, including river rafting, fishing, mountain biking, hiking, and hunting.

What to See and Do

The Angel of Shavano. Every spring the snow melts on the 14,239-foot slopes of Mount Shavano leaving an outline called "The Angel."

Arkansas Headwaters State Recreation Area. *307 W Sackett (81201). US 24, 285, and 50. Phone 719/539-7289.* Area of 5,000 acres, with an outstanding waterway that cuts its way through rugged canyons for 148 miles, from Leadville to Pueblo. One of the world's premier waterways for kayaking and whitewater rafting; fishing, boating (ramps); hiking, bridle trails; picnicking, camping. Interpretive programs. (Daily) **$**

Jeep tours. *Chamber of Commerce, 406 W Rainbow Blvd (81201).* To mountainous areas inaccessible by car, over trails, old railroad beds. Outfitters offer 1/2-hour, 1/2-day, and full-day trail rides; fishing, hunting, photography, and pack trips. Contact Chamber of Commerce for details.

Monarch Ski & Snowboard Area. *18 miles W on US 50 at Monarch Pass (11,312 feet). Phone 719/539-3573, 888/996-7669 (ski administration), 719/539-3573 (lodge), or 800/228-7943 (recorded information).* Four double chairlifts; patrol, school, rentals; cafeteria, restaurant, bar, nursery. Fifty-four runs; longest run 2 miles; vertical drop 1,160 feet. (Mid-Nov-mid-Apr, daily) Multiday, half-day rates. Cross-country skiing. **$$$$**

Mountain Spirit Winery. *201 F St. Phone 719/539-1175.* Family-operated boutique winery. Five acres with apple orchard, homestead. Tours, tastings (Memorial Day-Labor Day, weekends). **FREE**

Mount Shavano Fish Hatchery. *1/2 mile W on CO 291, US 50. Phone 719/539-6877.* State-operated hatchery. (Daily)

Salida Museum. *Hwy 50 at I St. Phone 719/539-7483.* Museum features mineral display, Native American artifacts, early pioneer household display, mining and railroad display. (Late May-early Sept, daily) **$$**

Tenderfoot Drive. *W on CO 291.* Spiral drive encircling Mount Tenderfoot. Views of surrounding mountain area and upper Arkansas Valley.

Special Events

Artwalk. *406 W Rainbow Blvd (81210). Downtown Historic District.* Local artisans, craftspeople, and entertainers display artwork. Last weekend in June.

Chaffee County Fair. *10165 County Rd 120 (81242). Phone 719/539-6151.* Five days last weekend in July.

Christmas Mountain USA. *406 W Rainbow Blvd (81210). Phone 719/539-2068.* Three-day season opener; more than 3,500 lights outline a 700-foot Christmas tree on Tenderfoot Mountain; parade. Day after Thanksgiving.

FIBArk River International Whitewater Boat Race. *240 N F St (81201). Phone 719/539-7997.* International experts compete in a 26-mile kayak race. Other events include slalom, raft, foot, and bicycle races. Father's Day weekend.

Motel/Motor Lodge

★ **TRAVELODGE.** *7310 W US Hwy 50 (81201). Phone 719/539-2528; toll-free 800/234-1077; fax 719/539-7235. www.salidatravelodge.com.* 27 rooms, 2 story. Pet accepted $3-$5. Check-out 11 am, check-in 2 pm. TV; cable (premium), VCR available. Outdoor pool, whirlpool. Downhill skiing, cross-country ski 18 miles. Fishing, rafting. Cr cds: A, C, D, DS, MC, V. **$**

B&B/Small Inn

★ ★ **TUDOR ROSE BED & BREAKFAST.** *6720 County Rd 104 (81201). Phone 719/539-2002; toll-free 800/379-0889; fax 719/530-0345. www.thetudorrose.com.* 6 rooms, 3 story. Children over 10 years only. Complimentary full breakfast; afternoon refreshments. Check-out 11 am, check-in 4 pm. TV; VCR (movies) in common room. In-room modem link. Whirlpool. Downhill ski 18 miles; cross-country ski 7 miles. Hiking trail. Overnight horse stabling $9.50/horse/day. Country manor located on hill. Totally nonsmoking. Cr cds: DS, MC, V. **$**

Restaurants

★ ★ **COUNTRY BOUNTY.** *413 W Rainbow Blvd (81201). Phone 719/539-3546; fax 719/539-6792.* American menu. Closed Thanksgiving, Dec 24-25. Breakfast, lunch, dinner. Children's menu. Casual attire. Totally nonsmoking. Cr cds: A, C, DS, MC, V. **$**

★ **WINDMILL.** *720 E Rainbow Blvd (81201). Phone 719/539-3594; fax 719/539-3479.* American menu. Closed Thanksgiving, Dec 25. Lunch, dinner. Bar. Children's menu. Casual attire. Cr cds: A, C, DS, ER, MC, V. **$$**

Silverton (F-2)

See also Durango, Ouray

Settled 1874 **Pop** 531 **Elev** 9,318 ft **Area code** 970 **Zip** 81433

Information Chamber of Commerce, 414 Greene St; 970/387-5654 or 800/752-4494

Web www.silverton.org

"The mining town that never quit" sits in the San Juan Mountains with other communities that provide reminders of Colorado's mining history; the last mine in Silverton closed in 1991. Tourists have now discovered the natural beauty, historic ghost towns, and many recreational opportunities of the area.

What to See and Do

Circle Jeep Tour. *414 Greene St. Phone 970/387-5654 or 800/752-4494.* Mapped Jeep route with historical information to many mines and ghost towns. Contact the Chamber of Commerce. **$**

Old Hundred Gold Mine Tour. *721 County Rd 4 A. Phone 970/387-5444. 5 miles E via CO 110.* Guided one-hour tour of underground mine offers view of mining equipment,

crystal pockets, veins; learn about methods of hardrock mining. (Memorial Day-Sept, daily).

San Juan County Historical Society Museum. *1315 Snowden. Phone 970/387-5838.* Located in old 3-story jail. Mining and railroad artifacts from Silverton's early days. (Memorial Day-mid-Oct, daily) **$$**

The Silverton. Narrow-guage train (see DURANGO). *Phone 970/347-2733.*

Special Events

Brass Band Festival. *414 Greene St (81433). Phone 800/752-4497.* Mid-Aug.

Hardrockers Holiday. *Chamber of Commerce, 414 Greene St (81433). Phone 800/752-4497.* Mining skills competition. Mid-Aug.

Iron Horse Bicycle Classic. *346 S Camino Del Rio (81301). Phone 970/259-4621.* Bicycles race the Silverton narrow-gauge train. Late May.

Silverton Jubilee Folk Music Festival. *Chamber of Commerce, 414 Greene St (81433). Phone 970/387-5737.* Late June.

B&B/Small Inns

★ ★ **ALMA HOUSE BED AND BREAKFAST.** *220 E 10th St (81433). Phone 970/387-5336; toll-free 800/267-5336; fax 970/387-5974.* 10 air-cooled rooms, 2 1/2 story, 6 with bath, 4 share bath. No room phones. S, D $79-$99; suites $130. Crib free. Pet accepted, some restrictions; $10. TV; cable (premium). Complimentary full breakfast. Check-out 11 am, check-in 2 pm. Business services available. Luggage handling. Built 1898. Victorian furnishings. Some fireplaces. Totally nonsmoking. Cr cds: A, DS, MC, V.

★ ★ ★ **WYMAN HOTEL.** *1371 Greene St (81433). Phone 970/387-5372; toll-free 800/609-7845; fax 970/387-5745. www.silverton.org/wymanhotel.* 18 air-cooled rooms, 2 story. Apr-Oct, Jan-Mar: S, D $100-$195; package plans; each additional $20, under 14 $15. Closed Nov, Dec, Mar, Apr. Crib free. Pet accepted; $15. Complimentary full breakfast. Check-out 10:30 am, check-in after 3-8 pm. TV; cable (premium), VCR (free movies). In-room modem link. Some refrigerators. Restaurant nearby. Street parking. Business services. Built 1902. Victorian furnishings. Totally nonsmoking. Cr cds: A, DS, MC, V.

Restaurant

★ **HANDLEBARS.** *117 W 13th (81433). Phone 970/387-5395; fax 970/387-5992. www.handlebarsco.com.* Hours: 10:30 am-10 pm. Closed Nov-Apr. No A/C. Bar to 2 am. Lunch $3.75-$8.95, dinner $5.95-$22.95. Specializes in baby back ribs, chicken-fried steak. Own chili and soup. Built in 1881; display of antique mining and museum wildlife artifacts. Cr cds: DS, MC, V.

[D]

Snowmass Village (D-4)

See also Aspen, Glenwood Springs

Pop 1,822 **Elev** 8,604 ft **Area code** 970 **Zip** 81615

Information Snowmass Resort Association, 38 Village Square, PO Box 5566; 970/923-2000 or 800/766-9627

All facilities of Snowmass Village are available to guests of the accommodations listed below. Year-round: nearly 50 outdoor heated pools and hot tubs, saunas. Children's and teen programs; sitter list. Convention facilities. More than 20 restaurants in village; bars. Free shuttle bus throughout village; local airport transportation. Summer: fishing (license, equipment available). Rafting, hiking, horseback riding, 18-hole golf, tennis (fees for all); jeep and bicycle tours; hot-air balloon rides. Winter: skiing (beginner-to-expert runs), instruction; cross-country skiing, barbecue sleigh rides, dogsled tours, guided snowshoe tours; swimming, indoor tennis.

What to See and Do

Bicycle trips and Jeep trips. *105 Snowmass Village Mall. Phone 970/923-4544.* Throughout the Snowmass/Aspen area. Transportation and equipment provided. (June-Sept) **$$$$**

Krabloonik Husky Kennels. *4250 Divide Rd. 5 miles SW of CO 82. Phone 970/923-3953.* Half-day dog-sled trips by reservations (Dec-Apr). Kennel tours (mid-June-Sept, Mon-Sat). **$$$$**

River rafting. *Snowmass Whitewater. 70 Snowmass Village Mall. Phone 970/923-4544; 800/282-7238.* Half-day, full-day, and overnight trips on the Arkansas, Roaring Fork, Colorado, Gunnison, and Dolores rivers. Trips range from scenic floats for beginners to exciting runs for experienced rafters. (May-Oct daily, depending on snow melt) Transportation to site. **$$$$**

Snowmass Ski Area. *40 Carriage Way (81615). Phone 970/923-1220.* Seven quad, two triple, six double chairlifts; two platter pulls; patrol, school, rentals, snowmaking; restaurants, bar, nursery. Eighty-three runs; longest run 5 miles, vertical drop 4,406 feet. (Late Nov-mid-Apr, daily) Cross-country skiing (50 miles). Shuttle bus service from Aspen. **$$$$**

Motels/Motor Lodges

★ ★ ★ **SILVERTREE HOTEL.** *100 Elbert Ln (81615). Phone 970/923-3520; toll-free 800/837-4255; fax 970/923-5192. www.silvertreehotel.com.* This year-round mountain resort provides skiing right from the hotel with over 5,000 acres of ski area. Summer brings balloon rides, hiking and jazz concerts. 260 rooms, 2-7 story story. No A/C. Pet accepted. Check-out 11 am. TV; cable (premium). In-room modem link. Coin laundry. Restaurant; entertainment. Room service. Children's activity center, babysitting services available. In-house fitness room, massage, steam room. Outdoor pool, children's pool, whirlpool, poolside service. Downhill/cross-country ski on site. Lawn games, bicycles. Free local airport transportation. Business center. Concierge. Cr cds: A, C, D, DS, MC, V. **$$$**

[D] [icons]

★ **STONEBRIDGE INN.** *300 Carrage Way (81615). Phone 970/923-2420; toll-free 800/213-3214; fax 970/923-5889. www.stonebridgeinn.com.* 92 rooms, 7 story. Closed mid-Apr-May. Complimentary continental breakfast. Check-out 10 am, check-in 4 pm. TV; cable (premium), VCR available (movies). Restaurant. In-house fitness room; massage, sauna. Outdoor pool, children's pool, whirlpool. Downhill ski on site, cross-country ski 1/2 mile. Free airport transportation. Concierge. Cr cds: A, D, MC, V. **$$**

[D] [icons]

Resorts

★ ★ **CRESTWOOD LODGE.** *400 Wood Rd (81615). Phone 970/923-2450; toll-free 800/356-5949; fax 970/923-5018. www.thecrestwood.com.* 124 rooms, 3 story. No elevator. Check-out 10 am, check-in 5 pm. TV; cable (premium), VCR (movies fee). In-room modem link. Fireplaces. Laundry services. Babysitting services available. In-house fitness room, sauna. Outdoor pool, whirlpool. Downhill, cross-country ski on site. Airport transportation. Cr cds: A, C, D, DS, MC, V. **$$$**

[D] [icons]

★ ★ ★ **SNOWMASS CLUB.** *0239 Snowmass Club Cir (81615). Phone 970/923-5600; toll-free 800/525-0710; fax 970/923-6944. www.snowmassclub.com.* This year-round resort is located in the Elk Mountain range area. 55 rooms, 4 story. Check-out 10 am, check-in 4 pm. TV; cable (premium), VCR available. Coin laundry. Restaurant. Room service. Supervised children's activities; ages 6 months-8 years. Babysitting services available. In-house fitness room, spa, massage, sauna, steam room. Children's pool, whirlpool, poolside service. Golf. Outdoor, indoor tennis, lighted courts. Downhill ski 1 mile, cross-country ski on site. Sleighing, Snowmobiling. Free valet parking. Free airport, ski area transportation. Business center. Concierge. Cr cds: A, D, DS, MC, V. **$$$**

★ ★ **WILDWOOD LODGE.** *40 Elbert Ln (81615). Phone 970/923-3550; toll-free 800/445-1642; fax 970/923-5494. www.wildwood-lodge.com.* 140 rooms, 3 story. Early April-May. Pet accepted. Complimentary continental breakfast (winter). Check-out 11 am, check-in 4 pm. TV; cable (premium), VCR available. In-room modem link. Coin laundry. Restaurant. Room service. Children's activity center, babysitting services available. Health club privileges. Outdoor pool, children's pool, whirlpool, poolside service. Downhill, cross-country ski 1 block. Free airport transportation. Concierge. Cr cds: A, C, D, DS, MC, V.

Restaurants

★ ★ ★ **KRABLOONIK.** *4250 Divide Rd (81615). Phone 970/923-3953; fax 970/923-0246. www.krabloonik.com.* This casual, elegant restaurant has a rustic décor and panoramic views of the mountains. Continental, seafood menu. Closed mid-Apr-May, Oct-Thanksgiving. Lunch, dinner. Children's menu. Casual attire. Reservations required. Totally nonsmoking. Cr cds: A, MC, V. **$$$**

★ ★ ★ **SAGE.** *239 Snowmass Cir (81615). Phone 970/923-0923; fax 970/923-6944.* In the summer, the patio offers unobstructed views of Mount Daly. Contemporary American menu. Hours: 7 am-10 pm. Breakfast $7-$10, lunch $7-$12, dinner $21-$29. Bar 10 am-midnight. Children's menu. Reservations accepted. Valet parking. Outdoor dining. Cr cds: A, C, D, DS, MC, V.

★ ★ **TOWER.** *45 Village Sq (81615). Phone 970/923-4650; fax 970/923-4651.* American, seafood menu. Lunch, dinner. Bar. Children's menu. Casual mountain-lodge décor; view of mountains. Outdoor seating, Totally nonsmoking. Cr cds: A, D, DS, MC, V. **$$**

South Fork (F-4)

See also Monte Vista

Pop 604 **Elev** 8,200 ft **Area code** 719 **Zip** 81154

Information Visitors Center, PO Box 1030; 719/873-5512 or 800/571-0881

Web www.southfork.org

Located at Wolf Creek Pass along US 160 in the heart of the San Juan Mountains, this resort community is popular for skiing, snowmobiling, biking, camping, hiking, fishing, and rafting, and for the Jeep trails in the surrounding area. The Silver Thread National Scenic Byway, a 75-mile drive, begins here and travels through the spectacular scenery of the Continental Divide, ending at Lake City (see).

What to See and Do

Rio Grande National Forest. *1803 US 160 W. Phone 719/852-5941.* This rugged forest surrounding the San Luis Valley includes Wolf Creek Pass (10,850 feet) (see PAGOSA SPRINGS). Within the forest is the rugged Sangre de Cristo backcountry and parts of Weminuche, South San Juan, and La Garita wildernesses. Fishing, boating; hunting, hiking, downhill and cross-country skiing, snowmobiling, picnicking, camping. In the forest are

Creede. *22 miles NW on CO 149.* (pop 653) Frontier mining town.

Wolf Creek Ski Area. (see). *18 miles SW on US 180.*

Special Events

Creede Repertory Theater. *124 N Main St (81130). Phone 719/658-2540. 21 miles NW on CO 149 in Creede.* Classic and modern comedies, drama, musicals. Advance reservations suggested. Nightly Tues-Sun; also Wed and Fri afternoons; children's matinee Sat in Aug. Early June-Labor Day.

Logger Days Festival. Logging competition, crafts, food, music. Third weekend in July.

Steamboat Springs (B-4)

Settled 1875 **Pop** 9,815 **Elev** 6,695 ft **Area code** 970 **Zip** 80477

Information Steamboat Springs Chamber Resort Association, PO Box 774408; 970/879-0880 or 800/922-2722

Web www.steamboat-chamber.com

Before the Ute retreated into Utah, Steamboat Springs was originally their summer home. The area's first white settlers were ranchers. Coal mining also became a very viable industry.

Skiing and Norwegian-style ski-jumping came to this area with the arrival of the Norseman Carl Howelsen in 1913, becoming two of the most popular winter sports in the area. Ten national ski-jumping records have been set on Steamboat Springs's Howelsen Hill; the area has produced 47 winter Olympians, which has helped earn it the name of "Ski Town USA." Summer activities include camping, fishing, hot-air ballooning, horseback riding, hiking, bicycling, river rafting, canoeing, and llama trekking. One of the largest elk herds in North America ranges near the town. There are more than 100 natural hot springs in the area. The headquarters and access routes to Routt National Forest are in or near Steamboat Springs.

What to See and Do

Howelsen Hill Ski Complex. *245 Howelsen Pkwy. Off US 40 on River Rd via 5th St bridge. Phone 970/879-4300.* International ski/jump complex includes a double chairlift, Pomalift, rope tow, five ski jumping hills; patrol; ice-skating, snowboarding. Evening skiing available. (Dec-Mar, daily) Also summer activities. **$$$$**

Routt National Forest. *925 Weiss Dr (80487). Phone 970/879-1722.* More than one million acres include the 139,898-acre Mount Zirkel Wilderness and 38,870 acres of the 235,230-acre Flat Tops Wilderness. Fishing; hunting, winter sports area, hiking, picnicking, camping.

Scenic drives. The following drives are accessible in summer and are well-maintained paved and gravel-surfaced roads. Impressive view of the valley and Howelsen Ski Complex. Fish Creek Falls (283 feet) 3 miles E. Picnic area. Buffalo Pass (10,180 feet) 15 miles NE. Impressive road atop Continental Divide leading to formerly inaccessible trout-filled lakes. Rabbit Ears Pass (9,680 feet) 22 miles SE. Additional information available at information centers.

Steamboat. *1475 Pine Grove Rd # 202. 3 miles E on US 40. Phone 800/922-2722.* Gondola; four high-speed quad, quad, six triple, seven double chairlifts; two surface tows; patrol, school, rentals, snowmaking; cafeterias, restaurants, bars, nursery. One hundred forty-two runs; longest run 3 miles; vertical drop 3,668 feet. (Late Nov-early Apr, daily) Cross-country skiing (14 miles). Multiday, half-day rates. Snowboarding. Gondola also operates mid-June-mid-Sept (daily; fee) **$$$$**

Steamboat Health & Recreation Association. *136 Lincoln Ave, east end of town. Phone 970/879-1828.* Three hot pools fed by 103°F mineral water; lap pool, saunas, exercise classes, massage, weight room, tennis courts (summer). (Daily). Also here is

Hot Slide Hydrotube. *136 Lincoln Ave (80477). Phone 970/879-1828.* Tube slide with 350 feet of hot water. (Daily) **$$$**

Steamboat Lake State Park. *61855 Routt County Rd 129. 26 miles N on County 129. Phone 970/879-3922.* Swimming, waterskiing, fishing, boating (ramps); picnicking, camping. Standard fees. (Daily) **$$**

Strawberry Park Natural Hot Springs. *44200 County Rd 36. 7 miles NE at 44200 County 36. Phone 970/879-0342.* Mineral springs feed four pools; water cooled from 160°F to 105°F. Changing area; picnicking, camping, cabins. (Daily)

Tread of Pioneers Museum. *800 Oak St. Phone 970/879-2214.* Victorian house with period rooms and furnishings. Pioneer and cattle ranching artifacts, Native American displays, permanent ski exhibit tracing the evolution of skiing. (Fall/Spring, Tues-Sat; Summer/Winter, Mon-Sat) **$$**

Special Events

Cowboy Roundup Days. Rodeos, parade, entertainment. July 4th weekend.

Mustang Round-Up. Mid-June.

Rainbow Weekend. Balloon rally, arts and crafts fair, concerts, rodeo. Mid-July.

Winter Carnival. Snow and ski competitions, parade. Early Feb.

Motels/Motor Lodges

★ **ALPINER LODGE.** *424 Lincoln Ave (80488). Phone 970/879-1430; toll-free 800/538-7519; fax 970/879-6044. www.steamboat-lodging.com.* 33 rooms, 2 story. Mid-Nov-Mar: S, D $69-$99; each additional $10; under 12 free; lower rates rest of year. Crib free. Pet accepted. Complimentary coffee in rooms. Check-out 10 am. TV; cable (premium). In-room modem link. Refrigerators, microwaves available. Restaurant opposite 6 am-10 pm. Downhill ski 1 mile, cross-country ski 1/2 mile. Business services. Cr cds: A, C, D, DS, MC, V.

★★ **BEST WESTERN PTARMIGAN INN.** *2304 Apres Ski Way (80477). Phone 970/897-1730; toll-free 800/538-7519; fax 970/879-6044. www.steamboat-lodging.com.* 77 rooms, 47 A/C, 3-4 story. Late Nov-mid-Apr: S, D $72-$234; each additional $10; under 18 free; higher rates late Dec; package plans; varied lower rates rest of year. Closed early Apr-late May. Crib free. Pet accepted. Complimentary coffee. Check-out 10 am. TV; cable, VCR. In-room modem link. Balconies. Refrigerators. Valet services, coin laundry. Bar 4-10 pm. Restaurant. Room service. Sauna. Heated pool, whirlpool. Downhill, cross-country ski on site, ski rentals, storage. Business services. View of Mount Werner, valley. Cr cds: A, C, D, DS, MC, V.

★★ **HOLIDAY INN.** *3190 S Lincoln Ave (80477). Phone 970/879-2250; toll-free 800/654-3944; fax 970/879-0251. www.holidayinnsteamboat.com.* 82 rooms, 2 story. Late Jan-Mar: S, D $129-$169; each additional $10; under 19 free; higher rates late Dec-early Jan; lower rates rest of year. Crib free. Pet accepted, some restrictions; $10/day. Check-out 11 am. TV; cable (premium), VCR available. In-room modem link. Some refrigerators. Microwaves available. Coffee in rooms. Valet services, coin laundry. Restaurant

6 am-11 pm. Bar 4-11 pm. Room service. Exercise equipment. Game room. Heated pool, wading pool, whirlpool. Downhill, cross-country ski 1 mile. Lawn games. Meeting room. Business services. Cr cds: A, C, D, DS, JCB, MC, V.

D ◨ ⊠ ⊠ 🛠 ⊠ SC

Hotel

★ ★ ★ **SHERATON STEAMBOAT SPRINGS RESORT AND CONFERENCE CENTER.** *2200 Village Inn Court (80477). Phone 970/879-2220; toll-free 800/848-8877; fax 970/879-7686. www.steamboat-sheraton.* 311 rooms, 8 story. S, D $99-$259; each additional $15; suites $249-$649; kitchen units $139-$580; under 17 free; ski, golf plans; varied lower rates June-mid-Sept, Thanksgiving-mid-Dec, Jan. Closed mid-Apr-mid-May, mid-Oct-mid-Nov. Complimentary coffee in rooms. Check-out 11 am, check-in 5 pm. TV; cable (premium). Private patios. Refrigerators. microwaves available. Coin laundry. Dining room 6:30 am-2 pm, 5:30-10 pm. Bar 2 pm-1 am. Room service. Health club privileges, exercise room, sauna. Game room. Heated pool, whirlpool. 18-hole golf privileges, greens fee $80, pro. Tennis privileges. Downhill, cross-country ski on site; rentals. Picnic tables. Business services. Convention center/facilities. Concierge. Cr cds: A, C, D, DS, ER, JCB, MC, V.

D ⊠ ⊠ ⊠ ⊠ ⊠ ⊠ 🛠

Resort

★ ★ **GLEN EDEN RESORT.** *54737 US 129 (80428). Phone 970/879-3906; toll-free 800/882-0854; fax 970/870-0858. www.glenedenresort.com.* 28 kitchen cottages, 1-2 story. Jan-Sept: cottages $115-$145; each additional $20; under 17 free; higher rates mid-Dec-early Jan; lower rates rest of year. Crib free. TV; VCR available (movies $2). Heated pool; whirlpools. Playground. Dining room 11:30 am-9 pm. Bar. Check-out 10 am, check-in 4 pm. Coin laundry. Grocery 1/2 mile. Meeting rooms. Business services available. Tennis. Downhill ski 20 miles; cross-country ski on site. Bicycles available. Lawn games. Microwaves. Balconies. Picnic tables, grills. Cr cds: A, DS, MC, V.

D ⊠ ⊠ ⊠ ⊠ ⊠ ⊠

B&B/Small Inn

★ ★ **SKY VALLEY LODGE.** *31490 US Hwy 40 (80477). Phone 970/879-7749; toll-free 800/499-4759; fax 970/879-7752. www.steamboat-lodging.com.* 24 rooms, 3 story. No A/C. No elevator. Late Nov-mid-Apr: S, D $69-$189; each additional $10; higher rates Christmas; lower rates rest of year. Crib free. Pet accepted, some restrictions. Complimentary breakfast. Check-out 11 am. TV; cable. In-room modem link. Dining room 7-10 am, noon-2 pm, 5-8 pm (in season). Bar 3-11 pm. Whirlpool.

Sauna. Downhill ski 7 miles, cross-country ski 5 miles. Meeting rooms. Business services. Totally nonsmoking. Cr cds: A, C, D, DS, MC, V.

◨ ⊠ ⊠ SC

Guest Ranches

★ ★ ★ **THE HOME RANCH.** *54880 Country Rd 129 (80428). Phone 970/879-1780; fax 970/879-1795.* Appropriately named, The Home Ranch makes everyone feel at home. Situated in the Elk River Valley with the majestic Rocky Mountains in the distance, the ranch is only 18 miles from the famed ski resort of Steamboat Springs. This natural paradise offers visitors an authentic guest ranch experience. Activities are plentiful, with more than 12 miles of snow-covered trails for snowshoeing and cross-country skiing in winter and mountain biking and hiking in summer. Horsemanship is the focus here, with cattle working and stockmanship lessons offered in addition to general riding. Eight cabins provide a secluded visit, while the rooms in the main lodge are convenient to the pool and dining room. Chef Clyde Nelson's culinary skills are highly praised, and the family-style meals are memorable. After dinner, guests listen to the sounds of the Ranch Hand Band, visit rodeos, or simply retire to the comfort of their Western-style rooms. 8 cottages, 6 lodge rooms. No room phones. AP, June-early Oct and mid-Dec-Mar, weekly: D $3,500-$4,600; each additional $1,650/week. Closed rest of year. Check-out 10 am, check-in 4 pm. Dining room 8-9 am, noon-1 pm, dinner (1 sitting) 7 pm; children's dinner 5:30 pm. Social director; entertainment nightly, movies. Supervised children's activities; ages 6-16. Petting zoo for children. Sauna. Heated pool; whirlpool. Downhill ski 20 miles; cross-country ski on site. Lawn games. Fishing guides. Fly-fishing instruction available. Guided hiking. Horse riding instruction available. Sleighing, tobogganing, ski instructor. Free local airport, bus depot transportation. Private porches. Ranch team roping, barbecue. Free local airport, bus depot transportation. Cr cds: A, MC, V.

D ⊠ ⊠ ⊠ ⊠ ⊠

★ ★ ★ **VISTA VERDE GUEST AND SKI RANCH.** *31100 Seedhouse Rd (80428). Phone 970/879-3858; toll-free 800/526-7433; fax 970/879-1413. www.vistaverde.com.* Situated on 500 acres in the Rocky Mountains, this wonderful ranch encourages guests to unwind while exploring the Old West. Private cabins and lodge rooms are decorated with a distinctive regional flair; the accommodations even feature furnishings handcrafted by the ranch's very own woodworker. Visitors are tempted by an array of on-property activities, from backcountry skiing and sleigh rides to fly fishing, hot-air ballooning, and hiking. Off the property, visitors enjoy dogsledding, whitewater rafting, and a host of other thrilling adventures. Naturally, horseback riding is the most popular activity at the ranch, and instruction is available for both children and adults. After a long day on the range, guests feast on gourmet meals at the lodge or on the sundeck while discussing the day's accomplishments with newly discovered friends. 8 cabins, 3 lodge rooms, 1-2 story. No A/C. Early June-late Sept, AP (7-day minimum): S, D $1,750-$1,850/person/week; under 8, $1,250-$1,350/week; lower rates June-Sept, Dec-Mar. Laundry services. Dining room. Entertainment; movies in lodge. Free supervised children's activities (late May-mid-Sept). Exercise equipment; sauna. Massage. Game room. Whirlpool. Cross-country ski on site. Lawn games. Mountain bikes. Guided hiking trips. Sleighing, tobogganing. Free airport, bus depot transportation. Float and backpack trips; gold-panning expeditions. Wood stoves. Private porches. Fish/hunt guides. Rock climbing with guide. Cattle drives. Dog sledding. Totally nonsmoking. No credit cards accepted.

Restaurants

★ ★ ★ **ANTARES.** *57 1/2 8th St (80477). Phone 970/879-9939; fax 970/879-0718.* Continental menu. Hours: 5:30-10 pm; hours vary off season. Closed Thanksgiving. Dinner $15-$35. Bar. Children's menu, 1909 building has Victorian-era furnishings; Victrola, large picture windows, stone fireplace. Reservations accepted. Cr cds: A, D, MC, V.

★ ★ ★ **L'APOGEE.** *911 Lincoln Ave (80487). Phone 970/879-1919; fax 970/879-2746. www.lapogee.com.* French menu. Menu changes every 3 months. Hours: 5:30-10:30 pm. Dinner $8-$32. Bar. Children's menu. Reservations accepted. Patio dining. Totally nonsmoking. 1886 building. Cr cds: MC.

★ ★ **LA MONTANA.** *2500 Village Dr (80487). Phone 970/879-5800; fax 970/879-5373. www.la-montana.com.* Southwestern, Mexican menu. Hours: 5:30-10 pm; summer from 6 pm. Closed Thanksgiving. Reservations accepted. Bar 5-10 pm. Dinner $9.25-$22.95. Children's menu. Parking. Outdoor dining. Cr cds: A, DS, MC, V.

★ ★ **ORE HOUSE AT THE PINE GROVE.** *1465 Pine Grove Rd (80477). Phone 970/879-1190; fax 970/879-0479. www.orehouseatthepinegrove.com.* Hours: 5-9:30 pm. Reservations accepted. Bar. Dinner $11.95-$29.50. Children's menu. Specializes in steak, prime rib, fresh seafood. Salad bar. Parking. Outdoor dining. Old ranch décor. Fireplaces; ranch antiques. Cr cds: A, DS, MC, V.

★ ★ **STEAMBOAT BREWERY.** *811 Yampa Ave (80477). Phone 970/879-4774; fax 970/879-1947.* Seafood, steak menu. Hours: 11:30 am-10 pm. Dinner $14.95-

$23.95. Bar. Children's menu. Reservations accepted. Outdoor dining overlooking river and ski jump. Cr cds: A; MC, V.

★ **WINONA'S DELI-BAKERY.** *617 Lincoln Ave (80477). Phone 970/879-2483; fax 970/879-3277.* Specializes in deli sandwiches, pastries. Hours: 7 am-9 pm. Closed Thanksgiving, Dec 25. Breakfast $1.95-$5.95, lunch $5-$8. Children's menu. Outdoor dining. Totally nonsmoking. Cr cds: MC, V.

Sterling (B-8)

Pop 11,360 **Elev** 3,939 ft **Area code** 970 **Zip** 80751

Information Logan County Chamber of Commerce, 109 N Front St, PO Box 1683; 970/522-5070 or 800/544-8609

Web www.logancountychamber.com

What to See and Do

Outdoor sculptures. Sterling is known as the "City of Living Trees" because of the unique carved trees found throughout town. A self-guided tour map shows where to find the 16 sculpted trees created by a local sculptor. Call the Logan County Chamber of Commerce for more information.

Overland Trail Museum. *21053 County Rd 26-1/2, just off I-76. Phone 970/522-3895.* Village of seven buildings. Collections of Native American artifacts, cattle brands, farm machinery; archaeological and paleontological exhibits, one-room schoolhouse, fire engine, children's displays; local historical items; park and picnic area. (Apr-Oct, daily; rest of year, Tues-Sat) **FREE**

Motels/Motor Lodges

★ **BEST WESTERN SUNDOWNER.** *Overland Trail St (80751). Phone 970/522-6265; toll-free 800/780-7234. www.bestwestern.com.* 30 rooms. S $70; D $79; each additional $7; under 12 free. Pet accepted; fee. Complimentary continental breakfast. Check-out 11 am. TV; cable (premium), VCR available. In-room modem link. Exercise equipment. Pool; whirlpool. Cr cds: A, C, D, DS, MC, V.

★ **COLONIAL MOTEL.** *915 S Division Ave (80751). Phone 970/522-3382; toll-free 888/522-2901.* 14 rooms. S $32; D $38-$44; each additional $3; under 10 free; weekly rates in winter. Pet accepted. Check-out 10 am. TV; cable (premium). In-room modem link. Some refrigerators. Microwaves available. Coffee in rooms. Cr cds: A, DS, MC, V.

★ ★ **RAMADA INN.** *22246 E Hwy 6 (80751). Phone 970/522-2625; toll-free 800/835-7275; fax 970/522-1321. www.ramada.com.* 100 rooms, 2 story. S $50-$72; D $57-$81; each additional $7; under 18 free. Crib free. Pet accepted, some restrictions. Complimentary coffee in rooms. Check-out noon. TV; cable (premium). In-room modem link. Valet services. Restaurant 6 am-10 pm. Bar 3:30-10 pm. Exercise equipment, sauna. Game room. Indoor pool, whirlpool. Meeting rooms. Business services. Cr cds: A, C, D, DS, ER, JCB, MC, V.

D ⊙ ⩦ ⩓ ⩘

B&B/Small Inn

★ ★ **ELK ECHO RANCH.** *47490 Weld County Rd 155 (80754). Phone 970/735-2426; fax 970/735-2427. www.wapiti.net/co/eer.htm.* This 5,200-square-foot log bed-and-breakfast offers guest rooms with a quiet atmosphere. Guests can enjoy watching over 500 head of elk and a small buffalo herd from the deck, or take advantage of the complimentary tour, which includes a guest photo. 4 rooms, 3 story. No room phones. S $89; D $99; each additional $10-$20. Complimentary full breakfast. Check-out 11 am, check-in 4 pm. Rustic log cabin lodge. Totally nonsmoking. Cr cds: MC, V.

⩘

Restaurant

★ **T.J. BUMMER'S.** *203 Broadway (80751). Phone 970/522-8397; fax 970/521-9554.* Steak menu. Hours: 5:30 am-9 pm; Oct-Apr to 8 pm. Closed most major holidays. Dinner $5.95-$14.95. Children's menu. Totally nonsmoking. Cr cds: A, DS, MC, V.

D ⩘ SC

Telluride (F-2)

See also Norwood

Settled 1878 **Pop** 2,221 **Elev** 8,800 ft **Area code** 970 **Zip** 81435

Information Telluride Visitor Services, 666 W Colorado Ave, Box 653; 970/728-4431 or 888/605-2578

Web www.telluride.com

Gray granite and red sandstone mountains surround this mining town named for the tellurium ore containing precious metals found in the area. Telluride, proud of its bonanza past, has not changed its façade. Because of its remoteness and small size, Telluride remains uncrowded and retains its history. Summer activities include fly-fishing, mountain biking, river rafting, hiking, Jeep trips, horseback riding, and camping, as well as many annual events and festivals from May to October.

What to See and Do

Bear Creek Trail. *S end of Pine St.* A 2-mile canyon walk with view of tiered waterfall. (May-Oct)

Bridal Veil Falls. *2 1/2 miles E on CO 145.* Highest waterfall in Colorado. Structure at top of falls was once a hydroelectric power plant, which served the Smuggler-Union Mine operations. It has been recently renovated and now provides auxiliary electric power to Telluride.

Telluride Gondola. *Four gondola terminals: Station Telluride, Oak St; Station St. Sophia, on the ski mountain; stations Mt Village and Village Parking in Mt Village.* Passengers are transported from downtown Telluride, over ski mountain, and to Mount Village. (Early June-early Oct and late Nov-mid-Apr, daily)

Telluride Historical Museum. *317 N Fir St. Phone 970/728-3344.* Built in 1893 as the community hospital, this historic building houses artifacts, historic photos, and exhibits that show what Telluride was like in its Wild West days. (Tues-Sun) **FREE**

Telluride Ski Resort. *565 Mt Village Blvd. Phone 800/801-4832.* Three-stage gondola; four quad, two triple, two double chairlifts; one surface lift; patrol, school, rentals; restaurants, nursery. Sixty-six runs; longest run 3 miles; vertical drop 3,522 feet. (Thanksgiving-early Apr, daily) Cross-country skiing, heliskiing, ice skating, snowmobiling, sleigh rides. Shuttle bus service and two in-town chairlifts. **$$$$**

Special Events

Balloon Rally. Early June.

Bluegrass Festival. *Town Park.* Late June.

Chamber Music Festival. *110 N Oak St (81435). Phone 970/728-6769.* Mid-Aug.

Jazz Celebration. *Town Park.* Early Aug.

Mountain Film Festival. *207 W Columbia Ave (81435). Phone 970/728-4401.* Labor Day weekend.

Telluride Airmen's Rendezvous & Hang Gliding Festival. Mid-Sept.

Telluride Bluegrass Festival. *Phone 800/624-2422.* For four days each June, thousands of music lovers flock to Telluride for what many agree is the nation's premier bluegrass festival. A tradition for more than 30 years, the festival draws some of the nation's top bluegrass and folk performers who pluck their stuff for the adoring throngs at Town Park. Spontaneous jams continue throughout the day and into the wee hours of the night at local eating and drinking spots. The festival includes amateur competitions and workshops. It is a favorite destination for campers wishing to experience the natural beauty of Telluride's mountain setting and the high-spirited fun of the festival. Mid-June. **$$$$**

Hotels

★ ★ **CAMEL'S GARDEN.** *250 W San Juan (81435). Phone 970/728-9300; toll-free 888/772-2635; fax 970/728-0433. www.camelsgarden.com.* 30 rooms, 3 story. Complimentary continental breakfast. Check-out 11 am, check-in 4 pm. TV; VCR available. Internet access. Restaurant. Whirlpool. **$$**

★ ★ ★ **COLUMBIA HOTEL.** *300 W San Juan Ave (81435). Phone 970/728-0660; toll-free 800/201-9505; fax 970/728-9249. www.columbiatelluride.com.* 21 rooms, 4 story. No A/C. D$230- $285. Pet accepted, some restrictions; $25. Check-out 11 am. TV; cable (premium), VCR (movies). In-room modem link. Fireplaces. Laundry. Restaurant, bar 4-9 pm. Room service. Exercise equipment. Downhill, cross-country ski/snowboard on site. Cr cds: A, MC, V.

Resort

★ ★ ★ **WYNDHAM – THE PEAKS RESORT.** *136 Country Club Dr (81435). Phone 970/728-6800; toll-free 800/789-2220; fax 970/728-6175. www.peaksresort.com.* 174 rooms, 6 story. Closed mid-Apr-mid-May, mid-Oct-mid-Nov. Pet accepted. Check-out noon, check-in 4 pm. TV; cable (premium), VCR. In-room modem link. Dining room. Room service. Bar. Supervised children's activities. Babysitting services available. In-house fitness room, spa, massage, sauna. Indoor, outdoor pool, children's pool, whirlpool, poolside service. Golf; greens fee $160 (including cart). Outdoor tennis, lighted courts. Downhill, cross-country ski on site; rentals. Hiking, sleighing, snowmobiles. Valet parking. Free airport transportation. Business center. Concierge. Cr cds: A, C, D, DS, MC, V. **$$$**

B&B/Small Inns

★ **MANITOU LODGE.** *333 S Fir St (80751). Phone 970/728-4011; toll-free 800/538-7754; fax 970/728-3716.* 12 rooms, 2 story. No A/C. Mid-Feb-Mar: S, D $140-$160; higher rates: festivals, holidays; lower rates rest of year. Complimentary continental breakfast. Check-out 10 am, check-in 4 pm. TV; cable (premium). Restaurant nearby. Downhill ski 1 block, cross-country ski on site. Cr cds: A, D, DS, MC, V.

★ ★ ★ **NEW SHERIDAN HOTEL.** *231 W Colorado Ave (81435). Phone 970/728-4351; toll-free 800/200-1891; fax 970/728-5024. www.newsheridan.com.* Built in 1891, this property is located in the heart of Telluride. Many of the elegant guest rooms feature mountain views and separate sitting rooms. Warm up with a hearty gourmet breakfast and relax in the afternoon with a complimentary glass of Pine Ridge wine at the New Sheridan Bar. 26 rooms, 3 story. Closed mid-Apr-mid-May. Complimentary continental breakfast. Check-out 11 am, check-in 2 pm. TV; cable (premium). In-room modem link. Restaurant. Babysitting services available. In-house fitness room. Game room. Whirlpool. Downhill, cross-country ski 2 blocks. Valet parking. Concierge. Totally nonsmoking. Cr cds: A, D, MC, V. **$$**

★ ★ ★ **THE SAN SOPHIA INN AND CONDOMINIUMS.** *330 W Pacific Ave (81435). Phone 970/728-3001; toll-free 800/537-4781; fax 970/728-6226. www.sansophia.com.* 16 rooms, 2 story. D $135-$300; each additional $25; higher rates: music and film festivals, Dec-Mar. Closed Apr, Nov. Children over 9 years only. Complimentary full breakfast. Check-out 11 am, check-in 3 pm. TV; cable (premium), VCR. Downhill ski 1 block, cross-country ski on site. Fishing, horses/riding. Modern frame structure built in Victorian style with octagon tower observatory; bay windows; library, sitting room. Interiors blend Victorian and modern Southwest design; stained and etched glass, period furnishings. Mountain views. Totally nonsmoking. Cr cds: A, MC, V.

★ **THE VICTORIAN INN.** *401 W Pacific St (81435). Phone 970/728-6601; toll-free 800/611-9893; fax 970/728-3233. www.tellurideinn.com.* 31 rooms, 2 story. No A/C. Late Nov-early Apr: D $88-$138; each additional $7; under 7 free; higher rates: mid-Dec-early Jan, Washington's birthday, special events; lower rates rest of year. Complimentary continental breakfast. Check-out 10 am, check-in 4 pm. TV. Restaurant nearby. Sauna. Downhill skiing, cross-country skiing. Totally nonsmoking. Cr cds: A, C, D.

Restaurants

★ ★ ★ **ALLRED'S.** *2 Coonskin Ridge (81435). Phone 970/728-7474.* American menu. Closed mid Apr-mid June, late Sept-mid-Dec. Dinner. Bar. Children's menu. Casual attire. Reservations required. **$$$**

★ ★ ★ **COSMOPOLITAN.** *300 W San Juan (81435). Phone 970/728-1292; fax 970/728-9249. www.cosmotelluride.com.* French, American menu. Closed mid Apr-mid May, last week Oct. Dinner. Bar. Entertainment. Children's menu. Casual attire. Reservations required. Nonsmoking. Cr cds: A, MC, V. **$$**

★ **FLORADORA.** *103 W Colorado Ave (81435). Phone 970/728-3888; fax 970/728-4846.* Hours: 11 am-10 pm. Southwestern, American menu. Bar to midnight. Lunch $5-$10, dinner $6.95-$18.95. Children's menu. Specializes in steak, pasta, fajitas. Stained-glass windows, Tiffany-style lamps. Totally nonsmoking. Cr cds: A, MC, V.

D ⊠

Thornton

Restaurant

★ **BRITTANY HILL.** *9350 Grant (80229). Phone 303/451-5151; fax 303/451-1013.* Hours: 11 am-2 pm, 4-9 pm; Fri, Sat to 11 pm; Sun 4-10 pm; Sun brunch 9 am-2:30 pm. Reservations accepted. Bar to 11 pm. Lunch $6.95-$8.95, dinner $13.95-$25.95. Sun brunch $17.95. Specializes in prime rib, steak, fresh seafood. Patio deck. Scenic view of city, mountains. Cr cds: A, C, D, DS, ER, MC, V.

D SC

Trinidad (G-6)

See also Walsenburg

Settled 1859 **Pop** 9,078 **Elev** 6,025 ft **Area code** 719 **Zip** 81082

Information Trinidad-Las Animas County Chamber of Commerce, 309 Nevada Ave; 719/846-9285

Web www.trinidadco.com

Bat Masterson was marshal and Kit Carson was a frequent visitor to Trinidad when it was a busy trading post along the Santa Fe Trail. Today the town specializes in small manufacturing and distribution, ranching, farming, and tourism. It is the seat of Las Animas County.

What to See and Do

A. R. Mitchell Memorial Museum of Western Art. *150 E Main St. Phone 719/846-4224.* Features Western paintings by Arthur Roy Mitchell, Harvey Dunn, Harold von Schmidt, and other famous artists; Western and Native American artifacts; Hispanic religious folk art. Housed in a 1906 former department store with original tin ceiling, wood floors, horseshoe-shaped mezzanine. (Apr-Sept, Mon-Sat; also by appointment; closed holidays) **FREE**

Trinidad History Museum. *300 E Main St, on the historic Santa Fe Trail. Phone 719/846-7217.* Colorado Historical Society administers this museum complex. The Baca House (1870) is a restored 9-room, 2-story adobe house purchased by a wealthy Hispanic sheep rancher. The Bloom House (1882) is a restored Victorian mansion and garden built by cattleman and banker Frank C. Bloom. The Santa Fe Museum is also here. Guided tours (Memorial Day-Sept, daily; rest of year, by appointment) **$$**

Trinidad Lake State Park. *32610 State Hwy 12 (81082). 3 miles W on CO 12. Phone 719/846-6951.* A 2,300-acre park with a 900-acre lake. Waterskiing, fishing, boating (ramps); nature trails, mountain biking, picnicking, playground, camping (electrical hookups, showers, dump station). Interpretive programs (Memorial Day-Labor Day, Fri, Sat, holidays Standard fees. (Daily) **$$**

Motels/Motor Lodges

★ **BUDGET HOST DERRICK MOTEL.** *10301 Santa Fe Trail (81082). Phone 719/846-3307; toll-free 800/BUDHOST; fax 719/846-3309. www.trinidadco.com/budgethost.* 26 rooms. June-mid-Sept: S $39.95-$59.95; D $49.95-$69.95; weekly rates; lower rates rest of year. Crib $3. Pet accepted; $5. Complimentary continental breakfast, coffee in rooms. Check-out 11 am. TV; cable. Refrigerators. Microwaves available. Coin laundry. Restaurant nearby. Whirlpool. Picnic tables. Lawn games. Free airport transportation. Features 107-foot oil derrick. Located along the Mountain Branch of the Santa Fe Trail. Cr cds: A, DS, MC, V.

D 🐾 🦮 ⊠ SC

★ **BUDGET SUMMIT INN.** *9800 Santa Fe Trail Dr (81082). Phone 719/846-2251.* 44 rooms, 21 with shower only, 2 story. Memorial Day-Labor Day: S $40-$60; D $45-$70; each additional $10; lower rates rest of year. Pet accepted; $3. TV; cable. Whirlpool. Complimentary continental breakfast. Restaurant adjacent open 24 hours. Check-out 11 am. Coin laundry. Meeting room. Business services available. In-room modem link. Gift shop. Recreation room. Lawn games. Some refrigerators; microwaves available. Cr cds: A, MC, V.

D 🐾 ⊠

★ ★ **HOLIDAY INN.** *3125 Toupal Dr (81082). Phone 719/846-4491; fax 719/846-2440. www.holiday-inn.com.* 113 rooms, 2 story. June-Sept: S $89-$109; D $99-$119; each additional $10; under 18 free; lower rates rest of year. Crib free. Pet accepted, some restrictions. Check-out noon. TV; cable (premium). In-room modem link. Some refrigerators, bathroom phones. Microwaves available. Coffee in rooms. Coin laundry. Restaurant 6 am-10 pm. Bar 5 pm-midnight. Room service from 7 am. Exercise equipment. Game room. Indoor pool, whirlpool, poolside service. Lawn games. Meeting rooms. Business services. Gift shop. Cr cds: A, C, D, DS, ER, JCB, MC, V.

D 🐾 🏊 🏋 ⊠

Restaurant

★ ★ **CHEF LIU'S CHINESE RESTAURANT.** *1423 Santa Fe Trail (81082). Phone 719/846-3333; fax 719/846-6688.* Chinese menu. Closed Thanksgiving; also Mon Thanksgiving-Mar. Dinner. Bar. Cr cds: A, MC, V. **$$**

D ⊠

Vail (C-4)

See also Dillon, Leadville

Pop 4,531 **Elev** 8,160 ft

Information Vail Valley Tourism & Convention Bureau, 100 E Meadow Dr; 970/476-1000 or 800/525-3875

Web visitvailvalley.com

A resort community in White River National Forest (see GLENWOOD SPRINGS), Vail offers activities including golf, tennis, bicycling, hiking, horseback riding, swimming, camping, Jeep trips, river rafting, and scenic gondola rides, hunting and fishing in season, and of course, skiing in winter.

What to See and Do

Beaver Creek/Arrowhead Resort. *137 Benchmark Rd (81620). 10 miles W on I-70, exit 167, then 3 miles S. Phone 970/949-5750.* Six quad, three triple, four double chairlifts; patrol, rentals, snowmaking; cafeteria, restaurants, bar, nursery. Longest run 2 3/4 miles; vertical drop 4,040 feet. (Late Nov-mid-Apr, daily) Cross-country trails and rentals (Nov-Apr), ice skating, snowmobiling, sleigh rides. Chairlift rides (July-Aug, daily; Sept, weekends; fee). **$$$$**

Colorado Ski Museum & Ski Hall of Fame. *231 S Frontage, in Vail Village Transportation Center. Phone 970/476-1876.* Skiing artifacts and photographs tracing the history of skiing in Colorado for more than 120 years. (Memorial Day-late Sept and late Nov-mid Apr, Tues-Sun; closed holidays) **$**

Gerald R. Ford Amphitheater/Betty Ford Gardens. *Phone 888/883-8245* The Gerald R. Ford Amphitheater Vilar Pavilion is an open-air stadium that gives music lovers of all ages the chance to enjoy a wide variety of shows while siting under Vail's crystal-clear, starlit skies. Surrounded by the Betty Ford Alpine Gardens, a public botanical garden with more than 500 varieties of wildflowers and alpine plants, the amphitheater combines natural beauty with top-quality entertainment. Performances throughout the summer normally include classical music, rock and roll, jazz, ballet, contemporary dance, and children's theater. (June-Aug)

Vail Ski Resort. *137 Benchmark Rd (81620). In town on I-70, exit 176. Phone 970/476-9090.* Gondola; thirteen high-speed quad, two fixed-grip quad, three triple, six double chairlifts; nine surface lifts; patrol, school, rentals, snowmaking; cafeterias, restaurants, bars, nursery. Longest run 4 1/2 miles; vertical drop 3,360 feet. (Late Nov-mid-Apr, daily) Cross-country trails, rentals (Nov-Apr; fee), ice skating, snowmobiling, sleigh rides. Gondola and Vista Bahn (June-Aug, daily; May and Sept, weekends; fee). **$$$$**

Special Event

Taste of Vail. *Phone 888/311-5665.* Early Apr.

Motel/Motor Lodges

★★ **BEST WESTERN VAILGLO LODGE.** *701 W Lionshead Cir (81658). Phone 970/476-5506; toll-free 800/541-9423; fax 970/476-3926. www.bestwestern.com.* 34 air-cooled rooms, 4 story. Feb-Mar, Dec: S, D $99-$250; each additional $25; under 8 free; lower rates rest of year. Crib free. Complimentary continental breakfast. Check-out noon. TV; cable (premium). In-room modem link. Balconies. Refrigerators. Valet services. Restaurant adjacent 7-3 am. Heated pool, whirlpool. Downhill, cross-country ski 1 block. Cr cds: A, C, D, DS, MC, V.

★ **VAIL'S MOUNTAIN HAUS.** *292 E Meadow Dr (81657). Phone 970/476-2434; toll-free 800/237-0922; fax 970/476-3007. www.mountainhaus.com.* 72 rooms, 5 story, 64 kitchen units. No A/C. Jan-Apr: S, D $120-$240; kitchen units $230-$600; weekly rates; higher rates holidays; lower rates rest of year. Crib available. Check-out 10 am. TV; cable (premium), VCR (movies). Many balconies. Fireplaces. Complimentary coffee in rooms. Coin laundry. Restaurant opposite 7 am-10 pm. Bar from 6 pm. Exercise equipment, massage, sauna. Pool, whirlpool. Downhill, cross-country ski 1 block. Garage parking $15. Meeting rooms. Business services. Concierge. Cr cds: A, C, D, DS, MC, V.

Hotels

★★ **HOTEL GASTHOF GRAMSHAMMER.** *231 E Gore Creek Dr (81657). Phone 970/476-5626; toll-free 800/610-7374; fax 970/476-8816. www.pepis.com.* 40 rooms, 4 story. No A/C. Late Apr-Late May. Complimentary continental breakfast. Check-out 11 am, check-in 3 pm. TV; VCR available. Fireplaces. Restaurant, bar. In-house fitness room. Health club privileges. Downhill ski 1 block. Austrian décor. Cr cds: A, D, DS, MC, V. **$$**

★ **SITZMARK LODGE.** *183 Gore Creek Dr (81657). Phone 970/476-5001; toll-free 888/476-5001; fax 970/476-8702.* 35 rooms, 3 story. Complimentary continental breakfast (winter). Check-out 11 am, check-in 4 pm. TV; cable (premium). In-room modem link. Some fireplaces. Sauna. Outdoor pool, whirlpool. Downhill, cross-country ski 1/2 block. Cr cds: DS, MC, V. **$$**

★ ★ **VAIL ATHLETIC CLUB HOTEL & SPA.** *352 E Meadow Dr (81657). Phone 970/476-0700; toll-free 800/822-4754; fax 970/476-6451. www.vailmountainlodge-spa.com.* 38 air-cooled rooms, 3 story, 9 suites, 7 kitchen units. Feb-Mar: S, D $350-$375; suites $765-$1,300; kitchen units $445; under 12 free; higher rates holidays; lower rates rest of year. Crib free. Complimentary continental breakfast, coffee in rooms. Check-out 11 am. TV; cable (premium), VCR available. In-room modem link. Balconies. Refrigerators, some microwaves. Valet services, coin laundry. Restaurant 7-10 am, 5:30-10 pm. Bar 5 pm-closing. Room service. Exercise room, spa, sauna. Indoor pool, whirlpool. Golf privileges, greens fee $85, pro, putting green, driving range. Tennis privileges. Downhill, cross-country ski 3 blocks. Beauty shop. Free covered parking. Meeting rooms. Business services. Concierge. Cr cds: A, C, D, DS, MC, V.

Resorts

★ ★ ★ **THE CHARTER AT BEAVER CREEK.** *120 Offerson Rd (81620). Phone 970/949-6660; toll-free 800/525-6660; fax 970/949-6709. www.thecharter.com.* 64 lodge rooms, 4-6 story, 156 condos. Late Nov-mid-Apr: S, D $140-$310; suites $210-$1,160; ski, golf plans; higher rates late Dec; lower rates rest of year. Crib $6. Check-out 11 am, check-in 4 pm. TV; cable (premium), VCR (movies). In-room modem link. Balconies. Refrigerators. Fireplace in condos. Coffee in rooms. Dining room 7-10:30 am, 11:30 am-2 pm, 5:30-9:30 pm; summer 7 am-2 pm, 5-11 pm. Bar 4-10 pm; summer 5-11 pm. Box lunches. Supervised children's activities (Jan-Apr); ages 4-12. Exercise room, massage, sauna, steam room. 2 pools, 1 indoor, wading pool, whirlpool. 18-hole golf privileges opp, pro. Tennis privileges, pro. Downhill, cross-country ski on site. Ski shop. Sleighing, snowmobiles. Beauty shop. Valet parking. Meeting rooms. Business services. Bellhops, concierge. Cr cds: A, MC, V.

★ ★ **CHATEAU AT VAIL.** *13 Vail Rd (81657). Phone 970/476-5631; toll-free 800/451-9840; fax 970/476-2508. www.chateauvail.com.* 120 rooms, 4 story. Nov-Mar, July-Sept: S $145; D $165; each additional $25; under 18 free; lower rates rest of year. Crib available. Pool; whirlpool. TV; cable. Complimentary coffee in rooms. Restaurant 7 am-9 pm. Bar. Check-out 11 am-3 pm. Meeting rooms. Free airport transportation. Sauna, steam room. Golf, 18 holes. Tennis, 4 courts. Downhill skiing. Hiking trail. Cr cds: A, D, DS, MC, V.

★ ★ ★ **THE INN AT BEAVER CREEK.** *10 Elk Track Ln (81620). Phone 970/845-7800; toll-free 800/859-8242; fax 970/845-5279. www.innatbeavercreek.com.* This ideal ski-in/ski-out location near the Strawberry Park Express chairlift is also within walking distance of Beaver Creek Resort shops and eateries. The rooms and suites have mountain lodge décor. Check-out 10 am. TV; cable (premium), VCR available. In-room modem link. Refrigerators, microwaves. Coffee in rooms. Valet services, free laundry. Restaurant nearby. Bar 3-10 pm. Health club privileges, exercise equipment, sauna, steam room. Heated pool, whirlpool. Downhill, cross-country ski on site. True ski in and ski out. Complimentary covered parking. Meeting rooms. Business services. Concierge. Cr cds: A, C, D, DS, MC, V. $$$

★ ★ **LION SQUARE LODGE.** *660 W Lionshead Pl (81657). Phone 970/476-2281; toll-free 800/525-5788; fax 970/476-7423. www.lionsquare.com.* 108 units, 3-7 story, 83 townhouses. No A/C. Nov-Apr: S $109-$400; D $189-$450; townhouses $260-$800; under 17 free; lower rates rest of year. Crib free. Check-out 10 am. TV; cable (premium), VCR available. Balconies. Refrigerators, microwaves. Coffee in rooms. Valet services, coin laundry. Restaurant 6-10 pm. Supervised children's activities (Nov-Apr); ages 5-12. Health club privileges, sauna. Heated pool, whirlpool. Downhill ski adjacent, cross-country ski on site. Ski shop. Picnic tables. Lawn games. Free garage parking. Meeting rooms. Business services. Concierge. On creek; adjacent to gondola. Cr cds: A, D, DS, MC, V.

★ ★ ★ **LODGE AND SPA AT CORDILLERA.** *2205 Cordillera Way, Edwards (81632). Phone 970/926-2200; toll-free 800/877-3529; fax 970/926-2486. www.cordillera-vail.com.* The French-chateau architecture and beautiful mountaintop location make this one of the most exclusive resorts in the Vail/Beaver Creek area. Part of a community that includes private homes and a golf club, this resort treats its guests to unparalleled intimacy. A lovely country style dominates the accommodations, where wood-burning or gas fireplaces add warmth and breathtaking mountain views set a sense of place. Award-winning golf and a sensational spa are at the doorstep, and world-class skiing is just down the road. Four restaurants garner praise from critics and gourmets, from the nightly works of art at Restaurant Picasso (see also RESTAURANT PICASSO) to the American dishes with a Western slant at the Timber Hearth Grille. Steaks and seafood are delicious at Chaparral, while the Grouse-on-the-Green, whose interiors were constructed in Ireland, is a true taste of the Emerald Isle. 56 rooms, 3 story. S $150-$495; D $150-$595; suites $275-$950; under 16 free. Check-out noon, check-in 4 pm. cable (premium), VCR available. In-room modem link. Many fireplaces, sleeping lofts. Restaurant. Bar; entertainment weekends. Room service 6 am-10 pm. Extensive exercise room; sauna, steam room. 2 pools, 1 indoor; indoor/outdoor whirlpool. 3 golf courses, two 18-hole, one 10-hole, greens fee $180. Tennis on premise. Downhill ski 8 miles; cross-country ski on site; rentals. Bicycle rentals. Hiking. Horseback riding. Business center. Concierge. Totally nonsmoking. Cr cds: A, D, DS, MC, V.

★ ★ ★ **THE LODGE AT VAIL.** *174 E Gore Creek Dr (81657). Phone 970/476-5011; fax 970/476-7425. www.vail.net/thelodge.* The Lodge at Vail is perfectly located in the heart of the pedestrian village, at the base of Vail Mountain. Skiers need to take only a few steps to the lift, while shoppers and diners walk out to enjoy the village's boutiques and cafés. Visitors reap the rewards of this Eden for outdoor enthusiasts. Summer adventures include whitewater rafting, golf, fishing, hot-air ballooning, and horseback riding, while winter is all about snowshoeing, skiing and snowboarding on the renowned slopes, and a host of other wintertime activities. Four hot tubs, one sauna, and an outdoor pool soothe weary muscles. Two restaurants satisfy hearty appetites, while Mickey's Piano Bar entertains. Individually decorated, the guest rooms are a perfect blend of European grace and Western aplomb. The Lodge marries the charm of an Alpine inn with the amenities of a world-class resort. 124 rooms, 2 story. Check-out 11 am, check-in 4 pm. TV; cable (premium). Restaurant, bar. In-house fitness room. Outdoor pool, children's pool, whirlpool. Concierge. Cr cds: A, C, D, DS, JCB, MC, V. **$$$**

★ ★ ★ **MARRIOTT VAIL MOUNTAIN RESORT.** *715 W Lionshead Cir (81657). Phone 970/476-4444; fax 970/476-1647. www.marriott.com.* The guest rooms range from a well-appointed standard to the Timberland Suite that has magnificent views of Vail Mountain. 350 units, 6 story, 40 kitchens Some A/C. Jan-Mar: S, D $175-$375; kitchen units, suites $300-$825; under 18 free; ski, package plans; higher rates Christmas holidays; lower rates rest of year. Crib free. TV; cable (premium). 2 pools, 1 indoor; whirlpool, poolside service (summer). Coffee in rooms. Restaurants 7 am-11 pm; summer to 10 pm. Bars to midnight. Check-out 11 am, check-in 4 pm. Coin laundry. Convention facilities. Business center. In-room modem link. Valet service. Concierge. Gift shop. Beauty shop. Tennis. Downhill/cross-country ski 1/4 mile. Ski rentals. Exercise room; steam room. Spa. Refrigerators; some microwaves, fireplaces. Balconies. Cr cds: A, C, D, DS, ER, JCB, MC, V.

★ ★ ★ **PARK HYATT BEAVER CREEK RESORT AND SPA.** *50 E Thomas Pl (81620). Phone 970/949-1234; fax 970/949-4164. www.hyatt.beavercreek .com.* Snuggled at the base of the Gore Mountains in the heart of the Beaver Creek Village, the ski-in/ski-out Park Hyatt Beaver Creek Resort and Spa is an alpine paradise. Three of the West's best ski resorts, Beaver Creek, Bachelor Gulch, and Arrowhead, are accessed from the hotel, and Vail is only 10 miles away. Skiers of all levels are accommodated, and the resort's Performance Skiing Program helps guests improve their level within days. This year-round resort delights visitors in any season, however, with championship golf, the Allegria Spa, six outdoor whirlpools, and a host of other activities. Five restaurants cover all the bases, with family dining places and romantic après-ski bars. From the giant chandelier crafted of antlers and the massive stone fireplaces to the pine furnishings in the guest rooms, this resort is Western country style at its best. 274 rooms, 6 story. Valet parking. Check-out noon, check-in 4 pm. TV; cable (premium), VCR available. In-room modem link. Laundry services. Restaurant, bar; entertainment. Room service. Children's activity center. Sauna, steam room, spa. Outdoor pool, children's pool, whirlpool. Golf, greens fee $80-$160. Outdoor tennis. Downhill, cross-country ski on site. Lawn games, bicycles, fishing, hiking. Business center. Concierge. Cr cds: A, C, D, DS, JCB, MC, V. **$$$**

★ ★ ★ **THE PINES LODGE.** *141 Scott Hill Rd (81620). Phone 970/845-7900; toll-free 800/859-8242; fax 970/845-7809.* Perched above the Beaver Creek Resort and golf course, this hotel, condo, and townhouse-complex has splendid views and a warm, mountain décor of pine, tapestries, and wild flowers. 60 rooms, 4 story. Complimentary continental breakfast. Check-out 10 am, check-in 4 pm. TV; cable (premium), VCR available. In-room modem link. Restaurant. Fireplaces. Babysitting services available. In-house fitness room, massage. Game room. Outdoor pool, whirlpool. Downhill, cross-country ski adjacent. Concierge. Cr cds: A, C, D, DS, MC, V. **$$$**

★ ★ ★ **SONNENALP RESORT OF VAIL.** *20 Vail Rd (81657). Phone 970/476-5656; toll-free 800/654-8312; fax 970/476-1639. www.sonnenalp.com.* All suites at this tranquil retreat in Vail have views, and soaking tubs with heated marble tiles. 149 rooms, 3 villas (3-4 story). Some A/C. Early Jan-early Apr: S $172-$497; D $190-$515; each additional $25; suite $370-$1,440; under 5 free; package plans; higher rates Christmas season; lower rates rest of year. TV; cable (premium), VCR available (movies available). 2 indoor/outdoor pools; whirlpool. Supervised children's activities; infant-6 years. Restaurant 7 am-10 pm. Room service. Bar. Check-out 11 am. Meeting rooms. Business center. In-room modem link. Bellhops. Valet service. Concierge. Free valet parking. Tennis privileges. 18-hole golf privileges, pro, putting green, driving range. Downhill/cross-country ski 1/4 mile. Exercise equipment;

sauna, steam room. Game room. Some balconies. Cr cds: A, D, DS, MC, V.

★ ★ ★ **VAIL CASCADE RESORT & SPA.** *1300 Westhaven Dr (81657). Phone 970/476-7111; fax 970/479-7020.* The Cascade Village chair lift is 10 feet from this European-style alpine village. 289 rooms, 4 story. Late Nov-mid-Apr: S, D $309-$429; suites $500-$995; under 18 free; package plans; lower rates rest of year. Crib free. Valet parking $12. TV; cable (premium), VCR available (movies). Heated pool; whirlpool, poolside service. Coffee in rooms. Restaurants 6:30 am-10 pm. Room service 24 hours. Bars 3:30 pm-1:30 am; entertainment. Check-out noon. Meeting rooms. Business center. In-room modem link. Concierge. Shopping arcade. Beauty shop. Tennis. Downhill/cross-country ski on site. Exercise room; sauna, steam room. Spa. Ski rentals. Mountain bike rentals. Refrigerators, minibars. Private patios, balconies. On river. Cr cds: A, C, D, DS, JCB, MC, V.

All Suite

★ ★ ★ **BEAVER CREEK LODGE.** *26 Avondale Ln (81620). Phone 970/845-9800; fax 970/845-8242. www. beavercreeklodge.net.* At the base of the Beaver Creek Resort, this lodge is close to the Centennial and Strawberry Park chairlifts. Each two-room suite offers Southwest-inspired décor. 77 suites, 6 story. Closed mid-Apr-mid-May, late Oct-early Nov. Check-out noon, check-in 3 pm. TV; cable (premium), VCR available. In-room modem link. Fireplaces. Restaurant. Babysitting services available. In-house fitness room, massage, sauna. Outdoor pool, whirlpool. Downhill, cross-country ski 1/2 block. Valet parking. Concierge. Cr cds: A, MC, V. **$$**

B&B/Small Inns

★ ★ ★ **CHRISTIANA AT VAIL.** *356 E Hanson Ranch Rd (81657). Phone 970/476-5641; fax 970/476-0470. www.christiania.com.* 22 air-cooled rooms, 3 story, 6 suites. Jan-Mar: S, D $185-$350; suites $250-$500; kitchen suite $375; Dec, Feb & Mar (7-day minimum); lower rates rest of year. Crib $10. Parking $5. TV; cable, VCR available. Heated pool. Sauna. Complimentary continental breakfast. Check-out 11 am, check-in 4 pm. Business services available. Luggage handling. Downhill/cross-country ski adjacent. Minibars; microwaves available. Bavarian-style inn. Some antiques, hand-carved furnishings. Totally nonsmoking. Cr cds: A, MC, V.

★ ★ **BLACK BEAR INN OF VAIL.** *2405 Elliott Rd (81657). Phone 970/476-1304; fax 970/476-0433. www.vail.net/blackbear.* 12 rooms, 2 story. Mid-Nov-mid-Apr: S, D $105-$200; each additional $35; higher rates Dec 25; lower rates mid-May-mid-Nov. Closed mid-Apr-mid May. Complimentary full breakfast. Check-out 11 am, check-in 3-7 pm. TV in sitting room; cable (premium). In-room modem link. Restaurant opposite 7 am-11 pm. Whirlpool. Game room. Downhill, cross-country ski 1 1/2 miles. Lawn games. Meeting room. Business services. On banks of Gore Creek. Totally nonsmoking. Cr cds: DS, MC, V.

Restaurants

★ **ALPENROSE.** *100 E Meadow Dr (81657). Phone 970/476-3194; fax 970/476-5184.* Hours: 11 am-10 pm; Mon to 5 pm. Closed Tues; also mid-Apr-late-May and mid-Oct-mid-Nov. Reservations accepted. No A/C. German, continental menu. Bar. Lunch $7-$9, dinner $19-$25. Specializes in veal, fresh fish, European pastries. Outdoor dining, two terraces. Cr cds: A, D, DS, MC, V.

★ ★ ★ **BEANO'S CABIN.** *PO Box 915 (81620). Phone 970/949-9090; fax 970/845-5769.* This restaurant is located amid the aspen trees on Beaver Creek Mountain. With reservations, guests can enjoy a winter moonlit sleigh ride to the restaurant. Seafood menu. Hours: 5-10 pm. Closed Mon, Tues in summer; also mid-Apr-May. Complete meals: dinner $89. Summer brunch 11 am-2 pm, $45-$65. Bar. Children's menu. Reservations required. Outdoor dining. Totally nonsmoking. Access by horse-drawn wagon, van or on horseback; winter months by sleigh. Cr cds: A, D, DS, MC, V.

★ **BLU'S.** *193 E Gore Creek Dr (81657). Phone 970/476-3113; fax 970/476-4319.* American, Eclectic, international menu. Breakfast, lunch, dinner. Bar. Children's menu. Casual attire. Outdoor seating. Non-smoking seating. Cr cds: A, D, DS, MC, V. **$$**

★ **CHILI WILLY'S.** *101 Main St, Minturn (81645). Phone 970/827-5887; fax 970/926-0886. www.chiliwilly.com.* Hours: 11 am-10 pm; Labor Day-Memorial Day 5-10 pm. Closed Thanksgiving, Dec 25. Bar. Lunch $4.95-$11.95, dinner $8.95-$16.95. Children's menu. Specializes in Tex-Mex and vegetarian dishes. Parking. Outdoor dining. Rustic décor; casual atmosphere. Cr cds: A, DS, MC, V.

★ ★ **GOLDEN EAGLE INN.** *118 Beaver Creek Pl (81620). Phone 970/949-1940; fax 970/949-6085.* American, international menu. Hours: 11:30 am-10 pm. Dinner

$12-$30. Bar. Children's menu. Casual attire. Outdoor dining. Cr cds: A, C, D, MC, V.

[D]

★ ★ ★ **GROUSE MOUNTAIN GRILL.** *141 Scott Hill Rd (81620). Phone 970/949-0600; fax 970/949-1221.* American menu. Closed Easter; mid-Apr-mid-May. Dinner. Bar. Entertainment. Casual attire. Free valet parking. Outdoor dining. Cr cds: A, MC, V. **$$**

[D]

★ ★ **LANCELOT INN.** *201 E Gore Creek Dr (81657). Phone 970/476-5828; fax 970/476-4746. www.lancelotinn.com.* Specializes in prime rib, Colorado beef, fresh seafood. Hours: 11:30 am-2:30 pm, 6-10 pm. Closed lunch except summer; also May. Dinner $20. Bar from 5 pm. Children's menu. Reservations accepted. Outdoor dining in summer. Totally nonsmoking. Cr cds: A, MC, V.

[D]

★ ★ ★ **LEFT BANK.** *183 Gore Creek Dr (81657). Phone 970/476-3696.* As the name suggests, this restaurant serves classic French cuisine with a friendly, casual elegance, right in the heart of the Village. Closed Wed; Memorial Day, Dec 25; mid-Apr-mid-June, Oct-mid-Nov. Closed. Dinner. Bar. Casual attire. Reservations accepted. Non-smoking seating. Cr cds: V. **$$$**

[D]

★ **MINTURN COUNTRY CLUB.** *131 Main St, Minturn (81645). Phone 970/827-4114.* Specializes in seafood, steak, chicken. Hours: 5:30-10 pm. Closed Dec 25. Reservations accepted. Wine, beer. Dinner $9.95-$30. Children's menu. Entertainment. Cr cds: MC, V.

[D]

★ ★ ★ ★ **MIRABELLE AT BEAVER CREEK.** *55 Village Rd (81657). Phone 970/949-7728; fax 970/845-9578. www.mirabelleatbeavercreek.com.* Set in a charming cottage in the mountains, Mirabelle at Beaver Creek appears to have dropped out of a fairy tale. The cottage, which dates to the 19th century, is perfect for quiet, intimate dining. Each of the restaurant's spacious, bright rooms are cozy and warm, while the outdoor porch, lined with colorful potted flowers, makes for ideal al fresco dining. A meal at Mirabelle is as magical as the surroundings. The kitchen offers sophisticated Belgian-tinged French food prepared with a modern sensibility. Signature dishes include Colorado lamb chops "My Grand Daddy Style" and roasted elk medallions with fruit compote. House-made ice creams are a special treat, so save room for several scoops if at all possible. Belgian menu. Closed Sun; also May, Nov. Dinner. Bar. Children's menu. Casual attire. Outdoor seating. Cr cds: A, DS, MC, V. **$$$**

[D]

★ ★ **MONTAUK SEAFOOD GRILL.** *549 W Lionshead Mall (81657). Phone 970/476-2601. www.montaukseafoodgrill.com.* Hours: 3-10 pm; summer months 5-9:30 pm. Closed Thanksgiving. Reservations accepted. Bar. Dinner $15.95-$21.95. Specializes in Hawaiian ahi, crispy calamari, tempura shrimp. Outdoor dining. View of mountains. Totally nonsmoking. Cr cds: A, DS, MC, V.

[D]

★ ★ ★ **RESTAURANT PICASSO.** *2205 Cordillera Way (81632). Phone 970/926-2200; fax 970/926-2486. www.cordillera-vail.com.* French menu. Hours: 7-10 am, 11:30 am-2 pm, 6-9 pm. Dinner $13.99-$34.95. Bar. Reservations accepted. Valet parking. Outdoor dining. Totally nonsmoking. Cr cds: A, C, D, DS, ER, MC, V.

[D]

★ ★ ★ **SPLENDIDO AT THE CHATEAU.** *17 Chateau Ln (81620). Phone 970/845-8808; fax 970/845-8961. www.splendidobeavercreek.com.* Special occasions draw many locals to this elegantly appointed, picturesque, chalet-style dining room tucked into the hills of Beaver Creek. Other guests come for the wonderful live piano, offered nightly. But truth be told, the food is Splendido's biggest draw, and for good reason. The menu is upscale and eclectic, merging ingredients from around the world with those of Colorado's native soil. Flavors balance, sauces glisten, and the mouth is treated to a magnificent meal. You'll be hard pressed to find a dish here that does not impress even the most discerning diner. The menu changes nightly, but seasonal signatures have included dishes like sesame-crusted Atlantic salmon with coconut basmati rice and cilantro-lemongrass sauce and grilled elk loin with braised elk osso buco. American menu. Closed mid-Apr-mid-June, mid-Oct-mid-Nov. Dinner. Bar. Piano. Children's menu. Reservations required. Valet parking. Cr cds: A, C, D, DS, MC, V. **$$$**

[D]

★ ★ ★ **SWEET BASIL.** *193 E Gore Creek Dr (81657). Phone 970/476-0125; fax 970/476-0137. www.sweetbasil-vail.com.* Eclectic, international menu. Lunch, dinner. Bar. Casual attire. Reservations required. Outdoor seating. Totally nonsmoking. Cr cds: A, DS, MC, V. **$$$**

★ ★ **THE TYROLEAN.** *400 E Meadow Dr (81657). Phone 970/476-2204; fax 970/476-3652. www.tyrolean.net.* Hours: 6-10 pm. Closed late Apr-May. Reservations accepted. Continental menu. Bar. Wine list. Dinner $16-$34. Children's menu. Specializes in wild game, steak, fresh seafood. Outdoor dining. Three-level dining area. Large logging sled chandelier. Austrian atmosphere. Cr cds: A, MC, V.

★★★ **THE WILDFLOWER.** *174 Gore Creek Dr (81657). Phone 970/476-5011; fax 970/476-7425. www.vail.net/thelodge.* If you're searching for a memorable dining experience—something more than just a night out—then make it over to The Wildflower, a beautiful restaurant that, as you might expect from its name, feels like spring in full bloom. Filled with baskets of wildflowers and massive floral arrangements, the room boasts wonderful views and tables lined with country-style Laura Ashley linens. The Wildflower's wonderful staff is skilled at the craft of service and is on hand to guide you through the eclectic American menu. You'll find a delicious and innovative selection of seafood, poultry, and game (Nebraska ostrich, anyone?) that is accented with global flavors like lemongrass, curry, and chilies and incorporates local fruits and vegetables, including herbs grown in The Wildflower's garden. An extensive, thoughtful, and reasonably priced wine list concentrates on Italy and matches up nicely with the distinctive global menu. Closed Mon in winter. Dinner. Casual attire. Valet parking. Outdoor seating. Cr cds: A, D, DS, MC, V. **$$$**

D

Walsenburg (F-6)

See also Trinidad

Founded 1873 **Pop** 4,182 **Elev** 6,182 ft **Area code** 719 **Zip** 81089

Information Chamber of Commerce, 400 Main St, Railroad Depot; 719/738-1065

Named after a German pioneer merchant, the present town was originally the small Spanish village of La Plaza de los Leones.

What to See and Do

Francisco Fort Museum. *16 miles SW on US 160 and CO 12 in La Veta. Phone 719/742-5501.* Original adobe trading fort (1862) now contains exhibits of pioneer cattle ranching and commercial mining. The site also has a saloon, blacksmith shop, one-room schoolhouse, and collection of Native American artifacts. (Late May-early Oct, Wed-Sun) **$$**

Lathrop State Park. *70 County Rd 502 (81089). 3 miles W on US 160. Phone 719/738-2376.* Swimming, waterskiing, fishing, boating (ramps); golf, picnicking (shelters), camping (dump station). Visitor Center. Standard fees. (Daily) **$$**

Walsenburg Mining Museum. *400 Main St, Old County Jail Building. Phone 719/738-1992.* Exhibits on the history of coal mining in Huerfano County, the Trinidad coal fields, and Raton basin. (May-Sept, Mon-Sat; rest of year, by appointment) **$**

Motel/Motor Lodge

★★ **BEST WESTERN RAMBLER MOTEL.** *I-25, exit 52 (81089). Phone 719/738-1121; fax 719/738-1093. www.bestwestern.com.* 35 rooms. Mid-May-early Sept: S $62-$77; D $77-$87; under 18 free; lower rates rest of year. Crib free. Pet accepted, some restrictions. Coffee in lobby. Check-out 11 am. TV. In-room modem link. Restaurant 6 am-9 pm. Heated pool. Cr cds: A, C, D, DS, MC, V.

D 🐾 ⌇ ⌇

Restaurant

★★ **IRON HORSE.** *503 W 7th St (81089). Phone 719/738-9966.* Hours: 11 am-2 pm, 4:30-10 pm; Sat and Sun from 4:30 pm. Winter hours vary. Closed Thanksgiving, Dec 24 and 25; 3 weeks in Feb. Bar. Lunch $4.25-$7.50, dinner $7.95-$15.95. Specializes in steak, ribs, chicken. Parking. Three dining rooms in turn-of-the-century armory. Cr cds: A, DS, MC, V.

D

Winter Park (C-5)

See also Central City, Georgetown, Granby, Idaho Springs

Pop 662 **Elev** 9,040 ft **Area code** 970 **Zip** 80482

Information Winter Park/Fraser Valley Chamber of Commerce, PO Box 3236; 800/903-7275

Web www.winterpark-info.com

Winter Park is part of the unique Denver Mountain Park System, located on the western slope of Berthoud Pass in the Arapaho National Forest (see DILLON).

What to See and Do

Winter Park Resort. *677 Winter Park Dr. 1 mile SE off US 40. Phone 970/726-5514.* Eight high-speed quad, five triple, seven double chairlifts; patrol, school, rentals, snowmaking; cafeterias, restaurants, bars. NASTAR and coin-operated race courses. (Mid-Nov-mid-Apr, daily) The five interconnected mountain areas include Winter Park, Mary Jane, and Vasquez Ridge. One hundred thirty-four runs; longest run 5 miles; vertical drop 2,610 feet. Half-day rates. Chairlift and alpine slide also operate late June-mid-Sept (daily). Bicycle rentals, miniature golf (summer, fee). Within the resort is

The Children's Center. *677 Winter Park Dr. Phone 970/726-5514.* An all-inclusive ski center for children (inquire about ages) with children's ski slopes, rentals, school, and day care (winter); human maze, 18-hole frisbee golf, indoor/outdoor climbing wall (summer). **$$$$**

Motels/Motor Lodges

★ **HIGH MOUNTAIN LODGE INC.** *425 County Rd 5001 (66211). Phone 970/726-5958; fax 970/726-9796. www.himtnlodge.com.* 12 air-cooled rooms, 2 story. Mid-Dec-early Apr: $80/person; weekly rates; higher rates special events; lower rates rest of year. Closed May. Crib available. Pet accepted, some restrictions. Complimentary full breakfast. Check-out 10 am. TV in recreation room; VCR available. Some balconies. Refrigerators, microwaves, fireplaces. Coin laundry. Restaurant nearby. Bar. Exercise equipment, massage, sauna. Game room. Indoor pool, whirlpool. Downhill, cross-country ski 9 miles. Picnic tables. Lawn games. Concierge. Opposite stream. Cr cds: MC, V.

★ **WOODSPUR LODGE.** *111 Van Anderson Dr (80482). Phone 970/726-8417; toll-free 800/626-6562; fax 970/726-8553.* 32 air-cooled rooms, 18 with shower only, 2 story. Mid-Dec-early Apr, MAP: S $95; D $156; under 3 free; lower rates rest of year. Crib free. TV in common room; cable. Complimentary coffee in lobby. Restaurant nearby. Bar (in season) 5-11 pm. Check-out 10 am. Meeting rooms. Business services available. Concierge. Free train station transportation. Downhill ski 3 miles; cross-country ski on site. Sauna. Whirlpools. Game room. Recreation room. Lawn games. Some balconies. Picnic tables. Cr cds: DS, MC, V.

Hotels

★ ★ **GASTHAUS EICHLER HOTEL.** *78786 US 40 (80482). Phone 970/726-4244; toll-free 800/543-3899; fax 970/726-5175.* 16 rooms. Mid-Nov-mid-Apr: D $69-$180; under 5 free; lower rates rest of year. Check-out 10 am. TV. Restaurant, bar 7:30 am-11 pm. Downhill, cross-country ski 2 miles. Concierge. Cr cds: A, D, DS, MC, V.

★ ★ **THE VINTAGE RESORT.** *100 Winter Park Dr (80482). Phone 970/726-8801; toll-free 800/472-7017; fax 970/726-9230. www.vintagehotel.com.* 170 rooms, 5 story. Mid-Nov-mid-Apr: S, D $60-$190; suites $180-$475; higher rates mid-Dec-early Jan; lower rates rest of year. Pet accepted. Check-out 11 am. TV; cable (premium). In-room modem link. Restaurant 7 am-10 pm. Bar 3 pm-midnight. Exercise equipment, sauna. Game room. Whirlpool. Downhill, cross-country ski. Cr cds: A, D, DS, MC, V.

★ **WINTER PARK MOUNTAIN LODGE.** *81699 US 40 (80482). Phone 970/726-6328; fax 970/726-1094.* 162 rooms, 5 story. Pet accepted. Complimentary continental breakfast. Check-out 10 am, check-in 4 pm. TV. Restaurant. Indoor pool, whirlpool. Cr cds: A, D, DS, MC, V. **$**

Resort

★ ★ **IRON HORSE RESORT.** *101 Iron Horse Way (80482). Phone 970/726-8851; toll-free 800/621-8190; fax 970/726-2321. www.ironhorse-resort.com.* 130 rooms, 5 story. Nov-Apr: $69-$399; higher rates Dec 25-Jan 1; lower rates rest of year. Check-out 10 am, check-in 4 pm. TV; cable (premium). Restaurant 7-10 am, 11:30 am-2:30 pm, 5-9:30 pm; summer hours vary. Bar 3 pm-midnight. Exercise equipment, steam room. Game room. Indoor/outdoor pool, whirlpool. Downhill, cross-country ski on site. Lawn games. Hiking. Business center. Concierge. On river. Cr cds: A, D, DS, MC, V.

B&B/Small Inns

★ ★ **ARAPAHOE SKI LODGE.** *78594 US 40 (80482). Phone 970/726-8222; toll-free 800/754-0094.* 11 rooms, 2 story. No A/C. No room phones. Mid-Dec-early Apr: D $54-$290; MAP available; holidays (5-day minimum); lower rates rest of year. Closed Apr, May, Oct. Complimentary full breakfast. Check-out 10 am. TV in lounge; cable (premium). Restaurant 7:30-9 am, 6-7:15 pm. Bar 3-10 pm. Sauna. Game room. Indoor pool, whirlpool. Downhill ski 3 miles, cross-country ski 10 miles. Concierge. Totally nonsmoking. Cr cds: A, DS, MC, V.

★ ★ **CREEKSIDE B & B.** *156 High Seasons Way (80482). Phone 970/726-8422.* 6 rooms, 2 story. Complimentary continental breakfast. Check-out noon, check-in 2 pm. Whirlpool. **$$**

★ ★ ★ **GRAND VICTORIAN AT WINTER PARK.** *78542 Fraser Valley Pkwy (80482). Phone 970/726-5881; toll-free 800/205-1170; fax 970/726-5602.* 10 rooms, 3 story. Mid-Dec-Mar: S, D $145-$245; lower rates Apr, June-mid-Dec. Closed May. Children over 12 years only. Complimentary breakfast. Check-out 11 am, check-in 4 pm. TV in some rooms. In-room modem link. Fireplaces. Restaurant nearby. Downhill ski 2 miles, cross-country ski 5 miles. Victorian architectural style. Room phones available. Totally nonsmoking. Cr cds: A, D, DS, MC, V.

Restaurants

★★ **DENO'S MOUNTAIN BISTRO.** *78911 US 40 (80482).* American menu. Lunch, dinner. Bar. Children's menu. Casual attire. Outdoor seating. Cr cds: A, D, DS, MC, V. **$**

★ ★ ★ **DINING ROOM AT SUNSPOT.** *Winter Park Ski Resort (80482). Phone 970/726-1446.* Hours: 11 am-2 pm, 5:30-8 pm; Sun-Wed to 2 pm. Closed May-Oct. Reservations accepted; required dinner. No A/C. Bar. Extensive wine list. Lunch $10-$15. Complete meals: dinner $49-$59. Children's menu. Own baking. Restaurant located at 10,700-foot altitude, reached by gondola; panoramic views of Continental Divide. Totally nonsmoking. Cr cds: A, D, DS, MC, V.

D ⊠

★ ★ **GASTHAUS EICHLER.** *78786 US 40 (80482). Phone 970/726-5133; fax 970/726-5175. www.gasthauseichler.com.* American, German menu. Hours: 7:30 am-2 pm, 5-9 pm; early-bird dinner 5-6 pm. Dinner $14-$26. Bar. No A/C. Children's menu. Casual attire. Outdoor dining. Cr cds: A, MC, V.

SC

★ ★ **RANDI'S IRISH SALOON.** *78521 US 40 (80482). Phone 970/726-1186.* Hours: 7:30-1:30 am. Irish menu. Bar. Prices: $6.95-$9.95. Children's menu. Specializes in Irish food; stew, steak, and mushroom pie. Outdoor dining. Chalet-style building with fireplace, early-American furnishings; patio has rock garden and fountain. Cr cds: A, C, D, DS, MC, V.

D SC

Nevada

Famous for gambling and glamorous nightlife, Nevada also has a rich history and tradition, magnificent scenery, and some of the wildest desert country on the continent.

Tourism is still the lifeblood of Nevada, with some 42 million visitors a year coming for vacation or conventions. Because of its central location and lack of inventory tax on goods bound out of state, Nevada is becoming increasingly important as a warehousing center for the western states.

Gambling (Nevadans call it "gaming") was first legalized in the Depression year of 1931, the same year residency requirements for obtaining a divorce were relaxed. Gaming is strictly controlled and regulated in Nevada, and casinos offer each bettor a fair chance to win. Taxes derived from the casinos account for nearly half of the state's revenue.

Most Nevadans feel that it is preferable to license, tax, and regulate gambling strictly than to tolerate the evils of bribery and corruption that inevitably accompany illegal gambling activities. While the state enforces numerous regulations, such as those barring criminals and prohibiting cheating, it does *not* control the odds on the various games.

Although Nevada has little rainfall and few rivers, water sports are popular on a few large lakes, both natural and man-made. These include Lakes Tahoe, Mead, and Lahontan; Pyramid Lake; and Walker Lake.

Mining and ranching have always been important facets of Nevada's economy. Sheep raising became important when millions of sheep were needed to feed the hungry miners working Nevada's Comstock Lode and California's Mother Lode. Most of these sheepherders were Basque. Although today's sheepherder is more likely Peruvian or Mexican, the Basques are still an important influence in the state.

Because of Nevada's arid land, cattle have to roam over a wide area; therefore, ranches average more than 2,000 acres in size. Most Nevada beef cattle are shipped to California or the Midwest for fattening prior to marketing.

Population: 1,998,257
Area: 110,567 square miles
Elevation: 470-13,143 feet
Peak: Boundary Peak (Esmeralda County)
Entered Union: October 31, 1864 (36th state)
Capital: Carson City
Motto: All for our country
Nickname: Silver State
Flower: Sagebrush
Bird: Mountain Bluebird
Tree: Piñon and Bristlecone Pine
Fair: August, in Reno
Time Zone: Pacific
Website: www.travelnevada.com
Fun Facts:
1. Nevada is the largest gold-producing state in the nation. It is second in the world behind South Africa.
2. In 1931, the Pair-O-Dice Club was the first casino to open on Highway 91, the future Las Vegas Strip.

Known for its precious metals, Nevada produces more than $2.6 billion worth of gold and silver a year. Eerie ghost towns still hint at the romantic early days of fabulous gold and silver strikes that made millionaires overnight and generated some of the wildest history in the world. In the southern part of the state, the deserted mining camps of Rhyolite, Berlin, Belmont, Goodsprings, and Searchlight, to name a few, still delight explorers. Industrial metals and minerals also have an impact on the economy.

The fur traders of the 1820s and 1830s, Jedediah Smith, Peter Ogden, and Joseph Walker and the Fremont expeditions, guided by Kit Carson in 1848, were the first to report on the area that is now Nevada.

The Mormons established a trading post in 1851. Now called Genoa, this was Nevada's first non-Indian settlement. Gold was found along the Carson River in Dayton Valley in May of 1850. A decade later the fabulous Comstock Lode (silver and gold ore) was discovered. The gold rush was on and Virginia City mushroomed into a town of 20,000. Formerly a part of Utah and New Mexico

Calendar Highlights

JANUARY
Cowboy Poetry Gathering (*Elko*). Phone 773/738-7508. Working cowpersons participate in storytelling verse. Demonstrations; country music.

MAY
Laughlin Riverdays (*Laughlin*). Contact Laughlin Chamber of Commerce, 800/227-5245. World's longest line dance, carnival, golf tournament.

JUNE
Fallon Air Show (*Fallon*). Fallon Naval Air Station. Phone 775/423-2544. Military exhibition flying, civilian aerobatics, aircraft displays; Blue Angels Demonstration Team.

Helldorado Days (*Las Vegas*). Phone 702/870-1221. Rodeos, parades, carnival, street dance, chili cook-off; Western theme throughout.

Kit Carson Rendezvous (*Carson City*). Contact Carson City Convention & Visitors Bureau, Phone 775/687-7410 or 800/638-2321. Mountain man encampment, Civil War camp, Native American village with competition dancing, music, arts and crafts, and food vendors.

Winnemucca Basque Festival (*Elko*). Phone 775/623-5071. Contests in weightlifting, sheephooking, other skills of mountaineers; dancing, feast.

AUGUST
Nevada State Fair (*Reno*). Phone 775/688-5767. Fairgrounds. Exhibits, entertainment, rides, games, and more.

SEPTEMBER
National Championship Air Races (*Reno*). Stead Air Field. Phone 775/972-6663. The world's longest-running air race, featuring 4 race classes: Unlimited, Formula One, AT-6, and Biplane. Skywriting, aerobatics, and displays.

OCTOBER
Invensys Classic (*Las Vegas*). PGA tournament with more than $4.5 million in prize money.

DECEMBER
National Finals Rodeo (*Las Vegas*). Thomas and Mack Center. Phone 702/895-3900. Nation's richest professional rodeo, featuring 15 finalists in 7 rodeo disciplines.

Territory, ceded by Mexico in 1848, Nevada became a territory in 1861, a state in 1864. Before Europeans arrived, Nevada was the home of the Paiute, the Shoshone, and the Washoe, and even earlier, the Basketmakers.

Note: It is illegal to pick many types of wildflowers in Nevada, as well as to gather rocks. Tossing away lighted cigarette butts is also illegal in this dry land.

When to Go/Climate

Temperatures vary greatly in Nevada—from scorching desert days in Death Valley to bone-chilling night freezes in the Sierra Nevada. The entire state is arid. You may want to avoid visiting Nevada in the hot summer months of June, July, and Aug, when daytime temperatures can remain above 100 degrees in many parts of the state.

AVERAGE HIGH/LOW TEMPERATURES (°F)

Elko

Jan 37/13	May 69/37	Sept 78/39
Feb 43/20	June 80/47	Oct 66/30
Mar 50/25	July 91/50	Nov 49/23
Apr 60/30	Aug 89/49	Dec 37/14

Las Vegas

Jan 57/34	May 88/60	Sept 95/66
Feb 63/39	June 100/69	Oct 82/54
Mar 69/44	July 106/76	Nov 67/43
Apr 78/51	Aug 103/74	Dec 58/34

Parks and Recreation

Water-related activities, hiking, riding, various other sports, picnicking, and visitor centers, as well as camping, are available in many of Nevada's parks. "Roughing it" may be necessary in remote areas. Camping on a first-come, first-served basis; $3-$9 per night. Boat launching $2-$6, except Lake Tahoe (covers all fees, including boat launching). Inquire locally about road conditions for areas off paved highways. Carry drinking water in remote areas. Pets on leash only. For detailed information, contact the Nevada Division of State Parks, 1300 S Curry St, Carson City 89703-5202; phone 775/687-4384.

FISHING AND HUNTING

Nevada's streams and lakes abound with trout, bass, mountain whitefish, and catfish. Most fishing areas are open year-round. Some exceptions exist; inquire locally. Nonresident license: $51 for 1 year or $12 for 1 day. Special use stamp ($3) for Lake Mead, Lake Mohave, and the Colorado River; $5 annual trout stamp required to take or possess trout.

There is an abundance of wildlife—mule deer, quail, ducks, geese, and partridges. Deer-hunting season lasts 4 to 5 weeks from the first 2 weekends in October; the season varies in some counties. Nonresident hunting license: $111 plus $155 for deer tag and processing. Deer hunting with bow and arrow: nonresidents $111 for license and $200 for deer tag and processing. Archery hunts usually held Aug 8-Sept 4, prior to rifle season.

For a digest of fishing and hunting regulations, write to the Nevada Division of Wildlife, PO Box 10678, Reno 89520; phone 775/688-1500.

Driving Information

Safety belts are mandatory for all persons anywhere in a vehicle. Children under 5 years and under 40 pounds in weight must be in an approved safety seat anywhere in the vehicle. For further information, call 877/368-7828.

Interstate Highway System

Use the following list as a guide to access interstate highways in Nevada. Always consult a map to confirm driving routes.

Highway Number	Cities/Towns within ten miles
Interstate 15	Las Vegas, Overton.
Interstate 80	Battle Mountain, Elko, Lovelock, Reno, Winnemucca.

Additional Visitor Information

Nevada Magazine, an illustrated bimonthly magazine, and *Nevada's Events Guide* (free), may be obtained by contacting the Nevada Commission on Tourism, 401 N Carson St, Carson City 89701; phone 775/687-4322 or 800/NEVADA-8.

For information about the Lake Mead area, write to the Public Affairs Officer, Lake Mead National Recreation Area, Boulder City 89005.

Information about camping, fishing and hunting, water sports, gambling, ghost towns, mining, agriculture, and the state capitol and museum may be obtained from the Commission on Tourism (see above).

Gambling

Gambling is limited to those 21 and older. Children are welcome in casino restaurants, however, and many casinos have childcare facilities.

SCENIC NEVADA

This tour from Reno, which can be accomplished over one or two days, combines the scenic beauty and recreational opportunities of Lake Tahoe with historic sites from Nevada's mining days. From Reno go south on US 395 to NV 431 (the Mount Rose Scenic Byway), which heads west and southwest as it climbs to an 8,911-foot pass and then drops down to Lake Tahoe, providing splendid panoramic views of the lake. Continue on NV 431 to NV 28 and Incline Village, a good base from which to enjoy the beach, swimming, fishing, and the spectacular views at Lake Tahoe Nevada State Park. The sandy beach at the park's Sand Harbor section is delightful but also very popular; those looking for more solitude can opt for Memorial Point and Hidden Beach, less-frequented areas of the state park. Those visiting from late July through August might want to experience the Lake Tahoe Shakespeare Festival, with shows at an outdoor theater at Sand Harbor. Also in Incline Village is the Ponderosa Ranch, a western theme park where the popular television series *Bonanza* was filmed from 1959 to 1973. Tours of the ranch house film set are given, and the ranch also includes an Old West town with a working blacksmith shop, a saloon, church, historic wagons and automobiles, a petting farm, pony rides, and staged gunfights.

From Incline Village, continue south on NV 28 along Lake Tahoe's eastern shore, then take US 50 east to Carson City. Part of the Lake Tahoe Scenic Byway, this route offers panoramic views of the lake and nearby mountains. Carson City, Nevada's capital, is roughly the half-way point of this tour and a good spot to spend the night. Founded in 1858, Carson City features numerous historic sites, including the handsome State Capitol, built in 1871, with a dome of silver. Attractions also include the 1864 Bowers Mansion, built of granite and furnished with many original pieces; the Warren Engine Company No. 1 Fire Museum, where you'll see a variety of historic firefighting equipment; and the Nevada State Railroad Museum, with three steam locomotives and numerous freight and passenger cars.

Carson City is also an especially family-friendly city, with lots of activities and attractions for children. There are several fun exhibits for kids at the Nevada State Museum, such as a full-size replica of a ghost town and an underground mine tunnel. Preteens especially enjoy the Children's Museum of Northern Nevada, which boasts numerous interactive exhibits including Musical Hands, in which a motion detector helps children "conduct" an orchestra; a small-scale grocery store; and a Show Box that produces body prints. The Children's Museum also has a fire engine that kids can climb on and the huge walk-on piano from the 1988 Tom Hanks movie *Big*.

Now head northeast on US 50 to NV 341, which you follow north to picturesque Virginia City, an historic mining town that had its heyday in the 1870s. Beautifully restored, Virginia City today offers a glimpse into its opulent and sometimes wicked past with historic buildings, a mine, and a working steam train. To see the epitome of 19th-century extravagance stop at The Castle, a 1868 Victorian mansion known for its marble fireplaces, crystal chandeliers, and silver doorknobs. Other attractions include Piper's Opera House, which hosted the major stars of the late 1800s, and the Mackay Mansion, built in 1860 as the headquarters of mining magnate John Mackay. Western history is highlighted at The Way It Was Museum and the Wild West Museum. Those interested in Virginia City's seamier side won't want to miss the Nevada Gambling Museum, with antique slot machines, cheating devices, and other gambling memorabilia; and the Bullette Red Light Museum, which features a mock bordello with Oriental art and vintage erotica, as well as a reproduction of a 19th-century doctor's office with antique medical equipment. Tours are offered at the Choller, a 1860's gold and silver mine, and steam train rides through the historic mining district are offered by the Virginia & Truckee Railroad. To return to Reno, take NV 341 north to US 395 north. **(Approximately 100 miles)**

Austin (E-3)

See also Battle Mountain

Settled 1862 **Pop** 350 **Elev** 6,525 ft **Area code** 775
Zip 89310

Information Chamber of Commerce, PO Box 212; 775/
964-2200

Austin was the mother town of central and eastern Nevada
mining. For a time its strike did not attract hordes because
of the phenomenal character of the Comstock Lode in
booming Virginia City. By 1867, however, the number of
ore-reduction mills had increased to 11, and 6,000 claims
had been filed.

Many of its old buildings have deteriorated and fallen
down, but Austin firmly denies that it is a ghost town.
Rather, it is a relic of Nevada's greatest days of fame and
glory, looking toward a future of renewed mining activity made possible through improved methods for using
low-grade ore.

A Ranger District office of the Toiyabe National Forest
(see RENO) is located here.

What to See and Do

Berlin-Ichthyosaur State Park. *NV 844 and Toiyabe For-
est. 50 miles SW via US 50, then 30 miles S on NV 361 to
Gabbs, then 22 miles E on NV 844, in Toiyabe National
Forest. Phone 775/964-2440.* Approximately 1,070 acres.
Fossilized remains of marine reptiles, some up to 50 feet
long, with fish-shaped bodies and long, narrow snouts.
The ghost town of Berlin is also here. Hiking and nature
trails, picnicking, camping facilities (fee, dump station).
(Daily) Standard fees. **$$**

Hickison Petroglyph Recreation Site. *US 50 and Monitor
Valley (89820). 24 miles E on US 50. Phone 775/635-4000.*
Native American drawings carved in stone (circa 1000
B.C.-A.D. 1500); near former Pony Express trail. Pic-
nicking, camping; no drinking water available. (Daily)
FREE

The Lander County Courthouse. Oldest county court-
house in the state and one of the plainest. Its sturdy con-
struction, without frills, suited the early residents.

Mountain biking. *610 SW Main St (89310). Phone 775/
964-1212; 775/964-2200 (Chamber of Commerce).* Many
miles of biking trails through central Nevada's varied ter-
rain. Brochure describing designated trails available from
Chamber of Commerce or Tyrannosaurus Rix Mountain
Bike & Specialties.

Other old buildings. *610 SW Main St (89310). Phone 775/
964-1133.* Stores, churches, hotels, and saloons. Stokes

Castle is a century-old, three-story stone building that can
be seen for miles.

The Reese River *Reveille*. Published from May 16, 1863,
to 1993; complete files are preserved.

Battle Mountain (C-4)

Settled 1868 **Pop** 2,871 **Elev** 4,512 ft **Area code** 775
Zip 89820

Motels/Motor Lodges

★ **BEST INN & SUITES.** *650 W Front St (89820).
Phone 775/635-5200; toll-free 800/237-8466; fax 775/
635-5699. www.bestinn.com.* 72 rooms, 2 story. S $49;
D $51; each additional $5; under 12 free. Pet accepted.
Check-out 11 am. TV; cable (premium). Some refrig-
erators. Restaurant adjacent open 24 hours. Picnic tables,
grills. Business services. Coffee in lobby. Western theme.
Cr cds: A, C, D, DS, MC, V.

D ⌖ ⊠

★ **COMFORT INN.** *521 E Front St (89820). Phone
775/635-5880; toll-free 800/228-5150; fax 775/635-5788.
www.comfortinn.com.* 72 rooms, 3 story. June-Aug: S,
D $56-$61; each additional $5; under 6 free. Crib $5.
Pet accepted; $20 deposit. TV; cable (premium). Heated
pool; whirlpool. Complimentary continental breakfast.
Restaurant adjacent 11 am-9 pm. Check-out 11 am.
Coin laundry. Meeting rooms. Business services available.
Refrigerators. Cr cds: A, C, D, DS, JCB, MC, V.

⌖ ⊠ ⊠ SC

Boulder City (I-6)

*See also Henderson, Lake Mead National Recreation Area,
Las Vegas*

Founded 1931 **Pop** 14,966 **Elev** 2,500 ft **Area code** 702

Information Chamber of Commerce, 1305 Arizona St;
702/293-2034

Web www.bouldercitychamber.com

Boulder City owes its birth to the construction of the
mighty Hoover Dam, which spans the Colorado River. A
movie on the project can be seen daily at the Hoover Dam
Museum; phone 702/294-1988.

This is a well-planned model city built by the federal
government to house personnel and serve as headquar-
ters for Reclamation, Park Service, and Bureau of Mines
forces operating in the area. It also serves as a gateway to
the Lake Mead National Recreation Area.

Special Events

Art in the Park. *Wilbur Square, Boulder Hwy and Colorado St. Phone 702/293-4111.* Bicentennial, and Escalante parks. First full weekend in Oct.

Boulder Damboree. *Central Park. 5th St and Ave B. Phone 702/293-9256.* July 4.

Motels/Motor Lodges

★ **EL RANCHO BOULDER.** *725 Nevada Hwy (89005). Phone 702/293-1085; fax 702/293-3021.* 39 rooms. S, D $60-$150; family, weekly rates. Complimentary coffee in lobby. Check-out 11 am. TV; cable (premium). Refrigerators. Restaurant adjacent 6 am-midnight. Pool. Airport transportation. Meeting rooms. Cr cds: A, D, DS, MC, V.

[D] [♦] [≈] [⊠]

★ **HACIENDA INN AND CASINO.** *US Hwy 93 (89005). Phone 702/293-5000; toll-free 800/245-6380; fax 702/293-5608.* 378 rooms, 17 story. S, D $29-$69; each additional $3.27; under 12 free. Crib $3. TV. Heated pool. Restaurant open 24 hours. Bar; entertainment Thurs-Sun. Check-out 11 am. Gift shop. Casino. Some private patios, balconies. View of Lake Mead. Cr cds: A, D, DS, MC, V.

[D] [≈] [⊠]

★ **SUPER 8 MOTEL.** *704 Nevada Hwy (89005). Phone 702/294-8888; toll-free 800/800-8000; fax 702/293-4344. www.super8.com.* 114 rooms, 3 story. S, D $42.88-$79.88; suites $75.88-$200.88; weekly, monthly rates. Crib $5. Check-out noon. TV; cable (premium). Restaurant 7 am-10 pm. Bar. Game room. Indoor pool, whirlpool. Picnic tables. Airport transportation. Meeting rooms. Cr cds: A, C, D, DS, MC, V.

[D] [≈] [⊠]

Caliente (G-6)

See also Las Vegas, Overton

Pop 1,123 **Elev** 4,395 ft **Area code** 775 **Zip** 89008

Information Chamber of Commerce, PO Box 553; 775/726-3129

Web www.lincolncountynevada.com

This is a ranch and recreation center situated in a fertile valley.

What to See and Do

Beaver Dam. *N. US 93 and Beaver Dam (89008).* 6 miles N on US 93, then 28 miles E on improved gravel road. *Phone 775/728-4460.* (Check conditions locally; trailers over 24 feet not recommended) More than 2,200 acres set amid pine forests and lofty cliffs. Fishing; hiking, picnicking, camping. (Apr-Oct)

Cathedral Gorge. *14 miles N on US 93. Phone 775/728-4460.* This 1,633-acre park is a long, narrow valley cut into tan bentonite clay formations. Peculiar erosion has created unique patterns, fluting the gorge walls and forming isolated towers that resemble cathedral spires. Hiking, picnicking, camping facilities.

Echo Canyon. *25 miles N on US 93, then 4 miles E on NV 322, then 10 miles SE on NV 323. Phone 775/728-4460.* A 920-acre park. Swimming, fishing on 65-acre reservoir (daily), boat launching; picnicking, camping (dump station).

Spring Valley. *26 miles N on US 93 to Pioche, then 18 miles E on NV 322. Phone 775/728-4460.* A 1,630-acre park. Boating and fishing on Eagle Valley Reservoir; picnicking, camping (dump station). (Daily)

Special Events

Lincoln County Fair and Rodeo. *Phone 775/962-5103.* Mid-Aug.

Lincoln County Homecoming. *Memorial Park (89008). Phone 775/726-3129.* Barbecue, celebrity auction, art show. Memorial Day weekend.

Meadow Valley Western Days. *Rodeo Grounds on Rowan Dr (89008). Phone 775/726-3129.* Hayrides, rodeo, talent show. Third weekend in Sept.

Carson City (E-1)

See also Incline Village, Reno, Stateline, Virginia City

Founded 1858 **Pop** 52,457 **Elev** 4,687 ft **Area code** 775 **Zip** 89701

Information Convention & Visitors Bureau, 1900 S Carson St, Suite 200; 775/687-7410 or 800/638-2321

Web www.carson-city.org

State capital and a county itself, Carson City is situated near the edge of the forested eastern slope of the Sierra Nevada in Eagle Valley. It was first called Eagle Ranch and later renamed for Kit Carson. It became the social center for nearby settlements and shared Wild West notoriety in the silver stampede days of the last century. Fitzsimmons knocked out Corbett here in 1897. Movies of the event (first of their kind) grossed $1 million.

A Ranger District office of the Toiyabe National Forest (see RENO) is located here.

What to See and Do

Bowers Mansion. *10 miles N in Washoe Valley. Phone 775/849-0201.* (1864) The Bowers built this $200,000 granite house with the profits from a gold and silver mine. Their resources were soon depleted, leaving them penniless

Mining and Money in Carson City

Home to Nevada's largest historical homes district and the State Capitol, a walking tour of Carson City offers a good viewpoint for investigating the heady days of the Old West's 19th-century mining boom. The legendary Comstock Lode, one of the era's richest silver strikes, was discovered in nearby Virginia City in 1859, creating the need for a US Mint in the area. As a result, Carson City was home to a US Mint from 1870 to 1895, pressing more than $50 million in coinage during that span. A half-century after it closed, the Mint building became the Nevada State Museum (600 North Carson Street), a good starting point for a tour of Carson City on foot. The museum mixes natural and cultural history in a collection of archaeological finds, dioramas, Indian baskets, and an antique—and operational—coin press. From the Nevada State Museum, it's only two blocks north on Carson Street to the Children's Museum of Northern Nevada (813 North Carson Street), the area's best attraction for kids. Backtracking south on Carson Street, you'll pass through Carson City's primary casino district in the vicinity of Spear and Telegraph streets. The casinos house the majority of the restaurants in downtown Carson City, so this is a good opportunity to grab a bite to eat. Continuing south on Carson Street for three blocks, the quarried sandstone Nevada State Capitol (just east of the intersection of Carson and Second streets) is the cornerstone of a beautifully landscaped plaza that is also home to the state's Supreme Court, Legislative Building, and Library and Archives Building (where Nevada Historic Marker Guides are available on the second floor). Just southeast of the Capitol plaza on Stewart Street is the Warren Engine Company No. 1 Museum (777 South Stewart Street), with exhibits, photographs, and memorabilia detailing the oldest continuously operating firefighting company in the West. From here, it is a just block north on Stewart Street to Fifth Street; take Fifth west to Nevada Street and walk three blocks north to King Street, on which you'll want to go west once again. At 449 West King Street is the Brewery Arts Center, a showcase for the work of local artists in the former Carson Brewing Company building, which was built in 1864 and is currently on the National Historic Register. The Arts Center is in the heart of Carson City's most historic neighborhood. A good way to cap the walking tour is to follow the Kit Carson Trail to get a peek at the city's "Talking Houses" by continuing west on King Street, turning right on Mountain Street, and going north to Robinson Street. At the Mountain-Robinson intersection are a pair of notable mansions: the Governor's Mansion and the Bliss Mansion. On the short walk back east on Robinson Street to the Nevada State Museum, you'll pass several more historic structures. (For information on the self-guided walking tour of the entire 2 1/2-mile Kit Carson Trail, contact the Carson City Convention and Visitor's Bureau.)

and forcing Mrs. Bower to become the "Washoe seeress," telling fortunes for a living. Half-hour guided tours of 16 rooms with many original furnishings. (Memorial Day-Labor Day, daily; May, Sept, and Oct, weekends). Swimming pool (Memorial Day-Labor Day; fee) and picnicking in adjacent park. **$$**

State Capitol. *Carson and Musser sts. 101 N Carson St. Phone 775/684-5700.* (1871) Large stone structure with Doric columns and a silver dome. Houses portraits of past Nevada governors. (Mon-Fri) Near the Capitol are

Nevada State Museum. *600 N Carson St. Phone 775/687-4810.* Former US Mint. Exhibits of Nevada's natural history and anthropology; life-size displays of Nevada ghost town, Native American camp with artifacts and walk-through "Devonian sea." A 300-foot mine tunnel with displays runs beneath the building. (Daily; closed Jan 1, Thanksgiving, Dec 25) **$$**

Nevada State Railroad Museum. *2180 S Carson St (89701). 2180 Carson at Fairview Dr. Phone 775/687-6953.* Exhibits 50 freight and passenger cars, as well as three steam locomotives that once belonged to the Virginia and Truckee railroad. Houses pictorial history gallery and artifacts of the famed Bonanza Rd. Motor car rides (summer weekends; fee) and steam-engine rides (summer holidays and some weekends; fee). Museum (daily). **$**

State Library Building. *100 N Stewart. Phone 775/684-3360.* Files of Nevada newspapers and books about the state. (Mon-Fri; closed holidays) **FREE**

Warren Engine Company No. 1 Fire Museum. *777 S Stewart St. Phone 775/887-2210.* Currier and Ives series "The Life of a Fireman," old photographs, antique firefighting equipment, state's first fire truck (restored), 1863 Hunneman handpumper, 1847 four-wheel cart. Children under 18 must be accompanied by adult. **FREE**

Special Events

Kit Carson Rendezvous. *Mills Park and Hwy 50 E (89701). Phone 775/687-7410.* Mountain man encampment, Civil War camp, Native American village with competition dancing, music, arts and crafts and food vendors. Second weekend in June.

Nevada Day Celebration. *Carson St. and Hwy 50 E (89701). Phone 775/687-7410.* Commemorates Nevada's admission to the Union. Grand Ball, parades, exhibits. Four days in late Oct.

Motels/Motor Lodges

★ **MILL HOUSE INN.** *3251 S Carson St (89701). Phone 775/882-2715; fax 775/882-2415.* 24 rooms. D $45-$85; each additional $5; under 12 free. Check-out 11 am. TV; cable. Heated pool (seasonal). Cr cds: A, D, DS, MC, V.

⬛ ⬛ ⬛

★ **PARK INN HARDMAN HOUSE.** *917 N Carson St (89701). Phone 775/882-7744; toll-free 800/626-0793; fax 775/887-0321. www.parkhtls.com.* 62 rooms, 3 story. D $79-$89; each additional $6. Check-out 11 am. TV. Cr cds: A, C, D, DS, ER, JCB, MC, V.

⬛ **SC**

Restaurants

★ ★ **ADELE'S.** *1112 N Carson St (89701). Phone 775/882-3353; fax 775/882-0437.* American menu. Hours: 11 am-midnight. Closed Sun; also week of Dec 31-mid-Jan. Lunch $7.95-$18.95, dinner $17.95-$44.95. Comstock Victorian décor in Second Empire house. Reservations accepted. Cr cds: A, DS, MC, V.

D

★ ★ **CARSON NUGGET STEAK HOUSE.** *507 N Carson St (89701). Phone 775/882-1626; fax 775/883-1106. www.nevada-events.net/rest_steakhouses.shtml.* Seafood, steak menu. Hours: 5-10 pm. Also on premises are buffet dining room and coffee shop open 24 hours. Dinner $9.95-$25.95. Bar open 24 hours. Children's menu. Reservations accepted. Valet parking available. Cr cds: A, D, DS, MC, V.

D **SC**

★ **SILVANA'S.** *1301 N Carson St (89701). Phone 775/883-5100.* Italian menu. Specializes in pasta, seafood, steak. Hours: 5-10 pm. Closed Sun, Mon; Dec 25. Dinner $10.95-$19.95. Bar. Reservations accepted. Cr cds: A, C, D, DS, MC, V.

D

Crystal Bay

(see Incline Village)

Elko (C-5)

Settled circa 1870 **Pop** 16,708 **Elev** 5,067 ft **Area code** 775 **Zip** 89801

Information Chamber of Commerce, 1405 Idaho St; 775/738-7135 or 800/428-7143

Web www.elkonevada.com

On the Humboldt River, Elko is the center of a large ranching area. Originally a stopping point for wagon trains headed for the West Coast, its main sources of revenue today are tourism, ranching, gold mining, gaming, and a large service industry.

What to See and Do

Humboldt National Forest. *2035 Last Chance Rd. (89801). 20 miles SE on NV 228 (Ruby Mountain District), or 70 miles N on NV 225 (Mountain City and Jarbridge Districts). Contact Supervisor, 976 Mountain City Hwy. Phone 775/738-5171.* Some of the features of this more than 2-million-acre forest are its eight wilderness areas, spectacular canyons, streams, and old mining camps. Fishing; hunting, picnicking, camping (May-Oct; fee). **$$**

Licensed casinos, nightclubs. *Idaho St (89801). Phone 775/738-2111.*

Northeastern Nevada Museum. *1515 Idaho St. Phone 775/738-3418.* Three galleries feature art, historical, Native American, and nature exhibits of area. Pioneer vehicles and original 1860 pony express cabin on grounds. (Daily; closed Jan 1, Thanksgiving, Dec 25) **$$**

Special Events

County Fair and Livestock Show. *13th and Cedar sts. (89801). Phone 775/738-7135.* Horse racing. Four days on Labor Day weekend.

Cowboy Poetry Gathering. *501 Railroad St (89801). Phone 775/738-7135.* Working cowpersons participate in storytelling verse. Demonstrations; music. Last full week in Jan.

National Basque Festival. *Basque House at Golf Course Rd. and Cedar St. (89801). Phone 775/738-7135.* Contests in weightlifting, sheephooking, other skills of mountaineers; dancing, feast. Weekend early in July.

Motels/Motor Lodges

★ **BEST WESTERN ELKO INN EXPRESS.** *837 Idaho St (89801). Phone 775/738-7261; toll-free 800/ 780-7234; fax 775/738-0118. www.bestwestern.com.* 49 rooms, 2 story. Mid-May-Sept: S $44-$54; D $54-$64; each additional $5; suites $79; higher rates during special events; varied lower rates rest of year. Complimentary continental breakfast. Check-outnoon. TV; cable (premium). Cr cds: A, D, DS, MC, V.

D 🐾 ☔ 🖎

★★ **RED LION HOTEL AND CASINO.** *2065 E Idaho St (89801). Phone 775/738-2111; fax 775/753-9859.* 223 rooms, 3 story. S $69-$79; D $79-$89; each additional $10; suites $259; under 18 free. Crib free. Pet accepted. TV; cable (premium). Heated pool. Coffee in rooms. Restaurant open 24 hours. Bar; entertainment. Check-out noon. Business services available. Gift shop. Barber, beauty shop. Free airport transportation. Game room. Casino. Cr cds: A, C, D, DS, ER, MC, V.

D 🐾 ☔ 🏋 🖎

★ **SHILO INN.** *2401 Mountain City Hwy (89801). Phone 775/738-5522; toll-free 800/222-2244; fax 775/ 738-6247. www.shiloinns.com.* 70 rooms, 16 kitchen units, 2 story. S, D $69.95-$129.95; kitchen units $69-$119; under 12 free; weekly rates; higher rates during special events. Pet accepted; fee. Complimentary continental breakfast. Check-out noon. TV; cable (premium), VCR available. In-room modem link. Laundry services. Exercise equipment, sauna. Indoor pool, whirlpool. Free transportation. Cr cds: A, C, D, DS, MC, V.

D 🐾 ⚡ ☔ 🏋 ✈ 🖎 SC

★ **SUPER 8 MOTEL.** *1755 Idaho St (89801). Phone 775/738-8488; toll-free 800/800-8000; fax 775/ 738-4637. www.super8.com.* 75 rooms, 2 story. Late May-Sept: S,D $40.88-$55.88; each additional $3; under 12 free; higher rates during special events; lower rates rest of year. Crib free. TV; cable (premium). Complimentary coffee in lobby. Restaurant nearby. Check-out 11 am. Business services available. Cr cds: A, C, D, DS, MC, V.

D 🖎 SC

Hotel

★★ **HIGH DESERT INN.** *3015 E Idaho St (89801). Phone 775/738-8425; toll-free 888/394-8303; fax 775/ 753-7906.* 170 rooms, 4 story. Apr-Oct: S $64-$84, D $74-$94; each additional $10; higher rates: Cowboy Poetry Gathering, Mining Exposition; lower rates rest of year. Crib free. Pet accepted. TV; cable. Indoor pool; whirlpool. Coffee in rooms. Restaurant 6 am-10 pm. Room service. Bar 4 pm-midnight. Check-out noon. Coin laundry. Meeting rooms. Valet service. Free airport, train station, bus depot transportation. Exercise equipment. Cr cds: A, D, DS, MC, V.

D 🐾 🏋 ☔ ✈ 🖎 SC

Ely (E-5)

Settled 1868 **Pop** 4,041 **Elev** 6,427 ft **Area code** 775 **Zip** 89301

Information White Pine Chamber of Commerce, 636 Aultman St; 775/289-8877

Although founded in 1868 as a silver mining camp, Ely's growth began in 1906 with the arrival of the Nevada Northern Railroad, which facilitated the development, in 1907, of large-scale copper mining. Gold and silver are still mined in Ely. The seat of White Pine County, it is the shopping and recreational center of a vast ranching and mining area. The city is surrounded by mountains that offer deer hunting, trout fishing, and winter skiing. High elevation provides a cool, sunny climate.

A Ranger District office of the Humboldt National Forest (see ELKO) is located here.

What to See and Do

Cave Lake State Park. *8 miles S on US 93, then 7 miles E on Success Summit Rd, NV 486. Phone 775/728-4467 or 775/728-4460.* A 1,240-acre area; 32-acre reservoir provides swimming, fishing (trout), boating; picnicking, camping (dump station, showers). (Daily; access may be restricted in winter) Standard fees.

Humboldt National Forest. (see ELKO) *Phone 775/578-3521.*

Nevada Northern Railway Museum. *1100 Ave A (89315). Phone 775/289-2085.* Located in the historic Nevada Northern Railway Depot (1906). **$$$$**

Ward Charcoal Ovens State Historic Park. *7 miles SE on US 6/50/93, then 11 miles W on Cave Valley Rd, a gravel road. Phone 775/728-4467.* Six stone beehive charcoal ovens used during the 1870 mining boom. Hunting in season. Picnicking.

White Pine Public Museum. *2000 Aultman St. Phone 775/ 289-4710.* 1905 stagecoach, early-day relics and mementos, mineral display. (Daily) **FREE**

Special Events

Auto races. *Hwy 318 Lund to Hiko (89301). Phone 775/ 289-8877.* Open road auto races. Third weekend in May and Sept.

Pony Express Days. *Hwy 50 and Pony Express Trail (89301). Phone 775/289-8877.* Pari-mutuel betting. Last two weekends in Aug.

White Pine County Fair. *McGill Hwy and Fairview Ln. Phone 775/289-8877.* Third weekend in Aug.

Motels/Motor Lodges

★ **JAIL HOUSE MOTEL & CASINO.** *211 5th St (89301). Phone 775/289-3033; toll-free 800/841-5430; fax 775/289-8709.* 47 rooms, 2 story. S $42; D $46-$51; each additional $5. Crib free. TV; cable (premium). Restaurant 5 am-9 pm. Check-out 11 am. Casino. Cr cds: A, C, D, DS, MC, V.

D ⌀ SC

★ ★ **RAMADA INN & COPPER QUEEN CASINO.** *805 E 7th St (89301). Phone 775/289-4884; toll-free 888/298-2054; fax 775/289-1492. www.ramada.com.* 65 rooms, 2 story. S $60-$70; D $65-$75; each additional $5. Crib free. Complimentary continental breakfast. Check-out noon. TV; cable (premium). Some refrigerators. Restaurant 11 am-10 pm. Bar. Indoor pool, whirlpool. Free airport transportation. Business services. Casino. Cr cds: A, C, D, DS, MC, V.

⚓ ⚒ ⌀ ✈ ⌀ SC

Fallon (E-2)

Pop 7,536 **Elev** 3,963 ft **Area code** 775 **Zip** 89406

Information Chamber of Commerce, 65 S Maine St, Ste C; 775/423-2544

Web www.fallonchamber.com

What to See and Do

Lahontan State Recreation Area. *16799 Lahontan Dr. 18 miles W on US 50. Phone 775/867-3500.* Approximately 30,000 acres with a 16-mile-long reservoir. Water sports, fishing, boating (launching, ramps); picnicking, camping (dump station). Standard fees.

Special Events

All Indian Rodeo. *65 S Maine St (89406). Phone 775/423-2544.* Rodeo events, parade, powwow, Native American dances, arts, games. Third weekend in July.

Fallon Air Show. *4755 Pasture Rd, Fallon Naval Air Station (89496). Phone 775/426-2880.* Military exhibition flying, civilian aerobatics, aircraft displays; Blue Angels Demonstration Team. Ground events and static displays of vintage and modern aircrafts. Late spring-early summer.

Motels/Motor Lodges

★ **BEST INN & SUITES.** *1830 W Williams Ave (89406). Phone 775/423-5554; toll-free 888/691-6388; fax 775/423-0663. www.bestinn.com.* 82 rooms, 2 story. Apr-Oct: S, D $51-$65; suites $75-$100; under 18 free; lower rates rest of year. Complimentary continental breakfast. Check-out noon. TV; cable; VCR available. Laundry services. Indoor pool. Cr cds: A, C, D, DS, ER, JCB, MC, V.

D ⌀ ⌀ SC

★ **BONANZA INN AND CASINO.** *855 W Williams Ave (89406). Phone 775/423-6031; fax 775/423-6282.* 75 rooms, 2 story. S $40; D $46; each additional $5; suite $59-$76; under 12 free. Crib $5. Pet accepted; $20. TV; cable (premium). Restaurant open 24 hours. Bar. Check-out 11 am. Business services available. Casino. RV park. Cr cds: A, C, D, DS, MC, V.

D ⚒ ⌀ SC

★ **WESTERN MOTEL.** *125 S Carson St (89407). Phone 775/423-5118; fax 775/423-4973.* 22 rooms, 2 story. S $39; D $43; each additional $5. Crib $4. Pet accepted, some restrictions; $3. Complimentary continental breakfast. Check-out 11 am. TV. Refrigerators. Restaurant nearby. Heated pool. Cr cds: A, MC, V.

⚒ ⌀ ⌀ SC

Gardnerville (E-1)

See also Carson City, Stateline

Pop 3,357 **Elev** 4,746 ft **Area code** 775 **Zip** 89410

Information Carson Valley Chamber of Commerce & Visitors Authority, 1513 US 395 N; 775/782-8144 or 800/727-7677

Web www.carsonvalleynv.org

Gardnerville lies just southeast of Minden, seat of Douglas County. The two are considered contiguous towns.

What to See and Do

Mormon Station State Historic Park. *4 miles N via US 395, then 4 miles W on NV 57 in Genoa. Phone 775/782-2590.* Fort/stockade. Museum exhibits relics of the early pioneer days and the first white settlement in state. Also picnicking, tables, grills. (Mid-May-mid-Oct, daily)

Special Events

Carson Valley Days. *North and South Hwy 395 (89410). Phone 775/782-8144.* Parade, arts and crafts, rodeo, sport tournaments. Second weekend in June.

Carson Valley Fine Arts & Crafts Street Celebration. *Esmeralda Street (89423). Phone 775/782-8144.* Street celebration with hundreds of crafters, treasures, entertainment, and food. Sept.

Hotel

★ ★ ★ **CARSON VALLEY INN HOTEL CASINO.**
*1627 US 395 N, Minden (89423). Phone 775/782-9711;
toll-free 800/321-6983; fax 775/782-4772. www.cvinn.com.*
Located just minutes from Lake Tahoe, this full-service
family resort offers a wide array of gaming, convention, and
recreation services. 153 rooms, 4 story. Apr-Oct: S, D $65-
$95; each additional $6; suites $129-$169; under 12 free; ski,
golf packages; higher rates: weekends, holidays; lower rates
rest of year. Crib free. Check-out noon. TV. Refrigerators,
bathroom phones. Valet services. Restaurant, bar; entertainment. Room service 6 am-10 pm. Supervised children's
activities; ages 4-12. Health club privileges. Game room.
Downhill ski 15 miles, cross-country ski 18 miles. Meeting rooms. Business services. Bellstaff. Gift shop. Casino.
Stained-glass wedding chapel. Cr cds: A, C, D, DS, MC, V.

D ⊠ ⊞ ⊟ SC

Great Basin National Park (E-6)

(5 miles W of Baker on NV 488)

Established as a national park in 1986, Great Basin
includes Lehman Caves (formerly Lehman Caves
National Monument), Wheeler Peak (elevation 13,063
feet), the park's only glacier, and Lexington Arch, a natural limestone arch more than six stories tall. The park
consists of 77,092 acres of diverse scenic, ecologic, and
geologic attractions.

Of particular interest in the park is Lehman Caves, a
large limestone solution cavern. The cave contains numerous limestone formations, including shields and helictites.
Temperature in the cave is 50°F; jackets are recommended.

The 12-mile Wheeler Peak Scenic Drive reaches to the
10,000-foot elevation mark of Wheeler Peak. From there,
you can hike to the summit. Backcountry hiking and
camping are permitted. The Lexington Arch is located at
the south end of the park.

Camping is allowed at three campgrounds located along
the Wheeler Peak Scenic Drive: the Wheeler Peak Campground, the Upper Lehman Creek Campground, and the
Lower Lehman Campground. Baker Creek Campground
is located approximately 5 miles from park headquarters.
Picnic facilities are available near park headquarters.

Park headquarters and the Visitor Center are located at
Lehman Caves (daily; closed Jan 1, Thanksgiving, Dec 25;
extended hours in summer). Also here is a souvenir and

snack shop (early Apr-mid-Oct; daily). For further information, contact the Superintendent, Great Basin National
Park, Baker 89311; phone 775/234-7331.

Hawthorne (F-2)

Pop 3,311 **Elev** 4,320 ft **Area code** 775 **Zip** 89415

Information Chamber of Commerce, 932 E St, PO Box
1635; 775/945-5896

Hawthorne, seat of Mineral County, is a truly Western desert town on a broad plain rimmed by beautiful mountains
where gold has been mined. The area is inviting to people
who like to explore the "old" Nevada.

What to See and Do

Walker Lake. *US 95 and Walker Lake (89415). 12 miles
N on US 95.* Phone 775/885-6000. Named for the trapper and scout Joseph Walker, this is a remnant of ancient
Lake Lahontan. It is 15 miles long and 5 miles wide.
Fishing is good for cutthroat trout in these alkaline and
saline waters; swimming, water skiing, boating (landing).
Camping sites. The US Bureau of Land Management
maintains one recreational area: Sportsman's Beach (boat
launching; camping; free). Also here is

> **Walker Lake State Recreation Area.** *US 95 and Walker
> Lake (89415). Phone 775/885-6000.* Approximately 280
> acres. Swimming, fishing, boating (launching ramp);
> picnicking, shade structures. **FREE**

Motels/Motor Lodges

★ **EL CAPITAN RESORT CASINO.** *540 F St (89415).
Phone 775/945-3321; toll-free 800/922-2311; fax 775/
945-2193.* 103 rooms, 1-2 story. S, D $41-$45; each
additional $7; under 12 free. Crib free. Pet accepted; $10
deposit. Check-out 1 pm. TV; cable. Refrigerators. Restaurant open 24 hours. Bar. Game room. Heated pool. Meeting rooms. Sundries. Casino. Cr cds: A, C, D, DS, MC, V.

D ⊠ ⊞ ⊠ ✈ ⊟

★ **SAND & SAGE LODGE.** *1301 E Fifth (89415).
Phone 775/945-3352; fax 775/945-3353.* 37 rooms, 2 story.
S $29.95; D $34.95; each additional $5; kitchen units $6
additional. Crib free. Pet accepted, some restrictions. TV;
cable (premium). Pool. Complimentary coffee in lobby.
Restaurant nearby. Check-out 11 am. Refrigerators,
microwaves. Cr cds: A, DS, MC, V.

⊠ ⊞ ✈

Henderson (I-5)

See also Boulder City, Lake Mead National Recreation Area, Las Vegas

Settled 1942 **Pop** 175,381 **Elev** 1,960 ft **Area code** 702 **Zip** 89015

Information Chamber of Commerce, 590 S Boulder Hwy; 702/565-8951

Web www.hendersonchamber.com

The industrial center of Nevada, Henderson is on level desert terrain, midway between Boulder City (see) and Las Vegas (see). It was originally created to provide housing for the employees of a wartime magnesium plant. The fastest growing city in Nevada, it has become the third-largest city in the state.

What to See and Do

Clark County Heritage Museum. *1830 S Boulder Hwy.* Phone 702/455-7955. Exhibit center with county "timeline." Railroad, early residence exhibits; commercial print shop, outdoor mining, farming display; gift shop. (Daily; closed Jan 1, Thanksgiving, Dec 25) **$**

Ethel M. Chocolates Factory & Cactus Garden. *1 Sunset Way at junction Mt Vista. (89014).* Phone 702/433-2500. Self-guided tours of famous chocolate factory and adjacent catcus garden. Free samples. Shops. (Daily, hours vary) **FREE**

Special Event

Heritage Days. *590 S Boulder Hwy (89015).* Phone 702/565-8951. Summer months.

Motel/Motor Lodge

★ **BEST WESTERN.** *85 W Lake Mead Dr (89015).* Phone 702/564-1712; toll-free 800/446-2994; fax 702/564-7642. www.bestwestern.com. 60 rooms, 2 story. D $51-$125; under 12 free. Complimentary continental breakfast. Check-out 11 am, check-in 3 pm. TV; cable (premium). Outdoor pool. Cr cds: A, C, D, DS, MC, V.

D ⊠ SC

Restaurants

★ **RAINBOW CLUB.** *122 Water St (89015).* Phone 702/565-9777; fax 702/565-4809. www.rainbowclubcasino.com. Hours: Open 24 hours. Dinner $1.39-$8.95. Bar. Casual attire. Reservations not accepted. In casino.

D

Incline Village

See also Stateline

Pop 9,952 **Elev** 6,360 ft **Area code** 775 **Zip** 89451

Information Lake Tahoe Incline Village/Crystal Bay Visitors Bureau, 969 Tahoe Blvd; 775/832-1606 or 800/GO-TAHOE

Web www.gotahoe.com

What to See and Do

Lake Tahoe Nevada State Park. *2005 Hwy 28 (89451). On NV 28.* Phone 775/831-0494. Approximately 14,200 acres on the eastern shore of beautiful Lake Tahoe consisting of five management areas. Gently sloping sandy beach, swimming, fishing, boating (ramp); hiking, mountain biking, cross-country skiing. Picnic tables, stoves. No camping. Standard fees. (Daily)

Ponderosa Ranch Western Studio and Theme Park. *100 Ponderosa Ranch Rd (89451). On Tahoe Blvd (NV 28).* Phone 775/831-0691. Cartwright House seen in the "Bonanza" television series. Frontier town with 1870 country church; vintage autos; breakfast hayrides (fee); amusements May-Oct. Convention facilities. (Daily) **$$$**

Skiing.

Diamond Peak Ski Resort. *1210 Ski Way (89451). Jct NV 28 and Country Club Dr.* Phone 775/832-1177. www.diamondpeak.com. Three quads, three double chairlifts; patrol, school, rentals, snowmaking; cafeteria, bar, lodge. Thirty runs; longest run approximately 2 1/2 miles; vertical drop 1,840 feet. (Mid-Dec-mid-Apr, daily) **$$$$**

Mount Rose Ski Area. *22222 Mt. Rose Hwy, Reno (89511). 12 miles NE on NV 431.* Phone 775/849-0704 or toll-free 800/SKI-ROSE (except in Nevada). www.mtrose.com. Two quads, two triple, one six-person chairlift; patrol, rentals, school; bar, cafeteria, deli; sport shop. Longest run 2 1/2 miles; vertical drop 1,440 feet. (Mid-Nov-mid-Apr, daily)

Special Event

Lake Tahoe Winter Games Festival. *1210 Ski Way, Diamond Peak Ski Resort (89451).* Phone 775/832-1177. Early Mar.

Hotels

★★ **CAL NEVA RESORT HOTEL, SPA AND CASINO.** *2 Stateline Rd, Crystal Bay (89402). Phone 775/832-4000; toll-free 800/225-6382; fax 775/831-9007. www.calnevaresort.com.* Visitors will enjoy the beauty of Lake Tahoe and the Sierra Mountains from this hotel. Every room has a view of the lake. 200 rooms, 9 story. S, D $79-$179; suites $199-$269; under 10 free; higher rates during holidays (2-4-day minimum). Check-out noon. TV; cable. Restaurant 7 am-11 pm; summer to 2 am. Bar. Exercise equipment, sauna. Heated pool, whirlpool. Tennis. Concierge. Cr cds: A, C, D, DS, ER, JCB, MC, V.

[icons]

★★ **TAHOE BILTMORE HOTEL AND CASINO.** *5 NV 28, Crystal Bay (89402). Phone 775/831-0660; toll-free 800/245-8667; fax 775/833-6715. www.tahoebiltmore.com.* 92 rooms, 4 story. June-Sept: S, D $59-$139; holidays (2-day minimum); lower rates rest of year. Crib $5. TV; cable (premium). Complimentary full breakfast. Restaurant open 24 hours. Bar; entertainment. Check-out 11 am. Meeting rooms. Business services available. Downhill/cross-country ski 5 miles. Pool. Some refrigerators, microwaves. Some balconies. Opposite beach. Cr cds: A, DS, MC, V.

[icons]

Resort

★★★ **HYATT REGENCY LAKE TAHOE RESORT & CASINO.** *1111 Country Club Dr (89450). Phone 775/832-1234; toll-free 800/533-3288; fax 775/831-7508. www.hyatt.com.* This property is a top pick for rustic, luxury accommodations on the North Shore of Lake Tahoe. Although it's not located on a ski mountain, the resort makes every effort to help you get to and enjoy the sites around the lake, including snow skiing, snowmobiling, hiking, tennis, golf, and water sports. Spa services are offered through the fitness center. The hotel itself houses a small but charmingly old-style casino, a private hotel beach, and a destination restaurant with arguably one of the best dining views of the lake. Three additional restaurants in the main resort building, Ciao Mein (an Italian and Asian bistro), Sierra Grill (American), and Cutthroat Saloon (Western saloon), round out the dining options. 449 rooms, 12 story. June-Sept, weekends, holidays: S, D $180-$350; each additional $25; suites $610-$1565; cottages $690-$1385; under 18 free; ski packages; lower rates rest of year. Crib free. TV; cable (premium). Heated pool; whirlpool, poolside service. Supervised children's activities (daily in season; Fri, Sat evenings off-season); ages 3-12. Restaurants. Room service. Bar. Check-out 11 am. Convention facilities. Business center. Concierge. Shopping arcade. Free valet parking. Downhill ski 1 1/2 miles; cross-country ski 6 miles. Children's arcade. Recreation room. Lawn games. Bicycles available. Minibars; refrigerators available. Wet bar in cottages. Cottages have balconies. Luxury level. Cr cds: A, C, D, DS, JCB, MC, V.

[icons]

B&B/Small Inns

★ **INN AT INCLINE AND CONDO.** *1003 Tahoe Blvd (NV 28) (89451). Phone 775/831-1052; toll-free 800/824-6391; fax 775/831-3016. www.innatincline.com.* 38 rooms, 2 story. No A/C. Mid-June-late Sept: S, D $99-$139; each additional $15; under 18 free; lower rates rest of year. Complimentary continental breakfast. Check-out 11 am. Check-in 4 pm. TV; cable (premium). Restaurant nearby. Sauna. Indoor pool, whirlpool. Downhill ski 1 mile, cross-country ski 6 miles. Cr cds: A, DS, MC, V.

[icons]

Restaurant

★ **LAS PANCHITAS.** *930 Tahoe Blvd, Incline Center (89451). Phone 775/831-4048.* Mexican menu. Hours: 1 am-10 pm; Sat, Sun from noon. Closed Thanksgiving, Dec 25. Lunch $5.25-$11.95, dinner $6.45-$10.95. Bar. Outdoor dining. Rustic Mexican décor. Cr cds: A, C, MC, V.

Lake Mead National Recreation Area (I-6)

See also Boulder City, Overton
(4 miles NE of Boulder City on US 93)

This 2,627-square-mile tract extends along the Colorado River from Grand Canyon National Park to a point below Davis Dam. It is a land of colorful deserts, high plateaus, narrow canyons, and two magnificent lakes. Lake Mead, impounded by Hoover Dam (726 feet high), is by volume the largest man-made reservoir; 110 miles long, with a shoreline of 550 miles when full, with a maximum depth of 500 feet. Lake Mohave, formed behind Davis Dam, is 67 miles long with a shoreline of 150 miles.

The dams are part of an irrigation, reclamation, and power project of the federal government. More than 10 million people use the recreational facilities yearly. The Alan Bible Visitor Center on US 93 is open daily except Jan 1, Thanksgiving, and Dec 25.

What to See and Do

Davis Dam. *Phone 702/293-8431.*

★ **Hoover Dam.** *US Hwy 93, Boulder City. Approximately 8 miles E of Boulder City on US 93. Phone 702/ 293-8421.* Tour of dam and powerhouse (daily; closed Dec 25). Old exhibit building houses a model of a generating unit and a topographical model of the Colorado River Basin. The new Visitor Center exhibits audiovisual presentation, theater, and lectures from guides. **$$$**

Lake Mead Cruises. *480 Lakeshore Rd, Boulder City. Lake Mead Marina. 7 miles E of Boulder City, at the Lake Mead Resort area. Phone 702/293-6180.* A 90-minute sightseeing cruise to Hoover Dam on the paddlewheeler *Desert Princess.* Breakfast and dinner cruises are available. (Daily except Dec 25) **$$$$**

Recreation. *Phone 702/293-8906.* Developed areas in Nevada: Boulder Beach on Lake Mead, 6 miles NE of Boulder City; Las Vegas Bay, 10 miles NE of Henderson; Callville Bay, 24 miles NE of Henderson; Overton Beach, 9 miles S of Overton; Echo Bay, 23 miles S of Overton; Cottonwood Cove, 14 miles E of Searchlight. Developed areas in Arizona: Willow Beach on Lake Mohave, 18 miles S of Hoover Dam (no camping); Temple Bar on Lake Mead, 50 miles E of Hoover Dam; Katherine on Lake Mohave, 3 miles N of Davis Dam (camping, stores, restaurants, motels, marinas, and boat ramps in these areas). All these sites, except Willow Beach and Overton Beach, have campgrounds, $10/site per night; stores, restaurants, marinas, and boat ramps. Contact the Superintendent, Lake Mead National Recreation Area, 601 Nevada Hwy, Boulder City 89005-2426.

Lake Tahoe

(see Lake Tahoe Area Side Trip on page 234)

Las Vegas (H-5)

See also Boulder City, Henderson

Settled 1905 **Pop** 478,434 **Elev** 2,020 ft **Area code** 702

Information Las Vegas Convention/Visitors Authority, Convention Center, 3150 Paradise Rd, 89109; 702/892-7575

Web www.lasvegas24hours.com

Las Vegas, Nevada's largest city, became a major entertainment center after World War II. Near Hoover Dam and Lake Mead National Recreation Area (see), the city has public buildings and entertainment facilities designed to attract vacationers. Famous for glittering nightclubs, bars, gambling casinos, and plush hotels, Las Vegas also offers tennis, racquetball, bowling, water sports, snow skiing, golf, fishing and hunting, hiking and riding trails, and tours to nearby points of interest. The townsite covers 53 square miles on a plain encircled by distant mountains. Beyond its suburban fringe lies the desert.

Two natural springs and green meadows made the Las Vegas valley a favorite camping place in the 1840s for caravans following the Old Spanish Trail from Santa Fe to California. It was first settled by the Spanish in 1829. American settlement began in 1855, when Brigham Young sent 30 settlers to build a fort and stockade here. The Mormons tried mining in the area but found that the ore was hard to smelt and the metal made poor bullets. Later this "lead" was discovered to be a galena ore carrying silver.

The Mormons abandoned the settlement in 1857; from 1862-99 it was operated as a ranch. Las Vegas was really born in 1905, with the advent of the railroad. A tent town sprang up; streets were laid out, and permanent buildings followed. In 1911 the city of Las Vegas was created by an act of the legislature.

A Ranger District office of the Toiyabe National Forest is located here.

What to See and Do

Bonnie Springs Old Nevada. *1 Gun Fighter Ln (89004). 20 miles W via W Charleston Blvd. Phone 702/875-4191. www.bonniesprings.com.* Historic Western mining town features a narrow-gauge railroad, museums, restaurants, shops, and entertainment, as well as 1880s melodramas, riding stables, and a petting zoo. (Daily; hours vary by season) Per vehicle **$** (some activities extra).

Boxing at Caesars Palace. *3570 Las Vegas Blvd S (89109). Phone 702/731-7110.* Nowhere is the sport of boxing cheered more vigorously than in Las Vegas, where bouts are often sponsored by Caesars Palace (even when the match takes place at another area, such as the UNLV's Thomas & Mack Center). Key title match-ups range from featherweight to heavyweight. Major boxing event weekends tend to flood Las Vegas with Saturday night visitors, making both beds and tickets hard to come by without advance planning.

Creative Cooking School. *7385 W Sahara Ave (89117). Phone 702/562-3900.* Boosting Las Vegas's growing reputation for cuisine, chef-author Catherine Margles opened the city's first cooking school, Creative Cooking. Classes are divided between shorter two- to three-hour demonstration classes, in which students watch an instructor, and longer hands-on affairs of four to five hours. Thirty-minute meals, French basics, and knife skills typify the range of instruction available here. While most of the courses are designed for avid or improving amateurs, Creative Cooking also offers children's classes.

Elvis-A-Rama Museum. *3401 Industrial Rd (89109). Phone 702/309-7200.* Viva Elvis Presley! The star of *Viva Las Vegas,* who came to spend his fading years playing Vegas showrooms, is immortalized at Elvis-A-Rama. The strip mall-lodged exhibit tucked behind the Fashion Show Mall enshrines the singer's life and music in memorabilia ranging from his blue-suede-shoes era to his rhinestone-jumpsuit era. The brainchild of Chris Davidson, owner of the largest private Elvis-related goods collection, the 2,000-piece collection features three of the King's cars, including his 1955 concert tour limo, as well as a speedboat, a guitar, an army uniform, personal letters, and half a million dollars in gems. Supplementing the exhibits, a roster of Elvis impersonators perform daily. Most performances are included with the price of admission, although evening concerts require a separate ticket. (Daily) **$$$**

Floyd Lamb State Park. *9200 Tule Springs Rd. 10 miles N via US 95.* Phone 702/486-5413. Approximately 2,000 acres. Small lakes; fishing. Picnicking. No overnight camping. **$$**

Guinness World Records Museum. *2780 Las Vegas Blvd S.* Phone 702/792-3766. www.guinnessmuseum.com. Interactive computers bring the famous Guinness book to life. Displays; rare videos; special exhibit on Las Vegas. Gift shop. (Daily) **$$**

Imperial Palace Auto Collection. *3535 Las Vegas Blvd, on 5th-floor parking area of hotel.* Phone 702/794-3174. Part museum, part sales floor, and all Vegas, the Auto Collections housed on the fifth floor of the parking lot at Imperial Palace behind the casino (yes, it's a trek) showcase vintage cars, most for ogling, many for sale. Still, it's a nice daytime diversion from the Strip's casinos and shops, drawing a million visitors annually. Models range from historic autos to muscle cars, with a few late-model luxury brands thrown in. Since some do sell, the 170-plus-car exhibit changes frequently, but examples like the 1962 red Alfa Romeo Spider, the 1954 Chevy Bel Air convertible, and the 1929 Duesenberg sedan generally wow the crowds. In addition to the autos and the occasional antiques and collectibles auction held here, look to the collection for vintage car parts and jukeboxes. (Daily) **$$$**

Las Vegas Art Museum. *9600 W Sahara Ave.* Phone 702/360-8000. An affiliate of Washington, DC's Smithsonian, the Las Vegas Art Museum serves primarily as a venue for traveling shows, including those mounted by the Smithsonian's traveling exhibition service. Other exhibits, sometimes locally curated by affiliates of the Guggenheim Hermitage in town, change roughly every two months, often showcasing modern or contemporary works. (Tues-Sat) **$$**

Las Vegas Convention/Visitors Authority. *1 Gun Fighter Lane. Paradise Rd, S of town.* Phone 702/892-0711. The largest single-level convention center in the country; 1.3 million square feet of exhibit and meeting space.

Las Vegas Motor Speedway. *7000 Las Vegas Blvd N.* Phone 702/644-4444. Motorsports complex covers 1,500 acres and features a 1 1/2-mile superspeedway, 2 1/2-mile road course, 1/2-mile dirt oval, drag strip, Go-Kart tracks, racing schools and fantasy camps, and other attractions. Home to NASCAR, IRL, and AMA racing. Tours. (Daily; event schedule varies)

Las Vegas Natural History Museum. *900 Las Vegas Blvd N.* Phone 702/384-3466. www.lvnhm.org. Wildlife collection featuring animated dinosaurs and shark exhibits. (Daily; closed Thanksgiving, Dec 25) **$$**

Liberace Foundation and Museum. *1775 E Tropicana Ave, 2 1/2 miles E of Strip.* Phone 702/798-5595. The flamboyance of late pianist Liberace shines on eternally at the Liberace Museum. From cars to capes, rhinestoned pianos to Russian antiques, all the glitz that made "Mr. Showman" who he was is enshrined in this kitschy collection. Now that Las Vegas has upscaled to the tasteful level with fine restaurants, top-notch spas, and groundbreaking shows, this tour recalls the good ol' tacky days when Liberace pulled up in a convertible Rolls painted red, white, and blue to play one of 39 pianos (18 shown here), including one festooned entirely in mini-mirror tiles, while wearing a 200-pound Neptune costume by the light of a rococo candelabra. In addition to costumes and a piano-shaped watch, Liberace's personal effects include fine French and Russian furnishings in a re-creation of his Palm Springs boudoir. Piped-in music and a gallery of Liberace photographs round out the trip down memory lane. (Daily; closed Jan 1, Thanksgiving, Dec 25) **$$$$**

Mount Charleston Recreation Area. *15 miles NW on US 95, then 21 miles W on NV 157, which leads to Toiyabe National Forest (see RENO).* Picnicking, camping (fee).

Nevada State Museum and Historical Society. *700 Twin Lakes Dr, in Lorenzi Park.* Phone 702/486-5205. Exhibits explore the growth of southern Nevada from Spanish explorers to present. The natural history of the area is presented in the Hall of Biological Science. Changing exhibits on art, history of the region. (Daily; closed Jan 1, Thanksgiving, Dec 25) **$**

⭐ **Red Rock Canyon National Conservation Area.** *700 Twin Lakes Dr. 17 miles W on W Charleston Blvd.* Phone 702/363-1922. Spectacular view of the area's steep canyons and red and white hues of the Aztec sandstone formation. Picnicking, hiking trails, rock climbing; 13-mile scenic drive (daylight hours only); limited primitive camping. Visitor center; nature walks led by Bureau of Land Management ranger-naturalists. **$$** Nearby is

Spring Mountain Ranch State Park. *Approximately 18 miles W on W Charleston Blvd.* Phone 702/875-4141. Visitor center at main ranch house (daily; closed Jan 1, Thanksgiving, Dec 25) has brochures with self-guided tours of park and interpretive trails. Guided tours of ranch buildings (daily). Picnicking. (Daily) **$$**

Scenic Airlines. *2105 Airport Dr.* Phone 702/736-8900 or toll-free 800/634-6801. Day trips to the Grand Canyon.

Southern Nevada Zoo. *1775 N Rancho Dr. Phone 702/647-4685.* Apes, monkeys, tiger, ostriches, exotic bird collection, and Southwestern desert animals. Also here is an endangered species breeding program. (Daily; closed Jan 1, Thanksgiving, Dec 25) **$$**

Sports Book at Mirage Hotel and Casino. *3400 Las Vegas Blvd S (89109). Phone 702/791-7111.* Most casinos have one, but sports books are shrinking in newer hotels, carving a scant 5,000 square feet out of the casino. The Mirage boasts a 10,000-square-foot sports betting palace. If there's a sport that can be bet on, it's on the busy tote boards and televisions here, easily accounting for the visual confusion of neophytes. If you don't understand the odds, ask the window clerks. Sports bookies have dreamed up myriad ways to bet: not just who wins, who loses, and the point spread, but who wins the coin toss, what the halftime score will be, and who will score more points today, an individual NBA star or the Green Bay Packers. Big events, including the Super Bowl, the Kentucky Derby, and the NBA Finals, are predictably jammed. But niche sports like NCAA basketball and World Cup soccer draw sizable contingents to the book as well, making seats scarce. (Open 24 hours) **FREE**

⭐ **The Strip.** *Las Vegas Blvd, S of town. Phone 702/735-1616.* Las Vegas's biggest attraction, with dazzling casinos, roulette wheels, luxurious hotels, glamorous chorus lines, and top entertainers. Some shows are free; some require buying food or drink. Make reservations.

Trader Joe's. *2101 S Decatur Blvd (89102). Phone 702/367-0227.* A link in the fast-growing LA-based chain of specialty grocers, Trader Joe's is part discounter, part gourmet emporium. Volume sales of such specialties as Norwegian smoked salmon, organic greens, Italian parmesan, and California wines helps Joe's cut prices. The shop's frozen meals, from cioppino to teriyaki rice bowls, regularly stock the cupboards of impatient gourmands. Rough wood shelves and bins aim to evoke a trader's ship, and staff wear Hawaiian shirts in keeping with the fun. (Daily; closed Jan 1, Thanksgiving, Dec 25)

University of Nevada, Las Vegas. *4505 Maryland Pkwy (89154). Phone 702/895-3443.* (1957) 19,500 students. Campus tours arranged in advance. On campus are

Artemus W. Ham Concert Hall. *4505 Maryland Pkwy (89154). Phone 702/895-3801 (box office).* A 1,900-seat theater featuring yearly Charles Vanda Master Series of symphony, opera, and ballet. Jazz and popular music concerts also performed here.

Donna Beam Fine Art Gallery. *4505 Maryland Pkwy (89154). Phone 702/895-3893.* Exhibits by professional artists, faculty, students; emphasis on contemporary art. (Mon-Fri; closed holidays) **FREE**

The Flashlight. A 38-foot-tall steel sculpture by Claes Oldenburg and Coosje von Bruggen.

Judy Bayley Theatre. *4505 Maryland Pkwy (89154). Phone 702/895-3801 (box office).* Varied theatrical performances all year.

Marjorie Barrick Museum of Natural History. *4505 Maryland Parkway (89154). Phone 702/895-3381.* Exhibits of the biology, geology, and archaeology of the Las Vegas area, including live desert animals. (Mon-Sat; closed holidays) **FREE**

Thomas and Mack Center. *4505 S Maryland Pkwy (89154). Phone 702/895-3761.* Events center (18,500-seat) features concerts, ice shows, rodeos, sporting events.

UNLV Performing Arts Center. *4505 S Maryland Pkwy (89154). Phone 702/895-3801.* Touring performers as diverse as Herbie Hancock, Yo-Yo Ma, the Shanghai Ballet, Regina Carter, and Andre Watts play at the Performing Arts Center found on the University of Nevada Las Vegas campus. In addition to classical musicians, jazz players, and world dance troops, the center stages lectures by visiting authors like John Irving and journalists such as Cokie Roberts. The UNLV departments of theater and performing arts also mount shows on the several stages here.

Wet 'n Wild Las Vegas. *2601 S Las Vegas Blvd (89154). Phone 702/737-3819.* Aquatic amusement park featuring 75-foot water slide; rafting (rentals), flumes, water cannons, whirlpools, whitewater rapids, waterfalls, pools, lagoon, four-foot waves, and children's activities. Picnicking; snack bars. (May-Sept, daily) **$$$$**

Special Events

Invensys Classic. *1700 Village Center Cir (89134). Phone 702/256-0111.* PGA tournament with more than $4.5 million in prize money. Oct.

Las Vegas Invitational. *1700 Village Center Circle (89134). Phone 702/242-3000.* A top Professional Golfer's Association tournament, autumn's annual Las Vegas Invitational draws the pro tour's elite to Sin City. Host of the PGA event since 1992, the Tournament Players Club at Summerlin was designed by architect Bobby Weed with input from player/consultant Fuzzy Zoeller. In addition to offering elevation changes and a variety of challenges, the course was built to accommodate spectators with natural amphitheaters and clear sightlines to the tees. **$$$$**

National Finals Rodeo. *4505 Maryland Pkwy (89154). Phone 702/895-3761. Thomas and Mack Center.* Nation's richest professional rodeo, featuring 15 finalists in seven rodeo disciplines. Dec.

Motels/Motor Lodges

★ **ARIZONA CHARLIE'S.** *740 S Decatur Blvd (89107). Phone 702/258-5111; toll-free 800/342-2695; fax 702/258-5192. www.arizonacharlies.com.* 257 rooms, 7 story. S, D $38.95-$138.95; suites $125-$300. Crib free. TV; cable (premium). Heated pool; lifeguard. Restaurant open 24 hours. Bar. Check-out 11 am, check-in 3 pm. Bellstaff. Business services available. Valet service. Gift shop. Game room. Airport transportation. Casino. Cr cds: A, C, D, DS, ER, JCB, MC, V.

D ⌦ ⌧

★ **BEST WESTERN MCCARRAN INN.** *4970 Paradise Rd (89119). Phone 702/798-5530; toll-free 800/626-7575; fax 702/798-7627. www.bestwestern.com.* 99 rooms, 3 story. S, D $49-$209; each additional $7; suites $90-$179; under 17 free; higher rates: national holidays, major events. Complimentary continental breakfast. Check-out noon, check-in 3 pm. TV. Laundry services. Heated pool. Free airport transportation. Cr cds: A, C, D, DS, ER, MC, V.

D ⌦ ⌦ ⌦ ⌦ ⌧ ⌦

★ ★ **COURTYARD BY MARRIOTT.** *3275 Paradise Rd (89109). Phone 702/791-3600; toll-free 800/321-2211; fax 702/796-7981. www.courtyard.com.* 161 rooms, 3 story. D $89-$349; higher rates: conventions, holiday weekends. Check-out noon, check-in 3 pm. TV; cable (premium). Internet access, in-room modem link. Restaurant 6:30 am-2 pm; 5-10 pm. Bar 5-11 pm. Exercise equipment. Outdoor pool, whirlpool. Free airport transportation. Cr cds: A, C, D, DS, ER, MC, V.

D ⌦ ⌧ ⌧ ⌦ SC

★ **FAIRFIELD INN.** *3850 Paradise Rd (89109). Phone 702/791-0899; toll-free 800/228-2800; fax 702/791-2705. www.fairfield.com.* 129 rooms, 4 story. Check-out noon, check-in 3 pm. TV; cable (premium). In-room modem link. Outdoor pool. Free airport transportation. Cr cds: A, C, D, DS, ER, JCB, MC, V. **$**

D ⌦ ⌧ ⌦

★ **LA QUINTA INN.** *3970 Paradise Rd (89109). Phone 702/796-9000; toll-free 800/531-5900; fax 702/796-3537. www.laquinta.com.* 251 units, 21 kitchen units, 3 story. Pet accepted, some restrictions. Complimentary continental breakfast. Check-out noon, check-in 3 pm. TV; cable (premium). In-room modem link. Laundry services. Heated pool. Free airport transportation. Cr cds: A, D, DS, JCB, MC, V. **$**

D ⌦ ⌦ SC

★ **TRAVELODGE.** *5075 Koval Ln (89119). Phone 702/736-3600; toll-free 800/578-7878; fax 702/736-0726. www.travelodge.com.* 106 rooms, 2 story. S, D $39-$159; under 18 free. Crib free. TV; cable (premium). Pool. Complimentary continental breakfast. Restaurant adjacent open 24 hours. Check-out 11 am, check-in 2 pm. Business services available. Cr cds: A, C, D, DS, ER, JCB, MC, V.

D ⌦ ⌧

Hotels

★ ★ ★ **BALLYS.** *3645 Las Vegas Blvd (89109). Phone 702/967-4111; toll-free 888/742-9248; fax 702/967-4405. www.ballyslv.com.* A neon-lit tunnel ushers you from the heart of the Strip into Bally's, offering good value in a prime location. At over 500 square feet, the recently renovated rooms are spacious and comfortable. The palm-fringed pool and spa, though small here, are musts for any Strip address. But what marquees Bally's is its showroom, where the showgirl-driven "Jubilee" is frequently named best of its kind by locals. While Bally's is old Las Vegas, it shares ownership, and a connecting walkway, with Paris Las Vegas, one of the Strip's newest and showiest corners, convenient for its many shopping and dining options. 2,832 rooms, 26 story. Pet accepted. Check-out 11 am. TV; cable (premium), VCR available. In-room modem link. Restaurant, bar; entertainment. In-house fitness room, sauna. Game room. Outdoor pool, children's pool. Outdoor tennis, lighted courts. Casino. Wedding chapel. Cr cds: A, C, D, DS, ER, JCB, MC, V. **$**

D ⌦ ⌦ ⌦ ⌧ ⌦

★ ★ ★ **BELLAGIO.** *3600 Las Vegas Blvd S (89109). Phone 702/693-7111; toll-free 888/967-6667; fax 702/693-8546. www.bellagiolasvegas.com.* The Bellagio Las Vegas is a visual masterpiece. From its bold designs and world-class artwork to its acclaimed entertainment and award-winning cuisine, the Bellagio delights the senses. The lobby draws attention with its dazzling bursts of color from the 2,000 hand-blown glass flowers by renowned artist Dale Chihuly. The rooms delightfully combine European élan with American comfort. A fantastic casino is only the beginning at this all-encompassing resort, which hosts an impressive swimming pool and fountain area, an arcade of fine shopping, and a Conservatory and Botanical Gardens under its roof. Discriminating diners will applaud the culinary works of art created in the resort's many fine dining establishments (see also AQUA, LE CIRQUE, PICASSO, and PRIME). Figuring largely in the Bellagio experience is its 8-acre lake, where mesmerizing fountains perform to a symphony of sounds and lights every half-hour or so. The Bellagio is also home to Cirque du Soleil's *O*, a heart-stopping aquatic performance that is simply not to be missed. 3,005 rooms, 36 story. D $159-$799; each additional $40. Adults only. TV; cable (premium). Restaurant. Exercise room. Spa. Massage. Heated pool; whirlpool, poolside service. Entertainment. Cr cds: A, C, D, DS, ER, JCB, MC, V.

D ⌦ ⌧ SC

★★ BINION'S HORSESHOE HOTEL & CASINO. 128 E Fremont (89125). Phone 702/382-1600; toll-free 800/937-6537; toll-free 888/967-6667; fax 702/382-1574. www.binionshorseshoe.com. 366 rooms, 22 story. S, D $19-$39 (2-night minimum weekends). Crib free. TV; cable (premium). Heated pool. Restaurant open 24 hours. Bar. Check-out noon, check-in 3 pm. Gift shop. Casino. Cr cds: A, C, D, DS, ER, JCB, MC, V.

★★★ CAESARS PALACE. 3570 Las Vegas Blvd S (89109). Phone 702/731-7110; toll-free 800/634-6001; fax 702/731-7172. www.caesars.com. The Roman-themed Caesar's was the Strip's first mega-resort when it opened in 1966. And though little lasts long in Vegas, Caesar's still reigns, constantly growing, and challenging competitors to keep up. To its Italian facade, Caesar's recently added a replica of Rome's Coliseum in which singer Celine Dion entertains. The hotel's swimming deck, modeled on Pompeii, trims three pools in marble statues. The confusing layout of the casino floor is an open play to keep you in house. But there's plenty to recommend it, including 808 and Bradley Ogden restaurants, as well as the high-end Forum Shops. Standard guest quarters include a couch as well as a marble bathroom. 2,500 rooms, 14-32 story. D $99-$500; each additional $15; under 13 free. Check-out noon, check-in 5 pm. TV; cable (premium), VCR available (movies). In-room modem link. Restaurant, bar; entertainment. Exercise room, massage, sauna, steam room. Game room. 3 pools, whirlpool. Handball. Racquetball. Free parking. Business center. Concierge. Casino. Cr cds: A, C, D, DS, ER, JCB, MC, V.

★★ CASTAWAYS. 2800 E Fremont St (89104). Phone 702/385-9123; toll-free 800/826-2800; fax 702/383-9238. www.castaways-lv.com. 453 rooms, 19 story. S, D $29-$89; suites $149-$195; under 12 free. Crib $5. Check-out noon. TV. Restaurant open 24 hours. Bar. Game room. Heated pool, lifeguard. 106-lane bowling. Barber, beauty shop. Free airport transportation. Meeting rooms. Business services. Gift shop. Casino. Cr cds: A, D, DS, MC, V.

★★ CIRCUS CIRCUS HOTEL & CASINO. 2880 Las Vegas Blvd S (89109). Phone 702/734-0410; toll-free 877/224-2287; fax 702/734-5897. www.circuscircus-lasvegas.com. 3,773 rooms, 100 suites, 35 story. Check-out 11 am, check-in 3 pm. TV. In-room modem link. Restaurant, bar; entertainment. In-house fitness room, health club privileges. Outdoor pool, children's pool. Casino. Cr cds: A, C, D, DS, ER, JCB, MC, V. $

★★ CLARION HOTEL & SUITES. 325 E Flamingo Rd (89109). Phone 702/732-9100; toll-free 800/424-6423; fax 702/731-9784. www.choicehotels.com. 150 rooms, 3 story. Check-out noon, check-in 3 pm. TV; cable (premium), VCR available. Restaurant, bar. In-house fitness room. Outdoor pool, children's pool. Concierge. Free transportation. Cr cds: A, C, D, DS, ER, JCB, MC, V.

★ EL CORTEZ HOTEL AND CASINO. 600 E Fremont St (89125). Phone 702/385-5200; toll-free 800/634-6703; fax 702/385-9765. www.elcortez.net. 303 rooms, 15 story. S, D $25-$40; each additional $3, suites $50. Crib free. TV; cable (premium). Restaurant 4:30-11 pm. Room service 7 am-7 pm. Bar open 24 hours. Check-out noon, check-in 2 pm. Meeting rooms. Shopping arcade. Barber, beauty shop. Free valet parking. Casino. Cr cds: A, D, DS, MC, V.

★ FIESTA RANCHO STATION CASINO HOTEL. 2400 N Rancho Dr (89130). Phone 702/631-7000; toll-free 800/731-7333; fax 702/631-6588. www.fiestacasinohotel.com. 100 rooms, 5 story. S, D $39-$100; under 18 free. Crib free. TV; cable. Restaurant open 24 hours (See also GARDUÑOS). No room service. Check-out noon, check-in 3 pm. Meeting rooms. Gift shop. Heated pool. Casino. Game room. Free airport transportation. Near North Las Vegas Airport. Cr cds: A, D, DS, ER, JCB, MC, V.

★ FLAMINGO. 3555 Las Vegas Blvd S (89109). Phone 702/733-3111; toll-free 800/308-8899; fax 702/733-3528. www.flamingolasvegas.com. This large, self-contained casino resort predates the recent explosion of megahotels on the Strip while bridging the old and new Vegas charm. Amenities include a water sports area and the new Radio City Music Hall Review, featuring the Rockettes. 3,655 rooms, 28 story. Pet accepted. Check-out noon, check-in 3 pm. TV; cable (premium). In-room modem link. Restaurant, bar. In-house fitness room, spa, sauna, steam room. Outdoor pool. Outdoor tennis. Valet parking. Business center. Casino. Cr cds: A, C, D, DS, ER, JCB, MC, V. $

★★ FOUR QUEENS HOTEL AND CASINO. 202 E Fremont St (89101). Phone 702/385-4011; toll-free 800/634-6045; fax 702/387-5160. www.fourqueens.com. 700 rooms, 19 story. S, D $49-$199; each additional $15; suites $99-$349; under 2 free. TV. Restaurant open 24 hours; dining room 6 pm-midnight. Bar; entertainment. Check-out noon. Meeting rooms. Business services available. Garage parking. Wet bar in suites. Casino. Cr cds: A, C, D, DS, MC, V.

★★★ FOUR SEASONS HOTEL. 3960 Las Vegas Blvd S (89119). Phone 702/632-5000; toll-free 877/632-5000; fax 702/632-5195. www.fourseasons.com. The Four Seasons Hotel is a palatial refuge in glittering Las Vegas.

Located on the southern tip of the famous strip, the Four Seasons remains close to the attractions of this dynamic city while providing a welcome respite from the hustle and bustle. This non-gaming hotel occupies the 35th through 39th floors of the Mandalay Bay Resort tower (see also MANDALAY BAY RESORT AND CASINO), yet it is distinctively Four Seasons with its sumptuous décor and inimitable service. Guests surrender to the plush furnishings in the stylish rooms, and floor-to-ceiling windows showcase exhilarating views of the strip's neon lights or the stark beauty of the Nevada desert. Steak lovers rejoice at Charlie Palmer Steak, while the sun-filled Verandah offers a casual dining alternative. The glorious pool is a lush oasis with its swaying palm trees and attentive poolside service. Lucky visitors retreat to the sublime spa, where JAMU Asian techniques soothe the weary. 424 rooms, 5 story. Pet accepted, some restrictions. Check-out noon, check-in 3 pm. TV; cable (premium). Room service 24 hours. Restaurant, bar. Spa. Outdoor pool; children's pool. Concierge. Cr cds: A, D, DS, JCB, MC, V. **$$**

D 🐾 ≈ SC

★ **FREMONT HOTEL & CASINO.** *200 E Fremont St (89125). Phone 702/385-3232; toll-free 800/634-6966; fax 702/385-6270. www.fremontcasino.com.* 423 rooms, 14 story. S, D $35-$110; suites $50-$150; package plan. Crib free. TV. Restaurant open 24 hours. Bars. Check-out noon. Gift shop. Casino. Cr cds: A, C, D, DS, ER, JCB, MC, V.

≈

★ ★ **FRONTIER HOTEL AND CASINO.** *3120 Las Vegas Blvd S (89109). Phone 702/794-8200; toll-free 800/634-6460; fax 702/794-8327. www.frontierlv.com.* 984 rooms, 416 suites, 16 story. Check-out noon, check-in 3 pm. TV. In-room modem link. Restaurant, bar. Outdoor pool. Business center. Concierge, casino. Cr cds: A, C, D, DS, ER, JCB, MC, V. **$**

D ≈ ≈

★ ★ ★ **GOLDEN NUGGET HOTEL AND CASINO.** *129 E Fremont St (89101). Phone 702/385-7111; toll-free 800/846-5336; fax 702/386-6970. www.goldennugget.com.* Downtown Las Vegas's star hotel, Golden Nugget is run by MGM Mirage, meaning that you get the same Strip-style amenities—including a cabana-ringed pool with a mist-cooled deck, fitness center, and full-service spa—at discount prices. Everything is cheaper downtown, including the gambling minimums, but the Nugget upholds elegant standards with a marble-trimmed lobby just off raucous Fremont Street. Among entertainment options, the International Beer Bar pours 40 foreign brands, and Zax serves an eclectic sushi-to-tostada menu through dinner, drinking, and dancing into the wee hours. 1,907 rooms, 18-22 story. D $59-$129. Check-out noon, check-in

11 am. TV; VCR available. In-room modem link. Restaurant, bar; entertainment. Exercise room, massage, sauna, steam room. Pool, whirlpool, poolside service. Business center. Casino. Cr cds: A, C, D, DS, ER, JCB, MC, V.

D ≈ 🏋 ≈ SC 🚶

★ ★ ★ **HARD ROCK HOTEL CASINO.** *4455 Paradise Rd (89109). Phone 702/693-5000; toll-free 888/ HRDROCK; fax 702/693-5010. www.hardrockhotel.com.* Rock-and-rollers play and stay at the Hard Rock, and so do their fans. A youthful party atmosphere prevails in the memorabilia-strewn complex run by the founder of the Hard Rock Café chain. About a mile off the Strip, Hard Rock generates its own fun, particularly when a big act is booked at The Joint concert hall. Then the swim-up blackjack tables by the pool, where rock music is piped underwater, get hot, and the lines for Nobu (see also), the celebrated sushi spot, lengthen. Hip room décor features French doors that open to neon-lit Strip views (preferred over mountain views). 340 rooms, 11 story. D $59-$329. Check-out noon, check-in 3 pm. TV; cable (premium). Restaurant. Exercise room. Pool. Airport transportation. Concierge. Cr cds: A, C, D, DS, ER, JCB, MC, V.

D ≈ 🏋 ✈ ≈

★ ★ ★ **HARRAH'S HOTEL AND CASINO.** *3475 Las Vegas Blvd S (89109). Phone 702/369-5000; toll-free 800/427-7247; fax 702/693-5010. www.harrahs.com.* The gaming powerhouse Harrah's runs this Strip hotel, where the emphasis, as you might expect, is on the casino. Bolstering the hotel and casino's carnival theme décor, an outdoor plaza showcases entertainers, trinket vendors, and snack booths. Spacious but rather bland rooms are lodged in a 35-story tower behind the gaming floor, although guests spend most of their time at the many tables, Olympic-size swimming pool, boutique spa, or 8 eateries. Popular entertainer Clint Holmes rules the showroom here with song and dance. 2,673 rooms, 35 story. Check-out noon, check-in 4 pm. TV. Laundry services. Restaurant, bar; entertainment. In-house fitness room, spa, massage, sauna. Game room. Outdoor pool. Valet parking. Casino. Wedding chapel. Cr cds: A, C, D, DS, ER, JCB, MC, V. **$**

D ≈ 🏋 ≈ SC

★ ★ **HOLIDAY INN FITZGERALDS CASINO.** *301 Fremont St (89101). Phone 702/388-2400; toll-free 800/274-5825; fax 702/388-2181. www.fitzgeralds.com.* 638 rooms, 34 story, 14 suites. S, D $25-$150; suites $150-$300; under 18 free. Crib $10. TV. Restaurant open 24 hours. Room service. Bar. Check-out noon. Business services available. Concierge. Gift shop. Casino. Cr cds: A, C, D, DS, JCB, MC, V.

D ≈ 🚶

★ **LADY LUCK CASINO HOTEL.** *206 N 3rd St (89101). Phone 702/477-3000; toll-free 800/634-6580; fax 702/477-7021. www.ladyluck.com.* 792 rooms, 17 and 25 story, 118 suites. Feb-Mar, Sept-Oct: S, D $39-$99; suites $49-$100; package plans; lower rates rest of year. TV. Heated pool; lifeguard. Restaurant open 24 hours. Bar. Check-out noon, check-in 3 pm. Free garage parking. Airport transportation. Refrigerators. Casino. Cr cds: A, D, DS, MC, V.

★★ **LAS VEGAS CLUB HOTEL AND CASINO.** *18 E Fremont St (89109). Phone 702/385-1664; toll-free 800/634-6532; fax 702/380-5793. www.vegasclubcasino.net.* 410 rooms, 16 story, 5 suites. S, D $29-$85; under 12 free; suites $150-$500; higher rates: holidays, special events. Crib free. TV; cable. Restaurant open 24 hours. Check-out noon, check-in 3 pm. Business services available. Shopping arcade. Cr cds: A, C, D, DS, MC, V.

★★★ **HILTON HOTEL.** *3000 Paradise Rd (89109). Phone 702/732-5111; toll-free 800/732-7117; fax 702/794-3611. www.lvhilton.com.* Play craps, get a massage, book a meeting or enjoy the food and entertainment at this popular Las Vegas destination adjacent to the Convention Center. Set upon 80 lushly landscaped acres, this 30-story hotel has several venues for fun beyond the casino, including the Race and Sports SuperBook, a "high-tech wonderland for the sports enthusiast" and a 1,600-seat theatre. 3,174 rooms, 30 story, 300 suites. S, D $55-$359; each additional $25; 1-2 bedroom suites $350-$1,200; lanai suites $330-$350. Crib free. TV. Rooftop pool; whirlpool, poolside service, lifeguard. Restaurant open 24 hours. Bars; entertainment. Check-out noon, check-in 3 pm. Convention facilities. Business center. In-room modem link. Shopping arcade. Barber, beauty shop. Free valet parking. Lighted tennis, pro. Exercise room; sauna. Massage. Game room. Some bathroom phones, refrigerators. Private patios, balconies. Casino. Cr cds: A, C, D, DS, ER, JCB, MC, V.

★★★ **LUXOR HOTEL AND CASINO.** *3900 Las Vegas Blvd S (89119). Phone 702/262-4000; toll-free 888/288-1000; fax 702/262-4857. www.luxor.com.* A 30-story glass pyramid in the desert, the thoroughly thematic Luxor emulates ancient Egypt, from its sphinx figurehead outdoors to gold-costumed employees within. Elevators travel the pyramid's incline to deposit guests at room hallways that overlook the world's largest atrium. Five pools, a fitness center, and a spa provide recreation, while an IMAX theater, two-story game room for the kids, and a museum devoted to King Tut entertain. The inventive performance artists Blue Man Group headline Luxor's stage options.

4,400 rooms, 30 story. Check-out 11 am, check-in 3 pm. TV; cable (premium), VCR available. Restaurant, bar; entertainment. In-house fitness room, spa, massage, sauna. Outdoor pool; children's pool. Business center. Concierge, casino. Cr cds: A, C, D, DS, ER, JCB, MC, V. **$**

★★ **MAIN STREET STATION.** *200 N Main St (89101). Phone 702/387-1896; toll-free 800/465-0711; fax 702/388-4421.* Despite its 28,000-square-foot game area, this Victorian-era property is more than just an award-winning casino. It is also home to downtown's only microbrewery and an antique collection that includes Buffalo Bill Cody's private rail car. 406 rooms, 15 story. S, D $37-$100; higher rates during holidays. Crib free. TV; cable (premium). Restaurant open 24 hours. Check-out noon, check-in 3 pm. Meeting rooms. Business center. In-room modem link. Concierge. Shopping arcade. Cr cds: A, C, D, DS, ER, JCB, MC, V.

★★★ **MANDALAY BAY RESORT AND CASINO.** *3950 Las Vegas Blvd S (89119). Phone 702/632-7777; toll-free 877/632-7000; fax 702/632-7234. www.mandalaybay.com.* Even in over-the-top Las Vegas, Mandalay Bay exceeds expectations. This all-encompassing resort captures the spirit of the tropics with its 11-acre sandy beach and three pools with lazy river ride. The stylish accommodations flaunt a tropical flavor, and the casino is a paradise of lush foliage and flowing water, yet this resort is perhaps best known for its mystifying Shark Reef. This facility goes far beyond the ordinary aquarium and takes the entire family on an unforgettable adventure. In true Vegas style, this resort has it all, including a 30,000-square-foot spa and terrific shopping. Thirteen restaurants offer a taste of the world, while an astounding variety of entertainment options include everything from live music to Broadway-style shows. 3,215 rooms, 403 suites, 36 story. Check-out 11 am, check-in 3 pm. TV; cable (premium). In-room modem link. Room service 24 hour. Restaurant, bar; entertainment. In-house fitness room, spa, massage. Beach. Outdoor pool; children's pool, whirlpool. Cr cds: A, C, D, DS, MC, V. **$**

★★★ **MGM GRAND HOTEL AND CASINO.** *3799 Las Vegas Blvd S (89109). Phone 702/891-7777; toll-free 877/880-0880; fax 702/891-1030. www.mgmgrand.com.* The largest hotel on the Strip, the MGM Grand virtually pulses with Las Vegas energy. If you've come for nonstop thrills, check in here, where the attractions work well to keep you out of your comfortable room. In the casino, a glassed-in lion habitat with waterfalls showcases a wild pride. The outdoor pool includes a current-fed lazy river, and the spa specializes in cutting-edge treatments. MGM eateries Coyote Café, NobHill, and Craftsteak are thought to be some of the best in the city. Big-name headliners like Cher and David Copperfield often play the MGM, and the French act Le Femme updates the showgirl revue. The party crowd crows for the dance club Studio 54 and the lounge Tabu. 5,005 rooms, 29 story. D $69.95-$399.95; under 12 free. Check-out 11 am. Check-in 3 pm. TV; cable (premium). Internet access. Restaurant, bar; entertainment. Supervised children's activities; ages 3-12. Exercise room, spa, steam room. Game room. Pool, whirlpool, poolside service. Free parking. Airport transportation. Business center. Concierge. Cr cds: A, C, D, DS, ER, JCB, MC, V.

⊡ ⩯ ⚹ ✈ ⊠ ⚶

★ ★ ★ **THE MIRAGE HOTEL AND CASINO.** *3400 Las Vegas Blvd S (89177). Phone 702/791-7111; toll-free 800/374-9000; fax 702/791-7446. www.mgm-mirage.com.* The Strip-side volcano—which erupts every 15 minutes at night—marks the Mirage and its exotic theme. Tropical fish tanks back the registration desks, the route to room elevators passes through a cascade of jungle foliage, and a lavish pool deck is ringed by towering palms. Among Mirage's many eateries, Renoir is one of town's tops for fine dining, while the Brazilian-style Samba makes a celebration of meat-eating. Two of Vegas' most popular shows—impersonator Danny Gans and lion-taming illusionists Seigfried & Roy—play the Mirage. Rooms, recently and smartly renovated, include spacious, marble-trimmed baths. 3,044 rooms, 30 story. D $79-$499. Check-out noon, check-in 2 pm. TV; VCR available. In-room modem link. Restaurant, bar; entertainment. Exercise room, massage. Pool, whirlpool. Valet parking. Business center. Concierge. Casino. Cr cds: A, C, D, DS, ER, JCB, MC, V.

⊡ ⩯ ⚹ ⚶

★ ★ ★ **MONTE CARLO RESORT & CASINO.** *3770 Las Vegas Blvd S (89030). Phone 702/730-7777; toll-free 800/311-8999; fax 702/730-7250. www.montecarlo.com.* Modeled on the sophisticated European republic of Monaco, this Strip resort is relatively toned down in comparison to its neighbor Bellagio. Its quiet opulence, replete with marble floors underfoot and chandeliers above, is its chief asset and a significant contrast to the party-hearty set. But the Monte Carlo couldn't claim a piece of Strip real estate without its considerable amenities: four pools, including a lazy river and a wave pool; a spa; and seven eateries. Standard rooms are bright and attractively furnished in cherry wood and Italian marble and granite. Crowd-pleasing magician Lance Burton is the house entertainer. 3,002 rooms, 32 story. $59-$299; under 12 free. Check-out 11 am, check-in 3 pm. TV; cable (premium), VCR available. In-room modem link. Restaurant. Exercise room. Pool, poolside service. Tennis. Business center. Concierge. Cr cds: A, D, DS, ER, JCB, MC, V.

⊡ ⚹ ⩯ ⚶ ⊠

★ ★ ★ **NEW YORK–NEW YORK HOTEL & CASINO.** *3790 Las Vegas Blvd S (89109). Phone 702/740-6969; toll-free 800/693-6763; fax 702/740-6920. www.nynyhotelcasino.com.* A hotel with a Manhattan skyline façade, New York—New York does a cheerful imitation of the Big Apple. Its main-floor casino models Central Park with trees, bridges, and brooks. Coney Island, New York—New York's upper-level midway, beckons with carnival games and the thrilling Manhattan Express roller-coaster. In perhaps a New York tradition the hotel didn't intend, standard rooms can feel cramped. Not that guests spend much time there, preferring the pool, a fairly straightforward affair relative to its Strip competitors. Among the many eateries, Il Fornaio does fine Italian amid the leafy casino. Wisecracking comedian Rita Rudner in the theater is a must-see. 2,033 rooms, 45 story. D $60-$200; under 12 free. Check-out noon. TV; cable (premium). In-room modem link. Restaurant, bar. Pool, whirlpool, poolside service. Free garage parking. Business center. Concierge. Cr cds: A, C, D, DS, ER, JCB, MC, V.

⊡ ⩯ ⊠ ⚶

★ ★ ★ **PARIS LAS VEGAS.** *3645 Las Vegas Blvd (89109). Phone 702/946-7000; toll-free 877/796-2096; fax 702/946-4405. www.parislasvegas.com.* A half-scale model of the Eiffel Tower landmarks Paris Las Vegas, an ode to French savoir faire, complete with a copy of the Arc de Triomphe and costumed landscape painters fronting the Strip-side pavilion. Its charms continue inside, where three legs of the Eiffel rest in the casino and a cobblestone street wends its way through the shopping arcade. Rooms underscore the theme with French fabrics and custom furniture. Request a Strip view to see the dancing Bellagio fountains across the street. Most of the restaurants here are French, including the charming Mon Ami Gabi, which features outdoor dining on a Las Vegas Boulevard terrace that offers prime people-watching. 2,916 rooms, 30 story. Pet accepted. Check-out 11 am, check-in 3 pm. TV. In-room modem link. Restaurant, bar; entertainment. In-house fitness room, massage, sauna. Outdoor pool, children's pool. Business center. Casino. Cr cds: A, C, D, DS, ER, JCB, MC, V. **$**

⊡ ⬚ ⩯ ⚹ ⊠ ⚶

★ ★ **PLAZA HOTEL.** *1 Main St (89125). Phone 702/386-2110; toll-free 800/634-6575; fax 702/386-2378. www.plazahotelcasino.com.* 1,037 rooms, 25 story. S, D $35-$125; suites $70-$250; under 12 free. Crib $8. TV; VCR available. Heated pool; wading pool. Restaurant open 24 hours. Bar. Check-out noon. Coin laundry. Convention facilities. Business services available. Shopping arcade. Barber. Tennis. Casino. Cr cds: A, C, D, DS, ER, JCB, MC, V.

⊡ ⚺ ⩯ ⚹ ⚶

★★ **RIVIERA HOTEL AND CASINO.** *2901 Las Vegas Blvd S (89109). Phone 702/734-5110; toll-free 800/634-5110; fax 702/794-9451. www.theriviera.com.* 2,072 rooms, 170 suites, 24 story. Check-out 11 am, check-in 3 pm. TV; cable (premium). In-room modem link. Restaurant, bar; entertainment. In-house fitness room, sauna, steam room. Outdoor pool; children's pool. Outdoor tennis, lighted courts. Business center. Casino. Cr cds: A, C, D, DS, ER, JCB, MC, V. **$**

D 🏊 ➷ 🖈 ➷

★★ **SAHARA HOTEL & CASINO.** *2535 Las Vegas Blvd S (89109). Phone 702/737-2111; toll-free 888/737-2111; fax 702/791-2027. www.saharavegas.com.* 1,720 rooms, 60 suites, 2-27 story. Check-out noon, check-in 3 pm. TV; cable (premium). In-room modem link. Restaurant, bar; entertainment. Outdoor pool; children's pool. Free parking. Business center. Casino. Cr cds: A, C, D, DS, ER, JCB, MC, V. **$**

D ➷ ➷ SC

★★ **SAM'S TOWN HOTEL & GAMBLING HALL.** *5111 Boulder Hwy (89122). Phone 702/456-7777; toll-free 800/897-8696; fax 702/454-8107. www.samstownlv.com.* Old West meets Las Vegas. Sound impossible? Just visit this western-style casino hotel which features a 25,000-square-foot atrium with a nightly laser show and a 56-lane bowling center. Visitors can buy their 10-gallon hats at the Western Emporium, attached to the casino, and join in the nightly Sunset Stampede. 648 rooms, 9 story. S, D $39.99-$140; suites $125-$225; under 12 free. Crib free. TV; cable. Heated pool; whirlpool, lifeguard. 10 restaurants (some open 24 hours). Check-out noon. Coin laundry. Convention facilities. Business services available. In-room modem link. Shopping arcade. Casino, bowling center. Old West décor; atrium. Cr cds: A, C, D, DS, ER, JCB, MC, V.

D ➷ ➷ 🖈

★★ **SAN REMO HOTEL CASINO AND RESORT.** *115 E Tropicana Ave (89109). Phone 702/739-9000; toll-free 800/522-7366; fax 702/736-1120. www.sanremolasvegas.com.* 711 rooms, 19 story. Check-out 11 am, check-in 4 pm. TV. In-room modem link. Restaurant, bar; entertainment. Outdoor pool; children's pool. Free parking. Casino. Cr cds: A, C, D, DS, ER, JCB, MC, V. **$**

D ➷ ➷

★★ **SANTA FE STATION HOTEL.** *4949 N Rancho Dr (89130). Phone 702/658-4900; toll-free 800/872-6823; fax 702/658-4919. www.stationcasino.com.* 200 rooms, 5 story. S, D $39.99-$79.99; each additional $5; under 13 free; higher rates some holidays. TV; cable. Heated pool; whirlpool. Supervised children's activities. Restaurant. Bar; entertainment. Check-out noon, check-in 3 pm. Meeting room. Business services available. Gift shop.

Game room. Bowling lanes. Ice rink. Cr cds: A, D, DS, ER, JCB, MC, V.

D 🍴 ➷ 🖈 ➷

★★ **SILVERTON HOTEL CASINO.** *3333 Blue Diamond Rd (89139). Phone 702/263-7777; toll-free 800/588-7711; fax 702/896-5635. www.silvertoncasino.com.* 300 rooms, 4 story. S, D $29-$45; suites $59-$89; under 12 free; higher rates during holidays. Crib free. TV; cable (premium). 2 pools; wading pool, whirlpool, poolside service, lifeguard. Restaurant open 24 hours. Room service. Check-out noon. Coin laundry. Meeting rooms. Business services available. In-room modem link. Shopping arcade. Game room. RV park. Cr cds: A, C, D, DS, ER, JCB, MC, V.

D ➷ 🍴 🖈 ➷ 🖈

★★ **STARDUST RESORT AND CASINO.** *3000 Las Vegas Blvd S (89109). Phone 702/732-6111; toll-free 800/634-6757; fax 702/732-6296. www.stardustlv.com.* 1,552 rooms, 161 suites, 32 story. Check-out noon, check-in 3 pm. TV. In-room modem link. Restaurant, bar; entertainment. In-house fitness room, health club privileges. Game room. Outdoor pool. Casino. Cr cds: A, C, D, DS, ER, JCB, MC, V. **$**

D ➷ 🍴 ➷

★★ **STRATOSPHERE HOTEL AND CASINO.** *2000 Las Vegas Blvd S (89104). Phone 702/380-7777; toll-free 800/634-6757; fax 702/380-7732. www.stratlv.com.* 2,444 rooms, 125 suites, 24 story. Check-out 11 am, check-in 3 pm. TV; cable (premium). Restaurant, bar. In-house fitness room, spa. Outdoor pool. Casino. Cr cds: A, C, D, DS, ER, JCB, MC, V. **$**

D ➷ ➷

★★★ **TREASURE ISLAND AT THE MIRAGE.** *3300 Las Vegas Blvd S (89109). Phone 702/894-7111; toll-free 800/288-7206; fax 702/894-7446. www.treasureisland.com.* Another MGM Mirage casino hotel, Treasure Island's South Seas pirate theme makes it appealing to travelers with children. Nightly, the sinking of a British frigate in Buccaneer Bay outside the hotel draws gawkers to Treasure Island, as does Cirque du Soleil's show "Mystére," staged here. For guests, there's a tropical pool deck with tiki accents and outdoor dining. Done in beige and gold hues, the guest rooms provide a tranquil respite from the hyper-theming. 2,679 rooms, 36 story. D $59-$400. Check-out noon. TV; cable; VCR available. In-room modem link. Restaurant, bar; entertainment. Exercise equipment. Pool, children's pool, poolside service. Business center. Casino. Cr cds: A, C, D, DS, ER, JCB, MC, V.

D ➷ 🍴 ➷ 🖈

★★ **TROPICANA HOTEL & CASINO.** *3801 Las Vegas Blvd S (89193). Phone 702/739-2222; toll-free 888/826-8767; fax 702/739-2492. www.tropicanalv.com.* Over

1,800 spacious guestrooms including two towers of suites overlook 5 acres of gardens and pools at this popular gaming city resort. Guests can enjoy the Folies Bergere, said to be Las Vegas's "longest running show." Don't miss a trip to The Comedy Spot for a couple of good laughs. 1,878 rooms, 22 story. Check-out 11 am, check-in 3 pm. TV; cable (premium). In-room modem link. Restaurant, bar; entertainment. Sauna. Outdoor pool. Business center. Casino. Cr cds: A, C, D, DS, ER, JCB, MC, V. **$**

★ ★ ★ ★ **THE VENETIAN RESORT HOTEL CASINO.** *3355 Las Vegas Blvd S (89109). Phone 702/414-1000; toll-free 877/283-6423; fax 702/414-4805. www.venetian.com.* strip. Guests amble down the winding alleys and glide past ornate architecture in gondolas in this perfect reproduction of the golden island that has inspired countless artists for centuries. Inside, the Venetian is glamorous and refined. This all-suite property ensures the comfort of its guests in its spacious and luxurious accommodations. After winning a hand in the casino, head for the upscale boutiques displaying world-famous brands alongside signature Murano glass and Carnival masks. Some of the biggest names in American cuisine operate award-winning restaurants here (see also LUTECE), while the Venetian's Guggenheim and Madame Tussaud's Wax Museums always delight. Guests soak away their sins at the Canyon Ranch Spa Club, the only outpost of the famous destination spa. 3,036 rooms, 35 story. Check-out noon, check-in 3 pm. TV; cable (premium). In-room modem link. Restaurant, bar; entertainment. In-house fitness room, sauna, spa. Outdoor pool, children's pool. Valet parking. Business center. Casino. Cr cds: A, C, D, DS, JCB, MC, V. **$$**

★ ★ **WESTWARD HO HOTEL & CASINO.** *2900 Las Vegas Blvd S (89109). Phone 702/731-2900; fax 702/731-3544. www.westwardho.com.* 776 rooms, 2-3 story. Check-out 11 am, check-in 3 pm. TV. Restaurant, bar; entertainment. Room service. Outdoor pool; children's pool. Casino. Free transportation. Cr cds: A, D, DS, ER, JCB, MC, V. **$**

Resort

★ ★ ★ **HYATT REGENCY LAKE LAS VEGAS RESORT.** *101 Montelago Blvd (89011). Phone 702/567-1234; toll-free 800/55HYATT; fax 702/567-6112. www.hyatt.com.* The Hyatt Regency Lake Las Vegas Resort takes guests on a magic carpet ride to seductive and mystical Morocco. Located in the heart of the Nevada desert on the white-sand shores of Lake Las Vegas, this 2,600-acre resort captures Morocco's exotic and sensuous essence. While the Hyatt Regency is a destination of its own, this romantic resort is also a perfect base for rolling the dice in

Sin City or exploring the nearby Hoover Dam, Lake Mead, and Red Rock Canyon. Guests can even helicopter to the Grand Canyon, only an hour away. North African touches, including hand-painted armoires and headboards, give the accommodations a unique flavor. The restaurants and lounges span the world for their influences, while the plentiful diversions at the Hyatt include two championship golf courses, a fabulous fitness center and spa, and an exciting casino. 496 rooms, 6 story. D $119-$319; each additional $25. Check-out noon. TV; cable (premium). In-room modem link. Restaurant open 24 hours. Bar; entertainment. Exercise room, spa, massage, sauna. Pool; whirlpool, poolside service. Golf, greens fee $210. Business center. Casino. Cr cds: A, C, D, DS, JCB, MC, V.

All Suites

★ ★ ★ **ALEXIS PARK ALL SUITE RESORT.** *375 E Harmon Ave (89109). Phone 702/796-3300; toll-free 800/582-2228; fax 702/796-3354. www.alexispark.com.* Clean, quiet, all-suite Alexis Park lacks a casino, an omission that bolsters its tranquil appeal. Two-story residence-style suites include a dining area and gas fireplace with one bedroom per floor, making this resort a good choice for families and longer stays. An on-site convention center encourages business affairs, while the freeform swimming pool, shallow children's pool, and full-service spa provide resort amenities. To get in on the gaming action, the Strip casinos and attractions are just several blocks away. 500 suites, 2 story. Check-out 11 am, check-in 3 pm. TV; cable (premium), VCR available. In-room modem link. Restaurant, bar; entertainment. Sauna, steam room. Outdoor pool; children's pool. Business center. Concierge. Cr cds: A, D, DS, MC, V. **$$**

★ ★ ★ **CROWNE PLAZA HOTEL.** *4255 S Paradise Rd (89109). Phone 702/369-4400; toll-free 800/227-6963; fax 702/369-3770. www.crowneplaza.com.* Conveniently located near the Las Vegas strip and the convention center, this non-gaming hotel offers a bit of piece and quiet for its guests. The lobby boasts an impressive glass atrium and working waterfall and guests can escape the heat of the desert sun with a swim in the outdoor pool. 201 suites, 6 story. Pet accepted; fee. Check-out noon, check-in 3 pm. TV; cable (premium), VCR available. In-room modem link. Restaurant, bar. Sauna. Outdoor pool; children's pool. Business center. Concierge. Free transportation. Cr cds: A, C, D, DS, ER, JCB, MC, V. **$**

★ ★ ★ **MARRIOTT SUITES.** *325 Convention Center Dr (89109). Phone 702/650-2000; toll-free 888/236-2427; fax 702/650-9466. www.marriott.com.* 278 rooms, 17 story. S, D $129-$269; each additional $25. Crib free. Check-out noon, check-in 3 pm. TV. In-room modem link. Restaurant 6 am-11 pm. Bar; entertainment. Exercise room, sauna. Game room. Heated pool, whirlpool. Airport transportation. Meeting rooms. Business center. Cr cds: A, C, D, DS, MC, V.

★ ★ ★ **RIO ALL-SUITE HOTEL AND CASINO.** *3700 W Flamingo Rd (89103). Phone 702/777-7777; toll-free 888/684-3746; fax 702/777-2360. www.playrio.com.* The all-suites Rio furnishes spacious, comfortable rooms with sitting areas supplementing its bed-and-bath arrangement. Off the Strip, its rooms offer expansive views of the Strip and the mountains beyond through floor-to-ceiling windows. Rio's Brazilian theme accounts for the carnival that parades above the casino floor seven times a day and the sand entries into Rio's four pools. Among attractions that draw guests as well as visitors, modern magicians Penn & Teller star in the showroom, and Rosemary's restaurant is acclaimed by local gourmets. 2,500 suites, 41 story. Check-out noon, check-in 4 pm. TV; cable (premium). Restaurant, bar; entertainment. Massage. Outdoor pool; children's pool. Concierge. Casino. Cr cds: A, C, D, DS, ER, JCB, MC, V. **$**

★ ★ ★ **ST. TROPEZ ALL SUITE HOTEL.** *455 E Harmon Ave (89109). Phone 702/369-5400; toll-free 800/666-5400; fax 702/369-1150. www.sttropezlasvegas.com.* Ideal for Las Vegas visitors who like the climate and excitement of the city but not the endless clanging of slot machines, the St. Tropez is a low-key respite off the Strip by a mile. Arrayed around the landscaped pool, standard suites combine both living and sleeping quarters in one spacious room. Complimentary breakfast is included in the room rate. For midnight duffers, the resort operates a 24-hour driving range. The closest casino to this nongaming hotel is the Hard Rock Hotel across the street. 149 suites, 2 story. Check-out noon, check-in 3 pm. TV; VCR available. In-room modem link. Outdoor pool; children's pool. Airport transportation. Concierge. Cr cds: A, C, D, DS, ER, JCB, MC, V. **$**

Extended Stay

★ ★ **RESIDENCE INN BY MARRIOTT.** *370 Hughes Center Dr (89109). Phone 702/650-0040; fax 702/650-5510. www.residenceinn.com.* Guests will enjoy the spacious guest rooms and the convenient location near the Las Vegas Strip. 256 kitchen suites, 11 story. Kitchen suites $139-$209. Crib available, pet accepted, some restrictions. Complimentary continental breakfast. Complimentary coffee in rooms. Check-out noon, check-in 4 pm. TV; cable (premium). In-room modem link. Refrigerators, microwaves. Valet services, coin laundry. Restaurant nearby. Exercise room. Outdoor pool, whirlpool. Meeting rooms. Business services. Cr cds: A, C, D, DS, ER, JCB, MC, V.

Restaurants

★ ★ **ANTONIO'S.** *3700 W Flamingo Rd (89103). Phone 702/252-7737.* If you are looking for romantic ambiance, the Rio (see also RIO ALL-SUITE HOTEL AND CASINO) might have your answer. Featuring one of the finest dining rooms in Vegas, Antonio's kitchen turns out fabulous specialties. Let the super-friendly waitstaff take care of you as you admire the marble and glass dome-ceiling surroundings. Italian menu. Hours: 5-11 pm. Bar. Live music. Casual attire. Reservations required. Valet parking. Cr cds: A, D, MC, V. **$$$**

★ ★ ★ ★ **AQUA.** *3600 Las Vegas Blvd S (89109). Phone 702/693-7223; fax 702/693-6512. www.bellagiolasvegas.com.* After strolling through the Bellagio Hotel's Conservatory & Botanical Gardens (See also BELLAGIO LAS VEGAS) on the way to dinner, guests find a luxurious, contemporary dining room bathed in blond wood, creamy neutral tones, and golden light. The menu here is in the care of a talented group of chef-creators trained and transported from the original Aqua in San Francisco. The kitchen is passionate about the sea; delicious dishes tend to concentrate on the creatures of the deep blue ocean jazzed up with California ingredients. The menu is extensive and offers à la carte selections in addition to a pair of five-course tasting menus, one vegetarian and one seasonal. The wine list focuses on American producers and contains some gems from small vineyards as well; you'll find lots of fish-friendly options. Contemporary American menu. Hours: 5:30-11 pm. Dinner $28-$90. Jacket required. Reservations required. Valet parking. Cr cds: A, C, D, MC, V.

★ ★ ★ ★ **AUREOLE.** *3950 Las Vegas Blvd (89119). Phone 702/632-7401; fax 702/632-7425. www.aureolerestaurant.com.* A branch of chef Charlie Palmer's New York original, Aureole wows patrons with its centerpiece four-story wine tower. Be sure to order a bottle just to see the catsuit-clad climber, suspended by ropes, locate your vintage. Its 12,000 bottles complement Palmer's seasonal contemporary American cuisine typified by dishes like Peking duck with foie gras ravioli and roast pheasant with sweet potato gnocchi. The modern but romantic room with encircling booths sets the stage for event dining at Mandalay Bay. Progressive American cuisine. Hours: 6-11 pm. Dinner $60-$95. Bar. Jacket required. Cr cds: A, C, D, DS, ER, JCB, MC, V.

★ **CAFE NICOLLE.** *4760 W Sahara Ave (89102). Phone 702/870-7675; fax 702/870-9502. www.cafenicolle.com.* American menu. Hours: 11 am-11 pm. Dinner $16-$25.

Bar. Entertainment. Live music. Casual attire. Outdoor dining. Cr cds: A, D, MC, V.

D

★ ★ **CAMELOT.** *3850 Las Vegas Blvd S (89109). Phone 702/597-7449. www.excalibur.com.* Located in the Excalibur Hotel and Casino. Camelot serves gourmet dishes in a romantic setting. A cigar room, wine cellar, a fireplace and an open kitchen are some of the classic elements found here. Open for dinner only Wednesday thru Sunday. Continental menu. Hours: 5-10 pm. Dinner $30-$60. Bar. Casual attire. Reservations accepted. Valet parking. Large fireplace. Cr cds: A, D, MC, V.

D

★ **CATHAY HOUSE.** *5300 W Spring Mountain Rd (89102). Phone 702/876-3838; fax 702/876-8208. www.cathayhouse.com.* Hours: 11 am-11 pm. Chinese menu. Bar. Lunch $8.25-$15.95, dinner $8.25-$26. Specialties: strawberry chicken, orange flavored beef. Chinese décor. Cr cds: A, DS, MC, V.

D

★ **CHAPALA.** *2101 S Decatur Blvd (89102). Phone 702/871-7805; fax 702/878-3181.* Dinner $5.25-$10.25. Bar. Children's menu. Reservations accepted. Closed some major holidays. Cr cds: A, D, MC, V.

D

★ ★ ★ **CHINOIS.** *3500 Las Vegas Blvd S (89109). Phone 702/737-9700; fax 702/737-9710. www.wolfgangpuck.com.* A spinoff of chef Wolfgang Puck's acclaimed Chinois on Main in Santa Monica, California, Las Vegas's Chinois features similar Asian fusion fare in the Forum Shops at Caesars Palace. The spare, artifact-decorated shop-level café, specializing in pan-Asian fare often lightened California style to please western palettes, is a well-located lunch spot. The broad-ranging menu includes sushi and sashimi, dim sum, wok-fried meat and vegetable recipes such as kung pao chicken, and Asian noodle dishes like pad Thai. Asian menu. Hours: 11:30 am-10 pm; Fri-Sun to midnight. Dinner $14.95-$30. Bar. Children's menu. Reservations required. Valet parking. Cr cds: A, D, DS, MC, V.

D

★ ★ ★ **CIRCO.** *3600 Las Vegas Blvd (89109). Phone 702/693-8150; fax 702/693-8106. www.bellagiolasvegas. com.* Though billed as the casual cousin to its neighbor and sibling Le Cirque, Circo is hardly less sophisticated. Its harlequin patterns and jewel tones reference the circus, and the windows frame ringside views of the Bellagio's dancing fountains (see also BELLAGIO). But the food is quite serious, focusing on Italian cuisine rather than Le

Cirque's French fare. Pastas are house-made, pizzas and often fish are wood-fired, and everything comes artfully arranged on the plate. Reservations are essential on most nights, particularly for diners seeking a table before the Cirque du Soleil *O* show across the casino at Bellagio. Northern Italian cuisine. Hours: 11:30 am-2:30 pm; 5:30-10:30 pm. Dinner $20-$85. Jacket required. Reservations required 60 days in advance. Cr cds: A, C, D, DS, MC, V.

D

★ ★ **COYOTE CAFE.** *3799 Las Vegas Blvd S (89109). Phone 702/891-7777; fax 702/891-7333. www.coyotecafe.com.* Hours: 7:30 am-11 pm. Reservations accepted. Southwestern menu. Bar. Breakfast $3-$8, lunch $8-$18, dinner $24-$42. Specialties: chicken tacos, black beans. Valet parking. Southwestern décor; artwork, cacti. Cr cds: A, D, DS, ER, JCB, MC, V.

D

★ ★ **DRAI'S OF LAS VEGAS.** *3595 Las Vegas Blvd S (89109). Phone 702/737-0555; fax 702/737-5557. www.draislasvegas.com.* Named after former movie producer Victor Drai, this restaurant brings the glamour of Hollywood to Las Vegas. Complete with leopard skin overstuffed chairs, this restaurant offers Provencal cuisine without the heavy ingredients. American menu. Hours: 5:30-11 pm; Sat, Sun to midnight. Dinner $14-$35. Bar. Reservations accepted. Valet parking. Cr cds: A, D, DS, ER, JCB, MC, V.

D

★ ★ ★ **EMERIL'S NEW ORLEANS.** *3799 Las Vegas Blvd (89109). Phone 702/891-7374; fax 702/891-7338. www.emerils.com.* Big Easy big-timer Emeril Lagasse runs this Louisiana kitchen at the MGM Grand. Wrought-iron gates, a stone courtyard, and French doors aim to evoke historic New Orleans. But the star, of course, is the bold food for which the gregarious chef of Food Network fame is renowned. Creole-spiced lobster, pecan-roasted redfish, and cedar plank steak typify Emeril's big flavors, while a raw bar and po' boys wave the regional flag. Finish off with the rave-worthy banana cream pie. Cajun/Creole menu. Hours: 11 am-2:30 pm, 5:30-10:30 pm. Dinner $19-$36. Bar. Cr cds: A, C, D, DS, ER, MC, V.

D

★ ★ ★ **EMPRESS COURT.** *3570 Las Vegas Blvd S (89109). Phone 702/731-7731. www.parkplace.com.* Native Hong Kong chefs distinguish themselves at Empress Court, frequently cited in local dining polls for authentic Chinese cuisine. Overlooking the Roman pool deck at Caesars Palace (see also CAESARS PALACE), Empress Court prepares a range of dishes from the Asian larder, including recipes from Malaysia, Thailand, and Indonesia, as well as China. Fresh and saltwater tanks stock cod, crab, and lobster. To splurge, opt for the multicourse, fixed-price meals made for two. Quality china, rare fare such as abalone, and the attention of knowledgeable servers justify the upmarket prices. Cantonese menu. Hours: 6-11 pm. Closed Mon, Tues. Dinner $30-$80. Bar. Jacket required. Valet parking available. Cr cds: A, C, D, DS, ER, MC, V.

D

★ ★ **FASOLINI'S PIZZA CAFE.** 222 S Decatur Blvd (89107). Phone 702/877-0071; fax 702/877-7144. Italian menu. Hours: noon-9 pm, closed Sun; Jan 1, Easter, Dec 25. Dinner $5.95-$16.95. Children's menu. Cr cds: A, D, MC, V.

D

★ ★ ★ **FERRARO'S.** 5900 W Flamingo Rd (89103). Phone 702/364-5300; fax 702/871-2721. www.ferraroslasvegas.com. Italian menu. Hours: 5:30-11 pm. Dinner $8.50-$38. Bar. Children's menu. Casual attire. Reservations accepted. Cr cds: A, D, MC, V.

D

★ **GARDUNOS.** 2400 N Rancho Dr (89130). Phone 702/631-7000; fax 702/631-7070. www.gardunosrestaurants.com. Mexican menu. Hours: 11 am-10 pm; Fri, Sat to 11 pm. Dinner $15-$35. Bar. Casual attire. Valet parking. Cr cds: A, D, DS, ER, MC, V.

D

★ **GOLDEN STEER STEAK HOUSE.** 308 W Sahara Ave (89109). Phone 702/384-4470. Steak menu. Hours: 5-11pm. Dinner $15-$45. Bar. Children's menu. Casual attire. Reservations accepted. Valet parking. Cr cds: A, D, MC, V.

D

★ ★ **HAMADA OF JAPAN.** 365 E Flamingo Rd (89119). Phone 702/733-3005; fax 702/733-7708. www.hamadaofjapan.com. Japanese menu. Hours: 11 am-4 pm; 5 pm-4 am. Lunch $7.95-$11.95, dinner $13.50-$47.50. Bar. Casual attire. Reservations accepted. Valet parking. Cr cds: A, D, MC, V.

D

★ ★ **IL FORNAIO.** 3790 Las Vegas Blvd S #13 (89109). Phone 702/650-6500; fax 702/740-2449. www.ilfornaio.com. Italian menu. Hours: 8:30 am-midnight. Dinner $11.50-$28.50. Bar. Casual attire. Valet parking. Cr cds: A, C, D, DS, JCB, MC, V.

D

★ ★ ★ **LE CIRQUE.** 3600 Las Vegas Blvd S (89109). Phone 702/693-8100; fax 702/693-8106. www.lecirque.com. The hallowed temple of cuisine for New York's financial elite has made it to Las Vegas. Restaurateur and charmer Sirio Maccioni, the face and creative force behind the Gotham power scene, brought a branch to the Bellagio (see also BELLAGIO LAS VEGAS). Like its New York City sibling, this Le Cirque is a shining jewel of a restaurant, awash in bold colors and warm fabrics, with a bright, silk-tented ceiling that brings a festive big-top feel to the intimate dining room. The three-course prix fixe menu features rustic French fare that includes something for everyone: snails, fish, lamb, beef, and game, as well as salads and pasta. In signature Maccioni style, each dish is prepared with precision and delivered with care. Caviar service is available for those seeking extreme luxury, and the wine list boasts several stellar choices. French menu. Hours: 5:30-10:30 pm. Dinner $28-$39; tasting menu $75-$120. Jacket required. Reservations required. Valet parking. Cr cds: A, C, D, MC, V.

D

★ ★ **LILY LANGTRY'S.** 129 E Fremont St (89101). Phone 702/385-7111. www.goldennugget.com. Presenting Cantonese and Szechwan favorites and mesquite-grilled steaks in a soft and surreal atmosphere. Specialties include Mongolian beef and stir-fried lobster. Open for dinner; reservations are suggested. In the Golden Nugget. Chinese, steak menu. Hours: 5-11 pm. Dinner $45-$100. Bar. Casual attire. Reservations required. Valet parking. Cr cds: A, D, DS, ER, JCB, MC, V.

D

★ ★ ★ **LUTECE.** 3355 Las Vegas Blvd S (89109). Phone 702/414-2220; fax 702/414-2221. www.lutece.com. A replica of the New York restaurant bearing the same name, Lutece is located in the luxurious Venetian (see also VENETIAN RESORT HOTEL & CASINO). The restaurant's Las Vegas outpost creates a new environment for a wonderful New York classic. In this bright new setting, the kitchen turns out an exciting selection of updated classic French recipes. You'll find high-end seasonal ingredients and a gentle flirtation with global flavors that brighten both the plate and the palate. This is a restaurant that will satisfy foodies and more conservative eaters alike. Divided into Appetizers, Caviar, Soup, Fish & Shellfish, and Meat & Poultry, the menu is like a classic navy blue pinstripe suit paired with a fun, bright tie: classic, with a sexy edge. Diners can choose from à la carte selections or a five-course tasting menu. The dessert list is impressive as well and includes three varieties of soufflé and a cheese course, among other lip-licking alternatives. Hours: 5:30-11 pm. Dinner $41-$55. Bar. Valet parking. Cr cds: A, DS, MC, V.

D

★ **MARRAKECH.** *3900 Paradise Rd (89109). Phone 702/737-5611; fax 702/737-4603. www.marrakech-lv.com.* Middle Eastern menu. Hours: 5:30-11 pm. Closed Dec 25. Dinner $26.95. Bar. Casual attire. Cr cds: A, D, MC, V.

D

★ ★ **MAYFLOWER CUISINIER.** *4750 W Sahara Ave (89102). Phone 702/870-8432; fax 702/259-8493. www.mayflowercuisinier.com.* Chinese menu. Hours: 11 am-3 pm, 5-10 pm; Sat to 11 pm. Closed Sun; major holidays. Dinner $8-$22. Bar. Reservations accepted. Outdoor dining, totally nonsmoking. Cr cds: A, D, MC, V.

D

★ ★ ★ **NOBU.** *4455 Paradise Rd (89109). Phone 702/693-5090. www.hardrockhotel.com.* The Zenlike décor of Nobu at the Hard Rock Hotel (see also HARD ROCK HOTEL AND CASINO)—bamboo-lined walls, seaweed-toned banquettes—brings a serene sense of peace to the otherwise frenetic pace of dining out in Las Vegas. This is a beautiful place to settle in for an evening. As at its sister restaurant in New York City's Tribeca, the quality of the sushi here is fantastic. Whether eaten as sashimi or sushi or tucked into fat, flavor-packed *maki* (rolls), the silky fish virtually melts in your mouth. Folks who shiver at the word *sushi* need not miss out on celebrity chef Nobu Matsuhisa's magnificent culinary talent (although you should at least try Nobu's sushi before swearing off of it based on fear alone). In addition to raw fish, the menu includes soup, *kushiyaki* (skewers of fish, chicken, vegetables, or beef), ceviches, salads, noodle bowls, teriyaki plates, and tempura, as well as a selection of hot entrées. An omakase (chef's choice) menu is also available for truly inspired (and adventurous) dining. Hours: 6-10 pm. Dinner $18-$30. Bar. Cr cds: A, MC, V.

D

★ ★ ★ **PALM.** *3500 Las Vegas Blvd S, Suite A (89109). Phone 702/732-7256; fax 702/732-0229. www.thepalm.com.* Another destination eatery in the Forum Shops at Caesars Palace, the Palm steakhouse is a branch of the New York power eatery. The woody surroundings lend a clubby feel to the dining room that specializes in healthy portions of meat supplemented by à la carte veggies and potatoes. Lunches of salads, pastas, and the house burger make this a more affordable midday option. Local notables like mayor Oscar Goodman and tennis pro Andre Agassi have been spotted dining here, as have many others; celebrity cartoon caricatures festoon the Palm's walls. Steak menu. Hours: 11:30 am-11 pm. Dinner $16-$64. Bar. Valet parking. Cr cds: A, C, D, DS, ER, JCB, MC, V.

D

★ ★ ★ **PEGASUS.** *375 E Harmon Ave (89109). Phone 702/796-3353; fax 702/796-4334.* Located half a mile off the Strip at the Alexis Park Resort, Pegasus brings formal dining to the lush Mediterranean hotel grounds. The service is notably attentive and the atmosphere, romantic, with cozy booths, hand-blown glass chandeliers, piano music, and views of the landscape. The restaurant's continental menu merges French and Italian cooking in fish, chicken, and meat dishes. Jackets are required, and reservations are strongly suggested, making Pegasus a special-occasion candidate. Continental menu. Hours: 6 am-10 pm. Dinner $12.95-$18.95. Bar. Jacket required. Valet parking available. Cr cds: A, D, MC, V.

D SC

★ ★ ★ ★ **PICASSO.** *3600 Las Vegas Blvd S (89109). Phone 702/693-7223. www.bellagiolasvegas.com.* The Bellagio Hotel (See also BELLAGIO LAS VEGAS) is home to some of the finest restaurants in Las Vegas. Le Cirque, Olives, Aqua, and Prime Steakhouse are all inside. But Picasso stands out among them. It offers exquisite food in a serene space, and it's one of those two-for-one experiences. If you're trying to decide between visiting a museum and having an elegant and inspired meal, you can do both at Picasso. The master painter's original works don the walls of this beautiful, cozy, country-style room with soaring wood-beamed ceilings, sage-toned upholstery, and a stunning view of the lake. The menu is also artwork. The kitchen uses French technique as a canvas for layering Spanish and Mediterranean flavor. (You can opt for a four-course tasting menu or a chef's degustation option as well.) To match the museum-worthy food, you'll be offered a rare and magnificent selection of international wines. If the weather is warm, you can also dine al fresco by the lake—nature's art. French cuisine with Spanish flair. Hours: 6-10 pm; Fri, Sat to 11 pm. Closed Wed. Dinner $69-$89. Jacket required. Reservations required. Valet parking. Cr cds: A, D, DS, MC, V.

D

★ ★ ★ **PRIME.** *3600 Las Vegas Blvd S (89109). Phone 702/693-7223; fax 702/693-7127. www.bellagiolasvegas.com.* Famed New York fusion chef Jean-Georges Vongerichten opened his first and only steakhouse with the stylish Prime. Located in the Bellagio with waterside views of the dancing fountains, Prime serves superior cuts of beef, veal, and lamb with a range of sauces, from standard béarnaise to very Vongerichten tamarind. Ample fish and chicken selections and creative appetizers entice lighter appetites. Elegant surrounds, including Baccarat crystal chandeliers and velvet draperies, distract from the expense-account prices. American menu. Hours: 5:30-10 pm. Dinner $24-$38. Reservations required 60 days in advance. Cr cds: A, D, MC, V.

D

★ ★ ★ **RENOIR.** *3400 Las Vegas Blvd S (89109). Phone 702/791-7223; fax 702/791-7437. www.mgm-mirage.com.* As you might expect from the restaurant's name, the works of French impressionist Pierre-Auguste Renoir are among the original works of art on display at Renoir, the Mirage Hotel's (See also THE MIRAGE HOTEL AND CASINO) opulent restaurant featuring contemporary French cuisine. Swathed in ornate silks and vintage tapestries, the room has an old-world elegance that is accented further by its dark-wood moldings and vintage brocade banquettes. Wear something neutral, or you are bound to clash with the room's elaborate design. The dining room is one of the most opulent and luxurious in Las Vegas, and it's worth taking in the plush surroundings with the fewest possible distractions. Fortunately, the food is as impressive as the décor. Inventive, modern French dishes focus on ingredients, revealing that the kitchen is of the "less is more" school of thought. Restraint pays off. Plates shine in their simplicity and make dinner at Renoir a winning experience. French cuisine. Dinner $29-$44; seasonal menu and vegetable tasting $95. Reservations required. Valet parking. Cr cds: A, C, D, DS, ER, MC, V.

D

★ ★ **SACRED SEA.** *3900 Las Vegas Blvd S (89119). Phone 702/262-4756; fax 702/262-4717. www.luxor.com.* Seafood, steak menu. Hours: 5-11 pm. Closed Wed, Thurs. Dinner $40-$80. Bar. Casual attire. Reservations accepted. Valet parking. Cr cds: A, D, DS, MC, V.

D

★ **SAM WOO BBQ.** *4215 Spring Mountain Rd (89102). Phone 702/368-7628; fax 702/368-7568.* Chinese menu. Hours: 10-5 am. Lunch $5-$10, dinner $10-$24.

★ **SHALIMAR.** *3900 S Paradise Rd (89109). Phone 702/796-0302; fax 702/796-6480.* Indian menu. Hours: 11:30 am-2:30 pm, 5:30-10 pm. Dinner $6.95-$15.95. Bar. Casual attire. Reservations accepted. Cr cds: A, D, MC, V.

D **SC**

★ ★ ★ **SMITH & WOLLENSKY.** *3767 Las Vegas Boulevard S (89109). Phone 702/862-4100; fax 702/933-3931. www.smithandwollensky.com.* This Las Vegas outpost of the growing Manhattan-based chain recreates the atmosphere of the original, right down to the chalk boards listing daily specials. Steak menu. Hours: 11:30-3 am. Dinner $30-$70. Bar. Casual attire. Reservations accepted. Valet parking. Cr cds: A, D, DS, ER, MC, V.

D

★ ★ ★ **SPAGO.** *3500 Las Vegas Blvd S (89109). Phone 702/399-6300; fax 702/369-0361. www.wolfgangpuck.com.* LA chef Wolfgang Puck was the first celebrity chef to open up shop in Las Vegas, and he did it here in Spago, a spinoff of his California original. Located in the Forum Shops at Caesars Palace, Spago specializes in Puck's signature California-Asian and California-Italian food, including Chinois chicken salad and salmon pizza, respectively. Creative salads make excellent lunch choices, while dinners are more elaborate. Owing to its location and fame, Spago is perpetually jammed. Try to phone ahead for a reservation. California-Asian, Italian menu. Hours: 11-12:30 am. Dinner $15-$30. Bar. Piano Sun. Cr cds: A, DS, MC, V.

D

★ **STAGE DELI.** *3500 Las Vegas Blvd S (89109). Phone 702/893-4045; fax 702/893-1241. www.arkrestaurants.com.* American, deli menu. Hours: 8:30 am-11 pm; Fri, Sat to 11:30 pm. Dinner $2.95-$13.75. Bar. Children's menu. Casual attire. Valet parking. Cr cds: A, D, DS, ER, MC, V.

D

★ ★ **THE STEAK HOUSE.** *2880 Las Vegas Blvd (89114). Phone 702/734-0410; fax 702/794-3874.* Steak menu. Hours: 5-10 pm. Dinner $25-$100, Sun brunch 10 am-2 pm; $19.95. Bar. Reservations accepted. Valet parking. Cr cds: A, D, DS, ER, JCB, MC, V.

D

★ ★ **TILLERMAN.** *2245 E Flamingo Rd (89109). Phone 702/731-4036; fax 702/731-1560. www.tillerman.com.* Serious seafood, fresh and simply prepared, has been served for years at this perennial favorite. American menu. Hours: 5-11 pm. Closed major holidays. Dinner $20-$49. Reservations accepted. Valet parking. Atrium, garden, loft dining areas. Cr cds: A, C, D, DS, ER, MC, V.

D

★ ★ ★ **TOP OF THE WORLD.** *2000 S Las Vegas Blvd (89104). Phone 702/380-7711. www.stratlv.com.* In a town of few casino windows and even fewer restaurant views, Top of the World atop the Stratosphere Hotel Tower stands out. The circular room revolves once every 90 minutes, offering 360-degree nighttime views of Vegas by neon. Few scenery-centric restaurants push the culinary envelope, and Top of the World is no exception, although it does a nice job with steaks and continental classics like lobster bisque. A mini Stratosphere in chocolate is a must for dessert, serving two. American menu. Hours: 11 am-11 pm; Fri Sat, Sun to midnight. Dinner $30-$100. Bar. Entertainment. Reservations required. Valet parking available. Cr cds: A, D, MC, V.

D

★ **VIVA MERCADOS.** *6182 W Flamingo Rd (89103). Phone 702/871-8826; fax 702/871-6915. www.vivamercados.com.* Mexican menu. Hours: 11 am-10 pm; Fri, Sat to 11 pm. Closed Sun; major holidays. Dinner $8.75-$18.95. Bar. Reservations accepted (dinner). Mexican décor. Cr cds: A, DS, MC, V.

D

★ **WOLFGANG PUCK CAFE.** *3799 Las Vegas Blvd S (89109). Phone 702/895-9653; fax 702/895-7571. www.mgmgrand.com.* Hours: 8 am-11 pm; Fri, Sat to 1 am. Bar. A la carte entrees: breakfast, lunch, dinner $5.95-$30.95. Specialties: wood-burning oven pizza, rotisserie chicken. Ultra modern décor. Cr cds: A, MC, V.

D

★ **XINH-XINH.** *220 W Sahara Ave (89102). Phone 702/471-1572.* Vietnamese menu. Hours: 11 am-11 pm. Dinner $3.50-$12.95. Bar. Casual attire. Cr cds: MC, V.

★**YOLIE'S BRAZILIAN STEAKHOUSE.** *3900 Paradise Rd (89109). Phone 702/794-0700; fax 704/794-0459. www.yoliesbraziliansteakhouse.com.* Steak menu. Hours: 11 am-11 pm; Sat from 5 pm. Dinner $15-$48. Bar. Reservations required. Outdoor dining. Cr cds: A, C, D, DS, ER, MC, V.

D

Laughlin (J-6)

See also Bullhead City, AZ; Kingman, AZ; Needles

Pop 7,076 **Elev** 520 ft **Area code** 702 **Zip** 89029

Information Chamber of Commerce, PO Box 77777; 800/227-5245

Web www.laughlinchamber.com

This resort community offers a pleasant change of pace from the dazzle of Las Vegas. In many ways, it resembles Las Vegas in its earlier days. Many hotels and casinos line the Colorado River; some provide ferry service to and from parking facilities on the Arizona side. But Laughlin offers other diversions as well; water sports such as fishing, waterskiing, and swimming in nearby Lake Mohave are popular.

Special Event

Laughlin Riverdays. *US 95 and Colorado River (89029). Phone 702/298-2214.* Rodeo, bull-riding, off-road racing, golf tournament. Mid-May.

Casino Hotels

★★**DON LAUGHLIN'S RIVERSIDE RESORT.** *1650 Casino Dr (89029). Phone 702/298-2535; fax 702/298-2695. www.riversideresort.com.* 1,404 rooms, 28 story. TV; cable. 2 pools. Restaurant open 24 hours. Bars; entertainment. Check-out 11 am, check-in 3 pm. Convention facilities. Business center. In-room modem link. Free airport transportation. Bathroom phones. Balconies. Movie theaters. Casino. Bus depot on premises. Boat dockage on Colorado River; RV spaces. Cr cds: A, C, D, DS, ER, JCB, MC, V. **$**

D 🐾 ⚓ 🏊 🏌

★ ★ ★ **FLAMINGO LAUGHLIN.** *1900 S Casino Dr (89029). Phone 702/298-5111; toll-free 800/FLAMINGO; fax 702/298-5116. www.laughlinflamingo.com.* The largest resort on the Colorado River, this enormous property offers activities for every member of the family. Visitors will enjoy the 350-seat showroom, 3,000-seat outdoor amphitheater, and 60,000-square-foot casino. 1,912 rooms, 18 story, 60 suites. Mar-Oct: S, D $29-$55; each additional $9; suites $170-$270; family rates; higher rates: weekends, holidays; lower rates rest of year. Crib free. TV; cable (premium). Heated pool. Restaurant open 24 hours. Room service 6 am-midnight. Bar; entertainment. Check-out 11 am. Meeting rooms. Business services available. Shopping arcade. Free garage parking. Free airport transportation. Lighted tennis. Game room. Wet bar in suites. Refrigerators available. Casino. On 18-acre site along Colorado River. Cr cds: A, C, D, DS, ER, JCB, MC, V.

D 🐾 🎾 🏌 🏊 🏌

★ ★ ★ **GOLDEN NUGGET.** *2300 S Casino Dr (89028). Phone 702/298-7222; toll-free 800/950-7700; fax 702/298-7122. www.gnlaughlin.com.* A jungle in the middle of the desert best describes this "tropical paradise" casino on the Colorado River. The rain forest-inspired lobby, tropical-themed guest rooms, and Tarzan's Night Club complete the illusion. 300 rooms, 4 story. S, D $29-$99; suites $150; under 12 free; higher rates weekends. Crib free. TV; cable. Pool; whirlpool, poolside service. Restaurants open 24 hours. Bar. Check-out noon, check-in 3 pm. Business services available. Shopping arcade. Free airport transportation. On Colorado River. Cr cds: A, DS, ER, JCB, MC, V.

D 🏊 🏌

★ **RIVER PALMS.** *2700 S Casino Dr (89029). Phone 702/298-2242; toll-free 800/835-7903; fax 702/298-2196. www.rvrpalm.com.* 1,003 rooms, 3-25 story. S, D $24-$65; suites $200-$250. Crib free. TV. Heated pool; whirlpool. Restaurant open 24 hours. Bar; entertainment. Check-out 11 am, check-in 2 pm. Convention facilities. Business services available. Shopping arcade. Free valet parking. Free airport transportation. Exercise equipment. Game room. Cr cds: A, D, DS, ER, JCB, MC, V.

D 🐾 🏊 🏌

Lovelock (D-2)

Settled early 1840s **Pop** 2,003 **Elev** 3,977 ft **Area code** 775 **Zip** 89419

Information Pershing County Chamber of Commerce, 25 W Marzen Lane, PO Box 821; 775/273-7213

The 49ers stopped in Lovelock Valley on their way west. There was plenty of feed for weary oxen and horses because beavers had dammed the Humboldt River, thus providing a steady water supply. The travelers mended their wagons and made other preparations for the 36-hour dash across the dreaded 40-mile desert to Hot Springs.

A deep layer of rich, black loam, left in the Lovelock Valley as the waters of an ancient lake receded, spreads over more than 40,000 acres. This soil, irrigated from the Rye Patch Reservoir, supports rich farms and productive ranches. Lovelock, the seat of Pershing County, was named for an early settler, George Lovelock, across whose ranch the original Central Pacific Railroad was built. Ore mines, mineral deposits, and a seed-processing plant in the area contribute to the growth of modern Lovelock.

What to See and Do

Courthouse Park. *1127 Central Ave (89419). Phone 775/273-7213.* The only round courthouse still in use. Shaded picnic grounds; swimming pool. (May-Aug, daily) **$**

Rye Patch State Recreation Area. *2505 Rye Patch Reservoir Rd (89419). 23 miles N on I-80. Phone 775/538-7321.* Approximately 27,500 acres on 200,000-acre reservoir; swimming, waterskiing, fishing, boating (launching ramps); picnicking, camping (dump station). Standard fees.

Special Event

Frontier Days. *1127 Central Ave. (Courthouse Park) (89419). Phone 775/273-7213.* Parade, races, rodeo. Late July or early Aug.

Lunar Crater

(Near US 6 between Tonopah and Ely)

This is a vast field of cinder cones and frozen lava. The crater is a steep-walled pit, 400 feet deep and three-quarters of a mile in diameter, created by volcanic action about 1,000 years ago. The earth exploded violently, heaving cinders, lava, and rocks the size of city blocks high into the air. Awed by the remains, pioneers named the pit Lunar Crater.

Overton (H-6)

See also Las Vegas

Pop 3,000 **Elev** 1,270 ft **Area code** 702 **Zip** 89040

An old Mormon settlement, Overton is located at the site of an ancient civilization that, 1,200 years ago, extended for 30 miles along the Muddy River. Some of this area is now covered by Lake Mead.

What to See and Do

Lost City Museum of Archaeology. *721 S. Moapa Valley Blvd. (89040). 1 miles S on NV 169. Phone 702/397-2193.* An agency of the state of Nevada, the museum is located on a restored portion of Pueblo Grande de Nevada. The museum has an extensive collection of ancient Native American artifacts, fossils, and semiprecious gems. There is also a picnic area. The curator and staff have travel tips and information on the area; gift shop. (Daily; closed Jan 1, Thanksgiving, Dec 25) **$**

Pyramid Lake (D-1)

See also Reno

(36 mi N of Reno on NV 445)

Surrounded by rainbow-tinted, eroded hills, this is a remnant of prehistoric Lake Lahontan, which once covered 8,400 square miles in western Nevada and northeastern California. The largest natural lake in the state, Pyramid is about 30 miles long and from 7 to 9 miles wide, with deep-blue sparkling waters. It is fed by scant water from the diverted Truckee River and by brief floods in other streams. Since the Newlands Irrigation Project deprives it of water, its level is receding.

General John C. Frémont gave the lake its name when he visited the area in 1844, apparently taking it from the tufa (porous rock) islands that jut up from the water. One, 475 feet high, is said by Native Americans to be a basket inverted over an erring woman. Though turned to stone, her "breath" (wisps of steam from a hot spring) can still be seen. Another island is called Stone Mother and Basket. At the north end there is a cluster of sharp spires known as the Needles. Anahoe Island, in the lake, is a sanctuary and breeding ground for more than 10,000 huge white pelicans.

An air of mystery surrounds the area, bred by the murmuring waves, the spires and domes with their wisps of steam, and the ever-changing tints of the folded, eroded hills. At nearby Astor Pass, railroad excavations uncovered a horse skull and fragmentary remains of an elephant, bison, and camel, all believed to have lived on the lakeshore in prehistoric times.

Pyramid Lake abounds with Lahonton cutthroat trout; it is one of the top trophy trout lakes in the United States. All rights belong to the Native Americans. For information about roads, fishing, and boat permits, contact the Sutcliffe Ranger Station or Pyramid Lake Fisheries, Star Rte, Sutcliffe 89510; 775/476-0500. Camping, boating, and fishing at Pyramid Lake are considered by many to be the best in the state. Day use $5-$10

Visitor centers, located in the hatcheries at Sutcliffe and between Nixon and Wadsworth, describe the land, lake, and people through photographs and displays (daily). **$$$**

Reno (E-1)

See also Carson City, Incline Village, Virginia City

Founded 1868 **Pop** 180,480 **Elev** 4,498 ft **Area code** 775

Information Chamber of Commerce, 1 E First St, 16th Floor, 89501 775/337-3030. For information on cultural events contact the Sierra Arts Foundation, 200 Flint St, 89501; 775/329-2787

Web www.reno-sparkschamber.org

Reno, "the biggest little city in the world," renowned as a gambling and vacation center, is an important distribution and merchandising area, the home of the University of Nevada-Reno, and a residential city. Between the steep slopes of the Sierra and the low eastern hills, Reno spills across the Truckee Meadows. The neon lights of the nightclubs, gambling casinos, and bars give it a glitter that belies its quiet acres of fine houses, churches, and schools. The surrounding area is popular for sailing, boating, horseback riding, and deer and duck hunting.

Reno was known as Lake's Crossing and was an overland travelers' camping place even before the gold rush. It grew with the exploitation of the Comstock Lode and became a city in May 1868, with a public auction of real estate by a railway agent. Within a month there were 100 houses. A railroad official named the town in honor of a Union officer of the Civil War, General Jesse Lee Reno. In 1871 it became the seat of Washoe County.

Many Nevadans resent Reno's reputation as a divorce capital. They point out that many more couples are married than divorced at the Washoe County Courthouse. A six-month divorce law had been on the books since 1861, before Nevada became a state. The six-week law became effective in the 1930s.

What to See and Do

National Automobile Museum. *10 Lake St S. Phone 775/333-9300. www.automuseum.org.* More than 200 vehicles on display. Theater presentation; period street scenes. (Daily; closed Thanksgiving, Dec 25) **$$**

Nevada Museum of Art. *100 S Virginia St. Phone 775/329-3333. www.nevadaart.org.* Changing art exhibits by international, national, regional, and local artists. (Tues-Sun 11 am-6 pm; closed holidays) **$$**

Pyramid Lake. (see) *55 N Main St. Phone 585/394-4975.* **$**

Sierra Nevada bus tours. *2050 Glendale Ave, Sparks 89431. Phone 775/331-1147.* To Virginia City, Ponderosa Ranch, Lake Tahoe, and other nearby points.

Toiyabe National Forest. *1200 Franklin Way, Sparks (89431). 10 miles W on I-80, then W on NV 27.* Approximately 3 million acres, partly in California. Trout fishing, big-game hunting, saddle and pack trips, camping (site fees vary), picnicking, and winter sports. Berlin-Ichthyosaur State Park (see AUSTIN), Lake Tahoe (see the Northern California book), and Mt Charleston Recreation Area (see LAS VEGAS) are in the forest. **FREE**

University of Nevada-Reno. *9th and Virginia sts (89557). Phone 775/784-4865.* (1874) 12,000 students. The campus covers 200 acres on a plateau overlooking the Truckee Meadows, in the shadow of the Sierra Nevada Mountains. Opened in Elko, it was moved to Reno and reopened in 1885. Tours of campus. On campus are

> **Fleischmann Planetarium and Science Center.** *1650 N. Virginia Street (89557). Phone 775/784-4812.* Northern Nevada's only planetarium, this facility features star shows, movies, astronomy museum, telescope viewing (Fri evenings), and more. (Daily; closed Jan 1, Thanksgiving, Dec 25) **$$**

> **Mackay School of Mines Museum.** *9th and Virginia sts (89557). Phone 775/784-6987.* Minerals, rocks, fossils, and mining memorabilia. (Mon-Fri; closed holidays) **FREE**

> **Nevada Historical Society Museum.** *1650 N Virginia St. Phone 775/688-1190.* Prehistoric and modern Native American artifacts; ranching, mining, and gambling artifacts. Carson City Mint materials; museum tours; research and genealogy library (Tues-Sat). Museum (Mon-Sat; closed holidays, Oct 31). **DONATION**

Special Events

National Championship Air Races. *4895 Texas Ave (89506). Reno/Stead Airport. Phone 775/972-6663.* Four days in mid-Sept.

Nevada State Fair. *1350 N Wells Ave (89512). Fairgrounds. Phone 775/688-5767.* Late Aug.

Rodeo. *1350 N Wells St (89512). Reno Livestock Events Center. Phone 775/329-3877.* Downtown contests and celebrations on closed streets. Late June.

Motels/Motor Lodges

★★ BEST WESTERN AIRPORT PLAZA HOTEL.
1981 Terminal Way (89502). Phone 775/348-6370; toll-free 800/648-3525; fax 775/348-9722. www.bestwestern.com. 270 rooms, 3 story. S $79-$99; D $79-$119; each additional $10; suites $125-$250; kitchen unit $275; under 12 free; higher rates: holidays, special events. Crib free. TV; cable (premium), VCR available. Pool; whirlpool. Restaurant 5:30 am-11 pm. Room service. Bar 11-1 am. Check-out noon. Meeting rooms. Business center. In-room modem link. Bellstaff. Valet service. Airport transportation. Putting green. Exercise equipment; sauna. Health club privileges. Refrigerators available. Some fireplaces. Mini-casino. Cr cds: A, C, D, DS, MC, V.

🔲 🏊 🎿 🏃

★ LA QUINTA INN.
4001 Market St (89502). Phone 775/348-6100; toll-free 800/531-5700; fax 775/348-8794. www.laquinta.com. 130 rooms, 2 story. S $61-$69; D $61-$77; each additional $8; under 18 free. Crib free. Pet accepted. TV; cable. Pool. Complimentary continental breakfast. Coffee in rooms. Check-out noon. Business services available. Free airport transportation. Cr cds: A, C, D, DS, MC, V.

🔲 🐾 🏊 🏊 ✈ 🔲

★ RODEWAY INN.
2050 Market St (89502). Phone 775/786-2500; toll-free 800/648-3800; fax 775/786-3884. www.choicehotels.com. 211 units, 4 story, 70 kit suites (no equipment). Late May-Oct: S $39, D $189; each additional $9; kitchen suites $64-$189; under 18 free; weekly rates; higher rates: weekends, holidays, special events; lower rates rest of year. Crib free. Pet accepted; $10/day. TV; cable. Pool; whirlpool. Sauna. Complimentary continental breakfast. Restaurant nearby. Check-out noon. Coin laundry. Business services available. Airport, casino transportation. Microwaves in kitchen units. Cr cds: A, C, D, DS, JCB, MC, V.

🔲 🐾 🏊 🎿 🔲

★ VAGABOND INN.
3131 S Virginia St (89502). Phone 775/825-7134; toll-free 800/522-1555; fax 775/825-3096. www.vagabondinns.com. 129 rooms, 2 story. May-Oct: S $45-$65; D $49-$69; each additional $5; under 18 free; higher rates special events, holidays; lower rates rest of year. Crib free. Pet accepted, some restrictions; $10/day. TV; cable (premium). Pool. Complimentary continental breakfast. Restaurant adjacent 11-4 am. Check-out 11 am. Business services available. Airport, train station, bus depot transportation.

Health club privileges. Some private patios, balconies. Cr cds: A, D, DS, MC, V.

🐾 🏊 🎿 🔲

Hotels

★★★ ATLANTIS CASINO RESORT.
3800 S Virginia St (89502). Phone 775/825-4700; toll-free 800/723-6500; fax 775/826-7860. www.atlantiscasino.com. Experience the mystery of a sunken city at this glass-enclosed casino. Full health spa facilities, 9-foot ceiling guest rooms, several restaurants and the Entertainment Fun Center with over 100 casino games add to the gaming experience. 973 rooms, 27 story. May-Sept: S, D $69-$125; each additional $10; suites $165-$275; under 18 free; ski, golf rates; higher rates: weekends, holidays, special events; lower rates rest of year. Crib free. TV; cable. Heated pool; whirlpool. Restaurant open 24 hours (see also ATLANTIS). Bar; entertainment. Check-out 11 am. Convention facilities. Business services available. Free valet parking. Free airport transportation. Spa. Some in-room whirlpools. Casino. Cr cds: A, C, D, DS, ER, JCB, MC, V.

🔲 🐾 🏊 🎿 🏃 🔲 🏃

★★★ CIRCUS CIRCUS HOTEL AND CASINO.
500 N Sierra St (89503). Phone 775/329-0711; toll-free 800/648-5010; fax 775/328-9652. www.circusreno.com. There is something for everyone at this family friendly casino: continually running circus acts from around the world, a midway to "test your skills" and more traditional casino games, as well as restaurants such as Art Gecko's Southwest Grill. 1,572 rooms, 23 and 28 story. Crib free. Check-out noon. TV; cable. Restaurant open 24 hours. Bar; entertainment. Health club privileges. Recreation room. S, D $39-$69; each additional $10; mini-suites $69-$99; under 13 free; ski/golf packages; higher rates: weekends, holidays, special events. Free covered valet parking. Airport transportation. Business services. Gift shop. Casino. Midway, arcade games. Free circus acts. Cr cds: A, C, D, DS, JCB, MC, V.

🔲 🔲

★★★ ELDORADO HOTEL & CASINO.
345 N Virginia St (89505). Phone 775/786-5700; toll-free 800/648-5966; fax 775/348-7513. www.eldoradoreno.com. In addition to the ten restaurants, extensive gaming facilities and sports bar with 80 beers from around the world, guests can enjoy live entertainment and a heated outdoor pool with a sun deck at this casino. 817 rooms, 26 story. July-Oct: S, D $69-$89; each additional $10; suites $110-$495; under 12 free; higher rates: weekends, holidays; lower rates rest of year. Crib free. TV; cable. Heated pool; whirlpool, poolside service. Restaurants open 24 hours. Room service 24 hours. Bar; entertainment. Check-out noon. Convention facilities. Business services available. In-room modem link. Concierge. Gift shop. Airport transportation. Garage; free valet parking. Health club privileges.

Wet bar in some suites; some bathroom phones, refrigerators. Casino. Cr cds: A, C, D, DS, JCB, MC, V.

★ ★ **FITZGERALD'S CASINO HOTEL.** *255 N Virginia St (89501). Phone 775/785-3300; fax 775/786-3686. www.fitzgeralds.com.* 351 rooms, 16 story. May-Oct: S, D $36-$88; each additional $10; suites $90-$140; under 13 free; higher rates: weekends, holidays; lower rates rest of year. TV; cable. Restaurants open 24 hours. Room service 6 am-9 pm. Bars; entertainment. Check-out 11 am. Free valet parking. Casino. Cr cds: A, D, DS, MC, V.

★ ★ ★ **GOLDEN PHOENIX HOTEL AND CASINO.** *255 N Sierra St (89501). Phone 775/ 322-1111; fax 775/785-7086.* Located in the heart of downtown Reno, this hotel with views of Reno and the Sierra Mountains, holds a 24-hour nonstop casino. There are five restaurants and a fitness center on property. Golf, driving range, putting green, bowling, horseback riding, and shopping are nearby attractions. 604 rooms, 20 story. May-Sept: S, D $52-$229; each additional $10; suites $145-$395; under 19 free; higher rates during holidays; lower rates rest of year. Crib free. TV; cable. Restaurants open 24 hours. Bars; entertainment. Room service 24 hours. Check-out 11 am. Convention facilities. Business center. In-room modem link. Gift shop. Free valet parking. Airport transportation. Exercise equipment. Casino. Cr cds: A, C, D, DS, JCB, MC, V.

★★★**HARRAH'S HOTEL.** *219 N Center St (89504). Phone 775/786-3232; toll-free 800/427-7247; fax 775/788-3274. www.harrahs.com.* 952 rooms, 26 story, no rooms on 1st 3 floors. May-Oct: S, D $79-$189; each additional $10; suites $210-$425; higher rates weekends; lower rates rest of year. Crib free. Pet accepted, some restrictions. TV; cable. Heated pool; whirlpool. Restaurant open 24 hours. Bars; entertainment. Check-out noon. Convention facilities. Business center. In-room modem link. Gift shop. Barber, beauty shop. Covered parking; valet. Free airport transportation. Sauna, steam room. Massage. Game room. Recreation room. Casino. Some bathroom phones. Some private patios. Cr cds: A, C, D, DS, JCB, MC, V.

★ ★ ★ **HILTON.** *2500 E Second St (89595). Phone 775/789-2000; fax 775/789-1678. www.hilton.com.* With a 40,000-square-foot Fun Quest Center and a recreational vehicle park, this casino resort is for the whole family. Other activities available include hang gliding, bungee jumping, sky diving, bowling, a health and fitness center, aquatic driving range, an indoor golf and sports center, six restaurants, a comedy club and swimming pool. 2,000

rooms, 27 story. S, D $69-$199; each additional $10; suites $149-$900; package plans. Crib free. TV; cable. Pool; whirlpool, poolside service, lifeguard. Restaurants open 24 hours. Bars; entertainment. Check-out 11 am. Convention facilities. Meeting rooms. Business center. Shopping arcade. Barber, beauty shop. Free valet parking. Free airport transportation. Driving range. Exercise room; sauna, steam room. Spa. Massage. Recreation room. Some bathroom phones, refrigerators; wet bars. Casino. Cr cds: A, C, D, DS, MC, V.

★ ★ ★ **JOHN ASCUAGA' S NUGGET.** *1100 Nugget Ave, Sparks (89431). Phone 775/356-3300; toll-free 800/648-1177; fax 775/356-4198. www.janugget.com.* This northern Nevada location has views of the Sierra Nevada mountains. The casino has more than 1,500 slot machines and there are eight restaurants to chose from. The "Best in the West Nugget Rib Cook Off" is a big draw on Labor Day weekend. 1,407 rooms, 29 story. S, D $99-$189; each additional $10; suites $145-$450; under 18 free. Crib free. Check-out 11 am. TV; cable. Restaurant open 24 hours. Bar; entertainment. Exercise equipment, massage. Indoor/outdoor pool; whirlpool, poolside service. Beauty shop. Free valet parking. Free airport transportation. Business center. Convention center/facilities. Concierge. Gift shop. Casino. Cr cds: A, C, D, DS, MC, V.

★ ★ **JOHN ASCUAGA'S NUGGET COURTYARD.** *1100 Nugget Ave, Sparks (89431). Phone 775/356-3300; toll-free 800/648-1177; fax 775/356-4198. www.janugget.com.* 157 rooms, 5 story. story. S, D $79-$119; under 18 free. Crib free. Complimentary coffee in lobby. Check-out 11 am. TV; cable. Some balconies. Health club privileges. Heated pool, poolside service. Free parking. Free airport transportation. Business services. Sundries. Wedding chapel. Cr cds: A, C, D, DS, MC, V.

★ ★ ★ **PEPPERMILL HOTEL AND CASINO.** *2707 S Virginia St (89502). Phone 775/826-2121; toll-free 800/648-6992; fax 775/689-7178. www.peppermillcasino .com.* Located downtown, this resort offers gaming and recreation activities. Choose from views of the Sierras, the large waterfall, or the city. 1,070 rooms, 16 story. S, D $49-$100; suites $109-$399; under 15 free. Crib free. Valet parking. TV; cable. 2 heated pools; whirlpool. Restaurant open 24 hours. Bars; entertainment. Check-out noon. Meeting rooms. Business services available. Gift shop. Barber, beauty shop. Free airport transportation. Exercise equipment; sauna. Minibars. Casino. Cr cds: A, C, D, DS, MC, V.

★★★**SIENA HOTEL SPA CASINO.** *One S Lake St (89505). Phone 775/337-6260. www.sienareno.com.* 214 rooms, 9 story. S, D $99-$189. Crib free. TV; cable. Restaurant open 24 hours. Bars; entertainment. Check-out noon. Business center. In-room modem link. Exercise room; sauna. Spa. Massage. Casino. Cr cds: A, C, D, DS, MC, V.

★★★**SILVER LEGACY RESORT CASINO.** *407 N Virginia St (89501). Phone 775/329-4777; toll-free 800/687-7733; fax 775/325-7474. www.silverlegacyresort. com.* One of the largest resorts in town, this property has a contemporary decor with Victorian accents. 1,720 rooms, 38 story. July-Oct: S, D $59-$119; each additional $10; suites $100-$200; under 12 free; lower rates rest of year. TV; cable. Pool; whirlpool, poolside service. Restaurant open 24 hours. Bar. Check-out 11 am. Convention facilities. Business services available. Barber, beauty shop. Valet service. Free airport transportation. Cr cds: A, C, D, DS, JCB, MC, V.

Restaurants

★★★**ATLANTIS.** *3800 S Virginia St (89502). Phone 702/825-4700. www.atlantis.reno.nv.us.* A wide variety of entrees and desserts are prepared tableside in this unique setting beneath the sea with a 1,100-gallon salt-water aquarium. Dance in the state-of-the art nightclub. Continental menu. Hours: 5-10 pm; Fri, Sat to 10:30 pm. Reservations accepted. Dinner $19.95-$28.95. Specialties: flaming coconut prawns, Alaskan king crab. Valet parking. Cr cds: A, C, D, DS, ER, MC, V.

★★**BRICKS RESTAURANT AND WINE BAR.** *1695 S Virginia St (89502). Phone 775/786-2277; fax 775/786-3377.* Continental menu. Hours: 11:30 am-2 pm, 5-10 pm; Sat from 5 pm. Closed Sun; major holidays. Reservations accepted. Bar 4-11 pm. Lunch $6.95-$12.95, dinner $11.95-$21.95. Specialties: shrimp scampi risotto, pork tenderloin, chicken pesto. Intimate atmosphere. Cr cds: A, DS, MC, V.

★★**FAMOUS MURPHY'S.** *3127 S Virginia St (89502). Phone 775/827-4111; fax 775/824-2599. www.famousmurphys.com.* Seafood, steak menu. Hours: 11 am-2 pm, 5-10 pm; Sat, 10 am-2 pm, closed Sunday. Lunch $5.95-15.95, dinner $10.95-$22.95. Bar to 3:30 am, Oyster bar. Children's menu. Reservations accepted. Cr cds: A, C, DS, ER, MC, V.

★★**PALAIS DE JADE.** *960 W Moana Ln #107 (89509). Phone 775/827-5233.* Chinese menu. Specialties: Jade crispy shrimp, sesame chicken, orange-flavored beef. Hours: 11 am-10 pm. Closed most major holidays. Lunch $5.95-$7.95, dinner $5.50-$17.95. Bar. Reservations accepted. Cr cds: A, MC, V.

★★**RAPSCALLION.** *1555 S Wells Ave (89502). Phone 775/323-1211; fax 775/323-6096. www.rapscallion.com.* Seafood menu. Closed Thanksgiving, Dec 25. Dinner $5.95-$18.95. Hours: 11:30 am-10 pm; Fri, Sat 5-10:30 pm; Sun brunch 10 am-2 pm. 6.95-$12.95. Bar 11-1 am; Sat to 2 am; Sun from 10 am. Reservations accepted. Outdoor dining. Cr cds: A, DS, MC, V.

★★**WASHOE GRILL.** *4201 W 4th St (89503). Phone 775/786-1323.* Specializes in steak, fresh seafood, chicken. Hours: 5-10:30 pm. Closed Thanksgiving. Dinner $16-$39. Bar. Salad bar. Cr cds: A, C, D, DS, ER, MC, V.

Sparks

(see Reno)

Stateline (E-1)

Pop 1,215 **Elev** 6,360 ft **Area code** 775 **Zip** 89449

This area is best known for its famous high-rise casino/hotels, cabarets, and fine dining, but as an integral part of Tahoe's "south shore", it is also appreciated for its spectacular natural beauty. Alpine beaches and Sierra forests afford visitors an endless variety of year-round recreation. There are several excellent public golf courses in the area.

Motel/Motor Lodge

★★**LAKESIDE INN & CASINO.** *Hwy 50 at Kingsbury Grade (89449). Phone 775/588-7777; toll-free 800/624-7980; fax 775/588-4092. www.lakesideinn.com.* 124 rooms, 2 story. Mid-June-mid-Oct: S, D $89-$119; each additional $10; suites $120-$235; package plans in winter; under 16 free; lower rates rest of year. Crib free. TV; cable. Pool. Complimentary coffee in rooms. Restaurant open 24 hours. Bars. Gift shop. Check-out noon. Sundries. Downhill ski 2 miles; cross-country. Game room. Wet bar in suites. Casino. Cr cds: A, C, D, DS, MC, V.

Hotels

★ ★ ★ **CAESAR'S TAHOE.** *55 US 50 (89449). Phone 775/588-3515; toll-free 888/829-7630; fax 775/586-2068. www.caesars.com.* All of the rooms at this casino hotel feature lake or mountain views. Guests can try their luck in the casino, or spend time relaxing by the lagoon-style pool or having treatments done in the spa. Don't miss a trip on *The Odyssey,* the hotel's private luxury yacht. 440 rooms, 15 story. S, D $89-$225; each additional $10; suites $300-$650; under 12 free; ski packages. Crib $10. TV; cable (premium). Indoor pool; whirlpools. Coffee in rooms. Restaurant open 24 hours. Bar; entertainment. Check-out noon. Convention facilities. Business center. Concierge. Shopping arcade. Barber, beauty shop. Free valet parking. Lighted tennis. Exercise equipment; steam room, sauna. Massage. Game room. Bathroom phones; some refrigerators, in-room whirlpools. Casino. Cr cds: A, C, D, DS, MC, V.

⬛ 🛗 💺 🎿 🖾 🐕 🏊 👤 🏃 🛖 🏃

★ ★ ★ **HARRAH'S LAKE TAHOE.** *Hwy 50 (89449). Phone 775/588-6611; toll-free 800/648-3773; fax 775/586-6607. www.harrahstahoe.com.* This property offers 18,000 square feet of function space and plenty of recreation options for leisure visitors. Shop at the Galleria, swim in the glass-domed pool, tan on the sun deck, or do the obvious at the casino. 532 rooms, 18 story. S, D $79-$209; each additional $20; suites $199-$950; ski packages; higher rates: weekends, holidays. Crib free. Pet accepted. TV; cable, VCR available. Indoor pool, whirlpool, poolside service. 6 restaurants with one open 24 hours (See also FRIDAY'S STATION and SUMMIT). Room service 24 hours. Bars; theater-restaurant; entertainment. Check-out noon. Convention facilities. Business services available. Concierge. Shopping arcade. Barber, beauty shop. Free covered valet parking. Exercise equipment; sauna, steam room. Massage. Game room. Casino. Microwaves, refrigerators available. Butler service in suites. Cr cds: A, C, D, DS, ER, JCB, MC, V.

⬛ 🐕 🛗 💺 🏃 🏊 🖾 👤 🏃

★ ★ ★ **HARVEY'S RESORT HOTEL AND CASINO.** *Stateline Ave (US 50) (89449). Phone 775/588-2411; toll-free 800/427-2789; fax 775/588-6643. www.harveys.com.* Most rooms at this property have a view of Lake Tahoe or the Sierra Nevada mountains. There is plenty of entertainment from the casino alone, however, should guests care to look for other activities, they are sure to be pleased. 740 rooms, 19 story. S, D $99-$229; each additional $20; suites $275-$725; package plans; higher rates weekends, holidays. Crib free. TV; cable. Pool; whirlpool. Poolside service. Eight restaurants (See also LEWELLYN'S and SAGE ROOM). Room service 24 hours. Six bars open 24 hours; entertainment. Check-out noon. Convention facilities. Business center. Concierge. Shopping arcade. Barber, beauty shop. Covered parking; free valet, self-park. Airport transportation (fee). Exercise room. Spa. Game room. Casino. Bathroom phones; minibars; wet bar in suites. Tahoe's first gaming establishment (1944). Cr cds: A, C, D, DS, JCB, MC, V.

⬛ 🏊 🏃 🖾 SC 🏃

★ **HORIZON CASINO RESORT.** *50 US 50 (89449). Phone 775/588-6211; toll-free 800/648-3322; fax 775/588-1344. www.horizoncasino.com.* 539 rooms, 15 story. Mid-June-mid-Sept: S, D $119-$169; each additional $10; suites $300-$600; higher rates: holidays, special events; lower rates rest of year. Crib free. Check-out noon. TV; cable. Some balconies. Wet bar in suites. Restaurant open 24 hours. Bar; entertainment. Exercise room, massage. Game room. Heated pool (seasonal); whirlpools, poolside service, lifeguard. Downhill ski 1 mile; cross-country ski 15 miles. Barber, beauty shop. Free garage parking. Business services. Convention center/facilities. Concierge. Gift shop. Casino. Cr cds: A, C, D, DS, JCB, MC, V.

⬛ 🏊 🖾 🏃 🖾 SC

Restaurants

★ ★ **CHART HOUSE.** *392 Kingsbury Grade (89449). Phone 775/588-6276; fax 775/588-4562. www.chart-house.com.* Hours: 5:30-10 pm; Sat 5-10:30 pm. Reservations accepted. Bar from 5 pm; Sat from 4:30 pm. Dinner $15.50-$31.95. Children's menu. Specialties: teriyaki sirloin, prime rib. Salad bar. Outdoor dining. View of lake. Cr cds: A, C, D, DS, ER, MC, V.

⬛

★ ★ ★ **FRIDAY'S STATION STEAK & SEAFOOD GRILL.** *US 50 (89449). Phone 775/588-6611. www.harrahs.com/our_casinos/tah/dining.* The view of the lake from this restaurant, located on the 18th floor, is truly breathtaking. Hours: 5:30-9:30 pm; Fri to 10 pm; Sat to 10:30 pm. Reservations accepted. Bar. A la carte entrees: dinner $16-$32. Specializes in hardwood-grilled seafood and steak. Overlooks Lake Tahoe. Cr cds: A, C, D, DS, ER, JCB, MC, V.

⬛

★ ★ ★ **LEWELLYN'S.** *US 50 (89449). Phone 775/588-2411; fax 775/586-6876.* High atop Harveys on the 19th floor, Llewellyn's offers a spectacular view of Lake Tahoe and an innovative menu with a beautiful presentation. International menu. Hours: 6-9:30 pm; Fri to 10 pm; Sat 5-10 pm. Sun 9:45-2 pm. Reservations accepted. Bar 5-11 pm. Wine list. Dinner $22-$36. Specialties:

abalone, rack of lamb, wild boar. Pianist Wed-Sun. Valet parking. Elegant dining room. Totally nonsmoking. Cr cds: A, C, DS, MC, V.

D

★ ★ ★ **SAGE ROOM.** *US 50 (89449). Phone 775/588-2411; fax 775/586-6854.* Since 1947, the Sage Room Steak House has been world renowned for its old western ambiance and fine cuisine. Dine among the works of Russell and Remington while enjoying traditional Steak House dining highlighted by tableside flambe service. Top off your meal with the Sage Room's famous Bananas Foster. Continental, American menu. Hours: 5:30-10 pm; Sat to 11 pm. Reservations accepted. Bar. Wine cellar. Dinner $18-$28. Specializes in steak, fresh seafood. Own baking. Valet parking. Dining room interior is part of original Wagon Wheel Saloon and Gambling Hall; hand-hewn beams, redwood ceilings, Remington bronzes, Western décor. Cr cds: A, C, D, DS, MC, V.

D

★ ★ ★ **SUMMIT.** *US 50 (89449). Phone 775/588-6611; fax 775/586-6643. www.harrahs.com/our_casinos/tah/dining/.* Located on the 16th and 17th floors of Harrah's, this restaurant has stunning views of the lake and mountains. Continental menu. Hours: 5:30-9:30 pm; Sat to 10 pm. Reservations accepted. Bar. Wine list. Dinner $22-$75. Specialties: rack of lamb, lobster Thermidor, abalone. Valet parking. Formal atmosphere; glass wine cases, views of lake. Totally nonsmoking. Cr cds: A, C, D, DS, ER, JCB, MC, V.

D

Tonopah (F-3)

Settled 1900 **Pop** 2,627 **Elev** 6,030 ft **Area code** 775 **Zip** 89049

Information Chamber of Commerce, 301 Brougher St, PO Box 869; 775/482-3859

Founded by prospector Jim Butler in 1900 and named by his wife, Tonopah was a high-spirited but unusually orderly camp in its early days. "Tono" is a shrub of the greasewood family, the roots of which can be eaten; "pah" means water in the Shoshone language. There are a couple of gold mines and a silver mine in the vicinity. The Tonopah Test Range is approximately 35 miles east. A Ranger District office of the Toiyabe National Forest (see RENO) is located here, as well as a detached area office of the Bureau of Land Management.

What to See and Do

Central Nevada Museum. *1900 Logan Field Rd. Phone 775/482-9676.* Historical, mining, and gem displays. (Daily; closed Dec 25) **DONATION**

Rock Collecting. *520 McCulloch (Mining Museum & Park) (89049). Phone 775/482-9274.* Historic mining park. Rich variety of minerals. (Daily)

Motels/Motor Lodges

★ ★ **BEST WESTERN HI-DESERT INN.** *320 Main St (89049). Phone 775/482-3511; toll-free 877/286-2208; fax 775/482-3300. www.bestwestern.com.* 62 rooms, 2 story. S $49; D $69; each additional $6. Crib $8. Pet accepted, some restrictions. TV; cable (premium). Pool; whirlpool. Complimentary continental breakfast. Restaurant nearby. Check-out 11 am. Cr cds: A, C, D, DS, ER, JCB, MC, V.

D 🔌 🏊 🏊 🏋 ✈ 🔌

★ **JIM BUTLER MOTEL.** *100 S Main St (89049). Phone 775/482-3577; toll-free 800/635-9455; fax 775/482-5240.* 24 rooms, 2 story. S, D $34-$42. Crib $5. Pet accepted, some restrictions. TV; cable (premium). Complimentary coffee in lobby. Restaurant adjacent 24 hours. Check-out 11 am. Some refrigerators. Cr cds: A, C, D, DS, MC, V.

🔌 🔌 **SC**

★ **SILVER QUEEN MOTEL.** *255 Erie Main (89049). Phone 775/482-6291; toll-free 800/210-9218; fax 775/482-3190.* 85 rooms, 1-2 story. No elevator. S $33; D $45; kitchen units $45. Crib $4. Pet accepted. TV; cable (premium), VCR available (movies). Pool. Restaurant adjacent 6 am-10 pm. Bar 11 am-midnight. Check-out 11 am. Some refrigerators, microwaves. Cr cds: A, C, D, DS, MC, V.

🔌 🏊 🔌 🏋

★ **STATION HOUSE HOTEL AND CASINO.** *1100 Erie Main St (89049). Phone 775/482-9777; fax 775/482-8762.* 78 rooms, 3 suites, 2 story. S $36; D $39; each additional $2; suites $58-$80; under 11 free. Crib free. TV; cable (premium). Complimentary coffee in rooms. Restaurant open 24 hours. Bar; entertainment except Mon. Check-out 11 am. Meeting rooms. Shopping arcade. Free bus depot transportation. Cr cds: A, D, DS, MC, V.

D 🔌 🏋

Valley of Fire State Park

(37 miles NE of Las Vegas on I-15, then 18 miles SE on NV 169)

This park, Nevada's oldest and largest state park, offers a geologically incredible 38,480-acre area that gained its name from the red Jurassic-period sandstone formed 150 million years ago. You may just feel like you've stepped onto another planet when you glimpse the otherworldly rock formations and striking vistas. Make sure to bring a camera to capture this unique and fascinating place. Fine examples of Native American petroglyphs can be seen throughout the park; Atlatl Rock is of particular interest. Picnic areas and campsites are available for those who wish to stick around awhile. The visitor center is open daily 8:30 am-4:30 pm.

Virginia City (E-1)
See also Carson City, Reno

Settled 1859 **Pop** 750 **Elev** 6,220 ft **Area code** 775 **Zip** 89440

Information Chamber of Commerce, South C Street, PO Box 464; 775/847-0311

Nevada's most famous mining town, Virginia City once had a population of about 35,000 people and was one of the richest cities in North America. Its dazzling career coincided with the life of the Comstock Lode, which yielded more than $1 billion worth of silver and gold. In the 1870s Virginia City had four banks, six churches, 110 saloons, an opera house, numerous theaters, and the only elevator between Chicago and San Francisco. Great fortunes, including those of Hearst and Mackay, were founded here.

Virginia City is perched on the side of Mount Davidson, where a diagonal slit marks the Comstock Lode. The site is beautiful and the air is so clear that the blue and purple masses of the Stillwater Range can be seen 120 miles away. Nearer are the green fields and cottonwoods along the Carson River and the white sands of Forty Mile Desert. Gold was found in this area in 1848, but the big silver strike was made in 1859.

Visitors can tour mines and old mansions, some of which have been restored (Easter week, Memorial Day-October, daily); visit several museums and saloons (daily); stroll through the local shops; and ride on the steam-powered V&T Railroad (May-Sept).

What to See and Do

The Castle. *70 South B St. Phone 775/847-0275.* (1868) Built by Robert N. Graves, a mine superintendent of the Empire Mine, the building was patterned after a castle in Normandy, France. It was once referred to as the "house of silver doorknobs." Filled with international riches; original furnishings. (Memorial Day weekend-Oct; daily) **$$**

Special Event

Camel Races. *Arena at Sutton and E sts (89440). Phone 775/847-0311.* Early Sept.

Wendover

(See Wendover, UT)

Winnemucca (C-3)

Settled circa 1850 **Pop** 7,174 **Elev** 4,299 ft **Area code** 775 **Zip** 89445

Information Humboldt County Chamber of Commerce, 30 W Winnemucca Blvd; 775/623-2225

Originally called French Ford, the town was renamed for the last great chief of the Paiutes, who ruled the area. Winnemucca was first settled by a Frenchman who set up a trading post. Many Basques live here. A Ranger District office of the Humboldt National Forest (see ELKO) is located here.

What to See and Do

Humboldt Museum. *175 W Jungo Rd. Jungo Rd and Maple Ave. Phone 775/623-2912.* Historical museum features Native American artifacts; bottles; pioneers' home items, tools, utensils; local history; antique auto display; old country store. (Mon-Fri, also Sat afternoons; closed holidays) **DONATION**

Motels/Motor Lodges

★**BEST INN.** *125 E Winnemucca Blvd (89445); toll-free 800/443-7777; fax 775/623-4722.* 80 rooms, 3 story. No elevator. Mid-May-Sept: S $45-$50; D $48-$57; each additional $5; lower rates rest of year. Crib $4. Pet accepted; $5. TV; cable (premium), VCR available. Heated pool. Sauna, steam room. Continental breakfast. Restaurant nearby. Check-out noon. Business services available. Cr cds: A, D, DS, MC, V.

D 🐾 🏊 ➿ SC 🏃

★ **BEST WESTERN GOLD COUNTRY INN.** *921 W Winnemucca Blvd (89445). Phone 775/623-6999; toll-free 800/346-5306; fax 775/623-9190. www.bestwestern.com.* 71 rooms, 2 story. June-Labor Day: S, D $65-$75; each additional $10; under 12 free; lower rates rest of year. Pet accepted, some restrictions. Check-out noon. TV; cable (premium). In-room modem link. Heated pool. Airport transportation. Cr cds: A, C, D, DS, MC, V.

D 🐾 ✈ 🏊 🏃 ✈ ➿

★★**RED LION HOTEL AND CASINO.** *741 W Winnemucca Blvd (89445). Phone 775/623-2565; toll-free 800/633-6435; fax 775/623-2527.* 105 units, 2 story. June-Oct: S, D $79-$89; each additional $10; suites $99-$150; under 12 free; lower rates rest of year. Crib $5. Pet accepted, some restrictions; $50 deposit. TV; cable (premium), VCR available. Heated pool. Restaurant open 24 hours. Bar. Check-out noon. Business services available. Airport transportation. Game room. Some balconies. Casino. Cr cds: A, C, D, DS, ER, JCB, MC, V.

★ **DAYS INN.** *511 W Winnemucca Blvd (89445). Phone 775/623-3661; toll-free 800/548-0531; fax 775/623-4234. www.daysinn.com.* 50 rooms, 2 story. June-Labor Day: S $60; D $65; each additional $5; lower rates rest of year. Crib $5. Pet accepted. TV; cable (premium). Heated pool. Coffee in lobby. Restaurant nearby. Check-out noon. Cr cds: A, C, D, DS, MC, V.

Hotel

★ **WINNERS HOTEL & CASINO.** *185 W Winnemucca Blvd (89445). Phone 775/623-2511; toll-free 800/648-4770; fax 775/623-3976. www.winnerscasino.com.* 37 rooms, 2 story. May-Labor Day: S, D $35; each additional $5; suites $70; lower rates rest of year. Pet accepted. Check-out 11 am. TV; cable (premium). Coin laundry. Restaurant nearby. Continental breakfast in lobby. Cr cds: A, C, D, DS, MC, V.

Restaurant

★ **ORMACHEA'S.** *180 Melarky St (89445). Phone 775/623-3455; fax 775/623-5208.* Basque, American menu. Hours: 4-10 pm. Closed Mon; some major holidays. Dinner $10-$12. Bar. Children's menu. Cr cds: A, C, D, DS, ER, MC, V.

Yerington (E-2)

Pop 2,883 **Elev** 4,384 ft

Information Mason Valley Chamber of Commerce, 227 S Main St; 775/463-2245

Web www.yerington.net

The town was once named Pizen Switch, presumably because of the bad whiskey being sold in a saloon. Wovoka, the Paiute messiah, grew up in this area. In 1889 Wovoka claimed to have had a vision in which he was instructed to teach a new dance that would oust the white intruders and restore to the Native Americans their lands and old way of life.

In 1894 the citizens saw the economic value of being on the route of the Carson and Colorado Railway. They decided to rename their town after the man with the power to decide the route—Henry Marvin Yerington. The railroad never did come to Yerington, instead established at nearby Wabuska.

What to See and Do

Fort Churchill State Historic Park. *10000 US 95A (89429). Phone 775/577-2345.* This post was established when the rush to the Comstock began as protection against the Paiutes. It was garrisoned from 1860-1869. Adobe walls of the old buildings exist in a state of arrested decay. The visitor center has displays. Picnicking, trails, and camping facilities on 1,232 acres. **$$$**

Lyon County Museum. *215 S Main. Phone 775/463-6576.* Complex includes a general store, natural history building, blacksmith shop, schoolhouse. (Thurs-Sun; closed Thanksgiving, Dec 25) **FREE**

Following the bright lights and late nights in the casinos in Nevada, a trip to connect with nature just might refresh your soul. Within a few hours, you could be sitting by Yosemite Falls at Yosemite National Park, checking out lava at Lava Beds National Monument, or wading in the water at Lake Tahoe, all of which are in California.

Death Valley National Park, CA

3 1/2 hours, 141 miles from Las Vegas, NV

Here, approximately 300 miles northeast of Los Angeles, are more than 5,200 square miles of rugged desert, peaks, and depressions—an unusual and colorful geography. The park is one vast geological museum, revealing secrets of ages gone by. Millions of years ago, this was part of the Pacific Ocean; then violent uplifts of the earth occurred, creating mountain ranges and draining water to the west. Today, 200 square miles of the valley are at or below sea level. The lowest point on the continent (282 feet below sea level) is here; Telescope Peak, at 11,049 feet, towers directly above it. The valley itself is about 140 miles long and 4-16 miles wide. The average rainfall is less than 2 inches a year. From Oct-May, the climate is very pleasant. In summer, it's extremely hot; a maximum temperature of 134°F in the shade has been recorded. If considered altogether, this is the lowest, hottest, and driest area in North America.

Death Valley was named in 1849 when a party of gold hunters took a shortcut here and were stranded for several weeks awaiting help. The discovery and subsequent mining of borax, hauled out by the famous 20-mule teams, led to development of the valley as a tourist attraction.

The visitor center at Furnace Creek is open daily. Guided walks, evening programs and talks (Nov-Apr). Golden Age, Golden Eagle, Golden Access passports (see MAKING THE MOST OF YOUR TRIP) are accepted. Phone 760/786-2331. Per vehicle $5-$10.

Note: Venturing off paved roads in this area in the summer months can be very dangerous. Carefully obey all National Park Service signs and regulations. Make sure that your vehicle has plenty of gas and oil. Carry water when you explore this park, especially in hot weather. For further information, contact Superintendent, Death Valley National Park, Death Valley 92328.

What to See and Do

20-Mule-Team Canyon. *Lone Pine.* Viewed from a twisting road on which RVs and trailers are not allowed. (This is an unpaved, one-way road; watch carefully for the entrance sign.)

Artist's Palette. A particularly scenic auto drive (9 miles one way) with spectacular colors. Because of difficult roads, RVs and trailers are advised not to drive here.

Badwater. At 279 feet below sea level, near the lowest spot on the North American continent; look for the sea level sign.

Camping. Developed and primitive camping in area; limited hookups. It is suggested that campers check with the visitors center for important information on camping facilities and road conditions. (Daily) **FREE**

Charcoal kilns. Beehive-shaped stone structures, formerly used to make charcoal for nearby mines. **Note:** The last mile of the access road is unpaved.

Dante's View. (5,475 feet) View of Death Valley with a steep drop to 279 feet below sea level at Badwater.

Devil's Golf Course. Vast beds of rugged salt crystals.

Golden Canyon. Offers a display of color ranging from deep red to rich gold. One-mile trail provides access.

Natural Bridge. A bridge spanning a rugged canyon in the Black Mountains; 1-mile walking trail.

Rhyolite Ghost Town. This was the largest town in the mining history of Death Valley in the early 1900s; 5,000 to 10,000 people lived here then. The town bloomed from 1905 to 1910; by 1911, it was a ghost town. One structure still standing from that era is the "bottle house," constructed of 12,000 to 50,000 beer and liquor bottles (depending on who does the estimating).

Sand dunes. Sand blown by the wind into dunes 5 to 100 feet high.

Scotty's Castle. A desert mansion (circa 1922-1931), designed and built to be viewed as a work of art as well as a house. The furnishings are typical of the period; many pieces were especially designed and hand-crafted for this house. Living history tours are led by costumed interpreters. **$$$**

Telescope Peak. Highest point in the Panamint Range (11,049 feet). There is a 14-mile round-trip hiking trail, but it is inaccessible in the winter months.

Ubehebe Crater. Colorful crater left by a volcanic steam explosion.

Zabriskie Point. View of Death Valley and the Panamint Range from the rugged badlands of the Black Mountains.

Motel/Motor Lodge

★**STOVEPIPE WELLS VILLAGE.** *Hwy 190 (92328). Phone 760/786-2387; fax 760/786-2389. www.stovepipewells.com.* 83 rooms, 5 buildings. No room phones. S, D $70-$92; each additional $10; under 13 free. Crib $20 deposit. Pet accepted; $20 refundable. Heated pool. Restaurant 7 am-2 pm, 6:30-10 pm. Bar 4:30-11 pm. Check-out 11 am. Sundries. Landing strip. Panoramic view of mountains, desert, dunes. Cr cds: A, D, DS, MC, V.

⊡ 🐾 ⚊ ⚊

Resort

★★★**FURNACE CREEK RANCH.** *CA 190 (92328). Phone 760/786-2345; toll-free 800/236-7916; fax 760/786-2423. www.furnacecreekresort.com.* 224 rooms, 1-2 story. S, D $102-$154; each additional $20; under 18 free. TV; cable. Bar noon-midnight. Natural thermal spring water pool. Playground. Dining rooms 6 am-9:30 pm. Check-out noon, check-in 4 pm. Grocery. Coin laundry. Package store. Gift shop. Lighted tennis. Golf, greens fee $40, pro, driving range. Volleyball, basketball courts. Museum. Some refrigerators. Cr cds: A, C, D, DS, JCB, MC, V.

⊡ ⚡ 🍴 ⚊ ⚊ 🏃 🐾 ⚊ SC

Guest Ranch

★★**FURNACE CREEK INN.** *CA 190 (92328). Phone 760/786-2345; toll-free 800/236-7916; fax 760/786-2307. www.furnacecreekresort.com.* This elegant and charming resort features the lowest golf course in the world, which seems like an oasis in these dead and desert surroundings of the national park. 66 units, 4 story. Feb-Apr S, D $102-$154; each additional $15; suites $155-$225; under 18 free; lower rates rest of year. Check-out noon. TV; cable. Private patios, balconies. Many refrigerators. Restaurant 6 am-9:30 pm (see also INN DINING ROOM). Bar noon-11 pm. Exercise equipment, sauna. Natural thermal spring water pool, poolside service. Golf privileges, greens fee $40, pro, driving range. Lighted tennis. Lawn games. Concierge. Gift shop. 1920s-30s décor; native stone in many areas. Cr cds: A, C, D, DS, JCB, MC, V.

[D] [symbols] [SC]

Restaurant

★★★**INN DINING ROOM.** *CA 190 (92328). Phone 760/786-2361. www.furnacecreekresort.com.* When you are in Death Valley and happen to have a jacket on you, visit the inn for some delicious food. Try their steaks while enjoying the 1930s decor under beamed ceilings. Continental menu. Hours: 7-10:30 am, 5:30-10 pm; also 11:30 am-2 pm Oct-May. Reservations accepted. Continental menu. Bar noon-11 pm. Wine list. A la carte entrees: breakfast $8.75-$12.50, lunch $8-$14, dinner $23-$30. Specializes in chicken, steak, seafood. Own baking. Valet parking. 1930s décor; beam ceilings. Jacket. Totally nonsmoking. Cr cds: A, DS, MC, V.

Lake Tahoe Area, CA

1 1/2 hours, 51 miles from Reno, NV

Lake Tahoe is one of the most magnificent mountain lakes in the world, with an area of about 200 square miles, an altitude of approximately 6,230 feet, and a maximum depth of more than 1,600 feet. Mostly in California, partly in Nevada, it is circled by paved highways edged with camp-grounds, lodges, motels, and resorts. The lake, with some fine beaches, is surrounded by forests of ponderosa, Jeffery and sugar pine, white fir, juniper, cedar, aspen, dogwood, and cottonwood, as well as a splendid assortment of wildflowers.

The Sierra Nevada, here composed mostly of hard granite, is a range built by a series of roughly parallel block faults along its eastern side, which have tipped the mountain-ous area to the west, with the eastern side much steeper than the western. Lake Tahoe lies in a trough between the Sierra proper and the Carson Range, similarly formed and generally regarded as a part of the Sierra, to its east.

There are spectacular views of the lake from many points on the surrounding highways. Eagle Creek, one of the thousands of mountain streams that feed the lake, cas-cades 1,500 feet over Eagle Falls into Emerald Bay at the southwestern part of the lake. Smaller mountain lakes are scattered around the Tahoe area; accessibility varies. Tahoe and El Dorado National Forests stretch north and west of the lake, offering many recreational facilities.

Public and commercial swimming (there are 29 public beaches), boating, and fishing facilities are plentiful. In winter the area is a mecca for skiers. There is legalized gambling on the Nevada side.

Note. Accommodations around Lake Tahoe are listed under South Lake Tahoe, Tahoe City, and Tahoe Vista. In this area many motels have higher rates in summer and during special events and holidays. Reservations advised. Phone 530/544-5050; 800/AT-TAHOE (reservations).

What to See and Do

Alpine Meadows. *2600 Alpine Meadows Rd. 6 miles NW of Tahoe City off CA 89. Phone 530/583-4232; 530/581-8374 (snow information).* Quad, two triple, seven double chair-lifts, one Pomalift; patrol, school, rentals; snowmaking; children's snow school; snack bar, cafeteria, restaurant, bars. Longest run 2 1/2 miles; vertical drop 1,800 feet. Snowboarding. (Mid-Nov-late May, daily) **$$$$**

Camp Richardson Corral. *4 Emerald Bay Rd. Phone 530/541-3113.* One- and two-hour rides, breakfast and steak rides (May-Oct, daily); sleigh rides (Dec-Mar). Contact PO Box 8335, South Lake Tahoe 96158. **$$$$**

D.L. Bliss State Park. *17 miles S of Tahoe City on CA 89. Phone 530/525-7277.* Sand beach; hiking, including Balancing Rock nature trail and start of Rubicon trail; camping (fee). **$$**

Emerald Bay State Park. *22 miles S of Tahoe City on CA 89. Phone 530/525-7232.* Swimming, fishing; picnicking, camping. Closed in winter. Standard fees. **$$** In Emerald Bay State Park is

> **Grover Hot Springs State Park.** *3415 Hot Springs Rd. 29 miles S of South Lake Tahoe on CA 89. Phone 530/694-2248.* Hot mineral pool, swimming; camping.

Heavenly Ski Resort. *3860 Saddle Rd (96150). 1 mile E of US 50 in South Lake Tahoe. Phone 775/586-7000.* Aerial Tramway to 8,200 feet. Five detachable quad, eight triple, five double chairlifts, eight surface lifts; patrol, school, rentals; snowmaking; snack bar, cafeteria, restaurant, bars; six lodges. Longest run 5 1/2 miles; vertical drop 3,500 feet. (Mid-Nov-mid-Apr, daily) Cross-country nearby. Gondola also operates May-Sept (fee). Observation platform, sun deck; hiking trail; picnic area. **$$$$**

Kirkwood Mountain Resort. *1501 Kirkwood Meadows Dr. 30 miles S off CA 88. Phone 209/258-6000; 877/KIRK-WOOD (snow conditions).* Two quads, seven triple, one double, two surface lifts; patrol, school, rentals; cafeteria, four restaurants, four bars. Longest run 2 1/2 miles; vertical drop 2,000 feet. (Mid-Nov-mid-May, daily) Cross-country skiing. Rentals, lessons; machine-groomed trails. (Nov-May; daily) Half-day rates. **$$$$**

Lake Tahoe Cruises. *900 Ski Run Blvd. Foot of Ski Run Blvd in South Lake Tahoe. Phone 530/541-3364.* Tahoe Queen, paddlewheeler, cruise boat to Emerald Bay (all year, departures daily, reservations required). **$$$$**

Lake Tahoe Historical Society Museum. *3058 US 50. Lake Tahoe Blvd. Phone 530/541-5458.* Displays of Lake Tahoe's Native American history, Fremont's discovery, and development as a resort center. (Late June-Labor Day, Tues-Sat afternoons; rest of year, weekends) **$**

MS *Dixie II* Cruises. *Leaves Zephyr Cove marina, 4 miles NE of Stateline, NV on US 50. Phone 775/588-3508 or 775/882-0786 (in CA).* Sightseeing. Tours of Lake Tahoe and Emerald Bay aboard paddlewheeler; sightseeing, breakfast and dinner cruises available. Champagne brunch cruise (Sun). Reservations recommended. **$$$$**

Ponderosa Ranch, Western Studio and Theme Park. *On Tahoe Blvd (NV 28). Phone 775/831-0691.* Cartwright House seen in the *Bonanza* television series. Frontier town with 1870 country church; vintage autos; breakfast hayrides (fee); amusements. Convention facilities. (Apr-Oct, daily) **$$$$**

Sierra at Tahoe. *1111 Sierra at Tahoe Rd. 12 miles W of South Lake Tahoe on US 50. Phone 530/659-7453; 530/659-7475 (snow conditions).* Three high-speed detachable quads, one triple, five double chairlifts; patrol, school, rentals; cafeterias. Longest run 2 1/2 miles; vertical drop 2,212 feet. (Nov-Apr, daily) Shuttle bus service. **$$$$**

Squaw Valley USA. *1960 Squaw Valley Rd. 7 miles NW of Tahoe City off CA 89. Phone 530/583-6985; 530/583-6955 (ski conditions).* Five high-speed quads, eight triple, eight double chairlifts, aerial cable car, gondola, five surface lifts; patrol, school, rentals; snack bars, cafeterias, restaurants, bars. Longest run 3.2 miles; vertical drop 2,850 feet. (Mid-Nov-mid-May, daily) Cross-country skiing (25 miles); rentals (Mid-Nov-late-May, daily). Aerial cable car also operates year-round (daily and evenings). **$$$$**

Tahoe State Recreation Area. *In Tahoe City on CA 28. Sugar Pine Point State Park. Phone 530/583-3074 (general information).* Cross-country skiing. Camping (fee). Pine Lodge is refurbished turn-of-century summer home (Ehrman Mansion), tours (July-Labor Day). Pier, picnicking, camping.

US Forest Service Visitor Center. *On CA 89, 3 miles NW of South Lake Tahoe. Contact US Forest Service, 870 Emerald Bay Rd, Suite 1, South Lake Tahoe 96150. Phone 530/573-2600.* Information, campfire programs, guided nature walks and self-guided trails. Visitors look into Taylor Creek from the Stream Profile Chamber; exhibits explain role of stream to Lake Clarity. (Memorial Day-Oct) **FREE**

Vikingsholm. *10 miles S of Tahoe City on CA 89. Phone 530/525-7277.* Old Scandinavian architecture and furnishings. Tours (mid-June-Labor Day, daily). Steep 1 mile walk from parking lot.

Special Events

American Century Investments Celebrity Golf Championship. *1156 Ski Run Blvd. Edgewood Tahoe Golf Course. Phone 530/544-5050.* More than 70 sports and entertainment celebrities compete for a $500,000 purse. July.

Great Gatsby Festival. *Hwy 50 and Hwy 89. Phone 530/541-5227.* Event at Tallac Historic Site re-creating the 1920s, with vintage clothing, music, cars, and children's games. Aug.

Lassen Volcanic National Park, CA

4 1/2 hours, 165 miles from Reno, NV

This 165-square-mile park was created to preserve the area including Lassen Peak (10,457 feet), a volcano last active in 1921. Lassen Park, in the southernmost part of the Cascade Range, contains glacial lakes, virgin forests, mountain meadows, and snow-fed streams. Hydrothermal features, the Devastated Area, and Chaos Jumbles can be seen from Lassen Park Road. Boiling mud pots and fumaroles (steam vents) can be seen a short distance off the road at Sulphur Works. At Butte Lake, colorful masses of lava and volcanic ash blend with the forests, meadows, and streams. The peak is named for Peter Lassen, a Danish pioneer who used it as a landmark in guiding immigrant trains into the northern Sacramento Valley.

The Devastated Area, after being denuded in 1915 by a mudflow and a hot blast, is slowly being reclaimed by small trees and flowers. The Chaos Crags, a group of lava plugs, were formed some 1,100 years ago. Bumpass Hell, a colorful area of mud pots, boiling pools, and steam vents, is a 3-mile round-trip hike from Lassen Park Road. Clouds of steam and sulfurous gases pour from vents in the thermal areas. Nearby is Lake Helen, named for Helen Tanner Brodt, first white woman to climb Lassen Peak (1864). At the northwest entrance is a visitor center (late June-Labor Day, daily) where one may find information on the park's human, natural, and geological history. There are guided walks during the summer; self-guided nature trails, and evening talks at some campgrounds. Camping (fee/site/night) at eight campgrounds; two-week limit except at Lost Creek and Summit Lake campgrounds (seven-day limit); check at the Ranger Stations for regulations.

Lassen Park Road is usually open mid-June to mid-October, weather permitting. Sulphur Works (south) and Manzanita Lake (northwest) entrances are open during winter months for winter sports.

Some facilities for the disabled (visitor center, comfort station, and amphitheater at Manzanita Lake; other areas in park). For information and descriptive folder contact the Superintendent, PO Box 100, Mineral 96063; phone 530/595-4444.

Lava Beds National Monument, CA

6 1/2 hours, 220 miles from Reno, NV

Seventy-two square miles of volcanic formations are preserved here in the extreme northeast part of the state. Centuries ago rivers of molten lava flowed here. In cooling, they formed a strange and fantastic region. Cinder cones dot the landscape—one rising 476 feet from its base. Winding trenches mark the collapsed roofs of lava tubes, an indicator of the 380 caves beneath the surface. Throughout the area are masses of lava hardened into weird shapes. Spatter cones may be seen where vents in the lava formed vertical tubelike channels, some only 3-feet in diameter but reaching downward 100 feet.

Outstanding caves include Sentinel Cave, named for a lava formation in its passageway; Catacombs Cave, with passageways resembling Rome's catacombs; and Skull Cave, with a broad entry cavern reaching approximately 80 feet in diameter. (The name comes from the many skulls of mountain sheep that were found here.) The National Park Service provides ladders and trails in the 24 caves easily accessible to the public.

One of the most costly Native American campaigns in history took place in this rugged, otherworldly setting. The Modoc War of 1872-73 saw a small band of Native Americans revolt against reservation life and fight a series of battles with US troops. Although obliged to care for their families and live off the country, the Modocs held off an army almost ten times their number for more than five months.

There is a campground at Indian Well (fee/site/night, water available mid-May-Labor Day) and picnic areas at Fleener Chimneys and Captain Jacks Stronghold (no water). Guided walks, audiovisual programs, cave trips,

and campfire programs are held daily, mid-June-Labor Day. Headquarters has a visitor center (daily). No gasoline is available in the park—fill gas tank before entering. Golden Eagle, Golden Age, and Golden Access passports accepted (see MAKING THE MOST OF YOUR TRIP). For further information, contact PO Box 867, Tulelake 96134; phone 530/667-2282. Per vehicle $2-$5

Yosemite National Park, CA

4 1/2 hours, 180 miles from Reno, NV

John Muir, the naturalist who was instrumental in the founding of this national park, wrote that here are "the most songful streams in the world . . . the noblest forests, the loftiest granite domes, the deepest ice sculptured canyons." More than 4 million people visit Yosemite year-round, and most agree with Muir. An area of 1,169 square miles, it is a park of lofty waterfalls, sheer cliffs, high wilderness country, alpine meadows, lakes, snowfields, trails, streams, and river beaches. There are magnificent waterfalls during spring and early summer. Yosemite's granite domes are unsurpassed in number and diversity. The entrance fee is $20 per car. Routes to Yosemite National Park involve some travel over steep grades, which may extend driving times. Tioga Pass (CA120) is closed in winter.

For general park information, contact Public Information Office, PO Box 577, Yosemite National Park; phone 209/372-0200. For lodging information, contact Yosemite Concession Services, Yosemite National Park; phone 559/252-4848. For recorded camping information, phone 209/372-0200. Camping reservations are taken by NPRS, the National Park Reservation System for Yosemite Valley (800/436-7275) and other campgrounds.

What to See and Do

Boating. No motors permitted.

Campfire programs. At several campgrounds; in summer, naturalists present nightly programs on park-related topics and provide tips on how to enjoy the park. Evening programs all year in the Valley only.

Camping. Limited to 30 days in a calendar year; May-mid-Sept, camping is limited to 7 days in Yosemite Valley, in the rest of the park to 14 days. Campsites in the Valley campgrounds, Hodgdon Meadow, Crane Flat, Wawona, and half of Tuolumne Meadows campgrounds may be reserved through NPRS. Other park campgrounds are on a first-come, first-served basis. Winter camping in the Valley, Hodgdon Meadow, and Wawona only.

Fishing. California fishing regulations pertain to all waters. A state license, inland waters stamp, and trout stamp are required. Special regulations for Yosemite Valley also apply.

The Giant Sequoias. Located principally in three groves. Mariposa Grove is near the south entrance to the park; toured on foot or by 50-passenger trams (May-early Oct; fee). Merced and Tuolumne groves are near Crane Flat, northwest of Yosemite Valley. The Grizzly Giant in Mariposa Grove is estimated to be 2,700 years old and is 209 feet high and 34.7 feet in diameter at its base.

Glacier Point. Offers one of the best panoramic views in Yosemite. From here the crest of the Sierra Nevada can be viewed, as well as Yosemite Valley 3,214 feet below. Across the valley are Yosemite Falls, Royal Arches, North Dome, Basket Dome, Mount Watkins, and Washington Column; up the Merced Canyon are Vernal and Nevada falls; Half Dome, Grizzly Peak, Liberty Cap, and the towering peaks along the Sierran crest and the Clark Range mark the skyline. (Road closed in winter)

The High Country. *For reservations information, phone 559/253-5674.* Tioga Rd (closed in winter) crosses the park and provides the threshold to a vast wilderness accessible via horseback or on foot to mountain peaks, passes, and lakes. Tuolumne Meadows is the major trailhead for this activity; one of the most beautiful and largest of the subalpine meadows in the High Sierra, 55 miles from Yosemite Valley by way of Big Oak Flat and Tioga rds. Organized group horse and hiking trips start from Tuolumne Meadows (except in winter), follow the High Sierra Loop, and fan out to mountain lakes and peaks. Each night's stop is at a High Sierra Camp; the pace allows plenty of time to explore at each camp.

Hiking and backpacking. *Phone 209/372-0740.* 840 miles of maintained trails. Wilderness permits are required for all overnight backcountry trips. Advance reservations for permits may be made up to 24 weeks in advance.

The Nature Center at Happy Isles. *E end of Yosemite Valley.* Exhibits on ecology and natural history. (Summer, daily)

Pioneer Yosemite History Center. A few miles from Mariposa Grove in Wawona. Has a covered bridge, historic buildings, wagons, and other exhibits. Living history program in summer.

Swimming. Prohibited at Hetch Hetchy Reservoir and in some areas of the Tuolumne River watershed. Swimming pools are maintained at Camp Curry, Yosemite Lodge, and Wawona.

Visitor Center. *At Park Headquarters in Yosemite Valley. Phone 209/372-0265.* Orientation slide program on Yosemite (daily). Exhibits on geology and ecology; naturalist-conducted walks and evening programs offered throughout the year on varying seasonal schedules. Native American cultural demonstrators (summer, daily).

The Indian Cultural Museum. Located in the building west of the Valley visitor center, the museum portrays the cultural history of the Yosemite Native Americans. Consult *Yosemite Guide* for hours. Adjacent is

Indian Village (Ahwahnee). Reconstructed Miwok-Paiute Village behind Visitor Center has self-guided trail.

Yosemite Fine Arts Museum. Gallery featuring contemporary art exhibits and the Yosemite Centennial. Consult *Yosemite Guide* for hours.

Walks and hikes. Conducted all year in the Valley and, during summer, at Glacier Point, Mariposa Grove, Tuolumne Meadows, Wawona, White Wolf, and Crane Flat.

⭐ **Waterfalls.** Reaching their greatest proportions in mid-May, they may, in dry years, dwindle to trickles or disappear completely by late summer. The **Upper Yosemite Fall** drops 1,430 feet; the lower fall drops 320 feet. With the middle Cascade they have a combined height of 2,425 feet and are the fifth highest waterfall in the world. Others are **Ribbon Fall,** 1,612 feet; **Vernal Fall,** 317 feet; **Bridalveil Fall,** 620 feet; **Nevada Fall,** 594 feet; and **Illilouette Fall,** 370 feet.

Winter sports. *Phone 209/372-1000 for snow conditions.* Centered around the **Badger Pass Ski Area,** 23 miles from Yosemite Valley on Glacier Point Rd. One triple, three double chairlifts, cable tow; patrol, rentals; snack stand, sun deck, nursery (minimum age 3 years); instruction (over 4 years). (Mid-Dec-mid-Apr, daily, weather permitting) Cross-country skiing. Ice skating (fee) in Yosemite Valley; scheduled competitions. Naturalists conduct snowshoe tours (fee) in the Badger Pass area. **$$$$**

Yosemite Mountain-Sugar Pine Railroad. *4 miles S of south park entrance on CA 41. For reservations and information, phone 559/683-7273.* Four-mile historic narrow-gauge steam train excursion through scenic Sierra National Forest. Picnic area. Museum; gift shops. Logger steam train (mid-May-Sept, daily; early May and Oct, weekends). Jenny Railcars (Mar-Oct, daily). Evening steam train, outdoor barbecue, live entertainment (late May-early Oct, Sat evenings; reservations advised). **$$$$**

Yosemite Valley. Surrounded by sheer walls, waterfalls, towering domes, and peaks. One of the most spectacular views is from Tunnel View, looking up the Valley to Clouds Rest. El Capitan (7,569 feet) is on the left, and Bridalveil Falls is on the right. The east end of the Valley, beyond Camp Curry, is closed to automobiles but is accessible by foot, bicycle, and, in summer, shuttle bus (free); special placards permit the disabled to drive in the restricted area when the route is drivable. The placards are available at visitor centers and entrance stations.

Motels/Motor Lodges

★ **COMFORT INN.** *4994 Bullion St, Mariposa (95338). Phone 209/966-4344; toll-free 800/228-5150; fax 209/966-4655.* 61 rooms, 2-3 story. Apr-Oct: S $75-$80; D $85-$90; each additional $6; suite $96-$185; kitchen units $140-$185; under 18 free; lower rates rest of year. Crib free. TV; cable (premium). Complimentary continental breakfast. Restaurant nearby. Check-out 11 am. Meeting rooms. Business services available. In-room modem link. Gift shop. Pool; whirlpool. Cr cds: A, C, D, DS, JCB, MC, V.

D ⛱ 🏊

★ **MINERS INN MOTEL.** *5181 Hwy 49 N, Mariposa (95338). Phone 209/742-7777; toll-free 888/646-2244; fax 209/966-2343. yosemite-rooms.com.* 78 rooms, 2 story. Apr-Oct: S $49-$59; D $59-$75; each additional $6; suites $149; kitchen units $125; under 6 free; lower rates rest of year. Crib free. Pet accepted; $6. Complimentary coffee in rooms. Check-out 11 am. TV; cable (premium). In-room modem link. Many balconies. Refrigerators, microwaves, fireplaces, in-room whirlpools, some bathroom phones. Restaurant 6:30 am-10 pm, bar; entertainment Fri, Sat. Pool, whirlpool. Business service available. Sundries. Gift shop. Cr cds: A, DS, MC, V.

D 🐾 ⛱ 🏊

★ ★ **PINES RESORT.** *54449 Rd 432, Bass Lake (93604). Phone 559/642-3121; toll-free 800/350-7463; fax 559/642-3902.* 104 units, 2 story. Apr-Oct: S, D $159-$279; family rates; weekends, holidays (2-3 day minimum); higher rates special events; lower rates rest of year. Crib free. Complimentary continental breakfast, complimentary coffee in rooms. Check-out 11 am. TV; cable (premium), VCR (movies available). Balconies, refrigerators, microwaves. Coin laundry. Restaurant 11 am-midnight, bar, entertainment Fri, Sat, room service. Split-level units on lake. Heated pool, whirlpool, poolside service. Tennis. Cross-country ski 5 miles. Meeting rooms. Business services. Cr cds: A, D, DS, MC, V.

D ⛷ ⛱ 🏊

★ ★ **YOSEMITE LODGE.** *On CA 41/140 (95389). Phone 559/252-4848; fax 209/372-1444. www.yosemitepark.com.* 226 rooms, 2 story. No A/C. Apr-Oct: S, D $73-$101; each additional $6-$12; lower rates rest of year. Crib $5. Heated pool; lifeguard. Supervised child's activities (June-Aug); ages over 3. Room service. Restaurant 6:30 am-7 pm. Bar noon-10 pm. Concierge. Barber, beauty shop. Check-out 11 am. Meeting rooms. Sundries. Gift shop. Valley tours. Cr cds: C, D, DS, JCB, MC, V.

D ⛷ ⛱ 🏊

★ **YOSEMITE RIVERSIDE INN.** *11399 Cherry Lake Rd, Groveland (95321). Phone 209/962-7408; toll-free 800/626-7408; fax 209/962-7400. www.yosemiteriversideinn.com.* 18 rooms, 2 kitchen units. No room phones. May-Sept: S $89; D $99; each additional $10; kit units $79-$275; under 5 free; weekly rates; lower rates rest of year. Crib free. Complimentary continental breakfast. Check-out 11 am. TV. Balconies, refrigerators available. Pool privileges. Picnic tables. On stream. Cr cds: A, C, D, DS, JCB, MC, V.

⛱ 🏊

★ ★ **YOSEMITE VIEW LODGE.** *11156 Hwy 140, El Portal (95318). Phone 209/379-2681; fax 209/379-2704. www.yosemite-motels.com.* 280 kitchen units, 2-3 story. Apr-Oct: S $99-$129; D $99-$139; each additional $10; ski plans; holidays (2-day minimum); lower rates rest of year. Crib $5. Pet accepted; $5. TV; cable (premium). Complimentary coffee in rooms. Restaurant 7 am-10 pm. Bar. Check-out 11 pm. Meeting rooms. Business services available. Sundries. Gift shop. Grocery store. Coin laundry. Downhill/cross-country ski 20 miles. 2 pools, 1 indoor; whirlpool. Many in-room whirlpools, fireplaces. Refrigerators, microwaves. Many balconies. On river. Cr cds: MC, V.

D 🐾 ⛷ ⛱ 🏊

Hotels

★ **BEST VALUE MARIPOSA LODGE.** *5052 Highway 140, Mariposa (95338). Phone 209/966-3607; toll-free 800/341-8000; fax 209/742-7038. www.mariposalodge.com.* 44 rooms, 13 rooms with shower only. Apr-Oct: S, D $65-$76; each additional $6; lower rates rest of year. Crib $6. Pet accepted, some restrictions; $6. TV; cable (premium), VCR available. Heated pool; whirlpool. Barber, beauty shop. In-room modem link. Complimentary coffee in rooms. Restaurant adjacent 7 am-9 pm. Check-out 11 am. Free airport transportation. Gazebo. Cr cds: A, C, D, DS, MC, V.

D 🐾 ⛱ 🏊

★ ★ **CEDAR LODGE.** *9966 Hwy 140, El Portal (95318). Phone 209/379-2612; toll-free 800/321-5261; fax 209/379-2712.* 211 rooms, 1-2 story. Mar-Nov: S $85; D $99; suites $120-$400; kitchen units $104; holidays (2-day minimum); lower rates rest of year. Crib $5. TV; cable (premium), VCR available (movies). Complimentary coffee in lobby. Restaurant adjacent 7 am-10 pm. Bar. Check-out 11 am. Meeting rooms. Business services available. In-room modem link. Sundries. Gift shop. 2 pools, 1 indoor; whirlpool. Many refrigerators, microwaves; some in-room whirlpools. Some balconies. Picnic tables, grills. On river. Cr cds: A, MC, V.

D ⛱ 🏊

★ ★ **GROVELAND HOTEL AT YOSEMITE NATIONAL PARK.** *18767 Main St, Groveland (95321). Phone 209/962-4000; toll-free 800/273-3314; fax 209/962-6674. www.groveland.com.* 17 rooms, 2 separate two-story buildings (one is California Monterey Colonial Adobe),

3 suites. S, D $135-$155; each additional $15 for under 12 years and $25 for over 12 years; suites $210. Crib free. Pet accepted. Complimentary innkeeper breakfast, complimentary coffee in rooms. Check-out noon, check-in 2 pm. TV in common room/bar/some rooms; cable, VCR available (movies). In-room modem link. Fireplace in suites, in-room whirlpool. Restaurant (see also THE VICTORIAN ROOM). Bar. Room service. Downhill skiing, cross-country ski 20 miles. Picnic tables. Conference/business services available. Concierge service. Built in 1849; European antiques. Open year-round. Totally nonsmoking. Cr cds: A, C, D, DS, JCB, MC, V.

★ **WAWONA HOTEL.** *Yosemite National Park, Wawona (95389). Phone 209/375-6556; fax 209/375-6601.* 104 rooms, 50 with bath, 1-2 story. No A/C. No room phones. Mid-Apr-late Dec: S, D $80-$110.55; each additional $13.75; under 12 free. Crib available. TV in lounge; VCR. Heated pool. Dining room 7:30-10:30 am, noon-1:30 pm, 5:30-9 pm. Check-out 11 am. Meeting room. Tennis. 9-hole golf, greens fee $13.75-$22, putting green. Gift shop. Free airport transportation. Saddle trips, stagecoach rides. Historic summer hotel. Cr cds: A, D, DS, JCB, MC, V.

Resorts

★ ★ ★ **THE AHWAHNEE.** *Yosemite Valley (95389). Phone 559/372-1407; reservations 559/252-4848; fax 559/456-0542. yosemitepark.com.* Built in 1927, this National Historic Landmark boasts striking beamed ceilings, a massive stone hearth, and beautifully appointed rooms. The hotel offers a perfect balance of refinement, grandness and hospitality. 123 rooms, 4 suites, 24 cottages, 6 story. No A/C in cottages. S, D $348-$359; each additional $20; suites $286-$510; 3-12 years free. Check-out noon. TV; VCR available. Some balconies, some fireplaces. Restaurant (reservation required), bar noon-10:30 pm; entertainment. Room service 6 am-11 pm. Heated pool. Tennis. Free valet parking. Meeting rooms. Concierge. Gift shops. Stone building with natural wood interior; Native American décor. Tire chains may be required by Park Service Nov-Mar to reach lodge. Cr cds: A, C, D, DS, JCB, MC, V.

★ ★ ★ **TENAYA LODGE AT YOSEMITE.** *1122 Highway 41, Fish Camp (93623). Phone 559/683-6555; toll-free 800/635-5807; fax 559/683-8684. www.tenayalodge.com.* At this deluxe mountain resort, you can enjoy the beauty of Yosemite National Park by horse or by foot. Enjoy such activities as shooting the rapids, bird-watching, biking or even a moonlight train ride. 244 rooms, 20 suites, 3-4 story. Mid-May-mid-Sept: S, D $149-$279; under 18 free; suites $289-$319; package plans; lower rates rest of year. Crib free. Pet accepted, some restrictions. Complimentary coffee in rooms. Check-out noon, check-in 3 pm. TV; cable (premium), VCR available. In-room modem link. Bathroom phones, minibars. Valet services, coin laundry. Dining room 6:30-11 am, 5:30-10 pm. Room service. Supervised children's activities; ages 3-12. Exercise equipment, massage, sauna, steam room. Game room. 2 pools, indoor pool, whirlpool. Cross-country ski on site. Bicycle rentals. Business center, convention facilities. Concierge. Gift shop. On river; water sports. Southwest, Native American décor; rustic with an elegant touch. June-Sept Western jamboree cookouts, wagon rides. Guided hikes and tours. Totally nonsmoking. Cr cds: A, C, D, DS, ER, JCB, MC, V.

B&B/Small Inns

★ **LITTLE VALLEY INN.** *3483 Brooks Rd, Mariposa (95338). Phone 209/742-6204; toll-free 800/889-5444; fax 209/742-5099. www.littlevalley.com.* 5 rooms, 1 cabin. No room phones. S, D $104; kitchen units $130; cabin $120; each additional $15. TV; VCR (movies). Complimentary full breakfast. Complimentary coffee in rooms. Check-out noon, check-in 4 pm. Concierge service. Picnic tables. Smoking on deck only. Cr cds: JCB, MC, V.

Restaurants

★ ★ **CHARLES STREET DINNER HOUSE.** *5043 Charles St, Mariposa (95338). Phone 209/966-2366. www.charlesstreetdinnerhouse.com.* Specialties: steak, fresh seafood. Own desserts. Hours: from 5 pm. Closed Mon, Tues; Thanksgiving, Dec 24, 25; also Jan. Dinner $15-$30. Reservations accepted. 19th-century house. Cr cds: A, DS, MC, V.

★ ★ **THE VICTORIAN ROOM.** *18767 Main St, Groveland (95321). Phone 209/962-4000; fax 209/962-6674. www.groveland.com.* California cuisine. Hours: 6-10 pm. Reservations accepted. Bar from noon. Dinner $12-$19. Specialties: baby back ribs, rack of lamb. Parking. Outdoor dining. Victorian décor. Totally nonsmoking. Cr cds: A, C, D, DS, MC, V.

New Mexico

Fray Marcos de Niza first saw what is now New Mexico in May, 1539. From a nearby mesa he viewed the Zuni pueblo of Hawikíuh, not far from the present Gallup. He returned to Mexico with tales of cities of gold which so impressed the Viceroy that in 1540 he dispatched Francisco Coronado with an army and Fray Marcos as his guide. They found no gold and very little of anything else. Coronado returned home two years later a broken man.

While others came to New Mexico before him for a variety of purposes, Don Juan de Oñate established the first settlement in 1598. Don Pedro de Peralta founded Santa Fe as the capital in 1609. Spanish villages were settled all along the Rio Grande until 1680, when the Pueblo, with Apache help, drove the Spaniards out of New Mexico in the famous Pueblo Revolt.

Twelve years later, Don Diego de Vargas reconquered the province with little resistance. The territory grew and prospered, though not entirely without conflict, since the Spanish were determined to maintain control at any cost. They forbade trade with the French of Louisiana, their nearest neighbors and rivals.

In 1810 Napoleon overran Spain; in 1821 Mexico won its independence and formed a republic. The following year, William Becknell of Missouri brought the first wagons across the plains and blazed what was later called the Santa Fe Trail. After the Mexican War of 1846, New Mexico became a US territory, joining the Union in 1912.

New Mexico is a land of contrasts. Traces of prehistoric Folsom Man and Sandia Man, whose ancestors may have trekked across the Bering Strait land bridge from Asia, have been found here. Working in the midst of antiquity, scientists at Los Alamos opened up the new atomic world.

Southern New Mexico has fascinating desert country and cool, green, high forests popular with campers, anglers, and vacationers. In the north, it also has desert lands, but most of this area is high mountain country with clear streams and snow which sometimes stays all

Population: 1,819,046
Area: 121,593 square miles
Elevation: 2,817-13,161 feet
Peak: Wheeler Peak (Taos County)
Entered Union: January 6, 1912 (47th state)
Capital: Santa Fe
Motto: It grows as it goes
Nickname: Land of Enchantment
Flower: Yucca
Bird: Chaparral (roadrunner)
Tree: Piñon
Fair: September in Albuquerque
Time Zone: Mountain
Website: www.newmexico.org

year. Spanish-speaking farmers mix with Native Americans and urban Americans in the plazas of Santa Fe and Albuquerque.

Where sheep and cattle were once the only industry, extractive industries—of which oil and uranium are a part—now yield nearly $5 billion a year.

NATIVE AMERICANS IN NEW MEXICO

Native Americans occupied New Mexico for centuries before the arrival of Europeans. The exploring Spaniards called them Pueblo Indians because their tightly clustered communities were not unlike Spanish pueblos, or villages. The Apache and Navajo, who arrived in New Mexico after the Pueblo people, were seminomadic wanderers. The Navajo eventually adopted many of the Pueblo ways, although their society is less structured and more individualistic than the Pueblo. The main Navajo reservation straddles New Mexico and Arizona (see SHIPROCK). The Apache, living closer to the Plains Indians, remained more nomadic.

The 19 Pueblo groups have close-knit communal societies and cultures, even though they speak six different languages. Their pueblos are unique places to visit. In centuries-old dwellings, craftspeople make and sell a variety of wares. The religious ceremonies, which include many dances and songs, are quite striking and not to be missed. While some pueblos are adamantly

Calendar Highlights

JANUARY

New Year's Celebration (*Albuquerque*). *Taos Pueblo.* Turtle dance. Contact Albuquerque Convention Center, phone 505/768-4575.

APRIL

Trinity Site Tour (*Alamogordo*). *Phone 505/437-6120 or 800/826-0294.* Visit the site of the first A-bomb explosion; only time the site is open to the public.

JUNE

New Mexico Arts & Crafts Fair (*Albuquerque*). *Fairgrounds. Phone 505/884-9043.* Exhibits and demonstrations by craftsworkers representing Spanish, Native American, and other North American cultures. Concerts in Popejoy Hall on the University of New Mexico campus.

JULY

Taos Pueblo Pow Wow (*Taos*). *Taos Pueblo. Phone 505/758-1028.* Intertribal dancers from throughout US, Canada, and Mexico participate; competition.

AUGUST

Fiesta at Santo Domingo Pueblo (*Santa Fe*). *Phone 505/465-2214.* Corn dance. This fiesta is probably the largest and most famous of the Rio Grande pueblo fiestas.

Indian Market (*Santa Fe*). *Santa Fe Plaza. Phone 505/983-5220 or 800/777-CITY.* One of largest juried displays of Native American art in the country. Dances, art. Make reservations at lodgings well in advance.

Inter-Tribal Indian Ceremonial (*Gallup*). *Red Rock State Park. Phone 505/863-3896 or 800/233-4528.* A major Native American festival; more than 50 tribes from the US, Canada, and Mexico participate in parades, rodeos, games, contests, dances, art and crafts sales.

SEPTEMBER

Enchanted Circle Century Bike Tour (*Red River*). Nearly 1,000 cyclists participate in a 100-mile tour around the Enchanted Circle (Red River, Angel Fire, Taos, Questa). Contact Chamber of Commerce, phone 505/754-2366 or 800/348-6444.

New Mexico State Fair (*Albuquerque*). *Phone 505/265-1791.* Horseracing, rodeo, midway; entertainment.

Santa Fe Fiesta (*Santa Fe*). *Sweeney Center. Phone 505/955-6200 or 800/777-2489.* This ancient folk festival, dating to 1712, features historical pageantry, religious observances, arts and crafts shows, street dancing. Celebrates the reconquest of Santa Fe by Don Diego de Vargas in 1692. Make reservations well in advance.

Southern New Mexico State Fair & Rodeo (*Las Cruces*). *Phone 505/524-8612.*

DECEMBER

Christmas Festivals (*Acoma Pueblo*). *San Estevan del Rey Mission, Old Acoma.* Dances, luminarias. Contact Tourist Visitation Center, phone 505/740-4966 or 800/747-0181.

Red Rock Balloon Rally (*Gallup*). Contact Convention & Visitors Bureau, phone 505/863-3841 or 800/242-4282.

---

uninterested in tourists, others are trying to find a way to preserve those aspects of their ancient culture they most value, while taking advantage of what is most beneficial to them in non-Native American culture and ways.

Tourists are welcome at all reservations in New Mexico on most days, although there are various restrictions. Since the religious ceremonies are sacred, photography is generally prohibited. This may also be true of certain sacred areas of the pueblo (in a few cases, the entire pueblo). Sometimes permission to photograph or draw is needed, and fees may be required. The ancient culture and traditions of these people hold great meaning; visitors should be as respectful of them as they would be of their own. Questions should be directed to the pueblo governor or representative at the tribal office.

More can be learned about New Mexico's Native Americans and their origins at the many museums and sites in Santa Fe (see), the visitor center at Bandelier National Monument (see), and the Indian Pueblo Cultural Center (see ALBUQUERQUE). For further information, contact the Office of Indian Affairs, 228 E Palace Ave, Santa Fe 87501; phone 505/827-6440.

When to Go/Climate

Extreme variations in elevation and terrain make New Mexico's weather unpredictable and exciting. One minute the sun may be shining, and the next could bring a cold, wind-whipping thunderstorm. Mountain temperatures can be freezing in winter; summers in the desert are hot and dry.

AVERAGE HIGH/LOW TEMPERATURES (°F)

Albuquerque

Jan 47/22	**May** 80/49	**Sept** 82/55
Feb 54/26	**June** 90/58	**Oct** 71/43
Mar 61/32	**July** 93/64	**Nov** 57/31
Apr 71/40	**Aug** 89/63	**Dec** 48/23

Roswell

Jan 54/25	**May** 85/55	**Sept** 86/59
Feb 60/29	**June** 94/62	**Oct** 77/47
Mar 68/36	**July** 95/67	**Nov** 66/35
Apr 77/45	**Aug** 92/65	**Dec** 56/26

Parks and Recreation

Water-related activities, hiking, riding, various other sports, picnicking, camping and visitor centers are available in many of New Mexico's parks. Most parks are open all year. Day-use fee per vehicle is $4 at most parks. Camping: $8-$10/day; electrical hookups $4 (where available); sewage hookups $4. Limit 14 consecutive days during any 20-day period; pets on leash only. Annual entrance passes and camping permits are available. For further information, contact the New Mexico State Park and Recreation Division, PO Box 1147, Santa Fe 87504-1147; phone 888/NM-PARKS.

FISHING AND HUNTING

New Mexico, with six of the seven life zones found on the North American continent, has a large number of wildlife species, among them four varieties of deer, as well as mountain lion, bear, elk, Rocky Mountain and Desert Bighorn sheep, oryx, antelope, javelina, Barbary sheep, ibex, wild turkey, goose, duck, quail, pheasant, and squirrel. There is good fishing for trout in mountain streams and lakes; bass, bluegill, crappie, walleye, and catfish can also be found in many of the warmer waters.

Nonresident fishing license (includes trout stamp): annual $40; 5-day $17; 1-day $9. Nonresident hunting license: deer $190-$310; bear $160; cougar $210; elk $281-$756; antelope $192; turkey $75. (Fees include $1 vendor fee.)

Hunting and fishing regulations are complex and vary from year to year. For detailed information, contact the New Mexico Game and Fish Department, Villagra Building, 408 Galisteo, Santa Fe 87503; phone 800/862-9310.

Driving Information

Safety belts are mandatory for all persons in the front seat of a vehicle. Children under 11 years must be in an approved passenger restraint anywhere in the vehicle. Children ages 5-10 may use a regulation seat belt. Children ages 1-4 may use a regulation seat belt in the back seat; however, in the front seat they must use an approved safety seat. Babies under age 1 must be in an approved safety seat. For more information, phone 505/827-0427.

INTERSTATE HIGHWAY SYSTEM

The following alphabetical listing of New Mexico towns in this book shows that these cities are within 10 miles of the indicated interstate highways. Check a highway map for the nearest exit.

Highway Number	Cities/Towns within ten miles
Interstate 10	Deming, Las Cruces.
Interstate 25	Albuquerque, Las Cruces, Las Vegas, Raton, Santa Fe, Socorro, Truth or Consequences.
Interstate 40	Albuquerque, Gallup, Grants, Santa Rosa, Tucumari.

Additional Visitor Information

For free information, contact the New Mexico Department of Tourism, Lamy Building, Room 751, 491 Old Santa Fe Trail, Santa Fe 87503; phone 505/827-7400 or 800/733-6396. *New Mexico*, a colorful, illustrated magazine, is published monthly; to order, contact *New Mexico Magazine* at the Lew Wallace Building, 495 Old Santa Fe Trail, Santa Fe 87501; phone 505/827-7447 or 800/435-0715.

There are several welcome centers in New Mexico; visitors who stop by will find information and brochures helpful when planning stops at points of interest. They are located in Anthony (24 miles S of Las Cruces on I-10); Chama (just off US 64/84); Gallup (I-40 exit 22); Glenrio (31 miles E of Tucumcari on I-40); La Bajada (11 miles S of Santa Fe on I-25); Lordsburg (on I-10); Raton (off I-25); Santa Fe (downtown); and Texico (7 miles E of Clovis on US 70/84).

THE WILD (AND NOT SO WILD) WEST

This two- to three-day tour from Las Cruces offers a combination of scenic and technological wonders, hiking and fishing opportunities, and a glimpse into the Wild West. From Las Cruces head northeast on US 70 to White Sands National Monument. This huge beach may lack an ocean, but it offers a seemingly endless expanse of sparkling white gypsum dunes. You'll drive among the dunes along a 16-mile scenic drive, which also provides access to the monument's four hiking trails. Or just take off on foot into the dunes, where kids will have endless hours of fun sliding down the mountains of sand on plastic saucers (available at the monument's gift shop). Visiting the monument is best either early or late in the day, when the dunes display mysterious and often surreal shadows.

Continue northeast on US 70 to Alamogordo, a good spot to spend the night. Attractions here include the Space Center, where you can test your skills as a pilot in a Space Shuttle simulator, explore the International Space Hall of Fame, and see a show at the Tombaugh Omnimax Theater. Also in town is the Alameda Park Zoo and the Toy Train Depot, a museum containing a fascinating collection of toy trains, some dating from the 1800s. The Depot is lots of fun for kids, but its biggest fans are probably baby boomers who reminisce about their childhood trains as they examine the best and sometimes the worst electric trains of the 40s and 50s, including Lionel's tremendous marketing flop—the pink train just for girls. About 12 miles south of Alamogordo via US 54 is Oliver Lee Memorial State Park, with a short, pleasant nature trail along a shaded stream, plus a rugged hiking trail that climbs up the side of a mountain and offers spectacular views. The park also includes the ruins of a pioneer cabin and a museum that tells the story of the site's often violent past.

From Alamogordo, go north on US 54 to Tularosa, where you can visit Tularosa Vineyards to sample the local wine and stop at the small but interesting Tularosa Basin Historical Society Museum. Then head east on US 70 up into the Sacramento Mountains to the resort community of Ruidoso, whose name (Spanish for "noisy") comes from the babbling Ruidoso Creek. Surrounded by the Lincoln National Forest, this picturesque town is a good base for hiking and fishing and is another possibility for overnight lodging. Nearby is the village of Ruidoso Downs, home of Ruidoso Downs Race Track, which offers quarter horse and thoroughbred racing, and the Hubbard Museum of the American West, with displays on horses, horse racing, and related items. Head east out of Ruidoso Downs to Hondo, then turn back to the northwest on US 380, which leads to Lincoln. This genuine Wild West town, which is preserved as a state monument, was the site of a jail break by famed outlaw Billy the Kid. It's also known for the notorious Lincoln County War, in which ranchers and merchants staged a lengthy and bloody battle for beef contracts for a nearby fort.

Continue west on US 380 to the town of Capitan for a visit to Smokey Bear Historical State Park, with exhibits and the grave of the orphaned bear cub who was found in a forest fire near here and became a symbol of forest fire prevention. Leaving Capitan, drive west on US 380 to the town of Carrizozo and cross US 54. Continue four miles to Valley of Fires National Recreation Site, where a short trail provides close-up views of numerous jet-black lava formations. Now return to Carrizozo and head south on US 54 to the turnoff to Three Rivers Petroglyph Site, one of the best places in the Southwest to see prehistoric rock art. An easy trail meanders along a hillside where there are thousands of images, ranging from geometric patterns to handprints to a variety of animals (some pierced by arrows or spears) created by the Mogollon people at least 1,000 years ago. To return to Las Cruces, take US 54 south through Tularosa and Alamogordo; turn southwest on US 70. **(Approximately 349 miles)**

Acoma Pueblo

See also Albuquerque, Grants

Pop 4,000 **Elev** 7,000 ft

Information Tourist Visitation Center, PO Box 309, Acoma 87034; 505/740-4966 or 800/747-0181

On a mesa rising 367 feet from the surrounding plain is perhaps the oldest continuously inhabited town in the United States. The exact date of establishment is not known, but archaeologists have dated occupation of the "Sky City" to at least 1150. Legend says it has been inhabited since the time of Christ.

Acoma is a beautiful pueblo with the mission church San Esteban del Rey. This mission probably includes part of the original built by Fray Ramirez in 1629. Beams 40 feet long and 14 inches square were carried from the mountains 30 miles away; even the dirt for the graveyard was carried up by Native Americans. They farmed on the plain below and caught water in rock basins on top. The Acoma are skilled potters and excellent stockbreeders.

The pueblo is about 12 miles south of I-40 and is accessible from exit 102. Tours leave from the base of the pueblo at the Visitor Center, where a shuttle bus takes visitors to the pueblo on top of the mesa (fee). Visitors may walk down the steep, narrow "stairway" to the Visitor Center after the tour.

There is a museum with Native American pottery and history exhibits (circa 1400 to the present). (Daily) **FREE**

Acoma-made crafts, native foods, tours, and a cultural and historical exhibit can be seen at the Visitor Center below Sky City.

Once or twice a year special religious ceremonials are held at which no outsiders are permitted, but there are several festivals (see SPECIAL EVENTS) to which the public is welcome. (Daily; closed pueblo holidays, mid-July, and first or second weekend in October) Your guide will explain the rules and courtesies of taking pictures (picture-taking fee; no video or movie cameras).

Approximately one mile north on NM 23 is the Enchanted Mesa, 400 feet high. According to an Acoma legend, the tribe lived on top of this mesa until a sudden, violent storm washed out the only way up. Visitors are not permitted to climb to the mesa.

Special Events

Christmas Festivals. *I-40 W and Acoma Pueblo exit. San Estevan del Rey Mission, Old Acoma. Phone 800/766-4405.* Dances, luminarias. Late Dec.

Feast of St. Estevan. *Old Acoma.* Harvest dance. Early Sept.

Fiesta (St. Lorenzo's) Day. *Acomita.* Mid-Aug.

Governor's Feast. *Old Acoma.* Dances. Early Feb.

Santa Maria Feast. *I-40 W and Acoma Pueblo exit. McCarty's Village Mission. Phone 800/766-4405.* First Sun in May.

Alamogordo (G-4)

See also Cloudcroft, Mescalero, Ruidoso

Founded 1898 **Pop** 35,582 **Elev** 4,350 ft **Area code** 505 **Zip** 88310

Information Chamber of Commerce, 1301 N White Sands Blvd, PO Box 518; 505/437-6120 or 800/826-0294

Web www.alamogordo.com

Alamogordo is a popular tourist destination because of its proximity to Mescalero Apache Indian Reservation, Lincoln National Forest, and White Sands National Monument. A branch of New Mexico State University is located here. Surrounded by desert and mountains, Alamogordo is the home of Holloman AFB and the 49th Fighter Wing, home of the Stealth fighter. The first atomic bomb was set off nearby.

What to See and Do

Alameda Park Zoo. *1021 N White Sands Blvd (US 54/70). Phone 505/439-4290.* A 7-acre zoo with more than 300 native and exotic animals. (Daily; closed Jan 1, Dec 25) **$$**

Lincoln National Forest. *3496 Hwy 82. E of town. Phone 505/434-7200.* Fishing; hunting, picnicking, camping, wild cave tours, and winter sports in the Sacramento, Capitan, and Guadalupe mountains. Backpack in the White Mountain Capitan Wildernesses. Some campsites in developed areas free, some require fee. Contact the Supervisor's Office, Federal Building, 1101 New York Ave.

⭐ **New Mexico Museum of Space History.** *New Mexico Hwy 2001. 2 miles E via US 54, Indian Wells and Scenic Dr. Phone 505/437-2840; toll-free 877/333-6589.* Museum features space-related artifacts and exhibits; self-guided tour (daily; closed Dec 25). Combination ticket includes

Tombaugh IMAX Theater. *Hwy 2001.* Planetarium with Omnimax movies (daily). Features laser light shows (Fri, Sat evenings). **$$$**

Oliver Lee State Park. *US 54 S and Dog Canyon Rd. 10 miles S via US 54, E on County A16. Phone 505/437-8284.* (Dog Canyon) Mecca for mountain climbers, photographers, and history buffs. Early Apache stronghold, site of at least five major battles; box canyon protected by 2,000-foot bluff; mossy bluffs, cottonwood trees; Frenchy's Place, a substantial rock house with miles of stone fence. Hiking, camping (hookups, dump station). Visitor center (daily), museum, tours of restored Lee Ranch House (Sat and Sun, mid-afternoon; also by appointment). **$$$**

Three Rivers Petroglyph Site. *29 miles N on US 54 to Three Rivers, then 5 miles E on county road. Phone 505/ 525-4300.* Twenty thousand rock carvings made between A.D. 900-1400 by the Jornada Branch of the Mogollon Indian Culture; semidesert terrain; interpretive signs; reconstructed prehistoric village; six picnic sites; tent and trailer sites (no hookups). **$$**

Toy Train Depot. *1991 N White Sands Blvd, N end of Alameda Park. Phone 888/207-3564.* Over 1,200 ft of model railroad track and hundreds of model and toy trains are on display in five-room, 100-year-old train depot. Also 2-mile outdoor miniature railroad track (rides). Gift and model shop. (Wed-Sun) **$**

Special Events

New Mexico Museum of Space History Induction Ceremonies. *Top of New Mexico Highway 2001 (88310). Phone 505/437-2840 or 877/333-6589.* Call for schedule.

Trinity Site Tour. *1301 N White Sands Blvd. Phone 505/ 437-6120.* Visit the site of the first A-bomb explosion; only time the site is open to the public. Phone 800/826- 0294. First Sat in Apr and Oct.

Motels/Motor Lodges

★ **BEST WESTERN DESERT AIRE HOTEL.** *1021 S White Sands Blvd (88310). Phone 505/437-2110; toll-free 800/780-7234; fax 505/437-1898. www.bestwestern.com.* 100 rooms, 2 story. S $47-$57; D $58; under 16 free. Pet accepted, some restrictions. Complimentary continental breakfast. Check-out noon. TV. Sauna. Game room. Whirlpool. Cr cds: A, C, D, DS, MC, V.

★ **COMFORT INN & SUITES.** *1020 S White Sands Blvd (88310). Phone 505/434-4200; fax 505/437-8872. www.nmohwy.com.* 16 suites, 2 story. S $42-$54; D $50- $65; each additional $5; suites $55; under 12 free. Complimentary continental breakfast. Check-out noon. TV; cable (premium). Whirlpool. Cr cds: A, C, D, DS, JCB, MC, V.

★ **DAYS INN.** *907 S White Sands Blvd (88310). Phone 505/437-5090; toll-free 800/329-7466; fax 505/434- 5667. www.daysinn.com.* 120 rooms, 2 story. S $38-$65;

D $46-$52; each additional $8. Complimentary continental breakfast. Check-out noon. TV; cable (premium). Pool. Cr cds: A, C, D, DS, ER, JCB, MC, V.

★ **SATELLITE INN.** *2224 N White Sands Blvd (88310). Phone 505/437-8454; toll-free 800/221-7690. www.satelliteinn.com.* 40 rooms, 1-2 story. S $32-$34; D $34-$38; each additional $2; kitchen unit $38-$46; family unit $36-$42. Crib free. Pet accepted. Check-out noon. TV; cable (premium), VCR available (movies). Refrigerators, microwaves available. Restaurant adjacent 6 am-9 pm. Pool. Cr cds: A, C, D, DS, MC, V.

Restaurant

★ **CHINA WEST.** *905 S White Sands Blvd (88310). Phone 505/437-8644.* Chinese menu. Specializes in seafood, chicken, beef. Hours: 11 am-9 pm. Reservations accepted. Bar. Lunch $3.95-$6.95, dinner $9.95-$22.95. Chinese decor. Cr cds: A, D, DS, MC, V.

Albuquerque (D-3)

Founded 1706 **Pop** 448,607 **Elev** 5,311 ft **Area code** 505

Information Convention & Visitors Bureau, 20 First Plaza NW, PO Box 26866, 87125; 505/842-9918 or 800/284- 2282

Web www.abqcvb.org

In 1706 Don Francisco Cuervo y Valdés, then governor of New Mexico, moved 30 families from Bernalillo to a spot some 15 miles south on the Rio Grande where there was better pasturage. He named this community after the Duke of Alburquerque, then Viceroy of New Spain. With a nice sense of diplomatic delicacy, the Viceroy renamed it San Felipe de Alburquerque (the first "r" was dropped later), in limited deference to King Philip V of Spain. He also named one of the first structures, a church (still standing), San Felipe de Nerí.

The pasturage proved good, and by 1790, the population grew to almost 6,000 (a very large city for New Mexico at the time). Today Albuquerque is the largest city in New Mexico.

Albuquerque was an important US military outpost from 1846 to 1870. In 1880, when a landowner near the Old Town refused to sell, the Santa Fe Railroad chose a route 2 miles east, forming a new town called New Albuquerque. It was not long before the new town had enveloped what is still called "Old Town," now a popular tourist shopping area.

Surrounded by mountains, Albuquerque continues to grow. The largest industry is Sandia National Laboratories, a laboratory engaged in solar and nuclear research and the testing and development of nuclear weapons. More than 100 firms are engaged in electronics manufacturing and research and development.

Dry air and plentiful sunshine (76 percent of the time) have earned Albuquerque a reputation as a health center. Adding to that reputation is the Lovelace Medical Center (similar to the Mayo Clinic in Rochester, Minnesota), which gave the first US astronauts their qualifying examinations. The University of New Mexico is also located in Albuquerque.

Additional Visitor Information

For further information and a list of sightseeing tours, contact the Convention & Visitors Bureau, 20 First Plaza NW, phone 505/842-9918 or toll-free 800/284-2282. For information about public transportation, phone 505/843-9200.

What to See and Do

Albuquerque Biological Park. *2601 Central Ave NW. Phone 505/764-6200.* Biological park consists of the Albuquerque Aquarium, the Rio Grande Botanic Garden, and the Rio Grande Zoo. The aquarium features a shark tank, eel tunnel, and shrimp boat. The Botanic Gardens displays formal walled gardens and a glass conservatory. The zoo exhibits include koalas, polar bears, sea lions, and other animals and features a variety of shows. (Daily 9 am-5 pm, until 6 pm in summer; closed Jan 1, Thanksgiving, Dec 25)

Albuquerque Little Theatre. *124 San Pasquale Ave SW (87104). Phone 505/242-4750.* Historic community theater troupe stages Broadway productions. Aug-May.

Albuquerque Museum. *2000 Mountain Rd NW (87103). Phone 505/243-7255.* Regional museum of art and history; traveling exhibits; solar-heated building. Across the street from the New Mexico Museum of Natural History and Science (See also). (Tues-Sun 9 am-5 pm; closed Mon, holidays) **$$**

Cibola National Forest. *2113 Osuna Rd NE (87113). Phone 505/346-3900.* More than 1 1/2 million acres located throughout central New Mexico. The park includes Mount Taylor (11,301 feet), several mountain ranges, and four wilderness areas: Sandia Mountain, Manzano Mountain, Apache Kid, and Withington. Scenic drives;

bighorn sheep in Sandia Mountains. Fishing; hunting, picnicking, and camping (some fees). La Cienega Nature Trail is for the disabled and visually impaired.

Coronado State Monument. *485 Kuaua Rd (87004). 15 miles N on I-25, then 1 mile W on NM 44. Phone 505/867-5351.* Coronado is said to have camped near this excavated pueblo in 1540 on his famous but unsuccessful quest for the seven golden cities of Cibola. Reconstructed, painted kiva; visitor center devoted to Southwestern culture and the Spanish influence on the area. Picnicking. (Wed-Mon 8:30 am-5 pm; closed Tues, holidays) **$**

Indian Pueblo Cultural Center. *2401 12th St NW (87192). 1 block N of I-40. Phone 505/843-7270.* Owned and operated by the 19 pueblos of New Mexico. Exhibits in the museum tell the story of the Pueblo culture; Pueblo Gallery showcasing handcrafted art; Native American dance and craft demonstrations (weekends). Restaurant. (Daily; closed holidays) **$**

Isleta Pueblo. *1905 Mountain Rd. Phone 505/869-3111.* (Population 1,703; altitude 4,885 feet) A prosperous pueblo with a church originally built by Fray Juan de Salas. The church was burned during the Pueblo Rebellion of 1680 and later rebuilt; beautiful sanctuary and altar. Recreation area 4 miles NE across the river includes stocked fishing lakes (fee); picnicking, camping (electricity, water available, two-week limit), concession. Pueblo (daily). **$$**

National Atomic Museum. *1905 Mountain Rd NW. Phone 505/245-2137.* This nuclear energy science center, the nation's only such museum, features exhibits depicting the history of the atomic age, including the Manhattan Project, the Cold War, and the development of nuclear medicine. Replicas of Little Boy and Fat Man, the world's first two atomic weapons deployed in Japan in World War II, fascinate visitors, as do the museum's outdoor exhibits of rockets, missiles, and B-52 and B-29 aircraft. Guided tours and audiovisual presentations are also offered. (Daily 9 am-5 pm; closed holidays) **$**

New Mexico Museum of Natural History and Science. *1801 Mountain Rd NW (87104). Phone 505/841-2800.* Fans of dinosaurs, fossils, volcanoes, and the like will love this museum, with exhibits on botany, geology, paleontology, and zoology. The LodeStar Astronomy Center gives museum-goers a view of the heavens in its observatory. Also on site are a naturalist center, the "Extreme Screen" DynaTheater, and a cafe. (Daily 9 am-5 pm; closed holidays) **$**

⭐ **Old Town.** *Old Town and Romero rds.* The original settlement is 1 block N of Central Ave, the city's main street, at Rio Grande Blvd. Old Town Plaza retains a lovely Spanish flavor with many interesting shops and restaurants.

Rio Grande Nature Center State Park. *2901 Candelaria Rd NW. E bank of Rio Grande. Phone 505/344-7240.* Glass-enclosed observation room overlooking a 3-acre pond that is home to birds and other wildlife, interpretive displays on the wildlife of the bosque (cottonwood groves) along the Rio Grande, 2 miles of nature trails. Guided hikes, hands-on activities. (Daily 8 am-5 pm; closed Jan 1, Thanksgiving, Dec 25) **$**

Rio Grande Zoo. *903 Tenth St SW. Phone 505/764-6200.* More than 1,200 exotic animals in exhibits among a grove of cottonwoods. Rain forest, reptile house, Ape Country, Cat Walk, white tigers. (Daily 9 am-5 pm, until 6 pm in summer; closed Jan 1, Thanksgiving, Dec 25) **$$**

Sandia Peak Tramway Ski Area. *10 Tramway Loop NE (87122). 16 miles E on I-40, then 7 miles N on NM 14, then 6 miles NW on NM 536, in Cibola National Forest, Crest Scenic Byway, Sandia Mountains. Phone 505/242-9133.* Area has four double chairlifts, surface lift; patrol, school, rentals, snowmaking, cafe, restaurant, bar. Aerial tramway on the west side of the mountain meets lifts at the top. Longest run is over 2 1/2 miles; vertical drop 1,700 feet. (Mid-Dec-Mar, daily.) Chairlift also operates July-Labor Day (Fri-Sun; fee). **$$$$**

Sandia Peak Aerial Tramway. *10 Tramway Loop NE (87122). 5 miles NE of city limits via I-25 and Tramway Rd. Phone 505/856-7325.* From the base at 6,559 feet, the tram travels almost 3 miles up the west slope of the Sandia Mountains to 10,378 feet, with amazing 11,000-square-mile views. Hiking trail, restaurant at summit, and Mexican grill at base. (Daily 9 am-9 pm in summer, shorter hours rest of year; closed two weeks in Apr and two weeks in Oct) **$$$$**

Telephone Pioneer Museum. *110 4th St NW. Phone 505/842-2937.* Displays trace the development of the telephone from 1876 to the present. More than 400 types of telephones, plus switchboards, early equipment, and old telephone directories, are available for viewing. (Mon-Fri 10 am-2 pm; weekends by appointment; closed holidays) **$**

University of New Mexico. *Central Ave and University Blvd. E of I-25, Central Ave exit. Contact the Visitor Center at the corner of Las Lomas and Redondo sts. Phone 505/277-1989.* (1889) 25,000 students. This campus shows both Spanish and Pueblo architectural influences. It is one of the largest universities in the Southwest. Special outdoor sports course for the disabled, N of Johnson Gym. On campus are

Fine Arts Center. *Just NW of university's Stanford Dr and Central Ave main entrance. Phone 505/277-4001.* Houses the University Art Museum, which features more than 23,000 pieces in its collection (Tues-Fri, also Sun afternoons; free); the Fine Arts Library, which contains the Southwest Music Archives; the Rodey

Theatre; and the 2,094-seat Popejoy Hall, home of the New Mexico Symphony Orchestra and host of the Best of Broadway International Theatre seasons of plays, dance, and music (phone 505/277-2111).

Jonson Gallery. *1909 Las Lomas NE (87131). Phone 505/277-4967.* This gallery, owned by the University of New Mexico and part of its art museums, houses the archives and work of modernist painter Raymond Jonson (1891-1982) and a few works by his contemporaries. Also has exhibitions on the arts in New Mexico. (Tues 9 am-8 pm, Wed-Fri 9 am-4 pm; closed Mon, weekends, holidays) **DONATION**

Maxwell Museum of Anthropology. *University Blvd and Central Ave (87131). Redondo Dr, in Anthropology Building. Phone 505/277-4405.* Permanent and changing exhibits of early man and Native American cultures with an emphasis on the Southwest. (Tues-Fri 9 am-4 pm, Sat 10 am-4 pm; closed Sun, Mon, holidays) **FREE**

Museum of Geology and Institute of Meteoritics Meteorite Museum. *200 Yale Blvd NE. Part of Earth and Planetary Science Dept, in Northrop Hall. Phone 505/277-4204.* The Museum of Geology contains numerous samples of ancient plants, minerals, rocks, and animals. The Meteorite Museum has a major collection of more than 550 meteorites. Both museums are part of the University of New Mexico. (Mon-Fri 9 am-4 pm; closed weekends, holidays) **DONATION**

Special Events

Albuquerque International Balloon Fiesta. *4401 Alameda Pl NE (87103). Phone 505/821-1000; toll-free 888/422-7277.* As many as 100,000 people attend this annual event, the largest of its kind in the world, that fills Albuquerque's blue skies with rainbows of color. Attendees can catch their own balloon rides from Rainbow Ryders, Inc. (Phone 505/823-1111). First Sat in Oct through the following Sun.

Founders Day. *In Old Town. Phone 505/768-3483.* Celebrates the city's founding in 1706 with traditional New Mexican festivities. Late Apr.

Musical Theater Southwest. *4804 Central Ave SE (87108). Phone 505/262-9301.* This troupe produces five Broadway-style musicals each season at the historic Hiland Theater in the Frank A. Peloso Performing Arts Center.

New Mexico Arts & Crafts Fair. *5500 San Mateo NE (87109). At the New Mexico State Fairgrounds. Phone 505/884-9043.* Exhibits and demonstrations by craftsworkers representing Spanish, Native American, and other North American cultures. Artists sell their wares, which range from paintings to sculpture to jewelry. Last weekend in June.

New Mexico State Fair. *300 San Pedro NE. Fairgrounds, San Pedro Dr between Lomas and Central blvds. Phone 505/265-1791.* Horse shows and racing, rodeo, midway, flea market; entertainment. Sept.

New Mexico Symphony Orchestra. *3301 Menaul Blvd NE (87190). Phone 505/881-9590; toll-free 800/251-NMSO.* Concerts in Popejoy Hall on the University of New Mexico campus. Sept-May.

Santa Ana Feast Day. *2401 12th St NW. Santa Ana and Taos Pueblos.* Corn dance. Late July.

St. Augustin's Feast Day. Dances at Isleta Pueblo. Late Aug.

Motels/Motor Lodges

★ ★ **BEST WESTERN RIO RANCHO INN AND CONFERENCE CENTER.** *1465 Rio Rancho Blvd (87124). Phone 505/892-1700; toll-free 800/658-9558; fax 505/892-4628. www.innatriorancho.com.* 121 rooms, 10 kitchen units. S $55-$73; D $61-$79; each additional $6; kitchen units $61-$67; under 12 free. Crib $6. Pet accepted, some restrictions; $6/day. Check-out 11 am. TV; cable (premium). In-room modem link. Some in-room whirlpools. Microwaves available. Coffee in rooms. Valet services, coin laundry. Restaurant 6:30 am-10 pm. Bar 11 am-midnight; Sun noon-midnight, entertainment. Room service. Exercise equipment. Pool, whirlpool, poolside service. Golf privileges, greens fee, pro, putting green, driving range. Downhill, cross-country ski 20 miles. Picnic tables, grills. Lawn games. Free airport, train, bus depot transportation. Meeting rooms. Business services. Sundries. Gift shop. Cr cds: A, C, D, DS, ER, MC, V.

★ **BEST WESTERN WINROCK INN.** *18 NE Winrock Ctr (87110). Phone 505/883-5252; toll-free 800/780-7234; fax 505/889-3206. www.bestwestern.com.* 173 rooms, 2 story. S, D $69-$99; each additional $10; suites $125; under 18 free. Complimentary breakfast buffet. Check-out noon. TV. Health club privileges. Cr cds: A, C, D, DS, MC, V.

★ **CLUBHOUSE INN.** *1315 Menaul Blvd NE (87107). Phone 505/345-0010; fax 505/344-3911. www.clubhouseinn.com.* 137 units, 17 kitchen suites, 2 story. S $74; D $84; each additional $10; kitchen suites $89-$105; under 16 free; weekly, weekend rates. Complimentary breakfast buffet. Check-out noon. TV; cable (premium). Health club privileges. Whirlpool. Cr cds: A, C, D, DS, MC, V.

★ **COMFORT INN EAST.** *13031 Central Ave NE (87123). Phone 505/294-1800; toll-free 800/748-3278; fax 505/293-1088. www.comfortinn.com.* 122 rooms, 2 story.

May-mid-Sept: S $49-$57; D $55-$63; each additional $6; under 18 free. Crib free. Pet accepted; $3/day. Complimentary full breakfast. Complimentary coffee in rooms. Check-out noon. TV; cable (premium). Refrigerators. Coin laundry. Restaurant 6-10 am, 5-8:30 pm; Sat, Sun 6-11 am, 5-8:30 pm. Pool; whirlpools. Downhill ski 9 miles. Picnic area. Meeting rooms. Business services. Cr cds: A, C, D, DS, JCB, MC, V.

★ ★ **COURTYARD BY MARRIOTT.** *1920 S Yale Blvd (87106). Phone 505/843-6600; toll-free 800/321-2211; fax 505/843-8740. www.courtyard.com.* 150 rooms, 4 story. S $61-$94; D $104; suites $115-$125; under 12 free; weekend rates. Crib free. TV; cable (premium). Indoor pool; whirlpool. Complimentary coffee in rooms. Restaurant 6 am-10 am, 5-10 pm; Sat, Sun 7 am-11 am. Room service. Bar 4-11 pm. Check-out noon. Meeting rooms. Business services available. In-room modem link. Valet service. Free airport transportation. Downhill/cross-country ski 15 miles. Exercise equipment. Refrigerator in suites. Balconies. Picnic tables. Cr cds: A, C, D, DS, JCB, MC, V.

★ **DAYS INN EAST.** *13317 NE Central Ave (87123). Phone 505/294-3297; toll-free 800/329-7466; fax 505/293-3973. www.daysinn.com.* 72 rooms, 2 story. S $52-$60; D $55-$65; each additional $5; under 12 free. Crib free. Check-out 11 am. TV; cable (premium). Restaurant adjacent open 24 hours. Sauna. Indoor pool, whirlpool. Business services. Cr cds: A, C, D, DS, ER, JCB, MC, V.

★ **DAYS INN WEST.** *6031 Iliff Rd NW (87123). Phone 505/836-3297; toll-free 800/329-7466; fax 505/836-1214. www.daysinn.com.* 80 rooms, 2 story. June-Oct: S $55-$75; D $60-$80; each additional $5; under 12 free. Pet accepted; $5/day. Complimentary continental breakfast. Check-out 11 am. TV; cable (premium). Guest laundry. Restaurant nearby. Sauna. Heated indoor pool; whirlpool. Downhill, cross-country ski 10 miles. Business services. Cr cds: A, C, D, DS, JCB, MC, V.

★ **HAMPTON INN.** *5101 Ellison NE (87109). Phone 505/344-1555; toll-free 800/426-7866; fax 505/345-2216. www.hamptoninn.com.* 125 rooms, 3 story. S $57-$62; D $62-$67; under 18 free. Crib free. Pet accepted, some restrictions. TV; cable (premium). Heated pool. Complimentary continental breakfast, coffee in rooms. Restaurant nearby. Check-out noon. Coin laundry. Health club privileges. Cr cds: A, C, D, DS, JCB, MC, V.

★ **HOLIDAY INN EXPRESS.** *10330 Hotel Ave NE (87123). Phone 505/275-8900; toll-free 800/465-4329; fax 505/275-6000. www.holidayinnexpress.com.* 104 rooms, 2 story. S $75; D $84; each additional $5; suites $95-$100; under 18 free; higher rates during special events. Crib free. Pet accepted; $5. Complimentary continental breakfast. Complimentary coffee in rooms. Check-out noon. TV; cable (premium), VCR available. In-room modem link. Balconies. Some in-room whirlpools. Microwaves, refrigerators, bathroom phones. Coin laundry. Restaurant 5 am-10 pm. Room service. Exercise equipment, sauna. Indoor pool, whirlpool. Downhill/cross-country ski 15 miles. Meeting rooms. Business services. Cr cds: A, D, DS, JCB, MC, V.

[D] [icons]

★ ★ ★ **HOLIDAY INN MOUNTAIN VIEW.** I-40 and I-25. 2020 Menaul NE (87107). Phone 505/884-2511; fax 505/884-5720. www.holiday-inn.com. This full-service hotel offers guests every service they may need. Parents can play virtual golf at the Sandia Springs golf course lounge, which features two full-swing golf simulators, while the kids play in the indoor pool and hot tub. 360 rooms, 4-5 story. S, D $99-$109; each additional $10; under 18 free. Crib free. Pet accepted; $25. Check-out noon. TV; cable (premium). Some private patios, balconies. Coffee in rooms. Valet services, coin laundry. Restaurant 6:30 am-2 pm, 5-10 pm. Bar 1 pm-1 am; Sun 11 am-midnight. Room service. Exercise equipment, sauna. Heated pool, whirlpool, poolside service. Downhill ski 15 miles. Free airport transportation. Meeting rooms, business services. Bellstaff. Sundries. Cr cds: A, D, DS, JCB, MC, V.

[D] [icons]

★ **HOWARD JOHNSON EXPRESS INN.** 411 Mcknight Ave NW (87102). Phone 505/242-5228; toll-free 800/446-4656; fax 505/766-9218. www.hojo.com. 100 rooms, 4 story. S $44-$62; D $49-$79; each additional $4; suites $57.59-$93.89; under 18 free. Crib free. Complimentary continental breakfast. Check-out noon. TV; cable (premium). Some minibars. Restaurant adjacent open 24 hrs; Sun to 11 pm. Heated pool, whirlpool. Meeting room. Business services. Cr cds: A, D, DS, JCB, MC, V.

[D] [icons] SC

★ **HOWARD JOHNSON INN.** 15 Hotel Cir NE (87123). Phone 505/296-4852; toll-free 800/446-4656; fax 505/293-9072. www.hojo.com. 150 rooms, 2 story. S, D $48-$88; each additional $5; under 18 free. Crib free. Complimentary continental breakfast. Complimentary coffee in rooms. Check-out noon. TV; cable (premium). In-room modem link. Some refrigerators, whirlpool suites. Valet services, coin laundry. Restaurant 6 am-10 pm. Room service. Exercise equipment. Heated pool, whirlpool. Free airport, train, bus depot transportation. Business services. Bellstaff. Cr cds: A, C, D, DS, ER, MC, V.

[D] [icons]

★ **LA QUINTA INN.** 2116 Yale Blvd SE (87106). Phone 505/243-5500; toll-free 800/531-5900; fax 505/247-8288. www.laquinta.com. 105 rooms, 3 story. S $69; D $75; each additional $7; suites $99; under 18 free. Crib free. Pet accepted, some restrictions. TV; cable (premium). Pool. Continental breakfast. Restaurant adjacent 6 am-10 pm. Check-out noon. Coin laundry. Business services available. Valet service. Free airport transportation. Downhill ski 20 miles. Microwave in suites. Cr cds: A, C, D, DS, MC, V.

[D] [icons] SC

★ **LE BARON COURTYARD AND SUITES.** 2120 Menaul Blvd NE (87107). Phone 505/884-0250; fax 505/883-0594. www.lebaronabq.com. 200 units, 33 suites, 2 story. S, D $55-$64; suites $76-$135; under 12 free. Complimentary continental breakfast. Check-out noon. TV; cable (premium). Downhill ski 15 miles. Free airport transportation. Cr cds: A, C, D, DS, MC, V.

[icons]

★ ★ **PLAZA INN.** 900 Medical Arts NE (87102). Phone 505/243-5693; toll-free 800/237-1307; fax 505/843-6229. www.plazainnabq.com. 120 rooms, 5 story. S, D $85-$117; each additional $10; under 18 free. Pet accepted. TV. Indoor pool; whirlpools. Restaurant 6 am-midnight. Bar 11-2 am; Sun noon-midnight. Check-out noon. Coin laundry. Meeting rooms. Business services available. Valet service. Free airport, train station, bus depot transportation. Downhill ski 14 miles. Exercise equipment. Health club privileges. Some refrigerators. Private patios, balconies. Cr cds: A, C, D, DS, JCB, MC, V.

[D] [icons]

★ ★ **RAMADA INN MOUNTAINVIEW.** 25 Hotel Cir NE (87123). Phone 505/271-1000; toll-free 888/298-2054; fax 505/291-9028. www.ramada.com. 205 rooms, 2 story. S $49-$85; D $59-$95; each additional $10; suites $89-$150; under 18 free; weekend rates. Crib free. Pet accepted. TV; cable (premium). Coffee in rooms. Heated pool. Restaurant 6 am-2 pm, 5-10 pm. Room service. Bar 2 pm-midnight; Sun from 1 pm. Check-out noon. Coin laundry. Meeting rooms. Business services available. Valet service. Free airport transportation. Downhill ski 10 miles. Refrigerators, microwaves. Cr cds: A, C, D, DS, JCB, MC, V.

[D] [icons] SC

★ **RAMADA LIMITED.** 1801 Yale Blvd SE (87106). Phone 505/242-0036; toll-free 888/298-2054; fax 505/242-0068. www.ramada.com. 76 rooms, 12 suites, 3 story. Apr-Oct: S $55-$95; D $65-$105; each additional $10; suites $99-$105; under 18 free; weekend rates; higher rates during special events; lower rates rest of year. Complimentary continental breakfast, coffee in rooms. Check-out 11 am. TV; cable. In-room modem link. Laundry services.

Exercise equipment, sauna. 2 pools, 1 indoor; whirlpool. Downhill- cross-country ski 20 miles. Free airport transportation. Cr cds: A, C, D, DS, JCB, MC, V.

[D] [⚡] [≈] [🏋] [✈] [⛷] [SC]

★ **TRAMWAY TRAVELODGE.** *13139 Central Ave NE (87123). Phone 505/292-4878; toll-free 800/515-6375; fax 505/299-1822. www.travelodge.com.* 41 rooms, 2 story. May-Dec: S, D $40-$60; each additional $5; under 17 free; lower rates rest of year. Crib free. Pet accepted, some restrictions; $5. TV; cable (premium). Complimentary continental breakfast. Complimentary coffee in rooms. Restaurant nearby. Check-out 11 am. Business services available. Downhill/cross-country ski 8 miles. Cr cds: A, C, D, DS, MC, V.

[D] [🐾] [⚡] [≈]

★★ **WYNDHAM GARDEN.** *6000 Pan American Fwy NE (87109). Phone 505/798-4300; toll-free 800/996-3426; fax 505/798-4305. www.wyndham.com.* 150 rooms, 5 story. S $69-$135; D $69-$145; each additional $10; under 18 free. Crib free. TV; cable. Indoor/outdoor pool; whirlpool. Coffee in rooms. Restaurant 6:30 am-2 pm, 5-10 pm. Room service. Bar 4 pm-midnight. Check-out noon. Meeting rooms. Business services available. Coin laundry. Exercise equipment. Some balconies. Cr cds: A, C, D, DS, MC, V.

[D] [⚡] [≈] [🏋] [✈] [⛷]

Hotels

★★★ **CROWNE PLAZA HOTEL.** *5151 San Francisco Rd NE (87109). Phone 505/821-3333; toll-free 800/227-6963; fax 505/828-0230. www.crowneplaza.com.* Located in Journal Center, the city's newest business complex, this pyramid-shaped hotel offers services for leisure and business travelers alike. The fitness center, indoor and outdoor pools, and hot tub are great for relaxation. The guest rooms feature dual phone lines with dataports, in-room coffee, high-speed Internet access, and Nintendo games. 311 units, 74 suites, 10 story. S, D $132-$152; each additional $20; suites $143-$275; under 18 free. Crib free. TV; cable (premium). Indoor/outdoor pool; whirlpool, poolside service. Coffee in rooms. Restaurant 6 am-10 pm. Bar 11-2 am. Check-out noon. Convention facilities. Business center. In-room modem link. Concierge. Shopping arcade. Downhill ski 8 miles. Exercise equipment. Some refrigerators. Private patios. Atrium lobby; waterfall. Luxury level. Cr cds: A, C, D, DS, JCB, MC, V.

[⛷] [≈] [🏋] [✈] [⛷]

★★ **DOUBLETREE HOTEL ALBUQUERQUE.** *201 Marquette NW (87102). Phone 505/247-3344; toll-free 888/222-4335; fax 505/247-7025. www.doubletree.com.* Connected to the Albuquerque Convention Center, this property is located in the heart of downtown. Guest rooms feature in-room coffee, dataports, work desks,

and hairdryers. Many suites offer views of the Sandia Mountains. Guests will enjoy the outdoor pool and fitness center. 295 rooms, 15 story. S, D $125-$145; each additional $10; suites $140-$475; under 18 free. Crib free. TV; cable (premium). Pool. Restaurant 6 am-10 pm. Bar 11:30-2 am; Sun from noon. Check-out noon. Convention facilities. Business services available. Gift shop. Downhill ski 15 miles. Exercise equipment. Health club privileges. Cr cds: A, C, D, DS, ER, JCB, MC, V.

[D] [⚡] [≈] [🏋] [⛷] [≈] [SC]

★★ **HILTON.** *1901 University NE (87102). Phone 505/884-2500; toll-free 800/932-3322; fax 505/880-1196. www.hilton.com.* With its arched doorways, Indian rugs, and local art, the Southwest comes alive in this conveniently located property. Guests will enjoy the indoor and outdoor heated pools, sauna, hot tubs, and lighted tennis courts. Accommodations feature two-line phones, dataports, in-room coffee and premium cable. 264 rooms, 12 story. S $89-139; D $99-$149; each additional $10; suites $395-$495; under 18 free. Check-out noon. TV; cable (premium). In-room modem link. Laundry services. Restaurant 6 am-11 pm. Bar 11-1 am; entertainment. Exercise equipment, sauna. Indoor pool, whirlpool, poolside service. Outdoor tennis. Downhill ski 15 miles. Business center. Concierge, luxury level. Cr cds: A, C, D, DS, ER, JCB, MC, V.

[D] [⚡] [🎾] [≈] [🏋] [⛷] [SC] [✈]

★★ **THE HOTEL BLUE.** *717 NW Central Ave (87102). Phone 505/294-2400; fax 505/924-2465. www.thehotelblue.com.* 135 rooms, 10 suites, 6 story. May-Oct: S $60-$70; D $65-$75; each additional $5; suites $75-$85; under 18 free; higher rates special events. Crib free. TV; cable (premium). Pool. Complimentary continental breakfast. Complimentary coffee in rooms. Restaurant 7 am-9 pm. Room service. Bar. Check-out noon. Meeting rooms. Business services available. In-room modem link. Bellstaff. Airport, train station transportation. Downhill ski 20 miles. Exercise equipment. Refrigerator in suites. Cr cds: A, C, D, DS, JCB, MC, V.

[≈] [≈] [🏋]

★★★ **HYATT REGENCY.** *330 Tijeras NW (87102). Phone 505/842-1234; toll-free 800/233-1234; fax 505/766-6710. www.hyatt.com.* Adjacent to the convention center, this 22-story tower is centrally located near Old Town and the Rio Grande Zoo and is only 5 miles from the airport. One of the city's newest high-rise hotels, the property offers a health club, sauna, and outdoor pool. Guest rooms include hairdryers, in-room coffee, and dataports. 395 rooms, 20 story. S $199; D $224; each additional $25; suites $375-$750; under 15 free. Crib free. Garage parking $8; valet $11. TV; cable (premium). Heated pool; lap pool; poolside service. Restaurant 6:30 am-10:30 pm. Bar 11 am-midnight; entertainment. Check-out noon. Convention facilities. Business services available. Concierge. Shopping arcade. Beauty shop. Downhill/cross-country ski 18 miles. Exercise equipment; sauna. Health club privileges. Refrigerator, wet bar in suites. Convention center adjacent. Cr cds: A, C, D, DS, ER, JCB, MC, V.

D ⭢ ⛝ ✕ ⬳ SC

★ ★ **LA POSADA DE ALBUQUERQUE.** *125 2nd St NW (87102). Phone 505/242-9090; toll-free 800/777-5732; fax 505/242-8664. www.laposada-abq.com.* 114 rooms, 10 story. S $115-$135; D $125-$145; each additional $15; suites $195-$275; under 17 free; weekend rates. Crib free. Check-out noon. TV; cable (premium). Refrigerators available. Restaurant (See also CONRAD'S DOWNTOWN). Bar 11 am-midnight. Health club privileges. Downhill ski 15 miles. Meeting rooms. Business services. Shopping arcade. Cr cds: A, C, D, DS, MC, V.

⬳

★ ★ ★ **MARRIOTT.** *2101 Louisiana Blvd NE (87110). Phone 505/881-6800; toll-free 800/228-9290; fax 505/888-2982. www.marriotthotels.com/abqnm/.* Located adjacent to Park Square in the uptown business district, this hotel is only steps away from shopping at the Winrock and Coronado Malls. The property offers both indoor and outdoor pools, a hot tub, sauna, health club, and free parking. Guest rooms feature in-room coffee, two-line phones with dataports, and hair dryers. 411 rooms, 17 story. S, D $129-$149; suites $250-$500; under 18 free; seasonal rates. Crib free. TV; cable (premium). Indoor/outdoor pool; whirlpool, poolside service. Coffee in rooms. Restaurant 6:30 am-11 pm. Bar 11 am-midnight; Sun from noon. Check-out noon. Coin laundry. Convention facilities. In-room modem link. Gift shop. Downhill ski 10 miles. Exercise equipment; sauna. Recreation room. Luxury level. Cr cds: A, C, D, DS, ER, JCB, MC, V.

D ⭢ ⛝ ✕ ⬳

★ ★ ★ **RADISSON INN.** *1901 University Blvd SE (87106). Phone 505/247-0512; toll-free 800/333-3333; fax 505/247-1063. www.radisson.com.* Located near the University of New Mexico, this recently redecorated hotel features a heated outdoor pool that is open year-round and a hot tub in the large Southwestern-style courtyard. Guest rooms offer in-room coffee, dataports, and an exercise room is available on the premises. 148 rooms, 2-3 story. S $75-$95; D $85-$105; each additional $10; under 18 free. Crib free. Pet accepted. Check-out noon. TV; cable (premium). In-room modem link. Restaurant 6 am-10 pm. Bar 2 pm-midnight. Room service. Health club privileges. Heated pool, whirlpool, poolside service. Downhill ski 20 miles. Free airport, train, bus depot transportation. Meeting rooms. Bellstaff. Cr cds: A, C, D, DS, ER, JCB, MC, V.

🐾 ⭢ ⛝ ✕ ⬳

★ ★ ★ **SHERATON.** *2600 Louisiana Blvd NE (87110). Phone 505/881-0000; toll-free 800/325-3535; fax 505/881-3736. www.sheratonuptown.com.* Located in Albuquerque's uptown business and financial district, this property is directly across from New Mexico's largest mall. Guest rooms feature refrigerators, hair dryers, speakerphones, and dataports. Enjoy a swim in the indoor heated pool, relax in the Jacuzzi and sauna or work out in the state-of-the-art fitness center. 296 rooms, 8 story. S $129; D $139; each additional $10; suites $150-$300; under 18 free; weekend rates. Crib free. TV; cable (premium). Indoor pool; whirlpool. Restaurant 6 am-11 pm. Bar 11-2 am. Check-out noon. Coin laundry. Convention facilities. Business services available. Gift shop. Downhill ski 7 miles. Exercise equipment. Refrigerators. Some whirlpool suites. Cr cds: A, C, D, DS, JCB, MC, V.

D ⭢ ⛝ ✕ ⬳ SC

★ ★ ★ **SHERATON OLD TOWN HOTEL.** *800 Rio Grande Blvd NW (87104). Phone 505/843-6300; toll-free 800/237-2133; fax 505/842-9863. www.sheraton.com.* With its large, open lobby and tiled floors, this property offers a casual yet elegant environment. Located in historic Old Town across from the New Mexico Museum of Natural History, it is close to over 200 specialty stores. All guest rooms feature furniture hand-made by local artists. 188 rooms, 11 story. S $110-$125; D $120-$130; each additional $10; suites $150-$170; under 18 free; weekend rates. Crib free. Check-out noon. TV; cable (premium). In-room modem link. Some balconies. Some refrigerators. Coffee in rooms. Restaurant 6 am-10:30 pm. Bar 4-11 pm. Exercise equipment. Heated pool, whirlpool, poolside service. Downhill ski 20 miles. Barber, beauty shop. Meeting rooms. Business center. Shopping arcade. Cr cds: A, C, D, DS, MC, V.

D ⭢ ⛝ ✕ ✕

★ ★ **WYNDHAM HOTEL.** *2910 Yale Blvd SE (87106). Phone 505/843-7000; toll-free 800/227-1117; fax 505/843-6307. www.wynatabq.com.* 276 rooms, 14 story. S $99-$169; D $109-$179; each additional $10; suites $189-$300; under 16 free; weekend rates. Crib free. TV; cable (premium). Heated pool; poolside service. Restaurant 6 am-11 pm. Bar 2 pm-1:30 am; Sun to midnight. Check-out noon. Meeting rooms. In-room modem link. Gift shop. Free airport transportation. Tennis. Downhill ski 15 miles. Exercise equipment. Some refrigerators. Balconies. Cr cds: A, C, D, DS, JCB, MC, V.

D ⭢ 🐾 ⛝ ✕ ✕ ⬳

All Suites

★ ★ **AMBERLEY SUITES HOTEL.** *7620 Pan American Fwy NE (87109). Phone 505/823-1300; toll-free 800/333-9806; fax 505/823-2896. www.amberleysuite.com.* 170 suites, 3 story. S, D $99-$138; each additional $10;

under 18 free; package plans. Crib free. Pet accepted; $5. Complimentary full breakfast, afternoon refreshments. Check-out noon. TV; cable (premium). In-room modem link. Microwaves, refrigerators. Coin laundry. Restaurant 6 am-10 pm. Bar 4 pm-midnight. Exercise equipment, sauna. Game room. Heated pool, whirlpool. Downhill ski 5 miles. Free airport, train, bus depot transportation. Meeting rooms. Business center. Gift shop. Courtyard; fountain. Cr cds: A, C, D, DS, ER, MC, V.

D ⊶ ⛱ ⊠ ⫟ ✈ ⊠ SC ⫟

B&B/Small Inns

★ ★ ★ **APACHE CANYON RANCH.** *4 Canyon Dr, Laguna (87026). Phone 505/836-7220; toll-free 800/808-8310; fax 505/836-2922. www.apachecanyon.com.* Surrounded by nature's beauty, guests can enjoy watching the antelope, cattle and coyotes roam freely. For more hands-on adventures, guests can explore the land by hiking on the nature trails or by horseback. 5 rooms, 2 share bath. Apr-Nov, MAP: S, D $90-$120; guest house $265; golf, package plans; lower rates rest of year. Complimentary full breakfast. Check-out 11 am, check-in 3 pm. TV; VCR available (movies). Some fireplaces. Exercise equipment, massage. Concierge service. View of mountains. Totally nonsmoking. Cr cds: A, MC, V.

D ⫟ ⊠ SC

★ ★ ★ **BRITTANIA W. E. MAUGER ESTATE B&B.** *701 Roma Ave NW (87102). Phone 505/242-8755; toll-free 800/719-9189; fax 505/842-8835. www.maugerbb.com.* "Mi Casa es Su Casa!" is the mantra of this warm bed and breakfast. The suites in this restored Queen Anne house (1897) offer fresh flowers, antique furniture, private baths, dataports with ISDN Internet connections, and air conditioning. Centrally located near the business district and Old Town. 10 rooms shower only, 3 story. S, D $89-$199; each additional $15. Pets accepted $30. Complimentary full breakfast; afternoon refreshments. Check-out 11 am, check-in 4-6 pm. TV; cable (premium), VCR available. In-room modem link. Restaurant nearby. Health club privileges. Downhill/cross-country ski 12 miles. Sun porch. Cr cds: A, C, D, DS, MC, V.

⊶ ⊠ ⊠

★ ★ ★ **CASA DEL GRANJERO B&B.** *414C De Baca Ln NW (87114). Phone 505/897-4144; toll-free 800/ 701-4144; fax 505/897-9788. www.innewmexico.com.* This 1880 bed and breakfast fits its Spanish name which translates as "farmer's house." Guests will enjoy the Old West decor, huge sculpted adobe fireplace, and Indian artifacts. Suites feature hand-painted murals, kiva fireplaces, and two headed showers. 7 rooms, 5 suites. No room phones. S $69-$99; D, suites, kitchen unit $89-$109; each additional $20; weekly, weekend, holiday rates; ski plans. Children of any age welcome. Complimentary full breakfast. Check-

out 11 am, check-in 11 am-2 pm. TV in common room; VCR (movies). Sauna. Whirlpool. Downhill, cross-country ski 10 miles. Lawn games. Business center. Concierge service. Hacienda built in 1880; carved Mexican furniture. Totally nonsmoking. Cr cds: A, DS, MC, V.

D ⊶ ⛱ ⊠ ⫟

★ ★ ★ **CASAS DE SUENOS OLD TOWN BED AND BREAKFAST INN.** *310 Rio Grande Blvd SW (87102). Phone 505/247-4560; toll-free 800/242-8987; fax 505/842-8493. www.casasdesuenos.com.* Situated in the valley of the Sandia Mountains just 3 blocks from the Historic Old Town Area, this inn features the art of local talents. Beautiful guest rooms offer private baths, private entrances, televisions and VCRs. Enjoy a full breakfast in the sunny garden room featuring such dishes as Southwestern frittatas. 17 rooms, S, D $85-$150; each additional $15; suites, kitchen units $110-$250; 3-day minimum during Balloon Fiesta. Children over 12 years only. Complimentary full breakfast. Check-out 11 am, check-in 3 pm. TV; cable (premium). In-room modem link. Restaurant nearby. Totally nonsmoking. Cr cds: A, D, DS, MC, V.

D ⊠ ⊠

★ ★ ★ **CHOCOLATE TURTLE B&B.** *1098 W Meadowlark, Corrales (87048). Phone 505/898-1800; toll-free 800/898-1842; fax 505/899-8734. www.collectorsguide.com/chocturtle.* Situated on 1 1/2 acres in Corrales, guests can enjoy the beautiful view of the mountains. Enjoy the homemade chocolates and gourmet breakfasts. 4 air-cooled rooms, 3 with shower only, 1 suite. No room phones. S, D $65-$115; each additional $10; suite $85-$90; package plans. Children over 6 years only. Complimentary full breakfast. Check-out 11 am, check-in 4-6 pm. TV in common rooms. cable (premium), VCR available (movies). Restaurant nearby. Whirlpool. Downhill ski 15 miles. Business services. Concierge service. Totally nonsmoking. Cr cds: MC, V.

⊶ ⊠

★ ★ ★ **HACIENDA ANTIGUA B&B.** *6708 Tierra Dr NW (87107). Phone 505/345-5399; toll-free 800/201-2986; fax 505/345-3855. www.haciendaantigua.com.* Built on the famous El Camino Real, this 200-year-old adobe is conveniently located in the North Valley area. The warm property features traditional kiva fireplaces and antique furnishings in the guest rooms. 8 rooms. S, D $149-$199; each additional $25; 3-day minimum during Balloon Fiesta. Complimentary full breakfast. Check-out 11 am, check-in 4-6 pm. TV in common room. Pool, whirlpool. Downhill, cross-country ski 12 miles. Spanish Colonial house built 1790 that once served as stagecoach stop; many antiques. Many room phones. Totally nonsmoking. Cr cds: A, MC, V.

⛱ ⊠ ⊠

★ ★ ★ **HACIENDA VARGAS B&B.** *1431 Hwy 313 Historical El Camino Real, Algodones (87001). Phone 505/867-9115; toll-free 800/261-0006; fax 505/867-0640. www.haciendavargas.com.* 7 rooms. No room phones. D $89-$149; each additional $15; Complimentary full breakfast. Check-out 11 am, check-in 4 pm. Totally non-smoking. Cr cds: A, MC, V.

★ ★ ★ **LA HACIENDA GRANDE.** *21 Baros Ln, Bernalillo (87004). Phone 505/867-1887; toll-free 800/ 353-1887; fax 505/771-1436. www.lahaciendagrande.com.* Cathedral ceilings, beautiful views and an open-air center courtyard grace this bed and breakfast. 6 rooms. D $109-$149; each additional $15; ski, golf plans. Complimentary full breakfast. Check-out 11 am, check-in 4-6 pm. TV; cable (premium), VCR available (movies). Greens fee $32. Downhill, cross-country ski 15 miles. Concierge. Spanish hacienda built in 1750s. Totally nonsmoking. Cr cds: A, D, DS, MC, V.

★ ★ ★ **RIVER DANCER B&B.** *16445 Hwy 4, Jemez (87025). Phone 505/829-3262; toll-free 800/809-3262. www.riverdancer.com.* Located near the village of Jemez Springs, the beauty of this 5-acre property is the natural landscaping. Guests will be treated to a relaxing and refreshing getaway. Enjoy Jemez Falls, natural hot springs and hot air ballooning. 6 rooms, 1 suite. D $99-$129; each additional $15; package plans. Complimentary full breakfast. Check-out 11 am, check-in 3-7 pm. TV; cable (premium), VCR available (movies). Restaurant nearby. Massage. Concierge service. On river. Totally nonsmoking. Cr cds: MC, V.

Restaurants

★ **66 DINER.** *1405 Central Ave NE (87106). Phone 505/ 247-1421; fax 505/247-0882. www.66diner.com.* Hours: 11 am-11 pm; Fri to midnight; Sat 8 am-midnight; Sun 8 am-10 pm. Closed major holidays. Breakfast $1.95-$4.25, lunch, dinner $3-$6.95. Children's menu. Outdoor dining. Cr cds: A, C, D, DS, ER, MC, V.

★★**ANTIQUITY.** *112 Romero St NW (87104). Phone 505/ 247-3545.* Continental, seafood, steak menu. Hours: 5-9 pm; Fri, Sat to 9:30 pm. Closed most major holidays. Dinner $14-$24. Reservations accepted. Cr cds: A, C, D, DS, MC, V.

★ ★ ★ **THE ARTICHOKE CAFE.** *424 Central St (87102). Phone 505/243-0200; fax 505/243-3365. www.artichokecafe.com.* A perennial favorite among the area's white-tablecloth restaurants, this pleasant eatery has beautiful fresh flowers and a menu that leans toward Italy. Specializes in pasta, fresh seafood, lamb. Hours: 11 am-2:30 pm, 5:30-10 pm; Sat from 5:30 pm. Closed Sun; Jan 1, Thanksgiving, Dec 25. Lunch $4.95-$10.95, dinner $14.95-$24.95. Children's menu. Reservations accepted. Outdoor dining. Cr cds: A, D, DS, MC, V.

★ ★ **BARRY'S OASIS.** *445 Osuna (87109). Phone 505/884-2324.* Greek, mediterranean menu. Hours: 11 am-2:30 pm, 5-9 pm; Fri to 10 pm; Sat noon-10 pm; Sun 5-9 pm. Closed Thanksgiving, Dec 25. Lunch $4-$6, dinner $8-$19.95. Bar. Children's menu. Reservations accepted. Outdoor seating. Cr cds: D, DS, MC, V.

★ ★ **CHEF DU JOUR.** *119 San Pasquale SW (87104). Phone 505/247-8998; fax 505/247-8998.* Eclectic/ International menu. Menu changes weekly. Own baking. Hours: 11 am-2 pm; Fri, Sat 5:30-8:30 pm. Closed Sun; major holidays. Lunch $2.25-$9. Reservations accepted. Outdoor dining. Totally nonsmoking. Cr cds: A, DS, MC, V.

★ **CHRISTY MAE'S.** *1400 San Pedro NE (87110). Phone 505/255-4740; fax 505/265-3511. www.christymaes.com.* Hours: 11 am-8 pm. Closed Sun; holidays. Lunch $5.29-$8.50. Dinner $5.95-$10.95. Children's menu. Cr cds: A, C, DS, ER, MC, V.

★ ★ **CONRAD'S DOWNTOWN.** *125 2nd St NW (87102). Phone 505/242-9090; fax 505/242-8664.* Southwestern menu. Breakfast, lunch, dinner. Bar. Valet parking. Cr cds: A, D, DS, MC, V. **$$**

★ **COOPERAGE.** *7220 Lomas Blvd NE (87110). Phone 505/255-1657; fax 505/266-0408.* Hours: 11 am-2:30 pm, 5-10pm; Fri to 11 pm; Sat noon-2:30 pm, 5-11; Sun noon-9 pm, closed Dec 25. Dinner $8.95-$37.95. Bar to 2 am, Sun to 9 pm. Entertainment Thurs-Sat. Children's menu. Built like an enormous barrel; circular rooms with many intimate corners, booths; atrium dining room. Reservations accepted. Cr cds: A, D, DS. **$$**

★ **EL PINTO.** *10500 4th St NW (87114). Phone 505/898-1771; fax 505/897-8147. www.elpinto.com.* Mexican menu. Closed Thanksgiving, Dec 25. Lunch, dinner. Bar. Children's menu. Outdoor seating. Cr cds: A, DS, MC, V. **$$**

★ **GARDUNO'S OF MEXICO.** *10551 Montgomery NE (87111). Phone 505/298-5000; fax 505/271-6628.*

www.gardunorestaurant.com. Contemporary Mexican menu. Specializes in enchiladas, fajitas. Hours: 11 am-10 pm; Fri, Sat to 10:30 pm; Sun from 10:30 am; Sun brunch to 3 pm. Closed Thanksgiving, Dec 25. Bar. Lunch $4.95-$11.95, dinner $7.50-$12.95. Sun brunch $9.95. Children's menu. Entertainment Thurs-Sun. Outdoor dining. Festive atmosphere; Mexican decor. Family-owned. Cr cds: A, D, DS, MC, V.

D

★ ★ **HIGH NOON.** 425 San Felipe St NW (87104). Phone 505/765-1455; fax 505/255-4505. Continental menu. Closed Jan 1, Dec 25. Lunch, dinner. Bar. Original 2 rooms built in 1785. Cr cds: A, C, D, DS, MC, V. **$$**

D

★ **LA HACIENDA DINING ROOM.** 302 San Felipe NW (87104). Phone 505/243-3131. American, Mexican menu. Hours: 11 am-9 pm; summer to 10 pm. Closed Thanksgiving, Dec 25. Dinner $8.95-$15.95. Bar. Entertainment Wed-Sun. Children's menu. Reservations accepted. Patio dining. Mexican décor in old hacienda; antiques, Native American art. Cr cds: A, C, D, DS, MC, V.

D

★ ★ **LE CAFE MICHE.** 1431 Wyoming Blvd NE (87112). Phone 505/299-6088; fax 505/332-8911. www.lecafemiche.com. Although the French-continental food is old-fashioned—think veal Orloff, chicken cordon bleu—this romantic, candlelit restaurant remains a favorite because of the attentive service and overall welcoming ambience. French country menu. Hours: 11 am-1:30 pm, 5:30-9 pm; Fri, Sat from 5 pm. Closed Sun, Mon (lunch only); major holidays. Lunch $7.50-$13.50, dinner $14.50-$28. Reservations accepted. Totally nonsmoking. Cr cds: A, D, DS, MC, V.

D

★ **M AND J.** 403 2nd St SW (87102). Phone 505/242-4890. Mexican menu. Specialties: tamales, carne adovada, blue corn enchilada plate. Hours: 9 am-4 pm. Closed Sun; major holidays. Lunch, dinner $5-$8.50. Children's menu. Cr cds: A, MC, V.

D SC

★ ★ **MARIA TERESA.** 618 Rio Grande Blvd NW (87104). Phone 505/242-3900. www.mariateresarestauant.com. Continental, Mexican menu. Hours: 11 am-2:30 pm, 5-9 pm; Sun brunch to 2:30 pm. Dinner $14.95-$24.95, Sun brunch $10.95-$16.95. Bar 11 am-9 pm. Children's menu. Reservations accepted. Restored adobe hacienda (1840); antique décor; art, fireplaces, walled gardens. Cr cds: A, C, D, ER, MC, V.

D

★ ★ **NEW CHINATOWN.** 5001 Central Ave NE (87108). Phone 505/265-8859; fax 505/266-3324. www.newchinatown.org. Chinese menu. Hours: 11 am-9:30 pm; Fri, Sat to 10:30 pm. Closed Thanksgiving, Dec 25. Lunch $3.25-$5.95, dinner $6.50-14.95. Bar to midnight. Piano bar. Children's menu. Reservations accepted. Cr cds: A, D, DS, MC, V.

D

★ **RAGIN' SHRIMP.** 3619 Copper NE (87108). Phone 505/254-1544. www.raginshrimp.com. Cajun menu. Hours: 11 am-9 pm; Fri to 10 pm; Sat 11:30 am-10 pm; Sun from 11:30 am. Closed most major holidays. Lunch $5.50-$7.95, dinner $5.50-$13.95. Children's menu, outdoor dining. Totally nonsmoking. Cr cds: A, D, DS, MC, V.

D

★ ★ ★ **SCALO.** 3500 Central Ave SE (87106). Phone 505/255-8782. Chef Enrique Guerrero has just taken over the kitchen of this northern Italian grill, and he's already brought back favorites such as chicken cooked under a brick. Italian menu. Hours: 11:30 am-2:30 pm, 5-11 pm; Sun 5-9 pm. Closed most major holidays. Reservations accepted. Bar. Lunch $4.95-$9.95, dinner $7.95-$19.95. Specialties: salmone alla Como, filet of beef, grilled fish. Own pasta. Patio dining. Dining areas on several levels. Cr cds: A, D, DS, MC, V.

D

★ ★ **TRATTORIA TROMBINO.** 5415 Academy Blvd NE (87109). Phone 505/821-5974. Italian menu. Specializes in pasta, seafood, steak. Hours: 11 am-2:30 pm, 5-10 pm; Fri, Sat 11 am-10:30 pm; Sun 4-9 pm. Closed Thanksgiving, Dec 25. and Superbowl Sunday. Lunch $5.50-$9.95, dinner $7.95-$16.95. Bar. Children's menu. Cr cds: A, D, DS, MC, V.

D

Angel Fire (B-5)

See also Cimarron, Red River, Taos

Pop 1,048 **Elev** 8,500 ft **Area code** 505 **Zip** 87710

Information Chamber of Commerce, PO Box 547; 505/377-6661 or 800/446-8117

Web www.angelfirechamber.org

This is a family resort area high in the Sangre de Cristo Mountains of northern New Mexico.

What to See and Do

Carson National Forest. *15160 State Rd 75 (87553). 3 miles W (see TAOS). Phone 505/587-2255.*

Cimarron Canyon State Park. *29519 US 64. 15 miles NE on US 64. Phone 505/377-6271.* Region of high mountains and deep canyons has scenic 200-foot palisades; winding mountain stream has excellent trout fishing; state wildlife area. Hiking, rock climbing, wildlife viewing, winter sports, camping. Standard fees. (Daily) **FREE**

Eagle Nest Lake. *12 miles N on US 64.* This 2,200-acre lake offers year-round fishing for rainbow trout and Kokonee salmon (fishing license required). **FREE**

Vietnam Veterans National Memorial. *3 miles N on US 64. Phone 505/377-6900.* This beautiful, gracefully designed building stands on a hillside overlooking Moreno Valley and the Sangre de Cristo Mountains. It is dedicated to all who fought in Vietnam. Chapel (daily). Visitor center (Daily). **FREE**

Artesia (G-6)

See also Carlsbad

Founded 1903 **Pop** 10,692 **Elev** 3,380 ft **Area code** 505 **Zip** 88210

Information Chamber of Commerce, 107 N First St, 88210; 505/746-2744 or 800/658-6251

Web www.artesiachamber.com

Artesia was named for the vast underground water supplies which once rushed up through drilled wells and are now used to irrigate the area's farmland. The first underground school in the United States, Abo Elementary School at 18th Street and Centre Avenue, was built here for safety from the radiation effects of fallout. Potash, natural gas, oil, and petroleum products are processed near here. Artesia is the home of the Federal Law Enforcement Training Center. The area offers wild turkey, deer, bear, and upland game for hunting enthusiasts.

What to See and Do

Historical Museum and Art Center. *503 and 505 W Richardson Ave. Phone 505/748-2390.* Pioneer and Native American artifacts; changing art exhibits. (Tues-Sat; closed holidays) **FREE**

Special Events

Bulldog Balloon Rally. *408 W Texas Ave.* Second weekend in Nov.

Eddy County Fair. *2707 S 1st St.* First week in Aug.

Motel/Motor Lodge

★ ★ **BEST WESTERN PECOS INN MOTEL.** *2209 W Main St (88210). Phone 505/748-3324; toll-free 800/780-7234; fax 505/748-2868. www.bestwestern.com.* 81 rooms, 2 story. S, D $48-$120; each additional $7; suites $100-$110. Crib free. Check-out 11 am. TV; cable. Some balconies. Refrigerators. Coin laundry. Restaurant 6 am-9 pm; Sun 5-8 pm. Bar 4 am-midnight; closed Sun. Room service. Sauna. Indoor pool, whirlpool. Meeting rooms. Cr cds: A, C, D, DS, MC, V.

B&B/Small Inns

★ ★ **HERITAGE INN.** *209 W Main St (88210). Phone 505/748-2552; toll-free 866/207-0222; fax 505/746-4981. www.artesiaheritageinn.com.* 9 rooms. No room phones. D $55-$65; each additional $10. Children over 15 years only. Complimentary continental breakfast; afternoon refreshments. Check-out 11 am, check-in 3 pm. TV; cable (premium). Restaurant nearby. Individually decorated rooms. Totally nonsmoking. Cr cds: A, DS, MC, V.

Restaurant

★★**LA FONDA.** *206 W Main (88210). Phone 505/746-9377.* American, Mexican menu. Hours: 11 am-9 pm, closed Jan 1, Thanksgiving, Dec 25. Buffet lunch $7.95, dinner $4.50-$9.25. Children's menu. Cr cds: A, D, DS, MC, V.

Aztec (B-2)

See also Farmington

Founded 1890 **Pop** 6,378 **Elev** 5,686 ft **Area code** 505 **Zip** 87410

Information Chamber of Commerce, 110 N Ash; 505/334-9551

Web www.cyberport.com/aztec

Aztec is the seat of San Juan County, a fruit-growing and cattle-grazing area. This town is filled with history; architectural and historic commentary for walking tours may be obtained at the Aztec Museum.

What to See and Do

Aztec Museum and Pioneer Village. *125 N Main. Phone 505/334-9829.* Main museum houses authentic pioneer artifacts, including mineral and fossil display, household items, farm and ranch tools, and Native American artifacts. Atwood Annex has authentically furnished pioneer rooms, farm equipment, sleighs, buggies, and wagons. Oil Field Museum has 1920s cable tool oil rig, oil well pumping unit, "doghouse," and tools. Pioneer Village has 12 reconstructed buildings, including doctor's and sheriff's offices, blacksmith shop and foundry, pioneer cabin (1880), general store and post office, original Aztec jail, and church. (Mon-Sat) $$

Navajo Lake State Park. *18 miles E via NM 173, 511. Phone 505/632-2278.* Surrounded by sandstone mesas and stands of piñon and juniper. Part of Colorado River Storage Project; reservoir extends 35 miles upstream into Colorado, totaling 15,000 surface acres of water. Standard fees. (Daily) $$ Also in the area are

> **Pine River Site.** *West side.* Swimming, waterskiing, fishing (panfish, catfish, bass, salmon, and trout), boating (ramps, rentals, marina); picnicking (fireplaces), concession, camping (hookups). Visitor center with interpretive displays.

> **San Juan River Recreation Area.** *Below the dam.* Fishing (trout); camping.

> **Sims Mesa Site.** *East side.* Boat ramp; camping (dump station). $$

Hotel

★ **STEP BACK INN.** *103 W Aztec Blvd (87410). Phone 505/334-1200; toll-free 800/334-1255; fax 505/334-9858.* 39 rooms, 2 story. Mid-May-mid-Oct: S, D $78; each additional $6; under 12 free; lower rates rest of year. Check-out 11 am. TV. Turn-of-the-century décor. Cr cds: A, MC, V.

D

Aztec Ruins National Monument (A-2)

See also National Monuments

1/2 miles N of US 550. Contact Superintendent, 84 County Rd 290, Aztec 87410.

One of the largest prehistoric Native American towns, it was occupied between A.D. 1100-1300. These are ancient Pueblo ruins, misnamed Aztec by early settlers in the 1800s. The partially excavated pueblo contains nearly 450 rooms, with its plaza dominated by the Great Kiva (48 feet in diameter). Instructive museum, interpretive programs in summer. Self-guided tours, trail guide available at visitor center for the 1/4-mile trail. Some portions accessible by wheelchair. (Daily; closed Jan 1, Dec 25)

Bandelier National Monument (C-4)

See also Los Alamos, Santa Fe

(From Los Alamos, 6 miles SW on NM 502, then 6 miles SE on NM 4 to turnoff sign)

A major portion of this 32,000-acre area is designated wilderness. The most accessible part is in Frijoles Canyon, which features cave dwellings carved out of the soft volcanic turf and houses built out from the cliffs. There is also a great circular pueblo ruin (Tyuonyi) on the floor of the canyon. These houses and caves were occupied from about 1150-1550. The depletion of resources forced the residents to abandon the area. Some of the modern pueblos along the Rio Grande are related to the prehistoric Anasazi people of the canyon and the surrounding mesa country. There is a paved 1-mile self-guided trail to walk and view these sites. The monument is named after Adolph Bandelier, ethnologist and author of the novel, *The Delight Makers,* which used Frijoles Canyon as its locale. There are 70 miles of trails (free permits required for overnight trips; no pets allowed on the trails). Visitor center with exhibits depicting the culture of the pueblo region (Daily; closed January 1, December 25), ranger-guided tours (summer), campfire programs (Memorial Day-Labor Day). Campground (March-November, daily) with tent and trailer sites (fee; no showers, hookups, or reservations); grills, tables, and water. Golden Access, Golden Age, Golden Eagle Passport (see MAKING THE MOST OF YOUR TRIP). Contact the Visitor Center, HCR 1, Box 1, Suite 15, Los Alamos 87544; 505/672-3861, ext 517 or 505/672-0343 (recording). Per vehicle $5-$10

Capulin Volcano National Monument (B-6)

29 miles E on US 64/87 to Capulin, then 3-1/2 miles N.

Dormant volcano that last erupted approximately 10,000 years ago. The strikingly symmetrical cinder cone rises more than 1,500 feet from plains, with a crater 1 mile in circumference and 415 feet deep. Visitors can spiral completely around the mountain on paved road to rim (daily); five states can be seen on clear days. Picnic area. Visitor center with exhibits of geology, flora, and fauna of the area (daily; closed January 1, December 25). Uniformed personnel on duty at the crater rim (summer only). Contact the Superintendent, Box 40, Capulin 88414.

Carlsbad (G-6)

See also Artesia

Founded 1893 **Pop** 25,625

Information Convention & Visitors Bureau, 302 S Canal, PO Box 910; 505/887-6516 or 800/221-1224 outside NM

Explorers such as Antonio de Espejo and Alvar Nuñez Cabeza de Vaca probably traveled through this area as they made their way down the Pecos River during the 1500s. Carlsbad is also on the famous Goodnight-Loving cattle drive trail.

Irrigation of the rich alluvial bottomland began with the earliest Spanish settlements in the early 1600s. In 1911 the US Bureau of Reclamation began its Carlsbad Project, building three dams and an intricate network of canals that now irrigate more than 25,000 acres. Cotton, alfalfa, and vegetables are the principal crops.

In 1925, potash was discovered by a company drilling for oil; six years later active mining began.

A Ranger District office of the Lincoln National Forest (see ALAMOGORDO) is located here.

What to See and Do

Brantley Lake State Park. *12 miles N on US 285, then 5 miles E on County Rd 30.* Phone 505/457-2384. This 3,000-acre park is adjacent to Brantley Lake on the Pecos River. Fishing, boating (ramps); picnicking (shelters), camping (hookups, dump station, showers). Visitor center. Standard fees. (Daily) **$$**

Carlsbad Museum & Art Center. *418 W Fox St, 1 block W of Canal St.* Phone 505/887-0276. Pueblo pottery, art, meteorite remains. Potash and mineral exhibits. Pioneer and Apache relics. McAdoo collection of paintings, bird carvings by Jack Drake, changing temporary exhibits. (Mon-Sat; closed holidays) **DONATION**

Lake Carlsbad Water Recreation Area. *Off Green St, on the Pecos River.* Phone 505/887-2702. Swimming, water sports, fishing, boating; tennis, golf (fee), picnic area.

Living Desert Zoo and Gardens State Park. *1504 Miehls Dr. 1 1/2 miles NW, off US 285.* Phone 505/887-5516. This 1,100-acre park is an indoor/outdoor living museum of the Chihuahuan Desert's plants and animals. The Desert Arboretum has an extensive cactus collection. Living Desert Zoo has over 60 animal species native to the region including mountain lions, bear, wolf, elk, bison, and an extensive aviary. (Daily; closed Dec 25) **$$**

Million Dollar Museum. *17 Carlsbad Cavern Hwy. 20 miles SW on US 62/180 to White's City, then W on NM 7.* Phone 505/885-6776. Early Americana collection; 31 antique European doll houses, $25,000 doll collection, first car

west of the Pecos, Whittlin' Cowboys Ranch. (Daily; closed Dec 25) **$$**

Sitting Bull Falls. *11 miles NW on US 285 to NM 137, then 30 miles SW, in Lincoln National Forest (see ALAMOGORDO).* Phone 505/885-4181. Day-use area near spectacular desert waterfall. Hiking trail to piñon and juniper forest, diverse vegetation along trail with scenic overlooks of canyons and plains. Picnicking. (Daily) **FREE**

Motels/Motor Lodges

★★ **BEST WESTERN STEVENS INN.** *1829 S Canal St (88220).* Phone 505/887-2851; toll-free 800/780-7234; fax 505/887-6338. www.bestwestern.com. 202 rooms, 1-2 story. S, D $52; suites $62-$85; each additional $5. Crib $5. Pet accepted. TV; cable (premium), VCR (movies $4). Pool. Playground. Comlimentary breakfast buffet. Restaurant 5:30 am-10 pm; Sun 6 am-9 pm. Room service 7 am-9 pm. Bar 11-2 am; entertainment except Sun. Check-out noon. Meeting rooms. Business services available. Sundries. Some refrigerators. Some patios. Cr cds: A, C, D, DS, JCB, MC, V.

D ⬛ 🐾 🏊 ✈ 🖂

★ **CONTINENTAL INN.** *3820 National Park Hwy (88220).* Phone 505/887-0341; toll-free 877/887-0341; fax 505/885-1186. 58 units, 2 story. S $35; D $45; each additional $5; suites $49.95-$79.95. Pet accepted, some restrictions; fee. Check-out 11 am. TV; cable (premium). In-room modem link. Cr cds: A, C, D, MC, V.

🏊 🖂

★★★ **HOLIDAY INN.** *601 S Canal St (88220).* Phone 505/885-8500; toll-free 800/456-4329; fax 505/887-5999. www.holiday-inn.com. Living Desert Zoo State Park and Brantley Lake State Park are just a few short minutes away. 100 rooms, 2 story. Mid-June-mid-Aug: S $79-$99; D $85-$105; each additional $5; suites $77-$87; under 19 free; lower rates rest of year. Crib free. Pet accepted; $25 deposit. Complimentary coffee in rooms. Check-out 11 am. TV; cable (premium), VCR available (movies). In-room modem link. Some refrigerators. Complimentary coffee in rooms. Valet services, guest laundry. Restaurant 6-10 am, 5:30-9:30 pm. Room service. Playground. Exercise equipment, sauna. Pool, whirlpool, poolside service. 36-hole golf privileges, greens fee $26, putting green, driving range. Tennis privileges. Picnic tables. Meeting rooms. Business services. Bellhops. Cr cds: A, C, D, DS, JCB, MC, V.

🐾 🏋 🏊 ✈ 🖂

★ **SUPER 8 MOTEL.** *3817 National Parks Hwy (88220).* Phone 505/887-8888; toll-free 800/800-8000; fax 505/885-0126. www.super8.com. 60 units, 3 story. S $40.88-$48.88; D $44.88-$48.88; each additional $4; under 12 free. Crib

$5. Complimentary breakfast. Check-out 11 am. TV; cable (premium). Coin laundry. Heated pool, whirlpool. Business services. Cr cds: A, C, D, DS, MC, V.

D ⊠ ⊠

Carlsbad Caverns National Park (H-6)

See also Carlsbad

(27 miles SW of Carlsbad on US 62/180)

One of the largest and most remarkable in the world, this cavern extends approximately 30 miles and is as deep as 1,037 feet below the surface.

It was once known as Bat Cave because of the spectacular bat flights, still a daily occurrence at sunset during the warmer months. Cowboy and guano miner Jim White first explored and guided people through the caverns in the early 1900s, later working for the National Park Service as the Chief Park Ranger. Carlsbad Cave National Monument was established in 1923, and in 1930 the area was enlarged and designated a national park. The park contains 46,755 acres and more than 80 caves. Carlsbad Cavern was formed by the dissolving action of acidic water in the Tansill and Capitan limestones of the Permian age. When an uplift drained the cavern, mineral-laden water dripping from the ceiling formed the stalactites and stalagmites.

The main cavern has two self-guided routes, a Ranger-guided Kings Palace tour, and several "off-trail" trips. The "Cavern Guide," an audio tour rented at the visitor center, enhances self-guided tours with interpretations of the caverns, interviews, and historic re-creations. Also available are tours in two backcountry caves: Slaughter Canyon Cave and Spider Cave. All guided tours require reservations.

Since the temperature in the cavern is always 56°F, be sure to carry a sweater even if it is hot outside; comfortable rubber-soled shoes are also recommended for safety. No pets; kennel available. Photography, including flash and time exposures, is permitted on self-guided trips and some guided tours. Wheelchairs can be accommodated in the elevator for a partial tour. Rangers patrol the cave. Holders of Golden Access and Golden Age passports (see MAKING THE MOST OF YOUR TRIP) receive a 50 percent discount. Picnic area at Rattlesnake Springs. Scenic 9 1/2-mile loop drive, hiking trails, observation tower, exhibits on surface, restaurant. No camping in park, but available nearby. Bat flight programs are held each evening during the summer at the cavern entrance amphitheater.

Visitor center and museum with educational exhibits and displays. For tour reservations and fees contact the Superintendent, 3225 National Parks Hwy, Carlsbad 88220. Phone 505/785-2232 (ext 429 for reservations).

Chaco Culture National Historical Park (C-2)

See also Farmington, Gallup, Grants

(From NM 44, 25 miles S on country road 7900; 3 miles S of Nageezi Trading Post; from I-40, 60 miles N of Thoreau on NM 57. Check road conditions locally; may be extremely difficult when wet)

From A.D. 900 to 1150, Chaco Canyon was a major center of Anasazi culture. A prehistoric roadway system, which included stairways carved into sandstone cliffs, extends for hundreds of miles in all directions. Ancient roads up to 30 feet wide represent the most developed and extensive road network of this period north of Central America. Researchers speculate that Chaco Canyon was the center of a vast, complex, and interdependent civilization in the American Southwest.

There are five self-guided trails with tours conducted (Memorial Day-Labor Day, times vary), as well as evening campfire programs in summer. Visitor center has museum (daily; closed Jan 1, Dec 25). Camping (fee). Contact Superintendent, PO Box 220, Nageezi, 87037-0220. Phone 505/786-7014. Per vehicle **$$$**

Chama (A-3)

See also Dulce

Pop 1,199 **Elev** 7,800 ft **Area code** 505 **Zip** 87520

What to See and Do

Cumbres & Toltec Scenic Railroad, New Mexico Express. *500 S Terrace Ave. Phone 888-CUMBRES.* The Colorado Limited runs to Osier from Antonito, CO (see ALAMOSA, CO). Round-trip excursion to Osier, CO on 1880s narrow-gauge steam railroad. Route passes through backwoods country and spectacular mountain scenery; including the 4-percent-grade climb to Cumbres Pass. Warm clothing advised due to sudden weather changes. (Memorial Day-mid-Oct, daily) Also through trips to Antonito, CO with van return. Reservations advised; contact PO Box 789. **$$$$**

El Vado Lake State Park. *15 miles S on US 84 to Tierra Amarilla, then 13 miles SW on NM 112. Phone 505/588-7247.* This park features an irrigation lake with fishing, ice fishing, boating (dock, ramps); hiking trail connects to Heron Lake, picnicking, playground, camping (hookups, dump station). Standard fees. (Daily)

Heron Lake State Park. *640 NM 95 (87551). 10 miles S on US 84, then 6 miles SW on NM 95. Phone 505/588-7470.* Region of tall ponderosa pines. Swimming, fishing (trout, salmon), ice fishing, boating (ramp, dock); hiking, winter sports, picnicking, camping (hookups; fee). Visitor center. (Daily) **$$**

Motel/Motor Lodge

★ **ELK HORN LODGE.** *HC 75 Box 45 (87520). Phone 505/756-2105; toll-free 800/532-8874; fax 505/756-2638. www.elkhornlodge.net.* 23 motel rooms, 1-2 story, 11 kitchen cottages. July-Oct: S $42-$62; D $55-$72; each additional $6; kitchen cottages $76-$108; weekly and lower rates rest of year. Crib $6. Pet accepted. TV; cable. Restaurant 6 am-10 pm. Check-out 11 am. Cross-country ski 5 miles. Balconies. Porches on cottages. Picnic tables, grills. On Chama River. Cr cds: A, C, D, DS, MC, V.

Cimarron (B-5)

See also Angel Fire, Raton, Red River

Pop 917 **Elev** 6,427 ft **Area code** 505 **Zip** 87714

Information Chamber of Commerce, PO Box 604; 505/376-2417 or 800/700-4298

This historic Southwestern town was part of Lucien B. Maxwell's land holdings on the Santa Fe Trail. The St. James Hotel (1872), where Buffalo Bill Cody held his Wild West Shows, the gristmill, the old jail (1872), and several other historic buildings still stand.

What to See and Do

Cimarron Canyon State Park. *10 miles W on US 64 (see ANGEL FIRE). Phone 505/377-6271.*

Old Aztec Mill Museum. *On NM 21, S of US 64 in Old Town. Phone 505/376-2913.* (1864) Built as gristmill. Chuckwagon, mill wheels, and local historical items. (Memorial Day-Labor Day, Fri-Wed; early May and late Sept, weekends) **$**

Philmont Scout Ranch. *Rte 1 and Hwy 21. Phone 505/376-2281.* A 138,000-acre camp for some 20,000 Boy Scouts. Villa Philmonte, former summer home of ranch's benefactor, offers tours (mid-June-Mid-Aug, daily; rest of year, call for schedule; fee). Ernest Thompson Seton Memorial Library and Philmont Museum include several thousand drawings, paintings, and Native American artifacts (Mon-Fri; closed holidays). Kit Carson Museum (7 miles S of headquarters; mid-June-Aug, daily; fee). Camp also has buffalo, deer, elk, bear, and antelope. Headquarters is 4 miles S on NM 21. **FREE**

Special Events

Cimarron Days. *Village Park Hwy 64 (87714). Phone 505/376-2417.* Crafts, entertainment. Labor Day weekend.

Maverick Club Rodeo. *Maverick Club Arena (87714). Phone 505/376-2417.* Rodeo for working cowboys. Parade, dance. July 4.

B&B/Small Inns

★★★ **CASA DEL GAVILAN.** *Hwy 21 S (87714). Phone 505/376-2246; fax 505/376-2247. www.casadelgavilan.com.* Peace and tranquility are the most appreciated features of this inn. Guests can relax in the library or on the porch while sipping tea or wine. The more adventurous guests can go hiking in the trails behind the inn. 5 rooms, 1 suite. No A/C. No room phones. D $75-$130; suite $125; under 10 free. Complimentary full breakfast. Check-out 11 am, check-in 3 pm. Restaurant nearby. Southwestern adobe built in 1912. Totally nonsmoking. Cr cds: A, DS, MC, V.

Cloudcroft (G-4)

See also Alamogordo, Mescalero, Ruidoso

Pop 749 **Elev** 8,700 ft **Area code** 505 **Zip** 88317

Information Chamber of Commerce, PO Box 1290; 505/682-2733

Web www.cloudcroft.net

One of the highest golf courses in North America is Cloudcroft's most publicized claim to distinction, but this is also a recreation area for non-golfers. It is at the crest of the Sacramento Mountains in the Lincoln National Forest (see ALAMOGORDO), among fir, spruce, pine, and aspen. A Ranger District office of the forest is located here. The area is popular with writers, photographers, and artists. Several art schools conduct summer workshops here. There are many miles of horseback trails through the mountains, and skiing, snowmobiling, and skating in winter. Deer, elk, turkey, and bear hunting is good in season. Several campgrounds are located in the surrounding forest. During the day temperatures seldom reach 80°F; nights are always crisp and cool.

What to See and Do

Sacramento Mountains Historical Museum. *1000 US Hwy 82. Phone 505/682-2333.* Exhibits depict 1880-1910 life in the Sacramento Mountains area. (Mon, Tues, Fri-Sun) **$**

Ski Cloudcroft. *2 1/2 miles E on US 82. Phone 505/682-2333.* Double chairlift, beginner tows; patrol, school, rentals, snowmaking, lodge, snack bar, cafeteria, restaurant. Vertical drop 700 feet. (Mid-Dec-mid-Mar, daily) Snowboarding. Elev 8,350-9,050 feet. **$$$$**

Special Event

Western Roundup. *1001 James Canyon Hwy. Phone 505/682-2733.* Contests, parade, street dance. Mid-June.

Resort

★ ★ ★ **LODGE AT CLOUDCROFT.** *1 Corona Pl (88317). Phone 505/682-2566; toll-free 800/395-6343; fax 505/682-2715. www.thelodge-nm.com.* 60 rooms, 7 suites, 3 story. No elevator. D $120; each additional $10; suites $139-$309; package plans. Crib free. Pet accepted; $100 deposit. Check-out noon, check-in after 4 pm. TV; cable (premium), VCR available. Restaurant (See also REBECCA'S). Bar 11-2 am; entertainment. Massage, sauna. Heated pool, whirlpool. 9-hole golf, greens fee, putting green, pro shop. Downhill ski 2 miles, cross-country ski on site. Meeting rooms. Business services. Gift shop. Historic building (1899). Cr cds: A, C, D, DS, MC, V.

D 🐾 🏊 👶 🏖 🏌

Restaurant

★ ★ ★ **REBECCA'S.** *1 Corona Pl (88317). Phone 505/682-2566; fax 505/682-2715. www.thelodge-nm.com.* This casual, fine-dining restaurant in The Lodge serves a Continental menu that includes beef, poultry and seafood. Hours: 7-10:30 am, 11:30 am-2 pm, 5:30-10 pm; Sun from 10 am; Sun brunch 11 am-2 pm. Reservations accepted. Continental menu. Bar 11 am-midnight. Wine list. Breakfast $3.25-$9.95, lunch $5.95-$9.95, dinner $12.95-$32.95. Sun brunch $16.95. Children's menu. Specializes in beef, chicken. Own pastries. Pianist. Mountain view; early 1900s atmosphere. Cr cds: A, C, D, DS, ER, MC, V.

D SC

Clovis (E-7)

See also Portales

Founded 1907 **Pop** 30,954 **Elev** 4,280 ft **Area code** 505 **Zip** 88101

Information Chamber of Commerce, 215 N Main; 505/763-3435

Web www.clovis.org

Established as a town for Santa Fe railroad stops, Clovis is named for the first Christian king of France, who ruled from A.D. 481-511. It is surrounded by cattle ranches and dairies, alfalfa, wheat, milo, and corn farms. Cannon Air Force Base is located 8 miles west on US 60. Clovis is also home of the Norman Petty Recording Studio, where Buddy Holly, Roy Orbison, and others recorded some of their first hits.

What to See and Do

Clovis Depot Model Train Museum. *221 W First St. Phone 505/762-0066.* Built in 1907 by the Atchison, Topeka, and Santa Fe Railway, the Depot has been restored to its condition in the 1950s era. Features working model train layouts, railroad memorabilia, historical displays, and an operating telegraph station. Real train operations along one of the busiest rail lines in the US can be viewed from platform. Gift shop. (Wed-Sun afternoons; closed holidays) **$$**

Hillcrest Park and Zoo. *Sycamore and 10th. Phone 505/769-7870.* Second-largest zoo in New Mexico; more than 500 animals, most of which are exhibited in natural environments. Informational programs. Park has kiddieland with amusement rides, outdoor and indoor swimming pool, golf course, picnic areas, sunken garden. **$$**

Special Events

Curry County Fair. *600 S Norris St. Phone 505/763-3435.* Mid-Aug.

Pioneer Days & PRCA Rodeo. *1002 W McDonald. Phone 505/763-3435.* Parade, Little Buckaroo Rodeo. First week in June.

Motels/Motor Lodges

★ **BEST WESTERN LA VISTA INN.** *1516 Mabry Dr (88101). Phone 505/762-3808; toll-free 800/780-7234; fax 505/762-1422. www.bestwestern.com.* 47 rooms. S $41-$51;

D $44-$54; each additional $4; under 12 free. Check-out 11 am. TV; cable (premium). Game room. Pool. Cr cds: A, C, D, DS, JCB, MC, V.

★ **CLOVIS INN AND SUITES.** *2912 Mabry Dr (88101). Phone 505/762-5600; toll-free 800/535-3440; fax 505/762-6803.* 97 rooms, 2 story. S $46; D $53; each additional $5; under 12 free. Complimentary continental breakfast. Check-out noon. TV. Whirlpool. Cr cds: A, C, D, DS, MC, V.

★ **COMFORT INN.** *1616 Mabry Dr (88101). Phone 505/762-4591; toll-free 800/228-5150; fax 505/763-6747. www.comfortinn.com.* 50 rooms, 2 story. S $33-$38; D $36-$47; each additional $5; under 12 free. Crib free. Check-out 11 am. TV; cable (premium). Restaurant adjacent 7 am-9 pm. Heated pool. Meeting room. Business services. Cr cds: A, C, D, DS, JCB, MC, V.

★ ★ **HOLIDAY INN.** *2700 E Mabry Dr (88101). Phone 505/762-4491; toll-free 800/465-4329; fax 505/769-0564. www.holiday-inn.com.* 120 rooms, 2 story. S $59-$95; D $64-$100; under 18 free. Crib free. Check-out noon. TV; cable. In-room modem link. Restaurant 6 am-2 pm, 5-10 pm. Bar 2-10 pm; closed Sun. Room service. Sauna. Game room. 2 pools, 1 indoor, whirlpool. Meeting rooms. Business services. Cr cds: A, C, D, DS, ER, JCB, MC, V.

★ **NUMBER ONE VALUE INN.** *1720 Mabry Dr (88101). Phone 505/762-2971; fax 505/762-2735.* 92 rooms, 1-2 story. S $31-$37; D $37-$44; each additional $6. Crib free. Complimentary coffee. Check-out 11 am. TV; cable (premium). Restaurant adjacent 7 am-9 pm. Pool. Business services. Cr cds: A, C, D, DS, MC, V.

Restaurants

★ **GUADLAJARA CAFE.** *916 L Casillas St (88101). Phone 505/769-9965.* Hours: 11 am-2 pm, 5-9 pm; Sat from 5 pm. Closed Sun. Mexican menu. Lunch, dinner $2.50-$7.55. Specialty: chile relleno con carne. Cr cds: MC, V.

★ **LEAL'S MEXICAN FOOD.** *3100 E Mabry Dr (88101). Phone 505/763-4075; fax 505/763-0791.* Hours: 10:30 am-9 pm; Sun to 8 pm. Closed Thanksgiving, Dec 25. Reservations accepted. Mexican, American menu. Lunch, dinner $3.25-$9.99. Children's menu. Specializes in enchiladas, tacos, tamales. Cr cds: A, DS, MC, V.

★ ★ **POOR BOY'S STEAKHOUSE.** *2115 N Prince (88101). Phone 505/763-5222; fax 505/769-1207. www.poorboyssteakhouse.com.* Hours: 11 am-9 pm; Fri, Sat to 10 pm. Reservations accepted. Closed Thanksgiving, Dec 25. Lunch $3.99-$18.99, dinner $3.99-$20.99. Children's menu. Specializes in steak, seafood. Salad bar. Antiques. Cr cds: A, DS, MC, V.

Deming (H-2)

See also Las Cruces

Founded 1881 **Pop** 14,116 **Elev** 4,335 ft **Area code** 505 **Zip** 88031

Information Chamber of Commerce, 800 E Pine St, PO Box 8; 505/546-2674 or 800/848-4955

Web www.cityofdeming.org

This is a livestock, cotton, chiles, onions, and feed grain town in the Mimbres Valley. The old Butterfield Trail, route of an early stagecoach line to California, passed about 12 miles north of here; there is a marker on US 180. Hunting enthusiasts will find deer, antelope, ibex, bear, and blue quail plentiful in the surrounding mountains.

What to See and Do

City of Rocks State Park. *28 miles NW on US 180, then E on NM 61. Phone 505/536-2800.* This 680-acre park features fantastic rock formations formed by a thick blanket of volcanic ash that hardened into tuff, and subsequently was sculpted by wind and water; extensive cactus garden. Hiking, picnicking, camping. Standard fees. (Daily) **$$**

Columbus Historical Museum. *Hwy 9 and Hwy 11. 32 miles S via NM 11 in Columbus. Phone 505/531-2620.* Housed in restored Southern Pacific Depot (1902). Memorabilia of 1916 Pancho Villa raid and Camp Furlong (Pershing expedition into Mexico); headquarters of Columbus Historical Society. (Daily; closed holidays) **FREE**

Deming-Luna Mimbres Museum. *301 S Silver St. Phone 505/546-2382.* Mining, military, ranching, railroad, Native American, and Hispanic artifacts of the Southwest. Mimbres pottery; Indian baskets; chuckwagon with equipment; photographic display; antique china, crystal; quilt room; antique dolls; bell and bottle collections; gems and minerals. Musical center; art gallery. (Daily; closed holidays) **FREE**

Pancho Villa State Park. *NM 9 and NM 11. 32 miles S on NM 11 near Columbus. Phone 505/531-2711.* Commemorates Pancho Villa's famous raid (Mar 9, 1916) into US territory. On site of Camp Furlong, from which Brigadier General John "Black Jack" Pershing pursued Villa into Mexico; the first US military action to employ motorized vehicles and airplanes. Some original buildings still stand. Garden of desert vegetation, hundreds of different cacti. Picnicking, playground, camping (hookups, dump station). Standard fees. Three miles south is Las Palomas, Mexico. (Daily) (For Border Crossing Regulations, see MAKING THE MOST OF YOUR TRIP.) **$$**

Rockhound State Park. *Highway 143. 5 miles S on NM 11, then 9 miles E on Access Rd 549. Phone 505/546-6182.* This 1,000-acre park is on the rugged western slope of the Little Florida Mountains. An abundance of agate, geodes, and other semiprecious stones for collectors (free; limit 15 lbs). Display of polished stones. Hiking, picnicking, playground, camping (hookups). Standard fees. (Daily) **$$**

Rock hunting. *Deming Gem and Mineral Society, Raymond Reed Blvd Southwestern NM Fair Grounds (88030). Phone 505/546-0348.* "Deming Agate," jasper, onyx, nodules, and many other types of semiprecious stones abound in area. Local gem and mineral society sponsors field trips (see SPECIAL EVENTS).

Special Events

Great American Duck Race. *101 N Copper. Courthouse Park.* Live duck racing; duck queen, darling duckling, best-dressed duck contests; hot-air balloon race; tortilla toss; parade. Fourth weekend in Aug.

Old West Gun Show. *800 E Pine. Fairgrounds. Phone 800/ 848-4955.* Western artifacts, jewelry; military equipment, guns, ammunition. Third weekends in Feb and Aug.

Rockhound Roundup. *3115 S Belen. Fairgrounds. Phone 505/544-4158.* More than 6,000 participants. Guided field trips for agate, geodes, candy rock, marble, honey onyx. Auctions; exhibitions; demonstrations. Contact Deming Gem & Mineral Society, PO Box 1459. Mid-Mar.

Southwestern New Mexico State Fair. *Fairgrounds. Phone 505/546-8694.* Livestock shows, midway, parade. Early-mid-Oct.

Motels/Motor Lodges

★ **DAYS INN.** *1601 E Pine St (88030). Phone 505/ 546-8813; toll-free 800/329-7466; fax 505/546-7095. www.daysinn.com.* 57 rooms, 2 story. S $36; D $44; each additional $4; suites $46-$58; under 12 free; weekly rates. Crib free. Pet accepted, some restrictions. TV; cable (premium). Pool. Complimentary continental breakfast. Check-out 11 am. Cr cds: A, C, D, DS, JCB, MC, V.

D 🔄 ➖

★ **GRAND MOTOR INN.** *1721 E Spruce St (88031). Phone 505/546-2632; fax 505/546-4446.* 62 rooms, 2 story.

S $42; D $45-$50; each additional $6; suites $65; under 12 free. Crib free. Pet accepted. TV; cable (premium). Heated pool; wading pool, poolside service. Restaurant 6 am-10 pm. Room service. Bar noon-12:30 am. Check-out noon. Meeting rooms. Business services available. Valet service. Free airport, train station, bus depot transportation. Golf privileges. Cr cds: A, C, D, DS, MC, V.

D 🔄 ➖ ➗ SC

★ ★ **HOLIDAY INN.** *I-10 E exit 85 (88031). Phone 505/546-2661; toll-free 888/546-2661; fax 505/546-6308. www.holiday-inn.com.* 120 rooms, 2 story. S, D $59; each additional $6; suites $79; under 19 free; higher rates last weekend Aug. Crib free. Pet accepted. TV; cable (premium). Pool. Restaurant 6 am-2 pm, 4-10 pm. Check-out 11 am. Coin laundry. Meeting rooms. Business services available. Sundries. Free airport, train station, bus depot transportation. Some in-room whirlpools. Cr cds: A, C, D, DS, JCB, MC, V.

D 🔄 ➖ ➗ SC

Dulce (A-3)

See also Chama

Pop 2,623 **Elev** 6,769 ft **Area code** 505 **Zip** 87528

A section of Carson National Forest (see TAOS) is located southwest on US 64.

What to See and Do

Jicarilla Apache Indian Reservation. *Seneca Dr. On US 64. Phone 505/759-3242.* The Jicarilla Apaches came from a group that migrated from southwestern Canada several centuries ago. The reservation is at an elevation of 6,500-8,500 feet and has excellent fishing and boating; hunting (guides available; tribal permit required; phone 505/759-3255 for information). **$$**

Special Events

Go-Jii-Ya. *Stone Lake. Phone 505/759-3242.* Rodeo, Pow Wow, foot races. Mid-Sept.

Little Beaver Roundup. *Jicarilla Apache Indian Reservation. Phone 505/759-3242.* Parade, rodeo, dances, arts and crafts, carnival, 62-mile pony express race; baseball tournament; archery. Mid-July.

Motel/Motor Lodge

★ ★ **BEST WESTERN JICARILLA INN.** *Jicarilla Blvd (87528). Phone 505/759-3663; toll-free 800/780-7234; fax 505/759-3170. www.bestwestern.com.* 42 units, 2 story. July-Jan: S $65; D $80; each additional $5; suites $90-$95; under 12 free; lower rates rest of year. TV. Restaurant 6:30 am-9 pm. Bar 4:30 pm-1:30 am. Complimentary continental breakfast. Check-out 11 am. Meeting rooms. Gift shop. Some refrigerators. Microwave in suites. Cr cds: A, C, D, DS, ER, JCB, MC, V.

D ⬛

El Malpais National Monument and National Conservation Area

S on NM 53; or 6 miles SE on I-40, then S on NM 117. Contact Information Center, 123 E Roosevelt.

These two areas total 376,000 acres of volcanic formations and sandstone canyons. Monument features splatter cones and a 17-mile-long system of lava tubes. Conservation area, which surrounds the monument, includes La Ventana Natural Arch, one of the state's largest freestanding natural arches; Cebolla and West Malpais wildernesses; and numerous Anasazi ruins. The Sandstone Bluffs Overlook, off NM 117, offers an excellent view of lava-filled valley and surrounding area. Facilities include hiking, bicycling, scenic drives, primitive camping (acquire Backcountry Permit at Information Center or Ranger Station). Lava is rough; caution is advised. Most lava tubes accessible only by hiking trails; check with Information Center in Grants before attempting any hikes. Monument, conservation area (daily). Information Center and visitor facility on NM 117 (daily; closed Jan 1, Thanksgiving, Dec 25).

El Morro National Monument (Inscription Rock) (D-2)

See also Gallup, Grants

(From I-40, 43 miles SW of Grants off NM 53)

Here, on the ancient trail taken by the Conquistadores from Santa Fe to Zuni, is the towering cliff that served as the guest book of New Mexico. Don Juan de Oñate carved his name here in 1605; others followed him in 1629 and 1632. Don Diego de Vargas, reconqueror of New Mexico after the Pueblo Rebellion of 1680, registered his passing in 1692, and scores of other Spaniards and Americans added their names to the cliff at later dates.

The rock is pale buff Zuni sandstone. The cliff, 200 feet high, has pueblo ruins on its top; pre-Columbian petroglyphs. Visitor center and museum (daily; closed January 1, December 25; free).

Trail (fee), picnic facilities. Ranger on duty. Golden Eagle and Golden Age passports (see MAKING THE MOST OF YOUR TRIP). Primitive camping (fee). Contact the Superintendent, El Morro National Monument, Rte 2, Box 43, Ramah 87321. Phone 505/783-4226.

Española (C-4)

See also Los Alamos, Santa Fe

Pop 9,688 **Elev** 5,585 ft **Area code** 505 **Zip** 87532

Information Española Valley Chamber of Commerce, 417 Big Rock Center; 505/753-2831

Web espanola.com/chamber

First settled 700 years ago by the Pueblo, then by Don Juan de Oñate in 1598, Española was claimed by the United States in 1846. Prosperity came with the railroad in the 1870s. A Ranger District office of the Santa Fe National Forest (see SANTA FE) is located here.

What to See and Do

Florence Hawley Ellis Museum. *Mile Post 224, Hwy 84. Phone 505/685-4333.* Exhibits of Native American/Spanish history. (Memorial Day-Labor Day, Tues-Sun; closed Dec; rest of year, Tues-Sat) **$$**

Ortega's Weaving Shop. *NM 76 and NM 520. 10 miles NE via NM 76, County Rd 98 in Chimayo. Phone 505/351-4215.* Near the Plaza del Cerro (plaza of the hill), an example of an old-style protected Spanish Colonial village. Generations of noted weavers make blankets, coats, vests, purses, rugs. (Mon-Sat) **FREE** Directly north of the shop is

> **Galeria Ortega.** *55 Plaza Del Cerro. Phone 800/743-5921.* Contains works by artists of northern New Mexico depicting the region's unique tri-cultural heritage. (May-Oct, daily; rest of year, Mon-Sat) **FREE**

Ruth Hall Museum of Paleontology. *Mile Post 224, Hwy 84. Phone 505/685-4333.* Exhibits on Triassic animals, Coelophysis, and New Mexico state fossils. (Memorial Day-Labor Day, Tues-Sun; rest of year, Tues-Sat) **$**

Special Events

Fiesta del Valle de Española. Celebrates establishment of New Mexico's first Spanish settlement in 1598. Torch relay, vespers, candlelight procession, street dancing, arts and crafts, food, entertainment, parade (Sun). Phone Chamber of Commerce. Second week in July.

Sainte Claire Feast Day. *South of Espanola, North of Santa Fe (87532).* Santa Clara Pueblo, 2 miles S via NM 30. Phone 505/753-7326. Dancing, food, market. Mid-Aug.

San Juan Feast Day. *San Juan Pueblo, 5 miles N via US 84, NM 68.* Phone 800/793-4955; 505/852-4400. Dancing, food, carnival. Late June.

Tri-cultural Arts Festival. *921 Paseo de Onte Rd (87532).* Northern New Mexico Community College. Features local artisans and their works; including potters, weavers, woodworkers, photographers, painters, singers, and dancers. Phone Chamber of Commerce. Usually first weekend in Oct.

White Water Race. *Phone 800/222-RAFT.* Canoe, kayak, raft experts challenge 14 miles of white water below Pilar. Mother's Day.

B&B/Small Inns

★ ★ ★ **INN AT DELTA.** *243 Paseo De Onate (87532). Phone 505/753-9466; toll-free 800/995-8599; fax 505/753-9446. www.innatthedelta.com.* This bed and breakfast is located between Sante Fe and Taos and is close to art studios, museums and local craft persons. The inn is also close to famous pueblos of New Mexico. 10 rooms, 2 story. S, D $100-$150; each additional $10; under 12 free; holiday plans. Crib available. Complimentary full breakfast. Check-out noon, check-in 3 pm. TV; cable. Fireplaces, in-room whirlpools. Restaurant adjacent 5-10 pm (see also ANTHONY'S AT THE DELTA). Concierge service. Adobe structure with Southwestern-style furnishings, hand-carved by local craftsmen. Cr cds: A, DS, MC, V.

D ⚡ ⊠

★ ★ ★ **RANCHO DE SAN JUAN COUNTRY INN.** *US Hwy 285, mile marker 340 (87533). Phone 505/753-6818; toll-free 800/726-7121; fax 505/753-6818. www.ranchodesanjuan.com.* Situated between Taos and Santa Fe, this inn offers many tranquil spots over its 225 scenic acres. Designed in the Spanish tradition, the decor is both rustic and refined with wildflower-filled courtyards, exposed beams, tile floors, and Southwestern art and antiques. The colorful mountain and river-valley views can be enjoyed from the rooms or the award-winning restaurant (see also RANCHO DE SAN JUAN COUNTRY INN). 14 suites, 3 std rooms, 3 kitchen units. D $225-$400. Children over 12 years only. Complimentary breakfast. Check-out 11 am, check-in 2 pm. Fireplaces. Restaurant. Concierge, totally nonsmoking. Cr cds: A, DS, MC, V.

D ⊠

Restaurants

★ ★ **ANTHONY'S AT THE DELTA.** *233 Paseo de Onate (87532).* Phone 505/753-4511. Hours: 5-9 pm; summer to 10 pm. Closed Jan 1, Thanksgiving, Dec 25. Reservations accepted. Bar. Dinner $10.95-$32. Specialties: prime rib, grilled salmon. Salad bar. 4 dining areas; 2 fireplaces; hand-carved wooden furniture; art collection displayed. Many plants; courtyard with rose bushes. Cr cds: A, C, D, DS, ER, MC, V.

D

★ ★ **EL PARAGUA.** *603 Santa Cruz Rd (87532). Phone 505/753-3211; fax 505/753-6749. www.elparagua.com.* Mexican menu. Stone building (1877); many antiques, Mexican tiles, stone fireplace. Hours: 11 am-9 pm; weekends to 9:30 pm. Closed most major holidays. Lunch $7-$9, dinner $8.50-$32. Bar. Children's menu. Reservations accepted. Cr cds: A, D, DS, MC, V.

D

★ ★ ★ **RANCHO DE SAN JUAN COUNTRY INN.** *US 285 (87533). Phone 505/753-6818 or 800/726-7121. www.ranchodesanjuan.com.* The elegant, cheerful dining room of this inn, situated between Taos and Santa Fe, overlooks the Ojo Caliente River valley and the Jemez Mountains. The tranquil setting is the perfect backdrop for chef/owner John H. Johnson III's Southwest-inspired, international cuisine. Each dish on the daily-changing prix fixe menu is artistically prepared and as beautiful as the patio sunsets. Sittings: Wed-Sat 6:30 and 8 pm; Tue sitting at 7 pm. Closed Sun, Mon; also Dec 25. Dinner $50-$95. Bar. Reservations required. Outdoor dining. Totally nonsmoking. Cr cds: A, DS, MC, V.

D

Farmington (B-2)

See also Aztec, Shiprock

Founded 1876 **Pop** 37,844 **Elev** 5,395 ft **Area code** 505

Information Chamber of Commerce, 203 W Main St, 87401; 505/326-7602 or 800/448-1240

Web www.farmingtonnm.org

The Navajos call it Totah, the meeting place at the convergence of three rivers in the colorful land of the Navajo, Ute, Apache, and Pueblo. Once the home of the ancient Anasazi, Farmington is now the largest city in the Four Corners area and supplies much of the energy to the Southwest. From Farmington, visitors may explore Mesa Verde, Chaco Canyon, and the Salmon and Aztec ruins.

Visitors to the area can also enjoy some of the best year-round fishing in the state at Navajo Lake State Park (see AZTEC) and in the San Juan River. Farmington is also the home of the Navajo Indian Irrigation Project, which encompasses more than 100,000 acres.

There are many shops offering traditional Native American crafts in the immediate area—baskets, jewelry, pottery, rugs, and sand paintings. Obtain a list of local art galleries and trading posts at the Convention and Visitors Bureau.

What to See and Do

Bisti Badlands. *Hwy 371. 37 miles S via NM 371. Phone 505/599-8900.* A federally protected wilderness area of strange geologic formations; large petrified logs and other fossils are scattered among numerous scenic landforms. No vehicles permitted beyond boundary. **FREE**

Chaco Culture National Historical Park. *75 miles S.*

⭐ **Four Corners Monument.** *Navajo Reservation (86514). 64 miles NW via US 64, NM 504, US 160. Phone 928/871-6647.* Only point in the country common to four states: Arizona, Colorado, New Mexico, and Utah.

San Juan County Archaeological Research Center & Library at Salmon Ruin. *6131 Hwy 64. 12 miles E on US 64 near Bloomfield. Phone 505/632-2013.* Archaeological remains of a 250-room structure built by the Pueblo (circa A.D. 1100). Museum and research center exhibit artifacts from excavation; historic structures; picnicking. (Daily; closed holidays) **$$**

Special Events

Black River Traders. *Pinon Hills & College. Lions Wilderness Park Amphitheater. Phone 505-325-0279.* Historical drama about the Southwest's multicultural heritage, presented in outdoor amphitheater. Contact Convention and Visitors Bureau for schedule. Mid-June-mid-Aug.

Connie Mack World Series Baseball Tournament. *1101 Fairgrounds Rd. Ricketts Park.* Seventeen-game series hosting teams from all over the US and Puerto Rico. Aug.

Farmington Invitational Balloon Rally. *3041 East Main. Phone 800/448-1240.* Hare and hound races; competitions. Memorial Day weekend.

San Juan County Fair. *41 Road 5568.* Parade; rodeo; fiddlers' contest; chili cook-off; exhibits. Mid-late Aug.

Totah Festival. *200 W Arrington.* Fine arts juried show. Rug auction; powwow. Labor Day weekend.

Motels/Motor Lodges

⭐⭐ **BEST WESTERN INN & SUITES.** *700 Scott Ave (87401). Phone 505/327-5221; toll-free 800/780-7234; fax 505/327-1565. www.bestwestern.com.* 194 rooms, 3 story. S, D $59-$69; each additional $10; under 12 free; weekend rates; golf plans. Crib free. Pet accepted. Check-out noon. TV; cable (premium), VCR available (movies $2). Some refrigerators. Coffee in rooms. Valet services, coin laundry. Restaurant 6-10 am, 11 am-2 pm, 5-10 pm. Bar 11:30 am-midnight. Room service. Exercise equipment, sauna. Recreation room. Indoor pool, whirlpool, poolside service. Free airport, bus depot transportation. Meeting rooms. Business services. Bellstaff. Cr cds: A, C, D, DS, MC, V.

D ⬤ 🛏 🏋 ✈ 🆘 SC

⭐ **COMFORT INN.** *555 Scott Ave (87401). Phone 505/325-2626; fax 505/325-7675. www.comfortinn.com.* 60 rooms, 2 story, 18 suites. May-Oct: S $54; D $62; each additional $6; suites $59-$69; under 18 free; lower rates rest of year. Crib $5. Pet accepted. TV; cable (premium). Pool. Complimentary continental breakfast. Complimentary coffee in rooms. Check-out 11 am. Business services available. In-room modem link. Health club privileges. Refrigerator in suites. Cr cds: A, C, D, DS, JCB, MC, V.

D ⬤ 🛏 🏋 🆘

⭐⭐ **HOLIDAY INN.** *600 E Broadway (87499). Phone 505/327-9811; toll-free 888/327-9812; fax 505/325-2288. www.holiday-inn.com.* 149 rooms, 2 story. S $69-$79; D $75-$85; each additional $8; under 19 free. Crib free. Pet accepted. TV; cable (premium). Pool; whirlpool. Restaurant 6 am-10 pm. Room service. Bar. Check-out noon. Business services available. Bellstaff. Free airport, bus depot transportation. Exercise equipment; sauna. Cr cds: A, D, DS, JCB, MC, V.

D ⬤ 🛏 🏋 ✈ 🆘 SC

⭐ **LA QUINTA INN.** *675 Scott Ave (87401). Phone 505/327-4706; toll-free 800/531-5900; fax 505/325-6583.* 106 rooms, 2 story. S, D $59-$74; each additional $8; under 18 free. Crib free. Pet accepted. Complimentary continental breakfast. Check-out noon. TV; cable (premium). Refrigerators available. Valet services. Restaurant adjacent open 24 hours. Heated pool. Picnic tables, grills. Cr cds: A, C, D, DS, MC, V.

D ⬤ 🛏 ✈ 🆘

★ ★ **RAMADA INN.** *601 E Broadway (87401). Phone 505/325-1191; toll-free 888/325-1191; fax 505/325-1223. www.ramada.com.* 75 rooms, 3 story. Apr-Sept: S, D $67; each additional $10; suites $175; under 12 free; family rates; lower rates rest of year. Crib free. TV; cable (premium), VCR available. Complimentary coffee in rooms. Restaurant 6:30 am-10:30 pm. Room service 7 am-10 pm. Check-out noon. Meeting rooms. Business services available. In-room modem link. Coin laundry. Free airport transportation. Heated pool; whirlpool. In-room whirlpool, microwave, wet bar in suites. Cr cds: A, D, DS, MC, V.

D ⊷ ⑂ ⊠

B&B/Small Inns

★ ★ ★ **CASA BLANCA.** *505 E La Plata St (87401). Phone 505/327-6503; toll-free 800/550-6503; fax 505/326-5680. www.4cornersbandb.com.* This property features manicured lawns and gardens on a bluff overlooking Farmington and the San Juan River. Guests can enjoy such activities as visiting the Anasazi sites, train rides, and golf and fly fishing. 4 rooms, 2 suites. D $75-$175. Complimentary full breakfast; afternoon refreshments. Check-out 11 am, check-in 4-7 pm. TV; cable, VCR (movies). Restaurant nearby. Concierge. Mission-style house built in the '50s. Totally nonsmoking. Free airport transportation. Cr cds: A, DS, MC, V.

⊠

Restaurants

★ **CLANCY'S PUB.** *2703 E 20th St (87402). Phone 505/325-8176; fax 505/325-9295. www.clancys.net.* Hours: 11-2 am; Sun noon-midnight. Closed Easter, Thanksgiving, Dec 25. Reservations accepted. Mexican, American menu. Bar. Lunch, dinner $2.50-$11.95. Children's menu. Specializes in prime rib, hamburgers. Outdoor dining. Casual dining. Cr cds: A, D, MC, V.

D

★ **LA FIESTA GRANDE.** *1916 E Main St (87401). Phone 505/397-1235.* Hours: 11 am-9:30 pm; Fri, Sat to 10 pm; Sun to 8 pm. Closed Jan 1, Thanksgiving, Dec 25. Mexican, American menu. Lunch $3-$4.95, dinner $3-$8.50. Lunch buffet $4.95, Sun $5.95. Children's menu. Specializes in fajitas, sopaipillas, green chili cheeseburgers. Salad bar. Cr cds: MC, V.

D SC

Fort Union National Monument (C-5)

20 miles NE on I-25 to Watrous/Fort Union exit 366, then 8 miles NW on NM 161. Contact Superintendent, PO Box 127, Watrous 87753.

Established at this key defensive point on the Santa Fe Trail in 1851, the third and last fort built here was the largest post in the Southwest and the supply center for nearly 50 other forts in the area. It was abandoned by the military in 1891; 100 acres of adobe ruins remain. Self-guided trail with audio stations, living history programs featuring costumed demonstrations (summer). Visitor center depicts the fort's history, artifacts. (Daily; closed Jan 1, Thanksgiving, Dec 25)

Gallup (C-1)

Founded 1881 **Pop** 20,209 **Elev** 6,600 ft **Area code** 505 **Zip** 87301

Information Gallup-McKinley County Chamber of Commerce, 103 W Hwy 66, 87301; 505/722-2228

Web www.gallupchamber.com

Gallup, originally a railroad town, was established to take advantage of the coal reserves nearby and has grown into a retail center serving a large area. The Navajo reservation is north and west of town. The Navajo, Zuni, Hopi, and Acoma trade here.

What to See and Do

Cultural Center. *201 US 66 E. Phone 505/863-4131.* Located in restored historic railroad station; ceremonial gallery, storyteller museum, Indian dances (Memorial Day-Labor Day, evenings), kiva cinema, visitor center, gift shop, café. (Summer, Mon-Sat; winter, Mon-Fri) **FREE**

McGaffey Recreation Area. *12 miles E on I-40, then 10 miles S on NM 400 in Cibola National Forest (see ALBUQUERQUE). Phone 505/287-8833.* Half mile to lake. Fishing, picnicking (fireplaces, tables), tent and trailer sites. Ranger District headquarters at Grants. Fees for some activities. (May-Sept, daily) **$**

Red Rock State Park. *5 miles E via I-40 and NM 566. Phone 505/722-3839.* Desert setting with massive red sandstone buttes. Nature trail, boarding stable. Picnicking, concession, camping (hookups; fee). Interpretive displays, auditorium/convention center, 7,000-seat arena; site of Inter-Tribal Indian Ceremonial (see SPECIAL EVENTS) and rodeos. In the park is

Red Rock Museum. *300 W Historic 66 Ave. Phone 505/ 863-1337.* Hopi, Navajo, and Zuni artifacts; gift shop. (Summer, Mon-Sat; winter, Mon-Fri; closed winter holidays) **DONATION**

Special Events

Inter-Tribal Indian Ceremonial. *226 W Coal Ave. Red Rock State Park. Phone 505/722-3839.* A major Native American festival; more than 50 tribes from the US, Canada, and Mexico participate in parades, rodeos, games, contests, dances, arts and crafts sales. Second week in Aug.

Navajo Nation Fair. *Fairgrounds in Window Rock, AZ. Phone 928/871-6478.* Dances, ceremonials, rodeo, arts and crafts, educational and commercial exhibits, food, traditional events. Contact PO Box 2370, Window Rock, AZ 86515. Five days beginning Wed after Labor Day.

Red Rock Balloon Rally. *Red Rock State Park. Phone 505/ 722-6274.* Contact Convention and Visitors Bureau for more information. First weekend in Dec.

Motels/Motor Lodges

★ **BEST VALUE INN.** *2003 W US 66 (87301). Phone 505/863-9385; toll-free 800/454-5444; fax 505/863-6532. www.bestvalueinn.com.* 92 rooms, 2 story. S, D $33.40-$44; each additional $4; weekly rates. Crib free. Pet accepted. TV; cable (premium). Heated pool; whirlpool. Sauna. Restaurant adjacent 6 am-10 pm. Check-out noon. Meeting room. Business services available. Cr cds: A, C, D, DS, ER, JCB, MC, V.

★ ★ **BEST WESTERN INN & SUITES.** *3009 W 66; I-40 (87301). Phone 505/722-2221; toll-free 800/780-7234; fax 505/722-7442. www.bestwestern.com.* 126 rooms, 2 story, 25 suites. June-Sept: S $64; D $72; each additional $8; suites $70; under 12 free; higher rates during special events; lower rates rest of year. Crib free. Pet accepted, some restrictions. TV; cable (premium). Indoor pool; whirlpool. Complimentary coffee in rooms. Restaurant 6-10 am, 5-9:30 pm. Room service. Bar 4:30-11 pm. Check-out noon. Meeting rooms. Sundries. Gift shop. Coin laundry. Exercise equipment; sauna. Game room. Microwave in suites. Cr cds: A, C, D, DS, MC, V.

★ **BEST WESTERN ROYAL HOLIDAY MOTEL.** *1903 W US 66 (87301). Phone 505/722-4900; toll-free 800/780-7234; fax 505/863-9952. www.bestwestern.com.* 50 rooms, 2 story. May-Oct: S $50-$65; D $55-$65; each additional $5; suites $64-$79; lower rates rest of year. Complimentary continental breakfast. Check-out 11 am. TV; cable (premium). Indoor pool, whirlpool. Cr cds: A, C, D, DS, MC, V.

★ **DAYS INN EAST.** *1603 W US 66 (87301). Phone 505/863-3891. www.daysinn.com.* 78 rooms, 2 story. Apr-Oct: S, D $50-$60; each additional $5; under 18 free; lower rates rest of year. Crib free. Pet accepted. TV; cable (premium). Heated pool. Playground. Complimentary continental breakfast. Restaurant nearby. Check-out 11 am. Business services available. Coin laundry. Cr cds: A, C, D, DS, JCB, MC, V.

★ ★ **EL RANCHO.** *1000 E US 66 (87301). Phone 505/863-9311; toll-free 800/543-6351; fax 505/722-5917.* 75 rooms, 6 kitchen units. S $46-$70; D $64-$70; suites $85-$95. Crib free. Pet accepted. Check-out noon. TV. Coin laundry. Restaurant 6:30 am-10 pm. Bar 5 pm-1 am. Meeting rooms. Business services. Gift shop. Cr cds: A, DS, MC, V.

★ ★ **HOLIDAY INN.** *2915 W US 66 (87301). Phone 505/722-2201; toll-free 800/432-2211; fax 505/722-9616. www.holiday-inn.com.* 212 rooms, 2 story. June-Aug: S, D $65-$73; each additional $5; under 19 free; lower rates rest of year. Crib free. Pet accepted. TV; cable (premium). Indoor pool; whirlpool. Complimentary full breakfast. Restaurant 6 am-10 pm. Room service. Bar 4 pm-12:30 am; closed Sun; entertainment. Check-out noon. Coin laundry. Meeting rooms. Business services available. Bellstaff. Valet service. Sundries. Free airport, train station, bus depot transportation. Exercise equipment; sauna. Game room. Cr cds: A, C, D, DS, JCB, MC, V.

Restaurants

★ **EARL'S.** *1400 E US 66 (87301). Phone 505/863-4201; fax 505/863-4073.* Hours: 6 am-9:30 pm; Fri, Sat to 10 pm; Sun to 9 pm. Closed most major holidays. Reservations accepted. Mexican, American menu. Breakfast $3.50-$5.50, lunch, dinner $4.50-$9.29. Children's menu. Salad bar. Casual family dining. Family-owned. Cr cds: A, D, MC, V.

★ **RANCH KITCHEN.** *3001 W US 66 (87301). Phone 505/722-2537; toll-free 800/717-8818; fax 505/722-2338. www.ranchkitchen.com.* Mexican, American menu. Specialties: beef chimichanga, Navajo taco, mesquite-smoked barbecue. Hours: 6 am-10 pm. Closed Dec 24, 25, Easter Sunday. Breakfast $2.95-$6, lunch $3.50-$7.95, dinner $5.95-$18. Children's menu. Reservations accepted. Cr cds: A, D, DS, MC, V.

D **SC**

Gila Cliff Dwellings National Monument (F-2)

See also Gila (HEE-la) National Forest

44 miles N of Silver City on NM 15.

There are 42 rooms in six caves (accessible by a 1-mile hiking trail), which were occupied by the Mogollon circa 1300. Well-preserved masonry dwellings in natural alcoves in the face of an overhanging cliff. Self-guided tour, camping. Forest naturalists conduct programs (Memorial Day-Labor Day). Ruins and visitor center (daily; closed Jan 1, Dec 25).

Grants (D-2)

Founded 1882 **Pop** 8,806 **Elev** 6,460 ft **Area code** 505 **Zip** 87020

Information Chamber of Commerce, 100 N Iron St, PO Box 297; 505/287-4802

Web www.grants.org

A Navajo named Paddy Martinez revolutionized the life of this town in 1950 when he discovered uranium ore. More than half the known domestic reserves of uranium ore are in this area.

About 4 miles east, I-40 (US 66) crosses one of the most recent lava flows in the continental United States. Indian pottery has been found under the lava, which first flowed about 4 million years ago from Mount Taylor, to the north. Lava also flowed less than 1,100 years ago from fissures that, today, are near the highway. The lava is sharp and hard; heavy shoes are advisable for walking on it. A Ranger District office of the Cibola National Forest (see ALBUQUERQUE) is located here.

What to See and Do

Acoma Pueblo. *32 miles SE via I-40, NM 23. Phone 800/747-0181.* Oldest continuously inhabited pueblo in North America. Provides a glimpse into well-preserved Native American culture.

Bluewater Lake State Park. *19 miles W on I-40, then 7 miles S on NM 412. Phone 505/876-2391.* Rolling hills studded with piñon and juniper trees encircle the Bluewater Reservoir. Swimming, waterskiing, fishing (trout, catfish), boating (ramps); ice-fishing, picnicking, camping (electrical hookups, dump station). Standard fees. (Daily) **$$**

El Morro National Monument (Inscription Rock). (see) *Approximately 43 miles SW off NM 53.*

Laguna Pueblo. *33 miles E off I-40. Phone 505/552-6654.* (Population approximately 7,000) This is one of the 19 pueblos located in the state of New Mexico. The people here speak the Keresan language. The pueblo consists of six villages: Encinal, Laguna, Mesita, Paguate, Paraje, and Seama. These villages are located along the western boundary of the pueblo. The Pueblo people sell their arts and crafts on the reservation; items such as Indian belts, pottery, jewelry, baskets, paintings, Indian kilts, and moccasins can be purchased. Visitors are welcomed to the pueblo throughout the year and may encounter various religious observances, some of which are open to the public. However, questions concerning social and religious ceremonies should be directed to the Governor of the Pueblo. As a general rule, photographs, sketches, and tape recordings of Pueblo ceremonials are strictly forbidden. Therefore, it is most important that visitors observe these restrictions and first obtain permission from the Governor of the Pueblo before engaging in such activities. Fiestas and dances are held throughout the year.

New Mexico Mining Museum. *100 N Iron St. Phone 505/287-4802 or 800/748-2142.* Only underground uranium mining museum in the world. Indian artifacts and relics; native mineral display. (Mon-Sat) **$$**

Motel/Motor Lodge

★ ★ **BEST WESTERN INN & SUITES.** *1501 E Santa Fe Ave (87020). Phone 505/287-7901; toll-free 800/780-7234; fax 505/285-5751. www.bestwestern.com.* 126 rooms, 2 story. S, D $60-$80; each additional $8; under 12 free; suites $65-$85. Crib free. Pet accepted, some restrictions. TV; cable (premium). Indoor pool; whirlpool. Sauna. Restaurant 6:30-9:30 am, 5-9:30 pm. Room service. Bar 3:30-11 pm; Fri, Sat to midnight; Sun to 11 pm. Check-out noon. Coin laundry. Meeting rooms. Business services available. Valet service. Sundries, Game room. Refrigerators available. Cr cds: A, C, D, DS, MC, V.

D **SC**

Hobbs (G-7)

Founded 1927 **Pop** 28,657 **Elev** 3,650 ft **Area code** 505
Zip 88240

Information Chamber of Commerce, 400 N Marland;
505/397-3202

Web www.hobbschamber.org

A chance meeting between two covered wagons on a trail across the Llano Estacado (Staked Plain) led to the founding of Hobbs. James Hobbs and his family were headed for Alpine, Texas when they met an eastbound wagon of pioneers returning from Alpine because they couldn't make a living there. Hearing this, James turned his wagon north and eventually settled in what is now Hobbs. This was primarily an agrarian community until the discovery of "black gold" turned it into a booming oil town.

Oil, natural gas, and potash are the big products here; however, Lea County has long been (and still is) an important cattle ranch and dairy territory. Because there is a plentiful supply of shallow water in the ground, cotton, alfalfa, grain, and vegetables have been grown successfully.

What to See and Do

Lea County Cowboy Hall of Fame & Western Heritage Center. *5317 N Lovington Hwy (88240). New Mexico Junior College. Phone 505/392-1275 or -5518.* Local memorabilia and artifacts with emphasis on the cowboy, Native American, and oil eras. Permanent displays of Lea County history. (Mon-Sat; closed holidays) **FREE**

Special Events

Lea County Fair. *101 S Commercial Ave. In Lovington, 20 miles NW on NM 18. Phone 505/396-5344.* Aug.

Noche de Espana Music Festival. *Main and Becker sts. Phone 505/864-2830.* Includes Mexican food booths, arts and crafts booths. May.

Motels/Motor Lodges

★★ **HOWARD JOHNSON INN.** *501 N Marland Blvd (88240). Phone 505/397-3251; fax 505/393-3065.* 75 rooms, 2 story. S $49; D $59; each additional $7; suites $95-$119; under 18 free. Crib free. Pet accepted, some restrictions; $25. Check-out 11 am. TV; cable. In-room modem link. Guest laundry. Restaurant 5 am-8 pm; dining room 5:30-10 pm. Bar 11-1:30 am; entertainment except Sun. Room service 6 am-10 pm. Heated pool. Meeting rooms. Business services. Sundries. Cr cds: A, C, D, DS, MC, V.

D 🔲 🔳 🔲

★ **TRAVELODGE.** *1301 E Broadway (88240). Phone 505/393-4101; toll-free 888/963-9663; fax 505/393-4101. www.travelodge.com.* 72 rooms. S $40-$48; D $50-$54; each additional $4. Crib $3. Pet accepted. Complimentary full breakfast. Check-out noon. TV; cable (premium). In-room modem link. Restaurant opposite 11 am-10 pm. Pool. Business services. Cr cds: A, C, D, DS, MC, V.

D 🔲 🔳 🔲

Restaurant

★★ **CATTLE BARON STEAK AND SEAFOOD.** *1930 N Grimes (88240). Phone 505/393-2800.* Hours: 11 am-9:30 pm; Fri, Sat to 10 pm; Sun to 9 pm. Closed Thanksgiving, Dec 25. Bar. Lunch $4.95-$8, dinner $7.25-$29.95. Children's menu. Specializes in steak, seafood, prime rib. Salad bar. Cr cds: A, D, DS, MC, V.

D

Las Cruces (G-3)

Founded 1849 **Pop** 74,627 **Elev** 3,896 ft **Area code** 505

Information Convention & Visitors Bureau, 211 N Water St, 88001; 505/541-2444 or 800/FIESTAS

Web www.lascrucescvb.org

In 1830 a group of people from Taos were traveling on the Spanish highway El Camino Real; they camped here and were massacred by the Apache. They were buried under a field of crosses; hence the name Las Cruces ("the crosses"). Situated in the vast farming area of the fertile lower Rio Grande Valley, this region is especially noted for its homegrown green chile as well as pecans, cotton, lettuce, and corn.

What to See and Do

Aguirre Spring Recreation Site. *17 miles E via US 70, 5 miles S on unnumbered road. Phone 505/525-4300.* Organ Mountain area formed by monzonite intrusions—molten rock beneath the surface. Wearing away of the crust left organ pipe rock spires. Baylor Pass and Pine Tree hiking trails. Picnicking, camping (centrally located rest rooms; no drinking water). Managed by the Department of the Interior, Bureau of Land Management, Las Cruces Field Office. (Daily) **$$**

Cultural Complex. *500 N Water St. Phone 505/541-2155.* Found at the north end of Downtown Mall, includes the Las Cruces Museum of Fine Art & Culture, and the Braningan Cultural Center, which oversees the Bicentennial Log Cabin Museum. Developing is a Volunteers Memorial

Sculpture Garden, five blocks west of the complex at the Historical Sante Fe Depot in the New Mexico Railroad and Transportation Museum. (Call for schedule)

Exploring by car. There are ghost mining towns, extinct volcanoes, frontier forts, mountains, and pecan orchards in the area.

Fort Selden State Monument. *12 miles N on I-25.* Phone 505/526-8911. Frontier fort established in 1865. General Douglas MacArthur lived here as a boy (1884-86) when his father was post commander. Famed Buffalo Soldiers were stationed here. Self-guided, bilingual trail. Visitor center has history exhibits. Picnicking. (Mon, Wed-Sun; closed winter holidays) **$$**

Gadsden Museum. *2 miles SW on W Barker Rd in Mesilla.* Phone 505/526-6293. Native American and Civil War artifacts; paintings; hand-painted china; Santo collection; history of the Gadsden Purchase. (Daily; closed holidays) **$**

Mesilla. *4100 Dripping Spring Rd (88011). 1 mile SW.* Phone 505/647-9698. Historic village that briefly served as the Confederate capital of the Territory of Arizona. Billy the Kid stood trial for murder here and escaped. La Mesilla consists of the original plaza and surrounding adobe buildings. There are numerous specialty shops, restaurants, art galleries, and museums.

New Mexico Farm and Ranch Heritage Museum. *4100 Dripping Springs Rd (88011). 1 1/2 miles E on University Ave.* Phone 505/522-4100. Interactive 47-acre museum that brings to life Mexico's 3,000-year history, and farming and ranching life. Hands-on exhibits including plowing, blacksmithing, and cow-milking. Outdoor animal and plant life. (Tues-Sun; closed holidays) **$$**

New Mexico State University. *University Ave.* Phone 505/646-3221. (1888) 15,500 students. On the 950-acre campus are a history museum (Tues-Sun; free), an art gallery, and an 18-hole public golf course.

White Sands Missile Range. *25 miles E on US 70.* Phone 505/678-1134. Missiles and related equipment tested here. Actual range closed to the public; visitors welcome at the outdoor missile park and museum. (Daily; closed holidays) **FREE**

Special Events

Our Lady of Guadalupe Fiesta. *3600 Parroquia St. Tortugas Village, adjacent to town.* Phone 505/526-8171. Evening Indian dances, vespers; daytime ascent of Mt Tortugas; Mass, bonfire, and torchlight descent; fiesta. Mid-Dec.

Renaissance Craftfaire. *224 N Campo St. Young Park.* Phone 505/524-6403. Juried fair with participants in Renaissance costume. Food, entertainment. Early Nov.

Southern New Mexico State Fair. *12125 Robert Larsen Blvd (88005).* First weekend in Oct.

Whole Enchilada Fiesta. *Main St and Las Cruces St (88005). Downtown Mall.* Phone 505/524-6832. Street dancing, entertainment, crafts, food including world's largest enchilada. Last weekend in Sept.

Motels/Motor Lodges

★ ★ **BEST WESTERN MESILLA VALLEY INN.** *901 Avenida De Mesilla (88005).* Phone 505/524-8603; toll-free 800/528-1234; fax 505/526-8437. www.bestwestern.com. 167 units, 2 story. S, D $59; each additional $7; under 12 free. Crib free. Pet accepted. TV; cable. Heated pool; whirlpool. Restaurant 6 am-10 pm. Room service. Bar 11-1:30 am; Sun noon-11 pm; entertainment. Check-out 11 am. Coin laundry. Meeting rooms. Business services available. Health club privileges. Some refrigerators; microwaves available. Cr cds: A, C, D, DS, JCB, MC, V.

⊡ 🐾 ➿ ⊠

★ **DAY'S END LODGE.** *755 N Valley Dr (88005).* Phone 505/524-7753; fax 505/541-0732. 32 rooms, 2 story. S $31; D $37-$41; each additional $3; family unit $43-$50; under 18 free. Crib free. Pet accepted. Complimentary continental breakfast. Check-out 11 am. TV; cable (premium). Pool. Business services. Cr cds: A, DS, MC, V.

⊡ 🐾 ➿ ⊠

★ **DAYS INN.** *2600 S Valley Dr (88005).* Phone 505/526-4441; toll-free 800/329-7466; fax 505/526-1980. www.daysinn.com. 130 rooms, 2 story. S $45-$50; D $49-$59; each additional $5; under 18 free. Pet accepted. TV; cable (premium). Indoor pool; poolside service. Sauna. Restaurant 6-10 am, 5:30-9 pm. Bar 11 am-11 pm; Sat, Sun noon-10 pm. Check-out noon. Coin laundry. Meeting rooms. Business services available. Health club privileges. Valet service. Some balconies. Cr cds: A, C, D, DS, MC, V.

⊡ 🐾 ➿ ⊠ SC

★ **FAIRFIELD INN.** *2101 Summit Ct (88011).* Phone 505/522-6840; toll-free 800/228-2800; fax 505/522-9784. www.fairfieldinn.com. 78 rooms, 3 story. S, D $54.95-$64.95. Crib free. TV; cable (premium), VCR available. Complimentary continental breakfast. Restaurant nearby. Check-out noon. Business services available. Coin laundry. Exercise equipment. Pool. Some refrigerators, microwaves. Cr cds: A, C, D, DS, MC, V.

⊡ ➿ 🏋 ⊠ SC

★ **HAMPTON INN.** *755 Avenida De Mesilla (88005).* Phone 505/526-8311; toll-free 888/846-6741; fax 505/527-2015. www.hamptoninn.com. 117 rooms, 2 story. S, D $61-$70; under 18 free. Crib free. Pet accepted. Complimentary continental breakfast. Check-out noon. TV; cable (premium). In-room modem link. Pool. Cr cds: A, C, D, DS, MC, V.

D 🐾 ⇌ SC

★ ★ **HOLIDAY INN.** *201 E University Ave (88005). Phone 505/526-4411; toll-free 800/465-4329; fax 505/ 524-0530. www.holiday-inn.com.* 114 rooms, 2 story. S $79-$150; D $84-$175; suites $150; under 18 free. Crib free. Pet accepted, some restrictions. Check-out noon. TV; cable (premium). Coin laundry. Restaurant 6 am-10 pm. Bar 11-1 am. Room service. Exercise equipment. Game room. Indoor pool, wading pool. Beauty shop. Free airport, bus depot transportation. Meeting rooms. Enclosed courtyard re-creates Mexican plaza. Cr cds: A, D, DS, JCB, MC, V.

D 🐾 ⇌ 🏋 ⛹ SC

Hotel

★ ★ ★ **HILTON.** *705 S Telshor Blvd (88011). Phone 505/522-4300; toll-free 800/445-8667; fax 505/521-4707. www.hilton.com.* This property is just minutes from New Mexico State University, Las Cruces International Airport, NASA, White Sands Missile Range and Historic Old Mesilla. Activities such as golfing, bowling, horseback riding and fishing just minutes away. 203 units, 7 story. S $85-$110; D $90-$115; each additional $10; suites $115-$300. Crib free. Pet accepted. TV; cable; VCR available (movies). Pool; whirlpool, poolside service. Coffee in rooms. Restaurant 6 am-2 pm, 5-10 pm. Room service. Bar 11-2 am; entertainment. Check-out 1 pm. Meeting rooms. Business services available. In-room modem link. Gift shop. Free airport, bus depot transportation. Tennis privileges. Golf privileges. Exercise equipment. Health club privileges. Some refrigerators. Overlooks valley. Cr cds: A, C, D, DS, MC, V.

D 🐾 🏋 ⇌ 🏋 ⛹ SC

Resort

★ ★ **MESON DE MESILLA RESORT HOTEL.** *1803 Avenida Demesilla (88046). Phone 505/525-9212; toll-free 800/732-6025; fax 505/527-4196. www.mesondemesilla.com.* 15 rooms, 2 story. S $45-$50; D $65-$70. Pet accepted. Complimentary full breakfast. Check-out 11 am, check-in 1 pm. TV; cable (premium). Balconies. Restaurant (See also MESON DE MESILLA). Bar 11:30 am-9:15 pm. Pool. Picnic tables. Antique furnishings, brass beds; fireplace. Scenic views. Totally nonsmoking. Cr cds: A, D, DS, MC, V.

🐾 ⇌ ⛹

B&B/Small Inns

★ ★ **LUNDEEN INN OF THE ARTS.** *618 S Alameda Blvd (88005). Phone 505/526-3326; toll-free 888/526-3326; fax 505/647-1334. www.innofthearts.com.* 21 units, 7 suites, 11 kitchen units, 2 story. D $77-$85; each additional $15. Pet accepted. Complimentary full breakfast. Check-out 11 am, check-in 4 pm. TV; in sitting room; cable (premium), VCR available. Restaurant nearby. Lawn games. Built in 1890; antique furnishings. Art gallery; each room named for an artist. Cr cds: A, D, DS, MC, V.

🐾

Restaurants

★ ★ **CATTLE BARON.** *790 S Telshor (88011). Phone 505/522-7533; fax 505/521-3300. www.cattlebaron.com.* Closed Thanksgiving Day, Dec 25. Lunch, dinner. Bar. Children's menu. Cr cds: A, C, D, DS, MC, V. **$$**

D

★ ★ ★ **MESON DE MESILLA.** *1803 Avenida de Mesilla (88005). Phone 505/525-9212; fax 505/527-4196. www.mesondemesilla.com.* This romantic restaurant in an adobe-style bed and breakfast is a haven of sophisticated dining. Swiss-trained chef Matthew Barton Mattox combines continental cuisine with Italian and Southwestern accents for an unusual and delicious menu. Continental menu. Menu changes. Hours: 5:30-9 pm; Sun brunch 11 am-1:45 pm, closed Mon; Jan 1, Dec 25. Dinner $23-$40, Sun brunch $16.95. Bar. Reservations accepted. Adobe building. Cr cds: A, C, D, DS, ER, MC, V.

Las Vegas (C-5)

See also Santa Fe

Founded 1835 **Pop** 14,565 **Elev** 6,470 ft **Area code** 505 **Zip** 87701

Information Las Vegas-San Miguel Chamber of Commerce, 727 Grand Ave, PO Box 128; 505/425-8631 or 800/832-5947

Web www.lasvegasnewmexico.com

Las Vegas once was a stopover on the old Santa Fe Trail. The town prospered as a shipping point, and after the arrival of the railroad in 1879 it began an active period of building and rebuilding. Consequently there are 918 historic buildings (1846-1938). A Ranger District office of the Santa Fe National Forest (see SANTA FE) is located here, as are New Mexico Highlands University and Armand Hammer United World College of the American West.

What to See and Do

City of Las Vegas Museum and Rough Riders' Memorial Collection. *Municipal Building, 727 Grand Ave.* Phone 505/425-8726. Artifacts and memorabilia from Spanish-American War and turn-of-the-century northern New Mexico life. (May-Oct, daily; Nov-Apr, Mon-Fri). **DONATION**

Las Vegas National Wildlife Refuge. *Storrie Project. 2 miles E via NM 104, then 4 miles S via NM 281.* Phone 505/425-3581. Nature trail, observation of wildlife, including migratory water fowl. Hunting for dove (permit required), Canada goose (permit required, limited drawing); user's fee for hunts. (Daily; some areas Mon-Fri) **FREE**

Morphy Lake State Park. *11 miles N on NM 518 to Sapello, then 16 miles NW off NM 94.* Phone 505/387-2328. Towering ponderosa pines surround 15-acre mountain lake in Carson National Forest. Primitive use area. Fishing (trout), restricted boating (oars or electric motors only; ramp); winter sports, primitive camping. Accessible to backpackers; four-wheel-drive vehicle advisable. No drinking water available. Standard fees. (Daily) **$$**

Storrie Lake State Park. *4 miles N on NM 518.* Phone 505/425-7278. Swimming, waterskiing, fishing, boating (ramp), windsurfing, picnicking, playground, camping (hookups). (Daily) Standard fees. **$$**

Motels/Motor Lodges

★ **BUDGET INN.** *1216 N Grand Ave (87701).* Phone 505/425-9357. 45 rooms, 2 story. May-Sept: S $40-$60; D $50-$80; each additional $5; under 3 free; lower rates rest of year. Crib $3. Pet accepted, some restrictions. Complimentary coffee in lobby. Check-out 11 am. TV; cable (premium). Restaurant adjacent. Cr cds: A, C, D, DS, MC, V.

★ **COMFORT INN.** *2500 N Grand Ave (87701).* Phone 505/425-1100; toll-free 800/716-1103; fax 505/454-8404. www.comfortinn.com. 101 rooms, 2 story. Mar-Oct: S $54-$65; D $59-$70; each additional $5; under 18 free; lower rates rest of year. Crib $5. TV; cable (premium). Indoor pool; whirlpool. Complimentary continental breakfast. Check-out 11 am. Meeting rooms. Business services available. Patio. Picnic tables. Cr cds: A, C, D, DS, JCB, MC, V.

Hotel

★★ **PLAZA HOTEL.** *230 Plaza (87701).* Phone 505/425-3591; toll-free 800/328-1882; fax 505/425-9659. www.plazahotel-nm.com. 37 rooms, 3 story. S $79; D $84; each additional $8; suites $138-$146; under 17 free; some weekend rates. Crib free. Pet accepted; $10/day. Check-out 11 am. TV; cable (premium). Coffee in rooms. Restaurant 7 am-2 pm, 5-9 pm. Bar noon-midnight. Health club privileges. Cross-country ski 5 miles. Meeting rooms. Business services. Historic hotel built 1882 in the Victorian Italianate-bracketed style; interior renovated; period furnishings, antiques. Cr cds: A, D, DS, MC, V.

Resort

★★ **INN ON THE SANTA FE TRAIL.** *1133 Grand Ave (87701).* Phone 505/425-6791; toll-free 888/448-8438; fax 505/425-0417. www.innonthesantafetrail.com. 42 rooms, 12 suites. May-Sept: S $64-$69; D $74-$79; each additional $5; suites $95-$145; weekly rates; lower rates rest of year. Crib free. Pet accepted; $5/day. Complimentary continental breakfast. Check-out 11 am. TV; cable (premium). In-room modem link. Refrigerator in suites, microwaves available. Restaurant opposite 6:30 am-9 pm. Heated pool, whirlpool. Lawn games. Business services available. Cr cds: A, DS, MC, V.

Restaurants

★ **EL RIALTO.** *141 Bridge St (87701).* Phone 505/454-0037. American, Mexican, seafood menu. Hours: 10:30 am-9 pm. Closed Sun; major holidays. Dinner $4.99-$24.99. Bar 11 am-midnight. Salad bar. Children's menu. Historic building (1890s); antiques. Reservations accepted. Cr cds: A, D, MC, V.

★ **PINOS TRUCK STOP.** *1901 N Grand Ave (87701).* Phone 505/454-1944. American, Mexican menu. Hours: 6 am-9 pm. Closed Thanksgiving, Dec 25. Dinner $15.95-$23.95. Salad bar. Children's menu. Casual dining. Cr cds: A, D, DS, MC, V.

Los Alamos (C-4)

See also Espanola, Santa Fe

Pop 11,909 **Elev** 7,410 ft **Area code** 505 **Zip** 87544

Information Los Alamos County Chamber of Commerce, 109 Central Park Sq, PO Box 460; 505/662-8105 or 800/444-0707

Web www.vla.com

On high mesas between the Rio Grande Valley floor and the Jemez Mountain peaks, Los Alamos offers spectacular views and outdoor activities. The city was originally the site of a boys' school; it was acquired by the government in 1942 to develop the first atomic bomb. In 1967, the city property was turned over to Los Alamos County. The scientific laboratory, where research continues, remains a classified installation.

What to See and Do

Bandelier National Monument. *296 N Main St. Phone 585/394-1472.*

Bradbury Science Museum. *15th St and Central Ave. Phone 505/667-4444.* Displays artifacts relating to the history of the laboratory and the atomic bomb. Exhibits on modern nuclear weapons; life sciences; materials sciences; computers; particle accelerators; geothermal, fusion, and fission energy sources. (Daily; closed holidays) **FREE**

Jemez State Monument. *18160 State Rd 4. 18 miles N on US 4, then 9 miles S in Jemez Springs. Phone 505/829-3530.* Stabilized Spanish mission (1621) built by Franciscan missionaries next to a prehistoric pueblo. Self-guided bilingual trail. Visitor center has anthropology and archaeology exhibits. Picnicking. (Daily; closed holidays) **$$**

Los Alamos Historical Museum. *1921 Juniper. Fuller Lodge Cultural Center. Phone 505/662-4493 or -6272.* Artifacts, photos, other material tracing local history from prehistoric to present times; exhibit on the Manhattan Project. (Daily; closed holidays) **FREE** Also here is

> **Fuller Lodge Art Center and Gallery.** *2132 Central Ave. Ground floor of Fuller Lodge's west wing. Phone 505/ 662-9331.* Historic log building provides setting for changing exhibits. Features arts and crafts of northern New Mexico. (Mon-Sat; closed holidays) **FREE**

Motel/Motor Lodge

★ ★ **BEST WESTERN HILLTOP HOUSE HOTEL.** *400 Trinity Dr at Central (87544). Phone 505/662-2441; toll-free 800/462-0936; fax 505/662-5913. www.vla.com/ hilltophouse.* 98 rooms, 3 story, 33 kitchens S $75; D $85; each additional $10; kitchen units $76-$86; suites $98-$275; under 12 free. Crib $10. Pet accepted; $25 deposit. TV; cable (premium). Indoor pool; whirlpool. Complimentary breakfast. Restaurant 6:30-9:30 am, 11: 30 am-2 pm, 5-9 pm. Room service. Check-out 11 am. Coin laundry. Meeting rooms. Business services available. In-room modem link. Airport transportation. Sauna. Downhill/cross-country ski 10 miles. Exercise equipment. Massage. Cr cds: A, C, D, DS, JCB, MC, V.

[D] 🐾 🖨 🏋 🛩 🖂

Hotel

★ **LOS ALAMOS INN.** *2201 Trinity Dr (87544). Phone 505/662-7211; toll-free 800/279-9279; fax 505/661-7714. www.losalamosinn.com.* 116 rooms, 2-3 story. S, D $79-$99; each additional $15; under 12 free. Crib free. TV; cable. Pool; whirlpool. Complimentary breakfast. Restaurant 6:30 am-2 pm, 5-9 pm; Sun from 7 am. Bar 11 am-midnight; Sun noon-9 pm. Check-out 12:30 pm. Meeting rooms. Business services available. Cr cds: A, D, DS, MC, V.

[D] 🖨 🖂 [SC]

B&B/Small Inns

★ **RENATA'S ORANGE STREET.** *3496 Orange St (87544). Phone 505/662-2651; toll-free 800/662-3180; fax 505/661-1538. www.losalamos.com/orangestreetinn.* 8 air-cooled rooms, 4 with bath, 2 story. S, D $55-$75; ski, golf plans. Children over 5 years only. TV in sitting room; cable. Complimentary full breakfast. Restaurant nearby. Room service. Check-out 11 am, check-in 4-7 pm. Business services available. Concierge service. Street parking. Airport transportation. Downhill/cross-country ski 8 miles. Lawn games. Picnic tables, grills. Southwest and country décor; antiques, library. Totally nonsmoking. Cr cds: A, D, DS, MC, V.

[D] 🖨 🖂

Restaurant

★ ★ **BLUE WINDOW BISTRO.** *813 Central Ave (87544). Phone 505/662-6305.* Continental menu. Specialty: Southwest chicken. Hours: 11 am-2 pm, 5-9 pm; Sat 5-9 pm , closed Sun; Jan 1, Thanksgiving, Dec 25. Lunch $5.75-$6.75, dinner $9.95-$15.95. Children's menu. Reservations accepted. Totally nonsmoking. Cr cds: A, C, D, DS, ER, MC, V.

[D] [SC]

Mescalero (F-4)

See also Alamogordo, Cloudcroft, Ruidoso

Pop 1,233 **Elev** 6,605 ft **Area code** 505 **Zip** 88340

What to See and Do

Mescalero Apache Reservation. *101 Central Mescalero Ave. Phone 505/671-4494.* Approximately 4,000 Native Americans live on this reservation. Timber, cattle, and recreation are sources of income. There is also a store, museum, and casino. Ceremonials may sometimes be observed (fee); inquire at the community center or at the Mescalero store. Most famous dances are on or around July 4 (see SPECIAL EVENT). Contact Main Tribal Office. Also on reservation are

> **Silver Lake, Mescalero Lake, and Ruidoso Recreation Areas.** *Phone 505/671-4494.* Fishing; hunting for elk,

deer, antelope, and bear (fall), picnicking, camping (except at Mescalero Lake; hookups at Silver and Eagle lakes only). Some fees. **$$$**

Special Event

Mescalero Apache Maidens' Ceremonial. *Phone 505/671-4494.* Colorful and interesting series of dances, Mountain Spirits dance at dusk, rodeo, parade. Four days including predawn ceremony July 4.

Pecos National Historical Park (C-4)

See also Santa Fe

25 miles SE via US 25

The ruins of Pecos Pueblo lie on a mesa along the Santa Fe Trail that served as a strategic trade route and crossroads between Pueblo and Plains Indian cultures. At its peak, the Pueblo housed a community of as many as 2,000 people, and was occupied for nearly 500 years. When the Spanish arrived it became an important missionary outpost that continued to be occupied until the 1800s when its last inhabitants relocated to Jemez Pueblo. Ruins of the original multi-story structures survive in the form of large stone walls and several ceremonial kivas that have been restored. The largest ruins are of two Spanish missionary churches that were destroyed in the Pueblo revolt of 1680. An easy 1.25-mile hike and self-guided tour allows visitors to explore the ruins at their own pace. The visitor center includes historical exhibits and shows an introductory film covering the area's history. (Daily 8 am-5 pm; closed Dec 25)

Petroglyph National Monument

See also Albuquerque

3 1/2 miles N of I-40.

Web www.nps.gov/petr

In the West Mesa area, this park contains concentrated groups of rock drawings believed to have been carved on lava formations by ancestors of the Pueblo. Three hiking trails wind along the 17-mile escarpment. (Daily 8 am-5 pm; closed Jan 1, Thanksgiving, Dec 25)

Portales (E-7)

See also Clovis

Founded 1890 **Pop** 11,131 **Elev** 4,000 ft **Area code** 505 **Zip** 88130

Information Roosevelt County Chamber of Commerce, 200 E 7th; 505/356-8541 or 800/635-8036

Web www.portales.com

Irrigated with water from several hundred wells, land near Portales produces a wide variety of crops. The county is the Valencia peanut capital of the United States.

What to See and Do

Blackwater Draw Museum. *7 miles N on US 70. Phone 505/562-2202.* Operated by Eastern New Mexico University. Includes 12,000-year-old artifacts and fossils from nearby archaeological site (Mar-Oct); displays, murals tell story of early inhabitants. Films, tours (by appointment). Museum (Memorial Day-Labor Day, Mon-Sat, also Sun afternoons; rest of year, Tues-Sat, also Sun afternoons). **$$**

Eastern New Mexico University. *1200 W University Ave (88130). SW corner of town. Phone 550/562-2178.* (1934) 4,000 students. On campus is the Roosevelt County Museum; exhibits depict daily lives of early Western pioneers (daily; closed holidays; museum phone 505/562-2592)

Oasis State Park. *1891 Oasis Rd (88130). 6 miles N, off NM 467. Phone 505/356-5331.* Shifting sand dunes and towering cottonwood trees, planted in 1902 by a homesteader, form an oasis. Fishing lake; picnicking, camping (hookups, dump station). Standard fees. (Daily) **$$**

Special Events

Peanut Valley Festival. *Phone 505/562-2242.* Late Oct.

Roosevelt County Fair. *705 E Lime St (88130). Phone 505/356-4417.* Mid-Aug.

Roosevelt County Heritage Days. *200 E 7th (88130). Phone 505/356-8541.* Rodeo, dance, barbecue, parade, contests, entertainment. June.

Motel/Motor Lodge

★**CLASSIC AMERICAN ECONOMY INN.** *1613 W 2nd St (88130). Phone 505/356-6668; toll-free 800/901-9466.* 40 units. S $40-$50; D $45-$60; suite $35-$50; under 18 free; weekly rates. Crib free. Pet accepted. Complimentary continental breakfast. Complimentary coffee in rooms. Check-out noon. TV; cable (premium), VCR available. In-room modem link. Refrigerators, microwaves. Coin laundry. Playground. Heated pool. Picnic tables, grills. Airport, bus depot transportation. Sundries. Adjacent to Eastern New Mexico University. Cr cds: A, C, D, DS, MC, V.

Raton (A-6)

See also Cimarron, Trinidad, CO

Founded 1880 **Pop** 7,282 **Elev** 6,666 ft **Area code** 505 **Zip** 87740

Information Chamber & Economic Development Council, 100 Clayton Rd, PO Box 1211; 505/445-3689 or 800/638-6161

Web www.ratonchamber.com

Raton is at the southern foot of famous Raton Pass, on the original Santa Fe Trail (the main road to Denver, now I-25). The road over the pass is a masterpiece of engineering; the view from several points is magnificent.

What to See and Do

Capulin Volcano National Monument. (see) *7 miles NW on NM 332 at the junction of NM 96; I-90, exit 44. Phone 585/924-3232.*

Folsom Museum. *29 miles E on US 64/87, then 10 miles N on NM 325, on Main St in Folsom. Phone 505/278-2122 or -3616.* Artifacts and fossils of Folsom Man (circa 12,000 B.C.). (Memorial Day-Labor Day, daily; May and Sept, weekends; winter, by appointment) **$**

Raton Museum. *218 S 1st St. Phone 505/445-8979.* Collections relating to the Native American, Hispanic, ranch, railroad, and mining cultures in New Mexico. (Memorial Day-Labor Day, Tues-Sat; rest of year, Wed-Sat or by appointment; closed holidays) **FREE**

Sugarite Canyon State Park. *Sugarite Canyon. 10 miles NE on NM 72 and NM 526. Phone 505/445-5607.* This park contains 3,500 acres on the New Mexico side and offers fishing, ice fishing, boating (oars or electric motors only), tubing; seasonal bow hunting for deer and turkey, cross-country skiing, ice-skating, riding trails (no rentals), picnicking, camping (fee). Visitor center. (May-Sept, daily; rest of year by appointment) **$$**

Motels/Motor Lodges

★★ **BEST WESTERN SANDS.** *300 Clayton Rd (87740). Phone 505/445-2737; toll-free 800/518-2581; fax 505/445-4053. www.bestwestern.com.* 50 rooms. June-Aug: S, D $49-$99; each additional $3; lower rates rest of year. Crib free. TV; cable (premium). Heated pool; whirlpool. Playground. Coffee in rooms. Restaurant 6:30 am-8 pm. Check-out 11 am. Business services available. In-room modem link. Free train station, bus depot transportation. Some refrigerators, microwaves. Cr cds: A, C, D, DS, MC, V.

★ **BUDGET HOST MELODY LANE.** *136 Canyon Dr (87740). Phone 505/445-3655; toll-free 800/283-4678; fax 505/445-3461. www.budgethost.com.* 27 rooms. May-early Oct: S $41-$49; D $46-$54; each additional $5; weekly rates; lower rates rest of year. Crib $5. Pet accepted. TV; cable (premium). Continental breakfast. Check-out 11 am. Meeting room. Train station transportation. Some in-room steam baths. Refrigerators, microwaves available. Cr cds: A, C, D, DS, MC, V.

Restaurant

★★ **PAPPAS' SWEET SHOP.** *1201 S 2nd St (87740). Phone 505/445-9811; fax 505/445-3080.* Specializes in prime rib, pasta, seafood. Hours: 9 am-2 pm, 5-9 pm. Closed Sun; most major holidays. Lunch $5.95-$9.95, dinner $9.95-$21.95. Bar. Children's menu. Reservations accepted. Cr cds: A, DS, MC, V.

Red River (B-5)

See also Angel Fire, Cimarron, Taos

Pop 484 **Elev** 8,676 ft **Area code** 505 **Zip** 87558

Information Chamber of Commerce, Main St, PO Box 870; 505/754-2366 or 800/348-6444

Web www.redrivernewmex.com

This was a gold mining boom town with a population of 3,000 in the early days of the twentieth century. Today it is a summer vacation and winter ski center. Trout fishing, hunting (deer, elk, and small game), snowmobiling, horseback riding, and backpacking are popular sports here.

What to See and Do

Red River Ski Area. *400 Pioneer Rd. Phone 505/754-2223.* Two triple, three double chairlifts, surface tow; patrol, school, rentals; snowmaking; snack bar, cafeteria. Fifty-seven runs, longest run over 2 1/2 miles; vertical drop 1,600 feet. (Thanksgiving-late Mar, daily) Chairlift also operates Memorial Day-Labor Day (daily; fee). **$$$$**

Special Events

Enchanted Circle Century Bike Tour. *100 E Main.* Nearly 1,000 cyclists participate in a 100-mile tour around the Enchanted Circle (Red River, Angel Fire, Taos, Questa). Sept.

Mardi Gras in the Mountains. Ski slope parades, Cajun food. Feb.

Motels/Motor Lodges

★ ★ **ALPINE LODGE.** *417 W Main (87558). Phone 505/754-2952; toll-free 800/252-2333; fax 505/754-6421. www.thealpinelodge.com.* 45 rooms, 15 kitchen units, 1-3 story. No A/C. No elevator. S, D from $46; kitchen units for 2-12, $35-$148. Crib $5. Check-out 10 am. TV; cable (premium). Some balconies. Restaurant 7 am-2 pm. Bar 4 pm-close. Playground. Downhill ski opposite, cross-country ski 2 miles. Business services. Cr cds: A, DS, MC, V.

🅳 ⬧ 🏊 🖂

★ **ARROWHEAD LODGE.** *405 Pioneer Rd (87558). Phone 505/754-2255; toll-free 800/299-6547; fax 505/754-2588. www.redrivernm.com/arrowhead.* 19 rooms, 12 kitchens No A/C. S, D $45-$70; each additional $10; kitchen units $50-$209. TV; cable. Complimentary coffee in lobby. Restaurant nearby. Check-out 10 am. Airport transportation. Downhill ski on site; cross-country ski 4 miles. Picnic tables, grill. Sun deck. On river. Cr cds: A, DS, MC, V.

🏊 🖂 SC

★ **THE LODGE AT RED RIVER.** *400 E Main St (87558). Phone 505/754-6280; toll-free 800/91LODGE; fax 505/754-6304. www.redriver.com/lodgeatrr/.* 26 rooms, 2 story. No A/C. No room phones. Mid-May-Sept, late Nov-Mar: S $46; D $78; each additional $11; ski plans; higher rates during holidays; lower rates rest of year. Check-out 11 am. Restaurant 7-11 am, 4:30-9 pm. Bar 5-10 pm. Downhill ski on site, cross-country ski 3 miles. Meeting rooms. Business services. Rustic lodge. Cr cds: A, D, DS, MC, V.

⬧ ⚡ 🏊 🖂

★ ★ **PONDEROSA LODGE.** *200 W Main St (87558). Phone 505/754-2988; toll-free 800/336-7787. www.redriver.com/ponderosa.* 17 rooms, 2 story, 17

kitchen apartments. No A/C. Dec-Mar: S, D $65-$79; each additional $10; suites $122-$245; under 12 free; higher rates Dec 25; lower rates rest of year. Crib free. TV; cable. Check-out 10 am. Downhill ski adjacent; cross-country ski 4 miles. Whirlpool. Sauna. Cr cds: A, D, DS, MC, V.

🅳 🏊 🖂

★ **RED RIVER INN.** *300 W Main St (87558). Phone 505/754-2930; toll-free 800/365-2930; fax 505/754-2943. www.redriverinn.com.* 14 rooms, 3 kitchen units. No A/C. June-Sept: S $37-$56; D $54-$64; kitchen units $60-$66; family, holiday rates; ski plans; higher rates during holidays; lower rates rest of year. Crib free. Complimentary coffee in lobby. Check-out 10 am. TV; cable (premium). Restaurant nearby. Whirlpool. Exercise equipment, sauna. Downhill ski 1 block, cross-country ski 1 mile. Picnic tables, grills. Gift shop. Totally nonsmoking. Cr cds: A, DS, MC, V.

🏊 🏃 🖂 SC

★ **TERRACE TOWERS LODGE.** *712 W Main St (87558). Phone 505/754-2962; toll-free 800/695-6343; fax 505/754-2990. www.redriver.com/terracetowers.* 26 kitchen suites, 2 story. S, D $55-$110; under 12 free; higher rates: Spring Break, Dec 25. Pet accepted. Check-out 10 am. TV; cable (premium), VCR available (movies $3). Coin laundry. Restaurant nearby. Playground. Whirlpool. Downhill, cross-country ski 1/2 mile. View of valley and mountains. Cr cds: A, D, DS, ER, MC, V.

🐾 🏊 🖂

Resort

★ **THE RIVERSIDE.** *201 Main (87558). Phone 505/754-2252; toll-free 800/432-9999; fax 505/754-2495. www.redriver-nm.com.* 8 rooms, 2 story, 30 winterized kitchen cabins. No A/C. Dec-Mar: S $50-$60; D $68-$80; each additional $10; kitchen units to 6, $115-$150; higher rates Dec 25, holidays; lower rates rest of year. Closed late Mar-Memorial Day. Check-out 10 am. TV. Some fireplaces. Downhill ski adjacent, cross-country ski 2 miles. Lawn games. Cr cds: DS, MC, V.

🅳 ⬧ 🏊 🖂

Restaurants

★ ★ ★ **BRETT'S HOMESTEAD STEAKHOUSE.** *102 High Cost Trl (87558). Phone 505/754-6136; fax 505/754-3319.* Prime aged beef with all the fixings is the draw at this casual steakhouse. Steak menu. Closed Easter-mid-May, Nov. Dinner. Children's menu. In Victorian house with duck pond. Cr cds: A, D, DS, MC, V. **$$**

🅳

★ **SUNDANCE.** *102 E High St (87558). Phone 505/754-2971. www.redrivernm.com/sundance.* Hours: 5-9 pm. Closed Apr-mid-May. Mexican menu. Wine, beer. Dinner

$7.50-$15.50. Children's menu. Specialties: stuffed sopaipilla, fajitas, super burrito. Southwestern décor; fireplace. Gift shop. Cr cds: A, D, MC, V.

[D]

★ ★ **TEXAS RED'S STEAK HOUSE.** *111 E Main St (87558). Phone 505/754-2964. www/texasreds.com.* Hours: 5-9:30 pm. Dinner $6-$28.50. Children's menu. Specialties: NY strip steak, smoked pork chops, char-broiled beef steak. Western décor. Family-owned. Cr cds: A, D, DS, MC, V.

[D]

Roswell (F-6)

See also Artesia

Founded 1871 **Pop** 45,293 **Elev** 3,981 ft **Area code** 505 **Zip** 88201

Information Chamber of Commerce, PO Box 70, 88202; 505/623-5695

Web www.roswellnm.org

Roswell was a cattle town in its early days, with the Goodnight-Loving cattle trail passing through and the Chisholm Trail starting here.

Farming, ranching, livestock feeding, oil and gas exploration and development as well as other industrial areas surround the town. The Roswell campus of Eastern New Mexico University is located here.

What to See and Do

Bitter Lake National Wildlife Refuge. *4065 Bitter Lakes Rd (88201). 13 miles NE, via US 70, 285, and US 380 exits. Phone 505/622-6755.* Wildlife observation, auto tour. Hunting in season with state license. (Daily) **FREE**

Bottomless Lakes State Park. *E Of City. 10 miles E on US 380, then 6 miles S on NM 409. Phone 505/624-6058.* Bordered by high red bluffs, 7 small lakes were formed when circulating underground water formed caverns that collapsed into sinkholes. Headquarters at Cottonwood Lake has displays and a network of trails. Beach and swimming at Lea Lake only, bathhouse, skin diving, some lakes have fishing (trout), paddleboat rentals; picnicking, camping. (Daily) **$$**

Dexter National Fish Hatchery and Technology Center. *7116 Hatchery Rd (88201). 20 miles SE via US 285 or NM 2. Phone 505/734-5910.* This facility is the US Fish and Wildlife Service's primary center for the study and culture of endangered fish species of the American Southwest. (Daily) Also visitor center (Apr-Oct, daily). **FREE**

Historical Center for Southeast New Mexico. *200 N Lea. Phone 505/622-8333.* Antiques, period rooms (early 1900s); turn-of-the-century furnishings, clothes; communications exhibits; research library, and archives. (Daily, afternoons; Fri, by appointment) Tours by appointment. **FREE**

★ **International UFO Museum & Research Center.** *114 N Main St. Phone 505/625-9495.* Museum includes exhibits on various aspects of UFO phenomena and a video viewing room. Various video tapes can be viewed upon request. (Daily) **FREE**

New Mexico Military Institute. *101 W College Blvd (88201). N Main St and College Blvd. Phone 505/624-8011 or 800/421-5376.* (1891) 1,000 cadets. State-supported high school and junior college. Alumni Memorial Chapel, near the entrance, has beautiful windows. Also here is the General Douglas L. McBride Military Museum with an interpretation of 20th-century American military history (Tues-Fri; free). Occasional marching formations and parades. Tours.

Roswell Museum and Art Center. *100 W 11th St. Phone 505/624-6744.* Southwest arts collection including Georgia O'Keeffe, Peter Hurd, Henriette Wyeth; Native American, Mexican American, and western arts; Dr. Robert H. Goddard's early liquid-fueled rocketry experiments. (Mon-Sat, also Sun and holiday afternoons; closed Jan 1, Thanksgiving, Dec 25) **FREE**

Spring River Park & Zoo. *1306 E College Blvd. Phone 505/624-6760.* Zoo and children's zoo area; small lake with fishing for children 11 and under only; miniature train; antique wooden-horse carousel. Picnicking, playground. (Daily; closed Dec 25) **FREE**

Special Events

Eastern New Mexico State Fair and Rodeo. *2500 N Main St. 2 miles S on US 285, at Fair Park. Phone 505/623-9411.* Sept-Oct.

UFO Encounters Festival. *114 Main St (88201). Phone 505/625-9495.* UFO Expo trade show, alien chase, alien parade, costume contest, guest speeches. July 4 weekend.

Motels/Motor Lodges

★ ★ **BEST WESTERN SALLY PORT INN & SUITES.** *2000 N Main St (88201). Phone 505/622-6430; toll-free 800/780-7234; fax 505/623-7631. www.bestwestern.com.* 124 rooms, 2 story. S, D $79; each additional $10; suites $90-$119; under 12 free. Crib free. Pet accepted. TV; cable (premium). Indoor pool; whirlpool. Complimentary full breakfast. Restaurant 6-10 am, 5-10 pm; Sun 6-11 am, 5-9 pm. Room service. Bar 4 pm-midnight; Fri, Sat to 1 am. Check-out noon.

Coin laundry. Meeting rooms. Business services available. Sundries. Beauty shop. Free airport, bus depot transportation. Tennis. 18-hole golf privileges adjacent, putting green, driving range. Exercise equipment. Refrigerators. Cr cds: A, C, D, DS, MC, V.

★ **FRONTIER MOTEL.** *3010 N Main St (88201). Phone 505/622-1400; toll-free 800/678-1401; fax 505/622-1405. www.frontiermotelroswell.com.* 38 rooms. S $28-$36; D $32-$40; each additional $4; higher rates during NMMI events. Pet accepted. TV; cable (premium). Pool. Complimentary continental breakfast. Restaurant adjacent 5:30 am-9 pm. Check-out 11 am. Some refrigerators. Cr cds: A, C, D, DS, MC, V.

★ **RAMADA LIMITED.** *2803 W 2nd St (88201). Phone 505/623-9440; toll-free 800/228-2828; fax 505/622-9708. www.ramada.com.* 61 rooms, 2 story. S $53; D $58; each additional $5; under 18 free. Pet accepted; fee. Check-out noon. TV. Cr cds: A, C, D, DS, MC, V.

★ ★ **ROSWELL INN.** *1815 N Main St (88202). Phone 505/623-4920. www.nmohwy.com.* 121 rooms, 2 story. S $62; D $65; each additional $7; suites $95-$145; under 18 free. Crib free. Check-out noon. TV; cable (premium). Balconies. Restaurant 6 am-9 pm. Bar 11-1 am. Room service. Heated pool, poolside service. 18-hole golf privileges. Free airport transportation. Meeting rooms. Cr cds: A, C, D, DS, MC, V.

Restaurant

★ **EL TORO BRAVO.** *102 S Main St (88201). Phone 505/622-9280.* Hours: 11 am-2:30 pm, 5-9 pm; Sat 11 am-9 pm; Sun to 2:30 pm. Reservations accepted. Closed most major holidays. Mexican menu. Wine, beer. Lunch, dinner $1.95-$10.95. Lunch buffet (Mon-Fri) $5.55. Children's menu. Specialties: chimichangas, chile Colorado, fajitas. Bullfighting and Mexican pictures. Cr cds: A, DS, MC, V.

Ruidoso (F-5)

See also Alamogordo, Cloudcroft, Mescalero

Pop 7,698 **Elev** 6,911 ft **Area code** 505 **Zip** 88345

Information Ruidoso Valley Chamber of Commerce, 720 Sudderth Dr, PO Box 698; 505/257-7395 or 800/253-2255

Web www.ruidoso.net

This resort town in the Sierra Blanca Mountains, surrounded by the trees of the Lincoln National Forests, has enjoyed spectacular growth. It is a thriving town and an all-year resort with skiing in winter and fishing and horseback riding in summer. If planning to visit during June, July, or August, secure confirmed reservations before leaving home. Few mountain resorts have such a variety of attractions. The forested mountain slopes and streams are idyllic, the air is clear and cool, especially at night, and there are many interesting ways to spend time. A Ranger District Office of the Lincoln National Forest (see ALAMOGORDO) is located here.

What to See and Do

Hubbard Museum of the American West. *841 Hwy 70 W. PO Box 40, 88346. Phone 505/378-4142.* Western-themed exhibits relating to horses and pioneer life. (Daily; closed Thanksgiving, Dec 25) **$$$**

Lincoln State Monument. *30 miles E on US 70, then 10 miles NW on US 380.* Lincoln was the site of the infamous Lincoln County War and a hangout of Billy the Kid. Several properties have been restored, including the Old Lincoln County Courthouse and the mercantile store of John Tunstall. Guided tours (summer, reservations required). (Daily; closed holidays) **$$**

Old Dowlin Mill. *Sudderth and Paradise Canyon Rd. In town. Phone 800/253-2255.* A 20-foot waterwheel still drives a mill more than 100 years old.

Ski Apache Resort. *NM 532. 16 miles NW on NM 48, 532 in Lincoln National Forests. Phone 505/336-4356 or (snow report) 505/257-9001.* Resort has four-passenger gondola; quad, five triple, two double chairlifts; surface lift; patrol, school, rentals; snack bars, cafeteria, bar. Fifty-two runs, longest run over 2 miles; vertical drop 1,900 feet. (Thanksgiving-Easter, daily) **$$$$**

Smokey Bear Historical State Park. *118 Smokey Bear Blvd. 22 miles N via NM 37/48 on US 380 in Capitan. Phone 505/354-2748.* Commemorates the history and development of the national symbol of forest fire prevention. The original Smokey, who was orphaned by a fire raging in the Lincoln National Forests, is buried here within sight of the mountain where he was found. Fire prevention exhibit, film. (Daily; closed Jan 1, Thanksgiving, Dec 25) **$** Nearby is

Smokey Bear Museum. *102 Smokey Bear Blvd. Phone 505/354-2298.* Features 1950s memorabilia of famed fire-fighting bear found in the nearby Capitan Mountains. (Daily; closed holidays) **FREE**

The Spencer Theater for the Performing Arts. *N of Ruidoso at Alto via NM 48. Phone 888/818-7872.* Stunning $22 million structure offers 514 seats for professional touring musical and theater productions. Created from 450 tons of Spanish limestone, the building's design calls forth images of pyramids, mountain peaks, and sci-fi star cruisers. Inside are multiple blown glass installations by Seattle artist Dale Chihuly. (Call for schedule) Tours (Tues, Thurs).

Special Events

Arts Festival. *Paradise Canyon Rd and Sudderth (88345). Phone 505/854-2261.* Last full weekend in July.

Aspenfest. *Phone 505/257-5121.* Includes motorcycle convention, official state chili cook-off, arts and crafts. Phone 505/253-2255 or 800/253-2255. Early Oct.

Horse racing. *1461 Hwy 70 W. Ruidoso Downs. Phone 505/378-4431.* Thoroughbred and quarter horse racing, pari-mutuel betting. Home of All-American Futurity, world's richest quarter horse race (Labor Day); All-American Derby and All-American Gold Cup. Thu-Sun and holidays. Early May-Labor Day.

Smokey Bear Stampede. *8 5th St (88316). 22 miles N via NM 48 in Capitan. Phone 505/354-2273.* Fireworks, music festival, parade, dances, barbecue. Early July.

Motels/Motor Lodges

★ ★ **BEST WESTERN SWISS CHALET.** *1451 Mechem Dr (88355). Phone 505/258-3333; toll-free 800/477-9477; fax 505/258-5325. www.ruidoso.net/swisschalet.* 81 rooms, 2 story. June-Sept: S $69-$99; D $79-$109; each additional $10; suites $99-$150; under 12 free; lower rates rest of year. Pet accepted, some restrictions. Check-out noon. TV; cable (premium), VCR available (movies). Balconies. Coin laundry. Restaurant 7-11 am, 5:30-9 pm; closed Mon. Bar 5-10 pm. Room service. Sauna. Indoor pool, whirlpool. Meeting rooms. Business services. Sundries. On hilltop. Cr cds: A, C, D, DS, ER, JCB, MC, V.

★ **INNSBRUCK LODGE.** *601 Sudderth Dr (88345). Phone 505/257-4071; toll-free 800/680-4447. www.ruidoso.com/innsbruck.* 48 rooms, 30 with A/C, 18 with shower only, 2 story. Mid-June-Sept: S, D $32-$60; under 10 free; weekly rates; higher rates during holidays; lower rates rest of year. Crib $4-$6. TV; cable. Restaurant nearby. Check-out 11 am. Business services available. Gift shop. Downhill ski 16 miles. Health club privileges. Cr cds: A, D, DS, MC, V.

★ **SUPER 8 MOTEL.** *100 Cliff Dr (88345). Phone 505/378-8180; toll-free 800/800-8000. www.super8.com.* 63 rooms, 2 story. May-Sept: S $45-$58; D $53-$62; each additional $4; suites $80.88-85.88; lower rates rest of year. Crib $3. TV; cable (premium), VCR available (movies). Whirlpool. Sauna. Check-out 11 am. Coin laundry. Business services available. Sundries. Picnic table. Cr cds: A, C, D, DS, MC, V.

★ **VILLAGE LODGE.** *1000 Mechem Dr (88345). Phone 505/258-5442; toll-free 800/722-8779; fax 505/258-3127. www.villagelodge.com.* 28 kitchen units, 2 story. Mid-May-mid-Sept, Nov-Easter: S, D $79-$109; each additional $10; under 13 free; higher rates holidays; lower rates rest of year. Check-out 11 am. TV; cable (premium). Downhill ski 14 miles. Cr cds: A, DS, MC, V.

Hotels

★ **ENCHANTMENT INN AND SUITES.** *307 Hwy 70 W (88355). Phone 505/378-4051; toll-free 800/435-0280; fax 505/378-5427. www.ruidoso.com/enchantment.* 81 rooms, 2 story, 33 suites. S, D $65-$80; suites, kitchen units $65-$185; under 18 free. TV; cable (premium). Indoor pool; whirlpool. Restaurant 7-11 am, 5-9 pm. Room service. Bar. Check-out 11 am. Coin laundry. Meeting rooms. Business services available. Downhill ski 20 miles. Picnic tables, grills. Cr cds: A, DS, MC, V.

★ ★ **SHADOW MOUNTAIN LODGE.** *107 Main Rd (88345). Phone 505/257-4886; toll-free 800/441-4331; fax 505/257-2000. www.smlruidoso.com.* 19 kitchen units. Memorial Day-Labor Day: S, D $67-$97; each additional $10; ski plans; lower rates rest of year. Complimentary coffee in rooms. Check-out 11 am. TV; cable (premium). Fireplaces, wet bars. Restaurant nearby. Downhill ski 18 miles. Grills. Business services. Opposite river. Cr cds: A, C, D, DS, MC, V.

Resorts

★ **HIGH COUNTRY LODGE.** *Hwy 48, Alto. Phone 505/336-4321; toll-free 800/845-7265; fax 505/336-8205. www.ruidoso.net.* 32 kitchen apartments (2-bedroom). No A/C. S, D $49-$119; each additional $10; higher rates during holiday weekends. Pet accepted. TV; cable (premium). Indoor pool; whirlpool. Playground. Check-out 11 am. Meeting rooms. Business services available. Tennis. Game room. Lawn games. Exercise room; sauna. Fireplaces. Picnic table, grills. Lake opposite. Cr cds: A, C, D, DS, JCB, MC, V.

★ ★ ★ **INN OF THE MOUNTAIN GODS.** *Caprizo Canyon Rd, Mescalero (88340). Phone 505/464-6173. toll-free 800/545-9011; www.innofthemountaingods.com.* 253 rooms, 2-5 story. June-Sep: S, D, suites $120-$150; each additional $14; under 12 free; package plans; lower rates rest of year. Crib $14. TV; cable (premium). Heated pool; wading pool, whirlpool, poolside service. Sauna. Dining room 7 am-10 pm. Box lunches. Room service. Bars 10-1 am; entertainment. Check-out noon, check-in 4 pm. Convention facilities. Business services available. Gift shop. Airport transportation. Lighted tennis, pro. 18-hole golf, pro, putting green. Dock; rowboats, paddleboats. Game room. Lawn games. Some refrigerators. Private patios, balconies. Casino. Cr cds: A, C, D, DS, MC, V.

B&B/Small Inns

★ ★ ★ **CASA DE PATRON BED AND BREAKFAST INN.** *Hwy 380 E, Lincoln. Phone 505/ 653-4676; toll-free 800/524-5202; fax 505/653-4671. www.casapatron.com.* 5 rooms, 2 suites. No A/C, no room phones. D $87-$117; each additional $6; casitas $97. Complimentary full breakfast. Check-out noon, check-in 3-8 pm. Restaurant nearby. Sauna. Built in 1860; antiques. This inn was the home of Juan Patron, the youngest Speaker of the House in the Territorial Legislature. Legendary figures such as Billy the Kid and Pat Garrett are said to have spent the night here. Totally nonsmoking. Cr cds: MC, V.

Salinas Pueblo Missions National Monument (E-4)

See also Socorro

(Approx 75 miles SE of Albuquerque via I-40, NM 337, 55)

This monument was established to explore European-Native American contact and the resultant cultural changes. The stabilized ruins of the massive 17th-century missions are basically unaltered, preserving the original design and construction. All three units are open and feature wayside exhibits, trails, and picnic areas (daily; closed January 1, December 25). Monument Headquarters, one block west of NM 55 on US 60 in Mountainair, has an audiovisual presentation and an exhibit depicting the Salinas story. (Daily; closed January 1, December 25) Contact the Superintendent, PO Box 517, Mountainair 87036; phone 505/847-2585. The three units of this monument are

Gran Quivira. *25 miles SE of Mountainair on NM 55. Phone 505/847-2770.* Here are the massive walls of the 17th-century San Buenaventura Mission (begun in 1659 but never completed), "San Isidro" Church (circa 1639), and 21 pueblo mounds, two of which have been excavated. A self-guided trail and museum/visitor center (exhibits,

seven-minute video, 40-minute video) combine to vividly portray Native American life and the cultural change that has occurred over the past 1,000 years. Various factors led to the desertion of the pueblo and the mission around 1671. Tompiro Indians occupied this and the Abó site. Picnicking.

Abó. *9 miles W of Mountainair on US 60, then 3/4 miles N on NM 513. Phone 505/847-2400.* Ruins of the mission church of San Gregorio de Abó (circa 1622), built by Native Americans under the direction of Franciscan priests. This is the only early church in New Mexico with 40-foot buttressed curtain walls—a style typical of medieval European architecture. The pueblo adjacent to the church was abandoned around 1673 because of drought, disease, and Apache uprisings. The Abó and others from the Salinas jurisdiction eventually moved south with the Spanish to El Paso del Norte, where they established the pueblo of Ysleta del Sur and other towns still in existence today. There are self-guided trails throughout the mission compound and pueblo mounds. Picnicking (no water).

Quarai. *8 miles N of Mountainair on NM 55, then 1 mile W on a county road from Punta. Phone 505/847-2290.* Ruins of the Mission de la Purísima Concepción de Cuarac, other Spanish structures, and unexcavated Native American mounds, all built of red sandstone. Built about 1630, it was abandoned along with the pueblo about 1677, most likely for the same reasons. Unlike the other two, this site was occupied by Tiwa-speaking people. Much of the history is related to the Spanish-Indian cultural conflict. The church ruins have been excavated, and it is the most complete church in the monument. The visitor center has a museum and interpretive displays. Wayside exhibits, trail guides. Picnicking.

Santa Fe (C-4)

See also Espanola, Las Vegas, Los Alamos

Settled 1607 **Pop** 62,203 **Elev** 7,000 ft **Area code** 505

Information Convention & Visitors Bureau, PO Box 909, 87504; 505/984-6760 or 800/777-2489

Web www.santafe.org

This picturesque city, the oldest capital in the United States, is set at the base of the Sangre de Cristo (Blood of Christ) Mountains. A few miles south these mountains taper down from a height of 13,000 feet to a rolling plain, marking the end of the North American Rocky Mountains. Because of the altitude, the climate is cool and bracing. Tourists and vacationers will find much to do and see here all year.

Santa Fe's Art and Architecture

Every tourist's Santa Fe exploration begins at the Plaza, plotted when the town was built in 1610. A square block planted with trees and grass, it's a place to sit on park benches to study a map or just watch the parade of visitors go by. Lining the Plaza on the east, south, and west are art galleries, Native American jewelry shops, boutiques, a vintage hotel, and restaurants. Facing the Plaza on the north is the Palace of the Governors, the first stop on your walking tour. Sheltered along the portal (porch) that spans the front of the block-long, pueblo-style building—which also dates from 1610—are dozens of craft and art vendors from the region's nearby pueblos. Only pueblo Indians can sell their jewelry, blankets, beadwork, pottery, and other goods here. Inside the palace, a museum exhibits nearly 20,000 historic objects, including pottery, books, documents, and artifacts.

One block west along Palace Avenue, the Museum of Fine Arts was built in 1917 and represents the Pueblo Revival style of architecture, also called Santa Fe style. Site of chamber music concerts, the museum exhibits work by local artists and by noted painters of the Santa Fe and Taos art colonies. Continue west on Palace another block, turning north on Grant Avenue one block, then west on Johnson Street one block. Stop inside the relatively new Georgia O'Keefe Museum to see the world's largest collection of the artist's work.

Backtrack to the Plaza, heading to the Catron Building, which forms the east "wall" of the Plaza. Inside the 1891 office building are several art galleries and stores. At the building's southern end, anchoring the southeast corner of the Plaza, is La Fonda, the oldest hotel in Santa Fe. The lobby's art and decor are worth a look, and the rooftop bar is a favorite gathering place. From the plaza, walk south two blocks on Old Santa Fe Trail to Loretto Chapel. The beautiful chapel has an irresistible story in its Miraculous Staircase. Now walk east on Water Street one block to Cathedral Place, turning left (north) on Cathedral one block to the magnificent St. Francis Cathedral, built over several years in the latter 1800s.

Directly across the street, see the Institute of American Indian Arts Museum, housing thousands of pieces of sculpture, basketry, paintings, and pottery. Cathedral ends here at Palace Avenue, which you'll follow east one long block to explore two excellent bookstores, Nicholas Potter Bookseller and Palace Avenue Books. Backtracking on Palace again to the west, Sena Plaza is on your right (on the north side of the street). Inside the lovely, flower-filled courtyard, you'll find a 19th-century hacienda that once belonged to the Sena family and is now filled with art galleries, shops and a restaurant. Wind up back at the Plaza by following Palace another long block to the west; head to the Ore House on the Plaza's west side to review the day over refreshments.

Santa Fe was founded by Don Pedro de Peralta, who laid out the plaza and built the Palace of the Governors in 1610. In 1680 the Pueblo revolted and drove the Spanish out. In 1692, led by General Don Diego de Vargas, the Spanish made a peaceful re-entry. Mexico gained its independence from Spain in 1821. This was followed by the opening of the Santa Fe Trail. In 1846 General Stephen Watts Kearny led US troops into the town without resistance and hoisted the American flag. During the Civil War Confederate forces occupied the town for two weeks before they were driven out.

In addition to its own attractions, Santa Fe is also the center of a colorful area, which can be reached by car. It is in the midst of the Pueblo country. The Pueblo, farmers for centuries, are also extremely gifted craftsworkers and painters. Their pottery, basketry, and jewelry are especially beautiful. At various times during the year, especially on the saint's day of their particular pueblo, they present dramatic ceremonial dances. Visitors are usually welcome. Since these are sacred rites, however,

visitors should be respectful. As a rule, photographs are forbidden. A list of many of these ceremonies is given under SPECIAL EVENTS.

The high altitude may cause visitors accustomed to lower altitudes to have a little shortness of breath for a day or two. A short walking tour taken slowly will be helpful; the tour covers many centrally located sights.

What to See and Do

Atalaya Mountain Hiking Trail. *From downtown Santa Fe take Alameda Ave eastbound. Turn right onto Camino Cabra and continue to the intersection with Camino Cruz Blanca where you will turn left. Look for the signs for St. John's College and the parking area for Atalaya Mountain Trailhead. For the shorter trail, keep driving 8 miles past the college on Camino Cruz Blanca to the small parking lot on the left side of the road. The Atalaya Mountain Trail, accessible from the parking lot at St. John's College, is one of the most popular and easily accessible hiking trails in*

Santa Fe. Hikers have the option of taking the longer route (Trail 174), which is approximately 7 miles roundtrip, or parking further up near the Ponderosa Ridge development and doing a 4.6-mile loop (Trail 170) instead. Both trials eventually join and take you towards the top of Atalaya mountain, a 9,121 foot peak. The first few miles of the trail are relatively easy but become increasingly steep and strenuous as you near the summit of Atalaya Mountain. Hikers who make it to the top will be afforded great views of the Rio Grande valley and city below.

⭐ **Canyon Road Tour.** *Go east on San Francisco St to the cathedral and bear right to the end of Cathedral Pl. Turn left on Alameda.* This tour totals about 2 or 3 miles, and there is no better way to savor the unique character of Santa Fe than to travel along its narrow, picturesque old streets. To the left on Alameda is

Camino del Monte Sol. Famous street on which many artists live and work. Turn left up the hill. Off this road are a number of interesting streets worth exploring. On Canyon Rd, down hill several miles is

Cristo Rey Church. This is the largest adobe structure in the US. It contains beautiful ancient stone reredos (altar screens). (Mon-Fri; closed holidays) Return on Canyon Rd to

Museum of Indian Arts and Culture. *710 Camino Lejo (87505). Phone 505/476-1250.* When the Spanish arrived in the Southwest in the 16th century they found many sprawling towns and villages which they referred to as Pueblos, a name that is still used to identify Indian communities in New Mexico to this day. The Museum of Indian Arts and Culture houses an extensive collection of historic and contemporary Pueblo art from throughout the Southwest. One of the highlights of the museum is an excellent interpretive section where you can encounter native Pueblo cultures from the viewpoint and narrative of modern-day Pueblo natives and exhibit designers. The museum itself is housed in a large, adobe-style building that blends architecturally into the surroundings, and also houses many outstanding examples of Pueblo textiles, pottery, jewelry, contemporary paintings, and other rotating exhibits. An adjacent building houses the Laboratory of Anthropology, which contains an extensive library and supports continuing research into Southwestern archeology and cultural studies. (Tues-Sun; closed Mon, holidays) **$$** Across the yard is

Museum of International Folk Art. *706 Camino Lejo (87502). Phone 505/476-1200.* The Museum of International Folk Art, first opened in 1953, contains more than 120,000 objects, billing itself as the world's largest folk museum dedicated to the study of traditional cultural art. Much of the massive collection was acquired when the late Italian immigrant, architect/designer Alexander Girard donated his 106,000-object collection of toys, figurines, figurative ceramics, miniatures, and religious/ceremonial art that he had collected from more than 100 countries around the world. In addition to the collection in the Girard wing, you'll also find a large collection of Hispanic art in the Hispanic Heritage Wing, as well as costumes and folk art from many cultures in the Neutrogena Collection. Several smaller collections and major temporary exhibits add to a rich museum experience that can easily take several hours to explore. Two museum shops offer a wide variety of folk-oriented books, clothing, and jewelry to choose from. (Tues-Sun; closed Mon, holidays) **$$$** On the same road, less than 1 long block beyond the museum, is the

National Park Service, Southwest Regional Office. *1100 Old Santa Fe Trail. Phone 505/988-6011.* (1939) Adobe building with central patio. (Mon-Fri; closed holidays) From here go west a short distance on Old Santa Fe Trail, and then south on Camino Lejo to the

St. Francis School. Turn right across first bridge and immediately bear left onto

St. John's College in Santa Fe. *On Camino Cruz Blanca, just W of Camino del Monte Sol. Phone 505/984-6000.* (1964) 400 students. The first campus of St. John's College is in Annapolis, MD (1696). Liberal arts. On the right is the

Wheelwright Museum. *704 Camino Lejo (87505). Phone 800/607-4636.* Founded in 1937 by Mary Cabot Wheelwright and Navajo singer/medicine man Hastiin Klah to help preserve Navajo art and traditions, the Wheelwright now devotes itself to hosting major exhibits of Native American artists from tribes throughout North America. The Case Trading Post in the basement sells pottery, jewelry, textiles, books, prints, and other gift items. (Daily; closed holidays) **DONATION** Shortest way back to town is via the Old Santa Fe Trail.

Cathedral of St. Francis. *Phone 505/982-5619.* (1869) French Romanesque cathedral built under the direction of Archbishop Lamy (prototype for Bishop Latour in Willa Cather's *Death Comes for the Archbishop*). La Conquistadora Chapel, said to be the country's oldest Marian shrine, is here. (Daily) Tours (summer).

College of Santa Fe. *1600 St. Michael's Dr (87505). 3 miles SW at Cerrillos Rd and St. Michael's Dr. Phone 505/473-6011.* (1947) 1,400 students. On campus are the Greer Garson Theatre Center, Communications Center, and Fogelson Library.

Dragon Room. *406 Old Santa Fe Trl (87501).* The rustic Dragon Room in the Pink Adobe Restaurant is one of the best places to mingle with locals, spot celebrities, and enjoy the Santa Fe ambience while sipping on house specialty drinks like the "Rosalita" or "Silver Coin Margarita."

The *Santa Fe Reporter* voted this the top bar in Santa Fe, and it's always a hot social spot on Friday and Saturday nights.

El Farol. *808 Canyon Rd (87501). Phone 505/983-9912.* El Farol ("The Lantern" in Spanish) is the oldest restaurant and cantina in Santa Fe, dating back to 1835. Located near the top of Canyon Road, it serves up award-winning Mediterranean food and continues to be one of the most popular late night watering holes, offering patrons live music and a usually packed dance floor Wednesday through Saturday nights. The music tends towards Flamenco, Latin, Jazz, Soul and Blues and usually gets hopping after 10 pm.

El Rancho de las Golondrinas. *334 Los Pinos Rd (87505). 13 miles S, off I-25. Phone 505/471-2261.* This living history museum is set in a 200-acre rural valley, and depicts Spanish Colonial life in New Mexico from 1700-1900. It was once a stop on the Camino Real, and is one of the most historic ranches in the Southwest. Original colonial buildings date from the 18th century, and special festivals and theme weekends offer visitors a glimpse of the music, dance, clothing, crafts, and celebrations of Spanish Colonial New Mexico. (June-Sept: Wed-Sun 10 am-4 pm) **$$**

Federal Court House. *Federal Pl and Paseo De Peralta.* There is a monument to Kit Carson in front.

Genoveva Chavez Recreation Center. *3221 Rodeo Rd (87507). Phone 505/955-4001.* The recently opened Chavez Recreation Center is housed in a massive, architecturally imposing solar complex covering several city blocks. Inside, for a small daily fee, visitors can get access to a 50 meter lap pool, leisure pool, spa, sauna, and therapy pool, competition-sized ice skating rink, basketball and racquetball courts, numerous fitness classes (extra charge), and a full line of state-of-the-art exercise equipment. **$$**

Georgia O'Keeffe Museum. *217 Johnson St (87501). Phone 505/946-1000.* One of the most important American artists of the 20th century, Georgia O'Keeffe lived and worked at Ghost Ranch near Abiqui for much of her career, drawing inspiration from the colors and forms of the surrounding desert environment. This museum houses the world's largest permanent collection of her artwork and is also dedicated to the study of American Modernism (1890- present), displaying special exhibits of many of her contemporaries. (Nov-June: Mon-Tues, Thurs-Sun; closed Wed; daily rest of year) **$$$**

Hyde Memorial State Park. *740 Hyde Park Rd (87501). 8 miles NE via NM 475. Phone 505/983-7175.* Perched 8,500 feet up in the Sangre de Cristo Mountains near the Santa Fe Ski Basin; used as base camp for backpackers and skiers in the Santa Fe National Forests. Cross-country skiing, rentals, picnicking (shelters), playground, concession, camping (electric hookups, dump station). Standard fees. (Daily) **$$**

Hyde Park Hiking/Biking Trails. *From the Santa Fe Plaza go north on Washington Ave, and continue several blocks to the light at Artist's Road and turn right. Continue on Artist's Rd for about 8.6 miles to a parking lot on the left side of the road just before you reach the Hyde Park RV campground.* One of the closest hiking opportunities to Santa Fe is available in the Hyde Park area on the road to the ski basin. From the Hyde Park parking lot, you can access a loop covering 3 different trails offering easy hiking that's popular with runners, hikers, dog walkers, and weekenders looking for a quick getaway. The loop consists of switchbacks, moderate grades, creek crossings, and fine views of the mixed conifer forest. If you come during the fall you can view the spectacularly colorful changing of the Aspen leaves. Start with the common trailhead at the far side of the parking lot. Look for the Borrego Trail (150), Bear Wallow Trail (182), and Winsor Trail (254) markings. A loop covering all 3 is about 4 miles long.

Institute of American Indian Arts Museum. *108 Cathedral Pl (87501). Phone 505/983-8900.* The Institute of American Indian Arts, established in 1962, runs a college in south Santa Fe in addition to a museum just off the Plaza. The museum is the only one in the country dedicated solely to collecting and exhibiting contemporary Native American art, much of it produced by the staff and faculty of the college. Inside you can view educational films, exhibits of contemporary artists, and outdoor sculptures in an enclosed courtyard. (June-Sept: Mon-Sat 9 am-5 pm, Sun from 10 am; Oct-May: Mon-Sat 10 am-5 pm, Sun from noon) **$$**

Kokopelli Rafting Adventures. *541 W Cordova Rd (87501). Phone 800/879-9035.* Kokopelli Rafting offers a full range of whitewater rafting trips to the Rio Grande and Rio Chama rivers as well as sea kayaking trips to Cochiti lake, Abiqui lake, and Big Bend National Park in Texas. Rafting trips cover Class II through IV rapids. Excursions include half-day, full-day, overnight and 2 to 8 day wilderness expeditions. Transportation from Santa Fe included. (Apr-Sept) **$$$$**

La Fonda Hotel. *100 E San Francisco St (87501).* A longtime center of Santa Fe social life. Former meeting place of trappers, pioneers, merchants, soldiers, and politicians; known as the "Inn at the End of the Trail."

Las Cosas School of Cooking. *181 Paseode Peralta (87501). Phone 505/988-3394.* Found within a beautiful store stocked with gourmet kitchen tools and elegant tableware, this cooking center offers hands-on culinary education experiences that fill a morning or evening. Taught by school director John Vollertsen and by chefs from New Mexico's leading restaurants, the classes cover a wide range of topics, such as artful risotto, Atkins diet dishes, soups and stocks, Oaxacan moles, the best in fish preparations, grilling, one-dish wonders, and fresh herb recipes. All kitchen supplies are provided, as are alcoholic beverages, and private classes can be arranged, too. (Classes usually at 10 am and 6 pm; closed Thanksgiving, Dec 25, Jan 1) **$$$$**

Lensic Performing Arts Center. *211 W San Francisco St (87501). Phone 505/988-7050; 505/988-1234 (box office).* The Lensic Theater is one of Santa Fe's historical and architectural gems, recently reopened after a full restoration completed in 2001. The structure was first built in 1931 in a Moorish/Spanish Renaissance style and has always been Santa Fe's premiere theater space, having played host to celebrities such as Roy Rogers and Judy Garland over the years. Since reopening, it has provided a constantly changing schedule of quality theater, symphony, and performing arts events.

Loretto Chapel. *207 Old Santa Fe Trail (87501). Phone 505/984-7971.* The Loretto Chapel was built in 1873 and is one of the few non adobe-style buildings in downtown Santa Fe. Modeled after St. Chapelle cathedral in Paris, it was the first Gothic building built west of the Missisippi. The chapel itself is not particularly impressive, but what draws countless tourists is the "miraculous stairway", a 2-story spiral wooden staircase built without any nails or central supports that seems to defy engineering logic. (Mon-Sat 9 am-5 pm, Sun 10:30 am-5 pm; closed Dec 25)

The Miraculous Staircase. *207 Old Santa Fe Tr, in Loretto Chapel (87501). Phone 505/984-7971.* A circular stairway 22 feet high, built without central support and, according to legend, put together with wooden pegs. It makes 2 complete 360-degree turns and has 33 steps. (Daily; closed Jan 1, Thanksgiving, Dec 25) **$**

Museum of Fine Arts. *107 W Palace Ave (87501). Phone 505/476-5072.* Designed by Isaac Hamilton Rapp in 1917, the museum is one of Santa Fe's earliest Pueblo revival structures and its oldest art museum. It contains over 20,000 holdings, with an emphasis on Southwest regional art and the artists of Santa Fe and Taos from the early 20th century. The St. Francis Auditorium inside the museum also presents lectures, musical events, plays, and various other performances. (Tues-Sun 10 am-5 pm) **$$$**

Museum of Spanish Colonial Art. *Phone 505/982-2226.* This small museum holds some 3,000 objects showcasing traditional Hispanic art in New Mexico dating from conquest to present day. The galleries are housed in a building designed in 1930 by famous local architect John Gaw Meem, gracefully restored with historically accurate appointments. The collection includes many early works in wood, tin, and other local materials as well as numerous works by contemporary New Mexican artists who continue the rich Hispanic artistic traditions to this day. (Tues-Sun; closed Mon, Thanksgiving, Dec 25) **$$$**

Oldest House. *De Vargas St and Old Santa Fe Tr.* Believed to be pre-Spanish; built by Native Americans more than 800 years ago.

Palace of the Governors. *105 Palace Ave (87501). Phone 505/476-5100.* Built in 1610, this is the oldest public building in continuous use in the US. It was the seat of government in New Mexico for more than 300 years. Lew Wallace, governor of the territory (1878-81), wrote part of *Ben Hur* here in 1880. It is now a major museum of Southwestern history. The Palace, Museum of Fine Arts, Museum of Indian Arts and Culture, Museum of International Folk Art, and state monuments all make up the Museum of New Mexico. (Tues-Sun 10 am-5 pm; closed holidays) **$$**

San Ildefonso Pueblo. *16 miles N on US 84, 285, then 6 miles W on NM 502. Phone 505/455-2273.* (Population: 447) This pueblo is famous for its beautiful surroundings and its black, red, and polychrome pottery, made famous by Maria Poveka Martinez. (Daily; closed winter weekends; visitors must register at the visitor center) Photography permit may be purchased at the visitor center (fee). Various festivals take place here throughout the year (see SPECIAL EVENTS). The circular structure with the staircase leading up to its rim is a kiva, or ceremonial chamber. There are two shops in the pueblo plaza, and a tribal museum adjoins the governor's office. One-half mile west is a fishing lake. Per vehicle **$$**

San Miguel Mission. *401 Old Santa Fe Trail (87501). Phone 505/983-3974.* Built in the early 1600s, this is the oldest church in the US still in use. Construction was overseen by Fray Alonso de Benavidez, along with a group of Tlaxcalan Indians from Mexico who did most of the work. The original adobe still remains beneath the stucco walls, and the interior has been restored along with Santa Fe's oldest wooden *reredos* (altar screen). Church services are still held on Sundays. (Daily; closed holidays) **DONATION**

Santa Fe Casino Hollywood and Hollywood Hills Speedway. *30 miles S of Santa Fe via I-25. Phone 877/529-2946* This multiuse complex situated midway between Santa Fe and Albuquerque on the San Felipe Pueblo brings something akin to Las Vegas-style entertainment to New Mexico. Within the casino, guests find abundant gaming opportunities, as well as showroom entertainment. (Sun-Thurs 8 am-4 pm, Fri-Sat 24 hours) Also on site is the Hollywood Hills Speedway, opened in 2002 and known as the state's premier venue of its kind. The 3/8-mile clay oval speedway for auto and motorcycle racing is viewed from a grandstand seating 10,000, as well as from sky boxes. Also look for monster truck shows, extreme sports events, and outdoor concerts, with entertainers ranging from country music acts to specialty cultural performers.

Santa Fe Children's Museum. *1050 Old Pecos Trail (87505). Phone 505/989-8359.* Happy activity fills a creative space that absorbs the attention of children of all ages. Hands-on exhibits invite kids to make magnetic structures, route water streams, create paintings, illustrate cartoon movies, discover plants on a greenhouse scavenger hunt, scale an 18-foot-high climbing wall, use an old-fashioned pitcher pump, and weave beads and fabric on a loom. Local artists and scientists make appearances to teach kids in playful, inventive ways. Especially interesting are regularly scheduled events like "Music Under the Big Top" and "Ice Cream Sunday." (Wed-Sat 10 am-5 pm, Sun noon-5 pm; closed Mon, Tues, Dec 25) **$**

Santa Fe National Forest. *1474 Radio Rd. (87501). Phone 505/438-7840.* This forest consists of over 1 1/2 million acres. Fishing is excellent in the Pecos and Jemez rivers and tributary streams. Hiking trails are close to unusual geologic formations. Hot springs in the Jemez Mountains. Four wilderness areas within the forest total more than 300,000 acres. Campgrounds are provided by the Forest Service at more than 40 locations; for reservations call 800/280-2267. There are user fees for many areas. Forest headquarters are located here.

Santa Fe Premium Outlets. *8380 Cerrillos Rd (87507). Phone 505/474-4000.* Shop for bargain-priced designer apparel, shoes, luggage, jewelry, housewares and other accessories at New Mexico's only outlet center. Located on the south side off Cerrillos road, the more than 40 stores include such well-known brands as Bass, Bose, Brooks Brothers, Dansk, Eddie Bauer, Liz Claiborne, Nautica, Samsonite, Van Hausen, and many more. (Daily)

Santa Fe Rafting Company. *1000 Cerrillos Rd (87505). Phone 505/998-4914; toll-free 800/222-RAFT.* The Rio Grande and Rio Chama rivers north of Santa Fe provide excellent opportunities for river running and white water rafting, offering Class II through Class IV rapids. Santa Fe Rafting Company offers several rafting trips including half-day, full-day and multi-day camping excursions, some of which include a boxed lunch. The biggest rapids are found on their Taos Box full-day trip, open to anyone over age 12. All trips include roundtrip transportation from Santa Fe. (Apr-Sept) **$$$$**

Santa Fe School of Cooking. *116 W San Francisco St. Phone 505/983-4511.* Sign up for classes offered several times weekly in traditional and contemporary Southwestern cuisine. Culinary tours involve classes with nationally renowned chefs with trips to local farms and wineries. Call for schedule.

Santa Fe Southern Railway. *410 Guadalupe St (87501). Phone 505/989-8600; toll-free 888/989-8600.* Made famous by the 1940's swing tune "Atchison, Topeka & Santa Fe," a small part of this historical rail line continues as the Santa Fe Southern Railway, which still carries freight and tourists between Santa Fe and nearby Lamy, an 18 mile trip. The start of the route is housed in the old Santa Fe Depot, where you can view vintage railcars and shop for gifts and memorabilia in the original mission-style train depot. Several scenic train rides in authentically restored vintage cars are offered to the public, following the original high desert route to and from Lamy. The rides cater to tourists and range from short scenic roundtrips to longer outings that include picnics, BBQs, and various holiday-themed events, such as the Halloween Highball Train and New Year's Eve Party Train.

The Santa Fe Plaza. *100 Old Santa Fe Trail.* The Santa Fe Plaza, steeped in a rich history, has been a focal point for commerce and social activities in Santa Fe since the early 17th century. The area is marked by a central tree-lined park surrounded by some of Santa Fe's most important historical landmarks, many of which survive from Spanish colonial times. The most important landmark is the Palace of the Governors, which was the original seat of local government and is the oldest public building in the US still in use. Native American artists from nearby Pueblos sell handmade artwork in front of the Palace and various museums, and shops, and dining establishments surround the Plaza, making it the top tourist destination in Santa Fe. Numerous festivals and activities are held in the Plaza throughout the year, including Spanish Market and Indian Market.

Santuario de Guadalupe. *100 Guadalupe St. Phone 505/988-2027.* Built in 1781, and the oldest shrine in America dedicated to Our Lady of Guadalupe, the Santuario has been converted into an art and history museum specializing in religious art and iconography. The holdings include a large collection of Northern New Mexican santos (carved wooden saints) and paintings in the Italian Renaissance and Mexican baroque styles. A famous rendering of Our Lady of Guadalupe by renowned Mexican artist Jose de Alzibar is also on display. (Mon-Fri 9 am-4 pm; May-Oct: Mon-Sat 9 am-4 pm; closed Sun, holidays) **DONATION**

Scottish Rite Temple. *463 Paseo De Peralta (87501).* Modeled after part of the Alhambra.

Sena Plaza and Prince Plaza. *Washington and Palace aves.* Small shops, formerly old houses, built behind portals and around central patios.

Shidoni Bronze Foundry and Gallery. *1508 Bishop's Lodge Rd. Phone 505/988-8001.* A fantastic resource for art collectors and sculptors, Shidoni consists of a bronze foundry, art gallery, and outdoor sculpture garden set in an 8-acre apple orchard 5 miles north of Santa Fe. Artists from around the country come to work at Shidoni's 14,000 square foot foundry, open to the general public for self-guided tours. Explore the lovely sculpture garden during daylight hours or shop for works of bronze and metal in the adjacent gallery. (Mon-Sat; closed Sun, Thanksgiving, Dec 25)

Ski Santa Fe. *Hyde Park Rd (Hwy 475). Take Paseo de Peralta to Bishop Lodge Rd and turn north onto Bishop Lodge Rd. Continue 1 block and turn right on Artist Rd (which becomes Hyde Park Rd) and follow to the top of the mountain (approximately 16 miles). Phone 505/982-4429; 505/983-9155 (snow conditions).* World-class skiing and snowboarding in the majestic Sangre de Cristo mountains is only a 20-minute drive from the downtown Santa Fe Plaza. Ski Santa Fe is a family-owned resort catering to skiers and snowboarders of all levels, from beginning to expert. In addition to breathtaking views of the city below, the 12,053-foot summit offers six lifts and 44 runs (20 percent easy, 40 percent more difficult, 40 percent most difficult), with a total of 660 acres of terrain. The longest run is 3 miles, and the mountain offers a vertical drop of 1,700 feet. The average yearly snowfall is 225 inches. A PSIA-certified ski school offers group and private lessons for adults and children, and there are restaurants, rental shops, and a clothing boutique on site. The Chipmunk Corner offers activities and lessons for children ages 4-9. (Late Nov-early Apr, daily) **$$$$**

State Capitol. *Old Santa Fe Tr and Pasco de Peralta (87501). Phone 505/986-4589.* (1966) This unique building, in modified Territorial style, is round and intended to resemble a Zia sun symbol. Self-guided tours. (Memorial Day-Labor Day, daily; rest of year, Mon-Sat; closed holidays). **FREE**

Swig. *135 W Palace Ave, Level 3 (87501). Phone 505/955-0400.* Santa Fe's newest bar/nightclub is also its swankiest. Swig offers four different bar areas (mostly nonsmoking) and a very red dance floor all set in an intoxicatingly contemporary atmosphere. Sip the expensive but refreshingly creative martinis (starting at $11) or sample the excellent pan-Asian tapas. The dance floor will keep you entertained while a fresh roster of rotating DJs spin. Be sure to dress the part: Swig does enforce a dress code. (Tues-Sat)

Ten Thousand Waves. *3451 Hyde Park Rd (87504). Take Paseo de Peralta to Bishop Lodge Rd and turn north onto Bishop Lodge Rd. Continue 1 block and turn right at Artist Rd (which becomes Hyde Park Rd) and follow to the sign on left side of winding road (approximately 4 miles). Phone 505/982-9304.* When you feel like being pampered, this exquisite Japanese-themed spa and bathhouse is a genuine treat. Located in a unique Zenlike setting in the Sangre de Cristo Mountains, Ten Thousand Waves offers soothing hot tubs, massages, facials, and other spa treatments to make you forget your cares. The choices here are endless: hand, foot, scalp, and full-body massages, herbal wraps, rejuvenating facials, and a variety of open-air hot tubs, including coed public hot tubs (where clothing is optional before 8:15 pm), a women-only tub, secluded private tubs, and large private tubs that can accommodate up to 20. Whichever you choose, you'll find all tubs clean and inviting (and chlorine-free), and amenities such as kimonos, towels, sandals, lotion, and lockers provided for you. Be sure to call ahead for reservations, especially for massage services. (Daily) **$$$$**

Special Events

AID and Comfort Gala. *309 W San Francisco St (87501). Phone 505/989-3399.* Since 1989, the organization Aid and Comfort has raised money to benefit those suffering from HIV and AIDS. The annual gala kicks off the holiday season on the Saturday after Thanksgiving with a lavish bash at the Eldorado Hotel, featuring live music for dancing, a buffet, and a silent auction.

Buffalo and Comanche dances. *2 Dove Rd (87004). Phone 505/867-3301.* Fiesta at San Ildefonso Pueblo. Late Jan.

Christmas Eve Canyon Road Walk. *Starts at the foot of Canyon Road near Paseo De Peralta.* Adorned with thousands of traditional luminaries (lights made of a single small candle inside a paper bag), the streets and homes around Canyon Road play host to a unique and colorful festival each Christmas Eve. Literally thousands of pedestrians stroll up and down the streets while singing Christmas carols, lighting bonfires and enjoying hot apple cider. A major Santa Fe tradition not to be missed. **FREE**

Christmas Eve Celebrations. In Santa Fe and nearby villages, with street fires and *farolitos* (paper bag lanterns) "to guide the Christ Child," candlelit *Nacimientos* (nativity scenes), and other events. Santo Domingo, Tesuque, Santa Clara, and other pueblos have Christmas dances the following three days.

Fiesta and Green Corn Dance. *San Felipe Pueblo.* Early May.

Fiesta at Santo Domingo Pueblo. Corn dance. This fiesta is probably the largest and most famous of the Rio Grande pueblo fiestas. Early Aug.

Indian Market. *125 E Palace Ave. Phone 505/983-5220.* Each year in late August the Santa Fe Indian Market attracts a swarm of national and international buyers and collectors to the largest and oldest Native American arts show and market in the world. Over 1,200 artists from over 100 North American tribes participate in the show, with around 600 outdoor booths set up in the middle of the ancient Santa Fe Plaza. The market is a great opportunity to meet the artists and buy directly from them instead of going through the usual galleries and other middlemen. Quality of work is stressed, as all sale items are strictly screened for quality and authenticity. Numerous outdoor booths sell food, and the event draws an estimated 100,000 visitors to Santa Fe during the weekend, so make your lodging reservations well in advance. Late Aug.

Invitational Antique Indian Art Show. *201 W Marcy (87501). Sweeney Center. Phone 505/984-6760.* Largest show of its kind in the country. Pre-1935 items; attracts dealers, collectors, museums. Two days in mid-Aug.

Mountain Man Rendezvous and Festival. *105 W Palace Ave (87504). Phone 505/476-5100.* In early August, costumed mountain men ride into town on horseback for the Museum of New Mexico's annual buffalo roast, part of a large gathering of trappers and traders from the pre-1840 wilderness. Participants sell primitive equipment, tools, and trinkets and compete in period survival skills such as knife and tomahawk throwing, muzzleloader rifle shooting, cannon firing, storytelling, and foot races.

Northern Pueblo Artist & Craftsman Show. Mid-July.

Santa Fe Chamber Music Festival. *239 Johnson St (87501). Phone 505/983-2075.* Since the first season of the festival in 1973, when Pablo Casals was the founding, honorary president, this artistic tradition has grown into a major event consisting of more than 80 performances, open rehearsals, concert previews, and roundtable discussions with composers and musicians during the annual summer season. The celebrated "Composer-in-Residence" Program has hosted luminaries such as Aaron Copland, Ellen Taafe Zwilich, and John Harbison, and the festival has sent ensembles on national tours since 1980. Performances are frequently heard on National Public Radio, and the festival fosters a significant outreach program to Santa Fe schools. Check for performances scheduled at St. Francis Auditorium, Museum of Fine Arts, and the Lensic Performing Arts Center. July-Aug.

Santa Fe Fiesta. *Phone 505/988-7575.* This ancient folk festival, dating back to 1712, features historical pageantry, religious observances, arts and crafts shows, and street dancing. Celebrates the reconquest of Santa Fe by Don Diego de Vargas in 1692. Make reservations well in advance. Second weekend in Sept.

Santa Fe Opera. *US Hwy 84 and 285 (87505). Drive N from Santa Fe about 7 miles via Hwy 84/285; the Opera is on the W side of the hwy. Phone 505/986-5900.* Founded in 1957, this opera company presents one of the world's most famous and respected opera festivals each summer from late June through late August. Each season, the company stages five works, including two classics, a lesser-known work by a well-known composer, a Richard Strauss offering, and a world premiere or new American staging. Possibly more dramatic and appealing, even to an opera novice, is the Santa Fe Opera's home, a breathtaking hilltop amphitheater found about 7 miles north of the city. Designed by Polshek & Partners of New York, who refurbished Carnegie Hall in Manhattan, the Opera incorporates bold, swooping lines with excellent sight lines and is known for superb acoustics. Featured stars frequently include those from New York's Metropolitan Opera, among many others, and the festival is known for offering an exemplary apprentice program to young opera hopefuls. (Performances begin at 9 pm) **$$$$**

Santa Fe Pro Musica. *320 Galisteo St # 502. Phone 505/988-4640.* Chamber orchestra and chamber ensemble perform classical and contemporary music, also performance of Messiah during Christmas season, Mozart Festival in Feb. Sept-May.

Santa Fe Rodeo. *2801 W Rodeo Rd (87502). Phone 505/471-4300.* The Santa Fe Rodeo offers the chance to see real live cowboys and bucking broncos in action at the outdoor rodeo fairgrounds. Various professional competitions and public exhibitions open to the public are put on during the brief summer season. Rodeo events generally happen during evening and weekend matinee hours. A downtown rodeo parade takes place in mid June at the start of the season. **$$$$**

Santa Fe Stages. *100 N Guadalupe St (87501). Phone 505/982-6683.* With presentations offered primarily at the wonderfully renovated, historic Lensic Performing Arts Center, Santa Fe Stages hosts a season of dance, music, and theater with national and regional appeal. The season typically begins before Memorial Day and ends in late September, and may offer Irish folk dance, classical ballet, opera, jazz, drama, comedy, or cabaret shows.

Santa Fe Symphony and Chorus. *211 W San Francisco St (87501). Phone 505/983-3530.* Recently marking its 20th anniversary, Santa Fe's orchestral company presents works in classical and jazz music, as well as specialty programs that may include the music of Spain and Mexico. Look for a blend of genres for the season-ender, which could include Copland's *Fanfare for the Modern Man,* Ellington's *The River,* and Dvorak's *Symphony No. 9 (New World).* The season generally runs from early October through Memorial Day, with matinee and evening performances at the Lensic Performing Arts Center. **$$$$**

Santa Fe Wine and Chile Fiesta. *551 W Cordova Rd (87505). Phone 505/438-8060.* Begun in 1991, this wildly popular festival honoring the best in food and drink brings in some 2,000 appreciative fans from around the state and across the country for 4 days of noshing and sipping on the last weekend in September. Roughly 30 local restaurants and 90 wineries from around the globe team up with a half-dozen or so of America's top celebrity chefs and cookbook authors to present a culinary extravaganza in a variety of venues around town. Wine seminars, cooking demonstrations, special vintners' lunches and dinners, and the gastronomic circus called the Grand Tasting, staged in mammoth tents on the Santa Fe Opera grounds, fill a palate-thrilling schedule. **$$$$**

Shakespeare in Santa Fe. *1516 Pacheco St (87505). Phone 505/982-2910.* Established in 1987, the Santa Fe Shakespeare Company is a professional group that presents classical and contemporary theater to the community, with an emphasis in bringing works to young people. Each season, one of the works by William Shakespeare is presented in an outdoor setting, but the majority of presentations are made at the Lensic Performing Arts Center, and a few are staged at venues like the Museum of Indian Arts and Culture. Classic Fairy Tales are among the presentations arranged specifically for Santa Fe families. Look for Shakespeare works to be presented in May and June. **$$$$**

Spanish Market. *750 Camino Lejo. Phone 505/983-4038.* The rich and colorful Hispanic art traditions of Northern New Mexico are celebrated twice a year during Spanish Market, the oldest and largest exhibition and sale of traditional Hispanic art in the US. The smaller winter market in December is held indoors in the Sweeney Convention Center (201 W Marcy St), while the larger summer market occupies the entire Santa Fe Plaza for one weekend in July. During the market as many as 300 vendors sell and display *santos* (carved saints), hide paintings, textiles, furniture, jewelry, tinwork, basketry, pottery, bonework, and other locally produced handicrafts reflecting the unique and deeply religious traditional art which still flourishes in this part of New Mexico. Sponsored by the Spanish Colonial Arts Society.

Spring Corn Dances. *Cochiti, San Felipe, Santo Domingo, and other pueblos. Phone 505/843-7270.* Races, contests. Late May-early June.

St. Anthony's Feast-Comanche Dance. *San Juan Pueblo.* Mid-June.

Tesuque Pueblo Flea Market. *From Santa Fe, take St. Francis Dr north, which turns into Hwy 84/285 as you leave town. Continue north for approx 5.5 miles. The Flea Market is located on the left side of the highway next to the Santa Fe Opera. Phone 505/995-8626; www.tesuquepuebloflea market. com.* At the Tesuque Pueblo outdoor flea market, you'll find hundreds of vendors offering antiques, gems, jewelry, pottery, rugs, and world folk art of all descriptions at very competitive prices. Plan on devoting a couple of hours to browse all the various treasures and myriad of vendor booths stretching for several acres. Even if you don't buy anything, it's a browser's paradise well worth the 15-minute drive from Santa Fe.

Zozobra Festival. *490 Washington Ave (87501).* Each year on the Thuday before Labor Day, the Kiwanis Club of Santa Fe hosts the burning of Zozobra, a 50-foot effigy of "Old Man Gloom", whose passing away is designed to dispel the hardships and travails of the previous year. As part of the Fiestas celebration, Zozobra started in 1924 when a local artist conceived a ritual based on a Yaqui Indian celebration from Mexico. Over the years Zozobra caught on

and the crowd sizes have grown, making Zozobra Santa Fe's largest, most colorful and most spectacular festival. Lasting for several hours, as many as 60,000 visitors crowd into a large grassy field in Fort Marcy Park to listen to live bands, watch spectacular fireworks displays and cheer the ritual burning. Fiestas celebrations continue during the Labor Day weekend with all day booths and activities setup in the nearby Plaza. Thu before Labor Day. **$$$**

Motels/Motor Lodges

★ **BEST WESTERN INN.** *3650 Cerrillos Rd (87505). Phone 505/438-3822; toll-free 800/780-7234; fax 505/438-3795. www.bestwestern.com.* 97 rooms, 3 story. Memorial Day-Labor Day: S $65-$105; D $66-$120; each additional $10; suites $95-$195; under 12 free; higher rates during special events; lower rates rest of year. Pet accepted, some restrictions. Complimentary continental breakfast. Check-out 11 am. TV; cable (premium). Laundry services. Indoor pool, whirlpool. Downhill, cross-country ski 20 miles. Cr cds: A, C, D, DS, MC, V.

🄳 ⊞ ⊞ ⊞ ⊞ ⊞

★★ **BEST WESTERN LAMPLIGHTER INN.** *2405 Cerrillos Rd (87505). Phone 505/471-8000; toll-free 800/767-5267; fax 505/471-1397. www.bestwestern.com.* 80 rooms, 2 story, 16 kitchens May-Oct: S, D $72-$85; suites $95; kitchen units $95; under 18 free; lower rates rest of year. Crib free. TV; cable (premium). Indoor pool. Sauna. Complimentary coffee in rooms. Restaurant 7 am-9 pm. Bar. Check-out 11 am. Guest laundry. Business services available. Refrigerators; some microwaves. Picnic tables. Cr cds: A, C, D, DS, MC, V.

⊞

★★ **COURTYARD BY MARRIOTT.** *3347 Cerrillos Rd (87505). Phone 505/473-2800; toll-free 800/777-3347; fax 505/473-4905. www.santafecourtyard.com.* 213 rooms, 3 story. May-Oct: S, D $69-$139; each additional $10; under 17 free; ski rates; higher rates: Dec 25, Indian Market; lower rates rest of year. Crib free. Check-out noon. TV; cable (premium). In-room modem link. Some private patios, balconies. Refrigerators. Microwaves available. Coffee in rooms. Coin laundry. Restaurant 7 am-1:30 pm, 5-9:30 pm. Bar. Exercise equipment. Indoor pool; whirlpools. Downhill, cross-country ski 17 miles. Free airport transportation. Meeting rooms. Business center. Gift shop. Cr cds: A, C, D, DS, MC, V.

🄳 ⊞ ⊞ ⊞ ⊞ SC ⊞

★ **GARRETTS DESERT INN.** *311 Old Santa Fe Tr (87501). Phone 505/982-1851; toll-free 800/888-2145; fax 505/989-1647.* 82 rooms, 2 story. July-Aug: S, D $111-$121; suites $131; lower rates rest of year. Check-out noon. TV; cable (premium). Restaurant 7 am-8 pm. Bar. Heated pool. Meeting rooms. Business services. Cr cds: A, D, DS, MC, V.

⊞

★ ★ **HOLIDAY INN.** *4048 Cerrillos Rd (87505). Phone 505/473-4646; toll-free 800/465-4329; fax 505/473-2186. www.holiday-inn.com.* 130 rooms, 4 story. Mid-June-Sept: S $89-$139; D $89-$149; each additional $10; under 18 free; lower rates rest of year. Crib free. Pet accepted, some restrictions. Complimentary coffee in rooms. Check-out noon. TV; cable (premium). In-room modem link. Private patios, balconies. Refrigerators. Restaurant 6:30 am-10 pm. Bar. Room service. Exercise equipment, sauna. Heated indoor/outdoor pool, whirlpool, poolside service. Downhill, cross-country ski 20 miles. Airport, bus depot transportation. Meeting rooms. Business services. Bellstaff. Sundries. Cr cds: A, D, DS, JCB, MC, V.

⊡ 🐾 ⇌ 🕍

★ ★ **HOTEL PLAZA REAL.** *125 Washington Ave (87501). Phone 505/988-4900; fax 505/983-9322.* 56 rooms, 3 story, 44 suites. June-Oct: S, D $149-$219; suites $199-$650; ski plans; lower rates rest of year. Garage parking $10. TV; cable (premium). Restaurant 7-11 am. Bar 4-11 pm. Check-out noon. Meeting rooms. Business services available. In-room modem link. Bellhops. Concierge. Health club privileges. Downhill/cross-country ski 15 miles. Wet bar in suites. Refrigerators. Some balconies. Territorial-style architecture; fireplaces, handcrafted Southwestern furniture. Cr cds: A, C, D, DS, JCB, MC, V.

⊡ ⇌ ⇌

★ **HOWARD JOHNSON EXPRESS INN.** *4044 Cerrillos Rd (87505). Phone 505/438-8950; toll-free 800/446-4656; fax 505/471-9129. www.hojo.com.* 47 rooms, 2 story. Mid-May-Aug: S $54-$98; D $65-$120; each additional $6; under 18 free; lower rates rest of year. Crib available. Complimentary continental breakfast. Check-out 11 am. TV; cable (premium). Restaurant adjacent 6:30 am-10 pm. Downhill, cross-country ski 20 miles. Business services. Near airport. Cr cds: A, C, D, DS, MC, V.

⊡ ⇌ ⇌

★ **LA QUINTA INN.** *4298 Cerrillos Road (87505). Phone 505/471-1142; toll-free 800/531-5900; fax 505/438-7219. www.laquinta.com.* 130 rooms, 3 story. Late June-Aug: S, D $89-$100; each additional $8; suites $120-$140; under 18 free; lower rates rest of year. Crib free. Pet accepted. Complimentary continental breakfast. Check-out noon. TV; cable (premium). Refrigerators, microwaves available. Coffee in rooms. Coin laundry. Restaurant adjacent open 24 hours. Pool. Downhill, cross-country ski 14 miles. Cr cds: A, C, D, DS, MC, V.

⊡ 🐾 ⇌ ⇌ ⇌

★ **LUXURY INN.** *3752 Cerrillos Rd (87505). Phone 505/473-0567; toll-free 800/647-1346; fax 505/471-9139.* 51 rooms, 2 story. May-Oct: S $35-$55; D $70-$90; under 10 free; weekly rates; ski plan; higher rates during special events; lower rates rest of year. Crib free. Complimentary

continental breakfast. Check-out 11 am. TV; cable (premium). Restaurant adjacent 11 am-9 pm. Pool, whirlpool. Cr cds: A, C, D, DS, MC, V.

⊡ ⇌ ⇌

★ **PARK INN AND SUITES SANTA FE.** *2907 Cerrillos Rd (87505). Phone 505/471-3000; fax 505/424-7561.* 101 rooms, 2 story. Mid-June-Oct: S $90; D $95; each additional $5; under 17 free; ski plan; lower rates rest of year. Crib free. Pet accepted. TV; cable (premium). Restaurant 7 am-2 pm, 6-9 pm. Bar. Health club privileges. Game room. Pool. Downhill, cross-country ski 20 miles. Meeting rooms. Business services. Cr cds: A, C, D, DS, ER, JCB, MC, V.

⊡ 🐾 ⇌ ⇌

★ ★ **QUALITY INN.** *3011 Cerrillos Rd (87505). Phone 505/471-1211; toll-free 800/228-5151; fax 505/438-9535. www.qualityinn.com.* 99 rooms, 2 story. May-Oct: S $55-$105; D $60-$105; each additional $10; under 18 free; lower rates rest of year. Crib free. Pet accepted, some restrictions. Check-out noon. TV; cable (premium). Balconies. Some refrigerators. Restaurant 7 am-9 pm. Room service. Heated pool. Downhill, cross-country ski 17 miles. Airport transportation. Meeting room. Business services, convention center/facilities. Cr cds: A, C, D, DS, ER, JCB, MC, V.

⊡ 🐾 ⇌ ⇌ 🕍 ⇌

★ **STAGE COACH INN.** *3360 Cerrillos Rd (87505). Phone 505/471-0707.* 15 rooms, 1-2 story. S, D $49-$89; each additional $10. TV; cable (premium). Restaurant nearby. Check-out 10 am. Downhill/cross-country ski 20 miles. Picnic tables, grills. Cr cds: A, MC, V.

⇌ ⇌ SC

Hotels

★ ★ ★ **ELDORADO HOTEL.** *309 W San Francisco (87501). Phone 505/988-4455; toll-free 800/286-6755; fax 505/995-4555. www.eldoradohotel.com.* The Eldorado Hotel's imposing pueblo-revival style building is one of Santa Fe's largest and most important landmarks. Its lobby and interiors are lavishly decorated with more than a quarter million dollars of original southwest art. The Lobby Lounge serves drinks and is a great spot for snacking, people watching and enjoying live entertainment. Sunday brunch is served in the cozy Eldorado Court, voted "Best Brunch" by the residents of Santa Fe. 219 rooms, 5 story. S, D $189-$269; suites $259-$2,000; under 18 free. Pet accepted. Garage parking $10. Check-out noon. TV; cable (premium), VCR available (movies). In-room modem link. Some fireplaces. Restaurant 7 am-9:30 pm (See also THE OLD HOUSE). Bar 11:30-2 am; entertainment. Exercise equipment; sauna. Massage.

Rooftop pool; whirlpool, poolside service. Downhill ski 16 miles, cross-country ski 7 miles. Business center. Concierge. Cr cds: A, C, D, DS, MC, V.

D ⊁ ⅀ ⚡ ⟟ ⟝ SC ⟟

★ ★ ★ **HILTON.** *100 Sandoval St. (87501). Phone 505/988-2811; toll-free 800/336-3676; fax 505/986-6439. www.hiltonofsantafe.com.* Located within walking distance of the Plaza in a 380-year-old family estate, this property embodies the history found in Santa Fe. Amenities include the city's largest pool, a hot tub, and an exercise room. Guest rooms feature locally handcrafted furnishings and include in-room coffee, hair dryers, and dataports. 157 rooms, 3 story. Mid-June-Oct: S $139-$249; D $159-$269; each additional $20; suites $275-$675; family rates; ski packages; lower rates rest of year. Crib free. Check-out noon. TV; cable (premium), VCR available (movies). In-room modem link. Minibars. Restaurant 6:30 am-midnight. Bar 11 am-11 pm. Room service. Exercise equipment. Heated pool, whirlpool. Downhill ski 15 miles. Airport transportation. Meeting rooms. Business center. Bellstaff. Concierge. Gift shop. Cr cds: A, C, D, DS, ER, JCB, MC, V.

D ⊁ ⅀ ⟟ SC ⟟

★ ★ ★ **HOTEL SANTA FE.** *1501 Paseo De Peralta (87501). Phone 505/982-1200; toll-free 800/825-9876; fax 505/955-7878.* This hotel features such extras as storytelling in front of the kiva fireplace, ceremonial dances and pottery/paintings. Guests can also relax in the swimming pool, whirlpool or with a massage. 129 rooms, 89 suites, 3 story. Late June-Aug: S, D $149-$209; suites $179-$219; under 17 free; ski plans; lower rates rest of year. Crib free. Check-out noon. TV; cable (premium). Balconies. Minibars. Valet services, coin laundry. Restaurant. Bar 4 pm-midnight, entertainment Fri, Sat. Health club privileges. Pool, whirlpool. Downhill, cross-country ski 10 miles. Airport transportation. Meeting rooms. Business services. Bellstaff. Concierge. Gift shop. Pueblo Revival architecture; original art by Native Americans. A Native American enterprise. Cr cds: A, C, D, DS, MC, V.

D ⅀ ⚡

★ ★ ★ **HOTEL ST. FRANCIS.** *210 Don Gaspar Ave (87501). Phone 505/983-5700; toll-free 800/529-5700; fax 505/989-7690. www.hotelstfrancis.com.* As part of the Historic Inns of America, this 83-room property was originally built in 1880 and then rebuilt in 1923 after a fire in 1922. Each room has a high ceiling and original windows, some with mountain views. The inn is one block from the historic plaza and close to museums, shops and galleries. Concierge services, an all day restaurant and afternoon tea service are available. 83 rooms, 3 story. S, D $80-$220; each additional $15; suites $205-$380; under 12 free. Crib free. Check-out 11 am. TV; cable. In-room modem link. Refrigerators. Restaurant 7-10 am,

11:30 am-2 pm, 5-10 pm; weekends 7 am-2 pm. Bar noon-2 am; Sun to midnight. Room service. Downhill ski 15 miles. Meeting rooms. Business services. Concierge. European ambience; antiques, original artwork. Cr cds: A, C, D, DS, JCB, MC, V.

D ⅀ ⚡ SC

★ ★ ★ **INN AT LORETTO.** *211 Old Santa Fe Tr (87501). Phone 505/988-5531; toll-free 800/727-5531; fax 505/984-7988. www.hotelloretto.com.* Built in 1975, this hotel offers guests a heated outdoor pool, 12 specialty shops, and galleries. Guests can also enjoy skiing, hiking, tennis and horseback riding. 140 rooms, 4 story. July-Aug: S, D $279-$349; each additional $15; under 18 free; lower rates rest of year. Crib free. Check-out noon. TV; cable (premium). Private patios, balconies. Refrigerators. Coffee in rooms. Guest laundry. Restaurant 7 am-9 pm; dining room from 5:30 pm. Bar 11-1 am; Sun noon-midnight; entertainment. Room service. Massage. Heated pool, poolside service. Downhill, cross-country ski 15 miles. Barber, beauty shop. Meeting rooms. Business services. Bellstaff. Concierge. Shopping arcade. Adobe building. Cr cds: A, C, D, DS, MC, V.

D ⚡ ⚥ ⅀ ⚡ ⟟ ⚡

★ ★ ★ ★ **INN OF THE ANASAZI.** *113 Washington Ave (87501). Phone 505/988-3030; toll-free 800/688-8100; fax 505/988-3277. www.innoftheanasazi.com.* Native American, Hispanic, and cowboy cultures collide at the Inn of the Anasazi, where a masterful blend of New Mexican legacies results in a stunning and unusual lodging. The true spirit of Santa Fe is captured here, where enormous handcrafted doors open to a world of authentic artwork, carvings, and textiles synonymous with the Southwest. The lobby sets a sense of place for arriving guests with its rough-hewn tables, leather furnishings, unique objects, and huge cactus plants in terracotta pots. Located just off the historic Plaza, the inn was designed to resemble the traditional dwellings of the Anasazi. The region's integrity is maintained in the guest rooms, where fireplaces and four-poster beds reside under ceilings of vigas and latillas, and guests discover toiletries made locally with native cedar extract. Artfully prepared, the meals of the Anasazi's restaurant earn praise for honoring the area's culinary heritage. 59 units, 3 story. Apr-Oct: S, D $249-$415; each additional $20; under 12 free; lower rates rest of year. Pet accepted, some restrictions; $30. Valet parking $12/day. Check-out noon. TV; cable (premium), VCR (movies $5). Restaurant. Exercise equipment. Massage. Health club privileges. 18-hole golf privileges. Tennis privileges. Downhill ski 13 miles; cross-country ski 7 miles. Concierge. Cr cds: A, D, DS, MC, V.

D ⊁ ⅀ ⟟ ⚡ ⟟ ⅀

★★★ **INN ON THE ALAMEDA.** *303 E Alameda (87501). Phone 505/984-2121; toll-free 800/984-2121; fax 505/986-8325. www.inn-alameda.com.* Sitting unassumingly behind adobe walls near the start of Canyon Road, this 69-room inn offers all the comforts of a luxury hotel but with the quiet elegance of a smaller bed and breakfast. Guest rooms feature Egyptian cotton sheets, fireplaces, robes, hairdryers, cable television, and dataports. Enjoy the two outdoor hot tubs and fully equipped exercise room. 69 rooms, 2-3 story. July-Oct: S, D $147-$197; each additional $15; suites $249-$334; lower rates rest of year. Pet accepted. Complimentary continental breakfast. Check-out noon. TV; cable (premium). In-room modem link. Private patios, balconies. Kiva fireplaces. Valet services. Restaurant nearby. Bar 2:30-11 pm. Whirlpools. Health club privileges, exercise equipment, massage. Downhill, cross-country ski 15 miles. Meeting room. Business services. Concierge, Library. Cr cds: A, C, D, DS, MC, V.

⊡ 🐾 ➤ 🏃 ☒

★★★ **LA POSADA DE SANTA FE RESORT AND SPA.** *330 E Palace Ave (87501). Phone 505/986-0000; toll-free 800/727-5276; fax 505/982-6850. www.laposadadesantafe.com.* Scattered over six beautifully landscaped acres, the hotel resembles a pueblo with its many cottages, secluded patios and bubbling fountains. The handsome public rooms in the historic Stabb House have been lovingly restored. 119 rooms, 1-2 story. May-Oct & hols: S, D $199-$279; suites $195-$395; under 12 free; package plans; lower rates rest of year. Crib $5. Check-out noon. TV; cable (premium). Many fireplaces. Restaurant (See also STAAB HOUSE). Bar 11 am-midnight; Sun noon-11 pm. Room service. Pool, poolside service. Downhill, cross-country ski 15 miles. Beauty shop. Meeting rooms. Business services. Bellstaff. Concierge. On 6 acres; gardens. Adobe casitas surround Victorian/Second Empire Staab mansion (1882); guest rooms either Pueblo Revival or Victorian in style. Cr cds: A, C, D, DS, MC, V.

⊡ ➤ 🏊 ☒

★★ **RADISSON.** *750 N St Francis Dr (87501). Phone 505/992-5800; toll-free 800/723-4776; fax 505/992-5865. www.radisson.com.* This beautifully landscaped hilltop property is centrally located near all of the city's major attractions. Guests will enjoy the large swimming pool and hot tub as well as their complimentary access to the next-door Santa Fe Spa. One and two bedroom condos offer kiva fireplaces and full kitchens. 141 rooms, 2 story. May-Dec: S, D, studio rooms $139; each additional $20; suites $169-$434; ski packages; lower rates rest of year. Pet accepted. Check-out noon. TV; cable (premium). Restaurant 6:30 am-2 pm, 5:30-10 pm. Bar 4 pm-midnight, entertainment. Room service. Health club privileges. Poolside service. Downhill, cross-country ski 18 miles. Cr cds: A, C, D, DS, ER, JCB, MC, V.

⊡ 🐾 ➤ 🏊 ☒ SC

Resorts

★★★ **BISHOPS LODGE.** *Bishop's Lodge Rd (87504). Phone 505/983-6377; toll-free 800/732-2240; fax 505/989-8739. www.bishopslodge.com.* Nestled in the foothills of the Sangre de Cristo Mountains, this resort offers a mix of traditional ranch experiences with luxurious accommodations. Activities include horseback riding, fishing, and hiking. Guests can take advantage of the fitness center, spa and swimming pool. The distinctive guest lodges feature dataports, in-room coffee, robes, and turndown service. 111 rooms in 1-3 story lodges. No elevator. July-Aug: S, D $299-$729; lower rates rest of year. Check-out noon, check-in 4 pm. TV; cable (premium), VCR available. In-room modem link. Some private patios. Many refrigerators, some fireplaces. Restaurant (See also BISHOP'S LODGE). Children's dining room. Bar 11:30 am-midnight; Sun from noon. Box lunches, picnics. Room service. Supervised children's activities (Memorial Day-Sept); ages 4-12. Playground. Exercise equipment, sauna. Sports director. Social director; entertainment. Recreation room. Heated pool, whirlpool, poolside service, lifeguard. 18-hole golf privileges. Tennis, pro. Downhill, cross-country ski 18 miles. Lawn games. Fishing pond for children. Business services. Concierge. Stocked pond. Skeet, trap shooting; pro. Riding instruction; breakfast and lunch rides; children's rides. Cr cds: A, D, DS, MC, V.

⊡ 🐕 ⛳ ➤ 🍴 🎿 ➤ 🏊 🏃 ☒

★★★ **HYATT REGENCY TAMAYA RESORT & SPA.** *1300 Tamaya Trail, Santa Ana Pueblo (87004). Phone 505/867-1234; toll-free 800/633-7313; www.hyatt.com.* 350 rooms, 4 story. S, D $195-$275; each additional $20; under 17 free. Crib available. Complimentary coffee in rooms. Check-out noon. TV; cable (premium), VCR available. Refrigerators, some minibars. Restaurant 6 am-10 pm. Exercise room, spa. Pool, whirlpool, poolside service. 18-hole golf. Meeting rooms. Business center. Gift shop. Cr cds: A, C, D, DS, JCB, MC, V.

⊡ ⛳ 🍴 ➤ 🏊 🏃 ☒ 🏃

★★★ **RANCHO ENCANTADO RESORT.** *198 State Rd 592 (87501). Phone 505/982-3537; toll-free 800/722-9339; fax 505/983-8269. www.nmhotels.com/html/sfranchencantado.html.* This ranch was built using a combination of Native American, Spanish, and Anglo-style architecture. The property is rich in history, offers finely decorated rooms with art work and antiques and is found tucked away on over 200 acres of land. 39 units, 16 cottages. Late June-mid-Oct: S, D $175-$375; each additional $10; cottages $210-$250; ski plan; lower rates rest of year. Crib available. TV. Pool; whirlpool. Complimentary coffee in rooms. Dining room 7-11 am, 11:30 am-2 pm, 5:30-9:30 pm. Box lunches. Picnics. Bar 11 am-11 pm. Check-out 11 am, check-in 3 pm. Gift shop. Grocery 3 miles. Coin laundry 8 miles. Meeting room. Business services available. Tennis; pro. Cross-country ski 12 miles. Hiking trails. Minibars. Picnic tables. Cr cds: A, C, D, DS, MC, V.

⊡ 🕭 🏊 🛬 🛶 🐾 🔌 SC

All Suites

★ ★ **VILLAS DE SANTA FE, NM.** *400 Griffin St (87501). Phone 505/988-3000; toll-free 800/869-6790; fax 505/988-4700. www.sunterra.com.* 100 kitchen suites, 4 story. May-Oct, Dec: S $155-$175, D $175-$310; lower rates rest of year. Crib free. Pet accepted; $10/day. Complimentary breakfast buffet. Complimentary coffee in rooms. Check-out noon. TV; cable (premium). In-room modem link. Many balconies. Microwaves. Coin laundry. Restaurant nearby. Exercise equipment. Heated pool, whirlpools. Picnic tables. Meeting rooms. Business services. Bellhops. Concierge. Cr cds: A, C, D, DS, MC, V.

⊡ 🕭 🛗 🔌 🏊 🛬 🔌 SC

B&B/Small Inns

★ ★ ★ **ADOBE ABODE.** *202 Chapelle St (87501). Phone 505/983-3133; fax 505/424-3027. www.adobeabode.com.* Built in 1905 as officer quarters for Fort Marcy, this property offers guests a unique stay in one of the finely decorated rooms. Visitors will enjoy the complimentary sherry and Santa Fe cookies in the afternoon. 6 rooms, 3 with shower only. S, D $120-$125; each additional $15; suite $145-$155. Complimentary full breakfast. Check-out 11 am, check-in 2 pm. TV; cable (premium). Luggage handling. Individually decorated rooms with antiques from all over the world. Cr cds: DS, MC, V.

🔌

★ ★ ★ **ALEXANDER'S INN.** *529 E Palace Ave (87501). Phone 505/986-1431; toll-free 888/321-5123; fax 505/982-8572. www.alexanders-inn.com.* With a location offering only a short walk to shopping, restaurants and galleries, this inn keeps a quiet and peaceful atmosphere. Built in 1903, the rooms are full of elegance with hardwood floors, stained-glass windows or lace curtains and more. 16 rooms, 2 share bath, 2 with shower only; 4 suites, 2 story. Mid-Mar-mid-Nov: S, D $100-$110; each additional $20; higher rates: Indian Market, Dec 25; lower rates rest of year. Pet accepted, some restrictions. TV; cable, VCR available. Whirlpool. Complimentary continental breakfast; afternoon refreshments. Check-out 11 am, check-in by arrangement. Business services available. Luggage handling. Concierge service. Downhill ski 17

miles; cross-country ski 10 miles. Health club privileges. Five rooms in renovated house built 1903. Totally nonsmoking. Cr cds: DS, MC, V.

🕭 🏊 🔌

★ ★ **DANCING GROUND OF THE SUN.** *711 Paseo De Peralta (87501). Phone 505/986-9797; toll-free 800/745-9910; fax 505/986-8082. www.dancingground.com.* 5 casitas, 5 kitchen units, 2 story. S, D $130-$219; each additional $20. Complimentary continental breakfast. Complimentary coffee in rooms. Check-out 11 am, check-in 3-6 pm. TV; cable. Patios. Microwaves. Restaurant nearby. Business services. Concierge. All rooms with Native American theme. Totally nonsmoking. Cr cds: A, D, DS, MC, V.

⊡ 🔌

★ ★ ★ **DOS CASAS VIEJAS.** *610 Agua Fria St (87501). Phone 505/983-1636; fax 505/983-1749. www.doscasasviejas.com.* Set in the heart of Sante Fe's Guadeloupe District, guests can enjoy all that Sante Fe has to offer. Available activities include opera, museums, art galleries, restaurants, hiking, skiing, horseback riding, shopping, and golfing. 8 rooms, 1 suite. S, D $185-$215; suite $265. Complimentary continental breakfast. Check-out noon, check-in 3-6 pm. TV; cable (premium). Refrigerators. Mexican-tiled floors and wood-burning kiva fireplaces. Coffee in rooms. Restaurant nearby. Heated pool. Business services. Two historical buildings in a 1/2-acre walled/gated compound; renovated to restore 1860s architecture. Totally nonsmoking. Cr cds: MC, V.

⊡ 🕭 🏊 🔌

★ ★ **EL PARADERO EN SANTA FE.** *220 W Manhattan Ave (87501). Phone 505/988-1177; fax 505/988-3577. www.elparadero.com.* 12 rooms, 2 kitchen suites. D $80-$150; each additional $15. Pet accepted; fee. Children over 3 years only. Complimentary full breakfast afternoon refreshments. Check-out 11 am, check-in 2-8 pm. TV in sitting room. Restaurant nearby. Downhill ski 18 miles, cross-country ski 9 miles. Renovated Spanish adobe house (circa 1820) with details from 1880 and 1912 remodelings. Cr cds: A, MC, V.

⊡ 🕭 🛗 🔌 🏊 🔌

★ ★ **EL REY INN.** *1862 Cerrillos Rd (87502). Phone 505/982-1931; toll-free 800/521-1349; fax 505/989-9249. www.elreyinnsantafe.com.* 86 rooms, 9 kitchen units, 1-2 story. May-Oct: S $85-$95; D $99-$105; each additional $12; kitchen suites $99-$185. Crib free. Complimentary continental breakfast. Check-out noon. TV; cable (premium). Some fireplaces. Coin laundry. Restaurant nearby. Playground. Health club privileges. Pool, whirlpool. Downhill/cross-country ski 17 miles. Picnic tables. Business services. Cr cds: A, C, D, DS, MC, V.

⊡ 🔌 🏊 🔌

★ ★ ★ **FORT MARCY SUITES.** *320 Artist Rd (87501). Phone 505/982-6636; toll-free 800/745-9910; fax 505/984-8682. www.territorialinn.com.* This charming 10-room Victorian home is located one block from the historic Santa Fe Plaza. Eight rooms offer private baths and all feature queen-size beds, alarm clocks, voice mail, cable televisions, and telephones. Relax in the rose garden or in the hot tub. 10 rooms, 1 with shower only, 2 share bath, 2 story. S $100-$120; D $120-$140; each additional $20. Children over 10 years only. Complimentary continental breakfast, evening refreshments. Check-out 11 am, check-in 3 pm. TV; cable (premium). Some fireplaces. Restaurant nearby. Whirlpool. Health club privileges. Downhill, cross-country ski 15 miles. Business services. House (circa 1895) blends New Mexico's stone and adobe architecture with pitched roof, Victorian-style interior; sitting room, antiques; garden and tree-shaded lawns more typical of buildings in the East. Cr cds: A, C, D, DS, MC, V.

D ⊳ ⌦ ⊠

★ ★ ★ **GALISTEO INN.** *9 La Vega, Galisteo (87540). Phone 505/466-8200; fax 505/466-4008. www.galisteoinn.com.* Guests can tour the area on mountain bikes, horseback, or by hiking. Located just a half hour from Pecos National Monument and nearby Santa Fe, guests can enjoy a true Southwestern vacation. 12 rooms. No A/C. No room phones. 4 TVs. D $110-$185; each additional $25. Children over 6 years only. Complimentary full breakfast. Check-out noon, check-in 4-6 pm. Restaurant Wed-Sun 6-8:30 pm. Massage, sauna. Pool, whirlpool. Hacienda on 8 acres built in 1750s. Totally nonsmoking. Cr cds: A, DS, MC, V.

D ⊹ ⌦ ⊠

★ ★ ★ **GRANT CORNER INN.** *122 Grant Ave (87501). Phone 505/983-6678; toll-free 800/964-9003; fax 505/983-1526. grantcornerinn.com.* Located two blocks from Santa Fe's historic Plaza and next to the Georgia O'Keeffe Museum, this 10-room Colonial Manor house (1905) is a picture of tranquility, with many gardens and large trees. The air-conditioned guest rooms feature hand-painted armoires, antique photographs, and four-poster beds. The full breakfast offers such dishes as Swedish pancakes. 12 rooms, 2 share bath, 3 story. June-Oct: S, D $145-$240; each additional $20. Children over 8 years only. Complimentary full breakfast, afternoon refreshments. Check-out noon, check-in 2-6 pm. TV; cable. Restaurant nearby. Massage. Downhill/cross-country ski 15 miles. Business services. Antiques. Totally nonsmoking. Cr cds: A, MC, V.

D ⊳ ⊠

★ ★ ★ **GUADALUPE INN.** *604 Agua Fria St (87501). Phone 505/989-7422. www.guadalupeinn.com.* A quiet inn offering rooms with unique style and decor. Local artists display their work in the rooms and many pieces are for sale. 12 rooms, 2 story. Mid-Apr-mid-Jan: S, D $125-$175; each additional $15; 4-day minimum during Indian Market; lower rates rest of year. Crib. TV; cable (premium). Whirlpool. Complimentary full breakfast. Restaurant adjacent. Check-out 11 am, check-in 3-6 pm. Concierge service. Business services available. Downhill ski 15 miles; cross-country ski 10 miles. Balconies. Picnic tables. Individually decorated rooms. Totally nonsmoking. Cr cds: A, DS, MC, V.

D ⊹ ⌦ ⊞ ⊠

★ ★ ★ **INN OF THE GOVERNORS.** *101 W Alameda (87501). Phone 505/982-4333; toll-free 800/234-4534; fax 505/989-9149. www.innofthegovernors.com.* Guests will enjoy relaxing at the piano bar or around the heated outdoor pool. Guests can venture into town for shopping, hiking, fine restaurants and even take in an opera or visit the museums. 100 rooms, 2-3 story. S, D $139-$330; each additional $15; under 18 free. Crib free. Complimentary continental breakfast. Check-out noon, check-in 4 pm. TV; cable (premium). In-room modem link. Balconies. Some fireplaces, minibars. Restaurant (See also MAÑANA). Bar 11:30 am-midnight; Sun from noon; entertainment. Room service. Pool. Downhill/cross-country ski 14 miles. Meeting room. Business services. Bellstaff. Concierge. Cr cds: A, C, D, DS, ER, JCB, MC, V.

D ⊳ ⌦ ⊠ SC

★ ★ ★ **INN ON THE PASEO.** *630 Paseo De Peralta (87501). Phone 505/984-8200; toll-free 800/457-9045; fax 505/989-3979. www.innonthepaseo.com.* Located on the Paseo de Peralta in the heart of downtown Santa Fe, this recently renovated 19-room inn offers a relaxing Southwest experience. Air-conditioned guest rooms feature down comforters, patchwork quilts, and private baths. The breakfast buffet is served on the sun deck and features a collection of healthy favorites like muffins, granola, and fresh fruit. 18 rooms, 2-3 story. July-Oct: S, D $105-$165; suite $165; summer weekends (2-day minimum), Indian market. TV; cable (premium). Complimentary breakfast buffet; afternoon refreshments. Restaurant nearby. Check-out 11 am, check-in 3 pm. Business services available. Sun decks. Totally nonsmoking. Cr cds: A, D, MC, V.

D ⊠

★ ★ ★ **LA TIENDA INN & DURAN HOUSE.** *445-447 and 511 W San Francisco St (87501). Phone 505/989-8259; toll-free 800/889-7611; fax 505/820-6931. www.latiendabb.com.* Located just four blocks from Santa Fe's Historic Plaza, this Territorial adobe farmhouse is over 100 years old (circa 1900) and offers southwestern decor with many antiques. Guest rooms feature private entrances and handcrafted furniture. 7 rooms. S, D $90-$160. Adults only. Complimentary continental breakfast.

Check-out 11 am, check-in 3-6 pm. TV; cable (premium). Restaurant nearby. Downhill, cross-country ski 17 miles. Luggage handling, concierge. House has 3 rooms; 4 rooms in Old Store adobe wing. Totally nonsmoking. Cr cds: A, MC, V.

D ☒

★ ★ ★ **THE MADELEINE.** *106 E Faithway St (87501). Phone 505/982-1431; toll-free 888/321-5123; fax 505/982-8572. www.madeleineinn.com.* This bed and breakfast is adorned with stained-glass windows, tile fireplaces and window seats. Enjoy shopping, museums, and galleries while strolling through Santa Fe. 8 rooms, 3 with shower only, 3 story, 1 suite. Apr-Oct, holidays: S, D $80-$180; each additional $25; lower rates rest of year. Pet accepted, some restrictions. Complimentary continental bkfst, afternoon refreshments. Check-out 11 am, check-in 3 pm. TV. Some fireplaces. Restaurant nearby. Downhill, cross-country ski 17 miles. Business services. Queen Anne house (1886) with antique furnishings and sitting room. Totally nonsmoking. Cr cds: DS, MC, V.

☜ ☒ ☒

★★**PUEBLO BONITO BED AND BREAKFAST INN.** *138 W Manhattan Ave (87501). Phone 505/984-8001; toll-free 800/461-4599; fax 505/984-3155. www.pueblobonitoinn.com.* 18 rooms, 7 suites, 6 kitchen units, 1-2 story. No A/C. May-Oct: S, D $115-$160; each additional $15; lower rates rest of year. Complimentary buffet breakfast. Check-out noon, check-in 2 pm. TV; cable. Some balconies. Fireplaces. Restaurant nearby. Whirlpool. Downhill/cross-country ski 18 miles. Antique furnishings, baskets. Renovated adobe casitas on 1880s estate; private courtyards, gardens, mature trees. Cr cds: A, DS, MC, V.

D ☒

★ ★ ★ **SPENCER HOUSE BED AND BREAKFAST INN.** *222 McKenzie St (87501). Phone 505/988-3024; toll-free 800/647-0530.* Taking a trip to this bed and breakfast is like taking a trip to the past. The inn is completely furnished in antiques and honeywood oak and has a hand-carved staircase. 6 air-cooled rooms. May-Oct: S, D $99-$165; lower rates rest of year. Children over 12 years only. Complimentary full breakfast. Check-out 10:30, check-in 3-5 pm. TV; cable (premium). Some fireplaces. Restaurant nearby. Downhill/cross-country ski 15 miles. Luggage handling. Country cottage atmosphere with antiques from England, Ireland and Wales. Cr cds: A, MC, V.

☒

★ ★ ★ **WATER STREET INN.** *427 W Water St (87501). Phone 505/984-1193; toll-free 800/646-6752; fax 505/984-6235. www.waterstreetinn.com.* Located just two blocks from Santa Fe's historic Plaza, this recently restored inn features Southwestern decor with art and photography lining its walls. Spacious brick-floored guest rooms have

private baths, cable TV with VCRs, air conditioning, and decks/patios. The courtyard offers a sundeck with great views and a large hot tub. 12 rooms. S, D $125-$225; each additional $15. Complimentary continental breakfast. Check-out 11 am, check-in 2-6 pm. TV; cable, VCR (movies $3). In-room modem link. Restaurant nearby. Whirlpool. Downhill/cross-country ski 17 miles. Business services. Restored adobe building; fireplaces, antique stoves. Totally nonsmoking. Cr cds: A, DS, MC, V.

D ☝ ☒ ☒ ☒

Restaurants

★ ★ ★ **THE ANASAZI.** *113 Washington Ave (87501). Phone 505/988-3236; fax 505/988-3277. www.innoftheanasazi.com.* The inn's dining room serves a wide variety of eclectic regional fare, including grilled cactus, crispy Thai shrimp dumplings, cinnamon-chile rubbed beef tenderloin and Alaskan halibut. There is a strong emphasis on organic meats, poultry and vegetables. Contemporary Southwestern menu. Menu changes seasonally. Hours: 7-10:30 am, 11:30 am-2:30 pm, 5:30-10 pm; Sun brunch 11 am-2:30 pm. Dinner $16-$32. Sun brunch. Bar 11 am-midnight. Children's menu. Casual attire. Cr cds: A, D, DS, MC, V.

D

★ ★ **ANDIAMO.** *322 Garfield (87501). Phone 505/995-9595.* Hours: 5:30-9:30 pm. Closed Tue. Reservations accepted. Italian menu. Wine, beer. Dinner $13.50-$17.50. Children's menu. Specializes in pasta. Outdoor dining. Three dining areas. Contemporary décor. Totally nonsmoking. Cr cds: A, DS, MC, V.

D

★ ★ ★ **BISHOP'S LODGE.** *Bishop's Lodge Rd (87504). Phone 505/983-6377; toll-free 800/732-2240; fax 505/989-8739. www.bishopslodge.com.* Named after the first bishop of Santa Fe, the lodge is nestled into the shadow of the Sangre de Cristo Mountains. Southwestern menu. Hours: 7:30-10 am, 11:30 am-2 pm, 6-9 pm; brunch 11 am-2 pm. Dinner $17-$30, Sun brunch. Bar. Entertainment Mon-Wed, Sat, Sun (seasonal). Children's menu. Adobe home was built in the early 1900s. Reservations required; (dinner). Outdoor dining. Cr cds: A, D, DS, MC, V.

D

★ **BLUE CORN CAFE.** *133 Water St (87501). Phone 505/984-1800.* New Mexican menu. Hours: 11 am-11 pm. Closed Thanksgiving, Dec 25. Lunch, dinner $7-$16. Bar to midnight. Children's menu. Casual attire. Southwestern décor; fireplace. Cr cds: A, C, D, DS, MC, V.

D

★ **THE BURRITO COMPANY.** *111 Washington Ave (87501). Phone 505/982-4453.* Mexican menu. Hours: 7:30 am-7 pm; Sun 10 am-5 pm. Closed Dec 25. Breakfast

$2-$3.50, lunch $4-$8. Children's menu. Fast-food style restaurant famous for breakfast burritos.

D

★ ★ **CAFE PARIS.** *31 Burro Alley (87501). Phone 505/986-9162; fax 505/995-0008.* French menu. Hours: 11:30 am-2:30 pm, 5:30-9:30 pm; Tues 11:30 am-2:30 pm. Closed Mon; also Jan 1, Dec 25. Dinner $25-$50. Casual attire. Cafe-style dining. Totally nonsmoking. Cr cds: DS, MC, V.

★ ★ **CAFE PASQUAL'S.** *121 Don Gaspar (87501). Phone 505/983-9340; fax 505/988-4645.* New Mexican, American menu. Hours: 7 am-3 pm, 6-10:30 pm; Sun brunch 8 am-2 pm. Closed Thanksgiving, Dec 25. Dinner $16-$34. Sun brunch. Casual attire. Totally nonsmoking. Cr cds: A, DS, MC, V.

★ ★ **CELEBRATIONS.** *613 Canyon Rd (87501). Phone 505/989-8904. www.celebrationscanyonroad.com.* Continental menu. Hours: 8:30 am-2:30 pm, 5-9 pm. Closed Jan 1, Thanksgiving, Dec 25. Dinner $12-$22. Bar. Casual attire. Outdoor dining. 3 dining areas; fireplaces. Cr cds: DS, MC, V.

D

★ **CHOW'S CUISINE BISTRO.** *720 St. Michaels Dr (87505). Phone 505/471-7120; fax 505/471-7120. www.mychows.com.* This little restaurant tucked away in a shopping mall offers some of the best Chinese food in Santa Fe. Offering mostly Szechwan dishes in a contemporary Asian atmosphere, Chow's consistently wins the *Santa Fe Reporter's* "Best of Santa Fe award". Enjoy numerous unique and tasty dishes all prepared without MSG. Chinese menu. Closed Sun. Lunch, dinner. Outdoor seating. Cr cds: MC, V. **$$**

D

★ ★ **CORN DANCE CAFE.** *1501 Paseo de Peralta (87501). Phone 505/982-1200. www.hotelsantafe.com.* Native Amercian menu. Hours: 11:30 am-2 pm, 5:30-9 pm. Dinner $14-$26. Bar to 10 pm; Fri, Sat to 11 pm. Casual attire. Outdoor dining. Southwestern décor; large fireplace; Native American art and artifacts. Totally nonsmoking. Cr cds: A, MC, V.

D

★ ★ **COYOTE CAFE.** *132 W Water St (87501). Phone 505/983-1615; fax 505/989-9026. www.coyote-cafe.com.* New Mexican menu. Hours: 6-9:30 pm; Sat, Sun 11 am-1:45 pm, 5:30-9:45 pm. Dinner $24-$35. Bar/cantina (May-Oct) 11:30 am-9:45 pm. Casual attire. Outdoor dining on rooftop cantina. Adobe structure; Southwestern décor; fireplace. Cr cds: A, C, D, DS, ER, MC, V.

D

★ **EL COMEDOR.** *727 Cerrillos Rd (87501). Phone 505/989-7575; fax 505/984-8879.* Southwestern menu. Hours: 7 am-9 pm; winter hours vary. Closed Thanksgiving, Dec 25. Dinner $8.40-$13.95. Children's menu. Casual attire. Outdoor dining. Cr cds: A, DS, MC, V.

D

★ ★ **EL MESON - LA COCINA DE ESPAÑA.** *213 Washington Ave (87501). Phone 505/983-6756; fax 505/983-1262. www.enchantedweb.com.* Hours: 11:30 am-2 pm, 5:30-10 pm. Closed Mon, Sun; also Jan 1, Thanksgiving, Dec 25. Reservations accepted. Spanish menu. Wine, beer. A la carte entrees: lunch $6-$9, dinner $15-$18. Children's menu. Specializes in tapas, paellas. Guitarist weekends. Street parking. Outdoor dining. Totally nonsmoking. Cr cds: A, C, D, DS, ER, MC, V.

D

★ ★ **GABRIEL'S.** *4 Banana Ln (87501). Phone 505/455-7000; fax 505/455-3866.* Southwestern, Mexican menu. Adobe building has four dining areas, two large fireplaces; Southwestern decor. Hours: 11:30 am-9 pm; Fri, Sat to 10 pm; closed Thanksgiving, Dec 25. Dinner $6.95-$17.95. Bar. Children's menu. Reservations accepted. Outdoor dining. Cr cds: A, D, DS, MC, V.

D SC

★ **GARDUNO'S.** *130 Lincoln Ave (87501). Phone 505/983-9797; fax 505/984-0332. www.gardunosrestaurants.com.* Mexican menu. Specializes in chimichangas, fajitas, seafood. Southwestern decor. Hours: 11 am-10 pm; Fri, Sat to 10:30 pm; Sun 10:30 am-10 pm; Sun brunch to 3 pm, closed Thanksgiving, Dec 25. Dinner $6.50-$13.95. Sun brunch $10.95. Bar. Entertainment. Children's menu. Cr cds: A, D, DS, MC, V.

D

★ ★ ★ **GERONIMO.** *724 Canyon Rd (87501). Phone 505/982-1500; fax 505/982-0106.* A break from gallery hopping around lunchtime. When it's warm outside, sit on the patio for prime Canyon Road people watching. Global menu. Hours: 11:30 am-2:30 pm, 6-10 pm. Dinner $20-$34. Bar to midnight. Casual attire. Outdoor dining. Cr cds: A, MC, V.

D

★ **GRANT CORNER INN.** *122 Grant Ave (87501). Phone 505/983-6678. www.grantcornerinn.com.* Hours: 8-9:30 am; Sat to 11 am; Sun to 1 pm. Brunch menu: $8.50-$10.50; Sun $10.50. Children's menu. Colonial-style house built 1905. Outdoor dining. Cr cds: A, MC, V.

D

★ ★ **IL PIATTO.** *95 W Marcy St (87501). Phone 505/984-1091; fax 505/983-6939.* Italian menu. Hours: 11:30 am-2 pm, 5:30-9:30 pm, Fri, Sat to 10 pm. Closed Jan

1, Thanksgiving, Dec 25. Dinner $8-$15. Bar. Children's menu. Casual attire. Outdoor dining. Cr cds: A, MC, V.

[D]

★ ★ **INDIA PALACE.** *227 Don Gaspar (87501). Phone 505/986-5859; fax 505/986-5856. www.indiapalace.com.* The multi-award-winning India Palace, conveniently located only a block from the Santa Fe Plaza, offers some of the best authentic Indian cuisine available in New Mexico. On the menu, you'll find an excellent selection of familiar Indian dishes, including a wide variety of meat and vegetarian offerings. The real deal, though, is the popular all-you-can eat lunch buffet, available for only $8.45. East Indian menu. Hours: 11:30 am-2:30 pm, 5-10 pm. Closed Super Bowl Sun. Dinner $6.95-$24.95. Outdoor seating. Cr cds: A, D, DS, MC, V.

[D]

★ ★ ★ **JULIAN'S.** *221 Shelby St (87501). Phone 505/988-2355; fax 505/988-5071. www.juliansofsantafe.com.* It would be hard to beat the menu for variety: entrées include cannelloni with veal, chicken and spinach; two versions of risotto; and veal sauteed with prosciutto, fontina and sage. Will there be room left for the "double chocolate cake"? Italian menu. Hours: 5:30-10 pm. Closed Thanksgiving. Dinner $14-$32. Bar. Reservations accepted. Outdoor dining. Elegant Italian ambience. Cr cds: A, D, DS, MC, V.

[D]

★ ★ **LITTLE ANITA'S.** *2811 Cerrillos Rd (87501). Phone 505/473-4505; fax 505/471-6441.* Mexican menu. Hours: 7 am-9 pm. Closed Dec 25. Dinner $5-$11.99. Children's menu. Casual attire. Cr cds: A, DS, MC, V.

[D] [SC]

★ ★ **MAÑANA.** *101 W Alameda (87501). Phone 505/982-4333; fax 505/989-9149. www.inn-gov.com.* Southwestern/Californian menu. Hours: 6:30 am-10 pm. Dinner $4.95-$12. Bar. Piano. Casual attire. Outdoor dining. Cr cds: A, D, DS, MC, V.

★ ★ **MARIA'S NEW MEXICAN KITCHEN.** *555 W Cordova Rd (87501). Phone 505/983-7929; fax 505/983-4700. www.marias-santafe.com.* If you love margaritas, this popular restaurant offers more 100 different varieties of REAL margaritas, made with some of the best and most exotic tequilas imported from Mexico. The margarita menu alone is bigger than most restaurants' food menus. Maria's also offers a great selection of Mexican beers and specializes in homemade, freshly cooked New Mexican cuisine. Try the BBQ ribs or any of the fajita dishes, along with the excellent homemade salsa. New Mexican, Southwestern menu. Hours: 11 am-10 pm; Sat, Sun from noon. Closed Thanksgiving, Dec 25. Dinner $8.95-$18.75. Bar. Children's menu. Casual attire. Outdoor seating. Cr cds: A, C, D, DS, MC, V.

[D]

★ **MU DU NOODLES.** *1494 Cerrillos Rd (87505). Phone 505/983-1411.* Popular with the locals, Mu Du Noodles serves up a well-prepared and eclectic Pan-Asian menu consisting of various noodle dishes, soups, and other yummy offerings. The setting is tasteful and contemporary in a colorful Zen kind of way. Despite the excellent food, the relatively high prices don't make for the best ethnic food value in town, but still worth a try for the non-budget conscious. Outdoor patio dining is available during summer hours. Hours: 11:30 am-2:30 pm, 5:30-9:30 pm; Sat from 5:30 pm. Closed Sun; some major holidays. Dinner $13-$17. Children's menu, totally nonsmoking. Asian menu. Cr cds: A, C, D, DS, MC, V.

[D]

★ ★ ★ **THE OLD HOUSE RESTAURANT.** *309 W San Francisco St (87501). Phone 505/988-4455; fax 505/995-4555. www.eldoradohotel.com.* Hidden away in the Hotel Eldorado, this gem of a restaurant features chef Martin Rios's imaginative New American/Southwestern cuisine. Knowledgeable, professional service and a well-developed wine list complement an inspired menu including an appetizer of grilled marinated quail with pear, savoy cabbage, and toasted walnuts. Don't miss the seared herbed scallops with crisped potato, sweet peppers, leeks, and roasted corn. Contemporary American menu. Hours: 5:30-10 pm. Closed Thanksgiving, Dec 25. Dinner $27-$33. Bar. Children's menu. Casual attire. Valet parking. Cr cds: A, D, DS, MC, V.

[D]

★ ★ **OLD MEXICO GRILL.** *2434 Cerrillos Rd (87501). Phone 505/473-0338; fax 505/424-0890.* Mexican menu. Hours: 11:30 am-2:30 pm, 5:30-9 pm. Closed Labor Day, Thanksgiving, Dec 25. Dinner $12-$20. Bar. Casual attire. Cr cds: DS, MC, V.

[D] [SC]

★ ★ **ORE HOUSE ON THE PLAZA.** *50 Lincoln Ave (87505). Phone 505/983-8687; fax 505/920-6892. www.orehouseontheplaza.com.* A perennial favorite on every list of great taverns in the City Different, this comfortable hangout is in its third decade of pleasing visitors with a menu of more than 40 custom-made margaritas and dozens of sipping tequila choices. The balcony, with its unbeatable setting above the historic Plaza, is open year-round, thanks to special heating during cooler weather. A regular custom of frequent pilgrims is to wind up the day over a cocktail, noshing on complimentary snacks, listening to the evening's guitarist, and watching the stars light the sky. Happy hour is from 4-6 pm daily. Seafood, steak menu. Hours: 11:30 am-2:30 pm, 5:30-10 pm; Sun noon-2:30 pm. Closed Thanksgiving, Dec 25. Dinner $14-$25. Bar to 1 am. Entertainment Fri-Sun. Children's menu. Casual attire. Outdoor dining. Cr cds: A, MC, V.

★ ★ **OSTERIA D'ASSISI.** *58 S Federal Pl (87501). Phone 505/986-5858; fax 505/986-3938. www.osteriadassisi.com.* Italian menu. Hours: 11 am-9 pm; Fri, Sat to 10 pm. Closed Jan 1, Thanksgiving, Dec 25. Dinner $10.95-$21. Casual attire. Outdoor dining. Totally nonsmoking. Cr cds: A, D, MC, V.

D

★ ★ ★ **PALACE RESTAURANT AND SALOON.** *142 W Palace Ave (87501). Phone 505/982-9891. www.palacerestaurant.com.* The menu offers a wide selection of meats (including tenderloin medallions, osso buco, and fresh fish), but the real delight is the homemade pastas: one example is the tortelloni filled with four cheese fondu and black truffles with a Pinot Grigio and mascarpone sauce. Continental menu. Hours: 11:30 am-3 pm, 5:30-10 pm; Sun from 5:30 pm. Closed Thanksgiving, Dec 25. Dinner $14.95-$34.50. Bar. Piano. Children's menu. Casual attire. Outdoor dining. Cr cds: A, D, DS, MC, V.

D

★ ★ ★ **PAUL'S.** *72 W Mary St, Pojoque Valley (87501). Phone 505/982-8738. www.paulsofsantafe.com.* This restaurant in a suburb of Santa Fe is known for fine service and elegant cooking. Hours: 11:30 am-2 pm, 5:30-9 pm. Closed July 4, Dec 25. Reservations accepted. Wine, beer. Lunch $5.95-$8.95, dinner $14-$19. Specializes in duck, seafood, lamb. Contemporary décor. Totally nonsmoking. Cr cds: A, D, DS, MC, V.

D

★ ★ **THE PINK ADOBE.** *406 Old Santa Fe Trl (87501). Phone 505/983-7712; fax 505/984-0691. www.thepinkadobe.com.* Southwestern, continental menu. Hours: 11:30 am-2:30 pm, 5:30-10 pm; Sat, Sun from 5:30 pm. Closed major holidays. Dinner $11.25-$23.75. Bar. Entertainment Tue-Thu, Sat. Children's menu. Historic pink adobe building circa 1700. Casual attire. Outdoor dining. Fireplace in dining rooms. Cr cds: A, D, DS, MC, V.

D

★ **PIZZERIA ESPIRITU.** *1722 St. Michaels Dr (87505). Phone 505/424-8000; fax 505/424-8001.* Hours: 11 am-9 pm. Closed Sun; also most major holidays. Reservations accepted. Italian menu. A la carte entrees: lunch $2.50-$8.95, dinner $2.50-$12.95. Children's menu. Specializes in gourmet pizzas, pastas, salads. Parking. Outdoor dining. Cr cds: A, D, DS, MC, V.

D

★ **PLAZA.** *54 Lincoln Ave (87501). Phone 505/982-1664.* Continental menu. Hours: 7 am-10 pm. Closed Thanksgiving, Dec 25. Dinner $9-$15. Children's menu. Century-old building with many original fixtures; stamped-tin ceiling; photos of early Santa Fe. Casual attire. Cr cds: A, D, MC, V.

★ ★ **PRANZO ITALIAN GRILL.** *540 Montezuma (87501). Phone 505/984-2645; fax 505/986-1123.* Pranzo, which translates from Italian as "main" or "favorite" meal of the day, consistently ranks as one of the best Italian restaurants in Santa Fe. Situated in the Sanbusco Center in an old 19th century lumberyard, its hardwood floors and casual ambience serve to transport diners back to Old World Italy. The experience is further enhanced by a superb menu of pastas, wood-oven pizzas, and succulent appetizers made with fresh ingredients such as goat cheese, sun-dried tomatoes, portabello mushrooms, roasted bell peppers, and plenty of garlic. You'll also find an excellent selection of wines. Late-nighters can enjoy pizza, salad, and appetizers, served in the lounge until midnight. During warm weather, patrons can dine on the rooftop patio, which offers great views of the surrounding mountains. Northern Italian menu. Hours: 11:30 am-3 pm, 5 pm-midnight; Sun from 5 pm. Closed July 4, Thanksgiving, Dec 25. Dinner $9.95-$23.85. Bar noon-midnight. Children's menu. Casual attire. Outdoor dining. Cr cds: A, C, D, DS, MC, V.

D

★ ★ ★ **RISTRA.** *548 Agua Fria (87501). Phone 505/982-8608. www.ristrarestaurant.com.* Three intimate dining rooms in a historic house spill out to patio dining during the season. French, Southwestern menu. Hours: 5:30-9:30 pm; Fri, Sat to 10 pm. Dinner $18-$28. Three intimate dining rooms in historic home. Reservations accepted. Outdoor dining. Cr cds: A, MC, V.

D

★ ★ ★ **ROCIADA.** *304 Johnson St (87501). Phone 505/983-3800; fax 505/983-8306.* Chef Nellie Maltezos and owner Eric Stapelman set out to bring an uncompromising French restaurant to Santa Fe. The result has exceeded all expectations. The deliciously creative Country French cooking bursts with Gallic tradition. The tiny renovated house with its crowded tables and bustling service and an extensive all-French wine list completes the picture. French menu. Hours: 5-10 pm. Closed Sun. Dinner $17-$32. Bar. Children's menu. Casual attire. Outdoor dining. Cr cds: A, MC, V.

D

★ ★ ★ **SANTACAFE.** *231 Washington Ave (87501). Phone 505/984-1788; fax 505/986-0110. www.santacafe.com.* Found within a striking, historic 150-year-old adobe structure (1850), the restaurant serves traditional entrees with a Southwestern flair, such as the grilled free range New Mexican chicken breast with chicken confit tamale and ancho mole. American menu. Hours: 11:30 am-2 pm, 5:30-10:30 pm; Sat, Sun from 5:30 pm. Dinner $19-$29. Bar. Landscaped courtyard. Casual attire. Outdoor dining. Cr cds: A, MC, V.

D

★ **SHED AND LA CHOZA.** *113 1/2 E Palace Ave (87501). Phone 505/982-9030; fax 505/982-0902. www.sfshed.com.* New Mexican menu. Hours: 11 am-2:30 pm, 5:30-9 pm; Mon, Tue to 2:30 pm. Closed Sun; major holidays. Dinner $5.95-$8.95. Children's menu. Casual attire. Outdoor dining. Totally nonsmoking. Cr cds: A, D, DS, MC, V.
D

★ ★ **SHOHKO-CAFE.** *321 Johnson St (87501). Phone 505/983-7288; fax 505/984-1853.* Japanese menu. Hours: 11: 30 am-2 pm, 6-9:30 pm; Fri, Sat to 10 pm. Closed holidays. Dinner $11.50-$32. Bar. Casual attire. Cr cds: A, D, MC, V.
D

★ ★ ★ **STAAB HOUSE.** *330 E Palace Ave (87501). Phone 505/986-0000; fax 505/982-6850. www. laposadadesantafe.com.* Located in the historic Staab House (1882), in the recently renovated La Posada de Santa Fe Resort, this beautiful Spanish Colonial dining room features New American cuisine with Carribbean influences. The patio is a popular dining spot in warm weather. Southwestern, French, American menu. Hours: 7 am-10:30 pm. Dinner $24-$34. Sun brunch. Bar 11-2 am; Sun from noon. Entertainment (seasonal). Children's menu. Hand-crafted furniture; fireplace. Casual attire. Outdoor dining. Cr cds: A, D, DS, MC, V.
D

★ ★ **STEAKSMITH AT EL GANCHO.** *Old Las Vegas Hwy (87505). Phone 505/988-3333; fax 505/988-3334. www.santafesteaksmith.com.* Hours: 5:30-10 pm; Sun 5-9 pm. Closed most major holidays. Reservations accepted. Continental menu. Bar from 4 pm. Complete meals: dinner $8.95-$32.95. Specializes in prime rib, fresh seafood, tapas. Southwestern décor. Cr cds: A, D, DS, MC, V.
D

★**TECOLOTE CAFE.** *1203 Cerrillos Rd (87501). Phone 505/988-1362.* Southwestern, American menu. Hours: 7 am-2 pm. Closed Mon; Thanksgiving, Dec 25. Lunch $5-$10. Children's menu. Casual attire. Cr cds: A, C, D, DS, MC, V.
D SC

★ ★ **TOMASITA'S.** *500 S Guadalupe (87501). Phone 505/983-5721; fax 505/983-0780.* An excellent choice for northern New Mexico cuisine, Tomasita's is housed in an old brick train station built in 1904. It's a great place to sample traditional sopapillas, puffy fried bread served with butter and honey (it comes with all entrees). Be warned about the chili, though; Tomasita's makes it HOT, whether you order it red, green, or Christmas. Other specialties include quesadillas, enchiladas, burritos, and various Mexican-inspired dishes prepared with a local twist. New Mexican menu. Closed Sun; Jan 1, Dec 25. Dinner $4.95-$10.95. Bar. Children's menu. Casual attire. Outdoor seating. Cr cds: MC, V.
D

★ ★ **VANESSIE OF SANTA FE.** *434 W San Francisco St (87501). Phone 505/982-9966; fax 505/982-1507.* Continental menu. Hours: 5:30-10 pm. Closed Easter, Thanksgiving, Dec 25. Dinner $14-$54. Bar to 2 am. Piano. Children's menu. Casual attire. Cr cds: A, C, D, DS, MC, V.
D

★ **WHISTLING MOON CAFE.** *402 N Guadalupe St (87501). Phone 505/983-3093; fax 505/983-9589.* Mediterranean, vegetarian menu. Hours: 11 am-9:30 pm. Closed July 4, Thanksgiving, Dec 25. Dinner $8.95-$13.95. Bar. Children's menu. Casual attire. Cr cds: D, DS, MC, V.
D

Santa Rosa (D-5)

Settled 1865 **Pop** 2,744 **Elev** 4,620 ft **Area code** 505 **Zip** 88435

Information Chamber of Commerce, 486 Parker Ave; 505/472-3763 or 800/450-7084

In grama-grass country on the Pecos River, Santa Rosa has several natural and man-made lakes.

What to See and Do

Billy the Kid Museum. *1601 E Sumner Ave, 44 miles SE via US 60/84, in Fort Sumner. Phone 505/355-2380.* Contains 60,000 items, including relics of the Old West, Billy the Kid, and Old Fort Sumner. On display is rifle once owned by Billy the Kid. (Daily; closed first 2 weekends Jan, major holidays) **$$**

City parks. *Phone 505/472-3404.* Fishing in stocked lakes; picnicking. (Daily) **FREE**

Blue Hole. *1 mile E on Blue Hole Rd.* Clear blue lake in rock setting fed by natural artesian spring, 81 feet deep; scuba diving (permit fee).

Janes-Wallace Memorial Park. *1 mile S on 3rd St.* Also camping, small trailers allowed.

Park Lake. *Park Lake Dr.* Also swimming, lifeguard (June-Aug), children's fishing only; paddleboats, canoe rentals; playground.

Santa Rosa Dam and Lake. *NM 91. 7 miles N via access road. Contact ACE, PO Box 345. Phone 505/472-3115.* Army Corps of Engineers project for flood control and irrigation. No permanent pool; irrigation pool is often available for recreation. Fishing, boating (ramp, launch); nature trails, also trail for the disabled; picnicking, camping (fee; electricity additional). Information center. Excellent area for photography. (Daily) **$$**

Tres Lagunas. *1/4 mile N of US 66, E end of town.* Fishing; hiking, 9-hole golf (fee).

Fort Sumner State Monument. *Rural Rte 1. 3 miles E on US 54/66, then 44 miles SE on US 84, near Fort Sumner. Phone 505/355-2573.* Original site of the Bosque Redondo, where thousands of Navajo and Mescalero Apache were held captive by the US Army from 1863-1868. The military established Fort Sumner to oversee the containment. (See SPECIAL EVENTS) Visitor center has exhibits relating to the period. (Mon, Wed-Sun; closed winter holidays) **$$**

Puerta de Luna. *10 miles S on NM 91. Phone 505/472-3763.* Founded approximately 1862, this Spanish-American town of 250 persons holds to old customs in living and working. Also here is

> **Grzelachowski Territorial House.** *Phone 505/472-5320.* Store and mercantile built in 1800; this house was visited frequently by Billy the Kid. Grzelachowski had a major role in the Civil War battle at Glorieta Pass. (Daily, mid-morning-early evening; closed holidays) **DONATION**

Rock Lake Rearing Station. *2 miles S off I-40. Phone 505/472-3690.* State fish hatchery, rearing rainbow trout and walleyed pike. (Daily) **FREE**

Sumner Lake State Park. *3 miles E on US 54/66, then 32 miles S on US 84, near Fort Sumner. Phone 505/355-2541.* A 4,500-surface-acre reservoir created by irrigation dam. Swimming, fishing (bass, crappie, channel catfish); picnicking, camping (hookups, dump station). (Daily) Standard fees. **$$**

Special Events

Old Fort Days. *Fort Sumner, downtown, and County Fairgrounds.* Parade, rodeo, bank robbery, barbecue, contests, exhibits. Second week in June.

Santa Rosa Day Celebration. Sports events, contests, exhibits. Memorial Day weekend.

Motels/Motor Lodges

★ **BEST WESTERN ADOBE INN.** *1501 Will Rogers Dr (88435). Phone 505/472-3446; toll-free 800/780-7234; fax 505/472-5759. www.bestwestern.com.* 58 rooms, 2 story. S $40-$52; D $62; each additional $2. Pet accepted. Complimentary continental breakfast. Check-out 11 am. TV; cable. In-room modem link. Heated pool. Airport transportation. Cr cds: A, C, D, DS, MC, V.

🔳 🔳 🔳 **SC**

★ **HOLIDAY INN EXPRESS.** *3202 Will Rogers Dr (88435). Phone 505/472-5411; toll-free 800/465-4329; fax 505/472-3537. www.holiday-inn.com.* 67 rooms, 2 story. S $55-$67; D $66-$77; each additional $10. Check-out 10 am. TV. Pool. Cr cds: A, C, D, DS, MC, V.

🔳 🔳 🔳

★ **LA QUINTA INN.** *1701 Will Rogers Dr (88435). Phone 505/472-4800; fax 505/472-4809. www.ramada.com.* 60 air-cooled rooms, 2 story. Mar-Aug: S $55-$65; D $60-$70; each additional $5-$10; under 18 free; package plans; lower rates rest of year. Crib free. Pet accepted; $10. TV; cable, VCR available (movies). Complimentary continental breakfast. Restaurant adjacent 6 am-10 pm. Meeting rooms. Business services available. In-room modem link. Indoor pool; whirlpool. Cr cds: A, D, DS, MC, V.

🔳 🔳 🔳 🔳 🔳 🔳 🔳

Shiprock (B-1)

See also Farmington

Founded 1904 **Pop** 8,156 **Elev** 4,903 ft **Area code** 505 **Zip** 87420

Named for a 1,865-foot butte rising out of the desert, Shiprock is on the Navajo Reservation. The tribe, largest in the United States, numbers about 200,000. Once almost exclusively shepherds and hunters, the Navajos have acquired some wealth by discoveries of oil, coal, and uranium on their lands—oil wells are found in the Four Corners area nearby and throughout San Juan County. The Navajo people are applying this income to urgent needs in educational and economic development. The Navajo Tribal Council has its headquarters at Window Rock, Arizona. Contact Navajo Tourism Department, PO Box 663, Window Rock, AZ 86515; phone 520/871-6659; or the Branch of Natural Resources, Shiprock Agency, PO Box 966; phone 505/368-3300.

Special Event

Shiprock Navajo Fair. *Phone 505/598-8213.* Powwow, carnival, parade. First weekend in Oct.

Silver City (G-2)

See also Deming

Founded 1870 **Pop** 10,545 **Elev** 5,895 ft **Area code** 505 **Zip** 88061

Information Chamber of Commerce, 201 N Hudson; 505/538-3785

Web www.silvercity.org

The rich gold and silver ores in the foothills of the Mogollon (pronounced MUG-ee-yone) Mountains are running low, but copper mining has now become important to the economy. Cattle ranching thrives on the plains. The forested mountain slopes to the north are the habitat of turkey, deer, elk, and bear, and the streams and lakes provide excellent trout fishing.

What to See and Do

⭐ **Gila (HEE-la) National Forest.** *Surrounds town on all borders except on southeast. Contact the Information Desk, 3005 E Camino del Bosque. Phone 505/388-8201.* Administers more than 3 million acres, including the New Mexico part of the Apache National Forest. Also includes Gila, Blue Range, and Aldo Leopold wildernesses. Hunting, backpacking, horseback riding. Lakes Quemado, Roberts, and Snow also have fishing, boating; picnicking, camping. Fees for some activities.

Angel Fire Ski Resort. *10 Miller Ln. 3 1/2 miles off US 64, NM 434. Phone 505/377-6401; 800/633-7463.* Resort has two high-speed quad, three double chairlifts; patrol, school, rentals; cafeteria, restaurants, bars. 67 runs, longest run over 3 miles; vertical drop 2,077 feet. (Thanksgiving-Mar, daily) Nordic center, snowmobiling. Summer resort includes fishing, boating, lake; 18-hole golf, tennis, mountain biking, riding stables. Conference center (all year). **$$$$**

Catwalk of Whitewater Canyon. *63 miles NW of Silver City via US 180, then 5 miles NE on NM 174. Phone 505/539-2481.* National recreation trail. Steel Causeway follows the course of two former pipelines that supplied water and water power in the 1890s to the historic gold and silver mining town of Graham. Causeway clings to sides of the sheer box canyon of Whitewater Creek. Access is by foot trail from Whitewater picnic ground (no water available); access also to Gila Wilderness. (Daily) **$$**

Mogollon Ghost Town. *75 miles NW of Silver City via US 180 on NM 159. (Note that NM 159 is closed Nov-Apr past the ghost town) Phone 505/539-2481.* (1878-1930s) Former gold-mining town. Weathered buildings, beautiful surroundings; nearby Whitewater Canyon was once the haunt of Butch Cassidy and his gang, as well as Vitorio and Geronimo. **FREE**

Phelps Dodge Copper Mine. *7 miles NE on NM 15. Phone 505/538-5331, 24 hrs in advance.* Historic mining town is home to fort and other historic buildings.

Silver City Museum. *312 W Broadway. Phone 505/538-5921.* In restored 1881 house of H. B. Ailman, owner of a rich silver mine; Victorian antiques and furnishings; Casas Grandes artifacts; memorabilia from mining town of Tyrone. (Tue-Sun; closed holidays) **FREE**

Western New Mexico University. *12th and Virginia sts. West part of town. Phone 505/538-6011.* (1893) 3,000 students. On campus is

Western New Mexico University Museum. *1000 College Ave, in Fleming Hall. Phone 505/538-6386.* Depicts contribution of Native American, Hispanic, black, and European cultures to history of region; largest display of Membres pottery in the nation; photography, archive, and mineral collections. (Daily; closed holidays) **FREE**

Special Event

Frontier Days. Parade, dances, exhibits, food. Western dress desired. July 4.

Motels/Motor Lodges

⭐ **COPPER MANOR MOTEL.** *710 Silver Heights Blvd (88062). Phone 505/538-5392; toll-free 800/853-2916; fax 505/538-5830.* 68 rooms, 2 story. S $42-$45; D $48-$52; each additional $4. Crib free. TV; cable. Indoor pool. Complimentary continental breakfast. Restaurant 6 am-2 pm. Check-out 11 am. Meeting room. Business services available. Valet service. Some refrigerators. Cr cds: A, C, D, DS, MC, V.

⭐ **DRIFTER MOTEL REST LOUNGE.** *711 Silver Heights Blvd (88061). Phone 505/538-2916; toll-free 800/853-2916; fax 505/538-5703.* 69 rooms, 2 story. No A/C. S $40-$45; D $44-$49; each additional $3; under 10 free. Crib free. TV; cable. Indoor/outdoor pool. Sauna. Complimentary continental breakfast. Complimentary coffee in lobby. Restaurant adjacent 6 am-2 pm. Bar 4 pm-2 am. Meeting rooms. Business services available. Recreation room. Cr cds: A, C, D, DS, JCB, MC, V.

⭐⭐ **HOLIDAY MOTOR HOTEL.** *3420 Hwy 180 E (88061). Phone 505/538-3711; toll-free 800/828-8291. www.holidayhotel.com.* 79 rooms, 2 story. S $42.20-$47.59; D $47.59; each additional $4; under 12 free. Pet accepted. TV; cable (premium). Pool. Restaurant 6 am-2 pm, 5-8:30 pm; Sun 7 am-2:30 pm, 5-8:30 pm. Room service. Check-out noon. Guest laundry. Meeting rooms. Business services available. Free airport transportation. Cr cds: A, C, D, DS, MC, V.

Restaurant

⭐⭐ **BUCKHORN SALOON.** *32 Main St, Pinos Altos (88053). Phone 505/538-9911.* Steak menu. Closed Sun; Jan 1, Thanksgiving, Dec 25. Dinner. Bar. Entertainment Thu-Sat. Four dining rooms in house designed to look like Western opera house; melodrama performed some weekends. Cr cds: DS, MC, V.

Socorro (E-3)

Pop 8,877 **Elev** 4,620 ft **Area code** 505 **Zip** 87801

Information Socorro County Chamber of Commerce, 103 Francisco de Avondo, PO Box 743; 505/835-0424

Originally a Piro Indian town, Socorro had a Franciscan mission as early as 1598. In 1817, a Spanish land grant brought ancestors of the present families here.

In an area once rich in silver, zinc, and other materials, Socorro was, in 1880, the largest city in New Mexico, with 44 saloons along its main street. Farming, stock raising, and research are the main income sources in this part of the Rio Grande Valley.

What to See and Do

Bosque del Apache National Wildlife Refuge. *18 miles S via I-25 and NM 1. Phone 505/835-1828.* A 12-mile self-guided auto tour loop allows visitors to view a variety of wildlife. Also walking trails. Nov-mid-Feb are best viewing months (see SPECIAL EVENTS). Visitor center has brochures and exhibits (daily). Tour loop (daily; phone for hours and fee).

Mineral Museum. *801 Leroy Pl (87801). 1 miles W of I-25 on campus of New Mexico Institute of Mining and Technology (College Ave and Leroy) at Workman Center. Phone 505/835-5154.* More than 12,000 mineral specimens from around the world. Free rockhounding and prospecting information. (Mon-Sat) **FREE**

National Radio Astronomy Observatory. *1003 Lopez Ville Rd (87801). 52 miles W on US 60, then S on NM 52. Phone 505/835-7000.* The VLA (Very Large Array) radio telescope consists of 27 separate antennas situated along three arms of railroad track. Self-guided walking tour of grounds and visitor center. (Daily) **FREE**

Old San Miguel Mission. *403 El Camino Real NW, 2 blocks N of the plaza. Phone 505/835-1620.* (1615-26) Restored; south wall was part of the original 1598 mission. Carved ceiling beams and corbels; walls are 5 feet thick. (Daily) Artifacts on display in church office (building south of church) (Mon-Fri). **FREE**

Special Events

Conrad Hilton Open Golf Tournament. *Olive Ln and Golf Course Rd (87801). Phone 505/835-0424.* Early June.

Festival of the Crane. *San Antonio Exit and Interstate 25 (87801). Bosque del Apache National Wildlife Refuge. Phone 505/835-0424.* Third weekend in Nov.

Socorro County Fair & Rodeo. *101 Plaza (87801). Phone 505/835-0424.* Labor Day weekend.

Motels/Motor Lodges

★ **DAYS INN.** *507 N California Ave (87801). Phone 505/835-0230; fax 505/835-1993. www.daysinn.com.* 41 rooms, 2 story. S $45; D $52; each additional $3. Crib $4. Pet accepted, some restrictions; $50 refundable. Check-out 11 am. TV; cable (premium). Microwaves. Restaurant 6 am-9 pm. Room service. Heated pool. Cr cds: A, C, D, DS, MC, V.

★ **SAN MIGUEL MOTEL.** *916 California Ave NE (87801). Phone 505/835-0211; toll-free 800/548-7938; fax 505/838-1516.* 40 rooms. S $45; D $49; each additional $3. Complimentary continental breakfast. Check-out noon. TV; cable (premium). Some refrigerators. Microwaves available. Coffee in rooms. Coin laundry. Restaurant opposite open 24 hours. Heated pool. Business services. Cr cds: A, C, D, DS, MC, V.

★ **SUPER 8 MOTEL.** *1121 Frontage Rd NW (87801). Phone 505/835-4626; toll-free 800/800-8000; fax 505/835-3988.* 88 rooms, 2 story. S $42.88-$46.88; D $49.88-$52.88; each additional $4; under 12 free. Crib $5. TV; cable (premium). Heated pool; whirlpool. Complimentary coffee in lobby. Restaurant nearby. Check-out 11 am. Coin laundry. Business services available. Refrigerator available. Cr cds: A, C, D, DS, MC, V.

★ **THE WESTERN.** *404 First St (87825). Phone 505/854-2417; fax 505/854-3217. www.thewesternmotel.com.* 6 rooms, shower only. No A/C. S $33-$36; D $41-$44; each additional $4; under 10 free; weekly rates. Pet accepted; $10. Complimentary coffee in rooms. Check-out 11 am. TV; TV; cable (premium). Cr cds: A, D, DS, MC, V.

Taos (B-5)

See also Angel Fire, Red River

Founded 1615 **Pop** 4,700 **Elev** 6,950 ft **Area code** 505 **Zip** 87571

Information Taos County Chamber of Commerce, 1139 Paseo Del Pueblo Sur, PO Drawer I; 505/758-3873 or 800/732-8267

Web www.taos.org

On a high plateau flanked by mountains, low, flat-roofed houses hug the ground. D. H. Lawrence said, "I think the skyline of Taos the most beautiful of all I have ever seen in my travels around the world."

Other artists and writers agree with him, for many now live and work amid this stimulating mixture of three peoples and three cultures: American Indian, Spanish-American, and Anglo-American. They like it for its clear air, magnificent surroundings, and exciting and congenial atmosphere.

Taos is actually three towns: the Spanish-American settlement into which Anglos have infiltrated, which is Taos proper; Taos Pueblo, 2 1/2 miles north; and Ranchos de Taos, 4 miles south. Each is distinct, yet all are closely allied. In the surrounding mountains are many other towns, Spanish-American farming communities, and fishing resorts. Taos Ski Valley, 19 miles northeast, is a popular ski resort.

As early as 1615 a handful of Spanish colonists settled in this area; in 1617 a church was built. After the Pueblo Rebellion of 1680 and the reconquest by De Vargas in 1692, the town was a farming center plagued by Apache raids and disagreements with the Taos Indians and the government of Santa Fe. The first artists came in 1898; since then it has flourished as an art colony.

What to See and Do

Carson National Forest. *208 Cruz Alta, Penasco (87571).* *Phone 505/758-6200.* On 1 1/2 million acres. Includes Wheeler Peak, New Mexico's highest mountain at 13,161 feet, and the Valle Vidal, home to Rocky Mountain elk. Fishing (good in the 425 miles of streams and numerous small mountain lakes); hunting, hiking, winter sports, picnicking, camping (some fees). (Daily)

Ernest L. Blumenschein Home. *222 Ledoux St (87571).* *Phone 505/758-0505.* Restored adobe house includes furnishings and exhibits of paintings by the Blumenschein family and other early Taos artists. Cofounder of Taos Society of Artists. (Daily, summer 9 am-5 pm; call for winter hours) Combination tickets to seven Taos museums available. **$$**

Fort Burgwin Research Center. *6580 Hwy 518 (87571).* *8 miles S on NM 518. Phone 505/758-8322.* Restored fort was occupied by First Dragoons of the US Calvary (1852-1860). Summer lecture series, music and theater performances. Operated by Southern Methodist University. (Schedule varies) **FREE**

Governor Bent House Museum and Gallery. *117A Bent St, 1 block N of plaza. Phone 505/758-2376.* Home of New Mexico's first American territorial governor; scene of his death in 1847. Bent family possessions, Native American artifacts, western American art. (Daily; closed Jan 1, Thanksgiving, Dec 25) **$**

Hacienda Martinez. *708 Ranchitos Rd. 2 miles W of plaza on NM 240. Phone 505/758-1000.* Contains early Spanish Colonial hacienda with period furnishings; 21 rooms, two large patios. Early Taos, Spanish culture exhibits. Used as a fortress during raids. Living museum demonstrations. (Daily) Combination tickets to seven Taos museums available. **$$**

Harwood Museum of Art. *238 Ledoux St. Phone 505/758-9826.* Founded in 1923; features paintings, drawings, prints, sculptures, and photographs by artists of Taos from 1800 to the present. (Tues-Sat 10 am-5 pm, Sun noon-5 pm; closed Mon, holidays) Combination tickets to seven Taos museums available. **$$**

Kit Carson Home and Museum. *113 Kit Carson Rd (87571). On US 64, 1/2 block E of Taos Plaza. Phone 505/758-4741.* (1825) Restored house with mementos of the famous scout, mountain man and trappers rooms, artifacts, gun exhibit. (Daily) Combination tickets to seven Taos museums available. **$$** Nearby is

> **Kit Carson Park.** *1005 Camino De Colores (87571). Phone 505/758-8234.* A 25-acre plot with bicycle/walking path. Picnic tables (grills), playground, sand volleyball pit. No camping. Graves of Kit Carson and his family. (Daily) **FREE**

> **Millicent Rogers Museum.** *1504 Millicent Roger Museum Rd. 4 miles N on NM 522. Phone 505/758-2462.* Native American and Hispanic arts and crafts. (Daily; closed holidays) **$$$**

Orilla Verde Recreation Area. *NM 570 and NM 68 (87571). 12 miles SW via NM 68. Phone 505/751-4899.* Offers spectacular views. Park runs along banks of the Rio Grande, offering some of the finest trout fishing in the state; whitewater rafting through deep chasm north of park. Hiking, picnicking. Standard fees. (Daily) **$$**

Ranchos de Taos. *60 Ranchos Plaza (87557). 4 miles S on NM 68. Phone 505/758-2754.* (circa 1800) This adobe-housed farming and ranching center has one of the most beautiful churches in the Southwest—the San Francisco de Asis Church. Its huge buttresses and twin bell towers only suggest the beauty of its interior. (Mon-Sat) **$$**

Rio Grande Gorge Bridge. *11 miles NW on US 64.* Bridge is 650 feet above the Rio Grande; observation platforms, picnic and parking areas.

Sipapu Area. *Hwy 518. 25 miles SE on NM 518, 3 miles W of Tres Ritos. Phone 505/587-2240.* Area has two triple chairlifts, two Pomalifts; patrol, school, rentals, snowmaking; accommodations, restaurant, lounge. 31 runs, the longest more than 1 mile; vertical drop 1,065 feet. (Mid-Dec-Mar, daily) Cross-country skiing on forest roads and trails. Snowboarding. **$$$$**

Taos Pueblo. *2 1/2 miles N. Phone 505/758-1028.* With a full-time population of 150, this is one of the most famous Native American pueblos and has been continuously inhabited for more than 1,000 years. Within the pueblo, a National Historic Landmark, is a double apartment house; the north and south buildings, separated by a river, are five stories tall and form a unique communal dwelling. Small buildings and corrals are scattered around these impressive architectural masterpieces. The residents here live without modern utilities such as electricity and plumbing and get their drinking water from the river. The people are independent, conservative, and devout in their religious observances. Fees are charged for parking and photography permits. Photographs of individual Native Americans may be taken only with their consent. Do not enter any buildings that do not indicate a shop. Pueblo (daily 8 am-5 pm; closed for special occasions in spring). (See also SPECIAL EVENTS) **$$**

Taos Ski Valley. *18 miles NE via NM 522, 150. Phone 505/776-2233 (reservations); 800/776-1111 (except NM) (reservations).* Bar. **$$$$**

Van Vechten-Lineberry Taos Art Museum. *501 N Pueblo Rd. Phone 505/758-2690.* Houses artwork of the Taos Founders and other local artists. (Wed-Sun) **$$$**

Special Events

Annual Pow Wow. *Taos Pueblo. Phone 505/758-1028.* Intertribal dancers from throughout US, Canada, and Mexico participate; competition. Second weekend in July.

Chamber Music Festival. *145 Paseo del Pueblo (87571). Taos Community Auditorium and Hotel St. Bernard in Taos Ski Valley. Phone 505/776-2388.* Mid-June-early Aug.

Fiestas de Santiago y Santa Ana. Traditional festival honoring the patron saints of Taos. Candlelight procession, parade, crafts, food, entertainment. Late July.

San Geronimo Eve Sundown Dance. *Taos Pueblo. Phone 505/758-1028.* Traditional men's dance followed next day by San Geronimo Feast Day, with intertribal dancing, trade fair, pole climb, footraces. Late Sept.

Spring Arts Festival. *Phone 800/732-8267.* Three-week festival featuring visual, performing, and literary arts. May.

Taos Arts Festival. *Phone 505/758-1028.* Arts and crafts exhibitions, music, plays, poetry readings. Mid-Sept-early Oct.

Taos Pueblo Dances. *2401 12th St NW (87104). Phone 505/758-1028. www.taospueblo.com.* Several Native American dances are held throughout the year. For a schedule of annual dances, contact the pueblo.

Taos Pueblo Deer or *Matachines* Dance. Symbolic animal dance or ancient Montezuma dance. Dec 25.

Taos Rodeo. *502 Los Pandos (87571). County Fairgrounds. Phone 800/732-8267.* Late June or early July.

Taos Talking Picture Festival. *1337 Gusdorf Rd. Phone 505/751-0637.* Four-day film festival showcasing independent productions. Mid-Apr.

Yuletide in Taos. *Phone 800/732-8267.* Ski area festivities, *farolito* (paper bag lantern) tours, food and craft fairs, art events, dance performances. Dec.

Motels/Motor Lodges

★ ★ **EL PUEBLO LODGE.** *412 Paseo Del Pueblo N (87571). Phone 505/758-8700; toll-free 800/433-9612; fax 505/758-7321.* 60 rooms, 16 kitchen units, 1-2 story. Mid-June-Oct, mid-Dec-early Apr: S $50; D $68; each additional $10; suites $105-$215; kitchen units $75; weekly rates; ski plans; lower rates rest of year. Crib free. Pet accepted. Complimentary continental breakfast. Check-out 11:30 am. TV; cable (premium). Some balconies. Refrigerators, some microwaves. Heated pool, whirlpool. Downhill ski 17 miles, cross-country ski 5 miles. Business services. Cr cds: A, DS, MC, V.

★ **HAMPTON INN.** *1515 Paseo Del Pueblo Sur (87571). Phone 505/737-5700; toll-free 800/426-7866; fax 505/737-5701. www.hamptoninn.com.* 71 rooms, 2 story. Memorial Day-Labor Day: S, D $74-$84; under 18 free; lower rates rest of year. Crib available. Pet accepted. Complimentary continental breakfast. Complimentary coffee in rooms. Check-out 11 am. TV; cable. In-room modem link. Restaurant opposite 7 am-10 pm. Indoor pool, whirlpool. Cross-country ski 10 miles. Meeting rooms. Business services. Cr cds: A, C, D, DS, ER, JCB, MC, V.

★ ★ ★ **HOLIDAY INN DON FERNANDO DE TAOS.** *1005 Paseo Del Pueblo Sur (87571). Phone 505/758-4444; toll-free 800/759-2736; fax 505/758-0055. www.holiday-inn.com.* The six buildings of this Pueblo Indian adobe-style property are connected by walkways leading through courtyards and landscaped grounds. The indoor/outdoor pool and hot tub are designed to provide a warm environment regardless of the weather. Guest rooms feature in-room ski storage, dataports, and hand-carved furnishings. 124 rooms, 2 story. S, D $99-$115; under 19 free; weekly rates; ski plans; higher rates during Christmas holidays. Crib free. Pet accepted; $75 deposit. Check-out 11 am. TV; cable, VCR available. Fireplace in suites. Restaurant 6:30 am-2 pm, 5-10 pm. Bar 3-11 pm; Fri, Sat to 1 am; Sun noon-11 pm. Room service. Indoor pool, whirlpool, poolside service. 18-hole golf privileges, greens fee $27-$35, pro, putting green, driving range. Tennis. Downhill ski 20 miles, cross-country ski 5 miles. Meeting room. Business services. Pueblo-style building; central courtyard. Cr cds: A, C, D, DS, JCB, MC, V.

★ ★ **QUALITY INN.** *1043 Paseo Del Pueblo Sur (87571). Phone 505/758-2200; toll-free 800/845-0648; fax 505/758-9009. www.qualityinn.com.* 99 rooms, 2 story. Mid-June-Oct: S, D $55-$99; each additional $7; suites $95-$175; under 18 free; ski plans; higher rates during Christmas holidays; lower rates rest of year. Crib free. Pet accepted. TV; cable (premium), VCR available. Heated pool; poolside service. Coffee in rooms. Restaurant 6:30 am-2 pm, 5-9 pm. Room service. Bar 11 am-11 pm. Check-out 11 am. Meeting rooms. Business services available. In-room modem link. Valet service. Downhill ski 20 miles; cross-country ski 5 miles. Health club privileges. Many microwaves; refrigerator, wet bar in suites. Picnic tables. Cr cds: A, C, D, DS, ER, JCB, MC, V.

D ⟦icons⟧ SC

★ **RAMADA INN.** *615 Paseo Del Pueblo Sur (87571). Phone 505/758-2900; toll-free 888/298-2054; fax 505/758-1662. www.ramada.com.* 124 rooms, 2 story. Mid-June-Sept, mid-Dec-mid-Apr: S, D $79-$120; each additional $10; under 18 free; package plans; lower rates rest of year. Check-out noon. TV; cable (premium). Some fireplaces. Indoor pool, whirlpool. Downhill ski 17 miles/cross-country ski 5 miles. Cr cds: A, C, D, DS, JCB, MC, V.

D ⟦icons⟧

Hotels

★ ★ ★ **FECHIN INN.** *227 Paseo del Pueblo Notre (87571). Phone 505/751-1000. www.fechin-inn.com.* 85 rooms, 2 story. S, D $149-$169; each additional $15. Crib available. Complimentary continental breakfast. Check-out noon. TV; cable (premium), VCR available. Exercise room. Whirlpool. Meeting rooms. Business services. Former home of Russian artist Nicolai Fechin. Southwestern décor. Cr cds: A, C, D, DS, MC, V.

D ⟦icons⟧

★ ★ ★ **SAGEBRUSH INN.** *1508 S Santa Fe Rd (87571). Phone 505/758-2254; toll-free 800/428-3626; fax 505/758-5077. www.sagebrushinn.com.* Built in 1929, this 100-room adobe inn houses a large collection of paintings, Indian rugs, and other regional art. The most recent addition, an 18,000 square foot conference center, features hand-hewn vigas and fireplaces. Visitors will enjoy the outdoor pool and two hot tubs. Guest rooms feature in-room coffee, handmade furniture, and cable television. 100 rooms, 2 story. S, D $65-$95; each additional $10; suites $90-$140; under 12 free. Crib $7. Pet accepted. Complimentary full breakfast. Check-out 11 am. TV; cable (premium). Some refrigerators, many fireplaces. Coffee in rooms. Restaurant 6:30-11 am, 5:30-10 pm. Bar 3 pm-midnight; entertainment. Pool; whirlpools. Cross-country ski 10 miles. Meeting rooms. Business center. Sundries. Built in 1929 of adobe in

Pueblo-Mission style; extensive art collection, antiques, Navajo rugs, pottery. Cr cds: A, C, D, DS, JCB, MC, V.

D ⟦icons⟧

Resort

★ ★ **QUAIL RIDGE INN RESORT.** *88 Ski Valley Rd (87571). Phone 505/776-2211; toll-free 800/624-4448; fax 505/776-2949. www.quailridgeinn.com.* 110 condos, 65 kitchen units. No A/C. S, D $72-$160; each additional $10; suites $170-$300; studio rooms $120-$140; under 18 free; tennis plans; higher rates ski season. Check-out 11 am. TV; cable (premium), VCR available. Balconies. Microwaves, fireplaces. Dining room 7-10 am, 6-9 pm. Bar from 4 pm. Supervised children's activities (June-Labor Day); ages 5-15. Exercise equipment, massage, saunas. Social director. Pool, whirlpools. Indoor tennis, pro. Meeting rooms. Business services. Cr cds: A, C, D, DS, MC, V.

D ⟦icons⟧

All Suites

★ **COMFORT SUITES.** *1500 Paseo Del Pueblo Sur (87571). Phone 505/751-1555; toll-free 888/751-1555; fax 505/751-1991. www.taoshotels.com//comfortsuites.* 60 suites, 2 story. S, D $60-$140; each additional $10; under 18 free; package plans. Crib free. Complimentary continental breakfast. Complimentary coffee in rooms. Check-out 11 am. TV; cable (premium). In-room modem link. Refrigerators, microwaves. Restaurant adjacent 6:30-11 am, 5:30-10 pm. Pool, whirlpool. Tennis. Cross-country ski 15 miles. Meeting rooms. Business services. Cr cds: A, C, D, DS, ER, JCB, MC, V.

D ⟦icons⟧

B&B/Small Inns

★ ★ ★ **ADOBE STARS BED AND BREAKFAST INN.** *584 NM 150 (87571). Phone 505/776-2776; toll-free 800/211-7076; fax 505/776-2872. www.taosadobe.com.* Located near the Historic Taos Plaza and the Taos Ski Valley, this Southwestern inn offers panoramic views of the Sangre de Christo Mountains. Guest rooms feature kiva fireplaces, private baths with terra-cotta tile, and ceiling fans. 8 rooms. No A/C. D $85-$185; each additional $20; Pet accepted, some restrictions. Complimentary full breakfast. Check-out 11 am, check-in 4 pm. TV in common room; VCR (movies). Downhill, cross-country ski 8 miles. Concierge service. Southwestern furnishings, regional art, kiva fireplaces. Totally nonsmoking. Cr cds: A, DS, MC, V.

⟦icons⟧ SC

★ ★ **AMERICAN ARTISTS GALLERY HOUSE.** *132 Frontier Ln (87571). Phone 505/758-4446; toll-free 800/532-2041; fax 505/758-0497. www.taosbedandbreakfast.com.* 10 rooms. No room phones. D $90-$225; each additional $25. Children over 8 years only. Complimentary full breakfast. Check-out 11 am, check-in 3-6 pm. Restaurant nearby. Downhill ski 18 miles/cross-country ski 8 miles. Concierge service. Art gallery located in main house. Cr cds: A, DS, MC, V.

★ ★ **AUSTING HAUS B&B.** *1282 NM 150, Taos Ski Valley (87525). Phone 505/776-2649; toll-free 800/748-2932; fax 505/776-8751. www.taoswebb.com/hotel/austinghaus.* 45 rooms, 2 story. No A/C. D $59-$75; each additional $20; under 5 free; ski plans. Mid-Apr-mid-May. Pet accepted. Complimentary continental breakfast. Check-out 10 am, check-in 2 pm. TV. Laundry facilities. Dining room 7:30-10 am; winter also 6-9 pm. Downhill ski 2 miles. Constructed of oak-pegged heavy timbers with beams exposed inside and out; built by hand entirely without nails or metal plates. Cr cds: A, DS, MC, V.

★ ★ ★ **BROOKS STREET INN.** *119 Brooks St (87571). Phone 505/758-1489; toll-free 800/758-1489; fax 505/758-7525. www.brooksstreetinn.com.* This casual 6-room inn offers a quiet environment where guests can relax while gazing at Taos Mountain. The elegant guest rooms feature fresh flowers, artwork, and handcrafted furniture, while the fireplace warms the common room. Breakfast includes an espresso bar and favorites like blue corn pancakes and pineapple salsa. 6 rooms. No A/C. No room phones. D $89-$140; each additional $20. Adults only. Complimentary full breakfast. Check-out 11 am, check-in 4-6 pm. Downhill ski 18 miles, cross-country ski 5 miles. Totally nonsmoking. Cr cds: A, DS, MC, V.

★ ★ ★ **CASA DE LAS CHIMENEAS.** *405 Cordoba Rd (87571). Phone 505/758-4777; toll-free 877/758-4777; fax 505/758-3976. www.visit-taos.com.* True to its Spanish name (The House of Chimneys), all guest rooms in this bed and breakfast have kiva fireplaces as well as brass and wooden beds, private entrances and baths, down pillows, and electric blankets or down comforters. Guests looking to relax will enjoy the inn's formal gardens and court-yards, fountains, and hot tub. 9 rooms. No A/C. D $165-$325; each additional $15. Complimentary full breakfast; afternoon refreshments. Check-out 11 am, check-in 3-6 pm. TV; cable (premium). Kiva fireplaces; hand-carved and antique furniture; regional art. Restaurant nearby. Exercise room; sauna. Massage. Totally nonsmoking. Cr cds: A, C, D, DS, MC, V.

★ ★ ★ **CASA EUROPA INN.** *840 Upper Ranchitos (87571). Phone 505/758-9798; toll-free 888/758-9798. www.casaeuropanm.com.* Set on six acres of land, this 17th-century Pueblo-style inn offers a soothing experience with its beautiful views and walls adorned with local art. The flowered courtyards feature a fountain as well as a sauna and hot tub. The seven spacious guest rooms offer private bathrooms, desks, and fans. 7 rooms, 2 story. No A/C. D $95-$145; each additional $20. Complimentary full breakfast. Check-out 11 am, check-in 3 pm. TV in sitting room; cable (premium). Sauna. Downhill/cross-country ski 16 miles. Old adobe structure with courtyard. Cr cds: A, MC, V.

★ ★ ★ **COTTONWOOD B&B INN.** *#2 State Rte 230 (87529). Phone 505/776-5826; toll-free 800/324-7120; fax 505/776-1141. www.taos-cottonwood.com.* Enjoy the beautiful Taos Mountains or the New Mexico sunsets at this Southwestern bed and breakfast. Guests can venture to Taos to enjoy hiking, whitewater rafting or even hot-air balloon rides. 8 rooms, 2 with shower only, 2 story. No A/C. No room phones. D $95-$175. Complimentary full breakfast. Check-out 11 am, check-in 4-7 pm. TV in common room. Many fireplaces. Restaurant nearby. Sauna. Downhill ski 11 miles. Lawn games. Concierge service. Built in 1947; renovated Pueblo-style adobe. Totally nonsmoking. Cr cds: A, DS, MC, V.

★ ★ **DREAMCATCHER B&B.** *416 La Lomita Rd (87571). Phone 505/758-0613; toll-free 888/758-0613; fax 505/751-0115. www.dreambb.com.* 7 rooms. No A/C. No room phones. D $89-$119; ski plans. Complimentary full breakfast. Check-out 11 am, check-in 4-6 pm. Downhill ski 18 miles, cross-country ski 5 miles. Cr cds: A, DS, MC, V.

★ ★ ★ **HACIENDA DEL SOL.** *109 Mabel Dodge Ln (87571). Phone 505/718-0287; toll-free 866/333-4459; fax 505/758-5895. www.taoshaciendadelsol.com.* This inn consists of three adobe buildings set on 1.2 acres of land overlooking the Taos Mountains. The romantic guest rooms feature thick adobe walls, original artwork, and corner fireplaces. 11 rooms, 2 with shower only, 2 suites. No A/C. No room phones. D $105-$265; suites $145-$189; under 3 free; 2-day minimum weekends, 3-day minimum holidays. Complimentary full breakfast. Check-out 11 am, check-in 3-6 pm. TV in common room; cable (premium). Restaurant opposite 11 am-9 pm. Downhill/cross-country ski 18 miles. Lawn games. Concierge. Adobe built in early 1800s. Totally nonsmoking. Cr cds: A, D, DS, MC, V.

★ ★ ★ **THE HISTORIC TAOS INN.** *125 Paseo Del Pueblo Norte (87571). Phone 505/758-2233; toll-free 800/826-7466; fax 505/758-5776. www.taosinn.com.* This historic inn offers a comfortable Old West experience with its blend of history and modern amenities. Guests will enjoy the outdoor heated pool and greenhouse hot tub. The unique guest rooms feature Southwestern decor, hair dryers, and voice mail; many offer kiva fireplaces. Be sure to dine at the acclaimed Doc Martin's Restaurant. 36 rooms. D $85-$225. Pet accepted. Check-out 11 am, check-in 3 pm. TV; cable (premium). Pueblo fireplaces; antique Taos-style furniture; Mexican tile. Restaurant, bar. Bar noon-10:30 pm; entertainment. Pool, whirlpool. Cross-country ski 15 miles. Inn consists of number of structures, some dating from 17th century. Some A/C. Meet-the-Artist Series in spring, fall. Cr cds: A, DS, MC, V.

D 🐾 🖾 🛏 🖫 SC

★ ★ ★ **INN ON LA LOMA PLAZA.** *315 Ranchitos Rd. (87571). Phone 505/758-1717; toll-free 800/530-3040; fax 505/751-0155. www.vacationtaos.com.* Formerly known as the Taos Hacienda Inn, this restored historic inn offers mountain views and spacious gardens. Visitors looking to relax can enjoy the large hot tub or take advantage of the complimentary spa, tennis, and health club privileges. Guest rooms feature private baths, fireplaces, phones, televisions, robes and slippers. 7 rooms, 2 kitchen units, 2 story. D $125-$275; each additional $10. Complimentary full breakfast. Check-out 11 am, check-in 4-9 pm. TV; cable (premium). Fireplaces. Whirlpool. Built in 1800; Pueblo Revival architecture. Totally nonsmoking. Cr cds: A, DS, MC, V.

D 🖾 🛏

★ ★ ★ **LA DONA LUZ INN, AN HISTORIC BED AND BREAKFAST.** *114 Kit Carson Rd (87571). Phone 505/758-4874; toll-free 800/758-9187; fax 505/758-4541. www.ladonaluz.com.* This 200-year-old pueblo-style adobe will delight visitors with its fascinating history and large collection of fine art. The unique guest rooms all have private baths and many feature fireplaces, mountain views, and art. Continental breakfast is served on the patio during the warm months. 15 rooms, 3 story. No room phones. D $59-$189; each additional $10-$15. Pet accepted; $10. Complimentary continental breakfast. Check-out 11 am, check-in 3 pm. TV; VCR (free movies). Many fireplaces. Restaurant nearby. Downhill ski 18 miles, cross-country ski 5 miles. Cr cds: A, DS, MC, V.

D 🐾 🔧 🖾 🛏

★ ★ **LA POSADA DE TAOS.** *309 Juanita Ln (87571). Phone 505/758-8164; toll-free 800/645-4803; fax 505/751-4696. www.laposadadetaos.com.* 6 rooms. D $99-$234; each additional $15. Complimentary full breakfast. Check-out 11 am, check-in 4-6 pm. TV in common room. Restaurant nearby. Old adobe structure with courtyard. Cr cds: A, DS, MC, V.

D 🖾

★ ★ ★ **SALSA DELI SALTO B&B INN.** *543 Highway 150 (87529). Phone 505/776-2422; toll-free 800/530-3097; fax 505/776-5734. www.bandbtaos.com.* With the inn conveniently located close to Taos Ski Valley and Taos, guests will have the option of skiing or shopping. After a game of tennis, guests can enjoy the mountain and sunset view from the hot tub. 10 rooms, 2 story. No A/C. No room phones. D $95-$180. Children over 6 years only. Complimentary full breakfast. Check-out 11 am, check-in 3-7 pm. TV in sitting room. Some fireplaces. Restaurant nearby. Whirlpool. Tennis. Downhill/cross-country ski 8 miles. Lawn games. Concierge service. View of mountains or mesas. Totally nonsmoking. Cr cds: A, DS, MC, V.

🖾 🎿 🛏 🖾

★ ★ **SAN GERONIMO LODGE.** *1101 Witt Rd (87571). Phone 505/751-3776; toll-free 800/894-4119; fax 505/751-1493. www.sangeronimolodge.com.* 18 rooms, 2 with shower only, 2 story. D $95-$150; each additional $10; under 5 free. Complimentary full breakfast. Check-out 11 am, check-in 3-7 pm. TV; cable (premium). Pool, whirlpool. Downhill ski 18 miles, cross-country 8 miles. Old adobe lodge with handcrafted furniture. Totally nonsmoking. Cr cds: A, D, DS, MC, V.

D 🖾 🛏 🖾

★ ★ ★ **TOUCHSTONE LUXURY B&B.** *110 Mabel Dodge Ln (87571). Phone 505/758-0192; toll-free 800/758-0192; fax 505/758-3498. www.touchstone.com.* This quiet, historic bed and breakfast is nestled among the trees on the edge of Taos Pueblo Lands. 7 rooms, 2 story. No A/C. D $135-$350; each additional $30. Complimentary full breakfast; afternoon refreshments. Check-out 11 am, check-in 4 pm. TV; cable (premium), VCR (movies). Downhill ski 15 miles; cross-country ski 10 miles. Totally nonsmoking. Cr cds: MC, V.

🖾 🖾

Restaurants

★ ★ **APPLE TREE.** *123 Bent St (87571). Phone 505/758-1900. www.appletreerestaurant.com.* Hours: 11:30 am-3 pm, 5:30-9 pm; Sun brunch 10 am-3 pm. Reservations accepted. Wine, beer. Lunch $5.95-$9.95, dinner $7.95-$19.95. Sun brunch $5.95-$9.95. Specializes in fresh seafood, New Mexican dishes. Outdoor dining. Cr cds: A, C, D, DS, MC, V.

D

★ ★ **CASA DE VALDEZ.** *1401 Paseo del Pueblo Sur (87571). Phone 505/758-8777.* Hours: 11:30 am-9:30 pm; Sun from 3:30 pm. Closed Wed; Easter, Thanksgiving, Dec 25; also 3 weeks after Thanksgiving. Reservations accepted. Southwestern menu. Service bar. Lunch $5.95-$9.95, dinner $8.95-$25.95. Specializes in barbecue, steak. Patio. Cr cds: A, D, DS, MC, V.

★ ★ ★ **DOC MARTIN'S.** *125 Paseo Del Pueblo (87571). Phone 505/758-1977; fax 505/758-5776. www.taoswebb.com/nmusa/hotel/taos.inn.* Chef Patrick Lambert serves nouvelle Southwestern in an adobe setting. Specialties include chipotle shrimp on corn cake and southwestern lacquered duck. The wine list is one of the best in the area. Hours: 7:30 am-2:30 pm, 5:30-9:30 pm. Reservations accepted. Continental, Southwestern menu. Wine list. Breakfast $4-$8, lunch $5.50-$10.50, dinner $14-$24. Specializes in fresh seafood. Own baking. In colorful, historic structure; fireplaces. Cr cds: A, D, MC, V.

D

★ ★ ★ **LAMBERT'S.** *309 Paseo Del Pueblo Sur (87571). Phone 505/758-1009.* Service is enthusiastic and friendly at this family-owned restaurant. Hours: 5:30-9 pm; Fri-Sun to 9:30 pm. Reservations accepted. No A/C. Wine list. Dinner $6-$20. Children's menu. Specialties: pepper-crusted loin of lamb with garlic glaze, San Francisco cheesecake. Own baking. Outdoor dining. Garden-like setting; 3 stone fireplaces. Cr cds: A, C, DS, MC, V.

D SC

★ **MICHAEL'S KITCHEN AND BAKERY.** *304 Paseo Del Pueblo N (87571). Phone 505/758-4178; fax 505/758-4088. www.michaelskitchen.com.* Hours: 7 am-8:30 pm. Closed most major holidays; also Nov. Mexican, American menu. Breakfast $2.55-$7.45, lunch $2.85-$7.55, dinner $6.05-$10.95. Children's menu. Specialties: stuffed sopapillas, Indian tacos. Cr cds: A, D, MC, V.

★ ★ **OGELVIE'S BAR AND GRILLE.** *103 E Plaza (87571). Phone 505/758-8866; fax 505/758-0728.* Specialties: fresh seafood, steaks, New Mexican dishes. Hours: 11 am-10 pm. Lunch $5.95-$18.50, dinner $6.95-$19.50. Bar. Children's menu. Outdoor dining. Eclectic Southwestern décor. Cr cds: A, MC, V.

★ ★ **STEAKOUT GRILL AND BAR.** *101 Stakeout Dr (87557). Phone 505/758-2042; fax 505/751-3815. www.stakeoutrestaurant.com.* Seafood, steak menu. Hours: 5-9:30 pm. Dinner $14-$29. Bar. Entertainment. Children's menu. Historically located adobe pueblo-style building. Reservations accepted. Outdoor dining May-Oct. Cr cds: A, C, D, DS, MC, V.

D

★ ★ **TIM'S CHILE CONNECTION.** *NM 150, MM 1 (87529). Phone 505/776-8787; fax 505/776-8018.* Hours: 11 am-10 pm. Mexican, New Mexican menu. Bar. Lunch $3.50-$9.25, dinner $3.50-$16.95. Children's menu. Specializes in tamales, chile, seafood. Entertainment. Outdoor dining. Hacienda-style furnishing. Fireplaces in each room. Cr cds: A, MC, V.

D

★ ★ ★ **VILLA FONTANA.** *NM 522 (87571). Phone 505/758-5800; fax 505/758-8301. www.villafontanahouse. com.* Italian-born chef and artist Carlo Gislimberti serves an authentic Italian menu, which includes fresh mozzarella, Parma ham, osso buco, and other favorites, in a comfortable setting. Northern Italian menu. Hours: 5:30 pm-closing. Closed Sun; also Sun-Wed mid-Apr-mid-May, mid-Nov-mid-Dec. A la carte entrees: dinner $19.50-$25. Bar. Reservations accepted. Outdoor dining. Cr cds: A, DS, MC, V.

D

Truth or Consequences (F-3)

Pop 7,289 **Elev** 4,240 ft **Area code** 505 **Zip** 87901

Information Truth or Consequences/Sierra County Chamber of Commerce, 201 S Foch St, PO Drawer 31; 505/894-3536

Formerly called Hot Springs, for the warm mineral springs, the town changed its name in 1950 to celebrate the tenth anniversary of Ralph Edwards' radio program, "Truth or Consequences."

In the early 1500s the Spanish Conquistadores came through this area, and legends of lost Spanish gold mines and treasures in the Caballo Mountains persist today. There are numerous ghost towns and old mining camps in the area. A Ranger District office of the Gila National Forest (see SILVER CITY) is located here.

What to See and Do

Caballo Lake State Park. *18 miles S on I-25. Phone 505/743-3942.* Caballo Mountains form a backdrop for this lake. Swimming, windsurfing, waterskiing, fishing (bass, crappie, pike, trout, catfish), boating (ramp); hiking, picnicking, playground, camping (hookups). Standard fees. (Daily) **$$**

Canoeing, boating, and tubing. *On the Rio Grande, which flows through the city.*

Elephant Butte Lake State Park. *NM 195. 5 miles N via I-25.* Phone 505/744-5421. This 40-mile-long lake was created in 1916 for irrigation; later adapted to hydroelectric power. Swimming, windsurfing, waterskiing, fishing (bass, crappie, pike, catfish), boating (ramp, rentals, slips, mooring, three marinas); hiking, picnicking, playground, concession, restaurant, lodge, camping (hookups), cabins. (Daily) Standard fees. **$$**

Geronimo Springs Museum. *211 Main St.* Phone 505/ 894-6600. Exhibits of Mimbres pottery, fossils, and photographs, and articles on local history. Ralph Edwards Room, Apache Room, Hispanic Room, and log cabin. Gift shop. (Mon-Sat; closed Jan 1, Thanksgiving, Dec 25) **$**

Motels/Motor Lodges

★ **ACE LODGE AND MOTEL.** *1302 N Date St (87901).* Phone 505/894-2151. 38 rooms. S $29-$32; D $34-$40; each additional $2; suites $50-$60; weekly rates. Crib $2. Pet accepted, some restrictions. Check-out 11 am. TV; cable. Restaurant 6 am-9 pm. Bar 5 pm-2 am. Playground. Heated pool. Golf privileges. Picnic tables. Free airport transportation. Cr cds: A, C, D, DS, JCB, MC, V.

★ **BEST WESTERN HOT SPRINGS MOTOR INN.** *2270 N Date St (87901).* Phone 505/894-6665; toll-free 800/780-7234; fax 505/894-6665. www.bestwestern.com. 40 rooms. S $55; D $60; each additional $5; under 12 free (2 max). Check-out noon. TV; cable (premium). Heated pool. Cr cds: A, C, D, DS, MC, V.

★ ★ **QUALITY INN ELEPHANT BUTTE.** *401 Hwy 195 Elephant Butte (87938).* Phone 505/744-5431; toll-free 800/228-5150; fax 505/744-5044. www.qualityinn.com. 48 rooms, 2 story. Apr-Aug: S, D $69-$79; each additional $5; under 12 free; weekly rates; lower rates rest of year. Crib $2. Pet accepted. Complimentary coffee in rooms. Check-out 11 am. TV; cable (premium). Many balconies. Restaurant 7 am-2 pm, 5-9 pm. Bar noon-midnight. Room service. Playground. Pool. 18-hole golf privileges. Tennis. Picnic tables. Meeting rooms. Business services. On lake. Cr cds: A, C, D, DS, JCB, MC, V.

Restaurant

★ ★ **LOS ARCOS STEAK HOUSE.** *1400 N Date St (87901).* Phone 505/894-6200; fax 505/894-9797. Mexican decor. Specializes in steak, lobster tail. Hours: 5-10:30 pm; Fri, Sat to 11 pm. Closed Thanksgiving, Dec 25. Dinner $11-$40. Bar to 2 am. Salad bar. Reservations accepted. Cr cds: A, D, DS, MC, V.

Tucumcari (D-7)

Settled 1901 **Pop** 5,989 **Elev** 4,096 ft **Area code** 505 **Zip** 88401

Information Tucumcari/Quay County Chamber of Commerce, 404 W Rt 66, PO Drawer E; 505/461-1694

Web www.tucumcarinm.com

A convenient stopping point between Amarillo, Texas, and Albuquerque, this is a trading center for a 45,000-acre irrigated and industrial water area. New energy is focused on carbon dioxide, petroleum, and natural gas. There is also a thriving cattle business. Tucumcari has become a transportation center with many trucking companies and much railroad traffic. Tucumcari Mountain (4,957 feet) is to the south. Born when the railroad reached its site, Tucumcari was once known as "six-shooter siding."

What to See and Do

Conchas Lake State Park. *33 miles NW via NM 104, 433.* Phone 505/868-2270. Lake is 25 miles long. Swimming, waterskiing, fishing, boating; picnicking, camping (hookups, dump station). Standard fees. (Daily) **$$**

Tucumcari Historical Museum. *416 S Adams St.* Phone 505/461-4201. Western Americana; Native American artifacts; gems, minerals, rocks, fossils; restored fire truck and caboose. (Tue-Sat) **$**

Ute Lake State Park. *1800 540 Loop. 22 miles NE on US 54, NM 540.* Phone 505/487-2284. Created by a dam on the Canadian River. Swimming, waterskiing, fishing (bass, crappie, channel catfish), boating (marina, ramp, slips, mooring); hiking trails, picnicking, camping (hookups, dump station). Standard fees. (Daily) **$$**

Special Event

Route 66 Festival. *404 W Tumcari Blvd (88401).* Rodeo, car show, parade, arts and crafts, entertainment. July.

Motels/Motor Lodges

★ **COMFORT INN.** *2800 E Tucumcari Blvd (88401).* Phone 505/461-4094; toll-free 800/228-5150; fax 505/461-4099. www.comfortinn.com. 59 rooms, 2 story. S $54-$60; D $61-$66; each additional $6; suites $66; under 18 free. Crib $6. Pet accepted; $6. TV. Pool. Complimentary continental breakfast. Restaurant nearby. Check-out noon. Meeting rooms. Cr cds: A, C, D, DS, JCB, MC, V.

★ **COUNTRY INN.** *1302 W Tucumcari Blvd (88401).* Phone 505/461-3140; fax 505/461-3143. 57 rooms, 2 story. S $38; D $48; each additional $10; under 18 free. Crib free. Pet accepted. Complimentary continental breakfast. Check-out noon. TV; cable (premium). Restaurant adjacent 6:30 am-9 pm. Pool. Meeting room. Cr cds: A, D, MC, V.

⊟ ⊠ ⊠

★ **ECONO LODGE.** *3400 Rte 66 E (88401). Phone 505/461-4194; fax 505/461-4911. www.econolodge.com.* 41 rooms, 2 story. S $31.95; D $43.95-$48.95; each additional $7; under 17 free. Crib free. Pet accepted. TV; cable. Complimentary coffee in lobby. Restaurant nearby. Check-out 11 am. Business services available. Cr cds: A, C, D, DS, JCB, MC, V.

D ⊟ ⊠

★ ★ **HOLIDAY INN TUCUMCARI.** *3716 E Tucumcari Blvd (88401). Phone 505/461-3780; toll-free 800/335-3780; fax 505/461-3931. www.holiday-inn.com.* 100 rooms, 2 story. S $45-$65; D $51-$72; each additional $6; under 18 free. Crib free. Pet accepted. Check-out noon. TV; cable. In-room modem link. Coin laundry. Restaurant 6 am-9 pm. Bar 5-10 pm. Room service. Playground. Exercise equipment. Heated pool, whirlpool. Meeting rooms. Business services. Sundries. Cr cds: A, D, DS, JCB, MC, V.

⊟ ⊠

★ **SUPER 8.** *4001 E Tucumcari Blvd (88401). Phone 505/461-4444; toll-free 800/800-8000; fax 505/461-4320. www.super8.com.* 63 rooms, 13 suites, 2 story. S $36.88-$42.88; D $47.88-$52.88; each additional $2; suites $45.88-$47.88; under 12 free. Check-out 11 am. TV. Coin laundry. Restaurant nearby. Indoor pool. Cr cds: A, DS, MC, V.

D ⊠ ⊠

White Sands National Monument (G-4)

See also Alamogordo

(15 miles SW of Alamogordo on US 70/82)

These shifting, dazzling white dunes are a challenge to plants and animals. Here, lizards and mice are white like the sand, helping them blend in with the background. (Similarly, mice are black in the black lava area only a few miles north.)

Plants elongate their stems up to 30 feet so that they can keep their leaves and flowers above the sand. When the sands recede, the plants are sometimes left on elevated pillars of hardened gypsum bound together by their roots. Even an ancient two-wheeled Spanish cart was laid bare when the sands shifted.

Beach sand is usually silica, but White Sands National Monument sand is gypsum, from which plaster of paris is made. Dunes often rise to 60 feet; White Sands is the largest gypsum dune field in the world.

White Sands National Monument encloses 143,732 acres of this remarkable area. The visitor center has an orientation video, exhibits concerning the dunes and how they were formed, and other related material (daily except Dec 25). Evening programs and guided nature walks in the dunes area are conducted (Memorial Day-mid-Aug). There is a 16-mile round-trip drive from the center; free printed guide leaflet. Picnic area with shaded tables and grills (no water); primitive backpackers' campsite (by permit only). Dunes Drive (daily except Dec 25).

For further information, contact the Superintendent, PO Box 1086, Holloman AFB, NM 88330-1086; phone 505/672-2599.

Zuni Pueblo

See also Gallop

Pop 6,367 **Elev** 6,283 ft **Area code** 505 **Zip** 87327

Thirty-nine miles south of Gallup, via NM 602 and west on NM 53, is one of Coronado's "Seven Cities of Cibola." Fray Marcos de Niza reported that these cities were built of gold. When looking down on the Zuni pueblo from a distant hilltop at sunset, it does seem to have a golden glow. Marcos' story was partly responsible for Coronado's expedition of the area in 1540, which found no riches for Spain.

Zuni is linguistically unique and distinct from other Rio Grande pueblos. The people here make beautiful jewelry, beadwork, and pottery. They also have a furniture and woodworking center with colorful and uniquely painted and carved items. Zuni works are available at **Pueblo of Zuni Arts and Crafts.** Phone 505/782-5531. **Ashiwi Awan Museum and Heritage Center** displays historical photos and exhibits. (Daily) Phone 505/782-4403. The pueblo, built mainly of stone, is one story high for the most part. The old Zuni mission church has been restored and its interior painted with murals of Zuni traditional figures. A tribal permit is required for photography; certain rules must be observed.

Picnicking and camping at Eustace, Ojo Caliente, Pescado, Nutria #2, and Nutria #4 Lakes. Lakes stocked by Tribal Fish & Wildlife Service; a tribal permit as well as a state fishing license is required. For further information contact the Pueblo of Zuni, PO Box 339; phone 505/782-4481.

Utah

Utah is named for the Ute people, a nomadic tribe that populated these regions before the days of westward expansion. The state presents many natural faces, with arid desert and the deep, jagged canyons of the Colorado and Green rivers dominating the west and south and high, rugged mountains in the east and north. Utah contains examples of almost all water and land forms, many unique to the state. This natural diversity, though stimulating to the artistic eye, created an environment inhospitable to early settlers. Tribes of Ute, Piute, and Shoshone were the only people living in the region when the first white men, two Franciscan priests, passed through the area in 1776 en route to California from New Mexico. In 1819, British fur trappers began voyaging into northern Utah; by 1824 mountain men—people like Canadians Étienne Provost and Peter Skene Ogden, for whom some of Utah's towns and rivers are named—were venturing into Utah's wilds. Although these men traversed and explored much of the state, it took the determination and perseverance of a band of religious fugitives, members of the Church of Jesus Christ of Latter-Day Saints, to conquer the wilderness that was Utah and permanently settle the land.

Brigham Young, leader of the Mormon followers, once remarked, "If there is a place on this earth that nobody else wants, that's the place I am hunting for." On July 24, 1847, upon entering the forbidding land surrounding the Great Salt Lake, Young exclaimed, "This is the place!" Immediately, the determined settlers began to plow the unfriendly soil and build dams for irrigation. Hard work and tenacity were put to the test as the Mormons struggled to convert the Utah wilderness into productive land. With little to work with—what the settlers did not have, they did without—the Mormons gradually triumphed over the land, creating the safe haven they were searching for.

The Mormon church was founded by Joseph Smith on April 6, 1830, in New York state. The religion, based on writings inscribed on golden plates said to have been delivered to Smith by an angel and translated by him into *The Book of Mormon*, drew a large following. Moving from New York to Ohio and Missouri, and then driven from Missouri and later Illinois, the church grew despite persecution and torture. When Smith was killed in Illinois, Young took over. With a zealot's determination, he headed farther west in search of a place of refuge. He found it in the Salt Lake area of Utah. Growing outward from their original settlement, Mormon pioneers and missionaries established colonies that were to become many of Utah's modern-day cities. During 1847, as many as 1,637 Mormons came to Utah, and by the time the railroad penetrated the region, more than 6,000 had settled in the state. Before his death in 1877, 30 years after entering the Salt Lake Valley, Brigham Young had directed the founding of more than 350 communities.

While the Mormon church undoubtedly had the greatest influence on the state—developing towns in an orderly fashion with wide streets, planting straight rows of poplar trees to provide wind breaks, and introducing irrigation throughout the desert regions—the church members were not the only settlers. In the latter part of the 19th century, the West's fabled pioneer era erupted. The gold rush of 1849-1850 sent gold seekers pouring through Utah on their way to California. The arrival of the Pony Express in Salt Lake City in 1860 brought more immigrants, and when the mining boom hit the state in the 1870s and 1880s, Utah's mining towns

Population: 1,722,850
Area: 84,990 square miles
Elevation: 2,200-13,528 feet
Peak: Kings Peak (Duchesne County)
Entered Union: January 4, 1896 (45th state)
Capital: Salt Lake City
Motto: Industry
Nickname: Beehive State
Flower: Sego Lily
Bird: California Gull
Tree: Blue Spruce
Fair: September in Salt Lake City
Time Zone: Mountain
Website: www.utah.com

Calendar Highlights

JANUARY

Sundance Film Festival *(Park City). www. sundance.org.* Week-long festival for independent filmmakers. Workshops, screenings, and special events.

JUNE

Utah Arts Festival *(Salt Lake City). Downtown. Phone 801/322-2428. www.uaf.org.* More than 1,000 participants, 90 performing groups; Children's Art Yard, juried show with demonstrations. Ethnic food.

Utah Summer Games *(Cedar City). Phone 435/ 865-8421. www.utahsummergames.org.* Olympic-style athletic events for amateur athletes.

JULY

Festival of the American West *(Logan). Phone 435/ 797-1143 or 800/225-FEST.* Ronald V. Jensen Living Historical Farm. Historical pageant; pioneer and Native American crafts fair, art exhibition, antique quilt show, frontier town, medicine man show, log construction; Dutch-oven cook-off.

Renaissance Fair *(Cedar City). Main St City Park.* Entertainment, food, and games in Renaissance style. Held in conjunction with the opening of the Utah Shakespearean Festival.

Ute Stampede Rodeo *(Nephi). Phone 435/623-7102.* Three-day festival featuring horse and mammoth parades, carnival, PRCA rodeo, contests, arts and crafts, concessions.

AUGUST

Bonneville National Speed Trials *(Wendover). Bonneville Speedway. Phone 805/526-1805.* Held since 1914 on the Bonneville Salt Flats, which has been used as a track for racing the world's fastest cars. Car racing in competition and against the clock.

Novell Showdown *(Park City). Contact Park Meadows Golf Club, phone 801/531-7029.* PGA invitational golf tournament.

Railroaders Festival *(Brigham City). Golden Spike National Historic Site. Contact Golden Spike National Historic Site, phone 435/471-2209. www.nps.gov/ gosp.* Relive the rush to complete the transcontinental railroad and watch professional railroaders pursue the world record in spike driving.

SEPTEMBER

Utah State Fair *(Salt Lake City). State Fair Park. Phone 801/538-FAIR.* Arts and crafts, live entertainment, horse show, and rodeo.

---

appeared almost overnight. In 1900, there were 277,000 Utahns; now the population stands at more than 1,700,000, with more than 75 percent living within 50 miles of Salt Lake City. The Mormon Church continues to play an important role, with close to 60 percent of the state's population being members.

Utah's natural diversity has made it a state of magnificent beauty, with more than 3,000 lakes, miles of mountains, acres upon acres of forests, and large expanses of deserts. Its main heights, 13,000 feet or more, are reached by plateaus and mountains lifted during the Cascade disturbance of the Cenozoic period. In northern Utah, the grandeur of the Wasatch Range, one of the most rugged mountain ranges in the United States, cuts across the state north to south; the Uinta Range, capped by the white peaks of ancient glaciers, is the only major North American range that runs east to west. In the western third of the state lies the Great Basin, a land-locked drainage area that, at one time, was half covered by a large, ancient sea. At its peak, Lake Bonneville was 1,050 feet deep, 145 miles wide, and 346 miles long. The Great Salt Lake and Sevier Lake are saltwater remnants of Bonneville, and Utah Lake is a freshwater remnant. To the east, the Bonneville Salt Flats lie where the ancient lake had retreated. To the east and west extends the Colorado River Plateau, or Red Plateau. This red rock country, renowned for its brilliant coloring and fantastic rock formations, is also home to one of the largest concentrations of national parks and monuments. With its many aspects, Utah is a land designed for the traveler who loves the Western outdoors and can appreciate the awesome accomplishments of the pioneers who developed it.

When to Go/Climate

Temperatures vary across the state, but in general, summer days are hot, summer nights cool; winters are cold and snowy except in the southwestern part of the state. The best time to visit Utah is in the spring or fall when temperatures are milder and the tourist crowds have thinned out.

AVERAGE HIGH/LOW TEMPERATURES (°F)

Salt Lake City

Jan 37/19	**May** 72/46	**Sept** 79/51
Feb 44/25	**June** 83/55	**Oct** 66/40
Mar 52/31	**July** 92/64	**Nov** 51/31
Apr 61/38	**Aug** 89/62	**Dec** 38/22

St. George

Jan 54/27	**May** 86/52	**Sept** 93/57
Feb 61/32	**June** 96/61	**Oct** 81/45
Mar 67/37	**July** 102/68	**Nov** 65/38
Apr 76/44	**Aug** 99/66	**Dec** 55/27

Parks and Recreation

Water-related activities, hiking, riding, various other sports, picnicking and visitor centers, as well as camping, are available in many of Utah's state parks. Day-use fee, including picnicking, boat launching, and museums: $5-$20 per vehicle. Camping (mid-Apr-Oct; some sites available rest of year), $7-$16/site per night; most sites 14-day maximum. Advance reservations may be obtained at most developed state parks; phone 801/322-3770 (Salt Lake City) or 800/322-3770. Pets on leash only. Senior citizen and disabled permit (free; UT residents only). For information on park facilities and permits, contact Utah State Parks & Recreation, 1594 W North Temple, Salt Lake City 84114; phone 801/538-7220.

FISHING AND HUNTING

Wildlife habitat authorization $6; nonresident deer permit $198; permit for bull elk $300; once-in-a-lifetime permit for moose, bison, desert bighorn sheep, Rocky Mountain goat $1,003. For special permits, write for information and apply from early-late Jan (bucks, bulls, and once-in-a-lifetime draw) and early June (antlerless draw). Small game licenses $40. Deer, elk, ducks, geese, pheasants, mourning doves, and grouse are favorite quarry.

More than 3,000 lakes and hundreds of miles of mountain streams are filled with rainbow, German brown, cutthroat, Mackinaw, and brook trout; there are also catfish, walleyed pike, bass, crappie, and bluegill. Nonresident season fishing license (14 years and over) $45; 7-day fishing license $27; 1-day fishing license $8.

Further information may be obtained from the Division of Wildlife Resources, 1594 W North Temple, Box 146301, Salt Lake City 84114-6301; phone 801/538-4700.

RIVER EXPEDITIONS

See Bluff, Green River, Moab, Salt Lake City, or Vernal. For a directory of professional outfitters and river runners, write to the Utah Travel Council, Council Hall, Capitol Hill, 300 N State St, Salt Lake City 84114; phone 801/538-1030 or toll-free 800/200-1160.

Driving Information

Safety belts are mandatory for all persons in the front seat of a vehicle. Children under age 8 must be in an approved passenger restraint anywhere in the vehicle: ages 2-7 may use a regulation safety belt; under age 2 must use an approved safety seat.

INTERSTATE HIGHWAY SYSTEM

Use the following list as a guide to access interstate highways in Utah. Always consult a map to confirm driving routes.

Highway Number	Cities/Towns within 10 Miles
Interstate 15	Beaver, Birmingham City, Cedar City, Fillmore, Nephi, Ogden, Payson, Provo, St. George, Salt Lake City.
Interstate 70	Green River, Salina.
Interstate 80	Salt Lake City, Wendover.

Additional Visitor Information

Utah Travel Council, Council Hall, Capitol Hill, 300 N State St, Salt Lake City 84114, will furnish excellent, extensive information about every section of the state and about special and annual events. Phone 801/538-1030 or 800/200-1160.

There are several visitor centers in Utah, with information and brochures about points of interest. Major centers may be found at the following locations: Utah Field House of Natural History, 235 E Main St, Vernal; St George Information Center, Dixie Center; Echo Information Center, 2 miles E of junction I-80 E, I-80 N; Thompson Information Center, on I-70, 45 miles W of Utah-Colorado border; and Brigham City Information Center, I-15, 5 miles N.

The Utah Fine Arts Council, 617 E South Temple, Salt Lake City 84102, phone 801/236-7555, provides information about local and statewide artists, museums, galleries, and exhibits.

WALLS OF STONE

This 3- to 4-day tour out of Moab includes magnificent vistas, whimsical rock formations, an early "newspaper," and the upper reaches of Lake Powell. From Moab, head south on US 191 to UT 211; follow 211 west to Newspaper Rock, a huge sandstone panel with petroglyphs up to 1,500 years old. Images etched into this wall of stone were left by prehistoric peoples such as the Fremonts and Ancestral Puebloans, as well as the Utes, Navajo, and European-American settlers from the 19th and early 20th centuries. From Newspaper Rock it is an easy drive west on UT 211 to the Needles District of Canyonlands National Park. You probably visited the Island in the Sky District of Canyonlands during your stay in Moab, but this section of the park offers a different perspective. Although best explored by mountain bike or in a high-clearance four-wheel-drive vehicle, there are several roadside viewpoints from which you can see the district's namesake red-and-white-striped rock pinnacles and other formations. Several easy hikes offer additional views.

Retrace your route back to US 191, and continue south to UT 95, where you will head west to Natural Bridges National Monument. This easy-to-explore monument has a scenic drive with overlooks that offer views of three awe-inspiring natural stone bridges and some 700-year-old Ancestral Puebloan cliff dwellings. There is also prehistoric rock art and a demonstration of how solar energy is used to produce the monument's electricity. The viewpoints are short walks from parking areas, and the more ambitious can also hike to all three of the natural bridges, which were created over millions of years as water cut through solid rock.

Returning to UT 95, head northwest to the Hite Crossing section of Glen Canyon National Recreation Area. Encompassing the northern end of Lake Powell, this is one of the least developed and also least crowded areas of the recreation area. Hite has scenic views, boat rentals, and plenty of available lodging (including houseboats). This is a good opportunity for kids who have spent too much time in the car to stretch their legs and play in the water.

From Hite, continue northwest on UT 95 across rock-studded terrain to Hanksville; head north on UT 24 to the turnoff to Goblin Valley State Park. This delightful little park—sure to be a favorite of anyone with a vivid imagination—is a fantasyland where whimsical stone goblins seem to be frozen in mid-dance. From Goblin Valley, return to UT 24 and continue north to I-70. Head east to the community of Green River, which offers an ample supply of motels. Here you'll discover Green River State Park, a good spot for a picnic under the Russian olive and cottonwood trees along the river or perhaps a round of golf at the park's 9-hole championship course. Nearby, the John Wesley Powell River History Museum tells the incredible story of explorer Powell, a one-armed Civil War veteran who did what was considered impossible when he charted the Green and Colorado rivers in the late 1800s. From Green River continue east on I-70 to US 191, which leads south back to Moab. **(Approximately 448 miles)**

Alta (C-4)

See also Heber City, Park City, Salt Lake City

Pop 370 **Elev** 8,600 ft **Area code** 435 **Zip** 84092

Founded around silver mines in the 1870s, Alta was notorious for constant shoot-outs in its 26 saloons. The town became the center of a noted ski area in 1937, with the opening of Utah's first ski resort. Historic markers identify the original townsite. Unusual wildflowers are found in Albion Basin.

What to See and Do

Alta Ski Area. *On UT 210 in Little Cottonwood Canyon. Phone 435/359-1078.* Three triple, five double chairlifts; four rope tows; patrol, school, rentals, snowmaking; lodges, restaurant, cafeteria. Longest run 3 1/2 miles, vertical drop 2,020 feet. (Mid-Nov-Apr, daily) Half-day rates. **$$$$**

Hotel

★ ★ **ALTA'S RUSTLER LODGE.** *Little Cottonwood Canyon (84092). Phone 435/742-2200; fax 435/742-3832. www.rustlerlodge.com.* 85 rooms, 5 story. No A/C. MAP: S $300-$400; D $350-$490; each additional $80; suites $520-$650/room; under 5 free; higher rates: Dec 19, mid-Mar. Closed May-Oct. Crib free. TV in recreation room; cable. Heated pool; whirlpool. Restaurant 7:30-9:45 am, 12:30-2 pm, 6:30-9 pm. Private club 3-11 pm. Check-out 1 pm. Coin laundry. Meeting rooms. Bellstaff. Downhill/cross-country ski on site. Exercise equipment. Recreation room. Cr cds: A, MC, V.

🄳 🏊 ⛵ 🏋 ✈ 🐾

Resort

★ **ALTA LODGE.** *State Road 210 (84092). Phone 435/742-3500; toll-free 800/707-2582; fax 435/742-3504. www.altalodge.com.* 57 rooms, 3 story. No elevator. MAP, Nov-Apr: S, D $103-$467; each additional $88-$97; men's, women's dorms $98-$108; under 4 free; EP available in summer; lower rates June-early-Oct. Closed rest of year. TV in common area; cable, VCR available (free movies). Supervised children's activities (Nov-Apr); ages 3-12. Restaurant 6:30-9 pm. Bar (winter). Check-out 11 am. Meeting rooms. Business services available. Coin laundry. Downhill/cross-country ski on site. Tennis. Whirlpool. Sauna. Some fireplaces. Some balconies. Sun deck. Cr cds: D, DS, MC, V.

🚴 🏊 ⛵ 🎿 🐾

Arches National Park (F-6)

See also Moab

(5 miles NW of Moab on US 191 to paved entrance road) Contact the Superintendent, PO Box 907, Moab 84532; phone 435/259-8161 or 435/259-5279 (TTY).

This timeless, natural landscape of giant stone arches, pinnacles, spires, fins, and windows was once the bed of an ancient sea. Over time, erosion laid bare the skeletal structure of the earth, making this 114-square-mile area a spectacular outdoor museum. This wilderness, which contains the greatest density of natural arches in the world, was named a national monument in 1929 and a national park in 1971. More than 2,000 arches have been cataloged, ranging in size from 3 feet wide to the 105-foot-high, 306-foot-wide Landscape Arch.

The arches, other rock formations, and views of the Colorado River canyon, with the peaks of the LaSal Mountains in the distance, can be reached by car, but hiking is the best way to explore. Petroglyphs from the primitive peoples who roamed this section of Utah from A.D. 700-1200 can be seen at the Delicate Arch trailhead. This is a wildlife sanctuary; no hunting is permitted. Hiking, rock climbing, or camping in isolated sections should not be undertaken unless first reported to a park ranger at the visitor center (check locally for hours). Twenty-four miles of paved roads are open year-round. Graded and dirt roads should not be attempted in wet weather. Devils Garden Campground, 18 miles north of the visitor center off US 191, provides 52 individual and 2 group camp sites (year-round; fee; water available only March-mid-October). There is an entrance fee of $10 for a 7-day permit; Golden Eagle, Golden Age, and Golden Access passports are accepted (see MAKING THE MOST OF YOUR TRIP).

Beaver (G-3)

See also Cedar City, Richfield

Settled 1856 **Pop** 2,454 **Elev** 5,898 ft **Area code** 435 **Zip** 84713

Information Chamber of Commerce, 1603 S Campground Rd, PO Box 760; 435/438-5081

The seat of Beaver County, this town is a national historic district with more than 200 houses of varied architectural styles and periods. It is also the birthplace of Butch Cassidy (1866).

Problems arose in Beaver's early days when tough gentile prospectors (in Utah, anyone not a Mormon was called a "gentile"), who came with a mining boom, derided the Mormons, who owned woolen mills. There was little harmony until the boom was over, but millions in gold, silver, lead, copper, tungsten, zinc, bismuth, and sulphur had been mined by then. Now, irrigation has brought farming to Beaver. Dairying and stock-raising, as well as recreation, hunting, and fishing, are important to the economy.

What to See and Do

Elk Meadows and Mount Holly Ski Area. *18 miles E on I-15. Phone 888/881-7669.* Quad, triple, three double chairlifts, one surface lift; school, rentals, shops, cafe, lodging. Longest run 2 1/2 miles; vertical drop 1,400 feet. (Mid-Dec-Apr, daily)

Fishlake National Forest. *115 East 900 North. E on UT 153. Phone 435/896-9233.* (See RICHFIELD) A Ranger District office of the forest is located in Beaver.

Special Event

Pioneer Days. *Phone 435/438-5081.* Features parade, entertainment, horse racing; other events. Late July.

Motels/Motor Lodges

★★ **BEST WESTERN BUTCH CASSIDY INN.** *161 South Main (84713). Phone 435/438-2438; fax 435/438-1053. www.bestwestern.com.* 35 rooms, 2 story. Mid-May-Oct: S $54-$60; D $63-$70; lower rates rest of year. Crib $3. Pet accepted, some restrictions; $5. Check-out 11 am. TV; cable (premium). In-room modem link. Coffee in rooms. Restaurant 7 am-10 pm. Sauna. Heated pool, whirlpool. Downhill ski 18 miles. Business services. Cr cds: A, C, D, DS, MC, V.

⊠ ⓒ ⊠ ⊠ ⊠

★ **DE LANO MOTEL.** *480 N Main St (84713). Phone 435/438-2418.* 11 rooms. May-Oct: S, D $34-$45; weekly rates; lower rates rest of year. Crib free. Pet accepted. TV; cable (premium). Restaurant nearby. Check-out 11 am. Business services available. Covered parking. Downhill ski 15 miles. Some refrigerators, microwaves. Cr cds: A, DS, MC, V.

⊠ ⊠ ⊠ SC

★ **QUALITY INN.** *781 W 1800 S (84713). Phone 435/438-5426; toll-free 800/228-5151; fax 435/438-2493. www.qualityinn.com.* 52 rooms, 2 story. June-Oct: S $54; D $60; each additional $6; under 18 free; ski plans; lower rates rest of year. Check-out 11 am. TV; cable. Indoor pool, whirlpool. Downhill, cross-country ski 18 miles. Cr cds: A, C, D, DS, JCB, MC, V.

Ⓓ ⊠ ⊠ SC

★ **SLEEPY LAGOON MOTEL.** *882 S Main St (84713). Phone 435/438-5681; fax 435/438-9991.* 20 rooms. May-Sept: S, D $40-$45; lower rates rest of year. Pet accepted. Complimentary continental breakfast (summer). Check-out 11 am. TV; cable. Heated pool. Small pond. Cr cds: A, DS, MC, V.

⊠ ⊠ ⊠ SC

Restaurant

★ **ARSHEL'S CAFE.** *711 N Main St (84713). Phone 435/438-2977.* Hours: 7 am-10 pm; Nov-Mar to 9 pm. Closed Thanksgiving, Dec 24, 25. Breakfast $4.10-$7.10, lunch, dinner $4.20-$11.50. Reservations accepted. Cr cds: DS, MC, V.

Ⓓ

Blanding (H-7)

See also Bluff, Monticello

Settled 1905 **Pop** 3,162 **Elev** 6,105 ft **Area code** 435 **Zip** 84511

Information San Juan County Visitor Center, 117 S Main St, Box 490, Monticello 84535; 435/587-3235 or 800/574-4386

Web www.southeastutah.org

In 1940, with a population of 600, Blanding was the largest town in a county the size of Connecticut, Rhode Island, and Delaware combined. Although surrounded by ranches and grazing areas, the city is a gateway to hunting and fishing grounds and national monuments. The sites can be explored by jeep or horseback along the many trails, or by boat through the waters of Glen Canyon National Recreation Area. A Pueblo ruin, inhabited between A.D. 800-1200, is now a state park within the city limits.

What to See and Do

Edge of the Cedars State Park. *660 W 400 North St. 1 mile NW off US 191. Phone 435/678-2238.* Excavated remnants of ancient dwellings and ceremonial chambers fashioned by the ancient Pueblo people. Artifacts and pictographs; museum of Native American history and culture. Visitor center. (Daily) **$**

Glen Canyon National Recreation Area/Lake Powell. *4 miles S on US 191, then 85 miles W on UT 95 and UT 276.* (See LAKE POWELL)

★ **Hovenweep National Monument.** *Approximately 13 miles S on US 191, then 9 miles E on UT 262 and 6 miles E on county roads to Hatch Trading Post, follow signs 16 miles to Hovenweep. Phone 970/562-4282.* Monument consists of six units of prehistoric ruins; the best preserved are the remains of pueblos (small cliff dwellings) and towers at Square Tower. Self-guided trail; park ranger on duty; visitor area (Daily; closed Jan 1, Thanksgiving, Dec 25). **$$$**

Natural Bridges National Monument. (see) *Off Rte 21 on Charlotte St. Phone 435/692-1234.* **$$$**

Bluff (I-7)

See also Blanding

Founded 1880 **Pop** 320 **Elev** 4,320 ft **Area code** 435 **Zip** 84512

Information San Juan County Visitor Center, 117 S Main St, Box 490, Monticello 84535; 435/587-3235 or 800/574-4386

Web www.southeasternutah.org

Bluff's dramatic location between the sandstone cliffs along the San Juan River, its Anasazi ruins among the canyon walls, and its Mormon pioneer past all combine to make it an interesting stop along scenic US 163 between the Grand Canyon and Mesa Verde National Parks.

What to See and Do

⭐ **Tours of the Big Country.** *US 191. Phone 435/672-2281.* Trips to Monument Valley, the Navajo Reservation, and into canyons of southeastern Utah explore desert plant and wildlife, history, geology, and Anasazi archaeology of this area. Naturalist-guided walking or four-wheel-drive tours. Llama rentals. Half-day, full-day, or overnight trips. (year-round) Contact Recapture Lodge. **$$$$**

Wild Rivers Expeditions. *101 Main Street (84512). Phone 435/672-2244 or 800/422-7654 (exc UT).* Fun and educational trips on the archaeologically rich San Juan River through Glen Canyon National Recreation Area (see LAKE POWELL) and Cataract Canyon of the Colorado River. Geological formations and fossil beds. (Apr-Oct) **$$$$**

Special Event

Utah Navajo Fair. *Phone 800/574-4FUN.* Third weekend in Sept.

Motel/Motor Lodge

★ **RECAPTURE LODGE.** *Hwy 191 (84512). Phone 435/672-2281; fax 435/672-2284. www.recapturelodge.com.* 28 rooms, 2 story. D $40-$50; each additional $2. Check-out noon, check-in 1 pm. TV; VCR available. Restaurant 7 am-9 pm. Whirlpool. Lawn games. Airport transportation. Also units for groups, families at Pioneer House (historic building). Totally nonsmoking. Cr cds: A, DS, MC, V.

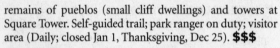

Brigham City (B-3)

See also Logan, Ogden

Settled 1851 **Pop** 17,411 **Elev** 4,439 ft **Area code** 435 **Zip** 84302

Information Chamber of Commerce, 6 N Main St, PO Box 458; 435/723-3931

Web www.bcareachamber.com

Renamed for Brigham Young in 1877, when he made his last public address here, this community was first known as Box Elder because of the many trees of that type that grew in the area. Main Street, which runs through the center of this city situated at the base of the towering Wasatch Mountains, is still lined with these leafy trees.

What to See and Do

Brigham City Museum-Gallery. *24 N 3rd W. Phone 435/723-6769.* Permanent history exhibits, rotating art exhibits; displays include furniture, clothing, books, photographs, and documents reflecting the history of the Brigham City area since 1851. (Tues-Fri, also Sat afternoons) **FREE**

⭐ **Golden Spike National Historic Site.** *6450 N 22000 W. 32 miles W via UT 83 and County Rd. Contact Chief Ranger, PO Box 897. Phone 435/471-2209.* Site where America's first transcontinental railroad was completed on May 10, 1869. Visitor center, movies, exhibits (daily; closed Jan 1, Thanksgiving, Dec 25). Self-guided auto tour along old railroad bed. Summer interpretive program includes presentations and operating replicas of steam locomotives "Jupiter" and "119" (May-early Oct, daily). (See SPECIAL EVENTS) Golden Eagle, Golden Age, Golden Access passports accepted (see MAKING THE MOST OF YOUR TRIP). **$$$**

Tabernacle. *251 S Main St. Phone 435/723-5376.* (1881) The tabernacle, one of the most architecturally interesting buildings in Utah, has been in continuous use since 1881. Guided tours (May-Sept, daily). **FREE**

Special Events

Box Elder County Fair. Late Aug.

Driving of Golden Spike. *Phone 435/471-2209.* At Promontory, site where the Central Pacific and Union Pacific met. Reenactment of driving of golden spike in 1869. Locomotive replicas used. Mid-May.

Peach Days Celebration. Parade, arts and crafts, carnival; car show, entertainment. First weekend after Labor Day.

Railroaders Festival. *6450 N 22000 W. Golden Spike National Historic Site.* Relive the rush to complete transcontinental railroad. Professional railroaders pursue world record in spike driving. Second Sat in Aug.

Motel/Motor Lodge

★ **HOWARD JOHNSON.** *1167 S Main St (84302). Phone 435/723-8511; toll-free 800/446-4656; fax 435/723-0957. www.hojo.com.* 44 rooms, 2 story. S $44-$54; D $51-$59; each additional $5; under 17 free. Crib free. Pet accepted, some restrictions. TV; cable (premium). Indoor pool; whirlpool. Complimentary continental breakfast. Restaurant adjacent. Business services available. Check-out noon. Cr cds: A, C, D, DS, ER, JCB, MC, V.

D ⬛ 🐾 ➰ ➚ SC

Restaurant

★★ **MADDOX RANCH HOUSE.** *1900 S UT 89 (84302). Phone 435/723-8545; fax 435/723-8547. www. maddoxranchhouse.com.* Specialties: chicken, beef, seafood. Hours: 11 am-9:30 pm. Closed Sun, Mon; Thanksgiving, Dec 25. Lunch, dinner $6.95-$19.95. Family-owned. Children's menu. Reservations accepted. Western décor. Cr cds: A, D, MC, V.

D

Bryce Canyon National Park (H-3)

See also Panguitch

(7 miles S of Panguitch on US 89, then 17 miles SE on UT 12 to UT 63, 3 miles to entrance)

Bryce Canyon is a 56-square-mile area of colorful, fantastic cliffs created by millions of years of erosion. Towering rocks worn to odd, sculptured shapes stand grouped in striking sequences. The Paiute, who once lived nearby, called this "the place where red rocks stand like men in a bowl-shaped canyon." Although termed a canyon, Bryce is actually a series of "breaks" in 12 large amphitheaters—some plunging as deep as 1,000 feet into the multicolored limestone. The formations appear to change color as the sunlight strikes from different angles and seem incandescent in the late afternoon. The famous Pink Cliffs were carved from the Claron Formation; shades of red, orange, white, gray, purple, brown, and soft yellow appear in the strata. The park road follows 17 miles along the eastern edge of the Paunsaugunt Plateau, where the natural amphitheaters are spread out below; plateaus covered with evergreens and valleys filled with sagebrush stretch away into the distance.

The visitor center at the entrance station has complete information about the park, including orientation shows, geologic displays, and detailed maps (daily; closed Jan 1, Thanksgiving, Dec 25). The park is open year-round; in winter, the park road is open to most viewpoints. Lodging is also available April to October. There is an entrance fee of $10 per vehicle; Golden Eagle, Golden Age, and Golden Access passports are accepted (see MAKING THE MOST OF YOUR TRIP). Shuttle system (fee, phone for information). Contact the Superintendent, PO Box 170001, Bryce Canyon 84717; phone 435/834-5322.

Motels/Motor Lodges

★★ **BEST WESTERN RUBY'S INN.** *UT 63 (84764). Phone 435/834-5341; fax 435/834-5265. www.rubysinn.com.* 368 rooms, 1-3 story. June-Sept: S, D $95-$130; each additional $5; lower rates rest of year. Crib free, Pet accepted, some restrictions; $100 deposit. Check-out 11 am, Check-in 4 pm. TV; VCR (movies). Coin laundry. Restaurant 6:30 am-9 pm; winter hours vary. Game room. Indoor/outdoor pool, whirlpool. Cross-country ski opposite. Picnic tables. Business services available. Shopping arcade. Rodeo in summer; general store. Lake on property. Trailer park. Cr cds: A, D, DS, MC, V.

🐾 🛥 ☇ ➚ ➰

★★ **BRYCE CANYON LODGE.** *1 Bryce Canyon Lodge (84717). Phone 435/834-5361; fax 435/834-5330. www.brycecanyonlodge.com.* 114 units in cabins, motel. Apr-Nov: motel units $110; cabin units $121; each additional $5; suites $135; each additional $10. Closed rest of year. Crib available. Restaurant 6:30-10 am, 11 am-3:30 pm, 5:30-9:30 pm. Check-out 11 am, check-in 4 pm. Coin laundry. Bellstaff. Sundries. Trail rides on mules, horses available. Private patios, balconies. Original 1925 building. Cr cds: A, D, DS, MC, V.

D ☇ ➚

Restaurant

★ **FOSTER'S STEAK HOUSE.** *UT 12 (84764). Phone 435/834-5227; fax 435/834-5304. www.brycecanyon country.com/dining/brycecanyonarea.html.* Hours: 7 am-10 pm; Dec-Mar from 2 pm. Beer. Breakfast $1.75-$5.99, lunch $2.99-$13.49, dinner $7.99-$22.50. Children's menu. Specializes in prime rib. Salad bar. Bakery adjacent. Cr cds: A, C, D, DS, ER, MC, V.

D

Canyonlands National Park (G-6)

See also Moab, Monticello

(N district: 12 miles N of Moab on US 191, then 21 miles SW on UT 313; S district: 12 miles N of Monticello on US 191, then 38 miles W on UT 211) Spectacular rock formations, canyons, arches, spires, pictograph panels, ancestral Puebloan ruins, and desert flora are the main features of this 337,570-acre area. Set aside by Congress in 1964 as a national park, the area is largely undeveloped. Road conditions vary; primary access roads are paved and maintained, while others are safe only for high-clearance four-wheel-drive vehicles. For backcountry road conditions and information, phone 801/259-7164.

Island in the Sky, North District, south and west of Dead Horse Point State Park (see MOAB), has Grand View Point, Upheaval Dome, and Green River Overlook. This section is accessible by passenger car via UT 313 and by four-wheel-drive vehicles and mountain bikes on dirt roads.

Needles, South District, has hiking trails and four-wheel-drive roads to Angel Arch, Chesler Park, and the confluence of the Green and Colorado rivers. Also here are prehistoric ruins and rock art. This section is accessible by passenger car via UT 211, by four-wheel-drive vehicle on dirt roads, and by mountain bike.

Maze, West District, is accessible by hiking or by four-wheel-drive vehicles using unimproved roads. The most remote and least visited section of the park, this area received its name from the many mazelike canyons. Horseshoe Canyon, a separate unit of the park nearby, is accessible via UT 24 and 30 miles of two-wheel-drive dirt road. Roads are usually passable only in mid-March through mid-November.

Canyonlands is excellent for calm-water and whitewater trips down the Green and Colorado rivers. Permits are required for private trips (fee; contact Reservation Office, 435/259-4351) and commercial trips (see MOAB). Campgrounds, with tent sites, are located at Island in the Sky (fee) and at Needles (fee); water is available only at Needles. Visitor centers are in each district and are open daily. There is an entrance fee of $10 per vehicle. Golden Eagle, Golden Age, Golden Access passports are accepted (see MAKING THE MOST OF YOUR TRIP). Contact Canyonlands NP, 2282 S West Resource Blvd, Moab 84532; phone 435/259-7164.

Capitol Reef National Park (G-5)

See also Loa

(10 miles E of Richfield on UT 119, then 65 miles SE on UT 24)

Capitol Reef, at an elevation ranging from 3,900–8,800 feet, is composed of red sandstone cliffs capped with domes of white sandstone. Located in the heart of Utah's slickrock country, the park is actually a 100-mile section of the Waterpocket Fold, an upthrust of sedimentary rock created during the formation of the Rocky Mountains. Pockets in the rocks collect thousands of gallons of water each time it rains. Capitol Reef was so named because the rocks formed a natural barrier to pioneer travel and the white sandstone domes resemble the dome of the US Capitol.

From A.D. 700–1350, this 378-square-mile area was the home of an ancient people who grew corn along the Fremont River. Petroglyphs can be seen on some of the sandstone walls. A schoolhouse, farmhouse, and orchards, established by early Mormon settlers, are open to the public in season.

The park can be approached from either the east or the west via UT 24, a paved road. There is a visitor center on this road about 7 miles from the west boundary and 8 miles from the east (daily; closed Dec 25). A 25-mile round-trip scenic drive, some parts unpaved, starts from this point. There are evening programs and guided walks (Memorial Day-Labor Day; free). Three campgrounds are available: Fruita, approximately 1 mile south off UT 24, provides 70 tent and trailer sites year-round (fee); Cedar Mesa, 23 miles south off UT 24, and Cathedral, 28 miles north off UT 24, offer five primitive sites with access depending on the weather (free; no facilities). There is an entrance fee of $4 per vehicle. Golden Eagle, Golden Age, Golden Access passports are accepted (see MAKING THE MOST OF YOUR TRIP). Contact the Superintendent, HC 70, Box 15, Torrey 84775; phone 435/425-3791.

★ **SUNGLOW MOTEL.** *63 E. Main, Bicknell (84715). 435/425-3821.* 12 rooms, 10 with A/C. Mar-mid-Nov: S, D $32-$37; each additional $2-$4. Closed rest of year. Crib $2. Pet accepted; $5. TV; cable. Restaurant 6:30 am-10 pm. Check-out 11 am, Cr cds: A, DS, MC, V.

D 🐾 ⚓ 🕎 🏖 🖼

Cedar Breaks National Monument (H-3)

See also Cedar City

(23 miles E of Cedar City via UT 14)

Cedar Breaks National Monument's major formation is a spectacular, multicolored, natural amphitheater created by the same forces that sculpted Utah's other rock formations. The amphitheater, shaped like an enormous coliseum, is 2,000 feet deep and more than 3 miles in diameter. It is carved out of the Markagunt Plateau and is surrounded by Dixie National Forest (see CEDAR CITY). Cedar Breaks, at an elevation of more than 10,000 feet, was established as a national monument in 1933. It derives its name from the surrounding cedar trees and the word "breaks," which means "badlands." Although similar to Bryce Canyon National Park, Cedar Breaks's formations are fewer but more vivid and varied in color. Young lava beds, resulting from small volcanic eruptions and cracks in the earth's surface, surround the Breaks area; the heavy forests include bristlecone pines, one of the oldest trees on the earth. Here, as soon as the snow melts, wildflowers bloom profusely and continue to bloom throughout the summer.

Rim Drive, a 5-mile scenic road through the Cedar Breaks High Country, provides views of the monument's formations from four different overlooks. The area is open late May to mid-October, weather permitting. Point Supreme Campground, 2 miles north of south entrance, provides 30 tent and trailer sites (mid-June-mid-September, fee; water, rest rooms). The visitor center offers geological exhibits (June-mid-October, daily); interpretive activities (mid-June-Labor Day). There is an entrance fee of $4 per vehicle. Golden Eagle, Golden Age, Golden Access passports accepted (see MAKING THE MOST OF YOUR TRIP). Contact the Superintendent, 2390 W Hwy 56, Suite 11, Cedar City 84720; phone 435/586-9451.

Cedar City (H-2)

Settled 1851 **Pop** 20,527 **Elev** 5,834 ft **Area code** 435
Zip 84720

Information Chamber of Commerce, 581 N Main St; 435/586-4484

Web www.chambercedarcity.org

In 1852, Cedar City produced the first iron made west of the Mississippi. The blast furnace operation was not successful, however, and stock-raising soon overshadowed it, though iron is still mined west of the city on a limited basis. A branch line of the Union Pacific entered the region in 1923 and helped develop the area. Now a tourist center because of its proximity to Bryce Canyon and Zion national parks (see both), Cedar City takes pride in its abundant natural wonders; streams and lakes have rainbow trout, and the Markagunt Plateau provides deer and mountain lion hunting. Headquarters and a Ranger District office of the Dixie National Forest are located here.

What to See and Do

Brian Head Ski Resort. *329 S UT 143. 19 miles NE on I-15 to Parowan, then 11 miles SE on UT 143, in Dixie National Forest.* Phone 435/677-2035. Five triple, double chairlift; patrol, school, rentals; restaurants, cafeterias, bars, nursery, ski shops, grocery, gift shops, lodging. Longest run 1/2 mile, vertical drop 1,700 feet. (Mid-Nov-early Apr, daily) Cross-country trails, rentals; snowmobiling, night skiing. Mountain biking (summer). **$$$$**

Dixie National Forest. *82 N and 100 E (84720). 12 miles E on UT 14 to forest boundary or 17 miles SW on I-15, then W.* Contact the Supervisor, PO Box 580, 84721. Phone 435/865-3200. Camping, picnicking, hiking, mountain biking, winter sports. (Daily) **FREE**

Iron Mission State Park. *585 N Main.* Phone 435/586-9290. Museum dedicated to the first pioneer iron foundry west of the Rockies; extensive collection of horse-drawn vehicles and wagons from Utah pioneer days. (Daily; closed Jan 1, Thanksgiving, Dec 25) **$**

Kolob Canyons Visitor Center. *3752 E Kolob Canyon Rd (84757). 17 miles S on I-15.* Phone 435/586-9548. This section of Zion National Park (see) provides a 14-mile round-trip hike to the Kolob Arch, world's second largest, with a span of 310 feet. A 5-mile scenic drive offers spectacular views of rugged peaks and sheer canyon walls 1,500 feet high. (Daily; closed Jan 1, Thanksgiving, Dec 25) **FREE**

Sightseeing trips. Cedar City Air Service. *2281 W Kitty Hawk Dr (84720).* Phone 435/586-3881. Trips include Cedar Breaks National Monument and Grand Canyon, Zion, and Bryce Canyon national parks (see all); other trips available. (Daily) **$$$$**

Southern Utah University. *351 W Center.* Phone 435/586-7700. (1897) 7,000 students. Braithwaite Fine Arts Gallery (Mon-Sat; free). (See SPECIAL EVENTS)

Zion National Park. (see) *60 miles SE via 1-15 and UT 9.*

Special Events

Renaissance Fair. *Main St. City Park.* Entertainment, food, and games, all in the style of the Renaissance. Held in conjunction with opening of Utah Shakespearean Festival. Early July.

Utah Shakespearean Festival. *351 W Center St. Phone 435/586-7878 (box office).* Southern Utah University campus. Shakespeare presented on outdoor stage (a replica of 16th-century Tiring House) and 750-seat indoor facility. Mon-Sat evenings; preplay activities. Children over 5 years only; babysitting at festival grounds. Late June-early Oct.

Utah Summer Games. *351 W Center St (84720). Phone 435/586-8421.* Olympic-style athletic events for amateur athletes. June.

Motels/Motor Lodges

★**ABBEY INN.** *940 W 200 N (01453). Phone 435/586-9966; toll-free 800/325-5411; fax 435/586-6522. www.abbeyinncedar.com.* 80 rooms, 2 story. June-mid-Sept: S, D $78-$96; each additional $5; suites $95-$150; under 12 free; lower rates rest of year. Complimentary continental breakfast. Check-out 11 am. TV; cable (premium), VCR available. In-room modem link. Laundry services. Indoor pool. Airport transportation. Near airport. Cr cds: A, C, D, DS, MC, V.

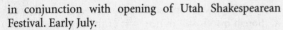

★★**BEST WESTERN TOWN AND COUNTRY INN.** *189 North Main (84720). Phone 435/586-9900; fax 435/586-1664. www.bwtowncountry.com.* 167 rooms, 2 story. S $71-$86; D $79-$94; suites $94-$115. Crib free. Complimentary continental breakfast. Check-out 11 am, check-in 2 pm. TV. Many refrigerators, microwaves. Laundry. Restaurant 7 am-10 pm. Game room. 2 pools, 1 indoor, whirlpool. Free airport transportation. Meeting rooms. Business services. Cr cds: A, C, D, DS, MC, V.

★**COMFORT INN.** *250 N 1100 W (84720). Phone 435/586-2082; toll-free 800/228-5750; fax 435/586-3193. www.comfortinn.com.* 93 rooms, 2 story. June-Sept: S, D $49-$106; each additional $5; under 12 free; lower rates rest of year. Crib free. Pet accepted. Complimentary continental breakfast. Check-out 11 am. TV; cable. Indoor pool, whirlpool. Free airport transportation. Business services. Cr cds: A, C, D, DS, JCB, MC, V.

Restaurant

★**MILT'S STAGE STOP.** *Hwy 14 Cedar Canyon Rd. (84720). Phone 435/586-9344.* Hours: 6-10 pm. Closed Thanksgiving, Dec 25. Dinner $12.75-$42. Bar. Salad bar. Children's menu. Reservations accepted. Cr cds: A, D, DS, MC, V.

Dinosaur National Monument (C-7)

See also Vernal

(7 miles N of Jensen on UT 149)

On August 17, 1909, paleontologist Earl Douglass discovered dinosaur bones in this area, including several nearly complete skeletons. Since then, this location has provided more skeletons, skulls, and bones of Jurassic-period dinosaurs than any other dig in the world. The dinosaur site comprises only 80 acres of this 325-square-mile park, which lies at the border of Utah and Colorado. The back country section, most of which is in Colorado, is a land of fantastic and deeply eroded canyons of the Green and Yampa rivers. Access to this backcountry section is via the Harpers Corner Road, starting at monument headquarters on US 40, 2 miles east of Dinosaur, Colorado. At Harpers Corner, the end of this 32-mile surfaced road, a 1-mile foot trail leads to a promontory overlooking the Green and Yampa rivers, more than 2,500 feet below. The entire area was named a national monument in 1915.

Utah's Dinosaur Quarry section can be entered from the junction of US 40 and UT 149, north of Jensen, 13 miles east of Vernal; approximately 7 miles north on UT 149 is the fossil exhibit. Another 5 miles north is Green River Campground, with 90 tent and trailer sites available mid-May to mid-September. A smaller campground, Rainbow Park, provides a small number of tent sites from May to November. Lodore, Deerlodge, and Echo Park campgrounds are available in Colorado. A fee is charged at Green River, Echo Park, and Lodore (water and rest rooms available).

Access to the Colorado back country section is via Harpers Corner Rd, starting at monument headquarters on US 40, 2 miles east of Dinosaur, Colorado. This 32-mile surfaced road ends at Harpers Corner. From there, a 1-mile foot trail leads to a promontory overlooking the Green and Yampa rivers, more than 2,500 feet below.

Because of snow, some areas of the monument are closed from approximately mid-Nov to mid-Apr. There is an entrance fee of up to $10 per vehicle. Golden Eagle, Golden Age, and Golden Access passports are accepted (see MAKING THE MOST OF YOUR TRIP). For more information, contact the Superintendent, 4545 E US 40, Dinosaur, CO 81610. Phone 970/374-3000.

What to See and Do

Backpacking. Backpacking is allowed by permit, obtainable at visitor centers; few marked trails exist.

⭐**Dinosaur Quarry Information Center.** Remarkable fossil deposit exhibit of 150 million-year-old dinosaur remains; preparation laboratory on display. (Daily; closed Jan 1, Thanksgiving, Dec 25)

Picnicking, hiking, fishing. *Phone 970/374-2468.* Harpers Corner area has picnic facilities, also picnicking at campgrounds. Self-guided nature trails (all year), guided nature walks. State fishing license required; boating permit required (obtainable by advance lottery at the Headquarters River Office). River rafting. On the Green and Yampa rivers, by advance permit from National Park Service or with concession-operated guided float trips. Information at River Office.

Fillmore (F-3)

See also Nephi, Richfield

Settled 1856 **Pop** 2,253 **Elev** 5,135 ft **Area code** 435
Zip 84631

Information Chamber of Commerce, City of Fillmore, 96 S Main St, PO Box 687; 435/743-6121

Fillmore, the seat of Millard County and Utah's territorial capital until 1856, is today a trading center for the surrounding farm and livestock region. It is a popular hunting and fishing area. A Ranger District office of the Fishlake National Forest is located here.

What to See and Do

Fishlake National Forest. *115 East 900 N. E on improved gravel road. Phone 435-896-9233.* (see RICHFIELD).

Territorial Statehouse State Park. *50 W Capitol Ave. Phone 435/743-5316.* Utah's first territorial capitol, built in the 1850s of red sandstone, is now a museum with an extensive collection of pioneer furnishings, pictures, Native American artifacts, and early documents; also rose garden. (Mon-Sat; closed Jan 1, Thanksgiving, Dec 25) **$**

Resort

⭐**BEST WESTERN PARADISE INN AND RESORT.** *905 N Main (84631). Phone 435/743-6895; fax 435/743-6892. www.bestwestern.com.* 80 rooms, 2 story. Mid-May-Oct: S, D $57-$63; each additional $3; lower rates rest of year. Crib $6. Pet accepted. TV; cable (premium). Heated pool; whirlpool. Restaurant 6 am-10 pm;

summer to 11 pm. Check-out 11 am. Business services available. Cr cds: A, C, D, DS, ER, MC, V.

🐾 🛏 ⚲ SC

Garden City (A-5)

See also Logan

Settled 1875 **Pop** 357 **Elev** 5,960 ft **Area code** 435
Zip 84028

Information Bear Lake Convention & Visitors Bureau, PO Box 26, Fish Haven, ID 83287; 208/945-2333 or 800/448-2327

Web www.bearlake.org

As was the case with many of Utah's towns, Garden City was settled by Mormon pioneers sent here from Salt Lake City. Today, it is a small resort town on the western shore of Bear Lake.

What to See and Do

Bear Lake. Covering 71,000 acres on the border of Utah and Idaho, this body of water is the state's second-largest freshwater lake. Approximately 20 miles long and 200 feet deep, it offers good fishing for mackinaw, rainbow trout, and the rare Bonneville Cisco. Boat rentals at several resorts. On the western shore is

> **Bear Lake State Park.** *147 W Logan Rd. 2 miles N on US 89. Phone 800/322-3770.* Three park areas include State Marina on west shore of lake, Rendezvous Beach on south shore, and Eastside area on east shore. Swimming, beach, waterskiing, fishing, ice fishing, boating (ramp, dock), sailing; hiking, mountain biking, cross-country skiing, snowmobiling, picnicking, tent and trailer sites (rest rooms, showers, hookups, dump station; fee). Visitor center. (Daily) **$$$**

Beaver Mountain Ski Area. *14 miles W via US 89. Phone 435/753-0921; 435/753-4822 (snow conditions).* Three double chairlifts, two surface lifts; patrol, school, rentals; day lodge, cafeteria. Twenty-two runs; vertical drop 1,600 feet. Half-day rates. (Dec-early Apr, daily) **$$$$**

Green River (F-6)

Settled 1878 **Pop** 973 **Elev** 4,079 ft **Area code** 435
Zip 84525

Information Green River Travel Council, 885 E Main St; 435/564-3526

Originally a mail relay station between Ouray, Colorado, and Salina, Utah, Green River now produces premium watermelons and cantaloupes on land irrigated by the Green River, one of Utah's largest rivers.

What to See and Do

Arches National Park. (see) *23 miles E on I-70 (US 50), then 54 miles S on US 191.*

Goblin Valley State Park. *450 S Green River Blvd. 50 miles W on I-70 (US 50), then 30 miles S on UT 24.* Phone 435/564-3633. Mile-wide basin filled with intricately eroded sandstone formations. Hiking, camping (rest rooms, showers, dump station). (Daily) **$$**

John Wesley Powell River History Museum. *885 E Main St.* Phone 435/564-3427. 20,000-square-foot museum sits on the banks of the Green River. Contains exhibits exploring geology and geography of area; auditorium with 20-minute multi-media presentation; river runner Hall of Fame. Green River Visitor Center (daily). Gift shop. Picnic area. (Daily; closed Jan 1, Thanksgiving, Dec 25) **$**

River trips. On the Colorado, Green, San Juan, and Dolores rivers.

    Colorado River & Trail Expeditions, Inc. *125 E and 1000 N sts (84525).* Phone 801/261-1789 or 800/253-7328. PO Box 57575, Salt Lake City 84157-0575. **$$$$**

    Holiday River and Bike Expeditions. *544 E 3900 S (84107).* Phone 801/266-2087 or 800/624-6323 (exc UT). 544 E 3900 S, Salt Lake City 84107. **$$$$**

    Moki Mac River Expeditions. *6006 S 1300 E.* Phone 801/268-6667 or 800/284-7280. PO Box 21242, Salt Lake City 84121. **$$$$**

Special Event

Melon Days. Third weekend in Sept.

Motels/Motor Lodges

★ **BEST WESTERN RIVER TERRACE MOTEL.** *880 E Main St (84525).* Phone 435/564-3401; fax 435/564-3403. www.bestwestern.com. 51 rooms, 2-3 story. No elevator. May-Oct: S, D $69-$79; higher rates some holidays and special events; lower rates rest of year. Check-out 11 am. TV; cable (premium). Whirlpool. On river. Cr cds: A, C, D, DS, MC, V.

D 🐾 ⊠

★ **RODEWAY INN WEST WINDS.** *525 E I-70 Business Loop (84525).* Phone 435/564-3421; toll-free 800/228-2000; fax 435/564-3282. www.rodeway.com. 42 rooms, 2 story. May-Oct: S, D $49-$55; each additional $5; suites $55-$65; under 18 free; lower rates rest of year. Crib free. TV; cable (premium). Restaurant adjacent open 24 hours. Check-out 11 am. Coin laundry. Meeting rooms. Cr cds: A, C, D, DS, ER, JCB, MC, V.

D ⊠ SC

Restaurant

★ **TAMARISK.** *870 E Main St (84525).* Phone 435/564-8109; fax 435/564-8590. American menu. Closed Thanksgiving, Dec 25. Buffet, breakfast, lunch, dinner. Children's menu. Totally nonsmoking. Cr cds: A, DS, MC, V. **$$**

D

Heber City (C-4)

See also Alta, Park City, Provo, Salt Lake City

Settled 1859 **Pop** 7,291 **Elev** 5,595 ft **Area code** 435 **Zip** 84032

Information Heber Valley Chamber of Commerce, 475 N Main St, PO Box 427; 435/654-3666

Web www.hebervalleycc.org

Located in a fertile, mountain-ringed valley, Heber City was once a commercial and livestock shipping center. Unusual crater mineral springs, called hot pots, are located 4 miles west near Midway. Mount Timpanogos, one of the most impressive mountains in the state, is to the southwest in the Wasatch Range. Good picnicking, fishing, and hunting areas abound. A Ranger District office of the Uinta National Forest (see PROVO) is located here.

What to See and Do

Deer Creek State Park. *Hwy 189. 8 miles SW on US 189.* Phone 435/654-0171. Swimming, fishing, boating (ramp); camping (fee; rest rooms, showers; dump and fish cleaning stations). (Daily) **$$$**

Heber Valley Railroad. *450 S 600 W, PO Box 609.* Phone 435/654-5601 or 801/581-9980 (in Salt Lake City). A 90-year-old steam-powered excursion train takes passengers through the farmlands of Heber Valley, along the shore of Deer Creek Lake and into Provo Canyon on various 1-hour to 4-hour trips. Restored coaches and open-air cars. Special trips some Fri, Sat evenings. Reservations required. (May-mid-Oct, Tue-Sun; mid-Oct-Nov, schedule varies; Dec-Apr, Mon-Sat) Contact **$$$$**

Timpanogos Cave National Monument. (see) *16 miles SW on US 189, then 12 miles NW on UT 92.*

Wasatch Mountain State Park. *1281 Warmsprings Dr. 2 miles NW off UT 224.* Phone 435/654-1791. Approximately 25,000 acres in Heber Valley. Fishing; hiking, 36-hole golf, snowmobiling, cross-country skiing, picnicking, restaurant, camping (fee; hookups, dump station). Visitor center. (Daily) Standard fees.

Special Events

Swiss Days. *55 S Center St. 4 miles W in Midway.* "Old country" games, activities, costumes. Fri and Sat before Labor Day.

Wasatch County Fair. *2843 S Daniels Rd.* Parades, exhibits, country market, livestock shows, rodeos, dancing. First weekend in Aug.

Motels/Motor Lodges

★ **DANISH VIKING LODGE.** *989 S Main St (84032). Phone 435/654-2202; toll-free 800/544-4066; fax 435/654-2770.* 34 rooms, 3 kitchen units, 1-2 story. Mid-May-mid-Sept and Christmas season: S $40-$49; D $49-$65; each additional $5; suite $99-$150; kitchen units $65-$95; under 18 free; package plans; lower rates rest of year. Crib $3. Pet accepted, some restrictions. Complimentary continental breakfast. Check-out 11 am. TV; cable (premium), VCR available. Refrigerators, microwaves. Coin laundry. Restaurant nearby. Playgrounds. Health club privileges, sauna. Pool, whirlpool. Downhill ski 12 miles, cross-country ski 7 miles. Picnic tables, grills. Cr cds: A, D, DS, MC, V.

★ **HIGH COUNTRY INN AND RV PARK.** *1000 S Main St (84032). Phone 435/654-0201; toll-free 800/345-9198.* 38 rooms. S $45-$55; D $65-$75; each additional $5; lower rates rest of year. Crib $5. TV; cable (premium). Heated pool; whirlpool. Playground. Complimentary continental breakfast. Restaurant adjacent. Check-out 11 am. Coin laundry. Downhill ski 20 miles; cross-country ski 5 miles. Refrigerators, microwaves. Picnic table. View of mountains. Cr cds: A, DS, MC, V.

Resort

★ ★ ★ **HOMESTEAD RESORT.** *700 N Homestead Dr, Midway (84049). Phone 435/654-1102; toll-free 800/327-7220; fax 435/654-5087. www.homesteadresort.com.* Surrounded by the Wasatch Mountains, this resort offers a truly delightful stay. Surrounded by lush gardens, this charming retreat welcomes guests with their country hospitality, quaint cottages, and rich history. 163 rooms, 1-2 story, 26 suites. S, D $130; suites $180-$325; condos $250-$600; ski, golf plans. TV; cable (premium), VCR available (movies). 2 pools, 1 indoor; whirlpool. Restaurant (See also SIMON'S FINE DINING). Bar. Check-out noon, check-in 4 pm. Meeting rooms. Business center. Gift shop. Lighted tennis. 18-hole golf. Cross-country ski 10 miles. Exercise equipment; sauna. Massage. Horse stables. Wagon and buggy rides. Lawn games. Historic country inn (1886); spacious grounds, gardens, duck ponds. Cr cds: A, C, D, DS, JCB, MC, V.

B&B/Small Inns

★ ★ ★ **THE BLUE BOAR INN.** *1235 Warm Springs Rd, Midway (84049). Phone 435/654-1400; toll-free 888/650-1400. www.theblueboarinn.com.* Utah's secluded and picturesque Heber Valley is home to the heartwarming Blue Boar Inn. The blissful quietude of this remote location is perfect for visitors wanting to unwind, yet be in relatively close proximity to the slopes and nightlife of the ski resorts of Deer Valley, The Canyons, and Sundance. During the summer months, nearby fly fishing and 54 holes of golf entertain guests. While the chandeliers are crafted of antlers and the furnishings are indicative of the region, the restaurant is a showpiece of fresh American cuisine. Decorated in a unique Austrian-influenced style, the guest rooms are enlivened with an amusing theme inspired by famous authors and poets. From the handmade willow bed of the Robert Frost and the whimsical design of the Lewis Carroll to the English cottage style of the William Butler Yeats and the exotic flavor of the Rudyard Kipling, each room attempts to capture its namesake's distinctive personality. 14 rooms, 2 story. D $150-$295. Restaurant 8 am-9 pm, closed Mon. Complimentary full breakfast. Check-out noon, check-in 3 pm. TV. cable (premium), VCR available. Golf. Tennis. Downhill skiing. Hiking trail. Business center. Concierge service. Free airport transportation. Cr cds: A, DS, MC, V.

Restaurants

★ ★ ★ **THE BLUE BOAR INN RESTAURANT.** *1235 Warm Springs Rd, Midway (84049). 435/654-1400. www.theblueboarinn.com.* Well worth the 20-minute drive from Park City, this charming Tyrolean chalet offers some of the best New American cuisine in Utah. Flavors are clean and fresh, as the chef endeavors to accentuate the natural quality of each ingredient. The menu changes periodically to capture the best produce and freshest seafood available. Specialties: rack of boar, duck, salmon. Hours: 11:30 am-2:30 pm, 5:30 pm-9:30 pm; Sun brunch 9 am-2 pm. Closed Mon. Lunch $6-$11; dinner $17-$28. Beer, wine. Reservations accepted. Cr cds: A, DS, MC, V.

★ ★ ★ **SIMON'S FINE DINING.** *700 N Homestead Dr, Midway (84032). Phone 435/654-1102; fax 435/654-5087.* Dine in an elegant country setting in the dining room or outside on the deck. Hours: 5:30-10 pm; Sun brunch 10 am-2 pm, closed Mon, Tues. Dinner, complete meals: $23-$34. Sun brunch $17.95. Children's menu. Reservations accepted. Outdoor seating. Daily specials. Credit cards accepted.

Kanab (I-3)

Founded 1870 **Pop** 3,564 **Elev** 4,909 ft **Area code** 435
Zip 84741

Information Kane County Office of Tourism, 78 E 100 S;
435/644-5033 or 800/733-5263

Web www.kaneutah.com

Located at the base of the Vermilion Cliffs, this city began
around Fort Kanab, built in 1864. Native Americans, however, forced the abandonment of the fort. Later, Mormon
missionaries made Kanab a permanent settlement. The
city's regular economy revolves around tourism. Since
1922, more than 200 Hollywood productions have used
the sand dunes, canyons, and lakes surrounding Kanab
as their settings. Some movie-set towns can still be seen.
Kanab is within a 1 1/2 hour drive from the north rim
of the Grand Canyon, Zion, and Bryce Canyon national
parks, Cedar Breaks and Pipe Spring national monuments,
and Glen Canyon National Recreation Area.

What to See and Do

Coral Pink Sand Dunes State Park. *Yellowjacket and Hancock rds. 8 miles NW on US 89, then 12 miles SW on county
road. Phone 435/648-2800.* Six square miles of very colorful, windswept sandhills. Hiking, picnicking, tent and
trailer sites (fee; showers, dump station). Off-highway
vehicles allowed; exploring, photography. (Daily) **$$**

Glen Canyon National Recreation Area/Lake Powell.
*68 miles E via US 89, at Wahweap Lodge and Marina.
Phone 928/608-6404.* (see PAGE, AZ); access in Utah at
Bullfrog Marina (see LAKE POWELL).

Grand Canyon Scenic Flights. *2 1/2 miles S on US 89 A.
Phone 435/644-2299.* Flights to Grand Canyon during
daylight hours; flight covering Bryce Canyon and Zion
national parks, Lake Powell, and Coral Pink Sand Dunes.
(All-year) **$$$$**

Pipe Spring National Monument. (see ARIZONA) *20
miles W on US 389, in Arizona. Phone 435/643-7105.*

Zion National Park. (see) *17 miles NW on US 89, then 25
miles W on UT 9.*

Motels/Motor Lodges

★ **BEST WESTERN RED HILLS.** *125 W Center St
(84741). Phone 435/644-2675; toll-free 800/830-2675; fax
435/644-5919. www.kanabbestwestern.com.* 75 rooms,
2 story. May-Oct: S, D $89; each additional $5; lower rates
rest of year. Check-out 11 am, check-in 3 pm. TV; cable.
Heated pool; whirlpool. Cr cds: A, C, D, DS, MC, V.

[D] [≈] [✕] [≋] [SC]

★ **FOUR SEASONS INN.** *36 N 300 W (84741). Phone
435/644-2635; fax 435/644-5895.* 41 rooms, 2 story. Apr-
Oct: S, D $68-$71; each additional $5; lower rates rest of
year. Crib $5. Pet accepted. Check-out 11 am. TV; cable.
Restaurant 6:30 am-10 pm. Pool, wading pool. Business
services. Gift shop. Cr cds: A, C, D, DS, MC, V.

[🐾] [≈] [SC]

★ **PARRY LODGE.** *89 E Center St (84741). Phone
435/644-2601; toll-free 800/748-4104; fax 435/644-2605.
www.infowest.com/parry.* 89 rooms, 1-2 story. May-Oct:
S $30-$60; D $35-$75; each additional $6; family rates;
lower rates rest of year. Closed Dec-mid-March. Crib $6.
Pet accepted; $5. Check-out 11 am. TV; cable. Laundry.
Restaurant 7 am-noon, 6-10 pm. Heated pool. Business
services. Autographed pictures of movie stars displayed in
lobby. Cr cds: A, DS, MC, V.

[D] [🐾] [≈] [≋]

★ **SHILO INN.** *296 W 100 N (84741). Phone 435/
644-2562; toll-free 800/222-2244; fax 435/644-5333.
www.shiloinns.com.* 118 rooms, 3 story. Mid-Apr-Sept:
S, D $69.95-$79.95; lower rates rest of year. Pet accepted;
fee. Complimentary continental breakfast. Check-out
noon. TV. Whirlpool. Free airport transportation.
Cr cds: A, C, D, DS, MC, V.

[D] [🐾] [⚡] [✕] [≋] [SC]

Restaurant

★ **HOUSTON'S TRAIL'S END.** *32 E Center St
(84741). Phone 435/644-2488; fax 435/644-8148.
www.redrockride.com.* Closed Thanksgiving-Mar 1.
Breakfast $2.65-$6.50, lunch $3.95-$9.95, dinner $5-$15.
Children's menu. Cr cds: A, C, D, DS, ER, MC, V.

[D]

Lake Powell (I-5)

See also Page, AZ

What to See and Do

Lake Powell. Lake Powell, formed by the Glen Canyon
Dam on the Colorado River, is located in Glen Canyon
National Recreation Area. It stretches 186 miles, has
more than 1,900 miles of shoreline, is the second-largest
man-made lake in the United States, and is located in the
second-largest canyon in the US. The lake is named for
John Wesley Powell, the one-armed explorer who, in 1869,
successfully navigated the Colorado River through Glen
Canyon and the Grand Canyon and later became director
of the US Geological Survey.

Boat trips on Lake Powell. *Bullfrog Marina on UT
276 (84531). From Bullfrog or Halls Crossing marinas,
both on UT 276. Phone 800/528-6154.* Trips include

Canyon Explorer tour (2 1/2 hours) and all-day Rainbow Bridge National Monument tour; also houseboat and powerboat rentals. Reservations advised. (Daily)

Glen Canyon National Recreation Area (Bullfrog Marina). *Bullfrog Marina on UT 276 (84533). Phone 435/684-2243.* Additional access and recreational activities available at Hite Marina, north end of lake. This boasts more than 1 million acres with year-round recreation area, swimming, fishing, boating, boat tours and trips, boat rentals and repairs; picnicking, camping, tent and trailer sites (full hookups; fee); lodgings. A ranger station and visitor center is located in Bullfrog on UT 276 (Apr-Oct, daily).

Lake Powell Ferry. *Bullfrog Marina on UT 276 (85431). Phone 435/538-1030 or 435/684-3000* (Lake Powell). Passenger vehicles. Approximately 3-mile trip between Bullfrog and Hall's Crossing saves 130 miles driving around lake. (Daily; reduced hours in winter) Contact Bullfrog Marina. **$$$$**

Motel/Motor Lodge

★**DEFIANCE HOUSE LODGE.** *Hwy 276. Phone 435/684-2233; toll-free 800/528-6154; fax 435/684-3114.* 48 units, 8 cottages, 2 story. S, D $115-$130; each additional $10; suites $59-$130; cottages $75-$175; boating tour plans; lower rates rest of year. Crib free. Pet accepted. Check-out 11 am, check-in 3 pm. TV; cable. Balconies. Coin laundry. Dining room 7 am-8 pm; summer to midnight. Bar 5-9 pm; summer to midnight. Playground. Airport transportation. Sundries, gift shop. Anasazi motif; décor, artifacts. On lake; swimming. Cr cds: A, C, D, DS, MC, V.

D 🐾 ⚓

Loa (G-4)

Pop 525 **Elev** 7,060 ft **Area code** 435 **Zip** 84747

This town was named Loa because of the volcano-like appearance of a nearby mountain. A Ranger District office of the Fishlake National Forest (see RICHFIELD) is located here.

What to See and Do

Capitol Reef National Park. (see) *Approximately 23 miles E via UT 24.*

Escalante State Park. *65 miles S via UT 12, then 1 mile W, near Escalante. Phone 435/826-4466.* Petrified forest; mineralized wood and dinosaur bones. Swimming, fishing, boating (ramps) at reservoir; hiking, bird-watching, picnicking, camping (fee; rest rooms, showers, dump station). (Daily) Standard fees. **$$**

Logan (A-4)

See also Brigham City, Garden City

Founded 1856 **Pop** 42,670 **Elev** 4,535 ft **Area code** 435 **Zip** 84321

Information Logan Convention & Visitors Bureau/Bridgerland Travel Region, 160 N Main; 435/752-2161 or 800/882-4433

Web www.bridgerland.com

Logan, situated in the center of beautiful Cache Valley, is surrounded by snowcapped mountains. The city received its name from an early trapper, Ephraim Logan. Begun by Mormons who were dedicated to living from fruits of the soil, little was sold in Logan's early days except timber and farm produce. The change to a more industrialized economic base came about slowly. Now the city of Logan is the location of Utah State University, five electronics plants, space technology, book printing, plastics, baking, and meat-packing plants, as well as specialized woodworking and locally made craft and collectible shops.

What to See and Do

Daughters of the Utah Pioneers Museum. *158 S 500 W St. Phone 435/752-5139.* Exhibits depict Utah's past. 160 N Main, in Chamber of Commerce Building. (Mon-Fri) **FREE**

Hyrum State Park. *405 W 300 S. 12 miles S, off US 89/90. Phone 435/245-6866.* A 450-acre reservoir with beach swimming, waterskiing, fishing, ice fishing, boating (ramp, dock), sailing; picnicking, camping (trailer parking). (Year-round) Standard fees. **$$**

Mormon Tabernacle. *50 N Main. Phone 435/755-5598.* (1891) Gray limestone example of early Mormon building; seats 1,800. Genealogy library. (Mon-Fri)

Mormon Temple. *175 N 300 E. Phone 435/752-3611.* (1884) The site for this massive, castellated limestone structure was chosen by Brigham Young, who also broke ground for it in 1877. Grounds are open all year, but the temple is closed to the general public.

Utah State University. *7th N and 7th E sts (84322). (Tours) Phone 435/797-1129.* (1888) 20,100 students. On campus is the Nora Eccles Harrison Museum of Art (Mon-Fri; closed holidays, also Thanksgiving weekend, Dec 22-Jan 2; free).

Wasatch-Cache National Forest, Logan Canyon. *1500 E US 89. Phone 435/755-3620.* Fishing, back country trails, hunting, winter sports, picnicking, camping. Fees charged at most recreation sites. (Daily) E on US 89 National Forest (scenic byway). A Ranger District office is located in Logan at 1500 E US 89.

Willow Park Zoo. *419 W 700 S. Phone 435/750-9893.* Small but attractive zoo with shady grounds and especially good bird-watching of migratory species. (Daily; closed Jan 1, Thanksgiving, Dec 25) **DONATION**

Special Events

American West Heritage Center. *7700 Old Main Hill. Hwy 8991 in Wellsville. Phone 435/245-6050.* Pioneer and Native American crafts fair, art exhibition, antique quilt show; frontier town; medicine man show; log construction; Dutch-oven cooking demonstration. Late July-early Aug.

Cache County Fair. *400 S 500 W.* Rodeo, horse races, exhibits. Early Aug.

Utah Festival Opera Company. *59 S 100 W.* July-Aug.

Motels/Motor Lodges

★ ★ **BEST WESTERN BAUGH MOTEL.** *153 S Main St (84321). Phone 435/752-5220; fax 435/752-3251. www.bestwestern.com.* 77 rooms, 1-2 story. S $59-$92; D $65-$75; each additional $6. Crib $4. Check-out 11 am. TV; cable (premium), VCR available. Refrigerators, microwaves, fireplaces. Restaurant 6 am-10 pm; Sun 8 am-2 pm. Room service. Health club privileges. Heated pool. Meeting rooms. Business services. Cr cds: A, C, D, DS, MC, V.

[D] [≈] [⊠] [SC]

★ **COMFORT INN.** *447 N Main St (84321). Phone 435/752-9141; fax 435/752-9723. www.comfortinn.com.* 83 rooms, 2 story. S $50-$63; D $58-$60; each additional $4; suites $89; under 18 free. Crib $5. Complimentary continental breakfast. Check-out noon. TV; cable. In-room modem link. Refrigerator in suites. Valet services. Coin laundry. Restaurant adjacent. Exercise equipment. Indoor pool, whirlpool. Cross-country ski 20 miles. Meeting rooms. Business services. Cr cds: A, C, D, DS, ER, JCB, MC, V.

[D] [≈] [≈] [☩] [✈] [⊠] [SC]

★ **DAYS INN.** *364 S Main (84321). Phone 435/753-5623. www.daysinn.com.* 64 rooms, 2 story, 20 kitchen units. S, D $36-$78; each additional $4; kitchen units $48-$56; under 12 free; weekly rates Sept-May. Crib free. Pet accepted. TV; cable. Indoor pool. Complimentary continental breakfast. Restaurant nearby. Check-out 11 am. Coin laundry. Cross-country ski 20 miles. Many refrigerators; some in-room whirlpools. Cr cds: A, C, D, DS, JCB, MC, V.

[D] [🐾] [⚓] [≈] [≈] [🎿] [⊠]

B&B/Small Inns

★ ★ ★ **THE ANNIVERSARY INN.** *169 E Center St (84321). Phone 435/752-3443; toll-free 800/574-7605; fax 435/752-8550. www.anniversaryinn.com.* This unique inn offers guests a truly remarkable stay. Guest rooms are all charmingly unique, each appointed with its own romantic theme. From the Jesse James Hideout to the Aphrodite's Court and the Space Odyssey, each room is guaranteed to tickle the senses. 21 rooms, 4 suites. S, D $99-$209; suites $159-$209. Adults only. Complimentary continental breakfast. Check-out noon, check-in 5 pm. TV; cable, VCR available. Microwaves. Restaurant nearby. Lobby in historic mansion (1879); Oriental rugs, period furniture. Special theme suites, such as Swiss family, and grand bridal suite, are uniquely decorated. Totally nonsmoking. Cr cds: A, DS, MC, V.

[≈] [⊠]

★ ★ ★ **LOGAN HOUSE INN.** *168 N 100 E (84321). Phone 435/752-7727; toll-free 800/478-7459; fax 435/752-0092. www.loganhouseinn.com.* This historic property, fully restored with leaded stained-glass windows over the main staircase, was built at the turn of the century. It services leisure or business travelers and is close to restaurants, theaters, and performing arts. The setting is landscaped with lilac bushes, evergreens, and maple trees. 6 rooms, 2 story. S, D $99-$175; each additional $15; golf, ski plans. Complimentary breakfast. Check-out 11 am, check-in 3-5 pm. TV; VCR available. In-room modem link. Fireplaces. Laundry services. Concierge. Built in 1898; totally nonsmoking. Cr cds: A, D, DS, JCB, MC, V.

[D] [⊠]

★ ★ ★ **PROVIDENCE INN.** *10 S Main (84332). Phone 435/752-3432; toll-free 800/480-4943; fax 435/752-3482. www.providenceinn.com.* As part of "The Old Rock Church" building, this historic bed and breakfast has rooms decorated in various periods: Early American, Victorian, and Georgian. A hearty breakfast is provided and guests may sit in the parlor and enjoy the fireplace and selection of reading material or wander through the landscaped grounds. 17 rooms, 3 story. June-Sept: S $69-$159; D $99-$229; each additional $10; suite $119-$149; under 5 free. TV; cable, VCR (movies). Complimentary full breakfast. Restaurant nearby. Check-out 11 am, check-in 4 pm. Business services available. In-room modem link. Coin laundry. Cross-country ski 5 miles. Whirlpools in rooms. Built in 1869; accurately restored. Totally nonsmoking. Cr cds: A, DS, MC, V.

[D] [⊠] [≈]

Restaurants

★ **BLUEBIRD.** *19 N Main St (84321). Phone 435/752-3155.* Hours: 11 am-9:30 pm; Fri, Sat to 10 pm. Closed Sun; Thanksgivng, Dec 25. Lunch $3-$10.45, dinner $7.50-$11. Children's menu. Cr cds: A, DS, MC, V.

[D]

★ ★ **GIA'S RESTAURANT AND DELI.** *119 S Main St (84321). Phone 435/752-8384; fax 435/750-6595.* Italian menu. Hours: 11 am-9:30 pm; Fri, Sat to 10 pm. Closed Dec 25. Lunch $6-$14.75. Dinner $6-$15.50. Children's menu. Reservations accepted. Cr cds: A, D, DS, MC, V.

D SC

Moab (F-6)

Founded 1879 **Pop** 4,779 **Elev** 4,025 ft **Area code** 435 **Zip** 84532

Information Moab Area Travel Council, PO Box 550; 435/259-8825, 435/259-1370, or 800/635-6622

Web www.discovermoab.com

The first attempt to settle this valley was made in 1855, but Moab, named after an isolated area in the Bible, was not permanently settled until 1880. Situated on the Colorado River at the foot of the LaSal Mountains, Moab was a sleepy agricultural town until after World War II, when uranium exploration and production and oil and potash development made it boom. Today, tourism and moviemaking help make it a thriving community. A Ranger District office of the Manti-LaSal National Forest is located here, as are headquarters for Canyonlands and Arches national parks.

What to See and Do

Arches National Park. *5 miles NW on US 191.*

Canyonlands By Night. *1861 S Hwy 191. PO Box 328. Leaves dock at bridge, 2 miles N on US 191. Phone 435/259-5261.* Two-hour boat trip with sound-and-light presentation highlights history of area. (Apr-mid-Oct, daily, leaves at sundown, weather permitting) Reservations required; tickets must be purchased at office. **$$$$**

Canyonlands Field Institute. *1320 S Hwy 191. Phone 435/259-7750.* Educational seminars/trips featuring geology, natural and cultural history, endangered species, Southwestern literature. Many programs use Canyonlands and Arches national parks as outdoor classrooms. (Mon-Fri) **$$$$**

Canyonlands National Park. *N district: 9 miles N on US 191, then 21 miles SW on UT 313.*

Dan O'Laurie Canyon Country Museum. *118 E Center St. Phone 435/259-7985.* Exhibits on local history, archaeology, geology, uranium, minerals of the area. Walking tour information. (Mon-Sat; closed holidays) **$**

Dead Horse Point State Park. *313 State Rd. 9 miles NW on US 191, then 22 miles SW on UT 313. Phone 435/259-2614.* Promontory rising 2,000 feet above the Colorado River, this island mesa offers views of the LaSal Mountains, Canyonlands National Park, and the Colorado River. Approximately 5,200 acres in region of gorges, cliffs, buttes, and mesas. Visitor center, museum. Picnicking,

limited drinking water, camping (fee; electricity, dump station). Trailer parking. (Daily) **$**

Hole 'n the Rock. *11037 S Hwy 191. 15 miles S via US 191. Phone 435/686-2250.* A 5,000-square-foot dwelling carved into huge sandstone rock. Picnic area with stone tables and benches. (Daily; closed Jan 1, Thanksgiving, Dec 25) **$$**

Manti-LaSal National Forest, LaSal Division. *2290 Resource Blvd. 8 miles S on US 191, then 5 miles E. Contact the Ranger District office, 125 W 200 S. Phone 435/259-7155; or the Forest Supervisor, 599 W Price River Dr, Price 84501, phone 435/637-2817.* The land of the forest's LaSal Division is similar in color and beauty to some parts of the Grand Canyon, but also includes high mountains nearing 13,000 feet and pine and spruce forests. Swimming, fishing; hiking, hunting. (See MONTICELLO, PRICE) **FREE**

Rim Tours. *1233 S Hwy 191. Phone 435/259-5223 or 800/626-7335.* Guided mountain bike tours in canyon country and the Colorado Rockies. Vehicle support for camping tours. Daily and overnight trips; combination bicycle/river trips available. **$$$$**

River trips. *Phone 435/259-8825.* On the Green and Colorado rivers, includes Canyonlands National Park, Lake Powell (see both), and Cataract Canyon.

Adrift Adventures. *378 N Main St. Phone 435/259-8594 or 800/874-4483.* Oar, paddle, and motorized trips available; 1 to 7 days. (Early Apr-late Oct) **$$$$**

Canyon Voyages. *211 N Main St. Phone 435/259-6007 or 800/733-6007.* Kayaking, whitewater rafting. (Early Apr-Oct) **$$$$**

Colorado River & Trail Expeditions, Inc. *5058 S 300 W.* **$$$$**

Sheri Griffith River Expeditions. *2231 S US 191. PO Box 1324. Phone 435/259-8229 or 800/332-2439.* Choice of rafts: oarboats, motorized rafts, paddleboats, or inflatable kayaks; 1- to 5-day trips; instruction available. (May-Oct) **$$$$**

Tex's Riverways. *691 N 500 W. PO Box 67. Phone 435/259-5101.* Flatwater canoe trips, 4 to 10 days. Confluence pick-ups available, jet boat cruises. (Mar-Oct) **$$$$**

Scenic Air Tours. *N Highway 191. 18 miles N on US 191, at Canyonlands Field. Contact Redtail Aviation. Phone 435/259-7421 or 435/564-3412.* Flights over Canyonlands National Park and various other tours. (All-year; closed Jan 1, Thanksgiving, Dec 25) **$$$$**

Tag-A-Long Expeditions. *452 N Main St. Phone 435/259-8946 or 800/453-3292.* One- to seven-day whitewater rafting trips on the Green and Colorado rivers; jetboat trips on the Colorado River; jetboat trips and four-wheel-drive tours into Canyonlands National Park; winter four-wheel-drive tours (Nov-Feb). Also Canyon Classics, 1-day jetboat trips with cultural performing arts programs. (Apr-mid-Oct). **$$$$**

Trail rides. Pack Creek Ranch. *La Sal Mountian Loop Rd. PO Box 1270. Phone 435/259-5505.* Horseback rides, ranging from one to 1 1/2 hours, in foothills of LaSal Mountain. Guided tours for small groups; reservations required. (Mar-Oct; upon availability) **$$$$**

Special Events

Butch Cassidy Days PRCA Rodeo. Second weekend in June.

Jeep Safari. Easter week and weekend.

Moab Music Festival. *59 S Main St.* First two weeks in Sept.

Motels/Motor Lodges

★**BEST WESTERN CANYONLANDS INN.** *16 S Main St (84532). Phone 435/259-2300; toll-free 800/780-7234; fax 435/259-2301. www.bestwestern.com.* 114 rooms, 2 story. D $99.95-$109.95; each additional $8; under 12 free; golf plan. Complimentary breakfast. Check-out 11 am, check-in 4 pm. TV; cable (premium), VCR available. In-room modem link. Laundry services. Restaurant noon-11 pm. Exercise equipment. Indoor/outdoor pool. Totally nonsmoking. Cr cds: A, C, D, DS, MC, V.

D 🏊 🐕 🖭 SC

★★**BEST WESTERN GREENWELL INN.** *105 S Main St (84532). Phone 435/259-6151; toll-free 800/780-7234; fax 435/259-4397. www.bestwestern.com.* 73 rooms, 1-2 story. D $69-$131; each additional $6; under 12 free. Check-out 11 am, check-in 3 pm. TV; cable (premium). In-room modem link. Restaurant 7 am-9 pm. Exercise equipment. Whirlpool. Cr cds: A, C, D, DS, JCB, MC, V.

🐕 🖭

★ **BOWEN MOTEL.** *169 N Main St (84532). Phone 435/259-7132; toll-free 800/874-5439; fax 435/259-6641. www.bowenmotel.com.* 40 rooms, 2 story. D $65-$75; each additional $6. Pet accepted; fee. Complimentary continental breakfast. Check-out 11 am, check-in 3 pm. TV; cable (premium). In-room modem link. Totally nonsmoking. Cr cds: A, D, DS, JCB, MC, V.

🐾 🖭

★ **LANDMARK INN.** *168 N Main St (84532). Phone 435/259-6147; toll-free 800/441-6147; fax 435/259-5556. www.moab-utah.com/landmark/motel.htm.* 36 rooms, 2 story. D $68-$86; each additional $4-$6. Complimentary continental breakfast. Check-out 11 am, check-in 2 pm. TV; cable (premium). In-room modem link. Restaurant 7 am-midnight. Whirlpool. Cr cds: A, C, D, DS, MC, V.

D 🖭

B&B/Small Inns

★ ★ ★ **CASTLE VALLEY INN.** *424 Amber Ln; HC 64 Box 2602 (84532). Phone 435/259-6012; toll-free 888/466-6012; fax 435/259-1501. www.castlevalleyinn.com.* Guests will enjoy watching the deer and a variety of birds which come to feed on the property. 5 rooms, 3 kitchen units. Apr-late Nov: S, D $100-$200; cabins $155. Complimentary breakfast. Check-out 11 am, check-in 3-9 pm. Lawn games. Cr cds: DS, MC, V.

🛴 ❄ 🖭

★ ★ **SUNFLOWER HILL BED AND BREAKFAST.** *185 N 300 E (84532). Phone 435/259-2974; fax 435/259-3065. www.sunflowerhill.com.* 15 rooms, 2 story. No room phones. D $139-$199; each additional $20. Children over 10 years only. Complimentary full breakfast. Check-out 11 am, check-in 3-6 pm. TV; VCR available. Turn-of-the-century adobe farmhouse, cottage amid gardens. Totally nonsmoking. Cr cds: A, DS, MC, V.

🖭 SC

Guest Ranch

★ ★ **PACK CREEK RANCH.** *Pack Creek Ranch Rd (84532). Phone 435/259-5505. www.packcreekranch.com.* 10 rooms. No room phones. D $180-$300. Pet accepted. Check-out 11 am, check-in 3 pm. Dining room 7-10 am, 6:30-8:30 pm. Sauna. Pool, whirlpool. Hiking. Cr cds: DS, MC, V.

D 🐾 🛴 ❄ 🏊 🏃 🖭

Restaurant

★ ★ **CENTER CAFE.** *60 N 100 W (84532). Phone 435/259-4295; fax 435/259-0158.* Hours: 5:30-10 pm. Closed Thanksgiving, Dec 25; also Jan. Reservations accepted. Continental menu. Service bar. A la carte entrees: dinner $16-$27. Specializes in fresh fish, grilled meats. Own pastries. Original artwork. Totally nonsmoking. Cr cds: DS, MC, V.

D

Monticello (H-7)

See also Blanding

Founded 1887 **Pop** 1,806 **Elev** 7,066 ft **Area code** 435 **Zip** 84535

Information San Juan County Visitor Center, 117 S Main St, PO Box 490; 435/587-3235 or 800/574-4386

Web www.southeastutah.org

The highest county seat in Utah (San Juan County), Monticello was named for Thomas Jefferson's Virginia home. On the east slope of the Abajo Mountains, the elevation makes the weather delightful but the growing season short. Livestock raising, dry farming, and tourism are the chief industries.

What to See and Do

Canyonlands National Park. (see) *S district: 14 miles N on US 191, then 35 miles W on UT 211 to Squaw Flats Campground Area.*

Canyon Rims Recreation Area. *82 E Dogwood St. 20 miles N on US 191.* Anticline and Needles overlooks into Canyonlands National Park are located here, as are Wind Whistle and Hatch campgrounds.

Manti-LaSal National Forest, LaSal Division. *2 1/2 miles W. Contact the Ranger District Office, 62 E 100 N. Phone phone 435/587-2041; or the Forest Supervisor, 599 W Price River Dr, Price 84501, phone 435/637-2817.* (See MOAB, PRICE) The forest land of this division ranges from red rock canyons to high alpine terrain. Ancient ruins and rock art contrast with pine and spruce forests and aspen-dotted meadows. Fishing; hiking, snowmobiling, Cross-country skiing, hunting, camping (fee). **FREE**

Special Events

Monticello Pioneer Days. Parade, booths, food, games, sports. Weekend nearest July 24.

San Juan County Fair & Rodeo. Second weekend in Aug.

Motel/Motor Lodge

★**BEST WESTERN WAYSIDE MOTOR INN.** *197 E Central Ave (84535). Phone 435/587-2261; toll-free 800/633-9700; fax 435/587-2920. www.bestwestern.com.* 38 rooms. D $69-$74; each additional $5; under 12 free. Pet accepted. Complimentary continental breakfast. Check-out 11 am, check-in 2 pm. TV; cable (premium). Restaurant. Cross-country ski 6 miles. Cr cds: A, C, D, DS, MC, V.

🐾 🕭 ⛷ 🖥 SC

Monument Valley

(see Kayenta, AZ)

Natural Bridges National Monument (H-6)

(4 miles S of Blanding on US 191, then 36 miles W on UT 95, then 4 miles N on UT 275)

This 7,439-acre area of fantastically eroded and colorful terrain, made a national monument in 1908, features three natural bridges, all with Hopi names: Sipapu, a 268-foot span, and Kachina, a 204-foot span, are in White Canyon, a major tributary gorge of the Colorado River; Owachomo, a 180-foot span, is near Armstrong Canyon, which joins White Canyon. Sipapu is the second-largest natural bridge in the world. From 650 to 2,000 years ago, the ancestral Puebloan people lived in this area, leaving behind cliff dwelling ruins and pictographs that can be viewed today. Bridge View Drive, a 9-mile-loop road, provides views of the three bridges from rim overlooks. There are hiking trails to each bridge within the canyon. In the park is a visitor center (daily; closed holidays in winter) and a primitive campground with 13 tent and trailer sites (all-year, fee; 26-foot combined-length limit). Car and passenger ferry service across Lake Powell is available (see LAKE POWELL). There is a $6 per vehicle entrance fee; Golden Eagle, Golden Age, Golden Access Passports are accepted (see MAKING THE MOST OF YOUR TRIP). Contact the Superintendent, Box 1, Lake Powell 84533; phone 435/692-1234.

Nephi (E-4)

See also Fillmore, Payson

Settled 1851 **Pop** 4,733 **Elev** 5,133 ft **Area code** 435

Information Juab Travel Council, 4 S Main, PO Box 71, 84648; 435/623-5203 or 435/623-2411

What to See and Do

Yuba State Park. *I-15, exit 202 (84639). 30 miles S via I-15, near Scipio. Phone 435/758-2611.* Waterskiing and walleyed pike fishing are the big attractions of this lake, as well as sandy beaches. Swimming, waterskiing, fishing, boating (ramps); picnicking, camping (fee; rest rooms, showers, dump station). (Daily) **$$$**

Special Event

Ute Stampede Rodeo. *795 S Main St. Phone 435/623-5608.* Three-day festival featuring horse and mammoth parades, carnival, PRCA rodeo, contests, arts and crafts, concessions. Second weekend in July.

Motels/Motor Lodges

★ **BEST WESTERN PARADISE INN.** *1025 S Main (84648). Phone 435/623-0624. www.bestwestern.com.* 40 rooms, 2 story. Mid-May-Oct: S $59; D $69; lower rates rest of year. Pet accepted, some restrictions. Complimentary continental breakfast. Check-out noon. TV; cable (premium). Heated pool; whirlpool. Cr cds: A, C, D, DS, MC, V.

🐾 ⛷ 🏊 📶

★ **ROBERTA'S COVE MOTOR INN.** *2250 S Main (84648). Phone 435/623-2629; toll-free 800/456-6460; fax 435/623-2245.* 43 air-cooled rooms, 2 story. S, D $39-$45; each additional $5; higher rates Ute Stampede. TV; cable (premium). Pool; whirlpool. Coffee in rooms. Restaurant opposite 6 am-9:30 pm. Check-out 11 am. Coin laundry. Cr cds: A, C, D, DS, MC, V.

🏊 📶

B&B/Small Inns

★ ★ **WHITMORE MANSION.** *110 S Main St (84648). Phone 435/623-2047. www.whitmoremansion.com.* 9 rooms, 5 with shower only, 3 story, 2 suites. No room phones. S, D $78-$128; suites $118. TV in common room, VCR available (movies). Complimentary continental breakfast. Restaurant nearby. Check-out 11 am, check-in 4-8 pm. Business services available. Street parking. Cross-country ski 10 miles. Recreation room. Built in 1898; antiques. Totally nonsmoking. Cr cds: A, DS, MC, V.

🎿 🏊 📶

Ogden (B-3)

See also Brigham City, Salt Lake City

Settled 1844 **Pop** 77,226 **Elev** 4,300 ft **Area code** 801

Information Convention & Visitors Bureau, 2501 Wall Ave, 84401; 801/627-8288 or 800/255-8824

Web www.ogdencvb.org

The streets of Ogden, fourth-largest city in Utah, were laid out by Brigham Young in traditional Mormon geometrical style: broad, straight, and bordered by poplar, box elder, elm, and cottonwood trees. In the 1820s and 1830s, Ogden was a rendezvous and wintering place for trappers, who wandered as far afield as California and Oregon. In 1846, Miles Goodyear, the first white settler, built a cabin and trading post, Fort Buenaventura, here. The next year he sold out to the Mormons. During the last 30 years of the 19th century, Ogden was an outfitting center for trappers and hunters heading north. Its saloons and gambling halls were typical of a frontier town, and there was considerable friction between the Mormons and the "gentiles." With the coming of the railroad, however, Ogden became one of the few cities in Utah whose inhabitants were not primarily Mormons.

Today, Ogden is a commercial and industrial center. Hill Air Force Base is nearby. Bernard DeVoto—American novelist, journalist, historian, and critic, best known for his history of the western frontier—was born in Ogden, as was John M. Browning, inventor of the automatic rifle. Mount Ben Lomond, north of the city in the Wasatch Range, was the inspiration for the logo of Paramount Pictures. A Ranger District office of the Wasatch-Cache National Forest (see SALT LAKE CITY) is located in Ogden.

What to See and Do

Daughters of Utah Pioneers Museum & Relic Hall. *2148 Grant Ave, in Tabernacle Sq. Phone 801/393-4460 or 801/621-5224.* Old handicrafts, household items, pioneer clothing, furniture, and portraits of those who came to Utah prior to the railroad of 1869. Also Miles Goodyear's cabin, the first permanent house built in Utah. (Mid-May-mid-Sept, Mon-Sat) **FREE**

Eccles Community Art Center. *2580 Jefferson Ave. Phone 801/392-6935.* A 19th-century castlelike mansion that hosts changing art exhibits, plus has a dance studio and an outdoor sculpture and floral garden. (Mon-Sat; closed holidays) **FREE**

Fort Buenaventura State Park. *2450 A Ave. Phone 801/621-4808.* The exciting era of mountain men is brought to life on this 32-acre site, where the actual fort, Ogden's first settlement, was built in 1846 by Miles Goodyear. The fort has been reconstructed according to archaeological and historical research: no nails have been used in building the stockade; wooden pegs and mortise and tenon joints hold the structure together. (Apr-Nov) **$$**

George S. Eccles Dinosaur Park. *1544 E Park Blvd. Phone 801/393-3466.* Outdoor display containing more than 100 life-size reproductions of dinosaurs and other prehistoric creatures, plus an educational building with a working paleontological lab and fossil and reptile displays. (Daily; closed Nov-Mar) **$$**

Hill Aerospace Museum. *7961 Wardleigh Rd. 4 miles S on I-15, exit 341, in Roy. Phone 801/777-6868.* More than 55 aircraft on display, some indoors and suspended from ceiling. Planes include B-29 Superfortress, SR-71 "Blackbird" reconnaissance plane, B-52 bomber, PT-71 Stearman; helicopters, jet engines, missiles; uniforms and other memorabilia. (Daily; closed Jan 1, Thanksgiving, Dec 25) **FREE**

Lagoon and Pioneer Village. *375 N Lagoon Dr (84025). Approximately 20 miles S on I-15, in Farmington. Phone 801/451-8000 or 800/748-5246, ext 5035.* Amusement park. Thrill rides, musical entertainment, water park, food, campground. (June-Aug, daily; late Apr-Memorial Day and Labor Day-Oct, weekends) **$$$$**

Nordic Valley. *7 miles E on UT 39, then N on UT 162. Phone 801/745-3511.* Two chairlifts; patrol, school, rentals; snack bar, lounge. Longest run 1 1/2 miles, vertical drop 1,000 feet. (Dec-Apr, daily) **$$$$**

Pine View Reservoir. *9 miles E on UT 39 in Ogden Canyon in Wasatch-Cache National Forest* (see SALT LAKE CITY). Boating, fishing, waterskiing; camping, picnicking. Fees for activities.

Powder Mountain. *8 miles E on UT 39, then 11 miles N on UT 158, in Eden. Phone 801/745-3772; 801/745-3771 (snow conditions).* Quad, triple, two double chairlifts; three surface tows; patrol, school, rentals; food service, lodging. (Mid-Nov-Apr, daily) Night skiing. **$$$$**

Snowbasin. *17 miles E-Ogden end of Route 26. 10 miles E on UT 39, then S on UT 226 in Wasatch-Cache National Forest* (see SALT LAKE CITY). *Phone 801/399-1135; 801/399-0198 (snow conditions).* Two gondolas; quad, four triple, double chairlifts; patrol, school, rentals; food service, lodges. Longest run 3 miles, vertical drop 2,940 feet. (Late Nov-mid-Apr, daily) **$$$$**

Union Station—the Utah State Railroad Museum. *2501 Wall Ave, center of Ogden. Phone 801/629-8444.* **Spencer S. Eccles Railroad Center** features some of the world's largest locomotives, model railroads, films, gem and mineral displays, guided tours by "conductors." **Browning-Kimball Car Museum** has classic American cars. **Browning Firearms Museum** contains the reconstructed original Browning gun shop and inventor's models. Also here is 500-seat theater for musical and dramatic productions and an art gallery; restaurant. Visitors Bureau for northern Utah located here. (June-Sept, daily; rest of the year, Mon-Sat; closed Jan 1, Thanksgiving, Dec 25) **$**

Weber State University. *3750 Harrison Blvd, off US 89. Phone 801/626-6000.* (1889) 17,000 students. On campus are Layton P. Ott Planetarium, with natural science museum and Foucault pendulum, shows (Wed; no shows summer; fee); and Stewart Bell Tower, with 183-bell electronic carillon, performances (daily; free). Campus tours.

Willard Bay State Park. *15 miles N via I-15, exit 360, near Willard. Phone 435/734-9494.* This park features a 9,900-acre lake. Swimming, fishing, boating (ramps), sailing; picnicking, tent and trailer sites (fee; showers, dump station). (Daily) **$$$**

Special Events

Pioneer Days. *1875 Monroe Blvd. Ogden Pioneer Stadium.* Rodeo, concerts, vintage car shows, fireworks, chili cookoff. Mon-Sat evenings. Mid-late July.

Utah Symphony Pops Concert. *1875 Monroe Blvd. Lindquist Fountain/Plaza.* Music enhanced by fireworks display. Late July.

Motel/Motor Lodge

★ **DAYS INN.** *3306 Washington Blvd (84401). Phone 801/399-5671; toll-free 800/999-6841; fax 801/621-0321. www.daysinn.com.* 109 rooms, 2 story. S $65-$70; D $80-$88; each additional $8; under 18 free. Crib free. TV; cable (premium). Indoor pool; whirlpool. Complimentary continental breakfast. Check-out noon. Coin laundry. Business services available. In-room modem link. Downhill/cross-country ski 15 miles. Microwaves available. Cr cds: A, C, D, DS, JCB, MC, V.

⧉ ✈ 🏊 ⓧ **SC**

Hotels

★★ **BEN LOMOND HISTORIC SUITE HOTEL.** *2510 Washington Blvd (84401). Phone 801/627-1900; toll-free 888/627-8897; fax 801/394-5342. www.benlomondhotel.com.* This beautiful historical building built in 1890, welcomes guests with warm and friendly service, and offers a comfortable stay. Located in the historic district of Ogden, this hotel provides a charming atmosphere, perfect for relaxing. 122 suites, 11 story. S $57-$64; D $64-$74; each additional $7; suites $129-$169; under 12 free; ski packages. Crib free. Pet accepted, some restrictions. Complimentary breakfast, coffee in rooms. Check-out noon. TV; cable (premium). Refrigerators, microwaves. Coin laundry. Restaurant 11 am-10 pm. Bar. Health club privileges, exercise equipment. Free covered parking. Meeting rooms. Business center. Cr cds: A, DS, MC, V.

⧉ 🐾 ♨ 🏊 ⓧ ⓧ 🏃

★★★ **MARRIOTT OGDEN.** *247 24th St (84401). Phone 801/627-1190; toll-free 888/825-3163; fax 801/394-6312. www.marriott.com.* This hotel is located in downtown Ogden and one block from the Eccles Convention Center and the Ogden Raptors baseball stadium. 292 rooms, 8 story. S, D $109; suites $150-$350; weekend rates; ski plans. TV; cable. Indoor pool; whirlpool. Coffee in rooms. Restaurant 6 am-10 pm. Private club 4:30 pm-midnight. Check-out noon. Coin laundry. Convention facilities. Business services available. Gift shop. Free parking. Exercise equipment. Refrigerator in suites. Cr cds: A, C, D, DS, JCB, MC, V.

⧉ 🏊 ⓧ ⓧ **SC**

Restaurants

★ ★ **BAVARIAN CHALET.** *4387 Harrison Blvd (84403). Phone 801/479-7561; fax 801/479-0212. www.bavarianchalet.com.* German menu. Hours: 5-10 pm. Closed Sun, Mon; some major holidays; also July. Dinner $9.95-$20.95. Children's menu. Reservations accepted. Outdoor seating. Totally nonsmoking. Cr cds: A, MC, V.

Ⓓ

★★**GRAY CLIFF LODGE.** *508 Ogden Canyon (84401). Phone 801/392-6775. www.graycliﬄodge.com.* Specialties: prime rib, fresh mountain trout, lamb chops. Own baking. Hours: 5-10 pm; Sat to 11 pm; Sun 3-8 pm; Sun brunch 10 am-2 pm. Closed Mon; most major holidays. Complete meal: dinner $12.95-$30.95. Sun brunch $8.95. Bar. Family-owned. Children's menu. Reservations accepted; required some holidays. Converted summer home with country atmosphere. Totally nonsmoking. Cr cds: A, D, DS, MC, V.

Ⓓ

★ ★ **YE LION'S DEN.** *3607 Washington Blvd (84403). Phone 801/399-5804; fax 801/399-4055.* Closed Jan 1, Dec 24, 25. Lunch, dinner. Service bar. Cr cds: DS, MC, V. **$$$**

Ⓓ

Panguitch (H-3)

See also Cedar City

Settled 1864 **Pop** 1,623 **Elev** 6,624 ft **Area code** 435 **Zip** 84759

Information Panguitch Chamber of Commerce, PO Box 400, 84759; 435/676-8585

Web www.infowest.com/panguitch

A livestock, lumbering, and farm town, Panguitch is also a center for summer tourists who come to see nearby Bryce Canyon National Park and Cedar Breaks National Monument. The Paiutes named the city, which means "big fish," because of the large fish they caught in nearby Panguitch Lake. A Ranger District office of the Dixie National Forest (see CEDAR CITY) is located here.

What to See and Do

Anasazi Indian Village State Park. *460 N Hwy 12. 75 miles E of Bryce Canyon National Park, in Boulder. Phone 435/335-7308.* Partially excavated village, believed to have been occupied from A.D. 1050-1200, is one of the largest ancient communities west of the Colorado River. Picnicking. Museum (daily; closed Jan 1, Thanksgiving, Dec 25). **$**

Cedar Breaks National Monument. (see) *35 miles SW on UT 143.*

Panguitch Lake. *17 miles SW on paved road in Dixie National Forest (see CEDAR CITY). Phone 435/676-2649.* This 8,000-foot-high lake, which fills a large volcanic basin, has fishing; resorts, public campgrounds (developed sites, fee), ice fishing, snowmobiling, cross-country skiing.

Paunsagaunt Wildlife Museum. *250 E Center St. Phone 435/676-2500.* More than 400 animals from North America in their natural habitat can be viewed here. Also exotic game animals from Africa, India, and Europe. (May-Oct, daily) **$$**

Motels/Motor Lodges

★ **BEST WESTERN NEW WESTERN MOTEL.** *180 E Center St (84759). Phone 435/676-8876; toll-free 800/780-7234. www.bestwestern.com.* 55 rooms. Apr-Oct: S, D $55-$85; each additional $5; suites $85-$125; lower rates rest of year. Pet accepted. Check-out 11 am. TV. Some rooms across street. Cr cds: A, C, D, DS, MC, V.

Ⓓ 🔁 🐾 ⬇ 🚫 ⤢

★ ★ **BRYCE CANYON PINES MOTEL.** *Hwy 12 (84764). Phone 435/834-5441; toll-free 800/892-7923; fax 435/834-5330. www.brycecanyonmotel.com.* 50 rooms, 1-2 story. May-Oct: S, D $55-$75; each additional $5; suites $85-$125; kitchen cottage $95; lower rates rest of year. Crib $5. TV; cable. Heated pool. Restaurant 6:30 am-9:30 pm. Check-out 11 am, check-in 2 pm. Some fireplaces, balconies. Early-American décor. Cr cds: A, D, DS, MC, V.

Ⓓ ⛱ SC

Restaurant

★ **FOY'S COUNTRY CORNER.** *80 N Main (84759). Phone 435/676-8851.* American menu. Closed Thanksgiving, Dec 25. Breakfast, lunch, dinner. Cr cds: A, D, DS, MC, V. **$**

SC

Park City (C-4)

See also Alta, Heber City, Salt Lake City

Founded 1868 **Pop** 7,371 **Elev** 7,080 ft **Area code** 435 **Zip** 84060

Information Park City Chamber/Visitors Bureau, 1910 Prospector Ave, PO Box 1630; or the Visitor Information Center, 750 Kearns Ave; 435/649-6100, 435/649-6104, or 800/453-1360

Web www.parkcityinfo.com

Soldiers struck silver here in 1868, starting one of the nation's largest silver mining camps, which reached a population of 10,000 before declining to a near ghost town when the silver market collapsed. Since then, however, Park City has been revived as a four-season resort area with skiing, snowboarding, golf, tennis, water sports, and mountain biking.

What to See and Do

Brighton Resort. *Approximately 10 miles SW via UT 190 in Big Cottonwood Canyon (see SALT LAKE CITY).*

The Canyons. *4000 The Canyons Resort Dr (84098). Phone 435/649-5400.* 16 high-speed quad, triple, double chairlifts; gondola; patrol, school, rentals; restaurant, cafeteria, bar, lodge. One hundred forty trails. (Thanksgiving-Apr, daily) **$$$$**

Deer Valley Resort. *2250 Deer Valley Dr S. 1 mile SE on Deer Valley Dr. Phone 435/649-1000.* Eight high-speed quad, eight triple, two double chairlifts; rental, patrol, school, snowmaking; restaurants, lounge, lodge, nursery. Approximately 1,750 skiable acres. Vertical drop 3,000 feet. (Dec-mid-Apr, daily) Summer activities include mountain biking, hiking, horseback riding, and scenic chairlift rides (fee). **$$$$**

Egyptian Theatre. *328 Main St. Phone 435/649-9371.* (1926) Originally built as a silent movie and vaudeville house, now a year-round performing arts center with a full semiprofessional theater season. (Thurs-Sat; some performances other days)

Factory Stores at Park City. *I-80 and UT 224 at Kimball Jct (84098). Phone 435/645-7078.* More than 45 outlet stores. (Daily)

Kimball Art Center. *638 Park Ave. Phone 435/649-8882.* Exhibits in various media by local and regional artists. (Mon, Wed-Sun) **FREE**

Park City Mountain Resort. *1310 Lowell Ave (84060). Phone 435/649-8111.* Gondola; quad, four double, five triple, three 6-passenger chairlifts; patrol, school, rentals, snowmaking; restaurants, cafeteria, bar. Approximately 2,200 acres; 100 novice, intermediate, expert slopes and trails; 750 acres of open-bowl skiing. Lighted snowboarding. (Mid-Nov-mid-Apr, daily) Alpine slide, children's park, miniature golf in summer (fees). **$$$$**

Rockport State Park. *N on UT 248 and US 40, then 8 miles NE on I-80, Wanship exit. Phone 435/336-2241.* Approximately 1,000-acre park along east side of Rockport Lake. Opportunity for viewing wildlife, including bald eagles (winter) and golden eagles. Swimming, waterskiing, sailboarding, fishing, boating (rentals, launch); picnicking, restaurant, concession, cross-country ski trail (6 miles), camping, tent and trailer sites. (Daily) Standard fees.

Solitude Resort. *W via I-80 to I-215 S, exit 6 in Big Cottonwood Canyon (see SALT LAKE CITY).*

Utah Winter Sports Park. *3000 Bear Hollow Dr. 4 miles N on Bear Hollow Dr. Phone 435/658-4233.* Recreational ski jumping in $25-million park built for 2002 Olympic Winter Games. Nordic, competition, freestyle, and training jumps. Lessons followed by 2-hour jumping session. Also Olympic bobsled and luge track (high-speed rides available). Day lodge, snack bar, gift shop. (Wed-Sun) **$$$$**

White Pine Touring Center. *201 Heber Ave. Approximately 1 mile N via UT 224 to Park City Golf Course. Phone 435/649-8710.* Groomed cross-country trails (20 km), school, rentals; guided tours. (Nov-Apr, daily) Summer mountain biking; rentals. **$$$$**

Special Events

Art Festival. *638 Park Ave.* Open-air market featuring work of more than 200 visual artists. Also street entertainment. First weekend in Aug.

Sundance Film Festival. *307 W 200 S # 5002.* Ten-day festival for independent filmmakers. Workshops, screenings, and special events. Mid-Jan.

Uniting Fore Care Classic presented by Novell PGA Tournament. *8 miles N on UT 224, at Park Meadows.* PGA Invitational Golf tournament. Aug.

Motels/Motor Lodges

★ **HAMPTON INN & SUITES.** *6609 Landmark Dr (84098). Phone 435/645-0900; toll-free 800/426-7866; fax 435/645-9672. www.hamptoninn.com.* 81 rooms, 20 suites, 4 story. Dec-Mar: S $135; D $210; suites $210; each additional $8; under 13 free; lower rates rest of year. Crib available. Check-out noon. TV; cable (premium), VCR available. Coin laundry, dry cleaning. Restaurant nearby. Exercise equipment. Indoor pool, whirlpool. Parking. Meeting rooms. Business services. Concierge. Cr cds: A, C, D, DS, MC, V.

★ **HOLIDAY INN EXPRESS HOTEL & SUITES.** *1501 West Ute Blvd (84098). Phone 435/658-1600. www.holiday-inn.com.* Conveniently located just off I-80 at the entrance to Park City, this hotel is well maintained and has a variety of accommodations. 76 rooms, 3 story, 12 suites. Jan-Apr, July-Sept: S, D $85; suites $129; under 18 free; lower rates rest of year. Crib available. Pet accepted, some restrictions. Parking lot. Indoor pool. TV; cable (premium), VCR available. Complimentary coffee in rooms. Restaurant nearby. Check-out noon, check-in

3 pm. Meeting room. Business services available. Dry cleaning, coin laundry. Exercise equipment, sauna, steam room. Golf, tennis nearby. Cr cds: A, D, DS, JCB, MC, V.

★ **THE LODGE AT MOUNTAIN VILLAGE.** *1415 Lowell Ave (84060). Phone 435/655-3315; toll-free 888/ PARK-CITY; fax 435/649-9162. www.davidhollands.com.* 123 rooms, 98 suites, some A/C, 3 story. Mid-Jan-Mar: S, D $55-$145; suites $145-$550; higher rates: Christmas, Presidents' Week; lower rates rest of year. Check-out 10 am. TV; cable (premium), VCR available (movies). Bar. Sauna. Indoor pool, outdoor pool, whirlpool. Downhill ski on site; cross-country ski 1 mile. Cr cds: A, C, D, DS, MC, V.

★ ★ **SHADOW RIDGE.** *50 Shadow Ridge St (84060). Phone 435/649-4300; toll-free 800/754-2002; fax 435/649-5951. www.davidhollands.com.* 150 rooms, 50 suites, 4 story. Mid-Jan-late-Mar: S, D $150-$175; condos $320-$450; ski, golf plans; higher rates mid-Dec-early Jan; lower rates rest of year. Crib free. Check-out 10 am. TV; cable, VCR available. Balconies; some refrigerators, microwaves, fireplaces. Valet services, laundry. Restaurant (seasonal). Exercise equipment, sauna. Heated pool, whirlpool. Golf 1/2 mile. Meeting rooms. Business services. Cr cds: A, C, D, DS, JCB, MC, V.

★ ★ ★ **THE YARROW RESORT HOTEL AND CONFERENCE CENTER.** *1800 Park Ave (84060). Phone 435/649-7000; fax 435/645-7007. www.yarrowresort.com.* Centrally located and within minutes to the ski resorts that hosted the competition for the 2002 Winter Olympic Games, this hotel offers all the charm of a resort. From the quiet luxury of their guest rooms to the overall elegance of the hotel, guests will appreciate the level of style and service that is offered. 181 rooms, 2 story. S, D $79-$249; each additional $15; suites $89-$249; under 13 free; package plans; higher rates mid-Dec-Mar. Crib free. TV; cable (premium). Heated pool; whirlpools. Coffee in rooms. Restaurant 6:30 am-10 pm. Room service. Bar. Check-out 11 am. Coin laundry. Meeting rooms. Business center. Bellstaff. Concierge. Downhill ski 1/4 mile; cross-country ski 1/2 mile. Exercise equipment. Refrigerators. Microwaves available. Balconies. Golf course adjacent. Cr cds: A, D, DS, JCB, MC, V.

Hotels

★★**INN AT PROSPECTOR SQUARE.** *2200 Sidewinder Dr (84060). Phone 435/649-7100; toll-free 800/ 453-3812; fax 435/649-8377. www.prospectorlodging.com.* 230 units, 125 kitchen units, 2-3 story. Late Nov-mid-Apr: S, D $79-$479; kitchen studio rooms $167-$187; 1-2-3-bedroom condos $175-$400; under 12 free; ski plan; lower rates rest of year. Check-out 11 am, check-in 4 pm. TV; VCR available. In-room modem link. Some balconies, refrigerators, microwaves. Valet services. Health club privileges. Pool. Picnic tables, grills. Bicycle rentals. Business services. Convention center/facilities. Cr cds: A, C, D, DS, MC, V.

★ ★ ★ **MARRIOTT PARK CITY.** *1895 Sidewinder Dr (84060). Phone 435/649-2900; toll-free 800/234-9003; fax 435/649-4852. www.parkcityutah.com.* This hotel is located just a mile from downtown Park City and historical Main Street. 200 rooms, 1-4 story. S, D $79-$269; each additional $15; suites $119-$400; under 18 free; ski, golf packages. Crib free. Check-out noon, check-in. TV; cable (premium). In-room modem link. Balconies. Restaurant 6:30 am-10 pm. Bar. Room service 11 am-10 pm. Exercise equipment, sauna. Indoor pool, whirlpool. Garage parking. Meeting rooms. Business center. Concierge. Gift shop. Cr cds: A, C, D, DS, JCB, MC, V.

Resorts

★ ★ ★ **THE CANYONS GRAND SUMMIT RESORT HOTEL AND CONFERENCE CENTER.** *4000 The Canyons Resort Dr (84098). Phone 435/649-5400; toll-free 888/226-9667; fax 435/649-7374. www.thecanyons.com.* This property has a spectacular location at the foot of the ski slopes in The Canyons area of Park City. Guest rooms have excellent views of the mountains and the valley below. 356 rooms, 65 suites, 8 story. Jan-Mar: S, D $119-$365; suites $300-900; lower rates rest of year. Crib available. Complimentary coffee and tea. Check-out 11 am. TV; cable (premium), VCR available. Laundry, dry cleaning. Restaurant 7 am-10 pm. Bar. Supervised children's activities. Video games. Exercise room, sauna, steam room. Pool, whirlpool. Golf nearby. Tennis. Downhill skiing. Bike rentals. Hiking trail. Valet parking available. Conference center/facilities. Concierge. Gift shop. Cr cds: A, D, DS, MC, V.

★ ★ **RADISSON INN.** *2121 Park Ave (84060). Phone 435/649-5000; toll-free 800/333-3333; fax 435/649-2122. www.radisson.com.* 125 rooms, 6 suites. Dec-Mar, July-Aug: S $89-$149; suites $109-$189; each additional $15; under 18 free; lower rates test of year. Crib free. Pet accepted; fee. Complimentary full breakfast. Check-out noon. TV; cable. Coffee. Coin laundry, dry cleaning. Restaurant 6:30 am-2 pm, 5-10 pm. Bar. Video games. Steam room. Indoor pool, outdoor pool, whirlpool. Golf.

Tennis. Downhill skiing. Bike rentals, Hiking trail. Garage parking. Meeting rooms. Business services. Concierge. Gift shop. Cr cds: A, C, D, DS, ER, JCB, MC, V.

★ ★ ★ **SILVER KING HOTEL.** *1485 Empire Ave (84060). Phone 435/649-5500; toll-free 800/331-8652; fax 435/649-6647. www.silverkinghotel.com.* This condominium hotel is close to the base of Park City Mountain Resort, which features over 2,000 acres of ski area. Guest rooms come with a washer and dryer. 64 kitchen suites, 5 story. Nov-Apr: S, $115-$385; D $195-$425; higher rates Sundance Film Festival; lower rates rest of year. Crib free. Garage parking free. TV; cable (premium), VCR (movies). Complimentary coffee in rooms. Restaurant nearby. Check-out 11 am. Meeting rooms. Business services available. Downhill/cross-country ski 1 mile. Sauna. Health club privileges. Indoor/outdoor pool; whirlpool. Refrigerators, microwaves, fireplaces. Some in-room whirlpools. Picnic tables, grills. Cr cds: A, DS, MC, V.

★ ★ ★ ★ **STEIN ERIKSEN LODGE.** *7700 Stein Way (84060). Phone 435/649-3700; toll-free 800/453-1302; fax 435/649-5825. www.steinlodge.com.* Stein Eriksen may be a skier's Valhalla, but this superb resort delights visitors year-round. Nestled mid-mountain at Utah's Deer Valley ski resort, this Scandinavian masterpiece enjoys a magnificent alpine setting. The resort offers visitors unparalleled levels of service. Heated sidewalks and walkways keep guests toasty, while the ski valet service is heaven-sent for skiers at the end of an adventurous day. The dining is equally outstanding, and the Sunday Jazz Brunch and Skiers Lunch Buffet are local sensations. The roaring fireplace and inviting ambience of the Troll Hallen Lounge make it a cozy place for après-ski or light fare. Guests rest weary muscles at the spa, work out at the well-equipped fitness center, or unwind in the year-round outdoor heated pool at this comprehensive, full-service resort. Rustically elegant, the Lodge proudly shows off its Norwegian heritage while incorporating design elements synonymous with the American West. 170 rooms rooms, 13 rooms in main lodge, 59 kitchen units, 2 story. Early Dec-early Apr: S, D from $350; each additional $25; kitchen suites from $615; under 12 free; summer rates; ski plans; higher rates holiday seasons; lower rates rest of year. Complimentary full breakfast (winter only). Check-out 11 am. TV; cable (premium), VCR, DVD available. In-room modem link. Some fireplaces; microwaves available. Dining rooms (See also THE GLITRETIND). Bar; pianist in winter. Room service 6:30 am-11 pm. Exercise equipment; sauna, steam room. Massage. Full service spa. Heated pool, whirlpool, poolside service. Golf privileges. Downhill ski on site; cross-country ski 3 miles. Lawn games. Hot air balloons; mountain bikes available. Sleighing. Snowmobiles. Valet parking. Business center. Concierge. Cr cds: A, D, DS, JCB, MC, V.

B&B/Small Inns

★ ★ **1904 IMPERIAL HOTEL B&B.** *221 Main St (84060). Phone 435/649-1904; toll-free 800/669-8824; fax 435/645-7421. www.1904imperial.com.* 12 rooms, 3 story. No A/C. D $140-$175;. Complimentary full breakfast. Check-out 11 am, check-in 4 pm. TV; cable. Restored boarding house (1904) in historic area. Cr cds: A, DS, MC, V.

★ ★ ★ **GOLDENER HIRSCH INN.** *7570 Royal St E (84060). Phone 435/649-7770; toll-free 800/252-3373; fax 435/649-7901. www.goldenerhirschinn.com.* Decorated with Austrian antiques and furnishings, this inn is located at the base of ski lifts at Deer Valley's Silver Lake Village. The restaurant serves both continental and Austrian cuisine. 20 rooms, 4 story; Dec-Jan: S, D $490-$950; lower rates rest of year; suites $950; $25 additional person. Crib free. TV; VCR. Restaurant. Bar; entertainment (winter 5 nights, summer weekend evenings). Limited room service. Valet. Conceirge. Gift shop. Exercise equipment. Business center. Fireplaces, bathroom phones. Cr cds: A, MC, V.

★ ★ ★ **OLD MINERS' LODGE.** *615 Woodside Ave (84060). Phone 435/645-8068; toll-free 800/648-8068; fax 435/645-7420. www.oldminerslodge.com.* Established in 1889, this charming inn is located within the National Historic District of Park City. Guest rooms are graciously appointed with antique furnishings and country charm and are named after historic society members of Park City. Guests will find service informative, friendly, and attentive. Located just blocks from the Town Lift and historic Main Street, this hotel offers something for everyone. 12 rooms, 3 suites, 2 story. No A/C. Mid-Nov-mid-Apr: S, D $130-$275; each additional $15; higher rates mid-Dec-early Jan; lower rates rest of year. Crib $5. Complimentary full breakfast. Check-out noon, check-in 2 pm. Restaurant nearby. Street parking. Business services. Renovated lodging house used by miners (1889); early Western décor, fireplace, antiques. Totally nonsmoking. Cr cds: A, C, D, DS, MC, V.

★ ★ ★ **WASHINGTON SCHOOL INN.** *543 Park Ave (84060). Phone 435/649-3800; toll-free 800/824-1672; fax 435/649-3802. www.washingtonschoolinn.com.* Built in 1889, this historic stone schoolhouse is charming and well appointed with turn-of-the-century country décor and replete with modern amenities. 12 rooms, 3 story. No A/C. D $145-$310. Complimentary full breakfast; afternoon refreshments. Check-out 11 am, check-in 3 pm. TV; cable. Sitting room with stone and carved wood fireplace, library, bell tower. Restaurant nearby. Sauna. Downhill ski 1 1/2 blocks; cross-country ski 1 1/2 miles. Street parking. Cr cds: A, D, DS, MC, V.

⊠ SC

Restaurants

★ ★ ★ **THE CABIN.** *4000 The Canyons Resort Dr (84098). Phone 435/615-8060; fax 435/615-8041. www.thecanyons.com.* Upscale rustic décor and a friendly staff bring warmth to this The Canyons Grand Summit Hotel dining room. The menu is frequently changing. Hours: 5:30-10 pm. Lunch $8-$15, dinner $14-$34. Children's menu. Reservations accepted. Garage. Cr cds: A, DS, MC, V.

D ⊠ SC

★ ★ ★ **CHEZ BETTY.** *1637 Short Line Rd (84060). Phone 435/649-8181; fax 435/649-0880. www.chezbetty.com.* The warm and understated elegance of the cozy dining room creates the setting for the chef's wonderfully imaginative cuisine. The featured menu items are enhanced by daily specials which capture the freshest ingredients the market has to offer that day. The combination of flavors and textures, as well as the visually stunning presentations, keep patrons returning again and again. Menu changes seasonally. Hours: 6-10 pm. Closed Tues, Wed. Reservations accepted. Wine, beer. Dinner $19-$30. Cr cds: A, DS, MC, V.

D ⊠

★ ★ ★ **CHIMAYO.** *368 Main St (84060). Phone 435/649-6222; fax 435/647-0844. www.chimayoresturant.com.* Park City's best venture into Southwestern cuisine. The warm colorful atmosphere is enhanced by a fireplace at one end of the dining room. Specializes in ribs, Chilean seabass. Hours: 5:30-10 pm. Closed Mon, Tues. Dinner $21-$32. Wine list. Reservations accepted. Cr cds: A, DS, MC, V.

D ⊠

★ ★ ★ **THE GLITRETIND.** *7700 Stein Way (84060). Phone 435/649-3700; fax 435/649-5825. www.steinlodge.com.* This rich, European dining room is housed at the Stein Eriksen Lodge perched in the Wasatch Mountains at Deer Valley Resort. The excellent wine list is nationally recognized and the American continental menu features first-rate preparations including mustard-crusted rack of lamb with lentil and arugula strudel. The upbeat Sunday jazz brunch draws a crowd for a good reason. Seafood menu. Breakfast, lunch, dinner, Sun brunch. Bar. Children's menu. Outdoor dining. Cr cds: A, D, DS, MC, V. **$$$$**

D

★ ★ ★ **GRAPPA.** *151 Main St (84060). Phone 435/645-0636. www.grapparestaurant.com.* Located in a former boarding house on Park City's historic Main Street, this upscale Italian restaurant offers dining on three levels. Many of the dishes feature just-picked herbs and flowers from the adjacent gardens. Italian menu. Specialties: pasta. Seasonal menu. Hours: 5-10 pm; summer 5:30-9:00 pm, closed Dec 24; also mid-Apr-mid-May. A la carte entrees: dinner $22-$36. Service bar. Children's menu. Reservations accepted. Outdoor dining. Rustic décor, stained-glass windows. Totally nonsmoking. Cr cds: A, D, MC, V.

★ ★ **KAMPAI.** *586 Main St (84060). Phone 435/649-0655; fax 435/277-2867.* Hours: 6-10 pm. Closed Thanksgiving, Dec 25; also 10 days in spring. Japanese menu. Service bar. Dinner $12.95-$24. Specializes in sushi, sashimi, tempura. Outdoor dining. Casual Japanese décor; extensive sushi bar. Totally nonsmoking. Cr cds: A, C, D, DS, ER, MC, V.

D

★ **MAIN STREET PIZZA AND NOODLE.** *530 Main St (84060). Phone 435/645-8878; fax 435/645-8895.* American, Italian menu. Hours: 11:30 am-10 pm; Fri, Sat to 11 pm. Closed Thanksgiving. Lunch $5-$8, dinner $8-$12. Bar. Casual décor. Totally nonsmoking. Cr cds: A, C, D, DS, ER, MC, V.

D

★ ★ ★ **RIVERHORSE CAFE.** *540 Main St (84060). Phone 435/649-3536; fax 435/649-2409. www.riverhorsegroup.com.* Visitors are just as likely to be drawn to this cafe by the nationally recognized musical guests as they are by the contemporary American cuisine featuring pasta, poultry, game, and seafood. Chef/manager Bill Hufferd welcomes guests—and the occasional celebrity—for dining, drinking, and dancing. Weather permitting, try to snag a second-story, balcony seat overlooking the Main Street scene. Hours: 5:30-10 pm. Closed Thanksgiving. Dinner $18.50-$29.50. Bar. Entertainment Thurs-Sun (summer), nightly (ski season). Children's menu. Reservations accepted. Outdoor dining. Cr cds: A, DS, MC, V.

★ **TEXAS RED'S PIT BARBECUE AND CAFE.** *440 Main St (84060). Phone 435/649-7337; fax 435/645-8408.* Barbecue menu. Lunch, dinner. Bar. Children's menu. Cr cds: A, C, D, DS, MC, V. **$$**

★ ★ **ZOOM ROADHOUSE GRILL.** *660 Main St (84060). Phone 435/647-0902; fax 435/649-7614. www.sundanceresort.com.* Lunch, dinner. Bar. Former train depot with original wood floor, high ceiling, fireplace. Outdoor dining. Cr cds: A, C, D, DS, MC, V. **$$**

D

Payson (D-4)

See also Nephi, Provo

Settled 1850 **Pop** 12,716 **Elev** 4,648 ft **Area code** 801
Zip 84651

Information Chamber of Commerce, 439 West Utah Ave;
801/465-5200 or 801/465-2634

Web www.paysonchamber.com

Payson sits at the foot of the Wasatch Mountains, near
Utah Lake. Mormons first settled the area after spending
a night on the banks of Peteneet Creek. The surrounding farmlands produce fruit, milk, grain, and row crops;
livestock is raised. Limestone and dolomite are dug in the
vicinity for use in smelting iron.

What to See and Do

Mount Nebo Scenic Loop Drive. This 45-mile drive
around the eastern shoulder of towering Mount Nebo
(elevation 11,877 feet) is one of the most thrilling in Utah;
Mount Nebo's three peaks are the highest in the Wasatch
range. The road travels south through Payson and Santa-
quin canyons and then climbs 9,000 feet up Mount Nebo,
offering a view of Devil's Kitchen, a brilliantly colored
canyon. (This section of the drive not recommended for
those who dislike heights.) The forest road continues S
to UT 132; take UT 132 E to Nephi, and then drive N on
I-15 back to Payson.

Payson Lake Recreation Area. *12 miles SE on unnumbered road in Uinta National Forest (see PROVO). Phone
801/798-3571.* Fishing, swimming; camping, hiking,
backpacking.

Special Event

Golden Onion Days. Includes community theater presentations, 5k and 10k runs, horse races, demolition derby,
parade, fireworks, and picnic. Labor Day weekend.

Motel/Motor Lodge

★ **COMFORT INN.** *830 N Main St (84651). Phone
801/465-4861; fax 801/465-7686. www.comfortinn.com.* 62
rooms, 2 story, 6 kitchens (no equipment). S $66-$76; D
$75-$85; each additional $6; suites $130; under 18 free.
Crib free. Pet accepted; $10 deposit. TV; cable (premium).
Indoor pool; whirlpool. Complimentary continental
breakfast. Restaurant adjacent open 24 hours. Check-out
11 am. Coin laundry. Meeting rooms. Business services
available. Exercise equipment; sauna. Cr cds: A, C, D, DS,
JCB, MC, V.

Price (E-5)

Settled 1879 **Pop** 8,402 **Elev** 5,567 ft **Area code** 435
Zip 84501

Information Carbon County Chamber of Commerce,
90 N 100 E, #3; 435/637-2788 or 435/637-8182

Web www.carboncountychamber.com

Price, the seat of Carbon County, bases its prosperity on
coal; more than 30 mine properties, as well as oil and natural gas fields, are within 30 miles. Farming and livestock
are also important. Price was one of the stopping places
for the Robbers Roost gang in the 1930s. Headquarters
and a Ranger District office of the Manti-LaSal National
Forest are located here.

What to See and Do

Cleveland-Lloyd Dinosaur Quarry. *155 E Main St (84501).
22 miles S on UT 10, then approximately 15 miles E on
unnumbered road. Phone 435/637-5060.* Since 1928,
more than 12,000 dinosaur bones, representing at least
70 different animals, have been excavated on this site.
Visitor center, nature trail, picnic area. (Memorial Day-
Labor Day, daily; Easter-Memorial Day, weekends only)
DONATION

College of Eastern Utah Prehistoric Museum. *155 E Main
St. Phone 435/637-5060.* Dinosaur displays, archaeology
exhibits; geological specimens. (Memorial Day-Labor
Day, daily; rest of year, Mon-Sat) **DONATION**

Geology tours. *90 N 100 E (84501). Phone 435/637-3009.*
Self-guided tours of Nine Mile Canyon, Native American
dwellings, paintings, San Rafael Desert, Cleveland-Lloyd
Dinosaur Quarry, Little Grand Canyon. Maps available at
Castle Country Travel Region or Castle Country Regional
Information Center, 155 E Main. Phone 800/842-0784.
FREE

Manti-LaSal National Forest, Manti Division. *21 miles
SW on UT 10, then NW on UT 31. Contact the Ranger
District office or the Forest Supervisor at 599 W Price River
Dr. Phone 435/637-2817.* (See MOAB, MONTICELLO)
Originally two forests—the Manti in central Utah and the
LaSal section in southeastern Utah—now under single
supervision. A 1,327,631-acre area partially in Colorado,
this forest has among its attractions high mountain sce-
nic drives, deep canyons, riding trails, campsites, winter
sports, fishing, and deer and elk hunting. Joe's Valley
Reservoir on UT 29 and Electric Lake on UT 31 have fishing and boating. Areas of geologic interest, developed as a

result of massive landslides, are near Ephraim. Some fees in developed areas. **FREE**

Price Canyon Recreation Area. *15 miles N on US 6, then 3 miles W on unnumbered road.* Scenic overlooks; hiking, picnicking, camping (fee). Roads have steep grades. (May-mid-Oct, daily) **FREE**

Scofield State Park. *US 6 and UT 96 (84501). 24 miles N on US 6, then 10 miles W and S on UT 96. Phone 435/448-9449.* Utah's highest state park has a 2,800-acre lake that lies at an altitude of 7,616 feet. Fishing, boating (docks, ramps); camping (rest rooms, showers), snowmobiling, ice fishing, cross-country skiing in winter. (May-Oct) Standard fees. **$$$**

Motels/Motor Lodges

★ **BEST WESTERN CARRIAGE HOUSE INN.** *590 E Main St (84501). Phone 435/637-5660; fax 435/637-5157. www.bestwestern.com.* 41 rooms, 2 story. S $51.95-$75.95; D $57.95-$75.95; each additional $6; suites $61.95-$75.95. Complimentary continental breakfast. Check-out noon. TV; cable. Indoor pool, whirlpool. Airport transportation. Cr cds: A, C, D, DS, MC, V.

D ⊠ ⊠

★ **GREENWELL INN & CONVENTION CENTER.** *655 E Main St (84501). Phone 435/637-3520; toll-free 800/666-3520; fax 435/637-4858. www.castlenet.com/greenwell.* 125 rooms, 1-2 story. May-Sept: S $34-$38; D $42-$46; each additional $5; suites $46.50-$51.50; under 18 free; lower rates rest of year. Crib $6. Pet accepted. Complimentary continental breakfast. Check-out 11 am. TV; cable. Refrigerators. Laundry. Restaurant adjacent 6 am-9 pm. Health club privileges, exercise equipment. Indoor pool. Meeting rooms. Gift shop. Cr cds: A, C, D, DS, ER, JCB, MC, V.

D ⊠ ⊠ ⊠ ⊠ ⊠ ⊠ ⊠ ⊠

★★ **HOLIDAY INN HOTEL & SUITES.** *838 Westwood Blvd (84501). Phone 435/637-8880; toll-free 800/465-4329; fax 435/637-7707. www.sunstonehotels.com.* 151 rooms, 2 story. S $84-$99; D $85-$106; each additional $6; suites $99-$126; under 17 free. Crib free. Check-out noon. TV. Refrigerators. Restaurant 6 am-10 pm. Bar. Room service. Health club privileges, exercise equipment. Indoor pool. Meeting rooms. Cr cds: A, C, D, DS, JCB, MC, V.

D ⊠ ⊠ ⊠ ⊠ SC

Restaurant

★ **CHINA CITY CAFE.** *350 E Main St (84501). Phone 435/637-8211.* Chinese, American menu. Closed Thanksgiving, Dec 25; also July. Lunch, dinner. Children's menu. Cr cds: A, C, D, DS, MC, V. **$$**

D

Provo (D-4)

See also Heber City, Payson, Salt Lake City

Settled 1849 **Pop** 105,166 **Elev** 4,549 ft **Area code** 801

Information Utah County Visitors Center, 51 S University Ave, 84601; 801/370-8394 or 800/222-8824

Web www.utahvalley.org/cvb

Provo received its name from French-Canadian trapper Etienne Provost, who arrived in the area in 1825. Provost and his party of mountain men set up camp near the mouth of the Provo River, but skirmishes with Native Americans forced them to escape to the mountains. It wasn't until 1849 that the first permanent settlement, begun by a party of Mormons, was established. The Mormon settlers erected Fort Utah as their first building, and despite famine, drought, hard winters, and the constant danger of attack, they persisted and the settlement grew. Today, Provo is the seat of Utah County and the state's third-largest city.

An important educational and commercial center, Provo's largest employer is Brigham Young University. Beyond that, the city boasts major steel and electronic component manufacturers, health care and municipal employers, and other educational facilities. Provo lies in the middle of a lush, green valley: to the north stands 12,008-foot Mount Timpanogos; to the south is the perpendicular face of the Wasatch Range; to the east Provo Peak rises 11,054 feet; and to the west lies Utah Lake, backed by more mountains. Provo is the headquarters of the Uinta National Forest, and many good fishing, boating, camping, and hiking spots are nearby.

What to See and Do

Brigham Young University. *Phone 801/378-4678 or 801/378-1211.* Buildings on campus (Mon-Fri; closed holidays). (1875) 27,000 students. Founded by Brigham Young and operated by the Church of Jesus Christ of Latter-day Saints. This is one of the world's largest church-related institutions of higher learning, with students from every state and more than 90 foreign countries. One-hour, free guided tours arranged at Hosting Center (Mon-Fri; also by appointment)

Earth Science Museum. *Phone 801/378-4678.* Geological collection, extensive series of minerals and fossils. **FREE**

Harris Fine Arts Center. *HFAC Campus Drive (84620). Phone 801/378-HFAC.* Houses B. F. Larsen Gallery and Gallery 303; periodic displays of rare instruments and music collection. Concert, theater performances. **FREE**

Monte L. Bean Life Science Museum. *Phone 801/378-5051.* Exhibits and collections of insects, fish, amphibians, reptiles, birds, animals, and plants. **FREE**

Museum of Art. *Phone 801/378-2787.* Exhibits from the BYU Permanent Collection; traveling exhibits (some fees). **$$$**

Museum of Peoples and Cultures. *Allen Hall, 710 N 100 E. Phone 801/378-6112.* Material from South America, the Near East, and the southwestern United States. **FREE**

Camp Floyd and Stagecoach Inn State Parks. *13 miles N on I-15 to Lehi, then 20 miles W on UT 73, in Cedar Valley. Phone 801/768-8932.* Only the cemetery and one commissary building remain as evidence of the pre-Civil War post that quartered the largest troop concentration in the US here between 1858-1861. Approximately 400 buildings were constructed for troops deployed to the west in expectation of a Mormon rebellion. The nearby Stagecoach Inn has been restored with original period furnishings. Visitor center. Museum. (Apr-Sept daily, mid-Oct-Mar, Mon-Sat) Standard fees. **$**

John Hutchings Museum. *17 miles NW via I-15 or UT 89/91, at 55 N Center St, in Lehi. Phone 801/768-7180.* Six main collections include archaeology, ornithology and zoology, paleontology, mineralogy, and pioneer artifacts. Most of the items are from the Great Basin area. Rare sea shells, fossils, Native American artifacts. (Tues-Sat; closed holidays) **$$**

Pioneer Museum. *500 W 500 N, on US 89. Phone 801/377-0995.* Outstanding collection of Utah pioneer relics and Western art. Pioneer Village. (June-early Sept, Wed, Fri, Sat afternoons; rest of year, by appointment) **FREE**

Springville Museum of Art. *7 miles SE via I-15 exit 263, at 126 E 400 S, in Springville. Phone 801/489-2727.* Contemporary artists. Changing exhibits. Competition in Apr, quilt show in July-Sept. Guided tours. (Hours vary with exhibit; closed Jan 1, Easter, Dec 25) **FREE**

Sundance Ski Area. *15 miles NE on US 189, North Fork Provo Canyon. Phone 801/225-4107.* Three chairlifts, rope tow; patrol, school, rentals; warming hut, restaurants. Longest run 2 miles, vertical drop 2,150 feet. (Late Nov-Apr, daily) Cross-country trails. **$$$$**

Uinta National Forest. *88 W and 100 N (84601). South and east of town. Phone 801/377-5780.* Scenic drives through the 950,000-acre forest; areas include Provo Canyon, Bridal Veil Falls, Deer Creek Dam and Reservoir, Diamond Fork Canyon, Hobble Creek Canyon, Strawberry Reservoir, and the Alpine and Mount Nebo Scenic Loop (see PAYSON); roads give an unsurpassed view of colorful landscapes, canyons, waterfalls. Stream and lake fishing; hunting for deer and elk, camping (fee), picnicking. Reservations accepted.

Utah Lake State Park. *4400 W Center St (84601). 2 miles W on Center St, off I-15. Phone 801/375-0733 or 801/375-0731.* Park situated on the eastern shore of Utah Lake, a 150-square-mile, freshwater remnant of ancient Lake Bonneville, which created the Great Salt Lake. Fishing (cleaning station), boating (ramp, dock); ice-skating (winter), roller-skating (summer), picnicking, play area, camping (dump station). Visitor center. (Daily) Standard fees.

Special Event

Freedom Festival. Bazaar, carnival, parades. Early July.

Motels/Motor Lodges

★**BEST WESTERN COTTONTREE INN.** *2230 N University Pkwy (84604). Phone 801/373-7044; toll-free 800/528-1234; fax 801/375-5240. www.bestwestern.com.* 80 rooms, 2 story. S $59-$64; D $64-$74; each additional $5; suites $150; under 18 free. Complimentary continental breakfast. Check-out noon. TV. Health club privileges. Indoor pool, whirlpool. View of river. Cr cds: A, C, D, DS, MC, V.

⬛🔧🔧🔧🔧🔧 SC

★ **COLONY INN NATIONAL 9.** *1380 S University Ave (84601). Phone 801/374-6800; fax 801/374-6803.* 80 kitchen suites, 2 story. May-Oct: S $42-$52; D $58-$72; each additional $5; weekly, monthly rates; lower rates rest of year. Crib $5. Pet accepted, some restrictions; $15 refundable and $5/day. TV; cable (premium). Heated pool. Complimentary continental breakfast. Restaurant adjacent. Check-out noon. Coin laundry. Business services available. In-room modem link. Downhill ski 20 miles. Cr cds: A, DS, MC, V.

🔧🔧🔧🔧🔧

★ **DAYS INN.** *1675 N 200 W (84604). Phone 801/375-8600; fax 801/374-6654. www.daysinn.com.* 49 rooms, 2 story. S $44-$54; D $46-$59; each additional $5; kitchen unit $65-$70; under 18 free. Crib free. Pet accepted, some restrictions. TV; cable. Heated pool. Complimentary continental breakfast. Coffee in rooms. Restaurant 11 am-11 pm. Check-out noon. Business services available. In-room modem link. Downhill/cross-country ski 15 miles. Some refrigerators, microwaves. Cr cds: A, C, D, DS, JCB, MC, V.

⬛🔧🔧🔧🔧

★ ★ **HOLIDAY INN.** *1460 S University Ave (84601). Phone 801/374-9750; fax 801/377-1615. www.holiday-inn.com.* 78 rooms, 2 story. S, D $65-$90; under 18 free. Crib $10. Complimentary continental breakfast. Check-out noon. TV; cable (premium). Restaurant 11 am-10 pm. Room service. Exercise equipment. Pool. Meeting rooms. Business center. Cr cds: A, C, D, DS, ER, JCB, MC, V.

⬛🔧🔧🔧🔧🔧🔧

★ **HOWARD JOHNSON.** *1292 S University Ave (84601). Phone 801/374-2500; toll-free 800/326-0025; fax 801/373-1146. www.hojo.com.* 116 rooms, 2 story. Apr-mid-Sept: S $49-$79; D $54-$85; each additional $6; suites $70-$75; cabin suite $195; family rates; lower rates rest of year. Crib free. TV; cable (premium). Heated pool; whirlpool. Restaurant. Check-out noon. Coin laundry. Meeting rooms. Business services available. Downhill ski 20 miles. Exercise equipment. Game room. Microwaves available. Cr cds: A, C, D, DS, MC, V.

Hotel

★ ★ ★ **MARRIOTT PROVO HOTEL AND CON-FERENCE CENTER.** *101 West 100 N (84601). Phone 801/377-4700; toll-free 800/777-7144; fax 801/377-4708. www.marriott.com.* Nearby attractions include two shopping malls, as well as the Seven Peaks Water Park and Ice Rink, where the ice hockey competition and practices for the 2002 Winter Olympics were held. 331 rooms, 9 story. S $89-$125; D $89-$130; each additional $8; suites $99-$289; under 18 free; ski, honeymoon packages. Crib free. TV; cable (premium). Heated pool; whirlpool. Complimentary coffee in rooms. Restaurant 6:30 am-10 pm. Private club 5 pm-midnight. Check-out noon. Meeting rooms. Business center. In-room modem link. Gift shop. Covered parking. Airport transportation; free train station, bus depot transportation. Downhill ski 14 miles. Exercise equipment; sauna. Some refrigerators, microwaves, wet bars. Cr cds: A, C, D, DS, MC, V.

Resort

★ ★ ★ **SUNDANCE.** *N Fork Provo Canyon (84604). Phone 801/225-4107; toll-free 800/892-1600; fax 801/226-1937. www.sundanceresort.com.* This rustic retreat is set amidst the lush wilderness and offers a truly delightful stay. Guests have a choice of charming mountain cottages to relax in, each a unique blend of elegance and rustic charm. This resort has something for everyone. 103 kitchen units. Mid-Dec-Mar: S $185-$235; D $235-$375; suites $425; 2-3-bedroom cottages $750-$950; ski plans; lower rates rest of year. TV; cable (premium), VCR available (free movies). Supervised children's activities (June-Sept); ages 6-12. Dining rooms (See also FOUNDRY GRILL). Check-out 11 am, check-in 3 pm. Meeting rooms. Business services available. Concierge. Downhill/cross-country ski on site. Exercise equipment. Some fireplaces;

microwaves available. Private patios. Handmade wooden furniture; Native American art. Rustic retreat surrounded by pristine wilderness. Cr cds: A, D, DS, MC, V.

Restaurants

★ **BOMBAY HOUSE.** *463 N University Ave (84601). Phone 801/373-6677; fax 801/373-9377. www.bombayhouse.com.* Indian menu. Hours: 4-10:30 pm. Closed Sun; Dec 25. Dinner $7.95-$16. Reservations accepted. Cr cds: A, D, DS, MC, V.

★ ★ **FOUNDRY GRILL.** *N Fork Provo Canyon (84604). Phone 801/223-4551; fax 801/223-4213. www.sundanceresort.com.* American menu, Southwestern menu. Specialties: pizza, pasta, steak, fish. Hours: 7 am-10 pm; Sun 9 am-10 pm; Sun brunch to 2:30pm. Breakfast $1.75-$12.95, lunch, dinner $6.95-$23.95. Sun brunch $22.95. Bar, service bar. Children's menu. Reservations accepted. Outdoor dining. Rustic, western décor; fireplace, bare wood floors. Totally nonsmoking. Cr cds: A, C, D, DS, ER, MC, V.

★ **MAGLEBY'S.** *1675 N 200 W (84604). Phone 801/374-6249; fax 801/374-0449.* Specialties: steak, seafood, deep-dish apple pie. Salad bar. Hours: 11 am-10 pm; Sat 4-11 pm. Closed Sun; Thanksgiving, Dec 24, 25. Lunch $7.95-$13.95, dinner $14.95-$26.95. Reservations accepted. Street lamps and high windows with flower-boxes; artwork for sale. Totally nonsmoking. Cr cds: A, DS, MC, V.

★ ★ ★ **THE TREE ROOM.** *N Fork Provo Canyon (84604). Phone 801/223-4200; toll-free 800/223-4107. www.sundanceresort.com.* Located at the base of the Sundance ski lift, this restaurant's two-story windows offer stunning views of the rugged mountains and surrounding wilderness. The upscale yet casual room is filled with beautiful displays of American Indian dolls and pottery. The sophisticated new American cuisine includes wild game, steaks, seafood, and herbs and vegetables from the resort's own organic gardens. Menu changes seasonally. Hours: 5-10 pm. Dinner $25-$40. Children's menu. Reservations required. Cr cds: A, C, D, DS, MC, V.

Rainbow Bridge National Monument (I-5)

(NW of Navajo Mountain, approachable from Arizona)

Rainbow Bridge, which rises from the eastern shore of Lake Powell, is the largest natural rock bridge in the world. It was named a national monument in 1910, one year after its sighting was documented. Carved by a meander of Bridge Creek, this natural bridge stands 290 feet tall, spans 275 feet, and stretches 33 feet at the top. One of the seven natural wonders of the world, Rainbow Bridge is higher than the nation's capitol dome and nearly as long as a football field. The monument is predominantly salmon pink in color, modified by streaks of iron oxide and manganese. In the light of the late afternoon sun, the bridge is brilliant to see. Native Americans consider the area a sacred place; legend holds that the bridge is a rainbow turned to stone.

The easiest way to reach Rainbow Bridge is a half-day round-trip boat ride across Lake Powell from Page, Arizona (see), or a full-day round-trip boat ride from Bullfrog and Halls Crossing marinas (see LAKE POWELL). The bridge also can be reached on foot or horseback via the Rainbow Trail through the Navajo Indian Reservation (see ARIZONA; permit required). Fuel and camp supplies are available at Dangling Rope Marina, accessible by boat only, 10 miles downlake (south). Contact the Superintendent, Glen Canyon National Recreation Area, PO Box 1507, Page, AZ 86040; phone 520/608-6404.

Richfield (F-3)

See also Beaver, Fillmore, Salina

Settled 1863 **Pop** 5,593 **Elev** 5,330 ft **Area code** 435 **Zip** 84701

Information Chamber of Commerce, PO Box 327; 435/896-4241

Brigham Young sent members of his church here to settle the area, but problems with Native Americans forced abandonment of the fledgling town for almost a year before the pioneers were able to regain their settlement. Located in the center of Sevier Valley, Richfield has become the commercial hub of the region. Today, some of the world's best beef is raised in and shipped from this area. Headquarters and a Ranger District Office of the Fishlake National Forest are located here.

What to See and Do

Big Rock Candy Mountain. *25 miles S on US 89, in Marysvale Canyon. Phone 435/896-4241.* Multicolored mountain that Burl Ives popularized in song.

Capitol Reef National Park. (see) *10 miles E on UT 119, then 76 miles SE on UT 24.*

Fishlake National Forest. *115 E and 900 N (84701). Phone 435/896-9233.* This 1,424,000-acre forest offers fishing; hunting, hiking, picnicking, camping (fee). Fish Lake, 33 miles SE via UT 119 and UT 24, then 7 miles NE on UT 25, offers high-altitude angling on 6-mile-long lake covering 2,600 acres. Campgrounds (mid-May-late Oct). Contact the Supervisor's Office.

Fremont Indian State Park. *20 miles SW via I-70, at 11550 W Clear Creek Canyon Rd, in Sevier. Phone 435/527-4631.* Museum and trails feature the Fremont people, who lived in the area from A.D. 300-1300 and then vanished. There is no explanation, only speculation, for their disappearance. Interpretive center highlights evolution of their culture; artifacts from nearby Five Fingers Ridge; nature trails lead to panels of rock art and a reconstructed pit house dwelling and granary. Fishing; camping (fee), picnicking. (Daily; closed Jan 1, Thanksgiving, Dec 25) Standard fees.

Motels/Motor Lodges

★★ **BEST WESTERN APPLE TREE INN.** *145 S Main St (84701). Phone 435/896-5481; fax 435/896-9465. www.bwappletree.com.* 62 rooms, 1-2 story. May-Oct: S $50-$65; D $55-$75; each additional $5; suites $58-$102; lower rates rest of year. Crib $4. Complimentary continental breakfast. Check-out noon. TV; cable. Restaurant nearby. Heated pool, whirlpool. Business services. Cr cds: A, C, D, DS, ER, JCB, MC, V.

D ⚡ ✈ ⌕ SC

★ **DAYS INN.** *333 N Main (84701). Phone 435/896-6476; toll-free 888/275-8513; fax 435/996-6476. www.daysinn.com.* 51 rooms, 3 story. No elevator. May-Oct: S $39-$75; D $59-$103; each additional $5; suites $85-$110; under 12 free; lower rates rest of year. Crib free. Pet accepted; $50 refundable. Check-out 11 am. TV; cable (premium). In-room modem link. Refrigerators. Restaurant 6 am-9:30 pm. Sauna. Heated pool, whirlpool. Meeting rooms. Business services. Sundries. Cr cds: A, C, D, DS, ER, JCB, MC, V.

⚡ 🐾 ⌕ ⌕

★★ **QUALITY INN.** *540 S Main St (84701). Phone 435/896-5465; fax 435/896-9005. www.qualityinn.com.* 79 rooms, 2 story. Mid-May-Oct: S, D $55-$80; suites $80-$110; under 18 free; lower rates rest of year. Crib free. TV; cable. Heated pool. Complimentary continental breakfast. Restaurant adjacent 6 am-11 pm. Check-out 11 am. Meeting rooms. Exercise equipment. Whirlpool in suites. Cr cds: A, C, D, DS, JCB, MC, V.

[icons]

★**ROMANICO INN.** *1170 S Main St (84701). Phone 435/896-8471.* 29 rooms, 2 story. S, D $36-$64; each additional $4; under 12 free. Crib free. Pet accepted. Check-out noon. TV; cable. Refrigerators, microwaves. Coin laundry. Restaurant adjacent 5:30-10 pm. Cr cds: A, C, DS, MC, V.

[icons]

★ **TRAVELODGE.** *647 S Main St (84701). Phone 435/896-9271; toll-free 800/549-8208; fax 435/896-6864. www.travelodge.com.* 40 rooms, 2 story. June-Sept: S, D $65-$77; each additional $4; under 12 free; lower rates rest of year. Crib free. Pet accepted. Complimentary continental breakfast. Check-out noon. TV; cable. Restaurant 5 am-10 pm. Room service. Indoor pool, whirlpool. Meeting rooms. Business services. Sundries. Cr cds: A, DS, MC, V.

[icons]

Roosevelt (D-6)

See also Vernal

Settled 1905 **Pop** 3,915 **Elev** 5,182 ft **Area code** 435 **Zip** 84066

Information Chamber of Commerce, 50 E 200 S 35-11, PO Box 1417; 435/722-4598

Roosevelt, in the geographical center of Utah's "dinosaur land," was settled when the opening of reservation lands prompted a flood of homesteaders to stake claims in the area. The town was named after Theodore Roosevelt, who had once camped on the banks of a nearby river. Nine Mile Canyon, with its Native American petroglyphs, can be reached from here. A Ranger District office of the Ashley National Forest (see VERNAL) is located in the town.

Motels/Motor Lodges

★ **BEST WESTERN INN.** *E Hwy 40 (84066). Phone 435/722-4644; fax 435/722-0179. www.bestwestern.com.* 40 rooms, 2 story. May-mid-Nov: S $55; D $60; lower rates rest of year. Check-out 11 am. TV; cable (premium). Exercise equipment. Heated pool; whirlpool. Cr cds: A, D, DS, MC, V.

[icons]

★ **FRONTIER MOTEL.** *75 S 200 E (98624). Phone 435/722-2201; fax 435/722-2212.* 54 units, 2 kitchens S $41-$45; D $49-$53; each additional $3; kitchen units $45-$50. Crib $3. Pet accepted. TV; cable (premium). Pool.

Restaurant 6 am-9:30 pm; Sun to 9 pm. Check-out 11 am. Business services available. Cr cds: A, D, DS, MC, V.

[icons] SC

St. George (I-1)

Founded 1861 **Pop** 49,663 **Elev** 2,761 ft **Area code** 435 **Zip** 84770

Information Washington County Travel & Convention Bureau, 425 S 700 E, Dixie Center, 84770; 435/634-5747 or 800/869-6635

Extending themselves to this hot, arid corner of southwest Utah, members of the Mormon Church built their first temple here and struggled to survive by growing cotton—hence the nickname "Dixie." With determination and persistence, members of the Church struggled against odds to construct the temple. The site, chosen by Brigham Young, turned out to be a bog, but another site was not selected. Instead, hundreds of tons of rocks were pounded into the mud until a stable foundation could be laid. Mormons from the north worked 40-day missions, and southern church members gave one day's labor out of every ten until the temple was complete. The workers quarried 17,000 tons of rock by hand. A team of oxen hauled the stones to the construction site, and for seven straight days, timber was hauled more than 80 miles from Mount Trumbull to build the structure. Made of red sandstone plastered to a gleaming white, the Mormon temple is not only the town's landmark, but also a beacon for passing aircraft.

In St. George, warm summers are balanced by mild winters and a long growing season. Tourists and sportspeople bring in important business. The seat of Washington County, St. George is the closest town of its size to Zion National Park (see). A Ranger District office of the Dixie National Forest (see CEDAR CITY) is located here.

What to See and Do

Brigham Young Winter Home. *200 N and 100 W sts. Phone 435/673-2517 or 435/673-5181.* (1873) Two-story adobe house where the Mormon leader spent the last four winters of his life; period furnishings, garden. (Daily) **FREE**

Daughters of Utah Pioneers Collection. *143 N 100 E, Memorial Building. Phone 435/628-7274.* Regional memorabilia. (Mon-Sat; closed holidays) **DONATION**

Gunlock State Park. *Hwy 8. 16 miles NW on Old Hwy 91. Phone 435/628-2255.* Approximately 450 undeveloped acres in scenic red rock country. A dam across the Santa Clara River has created a 240-acre lake, which offers swimming, waterskiing, fishing, boating (ramp); picnicking, primitive camping; no drinking water. (Daily) **FREE**

Jacob Hamblin Home. *490 S and 300 E. 5 miles W off I-15, in Santa Clara. Phone 435/673-2161 or 435/673-5181.* (1863) Native sandstone house of Hamblin, Mormon missionary to Native Americans for 32 years; pioneer furnishings. (Daily) **FREE**

Pine Valley Chapel. *30 miles N via UT 18, Central exit, in Dixie National Forest. Phone 435/634-5747.* White frame meeting house built in 1868 as an upside-down ship by Ebenezer Bryce, a shipbuilder by trade. The walls were completed on the ground, then raised and joined with wooden pegs and rawhide. Still in use, the chapel served as both church and schoolhouse until 1919. (Memorial Day-Labor Day, daily) **FREE**

Snow Canyon State Park. *Hwy 8. 10 miles N on UT 18. Phone 435/628-2255 or 800/322-3770 (reservations).* Flat-bottomed gorge cut into multicolored Navajo sandstone; massive erosional forms, sand dunes, Native American petroglyphs. Hiking, picnicking, improved camping areas (some hookups, dump station), trailer parking. (Daily) Standard fees.

St. George Temple. *490 S 300 E (84770). Main and Tabernacle sts. Phone 435/628-4072.* Red sandstone structure built 1863-1876 with local materials; resembles colonial New England church. (Daily; closed Dec 25) **FREE**

Tabernacle. *Main and Tabernacle sts. Phone 435/628-4072.* Red sandstone structure built in 1863-1876 with local materials; resembles colonial New England church. (Daily; closed Dec 25) **FREE**

Temple Visitor Center. *490 S 300 E. Phone 435/673-5181.* On grounds of temple; guided tour of center explains local history and beliefs of the Latter-day Saints; audiovisual program. (Daily; closed Dec 25) **FREE**

Motels/Motor Lodges

★ **AMBASSADOR INN.** *1481 S Sunland Dr (84790). Phone 435/673-7900; toll-free 877/373-7900; fax 435/673-8325. www.ambassadorinn.net.* 68 rooms, 2 story. Apr-Nov: S, D $43-$74; under 18 free; higher rates Easter; lower rates rest of year. Crib free. Complimentary continental breakfast. Check-out 11 am, TV; cable. Restaurant nearby. Heated pool, whirlpool. Business services. Cr cds: A, DS, MC, V.

★ **BEST WESTERN CORAL HILLS.** *125 E St. George Blvd (84770). Phone 435/673-4844; toll-free 800/542-7733; fax 435/673-5352. www.coralhills.com.* 98 rooms, 2 story. Feb-Oct: S, D $51-$79; each additional $5; suites $80-$121; under 18 free; lower rates rest of year. Complimentary continental breakfast. Check-out 11 am. TV; cable. Exercise equipment. 2 pools, 1 indoor; wading pool, whirlpool. Cr cds: A, C, D, DS, MC, V.

★ **CLARIDGE INN.** *1187 S Bluff St (84770). Phone 435/673-7222; toll-free 800/367-3790; fax 435/634-0773.* 50 rooms, 2 story. S, D $39-$49; higher rates holidays. Crib $3. TV; cable. Heated pool; whirlpool. Restaurant adjacent open 24 hours. Check-out 11 am, check-in 2 pm. Business services available. Totally nonsmoking. Cr cds: A, DS, MC, V.

★ **COMFORT SUITES.** *1239 S Main St (84770). Phone 435/673-7000; toll-free 800/517-4000; fax 435/628-4340. www.comfortsuites.net.* 122 units, 2 story. Feb-Aug: S, D $64-$119; under 18 free; higher rates: Easter, early Oct; lower rates rest of year. Crib free. Complimentary continental breakfast. Check-out 11 am. TV; cable. Refrigerators, microwaves. Restaurant opposite open 24 hours. Heated pool, whirlpool. Airport transportation. Meeting rooms. Business services. Cr cds: A, C, D, DS, JCB, MC, V.

★ **FOUR SEASONS HOWARD JOHNSON.** *747 E St. George (84771). Phone 435/673-6111; toll-free 800/635-4441; fax 435/673-0994.* 95 rooms, 2 story. S, D $45-$75; each additional $5; suites $80-$135; under 12 free. TV; cable (premium). Indoor/outdoor pool; whirlpool. Complimentary continental breakfast. Restaurant 5-10 pm. Check-out 11 am. Meeting rooms. Sun deck. Cr cds: A, DS, MC, V.

★★ **HOLIDAY INN.** *850 S Bluff St (84770). Phone 435/628-4235; toll-free 800/457-9800; fax 435/628-8157. www.holidayinnstgeorge.com.* 164 rooms, 2 story. S, D $89-$95; each additional $8; suites $100-$140; under 19 free. Crib free. Check-out 11 am. TV; cable (premium). In-room modem link. Balconies, refrigerators. Coin laundry. Restaurant 6 am-10 pm. Room service. Game room. Indoor, outdoor pools, whirlpool. Putting green. Lighted courts. Airport transportation. Meeting rooms. Business services. Cr cds: A, C, D, DS, JCB, MC, V.

★★ **SINGLETREE INN.** *260 E St. George Blvd (84770). Phone 435/673-6161; toll-free 800/528-8890; fax 435/673-7453.* 45 rooms, 2 story. S, D $47-$54. Crib $5. Pet accepted. Complimentary continental breakfast. Check-out 11 am. TV; cable. Restaurant adjacent 11:30 am-10 pm. Heated pool, whirlpool. Business services. Cr cds: A, D, DS, MC, V.

★**SUN TIME INN.** *420 E St. George Blvd (84770). Phone 435/673-6181; toll-free 800/656-3846. www.suntimeinn.com.* 46 rooms, 2 story. S, D $39-$89; each additional $4; under 16 free; weekly rates. Crib $5. Pet accepted. Complimentary continental breakfast. Check-out 11 am. TV; cable. Refrigerators, microwaves. Restaurant adjacent 10 am-9:30 pm. Heated pool, whirlpool. Cr cds: A, DS, MC, V.

[D] [⛺] [≈] [⊠] [SC]

B&B/Small Inns

★★★ **GREEN GATE VILLAGE.** *76 W Tabernacle St (84770). Phone 435/628-6999; toll-free 800/350-6999; fax 435/628-6989. www.greenegatevillage.com.* Situated in the historic district of St. George, this quaint village offers a delightful visit for guests who wish to enjoy modern elegance and nostalgic charm. Guests will find a delight waiting for them in one of the elegantly restored pioneer homes. 14 rooms, 3 kitchen units, 1-2 story. D $85-$189; Complimentary full breakfast. Check-out 11 am, check-in 3 pm. TV; cable (premium), VCR available (movies $2). Balconies; some fireplaces. Dining room Thurs-Sat 6-8 pm. Pool, whirlpool. Free airport, bus depot transportation. Consists of eight Victorian and pioneer houses from late 1800s; library, sitting room, antiques, tole-painted furnishings. Totally nonsmoking. Cr cds: A, DS, MC, V.

[≈] [⛷] [⊠]

Salina (F-4)

See also Richfield

Settled 1863 **Pop** 2,393 **Elev** 5,150 ft **Area code** 435 **Zip** 84654

What to See and Do

Palisade State Park. *2200 Palisade Rd (84665). 20 miles N via US 89, then 2 miles E, near Sterling. Phone 435/835-7275 or 800/322-3770 (camping res).* Day use. Approximately 200 acres. Swimming beaches, showers, fishing, nonmotorized boating, canoe rentals, nature trail, hiking, 18-hole golf, picnicking, camping (fee; dump station). Six Mile Canyon adjacent. **$$**

Special Event

Mormon Miracle Pageant. *4 N 100 E. 30 miles N via US 89 in Manti, on Temple grounds. Phone 435/835-3000.* Portrays historical events of the Americas; cast of 600. Early-mid-June. **FREE**

Motel/Motor Lodge

★ **BEST WESTERN SHAHEEN MOTEL.** *1225 S State St (84654). Phone 435/529-7455; toll-free 800/* WESTERN; fax 435/529-7257. www.bestwestern.com. 40 rooms, 2 story. May-Nov: S $69.95; D $74.95; each additional $7; lower rates rest of year. Complimentary continental breakfast. Check-out 11 am. TV; cable (premium). Cr cds: A, C, D, DS, MC, V.

[D] [⊠] [SC]

Restaurant

★ **MOM'S CAFE.** *10 E Main St (84654). Phone 435/529-3921; fax 435/529-3921.* Hours: 7 am-10 pm. Closed Thanksgiving, Dec 25. Breakfast $2.50-$8.95, lunch $3.90-$9.50, dinner $6.25-$13. Children's menu. Cr cds: DS, MC, V.

Salt Lake City (C-4)

See also Heber City, Ogden, Park City, Provo

Founded 1847 **Pop** 181,743 **Elev** 4,330 ft **Area code** 801

Information Convention & Visitors Bureau, 90 S West Temple, 84101-1406; 801/521-2822 or 801/534-4927

Web www.saltlake.org

On a hill at the north end of State Street stands Utah's classic capitol building. Three blocks south is Temple Square, with the famed Mormon Temple and Tabernacle. The adjacent block houses the headquarters of the Church of Jesus Christ of Latter-day Saints, whose members are often called Mormons. Salt Lake City, with its 10-acre blocks, 132-foot-wide, tree-lined streets, and mountains rising to the east and west, is one of the most beautifully planned cities in the country.

Once a desert wilderness, Salt Lake City was built by Mormon settlers who sought refuge from religious persecution. Neither the barrenness of the land, drought, nor a plague of crickets swayed these people from their purpose. Followers of Brigham Young arrived and named their new territory "Deseret." In these early days, the Mormons began a variety of experiments in farming, industry, and society, many of which were highly successful. Today, Salt Lake City is an industrious, businesslike city, a center for electronics, steel, missiles, and a hundred other enterprises.

West of the city is the enormous Great Salt Lake, stretching 48 miles one way and 90 miles the other. It is less than 35 feet deep and between 15 and 20 percent salt—almost five times as salty as the ocean. Humans bob like a cork and cannot sink in the water. The lake is what remains of ancient Lake Bonneville, once 145 miles wide, 350 miles long, and 1,000 feet deep. As Lake Bonneville water evaporated over thousands of years, a large expanse of perfectly flat, solid salt was left. Today, the Bonneville Salt Flats stretch west almost to Nevada.

Salt Lake City's Mormon Heritage

The centerpiece of downtown Salt Lake City is Temple Square, the city block bordered by three streets named Temple-West, North, and South-and Main Street on the east side. Utah's top tourist attraction, Temple Square, is the hub for the Church of Jesus Christ of the Latter-Day Saints, where guests are invited to join a free guided tour that offers a glimpse of several architectural and cultural landmarks, including the Mormon Tabernacle, the Museum of Church History and Art, and the Joseph Smith Memorial Building. (Tours start at the flagpole every few minutes.) If your timing is right, you can also take in a film, choir rehearsal, or organ recital here. From Temple Square, head east on South Temple to a pair of historic homes, the Lion House (63 East South Temple) and the Beehive House (67 East South Temple). No tours are available of the Lion House, which served as Brigham Young's abode during the mid-19th century, but there is a restaurant on the lower level that is a good spot for a lunch break. Next door, the Beehive House, another former Young residence and a National Historic Landmark, offers free tours every day. Just east of these houses on South Temple is Eagle Gate (at the intersection of State Street), an impressive arch capped by a 2-ton sculpture of an eagle with a 20-foot wingspan. Just south of Eagle Gate on the east side of State Street are two of Salt Lake City's standout cultural facilities, the Hansen Planetarium (15 South State Street) and the Social Hall Heritage Museum (39 South State Street). The former features daily star shows and a free space museum with hands-on exhibits; the latter includes remnants of Utah's first public building and the West's first theater. From the museum, it's best to reverse course and walk north on State Street, passing under Eagle Gate. Just beyond North Temple, hop on the paths that run through the lush City Creek Park for break from the urban bustle and head north to the adjoining Memory Grove Park. From here, it's only a 2-block walk west to the Utah State Capitol (just north of the intersection of State Street and 300 North Street), an exemplary Renaissance Revival-style structure built from Utah granite in 1915. The building is open to the public daily and guided tours are offered on weekdays. Two blocks west of the State Capitol is the Pioneer Memorial Museum (300 North Main Street), a majestic replica of the original Salt Lake Theater (demolished in 1928) with 38 rooms of relics from the area's past, including photographs, vehicles, dolls, and weapons. The museum is on the eastern edge of one of the city's oldest neighborhoods, the tree-lined Marmalade District (between 300 and 500 North streets to the north and south and Center and Quince streets to the east and west), a good place to meander and gaze at historic homes.

Headquarters and a Ranger District office of the Wasatch-Cache National Forest are located in Salt Lake City.

Salt Lake City was laid out in grid fashion, with Temple Square at the center. Most street names are coordinates on this grid: 4th South Street is four blocks south of Temple Square, 7th East is seven blocks east. These are written as 400 South and 700 East.

What to See and Do

Alta. *Phone 801/742-3333. 26 miles SE on UT 210 in Little Cottonwood Canyon in Alta (see).*

Arrow Press Square. *165 S West Temple St. Phone 801/531-9700.* Once the city's printing district, now buildings such as Arrow Press Building (1890), Upland Hotel (1910), and Midwest Office Building Supply (1910) have been reconstructed into a retail/restaurant complex.

Brigham Young Monument. *Main and South Temple sts, at north side of intersection. Phone 801-531-9700.* (1897)

Brighton Resort. *25 miles SE via I-215, exit 6 in Big Cottonwood Canyon. Phone 801/532-4731.* Three high-speed quad, one triple, three double chairlifts; patrol, school, rentals; lodge, restaurant, cafeteria. Sixty-four runs; longest run 3 miles, vertical drop 1,745 feet. (Mid-Nov-late-Apr, daily) Night skiing (Mon-Sat). Half-day rates. **$$$$**

The Canyons. *4000 The Canyons Resort Dr (84098). Phone 435/649-5400. 28 miles E and S via I-80, UT 224 in Park City (see).*

Council Hall. *Capitol Hill, 300 N State St, 84114. Phone 801/538-1900.* (1864-1866) Meeting place of territorial legislature and city hall for 30 years was dismantled and then reconstructed in 1963 at present location; Federal/Greek-Revival-style architecture. Visitor information center and office; memorabilia. (Daily; closed Jan 1, Thanksgiving, Dec 25) **FREE**

Deer Valley Resort. *Phone 435/521-2822. 34 miles E and S via I-80, UT 224 in Park City (see).*

Fort Douglas Military Museum. *3 miles NE, Building 32 Potter St. Phone 801/581-1710.* Army museum features history of military in Utah from arrival of Johnston's Army during the 1857 "Utah War" through Vietnam.

Also tours of fort (self-guided or guided, by appointment). (Tues-Sat; closed holidays)

Governor's Mansion. *603 E South Temple St. Phone 801/538-1005.* (1902) Restored mansion of Thomas Kearns, wealthy Utah senator of early 1900s; decorated with Italian marble. Tours. (Apr-mid-Dec, Tues and Thurs afternoons; closed holidays) **FREE**

Hansen Planetarium. *15 S State St. Phone 801/538-2104.* Space science museum and library. Seasonal star shows, stage plays (fee; schedule varies). (Daily; closed holidays) **FREE**

Hogle Zoological Garden. *2600 E Sunnyside Ave. Phone 801/582-1631.* Wildlife exhibits; Discovery Land; bird show; miniature train (summer). Picnicking, concession. (Daily; closed Jan 1, Dec 25) **$$$**

InnsBrook Tours. *3359 S Main, Suite 804 (84115). Phone 801/534-1001.*

Kennecott Bingham Canyon Mine. *8400 W Hwy U 111. Phone 801/569-6248 or 801/252-3234.* Open-pit copper mine 2 1/2 miles wide and 1/2 mile deep. Visitor center, observation deck, and audio presentation explain mining operations, which date from 1906. Gift shop.(Apr-mid-Oct, daily) **$$**

Lagoon Amusement Park, Pioneer Village and Water Park. *17 miles N on I-15, exit 325, then N to Lagoon Dr. Phone 800/748-5246.* Rides, water slides; re-creation of 19th-century Utah town; stagecoach and steam-engine train rides. Camping, picnicking. (Memorial Day-Aug, daily; mid-Apr-late May and Sept, Sat and Sun only) Parking (fee).

Liberty Park. *1300 South St. Phone 801/972-7800 (park) or 801/596-8500 (aviary).* In 100-acre park are Chase Mill (1852), Tracy Aviary, children's garden playground (Apr-Sept), amusement park. Swimming; lighted tennis, horseshoe courts, picnicking. (Daily) **FREE**

Lion House. *63 and 67 E South Temple. Phone 801/363-5466 (Lion House) or 801/240-2671 (Beehive House).* (1856) and Beehive House. (1854) Family residences, offices, and social centers for Brigham Young and his wives and children. Guided tours of Beehive House. (Daily; closed Jan 1, Thanksgiving, Dec 25) **FREE**

Maurice Abravanel Concert Hall. *123 W South Temple. Phone 801/533-6683 or 801/533-6407 (box office).* The home of the Utah Symphony, this building is adorned with more than 12,000 square feet of 24-karat gold leaf and a mile of brass railing. It has been rated one of the acoustically best halls in the US. Free tours (by appointment). The symphony has performances most weekends.

Park City Mountain Resort. *32 miles E and S via I-80, UT 224 in Park City.*

Pioneer Memorial Museum. *300 N Main St, west side of capitol grounds. Phone 801/538-1050.* Manuscripts, pioneer relics. Also here is **Carriage House,** with exhibits relating to transportation, including Brigham Young's wagon, mule-drawn vehicles, Pony Express items. One-hour guided tours (by appointment). (Mon-Sat; closed holidays) **FREE**

River trips. Moki Mac River Expeditions. *6006 S 1300 E. Phone 801/268-6667 or 800/284-7280.* Offers 1-14-day whitewater trips on the Green and Colorado rivers. Contact PO Box 71242, 84171. **$$$$**

Salt Lake Art Center. *20 S West Temple. Phone 801/328-4201.* Changing exhibits; school; lectures, seminars, films. (Tue-Sun; closed holidays) **DONATION**

Sightseeing USA. *553 W and 100 S sts. Phone 801/521-7060.*

Snowbird. *25 miles E and S via I-215, UT 210 in Little Cottonwood Canyon (see SNOWBIRD). Phone 801/521-2822.*

Solitude Resort. *12000 Big Cottonwood Canyon (84121). SE via I-215, in Big Cottonwood Canyon. Phone 801/534-1400.* Detachable quad, two triple, four double chairlifts; race course, patrol, school, rentals; day lodge, cafeteria, restaurants, bar. Longest run 3 1/2 miles, vertical drop 2,047 feet. (Nov-Apr, daily) Cross-country center. **$$$$**

State Capitol. *350 N Main St. Phone 801/538-1563.* (1914) Constructed of Utah granite and Georgia marble, with a modern annex, the capitol has a commanding view of the valley and Wasatch Mountains. Gold Room is decorated with bird's-eye marble and gold from Utah mines; ground floor has exhibits. Open daily. Guided tours every 30 minutes (Mon-Fri; hours vary). **FREE**

★ **Temple Square.** *Main and N,S, and W Temple sts (84101). N, S, Phone 801/240-1245.* (Daily) Visitor centers provide information, exhibits and guided tours (1/2- to 1-hour; daily, every 15 minutes). **FREE** Tour includes

Assembly Hall. *Phone 801/521-2822.* (1880) Tours (daily), concerts (Fri, Sat evenings).

Family History Library. *35 N W Temple. Phone 801/240-2331.* Largest genealogy library in the world aids in compilation of family histories. (Mon-Sat) **FREE**

Museum of Church History and Art. *45 N W Temple St. Phone 801/240-3310.* Exhibits of Latter-Day Saints church history from 1820 to present. (Daily; closed Jan 1, Easter, Thanksgiving, Dec 25) **FREE**

Seagull Monument. *Phone 801/521-2822.* (1913) Commemorates saving of the crops from crickets in 1848.

Tabernacle. *15 E South Temple. Phone 801/521-2822.* (1867) The self-supporting roof, an elongated dome, is 250 feet long and 150 feet wide. The tabernacle organ has 11,623 pipes, ranging from 5/8 inch to 32 feet in length. The world-famous Tabernacle Choir may be heard at rehearsal (Thu evening) or at broadcast time (Sun morning). Organ recitals (Mon-Sat noon, Sun afternoon). **FREE**

Temple. *N, S, and W Temple and Main sts. Phone 801-521-2822.* (1893) Used for sacred ordinances, such as baptisms and marriages. Closed to non-Mormons.

This is the Place Heritage Park. *2601 Sunnyside Ave. Phone 801/582-1847.* Day-use museum park at mouth of Emigration Canyon, where Mormon pioneers first entered the valley. In park are **"This Is the Place" Monument** (1947), commemorating Brigham Young's words upon first seeing the Salt Lake City site; visitor center with audio presentation and murals of the Mormon migration; and **Old Deseret Pioneer Village,** a living museum that depicts the 1847-1869 era and pioneer life. (June-Sept, daily) **$$**

Timpanogos Cave National Monument. (see) *26 miles S on I-15, then 10 miles E on UT 92.*

Trolley Square. *500 S st and 600 E sts. Bounded by 500 and 600 S sts and 600 and 700 E sts. Phone 801/521-9877.* Ten-acre complex of trolley barns converted into entertainment/shopping/dining center. (Daily)

University of Utah. *200 South St. 2 1/2 miles E, at head of 200 S St. Phone 801/581-6515.* (1850) 25,900 students. On campus are

Marriott Library. *Phone 801/581-8558.* Western Americana collection, rare books, manuscripts. (Daily; closed holidays, also July 24) **FREE**

Pioneer Theatre Company. *300 S and 1400 E sts. Phone 801/581-6270 or 801/581-6961 (box office).* Two auditoriums; dramas, musicals, comedies. (Sept-May; closed holidays)

Red Butte Garden and Arboretum. *On campus. Phone 801/581-4747.* More than 9,000 trees on 150 acres, representing 350 species; conservatory. Self-guided tours. Special events in summer. (Daily; closed Dec 25) **FREE**

Utah Museum of Fine Arts. *Art & Architecture Center, south of library. Phone 801/581-7332.* Representations of artistic styles from Egyptian antiquities to contemporary American paintings; 19th-century French and American paintings, furniture. (Daily; closed holidays) **FREE**

Utah Museum of Natural History. *Phone 801/581-4303.* Halls of anthropology, biology, mineralology, paleontology, geology; traveling exhibits. (Daily; closed holidays, also July 24) **$$**

Utah Fun Dome. *S on I-15, 53rd St S exit, W to 700 West, then N to 4998 S 360 W, in Murray. Phone 801/265-3866.* Enclosed mall with entertainment, rides, bowling, rollerskating, baseball, arcades, miniature golf; cafes. Fee for activities. (Daily)

Utah Jazz (NBA). *301 W South Temple. Delta Center. Phone 801/355-3865.*

Utah Opera Company. *50 W 200 South St. Phone 801/736-6868 or 801/355-ARTS (tickets).* Grand opera. (Oct-May)

Utah Starzz (WNBA). *301 W South Temple. Delta Center. Phone 801/355-DUNK.*

Wasatch-Cache National Forest. *E via I-80; or N via US 89; Lone Peak Wilderness Area, 20 miles SE. Contact the Supervisor, 8230 Federal Building, 125 S State St, 84138; Phone 801/524-3900.* High Uintas Wilderness Area has alpine lakes and rugged peaks; Big Cottonwood, Little Cottonwood, and Logan canyons. Forest (1 million acres) has fishing, boating; deer and elk hunting, winter sports, picnicking, camping (fees). **FREE**

Wheeler Historic Farm. *6351 S 900 East St, 15 miles SE on I-15, exit I-215. Phone 801/264-2241.* Living history farm (75 acres) depicts rural life from 1890 to 1918. Farmhouse, farm buildings; animals, crops; hay rides (fee; no rides Sun). Tour (fee). Visitors can feed animals, gather eggs, and milk cows. **$$**

ZCMI (Zion's Co-operative Mercantile Institution) Center. *36 S State St. Phone 801/321-8745.* Department store established in 1868 by Brigham Young anchors this 85-store, enclosed, downtown shopping mall. (Mon-Sat) **FREE**

Special Events

Days of '47 Celebration. *300 N Main St.* Mid-July.

Utah Arts Festival. *331 Pierpont Ave. Phone 801/322-2428. Downtown.* More than 1,000 participants, 90 performing groups; Children's Art Yard, juried show with demonstrations. Ethnic food. Last week in June.

Utah State Fair. *155 N 1000 W (84116). State Fair Park. Phone 801/538-FAIR.* Mid-Sept.

Motels/Motor Lodges

★**BEST WESTERN EXECUTIVE INN.** *280 W 72nd S (84047). Phone 801/566-4141; toll-free 800/253-0512; fax 801/566-5142. www.bestwesternexecinn.com.* 92 rooms, 2 story. Late Dec-Mar: S, D $59-$89; each additional $5; suites $79-$149; under 18 free; lower rates rest of year. Complimentary continental breakfast. Check-out noon. TV. In-room modem link. Laundry services. Health club privileges. Whirlpool. Cr cds: A, C, D, DS, JCB, MC, V.

D ⊠ ⊠ SC

★★**BEST WESTERN SALT LAKE PLAZA HOTEL.** *122 W S Temple St. (84101). Phone 801/521-0130; toll-free 800/366-3684; fax 801/322-5057. www.bestwestern.com.* 226 rooms, 13 story. S, D $69-$119; each additional $10; suites $159-$269; under 18 free. Crib free. Pet accepted; $10. Check-out noon. TV; cable. In-room modem link. Refrigerators, coffee. Valet services, laundry. Restaurant 6 am-11 pm.

Room service. Exercise equipment. Heated pool, whirlpool. Airport transportation. Meeting rooms. Business services. Concierge. Gift shop. Cr cds: A, C, D, DS, JCB, MC, V.

★BRIGHTON SKI RESORT. *Star Rte (84121). Phone 801/532-4731; toll-free 800/873-5512; fax 435/649-1787.* 22 rooms, 2 story. Mid-Nov-mid-Apr: S, D $50-$120; lower rates rest of year. TV room. Heated pool; whirlpool. Bar. Check-out 11:30 am. Downhill/cross-country ski on site. Refrigerators. Picnic tables, grills. On creek. Cr cds: A, DS, MC, V.

★ COMFORT INN. *200 N Admiral Byrd Rd (84116). Phone 801/537-7444; fax 801/532-4721. www.slccomfortinn.com.* 155 rooms, 4 story. S, D $69-$139; each additional $10; under 18 free. Crib free. Pet accepted; $15. TV. Heated pool; whirlpool. Restaurant 6:30-9:30 am, 11 am-2 pm, 5-11 pm. Room service. Check-out 11 am. Meeting rooms. Business services available. Valet service. Free airport transportation. Exercise equipment. Some refrigerators; microwaves available. Some balconies. Cr cds: A, C, D, DS, JCB, MC, V.

★ COMFORT INN. *8955 S 255 W (84070). Phone 801/255-4919; fax 801/255-4998. www.comfortinn.com.* 97 rooms, 2 story. S, D $64.99-$79.95; each additional $5; under 18 free. Crib $10. Complimentary continental breakfast. Check-out noon. TV; cable (premium), VCR (movies $2). In-room modem link. Indoor pool, whirlpool. Meeting rooms. Business services. Cr cds: A, C, D, DS, JCB, MC, V.

★ COUNTRY INN & SUITES. *3422 S Decker Lake Dr (84119). Phone 801/908-0311; fax 801/908-0315. www.countryinns.com.* 82 rooms, 49 suites, 3 story. S $79-$89; D $79-$97; each additional $8; suites $89-$97; under 18 free; weekend rates. Complimentary continental breakfast. Check-out noon. TV; cable. In-room modem link. Laundry services. Indoor pool; whirlpools. Free airport transportation. Cr cds: A, C, D, DS, JCB, MC, V.

★★COURTYARD BY MARRIOTT. *10701 S Holiday Park Dr (93515). Phone 801/571-3600; toll-free 800/321-2211; fax 801/572-1383. www.courtyard.com.* 124 rooms, 4 story. S, D $69-$109; each additional $10; suites $150-$155; under 18 free; weekend, holiday rates; ski plan. Crib free. TV; cable (premium). Indoor pool; whirlpool. Complimentary coffee in rooms. Restaurant 6:30-10:30 am, 5-10 pm. Room service. Bar 5-10 pm. Check-out noon. Coin laundry. Meeting rooms. Business services avail-

able. Exercise equipment. Health club privileges. Microwaves available. Some balconies. Cr cds: A, C, D, DS, MC, V.

★ DAYS INN AIRPORT. *1900 W North Temple (84116). Phone 801/539-8538; toll-free 800/329-7466; fax 801/595-1041. www.daysinn.com.* 110 rooms, 2 story. S, D $58-$105; each additional $7; suites $98-$125; under 17 free. Crib free. Pet accepted. TV; cable (premium). Indoor pool. Complimentary continental breakfast. Restaurant nearby. Check-out 11 am. Business services available. In-room modem link. Valet service. Guest laundry. Free airport, train station, bus depot transportation. Exercise equipment. Health club privileges. Refrigerators, microwaves. Cr cds: A, C, D, DS, JCB, MC, V.

★ HAMPTON INN. *2393 S 800 W (84087). Phone 801/296-1211; toll-free 888/834-4470; fax 801/296-1222. www.hamptoninn.com.* 60 rooms, 3 story. S $69; D $74; suites $129; under 18 free. Crib free. Pet accepted. TV; cable (premium). Indoor pool; whirlpool. Complimentary continental breakfast. Restaurant nearby. Check-out noon. Meeting rooms. Business services available. In-room modem link. Coin laundry. Free airport transportation. Health club privileges. Microwaves available. Cr cds: A, C, D, DS, MC, V.

★ HAMPTON INN. *10690 S Holiday Park Dr (84070). Phone 801/571-0800; fax 801/572-0708. www.hamptoninn.com.* 131 rooms, 4 story. S, D $78-$88; under 18 free; weekly rates, ski plans. Crib free. TV; cable (premium). Indoor pool; whirlpool. Complimentary continental breakfast. Restaurant adjacent 6 am-11 pm. Check-out noon. Coin laundry. Meeting rooms. Business services available. In-room modem link. Sundries. Free bus depot transportation. Downhill ski 14 miles. Exercise equipment. Health club privileges. Microwaves available. Shopping center adjacent. Cr cds: A, C, D, DS, MC, V.

★★HOLIDAY INN. *999 S Main Street (84111). Phone 801/359-8600; toll-free 800/933-9678; fax 801/359-7186. www.saltlakeholidayinn.com.* 292 rooms, 14 suites, 3 story. S, D $89; each additional $10; under 18 free. Crib free. Check-out noon. TV; cable, VCR available. Some refrigerators. Coin laundry. Restaurant 6 am-2 pm, 5-10 pm. Room service. Playgrounds. Exercise equipment, sauna. Pool, indoor pool, outdoor pool, whirlpool. Tennis. Lawn games. Free airport transportation. Business center. Convention center/facilities. Concierge. Gift shop. Cr cds: A, C, D, DS, JCB, MC, V.

★ **LA QUINTA.** *7231 S Catalpa Rd (84047). Phone 801/ 566-3291; fax 801/562-5943. www.laquinta.com.* 122 rooms, 2 story. S $69; D $77; each additional $8; under 18 free. Crib free. Pet accepted. TV; cable (premium). Heated pool. Continental breakfast. Complimentary coffee in rooms. Restaurant adjacent open 24 hours. Check-out noon. Coin laundry. In-room modem link. Downhill ski 15 miles; cross-country ski 20 miles. Health club privileges. Microwaves available. Cr cds: A, C, D, DS, JCB, MC, V.

D ⬛⬛⬛⬛⬛⬛⬛⬛

★ **QUALITY INN.** *4465 Century Dr S (84123). Phone 801/268-2533; fax 801/266-6206. www. sunbursthospitality.com.* 131 rooms, 2 story. Feb-Mar, July-Sept: S, D $65.95-$79.95; under 18 free; each additional $5; ski plan; lower rates rest of year. Pet accepted; fee. Complimentary continental breakfast. Check-out noon. TV; cable (premium). In-room modem link. Laundry services. Pool, whirlpool. Cr cds: A, C, D, DS, JCB, MC, V.

D ⬛⬛⬛⬛⬛

★★ **RAMADA INN DOWNTOWN.** *230 W 600 S (84101). Phone 801/364-5200; toll-free 800/595-0505; fax 801/359-2542. www.ramadainnslc.com.* 160 rooms, 2 story. S, D $59.95-$69.95; each additional $10; under 19 free. Crib free. Pet accepted, some restrictions; $10 deposit. Check-out noon. TV; cable. In-room modem link. Microwaves. Valet services, coin laundry. Restaurant 6 am-10 pm; Sun 6:30 am-9 pm. Room service. Exercise equipment, sauna. Game room, recreation room. Indoor pool, whirlpool. Free airport, train station, bus depot transportation. Meeting rooms. Business services. Private club from 5 pm. Cr cds: A, D, DS, MC, V.

D ⬛⬛⬛⬛⬛⬛⬛

★★ **SHILO INN.** *206 SW Temple St (84101). Phone 801/521-9500; toll-free 800/222-2244; fax 801/359-6527. www.shiloinns.com.* 200 rooms, 12 story. S, D $79.95-$125; each additional $12; suites $265-$425; under 12 free. Crib free. Complimentary full breakfast. Check-out noon. TV; cable (premium), VCR (movies $3). Refrigerators, microwaves, bathroom phones, Coffee in rooms. Coin laundry. Restaurant 6 am-10 pm. Exercise equipment, sauna. Heated pool, whirlpool. Free airport transportation. Meeting rooms. Business services. Gift shop. Cr cds: A, D, DS, MC, V.

D ⬛⬛⬛⬛⬛

★ **SLEEP INN.** *10626 S 300 W (84095). Phone 801/ 572-2020; toll-free 800/331-0073; fax 801/572-2459. www.sleepinn.com.* 68 rooms, 2 story. S $59-$69; D $65-$75; each additional $5; family rates. Crib free. Complimentary continental breakfast. Check-out noon. TV; cable (premium), VCR (movies). In-room modem link. Coin laundry. Restaurant nearby. Health club privileges. Indoor pool. Downhill ski 20 miles. Business services. Cr cds: A, DS, MC, V.

D ⬛⬛⬛⬛

★ **SUPER 8 MOTEL.** *616 S 200 W (84101). Phone 801/534-0808; fax 801/355-7735.* 120 rooms, 4 story. S $45.99; D $55.99; under 13 free; package plans; higher rates special events. Crib free. TV; cable (premium). Complimentary coffee in lobby. Restaurant nearby. Check-out 11 am. Business services available. Sundries. Coin laundry. Some refrigerators, microwaves. Cr cds: A, C, D, DS, MC, V.

D ⬛⬛⬛⬛⬛⬛⬛ SC

★ **TRAVELODGE.** *524 SW Temple St (84101). Phone 801/531-7100; toll-free 800/578-7878; fax 801/359-3814. www.travelodge.com.* 60 rooms, 3 story. S $50-$72; D $58-$79; each additional $6; under 18 free. Crib free. Pet accepted. TV; cable (premium). Heated pool; whirlpool. Complimentary coffee in rooms. Restaurant nearby. Check-out noon. Business services available. Cr cds: A, C, D, DS, JCB, MC, V.

⬛⬛⬛ SC

Hotels

★★ **CRYSTAL INN.** *2254 W City Center Ct (84119). Phone 801/736-2000; toll-free 888/977-9400; fax 801/ 736-2001. www.crystalinns.com.* 122 rooms, 3 story. S, D $69-$109; each additional $10; suites $129; under 18 free; weekend rates. Crib free. Complimentary breakfast, coffee and tea. Check-out noon. TV; cable, VCR available. In-room modem link. Refrigerators, microwaves, bathroom phones. Coin laundry. Indoor pool. Free airport, train station transportation. Meeting rooms. Business services. Cr cds: A, C, D, DS, MC, V.

D ⬛⬛⬛ SC

★★ **CRYSTAL INN.** *230 W 500 S (84101). Phone 801/328-4466; toll-free 800/366-4466; fax 801/328-4072. www.crystalinns.com.* 175 rooms, 4 story. S, D $89-$149; each additional $10; under 18 free; ski plan. Crib free. Complimentary breakfast. Check-out noon. TV; cable. In-room modem link. Refrigerators, microwaves. Valet services, laundry. Restaurant adjacent open 24 hours. Exercise equipment, sauna. Indoor pool, whirlpool. Free airport transportation. Meeting rooms. Business services. Sundries. Cr cds: A, C, D, DS, MC, V.

D ⬛⬛⬛ SC

★★ **FOUR POINTS BY SHERATON AIRPORT.** *307 N Admiral Byrd Rd (84116). Phone 801/530-0088; toll-free 800/325-3535.* 98 rooms, 3 story. S, D $145-$250; each additional $20; under 17 free. Crib $15. Check-out noon. TV; cable (premium), VCR available. Refrigerators. Restaurant 6 am-10 pm. Exercise room. Pool. Meeting rooms. Business center. Gift shop. Cr cds: A, C, D, DS, MC, V.

D ⬛⬛⬛⬛⬛⬛

★ ★ ★ ★ **THE GRAND AMERICA HOTEL.** *555 S Main St (84111). Phone 801/258-6000; toll-free 800/453-9450; fax 801/258-6811. www.grandamerica.com.* Set against the beautiful backdrop of the Wasatch Mountains, The Grand America is a tribute to the glory of old-world Europe. This esteemed hotel is the pinnacle of refinement. The details make the difference here, from intuitive service to extraordinary amenities. The guest rooms are classically French, with plush carpets, resplendent fabrics, fine art, and Richelieu furniture. Private balconies draw guests' attention to the splendid mountain views. Several dining establishments tantalize tastebuds in a variety of atmospheric settings. Afternoon tea, with its delicate sandwiches and flaky pastries, is particularly notable here, and the seasonally inspired cuisine of the Garden Cafe is matched by its lovely outdoor venue. The hotel's convenient location is perfect for exploring Utah's famous great outdoors, yet the two pools, spa, salon, and fine shopping persuade many to remain within this temple of luxury. 775 rooms, 24 story. S, D $195-$250; each additional; $20; under 17 free. Check-out noon. TV; cable (premium), VCR available. Restaurant 6 am-10 pm. Exercise room. Indoor pool. Golf on premises. Tennis on premises. Business center. Cr cds: A, C, D, DS, MC, V.

D 🐾 🏋 🍴 ⛽ 🏊 ✈ 🏃

★ ★ ★ **HILTON SALT LAKE CITY AIRPORT.** *5151 Wiley Post Way (84116). Phone 801/539-1515; toll-free 800/999-3736; fax 801/539-1113. www.hilton.com.* With views of the Wasatch and Oquirrh mountains this hotel is minutes from the airport. Amenities include an outdoor swiiming pool and hot tub, Other activities are paddle boats, a putting green, jogging path, fitness center and indoor pool. Grill 114 is a full service restaurant with seating outside and great panoramas. 287 rooms, 5 story. Jan-Oct: S $79-$169; D $89-$179; each additional $10; suites $189-$299; under 18 free; family rates; package plans; lower rates rest of year. Crib free. Pet accepted; $50 deposit. Complimentary coffee and tea. Check-out 1 pm. TV; cable, VCR available. Balconies, refrigerators, in-room whirlpools. Laundry. Restaurant 6 am-11 pm. Bar 4:30 pm-midnight. Exercise equipment. Indoor pool, whirlpool. 9-hole, putting green. Picnic tables. Free airport, train station transportation. Business center. Convention center/facilities. Concierge. Gift shop. Luxury level. Cr cds: A, C, D, DS, ER, JCB, MC, V.

D 🐾 🏋 🛢 🍴 🍽 🏊 🍴 ✈ 🏃

★ ★ ★ **HILTON SALT LAKE CITY CENTER.** *255 S W Temple (84101). Phone 801/328-2000; toll-free 800/445-8667; fax 801/238-4888. www.hilton.com.* Located in the heart of downtown, guests can enjoy all the comforts of home with spacious rooms and friendly service. 500 rooms, 18 story. S, D $129-$170; each additional $20; suites $300-$450; under 18 free; weekend rates; ski package. Crib free. Pet accepted. Complimentary coffee and tea. Check-out noon. TV; VCR available. In-room modem link. Some refrigerators. Restaurant (See also SPENCER'S). Exercise equipment, sauna. Indoor pool, whirlpool, poolside service. Valet parking, covered parking. Airport, train station, bus depot transportation available. Business center. Convention center/facilities. Concierge. Gift shop. Luxury level, private club. Cr cds: A, C, D, DS, ER, JCB, MC, V.

D 🐾 🏊 🍴 ✈ 🍽 SC 🏃

★ ★ ★ **HOTEL MONACO.** *15 W 200 S (84101). Phone 801/595-0000; toll-free 877/294-9710; fax 801/532-8500. www.monaco-saltlakecity.com.* Located in the heart of the city, within a short walk of many major attractions, this former bank building offers visually striking décor in the public areas and handsomely furnished guest rooms. 225 rooms, 15 story, 36 suites. Jan-Apr, June, Aug-Sept: S, D $129-$325; suites $225-$260; under 18 free; lower rates rest of year. Crib available. Pet accepted. Valet parking. TV; cable, CD available. Complimentary coffee in rooms. Restaurant 7 am-11 pm. Bar. Check-out noon, check-in 3 pm. Meeting rooms. Bellstaff. Dry cleaning. Exercise equipment. Golf. Tennis. Downhill skiing. Picnic facilities. Cr cds: A, C, D, DS, JCB, MC, V.

D 🐾 🏌 🎿 🍴 🏋 ✈ 🍽 SC 🏃

★ ★ ★ **INN AT TEMPLE SQUARE.** *71 W S Temple (84101). Phone 801/531-1000; toll-free 800/843-4668; fax 801/536-7272. www.theinn.com.* Nestled in the heart of downtown Salt Lake City and just blocks from the Symphony Hall and Temple Square, this Edwardian landmark offers guests a truly unique stay. From the warm and personal service to the elegant guest rooms, this hotel offers style and personal service that immediately welcomes guests and relaxes them. 90 rooms, 10 suites, 7 story. S, D $115-$130; each additional $10; suites $170; under 18 free. Crib free. Complimentary breakfast. Check-out noon. TV; cable, VCR available. Refrigerators, bathroom phones. Valet services. 6:30-9:30 am, 11:30 am-2:30 pm, 5-10 pm. Room service. Health club privileges. Pool. Free airport, train station, bus depot transportation. Business services. Concierge. Elegant inn built in 1930; antiques from old Hotel Utah. Opposite Temple Square. Totally nonsmoking. Cr cds: A, D, DS, MC, V.

D 🏊 🍴 ✈ 🍽

★ ★ ★ **LA EUROPA ROYALE.** *1135 Vine (84121). Phone 801/263-7999; toll-free 800/LAEUROPA; fax 801/263-8090. www.laeuropa.com.* Tucked away in a residential area, the large floor-to-ceiling windows in the public areas overlook the lovely landscaped grounds punctuated with fountains and small ponds. 9 rooms, 9 suites, 2 story. Dec-Apr: S, D $130-$230; lower rates rest of year. Crib $10. Complimentary full breakfast, coffee in rooms. Check-out noon. TV; cable (premium),

VCR available. Laundry, dry cleaning. Restaurant 7 am-10 pm. Bar. Exercise equipment. Downhill skiing. Picnic tables. Bike rentals, Hiking trail. Valet parking. Airport transportation available. Meeting rooms. Business center. Concierge. Cr cds: A, C, D, DS, MC, V.

★ ★ ★ **LITTLE AMERICA HOTEL.** *500 S Main St (84101). Phone 801/363-6781; toll-free 800/453-9450; fax 801/596-5911. www.littleamerica.com.* This hotel provides every possible amenity, along with elegant and spacious rooms. 850 rooms, 17 story. S $75; D $85; suites $800; under 13 free. Crib free. Check-out 1 pm. TV; cable (premium). Refrigerators, bathroom phones. Restaurant 5 am-midnight; dining room 7-10 am, 11 am-2 pm, 5-11 pm. Bar noon-midnight; entertainment. Health club privileges, exercise equipment, sauna. Indoor pool, wading pool, whirlpool. Barber, beauty shop. Parking, covered parking, free parking. Free airport, train station, bus depot transportation. Business services. Convention center/facilities. Cr cds: A, C, D, DS, MC, V.

★ ★ ★ **MARRIOTT CITY CENTER.** *220 South State St (84111). Phone 801/961-8700; fax 801/961-8704. www.marriott.com.* 359 rooms, 12 story. S, D $150-$225; each additional $20; under 17 free. Crib free. Indoor pool. TV; cable (premium), VCR available. Complimentary coffee in rooms. Restaurant 6 am-10 pm. Check-out noon. Meeting rooms. Business center. Gift shop. Exercise room. Golf, tennis nearby. Some refrigerators, minibars. Cr cds: A, C, D, DS, MC, V.

★ ★ ★ **MARRIOTT DOWNTOWN.** *75 S West Temple (84101). Phone 801/531-0800; fax 801/532-4127. www.marriott.com/slcut/.* Located across from the Salt Palace Convention Center this hotel caters to the business traveler and is close to the airport and major ski resorts. 515 rooms, 15 story. S $109-$135; D $119-$145; suites $250-$850; family rates; package plans. Crib free. Check-out noon. TV; cable (premium). In-room modem link. Balconies. Laundry. Restaurant 6:30 am-11 pm; Fri, Sat to midnight. Exercise equipment, sauna. Heated indoor/outdoor pool; whirlpool, poolside service. Valet parking, covered parking. Airport transportation available. Business center. Convention center/facilities. Concierge, luxury level, private club. Cr cds: A, C, D, DS, ER, JCB, MC, V.

★ ★ ★ **MARRIOTT UNIVERSITY PARK.** *480 Wakara Way (84108). Phone 801/581-1000; toll-free 800/637-4390; fax 801/584-3321. www.marriott.com.* Situated at the base of Wasatch Mountains in the scenic University of Utah Research Park, this well appointed hotel offers guests a very comfortable stay.

218 rooms, 7 story, 29 suites. S, D $125-$195; suites $145-$205; under 12 free. Crib free. TV; cable (premium). Indoor pool; whirlpool. Restaurant 6:30 am-10 pm. Bar 4 pm-midnight. Check-out noon. Meeting rooms. Business center. Gift shop. Free airport, train station, bus depot transportation. Downhill/cross-country ski 15 miles. Exercise equipment. Recreation room. Refrigerators, wet bar; microwave in suites. Cr cds: A, C, D, DS, ER, JCB, MC, V.

★ ★ **PEERY HOTEL.** *110 W 300 S (84101). Phone 801/521-4300; toll-free 800/331-0073; fax 801/575-5014. www.peeryhotel.com.* 73 rooms, 3 story. S, D $99-$149; under 16 free; weekend rates. Check-out 11 am. TV; cable (premium). Bar. Exercise equipment. Airport transportation. Meeting rooms. Concierge, Historic building (1910). Cr cds: A, C, DS, MC, V.

★ ★ ★ **RADISSON HOTEL AIRPORT.** *2177 W N Temple (84116). Phone 801/364-5800; fax 801/364-5823. www.radisson.com.* This hotel, set off the highway and near the airport, still manages to maintain a quiet elegance and sophisticated grace. Guests can get cozy in the French provincial-style rooms. 126 rooms, 46 suites, 3 story. S, D $89-$159; each additional $10; suites $109-$159; under 18 free; ski, golf plans. Crib free. Complimentary continental breakfast. Check-out noon. TV; cable (premium). Balconies, refrigerators, microwaves, fireplaces, bathroom phones. Restaurant 6:30-10 am, 11:30 am-2 pm, 5-10 pm; Sat, Sun 6:30-11 am. Room service. Exercise equipment. Heated pool. Free garage parking. Free airport, train station, bus depot transportation. Meeting rooms. Business services. Cr cds: A, C, D, DS, ER, JCB, MC, V.

★ ★ ★ **SHERATON CITY CENTRE.** *150 W 500 S (84101). Phone 801/401-2000; toll-free 800/421-7602; fax 801/531-0705. www.sheraton.com.* Located within walking distance of downtown attractions, guests are offered all the luxury of a full service hotel. This hotel offers a scenic view of the mountains. 362 rooms, 10 story. S, D $89-$159; each additional $10; suites $195-$399; ski plans. Crib free. Pet accepted, some restrictions; $50 deposit. TV; cable (premium), VCR available. Pool; whirlpool, poolside service. Restaurant 6 am-11:30 pm. Private club 11:30 am-midnight, Sun 5-10 pm. Check-out noon. Convention facilities. Business center. In-room modem link. Barber, beauty shop. Free airport transportation. Exercise equipment; sauna. Health club privileges. Ski rentals available. Balconies. Luxury level. Cr cds: A, C, D, DS, JCB, MC, V.

★ ★ **WYNDHAM HOTEL.** *215 W S Temple (84101). Phone 801/531-7500; toll-free 800/553-0075; fax 801/328-1289. www.wyndham.com.* 381 rooms, 15 story. S, D $79-$179; each additional $10; suites $179-$550; under 18 free; weekend, holiday rates; ski plans. TV; cable (premium). Indoor pool; whirlpool. Coffee in rooms. Restaurant 6 am-10 pm. Bar 3 pm-midnight. Check-out noon. Convention facilities. Business center. In-room modem link. Concierge. Gift shop. Airport, train station transportation available. Exercise equipment; sauna. Health club privileges. Microwaves available. Adjacent to Delta Center. Cr cds: A, C, D, DS, ER, JCB, MC, V.

D ⛵ 🎿 🏋 ⊠ SC

All Suite

★ ★ **CHASE SUITE HOTEL.** *765 E 400 S (84102). Phone 801/532-5511; toll-free 800/237-8811; fax 801/531-0416. www.woodfinsuitehotels.com.* 128 kitchen suites (1-2-bedroom) kitchen units, 2 story. S, D $99-$199; suites $159-$199; weekly, monthly rates;. Pet accepted. Complimentary continental breakfast. Check-out noon. TV; cable (premium). In-room modem link. Microwaves, fireplaces. Valet services, laundry. Heated pool. Free airport, train station, bus depot transportation. Business services. Sport court. Cr cds: A, C, D, DS, JCB, MC, V.

D 🐾 ⛵ 🎿 ⊠

★ ★ ★ **EMBASSY SUITES.** *110 W 600 S (84101). Phone 801/359-7800; toll-free 800/325-7643; fax 801/359-3753. www.embassy-suites.com.* Located in the heart of Salt Lake City, this downtown hotel offers guests spacious rooms, a relaxing atmosphere, and friendly service. Nearby attractions include the LDS Mormon Temple, Salt Lake City Convention Center, and guests are just 1/2 mile to the historic Trolley Square Plaza. 241 suites, 9 story. S $89-$149; each additional $15; under 18 free; weekend, ski rates. Crib free. TV; cable (premium). Indoor pool; whirlpool. Complimentary full breakfast, coffee in rooms. Restaurant 11 am-11 pm. Private club to 1 am. Check-out noon. Coin laundry. Meeting rooms. In-room modem link. Gift shop. Covered parking. Free airport, train station, bus depot transportation. Exercise equipment; sauna. Refrigerators, wet bars, microwaves. Atrium lobby. Cr cds: A, C, D, DS, JCB, MC, V.

D ⊠ 🎿 ⛵ 🏋 🛫 ⊠ SC

B&B/Small Inns

★ ★ ★ **ARMSTRONG MANSION.** *667 E 100 S (84102). Phone 801/531-1333; toll-free 800/708-1333; fax 801/531-0282. www.armstrongmansion.com.* This bed and breakfast is tastefully decorated with antiques and carved wood, creating a relaxing setting for guests. 13 rooms, 4 with shower only, 3 story. S, D $99-$229. TV; cable, VCR. Complimentary full breakfast. Restaurant nearby. Check-out 11 am, check-in 3 pm. Luggage handling. Downhill/cross-country ski 20 miles. Built in 1893; antiques. Totally nonsmoking. Cr cds: A, MC, V.

D ⊠ ⊠ SC

★ ★ ★ **BRIGHAM STREET INN.** *1135 E S Temple St (84102). Phone 801/364-4461; fax 801/521-3201. www.brightonstreetinn.citysearch.com.* This appealing bed and breakfast is located just blocks from the scenic area of downtown Salt Lake City. This remarkable inn offers guests a relaxing stay amidst elegant surroundings. 9 rooms, fireplace in 5 rooms, 3 story. D $85-$185; each additional $10. Complimentary continental breakfast. Check-out 11 am, check-in 3 pm. TV; cable, VCR available. Cross-country ski 15 miles. Cr cds: A, MC, V.

⊠ ⊠

★ ★ ★ **SALTAIR BED & BREAKFAST.** *164 S 900 E (84102). Phone 801/533-8184; toll-free 800/733-8184; fax 801/595-0332. www.saltlakebandb.com.* Minutes from the Salt Lake International Airport, guests can easily get to the ski slopes just 35 minutes away. Close-by, are the University of Utah, the Genealogy Library, Symphony Hall, and shopping. Complimentary breakfast and evening snacks, as well as down comforters, fresh flowers, robes and salt water taffy, are just a few of the amenities. 8 rooms, 3 share baths rooms, 3 suites, 2 story. S, D $55-$149; each additional $15; suites $129-$225. Complimentary breakfast. Check-out 11 am, check-in 3:30 pm. TV; cable (premium), VCR available (movies). Refrigerators, microwaves, fireplaces. Restaurant nearby. Health club privileges. Cross-country ski 15 miles. Built in 1903; antiques. Totally nonsmoking. Some room phones. Cr cds: A, D, DS, MC, V.

⊠ ⊠

★ ★ **WILDFLOWER BED & BREAKFAST.** *936 E 1700 S (84105). Phone 801/466-0600; toll-free 800/569-0009; fax 801/466-4728. www.wildflowersbb.com.* 5 rooms, 3 story. No elevator. S, D $85-$125; kitchen unit $130-$175; under 12 free. TV; cable (premium), VCR available. Crib free. Complimentary full breakfast. Restaurant nearby. Check-out 11 am, check-in 3 pm. Business services available. Built in 1891; antiques. Totally nonsmoking. Cr cds: A, DS, MC, V.

⊠ 🏋 ⊠

Restaurants

★ ★ **ABSOLUTE.** *52 W 200 S (84101). Phone 801/359-0899; fax 801/359-0559. www.citysearch.com/slc/absolute.* Hours: 11:30 am-10 pm, Sat 5-10 pm. Lunch $5-$12, dinner $13-$29. Bar. Entertainment. Children's menu. Reservations accepted. Cr cds: A, C, D, DS, MC, V.

D ⊠

★**ARGENTINE GRILL.** *6055 S 900 E (84121). Phone 801/265-0205; fax 801/265-0760. www.argentinegrill. citysearch.com.* Continental menu. Hours: 11:30 am-3 pm, 5:30-9 pm; Fri to 10:30 pm; Sun 10 am-9 pm. Lunch $7-$9, dinner $18-$23. Outdoor dining. Totally nonsmoking. Cr cds: A, D, DS, MC, V.

D SC

★★**BABA AFGHAN.** *55 E 400 S (84111). Phone 801/596-0786.* Hours: 11:30 am-2:30 pm, 5-9:30 pm; Mon to 2:30 pm; Sat, Sun from 5 pm. Closed some holidays. Lunch Buffet $7.52, dinner $10.95-$17.95. Reservations accepted. Totally nonsmoking. Cr cds: A, D, DS, MC, V.

D

★★**BACI TRATTORIA.** *134 W Pierpont Ave (84101). Phone 801/328-1500; fax 801/539-8783. www.gastronomyinc.com.* Italian menu. Closed Sun; major holidays. Lunch, dinner. Bar. Outdoor seating. Large stained-glass partitions. Cr cds: A, C, D, DS, MC, V. **$$**

★★**BAMBARA.** *202 S Main St (84101). Phone 801/363-5454; fax 801/363-5888. www.kimptongroup.com.* Menu changes monthly. Hours: 7-10 am, 11:30 am-2:30 pm, 5:30-10 pm; Fri, Sat 5:30-11 pm. Breakfast $4-$6; lunch $9-$11, dinner $13-$28. Reservations accepted. Cr cds: A, D, DS, MC, V.

D

★**COWBOY GRUB.** *2350 1/2 Foothill Blvd (84109). Phone 801/466-8334; fax 801/466-4114. www.cowboygrub.net.* Southwestern menu. Closed Sun; major holidays; also July 24. Lunch, dinner. Children's menu. Cr cds: A, D, DS, MC, V. **$$**

D SC

★★**CREEKSIDE AT SOLITUDE.** *12000 Big Cottonwood Canyon, Solitude (84121). Phone 435/649-8400; fax 435/649-5276. www.skisolitude.com.* Continental menu. Hours: open 24 hours. Lunch $7-$12, dinner $12-$20. Children's menu. Reservations accepted (dinner). Outdoor dining. Mediterranean décor; windows overlook pond, ski slopes. Cr cds: A, D, DS, MC, V.

D

★**CUCINA.** *1026 E 2nd Ave (84103). Phone 801/322-3055; fax 801/532-8360. www.cucinadeli.com.* American menu. Breakfast, lunch, dinner, brunch. Entertainment. Cr cds: A, MC, V. **$$**

D

★★**DESERT EDGE PUB.** *273 Charlie Sq (84102). Phone 801/521-8918; fax 801/521-8839.* Contemporary American menu. Closed Dec 25. Lunch, dinner. Bar. Outdoor seating. Cr cds: A, C, DS, ER, MC, V. **$$**

D

★★★**FRESCO ITALIAN CAFI.** *1513 S 1500 E (84105). Phone 801/486-1300.* A winding brick walkway lined with flowers leads the way to this charming neighborhood bistro, which offers a roaring fireplace indoors and al fresco dining during the summer. Guests will enjoy the fresh and authentic flavors of Italy. Menu changes seasonally. Specialties: polenta, gnocchi with crab. Hours: 5-10 pm. Dinner $17-$23. Service bar. Reservations accepted. Cr cds: A, C, D, DS, MC, V.

★★★**LA CAILLE.** *9565 S Wasatch Blvd (84092). Phone 801/942-1751; fax 801/944-8990. www.lacaille.com.* An impressive country French chateau surrounded by beautiful gardens populated by peacocks, llamas, ducks, and a host of other exotic creatures are just a prelude to the authentic French menu served by a friendly staff dressed in 18th-century costumes. Hours: 6-10 pm; Sun brunch 10 am-1 pm. Dinner $28-$62. Sun brunch $18-$32. Reservations accepted. Cr cds: A, C, D, DS, ER, MC, V.

D

★**LITZA'S FOR PIZZA.** *716 E 400 S St (84102). Phone 801/359-5352; fax 801/359-5352.* Italian menu. Hours: 11 am-11 pm; Fri, Sat to 12:30 am. Closed Sun; Thanksgiving, Dec 25. Lunch $5.15-$11, dinner $8-$15. Cr cds: A, MC, V.

★★★**LOG HAVEN.** *6451 E 3800 S (84109). Phone 801/272-8255; fax 801/272-6315. www.log-haven.com.* Chef David Jones revived this rustic log mansion into Utah's most innovative and elegant restaurant. His sophisticated and excellent fresh specialties change daily. Check out the wine and dine program. Continental menu. Hours: 5:30-9 pm; Sun 4:30-8:30 pm. Closed Jan 1, July 4, Dec 25. Dinner $17-$32. Bar. Children's menu. Renovated 1920 log mansion nestled among pine trees; views of waterfall, natural surroundings. Reservations accepted. Valet parking available. Outdoor seating. Cr cds: A, C, D, DS, ER, MC, V.

D

★★**MANDARIN.** *348 E 900 N, Bountiful (84010). Phone 801/298-2406; fax 801/294-2824. www.mandarinutah.com.* Hours: 5-9:30 pm; Fri, Sat to 10:30 pm. Closed Sun; most major holidays. Reservations accepted. Chinese menu. Wine, beer. Dinner $7-$13. Parking. Elegant atmosphere. Unique Chinese décor; murals. Glass atrium in garden room. Totally nonsmoking. Cr cds: A, MC, V.

D

★ ★ **MARKET STREET BROILER.** *260 S 1300 E (84102). Phone 801/583-8808; fax 801/582-8107. www.gastronomyinc.com.* Lunch, dinner. Bar. Children's menu. Modern décor in historic former fire station. Outdoor seating. Cr cds: A, D, MC, V. **$$**

D

★ ★ **MARKET STREET GRILL.** *48 Market St (84101). Phone 801/322-4668; fax 801/531-0730. www.gastronomyinc.com.* Closed Labor Day, Thanksgiving, Dec 25. Breakfast, lunch, dinner, Sun brunch. Bar. Children's menu. In renovated 1906 hotel. Cr cds: A, C, D, DS, ER, MC, V. **$$**

D

★ ★ ★ **METROPOLITAN.** *173 W Broadway (84110). Phone 801/364-3472; fax 801/364-8671. www.themetropolitan.citysearch.com.* Contemporary American menu. Hours: 5-10 pm; Fri, Sat to 11 pm (summer) 6-9:30 pm. Closed Mon, Sun; also Jan 1, Thanksgiving, Dec 25. Dinner $18-$28. Complete meal: $55. Bar. Reservations accepted. Totally nonsmoking. Cr cds: A, DS, MC, V.

D ⊠

★ ★ **MIKADO.** *67 W 100 S St (84101). Phone 801/328-0929; fax 801/328-0933.* Japanese menu. Closed major holidays. Dinner. Children's menu. Zashiki rooms. Cr cds: A, D, DS, JCB, MC, V. **$$**

D

★★★**NEW YORKER CLUB.** *60 W Market St (84101). Phone 801/363-0166; fax 801/363-0588. www.gastronomyinc.com.* Appetizers (including fruit, cheese, and seafood) are offered as guests arrive. Continental menu. Closed Sun; major holidays; July 4. Lunch, dinner. Bar. Valet parking available. Cr cds: A, C, D, DS, ER, MC, V. **$$**

★ ★ **PIERPONT CANTINA.** *122 W Pierpont Ave (84101). Phone 801/364-1222; fax 801/539-8783. www.gastronomyinc.com.* Mexican menu. Closed Jan 1, Thanksgiving, Dec 25. Lunch, dinner. Bar. Children's menu. Outdoor seating. Totally nonsmoking. Cr cds: A, C, D, MC, V. **$$**

D

★ **RAFAEL'S.** *889 E 9400 S (84094). Phone 801/561-4545; fax 801/561-9294.* Mexican, Indian and Aztec artwork. Mexican menu. Hours: 11:30 am-9 pm; Fri, Sat to 10 pm. Closed Sun; some major holidays. Lunch, dinner $4.50-$11. Cr cds: A, DS, MC, V.

D

★ ★ **RINO'S.** *2302 Parleys Way (84109). Phone 801/484-0901.* Italian, continental menu. Closed major holidays. Dinner. Outdoor seating. Bistro-style café. Cr cds: A, DS, MC, V. **$$$**

D

★ ★ **RIO GRANDE CAFE.** *270 S Rio Grande St (84101). Phone 801/364-3302; fax 801/364-1857. www.riograndecafe.citysearch.com.* Mexican menu. Closed major holidays. Lunch, dinner. Bar. Children's menu. In historic Rio Grande Depot also housing train museum and displays. Outdoor seating. Totally nonsmoking. Cr cds: A, D, DS, MC, V. **$$**

D

★ ★ ★ **SPENCER'S.** *255 SW Temple St (84101). Phone 801/238-4748; fax 801/714-8015. www.hilton.com.* Located in the Hilton, this sophisticated restaurant offers all the steakhouse staples including a bar that allows cigar smoking (there is a cover charge). Steak menu. Lunch, dinner. Bar. Children's menu. Valet parking available. Cr cds: A, D, DS, MC, V. **$$**

D

★ **SQUATTERS PUB BREWERY.** *147 W Broadway (84101). Phone 801/363-2739; fax 801/359-5426. www.squatters.com.* Specialties: burgers, sandwiches. Own baking, pasta. Hours: 11:30-12:30 am; Sun to 11:30 pm. Closed Thanksgiving, Dec 25. Lunch, dinner $6.99-$13.99. Bar. Turn-of-the-century building; microbrewery. Guitarist Sat-Sun. Children's menu. Totally nonsmoking. Cr cds: A, C, D, DS, ER, MC, V.

D

★ **SUGARHOUSE BARBECUE.** *2207 S 700 E St (84106). Phone 801/463-4800; fax 801/463-6875. www.sugarhousebbq.com.* Barbecue menu. Closed Jan 1, Thanksgiving, Dec 25. Lunch, dinner. Outdoor seating. Totally nonsmoking. Cr cds: A, C, D, DS, MC, V. **$$**

D

★ ★ **TUCCI'S CUCINA ITALIA.** *4835 S Highland Dr (84117). Phone 801/277-8338; fax 801/277-5240.* Italian menu. Closed Thanksgiving, Dec 25. Lunch, dinner. Bar. Children's menu. Outdoor seating. Totally nonsmoking. Cr cds: A, DS, ER, MC, V. **$$**

D

★ ★ ★ **TUSCANY.** *2832 E 6200 S (84121). Phone 801/277-9919; fax 801/277-0980. www.tuscanyslc.com.* This tremendously popular Italian place maintains a high quality of service. Italian menu. Lunch, dinner. Bar. Children's menu. Italian villa décor with several unique dining rooms; landscaped, wooded grounds near Big Cottonwood Canyon. Outdoor seating. Cr cds: A, C, D, DS, ER, MC, V. **$$**

D

★ ★ **XIAO LI.** *307 W 200 S #1000 (84101). Phone 801/328-8688; fax 801/328-9488.* Chinese menu. Closed July 4, Dec 25. Lunch, dinner. Totally nonsmoking. Cr cds: A, DS, MC, V. **$$**

D

Snowbird

See also Alta, Park City, Salt Lake City

Pop 150 **Area code** 435 **Zip** 84092

In 1971, a Texas oil man recognized the potential of Little Cottonwood Canyon in the Wasatch National Forest and developed the area as a ski resort. Once home to thriving mining communities, the resort village of Snowbird, 29 miles east of Salt Lake City, now offers year-round recreational activities.

What to See and Do

Snowbird Ski and Summer Resort. *On UT 210. Contact PO Box 929000. Phone 435/742-2222 or 800/453-3000 (res).* Lifts. Seven double chairlifts, high-speed quad, 125-passenger aerial tram; patrol, school, rentals; restaurants, cafeteria, bar, children's center, four lodges. Elevations of 7,900-11,000 feet. (Mid-Nov-early May, daily) Summer activities (June-Oct, daily) include rock climbing, hiking, mountain biking (rentals), tennis; tram rides; concerts (see SPECIAL EVENTS). **$$$$**

Special Event

Utah Symphony. *7350 S Wasatch Blvd (84092). Phone 800/385-2002.* Snowbird Ski and Summer Resort (see). Summer home of the orchestra. Several Sun afternoon concerts. July-Aug.

Motel/Motor Lodge

★ ★ ★ **LODGE AT SNOWBIRD.** *Snowbird Ski and Summer Resort (84092). Phone 801/933-2229; toll-free 800/453-3000; fax 801/933-2248. www.snowbird.com.* Lodging at this condominium building in the Snowbird resort ranges from single rooms to complete studios with lofts. The mountain views are spectacular. 123 rooms, 7 story, 61 kitchens No A/C. Late Nov-early May: S, D $229; suites $498; kitchen studio rooms $269; package plans. Crib free. TV; cable (premium), VCR available. Heated pool; whirlpool. Saunas. Playground. Restaurant 4-10 pm. Bar 3 pm-1 am. Check-out 11 am. Coin laundry. Business services available. Bellstaff. Valet service. Downhill ski on site; cross-country ski 1 mile. Fireplaces. Balconies. Cr cds: A, C, D, DS, MC, V.

D ⊡ ⊡ ⊡ ⊡ ⊡

Hotel

★ ★ ★ **IRON BLOSSOM LODGE.** *Cliff Lodge Entry # 4 (UT 210) (84092). Phone 801/742-2222; toll-free 800/ 232-9542; fax 801/933-2148. www.snowbird.com.* Nestled at the base of a mountain, this hotel with its beautiful Oriental rug collection, offers an unbeatable location with exhilarating slopes and panoramic views. 370 rooms, 13 story. Dec-Mar: S, D $229-$289; suites $389-$939; under 12 free; ski packages; lower rates rest of year. Check-out 10am. TV; cable, VCR available. Some private patios. Some refrigerators. Coin laundry. Restaurant. Private club noon-1 am; Supervised children's activities; ages infant-13. Exercise room, sauna, steam room. Game room, recreation room. Heated pool, whirlpool, poolside service. Tennis. Downhill ski on site, cross-country ski 1 mile. Picnic tables. Tram allows bicycles. Barber, beauty shop. Free garage, valet parking. Airport transportation. Business center. Convention center/facilities. Concierge. Cr cds: A, D, DS, MC, V.

D ⊡ ⊡ ⊡ ⊡ ⊡ ⊡

Restaurant

★ ★ **STEAK PIT.** *Snowbird Ctr (84092). Phone 801/ 933-2260; fax 801/933-2264. www.snowbird.com.* Hours: 6-10 pm. No A/C. Service bar. Dinner $14-$42. Children's menu. Specializes in steak, seafood, chicken. Mountain view. Cr cds: A, C, D, DS, MC, V.

D SC

Timpanogos Cave National Monument (C-4)

See also Heber City, Park City, Provo

(26 miles S of Salt Lake City on I-15, then 10 miles E on UT 92)

Timpanogos (tim-pa-NOH-gos) Cave National Monument consists of three small, beautifully decorated underground chambers within limestone beds. The cave entrance is on the northern slope of Mount Timpanogos, monarch of the Wasatch Range. Much of the cave's interior is covered by a filigree of colorful crystal formations where stalactites and stalagmites are common. However, what makes Timpanogos unique is its large number of helictites—formations that appear to defy gravity as they grow outward from the walls of the cave. Temperature in Timpanogos Cave is a constant 45°F, and the interior is electrically lighted.

The cave's headquarters are located on UT 92, 8 miles east of American Fork. There is picnicking at Swinging Bridge Picnic Area, 1/4 mile from the headquarters. The cave entrance is 1 1/2 miles from headquarters via a paved trail with a vertical rise of 1,065 feet. Allow 3 to 5 hours for guided tour. No pets, no strollers, walking shoes advised, jackets and sweaters needed. Tours limited to 20 people (late May-early September, daily). Purchase tickets in advance by calling 801/756-5238 or 801/756-1679, or at the Visitor Center. Golden Age and Golden Access passports accepted (see MAKING THE MOST OF YOUR TRIP). Contact the Superintendent, Rural Route 3, Box 200, American Fork 84003; 435/756-5238. Cave tours. **$$**

Vernal (C-6)

See also Roosevelt

Pop 7,714 **Elev** 5,336 ft **Area code** 435 **Zip** 84078

Information Dinosaurland Travel Board, 55 E Main St; 435/789-6932 or 800/477-5558

Web www.dinoland.com

This is the county seat of Uintah County in northeastern Utah, which boasts oil, natural gas, and many mineral deposits. A trading center for sheep and cattle, Vernal is in an area of ancient geologic interest. Nearby are beautiful canyons, striking rock formations, and majestic peaks. Headquarters and a Ranger District office of the Ashley National Forest are located here.

What to See and Do

Ashley National Forest. *15 miles N on US 191. Contact the Supervisor, 355 N Vernal Ave. Phone 435/789-1181.* The High Uinta Mountains—the only major east-west range in the US—runs through the heart of this nearly 1 1/2 million-acre forest. The 1,500-foot-deep Red Canyon, the 13,528-foot Kings Peak, and Sheep Creek Geological Area are also here. Swimming, fishing, boating (ramps, marinas), whitewater rafting, canoeing; hiking and nature trails, cross-country skiing, snowmobiling, improved or back country campgrounds (fee). Visitor centers. **FREE**

Daughters of Utah Pioneers Museum. *500 W 200 S. Phone 435/789-3890.* Relics and artifacts dating from before 1847, when pioneers first settled in Utah; period furniture, quilts, clothing, dolls; early doctor's, dentist's, and undertaker's instruments; restored Little Rock tithing office (1887). (June-weekend before Labor Day, Mon-Sat) **DONATION**

Dinosaur National Monument. (see) *122 Canal St. Phone 315/687-3451.* **DONATION**

Flaming Gorge Dam and National Recreation Area. *42 miles N on US 191, in Ashley National Forest. Contact the Ranger District office, PO Box 279, Manila 84046. Phone 435/784-3445.* Area surrounds 91-mile-long Flaming Gorge Reservoir and 502-foot-high Flaming Gorge Dam. Fishing on reservoir and river (all year), marinas, boat ramps, waterskiing; lodges, campgrounds (fee). River rafting below dam. Visitor centers at dam and Red Canyon (on secondary paved road 3 miles off UT 44).

Ouray National Wildlife Refuge. *30 miles SW on UT 88. Phone 435/789-0351.* Waterfowl nesting marshes; desert scenery; self-guided auto tour (limited route during hunting season). (Daily) **FREE**

Red Fleet State Park. *4335 N US 191. Phone 435/789-4432.* Scenic lake highlighted by red rock formations, boating, swimming, fishing; camping. Several hundred well-preserved dinosaur tracks. (Daily) **$$**

River trips. Guided whitewater trips on the Green and Yampa rivers.

> **Adrift Adventures of Dinosaur.** *Phone 800/824-0150.* **$$$$**

> **Hatch River Expeditions.** *55 E Main St. Phone 435/789-4316 or 800/342-8243.* **$$$$**

> **Holiday River and Bike Expeditions.** *Phone 435/266-2087 or 800/624-6323 (exc UT).* **$$$$**

Steinaker State Park. *7 miles N off US 191. Phone 435/789-4432.* Approximately 2,200 acres on west shore of Steinaker Reservoir. Swimming, waterskiing, fishing, boating (ramp, dock); picnicking, tent and trailer sites (fee). (Apr-Nov; fishing all year) **$$**

Utah Field House of Natural History and Dinosaur Gardens. *235 Main St. Phone 435/789-3799.* Guarded outside by three life-size cement dinosaurs, this museum has exhibits of fossils, archaeology, life zones, geology, and fluorescent minerals of the region. Adjacent Dinosaur Gardens contain 18 life-size model dinosaurs in natural surroundings. (Daily; closed Jan 1, Thanksgiving, Dec 25) **$**

Western Heritage Museum. *302 E 200 S. Phone 435/789-7399.* Houses memorabilia from Uintah County's "outlaw" past as well as other artifacts dealing with a western theme. Includes the Thorne Collection, photographs, and artifacts of the ancient people of Utah. (Mon-Sat; closed holidays) **FREE**

Special Events

Dinosaur Roundup Rodeo. *134 W Main St (84078). Phone 800/421-9635.* Mid-July.

Outlaw Trail Festival. Festivals, sporting events, entertainment, theatrical events. Late June-mid-Aug.

Uintah County Fair. *Phone 7810770.* Aug.

Motels/Motor Lodges

★ **WESTON'S LAMPLIGHTER INN.** *120 E Main St (84078). Phone 435/789-0312; fax 435/781-1480.* 167 rooms, 2 story. May-Aug: S $36; D $56; each additional $8; under 12 free; lower rates rest of year. TV; cable (premium). Heated pool. Playground. Restaurant hours vary. Check-out 11 am. Business services available. Picnic tables, grills. Cr cds: A, D, MC, V.

⬛⬛ **SC**

★ **WESTON PLAZA HOTEL.** *1684 W Hwy 40 (84078). Phone 435/789-9550; fax 435/789-4874.* 102 rooms, 3 story. S, D $52-$64; each additional $8; suites $149; under 12 free; weekend rates. TV; cable (premium). Indoor pool; whirlpool. Continental breakfast. Restaurant 11 am-10 pm. Bar to 1 am; entertainment except Sun (summer). Check-out 11 am. Meeting rooms. Business services available. Cr cds: A, D, MC, V.

⬛⬛⬛⬛⬛⬛

Restaurant

★ **7-11 RANCH.** *77 E Main St (84078). Phone 435/789-1170; fax 435/781-1130.* Hours: 6 am-11 pm. Closed Sun; Jan 1, Thanksgiving, Dec 25. Breakfast $2-$6.45, lunch $4-$7, dinner $7.50-$12.50. Children's menu. Gift shop. Reservations accepted. Western motif, totally nonsmoking. Cr cds: A, DS, MC, V.

⬛

Wendover (C-1)

Founded 1907 **Pop** 1,537 **Elev** 4,232 ft **Area code** 435 **Zip** 84083

Half in Utah, half in Nevada, Wendover lies on the western edge of the Great Salt Lake Desert. The town was settled to serve the Western Pacific Railroad, which cut a historic route through here across the Bonneville Salt Flats. Accommodations can be found on both sides of the state line, but gambling is allowed only in Nevada. Blue Lake, 30 miles south, provides water at a constant temperature of 75° F for scuba diving and is open to the public (no facilities).

What to See and Do

Bonneville Salt Flats. *East of town.* This approximately 100-square-mile area of perfectly flat salt, packed as solid as cement, is what remained after ancient Lake Bonneville, which once covered the entire area, retreated to the present-day Great Salt Lake. The area is part of the Great Salt Lake Desert.

Special Event

Bonneville National Speed Trials. *Phone 805/526-1805. Bonneville Speedway, approximately 15 miles E, then N.* Held since 1914 on the Bonneville Salt Flats (see), which has been used as a track for racing the world's fastest cars. Car racing in competition and against the clock. Aug or Sept.

Zion National Park (I-2)

See also, Cedar City, Kanab, St. George, Springdale

(42 miles NE of St. George on UT 9)

The spectacular canyons and enormous rock formations in this 147,551-acre national park are the result of powerful upheavals of the earth and erosion by flowing water and frost. Considered the grandfather of Utah's national parks, Zion is one of the nation's oldest national parks and one of the state's wildest, with large sections virtually inaccessible. The Virgin River runs through the interior of the park, and Zion Canyon, with its deep, narrow chasm and multicolored vertical walls, cuts through the middle, with smaller canyons branching from it like fingers. A paved roadway following the bottom of Zion Canyon is surrounded by massive rock formations in awe-inspiring colors that change with the light. The formations, described as temples, cathedrals, and thrones, rise to great heights, the loftiest reaching 8,726 feet. The canyon road runs 7 miles to the Temple of Sinawava, a natural amphitheater surrounded by cliffs. Another route, an extension of UT 9, cuts through the park in an east-west direction, taking visitors through the mile-long Zion-Mount Carmel Tunnel, and then descends through a series of switchbacks with viewpoints above Pine Creek Canyon. **Note:** Large vehicles must pay an escort fee to pass through the tunnel.

Zion's main visitor center is near the south entrance (daily). Check here for maps, information about the park, and schedules of naturalist activities and evening programs. Each evening, spring through fall, park naturalists give illustrated talks on the natural and human history of the area. Pets must be kept on leash and are not permitted on trails. Vehicle lights should be checked; they must be in proper condition for driving through the highway tunnel. The park is open year-round. There is an admission fee of $10/7-day stay per vehicle; Golden Eagle Passports are accepted (see MAKING THE MOST OF YOUR TRIP). Contact the Superintendent, Springdale 84767-1099; phone 435/772-3256.

What to See and Do

Bicycling. Permitted on roads in park, except through Zion-Mt Carmel tunnel. Roads are narrow and no designated bicycle routes exist.

Camping. At south entrance to par: South campground provides 140 tent or trailer sites (mid-Apr-mid-Sept); Watchman Campground provides 229 tent sites and 185 trailer sites (all year). Lava Point Campground, 26 miles N of Virgin off UT 9, provides a minimal number of tent sites (free; no facilities). South and Watchman Campgrounds **$$$**

Escorted horseback trips. *Phone 435/772-3967.* Special guide service may be obtained for other trips not regularly scheduled. Contact Bryce/Zion Trail Rides at Zion lodge. (Mar-Oct, daily)

"Grand Circle: A National Park Odyssey." *Phone 435/ 673-4811.* Multimedia presentation encompassing four states, 14 national parks and monuments, and numerous state parks and historic sites, plus Glen Canyon National Recreation Area (see PAGE, AZ, and LAKE POWELL, UT) and Monument Valley Navajo Tribal Park (see KAYENTA, AZ). One-hour show (Memorial Day-Labor Day). O.C. Tanner Amphitheatre in Springdale. **$$**

Guided trips, hiking tours. *Phone 435/772-3256.* Conducted by ranger naturalists, who explain geology, plant life, and history.

Kolob Canyons Visitor Center. (see Cedar City) *Phone 435/772-3256*

Mountain Climbing. *Phone 435/772-3256.* Should be undertaken with great care due to unstable sandstone. Climbers should consult with a ranger at the park visitor center.

Park Trails. *Phone 435/772-3256.* Trails lead to otherwise inaccessible areas: the Narrows (walls of this canyon are 2,000 feet high and as little as 50 feet apart at the stream), the Hanging Gardens of Zion, Weeping Rock, the Emerald Pools. Trails range from 1/2-mile trips to day-long treks, some requiring tested stamina. Trails in less-traveled areas should no be undertaken without first obtaining information from a park ranger. Back country permits required for travel through the Virgin River Narrows and other canyons, and on all overnight trips (fee/person/night).

Zion Nature Center. Junior Ranger program for children ages 6-12. (Memorial Day-Labor Day, Mon-Fri) Adjacent to South Campground. Phone 435/772-2356. **$**

Motels/Motor Lodges

★ **DRIFTWOOD LODGE.** *1515 Zion Park Blvd (84767). Phone 435/772-3262; toll-free 888/801-8811; fax 435/772-3702. www.driftwoodlodge.net.* 42 rooms, 1-2 story. S $82; D $90; each additional $4. Pet accepted; fee. Complimentary continental breakfast. Check-out 11 am. TV. Heated pool, whirlpool. Shaded grounds; good views of park. Cr cds: A, D, DS, MC, V.

★ ★ **FLANIGAN'S INN.** *428 Zion Park Blvd (84767). Phone 435/772-3244; toll-free 800/765-7787; fax 435/772-3396. www.flanigans.com.* 34 rooms, 2 story. Mid-Mar-mid-Nov: S, D $79-$119; each additional $5; lower rates rest of year. Crib free. TV; cable (premium). Heated pool; whirlpool. Restaurant 5-10 pm. Check-out 11 am, check-in 3 pm. Small local artists' gallery. Totally nonsmoking. Cr cds: A, DS, MC, V.

★ **TERRACE BROOK LODGE.** *990 Zion Park Blvd (84767). Phone 435/772-3932; toll-free 800/342-6779; fax 435/772-3596.* 26 rooms, 2 story. Apr-Oct: S $55; D $75; each additional $4; lower rates rest of year. Crib $4. TV; cable (premium). Heated pool. Restaurant nearby. Check-out 11 am, check-in 1 pm. Refrigerators available. Picnic tables, grills. Cr cds: DS, MC, V.

★ ★ **ZION LODGE.** *Zion National Park (84767). Phone 435/772-3213; toll-free 800/253-5896; fax 435/772-2001. www.zionlodge.com.* 75 rooms in motel, 1-2 story. 40 cabins. S, D $108-$136; each additional $5; suites $136; cabins $93. Crib $5. Restaurant 6:30-10 am, 11:30 am-3 pm, 6-10 pm. Check-out 11 am, check-in 4 pm. Business services available. Bellstaff. Sundries. Gift shop. Private porches. Cr cds: A, C, D, DS, JCB, MC, V.

Resort

★ ★ **CLIFFROSE LODGE AND GARDENS.** *281 Zion Park Blvd (84767). Phone 435/772-3234; toll-free 800/243-8824; fax 435/772-3900. www.cliffroselodge.com.* 36 rooms, 2 story. May-mid-Oct: S, D $119-$145; suites $145; each additional $10; under 18 free; lower rates rest of year. Crib $6. Pet accepted. TV; cable (premium), VCR available. Heated pool; whirlpool. Playground. Complimentary coffee in lobby. Restaurant nearby. Check-out 11 am, check-in 2 pm. Picnic tables. Cr cds: A, DS, MC, V.

B&B/Small Inns

★ ★ ★ **NOVEL HOUSE INN.** *73 Paradise Rd (84767). Phone 435/772-3650; toll-free 800/711-8400; fax 435/772-3651. www.novelhouse.com.* This bed-and-breakfast is set with the towering sandstone cliffs of Zion National Park on three sides. It is quiet but within walking distance of shops and restaurants. Complimentary breakfast and afternoon tea are served in the dining room with a view of West Temple Mountain. 10 rooms, 2 story. S $81; D $110. Children over 12 years only. Closed mid-Dec-late

Jan. TV; cable. Check-out 11 am, check-in 4-7 pm. Totally nonsmoking. Cr cds: A, DS, MC, V.

D ⚡ ⤢ ⤡ SC

★★ **RED ROCK INN.** *998 Zion Park Blvd (84767). Phone 435/772-3139. www.redrockinn.com.* 5 cottages, 1 story. No room phones. D $89-$150; each additional $10; under 14 free; Check-out 11 am, check-in 4 pm. TV; cable (premium), VCR available (movies). Restaurant nearby. Massage. Concierge service. Totally nonsmoking. Cr cds: A, DS, MC, V.

D ⤡

Index

Establishment names are listed in alphabetical order followed by their classificiaton and then city and state. The classification symbols are: [S] for Special Events, [W] for What to See and Do, [AS] for All Suites, [BB] for B&Bs/Small Inns, [CAS] for Casinos, [EX] for Extended Stays, [HOT] for Hotels, [MOT] for Motels/Motor Lodges, [RAN] for Guest Ranches, [RST] for Resorts, and [RES] for Restaurants.

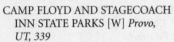

Notes

Notes

Notes

Notes

Notes

Notes

Notes

Notes

Notes

Notes

Notes

Notes